Creeds and Confessions of Faith in the Christian Tradition

Creeds & Confessions of Faith in the Christian Tradition

Volume II

Part Four: Creeds and Confessions of the
Reformation Era

edited by Jaroslav Pelikan and Valerie Hotchkiss

YALE UNIVERSITY PRESS   NEW HAVEN & LONDON

Designed by Sonia Shannon
Set in Sabon type by Tseng Information Systems, Inc.
Printed in the United States of America by Sheridan Books.

Library of Congress Cataloging-in-Publication Data
Creeds & confessions of faith in the Christian tradition /
edited by Jaroslav Pelikan and Valerie Hotchkiss.
p.   cm.
Includes bibliographical references and indexes.
Contents: v. 1. Rules of faith in the early church. Eastern Orthodox affirmations
of faith. Medieval Western statements of faith — v. 2. Creeds and confessions of
the Reformation era — v. 3. Statements of faith in modern Christianity —
v. [4]. Credo / Jaroslav Pelikan.
ISBN 0-300-09391-8 (set) (cloth : alk. paper)
ISBN 0-300-08435-8 (v. 2) (cloth : alk. paper)
ISBN 0-300-09916-9 (CD-ROM)
1. Creeds.   2. Creeds—History and criticism.   I. Title: Creeds and confessions
of faith in the Christian tradition.   II. Pelikan, Jaroslav Jan, 1923–
III. Hotchkiss, Valerie R., 1960–   IV. Pelikan, Jaroslav Jan, 1923–   Credo.
BT990.C64 2003
238—dc21
2003043067

A catalogue record for this book is available from the British Library.

The paper in this book meets the guidelines for permanence and durability
of the Committee on Production Guidelines for Book Longevity
of the Council on Library Resources.

10 9 8 7 6 5 4 3 2 1

Contents

Preface

Both for those who profess the name of Christian themselves and for those who are curious, whether in a friendly or in a hostile way, about what these people stand for or about what makes them different (from other people or from one another), creeds and confessions of faith have always been an indispensable resource. Therefore the conclusion of the Gospel of John, about books on the life and teachings of Jesus, "I suppose that the world itself could not contain the books that would be written" (Jn 21.25), though it was not referring explicitly to creeds and confessions of faith, might well have been. For from beginnings in the first century that can no longer be precisely traced to a veritable explosion of new creeds in the twentieth century, when almost every year saw one or more of them appear, the production of creeds and confessions has reached the point that, if not the world, then at any rate even these three stout volumes could not contain them all.

That has obliged the editors to practice a form of scholarly triage and to make difficult choices. Some of the choices were, of course, obvious and unavoidable: above all and in a class by itself, *The Niceno-Constantinopolitan Creed,* but then also, for the West, *The Apostles' Creed,* and, for most Christian churches of most centuries, the doctrinal decrees of the first seven ecumenical councils, as well as the confessional charters of the major groups coming out of the Reformation of the sixteenth century. That was the easy part. After initially casting our net as broadly as possible to assemble what we called a "maximal list" (which was quickly conflated into "maximalist"), and after consulting over a period of several years with scholars, theologians, and church leaders across the ecumenical spectrum and around the world, we gradually formulated, and then refined, additional criteria for deciding the ancient predestinarian question of *cur alii prae aliis*. One such criterion was definitional, although its application proved to be more complicated than it might have seemed to be initially: Does this text qualify as a creed or confession, rather than as a code of behavior or a set of ground rules for church administration, and has it been (or is it still) understood and employed as such a norm by some community that identifies itself as Christian? Once we came up with an affirmative answer to that question, what we dubbed "the Noah's ark principle" came into play: to strive to include (though not always necessarily in pairs) as many species as could fit into our capacious but nevertheless limited number of pages, species here being taken to mean ecclesiastical denominations, geographical regions, historical periods, theological styles, original languages, and literary genres. On that basis, some of these species that have manifested extraordinary fecundity in producing statements of faith (or have been the beneficiaries of unusually busy compilers and editors) have simply had to yield some of their space to assure fair, if not equal, representation for others. As earnestly as historical fairness and ecumenical sensitivity required and as human frailty permitted, each of us has made the effort not to let what we ourselves believe, teach, and confess—or where we pray—tip the scales for or against including any of the formularies, or color what we have said about them.

It would be too cumbersome to list all the editorial guidelines, rules, and exceptions we have worked with to bring some consistency to the presentation of these texts, but a few general comments may aid the reader. As a rule, biblical quotations (and paraphrases) are given as they appear in the creeds and translated accordingly. Biblical quotations in our commentary and notes are generally from the Revised Standard Version (RSV), which is therefore not usually identified. Sometimes they are from the New Revised Standard Version (NRSV). Scriptural citations that have been added by later editors (or by us) are placed in brackets. The citations appear either in the margins or, when numerous, as footnotes keyed to lowercase letters. For the sake of consistency, the spelling of proper names has been conformed to that of the third edition of *The Oxford Dictionary of the Christian Church (ODCC)*, with a few minor exceptions such as the *Council of Basel* (not "Basle"), John Hus (not "Huss"), and *The Smalcald Articles* (not "Schmalkaldic"). For names not found in the *ODCC*, we have followed Library of Congress authority records.

Finally, filial piety requires that we pay a special tribute here to the memory of Philip Schaff (1819–93), the émigré scholar who, in addition to publishing a veritable one-man library of other biblical, historical, patristic, and theological texts that total a hundred volumes or so, managed in 1877 to produce the three volumes of *Bibliotheca Symbolica Ecclesiae Universalis: The Creeds of Christendom*. As his son David said of it in his biography of his father, "Even in Germany such critics as [Isaak August] Dorner declared that it filled an unoccupied place in theological literature and satisfied a real need. 'The very conception of the work was a great thought which presupposed unusual courage and enterprise,' he wrote. . . . The work has been considered by some as his most valuable contribution to theological literature." With all its quirks (for example, *The Confession of Dositheus* in Greek and Latin but not in English, initially even his beloved *Second Helvetic Confession* left in the original Latin untranslated, with only a précis in English) and a Protestant partisanship that does sometimes seem to be excessive, Schaff's set proved to be so useful that for more than 125 years it has remained in print practically without interruption—and, except for a few supplementary texts, has remained fundamentally unrevised through six editions and numerous reprints. Our years of work on the ambitious project of replacing it for the twenty-first century have instilled in us an admiration for Schaff's enduring accomplishment.

Acknowledgments

The scope and duration of this project have required consultation with scholars from diverse fields, correspondence with churches and religious organizations around the world, and the goodwill of the people we work for and the people who work for us. First and foremost, we are indebted to the Lilly Endowment for its generous and continued support through research leaves, project support, and production assistance. We acknowledge with gratitude a special grant from the Virginia H. Farah Foundation that provided for the distribution of these volumes to libraries in Orthodox communities and in the developing world. We are also grateful to Yale University Press for taking on this massive task, and we thank in particular John Ryden, Laura Jones Dooley, Alex Schwartz, Otto Bohlmann, John Rollins, Lauren Shapiro, and Paul Royster. Further, we acknowledge the support of the other institutions that made our work possible: Yale University, Boston College, the Annenberg School for Communication of the University of Pennsylvania, the Library of Congress, and Southern Methodist University, especially the Perkins School of Theology and Bridwell Library. The many presses, denominations, and ecumenical bodies that made texts available for this collection are acknowledged elsewhere in this volume, but we offer here a general and heartfelt word of appreciation for their cooperation.

We express our gratitude to Colin Davey for the translation of *The Confession of Faith of Metrophanes Critopoulos* that he prepared for this project, and to Catharine P. Roth for her translations of *The Encyclical Letter of Photius*, the *Synodical Tomes* of 1341 and 1351, and the confessions of Gregory Palamas and Gennadius I. Through the years, several student researchers have assisted us and deserve thanks for their conscientious work: John Brown, Kirsten Christensen, Drew Cottle, James Ernst, Cinnamon Hearst, Caroline Huey, Brian Matz, Megan McLemore, and Amber Sturgess. We have also been aided by numerous librarians, church officials, and scholars, who helped us overcome various hurdles and whom we list here (in alphabetical order) with gratitude: Gerald H. Anderson, Metropolitan Anthony of Dardanelion/San Francisco, Urs von Arx, C. J. Dyck, Peter C. Erb, Ellen Frost, Brian A. Gerrish, Maria Habito, Ruben Habito, Duane Harbin, Susan Billington Harper, Patrick Henry, Linda Hervey, Sally Hoover, Seth Kasten, Karl Peter Koop, Robin Lovin, James McMillin, E. Ann Matter, Hermann Michaeli, James J. O'Donnell, Father George Papademetriou, Michael Pelikan, Russell Pollard, David Price, Helmut Renders, Charles C. Ryrie, Fred Sand, Lamin O. Sanneh, Barbara von Schlegell, Anthony Scott, Philip Shen, Joe A. Springer, Jane Stranz, Richard A. Taylor, Gayla

Tennison, Page A. Thomas, Bishop Kallistos Ware, Robert L. Wilken, Charles Willard, and Richard Wright.

David Price and Sylvia Pelikan deserve special mention here, though they have already earned a star in their heavenly crowns for their patience. And to son Samuel Price Hotchkiss and grandsons Stefan Daniel Pelikan and Nikolai Ivan Pelikan, who were not born when the project was conceived, we offer thanks for the joy you gave us when we closed our books at the end of the day.

Abbreviations for Creeds and Confessions

All citations of councils and synods—unless accompanied by "act" (= *Acts*), "can" (= *Canons*), "decr" (= *Decrees*), or some other abbreviation—refer specifically to their creedal or doctrinal formulations.

Abbreviation	Title and Date	Location
Abst Prin	*Abstract of Principles for Southern Baptist Seminary, 1858*	3:316–20; McBeth 1990, 304–15
Ad tuendam	*Ad tuendam fidem of Pope John Paul II, 1998*	3:871–76
Adv	*The Fundamental Beliefs of the Seventh-Day Adventist Church, 1872*	3:359–64
Afr Orth	*Doctrine of the African Orthodox Church, 1921*	3:435–36
A-L	*Anglican-Lutheran Pullach Report, 1972*	*Gr Agr II* 14–34
Alex	*The Creed of Alexander of Alexandria, c. 321–24*	1:79–81; Hahn, 15; *NPNF*–II 3:39–40
Am Bap	*The Statement of Faith of the American Baptist Association, 1905*	Lumpkin, 378–79
Ang Cat	*The Anglican Catechism, 1549/1662*	2:364–71; Schaff, 3:517–22
Ans	*The Evangelical Counsel of Ansbach [Ansbacher Evangelischer Ratschlag], 1524*	Schmidt-Schornbaum, 183–322
Ant 325	*The First Synod of Antioch, 325*	1:84–86
Ant 341	*The Second [Dedication] Synod of Antioch, 341*	1:87–89; Hahn, 153–56; *NPNF*–II 4:461
Ap	*The Apostles' Creed*	1:667–69; *BLK* 21–25; Cochrane, 303–4; Fabbri, 3;

Abbreviation	Title and Date	Location
		Gerrish, 56; Kolb-Wengert, 21–22; Leith, 24–25; Tappert, 18; *Triglotta* 2:30–31; Schaff, 2:45–55
Ap Const	The Apostolic Constitutions, c. 350–80	Hahn, 9–10, 129; Schaff, 2:39
Apol Aug	The Apology of the Augsburg Confession, 1531	CD-ROM; *BLK* 139–404; Fabbri, 58–328; Kolb-Wengert, 109–294; Tappert, 100–285; *Triglotta* 2:97–451
Ar	The Creeds of Arius and Euzoius, c. 320 and 327	1:75–78; Hahn, 186–87; Schaff, 2:28–29
Arist	The Creed of Aristides of Athens, 2d c.	1:51–52
Arm Ev	Armenian Evangelical Churches, 1846	3:261–63
Arn	The Arnoldshain Theses, 1957	3:558–61
Assem	The Statement of Fundamental Truths of the Assemblies of God, 1914	3:426–31
Ath	The Athanasian Creed [*Quicunque vult*]	1:673–77; *BLK* 28–30; Denzinger, 75–76; Fabbri, 6–8; Gerrish, 62–64; Hahn, 150; Kelly 1964, 17–20; Kolb-Wengert, 23–25; Schaff, 2:66–71; Tappert, 19–21; *Triglotta* 2:30–35
Aub	The Auburn Declaration, 1837	3:250–55; Schaff, 3:777–80
Aug	The Augsburg Confession	2:49–118; *BLK* 31–137; Fabbri, 11–57; Gerrish, 87–125; Kolb-Wengert, 30–105; Leith, 63–107; Noll, 81–121; Schaff, 3:3–73; Tappert, 23–96; *Triglotta* 2:37–95
Ger	German, 1530	
Lat	Latin, 1530	
Var	Variata, 1540	Reu, 2:398–411

Abbreviation	Title and Date	Location
Balamand	*Uniatism, Method of Union of the Past, and the Present Search for Full Communion:* Joint International Commission for Theological Dialogue Between the Catholic and Orthodox Church. Balamand, Lebanon, 1993	3:848-51; *Gr Agr II* 680-85
Bap Assoc	*The Doctrinal Statement of the North American Baptist Association,* 1950	Lumpkin, 377-81
Bap Aus	*Doctrinal Basis of the Baptist Union of Victoria, Australia,* 1888	Lumpkin, 416-20
Bap Conf	*The Statement of Beliefs of the North American Baptist Conference,* 1982	3:808-12
Bap Gr Br	*The Statement of the Baptist Union of Great Britain and Ireland,* 1888	Lumpkin, 344-46
Bap NZ	*The Doctrinal Basis of the New Zealand Baptist Union,* 1882	Lumpkin, 416
Barm	*The Barmen Declaration [Theologische Erklärung zur gegenwärtigen Lage der Deutschen Evangelischen Kirche],* 1934	3:504-8; Cochrane, 332-36; Leith, 517-22; Niesel, 333-37
Bas Bek	*The First Confession of Basel [Baseler Bekenntnis],* 1534	2:272-79; Augusti, 103-9; Böckel, 108-14; Cochrane, 89-96; Fabbri, 630-37; Niemeyer, 78-104
Bat	*The Confession of Faith of the Protestant Christian Batak Church (H. K. B. P.),* 1951	3:543-55; Anderson, 213-38; Leith, 555-66
BCP	*The Book of Common Prayer,* 1549, 1552, 1662, 1928, 1979	Blunt

Abbreviation	Title and Date	Location
BEC	*The Profession of Faith of the Salvadoran Basic Ecclesial Communities,* 1984	**3:844–45**
Belg	*The Belgic Confession,* 1561/1619	**2:405–26**; Augusti, 170–98; Bakhuizen van den Brink, 50–141; Böckel, 477–507; Cochrane, 185–219; Fabbri, 701–33; Niemeyer, 360–89; Niesel, 119–36; Schaff, 3:383–436
BEM	*Baptism, Eucharist, and Ministry* ["The Lima Text" of Faith and Order], 1982	**3:813–40**; *Gr Agr* 465–503
Bern	*The Ten Theses of Bern,* 1528	**2:215–17**; Böckel, 35–39; Cochrane, 45–50; Fabbri, 621–22; Leith, 129–30; Niemeyer, 14–15; Schaff, 3:208–10
Boh I	*The [First] Bohemian Confession,* 1535	**1:796–833**; Augusti, 273–326; Böckel, 777–827; Niemeyer, 771–818; Pelikan, 80–149
Boh II	*The [Second] Bohemian Confession,* 1575	CD-ROM; Böckel, 827–49; Niemeyer, 819–51; Reu, 2:424–33
Bonn I	*The Fourteen Theses of the Old Catholic Union Conference at Bonn with Greeks and Anglicans,* 1874	**3:365–67**; Schaff, 2:545–51
Bonn II	*The Old Catholic Agreement at Bonn on the Filioque Controversy,* 1875	Schaff, 2:552–54
Boston	*The Declaration of the Boston National Council,* 1865	Walker, 562–64
Brngr 1059	*The First Confession of Berengar,* 1059	**1:728–29**; Denzinger, 690
Brngr 1079	*The Second Confession of Berengar,* 1079	**1:728–29**; Denzinger, 700

Abbreviation	Title and Date	Location
Br St Luth	*The Brief Statement of the Doctrinal Position of the Evangelical Lutheran Synod of Missouri, Ohio, and Other States, 1932*	3:487–503; *Doct Dec* 42–57
Camb Dec	*The Cambridge Declaration of the Alliance of Confessing Evangelicals, 1996*	3:861–66
Camb Plat	*The Cambridge Platform, 1648*	3:63–91; Leith, 385–99; Walker, 194–237
Chal	*The Council of Chalcedon, 451*	1:172–81; COD-DEC 75–103; Denzinger, 300–303; Fabbri, 5; Gerrish, 65; Hahn, 146–47; Karmirēs, 1:173–76; Leith, 34–36; Mansi, 7:107–18; Michalcescu, 3–4; *NPNF*–II 14:243–95; Schaff, 2:62–65
Chile	*The Creed of the Evangelical Presbyterian Church of Chile, 1983*	3:841–43
Chin Man	*The Christian Manifesto of the Three-Self Patriotic Movement: "Directions of Endeavor for Chinese Christianity in the Construction of New China," 1950*	3:357–59; Anderson, 249–50
Chin Un	*The Bond of Union of the Church of Christ in China, 1927*	3:483–84; Anderson, 249
Chr Dec	*Common Christological Declaration Between the Catholic Church and the Assyrian Church of the East, 1994*	3:852–55; *Gr Agr II* 711–12
Chr Sci	*Tenets of the Mother Church of Christ, Scientist, 1879/1892/ 1906*	3:370–71

Abbreviation	Title and Date	Location
CNI	*The Church of North India/Pakistan, Plan of Church Union: The Doctrines of the Church*, 1965	**3:700–702**
Cologne	*The [Mennonite] Concept of Cologne*, 1591	**2:749–54**
Com Cr	*The "Commission" Creed of the Congregational Church*, 1883/ 1913	**3:372–74**; Walker, 577–82
Com Dec	*Common Declaration of Pope John Paul II and [Armenian] Catholicos Karekin I*, 1996	**3:867–70**; Gr Agr II 707–8
Confut	*The Confutation of the Augsburg Confession*, 1530	Reu, 2:348–83
Cons rep	*The Reaffirmed Consensus of the Truly Lutheran Faith [Consensus repetitus fidei vere lutheranae]*, 1655	Henke
Const	*The Council of Constance*, 1414–18	COD-DEC 403–51; Denzinger, 1151–1279
CP I	*The First Council of Constantinople*, 381	**1:160–63**; COD-DEC 21–35; Denzinger, 151; Karmirēs, 1:130–31; Michalcescu, 2; NPNF-II 14:162–90
CP II	*The Second Council of Constantinople*, 553	**1:183–215**; COD-DEC 105–22; Denzinger, 421–38; Hahn, 148; Karmirēs, 1:185–97; Leith, 45–50; Mansi, 9:367–90; Michalcescu, 5–7; NPNF-II 14:297–323
CP III	*The Third Council of Constantinople*, 680–81	**1:216–29**; COD-DEC 123–30; Denzinger, 550–59; Hahn, 149; Karmirēs, 1:221–24; Leith, 50–53; Mansi, 11:631–40; Michalcescu, 7–9; NPNF-II 14:344–46; Schaff, 2:72–73

Abbreviation	Title and Date	Location
CP 360	*The Creed of the Synod of Constantinople of 360*	Hahn, 167
CP 879-80	*The Synod of Constantinople of 879-80*	Karmirēs, 1:268–71
CP 1054	*The Edict of Michael Cerularius and of the Synod of Constantinople of 1054*	**1:309-17;** Karmirēs, 1:343–48; Mansi, 19:812–21; *PG* 151:679–82; Will, 155–68
CP 1341	*The Synod of Constantinople of 1341*	**1:318-33;** Karmirēs, 1:354–66; *PG* 151:679–82
CP 1347	*The Synod of Constantinople of 1347*	Karmirēs, 1:366–74
CP 1351	*The Synod of Constantinople of 1351*	**1:334-74;** Karmirēs, 1:374–407; *PG* 151:717–68
CP 1691	*The Synod of Constantinople of 1691*	Karmirēs, 2:779–83; Mansi, 37:463–72
CP 1838	*The Synod of Constantinople of 1838*	Karmirēs, 2:894–902; Mansi, 40:269–76
Craig	*Craig's Catechism, 1581*	Torrance, 97–165
Crg Sh Cat	*Craig's Short Catechism, 1592*	Torrance, 243–54
CSI 1929	*The Scheme of Union of the Church of South India, 1929/ 1942*	Schaff, 3:951
CSI 1947	*The Constitution of the Church of South India, 1947*	**3:517-24;** Anderson, 228–34
Cumb Pres	*The Confession of the Cumberland Presbyterian Church, 1814/1883*	**3:223-41;** Schaff, 3:771–76
Cum occas	*Cum occasione of Pope Innocent X, 1653*	**3:101-3;** Denzinger, 2001–7
Cyp	*The Creed of Cyprian of Carthage, 250*	Hahn, 12; Schaff, 2:20
Cyr Jer	*The Baptismal Creed of Jerusalem, c. 350*	**1:94-95;** Denzinger, 41; Hahn, 124; Schaff, 2:31–32
Czen	*The Hungarian Confession [Confessio Czengerina], 1570*	Augusti, 241–53; Niemeyer, 539–50
Dec Addr	Thomas Campbell, *Declaration and Address, 1809:* "Propositions"	**3:219-22**

Abbreviation	Title and Date	Location
Def Plat	*The Definite Platform* (Lutheran), 1855	**3:291–315**
Denck	*Hans Denck's Confession Before the Council of Nuremberg,* 1525	2:665–72; Bauman, 51–53
Dêr Bal	*The Dêr Balyzeh Papyrus,* c. 200–350	1:66–67; Denzinger, 2; Kelly, 89; Leith, 19
Design	*Christian Church (Disciples of Christ): The Design for the Christian Church,* 1968	3:726–29
Dict Pap	*The Dictatus Papae of Pope Gregory VII,* 1075	1:730–32
Did	*The Didache,* c. 60–150	**1:41–42**
Dordrecht	*The Mennonite Confession of Faith of Dordrecht,* 1632	2:768–87; Fabbri, 922–37; Gerrish, 218–34; Leith, 292–308; Loewen, 63–70; Lumpkin, 66–78
Dort	*The Canons of the Synod of Dort,* 1618–19	**2:569–600**; Augusti, 198–240; Bakhuizen van den Brink, 218–81; Böckel, 508–43; Bray, 455–78; Fabbri, 885–921; Niemeyer, 690–728; Schaff, 3:550–97
Dosith	*The Confession of Dositheus and of the Synod of Jerusalem,* 1672	**1:613–35**; Karmirēs, 2:746–73; Gerrish, 310–41; Kimmel, 1:425–88; Leith, 485–517; Mansi, 34:1723–62; Michalcescu, 123–82; Robertson; Schaff, 2:401–44
Ecth	*The Ecthesis of Emperor Heraclius,* 638	**1:150–54**; *BZ* 69:21–23; Mansi, 10:991–98
Edict	*The Edict of Emperor Justinian on the True Faith,* 551	**1:122–49**; Schwartz, 73–110; Wesche, 163–98
18 Diss	*Eighteen Dissertations Concerning the Entire Christian Life and of What It Consists, by Balthasar Hubmaier,* 1524	Lumpkin, 19–21

Abbreviation	Title and Date	Location
Eng Dec	The Declaration of the Congregational Union of England and Wales, 1833	Schaff, 3:730–34; Walker, 542–52
Ep Apost	The Epistula Apostolorum, c. 150	1:53–54; Denzinger, 1; Leith, 17
Eph 431	The Council of Ephesus, 431	1:164–71; COD-DEC 37–74; Denzinger, 250–68; Karmirēs, 1:138–56; Michalcescu, 2–3; NPNF-II 14:191–242
Form Un	The Formula of Union, 433	1:168–71; COD-DEC 69–70; Denzinger, 271–73
Epiph	The Creeds of Epiphanius, 373/374	1:100–101; Denzinger, 42–45; Hahn, 125–26; NPNF-II 14:164–65; Schaff, 2:32–38
Ess	Friends General Conference, Belief, 1900	3:399–401
Eun	The Confession of Eunomius to the Emperor, 383	1:105–9; Hahn, 190
Eus	The Creed of Eusebius of Caesarea, 325	1:82–83; Denzinger, 40; Hahn, 188; Leith, 27–28; NPNF-II 4:74; Schaff, 2:29–30
Ev All	The Nine Articles of the Evangelical Alliance, 1846	3:259–60; Schaff, 3:827–28
Fac	The Creed of Facundus of Hermiane, 6th c.	Hahn, 51
F&O Ban	Commission on Faith and Order of the World Council of Churches at Bangalore: A Common Statement of Our Faith, 1978	3:782–85
F&O Edin	Faith and Order Conference at Edinburgh: The Grace of Our Lord Jesus Christ; The Affirmation of Union, 1937	3:511–16; Leith, 569–74
F&O Laus	Faith and Order Conference at Lausanne: The Call to Unity, 1927	3:471–82

Abbreviation	Title and Date	Location
Fid cath	*On the Catholic Faith* [*De fide catholica*], by Boethius, c. 517–22	**1:699–706;** *LCL* 74:52–71
Fid rat	*A Reckoning of the Faith* [*Fidei ratio*], by Ulrich Zwingli, 1530	**2:249–71;** Böckel, 40–61; Niemeyer, 16–35
Flor	The Council of Basel-Ferrara-Florence-Rome	**1:751–65;** *COD-DEC* 523–91; Denzinger, 1300–1308
Arm	*The Bull of Union with the Armenians*, 1439	
Un	*The Decree of Union with the East*, 1439	
Form Conc	*The Formula of Concord*	**2:166–203;** *BLK* 735–1102;
Epit	*The Epitome*, 1577	Fabbri, 367–600; Kolb-Wengert, 486–660; Schaff, 3:93–180; Tappert, 464–636; *Triglotta* 2:774–1103
Sol Dec	*The Solid Declaration*, 1577	CD-ROM
42 Art	*The Forty-Two Articles of the Church of England*, 1553	Bray, 284–311; Niemeyer, 592–600
Free Meth	*Articles of Religion of the Free Methodist Church*, 1866	**3:335–40**
Free-Will Bap	*The Confession of the Free-Will Baptists*, 1834/1868/1948	Lumpkin, 367–76; Schaff, 3:749–56
Fréjus	*The Synod of Fréjus*, 796/797	**1:725–27;** Denzinger, 616–19
Friends I	*A Confession of Faith Containing XXIII Articles*, 1673	**3:136–48**
Friends II	*Theses Theologicae of Robert Barclay* [*The Confession of the Society of Friends, Commonly Called Quakers*], 1675	Schaff, 3:789–98
Gall	*The French Confession* [*Confessio Gallica*], 1559/1571	**2:372–86;** Augusti, 110–25; Böckel, 459–74; Cochrane, 137–58; Fabbri, 663–76; Gerrish, 150–63; Niemeyer, 311–39; Niesel, 65–79; Schaff, 3:356–82

Abbreviation	Title and Date	Location
Geloof	*The Doctrine of the True Mennonites or Baptists [De Geloofsleere der Waare Mennoniten of Dopgezinden] by Cornelis Ris, 1766/1895/1902*	3:155-200; Loewen, 85-103
Gen Bap	*General Baptists: The Faith and Practice of Thirty Congregations Gathered According to the Primitive Pattern, 1651*	3:92-100; Lumpkin, 171-88
Gennad	*The Confession of Faith of Gennadius II, 1455-56*	1:385-91; Karmirēs, 1:432-36; Michalcescu, 11-21; *PG* 160:333-52
Genv Cat	*The Geneva Catechism, 1541/1542*	2:320-63; Augusti, 460-531; Böckel, 127-72; Niemeyer, 123-90; Niesel, 1-41; Torrance, 3-65
Genv Con	*The Geneva Confession, 1536*	2:311-19; Cochrane, 117-26; Fabbri, 654-62; Noll, 123-32
Ghana	*Ghana Church Union Committee: The Faith of the Church, 1965*	3:703-8
Greg I	*The Creed of Pope Gregory I, d. 604*	Hahn, 231
Greg Palam	*The Confession of the Orthodox Faith by Gregory Palamas, 1351*	1:375-78; Karmirēs, 1:407-10; Michalcescu, 11-21; *PG* 160:333-52
Greg Thaum	*The Creed of Gregory Thaumaturgus (c. 213-c. 270)*	1:70-71; Hahn, 185; Schaff, 2:24-25
Heid	*The Heidelberg Catechism, 1563*	2:427-57; Augusti, 532-77; Bakhuizen van den Brink, 144-217; Böckel, 395-424; Cochrane, 305-31; Fabbri, 734-69; Niemeyer, 390-461; Niesel, 136-218; Noll, 133-64; Schaff, 3:307-55

Abbreviation	Title and Date	Location
Helv I	*The First Helvetic Confession* [*The Second Basel Confession*], 1536	**2:280-91**; Augusti, 94-102; Böckel, 115-26; Cochrane, 97-111; Fabbri, 638-51; Niemeyer, 105-23; Schaff, 3:211-31
Helv II	*The Second Helvetic Confession*, 1566	**2:458-525**; Augusti, 3-93; Böckel, 281-347; Cochrane, 220-301; Fabbri, 770-862; Leith, 131-92; Niemeyer, 462-536; Niesel, 219-75; Schaff, 3:233-306, 831-909
Hipp	*The Creeds of Hippolytus*, c. 170-236	**1:60-61**; Denzinger, 10; Hahn, 6; Leith, 23
Hond	*The Credo* from *The Mass of the Marginalized People*, Honduras, 1980	**3:795-97**; Link, 45
Horm	*The Confession of Hormisdas* [*Libellus fidei*], 515	Denzinger, 363-65
Hub Chr Cat	*The Christian Catechism of Balthasar Hubmaier*, 1526	**2:673-93**
Ign	*The Creeds of Ignatius of Antioch*, c. 107	**1:39-40**; *ANF* 1:69-70; Hahn, 1; Leith, 16-17; Schaff, 2:11-12
Ild	*The Confession of Ildefonsus of Toledo*, 7th c.	Denzinger, 23; Hahn, 55
Ineff	*Ineffabilis Deus of Pope Pius IX*, 1854	**3:289-90**; Denzinger, 2800-2804; Leith, 442-46; Schaff, 2:211-12
Iren	*The Creeds of Irenaeus of Lyons*, c. 180-c. 200	**1:48-50**; *ANF* 1:330-31; Hahn, 5; Leith, 20-21; Schaff, 2:12-16
Irish	*The Irish Articles of Religion*, 1615	**2:551-68**; Bray, 437-52; Fabbri, 865-84; Schaff, 3:526-44
Jer II 1	*The Reply of Ecumenical Patriarch Jeremias II to the Augsburg Confession*, 1576	**1:392-474**; Karmirēs, 1:443-503; Mastrantonis, 30-105

Abbreviation	Title and Date	Location
Jer II 2–3	*The Second and Third Replies to the Lutherans of Patriarch Jeremias II of Constantinople,* 1579, 1581	CD-ROM; Karmirēs, 2:435–89; Mastrantonis, 151–214, 288–307
Just	*The Creeds of Justin Martyr,* 155	1:45–47; Hahn, 3; Leith, 18
Korea	*The Theological Declaration by Christian Ministers in the Republic of Korea,* 1973	3:742–43; Anderson, 241–45
Lam	*Lamentabili of Pope Pius X,* 1907	3:402–8; Denzinger, 3401–66
Lamb Art	*The Lambeth Articles,* 1595	2:545–46; Bray, 399–400; Fabbri, 863–64; Schaff, 3:523–25
Lamb Quad	*The Lambeth Quadrilateral* [*The Chicago/Lambeth Quadrilateral*], 1886/1888	3:375–76; Fabbri, 1032–34
Lat 649	*The Lateran Synod of 649*	1:709–14; Denzinger, 500–522
Lat 1215	*The Fourth Lateran Council of 1215: The Lateran Creed*	1:739–42; COD-DEC 227–71; Denzinger, 800–820; Leith, 56–59
Laus Art	*The Lausanne Articles,* 1536	2:292–95; Cochrane, 113–16; Fabbri, 652–53
Laus Cov	*The Lausanne Covenant,* 1974	3:753–60
LDS	*The Articles of Faith of the Church of Jesus Christ of Latter-Day Saints (Mormons),* 1842	3:256–58
Leuen	*The Leuenberg Agreement* [*Konkordie reformatorischer Kirchen in Europa*], 1973	3:744–52; *ER* 25:355–59; Rusch-Martensen 1989, 144–54
Lit Chrys	*The Divine Liturgy According to Saint John Chrysostom*	1:269–95; Brightman, 353–99; Holy Cross 1–40; Kallis, 44–195; Karmirēs, 1:289–315; Kokkinakis, 86–143; Michalcescu, 277–98; OCA 29–87

Abbreviation	Title and Date	Location
Loll	*The Twelve Conclusions of the Lollards,* 1395	1:784–90
London I	*The [First] London Confession of the Particular Baptists,* 1644	3:47–62; Lumpkin, 144–71
London II	*The Assembly or Second London Confession,* 1677/1678	Lumpkin, 235–95
Lucar	*The Eastern Confession of the Christian Faith by Cyril Lucar,* 1629 (1633)	1:549–58; Bradow 1960, 190–204; Karmirēs, 2:565–70; Kimmel, 1:24–44; Michalcescu, 262–76
LuRC 4	*Lutheran-Roman Catholic Conversation 4: All Under One Christ,* 1980	Gr Agr 241–46
LuRC Just	*Lutheran-Roman Catholic Joint Declaration on the Doctrine of Justification,* 1999	3:877–88
Luth Lg Cat	*The Large Catechism of Martin Luther,* 1529	CD-ROM; *BLK* 543–733; Kolb-Wengert, 379–480; Tappert, 358–461; *Triglotta* 2:565–773
Luth Sm Cat	*The Small Catechism of Martin Luther,* 1529	2:29–48; *BLK* 499–541; Kolb-Wengert, 347–75; Leith, 107–26; Noll, 59–80; Schaff, 3:74–92; Tappert, 338–56; *Triglotta* 2:531–63
Lyons	*The Second Council of Lyons,* 1274	1:743–44; *COD-DEC* 314; Denzinger, 850–61
Madag	*The Statement of Faith of the Church of Jesus Christ in Madagascar,* 1958/1968	3:562–65
Marburg	*The Marburg Articles,* 1529	2:791–95; Reu, 2:44–47
Mark Eph	*The Confession of Faith of Mark of Ephesus,* 1439	1:379–84; Karmirēs, 1:422–25; *PG* 160:115–204
Masai	*The Masai Creed,* c. 1960	3:568–69; Donovan, 200; Marthaler, 417
Menn Con	*The Mennonite Confession of Faith,* 1963	3:674–85

Abbreviation	Title and Date	Location
Meros	*The Faith in Detail [Kata meros pistis]*, 6th c.?	Caspari, 18–21
Meth Art	*The Methodist Articles of Religion*, 1784/1804	3:201–7; Leith, 353–60; Schaff, 3:807–13
Meth Braz	*The Social Creed of the Methodist Church of Brazil*, 1971	3:732–35
Meth Kor	*The Doctrinal Statement of the Korean Methodist Church*, 1930	3:485–86; Anderson, 241
Metr Crit	*The Confession of Metrophanes Critopoulos*, 1625	1:475–548; Karmirēs, 2:498–561; Michalcescu, 183–252
Mogila	*The Orthodox Confession of the Catholic and Apostolic Eastern Church by Peter Mogila*, 1638/1642	1:559–612; Karmirēs, 2:593–686; Kimmel, 1:56–203; Malvy-Viller, 1–124; Michalcescu, 22–122; Overbeck, 6–162; Schaff, 2:275–400
Morav	*The Easter Litany of the Moravian Church*, 1749	3:149–54; Schaff, 3:799–806
Morav Am	*Moravian Church in America: The Ground of the Unity*, 1995	3:856–60
Munif	*Munificentissimus Deus of Pope Pius XII*, 1950	3:534–36; Denzinger, 3900–3904; Leith, 457–66; Schaff, 2:211–12
N	*The Creed of Nicaea*, 325	1:156–59; *COD-DEC* 5; Denzinger, 125–26; Hahn, 142; Gerrish, 59; Karmirēs, 1:122–23; Leith, 29–31; Mansi, 2:665–68; *NPNF*-II 14:3
Naz	*Articles of Faith of the Church of the Nazarene*, 1908	3:409–14
N-CP	*The Niceno-Constantinopolitan Creed ["The Nicene Creed"]*, 381	1:160–63; *COD-DEC* 24; Denzinger, 150; Gerrish, 59–60; Hahn, 144; Karmirēs, 1:130–31; Leith, 31–33; Mansi, 3:565–66; *NPNF*-II 14:163; Schaff, 2:57–58

Abbreviation	Title and Date	Location
Occ	*The Western [Occidental] Recension*	**1:670-72**; *BLK* 26-27; Cochrane, 303; Denzinger, 150; Fabbri, 4; Kolb-Wengert, 22-23; Schaff, 2:58-59; Tappert, 18-19; *Triglotta* 2:30-31
New Hamp	*The New Hampshire [Baptist] Confession*, 1833/1853	**3:242-49**; Leith, 334-39; Lumpkin, 360-77; Schaff, 3:742-48
Nic I	*The First Council of Nicaea*, 325	**1:156-59**; *COD-DEC* 1-19; Michalcescu, 1; *NPNF*-II 14:1-56; Schaff, 2:60-61
Nic II	*The Second Council of Nicaea*, 787	**1:230-41**; *COD-DEC* 133-38; Denzinger, 600-615; Karmirēs, 1:238-50; Leith, 53-56; Mansi, 13:373-80; Michalcescu, 10; *NPNF*-II 14:521-87
No Afr	*North African Creeds*	**1:110-12, 683-84**
Novat	*The Creeds of Novatian*, c. 240-50	**1:68-69**; Hahn, 11; Schaff, 2:21
Oberlin	*The Declaration of the Oberlin National Council*, 1871	Walker, 570-76
Orange	*The Synod of Orange*, 529	**1:692-98**; Denzinger, 370-97; Hahn, 174; Leith, 37-45
Origen	*The Creed of Origen*, c. 222-30	**1:62-65**; Hahn, 8; Schaff, 2:21-23
Pasc	*Pascendi dominici gregis of Pope Pius X*, 1907	Denzinger, 3475-3500
Patr	*The Profession of Faith of Patrick*, 5th c.	**1:690-91**
Petr Ab	*The Confession of Faith of Peter Abelard*, 1139-42	**1:735-38**; Gilson 1960, 107-8
Philad	*The Philadelphia Baptist Confession*, 1688/1689/1742	Lumpkin, 348-53; Schaff, 3:738-41

Abbreviation	Title and Date	Location
Philip Ind	*The Declaration of the Faith and Articles of Religion of the Philippine Independent Church,* 1947	3:525-31; Anderson, 255-60
Philip UCC	*The Statement of Faith of the United Church of Christ in the Philippines,* 1986/1992	3:846-47
Phot	*The Encyclical Letter of Photius,* 866	1:296-308; Karmirēs, 1:321-30; PG 102:721-41
Pol Br	*The Catechesis and Confession of Faith of the Polish Brethren,* 1574	2:709-44
Pol Nat Ch	*The Confession of Faith of the Polish National Catholic Church,* 1912/1914	3:423-25
Polyc	*The Creed of Polycarp of Smyrna,* c. 150	1:43-44
Prague	*The Four Articles of Prague,* 1420	1:791-95
Pres So Afr	*The Declaration of Faith of the Presbyterian Church in South Africa,* 1979/1981	3:793-94; Vischer, 27-28
Pres USA	*Confession of the United Presbyterian Church in the United States,* 1967	3:714-25
R	*The Roman Symbol,* 2d c.	1:681-82; Gerrish, 55
Rac	*The Racovian Catechism,* 1605	Rees
RCA	*Reformed Church in America: Our Song of Hope,* 1978	3:786-92
Ref All	*North American Area Council of the World Alliance of Reformed Churches: The Statement of Faith,* 1965	3:712-13
Ref Ep	*The Declaration of Principles of the Reformed Episcopal Church in America,* 1873/1875	Schaff, 3:814-26

Abbreviation	Title and Date	Location
Remon	The Remonstrance or Arminian Articles, 1610	2:547–50; Bakhuizen van den Brink, 282–87; Böckel, 544–640; Schaff, 3:545–49
Resp Non-Jur	The Responses of Eastern Orthodox Patriarchs to the Non-Jurors, 1718/1723	Karmirēs, 2:788–820; Mansi, 37:395–472
Resp Pius IX	The Response of Eastern Orthodox Patriarchs to Pope Pius IX, 1848	3:264–88; Karmirēs, 2:905–25; Mansi, 40:377–418
Richmond	The Richmond Declaration of Faith of the Friends Yearly Meeting, 1887	3:377–92
Ries	The [Mennonite] Short Confession of Faith of Hans de Ries, 1610	2:755–67; Dyck, 11–19
Rom Syn	The Creed of the Synod of Rome, 680	1:722–24; Denzinger, 546–48
Russ Cat	The Christian Catechism of the Orthodox Catholic Greco-Russian Church, 1839	Schaff, 2:445–542
Sacr ant	Sacrorum antistitum [Anti-Modernist Oath] of Pope Pius X, 1910	3:419–22; Denzinger, 3537–50
Salv Arm	Religious Doctrines of the Salvation Army, 1878	3:368–69
Sard	The Western Creed of Sardica, 343	1:90–93; Hahn, 157; NPNF–II 3:71–72
Sav	The Savoy Declaration of Faith and Order, 1658	3:104–35; Schaff, 3:707–29; Walker, 354–408
Sax	The Saxon Confession, 1551	Schaff, 3:181–89
Sax Vis	The Saxon Visitation Articles, 1592	Fabbri, 611–20; Schaff, 3:181–89
Schleit	The Schleitheim Confession, 1527	2:694–703; Leith, 281–92; Lumpkin, 22–31; Noll, 47–58
Scot I	The [First] Scots Confession, 1560	2:387–404; Augusti, 143–69; Böckel, 643–61; Cochrane, 159–84; Fabbri, 677–700;

Abbreviation	Title and Date	Location
		Niemeyer, 340–56; Niesel, 79–117; Schaff, 3:437–79
Scot II	*The King's Confession* [*The Second Scots Confession*], 1581	2:541–44; Böckel, 661–63; Niemeyer, 357–59; Schaff, 3:480–85
Send	*The Consensus of Sandomierz* [*Consensus Sendomiriensis*], 1570	Augusti, 254–64; Niemeyer, 553–61
Sens	*The Decrees of the Synod of Sens Against Abelard*, 1140/1141	1:733–34; Denzinger, 721–39
17 Art	*The Seventeen Articles for the Use of Visitors in Saxony*, 1527/1528	LW 40:263–320
Shema	*The Shema* of Dt 6.4–9, 11.13–21, Nm 15.37–41	1:29–31
Sheng Kung	*The Sheng Kung Hui Pastoral Letter of the Anglican Bishops of China*, 1950	3:540–42
Shkr	*The Concise Statement of the Principles of the [Shaker] Only True Church*, 1790	3:208–13
Sirm 357	*The Second [*"Blasphemy"*] Synod of Sirmium*, 357	Hahn, 161; *NPNF-II* 9:6–7
Sirm 359	*The Creed of the Fourth Synod of Sirmium*, 359, and *The Creed of Constantinople*, 360	1:96–99; Hahn, 165; *NPNF-II* 4:454
67 Art	*The Sixty-Seven Articles of Ulrich Zwingli*, 1523	2:207–14; Böckel, 3–9; Cochrane 33–44; Fabbri, 603–10; Niemeyer, 3–13; Noll, 37–46; Schaff, 3:197–207
Smal Art	*The Smalcald Articles* and *The Treatise on the Power and Primacy of the Pope*, 1537	2:119–65; *BLK* 405–68; Fabbri, 329–66; Kolb-Wengert, 297–328; Tappert, 288–318; *Triglotta* 2:453–529
Smyr	Confession of the Presbyters of Smyrna Against Noetus, c. 180–200	1:58–59

Abbreviation	Title and Date	Location
So Bap	*The Faith and Message of the Southern Baptist Convention, 1925*	3:437–44; Lumpkin, 390–400
Soc Ch	*The Social Creed of the Churches, 1908/1912/1933*	3:417–18
Socin	*Confession of Faith of Laelius Socinus [Lelio Sozini], 1555*	2:704–8
Soc Meth	*The Social Creed of Methodism, 1908*	3:415–16; *Meth Doct & Disc,* 479–81
Sri Lanka	*The Scheme of Church Union in Ceylon: Faith and Order, 1963*	3:686–99
Swed Bap	*The Confession of Faith of the Swedish Baptists, 1861*	3:321–23; Lumpkin, 407–10
Syl	*The Syllabus of Errors of Pope Pius IX, 1864*	3:324–34; Denzinger, 2901–80; *Dublin Review* (1865), 513–29; Schaff, 2:213–33
10 Art	*The Ten Articles, 1536*	2:296–310; Bray, 162–74
Tert	*The Creeds of Tertullian, c. 203–10*	1:55–57; *ANF* 3:598; Hahn, 7, 44; Leith, 21–22; Schaff, 2:16–20
Test Dom	*The Testamentum Domini, 4th–5th c.*	Denzinger, 61
Tetrapol	*The Tetrapolitan Confession, 1530*	2:218–48; Augusti, 327–68; Böckel, 363–94; Cochrane, 51–88; Niemeyer, 740–70
Thdr Mops	*The Creed of Theodore of Mopsuestia, c. 350–428*	Denzinger, 51
39 Art	*The Thirty-Nine Articles of the Church of England, 1571*	2:526–40; Augusti, 126–42; Böckel, 664–79; Bray, 285–311; Fabbri, 1017–31; Gerrish, 185–99; Leith, 266–81; Niemeyer, 601–11; Noll, 211–27; Schaff, 3:487–516
Am	*The American Revision, 1801*	
Thorn	*The Colloquy of Thorn [Collegium charitativum], 1645*	Augusti, 411–42; Niemeyer, 669–89

Abbreviation	Title and Date	Location
Tig	*The Zurich Consensus [Consensus Tigurinus]*, 1549	2:802–15; Böckel, 173–81; Niemeyer, 191–217
Togo	*The Evangelical Church of Togo: Our Faith*, 1971	3:736–37
Tol I	*The First Synod of Toledo*, 400/447	1:685–89; Denzinger, 188–208; Hahn, 168
Tol III	*The Third Synod of Toledo: The Profession of Faith of Recared*, 589	1:707–8; Denzinger, 470; Hahn, 176
Tol XI	*The Eleventh Synod of Toledo*, 675	1:715–21; Denzinger, 525–41; Hahn, 182
Tome	*The Tome of Pope Leo I*, 449	1:113–21; *COD-DEC* 77–82; Denzinger, 290–95; *NPNF*–II 14:254–58
Toraja	*Confession of the Church of Toraja*, 1981	3:798–807; Vischer, 48–58
Trans	*The Transylvanian Confession of Faith*, 1579	2:745–48; Williams, 1131–33
Trent	*The Council of Trent*, 1545–63	2:819–71; *COD-DEC* 657–799; Denzinger, 1500–1835; Gerrish, 259–92; Leith, 399–439; Noll, 165–205; Schaff, 2:77–206
Trid Prof	*The Tridentine Profession of Faith*, 1564	2:872–74; Denzinger, 1862–70; Leith, 439–42; Noll, 207–10; Schaff, 2:207–10
True Con	*A True Confession of the English Separatists (Brownists)*, 1596	3:31–46; Lumpkin, 79–97; Walker, 41–74
UCC	*The Statement of Faith of the United Church of Christ*, 1959/1981	3:566–67
Ulph	*The Confession of Ulphilas*, 383	1:102–4; Hahn, 198
Unam	*Unam Sanctam of Pope Boniface VIII*, 1302	1:745–47; Denzinger, 870–75
Un Ch Can: Crd	*New Creed of the United Church of Canada*, 1968/1980/1994	3:730–31

Abbreviation	Title and Date	Location
Un Ch Can: Union	*The Basis of Union of the United Church of Canada, 1925*	**3:445-52**; Schaff, 3:935-38
Un Ch Japan	*United Church of Christ in Japan: The Confession of Faith, 1954*	**3:556-57**; Anderson, 253-54
Un Pres	*The Confessional Statement of the United Presbyterian Church of North America, 1925*	**3:453-70**
Un Ref Ch	*United Reformed Church (The Reformed Association of the Church of Christ in Britain): The Basis of Union, 1972/ 1981/1997/2000*	**3:738-41**; Moss, 281-82
Utrecht	*The Old Catholic Declaration of Utrecht, 1889*	**3:393-96**
Vald	*The Profession of Faith of Valdes, 1180*	**1:769-73**
Vat I	*The First Vatican Council, 1869-70*	**3:341-58**; COD-DEC 811-16; Denzinger, 3000-3075; Leith, 447-57; Schaff, 2:234-71
Vat II	*The Second Vatican Council, 1962-65*	**3:570-673**; COD-DEC 817-1135; Denzinger, 4001-345
Vienne	*The Council of Vienne: Decree on the Foundation of the Catholic Faith, 1311-12*	**1:748-50**; COD-DEC 360-61; Denzinger, 900-904
Wald	*The Confession of the Waldenses, 1655*	**1:774-80**; Fabbri, 991-1016; Schaff, 3:757-70
Wash	*The Washington Profession of the Unitarian General Convention, 1935*	**3:509-10**; Robinson 1970, 160
WCC	*The Doctrinal Basis of the World Council of Churches, 1948/1961*	**3:532-33**; Leith, 574-77
West	*The Westminster Confession of Faith, 1647*	**2:601-49**; Bray, 487-520; Fabbri, 938-88; Leith, 192-230; Schaff, 3:600-673

Abbreviation	Title and Date	Location
Am	*The American Revision,* 1729	
West Sh Cat	*The Westminster Shorter Catechism,* 1648	**2:650–62**; Schaff, 3:674–703
Winch	*The Winchester [Universalist] Profession,* 1803	**3:217–18**
Witness	*Statement of Faith of the Jehovah's Witnesses,* 1918	**3:432–34**
Witt Art	*The Wittenberg Articles,* 1536	CD-ROM; Bray, 119–61
Witt Conc	*The Wittenberg Concord,* 1536	**2:796–801**
Wrt	*The Württemberg Confession,* 1552	Reu, 2:418–24
Wyclif	*John Wycliffe: A Confession on the Eucharist,* 1382	**1:781–83**
Zambia	*The Constitution of the United Church of Zambia,* 1965/1984	**3:709–11**

act	acts
anath	anathema
art	article
can	canon
ch	chapter
con	conclusion
decr	decree
def	definition
ecth	ecthesis
ep	epistle
int	introduction
par	paragraph
pr	preface
q	question
st	stanza
ttl	title

Editions, Collections, Journals, and Reference Works

ABD	*The Anchor Bible Dictionary.* Edited by David Noel Freedman. 6 vols. New York: Doubleday, 1992.
ACO	*Acta Conciliorum Oecumenicorum.* Series I edited by E. Schwartz and J. Straub. Strassburg: Wissenschaftliche Gesellschaft in Strassburg, 1914; Berlin: W. de Gruyter, 1922–84. Series II edited sub auspiciis Academiae Scientiarum Bavaricae. Berlin: 1984–.
ACW	*Ancient Christian Writers.* Edited by Johannes Quasten et al. 58 volumes to date. Westminster, Md.: Newman Press, 1946–.
Anderson	Anderson, Gerald H., ed. *Asian Voices in Christian Theology.* Maryknoll, N.Y.: Orbis Books, 1976.
ANF	*The Ante-Nicene Fathers.* Alexander Roberts and James Donaldson, editors. Reprint ed. 10 vols. Grand Rapids, Mich.: William B. Eerdmans, 1950, etc.
ARG	*Archiv für Reformationsgeschichte*
Augusti	Augusti, Johann Christian Wilhelm, ed. *Corpus Librorum Symbolicorum qui in Ecclesia Reformatorum auctoritatem publicam obtinuerunt.* Elberfeld: Bueschler, 1827.
Bakhuizen van den Brink	Bakhuizen van den Brink, J. N. *De Nederlandse Belijdenisgeschriften.* Amsterdam: Bolland, 1976.
Bauer-Arndt-Gingrich	Bauer, Walter. *A Greek-English Lexicon of the New Testament and Other Early Christian Literature.* Translated and adapted by William F. Arndt and F. Wilbur Gingrich. 2d ed. Chicago: University of Chicago Press, 1979.
Bauman	Bauman, Clarence, ed. *The Spiritual Legacy of Hans Denck.* Leiden: E. J. Brill, 1991.
Beck	Beck, Hans-Georg. *Kirche und theologische Literatur im byzantinischen Reich.* Munich: C. H. Beck'sche Verlagsbuchhandlung, 1959.
Blaise-Chirat	Blaise, Albert, and Henri Chirat. *Dictionnaire latin-français des auteurs chrétiens.* Strasbourg: Le Latin Chrétien.

Blass- Debrunner	Blass, Friedrich, and Albert Debrunner. *A Greek Grammar of the New Testament and Other Early Christian Literature.* Edited and translated by Robert W. Funk. Chicago: University of Chicago Press, 1961.
BLK	*Die Bekenntnisschriften der evangelisch-lutherischen Kirche.* 11th ed. Göttingen: Vandenhoeck und Ruprecht, 1992.
Blunt	Blunt, John Henry, ed. *The Annotated Book of Common Prayer, Being an Historical, Ritual, and Theological Commentary on the Devotional System of the Church of England.* Revised ed. New York: E. P. Dutton, 1903.
Böckel	Böckel, Ernst Gottfried Adolf, ed. *Die Bekenntniszschriften der evangelisch-reformirten Kirche.* Leipzig: F. A. Brockaus, 1847.
Bray	Bray, Gerald Lewis, ed. *Documents of the English Reformation.* Minneapolis, Minn.: Fortress Press, 1994.
Brightman	Brightman, Frank Edward, ed. *Liturgies Eastern and Western.* Oxford: Clarendon Press, 1896.
BZ	*Byzantinische Zeitschrift*
Caspari	Caspari, Carl Paul, ed. *Alte und neue Quellen zur Geschichte des Taufsymbols und der Glaubensregel.* Christiania: Mallingische Buchdruckerei, 1879.
CCCM	*Corpus Christianorum, Continuatio Mediaevalis.* 1953–. Turnhout: Brepols.
CCSL	*Corpus Christianorum, Series Latina.* Turnhout: Brepols, 1953–.
Chr Trad	*The Christian Tradition: A History of the Development of Doctrine.* By Jaroslav Pelikan. 5 vols. Chicago: University of Chicago Press, 1971–89.
Cochrane	Cochrane, Arthur C., ed. *Reformed Confessions of the Sixteenth Century.* Philadelphia: Westminster Press, 1966.
COD	*Conciliorum Oecumenicorum Decreta.* Edited by Joseph Alberigo et al. 3d ed. Bologna: Istituto per le scienze religiose, 1973. (Pagination identical with that of *DEC.*)
CR	*Corpus Reformatorum.* Edited by Carl Gottlieb Bretschneider. Berlin: C. A. Schwetschke, 1834–1900.
CSEL	*Corpus Scriptorum Ecclesiasticorum Latinorum.* Vienna: Hoelder-Pichler-Tempsky, 1866–.

CWS	*The Classics of Western Spirituality.* Edited by John Farina. 104 volumes to date. New York: Paulist Press, 1978–.
Day	Day, Peter D., ed. *The Liturgical Dictionary of Eastern Christianity.* Collegeville, Minn.: Liturgical Press, 1993.
DEC	*Decrees of the Ecumenical Councils.* Edited by Norman P. Tanner et al. 2 vols. Washington, D.C.: Georgetown University Press, 1990. (Pagination identical with that of *COD*.)
DECH	*Dictionary of English Church History.* 2d ed. by S. L. Ollard and G. Crosse. London: A. R. Mowbray, [1919].
DEM	*Dictionary of the Ecumenical Movement.* Edited by Nicholas Lossky, José Míguez Bonino, John Pobec, Tom Stransky, Geoffrey Wainwright, and Pauline Webb. Grand Rapids, Mich.: William B. Eerdmans, 1991.
Denzinger	Denzinger, Heinrich, ed. *Enchiridion symbolorum definitionum et declarationum de rebus fidei et morum.* [1854.] 37th ed. Edited by Peter Hünermann. Freiburg: Herder, 1991. (Cited by paragraph numbers.)
DNB	*Dictionary of National Biography*
Doct Dec	*Doctrinal Declarations of the Lutheran Churches.* Saint Louis, Mo.: Concordia, 1957.
Donovan	Donovan, Vincent J. *Christianity Rediscovered.* 2d ed. Maryknoll, N.Y.: Orbis Books, 1982.
Dossetti	Dossetti, Giuseppe Luigi, ed. *Il simbolo di Nicea e di Costantinopoli: Edizione critica.* Rome: Herder, 1967.
DTC	*Dictionnaire de théologie catholique.* Edited by Alfred Vacant, Emile Mangenot, and Emile Amann (15 vols., 1903–50); and "Tables Générales," edited by B. Loth and A. Michel (3 vols., 1951–72). Paris: Libraire Letouzey et Ané.
EC	*The Encyclopedia of Christianity.* Edited by Erwin Fahlbusch, Jan Milič Lochman, John Mbiti, Jaroslav Pelikan, and Lukas Vischer. Translated by Geoffrey W. Bromiley. Foreword by Jaroslav Pelikan. Grand Rapids, Mich.: William B. Eerdmans, 1999–.
EEC	*Encyclopedia of Early Christianity.* 2d ed. Edited by Everett Ferguson. New York: Garland, 1998.
EKL	*Evangelisches Kirchenlexikon: Internationale Theologische Enzyklopädie.* Edited by Erwin Fahlbusch. Göttingen: Vandenhoeck und Ruprecht, 1985–.

ER	*Ecumenical Review*
Fabbri	Fabbri, Romeo, ed. *Confessioni di fede delle chiese cristiane.* Bologna: Edizioni Dehoniane, 1996.
Fabricius	Fabricius, Cajus, ed. *Corpus Confessionum: Die Bekenntnisse der Christenheit.* Berlin: De Gruyter, 1928–43.
FC	*Fontes Christiani: Zweisprachige Neuausgabe christlicher Quellentexte aus Altertum und Mittelalter.* Edited by Norbert Brox, Wilhelm Geerlings, Gisbert Greshake, Rainer Ilgner, and Rudolf Schieffer. Freiburg, Basel, etc.: Herder, 1991–.
FOTC	*Fathers of the Church.* Washington, D.C.: Catholic University of America Press, 1947–.
Gass	Gass, Wilhelm. *Symbolik der griechischen Kirche.* Berlin: Reimer, 1872.
GCS	*Die griechischen christlichen Schriftsteller der ersten Jahrhunderte.* Leipzig and Berlin: Akademie-Verlag, 1897–.
Gerrish	Gerrish, Brian A., ed. *The Faith of Christendom: A Source Book of Creeds and Confessions.* New York: World Publishing, 1963.
GOTR	*Greek Orthodox Theological Review*
Gr Agr	*Growth in Agreement: Reports and Agreed Statements of Ecumenical Conversations on a World Level.* Edited by Harding Meyer and Lukas Vischer. Geneva: World Council of Churches; New York: Paulist Press, 1984.
Gr Agr II	*Growth in Agreement II: Reports and Agreed Statements of Ecumenical Conversations on a World Level, 1982–1988.* Edited by Jeffrey Gros, Harding Meyer, and William G. Rusch. Geneva: World Council of Churches; Grand Rapids, Mich.: William B. Eerdmans, 2000.
Hahn	Hahn, August. *Bibliothek der Symbole und Glaubensregeln der Alten Kirche.* 3d ed. Edited by G. Ludwig Hahn. Foreword by Adolf Harnack. [1897.] Reprint ed. Hildesheim: Georg Olms Verlagsbuchhandlung, 1962. (Cited by document numbers.)
Hefele	Hefele, Karl Joseph. *A History of the Councils of the Church from the Original Documents.* English translation of vols. 1–6 of 2d ed. by William Robinson Clark (vol. 1) and Henry Nutcombe Oxenham (vols. 2–6). Reprint, New York: AMS Press, 1972.

Hefele-Leclercq	Hefele, Charles Joseph, and Henri Leclercq. *Histoire des conciles d'après les documents originaux.* 11 vols. Paris: Letouzey et Ané, 1907–52.
Henke	Henke, Ernst Ludwig Theodor, ed. *Theologorum Saxonicorum consensus repetitus fidei vere Lutheranae.* Marburg: Typis Elwerti Academicis, 1846.
Holy Cross	*Hē Theia Leitourgia: The Divine Liturgy.* Brookline, Mass.: Holy Cross Orthodox Press, 1985.
Horst	Horst, Irvin B., ed. and tr. *Mennonite Confession of Faith Adopted April 21st, 1632, at Dordrecht, The Netherlands.* Lancaster, Pa.: Lancaster Mennonite Historical Society, 1988.
JTS	*Journal of Theological Studies*
Kallis	Kallis, Anastasios, ed. *Liturgie: Die Göttliche Liturgie der Orthodoxen Kirche Deutsch-Griechisch-Kirchenslawisch.* Mainz: Matthias-Grünewald-Verlag, 1989.
Karmirēs	Karmirēs, Ioannēs. *Ta dogmatika kai symbolika mnēmeia tēs orthodoxou katholikēs ekklēsias* [The dogmatic and symbolic monuments of the Orthodox Catholic Church]. 2 vols., 2d ed. Graz: Akademische Druck- und Verlagsanstalt, 1968. (Cited by page numbers of this edition.)
Kelly	Kelly, John Norman Davidson. *Early Christian Creeds.* 3d ed. London: Longman Group, 1972.
Kimmel	Kimmel, Ernst Julius, ed. *Libri symbolici ecclesiae orientalis; Appendix,* ed. H. J. C. Weissenborn. Jena: Apud Carolum Hochhausenium, 1843–50.
Kokkinakis	Kokkinakis, Athenagoras, ed. and tr. *The Liturgy of the Orthodox Church.* London: Mowbrays, 1979.
Kolb-Wengert	Kolb, Robert, and Timothy J. Wengert, eds. *The Book of Concord: The Confessions of the Evangelical Lutheran Church.* Minneapolis, Minn.: Fortress Press, 2000.
Lacoste	Lacoste, Jean-Yves, ed. *Dictionnaire critique de théologie.* Paris: Presses Universitaires de France, 1998.
Lampe	Lampe, Geoffrey W. H., ed. *A Patristic Greek Lexicon.* Oxford: Clarendon Press, 1961.
LCC	*Library of Christian Classics.* 26 vols. Philadelphia: Westminster Press, 1953–66.
LCL	*Loeb Classical Library*

Leith   Leith, John H., ed. *Creeds of the Churches: A Reader in Christian Doctrine from the Bible to the Present.* Garden City, N.Y.: Doubleday, 1963.

Link   Link, Hans-Georg, ed. *Confessing Our Faith Around the World.* 4 vols. Geneva: World Council of Churches, 1980–85.

Loewen   Loewen, Howard John, ed. *One Lord, One Church, One Hope, and One God: Mennonite Confessions of Faith.* Elkhart, Ind.: Institute of Mennonite Studies, 1985.

LTK   *Lexikon für Theologie und Kirche.* Edited by Josef Höfer and Karl Rahner. 2d ed. 10 vols. and index. Freiburg: Herder, 1957–67.

Lumpkin   Lumpkin, William L., ed. *Baptist Confessions of Faith.* Revised ed. Valley Forge, Pa.: Judson Press, 1969.

McGlothlin   McGlothlin, William Joseph, ed. *Baptist Confessions of Faith.* Philadelphia: American Baptist Publication Society, 1911.

Malvy-Viller   Malvy, Antoine, and Marcel Viller, eds. *La confession orthodoxe de Pierre Moghila.* Rome: Orientalia Christiana Analecta, 1927.

Mansi   Mansi, Giovanni Domenico, ed. *Sacrorum conciliorum nova et amplissima collectio.* 31 vols. Florence: Antonio Zatta, 1759–98.

Marthaler   Marthaler, Berard L. *The Creed.* Mystic, Conn.: Twenty-Third Publications, 1987.

Mastrantonis   Mastrantonis, George, ed. *Augsburg and Constantinople: The Correspondence Between the Tübingen Theologians and Patriarch Jeremiah II of Constantinople on the Augsburg Confession.* Brookline, Mass.: Holy Cross Orthodox Press, 1982.

ME   *The Mennonite Encyclopedia: A Comprehensive Reference Work on the Anabaptist-Mennonite Movement.* Hillsboro, Kans.: Mennonite Brethren Publishing House, 1955–90.

Meth Doct &   *The Doctrines and Discipline of the Methodist Episcopal*
   Disc   *Church.* New York: Eaton and Mains, 1908.

MGH   *Monumenta Germaniae Historica*

Michalcescu   Michalcescu, Jon, ed. *Thēsauros tēs Orthodoxias: Die Bekenntnisse und die wichtigsten Glaubenszeugnisse der griechisch-orientalischen Kirche.* Introduction by Albert Hauck. Leipzig: J. C. Hinrichs, 1904.

ML *Mennonitisches Lexikon.* Edited by Christian Hege and Christian Neff. 4 vols. Frankfurt: [n.p.], 1913–67.

MQR *Mennonite Quarterly Review*

Müller Müller, E. F. Karl. *Die Bekenntnisschriften der reformierten Kirche in authentischen Texten mit geschichtlicher Einleitung und Register.* Leipzig: A. Deichert, 1903. Reprint, Zurich: Theologische Buchhandlung, 1987.

Nestle/Aland *Greek-English New Testament.* Edited by Eberhard and Erwin Nestle, revised by Barbara and Kurt Aland. With English translation of the Revised Standard Version. Stuttgart: Deutsche Bibelstiftung, 1994.

Niemeyer Niemeyer, Hermann Agathon, ed. *Collectio Confessionum in Ecclesiis Reformatis Publicatarum.* Leipzig: Julius Klinkhardt, 1840.

Niesel Niesel, Wilhelm, ed. *Bekenntnisschriften und Kirchenordnungen der nach Gottes Wort reformierten Kirche.* Munich: Christian Kaiser Verlag, [1938].

Noll Noll, Mark A., ed. *Confessions and Catechisms of the Reformation.* Grand Rapids, Mich.: Baker Book House, 1991.

NPNF *A Select Library of the Nicene and Post-Nicene Fathers of the Christian Church.* First and Second Series. Reprint ed. 22 vols. Grand Rapids, Mich.: William B. Eerdmans, 1956.

NRSV *The Holy Bible: Containing the Old and New Testaments with the Apocryphal/Deuterocanonical Books.* Edited by the NRSV Bible Translation Committee, Bruce M. Metzger, Chair. New York: Oxford University Press, 1989.

OCA *The Divine Liturgy According to St. John Chrysostom, with Appendices.* The Orthodox Church in America. 2d ed. South Canaan, Pa.: St. Tikhon's Seminary Press, 1977.

ODCC *The Oxford Dictionary of the Christian Church.* 3d ed. Edited by F. L. Cross and E. A. Livingstone. Oxford: Oxford University Press, 1997.

OED *A New [Oxford] English Dictionary on Historical Principles.* Edited by J. A. H. Murray, H. Bradley, W. A. Craigie, and C. T. Onions. 12 vols. and 4 vols. of Supplement. Oxford: Oxford University Press, 1884–1933.

OER   *Oxford Encyclopedia of the Reformation*. Hans Hillerbrand,
                      editor-in-chief. 4 vols. Oxford: Oxford University Press,
                      1996.

Overbeck   Overbeck, J. J., ed. *The Orthodox Confession of the Catholic
                      and Apostolic Eastern Church from the Version of Peter Mogila*.
                      London: Thomas Baker, 1898.

Pelikan   Pelikan, Jaroslav. "Luther and the *Confessio Bohemica*." Ph.D.
                      diss., University of Chicago, 1946.

PG   *Patrologia Graeca*. Edited by Jacques Paul Migne. 162 vols.
                      Paris: Lutetiae Parisiorum, 1857–66.

PL   *Patrologia Latina*. Edited by Jacques Paul Migne. 221 vols.
                      Paris: Lutetiae Parisiorum, 1844–64.

PO   *Patrologia Orientalis*. Edited by René Graffin and François
                      Nau. Paris: Firmin-Didot, 1907–66.

Prav Slov   *Polnyj pravoslavný bogoslovský enciklopedičeský slovar'* [Com-
                      plete encyclopedic dictionary of Orthodox theology]. 1913.
                      Reprint ed. London: Variorum Reprints, 1971.

PRE   Johann Jakob Herzog and Albert Hauck, eds., *Realencyklopä-
                      die für protestantische Theologie und Kirche*. 3d ed. 21 vols.
                      and index. Leipzig: J. C. Hinrichs'sche Buchhandlung,
                      1896–1909.

Quasten   Quasten, Johannes, et al. *Patrology*. 4 vols. Westminster, Md.:
                      Newman Press and Christian Classics, 1951–86.

Raby   Raby, F. J. E., ed. *The Oxford Book of Medieval Latin Verse*.
                      Oxford: Clarendon Press, 1959.

Rahner-   Rahner, Karl, and Herbert Vorgrimler. *Theological Dictionary*.
  Vorgrimler   Edited by Cornelius Ernst. Translated by Richard Strachan.
                      New York: Herder and Herder, 1965.

Rees   Rees, Thomas, tr. *The Racovian Catechism, with Notes and
                      Illustrations*. London: Longman, Hurst, Rees, Orme, and
                      Brown, 1818.

Reu   Reu, J. Michael, ed. *The Augsburg Confession: A Collection
                      of Sources with an Historical Introduction*. 2 vols. Chicago:
                      Wartburg Publishing House, 1930.

Robertson   Robertson, J. N. W. B., ed. and tr. *The Acts and Decrees
                      of the Synod of Jerusalem, Sometimes Called the Council of
                      Bethlehem, Holden under Dositheus, Patriarch of Jerusalem in
                      1672*. London: Thomas Baker, 1899.

SC	*Sources chrétiennes.* Henri de Lubac and Jean Daniélou, founding eds. Paris: Editions du Cerf, 1942–.
Schaff	Schaff, Philip, ed. *Bibliotheca Symbolica Ecclesiae Universalis: The Creeds of Christendom.* 3 vols. New York: Harper and Brothers, 1877. 6th ed., by David S. Schaff. Reprint ed. Grand Rapids, Mich.: Baker Book House, 1990.
Schmidt-Schornbaum	Schmidt, Wilhelm Ferdinand, and Karl Schornbaum, eds. *Die fränkischen Bekenntnisse: Eine Vorstufe der Augsburgischen Konfession.* Munich: Christian Kaiser Verlag, 1930.
Schwartz	Schwartz, Eduard, ed. *Drei dogmatische Schriften Iustinians.* Munich: Bayerische Akademie der Wissenschaften, 1939.
Sophocles	Sophocles, Evangelinus Apostolides, ed. *Greek Lexicon of the Roman and Byzantine Periods (From B.C. 146 to A.D. 1100).* Boston: Little, Brown, 1870.
Tappert	Tappert, Theodore G., Jaroslav Pelikan, Robert H. Fischer, and Arthur Carl Piepkorn, ed. and tr. *The Book of Concord: The Confessions of the Evangelical Lutheran Church.* Philadelphia: Muhlenberg Press, 1959.
Torrance	Torrance, Thomas F., ed. *The School of Faith: The Catechisms of the Reformed Church.* New York: Harper and Brothers, 1959.
TRE	*Theologische Realenzyclopädie.* Edited by G. Krause, G. Müller, et al. Berlin: de Gruyter, 1976–.
Triglotta	*Concordia Triglotta.* Edited by G. Friedrich Bente. 2 vols. in 1. Saint Louis, Mo.: Concordia Publishing House, 1921.
Underhill	Underhill, Edward Bean, ed. *Confessions of Faith and Other Public Documents Illustrative of the History of the Baptist Churches of England in the Seventeenth Century.* London: Hanserd Knollys Society, 1854.
Vischer	Vischer, Lukas, ed. *Reformed Witness Today: A Collection of Confessions and Statements of Faith Issued by Reformed Churches.* Bern: Evangelische Arbeitsstelle Oekumene Schweiz, 1982.
WA	Luther, Martin. *Werke. Kritische Gesamtausgabe.* Weimar: Bohlau, etc., 1883–.
Walker	Walker, Williston, ed. *The Creeds and Platforms of Congregationalism.* [1893.] Reprint ed. Introduction by Douglas Horton. Boston: Pilgrim Press, 1960.

Wesche   Wesche, Kenneth Paul, ed. and tr. *On the Person of Christ:*
                The Christology of Emperor Justinian. Crestwood, N.Y.: Saint
                Vladimir's Seminary Press, 1991.
Will   Will, Cornelius, ed. *Acta et scripta quae de controversiis eccle-*
                siae Graecae et Latinae saeculo undecimo composita extant.
                [1861.] Reprint ed. Frankfurt: Minerva, 1963.
Williams   Williams, George Huntston. *The Radical Reformation.* 3d ed.
                Kirksville, Mo.: Sixteenth Century Journal Publishers, 1992.
ZfKT   *Zeitschrift für Katholische Theologie*
ZKG   *Zeitschrift für Kirchengeschichte*

IV

Creeds and Confessions of the Reformation Era

Introduction

When descendants of the Protestant Reformation use the word "creed," it is a designation for one or another of "the three creeds, Nicene Creed, Athanasius's Creed, and that which is commonly called the Apostles' Creed,"[1] which are listed in *The Thirty-Nine Articles of the Church of England* and in other confessions,[2] and which these churches share with Western Christendom generally. Most often, at least in common Protestant usage, "the Creed" has referred to the third of these, *The Apostles' Creed*, which *The Second Helvetic Confession* calls a "compendium" of Scripture.[3] But when Lutherans, Anglicans, or Presbyterians use the word "confession," or even "*the* confessions," that usually means the particular confession or confessions of their own church or branch of Protestantism, as when *The Canons of the Synod of Dort* make a cross-reference to "the confessions of the Reformed churches," which readers are urged to consult,[4] or when the Congregationalist *Declaration of the Boston National Council* speaks of "the confessions and platforms which our synods of 1648 and 1680 set forth or reaffirmed."[5] Specifically in the case of Lutherans, Anglicans, and Presbyterians, "confession" refers to *The Augsburg Confession* of 1530 (and the entire *Book of Concord* of 1580) for Lutherans, or to *The Thirty-Nine Articles of the Church of England* of 1571 for Anglicans (although this confession and its predecessors and successors are ordinarily designated by Anglicans as "the Articles"[6] rather than as "the confession"), or to *The Westminster Confession of Faith* of 1647 for Presbyterians. All three of these "confessions" are products of the Reformation era. Sometimes, however, both groups of authoritative texts, the universal "creeds" of the early church and the particular "confessions" of the Reformation churches, can be referred to together by the ancient title "symbols."[7]

Necessary though it is, this distinction between "creeds" and "confessions of faith," which also appears in the title of this set, is somewhat arbitrary and historically inconsistent, because the ancient creeds, too, can sometimes be called

---

1. *39 Art* 8.
2. *BLK* 21; *Form Conc Sol Dec* 12.37.
3. *Helv II* 17.17.
4. *Dort* con.
5. *Boston* pr.
6. *OED* 1–I:470; *ODCC* 112.
7. *Form Conc Epit* 1.2–3.

"confessions [*confessiones*],"[8] although the converse is not true and the Reformation confessions are not usually called "creeds."[9] In spite of some precedents in earlier formularies, most notably in such documents as *The Decree for the Armenians of the Council of Florence* of 22 November 1439, it was with the Reformation of the sixteenth century that "confession of faith" as a theological and literary form distinct from "creed" came into its own and achieved dominance. So dominant did it in fact become that in the seventeenth century Eastern Orthodoxy would employ the title *Confession [Homologia]* for the several systematizations of its own doctrinal position over against both Roman Catholicism and the various subdivisions of Protestantism (most of which by then had themselves formulated their doctrinal positions in such "confessions"). The so-called *Eastern Confession of the Christian Faith by Cyril Lucar* of 1629 was repudiated by the Orthodox for the Protestantizing tendencies of its teaching on such questions as the authority of Scripture alone and the number of the sacraments, but not for its appropriation of the Protestant style of setting forth a series of articles on the major doctrines, which, for example, *The Orthodox Confession of the Catholic and Apostolic Eastern Church by Peter Mogila* of 1638 and *The Confession of Dositheus* of 1672 also follow, as *The Confession of Metrophanes Critopoulos* of 1625 already does—all three of these latter being Eastern Orthodox "confessions" that were, and are, more or less officially approved.

Such comparisons suggest that in some respects it is possible, with a due measure of qualification and nuance, to treat the sixteenth and seventeenth centuries in all the Christian denominations, even beyond Protestantism, as a distinct historical period called "the confessional age."[10] The vertical divisions—between Eastern Orthodoxy and Western Christianity, or between Roman Catholicism and Protestantism, or between Lutheranism, Calvinism, and Anglicanism, or between Magisterial Protestantism and Radical Protestantism—do provide a natural taxonomy, and in some respects an unavoidable one, for presenting and studying confessions of faith, above all those from the period of the Reformation. But there are also horizontal differences from one historical period to another: in some decisive respects the era of Reformed Pietism bears greater similarities to the era of Lutheran Pietism than either of these does to the era of confessional scholasticism, which came before Pietism and after the Reformation in both Reformed and Lutheran churches. Such a schema of periodization does fit Roman Catholicism and Radical Protestantism less neatly than it does Calvinism and Lutheranism, and Eastern Orthodoxy less

8. *Form Conc Epit* pr 2.
9. One exception is Piepkorn 1993, 20.
10. Reinhard 1977.

neatly still, for a variety of reasons. But at any rate for the history of confessions of faith during the age of the Reformation, there is enough coherence in it to justify a treatment here that considers together the confessions coming from the several Western denominations during the same period.

The Proliferation of Confessions in the Age of the Reformation

The comparative page count of this Part Four of *Creeds and Confessions of Faith in the Christian Tradition* (which takes up a good deal of the total set), when set alongside any of the three preceding parts, or even alongside all of them together, is an indication of the quantum leap in the production of confessions of faith that took place during the sixteenth and seventeenth centuries. And what is collected here is only a fraction of the total number of Reformation confessions. The texts in three standard nineteenth- and twentieth-century collections of Reformation confessions in their original languages—the Reformed *Collectio Confessionum in Ecclesiis Reformatis Publicatarum* edited by H. A. Niemeyer and published in 1840, the Lutheran *Die Bekenntnisschriften der evangelisch-lutherischen Kirche* as prepared for the four-hundredth anniversary of *The Augsburg Confession* in 1930 and reissued with minor revisions several times since, and the Anglican *Documents of the English Reformation* edited by Gerald Bray in 1994—add up, with few overlapping documents between the three volumes, to almost three thousand pages; and the first and third of these, too, are also only a selection. For example, for the German territory of Franconia alone and only for the period leading up to *The Augsburg Confession* of 1530, Wilhelm Ferdinand Schmidt and Karl Schornbaum were able to compile five hundred pages of confessional texts.[11] As is evident from the collections of Ernst Gottfried Adolf Böckel and E. F. Karl Müller,[12] it is particularly for the Reformed churches that any collection of confessions must be only a selection. For the Dutch Reformation alone, and only for the sixteenth century, the detailed bibliography by Heijting comes to two solid volumes.[13] The importance of confessions for the age of the Reformation, and the importance of the age of the Reformation for confessions, may also be gauged from the prominence of references to Reformation confessions and quotations from them in any discussion of creeds and confessions. The issue of confessional subscription, for example, has been formulated and debated on the basis of the authority of confessions coming out of the sixteenth and seventeenth

11. Schmidt-Schornbaum, 157–655.
12. Böckel; Müller.
13. Heijting 1989.

centuries, even though the questions it raises are applicable to all creeds and confessions of faith from all centuries. It has also been in the interpretation of these same Reformation confessions that the principles and methods for interpreting confessions generally have been worked out.

Just as it must seem historically puzzling in many ways that there were so few creeds and confessions in the Orthodox East during the millennium preceding the appearance of the modern seventeenth-century texts bearing the title *Homologia,* so also there does not appear to be any easy or obvious explanation for the opposite phenomenon here, the rise of confessions and then their proliferation just at the time of the Protestant Reformation. Like the corollary phenomenon of the rise and proliferation of vernacular Bibles during the same period and under many of the same auspices in Germany, England, and elsewhere, it would not have been possible, or at any rate would not have been so successful, without the recent invention of printing in the fifteenth century. One need only imagine what a tedious and costly undertaking it would have been to produce by the copyist's hand the many sets that were circulated even of brief Reformation confessions,[14] not to speak of such compendious texts as *The Formula of Concord* in its *Solid Declaration* of 1577 or the entire *Book of Concord* of 1580 or *The Westminster Confession of Faith* of 1647 (also because the churches from which these confessions issued had meanwhile abolished the monastic communities on whose scriptoria such copying had depended in the Middle Ages). Both the confession as a printed book and the vernacular Bible as a printed book, moreover, were expressions of the fundamental Reformation conviction, as articulated by these confessions, that the correct interpretation of Scripture and the correct declaration of its doctrinal content are a right and a responsibility of the total church, of the laity as well as the clergy, not of the clergy or the theologians alone: the Bible has to speak *to* all the people, the confession has to speak *for* all the people. As each major shift in what was taken to be the correct interpretation of Scripture led in turn to a new form for the correct declaration of its doctrinal content, the result would often be the formulation of a new confession, either within the same Reformation church or party, or otherwise in a new movement or even a new church arising as a result of the controversy—a process that does not end in the period of the Reformation but continues into the modern era and spreads to all parts of the globe.

One possible negative explanation for this growth of confessions is the corresponding decline, just as the Reformation was erupting, in the credibility and standing of the institution of the church council, which in the classic period of

14. *Dordrecht* con.

Christian history had served as the primary agency for the church to affirm definitively what it believed, taught, and confessed. It had been such an agency preeminently between 325, the date of the First Council of Nicaea, and 787, the date of the Second Council of Nicaea: the doctrinal decrees of the first seven "ecumenical" councils remained the common foundation of church dogma for the Orthodox East and the Catholic West even after the two churches were separated by the schism; and in a special way, the first four of those seven councils (Nicaea I in 325, Constantinople I in 381, Ephesus in 431, and Chalcedon in 451),[15] albeit with a considerable amount of picking and choosing by the various groups, were held in common by the Magisterial Protestant churches not only with the Catholic West and the Orthodox East, but even with one another. After the schism between East and West, the East did not—and, in a real sense, could not, for theological, canonical, and political reasons—summon a truly "ecumenical" council on its own to deal with issues of doctrine or discipline.[16] During the Western Middle Ages, in sharp contrast, the West felt free to do just that on its own, convoking several such councils and identifying them as "ecumenical"; the most notable of all of these was the Fourth Lateran Council of 1215 under Pope Innocent III, at which several distinctively Western teachings, above all the doctrine of transubstantiation, achieved their binding form.[17] The four (or five) reform councils assembled by the Western church during the single century from 1409 to 1512 were an attempt, seen as a last chance by some but by others as no more than a quixotic and desperate effort,[18] to employ the instrumentality of the council for the solution of a range of doctrinal and disciplinary problems within Western Christendom, as well as for the most recent and ultimately unsuccessful attempts, after the failure of such medieval gatherings as the Council of Lyons in 1274, at healing the East-West schism: the Council of Pisa of 1409 (not usually counted as ecumenical in the West, because it was not convoked by a pope); the Council of Constance of 1414–18; the Council of Basel of 1431–49; the Council of Florence of 1438–45 (the canonically valid and therefore legitimately "ecumenical" sessions of Basel-Ferrara-Florence-Rome now usually being counted in Roman Catholic canon law as a single ecumenical council, the seventeenth); and the Fifth Lateran Council of 1512–17.[19] The "ecumenical" standing of some of these fifteenth-century reform councils, or in some cases of individual sessions of these

15. *10 Art* 1.5; *Helv II* 11.18.
16. Kartašev 1932.
17. *Lat 1215* 1.
18. *Chr Trad* 4:69–126.
19. Tierney 1998.

councils, has continued to be a matter of debate in Western theology and canon law, chiefly because of their legislation on the relative authority of pope and council.[20]

Regardless of how they are counted, however, there were more church councils held in the West during that one century before the Protestant Reformation than there have been ever since that time, even though the time span from the Reformation to the present is almost exactly the same as the period covered by all seven ecumenical councils between 325 and 787. The crisis of the Reformation had reawakened the hope among some Roman Catholics and even some Protestants that a truly universal council might be the forum for the adjudication of old and new doctrinal issues, as well as for the consideration of the new challenges being raised by Luther and the other Protestant Reformers.[21] In response to the condemnations of themselves and of their party by the pope, Reformation leaders repeatedly appealed from the actions of popes and bishops to such a council; and some of the early confessions, for example, Luther's *Smalcald Articles* of 1537, were part of that appellate process.[22] The repeated assertions by the decrees of such fifteenth-century reform councils as Constance and Basel that a council has ultimate authority even over the pope did little to commend the council to the papacy of the Reformation era as a mechanism for action or reform, and the project of another reform council moved from delays to fits and starts and back again. The opinions of theologians and churchmen in the sixteenth century, and of historians since the sixteenth century, vary greatly on the question of whether such a general council—if it had been called in timely fashion and if it had been permitted to become a forum for candid and fraternal debate—might conceivably have reversed the schism (or schisms) of the Reformation before it was too late; the modest achievements of the Fifth Lateran Council of 1512–17 do not support an unequivocally affirmative answer to that question. But the Council of Trent did not meet for its first session until 13 December 1545, just two months before Martin Luther died; and another eighteen years and twenty-five sessions were required until it adjourned on 4 December 1563, with many important issues left unsolved and in some instances even unaddressed. For these and other reasons, the church council did not serve as the principal venue for confessing what was believed and taught in the conflicts between Protestantism and Roman Catholicism, nor even in the continuing conflicts within Roman Catholicism: there was a hiatus of just over three centuries between the adjournment of the Council of Trent in 1563 and the assembling of the First Vatican Council in 1869—the very same cen-

20. Bogolepov 1963; Huizing and Walf 1983.
21. Jedin 1957–61, I.
22. *Smal Art* pr 1.

turies during which so many hundreds of confessions were being composed by the various Protestant churches in separation from the rest of the church, and usually in separation from one another.

The Diet of Augsburg assembled by Emperor Charles V in June 1530 was the occasion for the presentation not only of the Lutheran confession that now bears that name, *The Augsburg Confession,* which was written by Phillipp Melanchthon to summarize and vindicate the *magnus consensus* of "our churches"[23] and was presented to the diet and the emperor on 25 June, but also of the *Reckoning of the Faith* [*Fidei ratio*] of Ulrich Zwingli, which was presented to the diet and the emperor two weeks later, on 8 July, and of *The Tetrapolitan Confession,* which was written by Martin Bucer, Wolfgang Capito, and Caspar Hedio and was presented to the diet and the emperor on 11 July. The nearly simultaneous presentation of these three confessions—Melanchthon's and Zwingli's opposed to each other above all on the doctrine of the eucharist, and Bucer's intended to mediate between them on this and other points—dramatizes a problem that has attended the confessions of Protestantism ever since the Reformation: polemically, they have been intended simultaneously as a united front against Roman Catholicism and as a definition against other forms of Protestantism. These two purposes have not necessarily coincided: sometimes the interconfessionally Protestant (as with *The Wittenberg Concord* of 1536 and the *Variata* of *The Augsburg Confession* in 1540), sometimes the confessionally particularistic (as with *The Formula of Concord* in 1577 and *The Canons of the Synod of Dort* of 1618–19), predominated.

Another reason for the proliferation of confessions was also one of the differences that set the Reformed or Calvinist churches of the Reformation apart from the Lutheran. Many of the Reformed confessions bear national titles: *The [First] Bohemian Confession* of 1535; *The First Helvetic Confession* of 1536; *The French Confession* of 1559; *The [First] Scots Confession* of 1560; *The Belgic Confession* of 1561; *The Second Helvetic Confession* of 1566; *The [Second] Bohemian Confession* of 1575; *The Second Scots Confession* of 1581 (also called *The King's Confession*). And although no one of these confessions by itself could match the sheer bulk of *The Book of Concord,* all of them put together could, and (depending on which other Reformed confessions are included) would certainly exceed it. In spite of their essential agreement with one another on most points, each was obliged, as a separate confession, to rehearse most of the cardinal doctrines of the Reformed faith and to respond to the opponents of that faith. As a result of this pluralism of Reformed confessions, incredible though this must seem, it was impossible, even in the nineteenth century, to

23. *Aug Lat* 1.1.

find a copy of *The Westminster Confession of Faith* in Protestant and Reformed Germany, and the very existence of that confession was largely unknown; such is the report of a leading scholar and editor of the Reformed confessions.[24] Because, in the judgment of Wilhelm Niesel, "church order, too, bears a confessional character" for the Reformed churches and their confessions,[25] not only the differences over the sacraments within the Reformed family, between the Zwinglian and the Calvinist traditions, as reflected in the *Consensus Tigurinus* or *The Zurich Agreement* of 1549,[26] but the continuing and intensifying differences over church order among episcopal, presbyterian, and congregationalist doctrines of polity would go on calling forth a series of new Reformed confessions throughout the Reformed communion, above all in the English-speaking world.

Lutheran, Reformed, Roman Catholic, and Radical "Confessionalisms"

The term *confessional*, then, may serve as a designation for the entire era of the Reformation of the sixteenth and seventeenth centuries of Western Christian history. Even Eastern Orthodoxy during that same period can be included in the term. Nevertheless, each of the divided churches to emerge from the Reformation was "confessional" in its own special way.

What Claude Welch has said of the confessionalism of the nineteenth century was true already of the confessionalism of the sixteenth: "The paradigm . . . was without doubt the 'confessional' Lutheranism that appeared in Germany."[27] For, also in the era of the Reformation, "confessionalism" was probably emphasized by Lutheranism more persistently than it was by any other Protestant group; the nineteenth-century Lutheran champions of its "confessional principle"[28] and the nineteenth-century critics of the Lutheran "extreme of symbololatry and ultra-orthodoxy"[29] would agree on this, if not on other points. This was true of the requirement that ordinands and theological professors "subscribe" the confessions as a necessary condition of achieving and holding an official post. By contrast with Reformed ecclesiology, the Lutheran understanding of the church did not include

24. Müller, v.
25. Niesel, v.
26. *Tig* 7.
27. Welch 1972–85, 1:194.
28. Krauth [1899] 1963, 162–200.
29. Schaff, 1:222.

discipline as a "mark" of the church. Rather, *The Augsburg Confession* specified (in its Latin text): "For the true unity of the church it is enough to agree concerning the teaching of the gospel [*satis est consentire de doctrina evangelii*] and the administration of the sacraments."[30] The comparative indifference of Lutheranism to the issues of a normative church order and polity or of a fixed and prescribed liturgy, moreover, placed all of the weight on the confession of doctrine. As early as *The Marburg Articles* of 1529 and *The Wittenberg Concord* of 1536, the irenic theology of many in the Reformed camp put Luther and his followers on the defensive,[31] a situation that would continue in the Lutheranism of the nineteenth and twentieth centuries, both in Germany and in North America. The unchallenged standing of *The Augsburg Confession* of 1530 as amplified in *The Book of Concord* of 1580 made insistence on creedal conformity more enforceable, as did the arrangement of church-state relations in the Lutheran states of Northern Europe. Lutheran confessionalism eventuated in the acceptance and enforcement of a single standard of supreme confessional authority, *The Augsburg Confession* of 1530 and in most places the entire *Book of Concord* of 1580, of which *The Augsburg Confession* was the chief component; although *The Formula of Concord* did not become normative church law in some nations, on the ground that it was a local, German confession, as well as on the grounds of its theological content,[32] *The Augsburg Confession* was the uniform standard from one nation to another, even though additional statements did arise repeatedly in one or another nation to meet specific, and usually temporary, needs.

For the Reformed branch of Protestantism, however, "confessionalism" took the form of many confessions of faith, more or less equally authoritative, arising in many nations and cultures. To list only some of them, and in chronological order: *The [First] Bohemian Confession* of 1535; *The First Helvetic Confession* of 1536; *The [First] Scots Confession* of 1560; *The Belgic Confession* of 1561; *The Heidelberg Catechism* of 1563, as part of *The Church Order of the Palatinate* of that same year; *The Second Helvetic Confession* of 1566; *The Thirty-Nine Articles of the Church of England* of 1571; *The [Second] Bohemian Confession* of 1575; *The [Second] Scots Confession* of 1581; *The Irish Articles of Religion* of 1615. Only a few statements, notably *The Canons of the Synod of Dort*, acquired a transnational and even an international position, having been subscribed by delegates of the following churches, not alone from the Low Countries but also well beyond: "Great Britain, the Electoral Palatinate, Hessia, Switzerland, Wetteraw, the Republic and Church of Geneva, the Republic

---

30. *Aug Lat* 7.2.
31. *Marburg* 15; *Witt Conc* 3.
32. Spitz and Lohff 1977, 136–49.

and Church of Bremen, the Republic and Church of Emden, the Duchy of Gelderland, and of Zutphen, South Holland, North Holland, Zeeland, the Province of
Utrecht, Friesland, Transisalania, the State of Groningen, and Omland, Drent, and
the French Churches."[33] Therefore *The Confession of the Waldenses* of 1655 could affirm "that we do agree in sound doctrine with all the Reformed Churches of France,
Great Britain, the Low Countries, Germany, Switzerland, Bohemia, Poland, Hungary, and others, *as it is set forth by them in their confessions*"—meaning, by each of
them in its own confession, rather than by all of them in a single, normative body
of confessions.[34]

Although it is not as common to speak about "Roman Catholic confessionalism" in the period of the Reformation, such a term comports well with the
growing recognition of modern historiography that the traditional concept of "the
Counter-Reformation" is too restrictive and negative a label for the development of
Roman Catholicism during the sixteenth century, and that "the Catholic Reformation" is a more balanced and a more comprehensive designation, with important
implications also for the question of periodization.[35] This is not, of course, to deny
that there was a "Counter-Reformation," and that many of the changes within the
Roman Catholicism of the sixteenth and seventeenth centuries make sense chiefly
as a response and a reaction to the rise of Protestantism; these might include the
vigorous efforts, political as well as liturgical and theological, to reclaim lost territories or to compensate for their loss by an expansion of foreign missions. But it
is an oversimplification to assume that the reformatory impulse of the later Middle
Ages, as expressed in the reform councils of the fifteenth century, was completely
captured by the Protestant Reformation. Not only the continuing calls for reform
by Erasmus and other humanists, but theology and churchmanship from Nicholas
of Cusa to Girolamo Seripando (who died almost exactly a century apart) demonstrated the abiding power, also after the exit of the Protestants, of a deep-seated zeal
for reformation and renewal.[36] "Roman Catholic confessionalism" is part of that
phenomenon. In interpreting one section of *The Canons and Decrees of the Council
of Trent* after another, therefore, it is necessary to inquire both after the elements of
continuity with late medieval reform movements and after the reactions to Protestant doctrine and practice that were at work; the decree of the council itself defines

33. *Dort con.*
34. *Wald* 33; italics added.
35. Jedin 1946, 39–49.
36. *Chr Trad* 4:248–74, 69–126, 274–303.

"the dual purpose on account of which the council was primarily brought together" as "the rooting out of heresy" externally and "the reform of conduct" internally.[37] That applies even to the issues that were the most central to the doctrinal controversy with Protestantism: the doctrine of the relation between the authority of Scripture and the authority of the church, as reflected also in the problem of the biblical canon;[38] and the doctrine of justification as this had been an issue between Thomists and Scotists.[39] Of course the Council of Trent was reacting to the teachings of the Protestant Reformers on these two issues, but it was also addressing— if not really settling—the persistent and long-deferred need to sort out and clarify the unresolved state of the patristic and medieval tradition.[40] Addressing that need to manage the tradition has always been, in a special way, the historic assignment of a confession of faith.

The validity of the unconventional term "Roman Catholic confessionalism" is vindicated even more directly by the appearance of a confessional text like *The Tridentine Profession of Faith* of 1564: "I, N., with firm faith believe and profess [*credo et profiteor*] each and every article contained in the symbol of faith which the Holy Roman Church uses."[41] "Symbol" in that declaration of believing, teaching, and confessing refers to *The Niceno-Constantinopolitan Creed* in its *Western Recension*, which is also affirmed in many Protestant confessions of the time. But the confessional intent of *The Tridentine Profession of Faith* makes itself clear when it immediately goes on to affirm: "I most firmly accept and embrace the apostolic and ecclesiastical traditions, and all other observances and constitutions of the same church. I likewise accept Holy Scripture according to that sense which Holy Mother Church has held and does hold."[42] In addition to "each and every article contained in the symbol of faith," therefore, it goes on to enumerate the seven sacraments, original sin and justification, the sacrifice of the mass, purgatory, the intercession of the saints, and indulgences, all of these being seen as "the apostolic and ecclesiastical traditions, and all other observances and constitutions of the same church" (and, not incidentally, as doctrines not "contained in the symbol of faith" or confessed as such in *The Niceno-Constantinopolitan Creed*). In summary, one who subscribes the

---

37. *Trent* 3 decr.
38. Tavard 1959.
39. Rückert 1925, 134–43; Becker 1967.
40. Maichle 1929.
41. *Trid Prof* 1.
42. *Trid Prof* 2.

Profession "acknowledge[s] the holy, catholic, and apostolic Roman Church as the mother and teacher [*matrem et magistram*] of all the churches, and promise[s] and swear[s] true obedience" to the pope, as well as to the teachings of the ecumenical councils, especially the Council of Trent.[43] By promulgating such a confession after the relative paucity of confessions of faith in the medieval West, except for certain sacramental definitions, the Catholic Reformation (or Counter-Reformation) did represent a "confessionalization" that was not confined, as the conventional usage might lead one to suppose, to the Reformed and Lutheran confessions, but spanned the ecclesiastical and doctrinal spectrum.[44]

Within that spectrum, even the adherents of the Radical Reformation had what the Mennonite scholar Howard John Loewen identifies as "the confessional period,"[45] just as the Baptist scholar William L. Lumpkin can speak of "the rising interest in confessionalism and in the Baptist view of the Church" during the twentieth century.[46] The Anabaptists joined in the universal sixteenth-century practice of "mak[ing] known, in points and articles," as *The Schleitheim Confession* of 1527 puts it in its preface,[47] what sets them apart from others, both from Roman Catholics and from other Protestants; that confession goes on to present the Mennonite position on doctrines in controversy, including the sacraments, the ban, and the taking of oaths. Therefore even so untraditional and idiosyncratic a statement of faith as *Hans Denck's Confession Before the Council of Nuremberg* of 1525 is divided into separate articles, dealing in turn with faith, baptism, and the Lord's supper.[48] Indeed, as C. J. Dyck has described this ironic situation,

> It is generally true that the Anabaptists and later Mennonites have been and are non-creedal. Torture experienced because of doctrinal issues spelled out by representatives of the established churches, the stress of the learned clergy on doctrine at the expense of ethics, and particularly the desire to be biblical . . . led to clear antipathy to rational statements of faith. . . . So also spontaneity in worship eliminated the felt need for formal confessional recital.

43. *Trid Prof* 7–8.
44. Reinhard and Schilling 1995.
45. Loewen, 25.
46. Lumpkin, 5.
47. *Schleit* pr.
48. *Denck* 1–3.

It is surprising, therefore, to find that the Anabaptists and especially the Dutch Mennonites wrote many confessions, . . . probably
more than any of the other three Reformation traditions.[49]

The production of confessions by Mennonites, as well as by other Anabaptists,
would continue well beyond the era of the Reformation into the late twentieth century.[50]

Catholic Substance and Protestant Principle
in Reformation Confessions

In one way or another, almost every confession of the Protestant Reformation is
shaped both by the polemical efforts of Roman Catholic or other Protestant opponents to tar it with the brush of past heresy and by its own inner dynamics, in response to both of which it is obliged to cope with the relation between the Catholic
substance that it has inherited and the Protestant principle that it espouses. The
Anglican-Lutheran *Wittenberg Articles* of 1536 go further than most of them when
they open their first article, neither with the doctrine of one God as the Trinity nor
with the doctrine of the supreme and sole authority of Holy Scripture, which are the
usual alternatives, but with the declaration: "We confess simply and clearly, without
any ambiguity, that we believe, hold, teach, and defend everything which is in the
canon of the Bible and in the three creeds, i.e. the Apostles', Nicene, and Athanasian
Creeds, in the same meaning which the creeds themselves intend and in which the
approved holy fathers use and defend them." This oath of loyalty applies, moreover, to "the very form of words in those articles," which is to be "retained most
precisely."[51] The Reformed *Second Helvetic Confession* of 1566, for all of its determined adherence to the sole authority of the Bible over all ecclesiastical traditions,
including not only the councils but even the creeds, can nevertheless bracket Bible
and creed by speaking of "the truth of God presented in the Scriptures and in the
Apostles' Creed."[52]

For the epigram of Benjamin Breckenridge Warfield, who was a scholar
both of Augustine and of Calvin, that "the Reformation, inwardly considered, was

---

49. Foreword to Loewen, 16–17.
50. *Menn Con* (1963); *Menn Persp* (1995).
51. *Witt Art* 1.
52. *Helv II* 16.1.

just the ultimate triumph of Augustine's doctrine of grace over Augustine's doctrine of the church,"[53] does identify a stratification of the substance of the Catholic tradition that prevailed in the teachings of the Protestant Reformation and of its confessions. On portions of the Catholic substance such as the invocation of the saints, as the words of *The French Confession* of 1559 indicate, it is a Protestant principle shared by the confessions of all the Reformers that "as Jesus Christ is our only advocate, and as he commands us to ask of the Father in his name, and as it is not lawful for us to pray except in accordance with the model God has taught us by his word, . . . all imaginations of men concerning the intercession of dead saints are an abuse and a device of Satan to lead men from the right way of worship,"[54] even though these "imaginations of men" are in fact the unanimous teaching of the Catholic substance shared by both East and West. Even the effort of *The Augsburg Confession* and other confessions to lay claim to the Catholic substance, by insisting that "our churches dissent from the church catholic in no article of faith but only omit some few abuses which are new and have been adopted by the fault of the times although contrary to the intent of the canons,"[55] proved to be ineffectual. When it comes to the doctrine of grace, however, as Warfield's words suggest, Luther and Calvin, and the confessions issued in their name, consistently pit Augustine's glorification of the free and sovereign grace of God against what they denounce as the Pelagian or Semi-Pelagian tendencies in late medieval scholasticism. For the Protestant principle of *sola gratia*, therefore, the claim to be Augustinian and in that sense truly Catholic can, and does, supply chapter and verse especially from Augustine's anti-Pelagian writings. The Calvinist doctrine of predestination as reprobation as well as election to salvation is anticipated in some of the later works of Augustine.[56] By contrast, the identification with Augustine, and thus with a version of "Catholic substance," is considerably less successful in the confessions' defense of the Protestant principle of *sola fide* in the doctrine of justification by faith alone.

Even on what Warfield called "Augustine's doctrine of the church" as distinct from "Augustine's doctrine of grace," moreover, the confessions of the Reformation do lay claim to being Augustinian, in the sense of not being Donatist. Therefore it becomes a persistent refrain both of the Lutheran and of the Reformed confessions to dissociate the idea of "reform" as advocated by Luther, Zwingli, and Calvin from the Donatism of the earlier centuries, but likewise from the neo-

53. Warfield 1956, 322.
54. *Gall* 24.
55. *Aug Lat* 22 int.1.
56. *Chr Trad* 1:298–99.

Donatism consistently attributed, whether justly or not, to John Wycliffe and John Hus.[57] Already in *The Profession of Faith by Valdes,* known as a forerunner of the Reformation, the validity of the sacraments is affirmed "even though they be ministered by a sinful priest,"[58] a position that is reinforced in a confession by the followers of Hus in the sixteenth century.[59] Sometimes without mentioning the Donatists but sometimes identifying them by name, Reformed confessions frequently make a point of explaining that the well-known emphasis on the necessity of discipline as a mark of the church, especially in the confessions of the Reformed churches by contrast with the Lutheran confessions, does not, in spite of superficial similarities, mean that they have gone over into the Donatist camp. *The Second Helvetic Confession* of 1566 follows its insistence that "discipline is an absolute necessity in the church" with this disavowal in the very next paragraph: "We strongly detest the error of the Donatists."[60] Its predecessor of 1536, *The First Helvetic Confession,* identifies by name not the Donatists but the Anabaptists when it criticizes "all those who separate and cut themselves off from the holy fellowship and society of the church,"[61] but clearly the Donatists (and neo-Donatists) are included in the criticism. Even more clearly, the Swiss Protestants were insisting that they themselves were not guilty of such separatism. According to *The Thirty-Nine Articles of the Church of England,* because evil men ministering in the name of Christ "do minister by his commission and authority, we may use their ministry both in hearing the word of God and in the receiving of the sacraments. Neither is the effect of Christ's ordinance taken away by their wickedness, nor the grace of God's gifts diminished";[62] but it is obvious that this is intended to be a summary of the Augustinian case against Donatism, as is true also of a similar passage in *The Irish Articles of Religion* of 1615.[63] Even in the context of "condemn[ing] the papal assemblies, as the pure word of God is banished from them, their sacraments are corrupted, debased, falsified, or destroyed, and all superstitions and idolatries are in them," *The French Confession* of 1559 adds the Augustinian proviso that "the efficacy of baptism does not depend upon the person who administers it," not even, it would seem, when it is administered in those corrupted, superstitious, and idolatrous "papal as-

---

57. Spinka 1966.
58. *Vald.*
59. *Boh I* 11.7.
60. *Helv II* 18.20–21.
61. *Helv I* 25.
62. *39 Art* 26.
63. *Irish* 70.

semblies."[64] The neo-Donatism of the late Middle Ages and Reformation would likewise appear to be the reason behind the formulation of *The Augsburg Confession,* which *The Confutation of the Augsburg Confession* of the Roman Catholic opponents approves:[65] "Our churches condemn the Donatists *and others like them* who have denied that the ministry of evil men may be used in the church and who have thought the ministry of evil men to be unprofitable and without effect."[66]

The relation of the "Protestant principle" to the dogma of the Trinity as the central affirmation of the Catholic tradition, and therefore as the heart of "Catholic substance," evoked the assessment of Edward Gibbon that "after a fair discussion we shall rather be surprised by the timidity, than scandalized by the freedom, of our first reformers."[67] That "surprise"—or stricture—applies in even greater measure to the Reformation confessions than it does to the personal writings of these "first reformers." The confessions and other writings of the Antitrinitarians and Socinians of the Reformation period repeatedly charge that there is a blatant discrepancy between theory and practice in the confessions of the Magisterial Reformation, which, in the words of *The Augsburg Confession,* complain that on many points the "teaching of Paul has been almost wholly smothered by traditions,"[68] but which at the same time have no compunction about affirming, as that same confession does, that the most monumental tradition of them all, "the decree of the Nicene Synod concerning the unity of the divine essence and concerning the three persons, is true and should be believed without any doubting," complete with its entire conceptual apparatus and traditional Latin terminology of one essence, three persons, and all the rest.[69] This is, in the words of *The Marburg Articles,* bearing the signatures of Luther and his colleagues as well as of Zwingli and his colleagues, what is "sung and read in the Nicene Creed by the entire Christian church throughout the world."[70] Far from being a remnant of the Middle Ages or a mere political ploy, the trinitarianism of the mainline Protestant Reformers, whether Calvinist or Lutheran, is fundamental both to their theology and to their spirituality, as Thomas Torrance has shown.[71] So fundamental is it that, at least until the challenges of the Radical

64. *Gall* 28.
65. *Confut* 8.
66. *Aug Lat* 8.3; italics added.
67. Gibbon [1776–88] 1896–1900, 6:125 (ch 54).
68. *Aug Lat* 26.6.
69. *Aug Lat* 1.1.
70. *Marburg* 1.
71. Torrance, lxx–lxxii.

Reformation, it represents, within the circle of the Magisterial Reformation, what Whitehead once called one of those "fundamental assumptions which all the variant systems . . . unconsciously presuppose. Such assumptions appear so obvious that people do not know what they are assuming because no other way of putting things has ever occurred to them."[72]

In fact, so wholeheartedly and uncritically did the Magisterial Reformers make the Western version of the Nicene trinitarian tradition their own that the Filioque passed over unscathed from the Latin theology of the Middle Ages to the confessions of the Protestant Reformation. *The Belgic Confession* of 1561, which also argues for its list of the biblical canon by claiming that "the Holy Spirit testifies in our hearts that they are from God" and the Apocrypha are not,[73] argues for (among other trinitarian teachings) the Filioque by declaring: "*All these things* we know from the testimonies of Holy Scripture as well as from the effects of the persons [of the Trinity], especially from those we feel within ourselves."[74] Within this Protestant trinitarianism, the Filioque seems to be largely taken for granted as a "fundamental assumption"; this can be seen in the words of *The Augsburg Confession* about "the decree of the Nicene Synod," which, without mentioning the Filioque outright, are clearly referring not to *The Creed of Nicaea,* nor even to the original form of *The Niceno-Constantinopolitan Creed,* but to the *Western Recension of the Niceno-Constantinopolitan Creed* with the Filioque.[75] Teaching that "the Holy Spirit proceeds from him [the Son] as well as from the Father,"[76] *The Formula of Concord* reaffirms "the old, approved symbols, the Nicene and Athanasian Creeds," including the Filioque in both *The Niceno-Constantinopolitan Creed* and *The Athanasian Creed,*[77] as does *The Reaffirmed Consensus of the Truly Lutheran Faith* of 1655;[78] and both of these creeds in this form, together with *The Apostles' Creed,* lead the processions of creeds and confessions of faith in *The Book of Concord* of 1580, under the heading "The Three Chief Symbols or Creeds of the Christian Faith which Are Commonly Used in the Church."[79] Therefore in response to the presentation of the Lutheran theologians of Tübingen to the patriarch of Constantinople, Jeremias II,

72. Whitehead [1925] 1952, 49.

73. *Belg* 5.

74. *Belg* 9; italics added.

75. *Aug Lat* 1.1.

76. *Form Conc Sol Dec* 8.73.

77. *Form Conc Sol Dec* 12.37.

78. *Cons rep* 1.12.

79. *BLK* 21.

with its appeal to the creed supposedly held in common with his church, his second *Reply*, sent in 1579, opens with a full-length disquisition "On the Procession of the Holy Spirit," impeaching their claim to orthodoxy on the grounds of their adherence to the Filioque.[80]

According to article 8 of *The Belgic Confession*, the three persons of the one divine essence are "eternally distinct according to their incommunicable properties": it is the property of the Father in the Trinity to be "the cause, origin, and source of all things, visible as well as invisible," referring by that quotation from *The Niceno-Constantinopolitan Creed*[81] to the Father as the "origin [Greek *archē*, Latin *principium*]" of all creatures; it is the property of the Holy Spirit to be "the eternal power and might, proceeding from the Father *and the Son*."[82] Taking the unusual step of setting aside an entire separate article for the doctrine of the Holy Spirit, *The Belgic Confession* subsequently goes well beyond that perfunctory recitation of the Filioque: "We believe and confess also that the Holy Spirit proceeds eternally from the Father and the Son—neither made, nor created, nor begotten, but only proceeding from the two of them"; and in support it cites the standard Western proof texts for the Filioque.[83] *The French Confession* of two years earlier similarly speaks of the Father as "first cause, principle, and origin of all things," also referring to creatures, and of the Holy Spirit as "his [the Father's] virtue, power, and efficacy," but nonetheless as "proceeding eternally from them both."[84] *The Second Helvetic Confession* states that "the Holy Spirit truly proceeds from them both, and the same from eternity and is to be worshiped with both [*cum utroque adorandus*]."[85]

The British confessions of the Reformation, too, align themselves with the *Western Recension* and the Filioque. It is the teaching of *The Thirty-Nine Articles of the Church of England*, both in the Latin text of 1563 and in the English text of 1571, that "the Holy Ghost, proceeding from the Father and the Son, is of one substance, majesty, and glory with the Father and the Son, very and eternal God."[86] That language is repeated verbatim in *The Irish Articles of Religion* of 1615,[87] as it is again in

---

80. *Jer II* 2.1.1–42.
81. *N-CP* 1.
82. *Belg* 8; italics added.
83. *Belg* 11.
84. *Gall* 6.
85. *Helv II* 3.3.
86. *39 Art* 5.
87. *Irish* 10.

The Methodist Articles of Religion of 1784,[88] as well as in *The Articles of Religion of the Reformed Episcopal Church in America* of 1875.[89] In *The Westminster Confession of Faith* of 1647 the distinction "in the unity of the Godhead" between the "three persons, of one substance, power, and eternity" is said to be: "The Father is of none, neither begotten, nor proceeding; the Son is eternally begotten of the Father; the Holy Spirit eternally proceeding from the Father and the Son."[90] Similarly, *The Westminster Larger Catechism* confesses: "It is proper . . . to the Holy Spirit to proceed from the Father and the Son from all eternity."[91] In *The Scots Confession* of 1560 there is no reference to the Filioque at all; it contains no separate article on the doctrine of the Trinity, and its article entitled "Faith in the Holy Ghost" confines itself to the statement that "we confess [the Holy Spirit] to be God, equal with the Father and with his Son."[92] But it is evident from such texts as *Craig's Catechism* of 1581 that the confessions of the Scottish Reformation, too, retain and affirm the Filioque.[93] So does the Brownist *True Confession* of 1596.[94] As part of the Western confessional heritage, the Filioque goes on appearing in later confessions, also in such confessions of the Third World as *The Declaration of the Faith and Articles of Religion of the Philippine Independent Church* of 1947.[95] In this universal retention of the Filioque in the confessions of mainstream Protestantism, one exception deserves quoting in full, the confession of *The Easter Litany of the Moravian Church* of 1749: "I believe in the Holy Ghost, who *proceedeth* from the Father, and whom our Lord Jesus Christ *sent*, after he went away, that he should abide with us forever."[96] And the Mennonite *Concept of Cologne* of 1591 reverts to the formula of the Council of Florence by its confession of the Holy Spirit as "proceeding from the Father through the Son [*van den Vader door den Sone*]";[97] but *The Mennonite Short Confession of Faith* of 1610 retains the traditional Western version, "proceeding from the Father and the Son."[98]

88. *Meth Art* 4.
89. *Ref Ep* 4.
90. *West* 2.3.
91. *West Lg Cat* 10.
92. *Scot I* 12.
93. *Craig* 4.3.
94. *True Con* 2.
95. *Philip Ind* 1.3.
96. *Morav*; italics added.
97. *Cologne* 3; *Flor Un.*
98. *Ries* 3.

From Reformation Confessions to Confessional Scholasticism

Several of the confessions included here in Part Four of *Creeds and Confessions of Faith in the Christian Tradition* under the heading "Confessions of Faith in the Reformation Era" came from the first generation of Protestant Reformers, some of whom—including Luther the Augustinian, Bucer the Dominican, Thomas Cranmer, and John Knox—had received a more or less thorough training in scholastic theology and then had gone on to reject it. Among the first-generation Reformers who composed confessions were: Ulrich Zwingli (*The Sixty-Seven Articles* of 1523 and *Reckoning of the Faith* [*Fidei ratio*] of 1530); Martin Luther (*Small Catechism* of 1529, *Large Catechism* of 1529, and *Smalcald Articles* of 1537); Philipp Melanchthon (*The Augsburg Confession* of 1530 and *The Apology of the Augsburg Confession* of 1531); Martin Bucer (*The Tetrapolitan Confession* of 1530 and *The Wittenberg Concord* of 1536); Thomas Cranmer (*The Ten Articles* of the Church of England of 1536); John Calvin (*The Geneva Catechism* of 1541/1542); John Knox (*The Scots Confession* of 1560).

But many more of the Protestant confessions came from the second, third, and subsequent generations; those confessions, moreover, are not only more numerous, they are also usually much longer, than the earlier texts had been. Nor is the difference a matter only of comparative length as such. For it was, paradoxically, the writers of confessions who had not been trained in medieval, Roman Catholic scholasticism who laid the foundations for a new, Protestant "confessional scholasticism." As Horatius Bonar put it, speaking about *The Westminster Confession of Faith* from the seventeenth century in a description that could as readily have been applied also to *The Canons of the Synod of Dort* from the same century or to *The Formula of Concord* from late in the preceding century,

> It may be questioned whether the Church gained anything by the exchange of the Reformation standards for those of the seventeenth century. The scholastic mould in which the latter are cast has somewhat trenched upon the ease and breadth which mark the former; and the skilful metaphysics employed at Westminster [or in *The Formula of Concord*] in giving lawyer-like precision to each statement, have imparted a local and temporary aspect to the new which did not belong to the more ancient standards.[99]

99. Quoted in Torrance, xvii.

Bonar's term "scholastic," therefore, which in common usage ordinarily refers to Western Roman Catholic theology from the twelfth to the fourteenth century and to the revival of that theology in the modern era,[100] may also be applied to the Protestant "confessional scholasticism" of the sixteenth and seventeenth centuries, which manifested itself in both Lutheran and Reformed theology.

One presupposition for its rise, as it had been for the rise of medieval scholasticism, certainly was the cultivation of Aristotelian philosophy, which, after its rejection by Luther and other Reformers, enjoyed a strong revival of interest during subsequent generations of Lutheran and Reformed theologians: it had been Melanchthon's ambition to prepare a new edition of Aristotle. Aristotelianism helped to provide the Protestant dogmaticians of the seventeenth century with a precision in their vocabulary and with a capacity for making careful distinctions.[101] Partly as a consequence of this renewal of interest in the philosophy of Aristotle, another component of medieval scholasticism, the investigation of "natural theology," played a prominent part in this Protestant scholasticism, too; therefore an exploration of what the unaided human reason could know about God, including the traditional proofs for the existence of God, became the prolegomenon to the systematic exposition of the revealed doctrines of Scripture.[102]

But as Etienne Gilson, widely regarded as the leading historian of medieval philosophy in his generation, nevertheless complained, "During the past hundred years the general tendency among historians of medieval thought seems to have been to imagine the middle ages as peopled by philosophers rather than theologians."[103] It is likewise more important to pay attention to another presupposition of both pre-Reformation and post-Reformation scholasticism, the availability of the doctrinal tradition in a codified form.[104] In the works of Thomas Aquinas and his contemporaries, that had meant above all the compilation of patristic doctrine that had been produced in the *Sentences* of Peter Lombard.[105] A three-step process of explaining the apparent contradictions within the tradition—raising objections, formulating a positive answer on the basis of tradition, and then responding to the objections and apparent contradictions—set the pattern for the scholastic method.[106] But for the

100. *Chr Trad* 3:268–307.
101. Petersen [1921] 1964.
102. Troeltsch 1891, 194–206.
103. Gilson [1951] 1957, 156.
104. Grabmann [1909] 1957, 2:359–407.
105. Stegmüller 1947.
106. Chenu 1964, 93–96.

Protestant scholastics like Johann Gerhard, whose *Confessio catholica* of 1634–37 and invention of the word *patrology* in 1653 showed him to be a scholar of the patristic tradition in his own right,[107] it was the ancient creeds as seen through the prism of the more recent confessions that supplied the codification of the tradition. This they did in a form that gave it a special Reformation cast. For example, the tradition of the dogma of the person of Christ as represented by *The Creed of Chalcedon* was affirmed both by the Reformed confessions[108] and by the Lutheran confessions,[109] even as they disputed about its implication for eucharistic doctrine. But the concentration in both confessional traditions on the work of Christ rather than primarily on the person of Christ enabled seventeenth-century scholastic theologians to interpret *The Creed of Chalcedon* as a confirmation and a vindication of Reformation accents. In the celebrated formula of the first Protestant systematic theology, the *Loci communes* of Melanchthon first published in 1521, "to know Christ is to know the blessings he confers [*Hoc est enim Christum cognoscere, beneficia eius cognoscere*]."[110]

In spite of the continuing efforts throughout the sixteenth and seventeenth centuries to heal the separations in Western Christendom, above all the divisions between the several branches of Protestantism,[111] the "Creeds and Confessions of the Reformation Era" that make up this Part Four of *Creeds and Confessions of Faith in the Christian Tradition* had effectively made the separations permanent, at any rate until the nineteenth and twentieth centuries, when new and more successful movements for reconciliation would lead to new confessional statements. Polemics continued back and forth, also after the various confessions had been fixed. But the confessions, though they themselves became the occasion for it, as with the exchange between the *Concordia discors* of Rudolf Hospinian and the *Concordia concors* of Leonhard Hutter,[112] had meanwhile set the outcome of the controversies as a foundation on which a scholastic theology was able to build. This included the stabilization, at any rate within each of the confessional groups, of a technical theological vocabulary, an indispensable component of any scholasticism; prominent examples were the terminology of "the theology of the covenant [*foedus*]" within Reformed thought and of the christological "interchange of attributes [*idiomatum*

---

107. Quasten, 1:1.
108. *West* 8.2; *Fid rat* 1; *Wald* 13.
109. *Form Conc Sol Dec* 8.18.
110. *Chr Trad* 4:155–56.
111. McNeill 1964.
112. *PRE* 8:392–94; 497–500.

communicatio]" in Lutheran thought.[113] Similarly, as the systematization of the four-fold sense of Scripture had helped to make medieval scholasticism possible,[114] so also the confessions had worked out the distinctive principles of biblical interpretation that had come out of the exegetical work of the Reformation. Therefore when, for example, *The Second Helvetic Confession,* speaking in this case not for its own Reformed tradition alone but for Protestant theology generally, defines as "orthodox and genuine" only that interpretation "which is gleaned from the Scriptures themselves," it specifies the constituent elements for such an interpretation: first, "the nature of the language in which they were written"; second, "the circumstances in which they were set down"; third, "like and unlike passages and many and clearer passages"; fourth, "agree[ment] with the rule of faith and love"; and fifth, compatibility with "the glory of God and man's salvation."[115] Both in their exegetical writings on the books of Scripture and in the interpretations of individual biblical passages that were a continuing part of their works on dogmatics, the Protestant scholastics were able to capitalize on all of these accomplishments of "the confessional era." Conversely, however, when the attacks of Pietism, of the Enlightenment, and of modern thought and Liberal theology challenged this confessional scholasticism, the confessions of the Reformation era often became the objects of the attack as well.

113. *Chr Trad* 4:350–74.
114. Lubac 1959.
115. *Helv II* 2.1.

Lutheran Confessions

Although the Lutheran Confessions were written separately, and over a period of almost fifty years, between 1529 and 1577, the work of collecting them into *The Book of Concord* of 1580 has assured that they would mostly be read and studied together.

Among them, nevertheless, *The Augsburg Confession* of 1530 holds pride of place, as the one confession by which Lutherans have identified themselves, using, for example in *The Formula of Concord,* the designation "the theologians of *The Augsburg Confession.*" The *Catechisms* of Martin Luther were written before *The Augsburg Confession,* but not as confessional documents; by contrast, *The Apology of the Augsburg Confession* was explicitly intended as a defense and a commentary on *The Augsburg Confession.*

Because of its chronological priority and its political and theological importance, *The Augsburg Confession* therefore helped to define, not only for its followers but for many other groups, including some of its severest critics, what a "confession of faith" means. Its format of discrete "articles" and its way of stating a position became a standard methodology, and many of its individual formulations were echoed, even unconsciously, in later statements.

The Lutheran confessions have also played an important part in the later "reception" of confessions, because much (though by no means all) of the discussion and debate about confessional subscription came about through the enforcement of *The Book of Concord* as a requirement for ordination and a norm for fellowship and church union. The adherents of the Lutheran confessions expected others to issue similar formularies and to assign to them a similar place in the life and teaching of the church.

Because of all these considerations, it makes sense to open this Part Four, "Creeds and Confessions of the Reformation Era," with the documents that were eventually assembled into *The Book of Concord.*

The Small Catechism, 1529

In his preface to *The Small Catechism,* Luther explains that he wrote it in response to the "deplorable conditions" he encountered among laypeople during his visitations in Saxony and Meissen in 1528 and 1529. He complained that "although the people are supposed to be Christian, are baptized, and receive the holy sacrament, they do not know the Lord's Prayer, the Creed, or the Ten Commandments, they live as if they were pigs and irrational beasts."[1] *The Small Catechism* expounds upon these three texts in a question-and-answer format and includes discussion of the sacraments of baptism and the eucharist, as well as a "concise method of confessing" (expanded in later editions). It is worth noting that the practice of private confession remained important in Luther's theology.

Luther had common people in mind as the audience, and he prefaces the work with a plea to ministers to teach their congregations, especially the young, with the aid of the catechism. Indeed, he seems to prescribe the use of his catechism in his warning to pastors to avoid changes or variations in the wording of prayers or doctrinal explanations, for fear of confusing their flock. He also clearly intends *The Small Catechism* for family use, offering guidelines for prayers to be said by the head of the household. In the German edition it is also the *Hausvater* (as opposed to the later Latin version's pastor or schoolmaster) who is enjoined to teach his family the chief doctrines of the faith. Only Luther's Bible translation rivals *The Small Catechism* in its mastery of style and aptness of tone. As Schaff put it, here Luther expresses "the deepest things in the plainest language."[2] The work was an immediate bestseller and remains a popular and beloved text among Lutherans.

The catechism ends with a collection of scriptural passages defining such societal roles as pastor, teacher, husband, wife, and widow. In this, as in the very idea of a catechism, Luther was influenced by the works of Jean Gerson (1363–1429), whose catechetical and moral writings he knew well.[3] A marriage and baptismal manual were appended in later editions, but they were not prepared by Luther and are not reproduced here.

The Small Catechism first appeared in 1529 (Wittenberg: Nicholas Schir-

---

1. From the preface to *The Small Catechism.*
2. Schaff, 1:250. He also quotes Andreas Fabricius's enthusiastic praise: "A better book, next to the Bible, the sun never saw; it is the juice and the blood, the aim and the substance of the Bible" (Schaff, 1:251n).
3. In particular, Jean Gerson's *Tractatus de modo vivendi omnium fidelium.*

lentz) as a broadsheet, a format Luther refers to in his preface when he says that pastors "should have the tables and forms in front of them."[4] Later in 1529 the work appeared as an illustrated pamphlet with woodcuts by Lucas Cranach.[5] *The Small Catechism* is included in the Lutheran *Book of Concord* (1580).

Edition: *BLK* 501–27.

Translation: Tappert, 338–56.

Literature: Geisberg 1923; Grüneisen 1938; Harnack 1856, xi–lxii; Janetzki 1980; Johnston 1993; Kolb 1979; Kolb-Wengert, 345–47; Overduin 1980; Peters 1981; Raabe 1989; Reu 1929, esp. 62–93; Scaer and Preus 1979; Starke 1983, 536–37; Strauss 1978, 151–75; Tokuzen 1983; Vercruysse 1983; Voelz 1979; *WA* 30/1:559–85, 631–53, 666–819; Weismann 1995.

4. "[D]iese tafeln und forme für sich nemen." Luther is clearly referring to the practice of printing catechisms in broadsheet format. Only a fragment of a 1529 Low German broadsheet of his *Small Catechism* survives, but eight High German broadsheets are also recorded as having been printed in 1529. See *WA* 30/1:561, 666.
5. Ten of the woodcuts had already appeared in a 1527 broadside with Melanchthon's explication of the Ten Commandments. See Geisberg 1923; *Supplementa Melanchthoniana* 5/1:424–43; and *WA* 30/1:561–68, 631–35.

The Small Catechism, 1529

[Preface]

Grace, mercy, and peace in Jesus Christ, our Lord, from Martin Luther to all faithful, godly pastors and preachers.

[1] The deplorable conditions which I recently encountered when I was a visitor constrained me to prepare this brief and simple catechism or statement of Christian teaching. [2] Good God, what wretchedness I beheld! The common people, especially those who live in the country, have no knowledge whatever of Christian teaching, and unfortunately many pastors are quite incompetent and unfitted for teaching. [3] Although the people are supposed to be Christian, are baptized, and receive the holy sacrament, they do not know the Lord's Prayer, the Creed, or the Ten Commandments, they live as if they were pigs and irrational beasts, and now that the gospel has been restored they have mastered the fine art of abusing liberty.

[4] How will you bishops answer for it before Christ that you have so shamefully neglected the people and paid no attention at all to the duties of your office? May you escape punishment for this! [5] You withhold the cup in the Lord's supper and insist on the observance of human laws, yet you do not take the slightest interest in teaching the people the Lord's Prayer, the Creed, the Ten Commandments, or a single part of the word of God. Woe to you forever!

[6] I therefore beg of you for God's sake, my beloved brethren who are pastors and preachers, that you take the duties of your office seriously, that you have pity on the people who are entrusted to your care, and that you help me to teach the catechism to the people, especially those who are young. Let those who lack the qualifications to do better at least take this tablet and these forms and read them to the people word for word in this manner:

[7] In the first place, the preacher should take the utmost care to avoid changes or variations in the text and wording of the Ten Commandments, the Creed, the Lord's Prayer, the sacraments, etc. On the contrary, he should adopt one form, adhere to it, and use it repeatedly year after year. Young and inexperienced people must be instructed on the basis of a uniform, fixed text and form. They are easily confused if a teacher employs one form now and another form—perhaps with the intention of making improvements—later on. In this way all the time and labor will be lost.

[8] This was well understood by our good fathers, who were accustomed

to use the same form in teaching the Lord's Prayer, the Creed, and the Ten Commandments. We, too, should teach these things to the young and unlearned in such a way that we do not alter a single syllable or recite the catechism differently from year to year. Choose the form that pleases you, therefore, and adhere to it henceforth. [9] When you preach to intelligent and educated people, you are at liberty to exhibit your learning and to discuss these topics from different angles and in such a variety of ways as you may be capable of. But when you are teaching the young, adhere to a fixed and unchanging form and method. [10] Begin by teaching them the Ten Commandments, the Creed, the Lord's Prayer, etc., following the text word for word so that the young may repeat these things after you and retain them in their memory.

[11] If any refuse to receive your instructions, tell them that they deny Christ and are no Christians. They should not be admitted to the sacrament, be accepted as sponsors in baptism, or be allowed to participate in any Christian privileges. On the contrary, they should be turned over to the pope and his officials, and even to the devil himself. [12] In addition, parents and employers should refuse to furnish them with food and drink and should notify them that the prince is disposed to banish such rude people from his land.

[13] Although we cannot and should not compel anyone to believe, we should nevertheless insist that the people learn to know how to distinguish between right and wrong according to the standards of those among whom they live and make their living. For anyone who desires to reside in a city is bound to know and observe the laws under whose protection he lives, no matter whether he is a believer or, at heart, a scoundrel or knave.

[14] In the second place, after the people have become familiar with the text, teach them what it means. For this purpose, take the explanations in this booklet, or choose any other brief and fixed explanations which you may prefer, [15] and adhere to them without changing a single syllable, as stated above with reference to the text. [16] Moreover, allow yourself ample time, for it is not necessary to take up all the parts at once. They can be presented one at a time. When the learners have a proper understanding of the First Commandment, proceed to the Second Commandment, and so on. Otherwise they will be so overwhelmed that they will hardly remember anything at all.

[17] In the third place, after you have thus taught this brief catechism, take up a large catechism so that the people may have a richer and fuller understanding. Expound every commandment, petition, and part, pointing out their respective obligations, benefits, dangers, advantages, and disadvantages, as you will find all of this treated at length in the many books written for this purpose. [18] Lay the greatest

weight on those commandments or other parts which seem to require special attention among the people where you are. For example, the Seventh Commandment, which treats of stealing, must be emphasized when instructing laborers and shopkeepers, and even farmers and servants, for many of these are guilty of dishonesty and thievery. So, too, the Fourth Commandment must be stressed when instructing children and the common people in order that they may be encouraged to be orderly, faithful, obedient, and peaceful. Always adduce many examples from the Scriptures to show how God punished and blessed.

[19] You should also take pains to urge governing authorities and parents to rule wisely and educate their children. They must be shown that they are obliged to do so, and that they are guilty of damnable sin if they do not do so, for by such neglect they undermine and lay waste both the kingdom of God and the kingdom of the world and are the worst enemies of God and man. [20] Make very plain to them the shocking evils they introduce when they refuse their aid in the training of children to become pastors, preachers, notaries, etc., and tell them that God will inflict awful punishments on them for these sins. It is necessary to preach about such things. The extent to which parents and governing authorities sin in this respect is beyond telling. The devil also has a horrible purpose in mind.

[21] Finally, now that the people are freed from the tyranny of the pope, they are unwilling to receive the sacrament and they treat it with contempt. Here, too, there is need of exhortation, but with this understanding: No one is to be compelled to believe or to receive the sacrament, no law is to be made concerning it, and no time or place should be appointed for it. [22] We should so preach that, of their own accord and without any law, the people will desire the sacrament and, as it were, compel us pastors to administer it to them. This can be done by telling them: It is to be feared that anyone who does not desire to receive the sacrament at least three or four times a year despises the sacrament and is no Christian, just as he is no Christian who does not hear and believe the gospel. Christ did not say, "Omit this," or "Despise this," but he said, "Do this, as often as you drink it," etc. [1 Cor 11.25] Surely he wishes that this be done and not that it be omitted and despised. "Do this," he said.

[23] He who does not highly esteem the sacrament suggests thereby that he has no sin, no flesh, no devil, no world, no death, no hell. That is to say, he believes in none of these, although he is deeply immersed in them and is held captive by the devil. On the other hand, he suggests that he needs no grace, no life, no paradise, no heaven, no Christ, no God, nothing good at all. For if he believed that he was involved in so much that is evil and was in need of so much that is good, he would not neglect the sacrament in which aid is afforded against such evil and in which

such good is bestowed. It is not necessary to compel him by any law to receive the sacrament, for he will hasten to it of his own accord, he will feel constrained to receive it, he will insist that you administer it to him.

[24] Accordingly you are not to make a law of this, as the pope has done. All you need to do is clearly to set forth the advantage and disadvantage, the benefit and loss, the blessing and danger connected with this sacrament. Then the people will come of their own accord and without compulsion on your part. But if they refuse to come, let them be, and tell them that those who do not feel and acknowledge their great need and God's gracious help belong to the devil. [25] If you do not give such admonitions, or if you adopt odious laws on the subject, it is your own fault if the people treat the sacrament with contempt. How can they be other than negligent if you fail to do your duty and remain silent? So it is up to you, dear pastor and preacher! [26] Our office has become something different from what it was under the pope. It is now a ministry of grace and salvation. [27] It subjects us to greater burdens and labors, dangers, and temptations, with little reward or gratitude from the world. But Christ himself will be our reward if we labor faithfully. The Father of all grace grant it! To him be praise and thanks forever, through Christ, our Lord. Amen.

[1.] The Ten Commandments

in the plain form in which the head of the family shall teach them to his household

[1] THE FIRST

[Ex 20.3]   *"You shall have no other gods."*

[2] What does this mean?

Answer: We should fear, love, and trust in God above all things.

[3] THE SECOND

[Ex 20.7]   *"You shall not take the name of the Lord your God in vain."*

[4] What does this mean?

Answer: We should fear and love God, and so we should not use his name to curse, swear, practice magic, lie, or deceive, but in every time of need call upon him, pray to him, praise him, and give him thanks.

[5] THE THIRD

[Ex 20.8]   *"Remember the Sabbath day, to keep it holy."*

[6] What does this mean?

Answer: We should fear and love God, and so we should not despise his word and the preaching of the same, but deem it holy and gladly hear and learn it.

[7] THE FOURTH

"Honor your father and your mother."   [Ex 20.12]

[8] What does this mean?

Answer: We should fear and love God, and so we should not despise our parents and superiors, nor provoke them to anger, but honor, serve, obey, love, and esteem them.

[9] THE FIFTH

"You shall not kill."   [Ex 20.13]

[10] What does this mean?

Answer: We should fear and love God, and so we should not endanger our neighbor's life, nor cause him any harm, but help and befriend him in every necessity of life.

[11] THE SIXTH

"You shall not commit adultery."   [Ex 20.14]

[12] What does this mean?

Answer: We should fear and love God, and so we should lead a chaste and pure life in word and deed, each one loving and honoring his wife or her husband.

[13] THE SEVENTH

"You shall not steal."   [Ex 20.15]

[14] What does this mean?

Answer: We should fear and love God, and so we should not rob our neighbor of his money or property, nor bring them into our possession by dishonest trade or by dealing in shoddy wares, but help him to improve and protect his income and property.

[15] THE EIGHTH

"You shall not bear false witness against your neighbor."   [Ex 20.16]

[16] What does this mean?

Answer: We should fear and love God, and so we should not tell lies about our neighbor, nor betray, slander, or defame him, but should apologize for him, speak well of him, and interpret charitably all that he does.

[17] THE NINTH

[Ex 20.17] *"You shall not covet your neighbor's house."*

[18] What does this mean?

Answer: We should fear and love God, and so we should not seek by craftiness to gain possession of our neighbor's inheritance or home, nor to obtain them under pretext of legal right, but be of service and help to him so that he may keep what is his.

[19] THE TENTH

"You shall not covet your neighbor's wife, or his manservant, or his maidservant, or his
[Ex 20.17] *ox, or his ass, or anything that is your neighbor's."*

[20] What does this mean?

Answer: We should fear and love God, and so we should not abduct, estrange, or entice away our neighbor's wife, servants, or cattle, but encourage them to remain and discharge their duty to him.

[21] [CONCLUSION]

What does God declare concerning all these commandments?

[Ex 20.5–6] Answer: He says, "I the Lord your God am a jealous God, visiting the iniquity of the fathers upon the children to the third and the fourth generation of those who hate me, but showing steadfast love to thousands of those who love me and keep my commandments."

[22] What does this mean?

Answer: God threatens to punish all who transgress these commandments. We should therefore fear his wrath and not disobey these commandments. On the other hand, he promises grace and every blessing to all who keep them. We should therefore love him, trust in him, and cheerfully do what he has commanded.

[2.] The Creed

in the plain form in which the head of the family shall teach it to his household

[1] THE FIRST ARTICLE: CREATION

"I believe in God, the Father almighty, maker of heaven and earth."

[2] What does this mean?

Answer: I believe that God has created me and all that exists; that he has given me and still sustains my body and soul, all my limbs and senses, my reason and all the faculties of my mind, together with food and clothing, house and home, family and property; that he provides me daily and abundantly with all the necessities of life, protects me from all danger, and preserves me from all evil. All this he does out of his pure, fatherly, and divine goodness and mercy, without any merit or worthiness on my part. For all of this I am bound to thank, praise, serve, and obey him. This is most certainly true.

[3] THE SECOND ARTICLE: REDEMPTION

"And in Jesus Christ, his only Son, our Lord: who was conceived by the Holy Spirit, born of the Virgin Mary, suffered under Pontius Pilate, was crucified, dead, and buried: he descended into hell, the third day he rose from the dead, he ascended into heaven, and is seated on the right hand of God, the Father almighty, whence he shall come to judge the living and the dead."

[4] What does this mean?

Answer: I believe that Jesus Christ, true God, begotten of the Father from eternity, and also true man, born of the Virgin Mary, is my Lord, who has redeemed me, a lost and condemned creature, delivered me and freed me from all sins, from death, and from the power of the devil, not with silver and gold but with his holy and precious blood and with his innocent sufferings and death, in order that I may be his, live under him in his kingdom, and serve him in everlasting righteousness, innocence, and blessedness, even as he is risen from the dead and lives and reigns to all eternity. This is most certainly true.

[5] THE THIRD ARTICLE: SANCTIFICATION

"I believe in the Holy Spirit, the holy Christian church, the communion of saints, the forgiveness of sins, the resurrection of the body, and the life everlasting. Amen."

[6] What does this mean?

Answer: I believe that by my own reason or strength I cannot believe in Jesus Christ, my Lord, or come to him. But the Holy Spirit has called me through the gospel, enlightened me with his gifts, and sanctified and preserved me in true faith, just as he calls, gathers, enlightens, and sanctifies the whole Christian church on earth and preserves it in union with Jesus Christ in the one true faith. In this Christian church he daily and abundantly forgives all my sins, and the sins of all believers, and on the last day he will raise me and all the dead and will grant eternal life to me and to all who believe in Christ. This is most certainly true.

[3.] The Lord's Prayer

in the plain form in which the head of the family shall teach it to his household

[INTRODUCTION]

[Mt 6.9–13]   [1] *"Our Father who art in heaven."*

[2] What does this mean?

Answer: Here God would encourage us to believe that he is truly our Father and we are truly his children in order that we may approach him boldly and confidently in prayer, even as beloved children approach their dear father.

[3] THE FIRST PETITION

"Hallowed be thy name."

[4] What does this mean?

Answer: To be sure, God's name is holy in itself, but we pray in this petition that it may also be holy for us.

[5] How is this done?

Answer: When the word of God is taught clearly and purely and we, as children of God, lead holy lives in accordance with it. Help us to do this, dear Father in heaven! But whoever teaches and lives otherwise than as the word of God teaches, profanes the name of God among us. From this preserve us, heavenly Father!

[6] THE SECOND PETITION

"Thy kingdom come."

[7] What does this mean?

Answer: To be sure, the kingdom of God comes of itself, without our prayer, but we pray in this petition that it may also come to us.

[8] How is this done?

Answer: When the heavenly Father gives us his Holy Spirit so that by his grace we may believe his holy word and live a godly life, both here in time and hereafter forever.

[9] THE THIRD PETITION

"Thy will be done, on earth as it is in heaven."

[10] What does this mean?

Answer: To be sure, the good and gracious will of God is done without our prayer, but we pray in this petition that it may also be done by us.

[11] How is this done?

Answer: When God curbs and destroys every evil counsel and purpose of the devil, of the world, and of our flesh which would hinder us from hallowing his name and prevent the coming of his kingdom, and when he strengthens us and keeps us steadfast in his word and in faith even to the end. This is his good and gracious will.

[12] THE FOURTH PETITION

"Give us this day our daily bread."

[13] What does this mean?

Answer: To be sure, God provides daily bread, even to the wicked, without our prayer, but we pray in this petition that God may make us aware of his gifts and enable us to receive our daily bread with thanksgiving.

[14] What is meant by daily bread?

Answer: Everything required to satisfy our bodily needs, such as food and clothing, house and home, fields and flocks, money and property; a pious spouse and good children, trustworthy servants, godly and faithful rulers, good government; seasonable weather, peace and health, order and honor; true friends, faithful neighbors, and the like.

[15] THE FIFTH PETITION

"And forgive us our debts, as we also have forgiven our debtors."

[16] What does this mean?

Answer: We pray in this petition that our heavenly Father may not look upon our sins, and on their account deny our prayers, for we neither merit nor deserve those things for which we pray. Although we sin daily and deserve nothing but punishment, we nevertheless pray that God may grant us all things by his grace. And assuredly we on our part will heartily forgive and cheerfully do good to those who may sin against us.

[17] THE SIXTH PETITION

"And lead us not into temptation."

[18] What does this mean?

Answer: God tempts no one to sin, but we pray in this petition that God may so guard and preserve us that the devil, the world, and our flesh may not deceive us or mislead us into unbelief, despair, and other great and shameful sins, but that, although we may be so tempted, we may finally prevail and gain the victory.

[19] THE SEVENTH PETITION

"But deliver us from evil."

[20] What does this mean?

Answer: We pray in this petition, as in a summary, that our Father in heaven may deliver us from all manner of evil, whether it affect body or soul, property or reputation, and that at last, when the hour of death comes, he may grant us a blessed end and graciously take us from this world of sorrow to himself in heaven.

CONCLUSION

"Amen."

[21] What does this mean?

Answer: It means that I should be assured that such petitions are acceptable to our heavenly Father and are heard by him, for he himself commanded us to pray like this and promised to hear us. "Amen, amen" means "Yes, yes, it shall be so."

[4.] The Sacrament of Holy Baptism

in the plain form in which the head of the family shall teach it to his household

FIRST

[1] What is baptism?

[2] Answer: Baptism is not merely water, but it is water used according to God's command and connected with God's word.

[3] What is this word of God?

[4] Answer: As recorded in the last chapter of Matthew, our Lord Christ said, "Go therefore and make disciples of all nations, baptizing them in the name Mt 28[.19] of the Father and of the Son and of the Holy Spirit."

SECOND

[5] What gifts or benefits does baptism bestow?

[6] Answer: It effects forgiveness of sins, delivers from death and the devil, and grants eternal salvation to all who believe, as the word and promise of God declare.

[7] What is this word and promise of God?

[8] Answer: As recorded in Mark 16, our Lord Christ said, "He who be-
Mk 16[.16] lieves and is baptized will be saved; but he who does not believe will be condemned."

THIRD

[9] How can water produce such great effects?

[10] Answer: It is not the water that produces these effects, but the word of God connected with the water, and our faith which relies on the word of God connected with the water. For without the word of God the water is merely water and no baptism. But when connected with the word of God it is a baptism, that is, a gracious water of life and a washing of regeneration in the Holy Spirit, as St. Paul wrote to Titus in the third chapter, "He saved us by the washing of regeneration and renewal in the Holy Spirit, which he poured out upon us richly through Jesus Christ our Savior, so that we might be justified by his grace and become heirs in hope of eternal life." This saying is sure.   Ti 3[.5–8]

FOURTH

[11] What does such baptizing with water signify?

[12] Answer: It signifies that the old Adam in us, together with all sins and evil lusts, should be drowned by daily sorrow and repentance and be put to death, and that the new man should come forth daily and rise up, cleansed and righteous, to live forever in God's presence.

[13] Where is this written?

[14] Answer: In Romans 6, St. Paul wrote, "We were buried therefore with him by baptism into death, so that as Christ was raised from the dead by the glory of the Father, we too might walk in newness of life."   Rom 6[.4]

[5.] Confession and Absolution

HOW PLAIN PEOPLE ARE TO BE TAUGHT TO CONFESS[1]

[16] What is confession?

Answer: Confession consists of two parts. One is that we confess our sins. The other is that we receive absolution or forgiveness from the confessor as from God himself, by no means doubting but firmly believing that our sins are thereby forgiven before God in heaven.

[17] What sins should we confess?

[18] Answer: Before God we should acknowledge that we are guilty of all manner of sins, even those of which we are not aware, as we do in the Lord's Prayer.

---

1. This section first appears in the 1531 version, replacing the earlier "Short Method of Confession" of the 1529 version. See *WA* 30/2:342–45 for the 1529 text. See Tappert's notes for other variants in the 1531 edition and differences between the Latin and German versions.

Before the confessor, however, we should confess only those sins of which we have knowledge and which trouble us.

[19] What are such sins?

[20] Answer: Reflect on your condition in the light of the Ten Commandments: whether you are a father or mother, a son or daughter, a master or servant; whether you have been disobedient, unfaithful, lazy, ill-tempered, or quarrelsome; whether you have harmed anyone by word or deed; and whether you have stolen, neglected, or wasted anything, or done other evil.

[21] Please give me a brief form of confession.

Answer: You should say to the confessor: "Dear Pastor, please hear my confession and declare that my sins are forgiven for God's sake."

"Proceed."

[22] "I, a poor sinner, confess before God that I am guilty of all sins. In particular I confess in your presence that, as a manservant or maidservant, etc., I am unfaithful to my master, for here and there I have not done what I was told. I have made my master angry, caused him to curse, neglected to do my duty, and caused him to suffer loss. I have also been immodest in word and deed. I have quarreled with my equals. I have grumbled and sworn at my mistress, etc. For all this I am sorry and pray for grace. I mean to do better."

[23] A master or mistress may say: "In particular I confess in your presence that I have not been faithful in training my children, servants, and wife to the glory of God. I have cursed. I have set a bad example by my immodest language and actions. I have injured my neighbor by speaking evil of him, overcharging him, giving him inferior goods and short measure." Masters and mistresses should add whatever else they have done contrary to God's commandments and to their action in life, etc.

[24] If, however, anyone does not feel that his conscience is burdened by such or by greater sins, he should not worry, nor should he search for and invent other sins, for this would turn confession into torture; he should simply mention one or two sins of which he is aware. For example, "In particular I confess that I once cursed. On one occasion I also spoke indecently. And I neglected this or that," etc. Let this suffice.

[25] If you have knowledge of no sin at all (which is quite unlikely), you should mention none in particular, but receive forgiveness upon the general confession which you make to God in the presence of the confessor.

[26] Then the confessor shall say: "God be merciful to you and strengthen your faith. Amen."

[27] Again he shall say: "Do you believe that this forgiveness is the forgiveness of God?"

[28] Answer: "Yes, I do."

Then he shall say: "Be it done for you as you have believed. According to   [Mt 8.13]
the command of our Lord Jesus Christ, I forgive you your sins in the name of the
Father and of the Son and of the Holy Spirit. Amen. Go in peace."[a]

[29] A confessor will know additional passages of the Scriptures with
which to comfort and to strengthen the faith of those whose consciences are heavily
burdened or who are distressed and sorely tried. This is intended simply as an ordinary form of confession for plain people.

[6.] The Sacrament of the Altar

in the plain form in which the head of the family shall teach it to his household

[1] What is the sacrament of the altar?

[2] Answer: Instituted by Christ himself, it is the true body and blood of
our Lord Jesus Christ, under the bread and wine, given to us Christians to eat and
to drink.

[3] Where is this written?

[4] Answer: The holy evangelists Matthew, Mark, and Luke, and also St.
Paul, write thus: "Our Lord Jesus Christ, on the night when he was betrayed, took
bread, and when he had given thanks, he broke it, and gave it to the disciples and
said, 'Take, eat; this is my body which is given for you. Do this in remembrance
of me.' In the same way also he took the cup, after supper, and when he had given
thanks he gave it to them, saying, 'Drink of it, all of you. This cup is the new covenant in my blood, which is poured out for many for the forgiveness of sins. Do this,
as often as you drink it, in remembrance of me.'"[b]

[5] What is the benefit of such eating and drinking?

[6] Answer: We are told in the words "for you" and "for the forgiveness of
sin." By these words the forgiveness of sins, life, and salvation are given to us in the
sacrament, for where there is forgiveness of sins, there are also life and salvation.

[7] How can bodily eating and drinking produce such great effects?

[8] Answer: The eating and drinking do not in themselves produce them,
but the words "for you" and "for the forgiveness of sins." These words, when ac-

a. [Mk 5.34; Lk 7.50, 8.48]
b. [1 Cor 11.23; Mt 26.26–28; Mk 14.22–24; Lk 22.19–20]

companied by the bodily eating and drinking, are the chief thing in the sacrament, and he who believes these words has what they say and declare: the forgiveness of sins.

[9] Who, then, receives this sacrament worthily?

[10] Answer: Fasting and bodily preparation are a good external discipline, but he is truly worthy and well prepared who believes these words: "for you" and "for the forgiveness of sins." On the other hand, he who does not believe these words, or doubts them, is unworthy and unprepared, for the words "for you" require truly believing hearts.

[7.] Morning and Evening Prayers
HOW THE HEAD OF THE FAMILY SHALL TEACH HIS HOUSEHOLD TO SAY MORNING AND EVENING PRAYERS

[1] In the morning, when you rise, make the sign of the cross and say, "In the name of God, the Father, the Son, and the Holy Spirit. Amen."

[2] Then, kneeling or standing, say the Apostles' Creed and the Lord's Prayer. Then you may say this prayer:

"I give thee thanks, heavenly Father, through thy dear Son Jesus Christ, that thou hast protected me through the night from all harm and danger. I beseech thee to keep me this day, too, from all sin and evil, that in all my thoughts, words, and deeds I may please thee. Into thy hands I commend my body and soul and all that is mine. Let thy holy angel have charge of me, that the wicked one may have no power over me. Amen."

[3] After singing a hymn (possibly a hymn on the Ten Commandments) or whatever your devotion may suggest, you should go to your work joyfully.

[4] In the evening, when you retire, make the sign of the cross and say, "In the name of God, the Father, the Son, and the Holy Spirit. Amen."

[5] Then, kneeling or standing, say the Apostles' Creed and the Lord's Prayer. Then you may say this prayer:

"I give thee thanks, heavenly Father, through thy dear Son Jesus Christ, that thou hast this day graciously protected me. I beseech thee to forgive all my sin and the wrong which I have done. Graciously protect me during the coming night. Into thy hands I commend my body and soul and all that is mine. Let thy holy angels have charge of me, that the wicked one may have no power over me. Amen."

Then quickly lie down and sleep in peace.

[8.] Grace at Table

[6] HOW THE HEAD OF THE FAMILY SHALL TEACH HIS
HOUSEHOLD TO OFFER BLESSING AND THANKSGIVING AT TABLE
BLESSING BEFORE EATING

[7] When children and the whole household gather at the table, they should reverently fold their hands and say:

"The eyes of all look to thee, O Lord, and thou givest them their food in due season. Thou openest thy hand; thou satisfiest the desire of every living thing." [Ps 145.15–16]

[8] (It is to be observed that "satisfying the desire of every living thing" means that all creatures receive enough to eat to make them joyful and of good cheer. Greed and anxiety about food prevent such satisfaction.)

[9] Then the Lord's Prayer should be said, and afterwards this prayer:

"Lord God, heavenly Father, bless us, and these thy gifts which of thy bountiful goodness thou hast bestowed on us, through Jesus Christ our Lord. Amen."

[THANKSGIVING AFTER EATING]

[10] After eating, likewise, they should fold their hands reverently and say:

"O give thanks to the Lord, for he is good; for his steadfast love endures forever. He gives to the beasts their food, and to the young ravens which cry. His delight is not in the strength of the horse, nor his pleasure in the legs of a man; but the Lord takes pleasure in those who fear him, in those who hope in his steadfast love."[a]

[11] Then the Lord's Prayer should be said, and afterwards this prayer:

"We give thee thanks, Lord God, our Father, for all thy benefits, through Jesus Christ our Lord, who lives and reigns forever. Amen."

[9.] Table of Duties

[1] CONSISTING OF CERTAIN PASSAGES OF THE SCRIPTURES,
SELECTED FOR VARIOUS ESTATES AND CONDITIONS OF MEN,
BY WHICH THEY MAY BE ADMONISHED TO DO THEIR
RESPECTIVE DUTIES

[2] BISHOPS, PASTORS, AND PREACHERS

"A bishop must be above reproach, married only once, temperate, sensible, dignified, hospitable, an apt teacher, no drunkard, not violent but gentle, not quarrel-

a. [Ps 106.1, 136.26, 147.9–11]

some, and no lover of money. He must manage his own household well, keeping his children submissive and respectful in every way. He must not be a recent convert," etc., as in the first epistle to Timothy at the fourth chapter.

1 Tm [3.2–6]

[3] DUTIES CHRISTIANS OWE THEIR TEACHERS AND PASTORS[2]

"Remain in the same house, eating and drinking what they provide, for the laborer deserves his wages," Luke 10. "The Lord commanded that those who proclaim the gospel should get their living by the gospel," 1 Corinthians. "Let him who is taught the word share all good things with him who teaches. Do not be deceived; God is not mocked," Galatians 6. "Let the elders who rule well be considered worthy of double honor, especially those who labor in preaching and teaching; for the Scripture says, 'You shall not muzzle an ox when it is treading out the grain,' and 'The laborer deserves his wages,'" 1 Timothy 5. "We beseech you, brethren, to respect those who labor among you and who are over you in the Lord and admonish you, and to esteem them very highly in love because of their work. Be at peace among yourselves," 1 Thessalonians 5. "Obey your leaders and submit to them; for they are keeping watch over your souls, as men who will have to give account. Let them do this joyfully, and not sadly, for that would be of no advantage to you," Hebrews 13.

Lk 10[.7]

1 Cor 9[.14]

Gal 6[.6–7]

[Deut 25.4]

1 Tm 5[.17–18]

1 Thes 5[.12–13]

Heb 13[.17]

[4] GOVERNING AUTHORITIES

"Let every person be subject to the governing authorities. For there is no authority except from God, and those that exist have been instituted by God. Therefore he who resists the authorities resists what God has appointed, and those who resist will incur judgment. He who is in authority does not bear the sword in vain; he is the servant of God to execute his wrath on the wrongdoer." In Romans, the thirteenth chapter.

Rom 13[.1–4]

[5] DUTIES SUBJECTS OWE TO GOVERNING AUTHORITIES

Matthew 22: "Render therefore to Caesar the things that are Caesar's, and to God the things that are God's." Romans 13: "Let every person be subject to the governing authorities. Therefore one must be subject, not only to avoid God's wrath but also for the sake of conscience. For the same reason you also pay taxes, for the authorities are ministers of God, attending to this very thing. Pay all of them their dues, taxes to whom taxes are due, revenue to whom revenue is due, respect to whom

Mt 22[.21]

Rom 13[.1, 5–7]

2. Tappert notes that this section and the section below on "Governing Authorities" were not prepared by Luther but were probably added later with his consent.

respect is due, honor to whom honor is due." 1 Timothy 2: "I urge that supplica-   1 Tm 2[.1–2]
tions, prayers, intercessions, and thanksgivings be made for all men, for kings and
all who are in high positions, that we may lead a quiet and peaceable life, godly
and respectful in every way, etc." Titus 3: "Remind them to be submissive to rulers   Ti 3[.1]
and authorities, to be obedient, to be ready for any honest work." 1 Peter 2: "Be   1 Pt 2[.13–14]
subject for the Lord's sake to every human institution, whether it be to the emperor
as supreme, or to governors as sent by him to punish those who do wrong and to
praise those who do right."

[6] HUSBANDS

"You husbands, live considerately with your wives, bestowing honor on the woman
as the weaker sex, since you are joint heirs of the grace of life, in order that your
prayers may not be hindered," 1 Peter, chapter 3. "Husbands, love your wives, and   1 Pt 3[.7]
do not be harsh with them," in Colossians, chapter 3.   Col 3[.19]

[7] WIVES

"You wives, be submissive to your husbands, as Sarah obeyed Abraham, calling him
lord. And you are now her children if you do right and let nothing terrify you,"
1 Peter 3.   [1 Pt 3.1, 6]

[8] PARENTS

"Fathers, do not provoke your children to anger, lest they become discouraged, but
bring them up in the discipline and instruction of the Lord," Ephesians 6.   Eph 6[.4; Col 3.21]

[9] CHILDREN

"Children, obey your parents in the Lord, for this is right. 'Honor your father and
mother' (this is the first commandment with a promise) 'that it may be well with
you and that you may live long on the earth,'" Ephesians 6.   Eph 6[.1–3]

[10] LABORERS AND SERVANTS, MALE AND FEMALE

"Be obedient to those who are your earthly masters, with fear and trembling, with
singleness of heart, as to Christ; not in the way of eye-service, as men-pleasers, but
as servants of Christ, doing the will of God from the heart, rendering service with
a good will as to the Lord and not to men, knowing that whatever good anyone
does, he will receive the same again from the Lord, whether he is a slave or free,"
Ephesians 6.   Eph 6[.5–8]

[11] MASTERS AND MISTRESSES

"Masters, do the same to them, and forbear threatening, knowing that he who is both their Master and yours is in heaven, and that there is no partiality with him,"

Eph 6[.9]   Ephesians 6.

[12] YOUNG PERSONS IN GENERAL

"You that are younger, be subject to the elders. Clothe yourselves, all of you, with humility toward one another, for 'God opposes the proud, but gives grace to the humble.' Humble yourselves therefore under the mighty hand of God, that in due

1 Pt 5[.5–6]   time he may exalt you," 1 Peter 5.

[13] WIDOWS

"She who is a real widow, and is left all alone, has set her hope on God and continues in supplications and prayers night and day; whereas she who is self-indulgent

1 Tm 5[.5–6]   is dead even while she lives," 1 Timothy 5.

[14] CHRISTIANS IN GENERAL

The commandments are summed up in this sentence: "You shall love your neighbor

Rom 13[.9]   as yourself" from Romans 13. "I urge that supplications, prayers, intercessions, and

1 Tm 2[.1]   thanksgivings be made for all men," 1 Timothy 2.

> Let each his lesson learn with care
> And all the household well will fare.[3]

---

3. See *WA* 35:580 for a discussion of this couplet.

The Augsburg Confession, 1530, and The Apology of the Augsburg Confession, 1530-31

In a private letter to his wife, Emperor Charles V wrote that he had convened the Diet of Augsburg "to tear out heresy by the roots."[1] His public invitation, however, was more irenic. He expressed a desire "to allay divisions, to cease hostility, to surrender past errors to our Savior, and to display diligence in hearing, understanding, and considering with love and kindness the opinions and views of everybody, in order to reduce them to one single Christian truth."[2] Religious differences in Germany concerned the emperor, not only because he accepted the Catholic Church as the one true faith, but also because these differences had shattered political unity. In the face of Turkish advances in southeastern Europe—including the siege of Vienna in 1529—the emperor wanted assurances of support, both monetary and military, from the German princes.

In preparation for the diet, Elector John of Saxony asked Martin Luther, Justus Jonas, Johann Bugenhagen (1485–1558), and Philipp Melanchthon to prepare a statement of beliefs and a defense of church practices in Saxony. A confession of faith in the form of seventeen articles had been drawn up by Luther, Melanchthon, Jonas, and Johannes Brenz (1499–1570) for → *The Marburg Colloquy* in 1529 and adopted later that year at Schwabach. To these *Schwabach Articles* the Wittenberg theologians added a summary of ecclesiastical errors that they claimed to have corrected in Lutheran practice, such as clerical celibacy, the withholding of the chalice, compulsory confession, issues of authority, dietary rules, and monastic vows. This summary is known as *The Torgau Articles* because the theologians agreed upon the document—probably composed in final draft by Melanchthon—in the city of Torgau in March 1530.

The Augsburg Confession is a combination of the *Schwabach* and *Torgau Articles*, revised by Melanchthon in consultation with Luther for presentation to the emperor on 25 June 1530. The confession is written in a civil and conciliatory tone and emphasizes the moderate positions of the Lutherans, perhaps in an effort to divorce themselves from more radical reform movements. → *The Nicene Creed* and → *The Apostles' Creed* are cited as doctrinal standards under article 1 (God) and article 3 (Son of God), respectively. In the passage on justification (article 4),

---

1. Brandi 1965, 306.
2. Förstmann [1833] 1966, 1:8. Translation from *Triglotta*, "Historical Introduction," 18.

Melanchthon referred to "faith," but did not modify it with "sola" ("faith alone"), as Luther would have preferred.[3] He did, however, clearly express the belief that good works cannot reconcile humans with God (article 20). The Lutheran concept of "sola scriptura" is not explicitly stated in any of the twenty-eight articles, although Melanchthon says that all these beliefs are grounded in Holy Scriptures (article 21). He quickly adds, however, that they are not contrary to the teachings of the church, to tradition, or to patristic authorities.

Luther could not attend the Diet of Augsburg himself because he was technically an outlaw, but he corresponded with Melanchthon from Coburg. As drafts were exchanged, Luther sometimes complained that Melanchthon was too careful, but he eventually expressed approval of his work, even stating that he could not have done better himself, "denn ich so sanfft und leise nicht tretten kan" [for I cannot tread so gently and lightly].[4]

Before presentation to the emperor, six more German princes and two free cities (Reutlingen and Nuremberg) joined John of Saxony in signing *The Augsburg Confession,* making it a unified and authoritative statement of faith. After the reading before the diet (during which, some sources claim, the emperor fell asleep), four more free imperial cities signed the confession.[5] Other signatories followed, quickly establishing it as the chief confession of the Lutheran movement.

The Augsburg Confession was challenged in a *Confutation* prepared within a week by Roman Catholic theologians, among whom were Luther's bitter enemies Johannes Eck (1486–1543) and Johannes Cochlaeus (1479–1552). Even Charles V rejected the first draft of the *Confutation* as too polemical, and it was toned down somewhat before submission on 3 August. The emperor also wrote to Pope Clement VII, asking him to convene a council and to curb the abuses outlined by the

3. In two early versions of the German text, the phrase "allein durch den Glauben" appears, but Melanchthon seems to have removed "allein" from the final copy presented to the emperor. See *BLK* 56.

4. *WA Br* 5, no. 1568, 5–8. The letter was written on 15 May 1530. Delivery of correspondence was then delayed for three weeks, so that Luther did not see the final draft of the confession until it had been presented to the emperor. For a discussion of Luther's views during the drafting of *The Augsburg Confession* and thereafter, see Hägglund 1980; Klug 1980; and Lohse 1980a, 1983.

5. The cities of Windsheim, Heilbronn, Kempte, and Weißenburg im Nordgau signed in mid-July.

Protestants. But this was not to occur for another fifteen years, when Paul III convened the Council of Trent.

In reply to the *Confutation*, Melanchthon wrote his *Apology of the Augsburg Confession*, but Charles V refused to receive it. It was published in revised form in 1531. In 1537, Lutheran leaders and clergy signed the *Apology*, together with *The Augsburg Confession* and → *The Smalcald Articles*. It has a place in *The Book of Concord* as an official Lutheran confession.

The textual history of *The Augsburg Confession* is complex: it was based on the *Schwabach* and *Torgau Articles;* revised continuously in the spring and summer of 1530 before presentation; printed unofficially in 1530; published in an authorized imprint with minor changes in 1531; substantially modified by Melanchthon in a 1540 edition (known as the *Variata*);[6] and reconstructed in 1580 (the *Invariata* edition) to reflect more closely the text signed at Augsburg. The actual documents presented to the emperor do not survive, but there are several manuscripts from 1530, including copies of early drafts and manuscripts containing emendations made after 25 June 1530. Melanchthon's preface was replaced by a more obsequious introduction probably written by Gregor Brück, chancellor of electoral Saxony.[7] Further complicating the textual history is the bilingualism of the original, prepared in both Latin and German versions for presentation to the emperor.[8] The *editio princeps* appeared in 1531 at the Wittenberg press of Georg Rhau. The Latin text was issued first, together with the *Apology*. Within a few months, however, Rhau printed the German version by Justus Jonas and the two were sold as a dual-language edition.[9]

In recent years, *The Augsburg Confession* has been presented as a document with ecumenical significance. The claim arises from the fact that it was a major

6. For political as well as theological reasons, Melanchthon reworked *The Augsburg Confession*, particularly article 10 on the eucharist, to make it more palatable to the Reformed Church. See Lohse 1980a, esp. 413–15; and Maurer 1962. The text of *The Variata* is in Stupperich 1955, 6:12–79.

7. See *BLK* 33–43, for Melanchthon's original draft. There is also an earlier draft of his conclusion; see *BLK* 135–36.

8. Charles V requested that participants provide written texts of their views in both German and Latin. See Förstmann [1833] 1966, 1:309.

9. *Confessio Augustana. Confessio Fidei exhibita inuictiss. Imp. Carolo V. Caesari Aug. in Comicijs Augustae. Anno M.D.XXX. Addita est Apologia Confessionis. Beide, Deudsch vnd Latinisch* . . . (Wittemberg: Georg Rhau, 1531). The confession was printed in 1530 in an unauthorized German version; see Weber 1783–84, 353; and Kolb-Wengert, 29.

source for → *The Thirty-Nine Articles* of the Church of England, was accepted by John Calvin in 1541, and recognized by Reformed churches in Germany and Switzerland. In the 1970s, the Catholic Church even considered the possibility of recognizing *The Augsburg Confession* as a valid expression of Christian truth.[10] As Avery Dulles optimistically noted, "Everything in the *Confessio Augustana* was considered to be in agreement with the faith of the one catholic Church. [It] is therefore in principle an ecumenical document."[11] Although such discussions have contributed to better understanding of the commonality of belief between Lutherans and Roman Catholics, the realities of the Reformation make Roman Catholic recognition of this particular document difficult.

> **Edition:** *BLK* 44–137, with indications of the most significant changes in the *Variata* text, as edited by Stupperich 1955, 6:12–79. Edition of *The Apology*: *BLK* 141–404.

> **Translation:** Tappert, 23–96 (translations of both the Latin, at the bottom of the page, and German, at the top of the page). Translation of *The Apology* (from the first edition of the original Latin): Tappert, 98–285.

> **Note:** The Latin and German texts in the critical edition authorized by the Lutheran Church reflect the attempt—first made for *The Book of Concord* in 1580—to reconstruct the texts presented to the emperor in 1530. Versification follows the Latin text and is applied to the German version. Hence, the numbers do not always fall sequentially in the German version. For a translation of *The Apology* from the substantially altered second edition of 1531, see Kolb-Wengert, 109–294.

> **Literature:** Aalen 1981; Brandi 1965, 292–332; Brecht 1985–93, 2:387–97; Burgess 1980; *Chr Trad* 4:186; Dulles 1980; *EKL* 1:319–24; Förstmann [1833] 1966; Gritsch 1976; Gussmann 1911; Hägglund 1980; *Luther und die Bekenntnisschriften* 1981; Klug 1980; Kolb 1980; Kolb-Wengert, 27–29, 107–9; Lohse 1979, 1980a, 1983; Manns 1981; Maurer 1962, 1986; Pfnür 1970; Reu; Scheible 1997, 106–36, 153–58; *TRE* 4:616–39 (Sperl); Weber 1783–84.

10. See Burgess 1980.
11. Dulles 1980, 131.

The Augsburg Confession, 1530

A Confession of Faith Presented in Augsburg by Certain Princes and Cities to His Imperial Majesty Charles V

Psalms 119[.46]
"I will also speak of thy testimonies before kings,
and shall not be put to shame."

Preface

Most serene, most mighty, invincible Emperor, most gracious Lord:
[1] A short time ago Your Imperial Majesty graciously summoned a diet of the empire to convene here in Augsburg. In the summons Your Majesty indicated an earnest desire to deliberate concerning matters pertaining to the Turk, that traditional foe of ours and of the Christian religion, and how with continuing help he might effectively be resisted. [2] The desire was also expressed for deliberation on what might be done about the dissension concerning our holy faith and the Chris-

---

A Confession of Faith Presented in Augsburg to His Imperial Majesty Charles V at the Diet of Augsburg

Psalms 119[.46]
"I will also speak of thy testimonies before kings,
and shall not be put to shame."

Preface

[1] Most serene, most mighty, invincible Emperor, most gracious Lord: A short time ago Your Imperial Majesty graciously summoned a diet of the empire to convene here in Augsburg. In the summons Your Majesty indicated an earnest desire to deliberate concerning matters pertaining to the Turk, that traditional foe of ours and of the Christian religion, and how with continuing help he might effectively be resisted. [2] The desire was also expressed for deliberation on what might be done about the dissension concerning our holy faith and the Christian religion, and to

tian religion, and to this end it was proposed to employ all diligence amicably and charitably to hear, understand, and weigh the judgments, opinions, and beliefs of the several parties among us to unite the same in agreement on one Christian truth, [3] to put aside whatever may not have been rightly interpreted or treated by either side, [4] to have all of us embrace and adhere to a single, true religion and live together in unity and in one fellowship and church, even as we are all enlisted under one Christ. [5] Inasmuch as we, the undersigned elector and princes and our associates, have been summoned for these purposes, together with other electors, princes, and estates, we have complied with the command and can say without boasting that we were among the first to arrive.

[6] In connection with the matter pertaining to the faith and in conformity with the imperial summons, Your Imperial Majesty also graciously and earnestly requested that each of the electors, princes, and estates should commit to writing and present, in German and Latin, his judgments, opinions, and beliefs with reference to the said errors, dissensions, and abuses. [7] Accordingly, after due deliberation and counsel, it was decided last Wednesday that, in keeping with Your Majesty's wish, we should present our case in German and Latin today (Friday). [8] Wherefore, in dutiful obedience to Your Imperial Majesty, we offer and present a confes-

---

this end it was proposed to employ all diligence amicably and charitably to hear, understand, and weigh the judgments, opinions, and beliefs of the several parties among us to unite the same in agreement on one Christian truth, [3] to put aside whatever may not have been rightly interpreted or treated in the writings of either party, [4] to have all of us embrace and adhere to a single, true religion and live together in unity and in one fellowship and church, even as we are all enlisted under one Christ. [5] Inasmuch as we, the undersigned elector and princes and our associates, have been summoned for these purposes, together with other electors, princes, and estates, we have complied with the command and can say without boasting that we were among the first to arrive.

[6] In connection with the matter pertaining to the faith and in conformity with the imperial summons, Your Imperial Majesty also graciously and earnestly requested that each of the electors, princes, and estates should commit to writing and present, in German and Latin, his judgments, opinions, and beliefs with reference to the said errors, dissensions, and abuses. [7] Accordingly, after due deliberation and counsel, it was decided last Wednesday that, in keeping with Your Majesty's wish, we should present our case in German and Latin today (Friday). [8] Wherefore, in dutiful obedience to Your Imperial Majesty, we offer and present a confes-

sion of our pastors' and preachers' teaching and of our own faith, setting forth how and in what manner, on the basis of the Holy Scriptures, these things are preached, taught, communicated, and embraced in our lands, principalities, dominions, cities, and territories.

[9] If the other electors, princes, and estates also submit a similar written statement of their judgments and opinions, in Latin and German, [10] we are prepared, in obedience to Your Imperial Majesty, our most gracious lord, to discuss with them and their associates, in so far as this can honorably be done, such practical and equitable ways as may restore unity. Thus the matters at issue between us may be presented in writing on both sides, they may be discussed amicably and charitably, our differences may be reconciled, and we may be united in one, true religion, [11] even as we are all under one Christ and should confess and contend for Christ. All of this is in accord with Your Imperial Majesty's aforementioned summons. That it may be done according to divine truth we invoke almighty God in deepest humility and implore him to bestow his grace to this end. Amen!

[12] If, however, our lords, friends, and associates who represent the electors, princes, and estates of the other party do not comply with the procedure intended by Your Imperial Majesty's summons, if no amicable and charitable nego-

---

sion of our pastors' and preachers' teaching and of our own faith, setting forth how and in what manner, on the basis of the Holy Scriptures, these things are preached, taught, communicated, and embraced in our lands, principalities, dominions, cities and territories.

[9] If the other electors, princes, and estates also submit a similar written statement of their judgments and opinions, in Latin and German, [10] we are prepared, in obedience to Your Imperial Majesty, our most gracious lord, to discuss with them and their associates, in so far as this can honorably be done, such practical and equitable ways as may restore unity. Thus the matters at issue between us may be presented in writing on both sides, they may be discussed amicably and charitably, our differences may be reconciled, and we may be united in one, true religion, [11] even as we are all under one Christ and should confess and contend for Christ. All of this is in accord with Your Imperial Majesty's aforementioned summons. That it may be done according to divine truth we invoke almighty God in deepest humility and implore him to bestow his grace to this end. Amen.

[12] If, however, our lords, friends, and associates who represent the electors, princes, and estates of the other party do not comply with the procedure intended by Your Imperial Majesty's summons, if no amicable and charitable nego-

tiations take place between us, and if no results are attained, [13] nevertheless we on our part shall not omit doing anything, in so far as God and conscience allow, that may serve the cause of Christian unity. [14] Of this Your Imperial Majesty, our aforementioned friends (the electors, princes, and estates), and every lover of the Christian religion who is concerned about these questions will be graciously and sufficiently assured from what follows in the confession which we and our associates submit.

[15] In the past Your Imperial Majesty graciously gave assurance to the electors, princes, and estates of the empire, especially in a public instruction at the diet in Spires [Speyer] in 1526, [16] that for reasons there stated Your Imperial Majesty was not disposed to render decisions in matters pertaining to our holy faith but would diligently urge it upon the pope to call a council. [17] Again, by means of a written instruction at the last diet in Spires a year ago, [18] the electors, princes, and estates of the empire were, among other things, informed and notified by Your Imperial Majesty's viceroy (His Royal Majesty of Hungary and Bohemia, etc.) and by Your Imperial Majesty's orator and appointed commissioners, that Your Imperial Majesty's viceroy, administrators, and councilors of the imperial government (together with the absent electors, princes, and representatives of the estates) who

---

tiations take place between us, and if no results are attained, [13] nevertheless we on our part shall not omit doing anything, in so far as God and conscience allow, that may serve the cause of Christian unity. [14] Of this Your Imperial Majesty, our aforementioned friends (the electors, princes, and estates), and every lover of the Christian religion who is concerned about these questions will be graciously and sufficiently assured from what follows in the confession which we and our associates submit.

[15] In the past, not only once, but many times, Your Imperial Majesty graciously gave assurance to the electors, princes, and estates of the empire, especially in a public instruction at the diet in Speyer in 1526, [16] that for reasons there stated Your Imperial Majesty was not disposed to render decisions in matters pertaining to our holy faith but would diligently urge it upon the pope to call a council. [17] Again, by means of a written instruction at the last diet in Speyer a year ago, [18] the electors, princes, and estates of the empire were, among other things, informed and notified by Your Imperial Majesty's viceroy (His Royal Majesty of Hungary and Bohemia, etc.) and by Your Imperial Majesty's orator and appointed commissioners, that Your Imperial Majesty's viceroy, administrators, and councilors of the imperial government (together with the absent electors, princes, and representatives

were assembled at the diet convened in Regensburg had considered the proposal concerning a general council and acknowledged [19] that it would be profitable to have such a council called. Since the relations between Your Imperial Majesty and the pope were improving and were progressing toward a good, Christian understanding, Your Imperial Majesty was sure that the pope would not refuse to call a general council, [20] and so Your Imperial Majesty graciously offered to promote and bring about the calling of such a general council by the pope, along with Your Imperial Majesty, at the earliest opportunity and to allow no hindrance to be put in the way.

[21] If the outcome should be such as we mentioned above, we offer in full obedience, even beyond what is required, to participate in such a general, free, and Christian council as the electors, princes, and estates have with the highest and best motives requested in all the diets of the empire which have been held during Your Imperial Majesty's reign. [22] We have at various times made our protestations and appeals concerning these most weighty matters, and have done so in legal form and procedure. [23] To these we declare our continuing adherence, and we shall not be turned aside from our position by these or any following negotiations (unless the matters in dissension are finally heard, amicably weighed, charitably

---

of the estates) who were assembled at the diet convened in Regensburg had considered the proposal concerning a general council [19] and acknowledged that it would be profitable to have such a council called. Since the relations between Your Imperial Majesty and the pope were improving and were progressing toward a good, Christian understanding, Your Imperial Majesty was sure that the pope would not refuse to call a general council, [20] and so Your Imperial Majesty graciously offered to promote and bring about the calling of such a general council by the pope, along with Your Imperial Majesty, at the earliest opportunity and to allow no hindrance to be put in the way.

[21] If the outcome should be such that these differences between us and the other party should not be amicably settled, we offer in full obedience, even beyond what is required, to participate in such a general, free, and Christian council as the electors, princes, and estates have with the highest and best motives requested in all the diets of the empire which have been held during Your Imperial Majesty's reign. [22] We have at various times made our protestations and appeals concerning these most weighty matters, and have done so in legal form and procedure. [23] To these we declare our continuing adherence, and we shall not be turned aside from our position by these or any following negotiations (unless the matters in dissension are

settled, and brought to Christian concord in accordance with Your Imperial Majesty's summons) as we herewith publicly witness and assert. [24] This is our confession and that of our associates, and it is specifically stated, article by article, in what follows.

Articles of Faith and Doctrine
1. [GOD]¹

[1] We unanimously hold and teach, in accordance with the decree of the Council of Nicaea, [2] that there is one divine essence, which is called and which is truly God, and that there are three persons in this one divine essence, equal in power and alike eternal: God the Father, God the Son, God the Holy Spirit. [3] All three are one divine essence, eternal, without division, without end, of infinite power, wisdom, and goodness, one creator and preserver of all things visible and invisible. [4] The word "person" is to be understood as the fathers employed the term in this connection, not as a part or a property of another but as that which exists of itself.

---

finally heard, amicably weighed, charitably settled, and brought to Christian concord in accordance with Your Imperial Majesty's summons) as we herewith publicly witness and assert. [24] This is our confession and that of our associates, and it is specifically stated, article by article, in what follows.

Chief Articles of Faith
1. [GOD]

[1] Our churches teach with great unanimity that the decree of the Council of Nicaea concerning the unity of the divine essence and concerning the three persons is true and should be believed without any doubting. [2] That is to say, there is one divine essence, which is called and which is God, eternal, incorporeal, indivisible, of infinite power, wisdom, and goodness, the maker and preserver of all things, visible and invisible. [3] Yet there are three persons, of the same essence and power, who are also coeternal: the Father, the Son, and the Holy Spirit. [4] And the term "person" is used, as the ancient fathers employed it in this connection, to signify not a part or a quality in another but that which subsists of itself.

1. As Tappert notes, the headings of some articles (bracketed here) were inserted in 1533 or later.

[5] Therefore all the heresies which are contrary to this article are rejected. Among these are the heresy of the Manichaeans, who assert that there are two gods, one good and one evil; also that of the Valentinians, Arians, Eunomians, Mohammedans, and others like them; [6] also that of the Samosatenes, old and new, who hold that there is only one person and sophistically assert that the other two, the Word and the Holy Spirit, are not necessarily distinct persons but that the Word signifies a physical word or voice and that the Holy Spirit is a movement induced in creatures.

2. [ORIGINAL SIN]

[1] It is also taught among us that since the fall of Adam all men who are born according to the course of nature are conceived and born in sin. That is, all men are full of evil lust and inclinations from their mothers' wombs and are unable by nature to have true fear of God and true faith in God. [2] Moreover, this inborn sickness and hereditary sin is truly sin and condemns to the eternal wrath of God all those who are not born again through baptism and the Holy Spirit.

[3] Rejected in this connection are the Pelagians and others who deny that original sin is sin, for they hold that natural man is made righteous by his own powers, thus disparaging the sufferings and merit of Christ.

---

[5] Our churches condemn all heresies which have sprung up against this article, such as that of the Manichaeans, who posited two principles, one good and the other evil, and also those of the Valentinians, Arians, Eunomians, Mohammedans, and all others like these. [6] They also condemn the Samosatenes, old and new, who contend that there is only one person and craftily and impiously argue that the Word and the Holy Spirit are not distinct persons since "Word" signifies a spoken word and "Spirit" signifies a movement which is produced in things.

2. [ORIGINAL SIN]

[1] Our churches also teach that since the fall of Adam all men who are propagated according to nature are born in sin. That is to say, they are without fear of God, are without trust in God, and are concupiscent. [2] And this disease or vice of origin is truly sin, which even now damns and brings eternal death on those who are not born again through baptism and the Holy Spirit.

[3] Our churches condemn the Pelagians and others who deny that the vice of origin is sin and who obscure the glory of Christ's merit and benefits by contending that man can be justified before God by his own strength and reason.

3. [THE SON OF GOD]

[1] It is also taught among us that God the Son became man, born of the Virgin Mary, [2] and that the two natures, divine and human, are so inseparably united in one person that there is one Christ, true God and true man, who was truly born, suffered, was crucified, died, [3] and was buried in order to be a sacrifice not only for original sin but also for all other sins and to propitiate God's wrath. [4] The same Christ also descended into hell, truly rose from the dead on the third day, ascended into heaven, and sits on the right hand of God, that he may eternally rule and have dominion over all creatures, that through the Holy Spirit he may sanctify, purify, strengthen, and comfort all who believe in him, [5] that he may bestow on them life and every grace and blessing, and that he may protect and defend them against the devil and against sin. [6] The same Lord Christ will return openly to judge the living and the dead, etc., as stated in the Apostles' Creed.

4. [JUSTIFICATION]

[1] It is also taught among us that we cannot obtain forgiveness of sin and righteousness before God by our own merits, works, or satisfactions, but that we receive forgiveness of sin and become righteous before God by grace, for Christ's sake,

---

3. [THE SON OF GOD]

[1] Our churches also teach that the Word—that is, the Son of God—took on man's nature in the womb of the Blessed Virgin Mary. [2] So there are two natures, divine and human, inseparably conjoined in the unity of his person, one Christ, true God and true man, who was born of the Virgin Mary, truly suffered, was crucified, dead, and buried, [3] that he might reconcile the Father to us and be a sacrifice not only for original guilt but also for all actual sins of men. [4] He also descended into hell, and on the third day truly rose again. Afterward he ascended into heaven to sit on the right hand of the Father, forever reign and have dominion over all creatures, and sanctify those who believe in him by [5] sending the Holy Spirit into their hearts to rule, comfort, and quicken them and defend them against the devil and the power of sin. [6] The same Christ will openly come again to judge the living and the dead, etc., according to the Apostles' Creed.

4. [JUSTIFICATION]

[1] Our churches also teach that men cannot be justified before God by their own strength, merits, or works but are freely justified for Christ's sake through faith [2] when they believe that they are received into favor and that their sins are forgiven

through faith, [2] when we believe that Christ suffered for us and that for his sake our sin is forgiven and righteousness and eternal life are given to us. [3] For God will regard and reckon this faith as righteousness, as Paul says in Romans 3 and 4.[a]

5. [THE OFFICE OF THE MINISTRY]

[1] To obtain such faith God instituted the office of the ministry, that is, provided the gospel and the sacraments. [2] Through these, as through means, he gives the Holy Spirit, who works faith, when and where he pleases, in those who hear the gospel. [3] And the gospel teaches that we have a gracious God, not by our own merits but by the merit of Christ, when we believe this. [4] Condemned are the Anabaptists and others who teach that the Holy Spirit comes to us through our own preparations, thoughts, and works without the external word of the gospel.

6. [THE NEW OBEDIENCE]

[1] It is also taught among us that such faith should produce good fruits and good works and that we must do all such good works as God has commanded, but we

---

on account of Christ, who by his death made satisfaction for our sins. [3] This faith God imputes for righteousness in his sight,[a] Romans 3 and 4.

5. [THE MINISTRY OF THE CHURCH]

[1] In order that we may obtain this faith, the ministry of teaching the gospel and administering the sacraments was instituted. [2] For through the word and the sacraments, as through instruments, the Holy Spirit is given, and the Holy Spirit produces faith, where and when it pleases God, in those who hear the gospel. [3] That is to say, it is not on account of our own merits but on account of Christ that God justifies those who believe that they are received into favor for Christ's sake. "That we might receive the promise of the Spirit through faith." [Gal 3.14]

[4] Our churches condemn the Anabaptists and others who think that the Holy Spirit comes to men without the external word, through their own preparations and works.

6. [THE NEW OBEDIENCE]

[1] Our churches also teach that this faith is bound to bring forth good fruits and that it is necessary to do the good works commanded by God. We must do so be-

---

a. Rom 3[.21–26], 4[.5]

should do them for God's sake and not place our trust in them as if thereby to merit favor before God. [2] For we receive forgiveness of sin and righteousness through faith in Christ, as Christ himself says, "So you also, when you have done all that is [Lk 17.10]   commanded you, say, 'We are unworthy servants.'" [3] The fathers also teach thus, for Ambrose says, "It is ordained of God that whoever believes in Christ shall be saved, and he shall have forgiveness of sins, not through works but through faith alone, without merit."[2]

7. [THE CHURCH]

[1] It is also taught among us that one holy Christian church will be and remain forever. This is the assembly of all believers among whom the gospel is preached in its purity and the holy sacraments are administered according to the gospel. [2] For it is sufficient for the true unity of the Christian church that the gospel be preached in conformity with a pure understanding of it and that the sacraments be administered in accordance with the divine word. [3] It is not necessary for the true unity of the Christian church that ceremonies, instituted by men, should be observed uniformly in all places. [4] It is as Paul says in Ephesians 4: "There is one body and one

---

cause it is God's will and not because we rely on such works to merit justification before God, [2] for forgiveness of sins and justification are apprehended by faith, as Christ himself also testifies, "When you have done all these things, say, 'We are un- [Lk 17.10]   profitable servants.'" [3] The same is also taught by the fathers of the ancient church, for Ambrose says, "It is ordained of God that whoever believes in Christ shall be saved, not through works but through faith alone, and he shall receive forgiveness of sins by grace."[2]

7. [THE CHURCH]

[1] Our churches also teach that one holy church is to continue forever. The church is the assembly of saints in which the gospel is taught purely and the sacraments are administered rightly. [2] For the true unity of the church it is enough to agree concerning the teaching of the gospel and the administration of the sacraments. [3] It is not necessary that human traditions or rites and ceremonies, instituted by men, [Eph 4.5-6]   should be alike everywhere. [4] It is as Paul says, "One faith, one baptism, one God and Father of all," etc.

2. Ambrosiaster *The First Epistle to the Corinthians* 1.4.

Spirit, just as you were called to the one hope that belongs to your call, one Lord, one faith, one baptism."

Eph 4[.5–6]

8. [WHAT THE CHURCH IS]

[1] Again, although the Christian church, properly speaking, is nothing else than the assembly of all believers and saints, yet because in this life many false Christians, hypocrites, and even open sinners remain among the godly, the sacraments are efficacious even if the priests who administer them are wicked men, for as Christ himself indicated, "The Pharisees sit on Moses' seat, etc."

[Mt 23.2]

[3] Accordingly the Donatists and all others who hold contrary views are condemned.

9. BAPTISM

[1] It is taught among us that baptism is necessary and that grace is offered through it. [2] Children, too, should be baptized, for in baptism they are committed to God and become acceptable to him.

[3] On this account the Anabaptists, who teach that infant baptism is not right, are rejected.

---

8. [WHAT IS THE CHURCH?]

[1] Properly speaking, the church is the assembly of saints and true believers. However, since in this life many hypocrites and evil persons are mingled with believers, it is allowable to use the sacraments even when they are administered by evil men, according to the saying of Christ, "The scribes and Pharisees sit on Moses' seat,"

[Mt 23.2]

etc. [2] Both the sacraments and the word are effectual by reason of the institution and commandment of Christ even if they are administered by evil men.

[3] Our churches condemn the Donatists and others like them who have denied that the ministry of evil men may be used in the church and who have thought the ministry of evil men to be unprofitable and without effect.

9. BAPTISM

[1] Our churches teach that baptism is necessary for salvation, that the grace of God is offered through baptism, [2] and that children should be baptized, for being offered to God through baptism they are received into his grace.

[3] Our churches condemn the Anabaptists, who reject the baptism of children and declare that children are saved without baptism.

10. THE HOLY SUPPER

[1] Concerning the Lord's supper, we teach that the true body and blood of Christ are really present in the supper of our Lord under the form of bread and wine and are there distributed and received. [2] The contrary doctrine is therefore rejected.

11. CONFESSION

[1] It is taught among us that private absolution should be retained and not allowed to fall into disuse. However, in confession it is not necessary to enumerate all trespasses and sins, [2] for this is impossible, Psalm 18 [19]: "Who can discern

Ps [19.12]   his errors?"

12. REPENTANCE

[1] It is taught among us that those who sin after baptism receive forgiveness of sin whenever they come to repentance, [2] and absolution should not be denied them by the church. [3] Properly speaking, true repentance is nothing else than to have contrition and sorrow, or terror, on account of [5] sin, and yet at the same time to believe the gospel and absolution (namely, that sin has been forgiven and grace has been obtained through Christ), and this faith will comfort the heart and again set it at rest. [6] Amendment of life and the forsaking of sin would then follow, for these

---

10. LORD'S SUPPER

[1] Our churches teach that the body and blood of Christ are truly present and are distributed to those who eat in the supper of the Lord. [2] They disapprove of those who teach otherwise.

11. CONFESSION

[1] Our churches teach that private absolution should be retained in the churches. However, in confession an enumeration of all sins is not necessary, [2] for this is

[Ps 19.12]   not possible according to the Psalm, "Who can discern his errors?"

12. REPENTANCE

[1] Our churches teach that those who have fallen after baptism can receive forgiveness of sins whenever they are converted, [2] and that the church ought to impart absolution to those who return to repentance. [3] Properly speaking, repentance consists of these two parts: [4] one is contrition, that is, terror smiting the conscience with a knowledge of sin, [5] and the other is faith, which is born of the gospel, or of absolution, believes that sins are forgiven for Christ's sake, comforts the

must be the fruits of repentance, as John says in Matthew 3: "Bear fruit that befits
repentance." Mt 3[.8]

[7] Rejected here are those who teach that persons who have once become
godly cannot fall again. [9] Condemned on the other hand are the Novatians, who
denied absolution to such as had sinned after baptism.

[10] Rejected also are those who teach that forgiveness of sin is not obtained through faith but through the satisfactions made by man.

13. THE USE OF THE SACRAMENTS

[1] It is taught among us that the sacraments were instituted not only to be signs by
which people might be identified outwardly as Christians, but that they are signs
and testimonies of God's will toward us for the purpose of awakening and strengthening our faith. [2] For this reason they require faith, and they are rightly used when
they are received in faith and for the purpose of strengthening faith.

---

conscience, and delivers it from terror. [6] Then good works, which are the fruits
of repentance, are bound to follow.

[7] Our churches condemn the Anabaptists, who deny that those who have
once been justified can lose the Holy Spirit, [8] and also those who contend that
some may attain such perfection in this life that they cannot sin. [9] Also condemned
are the Novatians, who were unwilling to absolve those who had fallen after baptism although they returned to repentance. [10] Rejected also are those who do not
teach that remission of sins comes through faith but command us to merit grace
through satisfactions of our own.

13. THE USE OF THE SACRAMENTS

[1] Our churches teach that the sacraments were instituted not merely to be marks of
profession among men but especially to be signs and testimonies of the will of God
toward us, intended to awaken and confirm faith in those who use them. [2] Consequently the sacraments should be so used that faith, which believes the promises
that are set forth and offered, is added.

[3] [Our churches therefore condemn those who teach that the sacraments
justify by the outward act and who do not teach that faith, which believes that sins
are forgiven, is required in the use of the sacraments.][3]

---

3. Text in square brackets added later in the so-called *editio princeps*.

14. ORDER IN THE CHURCH

It is taught among us that nobody should publicly teach or preach or administer the sacraments in the church without a regular call.

15. CHURCH USAGES

[1] With regard to church usages that have been established by men, it is taught among us that those usages are to be observed which may be observed without sin and which contribute to peace and good order in the church, among them being certain holy days, festivals, and the like. [2] Yet we accompany these observances with instruction so that consciences may not be burdened by the notion that such things are necessary for salvation. [3] Moreover it is taught that all ordinances and traditions instituted by men for the purpose of propitiating God and earning grace are contrary to the gospel and the teaching about faith in Christ. [4] Accordingly monastic vows and other traditions concerning distinction of foods, days, etc., by which it is intended to earn grace and make satisfaction for sin, are useless and contrary to the gospel.

---

14. ECCLESIASTICAL ORDER

Our churches teach that nobody should preach publicly in the church or administer the sacraments unless he is regularly called.

15. ECCLESIASTICAL RITES

[1] Our churches teach that those rites should be observed which can be observed without sin and which contribute to peace and good order in the church. Such are certain holy days, festivals, and the like.

[2] Nevertheless, men are admonished not to burden consciences with such things, as if observances of this kind were necessary for salvation. [3] They are also admonished that human traditions which are instituted to propitiate God, merit grace, and make satisfaction for sins are opposed to the gospel and the teaching about faith. [4] Wherefore vows and traditions about foods and days, etc., instituted to merit grace and make satisfaction for sins, are useless and contrary to the gospel.

16. MAGISTRATES AND CIVIL GOVERNMENT

[1] It is taught among us that all government in the world and all established rule and laws were instituted and ordained by God for the sake of good order, [2] and that Christians may without sin occupy civil offices or serve as princes and judges, render decisions and pass sentence according to imperial and other existing laws, punish evildoers with the sword, engage in just wars, serve as soldiers, buy and sell, take required oaths, possess property, be married, etc.

[3] Condemned here are the Anabaptists, who teach that none of the things indicated above is Christian.

[4] Also condemned are those who teach that Christian perfection requires the forsaking of house and home, wife and child, and the renunciation of such activities as are mentioned above. Actually, true perfection consists alone of proper fear of God and real faith in God, for the gospel does not teach an outward and temporal but an inward and eternal mode of existence and righteousness of the heart. [5] The gospel does not overthrow civil authority, the state, and marriage but requires that all these be kept as true orders of God and that everyone, each according to his own calling, manifest Christian love and genuine good works in his station of life. [6] Accordingly Christians are obliged to be subject to civil authority and obey its commands and laws in all that can be done without sin. [7] But when commands of the civil authority cannot be obeyed without sin, we must obey God rather than men. Acts 5.   Acts 5[.29]

---

16. CIVIL AFFAIRS

[1] Our churches teach that lawful civil ordinances are good works of God [2] and that it is right for Christians to hold civil office, to sit as judges, to decide matters by the imperial and other existing laws, to award just punishments, to engage in just wars, to serve as soldiers, to make legal contracts, to hold property, to swear oaths when required by magistrates, to marry, to be given in marriage.

[3] Our churches condemn the Anabaptists, who forbid Christians to engage in these civil functions. [4] They also condemn those who place the perfection of the gospel not in the fear of God and in faith but in forsaking civil duties. The gospel teaches an eternal righteousness of the heart, but it does not destroy the state or the family. [5] On the contrary, it especially requires their preservation as ordinances of God and the exercise of love in these ordinances. [6] Therefore Christians are necessarily bound to obey their magistrates and laws except when commanded to sin, for then they ought to obey God rather than men. Acts 5.   Acts 5[.29]

17. [THE RETURN OF CHRIST TO JUDGMENT]

[1] It is also taught among us that our Lord Jesus Christ will return on the last day for judgment and will raise up all the dead, [2] to give eternal life and everlasting joy to believers and the elect [3] but to condemn ungodly men and the devil to hell and eternal punishment.

[4] Rejected, therefore, are the Anabaptists, who teach that the devil and condemned men will not suffer eternal pain and torment.

[5] Rejected, too, are certain Jewish opinions which are even now making an appearance and which teach that, before the resurrection of the dead, saints and godly men will possess a worldly kingdom and annihilate all the godless.

18. FREEDOM OF THE WILL

[1] It is also taught among us that man possesses some measure of freedom of the will which enables him to live an outwardly honorable life and to make choices among the things that reason comprehends. [2] But without the grace, help, and activity of the Holy Spirit man is not capable of making himself acceptable to God,

---

17. [THE RETURN OF CHRIST FOR JUDGMENT]

[1] Our churches also teach that at the consummation of the world Christ will appear for judgment and will raise up all the dead. [2] To the godly and elect he will give eternal life and endless joy, [3] but ungodly men and devils he will condemn to be tormented without end.

[4] Our churches condemn the Anabaptists, who think that there will be an end to the punishments of condemned men and devils. [5] They also condemn others who are now spreading Jewish opinions to the effect that before the resurrection of the dead the godly will take possession of the kingdom of the world, the ungodly being suppressed everywhere.

18. FREE WILL

[1] Our churches teach that man's will has some liberty for the attainment of civil righteousness and for the choice of things subject to reason. [2] However, it does not have the power, without the Holy Spirit, to attain the righteousness of God— that is, spiritual righteousness—because natural man does not perceive the gifts of the Spirit of God; [3] but this righteousness is wrought in the heart when the Holy Spirit is received through the word. [4] In book 3 of his *Hypognosticon* Augustine said these things in so many words: "We concede that all men have a free will which

[1 Cor 2.14]

of fearing God and believing in God with his whole heart, or of expelling inborn evil lusts from his heart. [3] This is accomplished by the Holy Spirit, who is given through the word of God, for Paul says in 1 Corinthians 2: "Natural man does not receive the gifts of the Spirit of God."   1 Cor 2[.14]

[4] In order that it may be evident that this teaching is no novelty, the clear words of Augustine on free will are here quoted from the third book of his *Hypognosticon:* "We concede that all men have a free will, for all have a natural, innate understanding and reason. However, this does not enable them to act in matters pertaining to God (such as loving God with their whole heart or fearing him), for it is only in the outward acts of this life that they have freedom to choose good or evil. [5] By good I mean what they are capable of by nature: whether or not to labor in the fields, whether or not to eat or drink or visit a friend, whether to dress or undress, whether to build a house, take a wife, engage in a trade, or do whatever else may be good and profitable. [6] None of these is or exists without God, but all things are from him and through him. [7] On the other hand, by his own choice man can also undertake evil, as when he wills to kneel before an idol, commit murder, etc."[4]

---

enables them to make judgments according to reason. However, this does not enable them, without God, to begin or (much less) to accomplish anything in those things which pertain to God, for it is only in acts of this life that they have freedom to choose good or evil. [5] By 'good' I mean the acts which spring from the good in nature, that is, to will to labor in the field, will to eat and drink, will to have a friend, will to clothe oneself, will to build a house, will to marry, will to keep cattle, will to learn various useful arts, or will to do whatever good pertains to this life. [6] None of these exists without the providence of God; indeed, it is from and through him that all these things come into being and are. [7] On the other hand, by 'evil' I mean such things as to will to worship an idol, will to commit murder," etc.[4]

[8] [Our churches condemn the Pelagians and others who teach that without the Holy Spirit, by the power of nature alone, we are able to love God above all things, and can also keep the commandments of God in so far as the substance of the acts is concerned. [9] Although nature is able in some measure to perform the outward works (for it can keep the hands from theft and murder), yet it cannot produce the inward affections, such as fear of God, trust in God, patience, etc.]

4. *Hypomnesticon contra Pelagianus et Coelestinianus* 3.4.5, attributed to Augustine in Luther's day.

19. THE CAUSE OF SIN

It is taught among us that although Almighty God has created and still preserves nature, yet sin is caused in all wicked men and despisers of God by the perverted will. This is the will of the devil and of all ungodly men; as soon as God withdraws his support, the will turns away from God to evil. It is as Christ says in John 8: "When the devil lies, he speaks according to his own nature."

Jn 8[.44]

20. FAITH AND GOOD WORKS

[1] Our teachers have been falsely accused of forbidding good works. [2] Their writings on the Ten Commandments, and other writings as well, show that they have given good and profitable accounts and instructions concerning true Christian estates and works. [3] About these little was taught in former times, when for the most part sermons were concerned with childish and useless works like rosaries, the cult of saints, monasticism, pilgrimages, appointed fasts, holy days, brotherhoods, etc. [4] Our opponents no longer praise these useless works so highly as they once did, [5] and they have also learned to speak now of faith, about which they did not preach at all in former times. [6] They do not teach now that we become

---

19. THE CAUSE OF SIN

Our churches teach that although God creates and preserves nature, the cause of sin is the will of the wicked, that is, of the devil and ungodly men. If not aided by God, the will of the wicked turns away from God, as Christ says in John 8, "When the devil lies, he speaks according to his own nature."

Jn 8[.44]

20. FAITH AND GOOD WORKS

[1] Our teachers are falsely accused of forbidding good works. [2] Their publications on the Ten Commandments and others of like import bear witness that they have taught to good purpose about all stations and duties of life, indicating what manners of life and what kinds of work are pleasing to God in the several callings. [3] Concerning such things preachers used to teach little. Instead, they urged childish and needless works, such as particular holy days, prescribed fasts, brotherhoods, pilgrimages, services in honor of saints, rosaries, monasticism, and the like. [4] Since our adversaries have been admonished about these things, they are now unlearning them and do not preach about such unprofitable works as much as formerly. [5] They are even beginning to mention faith, about which there used to be marvelous silence. [6] They teach that we are justified not by works only, but conjoining faith with works they say that we are justified by faith and works. [7] This

righteous before God by our works alone, but they add faith in Christ and say that faith and works make us righteous before God. [7] This teaching may offer a little more comfort than the teaching that we are to rely solely on our works.

[8] Since the teaching about faith, which is the chief article in the Christian life, has been neglected so long (as all must admit) while nothing but works was preached everywhere, our people have been instructed as follows:

[9] We begin by teaching that our works cannot reconcile us with God or obtain grace for us, for this happens only through faith, that is, when we believe that our sins are forgiven for Christ's sake, who alone is the mediator who reconciles the Father. [10] Whoever imagines that he can accomplish this by works, or that he can merit grace, despises Christ and seeks his own way to God, contrary to the gospel.

[11] This teaching about faith is plainly and clearly treated by Paul in many passages, especially in Ephesians 2: "For by grace you have been saved through faith; and this is not your own doing, it is the gift of God—not because of works, lest any man should boast," etc. Eph 2[.8]

[12] That no new interpretation is here introduced can be demonstrated

---

teaching is more tolerable than the former one, and it can afford more consolation than their old teaching.

[8] Inasmuch, then, as the teaching about faith, which ought to be the chief teaching in the church, has so long been neglected (for everybody must grant that there has been profound silence concerning the righteousness of faith in sermons while only the teaching about works has been treated in the church), our teachers have instructed our churches concerning faith as follows:

[9] We begin by teaching that our works cannot reconcile God or merit forgiveness of sins and grace but that we obtain forgiveness and grace only by faith when we believe that we are received into favor for Christ's sake, who alone has been ordained to be the mediator and propitiation through whom the Father is reconciled. [10] Consequently whoever trusts that he merits grace by works despises the merit and grace of Christ and seeks a way to God without Christ, by human strength, although Christ has said of himself, "I am the way, and the truth, and the life." [Jn 14.6]

[11] This teaching concerning faith is everywhere treated in Paul, as in Ephesians, "For by grace you have been saved through faith; and this is not because of works," etc. Eph 2[.8]

[12] Lest anyone should captiously object that we have invented a new in-

from Augustine, [13] who discusses this question thoroughly and teaches the same thing, namely, that we obtain grace and are justified before God through faith in Christ and not through works. His whole book, *De spiritu et litera,* proves this.

[15] Although this teaching is held in great contempt among untried people, yet it is a matter of experience that weak and terrified consciences find it most comforting and salutary. The conscience cannot come to rest and peace through works, but only through faith, that is, when it is assured and knows that for Christ's sake it has a gracious God, [16] as Paul says in Romans 5: "Since we are justified by faith, Rom 5[.1]   we have peace with God."

[19] In former times this comfort was not heard in preaching, but poor consciences were driven to rely on their own efforts, and all sorts of works were undertaken. [20] Some were driven by their conscience into monasteries in the hope that there they might merit grace through monastic life. [21] Others devised other works for the purpose of earning grace and making satisfaction for sins. [22] Many of them discovered that they did not obtain peace by such means. It was therefore necessary to preach this doctrine about faith in Christ and diligently to apply it in

---

terpretation of Paul, this whole matter is supported by testimonies of the fathers. [13] In many volumes Augustine defends grace and the righteousness of faith against the merits of works. [14] Ambrose teaches similarly in *De vocatione gentium* and elsewhere, for in his *De vocatione gentium* he says: "Redemption by the blood of Christ would become of little value and the preeminence of human works would not be superseded by the mercy of God if justification, which is accomplished by grace, were due to antecedent merits, for then it would be a reward for works rather than a free gift."[5]

[15] Although this teaching is despised by inexperienced men, God-fearing and anxious consciences find by experience that it offers the greatest consolation because the consciences of men cannot be pacified by any work but only by faith when they are sure that for Christ's sake they have a gracious God. [16] It is as Paul Rom 5[.1]   teaches in Romans 5, "Since we are justified by faith, we have peace with God." [17] This whole teaching is to be referred to that conflict of the terrified conscience, nor can it be understood apart from that conflict. [18] Accordingly inexperienced and profane men, who dream that Christian righteousness is nothing else than civil or philosophical righteousness, have bad judgment concerning this teaching.

[19] Consciences used to be plagued by the doctrine of works when consolation from the gospel was not heard. [20] Some persons were by their consciences

5. Pseudo-Ambrose *The Calling of the Gentiles* 1.17.

order that men may know that the grace of God is appropriated without merits, through faith alone.

[23] Instruction is also given among us to show that the faith here spoken of is not that possessed by the devil and the ungodly, who also believe the history of Christ's suffering and his resurrection from the dead, but we mean such true faith as believes that we receive grace and forgiveness of sin through Christ. [Jas 2.19]

[24] Whoever knows that in Christ he has a gracious God, truly knows God, calls upon him, and is not, like the heathen, without God. [25] For the devil and the ungodly do not believe this article concerning the forgiveness of sin, and so they are at enmity with God, cannot call upon him, and have no hope of receiving good from him. Therefore, as has just been indicated, the Scriptures speak of faith but do not mean by it such knowledge as the devil and ungodly men possess. Hebrews 11 teaches about faith in such a way as to make it clear that faith is not merely a knowledge of historical events but is a confidence in God and in the fulfillment of his promises. [26] Augustine also reminds us that we would understand the word "faith" in the Scriptures to mean confidence in God, assurance that God is gracious to us, and not merely such a knowledge of historical events as the devil also possesses.[6] [Heb 11[.1]]

---

driven into the desert, into monasteries, in the hope that there they might merit grace by monastic life. [21] Others invented works of another kind to merit grace and make satisfaction for sins. [22] Hence there was very great need to treat of and to restore this teaching concerning faith in Christ in order that anxious consciences should not be deprived of consolation but know that grace and forgiveness of sins are apprehended by faith in Christ.

[23] Men are also admonished that here the term "faith" does not signify merely knowledge of the history (such as is in the ungodly and the devil), but it signifies faith which believes not only the history but also the effect of the history, namely, this article of the forgiveness of sins—that is, that we have grace, righteousness, and forgiveness of sins through Christ. [Jas 2.19]

[24] Whoever knows that he has a Father reconciled to him through Christ truly knows God, knows that God cares for him, and calls upon God. [25] He is not without God, as are the heathen, for devils and ungodly men are not able to believe this article of the forgiveness of sins; hence they hate God as an enemy, do not call upon him, and expect no good from him. [26] Augustine, too, admonishes his readers in this way concerning the word "faith"[6] when he teaches that in the

6. Augustine *Homilies on the Epistle of John to the Parthians* 10.2.

[27] It is also taught among us that good works should and must be done, not that we are to rely on them to earn grace but that we may do God's will and glorify him. [28] It is always faith alone that apprehends grace and forgiveness of sin. [29] When through faith the Holy Spirit is given, the heart is moved to do good works. [31] Before that, when it is without the Holy Spirit, the heart is too weak. [32] Moreover, it is in the power of the devil, who drives poor human beings into many sins. [33] We see this in the philosophers who undertook to lead honorable and blameless lives; they failed to accomplish this, and instead fell into many great and open sins. [34] This is what happens when a man is without true faith and the Holy Spirit and governs himself by his own human strength alone. [35] Consequently this teaching concerning faith is not to be accused of forbidding good works but is rather to be praised for teaching that good works are to be done and for offering help as to how they may be done. [36] For without faith and without Christ human nature and human strength are much too weak to do good works, [37] call upon God, have patience in suffering, love one's neighbor, diligently engage in callings which are commanded, render obedience, avoid evil lusts, etc. [38] Such great and genuine works cannot be done without the help of Christ, [39] as he himself says in John 15: "Apart from me you can do nothing."

Jn 15[.5]

Scriptures the word "faith" is to be understood not as knowledge, such as is in the ungodly, but as confidence which consoles and lifts up terrified hearts.

[27] Our teachers teach in addition that it is necessary to do good works, not that we should trust to merit grace by them but because it is the will of God. [28] It is only by faith that forgiveness of sins and grace are apprehended, [29] and because through faith the Holy Spirit is received, hearts are so renewed and endowed with new affections as to be able to bring forth good works. [30] Ambrose says, "Faith is the mother of the good will and the right deed."[7] [31] For without the Holy Spirit man's powers are full of ungodly affections and are too weak to do works which are good in God's sight. [32] Besides, they are in the power of the devil, who impels men to various sins, impious opinions, and manifest crimes. [33] This we may see in the philosophers, who, although they tried to live honest lives, were not able to do so but were defiled by many manifest crimes. [34] Such is the feebleness of man when he governs himself by human strength alone without faith and without the Holy Spirit.

[35] Hence it may readily be seen that this teaching is not to be charged with forbidding good works. On the contrary, it should rather be commended for

7. Pseudo-Ambrose *The Calling of the Gentiles* 1.25.

21. THE CULT OF SAINTS

[1] It is also taught among us that saints should be kept in remembrance so that our faith may be strengthened when we see what grace they received and how they were sustained by faith. Moreover, their good works are to be an example for us, each of us in his own calling. So His Imperial Majesty may in salutary and godly fashion imitate the example of David in making war on the Turk, for both are incumbents of a royal office which demands the defense and protection of their subjects.

[2] However, it cannot be proved from the Scriptures that we are to invoke saints or seek help from them. "For there is one mediator between God and men, Christ Jesus," 1 Timothy 2, who is the only savior, the only high priest, advocate, and intercessor before God, Romans 8. He alone has promised to hear our prayers. [3] Moreover, according to the Scriptures, the highest form of divine service is sincerely to seek and call upon this same Jesus Christ in every time of need. "If anyone sins, we have an advocate with the [4] Father, Jesus Christ the righteous."

1 Tm 2[.5]

Rom 8[.34]

[1 Jn 2.1]

---

showing how we are enabled to do good works. [36] For without faith human nature cannot possibly do the works of the First or Second Commandments. [37] Without faith it does not call upon God, expect anything of God, or bear the cross, but it seeks and trusts in man's help. [38] Accordingly, when there is no faith and trust in God, all manner of lusts and human devices rule in the heart. [39] Wherefore Christ said, "Apart from me you can do nothing," John 15, [40] and the church sings,

Jn 15[.5]

> "Where Thou art not, man hath naught,
> Nothing good in deed or thought,
> Nothing free from taint of ill."[8]

21. THE CULT OF SAINTS

[1] Our churches teach that the remembrance of saints may be commended to us so that we imitate their faith and good works according to our calling. Thus the emperor may follow the example of David in waging war to drive the Turk out of his country, for like David the emperor is a king. [2] However, the Scriptures do not teach us to pray to the saints or seek their help, for the only mediator, propitiation, high priest, and intercessor whom the Scriptures set before us is Christ. [3] He is to be prayed to, and he has promised to hear our prayers. Such worship Christ especially approves, namely, that in all afflictions he be called upon. [4] "If anyone sins, we have an advocate with the Father," 1 John 2.

[1 Tm 2.5]

1 Jn 2[.1]

---

8. From the hymn *Veni sancte spiritus*.

[CONCLUSION OF PART 1]

[1] This is just about a summary of the doctrines that are preached and taught in our churches for proper Christian instruction, the consolation of consciences, and the amendment of believers. Certainly we would not wish to put our own souls and consciences in grave peril before God by misusing his name or word, nor should we wish to bequeath to our children and posterity any other teaching than that which agrees with the pure word of God and Christian truth. Since this teaching is grounded clearly on the Holy Scriptures and is not contrary or opposed to that of the universal Christian church, or even of the Roman church (in so far as the latter's teaching is reflected in the writings of the fathers), we think that our opponents cannot disagree with us in the articles set forth above. Therefore, those who presume to reject, avoid, and separate from our churches as if our teaching were heretical, act in an unkind and hasty fashion, contrary to all Christian unity and love, and do so without any solid basis of divine command or Scripture. [2] The dispute and dissension are concerned chiefly with various traditions and abuses. Since, then, there is nothing unfounded or defective in the principal articles and since this our confession is seen to be godly and Christian, the bishops should in all fairness act more leniently, even if there were some defect among us in regard to traditions, although we hope to offer firm grounds and reasons why we have changed certain traditions and abuses.

[CONCLUSION OF PART 1]

[1] This is about the sum of our teaching. As can be seen, there is nothing here that departs from the Scriptures or the Catholic Church or the Church of Rome, in so far as the ancient church is known to us from its writers. Since this is so, those who insist that our teachers are to be regarded as heretics judge too harshly. [2] The whole dissension is concerned with a certain few abuses which have crept into the churches without proper authority. Even if there were some difference in these, the bishops should have been so lenient as to bear with us on account of the confession which we have now drawn up, for even the canons are not so severe as to demand that rites should be the same everywhere, [3] nor have the rites of all the churches ever been the same. [4] Among us the ancient rites are for the most part diligently observed, for it is false and malicious to charge that all ceremonies and all old ordinances are abolished in our churches. [5] But it has been a common complaint that certain abuses were connected with ordinary rites. Because these could not be approved with a good conscience, they have to some extent been corrected.

Articles About Matters in Dispute in Which an Account Is Given of the Abuses Which Have Been Corrected

From the above it is manifest that nothing is taught in our churches concerning articles of faith that is contrary to the Holy Scriptures or what is common to the Christian church. However, inasmuch as some abuses have been corrected (some of the abuses having crept in over the years and others of them having been introduced with violence), we are obliged by our circumstances to give an account of them and to indicate our reasons for permitting changes in these cases in order that Your Imperial Majesty may perceive that we have not acted in an unchristian and frivolous manner but have been compelled by God's command (which is rightly to be regarded as above all custom) to allow such changes.

22. BOTH KINDS IN THE SACRAMENT

[1] Among us both kinds are given to laymen in the sacrament. The reason is that there is a clear command and order of Christ, Matthew 26: "Drink of it, all of you."   Mt 26[.27]

Articles in Which an Account Is Given of the Abuses Which Have Been Corrected

[1] Inasmuch as our churches dissent from the church catholic in no article of faith but only omit some few abuses which are new and have been adopted by the fault of the times although contrary to the intent of the canons, we pray that Your Imperial Majesty will graciously hear both what has been changed and what our reasons for such changes are in order that the people may not be compelled to observe these abuses against their conscience.

[2] Your Imperial Majesty should not believe those who disseminate astonishing slanders among the people in order to inflame the hatred of men against us. [3] By thus exciting the minds of good men, they first gave occasion to this controversy, and now they are trying by the same method to increase the discord. [4] Your Imperial Majesty will undoubtedly discover that the forms of teaching and of ceremonies observed among us are not so intolerable as those ungodly and malicious men represent. [5] The truth cannot be gathered from common rumors or the accusations of our enemies. [6] However, it can readily be judged that nothing contributes so much to the maintenance of dignity in public worship and the cultivation of reverence and devotion among the people as the proper observance of ceremonies in the churches.

[2] Concerning the chalice Christ here commands with clear words that all should drink of it.

[3] In order that no one might question these words and interpret them as if they apply only to priests, Paul shows in 1 Corinthians 11 that the whole assembly of the congregation in Corinth received both kinds. [4] This usage continued in the church for a long time, as can be demonstrated from history and from writings of the fathers. [5] In several places Cyprian mentions that the cup was given to laymen in his time. [6] Saint Jerome also states that the priests who administered the sacrament distributed the blood of Christ to the people.[9] [7] Pope Gelasius himself ordered that the sacrament was not to be divided.[10] [8] Not a single canon can be found which requires the reception of only one kind. Nobody knows when or through whom this custom of receiving only one kind was introduced, although Cardinal Cusanus mentions when the use was approved. [10] It is evident that such a custom, introduced contrary to God's command and also contrary to the ancient canons, is unjust. [11] Accordingly it is not proper to burden the consciences of those who desire to observe the sacrament according to Christ's institution or to compel them to act contrary to the arrangement of our Lord Christ. [12] Because

1 Cor 11[.26–28]

---

22. BOTH KINDS

[1] In the sacrament of the Lord's supper both kinds are given to laymen because this usage has the command of the Lord in Matthew 26, "Drink of it, all of you." [2] Christ has here manifestly commanded with reference to the cup that all should drink of it.

Mt 26[.27]

[3] Lest anybody should captiously object that this refers only to priests, Paul in 1 Corinthians 11 cites an example from which it appears that a whole congregation used both kinds. [4] This usage continued in the church for a long time. It is not known when or by whom it was changed, although Cardinal Cusanus mentions when the change was approved. [5] Cyprian in several places testifies that the blood was given to the people. [6] The same is testified by Jerome, who said, "The priests administer the eucharist and distribute the blood of Christ to the people."[9] [7] In fact, Pope Gelasius commanded that the sacrament should not be divided.[10] [8] It is only a custom of quite recent times that holds otherwise. [9] But it is evident that a custom introduced contrary to the commands of God is not to be approved, as the canons testify (distinction 3, chapter "Veritate" and the following chapters). [10] This custom has been adopted not only in defiance of the Scriptures but also in

1 Cor 11[.26–28]

9. Jerome *Commentary on Zephaniah* 3.
10. Gratian *Decretum* 3.2.12.

the division of the sacrament is contrary to the institution of Christ, the customary carrying about of the sacrament in processions is also omitted by us.

23. THE MARRIAGE OF PRIESTS

[1] Among all people, both of high and of low degree, there has been loud complaint throughout the world concerning the flagrant immorality and the dissolute life of priests who were not able to remain continent and who went so far as to engage in abominable vices. [3] In order to avoid such unbecoming offense, adultery, and other lechery, some of our priests have entered the married state. They have given as their reason that they have been impelled and moved to take this step by the great distress of their consciences, especially since the Scriptures clearly assert that the estate of marriage was instituted by the Lord God to avoid immorality, [4] for Paul says, "Because of the temptation to immorality, each man should have his own wife,"[a] and again, "It is better to marry than to be aflame with passion."[b] [5] Moreover, when Christ said in Matthew 19: "Not all men can receive this precept," Mt 19[.11] he indicated that few people have the gift of living in celibacy, and he certainly knew

---

contradiction to ancient canons and the example of the church. [11] Consequently, if any people preferred to use both kinds in the sacrament, they should not have been compelled, with offense to their consciences, to do otherwise. [12] Because the division of the sacrament does not agree with the institution of Christ, the processions which were hitherto held are also omitted among us.

23. THE MARRIAGE OF PRIESTS

[1] There has been common complaint concerning priests who have not been continent. [2] On this account Pope Pius is reported to have said that there were some reasons why priests were forbidden to marry but that there are now far weightier reasons why this right should be restored. Platina writes to this effect. [3] Since priests among us desired to avoid such open scandals, they took wives and taught that it was lawful for them to contract matrimony. [4] In the first place, this was done because Paul says, "Because of the temptation to immorality each man should have his own wife,"[a] and again, "It is better to marry than to be aflame with passion."[b] [5] In the second place, Christ said, "Not all men can receive this precept," [Mt 19.11] by which he declared that all men are not suited for celibacy because God created

a. [1 Cor 7.2]
b. [1 Cor 7.9]

Gn 1[.27]   man's nature. "God created man as male and female" according to Genesis 1. [6] Experience has made it all too manifest whether or not it lies in human power and ability to improve or change the creation of God, the supreme Majesty, by means of human resolutions or vows without a special gift or grace of God. What good has resulted? What honest and chaste manner of life, what Christian, upright, and honorable sort of conduct has resulted in many cases? It is well known what terrible torment and frightful disturbance of conscience many have experienced on their deathbeds on this account, and many have themselves acknowledged this. [8] Since God's word and command cannot be altered by any human vows or laws, [9] our priests and other clergy have taken wives to themselves for these and other reasons and causes.

[10] It can be demonstrated from history and from the writings of the fathers that it was customary for priests and deacons to marry in the Christian church of former times. [11] Paul therefore said in 1 Timothy 3: "A bishop must be above re-

1 Tm 3[.2]   proach, married only once." [12] It was only four hundred years ago that the priests in Germany were compelled by force to take the vows of celibacy. At that time there was such serious and strong resistance that an archbishop of Mainz who had published the new papal decree was almost killed during an uprising of the entire body of priests. The decree concerning celibacy was at once enforced so hastily and indecently that the pope at the time not only forbade future marriages of priests but also broke up the marriages which were of long standing. [13] This was of course not only contrary to all divine, natural, and civil law, but was also utterly opposed and contrary to the canons which the popes had themselves made and to the decisions of the most renowned councils.

Gn 1[.27]   man for procreation, Genesis 1. [6] Moreover, it is not in man's power to alter his creation without a singular gift and work of God. [7] Therefore those who are not suited for celibacy ought to marry, [8] for no law of man and no vow can nullify a commandment of God and an institution of God. [9] For these reasons our priests teach that it is lawful for them to have wives.

[10] It is also evident that in the ancient church priests were married men.

[1 Tm 3.2]   [11] Paul said that a married man should be chosen to be bishop, [11] and not until four hundred years ago were priests in Germany compelled by force to live in celibacy. In fact, they offered such resistance that the archbishop of Mainz, when about to publish the Roman pontiff's edict on this matter, was almost killed by the enraged priests in an uprising. [13] In such a harsh manner was the edict carried out that not only were future marriages prohibited but existing marriages were also dis-

Many devout and intelligent people in high station have expressed similar opinions and the misgiving that such enforced celibacy and such prohibition of marriage (which God himself instituted and left free to man) never produced any good but rather gave occasion for many great and evil vices and much scandal. As his biography shows, even one of the popes, Pius II, often said and allowed himself to be quoted as saying that while there may well have been some reasons for prohibiting the marriage of clergymen, there were now more important, better, and weightier reasons for permitting them to be married. There is no doubt that Pope Pius, as a prudent and intelligent man, made this statement because of grave misgivings.

[14] In loyalty to Your Imperial Majesty we therefore feel confident that, as a most renowned Christian emperor, Your Majesty will graciously take into account the fact that, in these last times of which the Scriptures prophesy, the world is growing worse and men are becoming weaker and more infirm.

Therefore it is most necessary, profitable, and Christian to recognize this fact in order that the prohibition of marriage may not cause worse and more disgraceful lewdness and vice to prevail in German lands. No one is able to alter or arrange such matters in a better or wiser way than God himself, [15] who instituted marriage to aid human infirmity and prevent unchastity.

[16] The old canons also state that it is sometimes necessary to relax severity and rigor for the sake of human weakness and to prevent and avoid greater offense.

In this case relaxation would certainly be both Christian and very necessary. How would the marriage of priests and the clergy, and especially of the pastors and others who are to minister to the church, be of disadvantage to the Christian church as a whole? [17] If this hard prohibition of marriage is to continue longer, there may be a shortage of priests and pastors in the future.

---

solved, although this was contrary to all laws, divine and human, and contrary even to the canons, both those made by the popes and those made by the most celebrated councils.

[14] Inasmuch as the world is growing old and man's nature is becoming weaker, it is also well to take precautions against the introduction into Germany of more vices.

[15] Besides, God instituted marriage to be a remedy against human infirmity. [16] The canons themselves state that in later times the old rigor should be relaxed now and then on account of man's weakness, and it is devoutly to be desired that this be done in the case of sacerdotal marriage. [17] And it seems that the churches will soon be lacking in pastors if marriage continues to be forbidden.

[18] As we have observed, the assertion that priests and clergymen may marry is based on God's word and command. Besides, history demonstrates both that priests were married and that the vow of celibacy has been the cause of so much frightful and unchristian offense, so much adultery, and such terrible, shocking immorality and abominable vice that even some honest men among the cathedral clergy and some of the courtiers in Rome have often acknowledged this and have complained that such vices among the clergy would, on account of their abomination and prevalence, arouse the wrath of God. It is therefore deplorable that Christian marriage has not only been forbidden but has in many places been swiftly punished, as if it were a great crime, [19] in spite of that fact that in the Holy Scriptures God commanded that marriage be held in honor. [20] Marriage has also been highly praised in the imperial laws and in all states in which there have been laws and justice. [21] Only in our time does one begin to persecute innocent people simply because they are married—and especially priests, who above all others should be spared—although this is done contrary not only to divine law but also to canon law. [22] In 1 Timothy 4, the Apostle Paul calls the teaching that forbids marriage a doctrine of the devil. [23] In John 8, Christ himself asserts that the devil is a murderer from the beginning. These two statements fit together well, for it must be a doctrine of the devil to forbid marriage and then to be so bold as to maintain such a teaching with the shedding of blood.

1 Tm 4[.1, 3]

Jn 8[.44]

[24] However, just as no human law can alter or abolish a command of God, neither can any vow alter a command of God. [25] Saint Cyprian therefore

---

[18] Although the commandment of God is in force, although the custom of the church is well known, and although impure celibacy causes many scandals, adulteries, and other crimes which deserve the punishments of just magistrates, yet it is a marvelous thing that nowhere is greater cruelty exercised than in opposition to the marriage of priests. [19] God has commanded that marriage be held in honor. [20] The laws of all well-ordered states, even among the heathen, have adorned marriage with the greatest praise. [21] But now men, and even priests, are cruelly put to death, contrary to the intent of the canons, for no other cause than marriage. [22] To prohibit marriage is called a doctrine of demons by Paul in 1 Timothy 4. [23] This can be readily understood now that the prohibition of marriage is maintained by means of such penalties.

1 Tm 4[.1, 3]

[24] Just as no human law can nullify a command of God, so no vow can do so. [25] Accordingly Cyprian advised that women who did not keep the chastity which they had promised should marry. His words in the first book of his letters,

offered the counsel that women who were unable to keep their vows of chastity should marry. He wrote in his eleventh letter, "If they are unwilling or unable to keep their chastity, it is better for them to marry than to fall into the fire through their lusts, and they should see to it that they do not give their brothers and sisters occasion for offense."[11]

[26] In addition, all the canons show great leniency and fairness toward those who have made vows in their youth—and most of the priests and monks entered into their estates ignorantly when they were young.

24. THE MASS

[1] We are unjustly accused of having abolished the mass. [9] Without boasting, it is manifest that the mass is observed among us with greater devotion and more earnestness than among our opponents. [7] Moreover, the people are instructed often and with great diligence concerning the holy sacrament, why it was instituted, and how it is to be used (namely, as a comfort for terrified consciences) in order that the people may be drawn to the communion and mass. The people are also given instruction about other false teachings concerning the sacrament. [2] Meanwhile no conspicuous changes have been made in the public ceremonies of the mass, except

---

Epistle 11, are these: "If they are unwilling or unable to persevere, it is better for them to marry than to fall into the fire through their lusts; at least they should give no offense to their brothers and sisters."[11]

[26] The canons show some consideration toward those who have made vows before attaining a proper age, and as a rule vows used to be so made in former times.

24. THE MASS

[1] Our churches are falsely accused of abolishing the mass. Actually, the mass is retained among us and is celebrated with the greatest reverence. [2] Almost all the customary ceremonies are also retained, except that German hymns are interspersed here and there among the parts sung in Latin. These are added for the instruction of the people, [3] for ceremonies are needed especially in order that the unlearned may be taught. [4] Paul prescribed that in church a language should be used which is understood by the people. [5] The people are accustomed to receive the sacrament together, in so far as they are fit to do so. [6] This likewise increases the reverence and devotion of public worship, for none are admitted unless they are first heard

[1 Cor 11.27]

[1 Cor 14.2, 9]

11. Cyprian *Epistles* 62.2.

that in certain places German hymns are sung in addition to the Latin responses for the instruction and exercise of the people. [3] After all, the chief purpose of all ceremonies is to teach the people what they need to know about Christ.

[10] Before our time, however, the mass came to be misused in many ways, as is well known, by turning it into a sort of fair, by buying and selling it, and by observing it in almost all churches for a monetary consideration. Such abuses were often condemned by learned and devout men even before our time. [12] Then when our preachers preached about these things and the priests were reminded of the terrible responsibility which should properly concern every Christian (namely, that [I Cor 11.27] whoever uses the sacrament unworthily is guilty of the body and blood of Christ), [13] such mercenary masses and private masses, which had hitherto been held under compulsion for the sake of revenues and stipends, were discontinued in our churches.

----

and examined. [7] The people are also admonished concerning the value and use of the sacrament and the great consolation it offers to anxious consciences, that they may learn to believe in God and ask for and expect whatever is good from God. [8] Such worship pleases God, and such use of the sacrament nourishes devotion to God. [9] Accordingly it does not appear that the mass is observed with more devotion among our adversaries than among us.

[10] However, it is evident that for a long time there has been open and very grievous complaint by all good men that masses were being shamefully profaned and applied to purposes of gain. [11] It is also well known how widely this abuse extends in all the churches, by what manner of men masses are celebrated only for revenues or stipends, and how many celebrate masses contrary to the canons. [12] But Paul severely threatened those who dealt unworthily with the eucharist when he said, "Whoever eats the bread or drinks the cup of the Lord in an unworthy manner [I Cor 11.27] will be guilty of profaning the body and blood of the Lord." [13] Accordingly when our priests were admonished concerning this sin, private masses were discontinued among us inasmuch as hardly any private masses were held except for the sake of gain.

[14] The bishops were not ignorant of these abuses. If they had corrected them in time, there would now have been less dissension. [15] By their own negligence they let many corruptions creep into the church. [16] Now when it is too late they are beginning to complain about the troubles of the church, although the disturbance was brought about by nothing else than those abuses which had become so manifest that they could no longer be borne. [17] Great dissensions have arisen

[21] At the same time the abominable error was condemned according to which it was taught that our Lord Christ has by his death made satisfaction only for original sin and had instituted the mass as a sacrifice for other sins. [22] This transformed the mass into a sacrifice for the living and the dead, a sacrifice by means of which sin was taken away and God was reconciled. [23] Thereupon followed a debate as to whether one mass held for many people merited as much as a special mass held for an individual. Out of this grew countless multiplication of masses, by the performance of which men expected to get everything they needed from God. Meanwhile faith in Christ and true service of God were forgotten.

[24] Demanded without doubt by the necessity of such circumstances, instruction was given so that our people might know how the sacrament is to be used rightly. [26] They were taught, first of all, that the Scriptures show in many places that there is no sacrifice for original sin, or for any other sin, except the one death of Christ. [27] For it is written in the Epistle to the Hebrews that Christ offered himself once and by this offering made satisfaction for all sin.ᵃ [25] It is an unprece-

---

concerning the mass, concerning the sacrament. [18] Perhaps the world is being punished for such long continued profanations of the mass as have been tolerated in the church for many centuries by the very men who were able to correct them and were under obligation to do so. [19] For in the Decalogue it is written, "The Lord will not hold him guiltless who takes his name in vain." [20] Since the beginning of the world nothing of divine institution seems ever to have been so abused for the sake of gain as the mass. [Ex 20.7]

[21] To all this was added an opinion which infinitely increased private masses, namely, that Christ had by his passion made satisfaction for original sin and had instituted the mass in which an oblation should be made for daily sins, mortal and venial. [22] From this has come the common opinion that the mass is a work which by its performance takes away the sins of the living and the dead. [23] Thus was introduced a debate on whether one mass said for many people is worth as much as special masses said for individuals, and this produced that infinite proliferation of masses to which reference has been made.

[24] Concerning these opinions our teachers have warned that they depart from the Holy Scriptures and diminish the glory of Christ's passion, [25] for the passion of Christ was an oblation and satisfaction not only for original guilt but also for other sins. [26] So it is written in the Epistle to the Hebrews,ᵃ "We have been

a. Heb [9.28, 10.10, 10.14]

dented novelty in church doctrine that Christ's death should have made satisfaction only for original sin and not for other sins as well. Accordingly it is to be hoped that everyone will understand that this error is not unjustly condemned.

[28] In the second place, St. Paul taught that we obtain grace before God through faith and not through works. [29] Manifestly contrary to this teaching is the misuse of the mass by those who think that grace is obtained through the performance of this work, for it is well known that the mass is used to remove sin and obtain grace and all sorts of benefits from God, not only for the priest himself but also for the whole world and for others, both living and dead.

[30] In the third place, the holy sacrament was not instituted to make provision for a sacrifice for sin—for the sacrifice has already taken place—but to awaken our faith and comfort our consciences when we perceive that through the sacrament grace and forgiveness of sin are promised us by Christ. Accordingly the sacrament requires faith, and without faith it is used in vain.

[34] Inasmuch, then, as the mass is not a sacrifice to remove the sins of others, whether living or dead, but should be a communion in which the priest and

---

sanctified through the offering of the body of Jesus Christ once for all," [27] and again, "By a single offering he has perfected for all time those who are sanctified."

[28] The Scriptures also teach that we are justified before God through faith in Christ. [29] Now, if the mass takes away the sins of the living and the dead by a performance of the outward act, justification comes from the work of the mass and not from faith. But the Scriptures do not allow this.

[30] Christ commands us to do this in remembrance of him.[a] Therefore the mass was instituted that faith on the part of those who use the sacrament should remember what benefits are received through Christ and should cheer and comfort anxious consciences. [31] For to remember Christ is to remember his benefits and realize that they are truly offered to us; [32] and it is not enough to remember the history, for the Jews and the ungodly can also remember this. [33] Consequently the mass is to be used to this end, that the sacrament is administered to those who have need of consolation. So Ambrose said, "Because I always sin, I ought always take the medicine."[12]

[34] Inasmuch as the mass is such a giving of the sacrament, one common mass is observed among us on every holy day, and on other days, if any desire the

a. [Lk 22.19; 1 Cor 11.25]

12. Pseudo-Ambrose *The Sacraments* 5.4.25.

others receive the sacrament for themselves, it is observed among us in the following manner: On holy days, and at other times when communicants are present, mass is held and those who desire it are communicated. [35] Thus the mass is preserved among us in its proper use, the use which was formerly observed in the church and which can be proved by St. Paul's statement in 1 Corinthians 11, and by many statements of the fathers. [36] For Chrysostom reports how the priest stood every day, inviting some to communion and forbidding others to approach.[13] [37] The ancient canons also indicate that one man officiated and communicated the other priests and deacons, [38] for the words of the Nicene canon [18] read, "After the priests the deacons shall receive the sacrament in order from the bishop or priest." 1 Cor 11[.20–34]

[40] Since, therefore, no novelty has been introduced which did not exist in the church from ancient times, and since no conspicuous change has been made in the public ceremonies of the mass except that other unnecessary masses which were held in addition to the parochial mass, probably through abuse, have been discontinued, this manner of holding mass ought not in fairness be condemned as heretical or unchristian. [41] In times past, even in large churches where there were many people, mass was not held on every day that the people assembled, for accord-

---

sacrament, it is also administered to those who ask for it. [35] Nor is this custom new in the church, for before the time of Gregory the ancients do not mention private masses but speak often of the common mass. [36] Chrysostom says that the priest stands daily at the altar, inviting some to communion and keeping others away.[13] [37] And it appears from the ancient canons that some one person or other celebrated mass and the rest of the presbyters and deacons received the body of the Lord from him, [38] for the words of the Nicene canon [18] read, "In order, after the presbyters, let the deacons receive holy communion from the bishop or from a presbyter." [39] Paul also commands concerning communion that one wait for another in order that there may be a common participation. [1 Cor 11.33]

[40] Since, therefore, the mass among us is supported by the example of the church as seen from the Scriptures and the fathers, we are confident that it cannot be disapproved, especially since the customary public ceremonies are for the most part retained. Only the number of masses is different, and on account of the great and manifest abuses it would certainly be of advantage to reduce the number. [41] In former times, even in churches most frequented, mass was not held every day; as the *Tripartite History* testifies in book 9, "Again, in Alexandria, the Scriptures are

13. John Chrysostom *Epistle to the Ephesians* 3.1.

ing to the *Tripartite History,* book 9, on Wednesday and Friday the Scriptures were read and expounded in Alexandria, and all these services were held without mass.

25. CONFESSION

[1] Confession has not been abolished by the preachers on our side. The custom has been retained among us of not administering the sacrament to those who have not previously been examined and absolved. [2] At the same time the people are carefully instructed concerning the consolation of the word of absolution so that they may esteem absolution as a great and precious thing. [3] It is not the voice or word of the man who speaks it, but it is the word of God, who forgives sin, for it is spoken in God's stead and by God's command. [4] We teach with great diligence about this command and power of keys and how comforting and necessary it is for terrified consciences. We also teach that God requires us to believe this absolution as much as if we heard God's voice from heaven, that we should joyfully comfort ourselves with absolution, and that we should know that through such faith we obtain forgiveness of sins. [5] In former times the preachers who taught much about confession never mentioned a word concerning these necessary matters but only tormented consciences with long enumerations of sins, with satisfactions, with indulgences, with pilgrimages and the like. [6] Many of our opponents themselves acknowledge that we have written about and treated of true Christian repentance in a more fitting fashion than had been done for a long time.

---

read and the doctors expound them on Wednesday and Friday, and all things are done except for the solemn remembrance of the sacrifice."

25. CONFESSION

[1] Confession has not been abolished in our churches, for it is not customary to administer the body of Christ except to those who have previously been examined and absolved. [2] The people are very diligently taught concerning faith in connection with absolution, a matter about which there has been profound silence before this time. [3] Our people are taught to esteem absolution highly because it is the voice of God and is pronounced by God's command. [4] The power of keys is praised, and people are reminded of the great consolation it brings to terrified consciences, are told that God requires faith to believe such absolution as God's own voice heard from heaven, and are assured that such faith truly obtains and receives the forgiveness of sins. [5] In former times satisfactions were immoderately extolled, but nothing was said about faith. Accordingly no fault is to be found with our churches on

[7] Concerning confession we teach that no one should be compelled to recount sins in detail, for this is impossible. [8] As the Psalm says, "Who can discern his errors?" Jeremiah also says, "The heart is desperately corrupt; who can understand it?" Our wretched human nature is so deeply submerged in sins that it is unable to perceive or know them all, [9] and if we were to be absolved only from those which we can enumerate we would be helped but little. On this account there is no need to compel people to give a detailed account of their sins. [10] That this was also the view of the fathers can be seen in distinction 1, *De poenitentia,* [11] where these words of Chrysostom are quoted: "I do not say that you should expose yourself in public or should accuse yourself before others, but obey the prophet who says, 'Show your way to the Lord.' Therefore confess to the Lord God, the true judge, in your prayer, telling him of your sins not with your tongue but in your conscience." Here it can be clearly seen that Chrysostom does not require a detailed enumeration of sins. [12] The marginal note in *De poenitentia,* distinction 5, also teaches that such confession is not commanded by the Scriptures, but was instituted by the church. [13] Yet the preachers on our side diligently teach that confession is to be retained for the sake of absolution (which is its chief and most important part), for the consolation of terrified consciences, and also for other reasons.

[Ps 19.12]

[Jer 17.9]

[Ps 37.5]

---

this point, [6] for even our adversaries are forced to concede to us that our teachers have shed light on the doctrine of repentance and have treated it with great care.

[7] Concerning confession they teach that an enumeration of sins is not necessary and that consciences should not be burdened with a scrupulous enumeration of all sins because it is impossible to recount all of them. So the Psalm testifies, "Who can discern his errors?" [8] Jeremiah also says, "The heart of man is corrupt and inscrutable." [9] But if no sins were forgiven except those which are recounted, our consciences would never find peace, for many sins can neither be perceived nor remembered. [10] The ancient writers also testify that such an enumeration is not necessary, [11] for Chrysostom is quoted in the canons as saying, "I do not say that you should expose yourself in public or should accuse yourself before others, but I wish you to obey the prophet who says, 'Show your way to the Lord.' Therefore, confess your sins to God, the true judge, in your prayer. Tell him of your sins not with your tongue but with the memory of your conscience." [12] The marginal note in *De poenitentia,* distinction 5, in the chapter "Consideret," admits that such confession is of human right. [13] Nevertheless, confession is retained among us on account of the great benefit of absolution and because it is otherwise useful to consciences.

[Ps 19.12]

[Jer 17.9]

[Ps 37.5]

26. THE DISTINCTION OF FOODS

[1] In former times men taught, preached, and wrote that distinctions among foods and similar traditions which had been instituted by men serve to earn grace and make satisfaction for sin. [2] For this reason new fasts, new ceremonies, new orders, and the like were invented daily, and were ardently and urgently promoted, as if these were a necessary service of God by means of which grace would be earned if they were observed and a great sin committed if they were omitted. [3] Many harmful errors in the church have resulted from this.

[4] In the first place, the grace of Christ and the teaching concerning faith are thereby obscured, and yet the gospel earnestly urges them upon us and strongly insists that we regard the merit of Christ as something great and precious and know that faith in Christ is to be esteemed far above all works. [5] On this account St. Paul contended mightily against the law of Moses and against human tradition so that we should learn that we do not become good in God's sight by our works but that it is only through faith in Christ that we obtain grace for Christ's sake. [6] This teaching has been almost completely extinguished by those who have taught that grace is to be earned by prescribed fasts, distinctions among foods, vestments, etc.

---

26. THE DISTINCTION OF FOODS

[1] It has been the common opinion not only of the people but also of those who teach in the churches that distinctions among foods and similar human traditions are works which are profitable to merit grace and make satisfactions for sins. [2] That the world thought so is evident from the fact that new ceremonies, new orders, new holy days, and new fasts were daily instituted, and the learned men in the churches exacted these works as a service necessary to merit grace and sorely terrified the consciences of those who omitted any of them. [3] From this opinion concerning traditions much harm has resulted in the church.

[4] In the first place, it has obscured the doctrine concerning grace and the righteousness of faith, which is the chief part of the gospel and ought above all else to be in the church, and to be prominent in it, so that the merit of Christ may be well known and that faith which believes that sins are forgiven for Christ's sake may be exalted far above works and above all other acts of worship. [5] Paul therefore lays the greatest weight on this article and puts aside the law and human traditions in order to show that the righteousness of a Christian is something other than works of this sort; it is faith which believes that for Christ's sake we are received into grace. [6] This teaching of Paul has been almost wholly smothered by traditions which have produced the opinion that it is necessary to merit grace and righteousness by

[8] In the second place, such traditions have also obscured the commands of God, for these traditions were exalted far above God's commands. [9] This also was regarded as Christian life: whoever observed festivals in this way, prayed in this way, fasted in this way, and dressed in this way was said to live a spiritual and Christian life. [10] On the other hand, other necessary good works were considered secular and unspiritual: the works which everybody is obliged to do according to his calling—for example, that a husband should labor to support his wife and children and bring them up in the fear of God, that a wife should bear children and care for them, that a prince and magistrates should govern land and people, etc. [11] Such works, commanded by God, were to be regarded as secular and imperfect, while traditions were to be given the glamorous title of alone being holy and perfect works. Accordingly there was no end or limit to the making of such traditions.

[12] In the third place, such traditions have turned out to be a grievous burden to consciences, for it was not possible to keep all the traditions, and yet the people were of the opinion that they were a necessary service of God. [13] Gerson writes that many fell into despair on this account, and some even committed sui-

---

distinctions among foods and similar acts of worship. [7] In treating of repentance no mention was made of faith; only works of satisfaction were proposed, and the whole of repentance was thought to consist of these.

[8] In the second place, these precepts obscured the commands of God, for traditions were exalted far above the commands of God. Christianity was thought to consist wholly in the observance of certain holy days, rites, fasts, and vestments. [9] Such observances claimed for themselves the glamorous title of comprising the spiritual life and the perfect life. [10] Meanwhile the commands of God pertaining to callings were without honor—for example, that a father should bring up his children, that a mother should bear children, that a prince should govern his country. These were regarded as secular and imperfect works, far inferior to those glittering observances. [11] This error greatly tormented the consciences of devout people who grieved that they were bound to an imperfect kind of life—in marriage, in the magistracy, or in other civil occupations—and admired the monks and others like them, falsely imagining that the observances of such men were more pleasing to God.

[12] In the third place, traditions brought great dangers to consciences, for it was impossible to keep all traditions, and yet men judged these observances to be necessary acts of worship. [13] Gerson writes that many fell into despair, and some even took their own lives, because they felt that they could not keep the tra-

cide, because they had not heard anything of the consolation of the grace of Christ. [14] We can see in the writings of the summists and canonists how consciences have been confused, for they undertook to collate the traditions and sought mitigations to relieve consciences, [15] but they were so occupied with such efforts that they neglected all wholesome Christian teachings about more important things, such as faith, consolation in severe trials, and the like. [16] Many devout and learned people before our time have also complained that such traditions caused so much strife in the church that godly people were thereby hindered from coming to a right knowledge of Christ. Gerson and others have complained bitterly about this. [17] In fact, Augustine was also displeased that consciences were burdened with so many traditions, and he taught in this connection that they were not to be considered necessary observances.[14]

[18] Our teachers have not taught concerning these matters out of malice or contempt of spiritual authority, [19] but dire need has compelled them to give instruction about the aforementioned errors which have arisen from a wrong estimation of tradition. [20] The gospel demands that the teaching about faith should

---

ditions and, meanwhile, they had never heard the consolation of grace and of the righteousness of faith. [14] We see that the summists and theologians gathered the traditions together and sought mitigations to relieve consciences; yet they did not altogether succeed in releasing them but rather entangled consciences even more. [15] Schools and sermons were so preoccupied with gathering traditions that they have had no time to treat the Scriptures and seek for the more profitable teachings concerning faith, the cross, hope, the importance of civil affairs, and the consolation of sorely tried consciences. [16] Hence Gerson and certain other theologians greatly lamented that they were so hindered by these bickerings about traditions that they were unable to devote their attention to a better kind of teaching. [17] Augustine also forbids the burdening of consciences with such observances and prudently admonishes Januarius that he should know that they are to be as things indifferent, for these are his words.[14]

[18] Our teachers, therefore, must not be looked upon as having taken up this matter rashly or out of hatred for the bishops, as some wrongly suspect. [19] There was great need to warn the churches of these errors which had arisen from misunderstanding of traditions. [20] For the gospel compels us to insist in the church on the teaching concerning grace and the righteousness of faith, and this

14. Augustine *Epistle 54 to Januarius* 2.2.

and must be emphasized in the church, but this teaching cannot be understood if it is supposed that grace is earned through self-chosen works.

[21] It is therefore taught that grace cannot be earned, God cannot be reconciled, and sin cannot be atoned for by observing the said human traditions. Accordingly they should not be made into a necessary service of God. [22] Reasons for this shall be cited from the Scriptures. In Matthew 15, Christ defends the apostles for not observing the customary traditions, and he adds, "In vain do they worship me, teaching as doctrines the precepts of men." [23] Since he calls them vain service, they must not be necessary. Thereupon Christ says, "Not what goes into the mouth defiles a man." [24] Paul also says in Romans 14: "The kingdom of God does not mean food and drink," [25] and in Colossians 2, he says, "Let no one pass judgment on you in questions of food and drink or with regard to a festival," etc. [27] In Acts 15, Peter says, "Why do you make trial of God by putting a yoke upon the neck of the disciples which neither our fathers nor we have been able to bear? But we believe that we shall be saved through the grace of the Lord Jesus, just as they will." [28] Here Peter forbids the burdening of consciences with additional outward

Mt 15[.1–20]

Mt 15[.9]

Mt 15[.11]

Rom 14[.17]

Col 2[.16]

Acts 15[.10, 11]

————————————

cannot be understood if men suppose that they merit grace by observances of their own choice.

[21] Accordingly our teachers have taught that we cannot merit grace or make satisfaction for sins by the observance of human traditions. Hence observances of this kind are not to be thought of as necessary acts of worship. [22] Our teachers add testimonies from the Scriptures. In Matthew Christ defends the apostles for not observing the customary tradition, a tradition which was seen to be legalistic and to have a relationship with the purifications of the law, and he says, "In vain do they worship me with the precepts of men." [23] So he does not require an unprofitable act of worship. Shortly afterward Christ says, "Not what goes into the mouth defiles a man." [24] It is also written in Romans 14, "The kingdom of God is not food and drink," [25] and in Colossians 2, "Let no one pass judgment on you in questions of food and drink or with regard to a festival or a sabbath."[15] [27] In Acts 15, Peter says, "Why do you make trial of God by putting a yoke upon the neck of the disciples which neither our fathers nor we have been able to bear? But

Mt 15[.1–20]

Mt 15[.9]

Mt 15[.11]

Rom 14[.17]

Col 2[.16]

15. The *editio princeps* (1531) here inserts: "If with Christ you died to the elemental spirits of the universe, why do you live as if you still belonged to the world? Why do you submit to regulations, 'Do not handle, Do not taste, Do not touch'?" (Col 2.20, 21). See *BLK*, 104.

1 Tm 4[.1, 3] ceremonies, whether of Moses or of another. [29] In 1 Timothy 4 such prohibitions as forbid food or marriage are called a doctrine of the devil, for it is diametrically opposed to the gospel to institute or practice such works for the purpose of earning forgiveness of sin or with the notion that nobody is a Christian unless he performs such services.

[30] Although our teachers are, like Jovinian, accused of forbidding mortification and discipline, their writings reveal something quite different. [31] They have always taught concerning the holy cross that Christians are obliged to suffer, [32] and this is true and real rather than invented mortification.

[33] They also teach that everybody is under obligation to conduct himself, with reference to such bodily exercise as fasting and other discipline, so that he does not give occasion to sin, but not as if he earned grace by such works. [34] Such bodily exercise should not be limited to certain specified days but should be practiced continually. [35] Christ speaks of this in Luke 21: "Take heed to yourselves

Lk 21[.34] lest your hearts be weighed down with dissipation," [36] and again, "This kind of
[Mk 9.29] demon cannot be driven out by anything but fasting and prayer." [37] Paul said that
[1 Cor 9.27] he pommeled his body and subdued it, [38] and by this he indicated that it is not

---

we believe that we shall be saved through the grace of the Lord Jesus, just as they
Acts 15[.10, 11] will." [28] Here Peter forbids the burdening of consciences with numerous rites,
1 Tm 4[.1, 3] whether of Moses or of others. [29] And in 1 Timothy 4 Paul calls the prohibition of foods a doctrine of demons, for it is in conflict with the gospel to institute or practice such works for the purpose of meriting grace through them or with the notion that Christian righteousness cannot exist without such acts of worship.

[30] Here our adversaries charge that our teachers, like Jovinian, forbid discipline and mortification of the flesh. But something different may be perceived in the writings of our teachers, [31] for they have always taught concerning the cross that Christians are obliged to suffer afflictions. [32] To be harassed by various afflictions and to be crucified with Christ is true and real, rather than invented, mortification.

[33] Besides, they teach that every Christian ought so to control and curb himself with bodily discipline, or bodily exercises and labors, that neither plenty nor idleness may tempt him to sin, but not in order to merit forgiveness of sins or satisfaction for sins by means of such exercises. [34] Such bodily discipline ought to be encouraged at all times, and not merely on a few prescribed days. [35] So Christ
[Lk 21.34] commands, "Take heed to yourselves lest your hearts be weighed down with dissi-

the purpose of mortification to merit grace but to keep the body in such a condition that one can perform the duties required by one's calling. [39] Thus fasting in itself is not rejected, but what is rejected is making a necessary service of fasts on prescribed days and with specified foods, for this confuses consciences.

[40] We on our part also retain many ceremonies and traditions (such as the liturgy of the mass and various canticles, festivals, and the like) which serve to preserve order in the church. [41] At the same time, however, the people are instructed that such outward forms of service do not make us righteous before God and that they are to be observed without burdening consciences, which is to say that it is not a sin to omit them if this is done without causing scandal. [42] The ancient fathers maintained such liberty with respect to outward ceremonies, [43] for in the East they kept Easter at a time different from that in Rome. When some regarded this difference a divisive of the church, they were admonished by others that it was not necessary to maintain uniformity in such customs. [44] Irenaeus said, "Disagreement in fasting does not destroy unity in faith,"[16] and there is a statement in distinction 12 that such disagreement in human ordinances is not in conflict with

---

pation," [36] and again, "This kind of demon cannot be driven out by anything but fasting and prayer." [37] Paul also said, "I pommel my body and subdue it." [38] [Mk 9.29] [1 Cor 9.27] By this he clearly shows that he pommeled his body not to merit forgiveness of sins by that discipline but to keep his body in subjection and fit for spiritual things and for discharging his duty according to his calling. [39] Condemned therefore is not fasting in itself, but traditions which with peril to conscience prescribe certain days and certain foods as if works of this sort were necessary acts of worship.

[40] Many traditions are nevertheless kept among us (such as the order of lessons in the mass, holy days, etc.) which are profitable for maintaining good order in the church. [41] At the same time men are warned that such observances do not justify before God and that no sin is committed if they are omitted without scandal. [42] Such liberty in human rites was not unknown to the fathers, [43] for Easter was kept in the East at a time different from that in Rome, and when on account of this difference the Romans accused the East of schism, they were admonished by others that such customs need not be alike everywhere. [44] Irenaeus says, "Disagreement about fasting does not destroy unity in faith,"[16] and Pope Gregory indicates in dis-

---

16. Quoted in Eusebius of Caesarea *Church History* 5.24.13 (*NPNF*-II 1:243).

the unity of Christendom. [45] Moreover, the *Tripartite History*, book 9, gathers many examples of dissimilar church usages and adds the profitable Christian observation, "It was not the intention of the apostles to institute holy days but to teach faith and love."

27. MONASTIC VOWS

[1] In discussing monastic vows it is necessary to begin by considering what opinions have hitherto been held concerning them, what kind of life was lived in the monasteries, and how many of the daily observances in them were contrary not only to the word of God but also to papal canons. [2] In the days of St. Augustine monastic life was voluntary. Later, when true discipline and doctrine had become corrupted, monastic vows were invented, and the attempt was made to restore discipline by means of these vows as if in a well-conceived prison.

[3] In addition to monastic vows many other requirements were imposed, [4] and such fetters and burdens were laid on many before they had attained an appropriate age.

[5] Many persons also entered monastic life ignorantly, for although they were not too young, they had not sufficiently appreciated or understood their capa-

---

tinction 12 that such diversity does not violate the unity of the church. [45] In the *Tripartite History*, book 9, many examples of dissimilar rites are gathered, and this statement is made: "It was not the intention of the apostles to enact binding laws with respect to holy days but to preach piety toward God and good conversation among men."

27. MONASTIC VOWS

[1] What is taught among us concerning monastic vows will be better understood if it is recalled what the condition of monasteries was and how many things were done in these monasteries every day that were contrary to the canons. [2] In Augustine's time they were voluntary associations. Afterward, when discipline fell into decay, vows were added for the purpose of restoring discipline, as in a carefully planned prison. [3] Many other observances were gradually added in addition to vows. [4] These fetters were laid on many, contrary to the canons, before they had attained a lawful age. [5] Many entered this kind of life through ignorance, for although they were not wanting in years, they were unable to judge their own strength. [6] Those who were thus ensnared were compelled to remain, though some could have been freed by appealing to the canons. [7] This was the case in convents of women more

bilities. [6] All of those who were thus ensnared and entangled were pressed and compelled to remain, in spite of the fact that even the papal canons might have set many of them free. [7] The practice was stricter in women's convents than in those of men, though it would have been seemly to show more consideration to women as the weaker sex. [8] Such severity and rigor displeased many devout people in the past, for they must have seen that both boys and girls were thrust into monasteries to provide for their maintenance. They must also have seen what evils came from this arrangement, what scandals and burdened consciences resulted. [9] Many people complained that in such a momentous matter the canons were not strictly adhered to. [10] Besides, monastic vows gained such a reputation, as is well known, that many monks with even a little understanding were displeased.

[11] It was claimed that monastic vows were equal to baptism, and that by monastic life one could earn forgiveness of sin and justification before God. [12] What is more, they added that monastic life not only earned righteousness and godliness, but also that by means of this life both the precepts and the counsels included in the gospel were kept, [13] and so monastic vows were praised more highly than baptism. They also claimed that more merit could be obtained by monastic life than by all other states of life instituted by God—whether the office of pastor and preacher, of ruler, prince, lord, or the like, all of whom serve in their appointed

---

than in those of men, although more consideration should have been given to the weaker sex. [8] Such rigor displeased many good men before our time when they saw that girls and boys were thrust into monasteries for their maintenance and saw what unfortunately resulted from this arrangement, what scandals were created, what snares were placed on consciences. [9] They regretted that in such a momentous matter the authority of the canons was utterly ignored and despised. [10] To these evils was added the fact that vows had such a reputation that it was clearly displeasing to those monks in former times who had a little more understanding.

[11] They said that vows were equal to baptism, and they taught that they merited forgiveness of sins and justification before God by this kind of life. [12] What is more, they added that monastic life merited not only righteousness before God but even more, for it was an observance not only of the precepts but also of the counsels of the gospel. [13] Thus they made men believe that the monastic profession was far better than baptism, and that monastic life was more meritorious than the life of magistrates, pastors, and the like who, without man-made observances, serve their calling in accordance with God's commands. [14] None of these things can be denied, for they appear in their own books.

calling according to God's word and command without invented spirituality. [14] None of these things can be denied, for they are found in their own books.

[15] Furthermore, those who were thus ensnared and inveigled into a monastery learned little about Christ. Formerly the monasteries had conducted schools of Holy Scripture and other branches of learning which are profitable to the Christian church, so that pastors and bishops were taken from monasteries. But now the picture is changed. [16] In former times people gathered and adopted monastic life for the purpose of learning the Scriptures, but now it is claimed that monastic life is of such a nature that thereby God's grace and righteousness before God are earned. In fact, it is called a state of perfection and is regarded as far superior to the other estates instituted by God. [17] All this is mentioned, without misrepresentation, in order that one may better grasp and understand what our teachers teach and preach.

[18] For one thing, it is taught among us with regard to those who desire to marry that all those who are not suited for celibacy have the power, right, and authority to marry, for vows cannot nullify God's order and command. [19] God's command in 1 Corinthians 7 reads, "Because of the temptation to immorality, each

1 Cor 7[.2]   man should have his own wife and each woman her own husband." [20] It is not alone God's command that urges, drives, and compels us to do this, but God's creation and order also direct all to marriage who are not endowed with the gift of

---

[15] What happened after such people had entered monasteries? Formerly there had been schools of the Holy Scriptures and other branches of learning which were profitable to the church, and pastors and bishops were taken from them. Now everything is different, and it is needless to rehearse what is well known. Formerly people came together in monasteries to learn. [16] Now they pretend that this kind of life was instituted to merit grace and righteousness. In fact, they assert that it is a state of perfection, and they put it far above all other kinds of life instituted by God. [17] We have rehearsed these things without odious exaggeration in order that our teaching on this topic may better be understood.

[18] In the first place, we teach concerning those who contract matrimony that it is lawful for all who are not suited for celibacy to marry, for vows can not nullify the command and institution of God. [19] This is the command of God, "Be-

[1 Cor 7.2]   cause of fornication let every man have his own wife." [20] Nor is it the command only, but God's creation and institution also compel those to marry who are not excepted by a singular work of God. This is according to the text in Genesis 2,

Gn 2[.18]   "It is not good that the man should be alone." [21] Therefore those who obey this command and institution of God do not sin.

virginity by a special act of God. This appears from God's own words in Genesis 2: "It is not good that the man should be alone; I will make him a helper fit for him."   Gn 2[.18]

[22] What objection may be raised to this? No matter how much one extols the vow and the obligation, no matter how highly one exalts them, it is still impossible to abrogate God's command. [23] Learned men say that a vow made contrary to papal canons is not binding. How much less must be their obligation, lawfulness, and power when they are contrary to God's command!

[24] If there were no reasons which allowed annulment of the obligation of a vow, the popes could not have dispensed and released men from such obligation, for no man has the right to cancel an obligation which is derived from divine law. [25] Consequently the popes were well aware that some amelioration ought to be exercised in connection with this obligation and have often given dispensations, [26] as in the case of the king of Aragon and many others. If dispensations were granted for the maintenance of temporal interests, how much more should dispensations be granted for necessities of men's souls!

[27] Why, then, do our opponents insist so strongly that vows must be kept without first ascertaining whether a vow is of the proper sort? For a vow must involve what is possible and voluntary and must be uncoerced. [28] Yet it is commonly known to what an extent perpetual chastity lies within human power and ability, [29] and there are few, whether men or women, who have taken monas-

---

[22] What objection can be raised to this? Exaggerate the obligation of a vow as much as one pleases, it cannot be brought about that a vow abrogates the command of God. [23] The canons state that every vow is subject to the right of a superior. How much less are those vows valid which are made contrary to God's commands!

[24] If the obligation of vows could not be changed for any reason at all, the Roman pontiffs would not have granted dispensations, for it is not lawful for a man to annul an obligation which is plainly derived from divine law. [25] But the Roman pontiffs have prudently judged that leniency should be observed in connection with this obligation. Therefore, we read that they often granted dispensation from vows. [26] Well known is the case of the king of Aragon, who was recalled from a monastery, and there is no want of examples in our time.

[27] In the second place, why do our adversaries exaggerate the obligation or effect of a vow while they remain silent concerning the nature of a vow, which ought to be voluntary and chosen freely and deliberately? [28] Yet it is not unknown to what an extent perpetual chastity lies in man's power. [29] How few there are

tic vows of themselves, willingly, and after due consideration. Before they came to a right understanding they were persuaded to take monastic vows, and sometimes have been compelled and forced to do so. [30] Accordingly it is not right to argue so rashly and insistently about the obligation of vows inasmuch as it is generally conceded that it belongs to the very nature and character of a vow that it should be voluntary and should be assumed only after due consideration and counsel.

[31] Several canons and papal regulations annul vows that are made under the age of fifteen years. They hold that before this age one does not possess sufficient understanding to determine or arrange the order of one's whole future life. [32] Another canon concedes still more years to human frailty, for it prohibits the taking of monastic vows before the eighteenth year. [33] On the basis of this provision most monastics have excuse and reason for leaving their monasteries inasmuch as a majority of them entered the cloister in their childhood, before attaining such age.

[34] Finally, although the breaking of monastic vows might be censured, it would not follow that the marriage of those who broke them should be dissolved. [35] For St. Augustine says in his *Nuptiarum,* question 27, chapter 1, that such a marriage should not be dissolved, and St. Augustine is no inconsiderable authority in the Christian church, even though some have subsequently differed from him.

---

who have taken the vow spontaneously and deliberately! Before they are able to judge, boys and girls are persuaded, and sometimes even compelled, to take the vow. [30] Accordingly it is not fair to argue so insistently about the obligation inasmuch as it is conceded by all that it is contrary to the nature of a vow to make a promise which is not spontaneous and deliberate.

[31] Many canons annul vows made before the age of fifteen on the ground that before that age a person does not seem to have sufficient judgment to make a decision involving the rest of his life. [32] Another canon, making a greater concession to human weakness, adds a few years and forbids making a vow before the eighteenth year. [33] Whether we follow one canon or the other, most monastics have an excuse for leaving the monastery because a majority of them took vows before they reached such an age.

[34] Finally, although the violation of vows might be rebuked, yet it seems not to follow of necessity that the marriages of persons who violated them ought to be dissolved. [35] For Augustine denies that they should be dissolved in *Nuptiarum,* question 27, chapter 1, and his authority is not inconsiderable, although others have subsequently differed from him.

[36] Although God's command concerning marriage frees and releases many from monastic vows, our teachers offer still more reasons why monastic vows are null and void. For all such service of God that is chosen and instituted by men to obtain righteousness and God's grace without the command and authority of God is opposed to God and the holy gospel and contrary to God's command. So Christ himself says in Matthew 15, "In vain do they worship me, teaching as doctrines the precepts of men." [37] Saint Paul also teaches everywhere that one is not to seek for righteousness in the precepts and services invented by men but that righteousness and godliness in God's sight come from faith and trust when we believe that God receives us into his favor for the sake of Christ, his only Son.   Mt 15[.9]

[38] It is quite evident that the monks have taught and preached that their invented spiritual life makes satisfaction for sin and obtains God's grace and righteousness. What is this but to diminish the glory and honor of the grace of Christ and deny the righteousness of faith? [39] It follows from this that the customary vows were an improper and false service of God. Therefore they are not binding, [40] for an ungodly vow, made contrary to God's command, is null and void. Even the canons teach that an oath should not be an obligation to sin.

[41] Saint Paul says in Galatians 5: "You are severed from Christ, you who would be justified by the law; you have fallen away from grace." [42] In the same way, those who would be justified by vows are severed from Christ and have fallen   Gal 5[.4]

---

[36] Although it appears that God's command concerning marriage frees many from their vows, our teachers offer still another reason to show that vows are void. Every service of God that is instituted and chosen by men to merit justification and grace without the command of God is wicked, for Christ says, "In vain do they worship me with the precepts of men." [37] Paul also teaches everywhere that righteousness is not to be sought for in observances and services devised by men but that it comes through faith to those who believe that they are received by God into favor for Christ's sake.   [Mt 15.9]

[38] It is evident that the monks have taught that their invented observances make satisfaction for sins and merit grace and justification. What is this but to detract from the glory of Christ and obscure and deny the righteousness of faith? [39] It follows, therefore, that the vows thus customarily taken were wicked services and on this account were void, [40] for a wicked vow, taken contrary to the commands of God, is invalid. As the canon says, no vow ought to bind men to iniquity.

[41] Paul says, "You are severed from Christ, you who would be justified by the law; you have fallen away from grace." [42] Therefore those who would be   [Gal 5.4]

away from God's grace, [43] for they rob Christ, who alone justifies, of his honor and bestow this honor upon their vows and monastic life.

[44] One cannot deny that the monks have taught and preached that they were justified and earned forgiveness of sins by their vows and their monastic life and observances. In fact, they have invented a still more indecent and absurd claim, namely, that they could apply their good works to others. [45] If one were inclined to count up all these claims for the purpose of casting them into their teeth, how many items could be assembled which the monks themselves are now ashamed of and wish had never occurred! [46] Besides all this, they persuaded the people that the invented spiritual estate of the orders was Christian perfection. [47] Certainly this is exaltation of works as a means of attaining justification. [48] Now, it is no small offense in the Christian church that the people should be presented with such a service of God, invented by men without the command of God, and should be taught that such a service would make men good and righteous before God. For righteousness of faith, which should be emphasized above all else in the Christian church, is obscured when man's eyes are dazzled with this curious angelic spirituality and sham of poverty, humility, and chastity.

[49] Besides, the commands of God and true and proper service of God are obscured when people are told that monks alone are in a state of perfection. For this

----

justified by vows are severed from Christ and fall away from grace, [43] for those who ascribe justification to their vows ascribe to their own works what properly belongs to the glory of Christ.

[44] It cannot be denied that the monks taught that they were justified and merited forgiveness of sins by their vows and observances. In fact, they invented greater absurdities when they claimed that they could transfer their works to others. [45] If out of hatred anybody should be inclined to enlarge on these claims, how many things could be collected of which even the monks are now ashamed! [46] Besides all this, they persuaded men that their invented observances were a state of Christian perfection. [47] Is not this attributing justification to works? [48] It is no light offense in the church to recommend to the people a certain service invented by men without the command of God and to teach that such service justifies men. For righteousness of faith, which ought especially to be taught in the church, is obscured when the eyes of men are blinded by these remarkable angelic observances and this pretense of poverty, humility, and chastity.

[49] Furthermore, the commands of God and true service of God are obscured when men hear that only monks are in a state of perfection. For this is Chris-

is Christian perfection: that we fear God honestly with our whole hearts, and yet have sincere confidence, faith, and trust that for Christ's sake we have a gracious, merciful God; that we may and should ask and pray God for those things of which we have need, and confidently expect help from him in every affliction connected with our particular calling and station in life; and that meanwhile we do good works for others and diligently attend to our calling. [50] True perfection and right service of God consist of these things and not of mendicancy or wearing a black or gray cowl, etc. [51] However, the common people, hearing the state of celibacy praised above all measure, draw many harmful conclusions from such false exaltation of monastic life, [52] for it follows that their consciences are troubled because they are married. [53] When the common man hears that only mendicants are perfect, he is uncertain whether he can keep his possessions and engage in business without sin. [54] When the people hear that it is only a counsel not to take revenge, it is natural that some should conclude that it is not sinful to take revenge outside of the exercise of their office. [55] Still others think that it is not right at all for Christians, even in the government, to avenge wrong.

[56] Many instances are also recorded of men who forsook wife and child, and also their civil office, to take shelter in a monastery. [57] This, they said, is fleeing from the world and seeking a life more pleasing to God than the other. They

---

tian perfection: honestly to fear God and at the same time to have great faith and to trust that for Christ's sake we have a gracious God; to ask of God, and assuredly to expect from him, help in all things which are to be borne in connection with our callings; meanwhile to be diligent in the performance of good works for others and to attend to our calling. [50] True perfection and true service of God consist of these things and not of celibacy, mendicancy, or humble attire. [51] The people draw many pernicious conclusions from such false commendations of monastic life. [52] They hear celibacy praised above measure, and therefore they engage in their married life with a troubled conscience. [53] They hear that only mendicants are perfect, and therefore they have a troubled conscience when they keep their possessions or engage in business. [54] They hear that it is an evangelical counsel not to take revenge, and therefore some are not afraid to take vengeance in their private life since they are told that this is prohibited by a counsel and not by a precept. [55] Others err still more, for they judge that all magistracy and all civil offices are unworthy of Christians and in conflict with the evangelical counsel.

[56] Cases can be read of men who, forsaking marriage and the administration of the state, withdrew into a monastery. [57] They called this "fleeing from

were unable to understand that one is to serve God by observing the commands God has given and not by keeping the commands invented by men. [58] That is a good and perfect state of life which has God's command to support it; on the other hand, that is a dangerous state of life which does not have God's command behind it. [59] About such matters it was necessary to give the people proper instruction.

[60] In former times Gerson censured the error of the monks concerning perfection and indicated that it was an innovation of his time to speak of monastic life as a state of perfection.

[61] Thus there are many godless opinions and errors associated with monastic vows: that they justify and render men righteous before God, that they constitute Christian perfection, that they are the means of fulfilling both evangelical counsels and precepts, and that they furnish the works of supererogation which we are not obligated to render to God. [62] Inasmuch as all these things are false, useless, and invented, monastic vows are null and void.

28. THE POWER OF BISHOPS

[1] Many and various things have been written in former times about the power of bishops, and some have improperly confused the power of bishops with the temporal sword. [2] Out of this careless confusion many serious wars, tumults, and up-

---

the world" and "seeking a holy kind of life." They did not perceive that God is to be served by observing the commands he has given and not by keeping the commands invented by men. [58] A good and perfect kind of life is one which has God's command in its favor. [59] Concerning such things it was necessary to admonish men.

[60] Before our times Gerson rebuked the error of the monks concerning perfection and testified that it was a novelty in his day to say that monastic life is a state of perfection.

[61] So there are many impious opinions which are associated with vows: that they justify, that they constitute Christian perfection, that the monks observe both the counsels and the precepts, and that monks do works of supererogation. [62] All these things, since they are false and useless, make vows null and void.

28. ECCLESIASTICAL POWER

[1] In former times there has been great controversy about the power of bishops, and some have improperly confused the power of the church with the power of the sword. [2] From this confusion great wars and tumults have resulted, while the pon-

risings have resulted because the bishops, under pretext of the power given them by Christ, have not only introduced new forms of worship and burdened consciences with reserved cases and violent use of the ban, but have also presumed to set up and depose kings and emperors according to their pleasure. [3] Such outrage has long since been condemned by learned and devout people in Christendom. [4] On this account our teachers have been compelled, for the sake of comforting consciences, to point out the difference between spiritual and temporal power, sword, and authority, and they have taught that because of God's command both authorities and powers are to be honored and esteemed with all reverence as the two highest gifts of God on earth.

[5] Our teachers assert that according to the gospel the power of keys or the power of bishops is a power and command of God to preach the gospel, to forgive and retain sins, and to administer and distribute the sacraments. [6] For Christ sent out the apostles with this command, John 20: "As the Father has sent me, even so I send you. Receive the Holy Spirit. If you forgive the sins of any, they are forgiven; if you retain the sins of any, they are retained." Jn 20[.21–23]

[8] This power of keys or of bishops is used and exercised only by teaching and preaching the word of God and by administering the sacraments (to many persons or to individuals, depending on one's calling). In this way are imparted not

———————————————

tiffs, relying on the power of keys, not only have instituted new forms of worship and burdened consciences with reservation of cases and violent excommunications but also have undertaken to transfer kingdoms of this world and take away the imperial power. [3] These wrongs have long since been rebuked in the church by devout and learned men. [4] Accordingly our teachers have been compelled, for the sake of instructing consciences, to show the difference between the power of the church and the power of the sword, and they have taught that on account of God's command both are to be held in reverence and honor as the chief gifts of God on earth.

[5] Our teachers hold that according to the gospel the power of keys or the power of bishops is a power or command of God to preach the gospel, to remit and retain sins, and to administer the sacraments. [6] For Christ sent out the apostles with this command. "As the Father has sent me, even so I send you. Receive the [Jn 20.21–23] Holy Spirit. If you forgive the sins of any, they are forgiven; if you retain the sins of any, they are retained." [7] According to Mark 16 he also said, "Go and preach the gospel to the whole creation." Mk 16[.15]

[8] This power is exercised only by teaching or preaching the gospel and by administering the sacraments either to many or to individuals, depending on one's

bodily but eternal things and gifts, namely, eternal righteousness, the Holy Spirit, and eternal life. [9] These gifts cannot be obtained except through the office of preaching and of administering the holy sacraments, for St. Paul says, "The gospel [Rom 1.16] is the power of God for salvation to everyone who has faith." [10] Inasmuch as the power of the church or of bishops bestows eternal gifts and is used and exercised only through the office of preaching, it does not interfere at all with government or temporal authority. [11] Temporal authority is concerned with matters altogether different from the gospel. Temporal power does not protect the soul, but with the sword and physical penalties it protects body and goods from the power of others.

[12] Therefore, the two authorities, the spiritual and the temporal, are not to be mingled or confused, for the spiritual power has its commission to preach the gospel and administer the sacraments. [13] Hence it should not invade the function of the other, should not set up and depose kings, should not annul temporal laws or undermine obedience to government, should not make or prescribe to the temporal power laws concerning worldly matters. [14] Christ himself said, "My kingship is not of this world,"[a] and again, [15] "Who made me a judge or divider over you?"[b]

---

calling. For it is not bodily things that are thus given, but rather such eternal things as eternal righteousness, the Holy Spirit, and eternal life. [9] These things cannot come about except through the ministry of word and sacraments, for Paul says, [Rom 1.16] "The gospel is the power of God for salvation to everyone who has faith," and Psalm [Ps 119.50] 118 states, "Thy word gives me life." [10] Inasmuch as the power of the church bestows eternal things and is exercised only through the ministry of the word, it interferes with civil government as little as the art of singing interferes with civil government. [11] For civil government is concerned with other things than the gospel. [11] The state protects not souls but bodies and goods from manifest harm, and constrains men with the sword and physical penalties, while the gospel protects souls from heresies, the devil, and eternal death.

[12] Therefore, ecclesiastical and civil power are not to be confused. The power of the church has its own commission to preach the gospel and administer the sacraments. [13] Let it not invade the other's function, nor transfer the kingdoms of the world, nor abrogate the laws of civil rulers, nor abolish lawful obedience, nor interfere with judgments concerning any civil ordinances or contracts, nor prescribe to civil rulers laws about the forms of government that should be established. [14] [Jn 18.36] Christ says, "My kingdom is not of this world," [15] and again, "Who made me a

a. [Jn 18.36]
b. [Lk 12.14]

[16] Paul also wrote in Philippians 3: "Our commonwealth is in heaven," [17] and   Phil 3[.20]
in 2 Corinthians 10: "The weapons of our warfare are not worldly but have divine
power to destroy strongholds and every proud obstacle to the knowledge of God."   2 Cor 10[.4–5]

[18] Thus our teachers distinguish the two authorities and the functions of
the two powers, directing that both be held in honor as the highest gifts of God on
earth.

[19] In cases where bishops possess temporal authority and the sword, they
possess it not as bishops by divine right, but by human, imperial right, bestowed
by Roman emperors and kings for the temporal administration of their lands. Such
authority has nothing at all to do with the office of the gospel.

[21] According to divine right, therefore, it is the office of the bishop to
preach the gospel, forgive sins, judge doctrine and condemn doctrine that is contrary to the gospel, and exclude from the Christian community the ungodly whose
wicked conduct is manifest. All this is to be done not by human power but by God's
word alone. [22] On this account parish ministers and churches are bound to be
obedient to the bishops according to the saying of Christ in Luke 10: "He who hears

---

judge or divider over you?" [16] Paul also wrote in Philippians 3, "Our common-   [Lk 12.14]
wealth is in heaven," [17] and in 2 Corinthians 10, "The weapons of our warfare   Phil 3[.20]
are not worldly but have divine power to destroy arguments," etc.   2 Cor 10[.4–5]

[18] In this way our teachers distinguish the functions of the two powers,
and they command that both be held in honor and acknowledged as gifts and blessings of God.

[19] If bishops have any power of the sword, they have this not as bishops
under a commission of the gospel, but by human right granted by kings and emperors for the civil administration of their lands. This, however, is a function other
than the ministry of the gospel.

[20] When one inquires about the jurisdiction of bishops, therefore, civil
authority must be distinguished from ecclesiastical jurisdiction. [21] Hence according to the gospel (or, as they say, by divine right) no jurisdiction belongs to the
bishops as bishops (that is, to those to whom has been committed the ministry of
word and sacraments) except to forgive sins, to reject doctrine which is contrary to
the gospel, and to exclude from the fellowship of the church ungodly persons whose
wickedness is known, doing all this without human power, simply by the word. [22]
Churches are therefore bound by divine law to be obedient to the bishops according
to the text, "He who hears you hears me."   [Lk 10.16]

[23] However, when bishops teach or ordain anything contrary to the gos-

Lk 10[.16]   you hears me." [23] On the other hand, if they teach, introduce, or institute anything contrary to the gospel, we have God's command not to be obedient in such
Mt 7[.15]   cases, for Christ says in Matthew 7: "Beware of false prophets." [24] Saint Paul
also writes in Galatians 1: "Even if we, or an angel from heaven, should preach to
Gal 1[.8]   you a gospel contrary to that which we preached to you, let him be accursed," [25]
and in 2 Corinthians 13: "We cannot do anything against the truth, but only for the
2 Cor 13[.8]   truth." [26] Again Paul refers to "the authority which the Lord has given me for
[2 Cor 13.10]   building up and not for tearing down." [27] Canon law requires the same in part 2,
question 7, in the chapters "Sacerdotes" and "Oves."

[28] Saint Augustine also writes in his reply to the letters of Petilian that
one should not obey even regularly elected bishops if they err or if they teach or
command something contrary to the divine Holy Scriptures.

[29] Whatever other power and jurisdiction bishops may have in various
matters (for example, in matrimonial cases and in tithes), they have these by virtue
of human right. However, when bishops are negligent in the performance of such
duties, the princes are obliged, whether they like to or not, to administer justice to
their subjects for the sake of peace and to prevent discord and great disorder in their
lands.

[30] Besides, there is dispute as to whether bishops have the power to introduce ceremonies in the church or establish regulations concerning foods, holy days,

---

pel, churches have a command of God that forbids obedience, Matthew 7: "Beware
Mt 7[.15]   of false prophets." Galatians 1: "If an angel from heaven should preach any other
Gal 1[.8]   Gospel, let him be accursed." [25] 2 Corinthians 13: "We cannot do anything against
2 Cor 13[.8]   the truth, but only for the truth," [26] and also, "Given to me is the authority for
2 Cor 13[.10]   building up and not for tearing down." [27] The canons require the same thing
(part 2, question 7, in chapters "Sacerdotes" and "Oves"). [28] Augustine also says
in reply to the letters of Petilian that not even Catholic bishops are to be obeyed if
they should happen to err or hold anything contrary to the canonical Scriptures of
God.

[29] If they have any other power or jurisdiction to decide legal cases (for
example, pertaining to matrimony, tithes, etc.), bishops have this by human right.
When the bishops are negligent in the performance of their duties, princes are
bound, even against their will, to administer justice to their subjects for the sake of
maintaining public peace.

[30] Besides, it is disputed whether bishops or pastors have the right to
introduce ceremonies in the church and make laws concerning foods, holy days,

and the different orders of the clergy. [31] Those who attribute such power to bishops cite Christ's saying in John 16: "I have yet many things to say to you, but you
cannot bear them now. When the Spirit of truth comes, he will guide you into all
the truth." [32] They also cite the example in Acts 15, where the eating of blood   Jn 16[.12–13]
and what is strangled was forbidden. [33] Besides, they appeal to the fact that the   Acts 15[.20, 29]
Sabbath was changed to Sunday—contrary, as they say, to the Ten Commandments.
No case is appealed to and urged so insistently as the change of the Sabbath, for
thereby they wish to maintain that the power of the church is indeed great because
the church has dispensed from and altered part of the Ten Commandments.

[34] Concerning this question our teachers assert that bishops do not have
power to institute or establish anything contrary to the gospel, as has been indicated
above and as is taught by canon law throughout the whole of the ninth distinction.
[35] It is patently contrary to God's command and word to make laws out of opinions or to require that they be observed in order to make satisfaction for sins and
obtain grace, [36] for the glory of Christ's merit is blasphemed when we presume
to earn grace by such ordinances. [37] It is also apparent that because of this notion
human ordinances have multiplied beyond calculation while teaching concerning
faith and righteousness of faith has almost been suppressed. Almost every day new
holy days and new fasts have been prescribed, new ceremonies and new venerations

---

grades or orders of ministers, etc. [31] Those who attribute this right to bishops cite
as evidence the passage, "I have yet many things to say to you, but you cannot bear
them now. When the spirit of truth comes, he will guide you into all the truth." [32]   [Jn 16.12–13]
They also cite the example of the apostles who commanded men to abstain from
blood and from what is strangled. [33] Besides, they cite the change from the Sab-   [Acts 15.20, 29]
bath to the Lord's Day—contrary to the Decalogue, it appears. No case is made
more of than this change of the Sabbath. Great, they say, is the power of the church,
for it dispensed from one of the Ten Commandments!

[34] Concerning this question our teachers assert, as has been pointed out
above, that bishops do not have power to institute anything contrary to the gospel.
The canons concede this throughout the whole of distinction 9. [35] Besides, it is
against Scripture to require the observance of traditions for the purpose of making
satisfaction for sins or meriting justification, [36] for the glory of Christ's merit is
dishonored when we suppose that we are justified by such observances. [37] It is
also evident that as a result of this notion traditions have multiplied in the church almost beyond calculation, while the teaching concerning faith and the righteousness
of faith has been suppressed, for from time to time more holy days were appointed,

of saints have been instituted in order that by such works grace and everything good might be earned from God.

[39] Again, those who institute human ordinances also act contrary to God's command when they attach sin to foods, days, and similar things and burden Christendom with the bondage of the law, as if in order to earn God's grace there had to be a service of God among Christians like the Levitical service, and as if God had commanded the apostles and bishops to institute it, as some have written. [40] It is quite believable that some bishops were misled by the example of the law of Moses. [41] The result was that countless regulations came into being—for example, that it is a mortal sin to do manual work on holy days (even when it does not give offense to others), that it is a mortal sin to omit the seven hours, that some foods defile the conscience, that fasting is a work by which God is reconciled, that in a reserved case sin is not forgiven unless forgiveness is secured from the person for whom the case is reserved, in spite of the fact that canon law says nothing of the reservation of guilt but speaks only about the reservation of ecclesiastical penalties.

[42] Where did the bishops get the right and power to impose such requirements on Christendom to ensnare men's consciences? In Acts 15, St. Peter forbids

---

more fasts prescribed, and new ceremonies and new orders instituted because the authors of these things thought that they would merit grace by these works. [38] So the penitential canons formerly increased, and we can still see some traces of these in the satisfactions.

[39] Again, the authors of traditions act contrary to the command of God when they attach sin to foods, days, and similar things and burden the church with the bondage of the law, as if in order to merit justification there had to be a service among Christians similar to the Levitical, and as if God had commissioned the apostles and bishops to institute it. [40] For thus some have written, and the pontiffs seem in some measure to have been misled by the example of the law of Moses. [41] This is the origin of such burdens as this, that it is a mortal sin to do manual work on holy days, even when it gives no offense to others, that certain foods defile the conscience, that fasting which is privative and not natural is a work that appeases God, that it is a mortal sin to omit the canonical hours, that in a reserved case a sin cannot be forgiven except by the authority of the person who reserved the case, although the canons themselves speak only of reserving ecclesiastical penalties and not of reserving guilt.

[42] Where did the bishops get the right to impose such traditions on the churches and thus ensnare consciences when Peter forbids putting a yoke on the

putting a yoke on the neck of the disciples. And St. Paul said in Corinthians that authority was given for building up and not for tearing down. Why, then, do they multiply sins with such requirements?

[43] Yet there are clear passages of Divine Scripture which forbid the establishment of such regulations for the purpose of earning God's grace or as if they were necessary for salvation. [44] Thus St. Paul says in Colossians 2: "Let no one pass judgment on you in questions of food and drink or with regard to a festival or a new moon or a Sabbath. These are only a shadow of what is to come; but the substance belongs to Christ." [45] And again, "If with Christ you died to the regulations of the world, why do you live as if you still belonged to the world? Why do you submit to regulations, 'Do not handle, Do not taste, Do not touch' (referring to things which all perish as they are used), according to human precepts and doctrines? These have an appearance of wisdom." [46] In Titus 1, St. Paul also forbids giving heed to Jewish myths or to commands of men who reject the truth.

[47] In Matthew 15, Christ himself says concerning those who urge human ordinances on people, "Let them alone; they are blind guides of the blind." [48] He rejects such service of God and says, "Every plant which my heavenly Father has not planted will be rooted up."

[49] If, then, bishops have the power to burden the churches with countless

Acts 15[.10]

2 Cor [10.8]

Col 2[.16–17]

[Col 2.20–23]
Ti 1[.14]

Mt 15[.14]

Mt 15[.13]

---

disciples and Paul says that authority was given for building up and not for tearing down? Why do they multiply sin with such traditions?

[43] Yet there are clear testimonies which prohibit the making of traditions for the purpose of appeasing God or as if they were necessary for salvation. [44] In Colossians 2, Paul says, "Let no one pass judgment on you in questions of food and drink or with regard to a festival or a new moon or a sabbath." [45] Again, "If with Christ you died to the elemental spirits of the universe, why do you live as if you still belonged to the world? Why do you submit to regulations, 'Do not handle, Do not taste, Do not touch' (referring to things which all perish as they are used), according to human precepts and doctrines? These have an appearance of wisdom." [46] In Titus 1, Paul also says, "Not giving heed to Jewish myths or to commands of men who reject the truth."

[47] In Matthew 15, Christ says concerning those who require traditions, "Let them alone; they are blind and leaders of the blind." [48] He rebukes such services and says, "Every plant which my heavenly Father has not planted will be rooted up."

[49] If bishops have the right to burden consciences with such traditions,

[Acts 15.10]

[2 Cor 10.8]

Col 2[.16]

[Col 2.20–23]

Ti 1[.14]

Mt 15[.14]

Mt 15[.13]

requirements and thus ensnare consciences, why does the Divine Scripture so frequently forbid the making and keeping of human regulations? Why does it call them [1 Tm 4.1] "doctrines of the devil"? Is it possible that the Holy Spirit warned against them for nothing?

[50] Inasmuch as such regulations as have been instituted as necessary to propitiate God and merit grace are contrary to the gospel, it is not at all proper for the bishops to require such services of God. [51] It is necessary to preserve the teaching of Christian liberty in Christendom, namely, that bondage to the law is not necessary for justification, [52] as St. Paul writes in Galatians 5: "For freedom Christ has set us free; stand fast, therefore, and do not submit again to a yoke of Gal 5[.1] slavery." For the chief article of the gospel must be maintained, namely, that we obtain the grace of God through faith in Christ without our merits; we do not merit it by services of God instituted by men.

[53] What are we to say, then, about Sunday and other similar church ordinances and ceremonies? To this our teachers reply that bishops or pastors may make regulations so that everything in the churches is done in good order, but not as a means of obtaining God's grace or making satisfaction for sins, nor in order to bind men's consciences by considering these things necessary services of God and counting it a sin to omit their observance even when this is done without offense. [54] So St. Paul directed in 1 Corinthians 11 that women should cover their heads in the

---

why does Scripture so often prohibit the making of traditions? Why does it call [1 Tm 4.1] them doctrines of demons? Was it in vain that the Holy Spirit warned against these?

[50] Inasmuch as ordinances which have been instituted as necessary or instituted with the intention of meriting justification are in conflict with the gospel, it follows that it is not lawful for bishops to institute such services or require them as necessary. [51] It is necessary to preserve the doctrine of Christian liberty in the churches, namely, that bondage to the law is not necessary for justification, [52] as it is written in the Epistle to the Galatians, "Do not submit again to a yoke of Gal [5.1] slavery." It is necessary to preserve the chief article of the gospel, namely, that we obtain grace through faith in Christ and not through certain observances or acts of worship instituted by men.

[53] What, then, are we to think about Sunday and about similar rites in our churches? To this our teachers reply that it is lawful for bishops or pastors to make regulations so that things in the church may be done in good order, but not that by means of these we make satisfaction for sins, nor that consciences are bound so as to regard these as necessary services. [54] So Paul ordained that women should cover

assembly. He also directed that in the assembly preachers should not all speak at   1 Cor 11[.5]
once, but one after another, in order.   1 Cor 11[.30]

[55] It is proper for the Christian assembly to keep such ordinances for the
sake of love and peace, to be obedient to the bishops and parish ministers in such
matters, and to observe the regulations in such a way that one does not give offense to another and so that there may be no disorder or unbecoming conduct in
the church. [56] However, consciences should not be burdened by contending that   [1 Cor 14.40]
such things are necessary for salvation or that it is a sin to omit them, even when
no offense is given to others, just as no one would say that a woman commits a sin
if without offense to others she goes out with uncovered head.

[57] Of like character is the observance of Sunday, Easter, Pentecost, and
similar holy days and usages. [58] Those who consider the appointment of Sunday
in place of the Sabbath as a necessary institution are very much mistaken, [59] for
the Holy Scriptures have abrogated the Sabbath and teach that after the revelation
of the gospel all ceremonies of the old law may be omitted. [60] Nevertheless, because it was necessary to appoint a certain day so that the people might know when
they ought to assemble, the Christian church appointed Sunday for this purpose,
and it was the more inclined and pleased to do this in order that the people might

---

their heads in the assembly and that interpreters in the church should be heard one   [1 Cor 11.5]
after another.   [1 Cor 14.30]

[55] It is proper that the churches comply with such ordinances for the sake
of love and tranquillity and that they keep them, in so far as one does not offend
another, so that everything in the churches may be done in order and without confusion. [56] However, consciences should not be burdened by suggesting that they   [1 Cor 14.40]
are necessary for salvation or by judging that those who omit them without offense
to others commit a sin, any more than one would say that a woman sins by going
out in public with her head uncovered, provided no offense is given.

[57] Of the same sort is the observance of Sunday, Easter, Pentecost, and
similar festivals and rites. [58] Those who hold that the observance of the Lord's Day
in place of the Sabbath was instituted by the church's authority as a necessary thing
are mistaken. [59] The Scriptures, not the church, abrogated the Sabbath, for after
the revelation of the gospel all ceremonies of the Mosaic law can be omitted. [60]
Nevertheless, because it was necessary to appoint a certain day so that the people
may know when they ought to assemble, it appears that the church designated the
Lord's Day for this purpose, and it seems that the church was the more pleased to
do this for the additional reason that men would have an example of Christian lib-

have an example of Christian liberty and might know that the keeping neither of the Sabbath nor of any other day is necessary.

[61] There are many faulty discussions of the transformation of the law, of the ceremonies of the New Testament, and of the change of the Sabbath, all of which have arisen from the false and erroneous opinion that in Christendom one must have services of God like the Levitical or Jewish services and that Christ commanded the apostles and bishops to devise new ceremonies which would be necessary for salvation. [62] Such errors were introduced into Christendom when the righteousness of faith was no longer taught and preached with clarity and purity. [63] Some argue that although Sunday must not be kept as of divine obligation, it must nevertheless be kept as almost of divine obligation, and they prescribe the kind and amount of work that may be done on the day of rest. [64] What are such discussions but snares of conscience? For although they undertake to lighten and mitigate human regulations, yet there can be no moderation or mitigation as long as the opinion remains and prevails that their observance is necessary. And this opinion will remain as long as there is no understanding of the righteousness of faith and Christian liberty.

[65] The apostles directed that one should abstain from blood and from
Acts 15[.20] what is strangled. Who observes this prohibition now? Those who do not observe it

---

erty and would know that the keeping neither of the Sabbath nor of any other day is necessary.

[61] There are monstrous discussions concerning the mutation of the law, concerning ceremonies of the new law, concerning the change of the Sabbath, all of which have arisen from the false notion that there must be a service in the church like the Levitical service and that Christ commissioned the apostles and bishops to devise new ceremonies which would be necessary for salvation. [62] These errors crept into the church when the righteousness of faith was not taught with sufficient clarity. [63] Some argue that the observance of the Lord's Day is not *indeed* of divine obligation but is *as it were* of divine obligation, and they prescribe the extent to which one is allowed to work on holy days. [64] What are discussions of this kind but snares of conscience? Although they try to mitigate the traditions, moderation can never be achieved as long as the opinion remains that their observance is necessary. And this opinion must remain where there is no understanding of the righteousness of faith and Christian liberty.

[Acts 15.20]   [65] The apostles commanded that one should abstain from blood, etc. Who observes this prohibition now? Those who do not observe it commit no sin, commit no sin, for the apostles did not wish to burden consciences with such bondage but forbade such eating for a time to avoid offense. [66] One must pay attention to the chief article of Christian doctrine, and this is not abrogated by the decree.

[67] Scarcely any of the ancient canons are observed according to the letter, and many of the regulations fall into disuse from day to day even among those who observe such ordinance most jealously. [68] It is impossible to give counsel or help to consciences unless this mitigation is practiced, that one recognizes that such rules are not to be deemed necessary and that disregard of them does not injure consciences.

[69] The bishops might easily retain the obedience of men if they did not insist on the observance of regulations which cannot be kept without sin. [70] Now, however, they administer the sacrament in one kind and prohibit administration in both kinds. Again, they forbid clergymen to marry and admit no one to the ministry unless he first swears an oath that he will not preach this doctrine, although there is no doubt that it is in accord with the holy gospel. [71] Our churches do not ask that the bishops should restore peace and unity at the expense of their honor and dignity (though it is incumbent on the bishops to do this, too, in the case of need), [72] but they ask only that the bishops relax certain unreasonable burdens which

---

for the apostles did not wish to burden consciences with such bondage but forbade such eating for a time to avoid offense. [66] In connection with the decree one must consider what the perpetual aim of the gospel is.

[67] Scarcely any of the canons are observed according to the letter, and many of them become obsolete from day to day even among those who favor traditions. [68] It is not possible to counsel consciences unless this mitigation is practiced, that one recognizes that canons are kept without holding them to be necessary and that no harm is done to consciences even if the usage of men changes in such matters.

[69] The bishops might easily retain the lawful obedience of men if they did not insist on the observance of traditions which cannot be kept with a good conscience. [70] But now they demand celibacy and will admit no one to the ministry unless he swears that he will not teach the pure doctrine of the gospel. [71] Our churches do not ask that the bishops restore concord at the expense of their honor (which, however, good pastors ought to do), [72] but ask only that they relax unjust burdens which are new and were introduced contrary to the custom of the church catholic. [73] Perhaps there were acceptable reasons for these ordinances

did not exist in the church in former times and which were introduced contrary to the custom of the universal Christian church. [73] Perhaps there was some reason for introducing them, but they are not adapted to our times. [74] Nor can it be denied that some regulations were adopted from want of understanding. Accordingly the bishops ought to be so gracious as to temper these regulations inasmuch as such changes do not destroy the unity of Christian churches. For many regulations devised by men have with the passing of time fallen into disuse and are not obligatory, as papal law itself testifies. [75] If, however, this is impossible and they cannot be persuaded to mitigate or abrogate human regulations which are not to be observed without sin, we are bound to follow the apostolic rule which commands us to obey

[Acts 5.29]   God rather than men.

[76] Saint Peter forbids the bishops to exercise lordship as if they had power

[1 Pt 5.2]   to coerce the churches according to their will. [77] It is not our intention to find ways of reducing the bishops' power, but we desire and pray that they may not coerce our consciences to sin. [78] If they are unwilling to do this and ignore our petition, let them consider how they will answer for it in God's sight, inasmuch as by their obstinacy they offer occasion for division and schism, which they should in truth help to prevent.

---

when they were introduced, but they are not adapted to later times. [74] It is also apparent that some were adopted out of misunderstanding. It would therefore befit the clemency of the bishops to mitigate these regulations now, for such change does not impair the unity of the church inasmuch as many human traditions have been changed with the passing of time, as the canons themselves show. [75] However, if it is impossible to obtain a relaxation of observances which cannot be kept without sin, we are bound to follow the apostolic injunction which commands us to obey

[Acts 5.29]   God rather than men.

[76] Peter forbids the bishops to be domineering and to coerce the

[1 Pt 5.2]   churches. [77] It is not our intention that the bishops give up their power to govern, but we ask for this one thing, that they allow the gospel to be taught purely and that they relax some few observances which cannot be kept without sin. [78] If they do not do this, they must see to it how they will answer for it before God that by their obstinacy they offer occasion for schism.

[CONCLUSION]

[1] These are the chief articles that are regarded as controversial. Although we could have mentioned many more abuses and wrongs, to avoid prolixity and undue length we have indicated only the principal ones. The others can readily be weighed in the light of these. [2] In the past there have been grave complaints about indulgences, pilgrimages, and misuse of the ban. Parish ministers also had endless quarrels with monks about the hearing of confessions, about burials, about sermons on special occasions, and about countless other matters. [3] All these things we have discreetly passed over for the common good in order that the chief points at issue may better be perceived.

[4] It must not be thought that anything has been said or introduced out of hatred or for the purpose of injuring anybody, [5] but we have related only matters which we have considered it necessary to adduce and mention in order that it may be made very clear that we have introduced nothing, either in doctrine or in ceremonies, that is contrary to Holy Scripture or the universal Christian church. For it is manifest and evident (to speak without boasting) that we have diligently and with God's help prevented any new and godless teaching from creeping into our churches and gaining the upper hand in them.

[6] In keeping with the summons, we have desired to present the above

---

[CONCLUSION]

[1] We have now reviewed the chief articles that are regarded as controversial. Although more abuses could be mentioned, to avoid undue length we have discussed only the principal ones. [2] There have been grave complaints about indulgences, pilgrimages, and misuse of excommunication. Parishes have been troubled in many ways by indulgence sellers. There have been endless quarrels between parish ministers and monks about parochial rights, confessions, burials, and countless other things. [3] We have passed over matters of this sort so that the chief points at issue, being briefly set forth, may more readily be understood.

[4] Nothing has here been said or related for the purpose of injuring anybody. [5] Only those things have been recounted which it seemed necessary to say in order that it may be understood that nothing has been received among us, in doctrine or in ceremonies, that is contrary to Scripture or to the church catholic. For it is manifest that we have guarded diligently against the introduction into our churches of any new and ungodly doctrines.

[6] In keeping with the edict of Your Imperial Majesty, we have desired to

articles as a declaration of our confession and the teaching of our preachers. [7] If anyone should consider that it is lacking in some respect, we are ready to present further information on the basis of the divine Holy Scripture. Your Imperial Majesty's most obedient servants:

John, Duke of Saxony, elector
George, Margrave of Brandenburg
Ernest, Duke of Lüneburg
Philip, Landgrave of Hesse
John Frederick, Duke of Saxony
Francis, Duke of Lüneburg
Wolfgang, Prince of Anhalt
Mayor and Council of Nuremberg
Mayor and Council of Reutlingen.

---

present the above articles in order that our confession may be exhibited in them and that a summary of the doctrine taught among us may be discerned. [7] If anything is found to be lacking in this confession, we are ready, God willing, to present ampler information according to the Scriptures.

Your Imperial Majesty's faithful subjects:
John, Duke of Saxony, elector
George, Margrave of Brandenburg
Ernest, with his own hand
Philip, Landgrave of Hesse, subscribes
John Frederick, Duke of Saxony
Francis, Duke of Lüneburg
Wolfgang, Prince of Anhalt
Senate and Magistrate of Nuremberg
Senate of Reutlingen

The Smalcald Articles, 1537, and The Treatise on the Power and Primacy of the Pope, 1537

> Pope Paul III called a council to meet in Mantua last year, in Whit-suntide. Afterwards he transferred the council from Mantua, and it is not yet known where it will or can be held. In any case, we had reason to expect that we might be summoned to appear before the council or be condemned without being summoned. I was therefore instructed [by John Frederick of Saxony] to draft and assemble articles of our faith to serve as a basis for possible deliberations and to indicate, on the one hand, what and in how far we were willing and able to yield to the papists and, on the other hand, what we intended to hold fast to and persevere in. Accordingly I assembled these articles and submitted them to our representatives. The latter accepted them, unanimously adopted them as their confession, and resolved that these articles should be presented publicly as the confession of our faith if the pope and his adherents ever became so bold as seriously, in good faith, and without deception or treachery to hold a truly free council.

Thus Luther explains the origins of *The Smalcald Articles* in his preface to the first printed edition (1538).[1] The church council did not meet in Mantua; it was delayed some eight years before it was finally convened as the Council of Trent (1545–63). Luther's articles of faith are quite unlike → *The Augsburg Confession,* which Melanchthon had prepared for the imperial Diet of 1530. Couched in polemical anti-papal language, his witness to the Lutheran faith is the product of a time when the moment had passed for reconciliation. Luther wrote the articles while suffering from a debilitating illness and perhaps thinking himself near death.[2]

The document was signed by more than forty ministers and theologians at a meeting of the Smalcald League in 1537, although it was not officially endorsed by the league's political leaders. Only Melanchthon qualified his approval of the articles, noting that he would concede to the pope's superiority over bishops for the

---

1. Tappert's translation, 288.
2. See Volz 1957; Hagen 1987, 245; and Russell 1991b. Several colleagues assisted in the composition. See Kolb-Wengert, 295.

sake of unity, "if he [the pope] would allow the gospel."[3] At the assembly's request, Melanchthon wrote an appendix (originally intended as a supplement to *The Augsburg Confession*), in which he took a less conciliatory position toward the papacy but used biblical and historical evidence instead of polemic to challenge the pope's primacy. This *Treatise on the Power and Primacy of the Pope* was also signed by the ministers gathered at Smalcald. Luther did not sign Melanchthon's text, apparently because illness prevented his presence; it was also omitted from the first edition of *The Smalcald Articles*.

Luther divided *The Smalcald Articles* into three sections. The first, on "Sublime Articles of Divine Majesty," acknowledges adherence to → *The Apostles' Creed* and → *The Athanasian Creed*. Luther notes that there is no disagreement with the Roman Catholic Church in these areas. In the second part, ostensibly on the "Office and Work of Jesus Christ" and redemption, Luther sharply criticizes Catholic practices, chastises priests for "unspeakable abuses," and declares the pope the Antichrist. He also rejects the mass, particularly masses for the dead, pilgrimages, relics, indulgences, the mediation of the saints, and monasteries. In the third part he turns to issues of church practice and pastoral care among Lutherans and is somewhat less polemical in tone.

Published as *Artikel christlicher Lehre* in 1538, the work became known as *The Smalcald Articles* only after Luther's death. In 1580 it was published as part of *The Book of Concord*, as was Melanchthon's *Treatise on the Power and Primacy of the Pope*.

Edition: *BLK* 407–98.

Translation: Tappert, 288–335.

Note: Luther's original was German, a Latin translation was made for the first edition of *The Book of Concord* in 1580 and revised for the 1584 edition. The German is given here. Melanchthon wrote *The Treatise on the Power and Primacy of the Pope* in Latin (which we give here), but it was translated immediately into German by Veit Dietrich of Nuremberg and signed in both forms at Smalcald. We include Tappert's footnote references to alternative readings in the Latin translation of Luther's text and in the German version of Melanchthon's text, as well as citations for quotations from early church authorities.

3. See Melanchthon's note after his signature below.

Literature: Bizer 1955–56, 1957; Bouman 1969; Hagen 1987; Hamann 1988; Johnson 1989; Jordan 1977; Jungkuntz 1977b; Kirchner 1983; Kolb 1988; Kolb-Wengert, 295–96; Lohse 1986; Russell 1991a, 1991b, 1994, 1995; Schaff, 1:253–57; Schaaf 1969; Schwarzwäller 1989; Seebass 1984; Volz 1957, 1963; Wolf 1962.

Articles of Christian doctrine
which were to have been presented by our party at the council in Mantua, or wherever
else the council was to have been convened, and which were to indicate what we could
or could not accept or yield. Written by Dr. Martin Luther in the year 1537

Preface of Dr. Martin Luther

[1] Pope Paul III called a council to meet in Mantua last year, in Whitsuntide. After-wards he transferred the council from Mantua, and it is not yet known where it will or can be held. In any case, we had reason to expect that we might be summoned to appear before the council or be condemned without being summoned. I was therefore instructed to draft and assemble articles of our faith to serve as a basis for possible deliberations and to indicate, on the one hand, what and in how far we were willing and able to yield to the papists and, on the other hand, what we intended to hold fast to and persevere in.

[2] Accordingly I assembled these articles and submitted them to our representatives. The latter accepted them, unanimously adopted them as their confession, and resolved that these articles should be presented publicly as the confession of our faith if the pope and his adherents ever became so bold as seriously, in good faith, and without deception or treachery to hold a truly free council, as indeed the pope is in duty bound to do.

[3] But the Roman court is dreadfully afraid of a free council and flees from the light in a shameful fashion. Even adherents of that party have lost hope that the Roman court will ever permit a free council, to say nothing of calling one. They are deeply offended, as well they might be, and are not a little troubled on this account, for they perceive that the pope prefers to see all Christendom lost and all souls damned rather than suffer himself and his adherents to be reformed a little and allow limitations to be placed on his tyranny.

Nevertheless, I have decided to publish these articles so that, if I should die before a council meets (which I fully expect, for those knaves who shun the light and flee from the day take such wretched pains to postpone and prevent the council), those who live after me may have my testimony and confession (in addition to the confession[1] which I have previously given) to show where I have stood until now and where, by God's grace, I will continue to stand.

1. Luther's "Confession Concerning the Holy Supper" (1528).

[4] Why do I say this? Why should I complain? I am still alive. I am still writing, preaching, and lecturing every day. Yet there are some who are so spiteful—not only among our adversaries, but also false brethren among those who profess to be adherents of our party—that they dare to cite my writings and teachings against me. They let me look on and listen, although they know very well that I teach otherwise. They try to clothe their venomous spirits in the garments of my labor and thus mislead the poor people in my name. Imagine what will happen after I am dead!

[5] I suppose I should reply to everything while I am still living. But how can I stop all the mouths of the devil? What, above all, can I do with those (for they are all poisoned) who do not pay attention to what I write and who keep themselves busy by shamefully twisting and corrupting my every word and letter? I shall let the devil—or ultimately the wrath of God—answer them as they deserve. [6] I often think of the good Gerson,[2] who doubted whether one ought to make good writings public. If one does not, many souls that might have been saved are neglected. On the other hand, if one does, the devil appears at once to poison and pervert everything by wagging countless venomous and malicious tongues and thus destroying the fruit. However, what such persons accomplish is manifest. [7] For although they slander us so shamefully and try by their lies to keep the people on their side, God has constantly promoted his work, has made their following smaller and smaller and ours ever larger, and has caused, and still causes, them and their lies to be put to shame.

[8] Let me illustrate this. There was a doctor here in Wittenberg, sent from France, who reported in our presence that his king had been persuaded beyond a doubt that among us there is no church, no government, and no state of matrimony, but that all live promiscuously like cattle and everybody does what he pleases. [9] Imagine how those will face us on the last day, before the judgment seat of Christ, who in their writings have urged such big lies upon the king and foreign peoples as if they were the unadulterated truth! Christ, the lord and judge of us all, knows very well that they lie and have lied. I am sure that he will pronounce sentence upon them. God convert those who are capable of conversion and turn them to repentance! As for the rest, wretchedness and woe will be their lot forever.

[10] But let us return to the subject. I should be very happy to see a true council assemble in order that many things and many people might derive benefit from it. Not that we ourselves need such a council, for by God's grace our churches have now been so enlightened and supplied with the pure word and the right use of the sacraments, with an understanding of the various callings of life, and with true

2. John Gerson in his *De laude scriptorum*, ch 11.

works, that we do not ask for a council for our own sake, and we have no reason to hope or expect that a council would improve our conditions. But in the dioceses of the papists we see so many vacant and desolate parishes everywhere that our hearts would break with grief. Yet neither the bishops nor the canons care how the poor people live or die, although Christ died for them too. Those people cannot hear

[Jn 10.12]   Christ speak to them as the true shepherd speaking to his sheep. [11] This horrifies me and makes me fear that he may cause a council of angels to descend on Germany and destroy us utterly, like Sodom and Gomorrah, because we mock him so shamefully with the council.[3]

[12] Besides such necessary concerns of the church, there are countless temporal matters that need reform. There is discord among princes and political estates. Usury and avarice have burst in like a deluge and have taken on the color of legality. Wantonness, lewdness, extravagance in dress, gluttony, gambling, vain display, all manner of vice and wickedness, disobedience of subjects, domestics, and laborers, extortion in every trade and on the part of peasants—who can enumerate everything?—these have gained the ascendancy to such an extent that ten councils and twenty diets would not be able to set things right again. [13] If members of a council were to consider such fundamental matters of the ecclesiastical and secular estates as are contrary to God, their hands would be so full that their trifling and tomfoolery with albs, great tonsures, broad cinctures, bishops' and cardinals' hats and crosiers, and similar nonsense would soon be forgotten. If we would first carry out God's commands and precepts in the spiritual and temporal estates, we would find enough time to reform the regulations concerning fasts, vestments, tonsures,

[Mt 23.24]   and chasubles. But if we are willing to swallow camels and strain out gnats, if we
[Mt 7.3–5]   let logs stand and dispute about specks, we might just as well be satisfied with such a council.

[14] I have drafted only a few articles, for, apart from these, God has laid so many tasks upon us in church, state, and family that we can never carry them out. What is the use of adopting a multitude of decrees and canons in a council, especially when the primary things, which are commanded by God, are neither regarded nor observed? It is as if we were to expect God to acquiesce in our mummeries while we trample his solemn commandments underfoot. But our sins oppress us and keep God from being gracious to us, for we do not repent and we even try to justify all our abominations.

[15] Dear Lord Jesus Christ, assemble a council of thine own, and by thy glorious advent deliver thy servants. The pope and his adherents are lost. They will

3. Latin: pretext of a council.

have nothing to do with thee. But help us, poor and wretched souls who cry unto thee and earnestly seek thee according to the grace which thou hast given us by thy Holy Spirit, who with thee and the Father liveth and reigneth, blessed forever. Amen.

[Part 1]

The first part of the articles treats the sublime articles of the divine majesty, namely:

1. That Father, Son, and Holy Spirit, three distinct persons in one divine essence and nature, are one God, who created heaven and earth, etc.

2. That the Father was begotten by no one, the Son was begotten by the Father, and the Holy Spirit proceeded from the Father and the Son.

3. That only the Son became man, and neither the Father nor the Holy Spirit.

4. That the Son became man in this manner: he was conceived by the Holy Spirit, without the cooperation of man, and was born of the pure, holy, and virgin Mary. Afterwards he suffered, died, was buried, descended to hell, rose from the dead, and ascended to heaven; and he is seated at the right hand of God, will come to judge the living and the dead, etc., as the Apostles' Creed, the Athanasian Creed, and the Catechism in common use for children teach.

These articles are not matters of dispute or contention, for both parties confess them. Therefore, it is not necessary to treat them at greater length.

[Part 2]

The second part treats the articles which pertain to the office and work of Jesus Christ, or to our redemption.

[ARTICLE 1. CHRIST AND FAITH]

[1] The first and chief article is this, that Jesus Christ, our God and Lord, "was put to death for our trespasses and raised again for our justification," Romans 4. [2] He alone is "the Lamb of God, who takes away the sin of the world," John 1. "God has laid upon him the iniquities of us all," Isaiah 53. [3] Moreover, "all have sinned," and "they are justified by his grace as a gift, through the redemption which is in Christ Jesus, by his blood," Romans 3.

[4] Inasmuch as this must be believed and cannot be obtained or apprehended by any work, law, or merit, it is clear and certain that such faith alone justifies us, as St. Paul says in Romans 3, "For we hold that a man is justified by faith

Rom 4[.25]

Jn 1[.29]

Is 53[.6]

Rom 3[.23–25]

Rom 3[.28]   apart from works of law," Romans 3, and again, "that he [God] himself is righteous
Rom 3[.26]   and that he justifies him who has faith in Jesus," Romans 3.

[5] Nothing in this article can be given up or compromised,[4] even if heaven
and earth and things temporal should be destroyed. For as St. Peter says, "There is
Acts 4[.12]   no other name under heaven given among men by which we must be saved," Acts 4.
Is 53[.5]   "And with his stripes we are healed," Isaiah 53.

On this article rests all that we teach and practice against the pope, the
devil, and the world. Therefore we must be quite certain and have no doubts about
it. Otherwise all is lost, and the pope, the devil, and all our adversaries will gain the
victory.

ARTICLE 2. [THE MASS]

[1] The mass in the papacy must be regarded as the greatest and most horrible
abomination because it runs into direct and violent conflict with this fundamental
article. Yet, above and beyond all others, it has been the supreme and most precious
of the papal idolatries, for it is held that this sacrifice or work of the mass (even
when offered by an evil scoundrel) delivers men from their sins, both here in this life
and yonder in purgatory, although in reality this can and must be done by the Lamb
of God alone, as has been stated above. There is to be no concession or compromise
in this article either, for the first article does not permit it.

[2] If there were reasonable papists, one would speak to them in the following friendly fashion:

"Why do you cling so tenaciously to your masses?

"1. After all, they are a purely human invention. They are not commanded
by God. And we can discard all human inventions, for Christ says, 'In vain do they
Mt 15[.9]   worship me, teaching as doctrines the precepts of men,' Matthew 15.

[3] "2. The mass is unnecessary, and so it can be omitted without sin and
danger.

[4] "3. The sacrament can be had in a far better and more blessed manner—
indeed, the only blessed manner—according to the institution of Christ. Why, then,
do you drive the world into wretchedness and woe on account of an unnecessary
and fictitious matter when the sacrament can be had in another and more blessed
way?

[5] "Let the people be told openly that the mass, as trumpery, can be omitted without sin, that no one will be damned for not observing it, and that one can be
saved in a better way without the mass. Will the mass not then collapse of itself—

---

4. Latin adds: nor can any believer concede or permit anything contrary to it.

not only for the rude rabble, but also for all godly, Christian, sensible, God-fearing people—especially if they hear that it is a dangerous thing which was fabricated and invented without God's word and will?

[6] "4. Since such countless and unspeakable abuses have arisen everywhere through the buying and selling of masses, it would be prudent to do without the mass for no other reason than to curb such abuses, even if it actually possessed some value in and of itself. How much the more should it be discontinued in order to guard forever against such abuses when it is so unnecessary, useless, and danger-ous and when we can obtain what is more necessary, more useful, and more certain without the mass.

[7] "5. The mass is and can be nothing else than a human work, even a work of evil scoundrels (as the canon and all books on the subject declare), for by means of the mass men try to reconcile themselves and others to God and obtain and merit grace and the forgiveness of sins. It is observed for this purpose when it is best ob-served. What other purpose could it have? Therefore, it should be condemned and must be abolished because it is a direct contradiction to the fundamental article, which asserts that it is not the celebrant of a mass and what he does but the Lamb of God and the Son of God who takes away our sin."   [Jn 1.29]

[8] Somebody may seek to justify himself by saying that he wishes to com-municate himself for the sake of his own devotion. This is not honest, for if he really desires to commune, he can do so most fittingly and properly in the sacrament ad-ministered according to Christ's institution. To commune by himself is uncertain and unnecessary, and he does not know what he is doing because he follows a false human opinion and imagination without the sanction of God's word. [9] Nor is it right (even if everything else is in order) for anyone to use the sacrament, which is the common possession of the church, to meet his own private need and thus trifle with it according to his own pleasure apart from the fellowship of the church.

[10] This article concerning the mass will be the decisive issue in the coun-cil. Even if it were possible for the papists to make concessions to us in all other articles, it would not be possible for them to yield on this article. It is as Campegio said in Augsburg: he would suffer himself to be torn to pieces before he would give up the mass. So by God's help I would suffer myself to be burned to ashes before I would allow a celebrant of the mass and what he does to be considered equal or su-perior to my Savior, Jesus Christ. Accordingly we are and remain eternally divided and opposed the one to the other. The papists are well aware that if the mass falls, the papacy will fall with it. Before they would permit this to happen, they would put us all to death.

[11] Besides, this dragon's tail—that is, the mass—has brought forth a brood of vermin and the poison of manifold idolatries.

[12] The first is purgatory. They were so occupied with requiem masses, with vigils, with the weekly, monthly, and yearly celebrations of requiems, with the common week, with All Souls' Day, and with soul-baths that the mass was used almost exclusively for the dead although Christ instituted the sacrament for the living alone. Consequently purgatory and all the pomp, services, and business transactions associated with it are to be regarded as nothing else than illusions of the devil, for purgatory, too, is contrary to the fundamental article that Christ alone, and not the work of man, can help souls. Besides, nothing has been commanded or enjoined upon us with reference to the dead. All this may consequently be discarded, apart entirely from the fact that it is error and idolatry.

[13] The papists here adduce passages from Augustine and some of the fathers who are said to have written about purgatory. They suppose that we do not understand for what purpose and to what end the authors wrote these passages. St. Augustine[5] does not write that there is a purgatory, nor does he cite any passage of the Scriptures that would constrain him to adopt such an opinion. He leaves it undecided whether or not there is a purgatory and merely mentions that his mother asked that she be remembered at the altar or sacrament. Now, this is nothing but a human opinion of certain individuals and cannot establish an article of faith. That is the prerogative of God alone. [14] But our papists make use of such human opinions to make men believe their shameful, blasphemous, accursed traffic in masses which are offered for souls in purgatory, etc. They can never demonstrate these things from Augustine. Only when they have abolished their traffic in purgatorial masses (which St. Augustine never dreamed of) shall we be ready to discuss with them whether statements of St. Augustine are to be accepted when they are without the support of the Scriptures and whether the dead are to be commemorated in the sacrament. [15] It will not do to make articles of faith out of the holy fathers' words or works. Otherwise what they ate, how they dressed, and what kind of houses they lived in would have to become articles of faith—as has happened in the case of relics. This means that[6] the word of God shall establish articles of faith and no one else, not

[Gal 1.8]   even an angel.

[16] The second is a consequence of this: evil spirits have introduced the knavery of appearing as spirits of the departed and, with unspeakable lies and cunning, of demanding masses, vigils, pilgrimages, and other alms. [17] We had to ac-

---

5. *Confessions* 9.11, 13.
6. Latin: We have another rule, namely, that.

cept all these things as articles of faith and had to live according to them. Moreover, the pope gave his approval to these things as well as to the mass and all the other abominations. Here, too, there can be no concession or compromise.

[18] The third are pilgrimages. Masses, forgiveness of sins, and God's grace were sought here, too, for masses dominated everything. It is certain that we have not been commanded to make pilgrimages, nor are they necessary, because we may obtain forgiveness and grace in a better way and may omit pilgrimages without sin and danger. Why do they neglect their own parishes, the word of God, their wives and children, etc., and pursue these unnecessary, uncertain, harmful will-o'-the-wisps of the devil? [19] They do so simply because the devil has possessed the pope to praise and approve of these practices in order that great multitudes of people may turn aside from Christ to their own merits and (what is worst of all) become idolaters. Besides, it is an unnecessary, uncommanded, abortive, uncertain, and even harmful thing. [20] Therefore there may be no concession or compromise here either.

[21] The fourth are fraternities. Here monasteries, chapters, and vicars have obligated themselves to transfer (by legal and open sale) all masses, good works, etc., for the benefit of the living and the dead. Not only is this mere human trumpery, utterly unnecessary and without command, but it is contrary to the first article, concerning redemption. Therefore, it is under no circumstances to be tolerated.

[22] The fifth are relics. In this connection so many manifest lies and so much nonsense has been invented about the bones of dogs and horses that even the devil has laughed at such knavery. Even if there were some good in them, relics should long since have been condemned. They are neither commanded nor commended. They are utterly unnecessary and useless. [23] Worst of all, however, is the claim that relics effect indulgences and the forgiveness of sin and that, like the mass, etc., their use is a good work and a service of God.

[24] The sixth place belongs to the precious indulgences, which are granted to the living and the dead (for money) and by which the pope sells the merits of Christ together with the superabundant merits of all the saints and the entire church. These are not to be tolerated. Not only are they unnecessary and without commandment, but they are also contrary to the first article, for the merits of Christ are obtained by grace, through faith, without our work or pennies. They are offered to us without our money or merit, not by the power of the pope but by the preaching of God's word.

The Invocation of Saints

[25] The invocation of saints is also one of the abuses of the Antichrist. It is in conflict with the first, chief article and undermines knowledge of Christ. It is neither commanded nor recommended, nor does it have any precedent in the Scriptures. Even if the invocation of saints were a precious practice (which it is not), we have everything a thousandfold better in Christ.

[26] Although angels in heaven pray for us (as Christ himself also does), and although saints on earth, and perhaps also in heaven, do likewise, it does not follow that we should invoke angels and saints, pray to them, keep fasts and festivals for them, say masses and offer sacrifices to them, establish churches, altars, and services for them, serve them in still other ways, regard them as helpers in time of need, and attribute all sorts of help to them, assigning to each of them a special function, as the papists teach and practice. This is idolatry. Such honor belongs to God alone. [27] As a Christian and a saint on earth, you can pray for me, not in one particular necessity only, but in every kind of need. However, I should not on this account pray to you, invoke you, keep fasts and festivals and say masses and offer sacrifices in your honor, or trust in you for my salvation. There are other ways in which I can honor, love, and thank you in Christ. [28] If such idolatrous honor is withdrawn from angels and dead saints, the honor that remains will do no harm and will quickly be forgotten. When spiritual and physical benefit and help are no longer expected, the saints will cease to be molested in their graves and in heaven, for no one will long remember, esteem, or honor them out of love when there is no expectation of return.

[29] In short, we cannot allow but must condemn the mass, its implications, and its consequences in order that we may retain the holy sacrament in its purity and certainty according to the institution of Christ and may use and receive it in faith.

ARTICLE 3. [CHAPTERS AND MONASTERIES]

[1] The chapters and monasteries which in former times had been founded with good intentions for the education of learned men and decent women should be restored to such purposes in order that we may have pastors, preachers, and other ministers in the church, others who are necessary for secular government in cities and states, and also well-trained girls to become mothers, housekeepers, etc.

[2] If they are unwilling to serve this purpose, it would be better to abandon them or tear them down rather than preserve them with their blasphemous services, invented by men, which claim to be superior to the ordinary Christian life and to the

offices and callings established by God. All this, too, is in conflict with the first, fundamental article concerning redemption in Jesus Christ. Besides, like other human inventions, all this is without commandment, unnecessary, and useless. Moreover, it causes dangerous and needless effort, and accordingly the prophets call such service of God *aven*, that is, vanity.[a]

ARTICLE 4. [THE PAPACY]

[1] The pope is not the head of all Christendom by divine right or according to God's word, for this position belongs only to one, namely, to Jesus Christ.[b] The pope is only the bishop and pastor of the churches in Rome and of such other churches as have attached themselves to him voluntarily or through a human institution (that is, a secular government). These churches did not choose to be under him as under [1 Pt 2.13] an overlord but chose to stand beside him as Christian brethren and companions, as the ancient councils and the time of Cyprian prove. [2] But now no bishop dares to call the pope "brother," as was then customary, but must address him as "most gracious lord," as if he were a king or emperor. This we neither will nor should nor can take upon our consciences. Those who wish to do so had better not count on us!

[3] Hence it follows that all the things that the pope has undertaken and done on the strength of such false, mischievous, blasphemous, usurped authority have been and still are purely diabolical transactions and deeds (except what pertains to secular government, where God sometimes permits much good to come to a people through a tyrant or scoundrel) which contribute to the destruction of the entire holy Christian church (insofar as this lies in his power) and come into conflict with the first, fundamental article which is concerned with redemption in Jesus Christ.

[4] All the pope's bulls and books, in which he roars like a lion (as the angel in Revelation 12 suggests), are available. Here it is asserted that no Christian can Rv [10.3] be saved unless he is obedient to the pope and submits to him in all that he desires, says, and does. This is nothing less than to say, "Although you believe in Christ, and in him have everything that is needful for salvation, this is nothing and all in vain unless you consider me your god and are obedient and subject to me." Yet it is manifest that the holy church was without a pope for more than five hundred years at the least and that the churches of the Greeks and of many other nationalities have never been under the pope and are not at the present time. [5] Manifestly (to repeat

---

a. [Zec 10.2; Hb 1.3; Is 1.13, 29.20, 41.29]
b. [Eph 1.22, 4.15; Col 1.18]

what has already been said often) the papacy is a human invention, and it is not commanded, it is unnecessary, and it is useless. The holy Christian church can exist very well without such a head, and it would have remained much better if such a head had not been raised up by the devil. [6] The papacy is of no use to the church because it exercises no Christian office. Consequently the church must continue to exist without the pope.

[7] Suppose that the pope would renounce the claim that he is the head of the church by divine right or by God's command; suppose that it were necessary to have a head, to whom all others should adhere, in order that the unity of Christendom might better be preserved against the attacks of sects and heresies; and suppose that such a head would then be elected by men and it remained in their power and choice to change or depose this head. This is just the way in which the Council of Constance acted with reference to the popes when it deposed three and elected a fourth. If, I say, the pope and the see of Rome were to concede and accept this (which is impossible), he would have to suffer the overthrow and destruction of his whole rule and estate, together with all his rights and pretensions. In short, he cannot do it. Even if he could, Christendom would not be helped in any way. [8] There would be even more sects than before because, inasmuch as subjection to such a head would depend on the good pleasure of men rather than on a divine command, he would very easily and quickly be despised and would ultimately be without any adherents at all. He would not always have to have his residence in Rome or some other fixed place, but it could be anywhere and in whatever church God would raise up a man fitted for such an office. What a complicated and confused state of affairs that would be!

[9] Consequently the church cannot be better governed and maintained than by having all of us live under one head, Christ,[a] and by having all the bishops equal in office (however they may differ in gifts)[b] and diligently joined together in unity of doctrine, faith, sacraments, prayer, works of love, etc. So St. Jerome writes[7] that the priests of Alexandria governed the churches together and in common. The apostles did the same, and after them all the bishops throughout Christendom, until the pope raised his head over them all.

a. [Eph 1.22, 4.15, 5.25; Col 1.18]
b. [1 Cor 12.4, 8–10; Rom 12.6–8]

7. Quoting from memory, Luther here combines two citations from Jerome that he was fond of quoting: *Commentary on the Epistle to Titus* 1.5, 6 and *Epistle to Euangelus the Presbyter* no. 146.

[10] This[8] is a powerful demonstration that the pope is the real Antichrist who has raised himself over and set himself against Christ, for the pope will not permit Christians to be saved except by his own power, which amounts to nothing since it is neither established nor commanded by God. [11] This is actually what St. Paul calls exalting oneself over and against God. Neither the Turks nor the Tar- [2 Thes 2.4] tars, great as is their enmity against Christians, do this; those who desire to do so they allow to believe in Christ, and they receive bodily tribute and obedience from Christians.

[12] However, the pope will not permit such faith but asserts that one must be obedient to him in order to be saved. This we are unwilling to do even if we have to die for it in God's name. [13] All this is a consequence of his wishing to be the head of the Christian church by divine right. He had to set himself up as equal to and above Christ and to proclaim himself the head, and then the lord of the church, and finally of the whole world. He went so far as to claim to be an earthly god and even presumed to issue orders to the angels in heaven.[9]

[14] When the teaching of the pope is distinguished from that of the Holy Scriptures, or is compared with them, it becomes apparent that, at its best, the teaching of the pope has been taken from the imperial, pagan law and is a teaching concerning secular transactions and judgments, as the papal decretals show. In keeping with such teaching, instructions are given concerning the ceremonies of churches, vestments, food, personnel, and countless other puerilities, fantasies, and follies without so much as a mention of Christ, faith, and God's commandments.

Finally, it is most diabolical for the pope to promote his lies about masses, purgatory, monastic life, and human works and services (which are the essence of the papacy) in contradiction to God, and to damn, slay, and plague all Christians who do not exalt and honor these abominations of his above all things. Accordingly, just as we cannot adore the devil himself as our lord or God, so we cannot suffer his apostle, the pope or Antichrist, to govern us as our head or lord, for deception, murder, and the eternal destruction of body and soul are characteristic of his papal government, as I have demonstrated in many books.

[15] In these four articles they will have enough to condemn in the council, for they neither can nor will concede to us even the smallest fraction of these

8. Latin: This doctrine.
9. The reference is to the allegedly spurious bull of Pope Clement VI, *Ad memoriam reducendo*, of 27 June 1346, in which the pope is said to have commanded the angels "to lead to heaven the souls of the pilgrims who might die on their way to Rome" during the "holy year" of 1350.

articles. Of this we may be certain, and we must rely on the hope that Christ, our Lord, has attacked his adversaries and will accomplish his purpose by his Spirit and his coming. Amen. [16] In the council we shall not be standing before the emperor or the secular authority, as at Augsburg, where we responded to a gracious summons and were given a kindly hearing, but we shall stand before the pope and the devil himself, who does not intend to give us a hearing but only to damn, murder, and drive us to idolatry. Consequently we ought not here kiss his feet or say, "You are my gracious lord," but we ought rather speak as the angel spoke to the devil in Zechariah, "The Lord rebuke you, O Satan."

[2 Thes 2.8]

Zec [3.2]

[Part 3]

The following articles treat matters which we may discuss with learned and sensible men, or even among ourselves. The pope and his court do not care much about these things; they are not concerned about matters of conscience but only about money, honor, and power.

1. SIN

Rom 5[.12]

[1] Here we must confess what St. Paul says in Romans 5, namely, that sin had its origin in one man, Adam, through whose disobedience all men were made sinners and became subject to death and the devil. This is called original sin, or the root sin.

[2] The fruits of this sin are all the subsequent evil deeds which are forbidden in the Ten Commandments, such as unbelief, false belief, idolatry, being without the fear of God, presumption, despair, blindness—in short, ignorance or disregard of God—and then also lying, swearing by God's name, failure to pray and call upon God, neglect of God's word, disobedience to parents, murder, unchastity, theft, deceit, etc.

[3] This hereditary sin is so deep a corruption of nature that reason cannot understand it. It must be believed because of the revelation in the Scriptures,[a] Psalm 50, Romans 5, Exodus 33, Genesis 3. What the scholastic theologians taught concerning this article is therefore nothing but error and stupidity, namely,

[4] 1. That after the fall of Adam the natural powers of man have remained whole and uncorrupted, and that man by nature possesses a right understanding and a good will, as the philosophers teach.

a. Ps 51[.7]; Rom 5[.12]; Ex 33[.20]; Gn 3[.6ff.]

[5] 2. Again, that man has a free will, either to do good and refrain from evil or to refrain from good and do evil.

[6] 3. Again, that man is able by his natural powers to observe and keep all the commandments of God.

[7] 4. Again, that man is able by his natural powers to love God above all things and his neighbor as himself.

[8] 5. Again, if man does what he can, God is certain to grant him his grace.

[9] 6. Again, when a man goes to the sacrament there is no need of a good intention to do what he ought, but it is enough that he does not have an evil intention to commit sin, for such is the goodness of man's nature and such is the power of the sacrament.

[10] 7. That it cannot be proved from the Scriptures that the Holy Spirit and his gifts are necessary for the performance of a good work.

[11] Such and many similar notions have resulted from misunderstanding and ignorance concerning sin and concerning Christ, our Savior. They are thoroughly pagan doctrines, and we cannot tolerate them. If such teachings were true, Christ would have died in vain, for there would be no defect or sin in man for which he would have had to die, or else he would have died only for the body and not for the soul inasmuch as the soul would be sound and only the body would be subject to death.

2. THE LAW

[1] Here we maintain that the law was given by God first of all to restrain sins by threats and fear of punishment and by the promise and offer of grace and favor. But this purpose failed because of the wickedness which sin has worked in man. [2] Some, who hate the law because it forbids what they desire to do and commands what they are unwilling to do, are made worse thereby. Accordingly, in so far as they are not restrained by punishment, they act against the law even more than before. These are the rude and wicked people who do evil whenever they have opportunity. [3] Others become blind and presumptuous, imagining that they can and do keep the law by their own powers, as was just said above concerning the scholastic theologians. Hypocrites and false saints are produced in this way.

[4] However, the chief function or power of the law is to make original sin manifest and show man to what utter depths his nature has fallen and how corrupt [Rom 7.7, 3.20] it has become. So the law must tell him that he neither has nor cares for God or that he worships strange gods—something that he would not have believed before without a knowledge of the law. Thus he is terror-stricken and humbled, becomes

despondent and despairing, anxiously desires help but does not know where to find it, and begins to be alienated from God, to murmur, etc. [5] This is what is meant

Rom [4.15]

by Romans 3 "The law brings wrath," and Romans 5, "Law came in to increase the

Rom 5[.20]

trespass."

3. REPENTANCE

[1] This function of the law is retained and taught by the New Testament. So Paul

Rom 1[.18]

says in Romans 1, "The wrath of God is revealed from heaven against all ungodliness and wickedness of men," and in Romans 3, "The whole world may be held

Rom 3[.19, 20]

accountable to God, for no human being will be justified in his sight." Christ also

Jn 16[.8]

says in John 16, "The Holy Spirit will convince the world of sin."

[2] This, then, is the thunderbolt by means of which God with one blow destroys both open sinners and false saints. He allows no one to justify himself. He drives all together into terror and despair. This is the hammer of which Jeremiah

Jer [23.29]

speaks, "Is not my word like a hammer which breaks the rock in pieces?" This is not *activa contritio* (artificial remorse), but *passiva contritio* (true sorrow of the heart, suffering, and pain of death).

[3] This is what the beginning of true repentance is like. Here man must hear such a judgment as this: "You are all of no account. Whether you are manifest sinners or saints,[10] you must all become other than you now are and do otherwise than you now do, no matter who you are and no matter how great, wise, mighty, and holy you may think yourselves. Here no one is godly," etc.

[4] To this office of the law the New Testament immediately adds the consoling promise of grace in the gospel. This is to be believed as Christ says in Mark 1,

Mk 1[.15]

"Repent and believe in the gospel," which is to say, "Become different, do otherwise, and believe my promise." [5] John, who preceded Christ, is called a preacher of repentance—but for the remission of sins. That is, John was to accuse them all and convince them that they were sinners in order that they might know how they stood before God and recognize themselves as lost men. In this way they were to be prepared to receive grace from the Lord and to expect and accept from him the forgiveness of sins. [6] Christ himself says this in Luke at the end, "Repentance and

Lk [24.47]

the forgiveness of sins should be preached in his name to all nations."

[7] But where the law exercises its office alone, without the addition of the gospel, there is only death and hell, and man must despair like Saul and Judas.[a] [8]

---

a. [1 Sm 28.20, 31.4; Mt 27.3–51]

10. Latin adds: in your opinion.

As St. Paul says, the law slays through sin. Moreover, the gospel offers consolation [Rom 7.10] and forgiveness in more ways than one, for with God there is plenteous redemption (as Psalm 129 puts it) from the dreadful captivity to sin, and this comes to us Ps [130.8] through the word, the sacraments, and the like, as we shall hear.

[9] Now we must compare the false repentance of the sophists with true repentance so that both may be better understood.

The False Repentance of the Papists

[10] It was impossible for them to teach correctly about repentance because they did not know what sin really is. For, as stated above, they did not have the right teaching concerning original sin but asserted that the natural powers of man have remained whole and uncorrupted, that reason is capable of right understanding and the will is capable of acting accordingly, and that God will assuredly grant his grace to the man who does as much as he can according to his free will.

[11] From this it follows that people did penance only for actual sins, such as wicked thoughts to which they consented (for evil impulses, lust, and inclinations they did not consider sin), wicked words, and wicked works which man with his free will might well have avoided. [12] Such repentance the sophists divided into three parts—contrition, confession, and satisfaction—with the added consolation that a man who properly repents, confesses, and makes satisfaction has merited forgiveness and has paid for his sins before God. In their teaching of penance the sophists thus instructed the people to place their confidence in their own works. [13] Hence the expression in the pulpit when the general confession was recited to the people: "Prolong my life, Lord God, until I make satisfaction for my sins and amend my life."

[14] There was no mention here of Christ or of faith. Rather, men hoped by their own works to overcome and blot out their sins before God. With this intention we, too, became priests and monks, that we might set ourselves against sin.

[15] As for contrition, this was the situation: Since nobody could recall all his sins (especially those committed during the course of a whole year), the following loophole was resorted to, namely, that when a hidden sin was afterwards remembered, it had also to be repented of, confessed, etc., but meanwhile the sinner was commended to the grace of God. [16] Moreover, since nobody knew how much contrition he had to muster in order to avail before God, this consolation was offered: If anybody could not be contrite (that is, really repentant), he should at least be attrite (which I might call halfway or partially repentant). They under-

stood neither of these terms, and to this day they are as far from comprehending their meaning as I am. Nevertheless, such attrition was reckoned as a substitute for contrition when people went to confession. [17] And when somebody said that he was unable to repent or be sorry for his sin (which might have been committed, let us say, in whoredom, revenge, or the like), such a person was asked if he did not wish or desire to be repentant. If he said Yes (for who but the devil himself would want to say No?) it was accounted as contrition and, on the basis of this good work of his, his sin was forgiven. Here the example of St. Bernard, etc., was cited.[11]

[18] Here we see how blind reason gropes about in matters which pertain to God, seeking consolation in its own works, according to its own inventions, without being able to consider Christ and faith. If we examine this in the light, we see that such contrition is an artificial and imaginary idea evolved by man's own powers without faith and without knowledge of Christ. A poor sinner who reflected on his lust or revenge in this fashion would sooner have laughed than wept, unless perchance he was really smitten by the law or vainly vexed with a sorrowful spirit by the devil. Apart from cases like this, such repentance surely was pure hypocrisy. It did not extinguish the lust for sin. The person involved was obliged to grieve, but he would rather have sinned if he had been free to do so.

[19] As for confession, the situation was like this: Everybody had to give an account of all his sins—an impossibility and the source of great torture. The sins which had been forgotten were pardoned only when a man remembered them and thereupon confessed them. Accordingly he could never know when he had made a sufficiently complete or a sufficiently pure confession. At the same time his attention was directed to his own works, and he was told that the more completely he confessed, the more he was ashamed, and the more he abased himself before the priest, the sooner and the better he would make satisfaction for his sins, for such humiliation would surely earn grace before God. Here, again, there was neither faith nor Christ. [20] A man did not become aware of the power of absolution, for his consolation was made to rest on his enumeration of sins and on his self-abasement. But this is not the place to recount the torture, rascality, and idolatry which such confession has produced.

[21] Satisfaction was even more complicated,[12] for nobody could know how much he was to do for one single sin, to say nothing of all his sins. Here the expedient was resorted to of imposing small satisfactions which were easy to render, like

11. Cf. Bernard of Clairvaux *Treatise on Grace and Free Will* 4.10.
12. Latin: perplexing.

saying five Our Fathers, fasting for a day, etc. For the penance that was still lacking man was referred to purgatory.

[22] Here, too, there was nothing but anguish and misery. Some thought that they would never get out of purgatory because, according to the ancient canons, seven years of penance were required for a single mortal sin. [23] Nevertheless, confidence was placed in man's own works of satisfaction. If the satisfaction could have been perfect, full confidence would have been placed in it, and neither faith nor Christ would have been of any value. But such confidence was impossible. Even if one had done penance in this way for a hundred years, one would still not have known whether this was enough. This is a case of always doing penance but never coming to repentance.

[24] Here the holy see in Rome came to the aid of the poor church and invented indulgences. By these satisfaction was remitted and canceled, first for seven years in a single case, then for a hundred, etc. The indulgences were distributed among the cardinals and bishops so that one could grant them for a hundred years, another for a hundred days, but the pope reserved for himself alone the right to remit the entire satisfaction.

[25] When this began to yield money and the bull market became profitable, the pope invented the jubilee year and attached it to Rome. This was called remission of all penalty and guilt, and the people came running, for everyone was eager to be delivered from the heavy, unbearable burden. Here we have the discovery and digging up of the treasures of the earth. The popes went further and quickly multiplied the jubilee years. The more money they swallowed, the wider became their maws. So they sent their legates out into all lands until every church and house was reached by jubilee indulgences. [26] Finally the popes forced their way into purgatory, first by instituting masses and vigils for the dead and afterwards by offering indulgences for the dead through bulls and jubilee years. In time souls got to be so cheap that they were released at six pence a head.

[27] Even this did not help, however, for although the pope taught the people to rely on and trust in such indulgences, he again introduced uncertainty when he declared in his bulls, "Whoever wishes to benefit from the indulgence or jubilee year must be contrite, make confession, and pay money." But the contrition and confession practiced by these people, as we have heard above, are uncertain and hypocritical. Moreover, nobody knew which soul was in purgatory, and nobody knew which of those in purgatory had truly repented and properly confessed. So the pope took the money, consoled the people with his power and indulgences, and once again directed attention to uncertain human works.

[28] There were some who did not think they were guilty of actual sins—that is, of sinful thoughts, words, and deeds. I and others like myself who wished to be monks and priests in monasteries and chapters fought against evil thoughts by fasting, vigils, prayers, masses, coarse clothing, and hard beds and tried earnestly and mightily to be holy, and yet the hereditary evil which is born in us did what is its nature to do, sometimes while we slept (as St. Augustine, St. Jerome, and others confess).[13] Each one, however, held that some of the others were, as we taught, without sin and full of good works, and so we shared our good works with others and sold them to others in the belief that they were more than we ourselves needed for heaven. This is certainly true, and there are seals, letters, and examples to show it. [29] Such persons did not need to repent, for what were they to repent of when they did not consent to evil thoughts? What should they confess when they refrained from evil words? What satisfaction should they render when they were innocent of evil deeds and could even sell their superfluous righteousness to other poor sinners? The scribes and Pharisees in Christ's time were just such saints.[14]

[Mt 11.10; Rv 10.1]

[Mt 3.2]

[30] Here the fiery angel St. John, the preacher of true repentance, intervenes. With a single thunderbolt he strikes and destroys both. "Repent," he says. On the one hand there are some who think, "We have already done penance," [31] and on the other hand there are others who suppose, "We need no repentance." [32] But John says: "Repent, both of you. Those of you in the former group are false penitents, and those of you in the latter are false saints. Both of you need the forgiveness of sins, for neither of you knows what sin really is, to say nothing of repenting and shunning sin. None of you is good. All of you are full of unbelief, blindness, and ignorance of God and God's will. For he is here present, and from

[Jn 1.16]

his fullness have we all received, grace upon grace. No man can be just before God without him. Accordingly, if you would repent, repent rightly. Your repentance accomplishes nothing. And you hypocrites who think you do not need to repent, you

[Mt 3.7]

brood of vipers, who has given you any assurance that you will escape the wrath to come?"

Rom 3[.10–12]

[33] Saint Paul teaches the same thing in Romans 3: "None is righteous, no, not one; no one understands, no one seeks for God. All have turned aside, together they have gone wrong." [34] And in Acts 17, "Now he commands all men every-

Acts [17.30]

where to repent." He says "all men," that is, excepting no one who is a man. [35] Such repentance teaches us to acknowledge sin—that is, to acknowledge that we are

13. Augustine *Confessions* 2.2, 10.30; Jerome *Epistle to Eustochius* 22.7.
14. Latin adds: and hypocrites.

all utterly lost, that from head to foot there is no good in us, that we must become altogether new and different men.

[36] This repentance is not partial and fragmentary like repentance for actual sins, nor is it uncertain like that. It does not debate what is sin and what is not sin, but lumps everything together and says, "We are wholly and altogether sinful." We need not spend our time weighing, distinguishing, differentiating. On this account there is no uncertainty in such repentance, for nothing is left that we might imagine to be good enough to pay for our sin. One thing is sure: We cannot pin our hope on anything that we are, think, say, or do. [37] And so our repentance cannot be false, uncertain, or partial, for a person who confesses that he is altogether sinful embraces all sins in his confession without omitting or forgetting a single one. [38] Nor can our satisfaction be uncertain, for it consists not of the dubious, sinful works which we do but of the sufferings and blood of the innocent Lamb of God who takes away the sin of the world. [Jn 1.29]

[39] This is the repentance which John preaches, which Christ subsequently preaches in the gospel, and which we also preach. With this repentance we overthrow the pope and everything that is built on our good works, for all of this is constructed on an unreal and rotten foundation which is called good works or the law, although no good work but only wicked works are there and although no one keeps the law (as Christ says in John 7) but all transgress it. Accordingly the entire building, even when it is most holy and beautiful, is nothing but deceitful falsehood and hypocrisy. Jn 7[.19]

[40] In the case of a Christian such repentance continues until death, for all through life it contends with the sins that remain in the flesh. As St. Paul testifies in Romans 7, he wars with the law in his members, and he does this not with his own powers but with the gift of the Holy Spirit which follows the forgiveness of sins. This gift daily cleanses and expels the sins that remain and enables man to become truly pure and holy. Rom 7[.23, 8.2]

[41] This is something about which the pope, the theologians, the jurists, and all men understand nothing. It is a teaching from heaven, revealed in the gospel, and yet it is called a heresy by godless saints.

[42] Some fanatics may appear (and perhaps they are already present, such as I saw with my own eyes at the time of the uprising)[15] who hold that once they have received the Spirit or the forgiveness of sins, or once they have become believers, they will persevere in faith even if they sin afterwards, and such sin will not

15. The Peasants' War in 1525.

harm them. They cry out, "Do what you will, it matters not as long as you believe, for faith blots out all sins," etc. They add that if anyone sins after he has received faith and the Spirit, he never really had the Spirit and faith. I have encountered many foolish people like this and I fear that such a devil still dwells in some of them.

[43] It is therefore necessary to know and to teach that when holy people, aside from the fact that they still possess and feel original sin and daily repent and strive against it, fall into open sin (as David fell into adultery, murder, and blas-

[2 Sm 11]   phemy), faith and the Spirit have departed from them. [44] This is so because the Holy Spirit does not permit sin to rule and gain the upper hand in such a way that sin is committed, but the Holy Spirit represses and restrains it so that it does not do what it wishes. If sin does what it wishes, the Holy Spirit and faith are not present,

1 Jn [3.9, 5.18]   [45] for St. John says, "No one born of God commits sin; he cannot sin." Yet it is also true, as the same St. John writes, "If we say we have no sin, we deceive ourselves,

1 Jn [1.8]   and the truth is not in us."

4. THE GOSPEL

We shall now return to the gospel, which offers counsel and help against sin in more than one way, for God is surpassingly rich in his grace: First, through the spoken word, by which the forgiveness of sin (the peculiar office of the gospel) is preached to the whole world: second, through baptism; third, through the holy sacrament of the altar; fourth, through the power of keys; and finally, through the mutual conver- sation and consolation of brethren. Matthew 18, "Where two or three are gathered,"

Mt 18[.20]   etc.

5. BAPTISM

[1] Baptism is nothing else than the word of God in water, commanded by the insti-

[Eph 5.26]   tution of Christ; or as Paul says, "the washing of water with the word"; or, again, as Augustine puts it, "The word is added to the element and it becomes a sacra- ment."[16] [2] Therefore we do not agree with Thomas[17] and the Dominicans who forget the word (God's institution) and say that God has joined to the water a spiri- tual power which, through the water, washes away sin. [3] Nor do we agree with Scotus[18] and the Franciscans who teach that baptism washes away sin through the assistance of the divine will, as if the washing takes place only through God's will and not at all through the word and the water.

16. *Tractate 80,* on Jn 3.
17. Cf. Thomas Aquinas *Summa theologica* 3.62.a.4.
18. Cf. Duns Scotus *Sentences* 4.1.2ff.

[4] As for infant baptism, we hold that children should be baptized, for they, too, are included in the promise of redemption which Christ made, and the church should administer baptism to them. [Mt 19.14]

6. THE SACRAMENT OF THE ALTAR

[1] We hold that the bread and the wine in the supper are the true body and blood of Christ and that these are given and received not only by godly but also by wicked Christians.

[2] We also hold that it is not to be administered in one form only. We need not resort to the specious learning of the sophists and the Council of Constance that as much is included under one form as under both. [3] Even if it were true that as much is included under one form as under both, yet administration in one form is not the whole order and institution as it was established and commanded by Christ. [4] Especially do we condemn and curse in God's name those who not only omit both forms but even go so far as autocratically to prohibit, condemn, and slander the use of both as heresy and thus set themselves against and over Christ, our Lord and God, etc.

[5] As for transubstantiation, we have no regard for the subtle sophistry of those who teach that bread and wine surrender or lose their natural substance and retain only the appearance and shape of bread without any longer being real bread, for that bread is and remains there agrees better with the Scriptures, as St. Paul himself states, "The bread which we break," and again, "Let a man so eat of [1 Cor 10.16] the bread." [1 Cor 11.28]

7. THE KEYS

[1] The keys are a function and power given to the church by Christ to bind and [Mt 16.19, 18.18] loose sins, not only the gross and manifest sins but also those which are subtle and secret and which God alone perceives. So it is written, "Who can discern his errors?" And Paul himself complains, Romans 7, that in his flesh he was a captive [Ps 19.13] to "the law of sin." [2] It is not in our power but in God's alone to judge which, Rom 7[.23] how great, and how many our sins are. As it is written, "Enter not into judgment with thy servant, for no man living is righteous before thee," [3] and Paul also says [Ps 143.2] in 1 Corinthians 4, "I am not aware of anything against myself, but I am not thereby acquitted." 1 Cor 4[.4]

8. CONFESSION

[1] Since absolution or the power of the keys, which was instituted by Christ in the gospel, is a consolation and help against sin and a bad conscience, confession and

absolution should by no means be allowed to fall into disuse in the church, especially for the sake of timid consciences and for the sake of untrained young people who need to be examined and instructed in Christian doctrine.

[2] However, the enumeration of sins should be left free to everybody to do or not as he will. As long as we are in the flesh we shall not be untruthful if we say, "I am a poor man, full of sin. I see in my members another law," etc., Romans 7. Although private absolution is derived from the office of the keys, it should not be neglected; on the contrary, it should be highly esteemed and valued, like all other functions of the Christian church.

Rom 7[.23]

[3] In these matters, which concern the external, spoken word, we must hold firmly to the conviction that God gives no one his Spirit or grace except through or with the external word which comes before. Thus we shall be protected from the enthusiasts—that is, from the spiritualists who boast that they possess the Spirit without and before the word and who therefore judge, interpret, and twist the Scriptures or spoken word according to their pleasure. Münzer did this, and many still do it in our day who wish to distinguish sharply between the letter and the spirit without knowing what they say or teach. [4] The papacy, too, is nothing but enthusiasm, for the pope boasts that "all laws are in the shrine of his heart,"[19] and he claims that whatever he decides and commands in his churches is spirit and law, even when it is above and contrary to the Scriptures or spoken word. [5] All this is the old devil and the old serpent who made enthusiasts of Adam and Eve. He led them from the external word of God to spiritualizing and to their own imaginations, and he did this through other external words. [6] Even so, the enthusiasts of our day condemn the external word, yet they do not remain silent but fill the world with their chattering and scribbling, as if the Spirit could not come through the Scriptures or the spoken word of the apostles but must come through their own writings and words. Why do they not stop preaching and writing until the Spirit himself comes to the people without and before their writings since they boast that the Spirit came upon them without the testimony of the Scriptures? There is no time to dispute further about these matters. After all, we have treated them sufficiently elsewhere.[20]

[7] Even those who have come to faith before they were baptized and those who came to faith in baptism came to their faith through the external word which preceded. Adults who have attained the age of reason must first have heard, "He who believes and is baptized will be saved," even if they did not at once believe and did not receive the Spirit and baptism until ten years later. [8] Cornelius in Acts 10

[Mk 16.16]

19. *Corpus juris canonici* 6.1.2.1.
20. E.g., Luther's "Against the Heavenly Prophets" (1525).

had long since heard from the Jews about the coming Messiah through whom he   Acts 10[.1ff.]
was justified before God, and his prayers and alms were acceptable to God in this
faith (Luke calls him "devout" and "God-fearing"), but he could not have believed   [Acts 10.2, 22]
and been justified if the word and his hearing of it had not preceded. However, St.
Peter had to reveal to him that the Messiah, in whose coming he had previously believed, had already come, and his faith concerning the coming Messiah did not hold
him captive with the hardened, unbelieving Jews, but he knew that he now had to
be saved by the present Messiah and not deny or persecute him as the Jews did.

[9] In short, enthusiasm clings to Adam and his descendants from the beginning to the end of the world. It is a poison implanted and inoculated in man by
the old dragon, and it is the source, strength, and power of all heresy, including that
of the papacy and Mohammedanism. [10] Accordingly, we should and must constantly maintain that God will not deal with us except through his external word
and sacrament. Whatever is attributed to the Spirit apart from such word and sacrament is of the devil. [11] For even to Moses God wished to appear first through the
burning bush and the spoken word, and no prophet, whether Elijah or Elisha, re-   [Ex 3.2, 4]
ceived the Spirit without the Ten Commandments. [12] John the Baptist was not
conceived without the preceding word of Gabriel, nor did he leap in his mother's
womb until Mary spoke. [13] Saint Peter says that when the prophets spoke, they   [Lk 1.13–44]
did not prophesy by the impulse of man but were moved by the Holy Spirit, yet as
holy men of God. But without the external word they were not holy, and the Holy   2 Pt [1.21]
Spirit would not have moved them to speak while they were still unholy. They were
holy, St. Peter says, because the Holy Spirit spoke through them.

9. EXCOMMUNICATION   [Mt 18.15ff.]

We consider the greater excommunication, as the pope calls it, to be merely a civil
penalty which does not concern us ministers of the church. However, the lesser (that
is, the truly Christian) excommunication excludes those who are manifest and impenitent sinners from the sacrament and other fellowship of the church until they
mend their ways and avoid sin. Preachers should not mingle civil punishments with
this spiritual penalty or excommunication.

10. ORDINATION AND VOCATION

[1] If the bishops were true bishops and were concerned about the church and the
gospel, they might be permitted (for the sake of love and unity, but not of necessity)
to ordain and confirm us and our preachers, provided this could be done without
pretense, humbug, and unchristian ostentation. However, they neither are nor wish
to be true bishops. [2] They are temporal lords and princes who are unwilling to

preach or teach or baptize or administer communion or discharge any office or work in the church. More than that, they expel, persecute, and condemn those who have been called to do these things. Yet the church must not be deprived of ministers on their account.

[3] Accordingly, as we are taught by the examples of the ancient churches and fathers, we shall and ought ourselves ordain suitable persons to this office. The papists have no right to forbid or prevent us, not even according to their own laws, for their laws state that those who are ordained by heretics shall also be regarded as ordained and remain so.[21] St. Jerome, too, wrote concerning the church in Alexandria that it was originally governed without bishops by priests and preachers in common.

11. THE MARRIAGE OF PRIESTS

[1] The papists had neither authority nor right to prohibit marriage and burden the divine estate of priests with perpetual celibacy. On the contrary, they acted like antichristian, tyrannical, and wicked scoundrels, and thereby they gave occasion for all sorts of horrible, abominable, and countless sins, in which they are still involved. [2] As little as the power has been given to us or to them to make a woman out of a man or a man out of a woman or abolish distinctions of sex altogether, so little have they had the power to separate such creatures of God or forbid them to live together honestly in marriage. [3] We are therefore unwilling to consent to their abominable celibacy, nor shall we suffer it. On the contrary, we desire marriage to be free, as God ordained and instituted it, and we shall not disrupt or hinder God's work, for [1 Tm 4.1–3] St. Paul says that to do so is a doctrine of demons.

12. THE CHURCH

[1] We do not concede to the papists that they are the church, for they are not. [2] Nor shall we pay any attention to what they command or forbid in the name of the church, for, thank God, a seven-year-old child knows what the church is, [Jn 10.3] namely, holy believers and sheep who hear the voice of their Shepherd. [3] So children pray, "I believe in one holy Christian church." Its holiness does not consist of surplices, tonsures, albs, or other ceremonies of theirs which they have invented over and above the Holy Scriptures, but it consists of the word of God and true faith.

21. Gratian *Decretum* 1.68.1, 3.4.107.

13. HOW MAN IS JUSTIFIED BEFORE GOD,
AND HIS GOOD WORKS

[1] I do not know how I can change what I have heretofore constantly taught on this subject, namely, that by faith (as St. Peter says) we get a new and clean heart   [Acts 15.9] and that God will and does account us altogether righteous and holy for the sake of Christ, our Mediator. Although the sin in our flesh has not been completely removed or eradicated, he will not count or consider it.

[2] Good works follow such faith, renewal, and forgiveness. Whatever is still sinful or imperfect in these works will not be reckoned as sin or defect for the sake of the same Christ. The whole man, in respect both of his person and of his works, shall be accounted and shall be righteous and holy through the pure grace and mercy which have been poured out upon us so abundantly in Christ. [3] Accordingly we cannot boast of the great merit in our works if they are considered apart from God's grace and mercy, but, as it is written, "Let him who boasts, boast of the Lord."[a] That is to say, all is well if we boast that we have a gracious God. To this we must add that if good works do not follow, our faith is false and not true.

14. MONASTIC VOWS

[1] Since monastic vows are in direct conflict with the first chief article, they must be absolutely set aside. It is of these that Christ says in Matthew 24, "I am the Christ," etc. Whoever takes the vows of monastic life believes that he is entering   Mt 24[.5] upon a mode of life that is better than that of the ordinary Christian and proposes by means of his work to help not only himself but also others to get to heaven. This is to deny Christ, etc. And on the authority of their St. Thomas, such people boast that a monastic vow is equal to baptism.[22] This is blasphemy.

15. HUMAN TRADITIONS

[1] The assertion of the papists that human traditions effect forgiveness of sins or merit salvation is unchristian and to be condemned. As Christ says, "In vain do they worship me, teaching as doctrines the precepts of men," and it is written in Titus 1,   [Mt 15.9] "They are men who reject the truth." [2] When the papists say that it is a mortal   Ti 1[.14] sin to break such precepts of men, this, too, is false.

---

a. [1 Cor 1.31; 2 Cor 10.17]

22. Thomas Aquinas *Summa theologica* 2.2.189.3.3.

[3] These are the articles on which I must stand and on which I will stand, God willing, until my death. I do not know how I can change or concede anything in them. If anybody wishes to make some concessions, let him do so at the peril of his own conscience.

[4] Finally, there remains the pope's bag of magic tricks which contains silly and childish articles, such as the consecration of churches, the baptism of bells, the baptism of altar stones, the invitation to such ceremonies of sponsors who might make gifts, etc. Such baptizing is a ridicule and mockery of holy baptism which should not be tolerated. [5] In addition, there are blessings of candles, palms, spices, oats, cakes, etc. These cannot be called blessings, and they are not, but are mere mockery and fraud. Such frauds, which are without number, we commend for adoration to their god and to themselves until they tire of them. We do not wish to have anything to do with them.

Dr. Martin Luther subscribed

Dr. Justus Jonas, rector, subscribed with his own hand

Dr. John Bugenhagen, of Pomerania, subscribed

Dr. Caspar Creutziger subscribed

Nicholas Amsdorf, of Magdeburg, subscribed

George Spalatin, of Altenburg, subscribed

I, Philipp Melanchthon, regard the above articles as right and Christian. However, concerning the pope I hold that, if he would allow the gospel, we, too, may concede to him that superiority over the bishops which he possesses by human right, making this concession for the sake of peace and general unity among the Christians who are now under him and who may be in the future.

John Agricola, of Eisleben, subscribed

Gabriel Didymus subscribed

I, Dr. Urban Rhegius, superintendent of the churches in the duchy of Lüneburg, subscribe in my own name and in the name of my brethren and of the church of Hanover

I, Stephen Agricola, minister in Hof, subscribe

Also I, John Drach, professor and minister in Marburg, subscribe

I, Conrad Figenbotz, for the glory of God subscribe that I have thus believed and am still preaching and firmly believing as above.

I, Andrew Osiander, minister in Nuremberg, subscribe

I, Master Veit Dietrich, minister in Nuremberg, subscribe

I, Erhard Schnepf, preacher in Stuttgart, subscribe

Conrad Oettinger, preacher of Duke Ulric of Pforzheim

Simon Schneeweiss, pastor of the church in Crailsheim

I, John Schlagenhaufen, pastor of the church in Köthen, subscribe

Master George Helt, of Forchheim

Master Adam of Fulda, preacher in Hesse

Master Anthony Corvinus

I, Dr. John Bugenhagen of Pomerania, again subscribe in the name of Master John Brenz, who on his departure from Smalcald directed me orally and by a letter which I have shown to these brethren who have subscribed

I, Dionysius Melander, subscribe the Confession, the Apology, and the Concord[23] in the matter of the eucharist

Paul Rhode, superintendent of Stettin

Gerard Oemcken, superintendent of the church in Minden

I, Brixius Northanus, minister of the church of Christ which is in Soest, subscribe the articles of the reverend father, Martin Luther, confess that I have hitherto thus believed and taught, and by the Spirit of Christ I will thus continue to believe and teach

Michael Caelius, preacher in Mansfeld, subscribed

Master Peter Geltner, preacher in Frankfurt, subscribed

Wendal Faber, pastor of Seeburg in Mansfeld

I, John Aepinus, subscribe

Likewise I, John Amsterdam, of Bremen

I, Frederick Myconius, pastor of the church in Gotha, Thuringia, subscribe in my own name and in that of Justus Menius, of Eisenach

I, Dr. John Lang, preacher of the church in Erfurt, in my own name and in the names of my other coworkers in the gospel, namely:

the Rev. Licentiate Louis Platz, of Melsungen

the Rev. Master Sigismund Kirchner

the Rev. Wolfgang Kiswetter

the Rev. Melchior Weitmann

the Rev. John Thall

the Rev. John Kilian

the Rev. Nicholas Faber

the Rev. Andrew Menser (I subscribe with my hand)

And I, Egidius Melcher, have subscribed with my hand

23. *The Wittenberg Concord* of 1536.

The Treatise on the Power and
Primacy of the Pope, 1537

[1] The Roman bishop arrogates to himself the claim that he is by divine right above all bishops and pastors. [2] Then he adds that by divine right he possesses both swords, that is, the authority to bestow and transfer kingdoms.[1] [3] Finally, he declares that it is necessary for salvation to believe these things, and for such reasons the bishop of Rome calls himself the vicar of Christ on earth.[2]

[4] These three articles we acknowledge and hold to be false, impious, tyrannical, and injurious to the church. [5] In order that the ground of this our assertion may be understood, we must at the outset define what the papists mean when they say that the Roman bishop is above all bishops by divine right. They mean that the pope is the universal bishop or, as they put it, the ecumenical bishop. That is, all bishops and pastors throughout the whole world should seek ordination and confirmation from him because he has the right to elect, ordain, confirm, and depose all bishops. [6] Besides this, he arrogates to himself the authority to make laws concerning worship, concerning changes in the sacraments, and concerning doctrine. He wishes his articles, his decrees, and his laws to be regarded as articles of faith or commandments of God, binding on the consciences of men, because he holds that his power is by divine right and is even to be preferred to the commandments of God. What is even more horrible is that he adds that it is necessary to salvation to believe all these things.

[TESTIMONY OF THE SCRIPTURES]

[7] 1. First of all, therefore, let us show from the Gospel that the Roman bishop is not by divine right above all other bishops and pastors. In Luke 22, Christ expressly

Lk 22[.24–27]

forbids lordship among the apostles. [8] For this was the very question the disciples were disputing when Christ spoke of his passion: Who was to be the leader and, as it were, the vicar of Christ after his departure? Christ reproved the apostles for this error and taught them that no one should have lordship or superiority among them but that the apostles should be sent forth as equals and exercise the ministry of the gospel in common. Accordingly he said, "The kings of the Gentiles exercise lordship over them. But not so with you; rather let the greatest among you become as

---

1. So especially in the bull → *Unam Sanctam* (1302) of Boniface VIII.
2. A designation used by popes after the time of Innocent III (1198–1216).

one who serves." The antithesis here shows that lordship is disapproved. The same thing is taught by a parable when, in a similar dispute concerning the kingdom, Christ put a child in the midst of the disciples, signifying thereby that there was to be no primacy among ministers, just as a child neither seeks nor takes preeminence for himself. [Mt 18.1–4]

[9] 2. According to John 20, Christ sent his disciples out as equals, without discrimination, when he said, "As the Father has sent me, even so I send you." He sent out each one individually, he said, in the same way in which he had himself been sent. Wherefore he granted to none a prerogative or lordship over the rest. [Jn 20[.21]]

[10] 3. In Galatians 2, Paul plainly asserts that he was neither ordained nor confirmed by Peter, nor does he acknowledge Peter as one from whom confirmation should be sought. From this fact he expressly argues that his call did not depend on the authority of Peter. But he should have acknowledged Peter as his superior if Peter had been his superior by divine right. He says, however, that he at once preached the gospel without consulting Peter. "What they were who were reputed to be something," he says, "makes no difference to me," and again, "Those who were of repute added nothing to me." Since Paul clearly testifies that he did not desire to seek confirmation from Peter, even after he had come to him, he teaches that the authority of the ministry depends on the word of God, that Peter was not superior to the other apostles, and that ordination or confirmation was not to be sought from Peter alone. [Gal 2[.2, 6]] [Gal 2[.6]]

[11] 4. In 1 Corinthians 3, Paul places ministers on an equality and teaches that the church is above the ministers. Therefore he does not attribute to Peter superiority or authority over the church or the other ministers. For he says, "All things are yours, whether Paul or Apollos or Cephas." This is to say that neither Peter nor the other ministers should assume lordship or authority over the church, nor burden the church with traditions, nor let anybody's authority count for more than the word, nor set the authority of Cephas over against the authority of the other apostles. At that time, however, they reasoned thus: "Cephas observes this. He is an apostle of superior rank. Therefore Paul and the others ought to observe this." Paul deprives Peter of this pretext and denies that Peter's authority is superior to that of the others and of the church. 1 Peter 5, "Not domineering over the clergy." [1 Cor 3[.4–8, 22]] [1 Cor 33.21–22] [1 Pt 5[.3]]

TESTIMONY FROM HISTORY

[12] 5. The Council of Nicaea decided that the bishop of Alexandria should administer the churches in the East and the bishop of Rome should administer the suburban

churches, that is, those that were in the Roman provinces in the West.[3] Originally, therefore, the authority of the Roman bishop grew out of a decision of a council and is of human right, for if the bishop of Rome had his superiority by divine right, it would not have been lawful for the council to withdraw any right from him and transfer it to the bishop of Alexandria. In fact, all the Eastern bishops should forever have sought ordination and confirmation from the Roman bishop.

[13] 6. Again, the Council of Nicaea decided that bishops should be elected by their own churches in the presence of one or more neighboring bishops.[4] [14] This was also observed in the West and in the Latin churches, as Cyprian and Augustine testify.[5] For Cyprian states in his fourth letter to Cornelius:[6] "Wherefore you must diligently observe and practice, according to divine tradition and apostolic usage, what is observed by us and in almost all provinces, namely, that for the proper celebration of ordinations the neighboring bishops of the same province should assemble with the people for whom a head is to be ordained, and a bishop should be elected in the presence of the people who are thoroughly acquainted with the life of each candidate (as we have seen it done among you in the ordination of our colleague Sabinus) in order that by the votes of all the brethren and by the judgment of the bishops assembled in their presence, the episcopate might be conferred and hands imposed on him." [15] Cyprian calls this custom a divine tradition and an apostolic usage, and he asserts that it was observed in almost all provinces. Since, therefore, neither ordination nor confirmation were sought from the bishop of Rome in the greater part of the world, whether in Greek or Latin churches, it is quite apparent that the churches did not attribute superiority and lordship to the bishop of Rome.

[16] 7. Such superiority is impossible, for it is not possible for one bishop to be the overseer of all the churches in the world or for churches situated in remote places to seek ordination from him alone. It is evident that the kingdom of Christ is scattered over all the earth and that there are many churches in the East today which do not seek ordination or confirmation from the bishop of Rome. Consequently, inasmuch as such superiority is impossible and the churches in the greater part of

---

3. *Nic I* can 6. The suburban bishoprics were those of the ten provinces of Italy, not the later suburbicarian dioceses around Rome.

4. *Nic I* can 4.

5. Cyprian *Epistles* 67 to Presbyter Felix and Deacon Aelius; Augustine *On Baptism Against the Donatists* 2.2.

6. In older editions Cyprian's Epistle 67, referred to above, was appended to a letter to Cornelius.

the world never recognized or acted in accordance with it, it is quite apparent that it was not instituted.[7]

[17] 8. Many ancient synods were called and held in which the bishop of Rome did not preside—as the Council of Nicaea and many others. This also shows that the church did not then acknowledge the primacy or superiority of the bishop of Rome.

[18] 9. Jerome says, "If it is authority that you want, the world is greater than the city.[8] Wherever there is a bishop—whether in Rome or Eugubium or Constantinople or Rhegium or Alexandria—he is of the same dignity and priesthood. It is the power of riches or the humility of poverty that makes a bishop superior or inferior."[9]

[19] 10. When writing to the patriarch of Alexandria, Gregory objected to having himself designated as universal bishop.[10] And in the records he states that at the Council of Chalcedon the primacy was offered to the bishop of Rome but he did not accept it.[11]

[20] 11. Finally, how can the pope be over the whole church by divine right when the church elects him and the custom gradually prevailed that the bishops of Rome were confirmed by the emperors?[12]

[21] Again, when there had for a long time been disputes between the bishops of Rome and Constantinople over the primacy, Emperor Phocas had finally decided that the primacy should be assigned to the bishop of Rome.[13] But if the ancient church had acknowledged the primacy of the Roman pontiff, this dispute could not have occurred, nor would a decree of the emperor have been necessary.

[ARGUMENTS OF OPPONENTS REFUTED]

[22] Here certain passages are quoted against us: "You are Peter, and on this rock I will build my church."[a] Again, "I will give you the keys."[b] Again, "Feed my sheep,"[c]

a. [Mt 16.18]
b. [Mt 16.19]
c. [Jn 21.17]

7. German: was not instituted by Christ and does not come from divine right.
8. German adds: That is, the world is greater than the city of Rome.
9. Jerome *Epistle to Euangelus* no. 146.
10. Gregory the Great *Epistles* bk. 8, no. 30, Epistle to Eulogius, bishop of Alexandria.
11. *Epistles* bk. 5, no. 43, Epistle to Eulogius and Anastasius.
12. Emperors Lothair I (824) and Otto I (962) concluded agreements with the popes providing for such confirmation.
13. In 607, Pope Boniface III received from the Byzantine Emperor Phocas an acknowledgment of Rome as "head of all the churches."

and certain other passages. Since this whole controversy has been treated fully and accurately in the books of our theologians [14] and all the details cannot be reviewed here once more, we refer to those writings and wish them to be regarded as re-iterated. [23] Nevertheless, we shall respond briefly by way of interpretation. In all these passages Peter is representative of the entire company of apostles, as is apparent from the text itself, for Christ did not question Peter alone but asked, "Who do

[Mt 16.15]   you say that I am?" And what is here spoken in the singular number ("I will give

[Mt 16.19]   you the keys" and "whatever you bind") is elsewhere given in the plural ("Whatever you bind"),[a] etc. In John, too, it is written, "If you forgive the sins," etc.[b] These words show that the keys were given equally to all the apostles and that all the apostles were sent out as equals. [24] In addition, it is necessary to acknowledge that the keys do not belong to the person of one particular individual but to the whole church, as is shown by many clear and powerful arguments, for after speak-

Mt 18[.19, 20]   ing of the keys in Matthew 18, Christ said, "If two or three of you agree on earth," etc.[15] Therefore, he bestows the keys especially and immediately on the church, and for the same reason the church especially possesses the right of vocation. So it is necessary in these passages to regard Peter as the representative of the entire company of apostles, on which account these passages do not ascribe to Peter any special prerogative, superiority, or power.

[Mt 16.18]   [25] As to the statement, "On this rock I will build my church," it is certain that the church is not built on the authority of a man but on the ministry of the confession which Peter made when he declared Jesus to be the Christ, the Son of God. Therefore Christ addresses Peter as a minister and says, "On this rock," that is, on this ministry. [26] Besides, the ministry of the New Testament is not bound to places and persons, as the Levitical priesthood is, but is spread abroad through the whole world and exists wherever God gives his gifts, apostles, prophets, pastors, teachers. Nor is this ministry valid because of any individual's authority but because of the word given by Christ.[16] [27] Most of the holy fathers (such as Ori-

---

a. [Mt 18.18]
b. Jn [20.23]

14. Luther dealt with these passages often—for example, in *WA*, 2:187–94, 6:309–11, 7:409–15.

15. Conflation of Mt 18.19, 20. German adds: Likewise Christ gives the supreme and final jurisdiction to the church when he says, "Tell it to the church" (Mt 18.17).

16. German adds: The person adds nothing to this word and office commanded by Christ. No matter who it is who preaches and teaches the word, if there are hearts that hear and ad-

gen,[17] Ambrose,[18] Cyprian,[19] Hilary,[20] and Bede[21]) interpret the statement "on this rock" in this way and not as applying to the person or superiority of Peter. [28] So Chrysostom declares that Christ says "on this rock" and not "on Peter," for he built his church not on the man but on the faith of Peter; and what was this faith other than "You are the Christ, the Son of the living God"?[22] [29] Hilary declares: "The Father revealed to Peter that he should say, 'You are the Son of the living God.' On this rock of confession, therefore, the church is built. This faith is the foundation of the church."

[30] As to the passages "Feed my sheep" and "Do you love me more than these?" it in no wise follows that they bestow a special superiority on Peter, for Christ bids Peter to pasture the sheep, that is, to preach the word or govern the church with the word. This commission Peter holds in common with the rest of the apostles.

[Jn 21.17]

[Jn 21.15]

[31] The second article is even clearer than the first because Christ gave the apostles only spiritual power, that is, the command to preach the gospel, proclaim the forgiveness of sins, administer the sacraments, and excommunicate the godless without physical violence. He did not give them the power of the sword or the right to establish, take possession of, or transfer the kingdoms of the world. For Christ said, "Go therefore and teach them to observe all that I have commanded you," and also, "As the Father has sent me, even so I send you." Moreover, it is manifest that Christ was not sent to wield a sword or possess a worldly kingdom, for he said, "My kingship is not of this world." Paul also said, "Not that we lord it over your faith,"[a] and again, "The weapons of our warfare are not worldly,"[b] etc.

[Mt 28.19, 20]

[Jn 20.21]

[Jn 18.36]

[32] That Christ in his passion was crowned with thorns and that he was led forth to be mocked in royal purple signified that the time would come after his spiritual kingdom was despised (that is, after the gospel was suppressed) when another

a. [2 Cor 1.24]
b. [2 Cor 10.4]

here to it, something will happen to them according as they hear and believe because Christ commanded such preaching and demanded that his promises be believed.

17. *Commentary on Matthew* 12.11.

18. Ambrosiaster *Commentary on the Epistle to the Ephesians* 2.20.

19. *The Unity of the Catholic Church* 4.

20. *The Trinity* 6.36, 37.

21. *Exposition of the Gospel of Matthew* 3.16.

22. The exact citation cannot be ascertained, but the reference may be to Chrysostom's *Homilies on Matthew* 54.

worldly kingdom would be set up on the pretext of ecclesiastical power. [33] Wherefore the constitution of Boniface VIII,[23] distinction 22 of the chapter "Omnes,"[24] and other similar statements which claim that the pope is by divine right lord of the kingdoms of the world are false and impious. [34] This notion has caused horrible darkness to descend over the church, and afterwards great disturbances to arise in Europe. The ministry of the gospel was neglected. Knowledge of faith and of a spiritual kingdom was extinguished. Christian righteousness was thought to be that external government which the pope had set up. [35] Then the popes began to seize kingdoms for themselves, transfer kingdoms, and harass the kings of almost all the nations of Europe, but especially the emperors of Germany, with unjust excommunications and wars, sometimes in order to occupy Italian cities and sometimes in order to make the German bishops subject to their power and deprive the emperors of the right to appoint bishops.[25] Indeed, it is even written in the Clementines, "When the imperial throne is vacant, the pope is the legitimate successor."[26] [36]

[Mk 10.42, 43] So the pope not only usurped dominion contrary to the command of Christ, but he even exalted himself tyrannically over all kings. In this matter the act itself is not to be deplored so much as the pretext is to be censured that he can transfer the keys of a worldly kingdom by the authority of Christ and that he can attach salvation to these impious and nefarious opinions by asserting that it is necessary for salvation to believe that such dominion belongs to the pope by divine right. [37] Since these monstrous errors obscure faith and the kingdom of Christ, they are under no circumstances to be ignored. The consequences demonstrate that they have been great plagues in the church.

[38] On the third article this must be added: Even if the bishop of Rome should possess primacy and superiority by divine right, obedience would still not be owing to those pontiffs who defend godless forms of worship, idolatry, and doctrines which conflict with the gospel. On the contrary, such pontiffs and such government ought to be regarded as accursed. So Paul clearly teaches, "If an angel from heaven should preach to you a gospel contrary to that which we preached to you, let him be accursed."[a] And it is written in Acts, "We must obey God rather than men."[b]

a. [Gal 1.8]
b. Acts [5.29]

23. *Unam.*
24. Gratian *Decretum* 1.22.1.
25. The reference is to the Investiture Controversy, which ended with the Concordat of Worms (1122).
26. *Corpus juris canonici Clementinae* 2.2.2.

The canons likewise clearly teach that a heretical pope is not to be obeyed.[27] The Levitical high priest was the supreme pontifex by divine right; nevertheless, godless high priests were not to be obeyed. So Jeremiah and other prophets dissented from them, and the apostles dissented from Caiaphas and were under no obligation to obey him.

[THE MARKS OF THE ANTICHRIST]

[39] But it is manifest that the Roman pontiffs and their adherents defend godless doctrines and godless forms of worship, and it is plain that the marks of the Antichrist coincide with those of the pope's kingdom and his followers. For in describing the Antichrist in his letter to the Thessalonians Paul calls him "an adversary of Christ who opposes and exalts himself against every so-called god or object of worship, so that he takes his seat in the temple of God, proclaiming himself to be God." He speaks therefore of one who rules in the church and not of the kings of nations, and he calls that man "an adversary of Christ" because he will devise doctrines which conflict with the gospel and will arrogate to himself divine authority. [2 Thes 2.3, 4]

[40] On the one hand, it is manifest that the pope rules in the church and that he has set up this kingdom for himself on the pretext of the authority of the church and the ministry, offering as pretext these words, "I will give you the keys." [Mt 16.19] On the other hand, the doctrine of the pope conflicts in many ways with the gospel, and the pope arrogates to himself a threefold divine authority. First, because he assumes for himself the right to change the doctrine of Christ and the worship instituted by God, and he wishes to have his own doctrine and worship observed as divine. Second, because he assumes for himself not only the power to loose and bind in this life but also the jurisdiction over souls after this life. Third, because the pope is unwilling to be judged by the church or by anybody, and he exalts his authority above the decisions of councils and the whole church. Such unwillingness to be judged by the church or by anybody is to make himself out to be God. Finally, he defends such horrible errors and such impiety with the greatest cruelty and puts to death those who dissent.

[41] Since this is the situation, all Christians ought to beware of becoming participants in the impious doctrines, blasphemies, and unjust cruelties of the pope. They ought rather to abandon and execrate the pope and his adherents as the kingdom of the Antichrist. Christ commanded, "Beware of false prophets." Paul also [Mt 7.15] commanded that ungodly teachers should be shunned and execrated as accursed, [Ti 3.10]

---

27. Gratian *Decretum* 1.40.6.

and he wrote in 2 Corinthians 6, "Do not be mismated with unbelievers, for what

2 Cor 6[.14]   fellowship has light with darkness?"

[42] To dissent from the consensus of so many nations and to be called schismatics is a serious matter. But divine authority commands us all not to be associated with and not to support impiety and unjust cruelty. Consequently our consciences are sufficiently excused. The errors of the pope's kingdom are manifest,

[1 Tm 4.1]   and the Scriptures unanimously declare these errors to be doctrines of demons and of the Antichrist. [43] The idolatry in the profanation of masses is manifest, for in addition to other abuses they are shamelessly employed to secure disgraceful profits. [44] The doctrine of repentance has been completely corrupted by the pope and his adherents, who teach that sins are forgiven on account of the worth of our work. Then they bid us to doubt whether forgiveness is obtained. Nowhere do they teach that sins are forgiven freely for Christ's sake and that by this faith we obtain the remission of sins. Thus they obscure the glory of Christ, deprive consciences of a firm consolation, and abolish true worship (that is, the exercise of faith struggling against despair).[28]

[45] They have obscured the teaching concerning sin and have invented a tradition concerning the enumeration of sins which has produced many errors and introduced despair. They have also invented satisfactions, by means of which they have further obscured the benefit of Christ. [46] Out of these arose indulgences, which are nothing but lies devised for the sake of gain. [47] Then there is the invocation of saints—how many abuses and what horrible idolatry it has produced! [48] How many profligate acts have sprung from the tradition of celibacy! With what darkness has the teaching about vows covered the gospel! Here they have feigned that vows produce righteousness before God and merit forgiveness of sins. Thus they have transferred merit from Christ to human traditions and have utterly extinguished the teaching concerning faith. They have pretended that the most trivial traditions are services of God and perfection, and they have preferred these to works performed in callings which God requires and ordained. Such errors are not to be taken lightly, for they detract from the glory of God and bring destruction to souls. Accordingly they cannot be overlooked.

[49] To these errors, then, two great sins must be added. The first is that the pope defends these errors with savage cruelty and punishment. The other is that the pope wrests judgment from the church and does not allow ecclesiastical controversies to be decided in the proper manner. In fact, he contends that he is above coun-

---

28. German: the exercise of faith which struggles against unbelief and despair over the promise of the gospel.

cils and can rescind the decrees of councils, as the canons sometimes impudently declare[29]—yet this was done much more impudently by the pontiffs, as examples show.[30] [50] The ninth question of the third canon states, "No one shall judge the supreme see, for the judge is judged neither by the emperor, nor by all the clergy, nor by kings, nor by the people."[31] [51] Thus the pope exercises a twofold tyranny: he defends his errors by force and murders, and he forbids a judicial examination. The latter does more harm than all the punishments, for when proper judicial process has been taken away, the churches are not able to remove impious teachings and impious forms of worship, and countless souls are lost generation after generation.

[52] Therefore, let the godly consider the enormous errors of the pope's kingdom and his tyranny. They should know, in the first place, that these errors must be rejected and that the true teaching must be embraced for the glory of God and the salvation of souls. [53] Then, in the second place, they should also know how great a crime it is to support unjust cruelty in the murder of saints, whose blood God will undoubtedly avenge.

[54] Especially does it behoove the chief members of the church, the kings and the princes, to have regard for the interests of the church and to see to it that errors are removed and consciences are healed. God expressly exhorts kings, "Now therefore, O kings, be wise; be warned, O rulers of the earth." For the first care of [Ps 2.10] kings should be to advance the glory of God. Wherefore it would be most shameful for them to use their authority and power for the support of idolatry and countless other crimes and for the murder of saints.

[55] Even if the pope should hold synods, how can the church be purified as long as the pope does not permit anything to be decreed contrary to his will and grants nobody the right to express an opinion, except his followers, whom he has bound by horrible oaths and curses to defend his tyranny and wickedness without any regard for the word of God? [56] Since decisions of synods are decisions of the church and not of the pontiffs, it is especially incumbent on the kings to restrain the license of the pontiffs and see to it that the church is not deprived of the power of making judgments and decisions according to the word of God. And as other Christians ought to censure the rest of the pope's errors, so they ought also to rebuke the pope when he evades and obstructs true understanding and true judgment on the part of the church.

[57] Accordingly, even if the bishop of Rome did possess the primacy by

---

29. E.g., Gratian *Decretum* 1.16, 17, 19, 21.

30. Cf. the bull *Execrabilis* by Pius II (1460).

31. Gratian *Decretum* 2.9.3.13.

divine right, he should not be obeyed inasmuch as he defends impious forms of worship and doctrines which are in conflict with the gospel. On the contrary, it is necessary to resist him as Antichrist.

[58] The errors of the pope are manifest, and they are not trifling. Manifest, too, is the cruelty which he employs against the godly. And it is the clear command of God that we should flee from idolatry, impious doctrines, and unjust cruelty. Therefore all the godly have weighty, compelling, and evident reasons for not submitting to the pope, and these urgent reasons are a comfort to the godly when, as often happens, they are reproached for scandal, schism, and discord. [59] On the other hand, those who agree with the pope and defend his doctrines and forms of worship defile themselves with idolatry and blasphemous opinions, make themselves guilty of the blood of the godly whom the pope persecutes, detract from the glory of God, and hinder the welfare of the church by so strengthening errors and other crimes as to impose them on all posterity.

THE POWER AND JURISDICTION OF BISHOPS

In the Confession and in the Apology[32] we have set forth in general terms what we have to say about ecclesiastical power.

[60] The gospel requires of those who preside over the churches that they preach the gospel, remit sins, administer the sacraments, and, in addition, exercise jurisdiction, that is, excommunicate those who are guilty of notorious crimes and absolve those who repent. [61] By the confession of all, even of our adversaries, it is evident that this power belongs by divine right to all who preside over the churches, whether they are called pastors, presbyters, or bishops. [62] Accordingly Jerome teaches clearly that in the apostolic letters all who preside over the churches are both bishops and presbyters. He quotes from Titus, "This is why I left you in Crete, that you might appoint presbyters in every town," and points out that these words

Ti [1.5-7]   are followed by, "A bishop must be married only once." Again, Peter and John call themselves presbyters.[a] And Jerome observes: "One man was chosen over the rest to prevent schism, lest several persons, by gathering separate followings around themselves, rend the church of Christ. For in Alexandria, from the time of Mark the Evangelist to the time of Bishops Heracles and Dionysius, the presbyters always chose one of their number, set him in a higher place, and called him bishop. Moreover, in the same way in which an army might select a commander for itself, the

a. [1]Pt [5.1]; [2] Jn [1]; [3] Jn [1]

32. *Aug 28; Apol Aug 28.*

deacons may choose from their number one who is known to be active and name him archdeacon. For, apart from ordination, what does a bishop do that a presbyter does not do?"[33]

[63] Jerome therefore teaches that the distinction between the grades of bishop and presbyter (or pastor) is by human authority. The fact itself bears witness to this, for the power is the same, as I have already stated. [64] Afterwards one thing made a distinction between bishops and pastors, and this was ordination, for it was decided that one bishop should ordain the ministers in a number of churches. [65] But since the distinction between bishop and pastor is not by divine right, it is manifest that ordination administered by a pastor in his own church is valid by divine right. [66] Consequently, when the regular bishops become enemies of the gospel and are unwilling to administer ordination,[34] the churches retain the right to ordain for themselves. [67] For wherever the church exists, the right to administer the gospel also exists. Wherefore it is necessary for the church to retain the right of calling, electing, and ordaining ministers.

This right is a gift given exclusively to the church, and no human authority can take it away from the church. It is as Paul testifies to the Ephesians when he says, "When he ascended on high he gave gifts to men." He enumerates pastors and teachers among the gifts belonging exclusively to the church, and he adds that they are given for the work of ministry and for building up the body of Christ. Where the true church is, therefore, the right of electing and ordaining ministers must of necessity also be. So in an emergency even a layman absolves and becomes the minister and pastor of another. It is like the example which Augustine relates of two Christians in a ship, one of whom baptized the other (a catechumen), and the latter, after his baptism, absolved the former.[35] [68] Here the words of Christ apply which testify that the keys were given to the church and not merely to certain individuals: "Where two or three are gathered in my name, there am I in the midst of them." Eph [4.8, 11, 12]

[Mt 18.20]

[69] Finally, this is confirmed by the declaration of Peter, "You are a royal priesthood." These words apply to the true church which, since it alone possesses the priesthood, certainly has the right of electing and ordaining ministers. [70] The most common custom of the church also bears witness to this, for there was a time when the people elected pastors and bishops. Afterwards a bishop, either of that church or of a neighboring church, was brought in to confirm the election with the [1] Pt [2.9]

---

33. Jerome *Epistle to Euangelus*. Following an old text Melanchthon wrote "Esdras" instead of "Heracles" in the quotation.

34. German: to ordain suitable persons.

35. Gratian *Decretum* 3.4.36, where a letter of Augustine to Fortunatus is cited.

laying on of hands; nor was ordination anything more than such confirmation. [71] Later on new ceremonies were added, many of which Dionysius describes; but he is a late and fictitious writer, whoever he may be,[36] just as the writings of Clement are spurious.[37] Still more recent writers added the words, "I give thee the power to sacrifice for the living and the dead."[38] But not even this is found in Dionysius!

[72] From all these facts it is evident that the church retains the right of electing and ordaining ministers. Wherefore, when the bishops are heretics or refuse to administer ordination, the churches are by divine right compelled to ordain pastors and ministers for themselves. And it is the wickedness and tyranny of the bishops that give occasion to schism and discord, for Paul commands that bishops who teach and defend impious doctrines and impious forms of worship should be re-
[Gal 1.7–9]   garded as anathema.

[73] We have spoken of ordination, which is the one thing (as Jerome states) that distinguishes bishops from the rest of the presbyters. There is no need, therefore, for discussion of the other functions of bishops. Nor is it necessary to speak about confirmation[39] or the blessings of bells, which are almost the only things they have retained for themselves. Something, however, must be said about jurisdiction.

[74] It is certain that the common jurisdiction of excommunicating those who are guilty of manifest crimes belongs to all pastors. This the bishops have tyrannically reserved for themselves alone and have employed for gain. For it is evident that the officials (as they are called) have exercised intolerable arbitrariness and, either on account of avarice or on account of other evil desires, have tormented men and excommunicated them without due process of law. What tyranny it is for civil officers to have the power to ban men arbitrarily without due process of law! [75] And in what kinds of cases they have abused this power! Not in punishing real offenses, but in dealing with nonobservance of fasts or festivals and similar trifles. To be sure, they sometimes punished persons involved in adultery, but in this connection they often harassed innocent and honest men. Besides, since this is a very seri-

---

36. Pseudo-Dionysius the Areopagite *The Celestial Hierarchy* 5. A writer of the fifth century; the genuineness of his writings was questioned by humanists.

37. The so-called *Recognitions,* attributed to Clement of Rome but probably written a century later.

38. This formula, by which Roman priests were given the power to offer the sacrifice of the mass, was introduced in the tenth century.

39. Here the reference is to the Roman sacrament of confirmation, not to the confirmation of elections, as above. The German text reads: confirmation [*Firmelung*], the blessing of the bells, and other humbug of this sort.

ous charge, nobody should be condemned without due process of law. [76] Since, therefore, the bishops have tyrannically reserved this jurisdiction for themselves and have shamefully abused it, there is no need, on account of this jurisdiction, to obey the bishops. And since we have good reason for not obeying, it is right to restore this jurisdiction to godly pastors and see to it that it is used properly for the reformation of morals and the glory of God.

[77] There remains jurisdiction in those cases which according to canon law pertain to ecclesiastical courts (as they call them), especially matrimonial cases. This, too, the bishops have by human right only, and they have not had it for long, for it appears from the *Codex* and *Novellae* of Justinian[40] that decisions in matrimonial cases had formerly belonged to the magistrate. By divine right temporal magistrates are compelled to make these decisions if the bishops are negligent. This is conceded by the canons.[41] Wherefore it is not necessary to obey the bishops on account of this jurisdiction either. [78] And since they have framed certain unjust laws concerning marriage and apply them in their courts, there is additional reason why other courts should be established. For the traditions concerning spiritual relationship are unjust,[42] and equally unjust is the tradition which forbids an innocent person to marry after divorce. Unjust, too, is the law that in general approves all clandestine and underhanded betrothals in violation of the right of parents. The law concerning the celibacy of priests is likewise unjust. There are also other snares of conscience in their laws, but it would not be profitable to enumerate all of them here.

It is enough to have pointed out that there are many unjust papal laws on matrimonial questions and that on this account the magistrates ought to establish other courts.

[79] Since therefore the bishops who are adherents of the pope defend impious doctrines and impious forms of worship and do not ordain godly teachers but rather support the cruelty of the pope; since, in addition, they have wrested jurisdiction from the pastors and tyrannically exercise it alone; and since, finally, they observe unjust laws in matrimonial cases; there are sufficiently numerous and compelling reasons why the churches should not recognize them as bishops. [80] They themselves should remember that riches have been given to bishops as alms for the administration and profit of the churches, as the rule states, "The benefice

40. Justinian Code 5.1–27.
41. Gregory *Decretum* 9.5.26.2.
42. German: the prohibition of marriage between sponsors is unjust.

is given because of the office."[43] Wherefore they cannot possess these alms with a good conscience. Meanwhile they defraud the church, which needs these means for the support of ministers, the promotion of education, the care of the poor, and the establishment of courts, especially courts for matrimonial cases. [81] The variety and number of matrimonial disputes are so great that they require special courts, but these cannot be established without the endowments of the church. [82] Peter [2] Pt [2.13, 15] predicted that there would be wicked bishops in the future who would consume the alms of the churches for luxuries and would neglect the ministry. Let those who defraud the church know that God will require them to pay for their crime.

LIST OF THE DOCTORS AND PREACHERS WHO SUBSCRIBED THE CONFESSION AND APOLOGY, 1537

According to the command of the most illustrious princes and of the estates and cities professing the doctrine of the gospel, we have re-read the articles of the Confession presented to the emperor in the Diet of Augsburg and, by the favor of God, all the preachers who have been present in this assembly in Smalcald unanimously declare that in their churches they believe and teach in conformity with the articles of the Confession and Apology. They also declare that they approve the article concerning the primacy of the pope and the power and jurisdiction of the bishops which was presented to the princes here in this assembly in Smalcald. Accordingly they subscribe their names.

I, Dr. John Bugenhagen, of Pomerania, subscribe the articles of the Augsburg Confession, the Apology, and the article concerning the papacy presented to the princes in Smalcald

I also, Dr. Urban Rhegius, superintendent of the churches in the duchy of Lüneburg, subscribe

Nicholas Amsdorf, of Magdeburg, subscribed

George Spalatin, of Altenburg, subscribed

I, Andrew Osiander, subscribe

Master Veit Dietrich, of Nuremberg, subscribes

Stephen Agricola, minister in Chur, subscribed with his own hand

John Drach, of Marburg, subscribed

Conrad Figenbotz subscribes to all throughout

Martin Bucer

I, Erhard Schnepf, subscribe

Paul Rhode, preacher in Stettin

---

43. *Corpus juris canonici* 6.1.3.15.

Gerard Oemcken, minister of the church in Minden

Brixius Northanus, minister in Soest

Simon Schneeweiss, pastor at Crailsheim

I, Pomeranus,[44] again subscribe in the name of Master John Brenz, as he commanded me

Philipp Melanchthon subscribes with his own hand

Anthony Corvinus subscribes with his own hand both in his name and in that of Adam of Fulda

John Schlagenhaufen subscribes with his own hand

George Helt, of Forchheim

Michael Caelius, preacher in Mansfeld

Peter Geltner, preacher in the church in Frankfurt

David Melander subscribed

Paul Fagius, of Strasbourg

Wendel Faber, pastor of Seeburg in Mansfeld

Conrad Oettinger, of Pforzheim, preacher of Ulric, duke of Württemberg

Boniface Wolfart, minister of the word in the church in Augsburg

John Aepinus, superintendent in Hamburg, subscribed with his own hand

John Amsterdam, of Bremen, did the same

John Fontanus, superintendent of Lower Hesse, subscribed

Frederick Myconius subscribed for himself and for Justus Menius

Ambrose Blaurer

44. John Bugenhagen, of Pomerania.

As second-generation Lutherans struggled to deal with such setbacks as the military defeat in the Smalcald War (1547) and the imposition of the Augsburg Interim (1548), divisions occurred within their own ranks as to the proper interpretation of doctrine. The so-called Gnesio-Lutherans claimed strict adherence to Lutheran doctrine and rejected any rapprochement with Catholics or Calvinists. Philippists, named for Philipp Melanchthon, took the view that Lutherans should be willing to make concessions on *adiaphora* ("matters of no consequence") in the interest of peace, as Melanchthon had done at the time of the Leipzig Interim (December 1548).

In addition to this Adiaphorist Controversy, the two sides could not agree on some basic issues concerning good works, free will and original sin, justification, and even the understanding of the Lord's supper. The struggle for dominance in the years after Luther's death involved polemical writings and political maneuvering. Almost from the beginning, however, there were also efforts at reconciliation.[1]

Proposals were made to end the conflict, most importantly by Jakob Andreae (1528–90), Martin Chemnitz (1522–86), Lucas Osiander (1534–1604), and Balthasar Bidembach (1533–78), whose various works formed the bases of *The Swabian-Saxon Concord* (1575) and *The Maulbronn Formula* (1576).[2] These documents were combined at a meeting of theologians in Torgau (28 May–7 June 1576). The resulting *Torgau Book,* as summarized by Jakob Andreae, is called *The Epitome.* The full text of the *Torgau Book* was revised in May 1577 at a meeting held at Bergen Abbey and became known as *The Solid Declaration.* These two texts, together with a preface, make up *The Formula of Concord* of 1577, a document intended to provide a definitive interpretation of → *The Augsburg Confession* acceptable to both strict Gnesio-Lutherans and moderate Philippists. For the most part, *The Formula of Concord* upholds more conservative positions. Some accommodations were made, however, as in the article on good works, which modifies the more negative formulations of the Gnesio-Lutherans—some of whom had gone so far as to declare good works deleterious to salvation—in favor of an interpretation closer to that of Luther and Melanchthon.

The Formula of Concord achieved its aim. Thousands of Lutheran ministers

---

1. See Spitz and Lohff 1977 and Tschackert [1910] 1979 for discussions of the various reconciliation attempts leading up to the *Formula.*
2. For a more detailed discussion of the controversies, see Kolb-Wengert, 481–85.

subscribed to the document, and it gained the support of most Lutheran communities and rulers in Germany.[3] In 1580, *The Formula of Concord* and other defining statements of Lutheran theology and doctrine were gathered in *The Book of Concord*. In addition to *The Formula of Concord*, *The Book of Concord* includes → *The Augsburg Confession*, its → *Apology*, → *The Smalcald Articles* and the appended → *Treatise on the Power and Primacy of the Pope*, and Luther's → *Large* and → *Small Catechisms*, as well as the chief creedal statements of the Western Church (→ *Apostles'*, → *Nicene*, and → *Athanasian Creeds*). *The Book of Concord* was printed simultaneously by several publishers and issued on 25 June 1580, the fiftieth anniversary of the reading of *The Augsburg Confession* before the emperor. It remains the confessional norm of doctrine for Lutherans.

Edition: *BLK* 767–1100 (German only).

Translation: Tappert (i.e., Piepkorn), 464–636.

Note: The original is in German. Five separate Latin translations were made between 1580 and 1584. Since 1584 the authorized text of *The Book of Concord* has included the text in both languages.

Literature: Bente [1921] 1965; Brecht and Schwartz 1980; Ebel 1978, 1980, 1981; Frank 1858–65; Green 1977; Hägglund 1981; Jungkuntz 1977a, 1977b; Kingdon 1977; Koelpin 1980; Kolb 1977; Kolb-Wengert, 481–85; Lohse 1980b; Manschreck 1957; Mehlhausen 1980; *OER* 2:117–21 (Kolb); Spitz and Lohff 1977; Themel 1973; *TRE* 19:472–83 (Koch); Wenz 1996.

---

3. Some notable exceptions were Braunschweig-Wolfenbüttel, Strasbourg, and Holstein.

[Part 1. Epitome]
A Summary Epitome of the Articles in Controversy Among the Theologians of the Augsburg Confession Expounded and Settled in Christian Fashion in Conformity with God's Word in the Recapitulation Here Following

THE COMPREHENSIVE SUMMARY, RULE, AND NORM
ACCORDING TO WHICH ALL DOCTRINES SHOULD BE JUDGED
AND THE ERRORS WHICH INTRUDED SHOULD BE
EXPLAINED AND DECIDED IN A CHRISTIAN WAY

[1] 1. We believe, teach, and confess that the prophetic and apostolic writings of the Old and New Testaments are the only rule and norm according to which all doctrines and teachers alike must be appraised and judged, as it is written in Psalms

Ps 119[.105] 119, "Thy word is a lamp to my feet and a light to my path." And St. Paul says in
Gal 1[.8] Galatians 1 "Even if an angel from heaven should preach to you a gospel contrary to that which we preached to you, let him be accursed."

[2] Other writings of ancient and modern teachers, whatever their names, should not be put on a par with Holy Scripture. Every single one of them should be subordinated to the Scriptures and should be received in no other way and no further than as witnesses to the fashion in which the doctrine of the prophets and apostles was preserved in postapostolic times.

[3] 2. Immediately after the time of the apostles—in fact, already during their lifetime—false teachers and heretics invaded the church. Against these the ancient church formulated symbols (that is, brief and explicit confessions) which were accepted as the unanimous, catholic, Christian faith and confessions of the orthodox and true church, namely, *The Apostles' Creed, The Nicene Creed,* and *The Athanasian Creed.* We pledge ourselves to these, and we hereby reject all heresies and teachings which have been introduced into the church of God contrary to them.

[4] 3. With reference to the schism in matters of faith which has occurred in our times, we regard, as the unanimous consensus and exposition of our Christian faith, particularly against the false worship, idolatry, and superstition of the papacy and against other sects, and as the symbol of our time, the first and unaltered *Augsburg Confession,* which was delivered to Emperor Charles V at Augsburg during the great diet in the year 1530, together with the *Apology* thereof and the *Articles* drafted at Smalcald in the year 1537, which the leading theologians approved by their subscription at that time.

[5] Since these matters also concern the laity and the salvation of their souls, we subscribe Dr. Luther's *Small* and *Large Catechisms* as both of them are contained in his printed works. They are "the layman's Bible" and contain everything which Holy Scripture discusses at greater length and which a Christian must know for his salvation.

[6] All doctrines should conform to the standards set forth above. Whatever is contrary to them should be rejected and condemned as opposed to the unanimous declaration of our faith.

[7] In this way the distinction between the Holy Scripture of the Old and New Testaments and all other writings is maintained, and Holy Scripture remains the only judge, rule, and norm according to which as the only touchstone all doctrines should and must be understood and judged as good or evil, right or wrong.

[8] Other symbols and other writings are not judges like Holy Scripture, but merely witnesses and expositions of the faith, setting forth how at various times the Holy Scriptures were understood in the church of God by contemporaries with reference to controverted articles, and how contrary teachings were rejected and condemned.

1. Original Sin

THE QUESTION AT ISSUE

[1] The principal question in this controversy is if, strictly and without any distinction, original sin is man's corrupted nature, substance, and essence, or indeed the principal and best part of his being (that is, his rational soul in its highest form and powers). Or if there is a distinction, even after the fall, between man's substance, nature, essence, body, and soul on the one hand, and original sin on the other hand, so that man's nature is one thing and original sin, which inheres in the corrupted nature and corrupts it, is something else.

AFFIRMATIVE THESES
The Pure Doctrine, Faith, and Confession According to the Aforesaid Standard and Comprehensive Exposition

[2] 1. We believe, teach, and confess that there is a distinction between man's nature and original sin, not only in the beginning when God created man pure and holy and without sin, but also as we now have our nature after the fall. Even after the fall our nature is and remains a creature of God. The distinction between our nature and original sin is as great as the difference between God's work and the devil's work.

[3] 2. We also believe, teach, and confess that we must preserve this distinction most diligently, because the view that admits no distinction between our corrupted human nature and original sin militates against and cannot coexist with the chief articles of our Christian faith, namely, creation, redemption, sanctification, and the resurrection of our flesh.

[4] God not only created the body and soul of Adam and Eve before the fall, but also our bodies and souls after the fall, even though they are corrupted, and God still acknowledges them as his handiwork, as it is written, Job 10, "Thy hands fashioned and made me, all that I am round about."

Jb 10[.8]

[5] Furthermore, the Son of God assumed into the unity of his person this same human nature, though without sin, and thus took on himself not alien flesh, but our own, and according to our flesh has truly become our brother. Hebrews 2, "Since therefore the children share in flesh and blood, he himself likewise partook of the same nature. . . . For surely it is not with angels that he is concerned but with the descendants of Abraham. Therefore he had to be made like his brethren in every respect," sin excepted.

Heb 2[.14–17]

[6] Thus Christ has redeemed our nature as his creation, sanctifies it as his creation, quickens it from the dead as his creation, and adorns it gloriously as his creation. But he has not created original sin, has not assumed it, has not redeemed it, has not sanctified it, will not quicken it in the elect, will not glorify it or save it. On the contrary, in the resurrection it will be utterly destroyed. [7] These points clearly set forth the distinction between the corrupted nature itself and the corruption which is in the nature and which has corrupted the nature.

[8] 3. On the other hand, we believe, teach, and confess that original sin is not a slight corruption of human nature, but that it is so deep a corruption that nothing sound or uncorrupted has survived in man's body or soul, in his inward or outward powers. It is as the church sings, "Through Adam's fall man's nature and essence are all corrupt."[1]

[9] This damage is so unspeakable that it may not be recognized by a rational process, but only from God's word.

[10] No one except God alone can separate the corruption of our nature from the nature itself. This will take place wholly by way of death in the resurrection. Then the nature which we now bear will arise and live forever, without original sin and completely separated and removed from it, as Job 19 asserts, "I shall be

Jb 19[.26–27]

---

1. "Durch Adams Fall ist ganz vorderbet menschlich Natur und Wesen," from a hymn by Lazarus Spengler (1524). See Wackernagel 1870, 3:48 (no. 71).

covered by this my skin, and in my flesh I shall see God; him I shall see for myself, and mine eyes shall behold him."

ANTITHESES
Rejection of the Contrary False Teaching

[11] 1. Accordingly we reject and condemn the teaching that original sin is only a debt which we owe because of someone else's wrongdoing, without any kind of corruption of our own nature.

[12] 2. Likewise the teaching that evil desires are not sin but concreated and essential properties of human nature, or the teaching that the cited defect and damage is not truly sin on account of which man outside of Christ is a child of wrath.

[13] 3. We likewise reject the Pelagian error which asserts that man's nature is uncorrupted even after the fall, and especially that in spiritual things its natural powers remained wholly good and pure.

[14] 4. Likewise the teaching that original sin is a slight, insignificant spot or blemish that has only been sprinkled or splashed on externally and that underneath man's nature has retained unimpaired its powers for good even in spiritual things.

[15] 5. Furthermore, that original sin is only an external impediment to man's good spiritual powers and not the complete deprivation or loss of the same, just as garlic juice, smeared upon a magnet, impedes but does not remove the natural powers of the magnet; likewise the view that this blemish may be removed as readily as a spot can be washed from the face or color from the wall.

[16] 6. Furthermore, that the human nature and essence in man is not entirely corrupted, but that man still has something good about him even in spiritual matters—for example, the capacity, skill, capability, or power to initiate, to effect, or to cooperate in something spiritual.

[17] 7. We also reject the Manichaean error that original sin is an essential, self-existing something which Satan infused into and mingled with human nature, as when poison and wine are mixed.

[18] 8. Likewise, that it is not the natural man himself who commits sin but something extraneous and alien within man, and that therefore not the nature of man but only the original sin which is in the nature is being accused.

[19] 9. We also reject and condemn as a Manichaean error the teaching that original sin is strictly and without any distinction corrupted man's substance, nature, and essence, so that no distinction should be made, even in the mind, be-

tween man's nature itself after the fall and original sin, and that the two cannot be differentiated in the mind.

[20] [10.] Luther calls original sin "nature-sin," "person-sin," "essential sin," not in order to identify without any distinction man's nature, person, or essence itself with original sin but by such terminology to indicate the difference between original sin, which inheres in human nature, and the other so-called actual sins.

[21] [11.] For original sin is not a sin which man commits; it inheres in the nature, substance, and essence of man in such a way that even if no evil thought would ever arise in the heart of corrupted man, no idle word were spoken, or no wicked act or deed took place, nevertheless man's nature is corrupted through original sin, innate in us through our sinful seed and the source of all other, actual sins, such as evil thoughts, words, and deeds, as it is written, "Out of the heart come evil thoughts,"[a] etc., and "The imagination of man's heart is evil from his youth."[b]

[22] [12.] It is important to observe that the word "nature" has several meanings. This enables the Manichaeans to conceal their error and to mislead many simple people. Sometimes the term means man's essence, as when we say, "God has created human nature." At other times the word means the good or bad quality which inheres in the nature or essence of a thing, as when we say, "It is the nature of a serpent to sting," and, "It is the nature or quality of a man to sin," or, "Man's nature is sin." Here the word "nature" does not mean the substance of man but something which inheres in the nature or substance.

[23] [13.] As far as the Latin words *substantia* and *accidens* are concerned, they are not biblical terms and, besides, they are unknown to the common man. They should therefore not be employed in sermons delivered to common, unlearned people, but simple folk should be spared them.

[24] [14.] In schools and learned circles these words can profitably be retained in the discussion of original sin because they are familiar and convey no false impressions, and they clearly show the distinction between the essence of a particular thing and that which pertains to it only accidentally.

[25] [15.] This terminology sets forth very clearly the distinction between God's work and Satan's work. Satan cannot create a substance; he can only, with God's permission, corrupt accidentally the substance which God has created.

a. [Mt 15.19]
b. [Gn 8.21, 6.5]

2. Free Will

THE QUESTION AT ISSUE IN THIS CONTROVERSY

The will of man may be discussed in four different states: (1) before the fall, (2) after the fall, (3) after regeneration, (4) after the resurrection of the flesh. In this controversy the primary question revolves exclusively about man's will and ability in the second state. The question is, What powers does man possess in spiritual matters after the fall of our first parents and before his regeneration? Can man by his own powers, before he is reborn through the Holy Spirit, dispose and prepare himself for the grace of God? Can he or can he not accept the grace of God offered in the word and the holy sacraments?

AFFIRMATIVE THESES

The Pure Teaching Concerning This Article on the Basis of God's Word

[2] 1. It is our teaching, faith, and confession that in spiritual matters man's understanding and reason are blind and that he understands nothing by his own powers, as it is written: "The unspiritual man does not receive the gifts of the Spirit of God, for they are folly to him, and he is not able to understand them" when he is examined [1 Cor 2.14] concerning spiritual things.

[3] 2. Likewise we believe, teach, and confess that man's unregenerated will is not only turned away from God, but has also become an enemy of God, so that he desires and wills only that which is evil and opposed to God, as it is written, "The imagination of man's heart is evil from his youth." Likewise, "The mind that is set [Gn 8.21] on the flesh is hostile to God; it does not submit to God's law, indeed it cannot." [Rom 8.7] As little as a corpse can quicken itself to bodily, earthly life, so little can man who through sin is spiritually dead raise himself to spiritual life, as it is written, "When we were dead through our trespasses, he made us alive together with Christ." There- [Eph 2.5] fore we are not of ourselves "sufficient to claim anything as coming from us; our sufficiency is from God," 2 Corinthians 3.   2 Cor 3[.5]

[4] 3. God the Holy Spirit, however, does not effect conversion without means; he employs to this end the preaching and the hearing of God's word, as it is written in Romans 1 that the gospel is a "power of God" for salvation; likewise,   Rom 1[.16] that faith comes from the hearing of God's word, Romans 10. [5] It is God's will   Rom 10[.17] that men should hear his word and not stop their ears. The Holy Spirit is present   [Ps 95.8] with this word and opens hearts so that, like Lydia in Acts 16, they heed it and thus   Acts 16[.14] are converted solely through the grace and power of the Holy Spirit, for man's conversion is the Spirit's work alone. [6] Without his grace our "will and effort," our   [Rom 9.16] planting, sowing, and watering are in vain unless he "gives the growth." Christ also   [1 Cor 3.7]

[Jn 15.5]   states, "Apart from me you can do nothing." In these few words he denies all power
              to free will and ascribes everything to the grace of God, so that no one might boast
[1 Cor 9[.16]   in the presence of God, 1 Corinthians 9.

ANTITHESES
Contrary False Doctrine

[7] Accordingly we reject and condemn all the following errors as being contrary
to the norm of the word of God:

[8] 1. The mad dream of the so-called Stoic philosophers and of Manichaeans, who taught that whatever happens must so happen and could not happen otherwise, that man always acts only under compulsion, even in his external acts, and
that he commits evil deeds and acts like fornication, robbery, murder, theft, and
similar sins under compulsion.

[9] 2. We also reject the error of the crass Pelagians, who taught that by his
own powers, without the grace of the Holy Spirit, man can convert himself to God,
believe the gospel, wholeheartedly obey God's law, and thus merit forgiveness of
sins and eternal life.

[10] 3. We also reject the error of the Semi-Pelagians, who teach that man
by virtue of his own powers could make a beginning of his conversion but could
not complete it without the grace of the Holy Spirit.

[11] 4. Likewise the teaching that while before his conversion man is indeed
too weak by his free will to make a beginning, convert himself to God, and wholeheartedly obey God's law by his own powers, yet after the Holy Spirit has made
the beginning through the preaching of the word and in it has offered his grace,
man's will is forthwith able by its own natural powers to add something (though
it be little and feeble) to help, to cooperate, to prepare itself for grace, to dispose
itself, to apprehend and accept it, and to believe the gospel.

[12] 5. Likewise that after his conversion man is able to keep the law of God
perfectly and entirely and that this fulfilling constitutes our righteousness before
God whereby we merit eternal life.

[13] 6. Likewise we reject and condemn the error of the Enthusiasts,[2] who
imagine that God draws men to himself, enlightens them, justifies them, and saves
them without means, without the hearing of God's word and without the use of the
holy sacraments.

---

2. A marginal note here: "Enthusiasts is the term for people who expect the Spirit's heavenly
illumination without the preaching of God's word."

[14] 7. Likewise that in conversion and rebirth God wholly destroys the substance and essence of the Old Adam, especially the rational soul, and that in conversion and rebirth he creates out of nothing a new essence of the soul.

[15] 8. Likewise when these statements are made without explanation that man's will before, in, and after conversion resists the Holy Spirit, and that the Holy Spirit is given to such as resist him purposely and persistently. For as Augustine says, in conversion God makes willing people out of unwilling people and dwells in the willing ones.[3]

[16] Some ancient and modern teachers have used expressions such as, "God draws, but draws the person who is willing," or, "Man's will is not idle in conversion, but does something." Since these expressions have been introduced to confirm the role of natural free will in conversion contrary to the doctrine of the grace of God, we hold that these expressions do not agree with the form of sound doctrine and that accordingly it is well to avoid them in a discussion of conversion to God.

[17] On the other hand, it is correct to say that in conversion, through the attraction of the Holy Spirit, God changes stubborn and unwilling people into willing people, and that after conversion, in the daily exercise of repentance, the reborn will of man is not idle but cooperates in all the works which the Holy Spirit performs through us.

[18] 9. Likewise Luther's statement that man's will in conversion behaves "altogether passively" (that is, that it does nothing at all) must be understood as referring to the action of divine grace in kindling new movements within the will, that is, when the Spirit of God through the word that has been heard or through the use of the holy sacraments takes hold of man's will and works the new birth and conversion. But after the Holy Spirit has performed and accomplished this and the will of man has been changed and renewed solely by God's power and activity, man's new will becomes an instrument and means of God the Holy Spirit, so that man not only lays hold on grace but also cooperates with the Holy Spirit in the works that follow.

[19] Prior to man's conversion there are only two efficient causes, namely, the Holy Spirit and the word of God as the Holy Spirit's instrument whereby he effects conversion. Man should hear this word, though he cannot give it credence and accept it by his own powers but solely by the grace and operation of God the Holy Spirit.

---

3. *Against Two Letters of the Pelagians* 1.19.37.

3. The Righteousness of Faith Before God
THE QUESTION AT ISSUE

[1] It is the unanimous confession of our churches according to the word of God and the content of *The Augsburg Confession* that we poor sinners are justified before God and saved solely by faith in Christ, so that Christ alone is our righteousness. He is truly God and man since in him the divine and human natures are personally united to one another, Jeremiah 23, 1 Corinthians 1, 2 Corinthians 5.[a] Because of the foregoing a question has arisen, According to which nature is Christ our righteousness? Two false and mutually contradictory teachings have invaded some churches.

[2] One party has held that Christ is our righteousness only according to his Godhead. When he dwells in us by faith, over against this indwelling Godhead, the sins of all men are esteemed like a drop of water over against the immense ocean. Others, however, held that Christ is our righteousness before God only according to the human nature.

AFFIRMATIVE THESES
The Pure Doctrine of the Christian Church Against Both These Errors

[3] 1. In opposition to these two errors just recounted, we believe, teach, and confess unanimously that Christ is our righteousness neither according to the divine nature alone nor according to the human nature alone. On the contrary, the entire Christ according to both natures is our righteousness solely in his obedience which as God and man he rendered to his heavenly Father into death itself. Thereby he won for us the forgiveness of sins and eternal life, as it is written, "For as by one man's disobedience many were made sinners, so by one man's obedience many will be made righteous," Romans 5.

Rom 5[.19]

[4] 2. Accordingly we believe, teach, and confess that our righteousness before God consists in this, that God forgives us our sins purely by his grace, without any preceding, present, or subsequent work, merit, or worthiness, and reckons to us the righteousness of Christ's obedience, on account of which righteousness we are accepted by God into grace and are regarded as righteous.

[5] 3. We believe, teach, and confess that faith is the only means and instrument whereby we accept Christ and in Christ obtain the "righteousness which avails before God,"[b] and that for Christ's sake such faith is reckoned for righteousness,[c] Romans 4.

a. Jer 23[.6]; 1 Cor 1[.30]; 2 Cor 5[.21]
b. [Rom 1.17]
c. Rom 4[.5]

[6] 4. We believe, teach, and confess that this faith is not a mere knowledge of the stories about Christ, but the kind of gift of God by which in the word of the gospel we recognize Christ aright as our redeemer and trust in him, so that solely because of his obedience, by grace, we have forgiveness of sins, are regarded as holy and righteous by God the Father, and shall be saved eternally.

[7] 5. We believe, teach, and confess that according to the usage of Scripture the word "justify" means in this article "absolve," that is, pronounce free from sin. "He who justifies the wicked and he who condemns the righteous are both alike an abomination to the Lord," Proverbs 17; likewise, "Who shall bring any charge against God's elect? It is God who justifies," Romans 8. [8] Sometimes, as in the Apology, the words *regeneratio* (rebirth) and *vivificatio* (making alive) are used in place of justification, and then they mean the same thing, even though otherwise these terms refer to the renovation of man and distinguish it from justification by faith.

Prv 17[.15]

Rom 8[.33]

[9] 6. We also believe, teach, and confess that, although the genuinely believing and truly regenerated persons retain much weakness and many shortcomings down to their graves, they still have no reason to doubt either the righteousness which is reckoned to them through faith or the salvation of their souls, but they must regard it as certain that for Christ's sake, on the basis of the promises and the word of the holy gospel, they have a gracious God.

[10] 7. We believe, teach, and confess that if we would preserve the pure doctrine concerning the righteousness of faith before God, we must give special attention to the "exclusive terms," that is, to those words of the holy apostle Paul which separate the merit of Christ completely from our own works and give all glory to Christ alone. Thus the holy apostle Paul uses such expressions as "by grace," "without merit," "without the law," "without works," "not by works," etc.[a] All these expressions say in effect that we become righteous and are saved "alone by faith" in Christ.

[11] 8. We believe, teach, and confess that the contrition that precedes justification and the good works that follow it do not belong in the article of justification before God. Nevertheless, we should not imagine a kind of faith in this connection that could coexist and co-persist with a wicked intention to sin and to act contrary to one's conscience. On the contrary, after a person has been justified by faith, a true living faith becomes "active through love," Galatians 5. Thus good works always follow justifying faith and are certainly to be found with it, since such faith is never alone but is always accompanied by love and hope.

Gal 5[.6]

a. [Rom 6.46, 3.20, 21, 24, 28, 11.6; Gal 2.16; Eph 2.9; Ti 3.5]

ANTITHESES
Rejection of the Contrary Doctrine

[12] Accordingly we reject and condemn all the following errors:

[13] 1. That Christ is our righteousness only according to the divine nature, etc.

[14] 2. That Christ is our righteousness only according to the human nature, etc.

[15] 3. That when the righteousness of faith is spoken of in the pronouncements of the prophets and apostles, the words "to justify" and "to be justified" do not mean to absolve or to be absolved from sin and to obtain the forgiveness of sins, but mean to be made righteous in fact before God on account of the love and virtue that the Holy Spirit has infused and the works resulting therefrom.

[16] 4. That faith does not look alone to Christ's obedience, but also to his divine nature (in so far as it dwells and works within us), and that by such indwelling our sins are covered up.

[17] 5. That faith is a kind of trust in the obedience of Christ that can exist and remain in a person though he does not truly repent and gives no evidence of resulting love, but continues to sin against his conscience.

[18] 6. That not God himself but only divine gifts dwell in believers.

[19] 7. That faith saves because by faith there is begun in us the renewal which consists in love toward God and our fellow man.

[20] 8. That faith indeed has the most prominent role in justification, but that also renewal and love belong to our righteousness before God, not indeed as if it were the primary cause of our righteousness, but that nevertheless our righteousness before God is incomplete and imperfect without such love and renewal.

[21] 9. That believers are justified before God and saved both by the righteousness of Christ reckoned to them and by the incipient new obedience, or in part by the reckoning to them of Christ's righteousness and in part by our incipient new obedience.

[22] 10. That the promise of grace becomes our own by faith in the heart and by the confession of the lips, along with other virtues.

[23] 11. That faith does not justify without good works, in such a way that good works are necessary for righteousness and that unless they are present a person cannot be justified.

4. Good Works

THE CHIEF ISSUE IN THE CONTROVERSY
CONCERNING GOOD WORKS

[1] 1. Two controversies have arisen in some churches concerning the doctrine of good works:

[2] The first division among some theologians was occasioned when one party asserted that good works are necessary to salvation; that it is impossible to be saved without good works; and that no one has ever been saved without good works. The other party asserted that good works are detrimental to salvation.

[3] 2. The second controversy arose among certain theologians concerning the use of the words "necessary" and "free." The one party contended that we should not use the word "necessary" when speaking of the new obedience, since it does not flow from necessity or coercion but from a spontaneous spirit. The other party held with reference to the word "necessary" that the new obedience is not a matter of our choice but that regenerated persons are bound to render such obedience.

[4] At first this was merely a semantic issue. Later on, a real controversy developed. The one party contended that the law should not be preached at all to Christians but that people should be admonished to do good works solely on the basis of the gospel. This the other party denied.

AFFIRMATIVE THESES
The Pure Doctrine of the Christian Church in This Controversy

[5] In order to explain this controversy from the ground up and to resolve it, this is our doctrine, faith, and confession:

[6] 1. That good works, like fruits of a good tree, certainly and indubitably follow genuine faith—if it is a living and not a dead faith.

[7] 2. We believe, teach, and confess that good works should be completely excluded from a discussion of the article of man's salvation as well as from the article of our justification before God. The apostle affirms in clear terms, "So also David declares that salvation pertains only to the man to whom God reckons righteousness apart from works, saying, 'Blessed are those whose iniquities are forgiven, and whose sins are covered,'" Romans 4. And again, "For by grace you have been saved through faith; and this is not your own doing, it is the gift of God—not because of works, lest any man should boast," Ephesians 2.

Rom 4[.6–8]

Eph 2[.8, 9]

[8] 3. We believe, teach, and confess further that all men, but especially those who are regenerated and renewed by the Holy Spirit, are obligated to do good works.

[9] 4. In this sense the words "necessary," "ought," and "must" are correctly and in a Christian way applied to the regenerated and are in no way contrary to the pattern of sound words and terminology.

[10] 5. However, when applied to the regenerated the words "necessity" and "necessary" are to be understood as involving not coercion but the due obedience which genuine believers, in so far as they are reborn, render not by coercion or compulsion of the law but from a spontaneous spirit because they are "no longer under the law but under grace."[a]

[11] 6. Therefore we also believe, teach, and confess that the statement, "The regenerated do good works from a free spirit," should not be understood as though it were left to the regenerated person's option whether to do or not to do good and that he might keep his faith even if he deliberately were to persist in sin.

[12] 7. This, however, should be understood exactly as our Lord and the apostles themselves explain it, as applying only to the liberated spirit which does good works not from a fear of punishment, like a slave, but out of a love of righ-

Rom 8[.15]   teousness, like a child, Romans 8.

[13] 8. However, in the elect children of God this spontaneity is not perfect, but they are still encumbered with much weakness, as St. Paul complains of himself in Romans 7 and Galatians 5.[b]

[14] 9. Nevertheless, for Christ's sake the Lord does not reckon this weakness against his elect, as it is written, "There is therefore now no condemnation for

Rom 8[.1]   those who are in Christ Jesus," Romans 8.

[15] 10. We also believe, teach, and confess that not our works but only the Holy Spirit, working through faith, preserves faith and salvation in us. The good works are testimonies of the Holy Spirit's presence and indwelling.

FALSE ANTITHESES

[16] 1. Accordingly we reject and condemn spoken and written formulations which teach that good works are necessary to salvation; likewise, that no one has ever been saved without good works; likewise, that it is impossible to be saved without good works.

[17] 2. We also reject and condemn as offensive and as subversive of Christian discipline that bald statement that good works are detrimental to salvation.

[18] Especially in these last times, it is just as necessary to exhort people to Christian discipline and good works, and to remind them how necessary it is

a. [Rom 6.14, 7.6, 8.14]
b. Rom 7[.14–25]; Gal 5[.17]

that they exercise themselves in good works as an evidence of their faith and their gratitude toward God, as it is to warn against mingling good works in the article of justification. Such an Epicurean dream concerning faith can damn people as much as a papistic and Pharisaic confidence in one's own works and merit.

[19] 3. We also reject and condemn the teaching that faith and the indwelling of the Holy Spirit are not lost through malicious sin, but that the holy ones and the elect retain the Holy Spirit even though they fall into adultery and other sins and persist in them.

5. Law and Gospel
THE CHIEF QUESTION AT ISSUE IN THIS CONTROVERSY

[1] The question has been, Is the preaching of the holy gospel strictly speaking only a preaching of grace which proclaims the forgiveness of sins, or is it also a preaching of repentance and reproof that condemns unbelief, since unbelief is condemned not in the law but wholly through the gospel?

AFFIRMATIVE THESES
The Pure Doctrine of God's Word

[2] 1. We believe, teach, and confess that the distinction between law and gospel is an especially glorious light that is to be maintained with great diligence in the church so that, according to St. Paul's admonition, the word of God may be divided rightly.[4]

[3] 2. We believe, teach, and confess that, strictly speaking, the law is a divine doctrine which teaches what is right and God-pleasing and which condemns everything that is sinful and contrary to God's will.

[4] 3. Therefore everything which condemns sin is and belongs to the proclamation of the law.

[5] 4. But the gospel, strictly speaking, is the kind of doctrine that teaches what a man who has not kept the law and is condemned by it should believe, namely, that Christ has satisfied and paid for all guilt and without man's merit has obtained and won for him forgiveness of sins, the "righteousness that avails before God,"[a] and eternal life.

[6] 5. The word "gospel" is not used in a single sense in Holy Scripture, and

---

a. [Rom 1.17; 2 Cor 5.21]

4. See 2 Tm 2.15, which Luther interpreted as "rightly dividing" law and gospel.

this was the original occasion of the controversy. Therefore we believe, teach, and confess that when the word "gospel" means the entire doctrine of Christ which he proclaimed personally in his teaching ministry and which his apostles also set forth (examples of this meaning occur in Mark 1ᵃ and Acts 20ᵇ), then it is correct to say or write that the gospel is a proclamation both of repentance and of forgiveness of sins.

[7] 6. But when law and gospel are opposed to each other, as when Moses is spoken of as a teacher of the law in contrast to Christ as a preacher of the gospel, then we believe, teach, and confess that the gospel is not a proclamation of contrition and reproof but is, strictly speaking, precisely a comforting and joyful message which does not reprove or terrify but comforts consciences that are frightened by the law, directs them solely to the merit of Christ, and raises them up again by the delightful proclamation of God's grace and favor acquired through the merits of Christ.

[8] 7. Now as to the disclosure of sin, as long as men hear only the law and [2 Cor 3.13–16] hear nothing about Christ, the veil of Moses covers their eyes; as a result they fail to learn the true nature of sin from the law, and thus they become either conceited hypocrites, like the Pharisees, or they despair, as Judas did, etc. Therefore Christ takes the law into his own hands and explains it spiritually, Matthew 5, Romans 7.ᶜ [Rom 1.8] Then "God's wrath is revealed from heaven" over all sinners and men learn how fierce it is. Thus they are directed back to the law, and now they learn from it for the first time the real nature of their sin, an acknowledgment which Moses could never have wrung from them.

[9] Therefore the proclamation of the suffering and death of Christ, the Son of God, is an earnest and terrifying preaching and advertisement of God's wrath which really directs people into the law, after the veil of Moses has been removed for them, so they now know for the first time what great things God demands of us in the law, none of which we could fulfill, and that we should now seek all our righteousness in Christ.

[10] 8. Nevertheless, as long as all this—namely, the passion and death of Christ—proclaims God's wrath and terrifies people, it is not, strictly speaking, the preaching of the gospel but the preaching of Moses and the law, and therefore it [Is 28.21] is an "alien work" of Christ by which he comes to his proper office—namely, to

a. Mk 1[.15]
b. Acts 20[.24]
c. Mt 5[.21–48]; Rom 7[.14]

preach grace, to comfort, to make alive. And this is the preaching of the gospel, strictly speaking.

ANTITHESIS
Rejected Contrary Doctrine

[11] 1. Hence we reject and deem it as false and detrimental when men teach that the gospel, strictly speaking, is a proclamation of conviction and reproof and not exclusively a proclamation of grace. Thereby the gospel is again changed into a teaching of the law, the merit of Christ and the Holy Scriptures are obscured, Christians are robbed of their true comfort, and the doors are again opened to the papacy.

6. The Third Function of the Law
THE CHIEF QUESTION AT ISSUE IN THIS CONTROVERSY

[1] The law has been given to men for three reasons: (1) to maintain external discipline against unruly and disobedient men, (2) to lead men to a knowledge of their sin, (3) after they are reborn, and although the flesh still inheres in them, to give them on that account a definite rule according to which they should pattern and regulate their entire life. It is concerning the third function of the law that a controversy has arisen among a few theologians. The question therefore is whether or not the law is to be urged upon reborn Christians. One party said yes, the other says no.

AFFIRMATIVE THESES
The Correct Christian Teaching in This Controversy

[2] 1. We believe, teach, and confess that although people who genuinely believe and whom God has truly converted are freed through Christ from the curse and the coercion of the law, they are not on that account without the law; on the contrary, they have been redeemed by the Son of God precisely that they should exercise themselves day and night in the law, Psalms 119. In the same way our first parents even Ps 119[.1] before the fall did not live without the law, for the law of God was written into their hearts when they were created in the image of God. [Gn 1.26, 2.16, 3.3]

[3] 2. We believe, teach, and confess that the preaching of the law is to be diligently applied not only to unbelievers and the impenitent but also to people who are genuinely believing, truly converted, regenerated, and justified through faith.

[4] 3. For although they are indeed reborn and have been "renewed in the spirit of their mind," such regeneration and renewal is incomplete in this world. In [Eph 4.25]

fact, it has only begun, and in the spirit of their mind the believers are in a constant war against their flesh (that is, their corrupt nature and kind), which clings to them until death. On account of this Old Adam, who inheres in people's intellect, will, and all their powers, it is necessary for the law of God constantly to light their way lest in their merely human devotion they undertake self-decreed and self-chosen acts of serving God. This is further necessary lest the Old Adam go his own [Rom 12.7–8] self-willed way. He must be coerced against his own will not only by the admonitions and threats of the law, but also by its punishments and plagues, to follow the Spirit and surrender himself a captive. 1 Corinthians 9, Romans 6, Galatians 6, Psalms 119, Hebrews 13.[a]

[5] 4. Concerning the distinction between works of the law and fruits of the Spirit we believe, teach, and confess that works done according to the law are, and are called, works of the law as long as they are extorted from people only under the coercion of punishments and the threat of God's wrath.

[6] 5. Fruits of the Spirit, however, are those works which the Spirit of God, who dwells in the believers, works through the regenerated, and which the regenerated perform in so far as they are reborn and do them as spontaneously as if they knew of no command, threat, or reward. In this sense the children of God live in the law and walk according to the law of God. In his epistles St. Paul calls it the law of Christ and the law of the mind. Thus God's children are "not under the law, but under grace,"[b] Romans 7, 8.

[7] 6. Therefore both for penitent and impenitent, for regenerated and unregenerated people the law is and remains one and the same law, namely, the unchangeable will of God. The difference, as far as obedience is concerned, rests exclusively with man, for the unregenerated man—just like the regenerated according to the flesh—does what is demanded of him by the law under coercion and unwillingly. But the believer without any coercion and with a willing spirit, in so far as he is reborn, does what no threat of the law could ever have wrung from him.

ANTITHESIS

[8] 1. Accordingly we condemn as dangerous and subversive of Christian discipline and true piety the erroneous teaching that the law is not to be urged, in the manner and measure above described, upon Christians and genuine believers, but only upon unbelievers, non-Christians, and the impenitent.

a. 1 Cor 9[.27]; Rom 6[.12]; Gal 6[.14]; Ps 119[.1]; Heb 13[.21]
b. Rom 7[.23], 8[.1, 14]

7. The Holy Supper of Christ

[1] The Zwinglian teachers cannot be numbered among the theologians identified with *The Augsburg Confession* since they separated themselves from the latter at the very outset when *The Augsburg Confession*[5] was being submitted. Nevertheless, they endeavored surreptitiously to insinuate themselves and to disseminate their errors under the name of this Christian confession, and therefore we have wished to report as far as necessary concerning this controversy also.

THE CHIEF QUESTION AT ISSUE BETWEEN OUR DOCTRINE AND THE SACRAMENTARIAN DOCTRINE IN THIS ARTICLE

[2] The question is, In the holy communion are the true body and blood of our Lord Jesus Christ truly and essentially present if they are distributed with the bread and wine and if they are received orally by all those who use the sacrament, be they worthy or unworthy, godly or godless, believers or unbelievers, the believers for life and salvation, the unbelievers for judgment? The sacramentarians say no; we say yes.

[3] In order to explicate this controversy, it is necessary to mention, first of all, that there are two kinds of sacramentarians. Some are crass sacramentarians who set forth in clear German words what they believe in their hearts, namely, that in the holy supper only bread and wine are present, distributed, and received orally. [4] Others, however, are subtle sacramentarians, the most harmful kind, who in part talk our language very plausibly and claim to believe a true presence of the true, essential, and living body and blood of Christ in the holy supper but assert that this takes place spiritually by faith. But under this plausible terminology they really retain the former crass opinion that in the holy supper nothing but bread and wine are present and received with the mouth.

[5] To them the word "spiritual" means no more than the presence of Christ's spirit, or the power of Christ's absent body, or his merit. They deny that the body of Christ is present in any manner or way, since in their opinion it is confined to the highest heaven above, whither we should ascend with the thoughts of our faith and there, but not in the bread and wine of the holy supper, seek the body and blood of Christ.

---

5. → *The Tetrapolitan Confession* and Ulrich Zwingli, *A Reckoning of the Faith*.

AFFIRMATIVE THESES
Confession of the Pure Doctrine of the Holy Supper
Against the Sacramentarians

[6] 1. We believe, teach, and confess that in the holy supper the body and blood of Christ are truly and essentially present and are truly distributed and received with the bread and wine.

[7] 2. We believe, teach, and confess that the words of the testament of Christ are to be understood in no other way than in their literal sense, and not as though the bread symbolized the absent body and the wine the absent blood of Christ, but that because of the sacramental union they are truly the body and blood of Christ.

[8] 3. Concerning the consecration we believe, teach, and confess that no man's work nor the recitation of the minister effects this presence of the body and blood of Christ in the holy supper, but it is to be ascribed solely and alone to the almighty power of our Lord Jesus Christ.

[9] 4. But at the same time we believe, teach, and confess with one accord that in the celebration of the holy supper the words of Christ's institution should under no circumstances be omitted, but should be spoken publicly, as it is written, 1 Cor [10.16] "the cup of blessing which we bless," 1 Corinthians 11. This blessing occurs through the recitation of the words of Christ.

[10] 5. The grounds on which we stand in this controversy with the sacramentarians are those which Dr. Luther proposed in his *Great Confession:*[6]

[11] "The first ground is this article of our Christian faith: Jesus Christ is true, essential, natural, complete God and man in one person, inseparable and undivided.

[12] "The second ground is: God's right hand is everywhere. Christ, really and truly set at this right hand of God according to his human nature, rules presently and has in his hands and under his feet everything in heaven and on earth. No other human being, no angel, but only Mary's son, is so set down at the right hand of God, whence he is able to do these things.

[13] "The third ground is that God's word is not false nor does it lie.

[14] "The fourth ground is that God has and knows various modes of being at a given place, and not only the single mode which the philosophers call *local* or spatial."

---

6. *Vom Abendmahl Christi, Bekenntnis,* in WA, 26:261–509.

[15] 6. We believe, teach, and confess that with the bread and wine the body and blood of Christ are received not only spiritually, by faith, but also orally—however, not in a Capernaitic manner, but because of the sacramental union in a supernatural and heavenly manner. The words of Christ teach this clearly when they direct us to take, eat, and drink, all of which took place in the case of the apostles, since it is written, "And they all drank of it," Mark 14. Likewise, St. Paul says, "The bread which we break, is it not a participation in the body of Christ?"—that is, whoever eats this bread eats the body of Christ. This has also been the unanimous teaching of the leading church fathers, such as Chrysostom, Cyprian, Leo I, Gregory, Ambrose, Augustine.[7]

Mk 14[.23]

[1 Cor 10.16]

[16] 7. We believe, teach, and confess that not only the genuine believers and those who are worthy but also the unworthy and the unbelievers receive the true body and blood of Christ; but if they are not converted and do not repent, they receive them not to life and salvation but to their judgment and condemnation.

[17] For although they reject Christ as a redeemer, they must accept him even contrary to their will as a strict judge. He is just as much present to exercise and manifest his judgment on unrepentant guests as he is to work life and consolation in the hearts of believing and worthy guests.

[18] 8. We believe, teach, and confess that there is only one kind of unworthy guest, namely, those who do not believe. Of such it is written, "He who does not believe is condemned already," John 3. The unworthy use of the holy sacrament increases, magnifies, and aggravates this condemnation, 1 Corinthians 11.

Jn 3[.18]

1 Cor 11[.27, 29]

[19] 9. We believe, teach, and confess that no genuine believer, no matter how weak he may be, as long as he retains a living faith, will receive the holy supper to his condemnation, for Christ instituted this supper particularly for Christians who are weak in faith but repentant, to comfort them and to strengthen their weak faith.

[20] 10. We believe, teach, and confess that the entire worthiness of the guests at this heavenly feast is and consists solely and alone in the most holy obedience and complete merit of Christ, which we make our own through genuine faith and of which we are assured through the sacrament. Worthiness consists not at all in our own virtues or in our internal and external preparations.

7. See Kolb and Wengert 2000, 603–4, n. 200, and 605, n. 203, for references as inserted in the Torgau Book.

ANTITHESES

The Contrary and Condemned Doctrine of the Sacramentarians

[21] On the other side, we unanimously reject and condemn all the following errors, which are contrary and contradictory to the doctrine set forth above and to our simple faith and confession about Christ's supper:

[22] 1. The papistic transubstantiation, when it is taught in the papacy that the bread and wine in the holy supper lose their substance and natural essence and are thus annihilated, in such a way that they are transmuted into the body of Christ and that only the exterior appearance remains.

[23] 2. The papistic sacrifice of the mass for the sins of the living and the dead.

[24] 3. The administration of only one kind of the sacrament to the laity and the withholding of the cup from them, contrary to the clear word of Christ's testament, so that they are deprived of the blood of Christ.

[25] 4. The teaching that the words of Christ's testament are not to be understood or believed in their simple sense, as they read, but that they are dark sayings whose meaning must first be sought in other passages.

[26] 5. That in the holy sacrament the body of Christ is not received orally with the bread, but that with the mouth we receive only bread and wine and that we receive the body of Christ only spiritually by faith.

[27] 6. That bread and wine in the holy supper are no more than tokens whereby Christians recognize one another.

[28] 7. That the bread and wine are only figures, images, and types of the far-distant body and blood of Christ.

[29] 8. That the bread and wine are no more than reminders, seals, and pledges to assure us that when our faith ascends into heaven, it there partakes of the body and blood of Christ as truly as we eat and drink bread and wine in the supper.

[30] 9. That the assurance and strengthening of our faith in the holy supper is effected solely by the external signs of bread and wine and not by the truly present body and blood of Christ.

[31] 10. That in the holy supper only the power, operation, and merit of the absent body and blood of Christ are distributed.

[32] 11. That the body of Christ is so enclosed in heaven that it can in no way be present at one and the same time in many places, still less in all places, where his holy supper is observed.

[33] 12. That Christ could not have promised that his body and blood would

be essentially present in the holy supper, nor could he have kept such a promise, since the nature and properties of his assumed human nature could neither permit nor admit this.

[34] 13. That God, even with all his omnipotence, is unable (a dreadful statement!) to cause his body to be essentially present at more than one place at a single given time.

[35] 14. That faith, and not the omnipotent words of Christ's testament, effect and cause the presence of the body and blood of Christ in the holy supper.

[36] 15. That the believers should not seek the body of Christ in the bread and wine of the holy supper, but should lift their eyes from the bread to heaven and there seek the body of Christ.

[37] 16. That in the holy supper unbelieving and impenitent Christians do not receive the body and blood of Christ, but only bread and wine.

[38] 17. That the worthiness of the guests at this heavenly meal does not consist only in true faith in Christ, but also depends on people's outward preparation.

[39] 18. That genuine believers, who have a genuine and living faith in Christ, can also receive this sacrament to their condemnation because they are still imperfect in their external behavior.

[40] 19. That the external visible elements of bread and wine in the holy sacrament should be adored.

[41] 20. By the same token we commend to the righteous judgment of God all presumptuous, sarcastic, and blasphemous questions and statements, which decency forbids us to recite and which the sacramentarians advance most blasphemously and offensively in a coarse, carnal, Capernaitic, and abhorrent way concerning the supernatural and celestial mysteries of this sacrament.

[42] 21. Accordingly, we herewith condemn without any qualification the Capernaitic eating of the body of Christ as though one rent Christ's flesh with one's teeth and digested it like other food. The sacramentarians deliberatly insist on crediting us with this doctrine, against the witness of their own consciences over our many protests, in order to make our teaching obnoxious to their hearers. On the contrary, in accord with the simple words of Christ's testament, we hold and believe in a true, though supernatural, eating of Christ's body and drinking of his blood, which we cannot comprehend with our human sense or reason. Here we take our intellect captive in obedience to Christ, as we do in other articles also, and accept [2 Cor 10.5] this mystery in no other way than by faith and as it is revealed in the word.

8. The Person of Christ

[1] In connection with the controversy on the holy supper a disagreement has arisen between the authentic theologians of *The Augsburg Confession* and the Calvinists (who have misled some other theologians also) concerning the person of Christ, the two natures in Christ, and their properties.

THE CHIEF QUESTION AT ISSUE IN THIS CONTROVERSY

[2] The chief question has been, Because of personal union in the person of Christ, do the divine and human natures, together with their properties, really (that is, in deed and truth) share with each other, and how far does this sharing extend?

[3] The sacramentarians have asserted that in Christ the divine and human natures are personally united in such a way that neither of the two really (that is, in deed and in truth) shares in the properties of the other but have in common only the name. They declare boldly that the "personal union makes merely the names common," so that God is called man and a man is called God, but that God really (that is, in deed and in truth) has nothing in common with the humanity and that the humanity really has nothing in common with the deity, its majesty, and its properties. Dr. Luther and his followers have contended for the opposite view against the sacramentarians.

AFFIRMATIVE THESES
The Pure Teaching of the Christian Church
Concerning the Person of Christ

[4] To explain and to settle this controversy according to our Christian faith we teach, believe, and confess the following:

[5] 1. That the divine and the human natures are personally united in Christ in such a way that there are not two Christs, one the Son of God and the other the Son of man, but a single individual is both the Son of God and the Son of man, Luke 1, Romans 9.

Lk 1[.35]; Rom 9[.5]

[6] 2. We believe, teach, and confess that the divine and the human nature are not fused into one essence and that the one is not changed into the other, but that each retains its essential properties and that they never become the properties of the other nature.

[7] 3. The properties of the divine nature are omnipotence, eternity, infinity, and (according to its natural property, by itself) omnipresence, omniscience, etc., which never become properties of the human nature.

[8] 4. The attributes of the human nature are to be a corporeal creature, to

be flesh and blood, to be finite and circumscribed, to suffer, to die, to ascend and to descend, to move from place to place, to endure hunger, thirst, cold, heat, and the like, which never become the properties of the divine nature.

[9] 5. Since both natures are united personally (that is, in one person) we believe, teach, and confess that this personal union is not a combination or connection of such a kind that neither nature has anything in common with the other personally (that is, on account of the personal union), as when two boards are glued together and neither gives anything to or takes anything from the other. On the contrary, here is the highest communion which God truly has with man. Out of this personal union and the resultant exalted and ineffable sharing there flows everything human that is said or believed about God and everything divine that is said or believed about Christ the man. The ancient fathers have illustrated this union and sharing of the natures by the analogy of incandescent iron and the union of body and soul in man.

[10] 6. Therefore we believe, teach, and confess that God is man and man is God, which could not be the case if the divine and human natures did not have a real and true communion with each other.

[11] For how could the man, Mary's son, truly be called or be God, or the Son of the most high God, if his humanity were not personally and truly united with the Son of God and hence really (that is, in deed and in truth) shared only the name of God with the divine nature?

[12] 7. Therefore we believe, teach, and confess that Mary conceived and bore not only a plain, ordinary, mere man but the veritable Son of God; for this reason she is rightly called, and truly is, the Mother of God.

[13] 8. Therefore we also believe, teach, and confess that it was not a plain, ordinary, mere man who for us suffered, died, was buried, descended into hell, rose from the dead, ascended into heaven, and was exalted to the majesty and omnipotent power of God, but a man whose human nature has such a profound and ineffable union and communion with the Son of God that it has become one person with him.

[14] 9. Therefore the Son of God has truly suffered for us, but according to the property of the human nature which he assumed into the unity of his divine person and made his own, so that he could suffer and be our high priest for our reconciliation with God, as it is written in 1 Corinthians 2, They have "crucified the Lord of glory," and in Acts 20, We are purchased with God's own blood. _{1 Cor 2[.8]} _{Acts 20[.28]}

[15] 10. Therefore we believe, teach, and confess that the Son of man according to his human nature is really (that is, in deed and in truth) exalted to the right hand of the omnipotent majesty and power of God, because he was assumed

into God when he was conceived by the Holy Spirit in his mother's womb and his human nature was personally united with the Son of the Most High.[8]

[16] 11. According to the personal union he always possessed this majesty. But in the state of his humiliation he dispensed with it and could therefore truly [Lk 2.52] increase in age, wisdom, and favor with God and men, for he did not always disclose this majesty, but only when it pleased him. Finally, after his resurrection he [Phil 2.7] laid aside completely the form of a slave (not the human nature) and was established in the full use, revelation, and manifestation of his divine majesty. Thus he entered into his glory in such a way that now not only as God, but also as man, he knows all things, can do all things, is present to all creatures, and has all things in heaven and on earth and under the earth beneath his feet and in his hands, as he himself [Mt 28.18] testifies, "All authority in heaven and on earth has been given to me," and as St. [Eph 4.10] Paul states, he ascended "far above all the heavens that he might fill all things." He exercises his power everywhere omnipresently, he can do everything, and he knows everything.

[17] 12. Therefore he is able and it is easy for him to impart to us his true body and blood which are present in the holy supper, not according to the mode or property of the human nature but according to the mode and property of God's right hand, as Dr. Luther says on the basis of our Christian faith as we teach this to our children. This presence is not mundane or Capernaitic although it is true and essential, as the words of Christ's testament declare, "This is, is, is my body," etc.[9]

[18] Our doctrine, faith, and confession do not divide the person of Christ, as Nestorius did. He denied the genuine sharing of the properties of the two natures in Christ and thus he actually divided the person, as Luther explains it in his treatise *On the Councils*.[10] Nor do we mingle the natures and their properties together in one essence, as Eutyches erroneously taught. Nor do we deny or abolish the human nature in the person of Christ, or change the one nature into the other. Christ is, and remains to all eternity, God and man in one indivisible person. Next to the Holy [1 Tm 3.16] Trinity this is the highest mystery, as the apostle testifies, and the sole foundation of our comfort, life, and salvation.

---

8. Andreae's original draft adds the following: "Accordingly he could not be exalted more highly after his resurrection, since he did not have to wait until after his resurrection to become God, or to have his human nature united personally with the Son of God, but he was God and man as soon as he was conceived in his mother's womb."

9. *WA*, 26:326ff., 23:131ff.

10. *Von den Konziliis und Kirchen* (1539), *WA*, 50:584–95.

ANTITHESES
Contrary False Doctrine Concerning the Person of Christ

[19] Accordingly we reject and condemn as contrary to the word of God and our simple Christian creed the following erroneous articles:

[20] 1. That in Christ God and man are not one person, but that the Son of God is one person and the Son of man another, as Nestorius foolishly asserted.

[21] 2. That the divine and human natures are mingled into one essence and that the human nature has been changed into the deity, as Eutyches dreamed.

[22] 3. That Christ is not true, natural, and eternal God, as Arius held.

[23] 4. That Christ did not have a true human nature with a body and a soul, as Marcion imagined.

[24] 5. That personal union achieves only common names and titles.

[25] 6. That it is only a verbalism and figure of speech when we say "God is man, man is God," since really (that is, in fact) the deity has nothing in common with the humanity, nor the humanity with the deity.

[26] 7. That it is a sheer matter of words when we say that the Son of God died for the sins of the world or that the Son of man has become almighty.

[27] 8. That Christ's human nature has become an infinite essence, like the divine nature; that it is omnipresent in the same manner as the divine nature, because this essential power and property has been severed from God and communicated to and infused into the human nature.

[28] 9. That the human nature has been raised to the level of, and has become equal to, the divine nature in its substance and essence, or in its essential properties.

[29] 10. That the human nature of Christ is locally extended to every place in heaven and earth (something that is not true of the divine nature either).

[30] 11. That because of the property of the human nature it is impossible for Christ to be present at the same time at more than one place, still less to be present with his body everywhere.

[31] 12. That only the mere humanity suffered for us and redeemed us, and that in the passion the Son of God had no communion with the human nature in fact, as though it did not concern him at all.

[32] 13. That Christ is present with us on earth in the word, in the sacraments, and in all our necessities only according to his deity, and that this presence does not at all concern his human nature; and that after Christ had redeemed us by his suffering and death he no longer has anything to do with us according to his human nature.

[33] 14. That the Son of God who assumed the human nature, after he laid aside the form of a slave, does not perform all works of his omnipotence in, through, and with his human nature, but only a few and only at the place where the human nature is locally present.

[Mt 28.18]

Col 2[.9]

[34] 15. That in spite of Christ's express assertion, "All authority in heaven and on earth has been given to me," and St. Paul's statement, "In him dwells the whole fullness of deity bodily," Colossians 2, Christ, according to the human nature, is wholly incapable of omnipotence and other properties of the divine nature.

[35] 16. That according to his human nature Christ has indeed been given greater power in heaven and on earth, that is, greater and more than all angels and other creatures; but that he does not share in the omnipotence of God, and that this has not been given to him. Therefore they invent an intermediate power (that is, a power that lies somewhere between God's omnipotence and the power of other creatures) and they imagine that through the exaltation the human nature of Christ received a power which is less than God's omnipotence but greater than the power of other creatures.

[36] 17. That according to his human spirit Christ has certain limitations as to how much he is supposed to know, and that he does not know more than is fitting and necessary to perform his office as judge.

[37] 18. That Christ does not as yet have a perfect knowledge of God and all his works, though it is written that in him are hid "all the treasures of wisdom and knowledge."

[Col 2.3]

[38] 19. That according to his human spirit Christ cannot know what has existed from eternity, what is happening everywhere today, nor what will yet take place in eternity.

[39] 20. They misinterpret and blasphemously pervert the words of Christ, "All authority has been given to me," Matthew 28, to mean that in the resurrection and his ascension all power in heaven and on earth was restored or again returned to Christ according to the divine nature, as though in the state of humiliation he had laid it aside and forsaken it even according to his deity. This doctrine not only perverts the words of Christ's testament, but it opens a way for the accursed Arian heresy. Hence, unless we refute these errors on the firm basis of the divine word and our simple Christian faith, we shall finally have Christ's eternal deity denied and we shall lose Christ altogether along with our salvation.

Mt 28[.18]

9. Christ's Descent into Hell

THE CHIEF QUESTION AT ISSUE IN THE
CONTROVERSY ABOUT THIS ARTICLE

[1] There has been a dispute among some theologians of *The Augsburg Confession* concerning this article also. The questions raised were: When and how, according to our simple Christian creed, did Christ go to hell? Did it happen before or after his death? Did it occur only according to the soul, or only according to the deity, or according to body and soul, spiritually or corporeally? Does this article belong to Christ's suffering or to his glorious victory and triumph?

[2] This article, like the preceding one, cannot be comprehended with our senses and reason, but must be apprehended by faith alone. Therefore it is our unanimous opinion that we should not engage in disputations concerning this article, [3] but believe and teach it in all simplicity, as Dr. Luther of blessed memory taught in his sermon preached at Torgau in the year 1533, where he explains this article in a wholly Christian manner, eliminates all unnecessary questions, and admonishes all Christians to simplicity of faith.[11]

[4] It is enough to know that Christ went to hell, destroyed hell for all believers, and has redeemed them from the power of death, of the devil, and of the eternal damnation of the hellish jaws. How this took place is something that we should postpone until the other world, where there will be revealed to us not only this point, but many others as well, which our blind reason cannot comprehend in this life but which we simply accept.

10. Church Usages, Called Adiaphora or Indifferent Things

[1] There has also been a division among theologians of *The Augsburg Confession* concerning those ceremonies or church usages which are neither commanded nor forbidden in the word of God but have been introduced into the church in the interest of good order and the general welfare.

THE CHIEF QUESTION AT ISSUE IN THIS CONTROVERSY

[2] The chief question has been, In times of persecution, when a confession is called for, and when the enemies of the gospel have not come to an agreement with us in doctrine, may we with an inviolate conscience yield to their pressure and demands, reintroduce some ceremonies that have fallen into disuse and that in themselves are indifferent things and are neither commanded nor forbidden by God, and thus come

11. WA, 37:62–67.

to an understanding with them in such ceremonies and indifferent things? One party said yes to this, the other party said no.

AFFIRMATIVE THESES
The Correct, True Doctrine and Confession About This Article

[3] 1. To settle this controversy we believe, teach, and confess unanimously that the ceremonies or church usages which are neither commanded nor forbidden in the word of God, but which have been introduced solely for the sake of good order and the general welfare, are in and for themselves no divine worship or even a part of it. "In vain do they worship me, teaching as doctrines the precepts of men," Matthew 15.

Mt 15[.9]

[4] 2. We believe, teach, and confess that the community of God in every locality and every age has authority to change such ceremonies according to circumstances, as it may be most profitable and edifying to the community of God.

[5] 3. But in this matter all frivolity and offenses are to be avoided, and particularly the weak in faith are to be spared.ª

[6] 4. We believe, teach, and confess that in time of persecution, when a clear-cut confession of faith is demanded of us, we dare not yield to the enemies in such indifferent things, as the apostle Paul writes, "For freedom Christ has set us free; stand fast therefore, and do not submit again to a yoke of slavery." "Do not be mismated with unbelievers, for what fellowship has light with darkness?" "To them we did not yield submission even for a moment, that the truth of the gospel might be preserved for you." In such a case it is no longer a question of indifferent things, but a matter which has to do with the truth of the gospel, Christian liberty, and the sanctioning of public idolatry, as well as preventing offense to the weak in faith. In all these things we have no concessions to make, but we should witness an unequivocal confession and suffer in consequence what God sends us and what he lets the enemies inflict on us.

[Gal 5.11]
[2 Cor 6.14]

[Gal 2.5]

[7] 5. We believe, teach, and confess that no church should condemn another because it has fewer or more external ceremonies not commanded by God, as long as there is mutual agreement in doctrine and in all its articles as well as in the right use of the holy sacraments, according to the familiar axiom, "Disagreement in fasting does not destroy agreement in faith."[12]

---

a. [1 Cor 8.9–13; Rom 14.13]

12. Irenaeus, "Epistle to Victor," quoted in Eusebius of Caesarea *Church History* 5.24.13.

ANTITHESES
False Doctrine Concerning This Article

[8] Therefore we reject and condemn as false and contrary to God's word the following teachings:

[9] 1. That human precepts and institutions in the church are to be regarded as in themselves divine worship or a part of it.

[10] 2. When such ceremonies, precepts, and institutions are forcibly imposed upon the community of God as necessary things, in violation of the Christian liberty which it has in external matters.

[11] 3. That in a time of persecution and when a public confession is required, one may make concessions to or come to an understanding with the enemies of the holy gospel (which serve to impair the truth) in such indifferent things and ceremonies.

[12] 4. When such external ceremonies and indifferent things are abolished in a way which suggests that the community of God does not have the liberty to avail itself of one or more such ceremonies according to its circumstances and as it may be most beneficial to the church.

11. God's Eternal Foreknowledge and Election

[1] No public dissension has developed among the theologians of *The Augsburg Confession* concerning this article. But since it is such a comforting article when it is correctly treated, we have included an explanation of it in this document, lest at some future date offensive dissension concerning it might be introduced into the church.

AFFIRMATIVE
Pure and True Doctrine Concerning This Article

[2] 1. To start with, the distinction between the foreknowledge and the eternal election of God is to be diligently noted.

[3] 2. God's foreknowledge is nothing else than that God knows all things before they happen, as it is written, "There is a God in heaven who reveals mysteries, and he has made known to King Nebuchadnezzar what will be in the latter days," Daniel 2.   Dn 2[.28]

[4] This foreknowledge extends alike over good people and evil people. But it is not a cause of evil or of sin which compels anyone to do something wrong; the original source of this is the devil and man's wicked and perverse will. Neither is it

the cause of man's perdition; for this man himself is responsible. God's foreknowledge merely controls the evil and imposes a limit on its duration, so that in spite of its intrinsic wickedness it must minister to the salvation of his elect.

[5] 4. Predestination or the eternal election of God, however, is concerned only with the pious children of God in whom he is well pleased. It is a cause of their salvation, for he alone brings it about and ordains everything that belongs to it. Our salvation is so firmly established upon it that the "gates of Hades cannot

[Jn 10.28; Mt 16.18]   prevail against" it.

[6] 5. We are not to investigate this predestination in the secret counsel of God, but it is to be looked for in his word, where he has revealed it.

[7] 6. The word of God, however, leads us to Christ, who is "the book of

[Phil 4.3; Rv 3.5]   life" in which all who are to be eternally saved are inscribed and elected, as it is

[Eph 1.4]   written, "He chose us in him before the foundation of the world."

[8] 7. This Christ calls all sinners to himself and promises them refreshment. He earnestly desires that all men should come to him and let themselves be

[Mt 11.28]   helped. To these he offers himself in his word, and it is his will that they hear the word and do not stop their ears or despise it. In addition he promises the power and operation of the Holy Spirit and divine assistance for steadfastness and eternal life.

[9] 8. Therefore we should not judge this election of ours to eternal life on the basis either of reason or of God's law. This would either lead us into a reckless, dissolute, Epicurean life, or drive men to despair and waken dangerous thoughts in their hearts. As long as men follow their reason, they can hardly escape such reflections as this: "If God has elected me to salvation I cannot be damned, do as I will." Or, "If I am not elected to eternal life, whatever good I do is of no avail; everything is in vain in that case."

[10] 9. We must learn about Christ from the holy gospel alone, which clearly testifies that "God has consigned all men to disobedience, that he may have mercy upon all,"[a] and that he does not want anyone to perish,[b] but that everyone

[1 Tm 2.6]   should repent and believe on the Lord Jesus Christ.

[11] 10. The doctrine of God's eternal election is profitable and comforting to the person who concerns himself with the revealed will of God and observes the order which St. Paul follows in the Epistle to the Romans. He there directs men first to repent, to acknowledge their sins, to believe in Christ, and to obey God, and only then does he speak of the mystery of God's eternal election.

[Mt 20.16]   [12] 11. The passage, "Many are called, but few are chosen," does not mean

a. [Rom 11.32]
b. [Ez 33.11, 18.23]

that God does not desire to save everyone. The cause of condemnation is that men either do not hear the word of God at all but willfully despise it, harden their ears and their hearts, and thus bar the ordinary way for the Holy Spirit, so that he cannot work in them; or, if they do hear the word, they cast it to the wind and pay no attention to it. The fault does not lie in God or his election, but in their own wickedness.[a]

[13] 12. The Christian is to concern himself with the doctrine of the eternal election of God only in so far as it is revealed in the word of God, which shows us Christ as the "book of life." Through the proclamation of the holy gospel, Christ opens and reveals this book for us, as it is written, "Those he predestined, he also called." In Christ we should seek the eternal election of the Father, who has decreed [Rom 8.30] in his eternal counsel that he would save no one except those who acknowledge his Son, Christ, and truly believe on him. The Christian should banish all other opinions since they do not proceed from God but are inspired by the evil foe in an attempt to weaken for us or to rob us entirely of the glorious comfort which this salutary doctrine gives us, namely, that we know that we have been elected to eternal life out of pure grace in Christ without any merit of our own, and that no one can pluck us out of his hand. God assures us of this gracious election not only in mere words, but also [Jn 10.28–29] with his oath, and has sealed it with his holy sacraments, of which we can remind ourselves and with which we can comfort ourselves in our greatest temptations and thus extinguish the flaming darts of the devil.

[14] 13. Furthermore, we are to put forth every effort to live according to the will of God and "to confirm our call," as St. Peter says. Especially are we to [2 Pt 1.10] abide by the revealed word which cannot and will not deceive us.

[15] 14. This brief exposition of the doctrine of God's eternal election gives God his glory entirely and completely, because he out of pure grace alone, without any merit of ours, saves us "according to the purpose" of his will. Nor will this doc- [Eph 1.11] trine ever give anyone occasion either to despair or to lead a reckless and godless life.

ANTITHESES
False Doctrine Concerning This Article

[16] Accordingly we believe and maintain that if anybody teaches the doctrine of the gracious election of God to eternal life in such a way that disconsolate Christians can find no comfort in this doctrine but are driven to doubt and despair, or in such

---

a. [2 Pt 2.9–15; Lk 11.47–52; Heb 12.15–17, 25]

a way that the impenitent are strengthened in their self-will, he is not teaching the doctrine according to the word and will of God, but in accord with his reason and under the direction of the devil, since everything in Scripture, as St. Paul testifies, was written for our instruction that by steadfastness and by the encouragement of [Rom 15.4] the Scriptures we might have hope. Therefore we reject the following errors:

[17] 1. The doctrine that God does not want all men to come to repentance and to believe the gospel.

[18] 2. Furthermore, the doctrine that God is not serious about wanting all men to come to him when he calls us to him.

[19] 3. Furthermore, that God does not want everybody to be saved, but that merely by an arbitrary counsel, purpose, and will, without regard for their sin, God has predestined certain people to damnation so that they cannot be saved.

[20] 4. Likewise that it is not only the mercy of God and the most holy merit of Christ, but that there is also within us a cause of God's election, on account of which he has elected us to eternal life.

[21] These are all blasphemous and terrible errors, for they rob Christians of all the comfort that they have in the holy gospel and in the use of the holy sacraments. Hence they should not be tolerated in God's church.

[22] This is a brief and simple explanation of the various articles which for a time the theologians of *The Augsburg Confession* have been discussing and teaching in mutually contradictory terms. From it, under the guidance of the word of God and the plain catechism, every simple Christian can understand what is right and what is wrong, since we have not only set forth the pure doctrine but have also exposed the contrary errors. In this way the offensive controversies that have developed receive a basic settlement.

May the Almighty God and Father of our Lord Jesus Christ grant us the [Jn 17.20–21] grace of his Holy Spirit that we may all be of one heart in him and constantly abide in this Christian and God-pleasing concord. Amen.

12. Other Factions and Sects Which Have Not Committed Themselves to the Augsburg Confession

[1] In the preceding explanation we have made no mention of the errors held by these factions. But lest as a result of our silence these errors be attributed to us, we wish here at the end merely to enumerate the articles in which they err and contradict our repeatedly cited Christian creed and confession.

ERRORS OF THE ANABAPTISTS

[2] The Anabaptists have split into many factions, some of which teach many errors, others teach fewer. But in general they profess doctrines of a kind that cannot be tolerated either in the church, or in the body politic and secular administration, or in domestic society.

Errors Which Cannot be Tolerated in the Church

[3] 1. That Christ did not assume his body and blood from the Virgin Mary, but brought them with him from heaven.

[4] 2. That Christ is not true God but that he only has more gifts of the Holy Spirit than any other holy person.

[5] 3. That our righteousness before God does not consist wholly in the unique merit of Christ, but in renewal and in our own pious behavior. For the most part this piety is built on one's own individual self-chosen spirituality, which in fact [Col 2.23] is nothing else but a new kind of monkery.

[6] 4. That in the sight of God unbaptized children are not sinners but are righteous and innocent, and that as long as they have not achieved the use of reason they will be saved in this innocence without baptism (which according to this view they do not need). They thus reject the entire doctrine of original sin and everything that pertains to it.

[7] 5. That children are not to be baptized until they have achieved the use of reason and can confess their faith personally.

[8] 6. That without and prior to baptism the children of Christian parents are holy and the children of God by virtue of their birth from Christian and pious parents. For this reason, too, the Anabaptists neither think highly of infant baptism nor encourage it, in spite of the expressed word of God's promise which extends only to those who keep his covenant and do not despise it, Genesis 17. Gn 17[.4–8, 19–21]

[9] 7. That a congregation is not truly Christian if sinners are still found in it.

[10] 8. That no one should hear sermons or attend services in those temples where formerly papistic masses were read and celebrated.

[11] 9. That one is to have nothing to do with clergymen who preach the gospel according to *The Augsburg Confession* and reprove the preaching and the errors of the Anabaptists; nor should one serve them or work for them in any way, but flee and avoid them as perverters of God's word.

Intolerable Articles in the Body Politic

[12] 1. That government is not a God-pleasing estate in the New Testament.

[13] 2. That no Christian can serve or function in any civic office with a good and clear conscience.

[14] 3. That as occasion arises no Christian, without violating his conscience, may use an office of the government against wicked people, and that subjects may not call upon the government to use the power that it possesses and that it has received from God for their protection and defense.

[15] 4. That a Christian cannot swear an oath with a good conscience nor pay oath-bound feudal homage to his territorial sovereign or liege-lord.

[16] 5. That in the New Testament the government cannot with a clear conscience inflict capital punishment upon criminals.

Intolerable Errors Which Undermine Domestic Society

[17] 1. That a Christian cannot with a good conscience hold or possess private property but is in conscience bound to put it into a common treasury.

[18] 2. That a Christian cannot with a good conscience be an innkeeper, a merchant, or a cutler.

[19] 3. That difference of faith is sufficient ground for married people to divorce one another, each go his own way, and marry someone else belonging to the same faith.

ERRORS OF THE SCHWENKFELDERS

[20] 1. That all who say that Christ according to the flesh is a creature do not have a right understanding of Christ as the reigning king of heaven.

[21] 2. That in Christ's glorification his flesh received all the divine properties in such a way that Christ as man is fully equal in rank and essential estates to the Father and to the Word as far as might, power, majesty, and glory are concerned, and that now both natures in Christ possess only one divine essence, property, will, and glory and that the flesh of Christ belongs to the essence of the Holy Trinity.

[22] 3. That the ministry of the church—the word preached and heard—is not a means through which God the Holy Spirit teaches people and creates in them the saving knowledge of Christ, conversion, repentance, faith, and new obedience.

[23] 4. That the water of baptism is not a means through which the Lord God seals the adoption of children and effects rebirth.

[24] 5. That bread and wine in the holy supper are not means through and by which Christ distributes his body and blood.

[25] 6. That a Christian who is truly born again through the Spirit of God can perfectly keep and fulfill the law of God in this life.

[26] 7. That it is no true Christian congregation in which public expulsion and the orderly process of excommunication do not take place.

[27] 8. That a minister of the church cannot teach profitably or administer true and genuine sacraments unless he is himself truly reborn, righteous, and pious.

ERROR OF THE NEW ARIANS

That Christ is not a true, essential, natural God, of one divine essence with God the Father and the Holy Spirit, but is merely adorned with divine majesty and is inferior to and beside God the Father.

ERROR OF THE ANTI-TRINITARIANS

[29] This is an entirely new sect, unknown in Christendom until now, which believes, teaches, and confesses that there is not only one eternal, divine essence, belonging to the Father, Son, and Holy Spirit, but as God the Father, Son, and Holy Spirit are three distinct persons, so each person has its distinct divine essence, separate from the other persons of the Deity. Some maintain that each of the three has the same power, wisdom, majesty, and glory, just like any three individual people who are essentially separate from one another. Others maintain that the three are unequal in essence and properties and that only the Father is rightly and truly God.

[30] All these and similar articles, together with their erroneous implications and conclusions, we reject and condemn as wrong, false, heretical, and contrary to the word of God, the three creeds, *The Augsburg Confession, The Apology, The Smalcald Articles,* and *The Catechisms* of Luther. All pious Christians, of high degree and low, must guard against these if they dearly love their soul's eternal welfare and salvation.

[31] In testimony that this is the doctrine, faith, and confession of all of us as we shall give account of it on the last day before the righteous judge, our Lord Jesus Christ, and that we shall neither secretly nor publicly say or write anything contrary to it but intend by the grace of God to abide by it, we have advisedly, in true fear and invocation of God, subscribed our signatures with our own hands. Done at Bergen, May 29, 1577.

Dr. Jakob Andreae subscribed

Dr. Nicholas Selnecker subscribed

Dr. Andrew Musculus subscribed

Dr. Christopher Körner subscribed

David Chytraeus

Dr. Martin Chemnitz

Reformed Confessions

The designation "reformed" (with a lowercase "r") applies to, and has been used by, confessions of churches of the Reformation that define themselves over against Roman Catholicism. For example, at the beginning of its *Solid Declaration,* the Lutheran *Formula of Concord* could refer to *The Augsburg Confession* as "the common confession of the reformed churches." The slogan, "the church is reformed and always in need of reformation [*ecclesia reformata et semper reformanda*]," speaks about (and for) all the churches of the Reformation.

But the designation "Reformed confessions" (with a capital "R") soon acquired a more technical significance, to identify those Reformation statements of faith that traced their ancestry to Zwingli and Calvin rather than to Luther: these confessions and churches were to be defined not negatively as "non-Lutheran" but positively as "Reformed in accordance with the word of God [*nach Gottes Wort reformiert*]." And the designation has stuck, having now gradually caught on even in the English-speaking world.

Unlike the Lutheran confessions, the Reformed confessions not only arose separately from one another but have been, for the most part, received and transmitted by their particular churches, with mutual recognition and even acceptance, but without a Reformed equivalent of *The Book of Concord.* In the conclusion of its *Canons* of 1619, the Synod of Dort could "plead with all who devoutly call on the name of our Savior Jesus Christ to form their judgment about the faith of the Reformed churches . . . on the bases of the churches' own official confessions," to which it now joined its own confession.

That decentralized quality of the Reformed confessions also accounts for the presence here of *The Thirty-Nine Articles of the Church of England;* for even those Anglicans who would not identify the Church of England as "Reformed" in the sense that the Presbyterian Church of Scotland is "Reformed" do acknowledge that the confession *is* Reformed; indeed, one non-Anglican scholar has called it "one of the most excellent symbols of the Reformed Church."[1]

1. Hofmann 1857, 269.

Ulrich Zwingli, *The Sixty-Seven Articles*, 1523

Ulrich Zwingli (1484–1531) prepared *The Sixty-Seven Articles* as topics for discussion with representatives of the bishop of Constance, under whose jurisdiction he served as pastor of the Grossmünster in Zurich. The meeting, known as the First Disputation of Zurich, took place in January 1523 before the city council and six hundred citizens.[1] Zwingli came armed with these articles and the Bible. The bishop's envoys, chief among them Johann Faber (1478–1541), did not wish to debate, however, preferring "to listen and not to dispute."[2] Faber suggested that a church council would be a more appropriate setting for such a discussion. But Zwingli tried to force the debate, attacking the mass, clerical celibacy, and church tradition, emphasizing at every possible point the authority of Scripture. Although patient and good-humored at first, Faber ultimately denounced *The Sixty-Seven Articles* as "not in harmony with the truth."[3] There are no official minutes of the Zurich disputation, but Erhard Hegenwald, a supporter of Zwingli, wrote an account of the proceedings that was published in 1523.[4] Zwingli's opponent Johann Faber also published his version of the disputation.[5]

As expected, the city council decided the matter in Zwingli's favor, declaring the Grossmünster outside episcopal control. It also mandated that all preaching must have its basis in Scripture.[6] After Zurich, such civic debates or "disputations"—often with predetermined outcomes—were used to introduce reforms into cities throughout Switzerland and southern Germany, most notably in Baden (1526) and Bern (1528). All were influenced by Zwingli, who is rightly called the founder of the Reformed tradition.

Several printings of *The Sixty-Seven Articles* exist from 1523; the earliest editions published the articles as they were presented to the city council. Editions

1. See Oberman 1981, 210–39, for a critical assessment of the First Disputation of Zurich.
2. Jackson [1901] 1972, 52.
3. Jackson [1901] 1972, 108.
4. See *CR* 93/1:114–68, for edition, and Jackson [1901] 1972, 40–117, for an English translation.
5. See Immenkötter 1979.
6. In fact, already on 22 July 1522, the Lesser Council of Zurich had mandated that all preaching must be from the Bible. This fact, combined with the refusal of the Catholic party to debate, led Oberman to observe that the event of 29 January was "neither the first nor the second disputation—it was no disputation at all" (Oberman 1981, 236).

after July 1523 add an exposition on the articles by Zwingli. The articles were written in Swiss German but were later translated into Latin for a broader audience by both Leo Juda (1482–1542) and Rudolf Gwalther (1519–86).[7]

Edition: *CR* 88:458–65.

Translation: Cochrane, 36–44 (with slight revisions).

Note: In his *Exposition of the Sixty-Seven Articles,* Zwingli offered copious biblical proof texts for each article; see Furcha 1984, 7–373, for an English translation. We have included the most significant biblical references from that work.

Literature: Baur 1883; Büsser 1985; Gäbler 1983a; Haas 1969; Immenkötter 1979; Jackson [1901] 1972; Lewis 1985; Locher 1978; Muralt 1969; Niemeyer, xv–xxii; Noll, 39–47; Oberman 1981, 210–39; *OER* 320–23 (Wandel); Pollet 1963; Potter 1976, 99–103; Schaff, 1:360–84; Stephens 1986 and 1992, 124–39; *450 Jahre Zürcher Reformation* 1969.

7. See Niemeyer, xv–xxii.

Ulrich Zwingli, *The Sixty-Seven Articles*, 1523

The following sixty-seven articles and opinions, I, Huldreich Zwingli, confess that I preached in the venerable city of Zurich on the basis of the Scripture which is called *theopneustos* [that is, inspired by God], and I offer to debate and defend them; and where I have not now correctly understood the said Scripture, I am ready to be instructed and corrected, but only from the aforesaid Scripture. [2 Tm 3.16]

1. All who say that the gospel is nothing without the approbation of the church err and slander God.

2. The sum of the gospel is that our Lord Jesus Christ, the true Son of God, has made known to us the will of his heavenly Father, and by his innocence has redeemed us from death and reconciled us unto God. [1 Pt 3.18]

3. Therefore Christ is the only way to salvation for all who ever lived, do live, or ever will live. [Jn 14.6]

4. Whoever seeks or points to another door errs—yea, is a murderer of souls and a robber. [Jn 10.1–5]

5. Therefore all who regard another doctrine as equal to or higher than the gospel err and do not know what the gospel is.

6. For Christ Jesus is the leader and captain whom God has promised and given to the whole human race. [Is 55.4]

7. That he [Christ] might be the eternal salvation and the head of all believers, who are his body, which, however, is dead and can do nothing without him. [Eph 1.22] [Jn 15.5]

8. From this it follows, first, that all who live in the head are his members and children of God.[a] And this is the church or fellowship of the saints, the bride of Christ, *ecclesia catholica*.

9. Secondly, that, just as the members of a physical body can do nothing without the guidance of the head, so now in the body of Christ no one can do anything without Christ, its head. [Jn 15.4]

10. Just as that person is demented whose members operate without his head, lacerating, wounding and harming himself, so also are the members of Christ demented when they undertake something without Christ, their head, tormenting and burdening themselves with foolish ordinances.

11. Therefore we perceive that the so-called clerical traditions with their

a. [Rom 12.5; 1 Cor 6.15]

pomp, riches, hierarchy, titles, and laws are a cause of all nonsense, because they are not in agreement with Christ, the head.

12. Thus they continue to rant and rave, not out of concern for the head (for that is what is being striven for now by the grace of God) but because they are not permitted to rave on and instead are required to listen to the head alone.

[Jn 6.44] 13. When we listen to the head, we acquire a pure and clear knowledge of the will of God, and we are drawn to him by his Spirit and are conformed to him.

14. Hence all Christians should do their utmost that everywhere only the gospel of Christ be preached.ᵃ

15. For our salvation is based on faith in the gospel, and our damnation on unbelief; for all truth is clear in it.

16. In the gospel we learn that human doctrines and traditions are of no avail to salvation.

CONCERNING THE POPE

17. That Christ is the one, eternal High Priest, from which it follows that those who have pretended to be high priests oppose the honor and authority of Christ—yea,
[Heb 7.26] they reject it.

CONCERNING THE MASS

[Heb 7.26–27] 18. That Christ, who offered himself up once and for all, is in eternity a perpetual sacrifice in payment of the sins of all believers, from which it follows that the mass is not a sacrifice but a recollection of the sacrifice and an assurance of the redemption
[Lk 22.19–20] which Christ has manifested to us.

CONCERNING THE INTERCESSION OF THE SAINTS

[Jn 14.6] 19. That Christ is the one Mediator between God and us.

20. That God wants to give us all things in his name, from which it follows that we need no mediator beyond this life but Christ.

21. That when we pray for one another on earth we do so in such wise that
[Mt 18.19] we trust that through Christ alone all things are given to us.

CONCERNING GOOD WORKS

22. That Christ is our righteousness, from which we conclude that our works are good in so far as they are of Christ; in so far as they are our works they are neither
[1 Cor 1.30] righteous nor good.

a. [Mk 16.15; Mt 24.14]

CONCERNING CLERICAL PROPERTY

23. That Christ condemns the possessions and pomp of this world, from which we conclude that those who heap up riches unto themselves in his name monstrously slander him, using him as a cloak to hide their own greed and arrogance.

CONCERNING THE PROHIBITION OF FOODS

24. That no Christian is bound to perform works which God has not commanded; [Mk 7.18] he is free to eat all foods at any time. From this we see that dispensations concerning fasting are a Roman fraud. [Col 2.16]

CONCERNING FESTIVALS AND PILGRIMAGES

25. That the Christian is not bound to times and places; rather they are subject to him. From this we learn that those who bind men to times and places rob Christians of their freedom. [Mt 12.6]

CONCERNING HOODS, DRESS, INSIGNIA

26. That nothing is more displeasing to God than hypocrisy. Hence we learn that everything which simulates holiness in the eyes of men is grievous hypocrisy and infamy. Under this head fall cowls, insignia, tonsures, etc.[a]

CONCERNING ORDERS AND SECTS

27. That all Christians are brothers of Christ and brothers one of another and no one on earth should be called father. Thus orders, sects, and fraternities are untenable. [Mt 12.50]

CONCERNING THE MARRIAGE OF MINISTERS

28. That everything which God permits or does not forbid is lawful. From this we learn that marriage is seemly for all men. [Rom 3.20]

29. That all who are called ministers sin when, having become convinced that God has denied them the gift of continence, they do not safeguard themselves by marrying. [Mt 19.11]

CONCERNING THE VOW OF CHASTITY

30. That those who take a vow of chastity foolishly or childishly undertake too much. From this we learn that those who accept such vows do violence to pious people.

a. [Jb 13.16; Mt 23.13, 24, 50–51]

CONCERNING EXCOMMUNICATION

31. That no single individual may impose a bann of excommunication upon anyone. Only the church may do it, which is the fellowship of those among whom the one worthy of excommunication dwells, together with the minister, who is their
[Mt 18.15–18]   watchman.

32. That only one who has committed a public offense may be excommunicated.

CONCERNING ILL-GOTTEN GAINS

33. That ill-gotten gain should not be given to temples, cloisters, monks, clerics, and
[Is 61.8]   nuns, but to the poor, provided it cannot be restored to the rightful owner.

CONCERNING AUTHORITY

[Mt 18.1–4]   34. The so-called spiritual power has no basis for its pomp in the teaching of Christ.

35. The temporal power, however, does have power and confirmation in the doctrine and work of Christ.

36. The so-called ecclesiastical estate pretends that the administration of justice rightfully belongs to it. But all this pertains to temporal rulers if they want to be Christians.

37. Moreover, all Christians, without exception, owe them obedience.[a]
[Acts 5.29]   38. That is, in so far as they do not require anything contrary to God.

39. For this reason, all their laws should conform to the divine will so that they protect the oppressed, even when he does not complain.

40. Only they [magistrates] may lawfully take life, and then only the lives of those who commit a public offense, without provoking God's wrath—unless God
[Rom 13.4]   has decreed otherwise.

41. When they [magistrates] offer counsel and help to those for whom they
[Rom 13.5–7]   will render an account to God, the latter owe to these magistrates bodily assistance.

42. But when they are unfaithful and do not act according to the rule of
[Acts 5.29]   Christ, they may be deposed in the name of God.

43. In a word, his kingdom is best and is the most stable who governs in the name of God alone; and his kingdom is the worst and the most insecure who governs according to his own will.

a. [Mt 22.21; Rom 13.1–2]

CONCERNING PRAYER

44. True worshipers call upon God in spirit and in truth without ostentation before men.

[Jn 4.24]

[Mt 6.7]

45. Hypocrites do their works in order to be seen of men, and they receive their reward in this world.

[Mt 23.5]

46. Thus it must follow that chanting and loud clamor which lack true devotion and are done only for the sake of reward, either seek the praise of men or material gain.

CONCERNING OFFENSE

47. A person should suffer physical death rather than offend or scandalize a fellow Christian.

48. Whoever through stupidity or ignorance wants to take offense without cause should not be permitted to remain in his weakness or ignorance but should be strengthened in order that he may not regard as sinful that which is not sinful.

[1 Cor 8.7–13]

49. I know of no greater offense than to forbid priests to have wives and then to allow them to hire prostitutes. Away with this shame!

CONCERNING THE REMISSION OF SINS

50. God alone remits sins, through Jesus Christ, his Son, our only Lord.

51. Whoever ascribes the remission of sins to a creature robs God of his honor and gives it to one who is not God. That is pure idolatry.[a]

[Is 43.25–27]

52. Consequently confession which is made to a priest or to a neighbor is not for the remission of sins, but for counseling.

53. Imposed works of penance stem from human counsel (with the exception of excommunication). They do not remit sin and are imposed to warn others.[b]

54. Christ has borne all our pain and misery. Whoever now attributes to works of penance what belongs to Christ alone, errs and blasphemes God.

[Jn 1.29]

55. Whoever refuses to remit any sin to a penitent person, would not be acting in the place of God or of Peter, but of the devil.

[Mt 12.31]

56. Whoever remits sins solely for the sake of money is the partner of Simon and Balaam and is really a messenger of the devil.

[Acts 8.18–19]

[Mt 10.8]

a. [Mt 9.6; Mk 2.10–12; Lk 5.24]
b. [Mt 9.22; Gal 2.16–21]

CONCERNING PURGATORY

57. The true Holy Scriptures know nothing of a purgatory after this life.

58. The judgment of those who have died is known only to God.

59. And the less God has let us know about it, the less should we try to know about it.

60. I do not condemn it when a person, concerned for the dead, calls upon God to show them mercy. But to stipulate the duration of purgatory (seven years for a mortal sin), and to lie for the sake of gain is inhuman and diabolical.

CONCERNING THE PRIESTHOOD

61. The Divine Scriptures know nothing of an indelible imprint [character] by consecration which the priests have invented in recent times.

[1 Tm 5.17] 62. Furthermore the Scriptures do not recognize any priests except those who proclaim God's word.

[1 Cor 9.13–15] 63. To such as do [proclaim God's word] Scripture commands us to show them honor and give support for their bodily needs.

CONCERNING THE CESSATION OF ABUSES

64. Those who recognize their error are not to be made to suffer for it, but are to be allowed to die in peace; afterward their bequests to the church are to be administered in a Christian manner.

[Mt 26.52] 65. God will deal with those who do not want to recognize their error. Therefore no violence is to be done to their bodies unless their conduct is so unseemly that it cannot be tolerated.

[Mt 3.10] 66. All officials in the church should forthwith humble themselves, and should exalt the cross of Christ alone and not the money chest. Otherwise they will perish; the ax is laid to the root of the tree.

67. If anyone wishes to have a discussion with me about usury, tithes, unbaptized children, or confirmation, I declare myself willing to respond.

Here let no one attempt to contend with sophistry or trifles, but let him come having Scripture as judge, in order that either the truth be found or, when it is found, as I hope it would be, that it be kept. Amen. May God grant it!

The Ten Theses of Bern, 1528

In preparation for a disputation on religious belief and practices, two reformed preachers in Bern, Berchtold Haller (1492–1536) and Franz Kolb (c. 1465–1535), wrote *The Ten Theses of Bern* in late 1527. Zwingli probably saw the document before the disputation and may have made minor revisions before it was printed (first published in 1528 in Zurich).[1] The Bern Disputation took place from 6 January to 26 January 1528. It was a carefully orchestrated assembly attended by important leaders of the Protestant movement in southwestern German-speaking lands, including Ambrosius Blaurer, Martin Bucer, Heinrich Bullinger, Conrad Pellican, Wolfgang Capito, Niklaus Manuel, Johannes Oecolampadius, and Zwingli himself. No Roman Catholic bishops attended, nor were their interests represented in any number or force. In addition to criticism of Catholic practices, the Bernese reformers objected to some Lutheran and Anabaptist views. The Bern Disputation led directly to the city council's mandate of 7 February 1528 giving *The Ten Theses* the force of law and effectively imposing the Reformation on the city. The success of the Bern Disputation was a major milestone in the progress of Zwinglian reform in the Swiss Confederation beyond the canton of Zurich.

The theses endorse biblicism (article 2) and solafideism (article 3). They also reject such religious practices as the Catholic mass (article 5), veneration of saints (article 6), and masses for the dead (article 7). Articles 9 and 10, which concern sexual morality, endorse marriage for the clergy. The eucharist is defined in a Zwinglian fashion (article 4), and there is a tentative formulation against the use of images in churches (article 8). This statement on religious images is, however, so moderate that it is technically in agreement with Luther's views.

Edition: *Aktensammlung* 1918–23, 1:518–21 (#1371).

Translation: Cochrane, 49–50 (with prefatory material added and slightly modified to reflect the edition used here).

Note: We include the Swiss-German version presented at the disputation as it was printed in the first edition (Zurich: Christoph Froschauer, 23 March 1528). *The Ten Theses* were also translated into Latin by Zwingli and into French by Guillaume Farel.

---

1. Potter 1976, 254.

Literature: Baker 1988; Cochrane, 45–48; Guggisberg 1958, 101–20; Hendricks 1978; Koch 1995; Lavater 1980; Locher 1980a, 1980b; Muralt 1930; *OER* 1:143–45 (Schmidt), 2:208–9 (Baker); Potter 1976, 244–66; Sladeczek 1988.

The Ten Theses of Bern, 1528

With these theses we, Franz Kolb and Berchtold Haller, preachers in Bern, along with others who confess the gospel, desire to give publicly and before God, an answer and account based on the Holy Scripture, the New and Old Testaments, in Bern on the Sunday after Circumcision in the year 1528.

1. The holy, Christian church, whose only head is Christ, is born of the word of God, abides in the same, and does not listen to the voice of a stranger. [Jn 10.5]

2. The church of Christ makes no laws or commandments without God's word. Hence all human traditions, which are called ecclesiastical commandments, are binding upon us only in so far as they are based on and commanded by God's word.

3. Christ is our only wisdom, righteousness, redemption, and payment for the sins of the whole world. Hence it is a denial of Christ when we acknowledge another merit for salvation and satisfaction for sin. [1 Cor 1.30]

4. It cannot be proved from biblical writings that the body and blood of Christ is essentially and corporeally received in the bread of the eucharist.

5. The mass as now in use, in which Christ is offered up to God the Father for the sins of the living and the dead, is contrary to Scripture, a blasphemy against the most holy sacrifice, passion, and death of Christ, and on account of its abuses, an abomination before God.

6. As Christ alone died for us, so he is to be worshiped as the only Mediator and Advocate between God the Father and us believers. Therefore, to propose the invoking of other mediators and advocates beyond this life is contrary to Scripture.

7. Scripture knows nothing of a purgatory after this life. Hence all offices for the dead such as vigils, masses, requiems, devotions repeated after the seventh or thirtieth day of each year, lamps, candles, and such like are in vain.

8. The making of images to be venerated is contrary to the word of God of the Old and New Testaments. Therefore when the setting up of images involves the danger of veneration, they are to be abolished.

9. Holy matrimony is not forbidden in Scripture to any class of men, but is granted to all in order to avoid adultery and fornication.

10. Since, according to Scripture, an open adulterer is to be excommunicated, it follows that because of the scandal involved, fornication and adultery are more pernicious for the clergy than for any other class of men.

May all things be to the honor of God and his holy word!

The Tetrapolitan Confession, 1530

The Augsburg Confession was not the only profession of faith submitted to Charles V at the Diet of Augsburg in the summer of 1530. Four southern German cities, Strasbourg, Memmingen, Constance, and Lindau, signed *The Tetrapolitan Confession*, which had been drawn up by representatives from Strasbourg, Martin Bucer (1491–1551) and Wolfgang Capito (1478–1541). It was delivered to the emperor's vice chancellor on 9 July 1530, two weeks after → *The Augsburg Confession* had been read before the diet and the day after Zwingli had submitted his → *Fidei ratio*.

In the places where *The Tetrapolitan Confession* diverges from *The Augsburg Confession* it emphasizes the concerns of the churches of southern Germany and Switzerland, particularly in its repeated insistence on the Bible as the sole source for preaching and teaching and in the rejection of images in worship. Substantial documentation exists from the period when Bucer and Capito were hurrying to compose the confession. Early drafts in Capito's hand expressly deny a real presence in the eucharist,[1] but the final version reflects Bucer's attempt to find a middle way between Luther and Zwingli: "To all those who sincerely have given their names among his disciples and receive this supper according to his institution, he deigns to give his true body and true blood to be truly eaten and drunk" (chapter 18). Elsewhere the text emphasizes the spiritual nature of any nourishment from the sacrament, as well as its function as a remembrance. In this way the authors tried to satisfy the spiritual or symbolic views of the four subscribing cities without alienating the politically powerful Lutheran princes and city governments.

The Tetrapolitan Confession lost its official status within a year. The city of Ulm, however, used it as the basis for its confession in 1531.[2] Moreover, *The Tetrapolitan Confession* remained an important document in religious discussions in Strasbourg from the time of the Synod of Strasbourg in 1532 to that city's adoption of the Lutheran *Formula of Concord* in 1598.

Edition: Niemeyer, 740–70.

Translation: Cochrane (from Jacobs 1893), 54–88.

---

1. See Bucer 1969, 3:122–34, esp. 128–31.
2. Endriss 1931, 94.

Note: The original Latin and German manuscripts presented to the emperor still exist (in the State Archives of Austria, Vienna, and the Austrian National Library). A critical edition, based on the manuscript sources with later variants in the apparatus, can be found in Bernd Moeller's edition in the *Opera Omnia* of Martin Bucer (Bucer 1969, 3:37–185). We have reproduced the Niemeyer edition, which has its basis in the first printed edition of 1531, with additional biblical citations from the manuscript sources and from Moeller's edition added where appropriate.

Literature: Brady 1973; Bucer 1969, 3:15–33 (introduction to edition by Bernd Moeller); Kittelson 1973, 1975, 154–68, and 1993; Seebass 1993; *TRE* 8:173–77 (Kittelson).

The Tetrapolitan Confession, 1530

Confession of the Four Cities, Strasbourg, Constance, Memmingen, and Lindau. Wherein They Set Forth Their Faith to His Imperial Majesty in the Diet of Augsburg.

Exordium

Thy Worshipful Majesty, Most Powerful and Most Clement Emperor, hath commanded that the orders and estates of the Holy Empire, so far as concerns each and each hopes to act toward tranquilizing the church, should present to him their opinion, reduced to writing in both languages, Latin and German, concerning religion, as well as concerning the errors and vices which have insinuated themselves in opposition thereto, for discussion and examination, to the end that thereby a mode and way may be found to restore to its place the pure doctrine, all errors being abolished. We desire, as is right, to obey this command, which has not so much originated from a religious design that has in view the profit of the church as it exhibits and savors of the unparalleled clemency and kindness whereby Thy Worshipful Majesty hath rendered himself so beloved by the entire world. For in these matters we have never sought anything else than that, those things being abrogated which are contrary to the Holy Gospels and to Christ's commands, it may be allowed not only us, but also all others who have professed Christ, to follow after his pure doctrine, which alone is vivifying. Wherefore we pray and most humbly beseech Thy Worshipful Majesty to be so disposed to us as to deign to hear and consider what we [1 Pt 3.15] will present as a reason for the hope that is in us, in order that concerning these matters there may be no doubt that it has been above all our desire to aim only at that whereby we may please, first of all, our Creator and Restorer Christ, and afterward also Thy Worshipful Majesty, and that in obedience to the summons we may show that we have embraced a doctrine varying somewhat from that in common use, influenced by no other purpose or hope than that, being persuaded as he who has fashioned and refashioned us requires, we promise ourselves as the result—and this especially because of the eminent praise whereby for a long time already thou hast been celebrated among us for thy religion, godliness, and piety—that His Worshipful Majesty will acknowledge the truth concerning all things which we have received for some time as Christ's doctrine and as the teaching of a purer religion, that he will absolutely approve our attempt, and number us among those who have endeavored to obey him with the greatest fidelity. For the renowned zeal of Thy

Most Worshipful Majesty for truth and justice and thy fervent godliness permit us not even to suspect that thou wilt prejudge us before we have as yet been heard, or wilt not hear us kindly and attentively, or when thou hast heard us, and weighed with thy devout deliberation what we present, God aiding thy spirit, as he has so successfully led Thy Most Worshipful Majesty in other matters, that thou wilt not immediately perceive that we have followed the very doctrines of Christ.

CHAPTER 1. OF THE SUBJECT-MATTER OF SERMONS

First, therefore, since about ten years ago, by the remarkable goodness of God, the doctrine of Christ began to be treated with somewhat more certainty and clearness than before everywhere throughout Germany, and hence among us, just as elsewhere, many doctrines of our religion were publicly controverted, and to a constantly increasing extent, among the learned, and those especially who held the position of teachers of Christ in the churches; and hence, as was necessary, while Satan was undoubtedly plying his work, so that the people were very dangerously divided by conflicting sermons, considering what St. Paul writes, that "divinely inspired Scripture is profitable for doctrine," that where there is sin "it may be detected and corrected, and every one be instructed in righteousness, that the man of God may be perfect, furnished for every good work"—we also, influenced and induced to avoid [2 Tm 3.16–17] all delay, not only from the fear of God, but from the certain peril to the state, at length enjoined our preachers to teach from the pulpit nothing else than is either contained in the Holy Scriptures or hath sure ground therein. For it seemed to us not improper to resort in such a crisis whither of old and always not only the most holy fathers, bishops, and princes, but also the children of God everywhere, have always resorted—that is, to the authority of the Holy Scriptures. For, to their praise, St. Luke mentions of some such that they were more noble than those of Thessalonica, since they examined the gospel of Christ, which they had heard according [Acts 17.11] to the Scriptures, in which Paul most earnestly desired that his scholar Timothy be exercised, and without which no pontiffs have ever required obedience to their decrees, nor fathers credit to their writings, nor princes authority to their laws, and from which only the great council of the Holy Empire assembled at Nuremberg in the year 1523 decreed that holy sermons should be derived. For if St. Paul has taught the truth when he said that by Holy Scripture the man of God is made perfect and furnished for every good work, he can lack nothing of Christian truth or sound [2 Tm 3.17] doctrine who strives religiously to ask counsel of Scripture.

CHAPTER 2. OF THE HOLY TRINITY AND THE
MYSTERY OF THE INCARNATE CHRIST

Since, therefore, holy sermons were derived from this source and dangerous contentions ceased, those in whom there was any desire after godliness have obtained a far more certain knowledge of Christ's doctrine and have begun to express it in their life. Just as they have withdrawn from those things which were improperly attached to the doctrines of Christ, so have they been confirmed in those that agree therewith. Among these is what the church of Christ has hitherto believed concerning the Holy Trinity—that is, that God the Father, the Son, and the Holy Ghost is one in substance, and admits no distinction other than of persons. Also that our Savior Jesus Christ, being true God, became likewise true man, the two natures not being confounded, but so united in the same person that they shall never throughout all ages be sundered. Nor do they vary in these particulars in any respect from what the church, taught out of the Holy Gospels, believes concerning our Savior Jesus Christ, conceived of the Holy Ghost, then born of the Virgin Mary, and who at length, after he had performed the office of preaching the gospel, having died on the cross and been buried, descended to hell, and was recalled the third day from the dead into immortal life; and when by various arguments he had proved this to witnesses hereunto appointed, was carried up to heaven to the right hand of his Father, whence we look for him as Judge of the quick and the dead. Meanwhile, we acknowledge that he is nevertheless present with his church, even to the end of the world; that he renews and sanctifies it and adorns it as his only beloved bride with all sorts of ornaments of virtues. In these points, since we vary nothing from the common consent of Christians, we think it sufficient in this manner to testify our faith.

CHAPTER 3. OF JUSTIFICATION AND FAITH

In regard to those things which were commonly taught concerning the manner in which we become partaker of the redemption made by Christ, and concerning the duties of a Christian, our preachers differ somewhat from the lately received dogmas. Those points which we have followed we will endeavor to explain most plainly to Your Most Worshipful Majesty, and at the same time to indicate in good faith the Scripture passages that have constrained us thereto. First, therefore, since for some years we were taught that man's own works are necessary for his justification, our preachers have taught that this whole justification is to be ascribed to the good pleasure of God and the merit of Christ, and to be received by faith alone. Among others, the following passages of Scripture have moved them thereto: "As many as received him, to them gave he power to become the sons of God, even to them that believe on his name: which were born not of blood, nor of the will of the flesh, but of God," John 1. "Verily, verily, I say unto thee, except a man be born again, he cannot see the kingdom of God," John 3. "No man knoweth the Son but the Father; neither knoweth any man the Father save the Son, and he to whomsoever the Son will reveal him," Matthew 11. "Blessed art thou, Simon Bar-Jona; for flesh and blood hath not revealed it unto thee," Matthew 16. "No man can come unto me, unless my Father draw him," John 6. "By grace are ye saved through faith; and that not of yourselves; it is the gift of God; not of works, lest any man should boast. For we are his workmanship, created in Christ Jesus unto good works, which God hath before ordained that we should walk in them," Ephesians 2. For since it is our righteousness and eternal life to know God and Jesus Christ our Savior, and this is so far from being a work of flesh and blood that it is necessary for this to be born again; neither can we come to the Son, unless the Father draw us; neither know the Father, unless the Son reveal him; and Paul writes so clearly, "not of us, nor of our works"—it is evident enough that our works can help us nothing, so that instead of unrighteous, as we are born, we may become righteous; because as we are by nature the children of wrath, and on this account unrighteous, so we are unable to do anything just or pleasing to God. But the beginning of all our righteousness and salvation must proceed from the mercy of the Lord, who from his own favor and the contemplation of the death of his Son first offers the doctrine of truth and his gospel, those being sent forth who are to preach it; and, secondly, since "the natural man receiveth not the things of the Spirit of God," as St. Paul says, Corinthians 2, he causes a beam of his light to arise at the same time in the darkness of our heart, so that now we may believe his gospel preached, being persuaded of the truth thereof by his Spirit from above, and then, relying upon the testimony of this Spirit, may call upon him with filial confidence and say, "Abba, Father," obtaining thereby sure salvation, according to the saying: "Whosoever shall call upon the name of the Lord shall be saved."[a]

Jn 1[.12–13]

Jn 3[.3]

Mt 11[.27]

Mt 16[.17]

Jn 6[.44]

Eph 2[.8–10]

Eph 2[.3]

1 Cor 2[.14]

[Rom 8.15]

CHAPTER 4. OF GOOD WORKS, PROCEEDING OUT OF FAITH THROUGH LOVE

These things we will not have men so to understand, as though we placed salvation and righteousness in slothful thoughts of the mind, or in faith destitute of love, which they call faith without form; seeing that we are sure that no man can be justified or saved except he supremely love and most earnestly imitate God. "For whom he did foreknow, he also did predestinate to be conformed to the image of his Son";

[Rom 8.29]

a. [Jer 33.3; Jl 2.32; Rom 10.13]

to wit, as in the glory of a blessed life, so in the cultivation of innocence and per-
[Eph 2.10]   fect righteousness; "for we are his workmanship, created unto good works." But
no one can love God above all things, and worthily imitate him, but he who indeed
knows him and expects all good things from him. Therefore, we cannot be otherwise justified—that is, become righteous as well as saved (for righteousness is even
our salvation)—than by being endued chiefly with faith, whereby, believing the gospel, and therefore being persuaded that God has adopted us as his children, and that
he will ever bestow his paternal kindness upon us, we wholly depend upon his pleasure. This faith St. Augustine in his book *De fide et operibus* calls "evangelical"—to
wit, that which is efficacious through love. By this only are we regenerated and the
image of God is restored in us. By this, although we are born corrupt, our thoughts
even from our childhood being altogether prone to evil, we become good and upright. For from this we, being fully satisfied with one God, the perennial fountain of
blessings that is copiously effluent, show ourselves to others as gods—that is, true
children of God—by love striving for their advantage so far as we are able. For "he
[1 Jn 4.7]   that loveth his brother abideth in the light" and "is born of God," and is wholly
given to the new, and at the same time old, commandment concerning mutual love.
And this love is the fulfilling of the whole law, as Paul says: "All the law is fulfilled
Gal 5[.14]   in one word: Thou shalt love thy neighbor as thyself," Galatians 5. For whatever the
law of God teaches has this end and requires this one thing, that at length we may
be reformed to the perfect image of God, being good in all things, and ready and
willing to serve the advantage of men; which we cannot do unless we be furnished
with virtues of every kind. For who can purpose and do all things, as the duty of a
Christian requires, to the true edifying of the church and the sound profit of all—
that is, according to God's law and for his glory—except he both think and speak
1 Cor [10.31]   and do everything in order and well, and therefore be very familiarly acquainted
with the whole company of virtues?

CHAPTER 5. TO WHOM GOOD WORKS ARE TO BE ASCRIBED, AND HOW THEY ARE NECESSARY

Rom 8[.14]   But since they who are the children of God are led by the Spirit of God, rather than
that they act themselves, Romans 8, and "of him, and through him, and to him, are
Rom 11[.36]   all things," Romans 11, whatsoever things we do well and holily are to be ascribed
to none other than to this one only Spirit, the Giver of all virtues. However it be, he
does not compel us, but leads us, being willing, working in us both to will and to
Phil 2[.13]   do, Philippians 2. Hence Augustine writes wisely that God rewards his own works
in us. By this we are so far from rejecting good works that we utterly deny that any

one can be saved unless by Christ's Spirit he be brought thus far, that there be in him no lack of good works, for which God has created him. For there are diverse members of the same body; therefore each of us has not the same office, 1 Corinthians 12. Inasmuch as it is so necessary for the law to be fulfilled that heaven and earth shall pass away before one iota or the least point thereof be remitted, yet because God alone is good, and has created all things out of nothing, and by his Spirit makes us altogether new, and wholly leads us (for in Christ nothing avails but a new creature), none of these things can be ascribed to human powers; and we must confess that all things are the mere gifts of God, who favors and loves us of his own accord, and not for any merit of ours. From the above it can be sufficiently known what we believe justification to be, by whom it is brought us, and in what way it is received of us, and by what passages of Scripture we are induced to so believe. For although of many we have cited a few, yet by these few any one who is even moderately versed in the Scriptures will be satisfied, and even more than satisfied, that passages of this kind that ascribe nothing but sin and perdition to us, as Hosea says, and all our righteousness and salvation to the Lord, meet readers of the Scriptures everywhere.

1 Cor 12

[Mt 5.18]

[Gal 6.15]

[Hos 13.9]

CHAPTER 6. OF THE DUTIES OF A CHRISTIAN

Now it cannot be doubted what be the duties of a Christian, and to what actions he should be chiefly devoted; namely, to all those whereby every one, for his part, may profit his neighbors—first, with respect to life eternal, that they may begin to know, worship, and fear God; and then with respect to the present life, that they may want nothing required by bodily necessity. For as the whole law of God, which is a most absolute commandment of all righteousness, is summed up in this one word: "Thou shalt love thy neighbor as thyself," Romans 13, so in rendering this love it is necessary that all righteousness be comprised and completed. Hence nothing at all is to be reckoned among the duties of a Christian which has not some force to profit our neighbor, and that every such work pertaineth the more to a Christian as more advantage may accrue to his neighbor. Therefore, after ecclesiastical functions we place among the chief duties of a Christian the administration of the government, obedience to magistrates (for these are of importance for the common profit), the care which is devoted to wife, children, and family, and the honor which is rendered parents, because without these the life of men cannot subsist; and, lastly, the professions of good arts and all honorable branches of learning, since without the cultivation of these we would necessarily be destitute of the greatest blessings, and those which are peculiar to mankind. Yet in these and all other duties of human life

Rom 13[.9]

no man must inconsiderately take anything to himself, but conscientiously consider whither God calls him. To conclude, let every man account that his duty, and that duty the more excellent, whereby he may confer the greatest advantage upon men.

CHAPTER 7. OF PRAYERS AND FASTS

We have prayers and fasts, actions nevertheless the most holy and such as are especially proper for Christians, to which our ecclesiastics most diligently exhort their hearers. For true fasting is, as it were, a renouncing of the present life, which is always subject to evil desires, and a meditation upon the future life, that is free from perturbations. Prayer, moreover, is a lifting up of the mind to God, and such conversation with him that no other thing so greatly inflames man with heavenly affections and more mightily conforms the mind to God's will. But however holy and necessary these exercises be to Christians, yet as one's neighbor is not so much served by them as man is prepared to serve his neighbor with profit, they are not to be preferred to holy doctrine, godly exhortations and admonitions, and other duties whereby our neighbor at once receives profit. Hence we read of the Savior that in the nighttime he gave himself to prayer, but in the daytime to doctrine and healing [1 Cor 13.13] the sick. For as love is greater than faith and hope, so we believe that those things which come nearest—that is, such as bring assured profit unto men—are to be preferred above all other holy functions. Hence St. Chrysostom wrote that in the whole company of virtues fasting had the last place.

CHAPTER 8. OF THE COMMANDING OF FASTS

But since no minds, unless they be very ardent and peculiarly influenced by inspiration from above, can either pray or fast aright and with profit, we believe that it is better, according to the example of the apostles and of the earlier and purer church, by holy exhortations to invite men to these things, rather than to exhort them by precepts, especially such as bind men under penalty of sin, as the priests that have been of late, since the order of priests had not a little degenerated, undertook to do. So we prefer to leave the place, time, and manner both of praying and of fasting to be determined by the Holy Ghost, without whom it is impossible for any one either to pray or to fast aright, rather than prescribe them by fixed laws, especially such as may not be broken without some atonement. Yet for the younger and less perfect our preachers do not disapprove of the appointment of a fixed time and mode for praying and fasting, whereby, as by holy introductions, they may be prepared hereunto, provided this be done without binding of the conscience. We were brought to this opinion not only because the nature of these actions conflicts with all ungrateful compulsion, but especially by the consideration that neither Christ himself nor any of his apostles have in any way mentioned such precepts. This St. Chrysostom also testifies. "Thou seest," says he, "that an upright life aids more than all other things. Now I term an upright life not the labor of fasting nor the bed of hair or ashes, but if thou despisest money no otherwise than thou shouldst; if thou burn with love; if thou nourish the hungry with thy bread; if thou overcome thy anger; if thou desire not vainglory; if thou be not possessed with envy. For these are his instructions. For he does not say that his fast must be imitated, although he could have laid down those forty days, but: 'Learn of me; for I am meek and lowly of heart.' Yea, rather he says, on the contrary: 'Whatsoever is set before you, eat.'" [1] [Mt 11.29] [Lk 10.8]

Moreover, we do not read that any solemn and set fast was appointed the ancient people of God, save that of one day. For the fasts which Scripture testifies were instituted by prophets and kings were evidently not set fasts, but enjoined only for their time, when certain calamities, either impending or already oppressing them, made such demands. Seeing, therefore, Scripture, as St. Paul distinctly affirms, instructs in every good work, but is ignorant of these fasts extorted by precepts, we do not see how it could be lawful for the successors of the apostles to oppress the church with so great and so dangerous a burden. Truly Irenaeus testifies that in time past the observance of fasts in the churches was diverse and free, as is read in the *Ecclesiastical History*, book 8, chapter 14. In the same book Eusebius mentions that one Apollonius, an ecclesiastical writer, among other arguments used this also to confute the doctrine of the heretic Montanus, that he was the first that made laws for fasts. So unworthy did he deem this of those professing the sound doctrine of Christ. Thereupon Chrysostom says somewhere: "Fasting is good, but let no man be compelled." [2] And in another place he exhorts him that is not able to fast to abstain from dainties, and affirms that this does not differ much from fasting, and that it is a strong weapon to repress the fury of the devil. Moreover, experience itself more than proves that such commandments concerning fasts have been a great hindrance to godliness. [2 Tm 3.16]

When, therefore, we saw very evidently that the chief men in the church beyond the authority of Scripture assumed this authority so to enjoin fasts as to bind men's consciences, we allowed consciences to be freed from these snares, but by the Scriptures, and especially Paul's writings, which with singular earnestness remove these rudiments of the world from the necks of Christians. For the saying of Paul ought not to have light weight with us: "Let no man, therefore, judge you in meat, or in drink, or in respect of an holy day, or of the new moon, or of the Sab- [Col 2[.16]]

1. John Chrysostom *Homilies on the Gospel of Matthew* 46.4 (*NPNF*–I 10:291).
2. Probably John Chrysostom *Concerning the Statues* Homily 3.8–11 (*NPNF*–I 9:357–59).

bath days." And again: "Wherefore if ye be dead with Christ from the rudiments
of the world, why, as though living in the world, are ye subject to ordinances?"
For if St. Paul (than whom no man at any time taught Christ more certainly) maintains that through Christ we have obtained such liberty in external things that he
not only allows no creature the right to burden those who believe in Christ, even
with those ceremonies and observances which God himself appointed, and wished
in their own time to be profitable, but also denounces as having fallen away from
Christ, and that Christ is of none effect to those who suffer themselves to be made
servant thereto, what verdict do we think should be passed on those commandments
which men have devised of themselves, not only without any oracle, but also without any example worthy of being followed, and which, therefore, are unto most not
only beggarly and weak, but also hurtful; not elements—that is, rudiments of holy
discipline—but impediments of true godliness? How much more unjust will it be
for any one to assume to himself this power over the inheritance of Christ, so as
to oppress it with such bondage, and how far shall it remove us from Christ if we
submit ourselves to these things! For who does not see that the glory of Christ (to
whom we ought wholly to live, as he has wholly redeemed us to himself and delivered us, and that, too, by his blood) is more obscured if without his authority
we bind our conscience to such laws as are the inventions of men, than to those
which have God as their author, even though they were once in their own time to
be observed? Certainly, it is less fault to play the Jew than the heathen. But it is the
custom of the heathen to receive laws for the worship of God which have originated
without God's advice, and from man's invention only. Wherefore, if ever elsewhere,
the saying of Paul is in place: "Ye are bought with a price; be not ye the servants of
men."

Col 2[.20]

1 Cor 7[.23]

CHAPTER 9. OF THE CHOICE OF FOODS

For the same cause was remitted also the selection of foods prescribed for certain
days, which St. Paul, writing to Timothy, calls a doctrine of demons. Nor is their
answer firmly grounded who maintain that these expressions were used only against
the Manichaeans, Encratites, Tatianites, and Marcionites, who wholly forbade certain kinds of foods and marriage. The apostle in this place condemned those who
command "to abstain from foods which God hath created to be received," etc. Now
they also who forbid the taking of certain foods on certain days nevertheless command men to abstain from foods which God created to be taken, and are akin to
the doctrines of demons, as is manifest from the reason that the apostle added. For
he says God has created everything that is good, and nothing is to be refused that
is received with thanksgiving. He excepts no times, although no one favored fru-

1 Tm [1.3]

1 Tm [4.3]

1 Tm [4.4]

gality, temperance, and also choice chastisements of the flesh and lawful fastings, more than he did. Certainly, a Christian must observe frugality, but at all times; and the flesh must sometimes be chastised by diminishing the accustomed diet, but plainness and moderation of foods conduce to this more than does the kind. To conclude: it is meet for Christians now and then to take upon themselves a due fast; but that must not be an abstinence from certain but from all foods; nor from foods only, but from all the dainties whatsoever of this life. For what kind of fast is this, what sort of abstinence, to change only the kind of dainties (as those who are regarded today more devout than others are wont to do), since St. Chrysostom does not regard it a fast if we continue even entirely without meats until evening, unless, together with abstinence from foods, we are continent also from those things that are hurtful, and bestow much leisure upon the pursuit of spiritual things?

CHAPTER 10. THAT BY PRAYERS AND FASTINGS WE MUST NOT LOOK TO MERIT ANYTHING

Moreover, our ecclesiastics have taught that this fault must be amended with respect to prayers and fasts—namely, that men are commonly taught to seek some sort of merit and justification by these their works. For just as we are saved by grace through faith, so also are we justified. And of the works of the law, among which prayers and fastings are reckoned, Paul has written thus: "Christ is become of none effect unto you, whosoever of you are justified by the law; you are fallen from grace. For we through the Spirit wait for the hope of righteousness by faith." Therefore we must pray, but to the end that we may receive of God, not that we may hereby confer anything upon him. We must fast, that we may the better pray and keep the flesh within duty, not that we may deserve anything for ourselves before God. This end and use alone of prayers and fasts both the Scripture and also the writings and examples of the fathers prescribe. Besides, our circumstances are such that although we could pray and fast with such devoutness, and perform all things that God has enjoined upon us, so that nothing more could be required (which hitherto no mortal has at any time performed), yet we must still confess that we are unprofitable servants. What merit, therefore, can we imagine?

Gal 5[.4]

[Lk 17.10]

CHAPTER 11. THAT ONE GOD IS TO BE WORSHIPED THROUGH CHRIST

Another abuse concerning these things has been rejected, by which some think by fastings and prayers they can so oblige the Virgin Mary that bare God, and other saints, as, by their intercession and merits, to be delivered from all evils, both of body and of soul, and to be enriched with every kind of good things. For our preachers teach that the heavenly Father alone is to be invoked through Christ as the only Mediator, and that we are to pray of him all things, as he himself has testified that he will refuse us nothing which we ask only in faith and in the name of Christ.

1 Tm 2[.5] Since, therefore, Paul proclaims this one man Jesus Christ as Mediator between God and men, and no one can love us more or have more influence with the Father, our preachers are accustomed to urge that this one advocate and intercessor with the Father is enough. Yet they teach the duty of honoring the most holy Virgin Mary, the Mother of God, and all saints, with the greatest devotion, but that this can be done only when we strive after those things that were especially pleasing to them—that is, innocency and godliness, of which they have afforded us such eminent examples. For since all godly persons love God with all the heart and soul and strength, we can in nothing please them better than together with them, as ardently as possible, both to love and to imitate God. For they do not ascribe their salvation to their own merits, much less ever think of aiding us thereby. For every one of them, when he lived here, said with Paul: "The life which I now live in the flesh I live by the faith

[Gal 2.20–21] of the Son of God, who loved me and gave himself for me. I do not make void the grace of God." Seeing, therefore, that they themselves ascribed all that they had received to the grace of God and the redemption of Jesus Christ, we can gratify them no better than if we also rely upon such assistance.

CHAPTER 12. OF MONKERY

For the same reason, that all our justification consists in faith in Jesus Christ, whence we derive liberty in all external things, we have permitted the bonds of monkery also among us to be relaxed. For we saw that this liberty of Christians was everywhere earnestly asserted by St. Paul, whereby every Christian, being of himself sure that all righteousness and salvation must be sought for only in Jesus Christ our Lord, and also that he must always use all things of this life as for the advantage of his neighbor, so also for the glory of God, freely permits himself and all that he has to be arbitrated and directed by the Holy Spirit of Christ, the bestower of true adoption and liberty, and also to be appointed and bestowed not only for the profit of his neighbors, but also to the glory of God. In retaining this liberty we show that we are servants of God; in betraying it to men, addicting ourselves to their inventions, we, like renegades, forsake Christ and flee to men. This we do the more wickedly as Christ has purchased us with no common price, as he has redeemed us by his blood from the deadly servitude of Satan. This is the reason why St. Paul, in writing to the Galatians, so greatly detested that they had bound themselves to the ceremonies of the law, although they were divine; yet, as we have shown above, the excuse for this was far better than to submit themselves to the yoke of those ceremonies which men devised of themselves. For he wrote, and of a truth, that those who admit the yoke of these ceremonies despise the grace of God and count the death of Christ as a thing of naught. And hence he says that he fears that he has labored for them in vain, and exhorts them to stand fast in that liberty wherewith Christ hath made them free, and not to be entangled again in the yoke of bondage.

Gal 2[.21]

Gal 4[.11]

Gal 5[.1]

Now, it is manifest that monkery is nothing else than a bondage of human traditions, and of such indeed as Paul has condemned by name in the passages which we have cited. For undoubtedly they who profess monkery consecrate themselves to these inventions of men in the hope of merits. Hence it is that they regard it so heinous an offense to desert these for the liberty of Christ. Therefore as our body as well as our spirit belongs to God (and that in a double respect—that is, of condition and of redemption), it cannot be lawful for Christians to make themselves slaves to this monastic servitude, much less than for temporal servants to change their masters. Besides, it cannot be denied that by such bondage and vows to live after the commandments of men a necessity, as it always used to be formerly, of transgressing God's law is occasioned, since God's law requires that, according to his ability, a Christian should be of service to the magistrate, parents, relatives, and all others whom God has made nearest to him and brought to him for assistance, in what place, time, or manner soever their profit demands. Then let him embrace that mode of living whereby he may chiefly provide for the affairs of his neighbors. Neither let him choose celibacy, unless it be given him for the kingdom of God— that is, in order to promote godliness and God's glory to renounce marriage and make himself a eunuch. For the commandment of God, published by Paul, abides, which no vows of men can render void: "To avoid fornication let every man" (he excepts no one) "have his own wife, and let every woman have her own husband." For all do not receive this word concerning adopting a single life for the kingdom of heaven, as Christ himself testifies, than whom no one more exactly knew and more faithfully taught either what is the power of human nature or what is acceptable to the Father. Now, it is well known that by these monastic vows they who assume them are so bound to a certain kind of men that they think it unlawful to be obedient and dutiful any longer to either the magistrate or their parents or any men (the head of the monastery alone excepted), or to relieve them with their substance, and least of all to marry, even when they greatly burn; and hence they necessarily fall into all sorts of disgraceful ways of life.

1 Cor [6]

[Mt 15.3]

[Mt 5]

[Mt 19.12]

[1 Cor 7.2]

Since, therefore, it is clear that these monastic vows render a man who is freed from the service of Christ subject not so much to the bondage of men as of Satan, and bring a necessity of transgressing God's law, as is the nature of all human traditions, and therefore conflict manifestly with God's commandments, we very properly believe that they are to be regarded void, as not only the written law, but also the law of nature, commands that a promise be disannulled if its observance hinder good morals, and much more if it hinder religion. Therefore we could not withstand any one who wished to exchange a monastic life—undoubtedly a bondage to Satan—for a Christian life. So also we could not withstand others of the ecclesiastical order who, marrying, embraced a kind of life wherefrom more advantage to their neighbors and greater purity of life could be expected than from that wherein they lived before. To conclude: neither did we undertake to prohibit from the right of marriage those among us who have persevered in the ministry of God, whatever were the vows of chastity that they had assumed. In this we were influenced by the reasons above specified, since St. Paul, the advocate of true chastity, assumes even a

[1 Tm 3.2, 12] bishop to be a married man. For we have justly preferred this one divine law above

[1 Cor 7.2] all human laws—that is: "To avoid fornication, let every man have his own wife." It is doubtless because this law has been rejected for so long a time that all kinds of lusts, even those that are unmentionable (with all reverence to Your Worshipful Majesty, Most Excellent Emperor), have more than overwhelmed the ecclesiastical order, so that today there is no kind of mortals more abominable than those who bear this name.

CHAPTER 13. OF THE OFFICE, DIGNITY, AND POWER OF MINISTERS IN THE CHURCH

Concerning the ministry and the dignity of the ecclesiastical order we teach: first,

2 Cor 12[.8–10] that there is no power in the church except for edification. Secondly, that we must not think otherwise of any man in this estate than Paul wished himself, Peter, Apol-

[1 Cor 4.1] los and others to be esteemed—namely, as ministers of Christ and stewards of the mysteries of God, in whom it is chiefly required that each one be found faithful. These have the keys of the kingdom of heaven, the power to bind and to loose, to remit and to retain sins, yet in such a manner that they be nothing else than ministers of Christ, whose right and prerogative alone this is. For as he is the only one who can renew souls, so he it is alone who by his power opens heaven to men and frees them from sins. Both of these come to us only when it is given us to be renewed in mind and to have our citizenship in heaven. It is the part of ministers to plant and to water,

1 Cor 3[.7] neither of which are efficacious of themselves, for it is God who giveth the increase. For no one is sufficient of himself to think anything as of himself, but his sufficiency is of God, who also hath made whom he wishes ministers of the New Testament, to render men properly convinced concerning Christ truly partakers of him; not to minister the dead letter—that is, doctrine that sounds forth only externally, with-

[2 Cor 3.6] out changing the heart—but that which quickens the spirit and renews the heart.

Thus they are at length coworkers with God, and truly open heaven and remit sins. 1 Cor 3[.9]
Hence it is that in delivering this power to the apostles Christ breathed upon them
and said: "Receive ye the Holy Ghost"; and then added: "Whosoever sins ye remit, they are remitted unto them." Therefore, what constitutes fit and properly con- [Jn 20.22–23]
secrated ministers of the church, bishops, teachers, and pastors, is that they have
been divinely sent ("for how will they preach unless they be sent?")—that is, that Rom 10[.15]
they have received the power and mind to preach the gospel and to feed the flock of
Christ, and also the Holy Ghost who cooperates—that is, persuades hearts. Other
virtues wherewith men of this order should be furnished St. Paul recounts. Those,
therefore, who are sent, anointed, and furnished in this sort have an earnest care for
the Lord's flock,[a] and labor faithfully in feeding it; and we acknowledge them in the
number of bishops, elders, and pastors, and as worthy of double honor, and every
Christian ought with the greatest promptness obey their commands. But those who
devote themselves to different things put themselves in a different place and are distinguished by a different name. Yet the life of no one should give such offence as that
Christians should hesitate to embrace whatever he may declare, either from Moses
or the chair of Christ; that is, either from the law or the gospel. But Christ's sheep
are not to hear the voice of such as introduce strange things. Moreover, they who Jn 10[.5]
in secular things have received power as it has been ordained of God have it in such
a way that he resists an ordinance of God who is unwilling to obey their direction
in matters that do not conflict with God's commands.

Therefore the charge against us by some is a calumny—namely, that our
preachers undermine the jurisdiction of ecclesiastics. The temporal jurisdiction
which they have has never been interfered with by our preachers. And the spiritual jurisdiction, whereby they ought by the word of God to free consciences and
to faithfully feed them on Christ's gospel, they have often invoked; so far are they
from ever resisting it. But the reason why we did not endure the doctrine of certain
ecclesiastics, and, according to our necessity, substituted others in their place, or,
as is manifest, have retained those who have been discharged by the episcopal authorities, is that the latter clearly proclaimed the voice of our Shepherd, while the
former declared that of strangers. For when the question is concerning the interests of the gospel and sound doctrine, those who truly believe in Christ must turn
themselves entirely to the Bishop of our souls, Jesus Christ, and in no way admit [1 Pt 2.25]
the voice of strangers. In this, injury can be inflicted on no one, since the words of
Paul are true: "For all things are yours; whether Paul, or Apollos, or Cephas, or the
world, or life, or death, or things present, or things to come; all are yours; and ye are

a. 1 Tm 3[.1–7]; Ti 1[.6–9]

1 Cor 3[.21–23]   Christ's; and Christ is God's." Certainly, if Peter and Paul, with the entire world, are hitherto ours, and we in no way theirs, but Christ's, and that just as he is his Father's—that in all things that we are we live to him alone, for this end using all things as ours—no one of the ecclesiastics can justly complain of us that we are not sufficiently obedient to them, while it has been manifest that we were following the will of God. These things are taught among us concerning the office, dignity and authority of ministers of the church, and the passages of Scripture which we have cited and others like them have influenced us to give our faith thereto.

CHAPTER 14. OF HUMAN TRADITIONS

Furthermore, concerning the traditions of the fathers or such as the bishops and churches at this day ordain, the opinion of our men is as follows: They reckon no traditions among human traditions (such, namely, as are condemned in the Scriptures) except those that conflict with the law of God, such as bind the conscience concerning meat, drink, times, and other external things, such as forbid marriage to those to whom it is necessary for an honorable life, and other things of that stamp. For such as agree with the Scripture, and were instituted for good morals and the profit of men, even though not expressed in Scripture in words, nevertheless, since they flow from the command of love, which orders all things most becomingly, are justly regarded divine rather than human. Of this sort were those of Paul—that

1 Cor 11[.4]   women should not pray in the church bareheaded or men with heads covered; that
1 Cor 11[.20]   they who are to commune should tarry one for the other; that no one should speak
1 Cor 14[.27]   with tongues in the congregation without an interpreter; that the prophets without
1 Cor 14[.29]   confusion should deliver their prophecies to be judged by those who sit by. Many such the church even today justly observes, and according to occasion frames anew, which he who rejects despises the authority, not of men, but of God, whose tradition whatsoever is profitable. For "whatever truth is said or written is said and written by his gift who is the truth itself," as St. Augustine has devoutly written. But oftentimes there is disputing about this as to what tradition is profitable, what not—that is, what promotes and what retards godliness. But he who shall seek nothing of his own, and consecrates himself entirely to the public profit, shall easily see what things correspond to God's law and what do not.

Furthermore, since the condition of Christians is such that they are even helped by injuries, the Christian will refuse to obey not even unjust laws, provided they make no godless command, according to the saying of Christ: "Whosoever
[Mk 5.14]   shall compel thee to go a mile, go with him two." Thus, undoubtedly, the Christian
[1 Cor 9.22]   ought to become all things unto all men, so that he may endeavor both to suffer and to do everything for the pleasure and profit of men, provided they be not opposed

to God's commands. Hence it is that every one obeys the civil laws that do not conflict with godliness, the more readily the more fully he is imbued with the faith of Christ.

CHAPTER 15. OF THE CHURCH

We must set forth now what we think concerning the church and the sacraments. The church of Christ, therefore, which is frequently called the kingdom of heaven, is the fellowship of those who have enlisted under Christ and committed themselves entirely to his faith; with whom, nevertheless, until the end of the world, those are mingled who feign faith in Christ, but do not truly have it. This the Lord has taught sufficiently by the parable of the tares; also by the net cast into the sea, which Mt 13[.24ff.]
brought bad fish in with the good; then, too, by the parable of the king who com-
manded all to be invited to the marriage of his son, and afterwards the one without Mt 22[.1]
the wedding garment to be cast out. Moreover, when the church is proclaimed the
bride of Christ, for whom he gave himself that she might be sanctified; also when Eph 5[.25]
it is called the house of God, the pillar and ground of the truth,[a] Mount Zion,[b] the
city of the living God, the heavenly Jerusalem, the church of the firstborn who are [Heb 12.22–23]
written in heaven,—these encomiums pertain only to those who have truly obtained
a place among the children of God because they firmly believe in Christ. Since in
these the Savior truly reigns, they are properly called this church and the communion—that is, society—of saints, as the term "church" is explained in the Apostles'
Creed. This the Holy Ghost rules, from this Christ is never absent, but he sanctifies it to present it at length to himself blameless, not having spot or wrinkle. This, [Eph 5.26]
finally, he that will not hear is to be regarded a heathen and a publican. [Mt 18.17]

  Although that whereby it is entitled to be called the church of Christ—namely, faith in Christ—cannot be seen, yet it can be seen and plainly known from its fruits. Of these fruits the chief are a courageous confession of the truth, a true love tendered to all, and a brave contempt of all things for Christ. These undoubtedly cannot be absent where the gospel and its sacraments are purely administered.

  Besides, since it is the church and kingdom of God, and for this reason all things must be done in the best order, it has various offices of ministers. For it is a body compacted of various members, whereof each has his own work. While they perform in good faith their ministry, laboring earnestly in word and doctrine, they truly represent the church, so that he who hears them is correctly said to hear the church.

a. 1 Tm 3[.15]
b. Heb 12[.22]

But with what spirit they should be moved and with what authority endowed we have declared above and given account when we explained our faith concerning the ministry of the church. For they who teach what conflicts with Christ's commands cannot represent the church of Christ; nevertheless, it may occur, and actually does occur frequently, that the wicked both prophesy in Christ's name and

[Mt 7.23] pass judgment in the church. But those who propose what differs from Christ's doctrines, even though they be within the church, nevertheless, because preoccupied with error, they do not proclaim the voice of the Shepherd, undoubtedly cannot

[Jn 10.5] represent the church, the bride of Christ. Therefore they are not to be heard in his name, since Christ's sheep follow not the voice of a stranger.

These things our theologians teach of the church, derived from the passages cited and similar passages.

CHAPTER 16. OF THE SACRAMENTS

Furthermore, since the church lives here in the flesh, even though not according to the flesh, it has pleased the Lord to teach, admonish and exhort it also by the outward word; and that this might be done the more conveniently he wished his people to maintain an external society among themselves. For this reason he has also given to them sacred symbols, which we call sacraments. Among these, baptism and the Lord's supper are the chief. These we believe were called sacraments by the ancients, not only because they are visible signs of invisible grace (to use the words of St. Augustine), but also because in them a profession of faith, as it were, is made.

CHAPTER 17. OF BAPTISM

Of baptism, therefore, we confess that which Scripture in various places declares of it: that by it we are buried into Christ's death,[a] are united into one body[b] and put on Christ;[c] that it is the washing of regeneration,[d] that it washes away sins[e] and saves

1 Pt 3[.21] us. All this we understand as St. Peter has interpreted when he says: "The like figure whereunto even baptism doth also now save us, not the putting away of the filth of

1 Pt 3[.21] the flesh, but the answer of a good conscience toward God." For without faith it is impossible to please God,[f] and we are saved by grace, not by our works.[g] But since

a. Rom 6[.4]
b. 1 Cor 12[.12]
c. Gal 3[.27]
d. Ti 3[.5]
e. Acts 22[.16]
f. Heb 11[.6]
g. Eph 2[.8]

baptism is the sacrament of the covenant that God makes with those who are his, promising to be their God and Protector, as well as of their seed, and to have them as his people, and finally, since it is a symbol of renewing through the Spirit, which occurs through Christ, our theologians teach that it is to be given infants also, no less than formerly under Moses they were circumcised. For we are indeed the children of Abraham. Therefore no less to us than to those of old pertains the promise: I will be thy God and the God of thy seed.

Gal 3[.7]
[Gn 17.7]

CHAPTER 18. OF THE EUCHARIST

Concerning this venerable sacrament of the body and blood of Christ, all that the evangelists, Paul, and the holy fathers have left in writing, our men, in the best faith, teach, commend, and inculcate. And hence with singular zeal they always publish this goodness of Christ to his people, whereby no less today than at that last supper, to all those who sincerely have given their names among his disciples and receive this supper according to his institution, he deigns to give his true body and true blood to be truly eaten and drunk for the food and drink of souls, for their nourishment unto life eternal, so that now he may live and abide in them, and they in him, to be raised up by him at the last day to new and immortal life, according to his words of eternal truth: "Take, eat; this is my body," etc.; "drink you all of it; for this is my blood," etc. Now, our ecclesiastics with especial diligence withdraw the minds of our people both from all contention and from all superfluous and curious inquiry to that which is alone profitable, and which was alone regarded by Christ our Savior—namely, that, fed upon him, we may live in and through him a life pleasing to God, holy, and therefore eternal and blessed, and that we who partake of one bread in the holy supper may be among ourselves one bread and one body. Hence indeed it occurs that the divine sacraments, the most holy supper of Christ, are administered and received among us very religiously and with singular reverence. From these things, which are truly in this manner, Thy Most Worshipful Majesty, Most Clement Emperor, doth know how falsely our adversaries proclaim that our men change Christ's words and do them violence by human glosses; that nothing save mere bread and mere wine is administered in our suppers; and thus that among us the Lord's supper has been despised and rejected. For with the greatest earnestness our men always teach and exhort that every man with simple faith embrace these words of the Lord, rejecting all devices and false glosses of men, and removing all wavering, apply his mind to their true meaning, and finally, with as great devotion as possible, receive these sacraments for the quickening nourishment of their souls and the grateful remembrance of so great a benefit; as is generally done now among us more frequently and devoutly than heretofore. Moreover, our

[1 Cor 11.24ff.]

ecclesiastics have always hitherto offered themselves, as they do today also, with all modesty and truth, in order to render an account of their faith and doctrine concerning all that they believe and teach touching this sacrament, as well as other things; and that not only to Thy Worshipful Majesty, but also to every one who demands it.

CHAPTER 19. THE MASS

Furthermore, since Christ has instituted his supper in this manner, which afterward began to be called the mass—to wit, that therein the faithful, being fed with his body and blood unto life eternal, should show forth his death, whereby they are redeemed—our ecclesiastics, by this means giving thanks and commending this salvation to others also, could not do otherwise than condemn, on the one hand, the general neglect of these things, and, on the other, the presumption of the celebrants of masses in offering Christ for the living and the dead, and in making the mass a work whereby almost alone the favor of God and salvation are obtained, without regard to what men either believe or live. Whence that shameful and twice and thrice impious buying and selling of this sacrament crept in, and the result was that today nothing is more a means of gain than the mass. Therefore they rejected private masses, because the Lord commanded this sacrament to his disciples to be used in common. Hence Paul also commands the Corinthians to wait for one another when going to the holy supper, and denies that they celebrate the Lord's supper when each one takes his own supper while they are eating. Moreover, their boast that they offer up Christ as a victim our men condemn, because the Epistle to the Hebrews plainly testifies that as men once die, so Christ was once offered to take away the sins of many, and can no more be offered again than die again; and on this account, as a perfect sacrifice for our sins, he sits for ever at the right hand of God, expecting what remains, until his enemies as a footstool may be placed beneath his feet. "For by one offering he hath perfected for ever them that are sanctified."

I Cor 11[.20]

Heb 9[.27–28]

Heb 10[.12–13]

But their making of the mass a good work, whereby something is obtained of God, our preachers have taught conflicts with the uniform declaration of Scripture that we are justified and receive God's favor by the Spirit of Christ and through faith, concerning which Scriptural testimonies have been cited above. So, too, our preachers have showed that the not commending in the mass the death of the Lord to the people is contrary to the command of Christ, to receive these sacraments in commemoration of himself, and to that of Paul, that thereby Christ's death is set forth until he come. And since many, without any desire of godliness, commonly celebrate the mass only for the purpose of nourishing the body, our preachers have shown that this is so execrable to God that even though the mass were in itself no hindrance to godliness, yet it should justly and by God's command be abolished.

[I Cor 11.25–26]

This is clear from Isaiah alone. For our God is spirit and truth, and therefore does [Is 1[.11]] not allow himself to be worshiped save in spirit and truth. Moreover, how griev- [Jn 4.24] ous to the Lord is this indecorous huckstering introduced with reference to these sacraments they have also taught should be conjectured from the fact that Christ so severely and altogether against his accustomed manner, taking to himself external vengeance, cast out of the temple those buying and selling, although they seemed [Mt 21.12–17] to be doing business only to further sacrifices that were made according to law.

Therefore, since the rite of the mass, as commonly celebrated, conflicts in so many ways with the Scripture of God, just as also it is diverse in many ways from that which the holy fathers observed, it has been very severely condemned among us from the pulpit, and by the word of God been made so detestable that many have abandoned it of their own accord, and others when it was abrogated by authority of the magistrate. This we have allowed for no other reason than because throughout the whole of Scripture the Spirit of God detests nothing so, and commands nothing so earnestly to be taken away, as a feigned and false worship of himself. Now, no one who is influenced in any way by religion is ignorant what an inevitable necessity is laid upon one who fears God when he is persuaded that God requires anything of him. For any one could easily foresee how many would endure that anything in so holy a rite as the mass should be changed by us; neither were there any who would not have preferred not only not to offend Thy Worshipful Majesty, but even any prince of the lowest rank. But since they did not doubt that by the common rite of the mass God was greatly provoked, and his glory, for which even life ought to be laid down, was obscured, they could not do otherwise than remove it, lest by their connivance they should render themselves liable for diminishing God's glory. Truly, if God is to be loved and worshiped above all, godly men must tolerate nothing less than what he abominates.

That this one cause has constrained us to change certain matters concerning these things we call him to witness from whom no secret is hid.

CHAPTER 20. OF CONFESSION

Since, indeed, also the confession of sins which arises from godliness can be ren- dered by no man whom his repentance and true grief of mind do not impel thereto, it cannot be extorted by any precept. Wherefore neither Christ himself nor the apos- tles would command it. For this cause, therefore, our ecclesiastics exhort men to confess their sins, and therewith show its fruit—that is, that a man should privately seek consolation, advice, doctrine, and instruction of one who is a Christian and wise—yet by commandments urge it upon no one, but affirm that such command- ments injure godliness. For the institution of confessing sins to a priest has driven innumerable souls into grievous despair, and is subject to so many other faults that it ought long since to have been abrogated; and doubtless would have been abrogated if the presidents of churches in the most recent times had glowed with the same zeal for removing stumbling blocks as in former times Nestorius, bishop of Constantinople, who abolished secret confession in his church, because a woman of the nobility, who went often to church as though to perform works of penance, was found to have lain frequently with a deacon. Undoubtedly innumerable sins of such kind were committed in many places. Besides, the pontifical laws require that the hearer and judge of confession should be of such character, so holy, learned, wise, and merciful, that one could scarcely determine to whom to confess among those who are commonly appointed to hear confessions. Moreover, the schoolmen also think that it is better to confess sins to a layman than to a priest as cannot be expected to afford edification. The sum of all is, that that confession which sound repentance and true grief of mind for sins does not produce brings more injury than good. Since, therefore, God alone can give repentance and true sorrow for our sins, nothing salutary in this matter can be accomplished by precepts, as experience itself has made too manifest.

CHAPTER 21. OF THE CHANTS AND PRAYERS OF ECCLESIASTICS

For the same reason—namely, that there should be no conniving at an offense to God, which might occur under pretext of his service, than which nothing can offend him more—our men have condemned most things in the chants and prayers of ecclesiastics. For it is clearly manifest that these have degenerated from the first institution of the fathers, since no one who has examined the writings of the ancients is ignorant that the custom was current among them to earnestly repeat and also expound a few psalms in connection with a chapter of Scripture; while now many of the psalms are chanted, but almost without thinking, and of the reading of Scripture only the beginnings of the chapters remain, and innumerable things are assumed one after another that serve for superstition rather than for godliness. First, therefore, our ministers have denounced the minglings with holy prayers and chants of not a few things that are contrary to the Scriptures, as they ascribe to some saints what pertains to Christ alone—namely, to free from sins and other evils—and not so much to obtain the favor of God and every kind of blessings by entreaty as to bestow it as a gift. Second, that they are increased so infinitely that they cannot be chanted or recited with an attentive mind. Last, that these are also made meritorious works, and are wont to be sold for no small price; to say nothing meanwhile [1 Cor 14.1–4] of what is contrary to the express command of the Holy Ghost—namely, that all

things are said and chanted in such a tongue as the people not only do not understand, but sometimes not even those who obtain their livelihood by these chants and
prayers.

CHAPTER 22. OF STATUES AND IMAGES

Finally, against statues and images our preachers have applied the holy oracles,
chiefly because they began to be worshiped and adored openly, and vain expenditure was devoted to them that was due the hungry, thirsty, and naked Christ; and [Mt 25.31–46]
lastly, because by their worship and the expenditure they required (both conflicting with God's word) they seek merits with God. Against this religious error they
have interposed also the authority of the ancient church, which undoubtedly abomi-
nated the sight of any image, whether painted or graven, in the church, as the deed
of Epiphanius, bishop of Salamis in Cyprus, that he reports of himself, abundantly
proves. For when he saw on a curtain in a certain church a painting of Christ or
some saint (for he writes that he does not exactly remember), he was inflamed with
such indignation because he saw an image of a man hanging in the church, contrary
to the authority of the Scriptures and to our faith and religion, that he at once tore
the curtain and ordered that the corpse of a poor man be wrapped therein. The letter in which this man of God narrates this of himself, writing to John, bishop of
Jerusalem, St. Jerome has translated as genuine into the Latin, nor has he uttered
a word in the least disapproving this judgment of Epiphanius concerning images.
From this it is clearly inferred that neither St. Jerome himself nor the bishop of Jerusalem to whom he wrote thought otherwise concerning images. For the declaration
that is commonly made that by statues and images the more rude are taught and instructed will not suffice to prove that they should be carried, especially where they
are adored by the populace. God's ancient people were of a ruder class, so that it
was needful to instruct them by numerous ceremonies; nevertheless, God did not
think that images were of such value to teach and instruct the more rude, since he
forbade them among the very chief things. If the answer be made that God forbade
such images as were worshiped, it immediately follows that when all have begun to
adore them they should be universally removed from the churches, on account of the
offense which they occasion. For all things in the church should be directed to edification, much less should anything be tolerated which may give occasion for ruin and
can contribute no advantage. Besides, as is generally objected concerning teaching,
St. Athanasius, refuting the heathen defending their idols by this argument, thus rejects it: "Let them say, I ask, in what way God is known through images? Whether
through the matter of which they consist or the form impressed upon the matter? If
on account of the matter, what necessity now of form, since God has shone forth in

the entire matter already, even before these were formed, since all things bear witness to this glory? Moreover, if the image that is produced is the cause of the divine knowledge, what need now of the picture and other material, for is not God known rather through those very animals whereof images are made? For God's glory would indeed be more clearly seen through animated beings, rational and irrational, than be manifested through the inanimate and motionless. When, therefore, for the purpose of understanding God, you carve or mold images, you make what is in no way worthy of him."[3] Thus far Athanasius. Lactantius has also said much in opposition to this pretext, *Divine Institutions,* book 2. For with him who can be taught with profit, in addition to the word of exhortation, the living and true works of God themselves are of far more service than the vain images that men prepare. Since in so many passages of Scripture God has most fully testified that this is his opinion concerning images, it will not be proper for us men to seek profit from objects the peril of which God has commanded us to shun, especially when we ourselves have learned by experience how greatly they hinder godliness.

Our men also confess that in itself the use of images is free, but, free as it may be, the Christian must consider what is expedient, what edifies, and should use images in such place and manner as not to present a stumbling block to any. For Paul was prepared to have both meat and wine prohibited him for his entire life if [1 Cor 8.13] he knew that either in any way injured the welfare of others.

CHAPTER 23. OF MAGISTRATES

We have above set forth that our ecclesiastics have assigned a place among good works of the first rank to the obedience which is rendered magistrates, and that they teach that every one ought the more diligently to adapt himself to the public laws to the degree that he is a more sincere Christian and richer in faith. They accordingly teach that to exercise the office of magistrate is the most sacred function that can be divinely given. Hence it has come to pass that they who exercise public [Ex 21.6; Ps 82.1, 6] power are called in the Scriptures *gods.* For when they discharge their duty aright and in order the people prosper both in doctrine and in life, because God is wont so to control our affairs that in great part both the welfare and the destruction of subjects depend upon those who are governors. Therefore none exercise the duties of magistrate more worthily than they who of all are the most Christian and holy; whence, beyond all doubt, it happened that bishops and other ecclesiastical men were formerly promoted by most godly emperors and kings to the external government of affairs. In this matter, although they were religious and wise, there was this

3. Athanasius *Against the Heathen* 1.20 (*NPNF*–II 4:14–15).

one fault—that they were not able to render what was needful for the proper administration of both offices, and they had to fail, either in their duty to the churches in ruling them by the word, or to the state in governing it with authority.

CONCLUSION

These are the chief points, most invincible and devout Emperor, wherein our men have somewhat receded from the common doctrine of ecclesiastics, being forced thereto by the authority alone of the Scriptures, which is justly to be preferred above all other traditions. These things being set forth as could be done by us in such short time, we wish to offer Thy Sacred Majesty, in order to give an account of our faith to thee, whom next to God we chiefly honor and reverence, and also to show how necessary it is speedily and earnestly to consult of a way and manner whereby a matter of so great importance may be known, weighed and discussed as in the first place respect for God requires, in whose highest interest we must act with fear and trembling; and in the second place, is worthy of Thy Holy Majesty, so greatly renowned for clemency and religion; and finally, the very means to attain the peace at which Thy Majesty aims demands—that certain and firm peace which, when there is dissent concerning faith and religion, cannot be acquired otherwise than when, before all other things, men's minds are plainly instructed concerning the truth.

Moreover, it might perhaps seem needless for us to mention so many things concerning these matters, since the most famous princes, the elector of Saxony and others, have very fully and thoroughly set forth the matters of present controversy in our holy religion. But because Thy Worshipful Majesty has required that all they who have any interest in this business declare to him their opinion concerning religion, we also thought it our duty to confess to Thy Majesty what is taught among us. Although the subject is so vast and embraces so many things that even what we have declared on both sides is too meagre and brief than to permit the hope of the determination of anything certain in these controversies, and such as may be approved, not of all, but at least of a good part of Christian people, so small in truth is the number of those who subscribe to the truth. Since, therefore, this is a matter of such vast importance, and is so varied and manifold, and cannot be decided profitably unless it be well known and examined by many, we beseech Thy Sacred Majesty, and most humbly request, by God and our Savior, whose glory undoubtedly thou dost chiefly seek, to cause as speedily as possible a general, free, and truly Christian council to be summoned, which hitherto has seemed so necessary both to Thy Sacred Majesty and other princes for pacifying the affairs of the church, that in almost all the assemblies of the empire which were held since the beginning of this dissent concerning religion both Thy Sacred Majesty's commissioners and other princes of the empire publicly testified that by no other way in these matters could that which is profitable be accomplished. Therefore, at the last assembly held at Spires Thy Sacred Majesty gave occasion to hope that the Roman pontiff would not prevent the speedy summoning of such a council.

But if the opportunity for a general council cannot in time be obtained, yet at least Thy Sacred Majesty might appoint a provincial assembly of the doctors of every degree and estate, whereunto all whom it is expedient to be present may freely and safety resort, every man may be heard, and all things may be weighed and judged by such men, who it is certain, being endowed with the fear of God, would prefer nothing to his glory. For it is not unknown with what dignity and diligence in times past both emperors and bishops conducted themselves in deciding controversies of faith, which were nevertheless frequently of much less importance than those that are now agitating Germany; so that they thought it worth while to assemble them to examine the same things the second and third time. Now he that shall consider how things are at present cannot doubt but that at this day there is need of greater fidelity, gravity, meekness, and skill than ever before, in order that the religion of Christ may be restored to its own place. For if the truth is with us, as we undoubtedly believe, how much time and labor, pray, is requisite that they also may know it without whose consent, or allowance at least, a solid peace cannot be prepared! But if we err, from which we have no doubt that we are far distant, the matter again will require no slothful diligence or short time that so many thousand men be called back again to the way. This diligence and time it will not be so unbecoming for Thy Majesty to bestow, as it is meet for thee to express toward us the mind of him in whose stead thou dost govern—namely, that of Jesus Christ, the Savior of us all. Since he came for the purpose of seeking and saving what had perished, there is no reason why Thy Worshipful Majesty, even though thou dost believe without doubt that we have fallen from the truth, should not refuse to leave the ninety-and-nine in the wilderness, and to seek for the hundredth and bring it [Mt 18.12–14] back into the sheepfold of Christ—that is, to prefer this business to all other matters, that the meaning of Christ in every one of these things which are at present in controversy may from the Scriptures be clearly and definitely explained to us, though we are but few and of an humble class. We certainly will be teachable, and will lay aside all obstinacy, provided we be permitted to hear the voice of our Shepherd Jesus Christ, and all things be supported by the Scriptures, that teach whatever is good. For if it should so occur that, the care of teaching us being rejected, compendious forms of edicts be sought (which while the matter is in the hands of Thy Worshipful Majesty we in no way fear), it cannot be said into what straits numberless thousands of men would be brought—that is, those who, being persuaded that

God is chiefly to be heard, and then that the dogmas that follow are supported upon the undoubted oracles of God, are always appalled by such sayings of the Savior as: "Fear not them which kill the body";[a] "He that loseth his life shall find it";[b] "If any one hate not his father and mother, etc., yea, and his own life also, he cannot be my disciple"; 'Whosoever shall be ashamed of me in this adulterous and sinful [Lk 14.26] generation, of him also shall I be ashamed before my Father and his angels"; and [Mk 8.38] the like.

Moved, indeed, by such thunderbolts, many men would cheerfully suffer every extremity. Many, too, the fear of death would indeed delay, yet only for an opportunity, if they be dealt with in this matter with power before doctrine, with violence before their error is indicated to them. For of what value a sound persuasion concerning religion is, and how it maketh men to take no account not only of property, but also of life, has been seen sufficiently, and even more than sufficiently, in many during the last ten years, to say nothing of former generations, who have suffered willingly not only exile and proscription, but even bonds, torture, and death itself, rather than suffer themselves to be withdrawn from the judgment they had conceived, and which they believed to be true. If now, when there is a disagreement concerning the matters of less importance, few are to be found whom one can bring to unfeigned concord unless persuaded of the law or equity of their conditions, how when the controversy is concerning religion are we to expect true peace and undoubted tranquillity of affairs, such as Thy Worshipful Majesty is seeking to establish, unless on both sides that be agreed upon which God approves and which harmonizes with the Scriptures? For as religion, by right and by the custom of nations, is preferred to all other things, so no controversy of mortals with one another could be more vehement and severe than that which is undertaken for altars and divinities. But since Thy Worshipful Majesty has used such inexpressible clemency towards enemies, and those too, who to be silent of other things, have omitted no kind of hostility, we have justly conceived the hope that thou wilt so moderate things in this matter also that in regard to us thou mayst seem to have sought much more the praise of goodness and kindness, since we have always been most desirous of thy welfare and honor, as we have actually testified and desire sincerely to testify further. For in this cause we have dealt so moderately as to all things that we have sufficiently declared to all good men that it has never been our purpose to hurt any one, or to provide for our advantage at the expense of that of others. Indeed, we have exposed ourselves to dangers and have made great outlays on this account; but

a. [Mt 10.28]
b. [Mt 10.39]

we have not even the smallest gain, with the one exception that, being better instructed concerning the goodness of God tendered through Christ, we have begun, by God's grace, to hope better of things to come. This is justly of such importance to us that we do not think that we have either done or suffered anything as yet that is worthy of it, since it is inestimable and should be preferred to all things that either heaven or earth contains. So far have we been from longing for the riches of ecclesiastics that when the husbandmen were in an uproar we defended these resources, in the interests of the ecclesiastics, with the greatest cost and danger. The gospel of our Lord Jesus Christ (may he so love us!) is the only thing that urges us and has induced us to do all those things which we seem to have introduced as innovations.

Let Thy Worshipful Majesty therefore prefer to follow the examples of the most mighty and truly happy emperors, Constantine, Jovinian, Theodosius, and the like, who by doctrine taught daily with all meekness by most holy and vigilant bishops, and also by councils lawfully assembled, and by a serious discussion of all things dealt with the erring and tried all means to bring them back into the way before they would determine anything against them more severe, than to follow the example of those who, it is certain, had such counsellors as were most unlike those ancient and truly holy fathers, and attained a result in no way corresponding to the godliness of the latter. Hence let not Thy Worshipful Majesty be withdrawn to this—namely, that most matters now in controversy were decided long ago, chiefly in the Council of Constance, especially since it may be seen of innumerable decrees of former councils that are not less holy than necessary that not the least point is observed by our ecclesiastics, and that all things among them have so degenerated that every one furnished with even ordinary sense must exclaim that there is need of a council for the restoration of religion and holiness of the ecclesiastical order. But if that which was decreed at Constance is so pleasing to them, how does it happen that meantime that which was then decreed has in no way been obtained—that every tenth year a Christian council be held? For in this way much godliness and faith might either be recovered or preserved.

For who does not confess that as often as a disease breaks out afresh a remedy must be applied, and that those who really have the truth think it much both that good men should teach it and defend it against the wicked where any fruit of this is to be hoped for? Now, when so many thousands are miserably perplexed with the doctrines of our religion, who can deny that there is hope of most plentiful fruit? And such as has justly impelled all whom the Spirit of Christ rules that, forsaking all other things and esteeming no labor or expense too great, they devote themselves with all their powers to this one thing—namely, that Christ's doctrine, the parent of all righteousness and salvation, may be properly considered, may be purged of all errors, and may be offered in its native form to all who love godliness and the true worship of God, whereby a holy and eternally firm peace and the true tranquillity of all things may be restored and confirmed to the sheep of Christ, for whom he has shed his blood, who are now so excessively harassed? As we have said, this peace can be restored and confirmed to them in no other way. For, while in other things they must sometimes yield, in a matter of godliness they must so cling to God's words and rely upon them that if they had a thousand lives they should offer them to be tortured to death, rather than yield a jot or tittle which they are persuaded has been divinely commanded. If, now, only one soul is of more value than the whole world, what should be done for the salvation of so many myriads? [Mt 16.26] Such hope indeed invites us, from the consideration that those who are accused to Thy Worshipful Majesty of error pray nothing else than that they be taught, and have applied themselves entirely to the Holy Scriptures, which are abundantly sufficient to confute every error, as well as from the fact that Christ our Savior has so clearly promised that where two or three are gathered together in his name he will be in their midst, and will grant them whatever they have agreed upon. [Mt 18.20]

These things, Most Godly Emperor, we here mention for no other reason than to show our obedience to thy wish that we should explain our opinion concerning the reformation of religion. For otherwise we have good hope that Thy Worshipful Majesty hast well considered and sees sufficiently what necessity urges us thereto, what fruit it invites, and finally how worthy a thing this is for Thy Worshipful Majesty, who is so much praised for religion and clemency, that, all the men in highest reputation for learning and godliness being assembled, the effort be made to learn what should be thought of each doctrine just now controverted, and then an explanation be made by suitable ministers of Christ, with all meekness and fidelity, to those who are believed to be detained in errors. Nevertheless, as it is at the same time to be feared that there are not those wanting who are endeavoring to draw Thy Worshipful Majesty otherwise, it has seemed good to us to reply to them in this sort, as though to Thy Worshipful Majesty himself; and all other things we have here set forth and confessed for no other purpose than, on our part, to maintain the glory of Christ Jesus our God, and to obey Thy Imperial Majesty, as is right—we beg thee, according to thy most excellent clemency, for which thou art renowned, to take and interpret in good part, and to deign to regard us among those who truly from the heart desire to show ourselves not less obedient and submissive with the greatest subjection than our illustrious ancestors, being ready in this cause, so far as it is lawful, to surrender both property and our lives. The King of kings, Jesus

Christ, grant Thy Worshipful Majesty in this matter, as well as in others, to do all things for his glory, and long preserve and happily advance thee in both health and prosperity, to the welfare of the entire Christian government! Amen.

Your Majesty's humble servants, the legates of the cities of:
Strasbourg
Constance
Memmingen
Lindau

Ulrich Zwingli, *A Reckoning of the Faith*, 1530

When Charles V's invitation to the Diet of Augsburg went out in January 1530, representatives of Swiss and southern German cities belonging to the Christian Civic Union (Burgrecht) met in Basel to decide how to respond.[1] They asked Johannes Oecolampadius (1482–1531) and Zwingli to compose a profession of faith for presentation to the emperor, and Oecolampadius did make a draft, but Zwingli does not seem to have done anything at that time. By May, the city of Strasbourg (a member of Christian Civic Union) had already sent two representatives to Augsburg. It appears that the cities of Strasbourg, Mühlhausen, and Constance were called to the diet but that Zwingli and the Swiss cities were included only in a general way in the emperor's desire to hear all opinions.[2] Zwingli may have been waiting for an official invitation that never came. One of the Strasbourg representatives, Jakob Sturm, kept Zwingli informed of the proceedings and urged him to submit an account of the beliefs of the Christian Civic Union. Sturm was particularly concerned that the Zwinglian view of the Lord's supper be represented. Although Sturm's motives are disputed, it is true that → *The Tetrapolitan Confession*, written by his fellow townsmen Bucer and Capito, addressed the nature of the eucharist in terms that could be interpreted as reflecting a more Lutheran position.[3]

In the course of two or three days, Zwingli composed his *Reckoning of the Faith (Fidei ratio)* for presentation to Charles V.[4] He professes belief in → *The Creed of Nicaea* and → *The Athanasian Creed*, expresses a Chalcedonian christology, and

1. At this time, the members of the Christian Civic Union were Zurich, Constance, Biel, Mühlhausen, Bern, Basel, Schaffhausen, Strasbourg, and St. Gall. See CR 93/2:790n.
2. See CR 93/2:754–56.
3. Sturm seems to have hoped that the Lutheran and Zwinglian views on the eucharist could coexist: "The two opinions on the Sacrament are nothing more than a verbal dispute (wortzank) from which each draws his own understanding and meaning" (quoted from Brady 1973, 187–88). Brady argues, however, that Sturm encouraged Zwingli to submit his own confession, not because he held the same beliefs, but rather in order to make *The Tetrapolitan Confession* seem moderate by comparison—and thereby to further Strasbourg's political aims in the Lutheran areas of Germany.
4. The speed with which it was prepared is impressive; evidence from letters shows that Zwingli began writing on 24 or 25 June and completed the work by 27 June. It was printed by 3 July and presented to Balthasar Merklin, bishop of Constance and vice chancellor to the emperor, on 8 July. See CR 93/2:755–56 (Blanke's introduction).

affirms orthodox views on the incarnation, the Trinity, and the universal church. But he diverges from Roman Catholic tenets when he comes to a discussion of the sacraments, of which he says, "I believe, yea I know that all the sacraments are so far from conferring grace that they do not even convey or distribute it" (article 7). In article 8, he calls the eucharist a sign of a sacred thing. He rejects both Lutheran and Catholic views, lumping the two together as "papists and some who long for the flesh-pots of Egypt." The concept of purgatory and, of course, the primacy of the pope are also dismissed. He defends himself against charges (made by Lutherans) of antitrinitarianism and Nestorianism and distances himself from the Anabaptist movement, which he claims he was the first to criticize. Zwingli provides copious proof texts from the Bible, upon which he claims to base all his beliefs, but he also cites patristic sources, including Ambrose and Augustine. His classical training is evident in the rhetorical style and his several allusions to Greek and Roman literature.

Although the *Reckoning of the Faith* was presented to the emperor on 8 July 1530, there was never a public reading or an official acknowledgment of the document. That is not to say that it was not read. Melanchthon had read it by 14 July, when he wrote to Luther that Zwingli had returned to his errors and seemed to be "insane."[5] He must have sent a copy of Zwingli's text to Luther, who had read it by 21 July, when he wrote an angry letter to Justus Jonas about it.[6] The Catholics were equally, if not more, annoyed, and Johannes Eck responded immediately with an attack, *Repulsio articulorum Zwinglii Caesari Maiestati oblatorum,* which was printed in Augsburg before the end of July. In his own circles, Zwingli's *Reckoning of the Faith* found some praise, but did not have as much influence as his → *Sixty-Seven Articles.* The year after the Diet of Augsburg—just before his death—Zwingli prepared another, similar statement of faith in *An Exposition of the Faith* addressed to Charles V's nemesis, François I, king of France.[7]

Edition: *CR* 93/2:790–817.

Translation: Jacobs 1893, 2:159–79 (slightly altered to reflect the edition used here).

5. *CR* 2:193 (no. 781).
6. *WA Br* 5, no. 1657.
7. English translation by G. W. Bromiley in *LCC* 24:239–79.

Note: Versification added at points in the original text where marginal notes introduce new topics.

Literature: Blanke 1966; Brady 1973; *Chr Trad* 4:194–201, 225–26; CR 93/2:193–94, 754–89; Eck 1530; Opitz 1995, 94–97; Potter 1976, 334–36; *WA Br* 5:495–96.

Ulrich Zwingli, *A Reckoning of the Faith*, 1530

We who were preaching the gospel in the cities of a Christian state were anxiously expecting, O Charles, holy emperor of right, the time when an account of the faith which we both have and confess would be sought of us also.

While we are standing in readiness for this, it is announced to us, rather by rumor than by any definite announcement, that many have already prepared an outline and summary of their religion and faith, which they are offering you. Here we are "between the victim and the knife"[1]; for on the one side the love of truth and the desire of public peace incite us the more to do what we see others doing; but, on the other, the shortness of the opportunity terrifies us, since, on account of your haste, all things must be done very rapidly, and, as it were, carelessly, for the report announces this also; and because we who are acting as preachers of the divine word in the cities and country of the state mentioned are situated and dispersed at too great a distance from one another to be able to assemble in so brief a time, and deliberate as to what is most fitting to write to Your Highness; also, as we have seen the confession of some, and even the confutation of the adversaries of the same, which seem to have been prepared before anything was demanded of them, I have believed that it would not be improper if I alone would forthwith set forth an account of my faith apart from the previous judgment of my nation. For if in any business one must hasten slowly, here we must hasten swiftly, lest by passing over the matter with apparent indifference we encounter the danger either of suspicious silence or arrogant negligence. You have here, then, O Emperor, a summary of my faith, presented under these circumstances in order that I may give in testimony my judgment not only concerning these articles, but concerning all that I have ever written, or, by God's goodness, will write, not merely to an individual or to any small number, but for the entire church of Christ, so far as it is determined by the command and inspiration of the word and Spirit of God to believe and accept.

[1] In the first place, I both believe and know that God is one and alone, and that he is by nature good, true, powerful, just, wise, the Creator and Preserver of all things, visible and invisible; that Father, Son, and Holy Ghost are indeed three persons, but that their essence is one and single. And I hold altogether according to the exposition of the Creed, the Nicene as well as the Athanasian, in all their details concerning the Godhead himself and the three names of persons.

1. Plautus *Captivi* verse 617.

I believe and understand that the Son assumed flesh, because he truly assumed of the immaculate and perpetual Virgin Mary the human nature, yea, the entire man, who consists of body and soul. But this in such a manner that the entire man was so assumed into the unity of the hypostasis, or person of the Son of God, that the man did not constitute a peculiar person, but was assumed into the inseparable, indivisible, and indissoluble person of the Son of God. Moreover, although both natures, the divine and the human, have so preserved their character and property that both are truly and naturally found in him, yet the distinct properties and works of the natures do not separate the unity of the person; no more than in man soul and body constitute two persons; for as they are of most diverse nature, so they operate by diverse properties and operations. Yet man, who consists of them, is not two persons, but one. So God and man is one Christ, the Son of God from eternity, and the Son of man from the dispensation of time to eternity; one person, one Christ; perfect God and perfect man; not because one nature becomes the other, or they are confused with one another, but because each remains itself; and, nevertheless, the united person is not separated by this property. Hence one and the same Christ, according to his human nature, cries in infancy, grows, increases in wisdom, hungers, thirsts, eats, drinks, is warm, is cold, is scourged, sweats, is wounded, is put to death, fears, is sad, and endures other things that pertain to the penalty and punishment of sin; for he is most remote from sin itself. But according to the property of his divine nature, with the Father he controls the highest and the lowest objects, pervades, sustains, and fosters all things, illumines the blind, restores the lame, awakens the dead, prostrates his enemies by a word, when dead resumes life, returns to heaven, and sends from himself the Holy Ghost. All these things, however diverse in nature and character, one and the same Christ does, remaining one person of the Son of God, so that even those things that pertain to his divine nature are sometimes ascribed, on account of the unity and perfection of the person, to the human nature, and those things that pertain to the human nature are sometimes spoken of the divine. He said that he was the Son of man in heaven, although he had not yet ascended into heaven with his body. Peter asserts [Jn 3.13] that Christ suffered for us, when the humanity alone could suffer. But on account [1 Pt 2.21] of the unity of the person it is truly said both "The Son of God suffered," and "The Son of man forgives sins." For he who is the Son of God and of man in one person [Mk 2.10] forgives sins, according to the property of the divine nature; as we say that man is wise, although consisting of body not less than soul, and a body most remote from wisdom, yea, a poison and hindrance to knowledge and intelligence. And again we say that he was mangled with wounds, when his body alone could receive wounds, but his spirit in no way. Here no one says that two persons are made of man when that which pertains to itself is ascribed to each part; and, again, no one says that the natures are confused when that is predicated of the entire man which, because of the unity of the person, belongs indeed to the entire man, but because of the property of the parts to only one. Paul says: "When I am weak, then am I strong." But who is it that is weak? Paul. Who at the same time is properly well? Paul. But is not this desperate, inconsistent, and intolerable? Not at all. For Paul is not one nature, although one person. When, therefore, he says, "I am weak," the person which speaks is undoubtedly Paul; but what is said is neither predicated nor understood of both natures, but of the weakness only of the flesh. And when he says, "I am strong and well," undoubtedly the person of Paul speaks, but only the soul is understood. So the Son of God dies, he undoubtedly who, according to the unity and simplicity of his person, is both God and man; yet he dies only with respect to his humanity. In this manner, concerning the divinity itself and concerning the persons and the assumed human nature, not only do I think, but so also all the orthodox, whether ancients or moderns, have thought; and so think those who even now acknowledge the truth.

[2 Cor 12.10]

[2] Secondly. — I know that this supreme divinity which is my God freely regulates all things, so that his purpose to determine anything does not depend upon the occasion of any creature, preceding reasoning or example; for this is peculiar to defective human wisdom. God, however, who from eternity to eternity regards all things with a single, simple view, has no need of any reasoning or expectation of events; but being equally wise, prudent, good, etc., he freely determines and disposes of all things, for whatever is, is his. Hence it is that, although knowing and foreseeing, he in the beginning formed man who should fall, and nevertheless determined to clothe in human nature his Son, who should restore him when fallen. For by this means his goodness in every way was manifested. For since he contains in himself mercy and justice, he exercised his justice when he expelled the transgressor from his happy home in paradise, when he bound him in the mill of human misery and with the fetters of diseases, when he shackled him with the law, which, although it was holy, he was never to fulfill. For here, twice miserable, he learned not only that the flesh had fallen into trouble, but that the mind also was tortured from dread of the transgressed law. For although, according to the Spirit, he saw that the law is holy and just and a declaration of the divine mind, so that it enjoined nothing but what equity taught, yet when at the same time he saw that by the deeds of the law the mind does not satisfy itself, condemned by his own judgment, with the hope of attaining happiness removed, departing in despair from God's sight, he thought of enduring nothing but the pain of eternal punishment. Thus far was manifested God's justice.

Moreover, when the time came to publish his goodness, which he had determined from eternity to display no less than his justice, God sent his Son to assume our nature in every part, whereby to outweigh the penalty of sin, in order that, being made our brother and equal, he could be a mediator to make a sacrifice for us to divine justice, which ought to remain holy and inviolate, no less than his goodness, whereby the world might be sure both of the appeased justice and the present kindness of God. For since he has given his Son to us and for us, how will he not with him and because of him give us all things? What is it that we ought not to promise [Rom 8.32] ourselves concerning him who humbled himself so as not only to be our equal, but to be altogether ours? Who can sufficiently admire the riches and grace of divine goodness, whereby he so loved the world, that is, the human race, as to give his Son [Jn 3.16] for its life? These I regard the springs and channels of the gospel; this the only medicine for the fainting soul, whereby it is restored both to God and self. For nothing save God himself can make it certain of God's grace. But now he has so liberally, abundantly, and wisely lavished himself upon us that nothing further is left for us to desire unless someone would venture to seek beyond what is highest and beyond overflowing abundance.

[3] Thirdly.—I know that there is no other victim for expiating crimes than Christ; for not even was Paul crucified for us; that there is no other name under the [1 Cor 1.13] sun in which we must be saved than that of Jesus Christ. Here, therefore, not only [Acts 4.12] the justification and satisfaction of our works are denied, but also the expiation or intercession of all saints, whether in earth or heaven, with reference to the goodness or mercy of God. For this is the one, sole Mediator between God and men, the [1 Tm 2.5] God and man Christ Jesus. Moreover, God's election is manifest and remains firm; for whom he has elected before the foundation of the world, he has so elected, as, [Eph 1.4] through his Son, to receive him to himself; for as he is kind and merciful, so also is he holy and just. All the works, therefore, of this mercy savor of mercy and judgment. Therefore, justly, his election also savors of both. It is of his goodness that he has elected whom he will; but it is of his justice to adopt and unite the elect to himself through his Son, who has been made a victim for satisfying divine justice for us.

[4] Fourthly.—I know that that remote ancestor, our first parent, was induced by self-love, at the pernicious advice suggested to him by the malice of the devil, to desire to become equal to God. [Gn 3.5]

When he had devised this crime he took the forbidden and deadly fruit, whereby he incurred the guilt of capital punishment, having become a public enemy and a foe of God himself. When, then, he could have destroyed him, as equity even [Jas 4.4] demanded, nevertheless, being better disposed, God commutes his penalty to the condition of making him a slave whom he could punish. Since this condition neither he himself nor any born of him could remove (for a slave can beget nothing but a slave), by a deadly taking of food he cast all his posterity into slavery. Hence, I think of original sin as follows: It is truly called sin when it is committed against law; for [Rom 4.15] where there is no law there is no transgression, and where there is no transgression there is no sin in the proper sense, inasmuch as sin is clearly enormity, crime, outrage, or guilt. I confess, therefore, that our father committed what is truly a sin—indeed, an enormity, a crime, an execrable deed. But those begotten of him have not sinned in this manner, for who of us destroyed with his teeth the forbidden fruit in paradise? Therefore, willing or unwilling, we are forced to admit that original sin, as it is in the children of Adam, is not properly sin, as has been explained: for it is no outrage upon any law. It is therefore, properly, a disease and condition—a disease, because just as he fell from self-love, so also do we; a condition, because just as he became a slave and subject to death, so also are we born slaves and children [Eph 2.3] of wrath and subject to death. Although I object not to this disease and condition [Rom 7.8] being called, after the manner of Paul, a sin; yea, such a sin that those born therein [Jas 4.4] are God's enemies and adversaries, for they are brought thereto by the condition of nativity, not by the perpetration of crime, unless so far as their first parent has perpetrated it.

The true cause, therefore, of the hostile conduct and death is the crime and wicked deed perpetrated by Adam. But this is truly sin. Yet it is such sin as clings to [Heb 12.1] us, and is truly a disease and a condition; yea, a necessity of death. Nevertheless, this would never have occurred by nativity, unless crime had depraved the nativity; therefore, the cause of human calamity is crime, and not nativity; it pertains to nativity no otherwise than as that which proceeds from a source and cause. The confirmation of this opinion is supported by authority and example. Paul, in the fifth chapter Rom 5[.17] of Romans, says: "If by one man's sin death reigned, by one," etc. Here we see that sin is properly understood. For Adam is the one by whose fault death hangs upon our shoulders. In the third chapter he says: "For all have sinned and come short of Rom 3[.23] the glory of God," that is, the goodness and liberality of God. Here sin is understood as disease, condition and nativity, so that we all are said to sin even before we come forth to the light; that is, we are in the condition of sin and death even before we sin in act. This opinion is irrefragably based upon the words of the same fifth chapter of Romans: "Death reigned from Adam unto Moses, even over them that Rom 5[.14] had not sinned after the similitude of Adam's transgression." So death is ours, even though we have not sinned as Adam. Why? Because he sinned. But why does death ravage us when we have not sinned in this way? Because he died on account of sin, and, having died, that is, being condemned to death, he begat us. Therefore we also die, but by his guilt, yet by our own condition and disease, or, if you prefer, by our sin, improperly so-called. An example is as follows: A captive in war by his perfidy and hostility has deserved to be held as a slave. Moreover, his descendants become native slaves, not by their fault, or guilt, or crime, but by their condition which has followed a fault; for the parent of whom they have been born has merited it by his crime. The children have no crime, but the punishment and penalty of the crime— namely, the condition, servitude, and workhouse.

If it be pleasing to call these a crime because they are inflicted for crime, I do not forbid. I acknowledge that this original sin, by condition and contagion, belongs by birth to all who are born from the love of man and woman; and I know that we are by nature the children of wrath, but I doubt not that we are received among [Eph 2.3] the sons of God by grace, which through the second Adam, Christ, has restored [1 Cor 15.45] what was lost in the fall. But this occurs in the following manner:

[5] Fifthly.—Hence it is evident, if in Christ, the second Adam, we are restored to life, as in the first Adam we were delivered to death, that in condemning children born of Christian parents, nay, even the children of heathen, we are inconsiderate. For if by sinning, Adam could ruin the entire race, and Christ by dying did not quicken and redeem the entire race from the calamity given by the former, the salvation given by Christ is no longer the same, and in like manner (which be it far from us to assert) is not true: "For as in Adam all die, even so in Christ shall all be made alive." But in whatever way this must be declared of the infants of the [1 Cor 15.22] heathen, this we must certainly maintain that by virtue of the salvation procured through Christ, it is irrelevant to pronounce them subject to an eternal curse, not only on account of the cause of restoration mentioned, but on account of God's free election, which does not follow faith, but faith follows election; of which we will treat in the article that follows. For those who have been elected from eternity have undoubtedly been elected even before faith. Therefore those who because of their age have not faith, should not be inconsiderately condemned by us; for although they do not as yet have it, yet God's election has been hidden from us; if before him they be elect, we judge precipitantly of what is unknown. But nevertheless of the infants of Christians we declare otherwise—namely, that as many as are infants of Christians are of the church of God's people and are parts and members of his church. This we prove in this way: It has been promised by the testimonies of almost all the prophets that the church is to be assembled from the heathen into the church of God's people. Christ himself says: "They shall come from the east and west, and shall sit down with Abraham, and Isaac, and Jacob"; and: "Go ye into the [Mt 8.11] world," etc. But to the church of the Jews their infants belonged equally as the Jews [Mk 16.15] themselves. Therefore our infants belong to Christ's church no less than, in former

times, did those of the Jews; for if it were otherwise the promise would not have been fulfilled, as then we would not sit down equally with God as did Abraham. For he was reckoned in the church with those also who were born of him according to the flesh. But if our children were not thus enumerated with the parents, Christ would be sordid and hostile to us in denying us what he had given to the ancients. It is godless to say this, for otherwise the entire prophecy concerning the call of the Gentiles would be vain. Therefore, since the infants of Christians, no less than the adults, are members of the visible church of Christ, it is manifest that they are no less than the parents of the number of those whom we judge elect. How godlessly and presumptuously, therefore, do they judge who execrate the infants of Christians, when so many clear testimonies of Scripture contradict, which declare that from the heathen there will be not merely an equal, but even a larger church than from the Jews. All this will be plainer when we explain our faith concerning the church.

[6] Sixthly. — Of the church, therefore, we thus think that in the Scriptures the word "church" is received in various significations. It is received for the elect who have been predestinated by God's will to eternal life. Of this Paul speaks when [Eph 5.27] he says that it has neither wrinkle nor spot. This is known to God alone, for, accord- [1 Kgs 8.39] ing to the word of Solomon, he alone knows the hearts of the children of men. But, nevertheless, those who are members of this church, since they have faith, know that they themselves are elect and are members of this first church, but are ignorant of the members other than themselves. For thus it is written in Acts: "And as Acts [13.48] many as were ordained to eternal life believed." Therefore, those who believe are ordained to eternal life. But no one, save he who truly believes, knows who truly believe. Here, therefore, he is already certain that he is elect of God. For, according [2 Cor 1.22] to the apostle's word, he has the seal of the Spirit, espoused and sealed, by which he knows that he is truly free, made a son of the family, and not a slave. For the Spirit cannot deceive. If he tells us that God is our Father, and we with certainty and confidence call him Father, secure of eternal inheritance, it is certain that God's Spirit [Ti 3.5–6] has been shed abroad in our hearts. It is therefore certain that he is elect who is so [Acts 13.48] secure and safe, for they who believe are ordained to eternal life. Yet many are elect who as yet have no faith. For were not the Mother of God, John, and Paul, while still infants, and even before the foundation of the world, elect? But this they knew neither from faith nor from revelation. Were not Matthew, Zacchaeus, the penitent thief, and Magdalene elect before the foundation of the world? Nevertheless, they were ignorant of this until they were illumined by God's Spirit and drawn to [Jn 6.44] Christ by the Father. From these facts, therefore, it is inferred that this first church

is known to God alone, and that they only who have firm and unwavering faith know that they are its members.

Again, the church is understood in a universal sense for all who are reckoned by Christ's name; that is, who have enlisted under Christ, a large number of whom sensibly acknowledge Christ by confession or participation in the sacraments, and yet in heart either are averse to him or ignorant of him. We believe, therefore, that all who confess Christ's name belong to this church. Thus Judas and all who have withdrawn from Christ belonged to Christ's church. For by the apostles Judas was regarded as belonging to Christ's church no less than Peter or John, although most remote from it. But Christ knew who were his and who were the devil's. This church, therefore, is perceptible to sense, however improperly in [Jn 13.11] this world the term be used; namely, all who confess Christ, although among them are many reprobates. For Christ has depicted this in the charming parable of the ten virgins, some of whom were wise and others foolish. This is also sometimes called [Mt 25.1–13] elect, although not that first elect which is without spot; but as in man's judgment it is the church of God, because of its confession which is perceptible to sense, thus in the same way is it called elect. For we judge that they who have enlisted under Christ are faithful and elect. Thus Peter spake: "To the elect scattered abroad throughout [1 Pt 1.1] Pontus," etc. Here by "elect" he means all who belonged to the churches to which he is writing, and not those only who were properly elect of God; for, as they were unknown to Peter, he could not have written to them.

Lastly on this point. — The church is received for every particular congregation of this universal and perceptible church, as the Church of Rome, of Augsburg, of Lyons. There are also other acceptations of "the church," which it is not worth while to enumerate here. Here, therefore, I believe that there is one church of those who have the same Spirit, who testifies to them that they are true children of God's family; and this is the first fruits of the church. I believe that this does not err in regard to the truth—namely, in those first foundations of the faith upon which everything depends. I believe also that there is one universal perceptible church while it maintains that true confession of which we have already spoken. I believe also that all belong to this church who enter into it according to the command and promise of God's word. I believe also that to this church belong the infants Isaac, Jacob, Judah, and all who were of the seed of Abraham, and also those infants whose parents among the first fruits of the church, under the preaching of the apostles, were won to the side of Christ. For if Isaac and the rest of the ancients had not belonged to the church, they would not have received the church's token. Since these, then, were members of the church, infants and children belonged to the primitive church.

Therefore I believe and know that they were sealed with the sacrament of baptism. For infants also confess when they are offered by their parents to the church, especially since the promise offers them to God, which is made to our infants no less, but even far more amply and abundantly than to the ancient infants of the Hebrews. These are the foundations for baptizing and commending infants to the church, against which all the weapons and machinations of the Anabaptists can effect nothing. For not only are they to be baptized who believe, but they who confess, and who from the promises of God's word belong to the church. For otherwise none of the apostles would have baptized anyone whatever, since there is certain evidence to none of the apostles concerning the faith of the one confessing and subscribing. For Simon the impostor, Ananias, Judas, and who not, were baptized when they gave their names, even though they had not faith. On the other hand, Isaac was circumcised as an infant, when he did not give in his name or believe, but the promise gave his name. But since our infants are in the same position as those of the Hebrews, the promise also gives their names to our church and makes confession. Truly, therefore, baptism just as circumcision (for we are speaking of the sacrament of baptism) requires nothing else than either, on the one hand, confession or the giving in of the name, or, on the other, a covenant or promise. And this will be somewhat clearer from what follows.

[7] Seventhly. — I believe, yea, I know, that all the sacraments are so far from conferring grace that they do not even convey or distribute it. In this matter, most powerful Caesar, I may seem to thee perhaps too bold. But my opinion is fixed. For as grace is produced or given by the Divine Spirit (for when I use the term "grace" I am speaking the Latin for pardon, that is, indulgence and gratuitous kindness), so this gift pertains to the Spirit alone.

Moreover, a channel or vehicle is not necessary to the Spirit, for he himself is the virtue and energy whereby all things are borne, and has no need of being borne; neither do we read in the Holy Scriptures that perceptible things, as are the sacraments, bear certainly with them the Spirit, but if perceptible things have ever been borne with the Spirit, it has been the Spirit, and not perceptible things, that [Acts 2.1–3]   has borne them. Thus, when the wind is violently agitated language is conveyed by force of the wind; the wind is not conveyed by force of the tongues. Thus, the wind [Nm 11.31]   brought quails, and carried away locusts, but no quails or locusts were ever so fleet as to bring the wind. Thus, when such a mighty wind passed before Elijah that it [1 Kgs 19.11]   could have even removed the mountains, the Lord was not borne in the wind, etc.

Briefly, the Spirit breathes wherever he wishes; that is, just as the wind bloweth where it listeth, and thou hearest the sound thereof, and canst not tell [Jn 3.8]   whence it cometh or whither it goeth, so is everyone that is born of the Spirit; that is, invisibly and imperceptibly illumined and drawn.[a] This the truth spake.[b] Therefore, the Spirit of grace is conveyed not by this mersion, not by this draught, not by this anointing; for if it were thus it would be known how, where, whence, and whither the Spirit is given.

For if the presence and efficacy of grace are bound to the sacraments, they work where these are conveyed; and where these are not applied all things languish. Neither is it the case that theologians allege this as material or subject, because the disposition for this is first required; that is, because the grace of baptism or the eucharist (for thus they speak) is conferred on one who is first prepared for this. For he who through the sacraments receives according to them this grace, either prepares himself for this or is prepared by the Spirit. If he prepares himself, we can do something of ourselves, and prevenient grace is nothing. If he be prepared by the Spirit for the reception of grace, I ask whether this be done through the sacrament as a channel or without the sacrament? If the sacrament intervene, man is prepared by the sacrament for the sacrament, and thus there will be a process ad infinitum; for a sacrament will always be required as a preparation for a sacrament. But if we be prepared without the sacrament for the reception of sacramental grace, the Spirit is present in his kindness before the sacrament, and hence grace is both rendered and is present before the sacrament is administered. From this it is inferred (as I willingly and gladly admit in regard to the subject of the sacraments) that the sacraments are given as a public testimony of that grace which is previously present to every individual. This baptism is administered in the presence of the church to one who before receiving it either confessed the religion of Christ, or has the word of promise whereby he is known to belong to the church. Hence it is that when we baptize an adult we ask him whether he believes. If he answers yes, then at length he receives baptism. Faith, therefore, has been present before he receives baptism. Faith, then, is not given in baptism. But when an infant is offered the question is asked whether its parents offer it for baptism. When they reply through witnesses that they wish it baptized, the infant is baptized. Here also God's promise precedes, that he regards our infants as belonging to the church no less than those of the Hebrews. For when they who are of the church offer it, the infant is baptized under the law that since it has been born of Christians it is regarded by the divine promise among the members of the church. By baptism, therefore, the church publicly receives one who had previously been received through grace. Baptism, therefore, does not bring grace, but testifies to the church that grace has been given for him to whom it is administered.

a. [Jn 6.44]
b. [Jn 14.6]

I believe, therefore, O Emperor, that a sacrament is a sign of a sacred thing —that is, of grace that has been given. I believe that it is a visible figure or form of invisible grace which has been provided and given by God's bounty; that is, a visible example which presents an analogy to something done by the Spirit. I believe that it is a public testimony. As when we are baptized the body is washed with the purest element, but by this it is signified that by the grace of divine goodness we have been drawn into the assembly of the church and God's people, wherein we ought to live pure and guiltless. Thus Paul explains the mystery in Romans 6. He testifies, there-

Rom 6[.1–11]   fore, that he who receives baptism is of the church of God, which worships its Lord in integrity of faith and purity of life. For this reason the sacraments, which are holy ceremonies (for the word is added to the element, and it becomes a sacrament), should be religiously cherished, that is, highly valued, and should be treated with respect; for while they are unable to give grace they nevertheless associate visibly with the church, us who have previously been received into it invisibly; and this should be esteemed with the highest devotion when declared and published in their administration, together with the words of the divine institution. For if we think otherwise of the sacraments, as that when externally used they cleanse internally, Judaism is restored, which believed that crimes were expiated, and grace, as it were, purchased and obtained, by various anointings, ointments, offerings, victims, and banquets. Nevertheless, the prophets, especially Isaiah and Jeremiah, always most steadfastly urged in their teaching that the promises and benefits of God are given by God's liberality, and not with respect to merits or external ceremonies. I believe also that the Anabaptists in denying baptism to the infants of believers are entirely wrong; and not here only, but also in many other things, of which there is no opportunity to speak. To avoid their folly or malice, relying upon God's aid, and not without danger, I have been the first to teach and write against them, so that now, by God's goodness, this pestilence among us has greatly abated; so far am I from receiving, teaching, or defending anything of this seditious faction.

[8] Eighthly.—I believe that in the holy eucharist—that is, the supper of thanksgiving—the true body of Christ is present by the contemplation of faith; that is, that they who thank the Lord for the kindness conferred on us in his Son acknowledge that he assumed true flesh, in it truly suffered, truly washed away our sins in his own blood; and thus everything done by Christ becomes present to them by the contemplation of faith. But that the body of Christ in essence and really— that is, the natural body itself—is either present in the supper or masticated with our mouth or teeth, as the papists and some who long for the fleshpots of Egypt as-

[Ex 16.3]   sert, we not only deny, but firmly maintain is an error opposed to God's word. This, with the divine assistance, I will in a few words, O Emperor, make as clear as the

sun. First, by citing the divine oracles; secondly, by attacking the adversaries with arguments derived therefrom, as with military engines; lastly, by showing that the ancient theologians held our opinion. Thou, meanwhile, Creator Spirit, be present, enlighten the minds of thy people, and fill with grace and light the hearts that thou hast created!

Christ himself, the mouth and the wisdom of God, has said: "The poor will always be with you, but me you will not always have." Here the presence of the [Mt 26.11; Jn 12.8] body alone is denied, for according to his divinity he is always present, because he is always everywhere, according to his word: "Lo, I am with you always, even unto the end of the world"; that is, according to divinity, truth, and goodness. Augustine [Mt 28.20] agrees with us. Neither is there any foundation for the assertion of the adversaries that the humanity of Christ is wherever the divinity is, and that otherwise the person is divided; for this would destroy Christ's true humanity.

For nothing but God can be everywhere. And that humanity is in one place, but divinity everywhere, does not thus divide the person; just as the Son's assumption of humanity does not divide the unity of essence. Yea, it would be more effectual for separating unity of essence if one person assumes to itself a creature which the rest do not at all assume, than it is for separating the person, that humanity is in one place, but divinity everywhere, since we see even in creatures that bodies are confined to one place, but their power and virtue are most widely diffused. The sun is an example, whose body is in one place, while his virtue pervades all things. The human soul also surmounts the stars and penetrates hell, but the body is nevertheless in one place.

Again he says: "Again I leave the world, and go to the Father." Here the [Jn 16.28] word "to leave" is used, just as "to have" before, so that the adversaries cannot say, "We do not have him *visibly*." For when he speaks of the visible withdrawal of his body, he says: "A little while and you shall not see me," etc. Neither would any- [Jn 11.19] thing but a delusion be supported if we were to contend that his natural body is present, but invisible. For why would he evade sight when he nevertheless would be here who so often manifested himself to the disciples after the resurrection? "But it is expedient for you," he says, "that I go away." But if he were here it would not [Jn 16.7] be expedient that we should not see him. For as often as the disciples were bewildered at seeing him, he himself openly manifested himself, so that neither sense nor thought might suffer in aught. "Handle me," he says; and, "Touch me not," "I am," [Lk 24.39] etc., and, "Mary, touch me not," etc.[a]

When in departing he commended the disciples to his Father, he said: "I

a. [Mt 14.27; Jn 20.17]

[Jn 17.11] am no more in the world." Here we have in "I am no more in the world" the sub-
[Mt 26.26] stantive verb, no less than in the words: "This is my body"; so that the adversaries
cannot say that there is a trope here, since they deny that substantives admit of the
trope. But the case has no need of such arguments, for there follows: "But these are
[Jn 17.11] in the world." The antithesis clearly teaches that he is not, according to his human
nature, in the world when his disciples are.

And that we may know when he took his departure—not, as they fabri-
cate rather than explain, when he rendered himself invisible—Luke says: "While he
[Lk 24.51] blessed them he was parted from them, and carried up into heaven." He does not
say: "He vanished" or "rendered himself invisible." Of this Mark says: "After the
Lord had spoken unto them he was received up into heaven, and sat at the right hand
[Mk 16.19] of God." He does not say: "He remained here, but rendered his body invisible."
Luke again says in Acts: "When he had spoken these things while they beheld, he
[Acts 1.9] was taken up and a cloud received him out of their sight." A cloud covered him,
whereof there would have been no need if he had only removed his appearance and
otherwise have continued present. Nor would there have been need of removal or
elevation. Again: "This same Jesus which is taken up from you into heaven shall so
[Acts 1.11] come in like manner as you have seen him go into heaven." What more clear than
this? "From you," he says, "he was taken up"; therefore, he was not with them,
either visibly or invisibly, according to his human nature. When, then, we will see
him return as he departed, we will know that he is present. Otherwise he sits, according to his human nature, at the right hand of his Father until he return to judge
[2 Tm 4.1] the quick and the dead.

But since there are some who deprive Christ of place, and say that he is not
in a place, let them see how clearly, although with shut eyes, they antagonize the
truth. He was in the manger, on the cross, at Jerusalem when his parents were on
their journey, in the sepulcher and out of the sepulcher; for the angel says: "He is
[Mk 16.6] risen; he is not here: behold the place where they laid him." And that they may not
[Jn 20.19] be able to say that his body is everywhere, let them hear: "When the doors were
shut, Jesus came and stood in their midst." What need had he of coming if his body
is everywhere, but invisibly? It would have been enough not to come, but only as
one who was present to manifest himself.

But let us bid farewell to such sophistical trifles that destroy for us the truth
both of Christ's humanity and of the Holy Scriptures. These testimonies deny the
presence of Christ's body anywhere else but in heaven by speaking canonically—
that is, so far as the Scripture is manifest with respect to the nature and properties of the assumed body. And whatever contradiction the things which we propose
to ourselves concerning God's power compel, yet this must not be so tortured as

to compel us to believe that God acts contrary to his word. For this would belong to impotency, and not to power. Moreover, that the natural body of Christ is not eaten with our mouth, he himself showed when he said to the Jews disputing concerning the corporeal eating of his flesh: "The flesh profiteth nothing"—that is, for   [Jn 6.63]
eating naturally, but for eating spiritually much, as it gives life.

"That which is born of the flesh is flesh; and that which is born of the   [Jn 3.6]
Spirit is spirit." If, therefore, the natural body of Christ is eaten by our mouth, what but flesh will be produced from flesh naturally masticated? And lest the argument should seem unimportant to anyone, let him hear the second part: "That which is born of the Spirit is spirit." Therefore, that which is spirit is born of the Spirit. If, then, the flesh of Christ is salutary to the soul, it should be eaten spiritually, not carnally. This also pertains to the substance of the sacraments, that Spirit is generated of spirit, and not of any corporeal matter, as we have previously indicated.

Paul teaches that if he once knew Christ according to the flesh, henceforth   [2 Cor 5.16]
he will know him no more according to the flesh.

By these passages we are compelled to confess that the words: "This is my body," should be received not naturally, but figuratively, just as the words: "This   [Mt 26.26]
is the passover." For the lamb that was eaten every year with the celebration of the   [Ex 12.11]
festival was not the passover, but signified that the passover and omission had been formerly made. To this is added the succession, since the passover was succeeded by the Lord's supper, which teaches that Christ used similar words; for succession observes imitation. The same composition of words is an additional argument. So is the time since, at the same supper, the old passover is discontinued, and the new eucharist is instituted. The proper signification of all memorials is a further confirmation which gives it its name, whereof they make mention as "commemoration."

Thus the Athenians named *seisaxtheia* [disburdening ordinance], not as though the debt were lowered every year, but because what Solon once did they continually celebrate; and this their celebration they dignify with the name of the thing itself. Thus those things are called the body and blood of Christ which are the symbols of the true body. Now follow the arguments:

As the body cannot be fed upon a spiritual substance, so the soul cannot be fed upon a bodily substance. But if the natural body of Christ is eaten, I ask whether it feed body or soul. Not the body; then the soul. If the soul, then the soul is nourished by meats, and it is not true that Spirit is born only of spirit.

In the second place, I ask: What does the body of Christ render naturally perfect? If the forgiveness of sins, as the one side claims, then the disciples obtained the forgiveness of sins in the holy supper, and Christ therefore died in vain. If that   [Gal 12.11]
which is eaten imparts the virtue of Christ's passion, as the same side claims, then

the virtue of the passion and redemption was imparted before it was acquired. If the body is fed for the resurrection, as another very ignorantly asserts, then would it much more heal and relieve of sickness our body. But Irenaeus wishes it to be understood otherwise when he says that our body is nourished by Christ's body for the resurrection. For he desires to show that the hope of our resurrection is strengthened by Christ's resurrection. An appropriate figure!

Thirdly. — If the natural body of Christ was given his disciples in the supper, it necessarily follows that they ate it such as it then was. But it was then susceptible of suffering; they ate, therefore, the vulnerable body, for it was not yet glorified. For when they say: They ate the same body, yet not susceptible to suffering as it was, but the same as it was after the resurrection, we object. Therefore he either had two bodies, of which one was glorified and the other was not, or the one and the same body was at the same time susceptible and unsusceptible to suffering. Thus, too, since he greatly dreaded death, he was undoubtedly willing not to suffer, and to use that bodily endowment whereby he was free from pain. Therefore he did not truly suffer, but in hypocrisy; whereby Marcion is recalled by these gladiators. Six hundred arguments, O Emperor, could be adduced, but we are content now with these.

Moreover, that the ancients agree with us on the last part of this article I will establish by two witnesses, and those, too, of the first rank:

By Ambrose, who in the First Epistle to the Corinthians says concerning [1 Cor 11.26] "You do show forth the Lord's death": "For as by the Lord's death we have been freed, mindful of this, in eating and drinking we declare the flesh and blood that were offered for us," etc. Ambrose, moreover, is speaking of the food and drink of the supper, and asserts that we declare those very objects that were offered for us.

By Augustine also, who in his thirtieth discourse on John says that the body of Christ that rose from the dead must be in one place. Here the printed copies have "can be" instead of "must be," but incorrectly, for in the Master of "Sentences" [Peter Lombard] and the canonical decrees, into which this judgment of Augustine was transferred, the word "must" is read. By this we clearly see that whatever they spake excellently concerning the supper, they understood not of the natural but of the spiritual eating of Christ's body. For when they knew that the body of Christ must be in one place, and that it is at the right hand of God, they did not withdraw it thence to submit it for mastication by the fetid teeth of men.

Augustine likewise teaches in the twelfth chapter "Against Adimantus" that the three expressions: "The blood is the life," and "This is my body," and "The rock was Christ," were spoken symbolically — that is, as he himself says, in a figure and figuratively. And among many other things he at length comes to these words: "I can interpret that command as prescribed for a sign. For the Lord did not hesitate to say: 'This is my body' when he gave a sign of his body." Thus far Augustine. Lo, a key for us whereby we can unlock all the declarations of the ancients concerning the eucharist! That which is only a sign of the body he says is called the body.

Let them who wish go now and condemn us for heresy, while they know that by the same work, contrary to the decrees of the pontiffs, they are condemning the support of theologians. For from these facts it becomes very manifest that the ancients always spoke symbolically when they attributed so much to the eating of the body of Christ in the supper; not that sacramental manducation could cleanse the soul, but faith in the Lord Jesus Christ, which is spiritual manducation, whereof these external things are symbol and shadow. And as bread sustains the body and wine enlivens and exhilarates, thus it strengthens the soul and assures it of God's mercy that he has given us his Son; thus it refreshes the mind by the confidence that, by his blood, the sins with which it was being consumed were destroyed. We will now be content with these passages, although anyone could compile entire volumes in explaining and confirming the fact that the ancients are of our opinion.

Neither can the pamphlet recently published concerning the opinion of the ancients, which it expressly promises to defend, move anyone. For in a short time we will see the refutation of our very learned brother (Oecolampadius), the province of whose exordium it is to insert the opinion of the ancients; and I think that we who are of this opinion have sufficiently exhibited in many volumes, written to different persons, what in this matter can be required for the clearer explanation or confutation of the adversaries.

[9] Ninthly.—I believe that ceremonies which are neither through superstition, contrary to faith or God's word (although I do not know whether such be found), can be tolerated by charity until the day-star arise. But at the same time I believe that by the same charity as mistress the ceremonies mentioned should be abolished when it can be done without great offense, however much they who are of a faithless mind may clamor. For Christ did not prohibit Magdalene from pouring out the ointment, although the avarice and dishonesty of Judas made a disturbance. [Mt 26.6–13] Images, moreover, that are prostituted for worship, I do not reckon among ceremonies, but among the number of those things that conflict diametrically with God's word. But I am so far from condemning those that are not offered for worship that I acknowledge both painting and statuary as God's gifts.

[10] Tenthly.—The work of prophecy or preaching I believe to be most holy, so that above any other duty it is in the highest degree necessary. For in speaking canonically or regularly we see that among all nations the outward preaching of evangelists or bishops has preceded faith, which we nevertheless say is received by

the Spirit alone. For, alas! We see very many who hear the outward preaching of the gospel, but believe not, because a dearth of the Spirit has occurred. Whithersoever, then, prophets or preachers of the word are sent, it is a sign of God's grace that he wishes to manifest the knowledge of himself to his elect; and where they are denied, it is a sign of impending wrath. This can be inferred from the prophets and the ex-

[Acts 16.6]   ample of Paul, who was sometimes forbidden to go to some and at other times was

[Acts 16.9]   called. But the laws themselves and the magistrates can be assisted in maintaining public justice by no means more effectually than by prophecy. For in vain is that which is just taught unless they upon whom it is enjoined have regard for what is just and love equity. But for this the minds are prepared by the prophets as ministers, and by the Spirit as the author both of teacher and of hearer. This kind of ministers—namely, they who teach, console, terrify, care for, and faithfully watch— we acknowledge among Christ's people. That also we acknowledge which baptizes, administers in the Lord's supper the body and blood (for thus we also by metonymy name the holy bread and wine of the supper), visits the sick, and feeds the poor from the resources and in the name of the church; that, finally, which reads, interprets, and makes confession of that whereby either they themselves or others are prepared for presiding at some time over the churches. But this mitered and withered race, which is a large number, born to consume food, we believe is a useless, spurious weight upon the earth, and that it is in the ecclesiastical, what humpbacks and scrofula are in the human body.

[Rom 13.2]   [11] Eleventhly.—I know that the magistrate, when properly inaugurated, holds God's place no less than the prophet. For as a prophet is a minister of heavenly wisdom and goodness, as he faithfully teaches and brings errors to light, so

[Rom 13.4]   the magistrate is the minister of goodness and justice. He is the minister of goodness, with fidelity and moderation like God, both to hear and to deliberate upon the affairs of the people—of justice, to restrain the wantonness of the ungodly and to guard the innocent. If a prince have these endowments, I believe that his conscience has nothing to fear. If he lack these, and yet render himself an object of fear and terror, I believe that his conscience can in no way be cleared upon the ground that he has been properly inaugurated. Yet, at the same time, I believe that a Christian should obey such a tyrant, even to the occasion whereof Paul says: "If thou mayst

[1 Cor 7.12]   be made free, use it rather." Nevertheless, I believe that this is indicated by God alone, and not by man; and this not obscurely, but as openly as when Saul was re-

[1 Sm 15–16]   jected and received David as successor. And with Paul I think concerning rendering

Rm 13[.7]   tribute and custom for protection, Romans 13.

[12] Twelfthly.—I believe that the figment of the purgatorial fire is as detrimental to the gratuitous redemption bestowed through Christ as it was lucrative to

its authors. For if it is necessary by punishments and tortures to expiate the merits of our crimes, Christ will have died in vain[a] and faith will have been made void.[b] What more wicked in a Christian can be imagined? Or what sort of Christ do they have who wish to be called Christians and yet dread this fire, which is no longer fire, but smoke? That there is a hell where the faithless and ignominious and public enemies are punished with Ixion and Tantalus I not only believe, but know. For when the truth speaks of the universal judgment, it asserts that after this judgment some [Jn 14.6] will go into everlasting fire. After the universal judgment, therefore, there will be [Mt 25.41] everlasting fire. That this is endless eternity the Anabaptists cannot disguise by their error that "for ever" does not last beyond the general judgment. For here Christ is speaking of everlasting fire that will burn after the judgment, and will torture the devil and his angels, and the ungodly who despise God, and the cruel who suppress the truth with falsehood and do not mercifully and faithfully aid the necessities of their neighbor.

The above I firmly believe, teach, and maintain, not from my own oracles, but from those of the divine word; and, God willing, I promise to do this "as long as life controls these members,"[2] unless someone from the declarations of Holy Scripture, properly understood, explain and establish the reverse as clearly and plainly as we have established the above. For it is no less grateful and delightful than fair and just for us to submit our judgments to the Holy Scriptures, and the church deciding according to them by the Spirit. We could explain all things more amply, but since there is no occasion, we are content with the above, which we regard such that while at them anyone can readily carp, as is so customary today, yet no one can overthrow. But if anyone make the attempt he will not escape unpunished. Then perhaps we will produce the arms we have in reserve. Now we have declared enough for the present.

Wherefore, most excellent Emperor and other princes, rulers, nobles, and deputies, and heads of states, I beseech and implore you, by Jesus Christ our Lord and Brother, by his goodness and justice, by the verdict which he will render all according to their merits, whom no deliberation escapes, who brings to confusion the designs of princes that take counsel and rule godlessly, who exalts the humble [Lk 1.52] and abases the proud, in the first place not to neglect the lowliness of the petitioner.

a. [Gal 2.21]
b. [1 Cor 1.17]

2. Virgil *Aeneid* 4.336.

For the foolish often have spoken opportunely, and the truth itself chooses for its

[1 Cor 1.27] publication weak men and those of the lowest class. Secondly, remember that you too are men, who yourselves also are capable of being deceived by others. For every

[Rom 3.4] man is a liar. And unless something else be taught by inspiration of God than what he himself either knows or desires, nothing is to be hoped of him than that he will be destroyed by his own arts and plans. For with too much truth the prophet Jere-

Jer [8.9] miah has said: "Lo, they have rejected the word of the Lord; and what wisdom is in them?" Wherefore, since ye are the priests of justice, none are so bound to thoroughly learn God's will. But whence can this be sought but from his oracles? Be not averse, therefore, to the opinions of those who rely upon God's word. For we see it generally happen that the more adversaries assail the truth, so much the more does it shine forth and is falsehood banished. But if, as it does not escape me, there are those with you who zealously defame us as ignorant, and, if God please, also as malicious, consider, in the first place, whether we who adopt this view of the gospel and the eucharist, have ever so conducted our lives that any good man would ever doubt as to whether we should be regarded as among good men. Secondly, whether from our very infancy talent and literary culture were so distant from us that all hope of our learning had to be rejected. Certainly we boast of neither of these, since

[1 Cor 15.10] even Paul was what he was by the grace of God. If even a very cheerful life has been our lot, nevertheless this has never deviated to luxury and shamelessness, nor, on the other hand, degenerated into cruelty, arrogance, or obstinacy; so that the designs of our adversaries, often confounded by the testimony of our life, have sounded a retreat. Our learning, although greater than our enemies either could bear or without conscience despise, is, notwithstanding, far less than our followers think we possess. However, that we may reach that towards which we are aiming, we have performed such service, not only in sacred, but also in profane literature, that what we teach is not at random. Let it be permitted us, moreover, to praise the grace and munificence of God so liberally communicated to our churches. The churches that hear the Lord God through us have indeed so received the word of God that falsehood and dishonesty are diminished, pride and luxury subdued, and reproaches and wrangling have departed. If these are not certainly true fruits of divine inspiration, what will they be? Consider, most excellent Emperor and all ye princes and nobles, what good fruit of human doctrine a person has produced for us. As the purchased masses increased the lust and impudence of both princes and people, so they both introduced and extended the luxury of the pontiffs and the excesses of the ministrants of the mass. Yea, what crime did they not kindle? For who will scatter the wealth accumulated by the mass if it be not stopped and held fast in their veins?

May God, therefore, who is far better than you all, whom we gladly both call and believe to be most excellent men, grant that you may undertake to extirpate the roots of all errors in the church, and to leave and desert Rome with her rubbish that she has obtruded upon the Christian world, and especially upon your Germany.

Whatever force, too, you have heretofore exerted against the purity of the gospel may you direct against the criminal attempts of ungodly papists, that justice to us which has been banished by your indifference, and our innocence which has been obscured by artful misrepresentations, may be established. Enough cruelty has been exercised, unless it be not savage and cruel without a just ground to make charges, to condemn—ay, to slaughter, kill, rob, interdict. Since success has not followed efforts made in this way, the attempt must certainly be made in another way. If this counsel is of the Lord, do not fight against God; but if from elsewhere, it will perish by its own rashness. For this reason permit God's word to be freely   [Acts 5.38–39] disseminated and to germinate, you sons of men, who can forbid not even a grain from growing. You see that this seed is abundantly watered by the rain from heaven, neither can it be checked by any heat from men so as to become parched.

Consider not what you most of all desire, but what the world requires in regard to the gospel. Take this, such as it is, in good part, and by your disposition show that you are children of God.

Huldreich Zwingli.

Most devoted to your Majesty and all believers. Zurich, July 3, 1530.

The First Confession of Basel, 1534

Although Evangelical practices had been introduced in the 1520s in Basel by such preachers as Wolfgang Capito and Caspar Hedio (1494–1552), the city did not officially abolish the mass until 1529. Frustrated by the delays of the city leaders, the townspeople, led by the guilds, staged a series of public protests beginning in 1528 and culminating on Ash Wednesday 1529 in one of the most destructive iconoclastic riots of the era. The town council capitulated, and the chief pastor of Basel, Johannes Oecolampadius (1482–1531), wrote formal guidelines for a reformed church order that were adopted by the city on 1 April 1529.

Oecolampadius, whom Schaff characterized as Zwingli's "Melanchthon," made a statement of faith at the Synod of Basel shortly before his death in 1531, upon which his successor, Oswald Myconius (1488–1552), based *The First Confession of Basel* in 1532. The confession was ratified by the city council on 21 January 1534, and all inhabitants of Basel were required to subscribe to it.

Although in his career Myconius sought compromise with the Lutherans on the issue of the Lord's supper, *The First Confession of Basel* is thoroughly Zwinglian in its theology. Reflecting the form of → *The Apostles' Creed*, it consists of twelve articles of faith. The central role of the Bible is expressed in the concatenated biblical citations that make up the text rather than a distinct *sola scriptura* article, as was common in other Evangelical professions of faith.

The confession is designated the "first" to distinguish it from → *The First Helvetic Confession* of 1536, which is also called *The Second Confession of Basel* because it was drawn up in that city. The confession of 1534, however, was not superseded by *The First Helvetic Confession* of 1536. It remained a formal confession of the Church of Basel until the late nineteenth century.

The first edition was issued by the city council and appeared in folio format in early 1534.[1] It was translated from the original Swiss-German into Latin in 1561.

---

1. *Bekantnuss unsers heyligen Christlichen Gloubens, wie es die Kilch z Basel haltet* ([Basel: Thomas Wolff, February 1534]). According to archival records, the city council commissioned Thomas Wolff to print the confession on 7 February 1534. The first edition of six hundred copies sold out immediately, and Wolff printed a second issue of two hundred copies in March 1534. See Burckhardt-Biedermann 1896, 359.

Edition: Müller, 95–100.

Translation: Cochrane, 89–96 (slightly altered to reflect Müller edition).

Literature: Burckhardt 1946; Burckhardt-Biedermann 1896; Guggisberg 1982; Hagenbach 1827; *OER* 1:125–27 (Burnett); Schaff, 1:385–88; Staehlin 1929.

The First Confession of Basel, 1534

1. CONCERNING GOD

We believe in God the Father, God the Son, God the Holy Spirit, one holy, divine Trinity, three persons and one single, eternal, almighty God, in essence and substance, and not three gods. We also believe that God has created all things by his eternal Word, that is, by his only-begotten Son, and preserves and strengthens all things by his Spirit, that is, by his power; and therefore, God sustains and governs all things as he created them.[a] [1]

Hence we confess that before he created the world God elected all those upon whom he willed to bestow the inheritance of eternal salvation.[b]

2. CONCERNING MAN

We confess that in the beginning God made man faultless in the likeness of righteousness and holiness. But he willfully fell into sin. Through this fall the whole human race was corrupted and made subject to damnation. Moreover, our nature was enfeebled and became so inclined to sin that, unless it is restored by the Spirit of God, man neither does nor wants to do anything good of himself.[c]

3. GOD'S CARE FOR US

Although man through the fall became subject to damnation and became God's enemy, yet God never ceased to care for the human race. Witnesses to this are the patriarchs, the promises before and after the flood, the law given by God through Moses, and the holy prophets.[d]

4. CONCERNING CHRIST, TRUE GOD AND TRUE MAN

We firmly believe and confess that Christ was given to us by the Father at the appointed time according to the promises of God, and that the eternal, divine Word

---

a. Gn 1[.1]; Jn 1[.3]; 1 Chr 29[.11–12]; Acts 2[.23]

b. Rom 8[.29–30], 9[.11–13], 11[.5–7]; Eph 1[.4–6]

c. Gn 1[.17, 26]; Eph 4[.24]; Gn 3[.6], 5[.3]; Rom 5[.12, 15, 19]; 1 Cor 15[.21–22]; Eph 2[.1–3]; Gn 6[.5], 8[.21]; Jn 3[.5–6]; Rom 3[.10–12]; Ps [143.1]; Eph 2[.1–5]

d. Rom 5[.16]; Gn 3[.15], 21[.15], 26[.3, 4, 24], 28[.13–15]

1. In margin: The universal faith. This is proved by the whole Scriptures of the Old and New Testaments in many passages.

became flesh, that is, the Son of God, united with human nature in one person, became our brother in order that we might become heirs of God through him.[a] [2]

Concerning this Jesus Christ, we believe that he was conceived by the Holy Spirit, born of the pure, undefiled Virgin Mary, suffered under Pontius Pilate, was crucified and died for our sins; and thus by offering up himself he made satisfaction to God for our sins and the sins of all believers and reconciled us to God, our heavenly Father, and by his death has conquered and overcome the world, death, and hell. Moreover, we believe that according to the flesh he was buried, descended into hell, on the third day rose from the dead, and when he had sufficiently shown himself, he ascended into heaven with body and soul where he sits at the right hand of God in the glory of God his heavenly Father, whence he will come to judge the living and the dead. Furthermore, as he had promised he sent to his disciples his Holy Spirit, in whom we believe even as we believe in the Father and the Son.[b]

5. CONCERNING THE CHURCH

We believe one holy, Christian church, the fellowship of the saints, the spiritual assembly of believers which is holy and the one bride of Christ, and in which all are citizens who truly confess that Jesus is the Christ, the Lamb of God who takes away the sin of the world, and who also confirm such faith by works of love.[c]

In this church one and the same sacrament is used, namely, baptism upon entering the church, and in due time in later life the Lord's supper, as a testimony to faith and brotherly love as was promised in baptism.[d]

This Christian church endeavors to keep the bonds of peace and love in unity, and therefore it has no fellowship with sects and the rules of religious orders which are determined to distinguish between days, food, clothing, and ecclesiastical pageantry.[e]

6. CONCERNING OUR LORD'S SUPPER

We confess that the Lord Jesus instituted his holy supper for the observance of his

---

a. Mt 1[.20–21]; Lk 2[.10]; Jn 1[.14]; Phil 2[.6–7]

b. Mt 1[.18, 20, 23]; Lk 2[.7]; Mt 20[.28]; Mt 26; Rom 5[.6–8]; 1 Cor 15[.3–4]; 1 Pt 2[.2–4]; Heb 9[.14–15, 26, 28], 10[.10, 12, 14]; Rom 6[.10]; 1 Pt 3[.18]; Jn 16[.11, 33]; Phil 2[.9–11]; Col 2[.14]; 1 Cor 15[.4, 15]; Mt 16[.19]; Lk 24; Acts 1[.9–11]; Mt 26[.34]; Eph 1[.20–22]; Col 3[.1]; Heb 1[.13], 10[.12], 12[.2]; Acts 2[.7]

c. Mt 16[.18]; Eph 1[.22–23], 5[.25–27]; Jn 3[.29]; 2 Cor 11[.2]; Eph 5; Heb 12[.22–23]; Jn 1[.29]; Gal 5[.6]

d. Mt 3[.11], 28[.19]; Acts 2[.41–42], 16[.15, 33]; Col 2[.12]; Mt 26[.26–29]; Mk 14[.22–25]; Lk 22[.19]; 1 Cor 11[.23–26]

e. Rom 12[.9–10]; Jn 15[.12, 17]; 1 Jn 3[.11, 14, 16, 23], 4[.7–8, 20–21]

2. In margin: We have one Father, namely God through Christ.

holy passion with thanksgiving, to proclaim his death, and also to attest Christian love and unity with true faith.[a]

And just as in baptism, in which the washing away of sins is offered to us by the ministers of the church but can only be effected by the Father, Son, and Holy Spirit, water remains truly water, so also does the bread and wine remain bread and wine in the Lord's supper, in which the true body and blood of Christ is portrayed and offered to us with the bread and wine of the Lord, together with the words of

Jn 6[.35, 47]   institution.[3]

We firmly believe, however, that Christ himself is the food of a believing soul unto eternal life, and that our souls are nourished through true faith in the crucified Christ with the flesh and blood of Christ,[b] [4] and that we, as members of his body of which he is our only Head, live in him and he in us, so that on the day of judgment we may be raised by him and in him to eternal joy and blessedness. Therefore we confess this: that Christ is present in his holy supper for all who truly believe.[5]

However, we do not enclose in the bread and wine of the Lord the natural, true, and essential body of Christ who was born of the pure Virgin Mary, suffered for us and has ascended into heaven.[c] Consequently we do not adore Christ in these signs of bread and wine which we commonly call sacraments of the body and blood of Christ, but in heaven at the right hand of God the Father, whence he will come to judge the living and the dead.[d]

7. CONCERNING THE USE OF EXCOMMUNICATION

Because weeds are mixed with the church of Christ, Christ has given his church authority to excommunicate such weeds when they show themselves by intolerable

---

a. Lk 22[.19]; 1 Cor 11[.23], 10[.16–17]
b. Jn 11[.25]; Eph 1[.22–23], 4[.15]; Col 1[.18–19]
c. Acts 1[.9–10], 7[.55–56]; Col 3[.1–2]; Heb 1[.3], 10[.19–20]
d. Acts 3[.21], 5; 2 Tm 4[.1]

3. In margin: A powerful parable against the enemies of truth, John 6.35ff. It is indeed a spiritual food and hence it has to be enjoyed by a believing soul.
4. In margin: That is, the souls are satisfied, made strong and robust, contented and at peace, cheerful and a match for anything, just as the body is nourished by bodily food. A man becomes a spiritual member of the spiritual body of Christ.
5. In margin: Sacramentally and through the contemplation of faith which raises a man in his thoughts to heaven, but does not draw Christ down in his human nature from the right hand of God.

crimes and sins against the commandment of the Lord, in order that as much as possible the church may keep her appearance unspotted. This is the reason we use excommunication in the church.[a]

But the Christian church excommunicates solely for the sake of the reclamation of offenders, and consequently it gladly receives them again after they have put away their scandalous life and have improved.[b]

8. CONCERNING GOVERNMENT

God has charged governments, his servants, with the sword and with the highest external power for the protection of the good and for vengeance upon and punishment of evildoers. For this reason, every Christian government with which we desire to be numbered, should do all in its power to see that God's name is hallowed among its subjects, God's kingdom extended, and his will observed by the assiduous extirpation of crimes.[c] [6]

9. CONCERNING FAITH AND WORKS

We confess that there is forgiveness of sins through faith in Jesus Christ the crucified. Although this faith is continually exercised, signalized, and thus confirmed by works of love, yet do we not ascribe to works, which are the fruit of faith, the righteousness and satisfaction for our sins. On the contrary, we ascribe it solely to a genuine trust and faith in the shed blood of the Lamb of God. For we freely confess that all things are granted to us in Christ, who is our righteousness, holiness, redemption, the way, the truth, the wisdom, and the life. Therefore the works of believers are not for the satisfaction of their sins, but solely for the purpose of showing in some degree our gratitude to the Lord God for the great kindness he has shown us in Christ.[d] [7]

a. Mt 18[.15, 18]; 1 Cor 5[.3]; 2 Thes 3[.6, 14]; 1 Tm 1[.19]

b. 2 Cor 2[.6, 11]; 1 Tm 1[.20]

c. Rom 13[.1–4]; 1 Pt 2[.13–17]

d. Mt 20[.28]; Mk 10[.45]; Lk 7[.48, 50]; Jn 3[.15–16, 36], 5[.24], 6[.28–47]; Rom 3[.21–28], 4, 10[.4–11]; Gal 2[.8–16]; Rom 3[.27–28], 10; Gal 2[.16, 21]; Eph 2[.8–16]; Jn 14[.6]

6. In margin: Pagan governments have always been charged with this office; how much more should a Christian government be required to be a true lieutenant of God!

7. In margin: Gratitude consists in recompensing blessings received. Now God cannot be recompensed at all since he does not lack anything. Hence we look to his demand, namely, faith and works of love. God demands faith for himself and love for our fellow man.

10. CONCERNING THE DAY OF JUDGMENT

We believe that there will be a day of judgment on which the resurrection of the flesh will take place, when every man will receive from Christ the Judge, according as he has lived in this life: eternal life, if out of true faith and with unfeigned love he has brought works of righteousness which are the fruit of faith; or everlasting fire if he has done either good[8] or evil without faith or with a feigned faith without love.[a]

11. CONCERNING THINGS COMMANDED AND NOT COMMANDED

We confess that just as no one may require things which Christ has not commanded, so in the same way no one may forbid what he has not forbidden. For this reason we hold that the confessional, fasting during Lent, holy days, and such things introduced by men are not commanded, and, on the other hand, that the marriage of priests is not forbidden.[b] [9]

Still less may anyone permit what God has forbidden. This is the reason we reject the veneration and invoking of departed saints,[10] the veneration and setting up of images, and such like. Moreover, no one may forbid what God has permitted. For this reason we do not think it is forbidden to enjoy food with thanksgiving.[c] [11]

12. AGAINST THE ERROR OF THE ANABAPTISTS

We publicly declare that we not only do not accept but reject as an abomination and as blasphemy the alien false doctrines which are among the damnable and wicked opinions uttered by these factious spirits, namely, that children (whom we baptize

a. Mt 24[.30], 25[.31–46]; 2 Tm 4[.1, 8]
b. Mt 17[.5]; Lk 9[.35]; Dt 18[.18–19]; Acts 7[.37]
c. Lv 18[.2]; Dt 10[.17]; 1 Tm 4[.1–5]

8. In margin: "Good" is to be understood as good according to human judgment.

9. In margin: It is written: "Hear him!"

10. In margin: Concerning them we confess, however, that they are with God, reigning with Christ in eternity, because they have confessed Christ by words and deeds as their Savior, their redemption and righteousness, without any assistance of human merit. Therefore we highly praise them as those who have been pardoned by God and are now heirs of an eternal kingdom, yet all to the honor of God and of Christ.

11. In margin: He says: "I am the Lord your God." He speaks through Moses: For the Lord your God is God of gods and Lord of lords, the great, the mighty, and the terrible God, etc. Therefore who would want to permit among his creatures what he has forbidden?

according to the custom of the apostles and the early church and because baptism has replaced circumcision) should not be baptized; that in no case may an oath be taken, even though the honor of God and love for one's neighbor require it;[12] and that Christians may not hold political offices;[13] together with all other doctrines which are opposed to the sound, pure teaching of Jesus Christ.

Finally, we desire to submit this our confession to the judgment of the divine biblical Scriptures. And should we be informed from the same Holy Scriptures of a better one, we have thereby expressed our readiness to be willing at any time to obey God and his holy word with great thanksgiving.

Enacted at a meeting of our council, Wednesday, January 21, in the year 1534 after the birth of Christ our only Savior.

Heinrich Ryhiner
Clerk of the City of Basel

12. In margin: An oath may be taken at appropriate times: for God has enjoined it in the Old Testament and Christ has not forbidden it in the New. Christ and also the apostles have themselves taken oaths.

13. In margin: Government is only then a true government when it is truly Christian.

The First Helvetic Confession, 1536

Pope Paul III's call for a church council to take place in Mantua in 1537 prompted both the Lutherans (→ *The Smalcald Articles*) and the Reformed churches to formulate statements of belief.[1] The Swiss did not have a broadly recognized standard of faith like the Lutheran *Augsburg Confession* because the Reformation had come to Switzerland city by city, with each locale adopting its own confession and ordinances on church government. In anticipation of a general council, however, the magistrates of most of the Reformed cities in Switzerland agreed to call upon their chief theologians to draw up a unified expression of belief. To that end, Heinrich Bullinger (1504–75) and Leo Juda of Zurich, Oswald Myconius and Simon Grynaeus (1493–1541) of Basel, Caspar Megander (1495–1545) of Bern, and representatives from Schaffhausen, St. Gall, and Mühlhausen gathered in Basel on 30 January 1536. Bucer and Capito of Strasbourg also joined the group, eager to urge their colleagues to produce a document that could mediate between the Lutheran and Reformed positions on the crucial issue of the eucharist.

The theologians quickly drafted twenty-eight articles of faith in Latin, which were then translated into Swiss-German by Leo Juda for wider distribution.[2] The Latin and German texts have equal authority, although the German version expands upon the Latin in places. The Latin version in particular expresses the understanding of the eucharist in terms more conciliatory to the Lutheran view, calling the bread and wine "symbols by which the true communication of his body and blood is exhibited [*exhibeatur*]" (article 22). The role of the Strasbourg participants in drafting this language was noted by Grynaeus, who, a few weeks after the meeting, wrote: "Bucer and Capito brought it about that we explicitly inserted into our confession those forms which Luther required."[3] Luther apparently reacted positively when Bucer presented the confession to him, but he soon rejected any rapprochement. Although the article on the eucharist is not purely Zwinglian, it does not appear to have been the intention of Bullinger and the other Swiss reformers (with the exception of the Strasbourgers) to surrender their symbolic understanding of the last supper.

1. The council was delayed until 1545, when it convened in Trent instead of Mantua.
2. Although overall a lengthier document, the German text has only twenty-seven articles because articles 13 and 14 are collapsed into one.
3. "Quas formas Lutherus requirit, eas ut in nostram confessionem expresse insereremus Bucerus et Capito obtinuerunt" (quoted from Niemeyer, xxxv).

The confession was drafted and agreed upon with astonishing alacrity. On 4 February, only five days after they had begun their work, the reformers sent their completed text to the leaders of the cities. On 27 March 1536, the cities of Basel, Bern, Biel, Constance, Mühlhausen, St. Gall, Schaffhausen, Strasbourg, and Zurich officially accepted the confession, and it remained the authoritative profession of faith of the Swiss Reformed Church until it was superseded in 1566 by → *The Second Helvetic Confession,* for which it served as a basis.

Edition: Niemeyer, 105–22 (Swiss-German); Schaff, 3:211–31 (Latin).

Translation: Cochrane, 100–111 (from the Swiss-German).

Note: The statement is also known as *The Second Confession of Basel.*

Literature: Camenisch 1920, 45–59; Hagenbach 1827, 26–54; Niemeyer, xxxiii–xxxvii; *OER* 2:219–20 (George); Schaff, 1:388–89.

The First Helvetic Confession, 1536

A Common Confession of the Holy, True, and Ancient Christian Faith and of Our Fellow-Citizens and Fellow-Christian Believers in Zurich, Bern, Basel, Schaffhausen, St. Gallen, Mühlhausen, and Biel, and Until Further Notice, Drawn Up, Ordered, and Delivered at Basel. — February 1, 2, 3, and 4, 1536.

The churches banded together in a confederacy, having accepted the gospel of Christ, present a short and common Confession of Faith to all believing and godly 1 Pt 3; 1 Jn 4   men for their consideration, evaluation, and judgment.

1. CONCERNING HOLY SCRIPTURE

The holy, divine, biblical Scripture, which is the word of God inspired by the Holy Spirit and delivered to the world by the prophets and apostles, is the most ancient, most perfect and loftiest teaching and alone deals with everything that serves the true knowledge, love, and honor of God, as well as true piety and the making of a godly, honest, and blessed life.[a]

2. CONCERNING THE INTERPRETATION OF SCRIPTURE

This holy, divine Scripture is to be interpreted in no other way than out of itself and is to be explained by the rule of faith and love.[b]

3. CONCERNING THE EARLY TEACHERS

Where the holy fathers and early teachers, who have explained and expounded the Scripture, have not departed from this rule, we want to recognize and consider them not only as expositors of Scripture, but as elect instruments through whom God has spoken and operated.[c]

4. CONCERNING DOCTRINES OF MEN

We regard all other human doctrines and articles which lead us away from God and true faith as vain and ineffectual, no matter how attractive, fine, esteemed, and of

a. Zec 7[.1ff.]; Mt 22[.29ff.]; 2 Pt 1[.19]; 1 Thes 4[.15]; 2 Tm 3[.15ff.]
b. 1 Jn 5[.9]; Rom 12[.7]; 1 Cor 13; Thus Christ in Mt 4[.4], 7[.10]
c. Jn 17[.11ff.]; Lk 10[.1ff.]; Mt 10[.5ff.]; 1 Thes 2[.4]

long usage they may be, as St. Matthew himself attests in chapter 15[.9] where he says: "In vain do they worship me, teaching as doctrines the precepts of men."[a]

5. THE PURPOSE OF HOLY SCRIPTURE AND THAT TO WHICH IT FINALLY POINTS

The entire biblical Scripture is solely concerned that man understand that God is kind and gracious to him and that he has publicly exhibited and demonstrated this his kindness to the whole human race through Christ his Son. However, it comes to us and is received by faith alone, and is manifested and demonstrated by love for our neighbor.[b]

6. CONCERNING GOD

Concerning God, we hold that there is one only, true, living, and almighty God, one in essence, threefold according to the persons, who has created all things out of nothing by his Word, that is, by his Son, and by his providence justly, truly, and wisely rules, governs, and preserves all things.[c]

7. CONCERNING MAN

Man, the most perfect image of God on earth and among visible creatures the most excellent and eminent, is composed of body and soul. The body is mortal, the soul immortal. This man, whom God made righteous and good, fell into sin through his own guilt, and dragged the whole human race into this fall with him and subjected it to such misery.[d]

8. CONCERNING ORIGINAL SIN

This original and inherited sin has so permeated the whole human race and has so ruined and poisoned it that man, who had become a child of wrath and an enemy of God, could not be saved or restored by anyone except God through Christ. Whatever good remained in him is continually enervated through daily faults and imperfections, so that it becomes even more wicked. For the power of sin and imperfection is so strong in us that reason cannot follow what it knows nor can the mind kindle a divine spark and fan it.[e]

a. Mt 15[.9]; Is 29[.13]; Mk 7[.6ff.]; 1 Tm 4; Ti 1[.10ff.]
b. Gn 3; Jn 4; Rom 8[.1ff.]; Eph 2[.4ff.]; 1 Jn 4[.16ff.]
c. Dt 6[.4]; Mt 28[.19]; Gn 1; Ps 33[.9]; Acts 17[.24ff.]
d. Gn 1[.26ff.], 2[.7]; Rom 8[.3ff.]
e. Eph 2; Ps 51[.3]; Rom 8[.3ff.]

9. CONCERNING FREEDOM OF CHOICE
WHICH IS CALLED FREE WILL

We ascribe freedom of choice to man because we find in ourselves that we do good and evil knowingly and deliberately. We are able to do evil of ourselves but we can neither embrace nor fulfill the good unless we are illumined, quickened, and impelled by the grace of Christ. For God is the one who effects in us the willing and the doing, according to his good pleasure. Our salvation is from God, but from ourselves there is nothing but sin and damnation.[a]

10. HOW GOD HAS SAVED MAN BY HIS ETERNAL COUNSEL

Although man through this his guilt and transgression is worthy of eternal damnation and has come under the righteous wrath of God, yet God, the gracious Father, has never ceased to be concerned about him. We can perceive and understand this sufficiently, clearly, and plainly from the first promise and from the whole law by which sin is awakened though not wiped out, and from Christ the Lord who was appointed and given for that purpose.[b]

11. CONCERNING CHRIST THE LORD,
AND WHAT WE HAVE THROUGH HIM

This Lord Christ, a true Son of God, true God and man, assumed a true human nature, with body and soul, in the time thereto appointed by God from eternity. He has two distinct, unmixed natures in one single, indissoluble person. The assumption of human nature took place in order that he might quicken us who were dead and make us joint heirs of God. This also is the reason he has become our brother.

From the undefiled Virgin Mary by the cooperation of the Holy Spirit, this Lord Christ, the Son of the living, true God, has assumed flesh which is holy through its unity with the Godhead in all things like unto our flesh yet without sin—since it was to be a pure, unblemished sacrifice, and has delivered it unto death for us as a payment, pardoning and washing away of all sins.[c]

And in order that we might have a perfect hope and trust in our immortal life, he has set his flesh, which he had raised again from death unto life, at the right
1 Cor 15; Acts 1   hand of his almighty Father.

This Lord Christ, who has overcome and conquered death, sin, and the whole power of hell, is our Forerunner, our Leader, and our Head. He is the true

a. Jn 15[.7], 14[.5]; Phil 2[.15]; Acts 17[.27ff.]; Hos 13[.2]
b. Eph 1[.4]; Gn 3[.15]; Rom 7[.7ff.]
c. Mt 1[.18]; Lk 1[.26ff.]; 1 Jn 2

High Priest who sits at God's right hand and always defends and promotes our cause, until he brings us back and restores us to the image in which we were created, and leads us into the fellowship of his divine nature.[a]

We await this Lord Jesus to come at the end of the world as a true, righteous Judge who will pass a true judgment upon flesh which he has raised to judgment. He will lead the godly and believing into heaven, and will condemn and thrust unbelievers with body and soul into eternal damnation.[b]

As this Lord Jesus is our only Mediator, Advocate, Sacrifice, High Priest, Lord, and King, we acknowledge him alone, and believe with all our hearts that he only is our reconciliation, our redemption, sanctification, payment, wisdom, defense, and deliverance. Here we reject everything that represents itself as the means, the sacrifice, and the reconciliation of our life and salvation, and we recognize none other than Christ the Lord alone.[c]

12. THE PURPOSE OF EVANGELICAL DOCTRINE

Consequently in all evangelical teaching the most sublime and the principal article and the one which should be expressly set forth in every sermon and impressed upon the hearts of men should be that we are preserved and saved solely by the one mercy of God and by the merit of Christ. However, in order that men may understand how necessary Christ is for their salvation and blessedness, the magnitude and gravity of sin should be most clearly and plainly pointed out, depicted, and held up before them by means of the law and Christ's death.[d]

13. HOW CHRIST'S GRACE AND MERIT ARE COMMUNICATED TO US AND THE FRUIT THAT FOLLOWS FROM IT

We do not obtain such sublime and great benefits of God's grace and the true sanctification of God's Spirit through our merits or powers but through faith which is a pure gift of God.

This faith is a sure, firm, and solid foundation for and a laying hold of all those things for which one hopes from God, and from which love and subsequently all virtues and the fruits of good works are brought forth.

And although godly believers constantly exercise themselves in such fruits of faith, yet we do not ascribe the piety and the salvation obtained to such works,

a. Eph 1[.20f.]; Rom 6[.23]; Eph 4[.8ff.]
b. Dn 7[.26ff.]; Jn 5[.26]; Mt 25[.31ff.]
c. 1 Tm 2[.5]; Heb 7; Rom 3[.23ff.]; 1 Cor 1[.30]
d. 1 Tm 1[.15]; Rom 3[.23ff.]

but only to the grace of God. Although this faith effects innumerable good works, it does not take comfort in them but in the mercy of God. Such a faith is the true and proper service with which a man is pleasing to God.[a]

14. CONCERNING THE CHURCH

We hold that from living stones built upon this living rock a holy, universal church is built and gathered together. It is the fellowship and congregation of all saints which is Christ's bride and spouse which he washes with his blood and finally presents to the Father without blemish or any spot. And although this church and congregation of Christ is open and known to God's eyes alone, yet it is not only known but also gathered and built up by visible signs, rites, and ordinances, which Christ himself has instituted and appointed by the word of God as a universal, public, and orderly discipline. Without these marks no one is numbered with this church (speaking generally and without a special permission revealed by God).[b]

15. CONCERNING THE MINISTERS OF GOD'S WORD AND THE FRUIT THAT FOLLOWS FROM IT

Therefore we also believe that the church's ministers are God's coworkers, as St. Paul calls them, through whom he imparts and offers to those who believe in him the knowledge of himself and the forgiveness of sins, converts, strengthens, and comforts men, but also threatens and judges them, yet with the understanding that in all things we ascribe all efficacy and power to God the Lord alone, and only the imparting to the minister. For it is certain that this power and efficacy never should or can be attributed to a creature, but God dispenses it to those he chooses according to his free will.[c]

16. CONCERNING THE AUTHORITY OF THE CHURCH

The authority to preach God's word and to tend the flock of the Lord, which properly speaking is the office of the keys, prescribes one pattern of life for all men whether of high or lowly station. Since it is commanded by God, it is a high and sacred trust which should not be violated. This administrative power should not be conferred upon anyone unless he has first been found and acknowledged to be qualified and fit for the office by divine calling and election and by those who after

---

a. Rom 3[.24]; Gal 2[.16]; Eph 2[.8]; Gal 5[.22]; Mi 6[.6ff.]

b. 1 Pt 2[.4ff.]; Mt 16[.18]; 1 Jn 1[.7]; 1 Pt 1[.3ff.]; Eph 5[.27]; Jn 6[.68f.]; 2 Tm 2[.19]; Acts 13[.39]; Mt 28[.18ff.]; Acts 10[.47ff.]

c. 1 Cor 3[.5ff.], 4[.1ff.]; 2 Cor 6[.4ff.]; Jn 20[.21ff.]; Lk 1[.51ff.]

careful deliberation have been appointed and elected as a committee of the church for that purpose.[a]

17. CONCERNING THE ELECTION OF
MINISTERS OF THE CHURCH

No one should be charged or entrusted with this office and ministry unless he has first been found and acknowledged by the ministers and elders of the church, and also by those Christian rulers elected to such office on behalf of the church, to be well instructed in the Holy Scriptures and in the knowledge of the will of God, blameless in piety and purity of life, and zealous and fervent in promoting the honor and name of Christ with diligence and earnestness. And because this is a true and proper election of God, it is reasonable and right that they should be recognized and accepted by the judgment of the church and the laying on of hands by the elders.[b]

18. WHO THE SHEPHERD AND HEAD OF THE CHURCH IS

Christ himself is the only true and proper Head and Shepherd of his church. He gives to his church shepherds and teachers who at his command administer the word and office of the keys in an orderly and regular fashion, as reported above. Consequently we do not acknowledge or accept the head [of the church] at Rome and those who are bishops in name only.[c]

19. WHAT THE OFFICE OF MINISTERS
AND OF THE CHURCH IS

The highest and chief thing in this office is that the ministers of the church preach repentance and sorrow for sins, improvement of life, and forgiveness of sins, and all through Christ. In addition they are to pray unceasingly for the people, to apply themselves earnestly and diligently to Holy Scripture and the word of God, in reading and devout meditation, and with God's word as with the sword of the Spirit to pursue the devil with deadly hatred by every means, and to crush and weaken his power so that they may defend Christ's stanch citizens and may warn, repel, and put away the wicked. And when the wicked in their sacrilege and shameless vices are forever determined to scandalize and destroy the church, they are to be expelled by the ministers of the word and the Christian government instituted for that pur-

a. Mt 16[.19]; Jn 20[.21ff.]; 1 Thes 4; Acts 13[.2ff.]

b. 1 Tm 3[.2ff.], 4[.12ff.]; Lk 12[.8ff.]; Acts 1[.15ff.]; Ti 1[.5ff.]; Nm 27[.28ff.]; Dt 34[.9]; Acts 6[.2ff.], 8[.14ff.], 13[.2ff.]; 1 Tm 1[.18]; Heb 6

c. Jn 10; Eph 1[.3ff.], 4, 5[.25ff.]; Col 1[.18], 2[.6ff.]; Jn 20[.28]; Zec 11[.15ff.]

pose, or they are to be punished and corrected in some other suitable and proper way until they confess their error, change and are restored. But when a citizen of Christ, who has been delinquent and derelict and has been expelled, is converted and earnestly confesses and admits his sin and error (for this is the purpose of the punishment), willingly seeks remedy for his failings, yields to spiritual discipline, and gladdens all the pious with his new diligence and zeal in the exercise of piety, he should be accepted again into the church.[a]

20. CONCERNING THE POWER AND EFFICACY OF THE SACRAMENTS

The signs, which are called sacraments, are two: baptism and the Lord's supper. These sacraments are significant, holy signs of sublime, secret things. However, they are not mere, empty signs, but consist of the sign and substance. For in baptism the water is the sign, but the substance and spiritual thing is rebirth and admission into the people of God. In the Lord's supper the bread and wine are the signs, but the spiritual substance is the communion of the body and blood of Christ, the salvation acquired on the cross, and forgiveness of sins. As the signs are bodily received, so these substantial, invisible, and spiritual things are received in faith. Moreover, the entire power, efficacy, and fruit of the sacraments lies in these spiritual and substantial things.

Consequently we confess that the sacraments are not simply outward signs of Christian fellowship. On the contrary, we confess them to be signs of divine grace by which the ministers of the church work with the Lord for the purpose and to the end which he himself promises, offers, and efficaciously provides. We confess, however, that all sanctifying and saving power is to be ascribed to God, the Lord, alone, as we said above concerning the servants of the word.

21. CONCERNING BAPTISM

According to the institution of the Lord, baptism is a bath of regeneration which the Lord offers and presents to his elect with a visible sign through the ministry of the church, as stated and explained above. We baptize our children in this holy bath because it would be unjust if we were to rob of the fellowship of God's people those who have been born of us for a people of God, for which they had been intended by the divine word and of whom it may be assumed that they have been elected by God.[b]

a. Lk 24[.25]; 1 Cor 11[.18ff.]; Acts 6; 1 Tm 4[.6ff.]; Eph 6[.13ff.]; 2 Tm 4; Ez 14[.3ff.]; 1 Cor 5; 2 Thes 3[.6]; 2 Cor 2[.24]
b. Mt 28[.18ff.]; Mk 16[.15ff.]; Ti 3[.5]; Gn 17[.10ff.]; Lk 18[.15ff.]

22. CONCERNING THE LORD'S SUPPER

In regard to the Lord's supper we hold, therefore, that in it the Lord truly offers his body and his blood, that is, himself, to his own, and enables them to enjoy such fruit that he lives ever more and more in them and they in him. We do not believe that the body and blood of the Lord is naturally united with the bread and wine or that they are spatially enclosed within them, but that according to the institution of the Lord the bread and wine are highly significant, holy, true signs by which the true communion of his body and blood is administered and offered to believers by the Lord himself by means of the ministry of the church—not as perishable food for the belly but the food and nourishment of a spiritual and eternal life. We frequently make use of this sublime and holy food in order that being thereby reminded, we may perceive with the eyes of faith the death and the blood of the crucified Christ, and, with a foretaste of the nature of heaven and with a genuine experience of eternal life, may aspire to our salvation. With this spiritual, quickening, inward food we are delighted and refreshed by its inexpressible sweetness and are overjoyed to find our life in Christ's death. Therefore, we shout for joy in our hearts and all the more break forth into thanksgiving for such a costly and sublime favor he has shown us.[a]

Therefore we are most unjustly blamed for attaching little value to these sublime signs. For these holy signs and sacraments are sacred and venerable things because they have been instituted and used by Christ the High Priest. Thus in the way discussed above they present and offer the spiritual things they signify. They bear witness to things that have happened. They portray and remind us of such high and holy things. And by means of a singular resemblance to the things they signify, they shed a great and glorious light upon sacred and divine matters. In addition they are something of an aid and support to faith, and are as much as an oath with which believers obligate and bind themselves to their head and to the church. Yet as highly as we prize these sacred and extremely meaningful signs, we ascribe the quickening and sanctifying power always to him alone who only is the life, to him be the praise forever and ever. Amen.   Acts 4[.12]

23. CONCERNING SACRED ASSEMBLIES AND MEETINGS OF BELIEVERS

We hold that the sacred assemblies and meetings of believers should be conducted in such a way that above all else God's word be placed before the people at a common place and reserved for that purpose alone; that the mysteries of Scripture be daily expounded and explained by qualified ministers; that the Lord's supper be ob-

a. Mt 26[.26ff.]; Jn 6[.48ff.], 10[.23]; 1 Cor 10[.16ff.]

served in order that the faith of believers be exercised continually; and that earnest prayer for the needs of all men be constantly made. Other ceremonies, which are innumerable, such as chalices, priestly gowns for the mass, choir robes, cowls, tonsures, flags, candles, altars, gold, and silver, to the extent they serve to hinder and pervert true religion and the proper worship of God, and especially the idols and pictures which are used for worship and are a scandal, and any more such ungodly things—these we want to have banished far from our holy congregations.[a]

24. CONCERNING THINGS WHICH ARE NEITHER COMMANDED NOR FORBIDDEN, BUT ARE ADIAPHORA AND VOLUNTARY

All things that are called, and properly speaking, are adiaphora, may be freely used by devout, believing Christians at all times and in all places, provided he does so judiciously and with love. For a believer is to use all things in such a way that God's honor is promoted and the church and his neighbor are not offended.[b]

25. CONCERNING THOSE WHO DIVIDE THE CHURCH OF CHRIST BY FALSE DOCTRINES OR SEPARATE THEMSELVES FROM IT AND CONSPIRE AGAINST IT

When all those who separate and cut themselves off from the holy fellowship and society of the church, introduce alien and ungodly doctrines into the church, or adhere to such doctrines—faults that in our day are chiefly evident in the Anabaptists—do not hear and heed the warning of the church and Christian instruction, but obstinately want to persist in their contention and error, with consequent injury to and seduction of the church, they should be punished and suppressed by the supreme power, in order that they may not poison, harm, or defile the flock of God with their false doctrine.[c]

26. CONCERNING THE TEMPORAL GOVERNMENT

Since all governmental power is from God, its highest and principal office, if it does not want to be tyrannical, is to protect and promote the true honor of God and the proper service of God by punishing and rooting out all blasphemy, and to exercise all possible diligence to promote and to put into effect what a minister of the church and a preacher of the gospel teaches and sets forth from God's word. However, in order that such true religion—a true service of God and propriety of conduct—may arise and flourish, a government will above all use every effort that the pure word

a. Acts 2[.41ff.]; 1 Tm 2; 1 Cor 14; Acts 8[.14ff.]; Ex 20[.4]; Is 40[.25]; 1 Cor 10[.7]; 1 Pt 4[.3]
b. Rom 14[.1ff.]; 1 Cor 8[.1ff.]; Whatever does not proceed from faith is sin: Rom 14[.23]; 1 Cor 10[.14ff.]
c. Is 5[.20]; Acts 3[.23]

of God be faithfully proclaimed to the congregation, and no one be prevented from hearing it; that schools be well regulated, the ordinary citizenry well taught, carefully instructed and disciplined; that the ministers of the church and the poor in the church be well taken care of, and their necessities properly and adequately be provided for. For this purpose the possessions of the church should serve.[a]

Furthermore, a government should rule the people according to just, divine laws. It should sit in judgment and administer justice, preserve the public peace and welfare, guard and defend the public interest, and with fairness punish wrongdoers according to the nature of their crimes against life and property. And when a government does this, it serves God its Lord as it ought to do and is obligated to do.

Although we are free in Christ, all of us should obey such supreme authority and be ready to serve with our lives, goods, and possessions. With sincere love and from faith we should show that we are subject to it, performing vows and oaths when its orders and commandments are manifestly not opposed to him for whose sake we honor and obey it.[b]

27. CONCERNING HOLY MATRIMONY

We contend that marriage has been instituted and prescribed by God for all men who are qualified and fit for it and who have not otherwise been called by God to live a chaste life outside marriage. No order or state is so holy and honorable that marriage would be opposed to it and should be forbidden. Since such marriage should be confirmed in the presence of the church by a public exhortation and vow in keeping with its dignity, the government should also respect it and see to it that a marriage is legally and decently entered into and given legal and honorable recognition, and is not lightly dissolved without serious and legitimate grounds.

Consequently we cannot commend cloisters and the impure and irregular chastity of all supposed clerics and the indolent and useless life they lead which certain people have instituted and arranged out of mistaken zeal. On the contrary, we reject it as an abominable and dreadful thing invented and devised by men in opposition to God's order.[c]

Basel, March 26, 1536.

Approved and unanimously adopted by the delegates from the above-mentioned cities.

---

a. 2 Chr 19[.8ff.]; Rom 13; Ps 82; Lv 24[.10]; Ex 18; Dn 3, 6[.10]; 1 Cor 9[.1ff.]; 1 Tm 5[.17ff.]; Rom 12[.13]; 1 Cor 16[.1ff.]

b. Ex 18[.13ff.]; Is 10; Rom 13[.5ff.]; Mt 17[.24ff.], 22[.21]; Acts 4[.19], 5[.29]

c. Mt 5[.27ff.], 19[.3ff.]; Heb 13[.4]; 1 Cor 7; 1 Tm 3[.2], 4[.1ff.]

The Lausanne Articles, 1536

In March 1536, the Swiss territory of Vaud, with the decisive help of Protestant Bern, freed itself from the rule of the Catholic house of Savoy. The Reformation had already taken hold in other cities of the region, notably in Geneva, through the work of Guillaume Farel (1489–1565), who had introduced reforms to Neuchâtel in 1530 and to Geneva in 1532, and his assistant Pierre Viret (1511–71), who later served as chief pastor in Lausanne. As the author of the *Sommaire*—the earliest explanation of the Protestant faith in French (1st ed., 1529)—and a charismatic preacher, Farel was the recognized Evangelical leader in French-speaking Switzerland. He presented these articles as topics for a disputation in Lausanne,[1] drawing on his experience at the public disputation in Basel in 1524 at which he had presented thirteen articles of faith for discussion, as well as the models of Zwingli's → *Sixty-Seven Articles* and → *The Ten Theses of Bern*—both prepared for similar introductions of reform in Zurich and Bern. *The Lausanne Articles* emphasize the centrality of the Bible in matters of faith and as the sole basis for preaching. They express a sacramentarian view of baptism and the eucharist as symbols or signs of divine grace and deny the efficacy of confession on the grounds that God alone pardons and remits sins. Celibacy, ceremony, and the use of images are rejected, but without harsh polemic against the Catholic Church.

   The disputation took place in the cathedral of Lausanne from 1 to 8 October 1536. No bishops or Roman Catholic theologians participated, and the local priests who attended offered little in the way of counterarguments. Farel and Viret dominated the discussions, although it is recorded that a young John Calvin was among the participants. In the discussions of articles 3 (on the church of believers) and 8 (on civil magistracy), Calvin took the liberty of expanding the issues to speak out with considerable fervor against the concept of transubstantiation and the power of the papacy.[2] Perhaps Farel remembered this when, later in the same year, he recruited Calvin for his mission in Geneva.

---

1. Locher 1988, 91–92, believes that the text shows little of the stylistic character of Farel's other writings and proposes that the final form of the theses may have been the work of a committee, perhaps headed by Farel, with the likely participation of Pierre Viret and Caspar Megander.
2. For Calvin's statements see Piaget 1928, 224–30, 330–31; for English translation see *LCC*, 22:38–46.

Edition: Bavaud 1956, 51–53.

Translation: *LCC* 22:35–37 (Reid; slightly revised to reflect Bavaud edition).

Note: The Latin and French texts have equal status and are both reproduced from Bavaud's edition. The translation is from the French text.

Literature: Bavaud 1956; Braekman 1988; Deluz and Meylan 1936, 9–22; Esser 1992; *Guillaume Farel* 1930; Higman 1988; *La Dispute de Lausanne 1536* 1988 (collection of articles, some cited separately here); Locher 1988; *OER* 2:403–4 (Higman); Peronnet 1988; Piaget 1928, 224–30, 330–31; Stauffer 1983; *TRE* 20:502–3 (Keller).

The Lausanne Articles, 1536

Issues to be discussed at Lausanne in the new province of Bern on the first day of October 1536

1.

Holy Scripture teaches no other way of justification, which is by faith in Jesus Christ once offered, and holds as nothing but a destroyer of all the virtue of Christ anyone who makes another satisfaction, oblation, or cleansing for the remission of sins.

2.

This Scripture acknowledges Jesus Christ, who is risen from the dead and sits in heaven at the right hand of the Father, as the only chief and true priest, sovereign mediator, and true advocate of his church.

3.

Holy Scripture names the church of God all who believe that they are received by the blood of Jesus Christ alone and who constantly and without vacillation believe and wholly establish and support themselves on the Word, who, having withdrawn from us in corporeal presence, nevertheless by the virtue of his Holy Spirit fills, sustains, governs, and vivifies all things.

4.

The said church contains certain who are known to the eyes of God alone. It possesses always ceremonies ordained by Christ, by which it is seen and known, that is to say baptism and the supper of our Lord, which are called sacraments, since they are symbols and signs of secret things, that is to say of divine grace.

5.

The said church acknowledges no ministry except that which preaches the word of God and administers the sacraments.

6.

Further this church itself receives no other confession than that which is made to God, no other absolution than that which is given by God for the remission of sins and which alone pardons and remits their sins who to this end confess their fault.

7.

Further this same church denies all other ways and means of serving God beyond that which is spiritually ordained by the word of God, which consists in the love of himself and of one's neighbor. Hence it rejects entirely the innumerable mockeries of all ceremonies which pervert religion, such as images and like things.

8.

Also it acknowledges the civil magistrate ordained by God only as necessary to preserve the peace and tranquillity of the state. To which end, it desires and ordains that all be obedient in so far as nothing contrary to God is commanded.

9.

Next it affirms that marriage, instituted by God for all persons as fit and proper for them, violates the sanctity of no one whatever.

10.

Finally as to things that are indifferent, such as foods, drinks, and the observation of days, it allows as many as the man of faith can use at all times freely, but not otherwise than wisdom and charity should do.

The Ten Articles, 1536

The first confessional document of the Church of England is commonly called *The Ten Articles*; its full title, however, better indicates its intent: *Articles to stablyshe Christian quietnes and unitie amonge us, and to avoyde contentious opinions.* In 1536, Henry VIII sent his vicar general, Thomas Cromwell (c. 1485–1540), to the convocation of clergy in southern England with a royal order that the body debate the religious controversies of the day and submit a document of common beliefs. The king was disturbed by the lack of uniformity in the reform movement or, as he described the situation: "Behold then what love and charitie is amongst you, when the one calleth another heretike and Anabaptist; and he calleth him againe Papist, hypocrite, and pharisey . . . I heare daily that you of the cleargie preach one against another, teach one contrary to another, envying one against another. . . . Thus all men, almost, be in variety and discord and fewe or none preach truly and sincerely the Word of God according as they ought to do."[1] In his preface to *The Ten Articles*, Henry implies that he had a hand in compiling the document, and it is possible that Cromwell arrived with a draft from the king that was worked over by a committee at the convocation. The king's place as head of the church is emphasized not only in his preface but also in the wording of most of the articles, which begin with the royal "we": "We will that all bishops and preachers shall . . . ."

Among the participants at the convocation was the bishop of Hereford, Edward Fox (1496?–1538), who had been representing England in conversations with the Wittenberg reformers. Consequently, on some doctrinal issues, in particular the articulation of justification and the understanding of the sacraments, *The Ten Articles* are influenced by Lutheran theology. In particular, they reveal a familiarity with → *The Augsburg Confession* and the unsuccessful alliance agreement that Bishop Fox and others concluded with the Lutherans known as *The Wittenberg Articles* of 1536.[2] Both Fox and Thomas Cranmer, who also had close ties to Lutheranism and was related by marriage to Andreas Osiander, probably had a hand in drafting *The Ten Articles*.[3]

Articles 1–5 of *The Ten Articles* deal with matters of faith, whereas the last five articles concern the ceremonies of the church. The first article declares the

1. Quoted from Stow's *Chronicle* in Hardwick 1876, 33n.
2. See Mentz [1905] 1968, 18–79, and Bray, 119–61.
3. Strype 1842–54, 1:57; Reardon 1989, 94.

Bible and the three creeds (→ *Apostles'*, → *Niceno-Constantinopolitan*, and → *Athanasian*) the only sources for the fundamentals of religion. Articles 2–4 affirm baptism, penance, and the eucharist as sacraments. Article 5 concerns justification, expressing the solafideism of Lutheranism without denying (just as Luther never denied) the importance of good works. Articles 6–8 take a moderate view on the use of images in worship and uphold the practice of honoring the saints, but deny their efficacy as mediators for obtaining grace, justification, or salvation. Article 9 defends the use of ceremony, albeit only "to put us in remembrance of those spiritual things that they do signify," not as acts with the power to remit sin or convey grace. The final article expresses a cautious view of the concept of purgatory, admitting the lack of scriptural evidence for it without denying the practice of praying for the souls of the dead, "trusting that God accepteth our prayers for them, referring the rest wholly to God." Papal pardons and other acts that promise delivery from punishment, however, are rejected as abuses.

The articles provide numerous proof texts from the Bible. Interestingly, the Bible quotations had to be given in Latin because there was no authorized translation of the English Bible in 1536.[4]

Edition: Hardwick 1876 (3d rev. ed.), 239–58.

Note: Paragraph numbering based on Bray's divisions of Hardwick's text.

Literature: Atkinson 1983; Bray, 162–74; *DECH* 30–32; Dugmore 1980; Hardwick 1876, 31–51.

4. Although Miles Coverdale had published the first complete English Bible in 1535 and had dedicated it to the king, it was not authorized.

The Ten Articles, 1536

Articles Devised by the Kinges Highnes Majestie, to Stablyshe Christian Quietnes and Unitie Amonge Us, and To Avoyde Contentious Opinions, Which Articles Be Also Approved by the Consent and Determination of the Hole Clergie of This Realme. Anno M.D.XXXVI.

The Preface

Henry the VIII. by the grace of God king of England and of France, defensor of the faith, lord of Ireland, and in earth supreme head of the Church of England, to all, and singular our most loving, faithful, and obedient subjects, greeting.

[1] Among other cures appertaining unto this our princely office, whereunto it hath pleased Almighty God of his infinite mercy and goodness to call us, we have always esteemed and thought, like as we also yet esteem and think, that it most chiefly belongeth unto our said charge diligently to foresee and cause, that not only the most holy word and commandments of God should most sincerely be believed, and most reverently be observed and kept of our subjects, but also that unity and concord in opinion, namely in such things as doth concern our religion, may increase and go forthward, and all occasion of dissent and discord touching the same be repressed and utterly extinguished.

[2] For the which cause, we being of late, to our great regret, credibly advertised of such diversity in opinions, as have grown and sprung in this our realm, as well concerning certain articles necessary to our salvation, as also touching certain other honest and commendable ceremonies, rites, and usages now of long time used and accustomed in our churches, for conservation of an honest policy and decent and seemly order to be had therein, minding to have that unity and agreement established through our said church concerning the premises, and being very desirous to eschew not only the dangers of souls, but also the outward unquietness which by occasion of the said diversity in opinions (if remedy were not provided) might perchance have ensued, have not only in our own person at many times taken great pains, study, labors, and travails, but also have caused our bishops, and other the most discreet and best learned men of our clergy of this our whole realm, to be assembled in our convocation, for the full debatement and quiet determination of the same. Where, after long and mature deliberation, and disputations had of and upon

the premises, finally they have concluded and agreed upon the most special points and articles, as well such as be commanded of God, and are necessary to our salvation, as also divers other matters touching the honest ceremonies and good and politic orders, as is aforesaid; which their determination, debatement, and agreement, for so much as we think to have proceeded of a good, right, and true judgment, and to be agreeable to the laws and ordinances of God, and much profitable for the establishment of that charitable concord and unity in our Church of England, which we most desire, we have caused the same to be published, willing, requiring, and commanding you, to accept, repute, and take them accordingly. And further we most heartily desire and pray Almighty God, that it may please him so to illumine your hearts, that you and every of you may have no less desire, zeal, and love to the said unity and concord, in reading, divulging, and following the same, than we have had, and have in causing them to be thus devised, set forth, and published.

[3] And, for because we would the said Articles and every of them should be taken and understanden of you after such sort, order, and degree, as appertaineth accordingly, we have caused, by the like assent and agreement of our said bishops and other learned men, the said Articles to be divided into two sorts; whereof the one part containeth such as be commanded expressly by God, and be necessary to our salvation; and the other containeth such things as have been of a long continuance for a decent order and honest policy, prudently instituted and used in the churches of our realm, and be for that same purpose and end to be observed and kept accordingly, although they be not expressly commanded of God, nor necessary to our salvation. Wherefore we will and require you to accept the same, after such sort as we have here prescribed them unto you, and to conform yourselves obediently unto the same. Whereby you shall not only attain that most charitable unity and loving concord, whereof shall ensue your incomparable commodity, profit, and lucre, as well spiritual as other, but also you shall not a little encourage us to take further travails, pains, and labors for your commodities, in all such other matters as in time to come may happen to occur, and as it shall be most to the honor of God, the profit, tranquillity, and quietness of all you our most loving subjects.

[1.] THE PRINCIPAL ARTICLES CONCERNING OUR FAITH
[2] First, As touching the chief and principal articles of our faith, since it is thus agreed as hereafter followeth by the whole clergy of this our realm, we will that all bishops and preachers shall instruct and teach our people, by us committed to their spiritual charge, that they ought and must most constantly believe and defend all those things to be true, which be comprehended in the whole body and canon of the Bible, and also in the three creeds or symbols, whereof one was made by the

apostles, and is the common creed, which every man useth; the second was made by the holy council of Nicaea, and is said daily in the mass; and the third was made by Athanasius, and is comprehended in the Psalm *Quicunque vult:* and that they ought and must take and interpret all the same things according to the selfsame sentence and interpretation, which the words of the selfsame creeds or symbols do purport, and the holy approved doctors of the church do entreat and defend the same.

[2] *Item,* That they ought and must repute, hold, and take all the same things for the most holy, most sure, and most certain, and infallible words of God, and such as neither ought, nor can be altered or convelled, by any contrary opinion or authority.

[3] *Item,* That they ought and must believe, repute, and take all the articles of our faith contained in the said creeds to be so necessary to be believed for man's salvation, that whosoever being taught will not believe them as is aforesaid, or will obstinately affirm the contrary of them, he or they cannot be the very members of Christ and his espouse the church, but be very infidels or heretics, and members of the devil, with whom they shall perpetually be damned.

[4] *Item,* That they ought and must most reverently and religiously observe and keep the selfsame words, according to the very same form and manner of speaking, as the articles of our faith be already contained and expressed in the said creeds, without altering in any wise, or varying from the same.

[5] *Item,* That they ought and must utterly refuse and condemn all those opinions contrary to the said Articles, which were of long time past condemned in the four holy councils, that is to say, in the Council of Nicaea, Constantinople, Ephesus, and Chalcedon, and all other since that time in any point consonant to the same.

[2.] THE SACRAMENT OF BAPTISM

[1] Secondly, As touching the holy sacrament of baptism, we will that all bishops and preachers shall instruct and teach our people committed by us unto their spiritual charge, that they ought and must of necessity believe certainly all those things, which hath been always by the whole consent of the church approved, received, and used in the sacrament of baptism; that is to say, that the sacrament of baptism was instituted and ordained in the New Testament by our Savior Jesu Christ, as a thing necessary for the attaining of everlasting life, according to the saying of Christ, *Nisi* [Jn 3.5] *quis renatus fuerit ex aqua et Spiritu Sancto, non potest intrare in regnum caelorum:* that is to say, No man can enter into the kingdom of heaven, except he be born again of water and the Holy Ghost.

[2] *Item,* That it is offered unto all men, as well infants as such as have the use of reason, that by baptism they shall have remission of sins, and the grace and favor of God, according to the saying of Christ, *Qui crediderit et baptizatus fuerit, salvus erit:* that is to say, Whosoever believeth and is baptized shall be saved.   [Mk 16.16]

[3] *Item,* That the promise of grace and everlasting life (which promise is adjoined unto this sacrament of baptism) pertaineth not only unto such as have the use of reason, but also to infants, innocents, and children; and that they ought therefore and must needs be baptized; and that by the sacrament of baptism, they do also obtain remission of their sins, the grace and favor of God, and be made thereby the very sons and children of God. Insomuch as infants and children dying in their infancy shall undoubtedly be saved thereby, and else not.

[4] *Item,* That infants must needs be christened because they be born in original sin, which sin must needs be remitted; which cannot be done but by the sacrament of baptism, whereby they receive the Holy Ghost, which exerciseth his grace and efficacy in them, and cleanseth and purifieth them from sin by his most secret virtue and operation.

[5] *Item,* That children or men once baptized, can, nor ought ever to be baptized again.

[6] *Item,* That they ought to repute and take all the Anabaptists' and the Pelagians' opinions contrary to the premises, and every other man's opinion agreeable unto the said Anabaptists' or the Pelagians' opinions in this behalf, for detestable heresies, and utterly to be condemned.

[7] *Item,* That men or children having the use of reason, and willing and desiring to be baptized, shall, by the virtue of that holy sacrament, obtain the grace and remission of all their sins, if they shall come thereunto perfectly and truly repentant and contrite of all their sins before committed, and also perfectly and constantly confessing and believing all the articles of our faith, according as it was mentioned in the first Article.

[8] And finally, if they shall also have firm credence and trust in the promise of God adjoined to the said sacrament, that is to say, that in and by this said sacrament, which they shall receive, God the Father giveth unto them, for his Son Jesu Christ's sake, remission of all their sins, and the grace of the Holy Ghost, whereby they be newly regenerated and made the very children of God, according to the saying of St. John and the apostle St. Peter, *Delictorum poenitentiam agite, et baptizetur unusquisque vestrum in nomen Jesu Christi in remissionem peccatorum, et accipietis*   [Acts 2.38] *donum Spiritus Sancti;* that is to say, Do penance for your sins, and be each of you baptized in the name of Jesu Christ, and you shall obtain remission of your sins, and shall receive the gift of the Holy Ghost. And according also to the saying of St. Paul,

Non ex operibus justitiae quae fecimus nos, sed secundum suam misericordiam, salvos nos fecit per lavacrum regenerationis et renovationis Spiritus Sancti, quem effudit in nos opulente per Jesum Christum Servatorem nostrum, ut justificati illius gratia haeredes efficiamur juxta spem vitae aeternae; that is to say, God hath not saved us for the works of justice which we have done, but of his mercy by baptism, and renovation of the Holy Ghost, whom he hath poured out upon us most plentifully, for the love of Jesu Christ our Savior, to the intent that we, being justified by his grace, should be made the inheritors of everlasting life, according to our hope.

[Ti 3.6–7]

[3.] THE SACRAMENT OF PENANCE

[1] Thirdly, Concerning the sacrament of penance, we will that all bishops and preachers shall instruct and teach our people committed by us unto their spiritual charge, that they ought and must most constantly believe, that that sacrament was instituted of Christ in the New Testament as a thing so necessary for man's salvation, that no man, which after his baptism is fallen again, and hath committed deadly sin, can, without the same, be saved, or attain everlasting life.

[2] *Item,* That like as such men which after baptism do fall again into sin, if they do not penance in this life, shall undoubtedly be damned; even so whensoever the same men shall convert themselves from their naughty life, and do such penance for the same as Christ requireth of them, they shall without doubt attain remission of their sins, and shall be saved.

[3] *Item,* That the sacrament of perfect penance which Christ requireth of such manner persons consisteth of three parts, that is to say, contrition, confession, and the amendment of the former life, and a new obedient reconciliation unto the laws and will of God, that is to say, exterior acts in works of charity according as they be commanded of God, which be called in Scripture, *fructus digni poenitentia,* the worthy fruits of penance.

[Mt 3.8]

[4] Furthermore, as touching contrition, which is the first part, we will that all bishops and preachers shall instruct and teach our people committed by us unto their spiritual charge, that the said contrition consisteth in two special parts, which must always be conjoined together, and cannot be dissevered; that is to say, the penitent and contrite man must first acknowledge the filthiness and abomination of his own sin (unto which knowledge he is brought by hearing and considering of the will of God declared in his laws), and feeling and perceiving in his own conscience that God is angry and displeased with him for the same; he must also conceive not only great sorrow and inward shame that he hath so grievously offended God, but also great fear of God's displeasure towards him, considering he hath no works or merits of his own which he may worthily lay before God, as sufficient satisfaction for

his sins; which done, then afterward with this fear, shame, and sorrow must needs succeed and be conjoined, the second part, that is to wit, a certain faith, trust, and confidence of the mercy and goodness of God, whereby the penitent must conceive certain hope and faith that God will forgive him his sins, and repute him justified, and of the number of his elect children, not for the worthiness of any merit or work done by the penitent, but for the only merits of the blood and passion of our Savior Jesu Christ.

[5] *Item,* That this certain faith and hope is gotten and also confirmed, and made more strong by the applying of Christ's words and promises of his grace and favor, contained in his gospel, and the sacraments instituted by him in the New Testament; and therefore to attain this certain faith, the second part of penance is necessary, that is to say, confession to a priest, if it may be had; for the absolution given by the priest was instituted of Christ to apply the promises of God's grace and favor to the penitent.

Wherefore as touching confession, we will that all bishops and preachers shall instruct and teach our people committed by us to their spiritual charge, that they ought and must certainly believe that the words of absolution pronounced by the priest, be spoken by authority given to him by Christ in the gospel.

[6] *Item,* That they ought and must give no less faith and credence to the same words of absolution so pronounced by the ministers of the church, than they would give unto the very words and voice of God himself if he should speak unto us out of heaven, according to the saying of Christ, *Quorumcunque remiseritis peccata,* [Jn 20.26] *remittuntur eis: quorumcunque retinueritis retenta sunt:* that is to say, Whose sins soever ye do forgive, shall be forgiven; whose sins soever ye do retain, shall be retained. And again in another place Christ saith, *Qui vos audit me audit,* etc.; that is [Lk 10.16] to say, Whosoever heareth you heareth me, etc.

[7] *Item,* That in no wise they do contemn this auricular confession which is made unto the ministers of the church, but that they ought to repute the same as a very expedient and necessary mean, whereby they may require and ask this absolution at the priest's hands, at such time as they shall find their consciences grieved with mortal sin, and have occasion so to do, to the intent they may thereby attain certain comfort and consolation of their consciences.

[8] As touching the third part of penance, we will that all bishops and preachers shall instruct and teach our people committed by us to their spiritual charge, that although Christ and his death be the sufficient oblation, sacrifice, satisfaction, and recompense, for the which God the Father forgiveth and remitteth to all sinners not only their sin, but also eternal pain due for the same; yet all men truly penitent, contrite, and confessed, must needs also bring forth the fruits of

penance, that is to say, prayer, fasting, almsdeeds, and must make restitution or satisfaction in will and deed to their neighbors, in such things as they have done them wrong and injury in, and also must do all other good works of mercy and charity, and express their obedient will in the executing and fulfilling of God's commandments outwardly, when time, power, and occasion shall be ministered unto them, or else they shall never be saved; for this is the express precept and commandment of God, *Agite fructus dignos poenitentiae;* that is to say, Do you the worthy fruits of penance: and St. Paul saith, *Quemadmodum praebuistis membra vestra serva immunditiae et iniquitati ad aliam atque aliam iniquitatem; sic et nunc praebete membra vestra serva justitiae ad sanctificationem,* etc.; that is to say, Like as in times past you have given and applied yourself and all the members of your body to all filthy living and wickedness, continually increasing the same, in like manner now you must give and apply yourself wholly to justice, increasing continually in purity and cleanness of life: and in another place he saith, *Castigo corpus meum, et in servitutem redigo;* that is to say, I chastise and subdue my carnal body, and the affections of the same, and make them obedient unto the spirit.

[Mt 3.8]

[Rom 6.19]

[1 Cor 9.27]

[9] *Item,* That these precepts and works of charity be necessary works to our salvation, and God necessarily requireth that every penitent man shall perform the same, whensoever time, power, and occasion shall be ministered unto him so to do.

[10] *Item,* That by penance and such good works of the same, we shall not only obtain everlasting life, but also we shall deserve remission or mitigation of these present pains and afflictions in this world, according to the saying of St. Paul, *Si nos ipsi judicaremus, non judicaremur a Domino;* that is to say, If we would correct and take punishment of ourselves, we should not be so grievously corrected of God: and Zacharias the prophet saith, *Convertimini ad me, et ego convertar ad vos;* that is to say, Turn yourselves unto me, and I will turn again unto you: and the prophet Esay saith, *Frange esurienti panem tuum, et egenos vagosque induc in domum tuam. Cum videris nudum operi eum et carnem tuam ne despexeris: tunc erumpet quasi mane lumen tuum, et sanitas tua citius orietur, et anteibit faciem tuam justitia tua, et gloria Dei colliget te: tunc invocabis et Dominus exaudiet te, clamabis, et dicet: Ecce adsum. Tunc orietur in tenebris lux tua et tenebrae tuae erunt sicut meridies, et requiem tibi dabit Dominus semper, et implebit splendoribus animam tuam, et ossa tua liberabit et eris quasi hortus irriguus et sicut fons aquarum, cujus non deficient aquae,* etc.; that is to say, Break and deal thy bread unto the hungry, bring into thy house the poor man, and such as want harbor; when thou seest a naked man, give him clothes to cover him with, and refuse not to succor and help the poor and needy, for he is thine

[1 Cor 11.31]

Zec [1.3]

Is [58.7-11]

own flesh. And if thou wilt thus do, then shall thy light glister out as bright as the
sun in the morning, and thy health shall sooner arise unto thee, and thy justice shall
go before thy face, and the glory of God shall gather thee up, that thou shalt not
fall: and whensoever thou shalt call upon God, God shall hear thee; and whensoever thou shalt cry unto God, God shall say, Lo, here I am, ready to help thee. Then
shall thy light overcome all darkness, and thy darkness shall be as bright as the sun
at noon day; and then God shall give unto thee continual rest, and shall fulfil thy
soul with brightness, and shall deliver thy body from adversity; and then thou shalt
be like a garden, that most plentifully bringeth forth all kind of fruits, and like a
well-spring that never shall want water.

[11] These things, and such other, should be continually taught and inculcated into the ears of our people to the intent to stir and provoke them unto good
works; and by the selfsame good works to exercise and confirm their faith and hope,
and look for to receive at God's hand mitigation and remission of the miseries,
calamities, and grievous punishments, which God sendeth to men in this world for
their sins.

[4.] THE SACRAMENT OF THE ALTAR

[1] Fourthly, As touching the sacrament of the altar, we will that all bishops and
preachers shall instruct and teach our people committed by us unto their spiritual
charge, that they ought and must constantly believe, that under the form and figure
of bread and wine, which we there presently do see and perceive by outward senses,
is verily, substantially, and really contained and comprehended the very selfsame
body and blood of our Savior Jesus Christ, which was born of the Virgin Mary, and
suffered upon the cross for our redemption; and that under the same form and figure
of bread and wine the very selfsame body and blood of Christ is corporally, really,
and in the very substance exhibited, distributed, and received unto and all of them
which receive the said sacrament; and that therefore the said sacrament is to be used
with all due reverence and honor, and that every man ought first to prove and examine himself, and religiously to try and search his own conscience, before he shall
receive the same: according to the saying of St. Paul, *Quisquis ederit panem hunc aut
biberit de poculo Domini indigne, reus erit corporis et sanguinis Domini; probet igitur
seipsum homo, et sic de pane illo edat et de poculo illo bibat; nam qui edit aut bibit*   [1 Cor 11.27–29]
indigne judicium sibi ipsi manducat et bibit, non dijudicans corpus Domini; that is to
say, Whosoever eateth this body of Christ unworthily, or drinketh of this blood of
Christ unworthily, shall be guilty of the very body and blood of Christ; wherefore
let every man first prove himself, and so let him eat of this bread, and drink of this

drink. For whosoever eateth it or drinketh it unworthily, he eateth and drinketh it to his own damnation; because he putteth no difference between the very body of Christ and other kinds of meat.

[5.] JUSTIFICATION

[1] Fifthly, As touching the order and cause of our justification, we will that all bishops and preachers shall instruct and teach our people committed by us to their spiritual charge, that this word Justification signifieth remission of our sins, and our acceptation or reconciliation into the grace and favor of God, that is to say, our perfect renovation in Christ.

[2] *Item,* That sinners attain this justification by contrition and faith joined with charity, after such sort and manner as we before mentioned and declared; not as though our contrition, or faith, or any works proceeding thereof, can worthily merit or deserve to attain the said justification; for the only mercy and grace of the Father, promised freely unto us for his Son's sake, Jesu Christ, and the merits of his blood and passion, be the only sufficient and worthy causes thereof: and yet that notwithstanding, to the attaining of the same justification, God requireth to be in us not only inward contrition, perfect faith and charity, certain hope and confidence, with all other spiritual graces and motions, which, as we said before, must necessarily concur in remission of our sins, that is to say, our justification; but also he requireth and commandeth us, that after we be justified we must also have good works of charity and obedience towards God, in the observing and fulfilling outwardly of his laws and commandments: for although acceptation to everlasting life be conjoined with justification, yet our good works be necessarily required to the attaining of everlasting life; and we being justified, be necessarily bound, and it is our necessary duty to do good works, according to the saying of St. Paul, *Debitores sumus non carni, ut secundum carnem vivamus. Nam si secundum carnem vixerimus, moriemur:*

[Rom 8.12–14] *sin autem spiritu facta corporis mortificaverimus, vivemus; etenim quicunque Spiritu Dei ducuntur, hi sunt filii Dei;* that is to say, We be bound not to live according to the flesh and to fleshly appetites; for if we live so, we shall undoubtedly be damned. And contrary, if we will mortify the deeds of our flesh, and live according to the Spirit, we shall be saved. For whosoever be led by the Spirit of God, they be the children

[Mt 19.17] of God. And Christ saith, *Si vis ad vitam ingredi, serva mandata;* that is to say, If ye will come to heaven, keep the commandments. And St. Paul, speaking of evil works,

[Gal 5.21] saith, *Qui talia agunt regnum Dei non possidebunt;* that is to say, Whosoever commit sinful deeds, shall never come to heaven. Wherefore we will that all bishops and preachers shall instruct and teach our people committed by us unto their spiritual charge, that God necessarily requireth of us to do good works commanded by him; and that not only outward and civil works, but also the inward spiritual motions and graces of the Holy Ghost; that is to say, to dread and fear God, to love God, to have firm confidence and trust in God, to invocate and call upon God, to have patience in all adversities, to hate sin, and to have certain purpose and will not to sin again, and such other like motions and virtues: for Christ saith, *Nisi abundaverit justitia vestra plusquam Scribarum et Pharisaeorum, non intrabitis in regnum coelorum;*   [Mt 5.20] that is to say, we must not only do outward civil good works, but also we must have these foresaid inward spiritual motions, consenting and agreeable to the law of God.[1]

Articles Concerning the Laudable Ceremonies Used in the Church

[6.] AND FIRST OF IMAGES

[1] As touching images, truth it is that the same have been used in the Old Testament, and also for the great abuses of them sometime destroyed and put down; and in the New Testament they have been also allowed, as good authors do declare. Wherefore we will that all bishops and preachers shall instruct and teach our people committed by us to their spiritual charge, how they ought and may use them. And first, that there may be attributed unto them, that they be representers of virtue and good example, and that they also be by occasion the kindlers and stirrers of men's minds, and make men oft to remember and lament their sins and offences, especially the images of Christ and our Lady; and that therefore it is meet that they should stand in the churches, and none otherwise to be esteemed: and to the intent the rude people should not from henceforth take such superstition, as in time past it is thought that the same hath used to do, we will that our bishops and preachers diligently shall teach them, and according to this doctrine reform their abuses, for else there might fortune idolatry to ensue, which God forbid. And as for censing of them, and kneeling and offering unto them, with other like worshipings, although the same hath entered by devotion, and fallen to custom; yet the people ought to be diligently taught that they in no wise do it, nor think it meet to be done to the same images, but only to be done to God, and in his honor, although it be done before the images, whether it be of Christ, of the cross, of our Lady, or of any other saint beside.

---

1. The literal translation from the Latin is: "Unless your justice exceed that of the Scribes and Pharisees, you shall not enter into the kingdom of heaven."

[7.] OF HONORING OF SAINTS

[1] As touching the honoring of saints, we will that all bishops and preachers shall instruct and teach our people committed by us unto their spiritual charges, that saints, now being with Christ in heaven be to be honored of Christian people in earth; but not with that confidence and honor which are only due unto God, trusting to attain at their hands that which must be had only of God: but that they be thus to be honored, because they be known the elect persons of Christ, because they be passed in godly life out of this transitory world, because they already do reign in glory with Christ; and most specially to laud and praise Christ in them for their excellent virtues which he planted in them, for example of and by them to such as yet are in this world to live in virtue and goodness, and also not to fear to die for Christ and his cause, as some of them did; and finally to take them, in that they may, to be advancers of our prayers and demands unto Christ. By these ways, and such like, be saints to be honored and had in reverence, and by none other.

[8.] OF PRAYING TO SAINTS

[1] As touching praying to saints, we will that all bishops and preachers shall instruct and teach our people committed by us unto their spiritual charge, that albeit grace, remission of sin, and salvation, cannot be obtained but of God only by the mediation of our Savior Christ, which is only sufficient Mediator for our sins; yet it is very laudable to pray to saints in heaven everlastingly living, whose charity is ever permanent, to be intercessors, and to pray for us and with us, unto Almighty God after this manner: "All holy angels and saints in heaven pray for us and with us, unto the Father, that for his dear Son Jesu Christ's sake, we may have grace of him and remission of our sins, with an earnest purpose, (not wanting ghostly strength,) to observe and keep his holy commandments, and never to decline from the same again unto our lives' end": and in this manner we may pray to our blessed Lady, to St. John Baptist, to all and every of the apostles or any other saint particularly, as our devotion doth serve us; so that it be done without any vain superstition, as to think that any saint is more merciful, or will hear us sooner than Christ, or that any saint doth serve for one thing more than another, or is patron of the same. And likewise we must keep holy-days unto God, in memory of him and his saints, upon such days as the church hath ordained their memories to be celebrated; except they be mitigated and moderated by the assent and commandment of us, the supreme head, to the ordinaries, and then the subjects ought to obey it.

[9.] OF RITES AND CEREMONIES

[1] As concerning the rites and ceremonies of Christ's church, as to have such vestments in doing God's service, as be and have been most part used, as sprinkling of holy water to put us in remembrance of our baptism and the blood of Christ sprinkled for our redemption upon the cross; giving of holy bread, to put us in remembrance of the sacrament of the altar, that all Christian men be one body mystical of Christ, as the bread is made of many grains, and yet but one loaf, and to put us in remembrance of the receiving of the holy sacrament and body of Christ, the which we ought to receive in right charity, which in the beginning of Christ's church men did more often receive than they use nowadays to do; bearing of candles on Candlemas-day in memory of Christ the spiritual light, of whom Simeon did prophesy, as is read in the church that day: giving of ashes on Ash-Wednesday, to put in remembrance every Christian man in the beginning of Lent and penance, that he is but ashes and earth, and thereto shall return, which is right necessary to be uttered from henceforth in our mother-tongue always on the same day; bearing of palms on Palm-Sunday, in memory of the receiving of Christ into Jerusalem, a little before his death, that we may have the same desire to receive him into our hearts; creeping to the cross, and humbling ourselves to Christ on Good Friday before the cross, and there offering unto Christ before the same, and kissing of it in memory of our redemption by Christ made upon the cross; setting up the sepulture of Christ, whose body after his death was buried; the hallowing of the font, and other like exorcisms and benedictions by the ministers of Christ's church; and all other like laudable customs, rites, and ceremonies be not to be contemned and cast away, but to be used and continued as things good and laudable, to put us in remembrance of those spiritual things that they do signify; not suffering them to be forgot, or to be put in oblivion, but renewing them in our memories from time to time. But none of these ceremonies have power to remit sin, but only to stir and lift up our minds unto God, by whom only our sins be forgiven.

[10.] OF PURGATORY

[1] Forasmuch as due order of charity requireth, and the Book of Maccabees, and divers ancient doctors plainly shew, that it is a very good and a charitable deed to pray for souls departed, and forasmuch also as such usage hath continued in the church so many years, even from the beginning, we will that all bishops and preachers shall instruct and teach our people committed by us unto their spiritual charge, that no man ought to be grieved with the continuance of the same, and that it standeth with the very due order of charity, a Christian man to pray for souls departed, and to commit them in our prayers to God's mercy, and also to cause other to pray

2 Mc [12.39–45]

for them in masses and exequies, and to give alms to other to pray for them, whereby they may be relieved and holpen of some part of their pain: but forasmuch as the place where they be, the name thereof, and kind of pains there, also be to us uncertain by Scripture; therefore this with all other things we remit to Almighty God, unto whose mercy it is meet and convenient for us to commend them, trusting that God accepteth our prayers for them, referring the rest wholly to God, to whom is known their estate and condition. Wherefore it is much necessary that such abuses be clearly put away, which under the name of purgatory hath been advanced, as to make men believe that through the bishop of Rome's pardons souls might clearly be delivered out of purgatory, and all the pains of it, or that masses said at *Scala Caeli*, or otherwhere, in any place, or before any image, might likewise deliver them from all their pain, and send them straight to heaven; and other like abuses.

The Geneva Confession, 1536, and
The Geneva Catechism, 1541/1542

Shortly before arriving in Geneva in 1536, John Calvin (1509–64) published the first edition of his *Institutes*. Later in the same year, after he had been persuaded to remain in Geneva by Guillaume Farel, he helped draft that city's articles of church order (adopted in January 1537) and prepared a confession of faith largely based on the *Institutes*. The confession has also been attributed to Farel, but Théodore de Bèze ascribed it to Calvin in his biography of the reformer.[1] What is known for certain, however, is that it was submitted jointly by Farel and Calvin to the city's Petit Conseil in November 1536, with the request "that all the inhabitants of the city be required to make a confession and give reason of their faith, in order to recognize those in harmony with the gospel, and those loving rather to be of the kingdom of the pope than of the kingdom of Jesus Christ."[2] It was, in part, Calvin's insistence on enforcing this requirement by withholding communion from those who did not take the oath that led to his expulsion from Geneva, together with Farel, in April 1538.

Calvin used the confession again in 1537 as part of his first catechism, the *Instruction et confession de foy dont on use en l'Eglise de Genève*, which also included an explication of doctrine in thirty-three brief chapters.[3] This version, in turn, became the basis for a more traditional catechism in the form of questions and answers published by Calvin in 1541 after his return to Geneva. The dialogue between a minister and a child covers issues of faith, including an exposition of → *The Apostles' Creed* (Questions 1–130); Christian duty, as outlined in the Ten Commandments (Questions 131–232); the importance of prayer, with an explication of the Lord's Prayer (Questions 233–95); and humankind's relations with God through the word and sacraments (Questions 296–373). This version of the *Geneva Catechism* influenced later Reformed catechisms throughout Europe, particularly after the original French was translated into Latin in 1545.

Edition: *Confession: CR* 37:693–700; *Catechism:* Niesel, 3–41.

1. See Backus and Chimelli 1986, 41–42.
2. *CR* 38:5–14; translation from Pont 1991, 107.
3. *CR* 22:33–74.

Translation: *Confession: LCC* 22:26-33 (with slight revisions); *Catechism:* Torrance, 5-65.

Literature: Backus and Chimelli 1986, 41-44; Bouwsma 1989; Eire 1986, 197-212; Hörcsik 1994; Kingdon 1974, 1985; McGrath 1990, 96-100; Oberman 1994; *OER* 1:278 (Janz), 2:160-63 (Kingdon); Pin 1979; Pont 1991; Torrance, xi-cxxvi.

The Geneva Confession, 1536

Confession of Faith which all the citizens and inhabitants of Geneva and the subjects of the country must promise to keep and hold

1. THE WORD OF GOD

First we declare that we desire to follow Scripture alone as rule of our faith and religion, without mixing with it any other thing which might be devised by the opinion of men without the word of God, and without claiming to accept for our spiritual government any other doctrine than what is conveyed to us by the same word, without addition or diminution, according to the command of our Lord.

2. ONE ONLY GOD

Following, then, the institution that is the content of Holy Scriptures, we acknowledge that there is one only God, whom we are both to worship and serve, and in whom we are to put all our confidence and hope: having this assurance, that in him alone is contained all wisdom, power, justice, goodness, and mercy. And since he is spirit, he is to be served in spirit and in truth. Therefore we think it an abomination to put our confidence or hope in any created thing, to worship anything else than him, whether angels or any other creatures, and to recognize any other Savior of our souls than him alone, whether saints or men living upon earth; and likewise to offer the service, which ought to be rendered to him, in external ceremonies or carnal observances, as if he took pleasure in such things, or to make an image to represent his divinity or any other image for adoration. [Jn 4.24]

3. THE LAW OF GOD ALIKE FOR ALL

Because he is the only Lord and Master who has dominion over our consciences, and because his will is the only principle of all justice, we confess that all our life ought to be ruled by the commandments of his holy law in which is contained all perfection of justice, and that we ought to have no other rule of good and just living, nor invent other good works to supplement it than those which are there contained as follows: Exodus 20: "I am the Lord thy God, who brought thee," and so on. Ex 20

4. NATURAL MAN

We acknowledge man in his nature to be blind, completely in darkness of understanding, and full of corruption and perversity of heart, so that of himself he has

313

no power to be able to comprehend the true knowledge of God as is proper, nor to apply himself to good works. But on the contrary, if he is left by God to his own nature, he is only able to live in ignorance and to be abandoned to all iniquity. Hence he has need to be illumined by God, so that he come to the right knowledge of his salvation, and thus to be redirected in his affections and reformed to the obedience of the righteousness of God.

5. MAN IN HIMSELF DAMNED

Since man is naturally (as has been said) deprived and destitute in himself of all the light of God and of all righteousness, we acknowledge that by himself he can only expect the wrath and malediction of God, and hence he must look outside himself for the means of his salvation.

6. SALVATION IN JESUS

We confess then that it is Jesus Christ who is given to us by the Father, in order that in him we should recover all of which in ourselves we are deficient. Yet all that Jesus Christ has done and suffered for our redemption, we veritably hold without any doubt, as it is contained in the creed, which is recited in the church, that is to say: "I believe in God the Father Almighty," and so on.

7. RIGHTEOUSNESS IN JESUS

Therefore we acknowledge the things which are consequently given to us by God in Jesus Christ: first, that being in our own nature enemies of God, subjects of his wrath and judgment, we are reconciled with him and received again in his grace through the intercession of Jesus Christ, so that by his righteousness and innocence we have remission of our sins, and by the shedding of his blood we are cleansed and purified from all our stains.

8. REGENERATION IN JESUS

Second, [we acknowledge] that by his Spirit we are regenerated into a new spiritual nature. That is to say that the evil desires of our flesh are mortified by grace, so that they rule us no longer. On the contrary, our will is rendered conformable to God's will, to follow in his way and to seek what is pleasing to him. Therefore we are by him delivered from the servitude of sin, under whose power we were of ourselves held captive, and by this deliverance we are made capable and able to do good works and not otherwise.

9. REMISSION OF SINS ALWAYS NECESSARY
FOR THE FAITHFUL

Finally, [we acknowledge] that this regeneration is so effected in us that, until we slough off this mortal body, there remains always in us much imperfection and infirmity, so that we always remain poor and wretched sinners before the face of God. And, however much we ought day by day to increase and grow in God's righteousness, there will never be plenitude or perfection while we live here. Thus we always have need of the mercy of God to obtain the remission of our faults and offenses. And so we ought always to look for our righteousness in Jesus Christ and not at all in ourselves, and rest in him, and be assured, attributing nothing to our works.

10. ALL OUR GOOD IN THE GRACE OF GOD

In order that all glory and praise be rendered to God (as is his due), and that we be able to have true peace and rest of conscience, we understand and confess that we receive all benefits from God, as said above, by his clemency and pity, without any consideration of our worthiness or the merit of our works, to which is due no other retribution than eternal confusion. Nonetheless, our Savior in his goodness, having received us into the communion of his Son Jesus, regards the works that we have done in faith as pleasing and agreeable; not that they merit it at all, but because, not imputing any of the imperfection that is there, he acknowledges in them nothing but what proceeds from his Spirit.

11. FAITH

We confess that the entrance which we have to such great treasures and riches of the goodness of God that is vouchsafed to us is by faith; inasmuch as, in certain confidence and assurance of heart, we believe in the promises of the gospel, and receive Jesus Christ as he is offered to us by the Father and described to us by the word of God.

12. INVOCATION OF GOD ONLY AND
INTERCESSION OF CHRIST

As we have declared that we have confidence and hope for our salvation and all good only in God through Jesus Christ, so we confess that we ought to invoke him in all necessities in the name of Jesus Christ, who is our mediator and advocate through whom we have access to him. Likewise we ought to acknowledge that all good things come from him alone, and render acts of thanks to him for them. On the other hand, we reject the intercession of the saints as a superstition invented by men contrary to Scripture, for the reason that it proceeds from mistrust of the sufficiency of the intercession of Jesus Christ.

13. PRAYER INTELLIGIBLE

Moreover since prayer is nothing but hypocrisy and fantasy unless it proceed from the interior affection of the heart, we believe that all prayers ought to be made with clear understanding. And for this reason, we hold the prayer of our Lord to show fittingly what we ought to ask of him: Our Father which art in heaven, . . . but deliver us from evil. Amen.[a]

14. SACRAMENTS

We believe that the sacraments which our Lord has ordained in his church are to be regarded as exercises of faith for us, both for fortifying and confirming it in the promises of God and for witnessing before men. Of them there are in the Christian church only two which are instituted by the authority of our Savior: baptism and the supper of our Lord; for what is held within the realm of the pope concerning seven sacraments, we condemn as fable and lie.

15. BAPTISM

Baptism is an external sign by which our Lord testifies that he desires to receive us for his children, as members of his Son Jesus. Hence in it there is represented to us the cleansing from our sin which we have in the blood of Jesus Christ, the mortification of our flesh which we have by his death that we may live in him by his Spirit. Now since our children belong to such an alliance with our Lord, we are certain that the external sign is rightly applied to them.

16. THE HOLY SUPPER

The supper of our Lord is a sign by which under bread and wine he represents to us the true spiritual communion which we have in his body and blood. And we acknowledge that according to his ordinance it ought to be distributed in the company of the faithful, in order that all those who wish to have Jesus for their life be partakers of it. In as much as the mass of the pope was a reprobate and diabolical ordinance subverting the mystery of the holy supper, we declare that it is execrable to us, an idolatry condemned by God, for so much is it itself regarded as a sacrifice for the redemption of souls that the bread is in it taken and adored as God. Be-

a. [Mt 6.9–13; Lk 11.2–4]

sides there are other execrable blasphemies and superstitions contained here, and the abuse of the word of God which is taken in vain without profit or edification.

17. HUMAN TRADITIONS

The ordinances that are necessary for the internal discipline of the church, and belong solely to the maintenance of peace, honesty, and good order in the assembly of Christians, we do not hold to be human traditions at all, in as much as they are comprised under the general command of St. Paul, where he desires that all be [1 Cor 14.40] done among us decently and in order. But all laws and regulations made binding on conscience which oblige the faithful to things not commanded by God, or establish another service of God than that which he demands, thus tending to destroy Christian liberty, we condemn as perverse doctrines of Satan, in view of our Lord's declaration that he is honored in vain by doctrines that are the commandment of men. It is in this estimation that we hold pilgrimages, monasteries, distinctions of [Mt 15.8; Mk 7.7] foods, prohibition of marriage, confessions, and other like things.

18. THE CHURCH

While there is one only church of Jesus Christ, we always acknowledge that necessity requires companies of the faithful to be distributed in different places. Of these assemblies each one is called church. But in as much as all companies do not assemble in the name of our Lord, but rather to blaspheme and pollute him by their sacrilegious deeds, we believe that the proper mark by which we rightly discern the church of Jesus Christ is that his holy gospel be purely and faithfully preached, proclaimed, heard, and kept, that his sacrament be properly administered, even if there be some imperfections and faults, as there always will be among men. On the other hand, where the gospel is not declared, heard, and received, there we do not acknowledge any form of the church. Hence the churches governed by the ordinances of the pope are rather synagogues of the devil than Christian churches.

19. EXCOMMUNICATION

Because there are always some who hold God and his sacred word in contempt, who take account of neither injunction, exhortation, nor remonstrance, thus requiring greater chastisement, we hold the discipline of excommunication to be a thing holy and salutary among the faithful, since truly it was instituted by our Lord with good reason. This is in order that the wicked would not by their damnable conduct corrupt the good and dishonor our Lord, and that being ashamed they may turn to penitence. Therefore we believe that it is expedient according to the ordinance of God that all manifest idolaters, blasphemers, murderers, thieves, lewd persons, false witnesses, sedition-mongers, quarrelers, those guilty of defamation or assault, drunkards, dissolute livers, when they have been duly admonished and if they do not make amendment, be separated from the communion of the faithful until their repentance is known.

20. MINISTERS OF THE WORD

We recognize no other pastors in the church than faithful pastors of the word of God, nourishing the flock of Jesus Christ on the one hand with instruction, admonition, consolation, exhortation, deprecation; and on the other resisting all false doctrines and deceptions of the devil, without mixing with the pure doctrines of the Scriptures their dreams or their foolish imaginings. To these we accord no other power or authority but to conduct, rule, and govern the people of God committed to them by the same word, in which they have the power to command, defend, promise, and warn, and without which they neither can nor ought to attempt anything. As we receive the true ministers of the word of God as messengers and ambassadors of God, it is necessary to listen to them as to him himself, and we hold their ministry to be a commission from God necessary in the church. On the other hand we hold that all seductive and false prophets, who abandon the purity of the gospel and deviate to their own inventions, ought not at all to be suffered or maintained, who are not the pastors they pretend, but rather, like ravening wolves, ought to be hunted and ejected from the people of God.

21. MAGISTRATES

We hold the supremacy and dominion of kings and princes as also of other magistrates and officers, to be a holy thing and a good ordinance of God. And since in performing their office they serve God and follow a Christian vocation, whether in defending the afflicted and innocent, or in correcting and punishing the malice of the perverse, we on our part also ought to accord them honor and reverence, to render respect and subservience, to execute their commands, to bear the charges they impose on us, so far as we are able without offense to God. In sum, we ought to regard them as vicars and lieutenants of God, whom one cannot resist without resisting God himself; and their office as a sacred commission from God which has been given them so that they may rule and govern us. Hence we hold that all Christians are bound to pray God for the prosperity of the superiors and lords of the country where they live, to obey the statutes and ordinances which do not contravene the commandments of God, to promote the welfare, peace, and public good, endeavoring to sustain the honor of those over them and the peace of the people, without contriving or attempting anything to inspire trouble or dissension. On the other hand we declare that all those who conduct themselves unfaithfully toward their superiors, and have not a right concern for the public good of the country where they live, demonstrate thereby their infidelity toward God.

The Geneva Catechism, 1541/1542

It has always been a matter which the church has held in singular commendation, to see that little children should be instructed in Christian doctrine. That this might be done, not only were schools opened in early times, and people enjoined to teach their families well, but it was also a public practice to examine children in the churches on articles of faith common to all Christians. That this might be carried out in order, a formulary was used which was called a catechism. Thereafter the devil rending the church, and making it a fearful ruin (the marks of which are still visible in most of the world), overthrew this sacred polity, and left nothing behind but certain remnants, which cannot but beget superstition, without any edification. This is "confirmation," as they call it, in which there is nothing but mimicry, and has no foundation. What we set before you, therefore, is nothing else than the use of things which from ancient times were observed among Christians, and which has never been neglected except when the church has been wholly corrupted.

1. FAITH

1. *Minister. What is the chief end of human life?*

    Child. To know God.

    2. *M. Why do you say that?*

    C. Because he created us and placed us in this world to be glorified in us. And it is indeed right that our life, of which he himself is the beginning, should be devoted to his glory.

    3. *M. What is the sovereign good of man?*

    C. The same thing.

    4. *M. Why do you hold that to be the sovereign good?*

    C. Because without it our condition is more miserable than that of brute beasts.

    5. *M. Hence, then, we see that nothing worse can happen to a man than to live without God.*

    C. It is so.

    6. *M. What is the true and right knowledge of God?*

    C. When we know him in order that we may honor him.

    7. *M. How do we honor him aright?*

    C. We put our reliance entirely on him, by serving him in obedience to his will, by calling upon him in all our need, seeking salvation and every good thing in him, and acknowledging with heart and mouth that all our good proceeds from him alone.

8. M. *To consider these things in order, and explain them more fully—what is the first point?*

C. It is to have our faith in God.

9. M. *How can we do that?*

C. First by knowing him as almighty and perfectly good.

10. M. *Is this enough?*

C. No.

11. M. *Why?*

C. Because we are unworthy that he should show his power in helping us, or employ his goodness toward us.

12. M. *What more then is required?*

C. That we be certain that he loves us, and desires to be our Father, and Savior.

13. M. *How do we know that?*

C. By his word, in which he declares his mercy to us in Christ, and assures us of his love toward us.

14. M. *Then the foundation for true faith in God is to know him in Jesus Christ?*   Jn 17[.3]

C. That is true.

15. M. *What then briefly is the substance of this knowledge?*

C. It is contained in the confession of faith used by all Christians. It is commonly called the Apostles' Creed, because it is a summary of the true faith which has always been held in Christianity, and was also derived from the pure doctrine of the apostles.

16. M. *Recite it.*

C. I believe in God the Father Almighty, Maker of heaven and earth; and in Jesus Christ, his only Son, our Lord, who was conceived by the Holy Ghost, born of the Virgin Mary, suffered under Pontius Pilate, was crucified, dead, and buried; he descended into hell; the third day he rose again from the dead; he ascended into heaven, and sitteth on the right hand of God the Father Almighty, from thence he shall come to judge the quick and the dead. I believe in the Holy Ghost; the holy catholic church; the communion of saints; the forgiveness of sins; the resurrection of the body; and the life everlasting.

17. M. *In order to expound this confession in detail, into how many parts do we divide it?*

C. Into four principal parts.

18. M. *What are they?*

C. The first is about God the Father; the second about his Son Jesus Christ, which also includes the whole history of our redemption; the third is about the Holy Spirit; the fourth is about the church, and the gracious gifts of God conferred on her.

19. M. *Since there is but one God, why do you mention the Father, Son, and Holy Spirit, who are three?*

C. Because in the one essence of God, we have to look on the Father as the beginning and origin, and the first cause of all things; then the Son, who is Eternal Wisdom; and the Holy Spirit, who is his virtue and power shed abroad over all creatures, but still perpetually resident in himself.

20. M. *You mean then that there is no objection to our understanding that these three persons are distinctly in one Godhead, and that God is not therefore divided?*

C. Just so.

21. M. *Now repeat the first part.*

C. "I believe in God the Father Almighty, Maker of heaven and earth."

22. M. *Why do you call him Father?*

C. It is with reference to Christ who is his eternal Word, begotten of him before all time, and being sent into this world was demonstrated and declared to be his Son. But since God is the Father of Jesus Christ, it follows that he is our Father also.

23. M. *In what sense do you mean that he is almighty?*

C. That does not only mean that he has a power which he does not exercise, but that he disposes all things by his providence, governs the world by his will, ruling all as it seems good to him.

24. M. *You mean that the power of God is not idle, but consider rather that his hand is always engaged in working, so that nothing is done except through him, with his permission and his decree.*

C. It is so.

25. M. *Why do you add that he is Creator of heaven and earth?*

Ps 104; Rom 1[.20]   C. Because he has manifested himself to us by works we ought to seek him in them. Our mind cannot comprehend his essence. But the world is for us like a mirror in which we may contemplate him in so far as it is expedient for us to know him.

26. M. *Do you not understand by "heaven and earth" all other creatures?*

C. Yes indeed; under these two words all are included, because they are all heavenly or earthly.

27. M. *But why do you call God a creator only, seeing that it is much more to uphold and preserve creatures in their state, than to have once created them?*

C. This term does not signify that God brought his works into being at a single stroke, and then left them without a care for them. We ought rather to understand, that as the world was made by God in the beginning, so now it is preserved by him in its estate, so that the heavens, the earth, and all creatures do not continue in their being apart from this power. Besides, seeing that he holds all things in his hand, it follows that the government and lordship over them belong to him. Therefore, in that he is Creator of heaven and earth, it is his to rule the whole order of nature by his goodness and power and wisdom. It is he who sends rain and drought, hail, tempest and fair weather, fruitfulness and barrenness, health and sickness. In short, all things are under his command, to serve him as it seems good to him.

28. M. *But what about wicked men and devils? Are they also subject to him?*

C. Although he does not guide them by his Holy Spirit, nevertheless he curbs them by his power, so that they cannot budge unless he permits them. He even constrains them to execute his will, although it is against their own intention and purpose.

29. M. *What good do you derive from the knowledge of this fact?*

C. Very much. It would go ill with us if devils and wicked men had power to do anything in spite of the will of God. Moreover we could never be at rest in our minds if we were exposed to them in danger, but when we know that they are curbed by the will of God, so that they can do nothing without his permission, then we may rest and breathe again, for God has promised to protect and defend us.

30. M. *Let us now come to the second part.*

C. "And in Jesus Christ his only Son our Lord," etc.

31. M. *What briefly does it comprehend?*

C. That we acknowledge the Son of God as our Savior, and the means by which he has redeemed us from death, and acquired salvation.

32. M. *What is the meaning of the name Jesus which you give to him?*

C. It means Savior, and was given to him by the angel at the command of God.   Mt 1[.21]

33. M. *Is this of more importance than if men had given it?*

C. Oh, yes. For since God wills that he be called so, he must be so in truth.

34. M. *What, next, is meant by the name Christ?*

C. By this title his office is still better expressed—for it signifies that he was anointed by the heavenly Father to be ordained king, priest, and prophet.

35. M. *How do you know that?*

C. Because according to the Scripture, anointing is used for these three things. Also, because they are attributed to him many times.

36. *M. But with what kind of oil was he anointed?*

C. Not with visible oil as was used for ancient kings, priests, and prophets, but this anointing was by the grace of the Holy Spirit, who is the reality signified by that outward anointing made in time past.

Is 61.1; Ps [45.8]

37. *M. But what is this kingdom of which you speak?*

C. It is spiritual, and consists in the word and Spirit of God, and includes righteousness and life.

38. *M. What of the priesthood?*

C. It is the office and prerogative of appearing in the presence of God to obtain grace and favor, and appease his wrath in offering a sacrifice which is acceptable to him.

39. *M. In what sense do you call Christ a prophet?*

C. Because on coming down into the world he was the sovereign messenger and ambassador of God his Father, to give a full exposition of God's will toward the world and so put an end to all prophecies and revelations.

40. *M. But do you derive any benefit from this?*

C. All this is for our good. For Jesus Christ has received all these gifts in order that he may communicate them to us, and that all of us may receive out of his fullness.

Jn 1[.16]

41. *M. Expound this to me more fully.*

C. He received the Holy Spirit in full perfection with all his graces, that he may lavish them upon us and distribute them, each according to the measure and portion which the Father knows to be expedient. Thus we may draw from him as from a fountain all the spiritual blessings we possess.

Eph 4[.7]

42. *M. What does his kingdom minister to us?*

C. By it, we are set at liberty in our conscience and are filled with his spiritual riches in order to live in righteousness and holiness, and we are also armed with power to overcome the devil, sin, the flesh, and the world—the enemies of our souls.

43. *M. What about his priesthood?*

C. First, by means of it he is the Mediator who reconciles us to God his Father; and secondly, through him we have access to present ourselves to God, and offer him ourselves in sacrifice with all that belongs to us. And in this way we are companions of his priesthood.

Heb 7-10, 13

44. *M. There remains his prophetic office.*

C. Since this office was given to the Lord Jesus to be the Master and Teacher of his own, its end is to bring us the true knowledge of the Father and of his truth, so that we may be scholars in the household of God.

45. M. *You would conclude, then, that the title of Christ includes three offices which God has given to his Son, in order to communicate virtue and fruit to his faithful people?*

C. That is so.

46. M. *Why do you call him the only Son of God, seeing that God calls us all his children?*

C. We are the children of God not by nature, but only by adoption and by grace, in that God wills to regard us as such. But the Lord Jesus who was begotten   Eph 1[.5] of the substance of his Father, and is of one essence with him, is rightly called the only Son of God for there is no other who is God's Son by nature.   Jn 1[.14]; Heb 1[.2]

47. M. *You mean to say, then, that this honor is proper to him alone, and belongs to him by nature, but it is communicated to us through a gratuitous gift, in that we are his members.*

C. That is so. Hence in regard to this communication he is called elsewhere "the First-born among many brethren."[a]

48. M. *What is meant by what follows?*

C. It declares how the Son of God was anointed by the Father to be our Savior. That is to say, he assumed human flesh, and accomplished all things necessary to our salvation, as enunciated here.

49. M. *What do you mean by the two clauses, "Conceived of the Holy Ghost, born of the Virgin Mary"?*

C. That he was formed in the womb of the Virgin Mary, of her proper substance, to be the seed of David, as had been foretold, and yet that this was wrought   Ps [132.11] by the miraculous operation of the Holy Spirit, without the cooperation of a man.   Mt 1[.18]; Lk 1[.35]

50. M. *Was it then required that he should put on our very flesh?*   Rom 5[.15]

C. Yes, because it was necessary that the disobedience committed by man against God should be redressed in human nature. And moreover he could not otherwise be our Mediator to reconcile us to God his Father.[b]

51. M. *You say that Christ had to become man, to fulfill the office of Savior, as in our very person.*

C. Yes, indeed. For we must recover in him all that we lack in ourselves, and this cannot be done in any other way.

a. Rom 8[.29]; Col 1[.15]
b. 1 Tm 2[.5]; Heb 4[.15]

52. *M. But why was that effected by the Holy Spirit, and not by the work of man according to the order of nature?*

C. As the seed of man is in itself corrupt, it was necessary that the power of the Holy Spirit should intervene in this conception, in order to preserve our Lord from all corruption, and to fill him with holiness.

53. *M. Thus we are shown that he who is to sanctify others was free from every stain, and from his mother's womb he was consecrated to God in purity from the very beginning, in order that he may not be subject to the universal corruption of the human race.*

C. So I understand it.

54. *M. How is he "our Lord"?*

C. Because he was appointed by the Father to have us under his government, to administer the kingdom and the lordship of God in heaven and on earth, and to be the head of men and believers.[a]

55. *M. Why do you go immediately from his birth to his death, passing over the whole history of his life?*

C. Because nothing is said here about what belongs properly to the substance of our redemption.

56. *M. Why is it not said simply and in a word that he died while Pontius Pilate is spoken of, under whom he suffered?*

C. That is not only to make us certain of the history, but is also meant to signify that his death involved condemnation.

57. *M. How is that?*

C. He died to suffer the punishment due to us, and thus to deliver us from it. However, because we were guilty before the judgment of God as evildoers, in order to represent us in person he was pleased to appear before the tribunal of an earthly judge, and to be condemned by his mouth, that we might be acquitted before the throne of the celestial Judge.

58. *M. But Pilate pronounced him innocent, and therefore did not condemn him as if he were worthy of death.*[b]

C. Both were involved. He was justified by the testimony of the judge, to show that he did not suffer for his own unworthiness but for ours and yet he was solemnly condemned by the sentence of the same judge, to show that he is truly our surety, receiving condemnation for us in order to acquit us from it.

59. *M. That is well said, for if he had been a sinner he could not have suffered*

a. Eph 5[.23]; Col 1[.18]
b. Mt 27[.24]; Lk 23[.14]

death for others; and yet in order that his condemnation might be our deliverance, he
had to be reckoned among transgressors.   Is 53[.12]

C. I understand so.

60. *M. Is there any greater importance in his having been crucified than if he*
had been put to death in another way?

C. Yes, as the apostle also shows us when he says that he hanged on a tree to
take our curse upon himself and acquit us of it. For that kind of death was accursed   Gal [3.13]
of God.   Dt 21[.23]

61. *M. What? Is it not to dishonor the Lord Jesus, to say he was subjected to*
the curse, and that before God?

C. By no means, for in taking it upon himself he abolished it, by his power,
yet in such a way that he did not cease to be blessed throughout in order that he
might fill us with his blessing.

62. *M. Explain the rest.*

C. Since death was the curse on man as a result of sin, Jesus Christ has
endured it, and in enduring it overcame it. And to show that he underwent a real
death, he chose to be placed in the tomb like other men.

63. *M. But nothing seems to redound to us from this victory, since we do not*
cease to die.

C. That is no obstacle. The death of believers is nothing else than a way of
entering into a better life.

64. *M. Hence it follows that we ought no longer to dread death as if it were a*
fearful thing, but we should willingly follow Jesus Christ our Head and Captain, who
precedes us, not in order to let us perish, but in order to save us.

C. That is so.

65. *M. What is the meaning of the additional clause: "He descended into hell"?*

C. That he not only suffered natural death, which is the separation of the
body from the soul, but also that his soul was pierced with amazing anguish, which
St. Peter calls the pains of death.   Acts 2[.24]

66. *M. Why and how did that happen to him?*

C. Because he presented himself to God in order to make satisfaction in
the name of sinners, it was necessary that he should suffer fearful distress of conscience, as if he had been forsaken by God, and even as if God had become hostile
to him. It was in this extremity that he cried, "My God, my God, why hast thou
forsaken me?"[a]

67. *M. Was his Father then opposed to him?*

a. Mt 27[.46]; Mk 15[.34]

C. No. But he had to be afflicted in this way in fulfillment of what had been foretold by Isaiah, that "he was smitten by the hand of God for our sins and wounded for our transgressions."

Is 53[.5]; 1 Pt 2[.24]

68. M. *But since he is God himself, how could he be in such dread, as if he were forsaken by God?*

C. We must hold that it was according to his human nature that he was in that extremity: and that in order to allow this, his deity held itself back a little, as if concealed, that is, did not show its power.

69. M. *How is it possible that Jesus Christ, who is the salvation of the world, should have been under such damnation?*

C. He was not to remain under it. For though he experienced the horror we have spoken of, he was by no means oppressed by it. On the contrary, he battled with the power of hell, to break and destroy it.

70. M. *Thus we see the difference between the torment which he suffered and that which sinners experience when God punishes them in his wrath. For what he suffered for a time in himself is perpetual in the others, and what was only a needle to sting him is to them a sword to deliver a mortal wound.*

C. It is so, for Jesus Christ, even in the midst of such distress, did not cease to hope in God. But sinners whom God condemns rush into despair, defy, and even blaspheme him.

71. M. *May we not gather from this what fruit we receive from the death of Jesus Christ?*

C. Yes, indeed. And, first, we see that it is a sacrifice by which he has made satisfaction for us before the judgment of God, and so has appeased the wrath of God and reconciled us to him. Secondly, that his blood is the laver by which our souls are cleansed from all stains. Finally, that by this death our sins are effaced, so as never to be remembered before God, and thus the debt which was against us is abolished.

72. M. *Do we not have any other benefit from it?*

C. Yes, we do. If we are true members of Christ, our old man is crucified, our flesh is mortified, so that evil desires no longer reign in us.

73. M. *Expound the next article.*

C. This is: "On the third day he rose again from the dead." By this he declared himself the conqueror of death and sin, for by his resurrection he swallowed up death, broke the fetters of the devil, and destroyed all his power.

1 Pt 3[.22]

74. M. *In how many ways does this resurrection benefit us?*

Rom 4[.24]

C. First, by it righteousness was fully acquired for us. Secondly, it is also a sure pledge to us that we shall rise again one day in immortal glory.

1 Cor 15[.20–23]

Thirdly, if we truly participate in his resurrection, even now we are raised in newness of life, to serve God and to live a holy life according to his pleasure.   Rom 6[.4]

75. M. *Continue.*

C. "He ascended into heaven."

76. M. *Did he ascend in such a way that he is no longer on earth?*

C. Yes. For after he had performed all that he was enjoined by the Father, and was required for our salvation, there was no need for him to remain longer on earth.

77. M. *What benefit do we obtain from this ascension?*

C. The benefit is twofold. For inasmuch as Jesus Christ entered heaven in our name, as he had descended for our sake, he has given us an entry, and assured us that the door, previously shut because of sin, is now open for us. Secondly, he   Rom 6[.8–11] appears before the face of the Father as our Intercessor and Advocate.   Heb 7[.25]

78. M. *But did Christ in going to heaven withdraw from us, in such a way that he has now ceased to be with us?*

C. No. On the contrary, he has promised that he will be with us to the end.   Mt 28[.20]

79. M. *Is it in bodily presence that he remains with us?*

C. No, for it is one thing to speak of his body which was taken up into heaven, and another to speak of his power, which is spread abroad everywhere.[a]

80. M. *How do you understand that he "sitteth on the right hand of the Father"?*

C. It means that he has received the dominion of heaven and earth, so that he reigns and rules over all.   Mt 28[.18]

81. M. *But what is meant by "right hand," and by "sitteth"?*

C. It is a similitude taken from earthly princes, who are wont to place on their right hand those whom they make their lieutenants to govern in their name.

82. M. *You do not mean anything more then than Paul when he says that Christ has been appointed head of the church, and raised above all principality, has secured a name which is above every name.*[b]

C. That is so.

83. M. *Continue.*

C. "From thence he will come to judge the quick and the dead." That is to say, he will appear again from heaven in judgment, as he was seen to ascend.   Acts 1[.11]

84. M. *As the judgment is not to be before the end of the world, how do you*

a. Lk 24[.51]; Acts 2[.33]

b. Eph [1.22, 4.15]; Phil 2[.9]

say that some men will then be alive, and thus will be dead, seeing it is appointed to all
Heb 9[.27–28] men once to die?

C. Paul answers this question when he says, that those who then survive
will suddenly be changed so that their corruption will be abolished, and their bodies
will put on incorruption.[a]

85. M. *You understand then that this change will be for them like a death, for
it will abolish their first nature, and raise them up in a new state.*

C. That is it.

86. M. *Does the fact that Christ is to come again to judge the world bring us
any consolation?*

C. Yes, indeed. For we are certain that he will appear only for our salvation.

87. M. *We should not then fear the last judgment, and have a horror of it?*

C. No, since we are not to come before any other judge than he who is our
Advocate, and who has taken our cause in hand to defend us.

88. M. *Let us come now to the third part.*

C. This is faith in the Holy Spirit.

89. M. *What do we gain by it?*

C. The knowledge that as God has redeemed and saved us by Jesus Christ,
he will also make us partakers of this redemption and salvation, through his Holy
Spirit.

90. M. *How?*

C. As the blood of Christ is our cleansing, the Holy Spirit must sprinkle
1 Pt 1[.19] our consciences with it that they may be cleansed.

91. M. *This requires a clearer explanation.*

C. I mean that the Holy Spirit, while he dwells in our hearts, makes us feel
Rom 5[.5] the virtue of our Lord Jesus. For he enlightens us to know his benefits; he seals and
Eph 1[.13] imprints them in our souls, and makes room for them in us. He regenerates us and
makes us new creatures, so that through him we receive all the blessings and gifts
which are offered to us in Jesus Christ.

92. M. *What follows?*

C. The fourth part, where it is said that we believe in the catholic church.

93. M. *What is the catholic church?*

C. The community of the faithful which God has ordained and elected to
eternal life.

M. *Is it necessary to believe this article?*

94. C. Yes, indeed, unless we want to make the death of Christ of none

---

a. 1 Cor 15[.52]; 1 Thes 4[.17]

effect, and all that has already been said. The fruit that proceeds from it is the church.

95. M. *You mean then that up to this point we have spoken of the cause and foundation of salvation, how God has received us in love through the mediation of Jesus, and has confirmed this grace in us through his Holy Spirit. But now the effect and ful-fillment of all this is explained in order to give us greater certainty.*

C. It is so.

96. M. *In what sense do you call the church holy?*

C. All whom God has chosen he justifies, and reforms to holiness and inno-cence, that his glory may be reflected in them. And so Jesus Christ sanctified the church which he redeemed, that it might be glorious and without blemish.   Rom 8[.30]
Eph 5[.25–27]

97. M. *What is meant by the word catholic or universal?*

C. It is meant to signify, that as there is only one head of the faithful, so they must all be united in one body, so that there are not several churches but one only, which is extended throughout the whole world.[a]

98. M. *And what is the meaning of what follows concerning the communion of saints?*

C. That is added to express more clearly the unity which exists among the members of the church. Moreover by this we are given to understand, that all the benefits that the Lord gives to the church, are for the good and salvation of every church, because they all have communion together.

99. M. *But is this holiness which you attribute to the church already perfect?*

C. Not as long as she battles in this world, for elements of imperfection always remain and will never be entirely removed, until she is united completely to Jesus Christ her head, by whom she is sanctified.

100. M. *Can this church be known in any other way than by believing in her?*

C. There is indeed the visible church of God, for the recognition of which he has certain signs, but here we speak properly of the fellowship of those whom he has elected to salvation which cannot be seen plainly by the eye.

101. M. *What comes next?*

C. I believe in "the forgiveness of sins."

102. M. *What do you understand by this word "forgiveness"?*

C. That God by his pure goodness forgives and pardons the sins of believ-ers, so that they are not brought to account before his judgment, in order to be punished.

a. Eph 4[.15]; 1 Cor 12[.12, 27]

103. M. *Hence it follows that it is not at all through our own satisfaction that we desire to have God's pardon?*

C. That is true; for the Lord Jesus has made payment and borne the punishment. We on our part could not make any recompense to God, but may only receive pardon for all our misdeeds through the pure generosity of God.

104. M. *Why do you insert this article after the church?*

C. Because no man obtains pardon for his sins without being previously incorporated into the people of God, persevering in unity and communion with the body of Christ in such a way as to be a true member of the church.

105. M. *And so outside the church there is nothing but damnation and death?*

C. Certainly, for all those who separate themselves from the community of the faithful to form a sect on its own, have no hope of salvation so long as they are in schism.

106. M. *What follows?*

C. I believe in "the resurrection of the flesh and the life everlasting."

107. M. *Why is this article inserted?*

C. To show us that our happiness is not situated on the earth. This serves a twofold end. We are to learn to pass through this world as though it were a foreign country, treating lightly all earthly things and declining to set our hearts on them.

Secondly, we are not to lose courage, no matter how much we fail to perceive as yet the fruit of the grace which the Lord has wrought for us in Jesus Christ, but wait patiently until the time of revelation.

108. M. *How will this resurrection take place?*

C. Those who were formerly dead will resume their bodies, but with another quality; that is, they will no longer be subject to death or corruption, even although their substance will remain the same. Those who will survive, God will 1 Cor 15[.52] miraculously raise up through a sudden change, as it is said.

109. M. *Will this resurrection not be common to the evil and the good?*

C. Yes indeed, but not in the same way. Some will rise to salvation and joy, others to condemnation and death.[a]

110. M. *Why then is eternal life only spoken of here, and hell not at all?*

C. Because nothing is set down in this summary that does not tend to the consolation of faithful consciences. It relates to us only the benefits which God performs for his servants. Accordingly no mention is made of the wicked, who are excluded from his kingdom.

a. Jn 5[.29]; Mt 25[.46]

111. M. *Since we have the foundation on which faith is laid, we should be quite able to gather from it what true faith is.*

C. Yes, indeed. It is a sure and steadfast knowledge of the love of God toward us, according as he declares in his gospel that he is our Father and Savior (through the mediation of Jesus Christ).

112. M. *Can we have this by ourselves, or does it come from God?*

C. Scripture teaches that it is the singular gift of the Holy Spirit, and experience also demonstrates it.

113. M. *How so?*

C. Our mind is too weak to comprehend the spiritual wisdom of God which is revealed to us by faith, and our hearts are too prone either to defiance or to a perverse confidence in ourselves or creaturely things. But the Holy Spirit enlightens us to make us capable of understanding what would otherwise be incomprehensible to us, and fortifies us in certitude, sealing and imprinting the promises of salvation on our hearts.

114. M. *What good comes to us from this faith, when we have it?*

C. It justifies us before God, and makes us obtain eternal life.

115. M. *How so? Is not man justified by good works in a holy life and in conformity to God?*

C. If any one be found so perfect, he might well be deemed righteous, but since we are all poor sinners, we must look elsewhere for a worthiness in which to make answer before the judgment of God.

116. M. *But are all our works so reprobate that they cannot merit grace before God?*

C. First, all that we do of ourselves, by our own nature, is vicious, and therefore cannot please God. He condemns them all.

117. M. *You say then that before God has received us in his grace, we can do nothing but sin, just as a bad tree cannot but produce bad fruit?*   Mt 7[.17]

C. It is so. For even if our works appear beautiful outwardly, yet they are evil, since the heart, to which God looks, is perverted.

118. M. *Hence you conclude, that we cannot by our merits anticipate God, and so induce him to be kind to us, but on the contrary that we do nothing but provoke him to be against us?*

C. Yes. And therefore I say: merely through his goodness, without any regard to our works, he is pleased to accept us freely in Jesus Christ, imputing his righteousness to us, and does not impute our sins to us.   Ti 3[.5-7]

119. M. *What do you mean then by saying that a man is justified by faith?*

C. That in believing the promises of the gospel and in receiving them in true affiance of the heart, we enter into this righteousness.

120. M. *You mean then that as God offers righteousness to us by the gospel, so it is by faith that we receive it?*

C. Yes.

121. M. *But after God has once received us, are the works which we do by his grace, not pleasing to him?*

C. Yes they are, in that he generously accepts them, not however in virtue of their own worthiness.

122. M. *How is that? Are they not accepted as worthy, seeing that they proceed from the Holy Spirit?*

C. No. For there is always some weakness in them, the weakness of our flesh, through which they are defiled.

123. M. *By what means, then, are they made acceptable?*

C. It is by faith. That is to say, that a person is assured in his conscience that God will not examine him harshly, but covering his defects and impurities by the purity of Jesus Christ, he will regard him as perfect.

124. M. *But can we say from this that a Christian man is justified by works after God has called him, or that through them he merits the love of God, and so obtains eternal life?*

Ps 143[.2]   C. No. On the contrary, it is said that no man living will be justified in his sight. Therefore we have to pray that he will not enter into judgment with us, nor call us to account.

125. M. *You do not mean therefore that the good works of believers are useless?*

C. No. For God promises to reward them fully, both in this world and in paradise. But this comes from his gratuitous love toward us: moreover he buries all our faults, so as never to remember them.

126. M. *But can we believe that we are justified, without doing good works?*

C. That is impossible. For to believe in Jesus Christ is to receive him as he has given himself to us. He promises not only to deliver us from death and to restore us to favor with God his Father, through the merit of his innocence, but also to regenerate us by his Spirit, that we may be enabled to live in holiness.

127. M. *Faith, then, not only does not make us careless of good works, but is the root from which they are produced.*

C. It is so, and for this reason the doctrine of the gospel is comprehended in these two points, faith and repentance.

128. M. *What is repentance?*

C. Dissatisfaction with and a hatred of evil and a love of good proceeding from the fear of God, and inducing us to mortify our flesh, so that we may be governed and led by the Holy Spirit, in the service of God.

129. M. *But this second point we have mentioned concerning the Christian life.*

C. Yes, and we said that the true and legitimate service of God is to obey his will.

130. M. *Why?*

C. Because he will not be served according to our own imagination, but in the way that pleases him.

2. THE LAW

131. M. *What rule has he given us by which we may direct our life?*

C. His law.

132. M. *What does it contain?*

C. It is divided into two parts: the first contains four commandments, the other six. Thus there are ten in all.

133. M. *Who made this division?*

C. God himself, who delivered it to Moses written on two tables, and declared that it was reduced into ten words.[a]

134. M. *What is the content of the first table?*

C. The way of the true worship of God.

135. M. *And the second?*

C. How we are to live with our neighbors, and what we owe them.

136. M. *Repeat the first commandment.*

C. Hear, O Israel, I am the Lord thy God, who brought thee out of the land of Egypt, out of the house of bondage: thou shalt have no other gods before me.[b]

137. M. *Explain the meaning.*

C. At first he makes a kind of preface for the whole law. For in calling himself the Eternal and the Creator of the world, he claims authority to command. Then he declares that he is our God, in order that we may esteem his doctrine. For if he is our Savior, that is good reason why we should be an obedient people to him.

138. M. *But is not that which he says after the deliverance from the land of Egypt, addressed particularly to the people of Israel?*

a. Ex 32[.15], 34[.29]; Dt 4[.13], 10[.1]
b. Ex 20[.2–3]; Dt 5[.6–7]

C. Yes, it does refer to the physical deliverance of Israel, but it also applies to us all in a general way, in that he has delivered our souls from the spiritual captivity of sin, and the tyranny of the devil.

139. *M. Why does he mention this at the beginning of his law?*

C. To remind us how much we are bound to obey his good pleasure, and what ingratitude it would be on our part if we do the contrary.

140. *M. And what does he require briefly in this first commandment?*

C. That we reserve for him alone the honor that belongs to him, and do not transfer it elsewhere.

141. *M. What is the honor due to him?*

C. To adore him alone, to call upon him, to have our affiance in him, and all similar things due to his majesty.

142. *M. Why is it said "Before my face"?*

C. Since he who sees and knows all is the Judge of the secret thoughts of men, it means that he wants to be worshiped as God, not only by outward confession, but also in pure trust and affection of heart.

143. *M. Turn to the second commandment.*

C. Thou shalt not make unto thee a graven image, nor any form that is in heaven above, or on the earth beneath, or in the water under the earth. Thou shalt not do honor to them.

144. *M. Does he entirely forbid us to make any image?*

C. No, but he forbids us to make any image with which to represent God, or to worship him.

145. *M. Why is it unlawful to represent God visibly?*

C. Because there is no resemblance between him who is eternal Spirit and incomprehensible, and corporal, dead, corruptible, and visible matter.[a]

146. *M. You think then that it does dishonor to his majesty to represent him in this way?*

C. Yes.

147. *M. What kind of worship is here condemned?*

C. When we come before an image intending to pray, or bow our knee before it; or make any other sign of reverence, as if God were there showing himself to us.

148. *M. This does not mean that all sculpture or painting is universally forbidden, but only all images used in the service of God, or in worshiping him in visible things, or indeed for any abuse of them in idolatry of any kind whatsoever.*

a. Dt 4[.15]; Is 40[.7]; Rom 1[.23]; Acts 17[.24–25]

C. That is so.

149. M. *Now to what end shall we refer this commandment?*

C. With the first commandment, God declared that he alone, and no one beside him, should be worshiped: so now he shows us the correct form of worship, in order that he may draw us away from all superstitions, and carnal ceremonies.

150. M. *Let us proceed.*

C. He adds a warning that he is the eternal, our God, strong and jealous, visiting the iniquity of the fathers upon the children of them who hate him, to the third and fourth generation.

151. M. *Why does he make mention of his might?*

C. To indicate that he has power to maintain his glory.

152. M. *What is meant by jealousy?*

C. That he cannot allow an associate. For as he has given himself to us out of his infinite goodness, so he would have us to be entirely his. And this is the chastity of our souls, to be consecrated and dedicated to him. On the other hand it is a spiritual whoredom for us to turn away from him to any superstition.

153. M. *How is this to be understood, that he punishes the sin of the fathers on their children?*

C. To give us greater fear of him. He says not only that he will inflict punishment on those who offend him, but that their offspring also will be cursed after them.

154. M. *But is it not contrary to the justice of God to punish someone for others?*

C. If we consider the condition of the human race, the question is answered. For by nature we are all cursed, and we cannot complain of God when he leaves us in this condition. Moreover as he manifests his grace and love toward his servants in blessing their children, so this is a testimony to his punishment of the wicked, when he leaves their seed accursed.

155. M. *What more does he say?*

C. To incite us by gentleness, he says that he will have mercy on all who love him and observe his commands, to a thousand generations.

156. M. *Does he mean that the obedience of a faithful man will save the whole of his race, even if they are still wicked?*

C. No, but that he will extend his goodness toward the faithful to such an extent, that in love for them he will make himself known to their children, not only to prosper them according to the flesh, but to sanctify them by his Spirit, that he might make them obedient to his will.

157. M. *But this is not always so.*

C. No. For as the Lord reserves for himself the freedom to show mercy to the children of the ungodly, so on the other hand he retains the power to elect or re-
Rom 9[.15–22] ject in the generation of the faithful as it seems good to him. However, he does this
Rom 2[.6–10] in such a way that men may acknowledge that this promise is not vain or fallacious.

158. M. *Why does he mention here a thousand generations, and in regard to punishment mention only three or four?*

C. To signify that it is his nature to exercise kindness and gentleness much more than strictness or severity, as he testifies, when he says that he is ready to show mercy, but slow to anger.[a]

159. M. *Let us come to the third commandment.*

C. Thou shalt not take the name of the Lord thy God in vain.

160. M. *What does this mean?*

C. He forbids us to abuse the name of God, not only in perjury, but also in superfluous and idle swearing.

161. M. *Can the name of God be used lawfully in oaths?*

C. Yes, when they are necessary, that is, in order to uphold the truth, when it requires it, and in maintaining love and concord among us.

162. M. *Does he reprove no other oaths, than those which are a dishonor to God?*

C. In this one case he gives us a general instruction never to utter the name of God except with fear and humility in order to glorify it. For since it is holy and honorable, we ought to guard against taking the name of God in such a way that we appear to hold it in contempt, or give others occasion to vilify it.

163. M. *How is this to be done?*

C. By never thinking or speaking of God and his works without honor and reverence.

164. M. *What follows?*

C. A warning, that he will not hold him guiltless, who takes his name in vain.

165. M. *Since elsewhere he gives a general warning that he will punish all transgressors, what is the advantage of this warning?*

C. He wants to declare how highly he regards the glory of his name, explicitly mentioning that he will not suffer anyone to despise it, so that we may be all the more careful to hold it in reverence.

166. M. *Let us come to the fourth commandment.*

C. Remember the Sabbath day, to keep it holy. Six days shalt thou labor,

a. Ex 34[.6–7]; Ps 103[.8]

and do all thy work: But the seventh is the Sabbath of the Lord thy God: in it thou shalt not do any work, thou, nor thy son, nor thy daughter, thy manservant, nor thy maidservant, nor thy cattle, nor thy stranger that is within thy gates: For in six days the Lord made heaven and earth, the sea, and all that in them is, and rested the seventh day: wherefore the Lord blessed the Sabbath day, and hallowed it.

167. *M. Does he order us to labor six days a week that we may rest on the seventh?*

C. Not precisely, but in allowing us to labor for six days, he excepts the seventh, on which it is not right to be engaged in work.

168. *M. Does he thus forbid us all work one day a week?*

C. This commandment has a particular reason, for the observance of rest is part of the ceremonies of the ancient law, which was abolished at the coming of Jesus Christ.

169. *M. Do you mean that this commandment properly belongs to the Jews, and that it was given for the time of the Old Testament?*

C. I do, in so far as it is ceremonial.

170. *M. How is that? Is there anything else in it besides the ceremony?*

C. It was given for three reasons.

171. *M. What are they?*

C. To represent spiritual rest, in aid of ecclesiastical polity, and for the relief of servants.

172. *M. What is this spiritual rest?*

C. It is to cease from our own works, that the Lord may work in us.

173. *M. How is that done?*

C. By mortifying our flesh, that is, renouncing our own nature, so that God may govern us by his Spirit.

174. *M. Is this to be done only one day a week?*

C. This is to be done continually. After we have once begun, we must continue all our life.

175. *M. Why, then, is a certain day appointed to represent this?*

C. It is not required that the representation should be altogether identical with the truth, but it is sufficient that there should be some resemblance.

176. *M. But why is the seventh day appointed rather than any other day?*

C. The number seven implies perfection in Scripture. Thus it is suited to denote perpetuity. It reminds us also that our spiritual rest is only begun in this life, and will not be perfect until we depart from this world.

177. *M. But what is meant when our Lord asserts that we must rest as he did?*

C. After having created all his works in six days, he dedicated the seventh to the contemplation of his works. And in order better to induce us to do this, he set before us his own example. For nothing is so desirable as to be conformed to him.

178. *M. Must we meditate continually on the works of God, or is it sufficient on one day out of seven?*

C. We must do it every hour, but because of our weakness, one day is specially appointed. And this is the polity of which I spoke.

179. *M. What order, then, is to be observed on that day?*

C. That the people meet to hear the doctrine of God, to engage in common prayer, and bear witness to their faith and religion.

180. *M. What do you mean by saying that this commandment is also given to provide for the relief of servants?*

C. To give some relaxation to those who are under the power of others. And likewise, this tends to maintain a common polity. For everyone accustoms himself to labor for the rest of the time, when there is one day for rest.

181. *M. Let us now see how this commandment addresses itself to us.*

C. As for the ceremony, it was abolished, for we have the accomplishment Col 2[.16] of it in Jesus Christ.

182. *M. How?*

C. Our old man is crucified, through the power of his death, and through Rom 6[.6] his resurrection we are raised up to newness of life.

183. *M. What else is there here for us?*

C. That we observe the order constituted in the church, to hear the word of God, to engage in public prayers and in the sacraments, and that we do not contravene the spiritual order among the faithful.

184. *M. And does the figure give us any further benefit?*

C. Yes, indeed. It should lead us to the truth, namely, that being true members of Christ, we should cease from our own works, and put ourselves under his government.

185. *M. Let us come to the second table.*

C. It begins, "Honor thy father and thy mother."

186. *M. What do you mean by "honor"?*

C. That children be humble and obedient toward their parents, doing them honor and reverence, helping them and being at their command, as they are bound.

187. *M. Proceed further.*

C. God adds a promise to the commandment, "That thy days may be prolonged on the land which the Lord thy God will give thee."

188. *M. What does that mean?*

C. That God will give long life to those who honor their father and mother as they ought.

189. M. *Seeing this life is so full of misery, why does God promise man as a favor that he will live long?*

C. However miserable it may be, life on earth is a blessing from God to the faithful, if only for this reason, that in it God testifies to his fatherly love in supporting them in it.

190. M. *Does it follow conversely, that the man who dies prematurely is cursed of God?*

C. By no means. Rather does it sometimes happen that the Lord withdraws from this world more quickly those whom he loves most.

191. M. *In so doing, how does he fulfill his promise?*

C. All that God promises us in earthly blessings, we must receive under this condition, namely, that it is expedient for our spiritual salvation. For it would be poor indeed if that did not have precedence.

192. M. *What of those who are rebellious against their father and mother?*

C. Not only will God punish them at the last judgment, but here also God will exercise vengeance on their bodies, it may be by letting them die before their time, or ignominiously, or in some other way.

193. M. *Does he not speak expressly of the land of Canaan in this promise?*

C. Yes, so far as the children of Israel are concerned, but the term ought to have a more general meaning for us. For seeing that the earth is the Lord's, whatever be the country we inhabit, he assigns it to us for our habitation.[a]

194. M. *Is that all there is to the commandment?*

C. Though father and mother only are mentioned, nevertheless all superiors are intended, as the reason is the same.

195. M. *What is the reason?*

C. That God has given them preeminence; for there is no authority whether of parents, or princes, or of any others who are over us, but what God has ordained.   Rom 13[.1]

196. M. *Repeat the sixth commandment.*

C. Thou shalt not kill.

197. M. *Does it forbid nothing but murder?*

C. Yes, indeed. For seeing it is God who speaks, he gives us law not only for outward deeds, but primarily for the affections of our heart.

198. M. *You mean then that there is some kind of inward murder which God forbids to us?*

a. Ps 24[.1], 89[.12], 115[.16]

C. I do: hatred and rancor, and desire to do evil to our neighbor.

199. M. *Is it sufficient for us not to hate or to bear ill will?*

C. No, for in condemning hatred God signifies that he requires us to love our neighbors and seek their salvation, and all this with true affection and without simulation.

200. M. *State the seventh commandment.*

C. Thou shalt not commit adultery.

201. M. *What is the essence of this?*

C. That all fornication is cursed by God, and therefore we must abstain from it if we do not want to provoke his anger against us.

202. M. *Does it not require anything else?*

C. We must always regard the nature of the Lawgiver, who does not halt at the outward act, but requires the affection of the heart.

203. M. *What more then does it mean?*

C. Since our bodies and our souls are temples of the Holy Spirit,[a] we must preserve them in uprightness. And so we must be chaste not only in deed, but also in desire, word, and gesture. Accordingly no part of us is to be polluted by unchastity.

204. M. *Let us come to the eighth commandment.*

C. Thou shalt not steal.

205. M. *Is it only meant to prohibit the thefts which are punished by justice, or does it extend further?*

C. It refers to all evil traffic and unscrupulous means of acquiring our neighbor's goods, whether by violence, or fraud, or in any other kind of way that God has not allowed.

206. M. *Is it enough to abstain from evil deeds, or is covetousness also included here?*

C. We must ever return to this, that the Lawgiver is spiritual, that he does not speak simply of outward thefts, but all schemes, wishes, and plans to enrich ourselves at the expense of our neighbor.

207. M. *What are we to do then?*

C. We must do our duty in preserving for every man his own.

208. M. *What is the ninth commandment?*

C. Thou shalt not bear false witness against thy neighbor.

209. M. *Does it forbid perjury in court, or any kind of lying against our neighbor?*

C. In mentioning this one case it gives a general instruction, that we are

---

a. 1 Cor 3[.16], 6[.15]; 2 Cor 6[.16]

not to speak evil of our neighbor falsely, nor by our slanders and lies are we to do him harm in his possessions, or in his reputation.

210. *M. But why does he expressly mention public perjury?*

C. That he may give us a greater abhorrence of this vice of evil speaking and slander, telling us that if a man accustom himself to slandering and defaming his neighbor, he will soon descend to perjury in court.

211. *M. Does he only forbid evil speaking, or does he also include evil thinking?*

C. Both of them, for the reason already stated. For whatever it is wrong to do before men, it is wrong to wish before God.

212. *M. Then summarize its meaning.*

C. He enjoins us not to be inclined to misjudge and defame our neighbors, but rather to esteem them highly, as far as the truth will permit, and to preserve their good reputation in our speech.

213. *M. Let us come to the last commandment.*

C. Thou shalt not covet thy neighbor's house, thou shalt not covet thy neighbor's wife, nor his manservant, nor his maidservant, nor his ox, nor his ass, nor any thing that is thy neighbor's.

214. *M. Seeing that the whole law is spiritual, as you have so often said before, and the other commandments are not only to order outward acts, but also the affections of the heart, what more is added here?*

C. The Lord wished by the other commandments to rule our affections and will, but here he imposes a law also on our thoughts which though charged with covetousness and desire, yet stop short of an active intention.

215. *M. Do you mean that the least temptation that enters into the thought of a believer is sin, even though he resists it and does not consent to it?*

C. It is certain that all evil thoughts proceed from the infirmity of our flesh, even though we do not consent to them. But I say that this commandment speaks of concupiscence which tickles and pierces the heart of man, without bringing him to a deliberate purpose.

216. *M. You say then that the evil affections which involve a definite act of will or resolution are already condemned, but now the Lord requires of us such integrity, that no wicked desire may enter our hearts, to solicit and incite them to evil.*

C. That is right.

217. *M. Can we not now give a short summary of the whole law?*

C. We can, reducing it to two articles—the first of which is that we are to love God with all our heart, and with all our soul, and with all our strength; the second that we love our neighbors as ourselves.

218. *M. What is meant by the love of God?*

C. To love him as God is to have and hold him as Lord, Savior, and Father, and this requires reverence, honor, faith, and obedience along with love.

219. M. *What does "with all our heart" signify, and "with all our soul, and all our strength"?*

C. Such a zeal and such a vehemence, that there is in us no desire, no will, no intention, and no thought contrary to this love.

220. M. *What is the meaning of the second article?*

C. As we are by nature so prone to love ourselves, that this affection overcomes all others, so love to our neighbor should be so predominant in our hearts, as to direct and govern us, and be the rule of all our thoughts and actions.

221. M. *What do you understand by "our neighbors"?*

C. Not only parents and friends, or those acquainted with us, but also those who are unknown to us, and even enemies.

222. M. *But what connection do they have with us?*

C. That which God has placed among all men on the earth, and is so inviolable, that it cannot be abolished by the malice of any man.

223. M. *You say, then, that if any man hate us, the blame is his own, and yet according to the order of God, he does not cease to be our neighbor, and we are to regard him as such?*

C. It is so.

224. M. *Seeing that the law of God comprises the form of worshiping him aright, should not the Christian man live according to its command?*

C. Yes indeed. But there is some infirmity in us, so that no man acquits himself perfectly in it.

225. M. *Why then does the Lord require a perfection which is beyond our ability?*

C. He requires nothing which we are not bound to perform. Nevertheless, provided we take care to conform our life to what we are told here, although we are very far from reaching perfection, the Lord does not impute our faults to us.

226. M. *Do you speak of all men in general, or of believers only?*

C. He who is not yet regenerated by the Spirit of God cannot begin to do the least of the commandments. Moreover, even if a person could be found who had fulfilled some part of the law, he would not acquit himself before God, for our Lord pronounces that all those who have not fulfilled all the things contained in it, will be accursed.[a]

---

a. Dt 27[.26]; Gal 3[.10]

227. *M. Hence we must conclude that the law has a twofold office, in accordance with the fact that there are two classes of men.*

C. Yes, in regard to unbelievers it seeks but to convict and make them inexcusable before God. And this is what Paul says, that it is the ministry of death and condemnation. In regard to believers, it has a very different use.

Rom 3[.3]

2 Cor 3[.6, 9]

228. *M. What?*

C. First, in that it shows them that they cannot justify themselves by their works, it humbles them and disposes them to seek their salvation in Jesus Christ. Secondly, inasmuch as it requires of them much more than they are able to perform, it admonishes them to pray unto the Lord, that he may give them strength and power, and at the same time reminds them of their perpetual guilt, that they may not presume to be proud. Thirdly it is a kind of bridle, by which they are kept in the fear of God.

Rom 5[.18–21]

Gal 4[.6]

229. *M. We say then that although during this mortal life we will never fulfill the law, such perfection is not required of us in vain, for it shows us the mark at which we ought to aim, that each of us, according to the grace God has bestowed on him, may strive continually to press toward it, and to advance day by day.*

C. That is as I understand it.

230. *M. Do we not have a perfect rule of goodness in the law?*

C. Yes, and therefore God demands nothing from us, but to follow it; and, on the other hand, repudiates and rejects all that a man undertakes to do beyond what it contains. The only sacrifice he requires is obedience.[a]

231. *M. What is the purpose then of all the admonitions, reproofs, commandments, and exhortations made both by prophets and apostles?*

C. They are nothing else than declarations of the law, leading us into obedience to it rather than turning us away from it.

232. *M. But nothing is said about particular vocations?*

C. When it is said that we are to render to every one his due, we may well infer what the duty of each is in his own vocation. Moreover as we have already said, this is expounded for us in the whole of Scripture, for what the Lord has set down in this summary, he treats of there, and with much fuller teaching.

3. PRAYER

233. *M. Since we have spoken sufficiently of the service of God, which is the second part of his worship, let us now speak of the third part.*

C. We said it was the invocation of God in all our needs.

a. 1 Sm [15.22]; Jer 7[.21–23]

234. M. *Do you think that he alone is to be invoked?*

C. Yes, for he requires this as the worship proper to his deity.

235. M. *If it is so, in what way is it legitimate for us to ask the aid of men?*

C. There is a great difference between these two things. For we call upon God to protest that we expect no good but from him, and that we have no refuge elsewhere, and yet we ask the assistance of men, as far as he permits, and has given them the power and means of helping us.

236. M. *You mean that when we seek the succor of men, there is nothing to prevent our calling upon God alone, seeing that we do not put our reliance on them, and do not seek their aid except in so far as God has ordained them to be ministers and dispensers of his blessings, in order to assist us.*

C. That is true. And indeed, every benefit that comes to us we should take as coming from God himself, as in truth it is he who sends it to us by their hands.

237. M. *Nevertheless, should we not give thanks to men for the kindness which they do to us?*

C. Certainly, if only for the reason that God honors them by communicating his blessings to us through their hands, for in this way he lays us under obligation to him, and wishes us to be mindful of them.

238. M. *Can we not conclude from this that it is wrong to invoke angels and saints who have departed from this world?*

C. Yes, indeed; for God has not assigned to saints this office of aiding and assisting us. And in regard to angels, though he employs their ministry for our salvation, nevertheless he does not wish us to invoke them, nor to address ourselves to them.

239. M. *You say, then, that all that conflicts with the order instituted by the Lord, contravenes his will?*

C. Yes, for it is a sure sign of infidelity if we are not contented with what the Lord gives to us. Moreover, if instead of having a refuge in God alone, in obedience to his command, we have recourse to them, putting something of our reliance on them, we fall into idolatry, seeing we transfer to them that which God has reserved for himself.

240. M. *Let us now speak of the way of prayer to God. Is it sufficient to pray with the tongue, or does prayer require also the spirit and the heart?*

C. The tongue is not always necessary, but there must be understanding and affection.

241. M. *How will you prove that?*

C. Since God is Spirit, he always requires the heart, and especially in prayer, in which we enter into communication with him, wherefore he promises to be near to those only who call upon him in truth. On the other hand, he curses all who pray to him in hypocrisy, and without affection.

Ps 145[.18]

Is 29[.13–14]

242. *M. All prayers, then, made only with the mouth are vain?*

C. Not only vain, but also displeasing to God.

243. *M. What kind of affection should we have in prayer?*

C. First, that we feel our misery and poverty, and that this feeling should beget sorrow and anguish in us. Secondly, that we have an earnest desire to obtain grace from God. This desire will also kindle our hearts, and engender in us an ardent longing to pray.

244. *M. Does this derive from our nature, or from the grace of God?*

C. Here God must come to our aid, for we are too dull, but the Spirit of God helps us with groanings that cannot be uttered, and forms in our hearts the affection and zeal that God requires, as Paul says.[a]

245. *M. Does this mean that we have not to incite and urge ourselves to pray?*

C. By no means. On the contrary, when we do not feel such a disposition within us we should beseech the Lord to put it into us, so as to make us capable and fit to pray as we ought.

246. *M. You do not, however, mean that the tongue is quite useless in prayer?*

C. Not at all, for sometimes it helps the mind, sustaining and keeping it from being drawn away from God so easily. Besides, since more than all the other members it was formed to the glory of God, it is very reasonable that it should be employed by all means for this purpose. Moreover, the zeal of the heart by its own ardor and vehemence often constrains the tongue to speak quite spontaneously.

247. *M. If so, what about prayer in an unknown tongue?*

C. It is a mockery of God, and a perverse hypocrisy.

1 Cor 14[.14]

248. *M. But when we pray to God, is it a venture in which we do not know whether we will succeed or not? Or ought we to be certain that our praying will be heard?*

C. The ground of our prayers should always be, that they will be received by God, and that we shall obtain what we request as far as it is expedient for us. And therefore St. Paul says that true prayer comes from faith. For if we have no reliance upon the goodness of God, it will be impossible for us to call upon him in truth.

Rom 10[.14]

249. *M. And what of those who doubt, not knowing if God hears or not?*

C. Their prayers are utterly void, since they have no promise, for he says that whatever we shall ask, believing, we shall receive.[b]

a. Rom 8[.26]; Gal 4[.6]
b. Mt 21[.22]; Mk 11[.24]

250. M. *It remains to learn how and in whose name we can have the boldness to present ourselves before God, seeing that we are so unworthy in ourselves.*

C. First we have the promises on which we must rest, without considering our worthiness.[a] Secondly, if we are children of God, he induces and urges us by his Holy Spirit to betake ourselves to him familiarly, as to our Father. And lest we, who are poor worms of the earth, and miserable sinners, should be afraid to appear before His glorious majesty, he gives us our Lord Jesus Christ as a Mediator,[b] that through him we may have access and have no doubt of finding grace.

Mt 9[.2, 22]

251. M. *Do you understand that we are to call upon God only, in the name of Jesus Christ?*

C. I understand so, for we have an express commandment about this. And in it we are promised that by his intercession our requests will be heard.

252. M. *It is not, then, temerity or foolish presumption on our part, if we presume to address God personally, seeing that we have Jesus Christ for our Advocate, and if we set him before us, that God may for his sake be gracious to us and accept us?*

C. No, for we pray as it were by his mouth, since he gives us entrance and audience, and intercedes for us.

Rom 8[.34]

253. M. *Let us now speak of the substance of our prayers. Can we ask for all that comes into our mind, or is there a certain rule to be observed about it?*

C. If we followed our own fantasy, our prayers would be very badly ordered. We are so ignorant that we cannot judge what it is good to ask: moreover, all our desires are so intemperate that it is necessary that we should not give them a loose rein.

254. M. *What is to be done, then?*

C. That God himself should instruct us, according to what he knows to be expedient; that we do nothing but follow him, as if he were leading us by the hand.

255. M. *What instructions has he given?*

C. He has given us ample instructions throughout Scripture; but that we may address ourselves the better to a definite end, he has given us a form in which he has briefly comprehended everything that is legitimate and expedient for us to pray for.

256. M. *Repeat it.*

C. Our Lord Jesus Christ, being asked by his disciples to teach them how to pray, answered that they should pray thus:[c]

a. Ps 50[.15], 91[.3], 145[.18]; Is 30[.15], 65[.24]; Jer 29[.12]; Jl 3[.5]
b. 1 Tm 2[.5]; Heb 4[.16]; 1 Jn 2[.1]
c. Mt 6[.9–13]; Lk 11[.1–4]

"Our Father, which art in heaven, hallowed be thy name. Thy kingdom come. Thy will be done in earth, as it is in heaven. Give us this day our daily bread. And forgive us our debts, as we forgive our debtors. And lead us not into temptation; but deliver us from evil: For thine is the kingdom, and the power, and the glory, for ever. Amen."

257. M. *To make it easier to understand, tell me how many sentences it contains.*

C. Six, of which the first three concern the glory of God alone, without any reference to ourselves; the other three are for us, and concern our blessing and profit.

258. M. *Are we then to ask God for anything from which no benefit redounds to us?*

C. It is true that God, by his infinite goodness, so arranges and orders things, that nothing tends to the glory of his name, without being also salutary to us. Therefore, when his name is sanctified, he turns it to our sanctification; when his kingdom comes, we are, in a way, sharers in it. But in desiring and asking all these things, we ought to have regard only for his glory, without thinking of ourselves, or seeking our own profit.

259. M. *According to what you say, the first three of these requests are expedient for us, and yet they ought not to be made with any other intention than of desiring that God may be glorified.*

C. It is so. And similarly, although the last three requests are appointed as prayers for what is expedient to us, yet even in them we ought to seek the glory of God, so that it may be the end of all our desires.

260. M. *Let us come to the exposition. And before we go any further, why is God called our Father, rather than some other name?*

C. Since it is essential that our consciences have a steadfast assurance, when we pray, our God gives himself a name, which suggests only gentleness and kindness, in order to take away from us all doubt and anxiety, and to give us boldness in coming to him personally.

261. M. *Shall we then dare to go to God familiarly, as a child to his father?*

C. Yes, in fact with greater assurance of obtaining what we ask. For if we, being evil, cannot refuse our children bread and meat, when they ask, how much less will our heavenly Father, who is not only good, but sovereign goodness itself?   Mt 7[.11]

262. M. *Can we not prove from this very name, what has been said, namely, that prayer should be grounded on the intercession of Jesus Christ?*

C. Yes, certainly. For God does not acknowledge us as his children, except in so far as we are members of his Son.

263. M. *Why do you not call God your God, but call him our Father together?*

C. Each believer may indeed call him his own Father, but in this formula Jesus Christ instructs us to pray together, to remind us that in our prayers we are to exercise charity towards our neighbors, and not only to care for ourselves.

264. M. *What is meant by the clause "who art in heaven"?*

C. It is just the same as if I were to call him exalted, mighty, incomprehensible.

265. M. *To what end, and for what reason?*

C. That when we call upon him, we may learn to lift up our thoughts on high, and not to have any carnal or earthly thoughts of him, not to measure him by our apprehension, nor to subject him to our will, but to adore his glorious majesty in humility. It teaches us also to have more reliance on him, since he is Governor and Master of all.

266. M. *Now expound the first petition.*

C. The name of God is his renown, with which he is celebrated among men. We pray then that his glory may be exalted above all, and in all things.

267. M. *Do you think that his glory can increase or decrease?*

C. Not in itself. But this means that it may be manifested, as it ought to be, that all the works which God performs may appear glorious, as indeed they are, so that he himself may be glorified in every way.

268. M. *What do you understand by the kingdom of God in the second petition?*

C. It consists principally of two things: that he leads his own, and governs them by his Spirit, and on the other hand casts down and confounds the reprobate who refuse to subject themselves to his rule, and so makes it clear that there is no power which can resist his power.

269. M. *In what sense do you pray that this kingdom may come?*

C. That day by day the Lord may increase the numbers of the faithful, that day by day he may increasingly bestow his graces upon them, until he has filled them completely; moreover, that he cause his truth to shine more and more and manifest his justice, so that Satan and the powers of darkness may be put to confusion, and all iniquity be destroyed and abolished.

270. M. *Is that not taking place today?*

C. Yes indeed—in part, but we pray that it may continually increase and advance, until at last it comes to its perfection in the day of judgment, in which God alone will be exalted, and every creature will be humbled before his majesty, and he 1 Cor 15[.28] will be all in all.

271. M. *What do you mean by asking that the will of God may be done?*

C. That all creatures may be brought under obedience to him, and so that everything may be done according to his good will.

272. M. *Do you mean that nothing can be done contrary to his will?*

C. We ask not only that he may bring all things to pass, as he has determined in his counsel, but also that, putting down all rebellion, he may bring all wills to conform to his own.

273. M. *In so doing, do we not renounce our own wills?*

C. We do, not only that he may overthrow our desires which are at variance with his own good will, bringing them all to nought, but also that he may create in us new spirits and new hearts, so that we may will nothing of ourselves, but rather that his Spirit may will in us, and bring us into full agreement with him.

274. M. *Why do you add "on earth as it is in heaven"?*

C. Since his heavenly creatures or his angels have it as their only object to obey him, promptly without any opposition, we desire that the same thing may be done on earth, that is, that all men may yield themselves in voluntary obedience.

275. M. *Let us come to the second part. What mean you by "the daily bread" you ask for?*

C. In general, everything that we need for our body, not only food and clothing, but all that God knows to be expedient for us, that we may be able to eat our bread in peace.

276. M. *But why do you ask God to give you your food, when he orders us to win it, by working with our hands?*

C. Though he commands us to work for our living, nevertheless it is not our labor, industry, and diligence, that provide us with food, but the blessing of God alone, which makes the labor of our hands to prosper. Moreover we ought to understand that it is not meat that nourishes us, although we have it owing to his command, but the power of the Lord alone who uses it as his instrument.   Dt 8[.3, 17]

277. M. *Why do you call it yours, when you ask God to give it to you?*

C. Because by the kindness of God it becomes ours, though it is by no means due to us. We are also reminded by this not to desire the bread of others, but only that which we acquire by legitimate means, according to the ordinance of God.

278. M. *Why do you say "daily" and "this day"?*

C. That we may learn to be content, and not to covet more than our need requires.

279. M. *Since this prayer is common to all, how can the rich, who have an abundance of good things, provided for a long time, ask for bread each day?*

C. The rich, as well as the poor, should understand that none of the things profit them, unless the Lord grant them the use of them, and by his grace make it profitable to them. Thus in having we have nothing, unless he gives it to us.

280. M. *What does the fifth petition contain?*

C. That it pleases God to pardon our sins.

281. M. *Is any man living so righteous, that he does not need to make this petition?*

C. No, for the Lord Jesus gave this form of prayer to his apostles for his church. Wherefore he who would exempt himself from this, must renounce the community of Christians. And indeed Scripture testifies to us that even the most perfect man seeking to justify himself before God in a single matter, will be found guilty in Jb 9[.3] a thousand. Thus the only refuge we may have is in his mercy.

282. M. *How do you think that such remission is granted to us?*

C. As the words Jesus Christ used declare: because our sins are debts, making us liable to eternal death, we pray that God will pardon us out of his sheer kindness.

283. M. *You mean, then, that it is by the gratuitous goodness of God that we obtain remission of sins?*

C. Yes, for we can offer no satisfaction for the smallest sin we commit, if God does not exercise his sheer kindness toward us in forgiving us them all.

284. M. *What gain and profit do we receive, when God pardons our sins?*

C. We are acceptable to him, just as if we were righteous and innocent, and our consciences are assured of his paternal love, from which comes salvation and life.

285. M. *When you pray that he may forgive us as we forgive our debtors, do you mean that in pardoning men we merit pardon from God?*

C. By no means, for then pardon would not be by grace, and would not be founded, as it ought to be, on the satisfaction which Jesus Christ made for us in his death. But since by forgetting the injuries done to ourselves, we follow his gentleness and clemency, and so demonstrate that we are his children, God has given us this as a sign in confirmation that we are his children. On the other hand, he indicates to us that we cannot expect anything at his judgment but utter severity and extreme rigor, if we are not ready to pardon and show mercy to others who are guilty toward us.

286. M. *Do you think, then, God refuses to have as his children those who cannot forget the offenses committed against them, so that they cannot hope to be partakers of his grace?*

C. Yes. And he intends that all men may know that with what measure they [Mt 7.2] mete to their neighbors, it shall be measured to them.

287. M. *What follows?*

C. "Lead us not into temptation, but deliver us from evil."

288. M. *Do you treat this as one petition?*

C. Yes, for the second part is an explanation of the first part.

289. M. *What is the substance of it?*

C. That God does not allow us to fall into evil, or permit us to be over- Rom 7[.23]
come by the devil, and the lustful desires of our flesh, which strive against us, but
he gives us strength to resist, sustains us by his hand, takes us into his safe keeping,
to defend and lead us.

290. M. *How is this done?*

C. When he governs us by his Spirit, to make us love the good, and hate the
evil, follow justice, and flee from sin. By the power of his Spirit, we may overcome
the devil, sin, and the flesh.

291. M. *Do we stand in need of this?*

C. Yes, for the devil continually watches for us, like a roaring lion ready
to devour us. We are so feeble and frail that he would immediately overcome us, if   1 Pt 5[.8]
God did not fortify us, that we might be victorious over him.

292. M. *What does the word "temptation" signify?*

C. The wiles and assaults of the devil, which he uses to attack us, seeing
that our natural judgment is prone to be deceived and to deceive us, and our will is
always ready to addict itself to evil rather than to good.

293. M. *But why do you pray God not to lead you into evil, when this is the
proper office of Satan the devil?*

C. As God by his mercy preserves the faithful, and does not permit the
devil to seduce them, or sin to overcome them, so those whom he means to punish
he not only abandons, and deprives of his grace, but also yields to the devil to be
subjected to his tyranny, blinds them, and delivers them over to a reprobate mind.

294. M. *What is intended by the addition, "For thine is the kingdom, and the
power, and the glory, for ever"?*

C. To remind us again that our prayers are altogether grounded on the
power and goodness of God, and not on ourselves, for we are not worthy to open
our mouth in prayer; and also that we may learn to close all our prayers in his praise.

295. M. *Is it lawful to ask anything else, not mentioned here?*

C. Although we are free to use other words, and another form and manner,
yet no prayer will ever please God which does not correspond to this as the only
rule of right prayer.

4. THE WORD AND SACRAMENTS

296. M. *It is time to come to the fourth part of the worship we are to render to God.*

C. We said that this consists in acknowledging with the heart and confirming with the mouth that God is the author of all good, that thereby we may glorify him.

297. M. *Has he given us any rule for this?*

C. All the praises and thanksgivings contained in Scripture ought to be our rule and guide.

298. M. *Is there nothing regarding this in the Lord's Prayer?*

C. Yes there is, for when we pray that his name may be hallowed, we pray that he may be glorified in all his works, as indeed he is—that he may be praised for his justice when he punishes, for his mercy when he pardons, and for his faithfulness when he fulfills his promises; in short, that there is nothing in which his glory does not shine forth. This is to ascribe to him the praise for all blessing.

299. M. *What shall we infer from all that we have said?*

C. What truth itself tells us, and was stated at the outset, namely, that this is eternal life to know one true God the Father, and Jesus Christ whom he has sent—to know him, I say, in order that we may worship him aright, that he may be not only our Master, but also our Father and Savior, and we be in turn his children and servants, and a people dedicated to his glory.

Jn 17[.3]

300. M. *How can we attain to such blessedness?*

C. For this end God has left us his holy word, which is, as it were, an entry into his heavenly kingdom.

301. M. *Where do you find this word?*

C. It is comprised for us in the Holy Scriptures.

302. M. *How are we to use it in order to profit by it?*

C. By receiving it with the full consent of our conscience, as truth come down from heaven, submitting ourselves to it in right obedience, loving it with a true affection by having it imprinted in our hearts, we may follow it entirely and conform ourselves to it.

303. M. *Is all this within our own power?*

C. None of it; but God works them in us in this way by his Holy Spirit.

304. M. *But are we not to take trouble and be diligent, and zealously strive by hearing and reading its teaching, as it is declared to us?*

C. Yes, indeed: first each one of us in particular ought to study it: and above all, we are frequently to attend the sermons in which this word is expounded in the assembly of the Christians.

305. M. *Do you mean that it is not enough for people to read it privately at home, without altogether hearing its teaching in common?*

C. That is just what I mean, while God provides the way for it.

306. M. *Why do you say that?*

C. Because Jesus Christ has established this order in his church, and he has   Eph 4[.11]
declared this to be the only means of edifying and preserving it. Thus we must keep
ourselves to it and not be wiser than our Master.

307. M. *Is it necessary, then, that there should be pastors?*

C. Yes; and that we should hear them, receiving the teaching of the Lord
in humility by their mouth. Therefore whoever despises them and refuses to hear
them, rejects Jesus Christ, and separates himself from the fellowship of the faithful.[a]

308. M. *But is it enough for a Christian man to have been instructed by them
once, or ought he to continue to do this?*

C. It is little to have begun, unless you go on and persevere. We must continue to be disciples of Christ right to the end. But he has ordained the ministers of
the church to teach in his name.

309. M. *Is there no other means than the word by which God communicates
himself to us?*

C. To the preaching of his word he has conjoined the sacraments.

310. M. *What is a sacrament?*

C. An outward attestation of the grace of God which, by a visible sign, represents spiritual things to imprint the promises of God more firmly in our hearts,
and to make us more sure of them.

311. M. *What? Does a visible and natural sign have this power to assure the
conscience?*

C. No, not of itself, but in so far as it is ordained of God for this end.

312. M. *Seeing it is the proper office of the Holy Spirit to seal the promises of
God in our hearts, how do you attribute this to the sacraments?*

C. There is a great difference between the one and the other. The Spirit of
God in very truth is the only one who can touch and move our hearts, enlighten
our minds, and assure our consciences; so that all this ought to be judged as his
own work, that praise may be ascribed to him alone. Nevertheless, the Lord himself makes use of the sacraments as inferior instruments according as it seems good
to him, without in any way detracting from the power of his Spirit.

313. M. *You think, then, that the efficacy of the sacraments does not consist in
the outward element, but proceeds entirely from the Spirit of God?*

C. Yes; for the Lord is pleased to work by these instruments which he has
instituted: without detracting from his own power.

314. M. *And what moves God to do that?*

C. For the alleviation of our weakness. If we were spiritual by nature, like

---

a. Mt 10[.40]; Lk 10[.16]

the angels, we could behold God and his graces. But as we are bound up with our bodies, it is needful for us that God should make use of figures to represent to us spiritual and heavenly things, for otherwise we could not comprehend them. At the same time, it is expedient for us to have all our senses exercised in his holy promises, in order to confirm us in them.

315. M. *Since God has introduced the sacraments to meet our need, it would be arrogance and presumption to think that we could dispense with them.*

C. Certainly: hence he who voluntarily abstains from using them thinks that he has no need of them, condemns Jesus Christ, rejects his grace, and quenches his Holy Spirit.

316. M. *But what assurance of grace can the sacraments give, seeing that good and bad both receive them?*

C. Although the unbelievers and the wicked make of none effect the grace offered to them through the sacraments, yet it does not follow that the proper nature of the sacraments is also made of none effect.

317. M. *How, then, and when do the sacraments produce this effect?*

C. When we receive them in faith, seeking Jesus Christ alone and his grace in them.

318. M. *Why do you say that we must seek Jesus Christ in them?*

C. I mean that we are not to be taken up with the earthly sign so as to seek our salvation in it, nor are we to imagine that it has a peculiar power enclosed within it. On the contrary, we are to employ the sign as a help, to lead us directly to the Lord Jesus, that we may find in him our salvation and all our well-being.

319. M. *Seeing that faith is required, why do you say that they are given to confirm us in faith, to assure us of the promises of God?*

C. It is not sufficient for faith once to be generated in us. It must be nourished and sustained, that it may grow day by day and be increased within us. To nourish, strengthen, and increase it, God gives us the sacraments. This is what Paul indicates when he says that they are used to seal the promises of God in our hearts.

Rom 4[.11]

320. M. *But is it not a sign of unbelief when the promises of God are not firm enough for us, without support?*

C. It is a sign of the smallness and weakness of faith, and such is indeed the faith of the children of God, who do not, however, cease to be faithful, although their faith is still imperfect. As long as we live in this world some elements of unfaithfulness remain in our flesh, and therefore we must always advance and grow in faith.

321. M. *How many sacraments are there in the Christian church?*

C. There are only two sacraments common to all which the Lord Jesus has instituted for the whole company of the faithful.

322. M. *What are they?*

C. Baptism and the holy supper.

323. M. *What likeness and difference is there between them?*

C. Baptism is for us a kind of entrance into the church of God, for it testifies that instead of our being strangers to him, God receives us as members of his family. The supper testifies that God as a good Father carefully feeds and refreshes the members of his household.

324. M. *That the meaning may be more clear to us, let us treat of them separately. First, what is the meaning of baptism?*

C. It consists of two parts. The Lord represents to us in it, first, the forgiveness of our sins,[a] and secondly, our regeneration or spiritual renewal.[b]

325. M. *What resemblance has water with these things in order to represent them?*

C. The forgiveness of sins is a kind of washing, by which our souls are cleansed from their defilements, just as the stains of the body are washed away by water.

326. M. *What about the other part?*

C. The beginning of our regeneration and its end is our becoming new creatures, through the Spirit of God. Therefore the water is poured on the head as a sign of death, but in such a way that our resurrection is also represented, for instead of being drowned in water, what happens to us is only for a moment.

327. M. *You do not mean that the water is a washing of the soul.*

C. By no means, for that pertains to the blood of Jesus Christ alone, which was shed in order to wipe away all our stains and render us pure and unpolluted before God. This is fulfilled in us when our consciences are sprinkled by the Holy Spirit. But by the sacrament that is sealed to us. 1 Jn 1[.7]; 1 Pt 1[.19]

328. M. *Do you think that the water is only a figure for us?*

C. It is such a figure that the reality is conjoined with it, for God does not promise us anything in vain. Accordingly it is certain that in baptism the forgiveness of sins is offered to us and we receive it.

329. M. *Is this grace fulfilled indiscriminately in all?*

C. No, for some make it of no effect by their perversity. Nevertheless, the sacrament loses nothing of its nature, although none but believers feel its efficacy.

a. Eph 5[.26–27]

b. Rom 6[.4]

330. M. *From what does regeneration get its power?*

C. From the death and resurrection of Christ. His death has had this effect, that through it our old Adam is crucified, and our evil nature is, as it were, buried, so that it no longer has the strength to rule over us. And the renewal of our life, in obedience to the righteousness of God, derives from the resurrection of Christ.

331. M. *How is this grace applied to us in baptism?*

C. In it we are clothed with Jesus Christ, and receive his Spirit, provided that we do not make ourselves unworthy of the promises given to us in it.

332. M. *What is the proper use of baptism on our part?*

C. It consists in faith and in repentance. That is, assurance that we have our spiritual purity in Christ, and in feeling within us, and declaring to our neighbors by our works, that his Spirit dwells in us to mortify our natural desires and bring us to follow the will of God.

333. M. *If this is required, how is it that we baptize little infants?*

C. It is not said that faith and repentance should always precede the reception of the sacrament, but they are only required from those who are capable of them. It is sufficient, then, if infants produce and manifest the fruit of their baptism after they come to the age of discretion.

334. M. *Can you show that there is nothing inconsistent in this?*

C. Circumcision was also a sacrament of repentance, as Moses and the prophets declare;[a] and was a sacrament of faith, as St. Paul says.[b] And yet God has not excluded little children from it.

335. M. *But can you show that they are now admitted to baptism for the same reason as in the case of circumcision?*

C. Yes, for the promises which God anciently gave to his people of Israel are now extended to the whole world.

336. M. *But does it follow from this that we are to use the sign also?*

C. That becomes evident when everything is considered. Jesus Christ has not made us partakers of his grace, which formerly had been bestowed on the people of Israel, in order to diminish it in us, or make it more obscure, but rather to manifest it and to bestow it upon us in increased abundance.

337. M. *Do you reckon that if we denied baptism to little infants, the grace of God would then be diminished by the coming of Christ?*

C. Yes; for the sign of the bounty and mercy of God toward our children,

a. Dt 10[.16], 30[.6]; Jer 4[.4]
b. Rom 4[.11–12]

which they had in ancient times, would be wanting in our case, the very sign which
ministers so greatly to our consolation, and to confirm the promise already given
in the command.

338. M. *You mean then that since God in ancient times declared himself to be
the Savior of little infants, and wanted to have this promise sealed on their bodies by an
external sacrament, it is right that confirmation of it should not be less after the advent
of Christ, since the same promise remains and indeed is more clearly attested by the
word and ratified in action.*

C. Yes. And besides, since it is quite evident that the power and the substance of baptism pertain to little children, to deny them the sign, which is inferior
to the substance, would be to do them injury.

339. M. *On what conditions should we baptize little children?*

C. As a sign and testimony that they are heirs of God's blessing promised
to the seed of the faithful, that when they come of age they are to acknowledge the
truth of their baptism, in order to derive benefit from it.

340. M. *Let us speak of the supper. And, first, what is its signification?*

C. Our Lord instituted it to assure us that by the communication of his
body and blood, our souls are nourished, in the hope of eternal life.

341. M. *But why does the Lord represent his body by the bread and his blood
by the wine?*

C. To signify that as it is the particular virtue of bread to nourish our bodies,
to refresh and sustain us in this mortal life, so it pertains to his body to act toward
our souls, that is, in nourishing and quickening them spiritually. Likewise as wine
strengthens, refreshes, and rejoices a man physically, so his blood is our joy, our
refreshing and our spiritual strength.

342. M. *Do you mean that we must truly communicate in the body and blood
of the Lord?*

C. I understand so. But since the whole affiance of our salvation rests in
the obedience which he has rendered to God, his Father, in order that it may be
imputed to us as if it were ours, we must possess him: for his blessings are not ours,
unless he gives himself to us first.

343. M. *But did he not give himself to us when he exposed himself to death, to
reconcile us to God his Father, and deliver us from damnation?*

C. That is true; but it is not enough for us unless we receive him, in order
that we may feel in ourselves the fruit and the efficacy of his death and passion.

344. M. *Is not the way to receive him by faith?*

C. Yes. Not only in believing that he died and rose again, in order to deliver us from eternal death, and acquire life for us, but also that he dwells in us, and is conjoined with us in a union as the head with the members, that by virtue of this conjunction he may make us partakers of all his grace.

      345. M. *Does this communion take place apart from the supper alone?*

1 Cor 1[.9]

      C. Yes, indeed, we have it through the gospel, as St. Paul declares: in that the Lord Jesus Christ promises us in it, that we are flesh of his flesh and bone of

Eph 5[.30]

his bone, that he is that living bread which came down from heaven to nourish our souls,[a] and that we are one with him, as he is one with the Father.[b]

      346. M. *What is the blessing that we have in the sacrament, and what more does it minister to us?*

      C. This communion is more abundantly confirmed in us, ratified as it were, for although Jesus Christ is truly communicated to us both by baptism and by the gospel, nevertheless this is only in part, and not fully.

      347. M. *What then fully do we have through the sign of the bread?*

      C. That the body of the Lord Jesus which was once offered to reconcile us to God, is now given to us, to certify to us that we have part in this reconciliation.

      348. M. *What do we have in the sign of wine?*

      C. That the Lord Jesus, who once shed his blood in payment and satisfaction for our offenses, gives it to us to drink, that we may have no doubt at all of receiving its fruit.

      349. M. *According to your replies, the supper takes us back to the death and passion of Jesus Christ, that we may communicate in its virtue?*

      C. Yes, for then the unique and perpetual sacrifice was offered for our redemption. Therefore there remains for us nought but to enjoy it.

      350. M. *The supper, then, was not instituted in order to offer up the body of Jesus the Son to his Father?*

      C. No, for this office pertains to none but him alone, since he is the eternal Priest.[c] But he commands us only to receive his body, not to offer it.[d]

      351. M. *Why is there a double sign?*

      C. Our Lord has appointed it for the sake of our weakness, in order to teach us that he is not only food to our souls, but drink also, so that we may seek our nourishment wholly and entirely in him, and not elsewhere.

      352. M. *Should all men equally use the second sign, that is the chalice?*

a. Jn 6[.51]
b. Jn 17[.21]
c. Heb 5[.5]
d. Mt 26[.26]

C. Yes, this is according to the commandment of Jesus Christ, against which nothing is to be attempted.

353. *M. Do we have in the supper simply the testimony of the things already mentioned, or are they truly given to us in it?*

C. Seeing that Jesus Christ is the Truth, there can be no doubt that the promises which he made at the supper, are actually fulfilled in it, and that what he figures in it is made true. Thus in accordance with what he promises and represents in the sacrament, I do not doubt that he makes us partakers of his very substance, in order to unite us with himself in one life.

354. *M. But how can this be, when the body of Jesus Christ is in heaven, and we are pilgrims on this earth?*

C. By the incomprehensible power of his Spirit, who conjoins things separated by distance.

355. *M. You do not think, then, either that the body is enclosed in the bread, or the blood in the chalice?*

C. No. On the contrary, in order to have the reality of the sacraments, we must lift up our hearts on high to heaven, where Jesus Christ is in the glory of his Father, from whence we expect him in our redemption, and do not seek him in these corruptible elements.

356. *M. You understand, then, that there are two things in this sacrament, material bread and wine, which we see by the eye, handle by the hands, and perceive by the taste, and Jesus Christ by whom our souls are inwardly nourished?*

C. Yes, but in such a way that we have in it also a testimony and a kind of pledge for the resurrection of our bodies, in that they are made partakers in the sign of life.

357. *M. What is the right use of this sacrament?*

C. That which St. Paul declares, namely that a man examine himself before he approach to it.   1 Cor 11[.28]

358. *M. In what is he to examine himself?*

C. Whether he is a true member of Jesus Christ.

359. *M. By what sign can he know this?*

C. If he has a true faith and repentance, if he loves his neighbor in true charity, and is not tainted by hatred or rancor or discord.

360. *M. But is it necessary to have perfect faith and charity?*

C. Both should be entire and unfeigned, but to have such a perfection, from which nothing is wanting, will not be found among men. Moreover the supper would have been instituted in vain if no one could receive it unless he were entirely perfect.

361. M. *Imperfection, then, does not prevent us from approaching it.*

C. On the contrary, the supper would be of no use to us, if we were not imperfect. It is an aid and support for our weakness.

362. M. *Do these two sacraments not serve any other end?*

C. Yes, they do. They are also signs and marks of our profession. That is to say, by them we declare that we are of the people of God, and make confession of our Christianity.

363. M. *How ought we to judge a man who never wishes to use it?*

C. He could not be regarded as a Christian, for in so doing he refuses to confess himself as such, and tacitly, as it were, disavows Jesus Christ.

364. M. *Is it sufficient to receive each once?*

C. Baptism is only ordered to be received once, and may not lawfully be repeated. But this is not so with the supper.

365. M. *What is the reason for that?*

C. By baptism God introduces and receives us into his church. After he has received us, he signifies by the supper that he wishes continually to nourish us.

366. M. *To whom does it belong truly to baptize and administer the supper?*

C. To those who are publicly charged to teach in the church. For the preaching of the word and the distribution of the sacraments are things conjoined.

367. M. *Is there any certain proof for this?*

Mt 28[.19] C. Yes, indeed. Our Lord specially charged his apostles to baptize as well as to preach. In regard to the supper, he ordered all to follow his example. Moreover, he performed the office of a minister in order to give it to others.

368. M. *But ought pastors, who are appointed to dispense the sacraments, to admit without discretion all who present themselves there?*

C. In regard to baptism, as it is administered today only to infants, there is no need for discrimination; but in the supper the minister ought to take heed not to give it to a man whom he recognizes to be entirely unworthy.

369. M. *Why so?*

C. Because it would pollute and dishonor the sacrament.

370. M. *But our Lord admitted Judas to the supper, impious though he was?*

C. His iniquity was still hidden, and although our Lord knew it, yet it was not evident to all.

371. M. *What then is to be done with hypocrites?*

C. The minister cannot exclude them as unworthy, but must wait until God has revealed their iniquity.

372. M. *But what if he knows or has been warned that someone is unworthy?*

C. That would not be sufficient to exclude him, unless there were a legitimate investigation and decision of the church.

373. M. *Then there ought to be some order and polity regarding this.*

C. Yes, if the church is to be well ordered. Some persons must be appointed to watch out for the offenses that may be committed. And they, with the authority of the church, should refuse communion to those who are quite unfit, and to whom communion cannot be given without dishonoring God and scandalizing the faithful.

The Anglican Catechism, 1549/1662

First included in the prayer book of Edward VI in 1549 as part of the order of confirmation, *The Anglican Catechism* underwent various revisions during the reign of Elizabeth I and was finally codified in its present form in the 1662 *Book of Common Prayer*. Archbishop Thomas Cranmer is generally given credit for the composition of the prayer book of Edward VI, which became the official doctrine of the Church of England with the Uniformity Act of 1549. A 1552 revision introduced a more Calvinist theology, until it was revised again under Elizabeth in 1559. It was further revised after the Restoration and issued in the 1662 *Book of Common Prayer*. This 1662 version remains the authorized text.

In the 1662 edition, the catechism's use is defined in some detail:

> The curate of every parish shall diligently upon Sundays and holy days, after the second lesson of evening prayer, openly in the church instruct and examine so many children of his parish sent unto him, as he shall think convenient, in some part of this catechism.
>
> And all fathers, mothers, masters, and dames, shall cause their children, servants and prentices (which have not learnt their catechism), to come to the church at the time appointed, and obediently to hear, and be ordered by the curate, until such time as they have learnt all that is here appointed for them to learn.

Among the antecedents for the catechism are *The Institution of a Christian Man* (1537) and its 1543 revision by Cranmer and Henry VIII, *A Necessary Doctrine and Erudition for Any Christian Man* (also called *The King's Book*). Later contributors to the composition of the catechism as it evolved probably include Alexander Nowell (c. 1507–1602), dean of St. Paul's, John Overall (1560–1619), bishop of Norwich, and John Ponet (1516?–1556), bishop of Rochester. The brief work guides the catechumen through five topics: (1) the nature and duties of a Christian; (2) → *The Apostles' Creed;* (3) the ten commandments; (4) the Lord's Prayer; and (5) the sacraments (baptism and the eucharist).

The Church of England sponsored a revision of the catechism in 1958, which modernized the language and added material on the Bible, Christian duty, and the church. This *Revised Catechism* was not intended to supersede the original catechism, but has been recommended for use in the Church of England since 1973. Several churches of the Anglican communion throughout the world, including the Episcopal Church of the United States, the Anglican Church in Korea, and the Church of England in Australia have also revised and rewritten the catechism.

Edition: *Anglican Book of Common Prayer* (1662), as authorized by the Anglican Church. The nineteenth-century American revisions are given in footnotes, as recorded by Schaff. The current *Book of Common Prayer* (1979) of the Episcopal Church, however, includes a new catechism.

Literature: *DNB* 42:375–77; Lankshear and Francis 1991; Müller, xliii–xliv; *Prayer Book Dictionary* [1918], 157–63; Schaff, 1:654–57, 3:517–22; Selwyn 1964; Wright 1988.

The Anglican Catechism, 1549/1662

A catechism,
that is to say, an instruction to be learned of every person,
before he be brought to be confirmed by the bishop

Question. What is your name?
Answer. N. or M.

Question. Who gave you this name?
Answer. My godfathers and godmothers[1] in my baptism; wherein I was made a member of Christ, the child of God, and an inheritor of the kingdom of heaven.

Question. What did your godfathers and godmothers[2] then for you?
Answer. They did promise and vow three things in my name. First, that I should renounce the devil and all his works, the pomps and vanity of this wicked world, and all the sinful lusts of the flesh. Secondly, that I should believe all the articles of the Christian faith. And thirdly, that I should keep God's holy will and commandments, and walk in the same all the days of my life.

Question. Dost thou not think that thou are bound to believe, and to do, as they have promised for thee?
Answer. Yes, verily; and by God's help so I will. And I heartily thank our heavenly Father that he hath called me to this state of salvation, through Jesus Christ our Savior. And I pray unto God to give me his grace, that I may continue in the same unto my life's end.

Catechist. Rehearse the articles of thy belief.
Answer. I believe in God the Father Almighty, Maker of heaven and earth: And in Jesus Christ his only Son our Lord, who was conceived by the Holy Ghost, born of the Virgin Mary, suffered under Pontius Pilate, was crucified, dead, and buried, he descended into hell; the third day he rose again from the dead, he ascended into heaven, and sitteth at the right hand of God the Father Almighty; from thence he shall come to judge the quick and the dead. I believe in the Holy Ghost; the holy

1. American edition reads: "my sponsors."
2. American edition reads: "sponsors."

catholick church; the communion of saints; the forgiveness of sins; the resurrection
of the body; and the life everlasting. Amen.

Question. What dost thou chiefly learn in these articles of thy belief?
Answer. First, I learn to believe in God the Father, who hath made me, and all the
world. Secondly, in God the Son, who hath redeemed me, and all mankind. Thirdly,
in God the Holy Ghost, who sanctifieth me and all the elect[3] people of God.

*Question. You said, that your godfathers and godmothers[4] did promise for you, that
you should keep God's commandments. Tell me how many there be?*
Answer. Ten.

Question. Which be[5] they?
Answer. The same which God spake in the twentieth chapter of Exodus, saying, I
am the Lord thy God, who brought thee out of the land of Egypt, out of the house
of bondage.

    I. Thou shalt have none other gods but me.   [Ex 20.3]

    II. Thou shalt not make to thyself any graven image, nor the likeness of   [Ex 20.4–6]
any thing that is in heaven above, or in the earth beneath, or in the water under
the earth. Thou shalt not bow down to them, nor worship them: for I the Lord thy
God am a jealous God, and visit the sins of the fathers upon the children unto the
third and fourth generation of them that hate me, and shew mercy unto thousands
in them that love me, and keep my commandments.

    III. Thou shalt not take the name of the Lord thy God in vain: for the Lord   [Ex 20.7]
will not hold him guiltless that taketh his name in vain.

    IV. Remember that thou keep holy the Sabbath day. Six days shalt thou   [Ex 20.8–11]
labor, and do all that thou hast to do; but the seventh day is the Sabbath of the Lord
thy God. In it thou shalt do no manner of work, thou, and thy son, and thy daughter, thy manservant, and thy maidservant, thy cattle, and the stranger that is within
thy gates. For in six days the Lord made heaven and earth, the sea, and all that in
them is, and rested the seventh day: wherefore the Lord blessed the seventh day,
and hallowed it.

    V. Honor thy father and thy mother, that thy days may be long in the land   [Ex 20.12]
which the Lord thy God giveth thee.

3. American edition omits "elect."
4. American edition reads: "sponsors."
5. American edition reads: "are."

[Ex 20.13]   VI. Thou shalt do no murder.

[Ex 20.14]   VII. Thou shalt not commit adultery.

[Ex 20.15]   VIII. Thou shalt not steal.

[Ex 20.16]   IX. Thou shalt not bear false witness against thy neighbor.

[Ex 20.17]   X. Thou shalt not covet thy neighbor's house, thou shalt not covet thy neighbor's wife, nor his servant, nor his maid, nor his ox, nor his ass, nor any thing that is his.

Question. What dost thou chiefly learn by these commandments?
Answer. I learn two things: my duty towards God, and my duty towards my neighbor.

Question. What is thy duty towards God?
Answer. My duty towards God, is to believe in him, to fear him, and to love him with all my heart, with all my mind, with all my soul, and with all my strength; to worship him, to give him thanks, to put my whole trust in him, to call upon him, to honor his holy name and his word, and to serve him truly all the days of my life.

Question. What is thy duty towards thy neighbor?
Answer. My duty towards my neighbor, is to love him as myself, and to do to all men, as I would they should do unto me: To love, honor, and succor my father and mother: To honor and obey the king, and all that are put in authority under him:[6]
To submit myself to all my governors, teachers, spiritual pastors, and masters: To order myself lowly and reverently to all my betters: To hurt no body by word nor deed: To be true and just in all my dealing: To bear no malice nor hatred in my heart: To keep my hands from picking and stealing, and my tongue from evil-speaking, lying, and slandering: To keep my body in temperance, soberness, and chastity: Not to covet nor desire other men's goods; but to learn and labor truly to get mine own living, and to do my duty in that state of life, unto which it shall please God to call me.

Catechist. My good child,[7] know this, that thou art not able to do these things of thyself, nor to walk in the commandments of God, and to serve him, without his special grace; which thou must learn at all times to call for by diligent prayer. Let me hear therefore, if thou canst say the Lord's Prayer.

6. American edition reads: "the civil authority."
7. Changed from "son" in the 1552 edition.

Answer. Our Father, which[8] art in heaven, hallowed be thy name. Thy kingdom come. Thy will be done, in earth as it is in heaven. Give us this day our daily bread. And forgive us our trespasses, As we forgive them that[9] trespass against us. And lead us not into temptation; but deliver us from evil. Amen.[a]

Question. What desirest thou of God in this prayer?
Answer. I desire my Lord God our heavenly Father, who is the giver of all goodness, to send his grace unto me, and to all people: that we may worship him, serve him, and obey him, as we ought to do. And I pray unto God, that he will send us all things that be needful both for our souls and bodies; and that he will be merciful unto us, and forgive us our sins; and that it will please him to save and defend us in all dangers ghostly and bodily;[10] and that he will keep us from all sin and wickedness, and from our ghostly[11] enemy, and from everlasting death. And this I trust he will do of his mercy and goodness, through our Lord Jesus Christ. And therefore I say, Amen, So be it.

Question. How many sacraments hath Christ ordained in his church?
Answer. Two only, as generally necessary to salvation, that is to say, baptism, and the supper of the Lord.

Question. What meanest thou by this word sacrament?
Answer. I mean an outward and visible sign of an inward and spiritual grace given unto us, ordained by Christ himself, as a means whereby we receive the same, and a pledge to assure us thereof.

Question. How many parts are there in a sacrament?
Answer. Two: the outward visible sign, and the inward spiritual grace.

Question. What is the outward visible sign or form in baptism?
Answer. Water: wherein the person is baptized in the name of the Father, and of the Son, and of the Holy Ghost.

---

a. [Mt 6.9-13; Lk 11.1-4]

8. American edition reads: "who."
9. American edition reads: "those who."
10. American edition reads: "both of soul and body."
11. American edition reads: "spiritual."

Question. What is the inward and spiritual grace?

Answer. A death unto sin, and a new birth unto righteousness: for being by nature born in sin, and the children of wrath, we are hereby made the children of grace.

Question. What is required of persons to be baptized?

Answer. Repentance, whereby they forsake sin: and faith, whereby they steadfastly believe the promises of God made to them in that sacrament.

Question. Why then are infants baptized, when by reason of their tender age they cannot perform them?

Answer. Because they promise them both by their sureties: which promise, when they come to age, themselves are bound to perform.

Question. Why was the sacrament of the Lord's supper ordained?

Answer. For the continual remembrance of the sacrifice of the death of Christ and of the benefits which we receive thereby.

Question. What is the outward part or sign of the Lord's supper?

Answer. Bread and wine, which the Lord hath commanded to be received.

Question. What is the inward part, or thing signified?

Answer. The body and blood of Christ, which are verily and indeed taken and received by the faithful in the Lord's supper.

Question. What are the benefits whereof we are partakers thereby?

Answer. The strengthening and refreshing of our souls by the body and blood of Christ, as our bodies are by the bread and wine.

Question. What is required of them who come to the Lord's supper?

Answer. To examine themselves, whether they repent them truly of their former sins, steadfastly purposing to lead a new life; have a lively faith in God's mercy through Christ, with a thankful remembrance of his death; and be in charity with all men.

The curate[12] *of every parish shall diligently upon Sundays and holy days, after the second lesson at evening prayer,*[13] *openly in the church instruct and examine so many*

12. American edition replaces "Curate" with "Minister."

13. American edition omits "after the second Lesson at Evening Prayer" and reads: "or on some other convenient occasion."

children of his parish sent unto him, as he shall think convenient, in some part of this catechism.

And all fathers, mothers, masters, and dames,[14] shall cause their children, servants, and prentices (which have not learned their catechism), to come to the church at the time appointed, and obediently to hear, and be ordered by the curate, until such time as they have learned all that is here appointed for them to learn.

So soon as children are come to a competent age, and can say, in their mother tongue,[15] the Creed, the Lord's Prayer, and the Ten Commandments; and also can answer to the other questions of this short catechism; they shall be brought to the bishop. And every one shall have a godfather, or a godmother, as a witness of their confirmation.[16]

And whensoever the bishop shall give knowledge for children to be brought unto him for their confirmation, the curate of every parish shall either bring, or send in writing, with his hand subscribed thereunto, the names of all such persons within his parish, as he shall think fit to be presented to the bishop to be confirmed. And, if the bishop approve of them, he shall confirm them in manner following.[17]

14. American edition reads: "mistresses."
15. American edition omits: "in their mother tongue."
16. American edition omits final sentence.
17. American edition omits final sentence.

The French Confession, 1559/1571

The French Confession of Faith or *Confession de foi,* the first French Protestant confession of faith, was the joint effort of French and Swiss Protestants. Although *The French Confession* reflects the teachings of John Calvin (1509–64), its roots go back to a profession of faith that persecuted reformers in Paris addressed to King Henri II of France in 1557. Calvin, probably in collaboration with Théodore de Bèze (1519–1605) and Pierre Viret, expanded upon the eighteen articles of faith in the original French text, drawing up thirty-five articles. This document was presented to the First National Synod of Protestants in Paris in 1559 and adopted in a revised form. The revision expanded the number of articles to forty (thirty-five in the shorter recension) and is generally credited to Calvin's student Antoine de la Roche Chandieu (1534–91). The confession was presented in 1560 to Henri's heir, King François II, and in 1561 to King Charles IX of France, who had succeeded his brother, although it did little to improve relations between Protestants and Catholics. The text was again ratified, in the longer recension, by the Seventh National Synod held in La Rochelle in 1571. It is *The Confession of La Rochelle* that is given here.

Edition: Fatio 1986, 115–27 (preface from Schaff, 3:356–59).

Translation: Schaff, 3:356–82 (Emily O. Butler; modified to reflect Fatio edition; biblical citations are from Fatio).

Note: For other sixteenth-century editions and translations, see Jahr 1964, 94–99.

Literature: Fatio 1986, 111–14; Jahr 1964; Leonard 1959; Marcel 1952; Mehl 1959; Niesel, 66–75; Pannier 1936.

The French Confession, 1559/1571

Confession of Faith made in one accord by the French people, who desire to live according to the purity of the gospel of our Lord Jesus Christ.

To the King

Sire, we thank God that hitherto having had no access to Your Majesty to make known the rigor of the persecutions that we have suffered, and suffer daily, for wishing to live in the purity of the gospel and in peace with our own consciences, he now permits us to see that you wish to know the worthiness of our cause, as is shown by the last edict given at Amboise in the month of March of this present year, 1559, which it has pleased Your Majesty to cause to be published. This emboldens us to speak, which we have been prevented from doing hitherto through the injustice and violence of some of your officers, incited rather by hatred of us than by love of your service. And to the end, Sire, that we may fully inform Your Majesty of what concerns this cause, we humbly beseech that you will see and hear our Confession of Faith, which we present to you, hoping that it will prove a sufficient answer to the blame and opprobrium unjustly laid upon us by those who have always made a point of condemning us without having any knowledge of our cause. In the which, Sire, we can affirm that there is nothing contrary to the word of God, or to the homage which we owe to you.

For the articles of our faith, which are all declared at some length in our Confession, all come to this: that since God has sufficiently declared his will to us through his prophets and apostles, and even by the mouth of his Son, our Lord Jesus Christ, we owe such respect and reverence to the word of God as shall prevent us from adding to it any thing of our own, but shall make us conform entirely to the rules it prescribes. And inasmuch as the Roman Church, forsaking the use and customs of the primitive church, has introduced new commandments and a new form of worship of God, we esteem it but reasonable to prefer the commandments of God, who is himself truth, to the commandments of men, who by their nature are inclined to deceit and vanity. And whatever our enemies may say against us, we can declare this before God and men, that we suffer for no other reason than for maintaining our Lord Jesus Christ to be our only Savior and Redeemer, and his doctrine to be the only doctrine of life and salvation.

And this is the only reason, Sire, why the executioners' hands have been stained so often with the blood of your poor subjects, who, sparing not their lives to maintain this same Confession of Faith, have shown to all that they were moved by some other spirit than that of men, who naturally care more for their own peace and comfort than for the honor and glory of God.

And therefore, Sire, in accordance with your promises of goodness and mercy toward your poor subjects, we humbly beseech Your Majesty graciously to examine the cause for which, being threatened at all times with death or exile, we thus lose the power of rendering the humble service that we owe you. May it please Your Majesty, then, instead of the fire and sword which have been used hitherto, to have our Confession of Faith decided by the word of God: giving permission and security for this. And we hope that you yourself will be the judge of our innocence, knowing that there is in us no rebellion or heresy whatsoever, but that our only endeavor is to live in peace of conscience, serving God according to his commandments, and honoring Your Majesty by all obedience and submission.

And because we have great need, by the preaching of the word of God, to be kept in our duty to him, as well as to yourself, we humbly beg, Sire, that we may sometimes be permitted to gather together, to be exhorted to the fear of God by his word, as well as to be confirmed by the administration of the sacraments which the Lord Jesus Christ instituted in his church. And if it should please Your Majesty to give us a place where any one may see what passes in our assemblies, we shall thereby be absolved from the charge of the enormous crimes with which these same assemblies have been defamed. For nothing will be seen but what is decent and well-ordered, and nothing will be heard but the praise of God, exhortations to his service, and prayers for the preservation of Your Majesty and of your kingdom. And if it do not please you to grant us this favor, at least let it be permitted us to follow the established order in private among ourselves.

We beseech you most humbly, Sire, to believe that in listening to this supplication which is now presented to you, you listen to the cries and groans of an infinite number of your poor subjects, who implore of your mercy that you extinguish the fires which the cruelty of your judges has lighted in your kingdom. And that we may thus be permitted, in serving Your Majesty, to serve him who has raised you to your power and dignity.

And if it should not please you, Sire, to listen to our voice, may it please you to listen to that of the Son of God, who, having given you power over our property, our bodies, and even our lives, demands that the control and dominion of our souls and consciences, which he purchased with his own blood, be reserved to him.

We beseech him, Sire, that he may lead you always by his Spirit, increasing with your age, your greatness and power, giving you victory over all your enemies, and establishing forever, in all equity and justice, the throne of Your Majesty: before whom, may it please him that we find grace, and some fruit of this our present supplication, so that having exchanged our pains and afflictions for some peace and liberty, we may also change our tears and lamentations into a perpetual thanksgiving to God, and to Your Majesty for having done that which is most agreeable to him, most worthy of your goodness and mercy, and most necessary for the preservation of your most humble and obedient subjects and servants.

1. We believe and confess that there is but one God,[a] who is one sole and simple essence,[b] spiritual,[c] eternal,[d] invisible,[e] immutable,[f] infinite,[g] incomprehensible,[h] ineffable, omnipotent; who is all-wise,[i] all-good,[j] all-just,[k] and all-merciful.[l]

2. As such this God reveals himself to men; firstly, in his works, in their creation, as well as in their preservation and control. Secondly, and more clearly, in his word,[m] which was in the beginning revealed through oracles,[n] and which was afterward committed to writing in the books which we call the Holy Scriptures.[o]   [Rom 1.19–20]

3. These Holy Scriptures are comprised in the canonical books of the Old and New Testaments, as follows: the five books of Moses, namely: Genesis, Exodus, Leviticus, Numbers, Deuteronomy; then Joshua, Judges, Ruth, the first and second books of Samuel, the first and second books of the Kings, the first and second books of the Chronicles, otherwise called Paralipomenon, the first book of Ezra; then Nehemiah, the book of Esther, Job, the Psalms of David, the Proverbs or Maxims of Solomon; the book of Ecclesiastes, called the Preacher, the Song of Solomon; then the book of Isaiah, Jeremiah, Lamentations of Jeremiah, Ezekiel, Daniel, Hosea, Joel, Amos, Obadiah, Jonah, Micah, Nahum, Habakkuk, Zephaniah, Haggai, Zechariah, Malachi; then the Holy Gospel according to St. Matthew,

a. [Dt 4.35, 39; 1 Cor 8.4, 6]
b. [Gn 1.3; Ex 3.14]
c. [Jn 4.24; 2 Cor 3.17]
d. [Rom 1.20]
e. [1 Tm 1.17]
f. [Mal 3.6; Nm 23.19]
g. [Rom 11.33; Acts 7.48, 17.23]
h. [Jer 10.7, 10; Lk 1.37]
i. [Rom 16.27]
j. [Mt 19.17]
k. [Jer 12.1; Ps 119.137]
l. [Ex 34.6–7]
m. [Rom 15.4; Jn 5.39; Heb 1.1]
n. [Gn 15.1, 3.15, 18.1]
o. [Ex 24.3–4; Rom 1.2]

according to St. Mark, according to St. Luke, and according to St. John; then the second book of St. Luke, otherwise called the Acts of the Apostles; then the Epistles of St. Paul: one to the Romans, two to the Corinthians, one to the Galatians, one to the Ephesians, one to the Philippians, one to the Colossians, two to the Thessalonians, two to Timothy, one to Titus, one to Philemon; then the Epistle to the Hebrews, the Epistle of St. James, the first and second Epistles of St. Peter, the first, second, and third Epistles of St. John, the Epistle of St. Jude; and then the Apocalypse, or Revelation of St. John.

[Ps 12.7, 19.8–9]   4. We know these books to be canonical, and the sure rule of our faith, not so much by the common accord and consent of the church, as by the testimony and inward illumination of the Holy Spirit, which enables us to distinguish them from other ecclesiastical books upon which, however useful, we can not base any articles of faith.

5. We believe that the word contained in these books has proceeded from God,[a] and receives its authority from him alone, and not from men.[b] And inasmuch as it is the rule of all truth, containing all that is necessary for the service of God and for our salvation,[c] it is not lawful for men, nor even for angels, to add to it, to take away from it, or to change it.[d] Whence it follows that no authority, whether of antiquity, or custom, or numbers, or human wisdom, or judgments, or proclamations, or edicts, or decrees, or councils, or visions, or miracles, should be opposed to these Holy Scriptures,[e] but, on the contrary, all things should be examined, regulated, and

[1 Cor 11.2, 23]   reformed according to them. And therefore we confess the three creeds, to wit: the Apostles', the Nicene, and the Athanasian, because they are in accordance with the word of God.

6. These Holy Scriptures teach us that in this one sole and simple divine essence, whom we have confessed, there are three persons: the Father, the Son, and the Holy Spirit.[f] The Father, first cause, principle, and origin of all things. The Son, his word and eternal wisdom. The Holy Spirit, his virtue, power, and efficacy. The Son begotten from eternity by the Father, the Holy Spirit proceeding eternally from them both; the three persons not confused, but distinct, and yet not separate, but of the same essence, equal in eternity and power.[g] And in this we confess that which has

a. [2 Tm 3.16–17; 1 Pt 1.11–12; 2 Pt 1.20–21]
b. [Jn 3.26–31; Jn 5.33–34; 1 Tm 1.15]
c. [Jn 15.15, 20.31; Acts 20.27]
d. [Dt 4.2, 12.32; Gal 1.8; Pr 30.6; Acts 22.18–19]
e. [Mt 15.9; Acts 5.28–29]
f. [Dt 4.12, 10.17; Mt 28.19; 1 Jn 5.7]
g. [Mt 28.19; Jn 1.1, 17.5; Acts 17.25; Rom 1.7; 1 Jn 5.7]

been established by the ancient councils, and we detest all sects and heresies which were rejected by the holy doctors, such as St. Hilary, St. Athanasius, St. Ambrose, and St. Cyril.

7. We believe that God, in three coworking persons, by his power, wisdom, and incomprehensible goodness, created all things, not only the heavens and the earth and all that is contained in them, but also invisible spirits,[a] some of whom have fallen away and gone into perdition, while others have continued in obedi- ence. That the first, being corrupted by evil, are enemies of all good, consequently of the whole church. The second, having been preserved by the grace of God, are ministers to glorify God's name, and to promote the salvation of his elect.[b]

    [2 Pt 2.4; Jude 6]

    [Ps 103.20–21]

    [Jn 8.44]

8. We believe that he not only created all things, but that he governs and directs them, disposing and ordaining by his sovereign will all that happens in the world;[c] not that he is the author of evil, or that the guilt of it can be imputed to him,[d] seeing that his will is the sovereign and infallible rule of uprightness and justice; but he has wonderful means of so making use of devils and sinners that he can turn to good the evil which they do, and of which they are guilty.[e] And thus, confessing that nothing takes place without the providence of God, we humbly bow before the secrets which are hidden to us, without questioning what is above our understand- ing;[f] but rather making use of what is revealed to us in Holy Scripture for our peace and safety, inasmuch as God, who has all things in subjection to him, watches over us with a Father's care, so that not a hair of our heads shall fall without his will.[g] And yet he restrains the devils and all our enemies, so that they can not harm us without his leave.[h]

    [Jb 1.22]

9. We believe that man was created pure and perfect in the image of God,[i] and that by his own guilt he fell from the grace which he received,[j] and is thus alien- ated from God, the fountain of justice and of all good, so that his nature is totally corrupt. And being blinded in mind, and depraved in heart, he has lost all integ- rity, and there is no good in him. And although he can still discern good and evil,[k]

    [Gn 6.5, 8.21]

a. [Gn 1.1, 3.1; Jn 1.3; Col 1.16; Heb 1.2]

b. [Heb 1.7–14; Ps 34.8, 91.11]

c. [Ps 104, 119.89–96, 147; Pr 16.4; Mt 10.29; Acts 2.23, 4.28, 17.24, 26, 28; Rom 9.11; Eph 1.11]

d. [Ps 5.5; Hos 13.9; 1 Jn 2.16, 3.8]

e. [Acts 2.23–24, 4.27–28]

f. [Rom 9.19–20, 11.33]

g. [Mt 10.30; Lk 21.18]

h. [Gn 3.15; Jb 1.12, 2.6; Mt 8.31; Jn 19.11]

i. [Gn 1.26; Ecc 7.29; Eph 4.24]

j. [Gn 3.17; Rom 5.12; Eph 2.2–3]

k. [Rom 1.20–21, 2.18–20]

we say, notwithstanding, that the light he has becomes darkness when he seeks for God, so that he can in nowise approach him by his intelligence and reason.[a] And although he has a will that incites him to do this or that, yet it is altogether captive to sin,[b] so that he has no other liberty to do right than that which God gives him.[c]

10. We believe that all the posterity of Adam is in bondage to original sin, which is an hereditary evil,[d] and not an imitation merely, as was declared by the Pelagians, whom we detest in their errors. And we consider that it is not necessary to inquire how sin was conveyed from one man to another, for what God had given Adam was not for him alone, but for all his posterity; and this in his person we have been deprived of all good things, and have fallen with him into a state of sin and misery.

11. We believe, also, that this evil is truly sin, sufficient for the condemnation of the whole human race, even of little children in the mother's womb, and that God considers it as such;[e] even after baptism it is still of the nature of sin, but the condemnation of it is abolished for the children God, out of his mere free grace and love. And further, that it is a perversity always producing fruits of malice and of [Rom 7.5] rebellion, so that the most holy men, although they resist it, are still stained with many weaknesses and imperfections while they are in this life.[f]

12. We believe that from this corruption and general condemnation in which all men are plunged, God, according to his eternal and immutable counsel, calls those whom he has chosen by his goodness and mercy alone in our Lord Jesus Christ, without consideration of their works,[g] to display in them the riches of his mercy;[h] leaving the rest in this same corruption and condemnation to show in them his justice.[i] For the ones are no better than the others, until God discerns them according to his immutable purpose which he has determined in Jesus Christ before [Eph 1.4; 2 Tm 1.9] the creation of the world. Neither can any man gain such a reward by his own virtue, as by nature we can not have a single good feeling, affection, or thought, except God has first put it into our hearts.[j]

a. [Rom 1.21; 1 Cor 2.14]
b. [Rom 6.16–17, 8.6–7]
c. [Jer 10.23; Jn 1.12, 3.6, 8.36, 15.5; Rom 7.18; 1 Cor 4.7; 2 Cor 3.5; Phil 2.13]
d. [Gn 6.5, 8.21; Jb 14.4; Ps 51.7; Mt 15.19; Rom 5.12–18]
e. [Ps 51.7; Rom 3.9–12, 23, 5.12; Eph 2.3]
f. [Rom 7.14–19; 2 Cor 12.7]
g. [Jer 1.5; Rom 3.28, 8.28–30, 9; Eph 1.4–5; 2 Tm 1.9; Ti 3.5]
h. [Eph 1.7; Rom 3.22–23, 9.23]
i. [Eph 1.7; Rom 3.22–23, 9.23]
j. [Jer 10.23; Rom 9.16; Eph 1.4–5; 2 Tm 1.9; Phil 2.13; Ti 3.3]

13. We believe that all that is necessary for our salvation was offered and communicated to us in Jesus Christ. He is given to us for our salvation, and "is made unto us wisdom, and righteousness, and sanctification, and redemption:[a] so that if we refuse him, we renounce the mercy of the Father, in which alone we can find a refuge.

[Jn 3.18; 1 Jn 2.23]

14. We believe that Jesus Christ, being the wisdom of God and his eternal Son, has put on our flesh, so as to be God and man in one person; indeed man, like unto us,[b] capable of suffering in body and soul, yet free from all stain of sin.[c] And as to his humanity, he was the true seed of Abraham and of David, although he was conceived by the secret power of the Holy Spirit.[d] In this we detest all the heresies that have of old troubled the church, and especially the diabolical conceits of Servetus, which attribute a fantastical divinity to the Lord Jesus, calling him the idea and pattern of all things, and the personal or figurative Son of God, and, finally, attribute to him a body of three uncreated elements, thus confusing and destroying the two natures.

[Jn 1.14; Phil 2.6–7]

[2 Cor 5.21]

15. We believe that in one person, that is Jesus Christ, the two natures are actually and inseparably joined and united, and yet each remains in its proper character: so that in this union the divine nature, retaining its attributes, remained uncreated, infinite, and all-pervading; and the human nature remained finite, having its form, measure, and attributes;[e] and although Jesus Christ, in rising from the dead, bestowed immortality upon his body, yet he did not take from it the truth of its nature,[f] and we so consider him in his divinity that we do not despoil him of his humanity.

16. We believe that God, in sending his Son, intended to show his love and inestimable goodness towards us, giving him up to die to accomplish all righteousness, and raising him from the dead to secure for us the heavenly life.[g]

17. We believe that by the perfect sacrifice that the Lord Jesus offered on the cross, we are reconciled to God, and justified before him;[h] for we can not be acceptable to him, nor become partakers of the grace of adoption, except as he pardons (all) our sins, and blots them out. Thus we declare that through Jesus Christ

[1 Pt 2.24–25]

a. [1 Cor 1.30; Eph 1.7; Col 1.13–14; 1 Tm 1.15; Ti 2.14]
b. [Heb 2.17]
c. [2 Cor 5.21]
d. [Lk 1.28, 31, 35, 2.11; Mt 1.18]
e. [Mt 1.20–21; Lk 1.31, 32, 35, 42, 43; Jn 1.14; Rom 9.5; 1 Tm 2.5, 3.16; Heb 5.8]
f. [Lk 24.38–39; Rom 1.4; Phil 2.6–11, 3.21]
g. [Jn 3.16, 15.13; 1 Jn 4.9; Rom 4.25; 1 Tm 1.14–15]
h. [2 Cor 5.19; Eph 5.2; Heb 5.7–9, 9.14, 10.10, 12, 14; 1 Tm 1.15]

[Eph 5.26; Ti 3.5] we are cleansed and made perfect; by his death we are fully justified, and through him only can we be delivered from our iniquities and transgressions.[a]

18. We believe that all our justification rests upon the remission of our sins, in which also is our only blessedness, as the Psalmist says.[b] We therefore reject all [Rom 3.19] other means of justification before God, and without claiming any virtue or merit, we rest simply in the obedience of Jesus Christ, which is imputed to us as much to blot out all our sins as to make us find grace and favor in the sight of God.[c] And, in fact, we believe that in falling away from this foundation, however slightly, we [Acts 4.12] could not find rest elsewhere, but should always be troubled. Forasmuch as we are never at peace with God till we resolve to be loved in Jesus Christ, for of ourselves we are worthy of hatred.

19. We believe that by this means we have the liberty and privilege of calling upon God, in full confidence that he will show himself a Father to us.[d] For we would have no access to the Father if we were not recommended by this Mediator. And to be heard in his name, it is fitting that our life takes after his as our leader.[e]

20. We believe that we are made partakers of this justification by faith alone, as it is written: "He suffered for our salvation, that whosoever believes on [Jn 3.16] him should not perish." And this is done inasmuch as we appropriate to our use the promises of life which are given to us through him, and feel their effect when we accept them, being assured that we are established by the word of God and shall not be deceived. Thus our justification through faith depends upon the free promises by which God declares and testifies his love to us.[f]

21. We believe that we are enlightened in faith by the secret power of the Holy Spirit,[g] that it is a gratuitous and special gift which God grants to whom he will,[h] so that the elect have no cause to glory,[i] but are bound to be doubly thankful that they have been preferred to others. We believe also that faith is not given to the elect only to introduce them into the right way, but also to make them con-

a. [Heb 9.14; 1 Pt 1.18–19; 1 Jn 1.7; Rom 3.26]
b. [Ps 32.1–2; Rom 4.7–8]
c. [Rom 5.19; 1 Tm 2.5; 1 Jn 2.1–2; Rom 1.16]
d. [Rom 5.1, 8.15; Gal 4.6; Eph 3.12]
e. [Jn 15.16; Rom 5.2; Eph 2.13–15; 1 Tm 2.5; Heb 4.14]
f. [Rom 3.24, 25, 27, 28, 30, 1.16–17, 4.3, 9.30–32, 11.6; Gal 2.16, 21, 3.9, 10, 18, 24, 5.4; Phil 3.9; 2 Tm 1.9; Ti 3.5–6; Heb 11.7; Acts 10.43; Jn 17.23–26]
g. [Eph 1.17–18; 1 Thes 1.5; 2 Pt 1.3–4]
h. [Rom 9.16, 18, 24, 25; 1 Cor 4.7]
i. [Eph 2.8]

tinue in it to the end.[a] For as it is God who has begun the work, he will also perfect it.[b]

22. We believe that by this faith we are regenerated in newness of life, being
by nature subject to sin.[c] Now we receive by faith grace to live in a holy way and in
the fear of God, in accepting the promise which is given to us by the gospel, namely:
that God will give us his Holy Spirit. This faith not only does not hinder us from
holy living, or turn us from the love of righteousness, but of necessity begets in us [Jas 2.17, 26]
all good works.[d] Moreover, although God works in us for our salvation, and renews our hearts, determining us to that which is good, yet we confess that the good [Dt 30.6; Jn 3.5]
works which we do proceed from his Spirit, and can not be accounted to us for justification, neither do they entitle us to adoption as children,[e] for we should always
be doubting and restless in our hearts, if we did not rest upon the atonement by
which Jesus Christ hath acquitted us. [Rom 5.1–2]

23. We believe that the ordinances of the law come to an end at the advent
of Jesus Christ;[f] but, although the ceremonies are no more in use, yet their substance
and truth remain in the person of him in whom they are fulfilled.[g] And, moreover,
we must seek aid from the law and the prophets for the ruling of our lives, as well
as for our confirmation in the promises of the gospel.[h]

24. We believe, as Jesus Christ is our only advocate,[i] and as he commands
us to ask of the Father in his name, and as it is not lawful for us to pray except in [Jn 16.23–24]
accordance with the model God has taught us by his word,[j] that all imaginations of
men concerning the intercession of dead saints are an abuse and a device of Satan to
lead men from the right way of worship.[k] We reject, also, all other means by which
men hope to redeem themselves before God, as derogating from the sacrifice and
passion of Jesus Christ.

Finally, we consider purgatory as an illusion proceeding from the same
shop, from which have sprung monastic vows, pilgrimages, the prohibition of marriage, and of eating meat, the ceremonial observance of days, auricular confession,

a. [1 Cor 1.8–9]
b. [Phil 1.6, 2.13]
c. [Ti 3.5; 1 Pt 1.3; Rom 6.17–20; Col 2.13, 3.10]
d. [Gal 5.6, 22; 1 Jn 2.3–4; 2 Pt 1.5–8]
e. [Lk 17.10; Ps 6.2; Rom 3.19–20, 4.3–5]
f. [Rom 10.4; Gal 3, 4; Col 2.17; Jn 1.17]
g. [Gal 4.3, 9; 2 Pt 1.19; Lk 1.70; Jas 5.10]
h. [2 Tm 3.16; 2 Pt 3.2]
i. [1 Jn 2.1–2; 1 Tm 2.5; Acts 4.12]
j. [Mt 6.9ff; Lk 11.2ff.]
k. [Acts 10.25–26, 14.15, 19.10, 22.8–9]

indulgences, and all such things by which they hope to merit forgiveness and salvation.ᵃ These things we reject, not only for the false idea of merit which is attached to them, but also because they are human inventions imposing a yoke upon the conscience.

25. Now because we enjoy Jesus Christ only through the gospel,ᵇ we believe that the order of the church, established by his authority, ought to be sacred and inviolable,ᶜ and that, therefore, the church can not exist without pastors for instruction, whom we should respect and reverently listen to, when they are properly called and exercise their office faithfully.ᵈ Not that God is bound to such aid and subordinate means, but because it pleases him to govern us by such restraints. In this we detest all visionaries who would like, so far as lies in their power, to destroy the ministry and preaching of the word and sacraments.

26. We believe that no one ought to seclude himself and be contented to be alone; but that all jointly should keep and maintain the union of the church, and submit to the public teaching, and to the yoke of Jesus Christ,ᵉ wherever God shall have established a true order of the church even if the magistrates and their edicts are contrary to it. For if they do not take part in it, or if they separate themselves from it, they do contrary to the word of God.ᶠ

27. Nevertheless we believe that it is important to discern with care and prudence which is the true church, for this title has been much abused.ᵍ We say, then, according to the word of God, that it is the company of the faithful who agree to follow his word, and the pure religion which it teaches; who thrive in it all their lives, growing and becoming more confirmed in the fear of God depending on their need to commit and press onward.ʰ Even though they strive continually, they can [Rom 3] have no hope save in the remission of their sins. Nevertheless we do not deny that among the faithful there may be hypocrites and reprobates, but their wickedness can not destroy the title of the church.ⁱ

28. In this belief we declare that, properly speaking, there can be no church where the word of God is not received, nor profession made of subjection to it, nor

a. [Mt 15.11, 6.16–18; Acts 10.14–15; Rom 14.2; Gal 4.9–10; Col 2.18–23; 1 Tm 4.2–5]
b. [Mt 10.27; Rom 1.16–17, 10.17]
c. [Mt 18.20; Eph 1.22–23]
d. [Mt 10.40; Jn 13.20; Lk 10.16; Rom 10.14–15; Eph 4.11–12]
e. [Ps 5.8, 22.23, 42.5; Eph 4.12; Heb 2.12]
f. [Acts 4.17, 19, 20; Heb 10.25]
g. [Jer 7.4, 8, 11, 12; Mt 3.8–10, 7.22, 24; 1 Cor 3.10–11; Mi 2.10–12]
h. [Eph 2.19–20, 4.11–12; 1 Tm 3.15; Dt 31.12]
i. [Mt 13; 2 Tm 2.18–20]

use of the sacraments. Therefore we condemn the papal assemblies, as the pure word of God is banished from them, their sacraments are corrupted, debased, falsified, or destroyed, and all superstitions and idolatries are in them. We hold, then, that all who take part in these acts, and commune in that church, separate and cut themselves off from the body of Christ.[a] Nevertheless, as some trace of the church is left in the papacy, and the virtue and substance of baptism remain, and as the efficacy of baptism does not depend upon the person who administers it,[b] we confess that those baptized in it do not need a second baptism. But, on account of its corruptions, we can not present children to be baptized in it without incurring pollution.

29. As to the true church, we believe that it should be governed according to the order established by our Lord Jesus Christ.[c] That there should be pastors, overseers, and deacons, so that true doctrine may have its course, that errors may be corrected and suppressed, and the poor and all who are in affliction may be helped in their necessities; and that assemblies may be held in the name of God, so that great and small may be edified.

30. We believe that all true pastors, wherever they may be, have the same authority and equal power under one head, only one sovereign and universal bishop, Jesus Christ;[d] and that consequently no church shall claim any authority or dominion over any other.

31. We believe that no person should undertake to govern the church upon his own authority, but that this should be derived from election,[e] as much as it is possible, and as God will permit. And we make this exception especially, because sometimes, and even in our own days, when the state of the church has been interrupted, it has been necessary for God to raise men in an extraordinary manner to restore the church which was in ruin and desolation. But, notwithstanding, we believe that this rule must always be binding: that all pastors, overseers, and deacons should have evidence of being called to their office.[f]

32. We believe, also, that it is desirable and useful that those elected to be superintendents devise among themselves what means should be adopted for the government of the whole body,[g] and yet that they should never depart from that

a. [Mt 10.14–15; Jn 10; 1 Cor 3.10–13; Eph 2.19–21]
b. [Mt 3.11, 28.19; Mk 1.8; Acts 1.5, 11.15–17, 19.4–5; 1 Cor 1.13]
c. [Acts 6.34; Eph 4.11; 1 Tm 3.1–13; Ti 1.5–9; 1 Cor 12]
d. [Mt 20.20–28; 1 Cor 3.4–9, 4.1; Eph 1.22; Col 1.18–19]
e. [Mt 28.19; Mk 16.15; Jn 15.16; Acts 1.21, 6.1–3; Rom 10.15; Ti 1.5]
f. [Gal 1.15; 2 Tm 3.7–10, 15]
g. [Acts 15.6–7, 25, 28; Rom 12.6–8]

which was ordained by our Lord Jesus Christ.[a] Which does not prevent there being some special ordinances in each place, as convenience may require.

33. However, we reject all human inventions, and all laws which men may introduce under the pretense of serving God, by which they wish to bind consciences;[b] and we receive only that which conduces to concord and holds all in obedience, from the greatest to the least. In this we must follow that which the Lord Jesus Christ declared as to excommunication, which we approve and confess to be necessary with all its antecedents and consequences.[c]

34. We believe that the sacraments are added to the word for more ample confirmation, that they may be to us pledges and seals of the grace of God, and by this means aid and comfort our faith, because of the infirmity which is in us,[d] and that they are outward signs through which God operates by his Spirit, so that he may not signify any thing to us in vain.[e] Yet we hold that their substance and truth is in Jesus Christ, and that of themselves they are only smoke and shadow.

35. We confess only two sacraments common to the whole church, of which the first, baptism, is given as a pledge of our adoption; for by it we are grafted into the body of Christ, so as to be washed and cleansed by his blood, and then renewed in purity of life by his Holy Spirit.[f] We hold, also, that although we are baptized only once, yet the gain that it symbolizes to us reaches over our whole lives and to our death, so that we have a lasting witness that Jesus Christ will always be our

[Rom 4, 6.22–23] justification and sanctification. Nevertheless, although it is a sacrament of faith and penitence,[g] yet as God receives little children into the church with their fathers,[h] we say, upon the authority of Jesus Christ, that the children of believing parents should be baptized.

36. We confess that the Lord's supper, which is the second sacrament, is a witness of the union which we have with Christ,[i] inasmuch as he not only died and rose again for us once, but also feeds and nourishes us truly with his flesh and blood, so that we may be one in him, and that our life may be in common.[j] Although

---

a. [1 Cor 14.40; 1 Pt 5.1–3]

b. [Rom 16.17–18; 1 Cor 3.11; Gal 5.1; Col 2.8]

c. [Mt 18.17; 1 Cor 5.45; 1 Tm 1.20]

d. [Ex 12; Mt 26.26–27; Rom 4.11; 1 Cor 11.23–24]

e. [Acts 22.16; Gal 3.27; Eph 5.26]

f. [Rom 6.3–4; Acts 22.16; Ti 3.5; Eph 5.26]

g. [Mt 3.11; Mk 1.4, 16.16; Lk 3.3; Acts 13.24, 19.4]

h. [Mt 19.14; 1 Cor 7.14]

i. [1 Cor 10.16–17, 11.24]

j. [Jn 6.55–57, 17.21; Rom 8.32]

he remains in heaven until he will come to judge all the earth,[a] still we believe that by the secret and incomprehensible power of his Spirit he feeds and strengthens us with the substance of his body and of his blood.[b] We hold that this is done spiritually, not because we put imagination and fancy in the place of fact and truth, but because the greatness of this mystery exceeds the measure of our senses and the laws of nature. In short, because it is heavenly, it can only be apprehended by faith.

37. We believe, as has been said, that in the Lord's supper, as well as in baptism, God gives us really and in fact that which he there sets forth to us; and that consequently with these signs is given the true possession and enjoyment of that which they present to us. And thus all who bring a pure faith, like a vessel, to the sacred table of Christ, receive truly that of which it is a sign; for the body and the blood of Jesus Christ give food and drink to the soul, no less than bread and wine nourish the body.[c]

38. Thus we hold that water, being a feeble element, still testifies to us in truth the inward cleansing of our souls in the blood of Jesus Christ by the efficacy of his Spirit,[d] and that the bread and wine given to us in the sacrament serve to our spiritual nourishment, inasmuch as they show, as to our sight, that the body of Christ is our meat, and his blood our drink.[e] And we reject the enthusiasts and sacramentarians, who will not receive such signs and marks, although our Savior said: "This is my body, and this cup is my blood."[f]

39. We believe that God wishes to have the world governed by laws and magistrates, so that some restraint may be put upon its disordered appetites.[g] And as he has established kingdoms, republics, and all sorts of principalities, either hereditary or otherwise, and all that belongs to a just government, and wishes to be considered as their author, so he has put the sword into the hands of magistrates to suppress crimes against the first as well as against the second table of the commandments of God. We must therefore, on his account, not only submit to them as superiors, but honor and hold them in all reverence as his lieutenants and officers, whom he has commissioned to exercise a legitimate and holy authority.[h]

a. [Mk 16.19; Acts 1.2–11, 3.21]
b. [1 Cor 10.16; Jn 6.35]
c. [Mt 26.26–29; Jn 6.51, 56; 1 Cor 11.23–26]
d. [Rom 6.3–4; 1 Cor 6.11; Eph 5.26]
e. [Jn 6.51; 1 Cor 11.24]
f. [Mt 26.26; 1 Cor 11.24–25]
g. [Ex 18.20–21; Mt 17.24–27; Rom 13.1–7]
h. [1 Pt 2.13–14; 1 Tm 2.2]

40. We hold, then, that we must obey their laws and statutes, pay customs, taxes, and other dues, and bear the yoke of subjection with a good and free will, even if they are unbelievers, provided that the sovereign empire of God remain intact.[a] Therefore we detest all those who would like to reject authority, to establish community and confusion of property, and overthrow the order of justice.

a. [Mt 17.24; Acts 4.17-19]

The Scots Confession, 1560

It is an indication of the turbulence and shifting fortunes of the Reformation that the first confession of faith of the Reformed Church of Scotland was adopted by that country's parliament in the same year that saw the first edition of the Geneva Bible. The Bible was the product of English and Scottish exiles in Switzerland who had fled Mary Tudor's England. After Queen Mary's death (1558), however, John Knox (c. 1513–72) and other Protestants who had been living abroad began returning to Scotland. In 1560 the Scottish Parliament commissioned Knox and five other ministers to compose a profession of the reformed faith.[1] In only four days, according to Knox, the document was prepared and accepted by Parliament with almost no objections.[2]

The twenty-five articles of *The Scots Confession* draw upon the theology of John Calvin, influenced by his *Institutes*, and → *The French Confession*, as well as such Reformed confessions as → *The First Helvetic Confession*, and Lutheran thought, especially as expressed in → *The Augsburg Confession*.[3] Among the principles of belief are a Nicene view of the Trinity, justification by faith alone, the supreme authority of Scripture, a Calvinist understanding of the Lord's supper, the acceptance of baptism and the eucharist as sacraments, the concept of the elect, the central role of the congregation, and the understanding of good works as being instigated by faith. In the doctrine of civil authority, one senses some concern about the shifting religious landscape in England and the Catholic queen of Scotland, Mary Stuart (who would return to Scotland in 1561). Although article 24 states that rulers are ordained by God to govern and to "maintain true religion," article 14 counts the repression of tyranny among good works.

The Scots Confession was adopted on 17 August 1560 and printed in three

1. The others were John Winram, John Spottiswood, John Douglas, John Row, and John Willock. See *OER* 4:33–34 (Kirk).
2. Knox records that only three lords dissented and the bishops said nothing. The record shows that the number was probably closer to nine, with five lords, three bishops, and one commendator either abstaining or disagreeing out of the body of 191 members. See Hazlett 1987, 289–90. For Knox's account, see his *History of the Reformation*, Dickinson ed., 1949, 1:338–42.
3. Other sources commonly cited are *The Confession of Faith Used in the English Congregation in Geneva* (1556), → *The First Confession of Basel*, → *The Geneva Catechism*, and *The Forty-Two Articles* of the Church of England (1553).

editions in 1561, but it was not ratified until after Mary Stuart abdicated in 1567. The Parliament of her infant son, James VI, authorized it "as a doctrin grounded upon the infallable wourd of God."[4]

Edition: Henderson 1960, 31–53.

Translation: Henderson 1960 (by James Bulloch), 59–80.

Literature: Cowan 1982, 89–130; Donaldson 1960, 29–75; Hazlett 1987; Henderson 1960; Knox 1949, 1:338–42; Niesel, 79–83; *OER* 4:33–36 (Kirk).

4. From the title page of the first edition (Edinburgh: Robert Lekprewik, 1561).

The Scots Confession, 1560

The Confession of the Faith and Doctrine Believed and Professed by the Protestants of Scotland, Exhibited to the Estates of Scotland in Parliament in August 1560 and Approved by Their Public Vote as Doctrine Founded upon the Infallible Word of God, And Afterwards Established and Publicly Confirmed by Various Acts of Parliaments, and of Lawful General Assemblies.

The Preface

The Estates of Scotland, with the inhabitants of Scotland who profess the holy evangel of Jesus Christ, to their fellow countrymen and to all other nations who confess the Lord Jesus with them, wish grace, mercy, and peace from God the Father of our Lord Jesus Christ, with the Spirit of righteous judgment, for salvation.

Long have we thirsted, dear brethren, to have made known to the world the doctrine which we profess and for which we have suffered abuse and danger; but such has been the rage of Satan against us, and against the eternal truth of Christ now recently reborn among us, that until this day we have had neither time nor opportunity to set forth our faith, as gladly we would have done. For how we have been afflicted until now the greater part of Europe, we suppose, knows well.

But since by the infinite goodness of God (who never suffers his afflicted to be utterly confounded) we have received unexpected rest and liberty, we could not do other than set forth this brief and plain confession of that doctrine which is set before us, and which we believe and confess; partly to satisfy our brethren whose hearts, we suspect, have been and are grieved by the slanders against us; and partly to silence impudent blasphemers who boldly condemn that which they have not heard and do not understand.

We do not suppose that such malice can be cured merely by our confession, for we know that the sweet savor of the gospel is, and shall be, death to the sons of perdition; but we are considering chiefly our own weaker brethren, to whom we would communicate our deepest thoughts, lest they be troubled or carried away by the different rumors which Satan spreads against us to defeat our godly enterprise, protesting that if any man will note in our confession any chapter or sentence contrary to God's holy word, that it should please him of his gentleness and for Christian charity's sake to inform us of it in writing; and we, upon our honor, do promise him that by God's grace we shall give him satisfaction from the mouth of

God, that is, from Holy Scripture, or else we shall alter whatever he can prove to be wrong. For we call on God to record that from our hearts we abhor all heretical sects and all teachers of false doctrine, and that with all humility we embrace the purity of Christ's gospel, which is the one food of our souls and therefore so precious to us that we are determined to suffer the greatest of worldly dangers, rather than let our souls be defrauded of it. For we are completely convinced that whoever denies Christ Jesus, or is ashamed of him in the presence of men, shall be denied be-

[Mk 8.38]   fore the Father and before his holy angels. Therefore by the aid of the mighty Spirit of our Lord Jesus Christ we firmly intend to endure to the end in the confession of our faith, as in the following chapters.

ARTICLE 1. GOD

We confess and acknowledge one God alone, to whom alone we must cleave, whom alone we must serve, whom only we must worship, and in whom alone we put our trust. Who is eternal, infinite, immeasurable, incomprehensible, omnipotent, invisible; one in substance and yet distinct in three persons, the Father, the Son, and the Holy Ghost. By whom we confess and believe all things in heaven and earth, visible and invisible, to have been created, to be retained in their being, and to be ruled and guided by his inscrutable providence for such end as his eternal wisdom, goodness, and justice have appointed, and to the manifestation of his own glory.

ARTICLE 2. THE CREATION OF MAN

We confess and acknowledge that our God has created man, that is, our first father, Adam, after his own image and likeness, to whom he gave wisdom, lordship, justice, free will, and self-consciousness, so that in the whole nature of man no imperfection could be found. From this dignity and perfection man and woman both fell; the woman being deceived by the serpent and man obeying the voice of the woman, both conspiring against the sovereign majesty of God, who in clear words had previously

[Gn 2.17]   threatened death if they presumed to eat of the forbidden tree.

ARTICLE 3. ORIGINAL SIN

By this transgression, generally known as original sin, the image of God was utterly defaced in man, and he and his children became by nature hostile to God, slaves to Satan, and servants to sin. And thus everlasting death has had, and shall have, power and dominion over all who have not been, are not, or shall not be born from above. This rebirth is wrought by the power of the Holy Ghost creating in the hearts of God's chosen ones an assured faith in the promise of God revealed to us in his word; by this faith we grasp Christ Jesus with the graces and blessings promised in him.

ARTICLE 4. THE REVELATION OF THE PROMISE

We constantly believe that God, after the fearful and horrible departure of man from his obedience, did seek Adam again, call upon him, rebuke and convict him of his sin, and in the end made unto him a most joyful promise, that "the seed of the woman should bruise the head of the serpent," that is, that he should destroy [Gn 3.15] the works of the devil. This promise was repeated and made clearer from time to time; it was embraced with joy, and most constantly received by all the faithful from Adam to Noah, from Noah to Abraham, from Abraham to David, and so onwards to the incarnation of Christ Jesus; all (we mean the believing fathers under the law) did see the joyful day of Christ Jesus, and did rejoice. [Jn 8.56]

ARTICLE 5. THE CONTINUANCE, INCREASE, AND PRESERVATION OF THE KIRK

We most surely believe that God preserved, instructed, multiplied, honored, adorned, and called from death to life his kirk in all ages since Adam until the coming of Christ Jesus in the flesh. For he called Abraham from his father's country, instructed him, and multiplied his seed; he marvelously preserved him, and more marvelously delivered his seed from the bondage and tyranny of Pharaoh; to them he gave his laws, constitutions, and ceremonies; to them he gave the land of Canaan; after he had given them judges, and afterwards Saul, he gave David to be king, to whom he gave promise that of the fruit of his loins should one sit forever upon his royal throne. To this same people from time to time he sent prophets, to recall them [2 Sm 7.12] to the right way of their God, from which sometimes they strayed by idolatry. And although, because of their stubborn contempt for righteousness he was compelled to give them into the hands of their enemies, as had previously been threatened by the mouth of Moses, so that the holy city was destroyed, the temple burned with fire, and the whole land desolate for seventy years, yet in mercy he restored them again to Jerusalem, where the city and the temple were rebuilt, and they endured against all temptations and assaults of Satan till the Messiah came according to the promise.

ARTICLE 6. THE INCARNATION OF CHRIST JESUS

When the fullness of time came God sent his Son, his eternal wisdom, the substance of his own glory, into this world, who took the nature of humanity from the substance of a woman, a virgin, by means of the Holy Ghost. And so was born the "just

[Rom 1.3] seed of David," the "angel of the great counsel of God," the very Messiah promised, whom we confess and acknowledge to be Emmanuel, true God and true man, two perfect natures united and joined in one person. So by our confession we condemn the damnable and pestilent heresies of Arius, Marcion, Eutyches, Nestorius, and such others as did either deny the eternity of his Godhead, or the truth of his humanity, or confounded them, or else divided them.

ARTICLE 7. WHY THE MEDIATOR HAD TO BE TRUE GOD AND TRUE MAN

We acknowledge and confess that this wonderful union between the Godhead and the humanity in Christ Jesus did arise from the eternal and immutable decree of God from which all our salvation springs and depends.

ARTICLE 8. ELECTION

That same eternal God and Father, who by grace alone chose us in his Son Christ Jesus before the foundation of the world was laid, appointed him to be our head, our brother, our pastor, and the great bishop of our souls. But since the opposition between the justice of God and our sins was such that no flesh by itself could or might have attained unto God, it behooved the Son of God to descend unto us and take himself a body of our body, flesh of our flesh, and bone of our bone, and so become the mediator between God and man, giving power to as many as believe in him to be the sons of God; as he himself says, "I ascend to my Father and to your

[Jn 20.17] Father, to my God and to your God." By this most holy brotherhood whatever we have lost in Adam is restored to us again. Therefore we are not afraid to call God our Father, not so much because he has created us, which we have in common with the reprobate, as because he has given unto us his only Son to be our brother, and given us grace to acknowledge and embrace him as our only Mediator. Further, it behooved the Messiah and Redeemer to be true God and true man, because he was able to undergo the punishment of our transgressions and to present himself in the presence of his Father's judgment, as in our stead, to suffer for our transgression and disobedience, and by death to overcome him that was the author of death. But because the Godhead alone could not suffer death, and neither could manhood overcome death, he joined both together in one person, that the weakness of one should suffer and be subject to death—which we had deserved—and the infinite and invincible power of the other, that is, of the Godhead, should triumph, and purchase for us life, liberty, and perpetual victory. So we confess, and most undoubtedly believe.

ARTICLE 9. CHRIST'S DEATH, PASSION, AND BURIAL

That our Lord Jesus offered himself a voluntary sacrifice unto his Father for us, that he suffered contradiction of sinners, that he was wounded and plagued for our transgressions, that he, the clean innocent Lamb of God, was condemned in the presence of an earthly judge, that we should be absolved before the judgment seat of our God; that he suffered not only the cruel death of the cross, which was accursed by the sentence of God; but also that he suffered for a season the wrath of his Father which sinners had deserved. But yet we avow that he remained the only, well beloved, and blessed Son of his Father even in the midst of his anguish and torment which he suffered in body and soul to make full atonement for the sins of his people. From this we confess and avow that there remains no other sacrifice for sin; if any affirm so, we do not hesitate to say that they are blasphemers against Christ's death and the everlasting atonement thereby purchased for us.

ARTICLE 10. THE RESURRECTION

We undoubtedly believe, since it was impossible that the sorrows of death should retain in bondage the author of life, that our Lord Jesus crucified, dead, and buried, who descended into hell, did rise again for our justification, and the destruction of him who was the author of death, and brought to life again to us who were subject to death and its bondage. We know that his resurrection was confirmed by the testimony of his enemies,[a] and by the resurrection of the dead,[b] whose sepulchers did open, and they did rise and appear to many within the city of Jerusalem. It was also confirmed by the testimony of his angels, and by the senses and judgment of   [Mt 28.5–6] his apostles and of others, who had conversation, and did eat and drink with him after his resurrection.

ARTICLE 11. THE ASCENSION

We do not doubt but that the selfsame body which was born of the Virgin, was crucified, dead, and buried, and which did rise again, did ascend into the heavens, for the accomplishment of all things, where in our name and for our comfort he has received all power in heaven and earth, where he sits at the right hand of the Father, having received his kingdom, the only Advocate and Mediator for us. Which glory, honor, and prerogative, he alone amongst the brethren shall possess till all his enemies are made his footstool, as we undoubtedly believe they shall be in the

a. [Mt 28.4]
b. [Mt 27.52–53]

last judgment. We believe that the same Lord Jesus shall visibly return for this last judgment as he was seen to ascend. And then, we firmly believe, the time of refreshing and restitution of all things shall come, so that those who from the beginning have suffered violence, injury, and wrong, for righteousness's sake, shall inherit that blessed immortality promised them from the beginning. But, on the other hand, the stubborn, disobedient, cruel persecutors, filthy persons, idolaters, and all sorts of the unbelieving, shall be cast into the dungeon of utter darkness, where their worm shall not die, nor their fire be quenched. The remembrance of that day, and of the judgment to be executed in it, is not only a bridle by which our carnal lusts are restrained but also such inestimable comfort that neither the threatening of worldly princes, nor the fear of present danger or of temporal death, may move us to renounce and forsake that blessed society which we, the members, have with our Head and only Mediator, Christ Jesus: whom we confess and avow to be the promised Messiah, the only Head of his kirk, our just Lawgiver, our only High Priest, Advocate, and Mediator. To which honors and offices, if man or angel presume to intrude themselves, we utterly detest and abhor them, as blasphemous to our sovereign and supreme governor, Christ Jesus.

ARTICLE 12. FAITH IN THE HOLY GHOST

Our faith and its assurance do not proceed from flesh and blood, that is to say, from natural powers within us, but are the inspiration of the Holy Ghost; whom we confess to be God, equal with the Father and with his Son, who sanctifies us, and brings us into all truth by his own working, without whom we should remain forever enemies to God and ignorant of his Son, Christ Jesus. For by nature we are so dead, blind, and perverse, that neither can we feel when we are pricked, see the light when it shines, nor assent to the will of God when it is revealed, unless the Spirit of the Lord Jesus quicken that which is dead, remove the darkness from our minds, and bow our stubborn hearts to the obedience of his blessed will. And so, as we confess that God the Father created us when we were not, as his Son our Lord Jesus redeemed us when we were enemies to him, so also do we confess that the Holy Ghost does sanctify and regenerate us, without respect to any merit proceeding from us, be it before or after our regeneration. To put this even more plainly; as we willingly disclaim any honor and glory for our own creation and redemption, so do we willingly also for our regeneration and sanctification; for by ourselves we are not capable of thinking one good thought, but he who has begun the work in us alone continues us in it, to the praise and glory of his undeserved grace.

ARTICLE 13. THE CAUSE OF GOOD WORKS

The cause of good works, we confess, is not our free will, but the Spirit of the Lord Jesus, who dwells in our hearts by true faith, brings forth such works as God has prepared for us to walk in. For we most boldly affirm that it is blasphemy to say that Christ abides in the hearts of those in whom is no spirit of sanctification. Therefore we do not hesitate to affirm that murderers, oppressors, cruel persecutors, adulterers, filthy persons, idolaters, drunkards, thieves, and all workers of iniquity have neither true faith nor anything of the Spirit of the Lord Jesus, so long as they obstinately continue in wickedness. For as soon as the Spirit of the Lord Jesus, whom God's chosen children receive by true faith, takes possession of the heart of any man, so soon does he regenerate and renew him, so that he begins to hate what before he loved and to love what he hated before. Thence comes that continual battle which is between the flesh and Spirit in God's children, while the flesh and the natural man, being corrupt, lust for things pleasant and delightful to themselves, are envious in adversity and proud in prosperity, and every moment prone and ready to offend the majesty of God. But the Spirit of God, who bears witness to our spirit that we are the sons of God, makes us resist filthy pleasures and groan in God's presence for deliverance from this bondage of corruption, and finally to triumph over sin so that it does not reign in our mortal bodies. Other men do not share this conflict since they do not have God's Spirit, but they readily follow and obey sin and feel no regrets, since they act as the devil and their corrupt nature urge. But the sons of God fight against sin; sob and mourn when they find themselves tempted to do evil; and, if they fall, rise again with earnest and unfeigned repentance. They do these things, not by their own power, but by the power of the Lord Jesus, apart from whom they can do nothing.

ARTICLE 14. THE WORKS WHICH ARE COUNTED
GOOD BEFORE GOD

We confess and acknowledge that God has given to man his holy law, in which not only all such works as displease and offend his godly majesty are forbidden, but also those which please him and which he has promised to reward are commanded. These works are of two kinds. The one is done to the honor of God, the other to the profit of our neighbor, and both have the revealed will of God as their assurance. To have one God, to worship and honor him, to call upon him in all our troubles, to reverence his holy name, to hear his word and to believe it, and to share in his holy sacraments, belong to the first kind. To honor father, mother, princes, rulers, and superior powers; to love them, to support them, to obey their orders if they are not contrary to the commands of God, to save the lives of the innocent, to repress tyranny, to defend the oppressed, to keep our bodies clean and holy, to live in soberness and temperance, to deal justly with all men in word and deed, and, finally, to repress any desire to harm our neighbor, are the good works of the second kind, and these are most pleasing and acceptable to God as he has commanded them himself. Acts to the contrary are sins, which always displease him and provoke him to anger, such as, not to call upon him alone when we have need, not to hear his word with reverence, but to condemn and despise it, to have or worship idols, to maintain and defend idolatry, lightly to esteem the reverend name of God, to profane, abuse, or condemn the sacraments of Christ Jesus, to disobey or resist any whom God has placed in authority, so long as they do not exceed the bounds of their office, to murder, or to consent thereto, to bear hatred, or to let innocent blood be shed if we can prevent it. In conclusion, we confess and affirm that the breach of any other commandment of the first or second kind is sin, by which God's anger and displeasure are kindled against the proud, unthankful world. So that we affirm good works to be those alone which are done in faith and at the command of God who, in his law, has set forth the things that please him. We affirm that evil works are not only those expressly done against God's command, but also, in religious matters and the worship of God, those things which have no other warrant than the invention and opinion of man. From the beginning God has rejected such, as we learn from the words of the prophet Isaiah and of our master, Christ Jesus, [Mk 7.7] "In vain do they worship me, teaching the doctrines and commandments of men."

ARTICLE 15. THE PERFECTION OF THE LAW AND THE IMPERFECTION OF MAN

We confess and acknowledge that the law of God is most just, equal, holy, and perfect, commanding those things which, when perfectly done, can give life and bring man to eternal felicity; but our nature is so corrupt, weak, and imperfect, that we are never able perfectly to fulfill the works of the law. Even after we are reborn, if we say that we have no sin, we deceive ourselves and the truth of God is not in us. It is therefore essential for us to lay hold on Christ Jesus, in his righteousness and his atonement, since he is the end and consummation of the law and since it is by him that we are set at liberty so that the curse of God may not fall upon us, even though we do not fulfill the law in all points. For as God the Father beholds us in the body of his Son Christ Jesus, he accepts our imperfect obedience as if it were perfect, and covers our works, which are defiled with many stains, with the righteousness of his Son. We do not mean that we are so set at liberty that we owe no obedience to the law—for we have already acknowledged its place—but we affirm that no man on earth, with the sole exception of Christ Jesus, has given, gives, or shall give in action that obedience to the law which the law requires. When we have done all things we must fall down and unfeignedly confess that we are unprofitable servants. Therefore, whoever boasts of the merits of his own works or puts his trust in works of supererogation, boasts of what does not exist, and puts his trust in damnable idolatry.

ARTICLE 16. THE KIRK

As we believe in one God, Father, Son, and Holy Ghost, so we firmly believe that from the beginning there has been, now is, and to the end of the world shall be, one kirk, that is to say, one company and multitude of men chosen by God, who rightly worship and embrace him by true faith in Christ Jesus, who is the only Head of the kirk, even as it is the body and spouse of Christ Jesus. This kirk is catholic, that is, universal, because it contains the chosen of all ages, of all realms, nations, and tongues, be they of the Jews or be they of the Gentiles, who have communion and society with God the Father, and with his Son, Christ Jesus, through the sanctification of his Holy Spirit. It is therefore called the communion, not of profane persons, but of saints, who, as citizens of the heavenly Jerusalem, have the fruit of inestimable benefits, one God, one Lord Jesus, one faith, and one baptism. Out of this kirk there is neither life nor eternal felicity. Therefore we utterly abhor the blasphemy of those who hold that men who live according to equity and justice shall be saved, no matter what religion they profess. For since there is neither life nor salvation without Christ Jesus; so shall none have part therein but those whom the Father has given unto his Son Christ Jesus, and those who in time come to him, avow his doctrine, and believe in him. (We include the children with the believing parents.) This kirk is invisible, known only to God, who alone knows whom he has chosen, and includes both the chosen who are departed, the kirk triumphant, those who yet live and fight against sin and Satan, and those who shall live hereafter.

ARTICLE 17. THE IMMORTALITY OF SOULS

The chosen departed are in peace, and rest from their labors; not that they sleep and are lost in oblivion as some fanatics hold, for they are delivered from all fear and torment, and all the temptations to which we and all God's chosen are subject in this life, and because of which we are called the kirk militant. On the other hand, the reprobate and unfaithful departed have anguish, torment, and pain which cannot be expressed. Neither the one nor the other is in such sleep that they feel no joy or torment, as is testified by Christ's parable in St. Luke 16,[a] his words to the thief,[b] and the words of the souls crying under the altar, "O Lord, you who are righteous and just, how long shall you not revenge our blood upon those that dwell in the earth?"

[Rv 6.9–10]

ARTICLE 18. THE NOTES BY WHICH THE TRUE KIRK SHALL BE DETERMINED FROM THE FALSE, AND WHO SHALL BE JUDGE OF DOCTRINE

Since Satan has labored from the beginning to adorn his pestilent synagogue with the title of the kirk of God, and has incited cruel murderers to persecute, trouble, and molest the true kirk and its members, as Cain did to Abel, Ishmael to Isaac, Esau to Jacob, and the whole priesthood of the Jews to Christ Jesus himself and his apostles after him. So it is essential that the true kirk be distinguished from the filthy synagogues by clear and perfect notes lest we, being deceived, receive and embrace, to our own condemnation, the one for the other. The notes, signs, and assured tokens whereby the spotless bride of Christ is known from the horrible harlot, the false kirk, we state, are neither antiquity, usurped title, lineal succession, appointed place, nor the numbers of men approving an error. For Cain was before Abel and Seth in age and title; Jerusalem had precedence above all other parts of the earth, for in it were priests lineally descended from Aaron, and greater numbers followed the scribes, pharisees, and priests, than unfeignedly believed and followed Christ Jesus and his doctrine. And yet no man of judgment, we suppose, will hold that any of the forenamed were the kirk of God. The notes of the true kirk, therefore, we believe, confess, and avow to be: first, the true preaching of the word of God, in which God has revealed himself to us, as the writings of the prophets and apostles declare; secondly, the right administration of the sacraments of Christ Jesus, with which must be associated the word and promise of God to seal and confirm them in our hearts; and lastly, ecclesiastical discipline uprightly ministered, as God's word prescribes, whereby vice is repressed and virtue nourished. Then wherever these notes are seen and continue for any time, be the number complete or not, there, beyond any doubt, is the true kirk of Christ, who, according to his promise, is in its midst. This is not that universal kirk of which we have spoken before, but particular kirks, such as were in Corinth, Galatia, Ephesus, and other places where the ministry was planted by Paul and which he himself called kirks of God. Such kirks, we the inhabitants of the realm of Scotland confessing Christ Jesus, do claim

a. [Lk 16.22–26]
b. [Lk 23.43]

to have in our cities, towns, and reformed districts because of the doctrine taught in our kirks, contained in the written word of God, that is, the Old and New Testaments, in those books which were originally reckoned canonical. We affirm that in these all things necessary to be believed for the salvation of man are sufficiently expressed. The interpretation of Scripture, we confess, does not belong to any private or public person, nor yet to any kirk for preeminence or precedence, personal or local, which it has above others, but pertains to the Spirit of God by whom the Scriptures were written. When controversy arises about the right understanding of any passage or sentence of Scripture, or for the reformation of any abuse within the kirk of God, we ought not so much to ask what men have said or done before us, as what the Holy Ghost uniformly speaks within the body of the Scriptures and what Christ Jesus himself did and commanded. For it is agreed by all that the Spirit of God, who is the Spirit of unity, cannot contradict himself. So if the interpretation or opinion of any theologian, kirk, or council, is contrary to the plain word of God written in any other passage of the Scripture, it is most certain that this is not the true understanding and meaning of the Holy Ghost, although councils, realms, and nations have approved and received it. We dare not receive or admit any interpretation which is contrary to any principal point of our faith, or to any other plain text of Scripture, or to the rule of love.

ARTICLE 19. THE AUTHORITY OF THE SCRIPTURES

As we believe and confess the Scriptures of God sufficient to instruct and make perfect the man of God, so do we affirm and avow their authority to be from God, and not to depend on men or angels. We affirm, therefore, that those who say the Scriptures have no other authority save that which they have received from the kirk are blasphemous against God and injurious to the true kirk, which always hears and obeys the voice of her own Spouse and Pastor, but takes not upon her to be mistress over the same.

ARTICLE 20. GENERAL COUNCILS, THEIR POWER, AUTHORITY, AND THE CAUSE OF THEIR SUMMONING

As we do not rashly condemn what good men, assembled together in general councils lawfully gathered, have set before us; so we do not receive uncritically whatever has been declared to men under the name of the general councils, for it is plain that, being human, some of them have manifestly erred, and that in matters of great weight and importance. So far then as the council confirms its decrees by the plain word of God, so far do we reverence and embrace them. But if men, under the name of a council, pretend to forge for us new articles of faith, or to make decisions contrary to the word of God, then we must utterly deny them as the doctrine of devils, drawing our souls from the voice of the one God to follow the doctrines and teachings of men. The reason why the general councils met was not to make any permanent law which God had not made before, nor yet to form new articles for our belief, nor to give the word of God authority; much less to make that to be his word, or even the true interpretation of it, which was not expressed previously by his holy will in his word; but the reason for councils, at least of those that deserve that name, was partly to refute heresies, and to give public confession of their faith to the generations following, which they did by the authority of God's written word, and not by any opinion or prerogative that they could not err by reason of their numbers. This, we judge, was the primary reason for general councils. The second was that good policy and order should be constituted and observed in the kirk where, as in the house of God, it becomes all things to be done decently and in order. Not that we think any policy or order of ceremonies can be appointed for all ages, times, and places; for as ceremonies which men have devised are but temporal, so they may, and ought to be, changed, when they foster superstition rather than edify the kirk.

ARTICLE 21. THE SACRAMENTS

As the fathers under the law, besides the reality of the sacrifices, had two chief sacraments, that is, circumcision and the Passover, and those who rejected these were not reckoned among God's people; so do we acknowledge and confess that now in the time of the gospel we have two chief sacraments, which alone were instituted by the Lord Jesus and commanded to be used by all who will be counted members of his body, that is, baptism and the supper or table of the Lord Jesus, also called the communion of his body and blood. These sacraments, both of the Old Testament and of the New, were instituted by God not only to make a visible distinction between his people and those who were without the covenant, but also to exercise the faith of his children and, by participation of these sacraments, to seal in their hearts the assurance of his promise, and of that most blessed conjunction, union, and society, which the chosen have with their Head, Christ Jesus. And so we utterly condemn the vanity of those who affirm the sacraments to be nothing else than naked and bare signs. No, we assuredly believe that by baptism we are engrafted into Christ Jesus, to be made partakers of his righteousness, by which our sins are covered and remitted, and also that in the supper rightly used, Christ Jesus is so joined with us that he becomes the very nourishment and food for our souls. Not that we imagine any transubstantiation of bread into Christ's body, and of wine into his natural blood, as the Romanists have perniciously taught and wrongly believed; but this union and conjunction which we have with the body and blood of Christ Jesus in the right use of the sacraments is wrought by means of the Holy Ghost, who by true faith carries us above all things that are visible, carnal, and earthly, and makes us feed upon the body and blood of Christ Jesus, once broken and shed for us but now in heaven, and appearing for us in the presence of his Father. Notwithstanding the distance between his glorified body in heaven and mortal men on earth, yet we must assuredly believe that the bread which we break is the communion of Christ's body and the cup which we bless the communion of his blood. Thus we confess and believe without doubt that the faithful, in the right use of the Lord's table, do so eat the body and drink the blood of the Lord Jesus that he remains in them and they in him; they are so made flesh of his flesh and bone of his bone that as the eternal Godhood has given to the flesh of Christ Jesus, which by nature was corruptible and mortal, life and immortality, so the eating and drinking of the flesh and blood of Christ Jesus does the like for us. We grant that this is neither given to us merely at the time nor by the power and virtue of the sacrament alone, but we affirm that the faithful, in the right use of the Lord's table, have such union with Christ Jesus as the natural man cannot apprehend. Further we affirm that although the faithful, hindered by negligence and human weakness, do not profit as much as they ought in the actual moment of the supper, yet afterwards it shall bring forth fruit, being living seed sown in good ground; for the Holy Spirit, who can never be separated from the right institution of the Lord Jesus, will not deprive the faithful of the fruit of that mystical action. Yet all this, we say again, comes of that true faith which apprehends Christ Jesus, who alone makes the sacrament effective in us. Therefore, if anyone slanders us by saying that we affirm or believe the sacraments to be symbols and nothing more, they are libelous and speak against the plain facts. On the other hand we readily admit that we make a distinction between Christ Jesus in his eternal substance and the elements of the sacramental signs. So we neither worship the elements, in place of that which they signify, nor yet do we despise them or undervalue them, but we use them with great reverence, examining ourselves diligently before we participate, since we are assured by the mouth of the apostle that "whosoever shall eat this bread, and drink this cup of the Lord, unworthily, shall be guilty of the body and blood of the Lord."   [1 Cor 11.27–29]

ARTICLE 22. THE RIGHT ADMINISTRATION OF THE SACRAMENTS

Two things are necessary for the right administration of the sacraments. The first is that they should be ministered by lawful ministers, and we declare that these are men appointed to preach the word, unto whom God has given the power to preach the gospel, and who are lawfully called by some kirk. The second is that they should be ministered in the elements and manner which God has appointed. Otherwise they cease to be the sacraments of Christ Jesus. This is why we abandon the teaching of the Roman Church and withdraw from its sacraments; firstly, because their ministers are not true ministers of Christ Jesus (indeed they even allow women, whom the Holy Ghost will not permit to preach in the congregation, to baptize) and, secondly, because they have so adulterated both the sacraments with their own additions that no part of Christ's original act remains in its original simplicity. The addition of oil, salt, spittle, and such like in baptism, are merely human additions. To adore or venerate the sacrament, to carry it through streets and towns in procession, or to reserve it in a special case, is not the proper use of Christ's sacrament but an abuse of it. Christ Jesus said, "Take, eat," and "Do this in remembrance of me."[a] By these words and commands he sanctified bread and wine to be the sacrament of his holy body and blood, so that the one should be eaten and that all should drink of the other, and not that they should be reserved for worship or honored as God, as the Romanists do. Further, in withdrawing one part of the sacrament—the blessed cup—from the people, they have committed sacrilege. Moreover, if the sacraments are to be rightly used it is essential that the end and purpose of their institution should be understood, not only by the minister but also by the recipients. For if the recipient does not understand what is being done, the sacrament is not being rightly used, as is seen in the case of the Old Testament sacrifices. Similarly, if the teacher teaches false doctrine which is hateful to God, even though the sacraments are his own ordinance, they are not rightly used, since wicked men have used them for another end than what God had commanded. We affirm that this has been done to the sacraments in the Roman Church, for there the whole action of the Lord Jesus is adulterated in form, purpose, and meaning. What Christ Jesus did, and commanded to be done, is evident from the Gospels and from St. Paul; what the priest does at the altar we do not need to tell. The end and purpose of Christ's institution, for which it should be used, is set forth in the words, "Do this in remembrance of me,"[b] and "For as often as ye eat this bread and drink this cup ye

[1 Cor 11.24, 26] do show"—that is, extol, preach, magnify, and praise—"the Lord's death, till he come." But let the words of the mass, and their own doctors and teachings witness, what is the purpose and meaning of the mass; it is that, as mediators between Christ and his kirk, they should offer to God the Father, a sacrifice in propitiation for the sins of the living and of the dead. This doctrine is blasphemous to Christ Jesus and

a. [Mt 26.26; Mk 14.22; Lk 22.19; 1 Cor 11.24]
b. [Lk 22.19; 1 Cor 11.24]

would deprive his unique sacrifice, once offered on the cross for the cleansing of all who are to be sanctified, of its sufficiency; so we detest and renounce it.

ARTICLE 23. TO WHOM SACRAMENTS APPERTAIN

We hold that baptism applies as much to the children of the faithful as to those who are of age and discretion, and so we condemn the error of the Anabaptists, who deny that children should be baptized before they have faith and understanding. But we hold that the supper of the Lord is only for those who are of the household of faith and can try and examine themselves both in their faith and their duty to their neighbors. Those who eat and drink at that holy table without faith, or without peace and goodwill to their brethren, eat unworthily. This is the reason why ministers in our kirk make public and individual examination of those who are to be admitted to the table of the Lord Jesus.

ARTICLE 24. THE CIVIL MAGISTRATE

We confess and acknowledge that empires, kingdoms, dominions, and cities are appointed and ordained by God; the powers and authorities in them, emperors in empires, kings in their realms, dukes and princes in their dominions, and magistrates in cities, are ordained by God's holy ordinance for the manifestation of his own glory and for the good and well being of all men. We hold that any men who conspire to rebel or to overturn the civil powers, as duly established, are not merely enemies to humanity but rebels against God's will. Further, we confess and acknowledge that such persons as are set in authority are to be loved, honored, feared, and held in the highest respect, because they are the lieutenants of God, and in their councils God himself sits and judges. They are the judges and princes to whom God has given the sword for the praise and defense of good men and the punishment of all open evildoers. Moreover, we state the preservation and purification of religion is particularly the duty of kings, princes, rulers, and magistrates. They are not only appointed for civil government but also to maintain true religion and to suppress all idolatry and superstition. This may be seen in David, Jehosaphat, Hezekiah, Josiah, and others highly commended for their zeal in that cause.

Therefore we confess and avow that those who resist the supreme powers, so long as they are acting in their own spheres, are resisting God's ordinance and cannot be held guiltless. We further state that so long as princes and rulers vigilantly fulfill their office, anyone who denies them aid, counsel, or service, denies it to God, who by his lieutenant craves it of them.

ARTICLE 25. THE GIFTS FREELY GIVEN TO THE KIRK

Although the word of God truly preached, the sacraments rightly ministered, and discipline executed according to the word of God, are certain and infallible signs of the true kirk, we do not mean that every individual person in that company is a chosen member of Christ Jesus. We acknowledge and confess that many weeds and tares are sown among the corn and grow in great abundance in its midst, and that the reprobate may be found in the fellowship of the chosen and may take an outward part with them in the benefits of the word and sacraments. But since they only confess God for a time with their mouths but not with their hearts, they lapse, and do not continue to the end. Therefore they do not share the fruits of Christ's death, resurrection, and ascension. But such as unfeignedly believe with the heart and boldly confess the Lord Jesus with their mouths shall certainly receive his gifts. Firstly, in this life, they shall receive remission of sins and that by faith in Christ's blood alone; for though sin shall remain and continually abide in our mortal bodies, yet it shall not be counted against us, but be pardoned, and covered with Christ's righteousness. Secondly, in the general judgment, there shall be given to every man and woman resurrection of the flesh. The seas shall give up her dead, and the earth those who are buried within her. Yea, the Eternal, our God, shall stretch out his hand on the dust, and the dead shall arise incorruptible, and in the very substance of the selfsame flesh which every man now bears, to receive according to their works, glory or punishment. Such as now delight in vanity, cruelty, filthiness, superstition, or idolatry, shall be condemned to the fire unquenchable, in which those who now serve the devil in all abominations shall be tormented forever, both in body and in spirit. But such as continue in well doing to the end, boldly confessing the Lord Jesus, shall receive glory, honor, and immortality, we constantly believe, to reign forever in life everlasting with Christ Jesus, to whose glorified body all his chosen shall be made like, when he shall appear again in judgment and shall render up the kingdom to God his Father, who then shall be and ever shall remain, all in all things, God blessed forever. To whom, with the Son and the Holy Ghost, be all honor and glory, now and ever. Amen.

Arise, O Lord, and let your enemies be confounded; let them flee from your presence that hate your godly name. Give your servants strength to speak your word with boldness, and let all nations cleave to the true knowledge of you. Amen.

These acts and articles were read in the face of the Parliament and ratified by the Three Estates, at Edinburgh the 17 day of August the year of God, 1560 years.

The Belgic Confession, 1561

The Belgic Confession is the oldest of the three statements of faith that define the doctrine of the Dutch Reformed Church and its American and South African descendants. It was written as a defense of the Reformed faith in the Netherlands by Guido de Brès (c. 1522–67), a minister who prepared this apology while in prison for having sung the Psalms with his congregation in the Calvinist translations of de Bèze and Clement Marot. The confession is mild in its critique of Catholicism and supportive of civil authority. Originally written in French, the first edition is prefaced with a plea for tolerance addressed to Phillipp II, to whom those professing this faith offer support and obedience. But rather than deny their beliefs, they would "offer their backs to blows, their tongues to knives, their mouths to gags, and their whole bodies to the fire."[1]

First published in Rouen in 1561, nearly every copy was destroyed by official order (only two copies still exist).[2] In 1567, Guido de Brès suffered the kind of martyr's death he had described in the confession. Political fortunes soon shifted, however, leading to the ascendance of the Reformed faith in the Netherlands, and The Belgic Confession became the doctrinal standard. It was modified and adopted at local synods in Antwerp (1566), Wessel (1568), Emden (1571), Dort (1574), and Middleburg (1581). At the national Synod of Dort in 1618–19, the text was again revised and formally adopted, along with → The Heidelberg Catechism and → The Canons of Dort as a defining statement of faith for the Dutch church. It was issued simultaneously in Latin, French, and Dutch.

In its theology the confession has much in common with → The French Confession of 1559. The thirty-seven articles emphasize the authority of Scripture, divine providence, and justification by faith alone, with a Calvinist view of election. The three traditional creeds of Western Christianity are affirmed, as are all patristic writings that conform to them. The eucharist connects the faithful (but not the unworthy) to the sacrifice of Christ and is the "true body and true blood of Christ," but it is consumed spiritually, by faith (article 35). The final article looks forward to the day of judgment, "when the number of the elect is complete."

1. Bakhuizen van den Brink, 64: "nous tendons le dos aux coups, langues aux cousteaux, la bouche aux baillons et tout le corps au feu."
2. See Bakhuizen van den Brink, 11–26, for a discussion of early editions. See also Brackman and Gilmont 1971 for a detailed discussion of the first edition.

Ministers and officeholders of the Dutch Reformed Church, the Christian Reformed Church, the Reformed Church in America, and the South African Reformed Church accept *The Belgic Confession, The Heidelberg Catechism,* and *The Canons of Dort* as doctrinal standards of the faith.[3]

Edition: Bakhuizen van den Brink, 70–146 (Latin, French, and Dutch).

Translation: *Ecumenical Creeds and Reformed Confessions* 1988, 78–120. Authorized translation (from the French 1619 version) adopted by the Christian Reformed Church in 1985 and also used by the Reformed Church in America.

Note: The biblical citations of the authorized translation sometimes differ from those given in the French version.

Literature: Bakhuizen van den Brink, 1–27; Bangs 1985; Duke 1990, 269–93; Hoenderdaal 1969; Jacobs 1959, 47–50; *OER* 1:137–39 (Hakkenberg); *TRE* 7:181–83; Van Halsema 1961; Zimmerman 1989, esp. 363–74.

---

3. In 1978 the Reformed Church in America added → *Our Song of Hope* as a contemporary statement of faith, and in 1986, a synod of the Christian Reformed Church approved *Our World Belongs to God* as "a testimony of faith for our times, subordinate to our creeds and confessions." See Part Five of this edition.

The Belgic Confession, 1561

ARTICLE 1. THE ONLY GOD

We all believe in our hearts and confess with our mouths that there is a single and simple spiritual being, whom we call God—eternal, incomprehensible, invisible, unchangeable, infinite, almighty; completely wise, just, and good, and the overflowing source of all good.

ARTICLE 2. THE MEANS BY WHICH WE KNOW GOD

We know him by two means: First, by the creation, preservation, and government of the universe, since that universe is before our eyes like a beautiful book in which all creatures, great and small, are as letters to make us ponder the invisible things of God: his eternal power and his divinity, as the apostle Paul says in Romans 1.20. Rom 1.20
All these things are enough to convict men and to leave them without excuse.

Second, he makes himself known to us more openly by his holy and divine word, as much as we need in this life, for his glory and for the salvation of his own.

ARTICLE 3. THE WRITTEN WORD OF GOD

We confess that this word of God was not sent nor delivered by the will of men, but that holy men of God spoke, being moved by the Holy Spirit, as Peter says. 2 Pt 1.21
Afterwards our God—because of the special care he has for us and our salvation—commanded his servants, the prophets and apostles, to commit this revealed word to writing. He himself wrote with his own finger the two tables of the law. Therefore we call such writings Holy and Divine Scriptures.

ARTICLE 4. THE CANONICAL BOOKS

We include in the Holy Scripture the two volumes of the Old and New Testaments. They are canonical books with which there can be no quarrel at all. In the church of God the list is as follows:

In the Old Testament, the five books of Moses—Genesis, Exodus, Leviticus, Numbers, Deuteronomy; the books of Joshua, Judges, and Ruth; the two books of Samuel, and two of Kings; the two books of Chronicles, called Paralipomenon; the first book of Ezra; Nehemiah, Esther, Job; the Psalms of David; the three books of Solomon—Proverbs, Ecclesiastes, and the Song; the four major prophets—Isaiah, Jeremiah, Ezekiel, Daniel; and then the other twelve minor prophets—Hosea, Joel,

Amos, Obadiah, Jonah, Micah, Nahum, Habakkuk, Zephaniah, Haggai, Zechariah, Malachi.

In the New Testament, the four Gospels — Matthew, Mark, Luke, and John;
the Acts of the Apostles; the fourteen letters of Paul — to the Romans; the two letters to the Corinthians; to the Galatians, Ephesians, Philippians, and Colossians;
the two letters to the Thessalonians; the two letters to Timothy; to Titus, Philemon,
and to the Hebrews; the seven letters of the other apostles — one of James; two of
Peter; three of John; one of Jude; and the Revelation of the apostle John.

ARTICLE 5. THE AUTHORITY OF SCRIPTURE

We receive all these books and these only as holy and canonical, for the regulating,
founding, and establishing of our faith. And we believe without a doubt all things
contained in them — not so much because the church receives and approves them as
such but above all because the Holy Spirit testifies in our hearts that they are from
God, and also because they prove themselves to be from God. For even the blind
themselves are able to see that the things predicted in them do happen.

ARTICLE 6. THE DIFFERENCE BETWEEN CANONICAL
AND APOCRYPHAL BOOKS

We distinguish between these holy books and the apocryphal ones, which are the
third and fourth books of Esdras; the books of Tobit, Judith, Wisdom, Jesus Sirach,
Baruch; what was added to the Story of Esther; the Song of the Three Children in
the Furnace; the Story of Susannah; the Story of Bel and the Dragon; the Prayer of
Manasseh; and the two books of Maccabees. The church may certainly read these
books and learn from them as far as they agree with the canonical books. But they
do not have such power and virtue that one could confirm from their testimony
any point of faith or of the Christian religion. Much less can they detract from the
authority of the other holy books.

ARTICLE 7. THE SUFFICIENCY OF SCRIPTURE

We believe that this Holy Scripture contains the will of God completely and that
everything one must believe to be saved is sufficiently taught in it. For since the entire manner of service which God requires of us is described in it at great length, no
Gal 1.8   one — even an apostle or an angel from heaven, as Paul says — ought to teach other
than what the Holy Scriptures have already taught us. For since it is forbidden to
add to or subtract from the word of God,ᵃ this plainly demonstrates that the teach-

a. Dt 12.32; Rv 22.18–19

ing is perfect and complete in all respects. Therefore we must not consider human writings—no matter how holy their authors may have been—equal to the divine writings; nor may we put custom, nor the majority, nor age, nor the passage of time or persons, nor councils, decrees, or official decisions above the truth of God, for truth is above everything else. For all human beings are liars by nature and more vain than vanity itself. Therefore we reject with all our hearts everything that does not agree with this infallible rule, as we are taught to do by the apostles when they say, "Test the spirits to see if they are of God," and also, "If anyone comes to you   1 Jn 4.1
and does not bring this teaching, do not receive him into your house."   2 Jn 10

ARTICLE 8. THE TRINITY

In keeping with this truth and word of God we believe in one God, who is one single essence, in whom there are three persons, really, truly, and eternally distinct according to their incommunicable properties—namely, Father, Son, and Holy Spirit. The Father is the cause, origin, and source of all things, visible as well as invisible. The Son is the Word, the Wisdom, and the Image of the Father. The Holy Spirit is the eternal power and might, proceeding from the Father and the Son. Nevertheless, this distinction does not divide God into three, since Scripture teaches us that the Father, the Son, and the Holy Spirit each has his own subsistence distinguished by characteristics—yet in such a way that these three persons are only one God. It is evident then that the Father is not the Son and that the Son is not the Father, and that likewise the Holy Spirit is neither the Father nor the Son. Nevertheless, these persons, thus distinct, are neither divided nor fused or mixed together. For the Father did not take on flesh, nor did the Spirit, but only the Son. The Father was never without his Son, nor without his Holy Spirit, since all these are equal from eternity, in one and the same essence. There is neither a first nor a last, for all three are one in truth and power, in goodness and mercy.

ARTICLE 9. THE SCRIPTURAL WITNESS ON THE TRINITY

All these things we know from the testimonies of Holy Scripture as well as from the effects of the persons, especially from those we feel within ourselves. The testimonies of the Holy Scriptures, which teach us to believe in this Holy Trinity, are written in many places of the Old Testament, which need not be enumerated but only chosen with discretion. In the book of Genesis God says, "Let us make man in our image, according to our likeness." So "God created man in his own image"—indeed, "male and female he created them." "Behold, man has become like one of   Gn 1.26–27
us." It appears from this that there is a plurality of persons within the Deity, when   Gn 3.22

he says, "Let us make man in our image"—and afterwards he indicates the unity when he says, "God created." It is true that he does not say here how many persons there are—but what is somewhat obscure to us in the Old Testament is very clear in the New.

For when our Lord was baptized in the Jordan, the voice of the Father was

Mt 3.17   heard saying, "This is my dear Son"; the Son was seen in the water; and the Holy Spirit appeared in the form of a dove. So, in the baptism of all believers this form was prescribed by Christ: "Baptize all people in the name of the Father, and of the

Mt 28.19   Son, and of the Holy Spirit." In the Gospel according to Luke the angel Gabriel says to Mary, the mother of our Lord: "The Holy Spirit will come upon you, and the power of the Most High will overshadow you; and therefore that holy one to

Lk 1.35   be born of you shall be called the Son of God." And in another place it says: "The grace of our Lord Jesus Christ, and the love of God, and the fellowship of the Holy

2 Cor 13.14   Spirit be with you." "There are three who bear witness in heaven—the Father, the

1 Jn 5.7 (AV)   Word, and the Holy Spirit—and these three are one." In all these passages we are fully taught that there are three persons in the one and only divine essence. And although this doctrine surpasses human understanding, we nevertheless believe it now, through the word, waiting to know and enjoy it fully in heaven.

Furthermore, we must note the particular works and activities of these three persons in relation to us. The Father is called our Creator, by reason of his power. The Son is our Savior and Redeemer, by his blood. The Holy Spirit is our Sanctifier, by his living in our hearts.

This doctrine of the Holy Trinity has always been maintained in the true church, from the time of the apostles until the present, against Jews, Muslims, and certain false Christians and heretics, such as Marcion, Mani, Praxeas, Sabellius, Paul of Samosata, Arius, and others like them, who were rightly condemned by the holy fathers. And so, in this matter we willingly accept the three ecumenical creeds—the Apostles', Nicene, and Athanasian—as well as what the ancient fathers decided in agreement with them.

ARTICLE 10. THE DEITY OF CHRIST

We believe that Jesus Christ, according to his divine nature, is the only Son of God— eternally begotten, not made nor created, for then he would be a creature. He is one in essence with the Father; coeternal; the exact image of the person of the Father

Col 1.15; Heb 1.3   and the "reflection of his glory," being in all things like him. He is the Son of God not only from the time he assumed our nature but from all eternity, as the following testimonies teach us when they are taken together. Moses says that God "created

the world";ᵃ and John says that "all things were created by the Word,"ᵇ which he
calls God. The apostle says that "God made the world by his Son." He also says Heb 1.2
that "God created all things by Jesus Christ." And so it must follow that he who Col 1.16
is called God, the Word, the Son, and Jesus Christ already existed when all things
were created by him. Therefore the prophet Micah says that his origin is "from ancient times, from eternity." And the apostle says that he has "neither beginning of Mi 5.2
days nor end of life." So then, he is the true eternal God, the Almighty, whom we Heb 7.3
invoke, worship, and serve.

ARTICLE 11. THE DEITY OF THE HOLY SPIRIT

We believe and confess also that the Holy Spirit proceeds eternally from the Father
and the Son—neither made, nor created, nor begotten, but only proceeding from
the two of them. In regard to order, he is the third person of the Trinity—of one
and the same essence, and majesty, and glory, with the Father and the Son. He is
true and eternal God, as the Holy Scriptures teach us.

ARTICLE 12. THE CREATION OF ALL THINGS

We believe that the Father created heaven and earth and all other creatures from
nothing, when it seemed good to him, by his Word—that is to say, by his Son. He
has given all creatures their being, form, and appearance, and their various functions
for serving their Creator. Even now he also sustains and governs them all, according to his eternal providence, and by his infinite power, that they may serve man, in
order that man may serve God. He has also created the angels good, that they might
be his messengers and serve his elect. Some of them have fallen from the excellence
in which God created them into eternal perdition; and the others have persisted and
remained in their original state, by the grace of God. The devils and evil spirits are
so corrupt that they are enemies of God and of everything good. They lie in wait
for the church and every member of it like thieves, with all their power, to destroy
and spoil everything by their deceptions. So then, by their own wickedness they are
condemned to everlasting damnation, daily awaiting their torments. For that reason
we detest the error of the Sadducees, who deny that there are spirits and angels, and
also the error of the Manichaeans, who say that the devils originated by themselves,
being evil by nature, without having been corrupted.

a. Gn 1.1
b. Jn 1.3

ARTICLE 13. THE DOCTRINE OF GOD'S PROVIDENCE

We believe that this good God, after he created all things, did not abandon them to chance or fortune but leads and governs them according to his holy will, in such a way that nothing happens in this world without his orderly arrangement. Yet God is not the author of, nor can he be charged with, the sin that occurs. For his power and goodness are so great and incomprehensible that he arranges and does his work very well and justly even when the devils and wicked men act unjustly. We do not wish to inquire with undue curiosity into what he does that surpasses human understanding and is beyond our ability to comprehend. But in all humility and reverence we adore the just judgments of God, which are hidden from us, being content to be Christ's disciples, so as to learn only what he shows us in his word, without going beyond those limits.

This doctrine gives us unspeakable comfort since it teaches us that nothing can happen to us by chance but only by the arrangement of our gracious heavenly Father. He watches over us with fatherly care, keeping all creatures under his control, so that not one of the hairs on our heads (for they are all numbered) nor even Mt 10.29-30 a little bird can fall to the ground without the will of our Father. In this thought we rest, knowing that he holds in check the devils and all our enemies, who cannot hurt us without his permission and will.

For that reason we reject the damnable error of the Epicureans, who say that God involves himself in nothing and leaves everything to chance.

ARTICLE 14. THE CREATION AND FALL OF MAN

We believe that God created man from the dust of the earth and made and formed him in his image and likeness—good, just, and holy; able by his own will to conform Ps 49.20 in all things to the will of God. But when he was in honor he did not understand it and did not recognize his excellence. But he subjected himself willingly to sin and consequently to death and the curse, lending his ear to the word of the devil. For he transgressed the commandment of life, which he had received, and by his sin he separated himself from God, who was his true life, having corrupted his entire nature. So he made himself guilty and subject to physical and spiritual death, having become wicked, perverse, and corrupt in all his ways. He lost all his excellent gifts which he had received from God, and he retained none of them except for small traces which are enough to make him inexcusable. Moreover, all the light in us is turned to darkness, as the Scripture teaches us: "The light shone in the darkness, Jn 1.5 and the darkness did not receive it." Here John calls men "darkness."

Therefore we reject everything taught to the contrary concerning man's free will, since man is nothing but the slave of sin and cannot do a thing unless it is

"given him from heaven." For who can boast of being able to do anything good *Jn 3.27*
by himself, since Christ says, "No one can come to me unless my Father who sent
me draws him"? Who can glory in his own will when he understands that "the *Jn 3.27, 6.44*
mind of the flesh is enmity against God"? Who can speak of his own knowledge in *Rom 8.7*
view of the fact that "the natural man does not understand the things of the Spirit
of God"? In short, who can produce a single thought, since he knows that we are *1 Cor 2.14*
"not able to think a thing" about ourselves, by ourselves, but that "our ability is
from God"? And therefore, what the apostle says ought rightly to stand fixed and *2 Cor 3.5*
firm: "God works within us both to will and to do according to his good pleasure." *Phil 2.13*
For there is no understanding nor will conforming to God's understanding and will
apart from Christ's involvement, as he teaches us when he says, "Without me you
can do nothing." *Jn 15.5*

ARTICLE 15. THE DOCTRINE OF ORIGINAL SIN

We believe that by the disobedience of Adam original sin has been spread through
the whole human race. It is a corruption of all nature—an inherited depravity which
even infects small infants in their mother's womb, and the root which produces in
man every sort of sin. It is therefore so vile and enormous in God's sight that it is
enough to condemn the human race, and it is not abolished or wholly uprooted even
by baptism, seeing that sin constantly boils forth as though from a contaminated
spring. Nevertheless, it is not imputed to God's children for their condemnation but
is forgiven by his grace and mercy—not to put them to sleep but so that the awareness of this corruption might often make believers groan as they long to be set free
from the "body of this death." Therefore we reject the error of the Pelagians, who *Rom 7.24*
say that this sin is nothing else than a matter of imitation.

ARTICLE 16. THE DOCTRINE OF ELECTION

We believe that—all Adam's descendants having thus fallen into perdition and ruin
by the sin of the first man—God showed himself to be as he is: merciful and just.
He is merciful in withdrawing and saving from this perdition those whom he, in
his eternal and unchangeable counsel, has elected and chosen in Jesus Christ our
Lord by his pure goodness, without any consideration of their works. He is just in
leaving the others in their ruin and fall into which they plunged themselves.

ARTICLE 17. THE RECOVERY OF FALLEN MAN

We believe that our good God, by his marvelous wisdom and goodness, seeing that
man had plunged himself in this manner into both physical and spiritual death and
made himself completely miserable, set out to find him, though man, trembling all

over, was fleeing from him. And he comforted him, promising to give him his Son, "born of a woman,"[a] to crush the head of the serpent,[b] and to make him blessed.

ARTICLE 18. THE INCARNATION

So then we confess that God fulfilled the promise which he had made to the early fathers by the mouth of his holy prophets when he sent his only and eternal Son into the world at the time set by him. The Son took the "form of a servant" and Phil 2.7   was made in the "likeness of man," truly assuming a real human nature, with all its weaknesses, except for sin; being conceived in the womb of the Blessed Virgin Mary by the power of the Holy Spirit, without male participation. And he not only assumed human nature as far as the body is concerned but also a real human soul, in order that he might be a real human being. For since the soul had been lost as well as the body he had to assume them both to save them both together. Therefore we confess, against the heresy of the Anabaptists, who deny that Christ assumed Heb 2.14   human flesh from his mother, that he "shared the very flesh and blood of children"; Acts 2.30   that he is "fruit of the loins of David" according to the flesh; "born of the seed of David" according to the flesh;[c] "fruit of the womb of the Virgin Mary";[d] "born of a woman";[e] "the seed of David";[f] "a shoot from the root of Jesse";[g] "the offspring Heb 7.14   of Judah," having descended from the Jews according to the flesh; "from the seed of Abraham"—for he "assumed Abraham's seed" and was "made like his brothers except for sin."[h] In this way he is truly our Immanuel—that is: "God with us."[i]

ARTICLE 19. THE TWO NATURES OF CHRIST

We believe that by being thus conceived the person of the Son has been inseparably united and joined together with human nature, in such a way that there are not two sons of God, nor two persons, but two natures united in a single person, with each nature retaining its own distinct properties. Thus his divine nature has always re-Heb 7.3   mained uncreated, without beginning of days or end of life, filling heaven and earth. His human nature has not lost its properties but continues to have those of a crea-

a. Gal 4.4
b. Gn 3.15
c. Rom 1.3
d. Lk 1.42
e. Gal 4.4
f. 2 Tm 2.8
g. Rom 15.12
h. Heb 2.17, 4.15
i. Mt 1.23

ture—it has a beginning of days; it is of a finite nature and retains all that belongs to a real body. And even though he, by his resurrection, gave it immortality, that nonetheless did not change the reality of his human nature; for our salvation and resurrection depend also on the reality of his body. But these two natures are so united together in one person that they are not even separated by his death. So then, what he committed to his Father when he died was a real human spirit which left his body. But meanwhile his divine nature remained united with his human nature even when he was lying in the grave; and his deity never ceased to be in him, just as it was in him when he was a little child, though for a while it did not show itself as such.

These are the reasons why we confess him to be true God and true man—true God in order to conquer death by his power, and true man that he might die for us in the weakness of his flesh.

ARTICLE 20. THE JUSTICE AND MERCY OF GOD IN CHRIST

We believe that God—who is perfectly merciful and also very just—sent his Son to assume the nature in which the disobedience had been committed, in order to bear in it the punishment of sin by his most bitter passion and death. So God made known his justice toward his Son, who was charged with our sin, and he poured out his goodness and mercy on us, who are guilty and worthy of damnation, giving to us his Son to die, by a most perfect love, and raising him to life for our justification, in order that by him we might have immortality and eternal life.

ARTICLE 21. THE ATONEMENT

We believe that Jesus Christ is a high priest forever according to the order of Melchizedek—made such by an oath—and that he presented himself in our name before his Father, to appease his wrath with full satisfaction by offering himself on the tree of the cross and pouring out his precious blood for the cleansing of our sins, as the prophets had predicted. For it is written that "the chastisement of our peace" was placed on the Son of God and that "we are healed by his wounds." He was "led to death as a lamb"; he was "numbered among sinners" and condemned as a criminal by Pontius Pilate, though Pilate had declared that he was innocent. So he paid back what he had not stolen,[a] and he suffered—the "just for the unjust,"[b] in both his body and his soul—in such a way that when he sensed the horrible punishment required by our sins his sweat became like "big drops of blood falling on the ground." He

Is 53.4–12

Lk 22.44

a. Ps 69.4
b. 1 Pt 3.18

Mt 27.46   cried, "My God, my God, why have you abandoned me?" And he endured all this
for the forgiveness of our sins. Therefore we rightly say with Paul that we "know

1 Cor 2.2   nothing but Jesus and him crucified"; we consider all things as "dung for the ex-

Phil 3.8   cellence of the knowledge of our Lord Jesus Christ." We find all comforts in his
wounds and have no need to seek or invent any other means to reconcile ourselves
with God than this one and only sacrifice, once made, which renders believers perfect forever. This is also why the angel of God called him Jesus—that is, "Savior"—

Mt 1.21   because he would save his people from their sins.

ARTICLE 22. THE RIGHTEOUSNESS OF FAITH

We believe that for us to acquire the true knowledge of this great mystery the Holy
Spirit kindles in our hearts a true faith that embraces Jesus Christ, with all his mer-
its, and makes him its own, and no longer looks for anything apart from him. For
it must necessarily follow that either all that is required for our salvation is not in
Christ or, if all is in him, then he who has Christ by faith has his salvation entirely.
Therefore, to say that Christ is not enough but that something else is needed as well
is a most enormous blasphemy against God—for it then would follow that Jesus
Christ is only half a Savior. And therefore we justly say with Paul that we are jus-

Rom 3.28   tified "by faith alone" or by faith "apart from works." However, we do not mean,
properly speaking, that it is faith itself that justifies us—for faith is only the instrument by which we embrace Christ, our righteousness. But Jesus Christ is our
righteousness in making available to us all his merits and all the holy works he has
done for us and in our place. And faith is the instrument that keeps us in communion with him and with all his benefits. When those benefits are made ours they are
more than enough to absolve us of our sins.

ARTICLE 23. THE JUSTIFICATION OF SINNERS

We believe that our blessedness lies in the forgiveness of our sins because of Jesus
Christ, and that in it our righteousness before God is contained, as David and Paul
teach us when they declare that man blessed to whom God grants righteousness

Ps 32.1; Rom 4.6   apart from works. And the same apostle says that we are justified "freely" or "by

Rom 3.24   grace" through redemption in Jesus Christ. And therefore we cling to this foundation, which is firm forever, giving all glory to God, humbling ourselves, and recognizing ourselves as we are; not claiming a thing for ourselves or our merits and
leaning and resting on the sole obedience of Christ crucified, which is ours when we
believe in him. That is enough to cover all our sins and to make us confident, freeing
the conscience from the fear, dread, and terror of God's approach, without doing
what our first father, Adam, did, who trembled as he tried to cover himself with

fig leaves. In fact, if we had to appear before God relying—no matter how little—on ourselves or some other creature, then, alas, we would be swallowed up. Therefore everyone must say with David: "Lord, do not enter into judgment with your servants, for before you no living person shall be justified." Ps 143.2

ARTICLE 24. THE SANCTIFICATION OF SINNERS

We believe that this true faith, produced in man by the hearing of God's word and by the work of the Holy Spirit, regenerates him and makes him a "new man," causing him to live the "new life" and freeing him from the slavery of sin. Therefore, far from making people cold toward living in a pious and holy way, this justifying faith, quite to the contrary, so works within them that apart from it they will never do a thing out of love for God but only out of love for themselves and fear of being condemned. So then, it is impossible for this holy faith to be unfruitful in a human being, seeing that we do not speak of an empty faith but of what Scripture calls "faith working through love," which leads a man to do by himself the works that God has commanded in his word. These works, proceeding from the good root of faith, are good and acceptable to God, since they are all sanctified by his grace. Yet they do not count toward our justification—for by faith in Christ we are justified, even before we do good works. Otherwise they could not be good, any more than the fruit of a tree could be good if the tree is not good in the first place. So then, we do good works, but not for merit—for what would we merit? Rather, we are indebted to God for the good works we do, and not he to us, since it is he who "works in us both to will and do according to his good pleasure"—thus keeping in mind what is written: "When you have done all that is commanded you, then you shall say, 'We are unworthy servants; we have done what it was our duty to do.'"

2 Cor 5.17

Rom 6.4

Gal 5.6

Phil 2.13

Lk 17.10

Yet we do not wish to deny that God rewards good works—but it is by his grace that he crowns his gifts. Moreover, although we do good works we do not base our salvation on them; for we cannot do any work that is not defiled by our flesh and also worthy of punishment. And even if we could point to one, memory of a single sin is enough for God to reject that work. So we would always be in doubt, tossed back and forth without any certainty, and our poor consciences would be tormented constantly if they did not rest on the merit of the suffering and death of our Savior.

ARTICLE 25. THE FULFILLMENT OF THE LAW

We believe that the ceremonies and symbols of the law have ended with the coming of Christ, and that all foreshadowings have come to an end, so that the use of them ought to be abolished among Christians. Yet the truth and substance of these things remain for us in Jesus Christ, in whom they have been fulfilled. Nevertheless, we continue to use the witnesses drawn from the law and prophets to confirm us in the gospel and to regulate our lives with full integrity for the glory of God, according to his will.

ARTICLE 26. THE INTERCESSION OF CHRIST

We believe that we have no access to God except through the one and only Media-

1 Jn 2.1

tor and Intercessor: Jesus Christ the righteous. He therefore was made man, uniting together the divine and human natures, so that we human beings might have access to the divine Majesty. Otherwise we would have no access. But this Mediator, whom the Father has appointed between himself and us, ought not terrify us by his greatness, so that we have to look for another one, according to our fancy. For neither in heaven nor among the creatures on earth is there anyone who loves us more than Jesus Christ does. Although he was "in the form of God," he nevertheless

Phil 2.6–8

"emptied himself," taking the form of "a man" and "a servant" for us; and he made

Heb 2.17

himself "completely like his brothers." Suppose we had to find another intercessor. Who would love us more than he who gave his life for us, even though "we were

Rom 5.10

his enemies"? And suppose we had to find one who has prestige and power. Who

Rom 8.34; Heb 1.3

has as much of these as he who is seated "at the right hand of the Father," and who

Mt 28.18

has all power "in heaven and on earth"? And who will be heard more readily than God's own dearly beloved Son?

So then, sheer unbelief has led to the practice of dishonoring the saints, instead of honoring them. That was something the saints never did nor asked for, but which in keeping with their duty, as appears from their writings, they consistently refused. We should not plead here that we are unworthy—for it is not a question of offering our prayers on the basis of our own dignity but only on the basis of the excellence and dignity of Jesus Christ, whose righteousness is ours by faith. Since the apostle for good reason wants us to get rid of this foolish fear—or rather, this unbelief—he says to us that Jesus Christ was "made like his brothers in all things," that he might be a high priest who is merciful and faithful to purify the sins of the

Heb 2.17

people. For since he suffered, being tempted, he is also able to help those who are

Heb 2.18

tempted. And further, to encourage us more to approach him he says, "Since we have a high priest, Jesus the Son of God, who has entered into heaven, we maintain our confession. For we do not have a high priest who is unable to have compassion for our weaknesses, but one who was tempted in all things, just as we are, except for sin. Let us go then with confidence to the throne of grace that we may obtain

Heb 4.14–16

mercy and find grace, in order to be helped."

The same apostle says that we "have liberty to enter into the holy place

by the blood of Jesus. Let us go, then, in the assurance of faith . . . ." Likewise, Heb 10.19, 22
"Christ's priesthood is forever. By this he is able to save completely those who draw
near to God through him who always lives to intercede for them." What more do Heb 7.24–25
we need? For Christ himself declares: "I am the way, the truth, and the life; no one
comes to my Father but by me." Why should we seek another intercessor? Since it Jn 14.6
has pleased God to give us his Son as our Intercessor, let us not leave him for another—or rather seek, without ever finding. For when God gave him to us he knew
well that we were sinners.

Therefore, in following the command of Christ we call on the heavenly
Father through Christ, our only Mediator, as we are taught by the Lord's Prayer,
being assured that we shall obtain all we ask of the Father in his name.

ARTICLE 27. THE HOLY CATHOLIC CHURCH

We believe and confess one single catholic or universal church—a holy congregation and gathering of true Christian believers, awaiting their entire salvation in Jesus
Christ, being washed by his blood, and sanctified and sealed by the Holy Spirit.

This church has existed from the beginning of the world and will last until
the end, as appears from the fact that Christ is eternal King who cannot be without
subjects. And this holy church is preserved by God against the rage of the whole
world, even though for a time it may appear very small in the eyes of men—as
though it were snuffed out. For example, during the very dangerous time of Ahab
the Lord preserved for himself seven thousand men who did not bend their knees
to Baal. 1 Kgs 19.18

And so this holy church is not confined, bound, or limited to a certain
place or certain persons. But it is spread and dispersed throughout the entire world,
though still joined and united in heart and will, in one and the same Spirit, by the
power of faith.

ARTICLE 28. THE OBLIGATIONS OF CHURCH MEMBERS

We believe that since this holy assembly and congregation is the gathering of those
who are saved and there is no salvation apart from it, no one ought to withdraw
from it, content to be by himself, regardless of his status or condition. But all people
are obliged to join and unite with it, keeping the unity of the church by submitting to its instruction and discipline, by bending their necks under the yoke of Jesus
Christ, and by serving to build up one another, according to the gifts God has given
them as members of each other in the same body. And to preserve this unity more
effectively, it is the duty of all believers, according to God's word, to separate themselves from those who do not belong to the church, in order to join this assembly

wherever God has established it, even if civil authorities and royal decrees forbid and death and physical punishment result.

And so, all who withdraw from the church or do not join it act contrary to God's ordinance.

ARTICLE 29. THE MARKS OF THE TRUE CHURCH

We believe that we ought to discern diligently and very carefully, by the word of God, what is the true church—for all sects in the world today claim for themselves the name of "the church."

We are not speaking here of the company of hypocrites who are mixed among the good in the church and who nonetheless are not part of it, even though they are physically there. But we are speaking of distinguishing the body and fellowship of the true church from all sects that call themselves "the church." The true church can be recognized if it has the following marks: The church engages in the pure preaching of the gospel; it makes use of the pure administration of the sacraments as Christ instituted them; it practices church discipline for correcting faults. In short, it governs itself according to the pure word of God, rejecting all things contrary to it and holding Jesus Christ as the only Head.

By these marks one can be assured of recognizing the true church—and no one ought to be separated from it. As for those who can belong to the church, we can recognize them by the distinguishing marks of Christians: namely by faith, and by their fleeing from sin and pursuing righteousness, once they have received the one and only Savior, Jesus Christ. They love the true God and their neighbors, without turning to the right or left, and they crucify the flesh and its works. Though great weakness remains in them, they fight against it by the Spirit all the days of their lives, appealing constantly to the blood, suffering, death, and obedience of the Lord Jesus, in whom they have forgiveness of their sins, through faith in him.

As for the false church, it assigns more authority to itself and its ordinances than to the word of God; it does not want to subject itself to the yoke of Christ; it does not administer the sacraments as Christ commanded in his word; it rather adds to them or subtracts from them as it pleases; it bases itself on men, more than on Jesus Christ; it persecutes those who live holy lives according to the word of God and who rebuke it for its faults, greed, and idolatry. These two churches are easy to recognize and thus to distinguish from each other.

ARTICLE 30. THE GOVERNMENT OF THE CHURCH

We believe that this true church ought to be governed according to the spiritual order that our Lord has taught us in his word. There should be ministers or pastors to preach the word of God and administer the sacraments. There should also be elders and deacons, along with the pastors, to make up the council of the church. By this means true religion is preserved; true doctrine is able to take its course; and evil men are corrected spiritually and held in check, so that also the poor and all the afflicted may be helped and comforted according to their need. By this means everything will be done well and in good order in the church, when such persons are elected who are faithful and are chosen according to the rule that Paul gave to Timothy.   1 Tm 3

ARTICLE 31. THE OFFICERS OF THE CHURCH

We believe that ministers of the word of God, elders, and deacons ought to be chosen to their offices by a legitimate election of the church, with prayer in the name of the Lord, and in good order, as the word of God teaches. So everyone must be careful not to push himself forward improperly, but he must wait for God's call, so that he may be assured of his calling and be certain that he is chosen by the Lord.

As for the ministers of the word, they all have the same power and authority, no matter where they may be, since they are all servants of Jesus Christ, the only universal Bishop, and the only Head of the church.

Moreover, to keep God's holy order from being violated or despised, we say that everyone ought, as much as possible, to hold the ministers of the word and elders of the church in special esteem, because of the work they do, and be at peace with them, without grumbling, quarreling, or fighting.

ARTICLE 32. THE ORDER AND DISCIPLINE OF THE CHURCH

We also believe that although it is useful and good for those who govern the churches to establish and set up a certain order among themselves for maintaining the body of the church, they ought always to guard against deviating from what Christ, our only Master, has ordained for us.

Therefore we reject all human innovations and all laws imposed on us, in our worship of God, which bind and force our consciences in any way. So we accept only what is proper to maintain harmony and unity and to keep all in obedience to God. To that end excommunication, with all it involves, according to the word of God, is required.

ARTICLE 33. THE SACRAMENTS

We believe that our good God, mindful of our crudeness and weakness, has ordained sacraments for us to seal his promises in us, to pledge his good will and grace toward us, and also to nourish and sustain our faith. He has added these to the word of the gospel to represent better to our external senses both what he enables us to understand by his word and what he does inwardly in our hearts, confirming in us the salvation he imparts to us. For they are visible signs and seals of something internal and invisible, by means of which God works in us through the power of the Holy Spirit. So they are not empty and hollow signs to fool and deceive us, for their truth is Jesus Christ, without whom they would be nothing.

Moreover, we are satisfied with the number of sacraments that Christ our Master has ordained for us. There are only two: the sacrament of baptism and the holy supper of Jesus Christ.

ARTICLE 34. THE SACRAMENT OF BAPTISM

We believe and confess that Jesus Christ, in whom the law is fulfilled, has by his shed blood put an end to every other shedding of blood, which anyone might do or wish to do in order to atone or satisfy for sins. Having abolished circumcision, which was done with blood, he established in its place the sacrament of baptism. By it we are received into God's church and set apart from all other people and alien religions, that we may be dedicated entirely to him, bearing his mark and sign. It also witnesses to us that he will be our God forever, since he is our gracious Father. Therefore he has commanded that all those who belong to him be baptized with Mt 28.19 pure water in the name of the Father, and the Son, and the Holy Spirit. In this way he signifies to us that just as water washes away the dirt of the body when it is poured on us and also is seen on the body of the baptized when it is sprinkled on him, so too the blood of Christ does the same thing internally, in the soul, by the Holy Spirit. It washes and cleanses it from its sins and transforms us from being the children of wrath into the children of God. This does not happen by the physical water but by the sprinkling of the precious blood of the Son of God, who is our Red Sea, through which we must pass to escape the tyranny of Pharaoh, who is the devil, and to enter the spiritual land of Canaan. So ministers, as far as their work is concerned, give us the sacrament and what is visible, but our Lord gives what the sacrament signifies—namely the invisible gifts and graces; washing, purifying, and cleansing our souls of all filth and unrighteousness; renewing our hearts and filling them with all comfort; giving us true assurance of his fatherly goodness; clothing us with the "new man" and stripping off the "old," with all its works.

For this reason we believe that anyone who aspires to reach eternal life ought to be baptized only once without ever repeating it—for we cannot be born twice. Yet this baptism is profitable not only when the water is on us and when we receive it but throughout our entire lives. For that reason we detest the error of the Anabaptists, who are not content with a single baptism once received and also condemn the baptism of the children of believers. We believe our children ought to be baptized and sealed with the sign of the covenant, as little children were circumcised in Israel on the basis of the same promises made to our children. And truly, Christ has shed his blood no less for washing the little children of believers than he did for adults. Therefore they ought to receive the sign and sacrament of what Christ has done for them, just as the Lord commanded in the law that by offering a lamb for them the sacrament of the suffering and death of Christ would be granted them shortly after their birth. This was the sacrament of Jesus Christ. Furthermore, baptism does for our children what circumcision did for the Jewish people. That is why Paul calls baptism the "circumcision of Christ." Col 2.11

ARTICLE 35. THE SACRAMENT OF THE LORD'S SUPPER

We believe and confess that our Savior Jesus Christ has ordained and instituted the sacrament of the holy supper to nourish and sustain those who are already born again and ingrafted into his family: his church. Now those who are born again have two lives in them. The one is physical and temporal—they have it from the moment of their first birth, and it is common to all. The other is spiritual and heavenly, and is given them in their second birth; it comes through the word of the gospel in the communion of the body of Christ; and this life is common to God's elect only. Thus, to support the physical and earthly life God has prescribed for us an appropriate earthly and material bread, which is as common to all as life itself also is. But to maintain the spiritual and heavenly life that belongs to believers he has sent a living bread that came down from heaven: namely Jesus Christ, who nourishes and maintains the spiritual life of believers when eaten—that is, when appropriated and received spiritually by faith. To represent to us this spiritual and heavenly bread Christ has instituted an earthly and visible bread as the sacrament of his body and wine as the sacrament of his blood. He did this to testify to us that just as truly as we take and hold the sacraments in our hands and eat and drink it in our mouths, by which our life is then sustained, so truly we receive into our souls, for our spiritual life, the true body and true blood of Christ, our only Savior. We receive these by faith, which is the hand and mouth of our souls.

Now it is certain that Jesus Christ did not prescribe his sacraments for us in vain, since he works in us all he represents by these holy signs, although the manner in which he does it goes beyond our understanding and is incomprehensible to us, just as the operation of God's Spirit is hidden and incomprehensible. Yet we do not go wrong when we say that what is eaten is Christ's own natural body and what is drunk is his own blood—but the manner in which we eat it is not by the mouth but by the spirit, through faith. In that way Jesus Christ remains always seated at the right hand of God the Father in heaven—but he never refrains on that account to communicate himself to us through faith. This banquet is a spiritual table at which Christ communicates himself to us with all his benefits. At that table he makes us enjoy himself as much as the merits of his suffering and death, as he nourishes, strengthens, and comforts our poor, desolate souls by the eating of his flesh, and relieves and renews them by the drinking of his blood.

Moreover, though the sacraments and thing signified are joined together, not all receive both of them. The wicked person certainly takes the sacrament, to his condemnation, but does not receive the truth of the sacrament, just as Judas and Simon the sorcerer both indeed received the sacrament, but not Christ, who was signified by it. He is communicated only to believers. Finally, with humility and reverence we receive the holy sacrament in the gathering of God's people, as we engage together, with thanksgiving, in a holy remembrance of the death of Christ our Savior, and as we thus confess our faith and Christian religion. Therefore no one should come to this table without examining himself carefully, lest "by eating this

1 Cor 11.27   bread and drinking this cup he eat and drink to his own judgment." In short, by the use of this holy sacrament we are moved to a fervent love of God and our neighbors.

Therefore we reject as desecrations of the sacraments all the muddled ideas and damnable inventions that men have added and mixed in with them. And we say that we should be content with the procedure that Christ and the apostles have taught us and speak of these things as they have spoken of them.

ARTICLE 36. THE CIVIL GOVERNMENT

We believe that because of the depravity of the human race our good God has ordained kings, princes, and civil officers. He wants the world to be governed by laws and policies so that human lawlessness may be restrained and that everything may be conducted in good order among human beings. For that purpose he has placed the sword in the hands of the government, to punish evil people and protect the good. And the government's task is not limited to caring for and watching over the public domain but extends also to upholding the sacred ministry, with a view to removing and destroying all idolatry and false worship of the Antichrist; to promoting the kingdom of Jesus Christ; and to furthering the preaching of the gospel everywhere; to the end that God may be honored and served by everyone, as he requires in his word.[1]

1. The Christian Reformed Church Synod of 1958, in line with the Synods of 1910 and 1938, deemed this sentence unbiblical and replaced it with following statement: "And being called in this manner to contribute to the advancement of a society that is pleasing to God, the civil

Moreover everyone, regardless of status, condition, or rank, must be subject to the government, and pay taxes, and hold its representatives in honor and respect, and obey them in all things that are not in conflict with God's word, praying for them that the Lord may be willing to lead them in all their ways and that we may live a peaceful and quiet life in all piety and decency.

And on this matter we denounce the Anabaptists, other anarchists, and in general all those who want to reject the authorities and civil officers and to subvert justice by introducing common ownership of goods and corrupting the moral order that God has established among human beings.[2]

ARTICLE 37. THE LAST JUDGMENT

Finally we believe, according to God's word, that when the time appointed by the Lord is come (which is unknown to all creatures) and the number of the elect is complete, our Lord Jesus Christ will come from heaven, bodily and visibly, as he ascended, with great glory and majesty, to declare himself the judge of the living and the dead. He will burn this old world, in fire and flame, in order to cleanse it. Then all human creatures will appear in person before the great judge—men, women, and children, who have lived from the beginning until the end of the world. They will be summoned there by the voice of the archangel and by the sound of the divine trumpet. For all those who died before that time will be raised from the earth, their   1 Thes 4.16
spirits being joined and united with their own bodies in which they lived. And as for those who are still alive, they will not die like the others but will be changed "in the twinkling of an eye" from "corruptible to incorruptible."   1 Cor 15.51–53

Then "the books" (that is, the consciences) will be opened, and the dead will be judged according to the things they did in the world, whether good or evil.   Rv 20.12
Indeed, all people will give account of all the idle words they have spoken, which   Mt 12.36
the world regards as only playing games. And then the secrets and hypocrisies of men will be publicly uncovered in the sight of all.

Therefore, with good reason the thought of this judgment is horrible and

rulers have the task, subject to God's law, of removing every obstacle to the preaching of the gospel and to every aspect of divine worship. They should do this while completely refraining from every tendency toward exercising absolute authority and while functioning in the sphere entrusted to them, with the means belonging to them. They should do it in order that the word of God may have free course; the kingdom of Jesus Christ may make progress; and every anti-Christian power may be resisted."
2. The Synod of 1985 directed that the statement on the Anabaptists be taken from the body of the text and be placed in a footnote.

dreadful to wicked and evil people. But it is very pleasant and a great comfort to the righteous and elect, since their total redemption will then be accomplished. They will then receive the fruits of their labor and of the trouble they have suffered; their innocence will be openly recognized by all; and they will see the terrible vengeance that God will bring on the evil ones who tyrannized, oppressed, and tormented them in this world. The evil ones will be convicted by the witness of their own consciences, and shall be made immortal—but only to be tormented in the everlasting fire prepared for the devil and his angels.

Mt 25.14

In contrast, the faithful and elect will be crowned with glory and honor. The Son of God will "confess their names" before God his Father and the holy and elect angels; all tears will be "wiped from their eyes"; and their cause—at present condemned as heretical and evil by many judges and civil officers—will be acknowledged as the "cause of the Son of God." And as a gracious reward the Lord will make them possess a glory such as the heart of man could never imagine.

Mt 10.32

Rv 7.17, 21

So we look forward to that great day with longing in order to enjoy fully the promises of God in Christ Jesus, our Lord. Amen.

The Heidelberg Catechism, 1563

In *The Heidelberg Catechism,* Frederick III, elector of the Palatinate, sought to have the beliefs of the Reformed Church of the Palatinate defined in a way that reflected the core of Evangelical faith and also eschewed the scholastic quibbling of the Gnesio-Lutherans and the Philippists (also called Crypto-Calvinists by their enemies). Although more Reformed than Lutheran in his theology, Frederick consulted Melanchthon for advice and never rejected → *The Augsburg Confession.* In an attempt to bring together the best of Reformed and Lutheran doctrine, he asked the theological faculty and local ministers of Heidelberg to compose a catechism for teaching the youth of the region. Zacharias Ursinus (1534–83), a student of both Calvin and Melanchthon and a professor of theology at the University of Heidelberg, is generally credited with providing the first drafts of the catechism in his *Summa Theologiae* (323 questions) and in the condensed version of the *Summa,* his *Catechesis Minor* (108 questions).[1] A committee of Frederick III's theologians, however, prepared the official text of the catechism and clearly drew upon such other sources as Luther's → *Small Catechism,* Melanchthon's *Examen Ordinandorum,* and Leo Juda's catechism. *The Heidelberg Catechism* was approved by the Palatinate synod in January 1563 and printed with a preface by the elector in February.[2] Although Kaspar Olevianus (1536–87), a student of Calvin and de Bèze and pastor of the main church in Heidelberg, certainly participated in the deliberations about the final form of the catechism, he probably played a less prominent role than earlier scholarship has suggested.[3] In the catechism, Calvinist doctrine is couched in moderate tones and predestination is not even mentioned. Schaff described *The Heidelberg Catechism* as a union of Melanchthonian and Calvinist thought.[4]

Four German editions and a Latin translation appeared in 1563. Changes were made in the second and third editions, most notably by the addition to the third edition of a sharp condemnation of the mass in article 80—a direct response

---

1. Further evidence for Ursinus's leading role in its composition is the fact that he was also asked to compose an apology after it had been criticized as "Calvinist" or even "Zwinglian" by Lutheran theologians. The *Apologia Catechismi* was published in 1564 in the name of the entire theological faculty of Heidelberg. See Klooster 1986, 78.

2. Frederick championed the catechism and even defended it before the imperial Diet of Augsburg in 1566 as professing a faith compatible with *The Augsburg Confession.*

3. See Hollweg 1968 and Klooster 1986.

4. Schaff, 1:531.

to the Council of Trent, which had anathematized all who denied the sacrament of the mass in 1562 (Session 22). It is the third edition that has become the standard text. In 1618–19, the Synod of Dort adopted the catechism, and it remains an authorized doctrinal statement in most Presbyterian and Reformed churches, as well as numerous Congregational churches throughout the world.

Like Luther's *Small Catechism, The Heidelberg Catechism* explains the Decalogue, the Lord's Prayer, and tenets of the faith in a congenial question-and-answer style.[5] It also shares with Luther's work an ability to present sophisticated theological concepts in a straightforward manner, a characteristic that undoubtedly has contributed to the staying power of both catechisms.

Edition: Niesel, 149–81.

Translation: Miller and Osterhaven 1963, 9–127 (slightly altered to reflect German text but with biblical references as given there).

Note: The translation of Miller and Osterhaven is authorized by most Presbyterian churches and appears in *The Book of Confessions* of the Presbyterian Church (USA) without biblical references. A different translation was adopted by the Synod of the Christian Reformed Church in 1975 and has since been authorized by the Canadian and American Reformed Churches as well. See *Ecumenical Creeds and Reformed Confessions* 1988, 12–77, for this text.

Literature: Barth 1948a; Benrath 1963; Berkhof 1963; Bierma 1982; Burchill 1986; Hollweg 1968; Klooster 1986, 1994; Niemeyer, lvii–lxiii; Péry 1959; Plantinga 1979; Staedtke 1965; Thompson 1963; Torrance, 67–96; *TRE* 14:582–86 (Metz); Visser 1983, 116–19, and 1986.

5. Torrance, xiii, divides the catechism into three thematic parts: (1) the misery of man, (2) redemption, and (3) thankfulness.

The Heidelberg Catechism, 1563

Question 1. What is your only comfort, in life and in death?

That I belong—body and soul, in life and in death[a]—not to myself[b] but to my faithful Savior, Jesus Christ,[c] who at the cost of his own blood[d] has fully paid for all my sins[e] and has completely freed me from the dominion of the devil;[f] that he protects me so well that without the will of my Father in heaven not a hair can fall from my head; indeed, that everything must fit his purpose for my salvation.[g] Therefore, by his Holy Spirit, he also assures me of eternal life,[h] and makes me wholeheartedly willing and ready from now on to live for him.

Jn 6.35, 39

Mt 10.29–31

Rom 8.14, 17

Question 2. How many things must you know that you may live and die in the blessedness of this comfort?

Three.[i] First, the greatness of my sin and wretchedness.[j] Second, how I am freed from all my sins and their wretched consequences.[k] Third, what gratitude I owe to God for such redemption.[l]

Part I

LORD'S DAY 2

Question 3. Where do you learn of your sin and its wretched consequences?

From the law of God.

Rom 3.20, 7.7–25

Question 4. What does the law of God require of us?

Jesus Christ teaches this in a summary in Matthew 22.37–40: "You shall love the Lord your God with all your heart, and with all your soul, and with all your mind. This is the great and first commandment. And a second is like it, you

Mt 22.37–40

Dt 6.5

a. Rom 14.8
b. 1 Cor 6.19–20
c. 1 Cor 3.23
d. 1 Pt 1.18–19
e. 1 Jn 1.7, 2.2
f. 1 Jn 3.8
g. Rom 8.28
h. 2 Cor 1.21–22
i. Ti 3.3–8
j. Jn 9.41; Rom 1.18–3.20
k. Jn 17.1–3; Rom 3.21–8.39; Phil 2.5–11; Acts 10.34–43
l. 1 Pt 2.9–10; Rom 12–14; Eph 5.8–10

Lv 19.18   shall love your neighbor as yourself. On these two commandments depend all the
law and the prophets."

Question 5. Can you keep all this perfectly?

No,[a] for by nature I am prone to hate God and my neighbor.[b]

LORD'S DAY 3

Question 6. Did God create man evil and perverse like this?

No.[c] On the contrary, God created man good and in his image,[d] that is,

Eph 4.24; Col 3.10   in true righteousness and holiness, so that he might rightly know God his Creator,
love him with his whole heart, and live with him in eternal blessedness, praising and

Rv 21.3   glorifying him.

Question 7. Where, then, does this corruption of human nature come from?

From the fall and disobedience of our first parents, Adam and Eve, in the
garden of Eden;[e] whereby our human life is so poisoned[f] that we are all conceived

Ps 51.5   and born in the state of sin.

Question 8. But are we so perverted that we are altogether unable to do
good and prone to do evil?

Yes,[g] unless we are born again through the Spirit of God.[h]

LORD'S DAY 4

Question 9. Is not God unjust in requiring of man in his law what he cannot do?

Gn 1.31   No, for God so created man that he could do it. But man, upon the in-

Jn 8.44   stigation of the devil, by deliberate disobedience, has cheated himself and all his
descendants out of these gifts.[i]

Question 10. Will God let man get by with such disobedience and defec-
tion?

Certainly not, for the wrath of God is revealed from heaven, both against

Rom 1.18   our inborn sinfulness and our actual sins, and he will punish them according to his

a. Rom 3.10, 23; 1 Jn 1.8
b. Rom 8.7; Eph 2.1–3; Ti 3.3
c. Gn 1.31
d. Gn 1.27, 2.7
e. Gn 3.1–6
f. Rom 5.12
g. Gn 6.5; Is 53.6; Jb 14.4; Jn 3.6
h. Jn 3.5
i. Rom 5.12, 18–19; Gn 3

righteous judgment in time and in eternity, as he has declared: "Cursed be everyone who does not abide by all things written in the book of the law, and do them."[a]

Question 11. But is not God also merciful?

God is indeed merciful[b] and gracious, but he is also righteous.[c] It is his righteousness which requires that sin committed against the supreme majesty of God be punished with extreme, that is, with eternal punishment of body and soul.

Mt 25.45-46

Part II
LORD'S DAY 5

Question 12. Since, then, by the righteous judgment of God we have deserved temporal and eternal punishment, how may we escape this punishment, come again to grace, and be reconciled to God?

God wills that his righteousness be satisfied;[d] therefore, payment in full must be made to his righteousness, either by ourselves or by another.

Rom 8.3-4

Question 13. Can we make this payment ourselves?

By no means. On the contrary, we increase our debt each day.[e]

Question 14. Can any mere creature make the payment for us?

No one. First of all, God does not want to punish any other creature for man's debt.[f] Moreover, no mere creature can bear the burden of God's eternal wrath against sin and redeem others from it.

Ps 130.3; Ps 49.7

Question 15. Then, what kind of mediator and redeemer must we seek?

One who is a true[g] and righteous man[h] and yet more powerful than all creatures, that is, one who is at the same time true God.

Is 9.6; Jer 23.5-6

LORD'S DAY 6

Question 16. Why must he be a true and righteous man?

Because God's righteousness requires that man who has sinned should make reparation for sin, but the man who is himself a sinner cannot pay for others.[i]

Rom 5.12, 15

a. Gal 3.10; Dt 27.26, 28.15

b. Ex 34.6-7

c. Ex 20.5; Ps 5.4-6

d. Ex 23.7, 20.5, 34.7; Dt 7.9-11

e. Jb 9.3; Rom 2.4-5; Mt 6.12

f. Ez 18.20; Heb 2.14-15

g. 1 Cor 15.21

h. Is 53.9; Heb 7.26; 2 Cor 5.21

i. 1 Pt 3.18; Is 53.3-5, 10-11

Question 17. Why must he at the same time be true God?

So that by the power of his divinity he might bear as a man the burden of God's wrath,[a] and recover for us[b] and restore to us righteousness and life.[c]

Question 18. Who is this mediator who is at the same time true God and a true and perfectly righteous man?

Our Lord Jesus Christ,[d] who is freely given to us for complete redemption and righteousness.

1 Cor 1.30

Question 19. Whence do you know this?

From the holy gospel, which God himself revealed in the beginning in the garden of Eden,[e] afterward proclaimed through the holy patriarchs[f] and prophets[g] and foreshadowed through the sacrifices and other rites of the old covenant,[h] and finally fulfilled through his own well-beloved Son.[i]

LORD'S DAY 7

Question 20. Will all men, then, be saved through Christ as they became lost through Adam?

No. Only those who, by true faith, are incorporated into him and accept all his benefits.[j]

Question 21. What is true faith?

It is not only a certain knowledge by which I accept as true all that God has revealed to us in his word, but also a wholehearted trust which the Holy Spirit creates in me[k] through the gospel,[l] that, not only to others, but to me also God has given the forgiveness of sins, everlasting righteousness, and salvation, out of sheer grace solely for the sake of Christ's saving work.[m]

Jn 17.3; Jas 1.18

Question 22. What, then, must a Christian believe?

a. Is 53.8
b. Acts 2.23–24; Jn 1.4
c. Jn 3.16; 2 Cor 5.21
d. Mt 1.23; Lk 2.11; 1 Tm 3.16
e. Gn 3.14–15
f. Gn 22.18; Gn 49.10
g. Heb 1.1–2; Acts 10.43; Rom 1.1–6; Acts 3.22–26
h. Heb 9.13–15, 9.1–10.10
i. Gal 4.4–5; Rom 10.4
j. Jn 1.11–13; Rom 11.17–20; Heb 4.2, 10.39; Is 53.11; Heb 11
k. Rom 4.13, 16; Mt 16.15–17; 2 Cor 1.21–22
l. Rom 1.16, 10.17
m. Rom 3.21–26; Eph 2.4–9; Gal 2.15–16

All that is promised us in the gospel,[a] a summary of which is taught us in the articles of the Apostles' Creed, our universally acknowledged confession of faith.

Question 23. What are these articles?

I believe in God the Father Almighty, Maker of heaven and earth;

And in Jesus Christ, his only-begotten Son, our Lord: who was conceived by the Holy Spirit, born of the Virgin Mary; suffered under Pontius Pilate, was crucified, dead, and buried; he descended into hell, the third day he rose again from the dead; he ascended into heaven and sits at the right hand of God the Father Almighty; from thence he shall come to judge the living and the dead.

I believe in the Holy Spirit; the holy catholic church; the communion of saints; the forgiveness of sins; the resurrection of the body; and the life everlasting.

LORD'S DAY 8

Question 24. How are these articles divided?

Into three parts: The first concerns God *the Father* and our *creation*; the second, God *the Son* and our *redemption*; and the third, God *the Holy Spirit* and our *sanctification*.

Question 25. Since there is only one Divine Being, why do you speak of three, Father, Son, and Holy Spirit?   Dt 6.4

Because God has thus revealed himself in his word, that these three distinct persons are the one, true, eternal God.[b]

LORD'S DAY 9

Question 26. What do you believe when you say: "I believe in God the Father Almighty, Maker of heaven and earth"?

That the eternal Father of our Lord Jesus Christ, who out of nothing created heaven and earth with all that is in them,[c] who also upholds and governs them by his eternal counsel and providence,[d] is for the sake of Christ his Son my God and my Father.[e] I trust in him so completely that I have no doubt that he will provide me with all things necessary for body and soul.[f] Moreover, whatever evil he sends

a. Jn 20.31; Mt 28.18–20; Acts 10.34–43

b. Mt 3.16–17, 28.19; 2 Cor 13.14

c. Ps 90.1–2; Is 44.24; Gn 1; Jn 1.1–5; Ps 33.6

d. Mt 10.29; Ps 104; Heb 1.1–3

e. Rom 8.15–16; Jn 1.12–13; Gal 4.4–7

f. Lk 12.22; Mt 6.25–44

Rom 8.28   upon me in this troubled life he will turn to my good, for he is able to do it, being
Mt 7.9–11   Almighty God, and is determined to do it, being a faithful Father.

LORD'S DAY 10

Question 27. What do you understand by the providence of God?

Heb 1.3   The almighty and ever-present power of God[a] whereby he still upholds, as
it were by his own hand, heaven and earth together with all creatures, and rules in
such a way that leaves and grass, rain and drought, fruitful and unfruitful years,
food and drink,[b] health and sickness,[c] riches and poverty,[d] and everything else, come
Eph 1.11   to us not by chance but by his fatherly hand.

Question 28. What advantage comes from acknowledging God's creation
and providence?

We learn that we are to be patient in adversity,[e] grateful in the midst of
Dt 8.10   blessing, and to trust our faithful God and Father for the future, assured that no
Rom 8.38–39 creature shall separate us from his love, since all creatures are so completely in his
hand that without his will they cannot even move.[f]

LORD'S DAY 11

Question 29. Why is the Son of God called Jesus, which means Savior?

Mt 1.21; Heb 7.25   Because he saves us from our sins, and because salvation is to be sought or
Acts 4.12   found in no other.

Question 30. Do those who seek their salvation and well-being from saints,
by their own efforts, or by other means really believe in the only Savior Jesus?

No. Rather, by such actions they deny Jesus, the only Savior and Redeemer,
even though they boast of belonging to him.[g] It therefore follows that either Jesus
is not a perfect Savior, or those who receive this Savior with true faith must possess
in him all that is necessary for their salvation.[h]

LORD'S DAY 12

Question 31. Why is he called Christ, that is, the Anointed One?

a. Acts 17.24–25, 26–28
b. Acts 14.15–17; Jer 5.24
c. Jn 9.3
d. Prv 22.2; Mt 10.29–31
e. Rom 5.3–4; Jas 1.3; Jb 1.21
f. Acts 17.28, 25; Jb 1.12; Prv 21.1
g. 1 Cor 1.12–13; Gal 5.4
h. Col 1.19–20; Is 9.6–7; Jn 1.16

Because he is ordained by God the Father and anointed with the Holy Spirit[a] to be *our chief Prophet* and *Teacher*,[b] fully revealing to us the secret purpose and will of God concerning our redemption;[c] to be *our only High Priest*,[d] having redeemed us by the one sacrifice of his body and ever interceding for us with the Father;[e] and to be *our eternal King*, governing us by his word and spirit, and defending and sustaining us in the redemption he has won for us.[f]

Question 32. But why are you called a Christian?

Because through faith I share in Christ[g] and thus in his anointing,[h] so that I may confess his name,[i] offer myself a living sacrifice of gratitude to him,[j] and fight against sin and the devil with a free and good conscience throughout this life and hereafter rule with him in eternity over all creatures.

1 Tm 1.18–19

2 Tm 2.11–13

LORD'S DAY 13

Question 33. Why is he called God's only-begotten Son, since we also are God's children?

Because Christ alone is God's own eternal Son,[k] whereas we are accepted for his sake as children of God by grace.[l]

Question 34. Why do you call him our Lord?

Because, not with gold or silver but at the cost of his blood,[m] he has redeemed us body and soul from sin and all the dominion of the devil, and has bought us for his very own.

1 Cor 7.23, 6.20

LORD'S DAY 14

Question 35. What is the meaning of: "Conceived by the Holy Spirit, born of the Virgin Mary"?

That the eternal Son of God, who is and remains true and eternal God,

Jn 1.1

a. Lk 3.21–22, 4.14–19 (Is 61.1–2); Heb 1.9

b. Acts 3.22; Dt 18.15, 18

c. Jn 1.18, 15.15

d. Heb 7.17

e. Heb 9.12, 28; Rom 8.34

f. Lk 1.32–33; Zec 9.9; Mk 11.1–10; Mt 21.1–11, 28.18

g. Acts 11.26; 1 Cor 12.27

h. Acts 2.17; Jl 2.28; 1 Jn 2.27

i. Mt 10.5, 32

j. Rom 12.1; 1 Pt 2.5, 9

k. Jn 1.1–3, 14, 18; Heb 1.2

l. Eph 1.5–6; Jn 1.12; Rom 8.15–17

m. 1 Pt 1.18–19, 2.9–10

Jn 1.14; Gal 4.4   took upon himself our true manhood from the flesh and blood of the Virgin Mary
Lk 1.35; Mt 1.18, 20   through the action of the Holy Spirit, so that he might also be the true seed of
David,[a] like his fellow men in all things,[b] except for sin.[c]

Question 36. What benefit do you receive from the holy conception and birth of Christ?

1 Tm 2.5–6   That he is our Mediator, and that, in God's sight, he covers over with his innocence and perfect holiness the sinfulness in which I have been conceived.[d]

LORD'S DAY 15

Question 37. What do you understand by the word "suffered"?

That throughout his life on earth, but especially at the end of it, he bore in
Is 53.12; 1 Pt 2.24   body and soul the wrath of God against the sin of the whole human race, so that by his suffering, as the only expiatory sacrifice, he might redeem our body and soul from everlasting damnation, and might obtain for us God's grace, righteousness, and eternal life.[e]

Question 38. Why did he suffer "under Pontius Pilate" as his judge?

That he, being innocent, might be condemned by an earthly judge,[f] and thereby set us free from the judgment of God which, in all its severity, ought to fall upon us.[g]

Question 39. Is there something more in his having been crucified than if he had died some other death?

Yes, for by this I am assured that he took upon himself the curse which lay
Gal 3.13; Dt 21.23   upon me, because the death of the cross was cursed by God.

LORD'S DAY 16

Question 40. Why did Christ have to suffer "death"?

Because the righteousness and truth of God are such that nothing else could make reparation for our sins except the death of the Son of God.[h]

Question 41. Why was he "buried"?

a. Rom 1.1–3; Ps 132.11; 2 Sm 7.12–17
b. Phil 2.5–7
c. Heb 4.15
d. Rom 4.7; Ps 32.1; 1 Cor 1.30
e. Rom 3.24–25; 1 Jn 2.2
f. Jn 19.13–16; Lk 23.13–24; Acts 4.27–28
g. Is 53.4–5; Rom 5.6; 2 Cor 5.21; Gal 3.13
h. Heb 2.9; Rom 8.3–4

To confirm the fact that he was really dead.ᵃ

Question 42. Since, then, Christ died for us, why must we also die?

Our death is not a reparation for our sins, but only a dying to sin and an entering into eternal life.ᵇ

Rom 7.24; Ps 49.7

Question 43. What further benefit do we receive from the sacrifice and death of Christ on the cross?

That by his power our old self is crucified, put to death, and buried with him,ᶜ so that the evil passions of our mortal bodies may reign in us no more,ᵈ but that we may offer ourselves to him as a sacrifice of thanksgiving.

Rom 12.1

Question 44. Why is there added: "He descended into hell"?

That in my severest tribulations I may be assured that Christ my Lord has redeemed me from hellish anxieties and torment by the unspeakable anguish, pains, and terrors which he suffered in his soul both on the cross and before.

Is 53.5; Mt 27.46

LORD'S DAY 17

Question 45. What benefit do we receive from "the resurrection" of Christ?

First, by his resurrection he has overcome death that he might make us share in the righteousness which he has obtained for us through his death.ᵉ Second, we too are now raised by his power to a new life.ᶠ Third, the resurrection of Christ is a sure pledge to us of our blessed resurrection.

Rom 8.11; 1 Cor 15

LORD'S DAY 18

Question 46. How do you understand the words: "He ascended into heaven"?

That Christ was taken up from the earth into heaven before the eyes of his disciplesᵍ and remains there on our behalfʰ until he comes again to judge the living and the dead.ⁱ

Question 47. Then, is not Christ with us unto the end of the world, as he has promised us?

Mt 28.20

a. Acts 13.29; Mt 27.59–60; Lk 23.50–55; Jn 19.38–42

b. 1 Thes 5.9–10; Jn 5.24

c. Rom 6.6; Col 2.12

d. Rom 6.12

e. Rom 4.24–25; Heb 2.14–15; 1 Pt 1.3, 21

f. Rom 6.3–4; Col 3.1–5; Eph 2.4–6

g. Lk 24.50–51; Acts 1.9

h. Heb 9.24; Rom 8.34; Eph 4.8

i. Acts 1.11, 10.42; Mt 25.31–46

Jn 17.11, 16.28
Jn 14.18–19

Christ is true man and true God. As a man he is no longer on earth, but in his divinity, majesty, grace, and Spirit, he is never absent from us.

Question 48. But are not the two natures in Christ separated from each other in this way, if the humanity is not wherever the divinity is?

Not at all; for since divinity is incomprehensible and everywhere present,[a] it must follow that the divinity is indeed beyond the bounds of the humanity which it has assumed, and is nonetheless ever in that humanity as well, and remains personally united to it.

Jn 3.13; Col 2.9

Question 49. What benefit do we receive from Christ's ascension into heaven?

Rom 8.34; 1 Jn 2.1

First, that he is our Advocate in the presence of his Father in heaven. Second, that we have our flesh in heaven as a sure pledge that he, as the head, will also take us, his members, up to himself.[b] Third, that he sends us his Spirit as a counter-pledge[c] by whose power we seek what is above, where Christ is, sitting at the right hand of God, and not things that are on earth.

Col 3.1; Phil 3.20

LORD'S DAY 19

Question 50. Why is there added: "And sits at the right hand of God"?

Because Christ ascended into heaven so that he might manifest himself there as the head of his church,[d] through whom the Father governs all things.[e]

Question 51. What benefit do we receive from this glory of Christ, our head?

Acts 2.33; Eph 4.8
Jn 10.28

First, that through his Holy Spirit he pours out heavenly gifts upon us, his members. Second, that by his power he defends and supports us against all our enemies.

Question 52. What comfort does the return of Christ "to judge the living and the dead" give you?

Lk 21.28; Phil 3.20
Mt 25.41–43
Mt 25.34

That in all affliction and persecution I may await with head held high the very judge from heaven who has already submitted himself to the judgment of God for me and has removed all the curse from me; that he will cast all his enemies and mine into everlasting condemnation, but he shall take me, together with all his elect, to himself into heavenly joy and glory.

a. Jer 23.23–24; Ps 139.7–10
b. Jn 14.2, 17.24, 20.17
c. Jn 14.16–17; Acts 2; 2 Cor 1.22, 5.5
d. Eph 1.20–23; Col 1.18
e. Mt 28.18; Jn 5.22

LORD'S DAY 20

Question 53. What do you believe concerning "the Holy Spirit"?

First, that, with the Father and the Son, he is equally eternal God;[a] second, that God's Spirit is also given to me,[b] preparing me through a true faith to share in Christ and all his benefits,[c] that he comforts me[d] and will abide with me forever.[e]

LORD'S DAY 21

Question 54. What do you believe concerning "the holy catholic church"?

I believe that, from the beginning to the end of the world, and from among the whole human race,[f] the Son of God,[g] by his Spirit and his word,[h] gathers, protects, and preserves for himself, in the unity of the true faith,[i] a congregation chosen for eternal life. Moreover, I believe that I am and forever will remain a living member of it.[j]

Question 55. What do you understand by "the communion of saints"?

First, that believers one and all, as partakers of the Lord Christ, and all his treasures and gifts, shall share in one fellowship.[k] Second, that each one ought to know that he is obliged to use his gifts freely and with joy for the benefit and welfare of other members.[l]

Question 56. What do you believe concerning "the forgiveness of sins"?

That, for the sake of Christ's reconciling work,[m] God will no more remember my sins or the sinfulness with which I have to struggle all my life long;[n] but that he graciously imparts to me the righteousness of Christ so that I may never come into condemnation.

Jn 3.17-18

a. Gn 1.1-2; Jn 4.24, 14.7-17; Acts 5.3-4
b. Mt 28.19; 1 Cor 3.16; 2 Cor 1.22
c. 1 Cor 6.17, 19; Gal 4.6-7
d. Acts 9.31
e. Jn 14.16
f. Gn 26.3-4; Rv 5.9
g. Col 1.18
h. Is 59.21; Rom 1.16-18, 10.14-17
i. Acts 13.47-48; Is 49.6; Eph 4.3-6, 5.25-27
j. Jn 10.28; Rom 8.29-39
k. 1 Cor 1.9, 12.4-7, 12-13
l. 1 Cor 12.14, 21, 26-27, 13.4-5; Phil 2.1-11; 1 Cor 12-13
m. 2 Cor 5.19, 21; 1 Jn 1.7; 2.2
n. Jer 31.34; Ps 103; Rom 8.1-2

LORD'S DAY 22

Question 57. What comfort does "the resurrection of the body" give you?

That after this life my soul shall be immediately taken up to Christ, its Head, and that this flesh of mine, raised by the power of Christ, shall be reunited with my soul, and be conformed to the glorious body of Christ.[a]

Lk 23.43; Phil 1.21

Question 58. What comfort does the article concerning "the life everlasting" give you?

Rom 14.17

That, since I now feel in my heart the beginning of eternal joy, I shall possess, after this life, perfect blessedness, which no eye has seen, nor ear heard, nor the heart of man conceived,[b] and thereby praise God forever.[c]

LORD'S DAY 23

Question 59. But how does it help you now that you believe all this?

That I am righteous in Christ before God, and an heir of eternal life.[d]

Question 60. How are you righteous before God?

Only by true faith in Jesus Christ.[e] In spite of the fact that my conscience accuses me that I have grievously sinned against all the commandments of God, and have not kept any one of them,[f] and that I am still ever prone to all that is evil,[g] nevertheless, God, without any merit of my own,[h] out of pure grace,[i] grants me the benefits of the perfect expiation of Christ, imputing to me his righteousness and holiness as if I had never committed a single sin or had ever been sinful, having fulfilled myself all the obedience which Christ has carried out for me,[j] if only I accept such favor with a trusting heart.

1 Jn 2.1–2

Rom 4.3–5

Rom 3.24–25

Question 61. Why do you say that you are righteous by faith alone?

Not because I please God by virtue of the worthiness of my faith, but because the satisfaction, righteousness, and holiness of Christ alone are my righteousness before God, and because I can accept it and make it mine in no other way than by faith alone.

1 Cor 1.30, 2.2

a. 1 Cor 15.20, 42–46, 54; Jb 19.25; 1 Jn 3.2; Phil 3.21
b. 1 Cor 2.9
c. Jn 17.3
d. Rom 1.17; Hb 2.4; Rom 5.1; Jn 3.36
e. Rom 3.21–22; Phil 3.8–11
f. Rom 3.9–10
g. Rom 7.23
h. Ti 3.5
i. Eph 2.8; Rom 3.24
j. Rom 4.24; 2 Cor 5.21

LORD'S DAY 24

Question 62. But why cannot our good works be our righteousness before God, or at least a part of it?

Because the righteousness which can stand before the judgment of God must be absolutely perfect and wholly in conformity with the divine law. But even our best works in this life are all imperfect and defiled with sin.

Gal 3.10; Dt 27.26
Is 64.6

Question 63. Will our good works merit nothing, even when it is God's purpose to reward them in this life, and in the future life as well?

This reward is not given because of merit, but out of grace.

Lk 17.10

Question 64. But does not this teaching make people careless and sinful?

No, for it is impossible for those who are engrafted into Christ by true faith not to bring forth the fruit of gratitude.

Mt 7.16–17; Jn 15.5

LORD'S DAY 25

Question 65. Since, then, faith alone makes us share in Christ and all his benefits, where does such faith originate?

The Holy Spirit creates it in our hearts by the preaching of the holy gospel,[a] and confirms it by the use of the holy sacraments.

Eph 2.8; Jn 3.5

Question 66. What are the sacraments?

They are visible, holy signs and seals[b] instituted by God in order that by their use he may the more fully disclose and seal to us the promise of the gospel, namely, that because of the one sacrifice of Christ accomplished on the cross he graciously grants us the forgiveness of sins and eternal life.[c]

Question 67. Are both the word and the sacraments designed to direct our faith to the one sacrifice of Jesus Christ on the cross as the only ground of our salvation?

Yes, indeed, for the Holy Spirit teaches in the gospel and confirms by the holy sacraments that our whole salvation is rooted in the one sacrifice of Christ offered for us on the cross.[d]

Question 68. How many sacraments has Christ instituted in the New Testament?

Two, holy baptism and the holy supper.

a. 1 Pt 1.23, 25; Mt 28.19–20
b. Rom 4.11; Gn 17.11; Dt 30.6
c. Acts 2.38, 22.16; Mt 26.28; Heb 9
d. Rom 6.3; Gal 3.27; 1 Cor 11.26

LORD'S DAY 26

Question 69. How does holy baptism remind and assure you that the one sacrifice of Christ on the cross avails for you?

Mt 28.19; Acts 2.38   In this way: Christ has instituted this external washing with water and by it has promised[a] that I am as certainly washed with his blood and Spirit from the uncleanness of my soul and from all my sins, as I am washed externally with water
1 Pt 3.21   which is used to remove the dirt from my body.

Question 70. What does it mean to be washed with the blood and Spirit of Christ?

It means to have the forgiveness of sins from God, through grace, for the sake of Christ's blood which he shed for us in his sacrifice on the cross,[b] and also to be renewed by the Holy Spirit and sanctified as members of Christ, so that we may more and more die unto sin and live in a consecrated and blameless way.[c]

Question 71. Where has Christ promised that we are as certainly washed with his blood and Spirit as with the water of baptism?

In the institution of baptism which runs thus: "Go therefore and make disciples of all nations, baptizing them in the name of the Father and of the Son and of
Mt 28.19   the Holy Spirit." "He who believes and is baptized will be saved: but he who does
Mk 16.16   not believe will be condemned." This promise is also repeated where the Scriptures call baptism "the water of rebirth"[d] and the washing away of sins.[e]

LORD'S DAY 27

Question 72. Does merely the outward washing with water itself wash away sins?

No;[f] for only the blood of Jesus Christ and the Holy Spirit cleanse us from
1 Jn 1.7; 1 Cor 6.11   all sins.

Question 73. Then why does the Holy Spirit call baptism the water of rebirth and the washing away of sins?

God does not speak in this way except for a strong reason. Not only does he teach us by baptism that just as the dirt of the body is taken away by water, so
Rv 7.14; 1 Cor 6.11   our sins are removed by the blood and Spirit of Christ; but more important still, by the divine pledge and sign he wishes to assure us that we are just as truly washed
Gal 3.27   from our sins spiritually as our bodies are washed with water.

a. Mt 3.11; Rom 6.3–10
b. Eph 1.7; Heb 12.24; 1 Pt 1.2; Rv 1.5–6
c. 1 Cor 6.11; Rom 6.4; Jn 1.33; Col 2.12
d. Ti 3.5
e. Acts 22.16
f. Mt 3.11; Eph 5.25–26; 1 Pt 3.21

Question 74. Are infants also to be baptized?

Yes, because they, as well as their parents, are included in the covenant and belong to the people of God. Since both redemption from sin through the blood of Gn 17.7; Mt 19.14 Christ and the gift of faith from the Holy Spirit are promised to these children no less than to their parents,[a] infants are also by baptism, as a sign of the covenant, to be incorporated into the Christian church and distinguished from the children of un-believers.[b] This was done in the old covenant by circumcision.[c] In the new covenant baptism has been instituted to take its place. Col 2.11–13

LORD'S DAY 28

Question 75. How are you reminded and assured in the holy supper that you par-ticipate in the one sacrifice of Christ on the cross and in all his benefits?

In this way: Christ has commanded me and all believers to eat of this bro-ken bread, and to drink of this cup in remembrance of him. He has thereby prom-ised[d] that his body was offered and broken on the cross for me, and his blood was shed for me, as surely as I see with my eyes that the bread of the Lord is broken for me, and that the cup is shared with me. Also, he has promised that he himself as certainly feeds and nourishes my soul to everlasting life with his crucified body and shed blood as I receive from the hand of the minister and actually taste the bread and the cup of the Lord which are given to me as sure signs of the body and blood of Christ.

Question 76. What does it mean to eat the crucified body of Christ and to drink his shed blood?

It is not only to embrace with a trusting heart the whole passion and death of Christ, and by it to receive the forgiveness of sins and eternal life. In addition, Jn 6.35, 40, 53–54 it is to be so united more and more to his blessed body by the Holy Spirit dwell-ing both in Christ and in us[e] that, although he is in heaven[f] and we are on earth, we are nevertheless flesh of his flesh and bone of his bone,[g] always living and being governed by one Spirit, as the members of our bodies are governed by one soul.[h]

Question 77. Where has Christ promised that he will feed and nourish be-

a. Acts 2.38–39; Is 44.1–3; Lk 1.15
b. Acts 10.47; 1 Cor 7.14
c. Gn 17.9–14
d. See Question 77 below
e. Jn 6.56
f. Acts 3.20–21, 1.9–11; 1 Cor 11.26
g. Eph 5.30; 1 Cor 6.15, 17, 19
h. 1 Jn 3.24; Eph 4.15–16; Jn 6.56–58, 15.1–6

lievers with his body and blood just as surely as they eat of this broken bread and drink of this cup?

In the institution of the holy supper which reads: The Lord Jesus on the night when he was betrayed took bread, and when he had given thanks, he broke it, and said, "This is my body which is for you. Do this in remembrance of me." In the same way also the cup, after supper, saying, "This cup is the new covenant in my blood. Do this, as often as you drink it, in remembrance of me." For as often as you eat this bread and drink the cup, you proclaim the Lord's death until he comes.[a]

This promise is also repeated by the apostle Paul: When we bless "the cup of blessing," is it not a means of sharing in the blood of Christ? When we break the bread, is it not a means of sharing the body of Christ? Because there is one loaf, we,

1 Cor 10.16–17   many as we are, are one body; for it is one loaf of which we all partake.

LORD'S DAY 29

Question 78. Do the bread and wine become the very body and blood of Christ?

No, for as the water in baptism is not changed into the blood of Christ, nor becomes the washing away of sins by itself, but is only a divine sign and confirma-

Mt 26.26–29   tion of it, so also in the Lord's supper the sacred bread does not become the body of Christ itself,[b] although, in accordance with the nature and usage of sacraments,[c] it is called the body of Christ.

Question 79. Then why does Christ call the bread his body, and the cup his blood, or the new covenant in his blood, and why does the apostle Paul call the supper "a means of sharing" in the body and blood of Christ?

Christ does not speak in this way except for a strong reason. He wishes to teach us by it that as bread and wine sustain this temporal life so his crucified

Jn 6.51, 55   body and shed blood are the true food and drink of our souls for eternal life. Even more, he wishes to assure us by this visible sign and pledge that we come to share in his true body and blood through the working of the Holy Spirit as surely as we

1 Cor 10.16–17   receive with our mouth these holy tokens in remembrance of him, and that all his sufferings and his death are our own as certainly as if we had ourselves suffered and rendered satisfaction in our own persons.

a. 1 Cor 11.23–26; Mt 26.26–28; Mk 14.22–24; Lk 22.19
b. 1 Cor 11.26–28
c. 1 Cor 10.1–4; Gn 17.10–19; Ex 12.27, 43, 48

LORD'S DAY 30

Question 80.[1] What difference is there between the Lord's supper and the papal mass?

The Lord's supper testifies to us that we have complete forgiveness of all our sins through the one sacrifice of Jesus Christ which he himself has accomplished on the cross once for all;[a] (and that through the Holy Spirit we are incorporated into Christ,[b] who is now in heaven with his true body at the right hand of the Father[c] and is there to be worshiped[d]). But the mass teaches that the living and the dead do not have forgiveness of sins through the sufferings of Christ unless Christ is again offered for them daily by the priest (and that Christ is bodily under the form of bread and wine and is therefore to be worshiped in them). Therefore the mass is fundamentally a complete denial of the once for all sacrifice and passion of Jesus Christ[e] (and as such an idolatry to be condemned).

Question 81. Who ought to come to the table of the Lord?

Those who are displeased with themselves for their sins, and who neverthe-less trust that these sins have been forgiven them and that their remaining weakness is covered by the passion and death of Christ, and who also desire more and more to strengthen their faith and improve their life.[f] The impenitent and hypocrites, however, eat and drink judgment to themselves.

Mt 5.3

Ps 103.2–3; Eph 1.7

1 Cor 10.21, 11.28

Question 82. Should those who show themselves to be unbelievers and ene-mies of God by their confession and life be admitted to this supper?

No, for then the covenant of God would be profaned and his wrath pro-voked against the whole congregation.[g] According to the ordinance of Christ and his apostles, therefore, the Christian church is under obligation, by the office of the keys, to exclude such persons until they amend their lives.

a. Heb 7.27, 9.12, 25–28, 10.10–18

b. 1 Cor 6.17

c. Heb 1.3, 8.1

d. Jn 20.17; Acts 7.55–56; Col 3.1; Jn 4.21–24; Phil 3.20; 1 Thes 1.10

e. Heb 9.25–26, 10.11–14

f. Mt 5.5; Ps 116.12–14

g. 1 Cor 11.20, 26–29, 34; Is 1.11–15, 66.3; Ps 50.16

1. This question first appeared in part in the second edition. The sections in parentheses were added in the third. Both editions appeared in 1563.

LORD'S DAY 31

Question 83. What is the office of the keys?

Mt 16.19; Jn 20.23   The preaching of the holy gospel and Christian discipline. By these two means the kingdom of heaven is opened to believers and shut against unbelievers.

Question 84. How is the kingdom of heaven opened and shut by the preaching of the holy gospel?

In this way: The kingdom of heaven is opened when it is proclaimed and openly testified to believers, one and all, according to the command of Christ, that as often as they accept the promise of the gospel with true faith all their sins are truly forgiven them by God for the sake of Christ's gracious work. On the contrary, the wrath of God and eternal condemnation fall upon all unbelievers and hypocrites as long as they do not repent.[a] It is according to this witness of the gospel that God will judge the one and the other in this life and in the life to come.

Question 85. How is the kingdom of heaven shut and opened by Christian discipline?

In this way: Christ commanded that those who bear the Christian name in an unchristian way either in doctrine or in life should be given brotherly admonition. If they do not give up their errors or evil ways, notification is given to the church or to those ordained for this by the church. Then, if they do not change after this warning, they are forbidden to partake of the holy sacraments and are thus excluded from the communion of the church and by God himself from the kingdom of Christ.[b] However, if they promise and show real amendment, they are received again as members of Christ and of the church.[c]

Part III

LORD'S DAY 32

Question 86. Since we are redeemed from our sin and its wretched consequences by grace through Christ without any merit of our own, why must we do good works?

Because just as Christ has redeemed us with his blood he also renews us through his Holy Spirit according to his own image, so that with our whole life we may show ourselves grateful to God for his goodness[d] and that he may be glorified

a. Mt 28.19; Jn 20.21–23; Mt 16.19; Jn 3.18–36; Rom 2.2–17
b. Mt 18.15–18; 1 Cor 5.11–13; 2 Thes 3.14; 2 Jn 10–11
c. Lk 15.18; 2 Cor 2.6–11
d. Rom 6.13, 12.1; 1 Pt 2.5–10

through us;[a] and further, so that we ourselves may be assured of our faith by its fruits[b] and by our reverent behavior may win our neighbors to Christ.[c]

Question 87. Can those who do not turn to God from their ungrateful, impenitent life be saved?

Certainly not! Scripture says, "Surely you know that the unjust will never come into possession of the kingdom of God. Make no mistake: no fornicator or idolater or adulterer or thief or grabber or drunkard or slanderer or swindler will possess the kingdom of God."[d]

LORD'S DAY 33

Question 88. How many parts are there to the true repentance or conversion of man?

Two: the dying of the old self and the birth of the new.[e]

Question 89. What is the dying of the old self?

Sincere sorrow over our sins and more and more to hate them and to flee from them.[f]

Question 90. What is the birth of the new self?

Complete joy in God through Christ[g] and a strong desire to live according to the will of God in all good works.[h]

Question 91. But what are good works?

Only those which are done out of true faith, in accordance with the law of God,[i] and for his glory,[j] and not those based on our own opinion or on the traditions of men.[k]

Rom 14.20, 22–23

LORD'S DAY 34

Question 92. What is the law of God?

God spoke all these words saying:

a. Mt 5.16; 1 Cor 6.19–20; 1 Pt 2.12

b. Mt 7.17; Lk 13.6–9; Gal 5.22–24

c. 1 Pt 3.1–2

d. 1 Cor 6.9–10; Gal 5.19–21; Eph 5.5–33; 1 Jn 3.14–24

e. Rom 6.4–6; 2 Cor 5.17; Eph 4.22–24; Col 3.5–10; 1 Cor 5.7

f. Rom 8.13; 2 Cor 7.10; Jl 2.13; Ps 51.3, 8, 17

g. Rom 5.1, 14.17; Is 57.15

h. Gal 2.20; Rom 6.10–11

i. 1 Sm 15.22; Eph 2.10

j. 1 Cor 10.31

k. Dt 12.32; Mt 15.9; Is 29.13; Ez 20.18–19

First Commandment

"I am the Lord your God, who brought you out of the land of Egypt, out of the house of bondage. You shall have no other gods before me."

Second Commandment

"You shall not make yourself a graven image, or any likeness of anything that is in heaven above, or that is in the earth beneath, or that is in the water under the earth; you shall not bow down to them or serve them; for I the Lord your God am a jealous God, visiting the iniquity of the fathers upon the children to the third and the fourth generation of those who hate me, but showing steadfast love to thousands of those who love me and keep my commandments."

Third Commandment

"You shall not take the name of the Lord your God in vain; for the Lord will not hold him guiltless who takes his name in vain."

Fourth Commandment

"Remember the sabbath day, to keep it holy. Six days you shall labor, and do all your work; but the seventh day is a Sabbath to the Lord your God; in it you shall not do any work, you, or your son, or your daughter, your manservant, or your maidservant, or your cattle, or the sojourner who is within your gates; for in six days the Lord made heaven and earth, the sea, and all that is in them, and rested the seventh day; therefore the Lord blessed the Sabbath day and hallowed it."

Fifth Commandment

"Honor your father and your mother, that your days may be long in the land which the Lord your God gives you."

Sixth Commandment

"You shall not kill."

Seventh Commandment

"You shall not commit adultery."

Eighth Commandment

"You shall not steal."

Ninth Commandment

"You shall not bear false witness against your neighbor."

Tenth Commandment

"You shall not covet your neighbor's house; you shall not covet your neighbor's wife, or his manservant, or his maidservant, or his ox, or his ass, or anything that is your neighbor's."[a]

Question 93. How are these commandments divided?

a. Ex 20.1–17; Dt 5.6–21

Into two tables,[a] the first of which teaches us in four commandments how we ought to live in relation to God; the other, in six commandments, what we owe to our neighbor.

Mt 22.37-39

Question 94. What does the Lord require in the first commandment?

That I must avoid and flee all idolatry,[b] sorcery, enchantments,[c] invocation of saints or other creatures[d] because of the risk of losing my salvation. Indeed, I ought properly to acknowledge the only true God,[e] trust in him alone,[f] in humility[g] and patience[h] expect all good from him only,[i] and love,[j] fear[k] and honor[l] him with my whole heart. In short, I should rather turn my back on all creatures than do the least thing against his will.[m]

Question 95. What is idolatry?

It is to imagine or possess something in which to put one's trust in place of or beside the one true God who has revealed himself in his word.[n]

LORD'S DAY 35

Question 96. What does God require in the second commandment?

That we should not represent[o] him or worship him in any other manner than he has commanded in his word.[p]

Question 97. Should we, then, not make any images at all?

God cannot and should not be pictured in any way. As for creatures, although they may indeed be portrayed, God forbids making or having any likeness of them in order to worship them, or to use them to serve him.[q]

a. Ex 34.28-29; Dt 4.13, 10.3

b. 1 Cor 10.5-14, 6.9-10

c. Lv 19.31; Dt 18.10-12

d. Mt 4.10; Rv 19.10, 22.8-9

e. Jn 17.3

f. Jer 17.5, 7

g. 1 Pt 5.5-6

h. Heb 10.36; Rom 5.3-4; Phil 2.14; Col 1.11-12

i. Jas 1.17; Ps 104.27-28

j Dt 6.5; Mt 22.37

k. Dt 6.2; Ps 111.10; Prv 1.7, 9.10; Mt 10.28

l. Rv 5.13

m. Mt 10.37, 5.29-30; Acts 5.29

n. Gal 4.8-9; 1 Chr 16.26; 2 Chr 16.12; Phil 3.18-19; Eph 2.12; 2 Jn 1.9

o. Acts 17.29; Dt 4.15-19; Is 40.18-25; Rom 1.23

p. 1 Sm 15.23; Dt 12.30-32; Mt 15.9

q. Ex 23.24, 34.13-14; Nm 33.52; Dt 4.15-16, 7.5, 12.3-4; 2 Kgs 18.3-4

Question 98. But may not pictures be tolerated in churches in place of books for unlearned people?

No, for we must not try to be wiser than God, who does not want his people to be taught by means of lifeless idols,ᵃ but through the living preaching of his word.ᵇ

LORD'S DAY 36

Question 99. What is required in the third commandment?

Lv 24.11, 13, 16   That we must not profane or abuse the name of God by cursing, by perjury,ᶜ or by unnecessary oaths.ᵈ Nor are we to participate in such horrible sins by keeping quiet and thus giving silent consent. In a word, we must not use the holy name of God except with fear and reverenceᵉ so that he may be rightly confessedᶠ and addressedᵍ by us, and be glorified in all our words and works.ʰ

Question 100. Is it, therefore, so great a sin to blaspheme God's name by cursing and swearing that God is also angry with those who do not try to prevent and forbid it as much as they can?

Lv 5.1   Yes, indeed; for no sin is greater or provokes his wrath more than the pro-
Lv 24.15–16   faning of his name. That is why he commanded it to be punished with death.

LORD'S DAY 37

Question 101. But may we not swear oaths by the name of God in a devout manner?

Yes, when the civil authorities require it of their subjects, or when it is otherwise needed to maintain and promote fidelity and truth, to the glory of God and the welfare of our neighbor. Such oath-taking is grounded in God's wordⁱ and has therefore been rightly used by God's people under the old and new covenants.ʲ

Question 102. May we also swear by the saints or other creatures?

No; for a lawful oath is a calling upon God, as the only searcher of hearts,
2 Cor 1.23   to bear witness to the truth, and to punish me if I swear falsely. No creature deserves
Mt 5.34–35   such honor.

a. Hb 2.18–20; Jer 10.8
b. 2 Tm 3.16–17; 2 Pt 1.19
c. Lv 19.12
d. Mt 5.37; Jas 5.12
e. Ps 99.3; Dt 28.58
f. Mt 10.32
g. 1 Tm 2.8
h. Col 3.17; Rom 2.24; 1 Tm 6.1
i. Dt 6.13, 10.20; Is 48.1; Heb 6.16
j. Gn 21.24, 31.53–54; Jos 9.15, 19; 1 Sm 24.22; 2 Sm 3.35; 1 Kgs 1.28–30; Rom 1.9; 2 Cor 1.23

LORD'S DAY 38

Question 103. What does God require in the fourth commandment?

First, that the ministry of the gospel and Christian education be maintained,[a] and that I diligently attend church, especially on the Lord's day,[b] to hear the word of God,[c] to participate in the holy sacraments,[d] to call publicly upon the Lord,[e] and to give Christian service to those in need.[f] Second, that I cease from my evil works all the days of my life, allow the Lord to work in me through his Spirit, and thus begin in this life the eternal sabbath.

Is 66.23

LORD'S DAY 39

Question 104. What does God require in the fifth commandment?

That I show honor, love, and faithfulness to my father and mother and to all who are set in authority over me; that I submit myself with respectful obedience to all their careful instruction and discipline;[g] and that I also bear patiently their failures,[h] since it is God's will to govern us by their hand.[i]

LORD'S DAY 40

Question 105. What does God require in the sixth commandment?

That I am not to abuse, hate, injure, or kill my neighbor, either with thought, or by word or gesture, much less by deed, whether by myself or through another,[j] but to lay aside all desire for revenge;[k] and that I do not harm myself or willfully expose myself to danger. This is why the authorities are armed with the means to prevent murder.[l]

Mt 4.7

Question 106. But does this commandment speak only of killing?

In forbidding murder God means to teach us that he abhors the root of

a. 2 Tm 2.2, 3.15; 1 Tm 4.13–16, 5.17; 1 Cor 9.13–14

b. Lv 23.3; Acts 2.42, 46; Ps 68.26

c. Rom 10.17; 1 Cor 14.19, 14.29, 31

d. 1 Cor 11.24

e. 1 Tm 2.1

f. 1 Cor 16.2

g. Eph 6.1–4; Rom 13.1–2; Prv 1.8, 4, 20.20; Dt 6.6–9

h. Prv 23.22; 1 Pt 2.18

i. Col 3.18–21; Eph 6.1–9; Rom 13.1–8; Mt 22.21

j. Mt 5.21–22

k. Rom 12.19; Eph 4.26; Mt 5.25, 39–40, 18.35

l. Rom 13.4; Gn 9.6; Mt 26.52

murder, which is envy,[a] hatred,[b] anger, and desire for revenge,[c] and that he regards

1 Jn 3.15 all these as hidden murder.

Question 107. Is it enough, then, if we do not kill our neighbor in any of these ways?

No; for when God condemns envy, hatred, and anger, he requires us to love our neighbor as ourselves,[d] to show patience, peace, gentleness,[e] mercy,[f] and friendliness[g] toward him, to prevent injury to him as much as we can,[h] also to do good to our enemies.[i]

LORD'S DAY 41

Question 108. What does the seventh commandment teach us?

Gal 5.19–21 That all unchastity is condemned by God, and that we should therefore detest it from the heart,[j] and live chaste and disciplined lives,[k] whether in holy wedlock or in single life.[l]

Question 109. Does God forbid nothing more than adultery and such gross sins in this commandment?

Since both our body and soul are a temple of the Holy Spirit, it is his will that we keep both pure and holy. Therefore he forbids all unchaste actions, gestures, words,[m] thoughts, desires,[n] and whatever may excite another person to them.[o]

LORD'S DAY 42

Question 110. What does God forbid in the eighth commandment?

1 Cor 6.10, 5.9–13 He forbids not only the theft and robbery which civil authorities punish, but God also labels as theft all wicked tricks and schemes by which we seek

---

a. Gal 5.19–21; Rom 1.29

b. 1 Jn 2.9

c. Rom 12.19

d. Mt 22.39, 7.12

e. Rom 12.10; Eph 4.2; Gal 6.1–2; Mt 5.5

f. Mt 5.7; Lk 6.36

g. Rom 12.15–18

h. Mt 5.45

i. Mt 5.44; Rom 12.20–21

j. Jude 23

k. 1 Thes 4.3–4

l. Heb 13.4; 1 Cor 7.1–9, 25–28

m. Eph 5.3–4; 1 Cor 6.18–20

n. Mt 5.27–29

o. Eph 5.18; 1 Cor 15.33

to get for ourselves our neighbor's goods, whether by force or under the pretext of right,[a] such as false weights[b] and measures,[c] deceptive advertising or merchandising,[d] counterfeit money, exorbitant interest, or any other means forbidden by God. He also forbids all greed[e] and misuse and waste of his gifts.[f]

Lk 6.35; Ps 15.5

Question 111. But what does God require of you in this commandment?

That I work for the good of my neighbor wherever I can and may, deal with him as I would have others deal with me, and do my work well so that I may be able to help the poor in their need.

Mt 7.12
Eph 4.28; Phil 2.4

LORD'S DAY 43

Question 112. What is required in the ninth commandment?

That I do not bear false witness against anyone,[g] twist anyone's words,[h] be a gossip or a slanderer,[i] or condemn anyone lightly without a hearing.[j] Rather I am required to avoid, under penalty of God's wrath, all lying and deceit as the works of the devil himself.[k] In judicial and all other matters I am to love the truth, and to speak and confess it honestly. Indeed, insofar as I am able, I am to defend and promote my neighbor's good name.

Eph 4.25; 1 Cor 13.6
1 Pt 4.8

LORD'S DAY 44

Question 113. What is required in the tenth commandment?

That there should never enter our heart even the least inclination or thought contrary to any commandment of God, but that we should always hate sin with our whole heart and find satisfaction and joy in all righteousness.

Rom 7.7

Question 114. But can those who are converted to God keep these commandments perfectly?

No, for even the holiest of them make only a small beginning in obedience in this life. Nevertheless, they begin with serious purpose to conform not only to some, but to all the commandments of God.

1 Jn 1.8; Rom 7.14
Rom 7.22; Jas 2.10

a. Lk 3.14; 1 Thes 4.6
b. Prv 11.1
c. Ez 45.10; Dt 25.13–16
d. Prv 12.22
e. Lk 12.15; 1 Cor 6.10
f. Lk 16.1–2
g. Prv 19.5
h. Ps 15.3, 5
i. Rom 1.29–30
j. Mt 7.1; Lk 6.37
k. Jn 8.44; Prv 12.22, 13.5; Lv 19.11–12

Question 115. Why, then, does God have the ten commandments preached so strictly since no one can keep them in this life?

First, that all our life long we may become increasingly aware of our sinfulness,[a] and therefore more eagerly seek forgiveness of sins and righteousness in Christ. Second, that we may constantly and diligently pray to God for the grace of the Holy Spirit, so that more and more we may be renewed in the image of God, until we attain the goal of full perfection after this life.[b]

Rom 7.24-25

LORD'S DAY 45

Question 116. Why is prayer necessary for Christians?

Ps 50.14-15

Because it is the chief part of the gratitude which God requires of us, and because God will give his grace and Holy Spirit only to those who sincerely beseech him in prayer without ceasing, and who thank him for these gifts.[c]

Question 117. What is contained in a prayer which pleases God and is heard by him?

First, that we sincerely call upon the one true God, who has revealed himself to us in his word,[d] for all that he has commanded us to ask of him.[e] Then, that we thoroughly acknowledge our need and evil condition so that we may humble ourselves in the presence of his majesty.[f] Third, that we rest assured[g] that, in spite of our unworthiness, he will certainly hear our prayer for the sake of Christ our Lord, as he has promised us in his word.[h]

Is 66.2; 2 Chr 20.12

Question 118. What has God commanded us to ask of him?

Jas 1.17; Mt 6.33

All things necessary for soul and body which Christ the Lord has included in the prayer which he himself taught us.

Question 119. What is the Lord's Prayer?

"Our Father who art in heaven, hallowed be thy name. Thy kingdom come, thy will be done, on earth as it is in heaven. Give us this day our daily bread; and forgive us our debts, as we also have forgiven our debtors; and lead us not into temp-

a. 1 Jn 1.9; Ps 32.5; Rom 3.19, 7.7
b. 1 Cor 9.24; Phil 3.12-14
c. Mt 7.7-8; Lk 11.9-13
d. Ps 145.18; Jn 4.24
e. 1 Jn 5.14; Jas 1.5; Rom 8.26
f. 2 Chr 7.14
g. Jas 1.6
h. Mt 7.8; Jn 14.13-14; Dn 9.17-18; Rom 10.13

tation, but deliver us from evil, for thine is the kingdom and the power and the glory, forever. Amen."[a]

LORD'S DAY 46

Question 120. Why has Christ commanded us to address God: "Our Father"?

That at the very beginning of our prayer he may awaken in us the child-like reverence and trust toward God which should be the motivation of our prayer, which is that God has become our Father through Christ and will much less deny us what we ask him in faith than our human fathers will refuse us earthly things.[b]

Question 121. Why is there added: "who art in heaven"?

That we may have no earthly conception of the heavenly majesty of God,[c] but that we may expect from his almighty power all things that are needed for body and soul.   Rom 8.32, 10.12

LORD'S DAY 47

Question 122. What is the first petition?

"Hallowed be thy name." That is: help us first of all to know thee rightly,[d] and to hallow, glorify, and praise thee in all thy works through which there shine thine almighty power, wisdom, goodness, righteousness, mercy, and truth.[e] And so order our whole life in thought, word, and deed that thy name may never be blasphemed on our account, but may always be honored and praised.   Ps 71.8, 115.1

LORD'S DAY 48

Question 123. What is the second petition?

"Thy kingdom come." That is: so govern us by thy word and Spirit that we may more and more submit ourselves unto thee.[f] Uphold and increase thy church.[g] Destroy the works of the devil, every power that raises itself against thee, and all wicked schemes thought up against thy holy word, until the full coming of thy king-   1 Jn 3.8; Rom 16.20
dom[h] in which thou shalt be all in all.[i]

a. Mt 6.9–13; Lk 11.2–4
b. Mt 7.9–11; Lk 11.11–13
c. Jer 23.23–24; Acts 17.24–25
d. Jn 17.3; Jer 9.23–24; Mt 16.17; Ps 119.105; Jas 1.5
e. Ps 119.137; Rom 11.33–36
f. Mt 6.33; Ps 119.5
g. Ps 51.18
h. Rv 22.17; Rom 8.22–24
i. 1 Cor 15.20, 28

LORD'S DAY 49

Question 124. What is the third petition?

"Thy will be done, on earth, as it is in heaven." That is: grant that we and
all men may renounce our own will and obey thy will, which alone is good, without
grumbling,[a] so that everyone may carry out his office and calling as willingly and
faithfully[b] as the angels in heaven.[c]

Mt 16.24; Ti 2.12

LORD'S DAY 50

Question 125. What is the fourth petition?

"Give us this day our daily bread." That is: be pleased to provide for all our
bodily needs[d] so that thereby we may acknowledge that thou art the only source
of all that is good, and that without thy blessing neither our care and labor nor thy
gifts can do us any good.[e] Therefore, may we withdraw our trust from all creatures
and place it in thee alone.[f]

Acts 14.17, 17.25

LORD'S DAY 51

Question 126. What is the fifth petition?

"And forgive us our debts, as we also have forgiven our debtors." That is:
be pleased, for the sake of Christ's blood, not to charge to us, miserable sinners, our
many transgressions, nor the evil which still clings to us.[g] We also find this witness
of thy grace in us, that it is our sincere intention heartily to forgive our neighbor.

Mt 6.14–15

LORD'S DAY 52

Question 127. What is the sixth petition?

"And lead us not into temptation, but deliver us from evil." That is: since
we are so weak that we cannot stand by ourselves for one moment,[h] and besides,
since our sworn enemies, the devil,[i] the world,[j] and our own sin,[k] ceaselessly assail
us, be pleased to preserve and strengthen us through the power of thy Holy Spirit so

a. Lk 22.42; Rom 12.2; Eph 5.10
b. 1 Cor 7.24
c. Ps 103.20
d. Ps 104.27–28; Mt 6.25–34
e. 1 Cor 15.58; Dt 8.3; Ps 37.3–11, 16–17, 127.1–2
f. Ps 55.22, 62.8, 10, 146.3
g. 1 Jn 2.1–2; Ps 51.1–7
h. Jn 15.5; Ps 103.14; Rom 8.26
i. 1 Pt 5.8
j. Jn 15.19; Eph 6.12
k. Rom 7.23; Gal 5.17

that we may stand firm against them, and not be defeated in this spiritual warfare, Mt 26.41; Mk 13.33

until at last we obtain complete victory. 1 Thes 3.13, 5.23

Question 128. How do you close this prayer?

"For thine is the kingdom and the power and the glory, forever." That is: we ask all this of thee because, as our King, thou art willing and able to give us all that is good since thou hast power over all things,[a] and that by this not we ourselves but thy holy name may be glorified forever. Jn 14.13; Ps 115.1

Question 129. What is the meaning of the little word "Amen"?

Amen means: this shall truly and certainly be. For my prayer is much more certainly heard by God than I am persuaded in my heart that I desire such things from him.[b]

a. Rom 10.12–13; 2 Pt 2.9
b. 2 Cor 1.20; 2 Tm 2.13; Is 65.24; Jer 28.6

The Second Helvetic Confession, 1566

This long-lived and widely accepted Reformed confession is the work of Heinrich Bullinger (1504–75), Zwingli's successor in Zurich. A strong proponent of sacramentarianism, Bullinger had successfully negotiated → *The Consensus Tigurinus* with Calvin in 1549. He apparently wrote the first draft of what is now called *The Second Helvetic Confession* as a private statement of belief in 1561.[1] Later, Bullinger revised and expanded that text in response to a request from Frederick III, elector of the Palatinate, for a comprehensive confession of faith that would reflect his Reformed views. Frederick had earlier called upon Bullinger to draw up a defense of → *The Heidelberg Catechism* in response to objections from his Lutheran allies. The elector also discussed the need for a Reformed confession with Theodore de Bèze in Geneva. De Bèze, however, suggested that the Reformed areas of Switzerland adopt Bullinger's text (which de Bèze seems to have revised in a few places on the matter of predestination). Before the end of 1566, not only Geneva but also Bern, Chur, Biel, and Mühlhausen—in short, almost all of Protestant Switzerland[2]—had accepted Bullinger's confession.

Although the confession was positively received in Heidelberg in 1566, political necessities prevented the Palatinate from adopting *The Second Helvetic Confession*, and they subscribed instead to → *The Augsburg Confession*, which by then had become obligatory in Protestant Germany. In other European countries, however, *The Second Helvetic Confession* became a standard. It was officially recognized by Protestants in Scotland and Austria, and became a chief confession of the Reformed Church of Hungary (1567) and of Poland (1566/1570). Though not officially adopted, the confession also enjoyed wide circulation in France, England, and the Netherlands. It remains an official confession of the Reformed Church of Hungary, the Bohemian Brethren in the Czech Republic, and several Protestant groups in America, including the Presbyterian Church (USA), the Christian Reformed Church, and the Reformed Church in America.

The textual history of the confession is extremely complicated, and unfortunately, there is no modern critical edition to sort out all the variants. Even as the first pages were coming off the printing press in Zurich, Bullinger introduced

---

1. Under the title: *Expositio brevis ac dilucida orthodoxae fidei.* See TRE 8:169 and Koch 1966, 19.
2. Basel withheld approval until 1642.

revisions—probably at de Bèze's insistence—so that the first edition exists in two issues or versions. Manuscripts of the text circulating in 1566 also contained textual variants—some minor, some substantive. Thus, the various Swiss cities and regions that declared their agreement with the confession were all signing slightly different documents. Compounding the complexity is that Bullinger wrote the text in Latin and immediately translated it into German, introducing variations due to language and, interestingly, reintroducing some concepts and phrases edited out by his French colleagues in the Latin edition signed in Geneva.[3] Then, almost immediately, the text was translated into French (by de Bèze), English, Polish, Hungarian, Dutch, and several other languages.

Edition: Niesel, 222–75.

Translation: Cochrane, 220–301.

Note: The text in Niesel follows the first edition (March 1566) with variant readings from the 1568 edition. Marginal subtitles are incorporated into the English translation, but set off in italics. The versification follows Schaff, 3:237–306.

Literature: Biel 1991, 204–5; Blanke and Leuschner 1990, 250–72; Courvoisier 1944, 7–29; Dowey 1966; Koch 1966, 1968, esp. 9–53, and 1992; Linde 1966; *ODCC* 749; Pfister 1966; Schaff, 3:233–306; Schummer 1982; Staedtke 1963, 1966; Staedtke and Locher 1967; *TRE* 8:169–73 (Zsindeley); Zimmermann and Hildebrandt 1967, 139–64.

---

3. See Staedtke 1963 and 1966 for a discussion of the early textual history.

Confession and Simple Exposition of the Orthodox Faith and Catholic Articles of the Pure Christian Religion

CHAPTER 1. OF THE HOLY SCRIPTURE BEING THE TRUE WORD OF GOD

[1.] *Canonical Scripture.* We believe and confess the canonical Scriptures of the holy prophets and apostles of both Testaments to be the true word of God, and to have sufficient authority of themselves, not of men. For God himself spoke to the fathers, prophets, apostles, and still speaks to us through the Holy Scriptures.

[2.] And in this Holy Scripture, the universal church of Christ has the most complete exposition of all that pertains to a saving faith, and also to the framing of a life acceptable to God; and in this respect it is expressly commanded by God that nothing either be added to or taken from the same.

[3.] *Scripture Teaches Fully All Goodness.* We judge, therefore, that from these Scriptures are to be derived true wisdom and godliness, the reformation and government of churches; as also instruction in all duties of piety; and, to be short, the confirmation of doctrines, and the rejection of all errors, moreover, all exhortations according to that word of the apostle, "All Scripture is inspired by God and profitable for teaching, for reproof," etc. Again, "I am writing these instructions to you," says the apostle to Timothy, "so that you may know how one ought to behave in the household of God," etc. *Scripture Is the Word of God.* Again, the self-same apostle to the Thessalonians: "When," says he, "you received the word of God which you heard from us, you accepted it, not as the word of men but as what it really is, the word of God," etc. For the Lord himself has said in the Gospel, "It is not you who speak, but the Spirit of my Father speaking through you"; therefore "he who hears you hears me, and he who rejects me rejects him who sent me."[a]

[4.] *The Preaching of the Word of God Is the Word of God.* Wherefore when this word of God is now preached in the church by preachers lawfully called, we believe the very word of God is proclaimed, and received by the faithful; and that neither any other word of God is to be invented nor is to be expected from heaven: and that now the word itself which is preached is to be regarded, not the minister that preaches; for even if he be evil and a sinner, nevertheless the word of God remains still true and good.

[5.] Neither do we think that therefore the outward preaching is to be

2 Tm 3.16–17

1 Tm 3.14–15

1 Thes 2.13

a. Mt 10.20; Lk 10.16; Jn 13.20

thought as fruitless because the instruction in true religion depends on the inward illumination of the Spirit, or because it is written "And no longer shall each man teach his neighbor . . . , for they shall all know me," and "Neither he who plants nor he who waters is anything, but only God who gives the growth." For although "no one can come to Christ unless he be drawn by the Father," and unless the Holy Spirit inwardly illumines him, yet we know that it is surely the will of God that his word should be preached outwardly also. God could indeed, by his Holy Spirit, or by the ministry of an angel, without the ministry of St. Peter, have taught Cornelius in the Acts; but, nevertheless, he refers him to Peter, of whom the angel speaking says, "He shall tell you what you ought to do." Jer 31.34
1 Cor 3.7
Jn 6.44

Acts 10

[6.] *Inward Illumination Does Not Eliminate External Preaching.* For he that illuminates inwardly by giving men the Holy Spirit, the same one, by way of commandment, said unto his disciples, "Go into all the world, and preach the gospel to the whole creation." And so in Philippi, Paul preached the word outwardly to Lydia, a seller of purple goods; but the Lord inwardly opened the woman's heart. And the same Paul, after a beautiful development of his thought, in Romans 10.17 at length comes to the conclusion, "So faith comes from hearing, and hearing from the word of God by the preaching of Christ." Mk 16.15
Acts 16.14

Rom 10.17

[7.] At the same time we recognize that God can illuminate whom and when he will, even without the external ministry, for that is in his power; but we speak of the usual way of instructing men, delivered unto us from God, both by commandment and examples.

[8.] *Heresies.* We therefore detest all the heresies of Artemon, the Manichaeans, the Valentinians, of Cerdon, and the Marcionites, who denied that the Scriptures proceeded from the Holy Spirit; or did not accept some parts of them, or interpolated and corrupted them.

[9.] *Apocrypha.* And yet we do not conceal the fact that certain books of the Old Testament were by the ancient authors called *Apocryphal,* and by others *Ecclesiastical;* inasmuch as some would have them read in the churches, but not advanced as an authority from which the faith is to be established. As Augustine also, in his *City of God,* book 18, chapter 38, remarks that "in the books of the Kings, the names and books of certain prophets are cited"; but he adds that "they are not in the canon"; and that "those books which we have suffice unto godliness."

CHAPTER 2. OF INTERPRETING THE HOLY SCRIPTURES; AND OF FATHERS, COUNCILS, AND TRADITIONS

[1.] *The True Interpretation of Scripture.* The apostle Peter has said that the Holy Scriptures are not of private interpretation, and thus we do not allow all possible 2 Pt 1.20

interpretations. Nor consequently do we acknowledge as the true or genuine interpretation of the Scriptures what is called the conception of the Roman Church, that is, what the defenders of the Roman Church plainly maintain should be thrust upon all for acceptance. But we hold that interpretation of the Scriptures to be orthodox and genuine which is gleaned from the Scriptures themselves (from the nature of the language in which they were written, likewise according to the circumstances in which they were set down, and expounded in the light of like and unlike passages and of many and clearer passages) and which agrees with the rule of faith and love, and contributes much to the glory of God and man's salvation.

[2.] *Interpretations of the Holy Fathers.* Wherefore we do not despise the interpretations of the holy Greek and Latin fathers, nor reject their disputations and treatises concerning sacred matters as far as they agree with the Scriptures; but we modestly dissent from them when they are found to set down things differing from, or altogether contrary to, the Scriptures. Neither do we think that we do them any wrong in this matter; seeing that they all, with one consent, will not have their writings equated with the canonical Scriptures, but command us to prove how far they agree or disagree with them, and to accept what is in agreement and to reject what is in disagreement.

[3.] *Councils.* And in the same order also we place the decrees and canons of councils.

[4.] Wherefore we do not permit ourselves, in controversies about religion or matters of faith, to urge our case with only the opinions of the fathers or decrees of councils; much less by received customs, or by the large number who share the same opinion, or by the prescription of a long time. *Who Is the Judge?* Therefore, we do not admit any other judge than God himself, who proclaims by the Holy Scriptures what is true, what is false, what is to be followed, or what to be avoided. So we do assent to the judgments of spiritual men which are drawn from the word of God. Certainly Jeremiah and other prophets vehemently condemned the assemblies of priests which were set up against the law of God; and diligently admonished us that we should not listen to the fathers, or tread in their path who, walking in their own inventions, swerved from the law of God.

[5.] *Traditions of Men.* Likewise we reject human traditions, even if they be adorned with high-sounding titles, as though they were divine and apostolical, delivered to the church by the living voice of the apostles, and, as it were, through the hands of apostolical men to succeeding bishops which, when compared with the Scriptures, disagree with them; and by their disagreement show that they are not apostolic at all. For as the apostles did not contradict themselves in doctrine, so the apostolic men did not set forth things contrary to the apostles. On the contrary, it would be wicked to assert that the apostles by a living voice delivered anything contrary to their writings.

[6.] Paul affirms expressly that he taught the same things in all churches. And, again, "For we write you nothing but what you can read and understand." Also, in another place, he testifies that he and his disciples — that is, apostolic men — walked in the same way, and jointly by the same Spirit did all things. Moreover, the Jews in former times had the traditions of their elders; but these traditions were severely rejected by the Lord, indicating that the keeping of them hinders God's law, and that God is worshiped in vain by such traditions.

1 Cor 4.17

2 Cor 1.13

2 Cor 12.18

Mt 15.1ff.; Mk 7.1ff.

CHAPTER 3. OF GOD, HIS UNITY AND TRINITY

[1.] *God Is One.* We believe and teach that God is one in essence or nature, subsisting in himself, all sufficient in himself, invisible, incorporeal, immense, eternal, Creator of all things both visible and invisible, the greatest good, living, quickening and preserving all things, omnipotent and supremely wise, kind and merciful, just and true. [2.] Truly we detest many gods because it is expressly written: "The Lord your God is one Lord." "I am the Lord your God. You shall have no other gods before me."ª "I am the Lord, and there is no other god besides me. Am I not the Lord, and there is no other God beside me? A righteous God and a Savior; there is none besides me." "The Lord, the Lord, a God merciful and gracious, slow to anger, and abounding in steadfast love and faithfulness."

Dt 6.4

Is 45.5, 21

Ex 34.6

[3.] *God Is Three.* Notwithstanding we believe and teach that the same immense, one, and indivisible God is in person inseparably and without confusion distinguished as Father, Son, and Holy Spirit so, as the Father has begotten the Son from eternity, the Son is begotten by an ineffable generation, and the Holy Spirit truly proceeds from them both, and the same from eternity, and is to be worshiped with both. Thus there are not three gods, but three persons, consubstantial, coeternal, and coequal; distinct with respect to *hypostases*, and with respect to order, the one preceding the other yet without any inequality. For according to the nature or essence they are so joined together that they are one God, and the divine nature is common to the Father, Son, and Holy Spirit. [4.] For Scripture has delivered to us a manifest distinction of persons, the angel saying, among other things, to the Blessed Virgin, "The Holy Spirit will come upon you, and the power of the Most High will overshadow you; therefore the child to be born will be called holy, the Son of God." And also in the baptism of Christ a voice is heard from heaven concerning Christ, saying, "This is my beloved Son." The Holy Spirit also appeared in

Lk 1.35

Mt 3.17

a. Ex 20.2–3; [Dt 5.6–7]

Jn 1.32   the form of a dove. And when the Lord himself commanded the apostles to baptize, he commanded them to baptize "in the name of the Father, and the Son, and the
Mt 28.19   Holy Spirit." Elsewhere in the Gospel he said: "When the Counselor comes, whom I shall send to you from the Father, even the Spirit of truth, who proceeds from the
Jn 15.26   Father, he will bear witness to me," etc. In short, we receive the Apostles' Creed because it delivers to us the true faith.

[5.] *Heresies.* Therefore we condemn the Jews and Mohammedans, and all those who blaspheme that sacred and adorable Trinity. We also condemn all heresies and heretics who teach that the Son and Holy Spirit are God in name only, and also that there is something created and subservient, or subordinate to another in the Trinity, and that there is something unequal in it, a greater or a lesser, something corporeal or corporeally conceived, something different with respect to character or will, something mixed or solitary, as if the Son and Holy Spirit were the affections and properties of one God the Father, as the Monarchians, Novatians, Praxeas, Patripassians, Sabellius, Paul of Samosata, Aetius, Macedonius, Anthropomorphites, Arius, and such like have thought.

CHAPTER 4. OF IDOLS OR IMAGES OF GOD, CHRIST, AND THE SAINTS

[1.] *Images of God.* Since God as Spirit is in essence invisible and immense, he cannot really be expressed by any art or image. For this reason we have no fear pronouncing with Scripture that images of God are mere lies. [2.] Therefore we reject not only the idols of the Gentiles, but also the images of Christians.

Images of Christ. Although Christ assumed human nature, yet he did not on that account assume it in order to provide a model for carvers and painters. He
Mt 5.17   denied that he had come "to abolish the law and the prophets." But images are
Dt 4.15; Is 44.9   forbidden by the law and the prophets. He denied that his bodily presence would be profitable for the church, and promised that he would be near us by his Spirit
Jn 16.7   forever. [3.] Who, therefore, would believe that a shadow or likeness of his body
2 Cor 5.5   would contribute any benefit to the pious? Since he abides in us by his Spirit, we
2 Cor 3.16   are therefore the temple of God. But "what agreement has the temple of God with
2 Cor 6.16   idols?" *Images of Saints.* And since the blessed spirits and saints in heaven, while they lived here on earth, rejected all worship of themselves[a] and condemned images, shall anyone find it likely that the heavenly saints and angels are pleased with their own images before which men kneel, uncover their heads, and bestow other honors?

[4.] But in fact in order to instruct men in religion and to remind them of divine things and of their salvation, the Lord commanded the preaching of the

a. Acts 3.12ff., 14.11ff.; Rv 14.7, 22.9

gospel—not to paint and to teach the laity by means of pictures. Moreover, he insti- Mk 16.15
tuted sacraments, but nowhere did he set up images. [5.] *The Scriptures of the Laity.*
Furthermore, wherever we turn our eyes, we see the living and true creatures of God
which, if they be observed, as is proper, make a much more vivid impression on the
beholders than all the images or vain, motionless, feeble, and dead pictures made
by men, of which the prophet truly said: "They have eyes, but do not see." Ps 115.5

[6.] *Lactantius.* Therefore we approved the judgment of Lactantius, an ancient writer, who says: "Undoubtedly no religion exists where there is an image."[1]

Epiphanius and Augustine. We also assert that the blessed bishop Epiphanius did right when, finding on the doors of a church a veil on which was painted
a picture supposedly of Christ or some saint, he ripped it down and took it away,
because to see a picture of a man hanging in the church of Christ was contrary
to the authority of Scripture. Wherefore he charged that from henceforth no such
veils, which were contrary to our religion, should be hung in the church of Christ,
and that rather such questionable things, unworthy of the church of Christ and the
faithful people, should be removed. Moreover, we approve of this opinion of St.
Augustine concerning true religion: "Let not the worship of the works of men be a
religion for us. For the artists themselves who make such things are better; yet we
ought not to worship them" *(De Vera Religione,* cap. 55).

CHAPTER 5. OF THE ADORATION, WORSHIP, AND INVOCATION
OF GOD THROUGH THE ONLY MEDIATOR JESUS CHRIST

[1.] *God Alone Is to Be Adored and Worshiped.* We teach that the true God alone
is to be adored and worshiped. This honor we impart to none other, according to
the commandment of the Lord, "You shall worship the Lord your God and him
only shall you serve." Indeed, all the prophets severely inveighed against the people Mt 4.10
of Israel whenever they adored and worshiped strange gods, and not the only true
God. [2.] But we teach that God is to be adored and worshiped as he himself has
taught us to worship, namely, "in spirit and in truth," not with any superstition, but Jn 4.23-24
with sincerity, according to his word; lest at any time he should say to us: "Who
has required these things from your hands?" For Paul also says: "God is not served Is 1.12; Jer 6.20
by human hands, as though he needed anything," etc. [3.] *God Alone Is To Be In-* Acts 17.25
voked Through the Mediation of Christ Alone. In all crises and trials of our life we call
upon him alone, and that by the mediation of our only Mediator and Intercessor,
Jesus Christ. For we have been explicitly commanded: "Call upon me in the day
of trouble; I will deliver you, and you shall glorify me." Moreover, we have a most [Ps 50.15]
generous promise from the Lord who said: "If you ask anything of the Father, he

1. *CSEL* 19.175.1.

Jn 16.23   will give it to you," and: "Come to me, all who labor and are heavy laden and I will
Mt 11.28   give you rest." And since it is written: "How are men to call upon him in whom
Rom 10.14 they have not believed?" and since we do believe in God alone, we assuredly call
           upon him alone, and we do so through Christ. For as the apostle says, "There is
1 Tm 2.5   one God and there is one mediator between God and men, the man Christ Jesus,"
           and, "If any one does sin, we have an advocate with the Father, Jesus Christ the
1 Jn 2.1   righteous," etc.

[4.] *The Saints Are Not to Be Adored, Worshiped, or Invoked.* For this reason
we do not adore, worship, or pray to the saints in heaven, or to other divine beings,
and we do not acknowledge them as our intercessors or mediators before the Father
in heaven. For God and Christ the Mediator are sufficient for us; neither do we give
to others the honor that is due to God alone and to his Son, because he has expressly
Is 42.8   said: "My glory I give to no other," and because Peter has said: "There is no other
           name under heaven given among men by which we must be saved," except the name
Acts 4.12 of Christ. In him, those who give their assent by faith do not seek anything outside
           Christ.

[5.] *The Due Honor to Be Rendered to the Saints.* At the same time we do not
despise the saints or think basely of them. For we acknowledge them to be living
members of Christ and friends of God who have gloriously overcome the flesh and
the world. Hence we love them as brothers, and also honor them; yet not with any
kind of worship but by an honorable opinion of them and just praises of them. We
also imitate them. For with ardent longings and supplications we earnestly desire to
be imitators of their faith and virtues, to share eternal salvation with them, to dwell
eternally with them in the presence of God, and to rejoice with them in Christ. And
in this respect we approve of the opinion of St. Augustine in *De Vera Religione:* "Let
not our religion be the cult of men who have died. For if they have lived holy lives,
they are not to be thought of as seeking such honors; on the contrary, they want us
to worship him by whose illumination they rejoice that we are fellow servants of his
merits. They are therefore to be honored by way of imitation, but not to be adored
in a religious manner," etc.

[6.] *Relics of the Saints.* Much less do we believe that the relics of the saints
are to be adored and reverenced. Those ancient saints seemed to have sufficiently
honored their dead when they decently committed their remains to the earth after
the spirit had ascended on high. And they thought that the most noble relics of their
ancestors were their virtues, their doctrine, and their faith. Moreover, as they commend these "relics" when praising the dead, so they strive to copy them during their
life on earth.

[7.] *Swearing by God's Name Alone.* These ancient men did not swear except

by the name of the only God, Yahweh, as prescribed by the divine law. Therefore, as
it is forbidden to swear by the names of strange gods, so we do not perform oaths to   Ex 23.13; Dt 10.20
the saints that are demanded of us. We therefore reject in all these matters a doctrine
that ascribes much too much to the saints in heaven.

CHAPTER 6. OF THE PROVIDENCE OF GOD

[1.] *All Things Are Governed by the Providence of God.* We believe that all things in
heaven and on earth, and all creatures, are preserved and governed by the providence of this wise, eternal, and almighty God. For David testifies and says: "The
Lord is high above all nations, and his glory above the heavens! Who is like the
Lord our God, who is seated on high, who looks far down upon the heavens and
the earth?" Again: "Thou searchest out . . . all my ways. Even before a word is on   Ps 113.4-6
my tongue, lo, O Lord, Thou knowest it altogether." Paul also testifies and declares: Ps 139.3-4
"In him we live and move and have our being," and "from him and through him   Acts 17.28
and to him are all things." [2.] Therefore Augustine most truly and according to   Rom 11.36
Scripture declared in his book *De agone Christi*, cap. 8, "The Lord said, 'Are not
two sparrows sold for a penny? And not one of them will fall to the ground without
your Father's will.'" By speaking thus, he wanted to show that what men regard as   Mt 10.29
of least value is governed by God's omnipotence. For he who is the truth says that
the birds of the air are fed by him and the lilies of the field are clothed by him; he
also says that the hairs of our head are numbered.   Mt 6.26ff.

[3.] *The Epicureans.* We therefore condemn the Epicureans, who deny the
providence of God, and all those who blasphemously say that God is busy with the
heavens and neither sees nor cares about us and our affairs. David, the royal prophet,
also condemned this when he said: "O Lord, how long shall the wicked exult? They
say, 'The Lord does not see; the God of Jacob does not perceive.' Understand, O
dullest of the people! Fools, when will you be wise? He who planted the ear, does
he not hear? He who formed the eye, does he not see?"   Ps 94.3, 7-9

[4.] *Means Not to Be Despised.* Nevertheless, we do not spurn as useless
the means by which divine providence works, but we teach that we are to adapt
ourselves to them in so far as they are recommended to us in the word of God.
Wherefore we disapprove of the rash statements of those who say that if all things
are managed by the providence of God, then our efforts and endeavors are in vain. It
will be sufficient if we leave everything to the governance of divine providence, and
we will not have to worry about anything or do anything. For although Paul understood that he sailed under the providence of God who had said to him: "You must
bear witness also at Rome," and in addition had given him the promise, "There   Acts 23.11
will be no loss of life among you . . . and not a hair is to perish from the head of

Acts 27.22, 34   any of you," yet when the sailors were nevertheless thinking about abandoning ship
                 the same Paul said to the centurion and the soldiers: "Unless these men stay in the
Acts 27.31   ship, you cannot be saved." For God, who has appointed to everything its end, has
                 ordained the beginning and the means by which it reaches its goal. The heathen as-
                 cribe things to blind fortune and uncertain chance. But St. James does not want us
                 to say: "Today or tomorrow we will go into such and such a town and trade," but
                 adds: "Instead you ought to say, 'If the Lord wills, we shall live and we shall do
Jas 4.13, 15   this or that.'" And Augustine says: "Everything which to vain men seems to hap-
                 pen in nature by accident, occurs only by his word, because it happens only at his
                 command" (*Enarrationes in Psalmos* 148). Thus it seemed to happen by mere chance
                 when Saul, while seeking his father's asses, unexpectedly fell in with the prophet
                 Samuel. But previously the Lord had said to the prophet: "Tomorrow I will send to
1 Sm 9.16   you a man from the land of Benjamin."

CHAPTER 7. OF THE CREATION OF ALL THINGS:
OF ANGELS, THE DEVIL, AND MAN

[1.] *God Created All Things.* This good and almighty God created all things, both
visible and invisible, by his coeternal Word, and preserves them by his coeternal
Spirit, as David testified when he said: "By the Word of the Lord the heavens were
Ps 33.6   made, and all their host by the breath of his mouth." And, as Scripture says, every-
           thing that God had made was very good, and was made for the profit and use of man.
[2.] Now we assert that all those things proceed from one beginning. *Manichaeans
and Marcionites.* Therefore, we condemn the Manichaeans and Marcionites, who
impiously imagined two substances and natures, one good, the other evil; also two
beginnings and two gods contrary to each other, a good one and an evil one.

[3.] *Of Angels and the Devil.* Among all creatures, angels and men are most
excellent. Concerning angels, Holy Scripture declares: "Who makest the winds thy
Ps 104.4   messengers, fire and flame thy ministers." Also it says: "Are they not all minister-
Heb 1.14   ing spirits sent forth to serve, for the sake of those who are to obtain salvation?"
           Concerning the devil, the Lord Jesus himself testifies, "He was a murderer from the
           beginning, and has nothing to do with the truth, because there is no truth in him.
           When he lies he speaks according to his own nature, for he is a liar and the father
Jn 8.44   of lies." [4.] Consequently we teach that some angels persisted in obedience and
           were appointed for faithful service to God and men, but others fell of their own
           free will and were cast into destruction, becoming enemies of all good and of the
           faithful, etc.

[5.] *Of Man.* Now concerning man, Scripture says that in the beginning he
was made good according to the image and likeness of God; that God placed him in

paradise and made all things subject to him. This is what David magnificently sets   Gn 2
forth in Psalm 8. Moreover, God gave him a wife and blessed them. [6.] We also affirm that man consists of two different substances in one person: an immortal soul
which, when separated from the body, neither sleeps nor dies, and a mortal body
which will nevertheless be raised up from the dead at the last judgment in order
that then the whole man, either in life or in death, abide forever.

[7.] *The Sects*. We condemn all who ridicule or by subtle arguments cast
doubt upon the immortality of souls, or who say that the soul sleeps or is a part of
God. In short, we condemn all opinions of all men, however many, that depart from
what has been delivered unto us by the Holy Scriptures in the apostolic church of
Christ concerning creation, angels, and demons, and man.

CHAPTER 8. OF MAN'S FALL, SIN, AND THE CAUSE OF SIN

[1.] *The Fall of Man*. In the beginning, man was made according to the image of
God, in righteousness and true holiness, good and upright. But when at the instigation of the serpent and by his own fault he abandoned goodness and righteousness,
he became subject to sin, death, and various calamities. And what he became by the
fall, that is, subject to sin, death, and various calamities, so are all those who have
descended from him.

[2.] *Sin*. By sin we understand that innate corruption of man which has
been derived or propagated in us all from our first parents, by which we, immersed
in perverse desires and averse to all good, are inclined to all evil. Full of all wickedness, distrust, contempt, and hatred of God, we are unable to do or even to think
anything good of ourselves. [3.] Moreover, even as we grow older, so by wicked
thoughts, words, and deeds committed against God's law, we bring forth corrupt
fruit worthy of an evil tree. For this reason by our own deserts, being subject to the   Mt 12.33ff.
wrath of God, we are liable to just punishment, so that all of us would have been
cast away by God if Christ, the Deliverer, had not brought us back.

[4.] *Death*. By death we understand not only bodily death, which all of us
must once suffer on account of sins, but also eternal punishment due to our sins and
corruption. For the apostle says: "We were dead through trespasses and sins . . . and
were by nature children of wrath, like the rest of mankind. But God, who is rich in
mercy . . . even when we were dead through our trespasses, made us alive together
with Christ." Also: "As sin came into the world through one man and death through   Eph 2.1, 3–5
sin, and so death spread to all men because all men sinned."   Rom 5.12

[5.] *Original Sin*. We therefore acknowledge that there is original sin in all
men.

Actual Sins. We acknowledge that all other sins which arise from it are called and truly are sins, no matter by what name they may be called, whether mortal, venial, or that which is said to be the sin against the Holy Spirit which is never

Mk 3.29; 1 Jn 5.16 forgiven. [6.] We also confess that sins are not equal; although they arise from the same fountain of corruption and unbelief, some are more serious than others. As the Lord said, it will be more tolerable for Sodom than for the city that rejects the

Mt 10.14f., 11.20ff. word of the gospel.

[7.] *The Sects.* We therefore condemn all who have taught contrary to this, especially Pelagius and all the Pelagians, together with the Jovinians, who, with the Stoics, regard all sins as equal. In this whole matter we agree with St. Augustine, who derived and defended his view from Holy Scriptures. [8.] Moreover, we condemn Florinus and Blastus, against whom Irenaeus wrote, and all who make God the author of sin.

God Is Not the Author of Sin, and How Far He Is Said to Harden. It is expressly written: "Thou art not a God who delights in wickedness. Thou hatest all

Ps 5.4ff. evildoers. Thou destroyest those who speak lies." And again: "When the devil lies,

Jn 8.44 he speaks according to his own nature, for he is a liar and the father of lies." Moreover, there is enough sinfulness and corruption in us that it is not necessary for God to infuse into us a new or still greater perversity. [9.] When, therefore, it is said in Scripture that God hardens, blinds, and delivers up to a reprobate mind, it is to be understood that God does it by a just judgment as a just Judge and Avenger. Finally, as often as God in Scripture is said or seems to do something evil, it is not thereby said that man does not do evil, but that God permits it and does not prevent it, according to his just judgment, who could prevent it if he wished, or because he turns man's evil into good, as he did in the case of Joseph's brethren, or because he governs sins lest they break out and rage more than is appropriate. St. Augustine writes in his *Enchiridion* [c. 100]: "What happens contrary to his will occurs, in a wonderful and ineffable way, not apart from his will. For it would not happen if he did not allow it. And yet he does not allow it unwillingly but willingly. But he who is good would not permit evil to be done, unless, being omnipotent, he could bring good out of evil." Thus wrote Augustine.

[10.] *Curious Questions.* Other questions, such as whether God willed Adam to fall, or why he did not prevent the fall, and similar questions, we reckon among curious questions (unless perchance the wickedness of heretics or of other churlish men compels us also to explain them out of the word of God, as the godly teachers of the church have frequently done), knowing that the Lord forbade man to eat of the forbidden fruit and punished his transgression. We also know that what things are done are not evil with respect to the providence, will, and power of God, but in respect of Satan and our will opposing the will of God.

CHAPTER 9. OF FREE WILL, AND THUS OF HUMAN POWERS

[1.] In this matter, which has always produced many conflicts in the church, we teach that a threefold condition or state of man is to be considered. [2.] *What Man Was Before the Fall.* There is the state in which man was in the beginning before the fall, namely, upright and free, so that he could either continue in goodness or decline toward evil. However, he declined to evil, and has involved himself and the whole human race in sin and death, as has been said already. *What Man Was After the Fall.* Then we are to consider what man was after the fall. To be sure, his reason was not taken from him, nor was he deprived of will, and he was not entirely changed into a stone or a tree. But they were so altered and weakened that they no longer can do what they could before the fall. For the understanding is darkened, and the will which was free has become an enslaved will. [3.] Now it serves sin, not unwillingly but willingly. And indeed, it is called a will, not an unwilling.

Man Does Evil by His Own Free Will. Therefore, in regard to evil or sin, man is not forced by God or by the devil but does evil by his own free will, and in this respect he has a most free will. But when we frequently see that the worst crimes and designs of men are prevented by God from reaching their purpose, this does not take away man's freedom in doing evil, but God by his own power prevents what man freely planned otherwise. Thus Joseph's brothers freely determined to get rid of him, but they were unable to do it because something else seemed good to the counsel of God.

[4.] *Man Is Not Capable of Good per se.* In regard to goodness and virtue man's reason does not judge rightly of itself concerning divine things. For the evangelical and apostolic Scripture requires regeneration of whoever among us wishes to be saved. Hence our first birth from Adam contributes nothing to our salvation. Paul says: "The unspiritual man does not receive the gifts of the Spirit of God," etc.   1 Cor 2.14
And in another place he denies that we of ourselves are capable of thinking anything good. [5.] Now it is known that the mind or intellect is the guide of the will, and   2 Cor 3.5
when the guide is blind, it is obvious how far the will reaches. Wherefore, man not yet regenerate has no free will for good, no strength to perform what is good. The Lord says in the Gospel: "Truly, truly, I say to you, everyone who commits sin is a slave to sin." And the apostle says: "The mind that is set on the flesh is hostile   Jn 8.34
to God; it does not submit to God's law, indeed it cannot." [6.] Yet in regard to   Rom 8.7
earthly things, fallen man is not entirely lacking in understanding.

Understanding of the Arts. For God in his mercy has permitted the powers of the intellect to remain, though differing greatly from what was in man before the fall. God commands us to cultivate our natural talents, and meanwhile adds both gifts and success. And it is obvious that we make no progress in all the arts without

God's blessing. In any case, Scripture refers all the arts to God; and, indeed, the heathen trace the origin of the arts to the gods who invented them.

[7.] *Of What Kind Are the Powers of the Regenerate, and in What Way Their Wills Are Free*. Finally, we must see whether the regenerate have free wills, and to what extent. In regeneration the understanding is illumined by the Holy Spirit in order that it may understand both the mysteries and the will of God. And the will itself is not only changed by the Spirit, but it is also equipped with faculties so that it wills and is able to do the good of its own accord. Unless we grant this, we will deny Christian liberty and introduce a legal bondage. But the prophet has God saying: "I will put my law within them, and I will write it upon their hearts." The Lord also says in the Gospel: "If the Son makes you free, you will be free indeed." Paul also writes to the Philippians: "It has been granted to you that for the sake of Christ you should not only believe in him but also suffer for his sake." Again: "I am sure that he who began a good work in you will bring it to completion at the day of Jesus Christ." Also: "God is at work in you, both to will and to work for his good pleasure."

Rom 8.1ff.

Jer 31.33; Ez 36.26f.

Jn 8.36

Phil 1.29

Phil 1.6

Phil 2.13

[8.] *The Regenerate Work Not Only Passively but Actively*. However, in this connection we teach that there are two things to be observed: First, that the regenerate, in choosing and doing good, work not only passively but actively. For they are moved by God that they may do themselves what they do. For Augustine rightly adduces the saying that "God is said to be our helper. But no one can be helped unless he does something." The Manichaeans robbed man of all activity and made him like a stone or block of wood.

[9.] *The Free Will Is Weak in the Regenerate*. Secondly, in the regenerate a weakness remains. For since sin dwells in us, and in the regenerate the flesh struggles against the Spirit till the end of our lives, they do not easily accomplish in all things what they had planned. These things are confirmed by the apostle in Romans 7, and Galatians 5. [10.] Therefore that free will is weak in us on account of the remnants of the old Adam and of innate human corruption remaining in us until the end of our lives. Meanwhile, since the power of the flesh and the remnants of the old man are not so efficacious that they wholly extinguish the work of the Spirit, for that reason the faithful are said to be free, yet so that they acknowledge their infirmity and do not glory at all in their free will. For believers ought always to keep in mind what St. Augustine so many times inculcated according to the apostle: "What have you that you did not receive? If then you received, why do you boast as if it were not a gift?" To this he adds that what we have planned does not immediately come to pass. For the issue of things lies in the hand of God. This is the reason Paul prayed to the Lord to prosper his journey. And this also is the reason the free will is weak.

Rom 7; Gal 5

1 Cor 4.7

Rom 1.10

[11.] *In External Things There Is Liberty.* Moreover, no one denies that in external things both the regenerate and the unregenerate enjoy free will. For man has in common with other living creatures (to which he is not inferior) this nature to will some things and not to will others. Thus he is able to speak or to keep silent, to go out of his house or to remain at home, etc. However, even here God's power is always to be observed, for it was the cause that Balaam could not go as far as he wanted, and Zacharias upon returning from the temple could not speak as he wanted.

Num 24
Luke 1

[12.] *Heresies.* In this matter we condemn the Manichaeans, who deny that the beginning of evil was for man [created] good, from his free will. We also condemn the Pelagians, who assert that an evil man has sufficient free will to do the good that is commanded. Both are refuted by Holy Scripture, which says to the former, "God made man upright," and to the latter, "If the Son makes you free, you will be free indeed."

Eccl 7.29
Jn 8.36

CHAPTER 10. OF THE PREDESTINATION OF GOD AND
THE ELECTION OF THE SAINTS

[1.] *God Has Elected Us out of Grace.* From eternity God has freely, and of his mere grace, without any respect to men, predestinated or elected the saints whom he wills to save in Christ, according to the saying of the apostle, "God chose us in him before the foundation of the world." And again: "Who saved us and called us with a holy calling, not in virtue of our works but in virtue of his own purpose and the grace which he gave us in Christ Jesus ages ago, and now has manifested through the appearing of our Savior Christ Jesus."

Eph 1.4

2 Tm 1.9–10

[2.] *We Are Elected or Predestinated in Christ.* Therefore, although not on account of any merit of ours, God has elected us, not directly, but in Christ, and on account of Christ, in order that those who are now engrafted into Christ by faith might also be elected. But those who were outside Christ were rejected, according to the words of the apostle, "Examine yourselves, to see whether you are holding to your faith. Test yourselves. Do you not realize that Jesus Christ is in you?—unless indeed you fail to meet the test!"

2 Cor 13.5

[3.] *We Are Elected for a Definite Purpose.* Finally, the saints are chosen by God for a definite purpose, which the apostle himself explains when he says, "He chose us in him for adoption that we should be holy and blameless before him in love. He destined us for adoption to be his sons through Jesus Christ that they should be to the praise of the glory of his grace."

Eph 1.4–6

[4.] *We Are to Have a Good Hope for All.* And although God knows who are his, and here and there mention is made of the small number of elect, yet we must hope well of all, and not rashly judge any man to be a reprobate. For Paul says to the Philippians, "I thank my God for you all" (now he speaks of the whole church in Philippi), "because of your fellowship in the gospel, being persuaded that he who began a good work in you will bring it to completion at the day of Jesus Christ. It is also right that I have this opinion of you all."

Phil 1.3, 5-7

[5.] *Whether Few Are Elect.* And when the Lord was asked whether there were few that should be saved, he does not answer and tell them that few or many should be saved or damned, but rather he exhorts every man to "strive to enter by the narrow door": as if he should say, It is not for you curiously to inquire about these matters, but rather to endeavor that you may enter into heaven by the straight way.

Lk 13.24

[6.] *What in This Matter Is to Be Condemned.* Therefore we do not approve of the impious speeches of some who say, "Few are chosen, and since I do not know whether I am among the number of the few, I will enjoy myself." Others say, "If I am predestinated and elected by God, nothing can hinder me from salvation, which is already certainly appointed for me, no matter what I do. But if I am in the number of the reprobate, no faith or repentance will help me, since the decree of God cannot be changed. Therefore all doctrines and admonitions are useless." Now the saying of the apostle contradicts these men: "The Lord's servant must be ready to teach, instructing those who oppose him, so that if God should grant that they repent to know the truth, they may recover from the snare of the devil, after being held captive by him to do his will."

2 Tm 2.23-26

[7.] *Admonitions Are Not in Vain Because Salvation Proceeds from Election.* Augustine also shows that both the grace of free election and predestination, and also salutary admonitions and doctrines, are to be preached (*Liber de Dono Perseverantiae,* cap. 14ff.).

Whether We Are Elected. We therefore find fault with those who outside of Christ ask whether they are elected.[2] And what has God decreed concerning them before all eternity? [8.] For the preaching of the gospel is to be heard, and it is to be believed; and it is to be held as beyond doubt that if you believe and are in Christ, you are elected. For the Father has revealed unto us in Christ the eternal purpose of his predestination, as I have just now shown from the apostle in 2 Timothy 1. This is therefore above all to be taught and considered, what great love of the Father toward us is revealed to us in Christ. We must hear what the Lord himself daily preaches to us in the Gospel, how he calls and says: "Come to me all who labor and are heavy-laden, and I will give you rest." "God so loved the world, that he gave

2 Tm 1[.9-10]

Mt 11.28

2. The 1568 edition reads: "whether they are elected from eternity?"

his only Son, that whoever believes in him should not perish, but have eternal life."   Jn 3.16
Also, "It is not the will of my Father that one of these little ones should perish."   Mt 18.14

[9.] Let Christ, therefore be the looking glass, in whom we may contemplate our predestination. We shall have a sufficiently clear and sure testimony that we are inscribed in the book of life if we have fellowship with Christ, and he is ours and we are his in true faith.

Temptation in Regard to Predestination. In the temptation in regard to predestination, than which there is scarcely any other more dangerous, we are comforted by the fact that God's promises apply to all the faithful, for he says: "Ask, and everyone who seeks, shall receive." [10.] This finally we pray, with the whole   Lk 11.9
church of God, "Our Father who art in heaven," both because by baptism we are en-   Mt 6.9
grafted into the body of Christ, and we are often fed in his church with his flesh and blood unto life eternal. Thereby, being strengthened, we are commanded to work out our salvation with fear and trembling, according to the precept of Paul.   [Phil 2.12]

CHAPTER 11. OF JESUS CHRIST, TRUE GOD AND MAN, THE ONLY SAVIOR OF THE WORLD

[1.] *Christ Is True God.* We further believe and teach that the Son of God, our Lord Jesus Christ, was predestinated or foreordained from eternity by the Father to be the Savior of the world. And we believe that he was born, not only when he assumed flesh of the Virgin Mary, and not only before the foundation of the world was laid, but by the Father before all eternity in an inexpressible manner. For Isaiah said: "Who can tell his generation?" And Micah says: "His origin is from of old,   Is 53.8
from ancient days." And John said in the Gospel: "In the beginning was the Word,   Mi 4.2
and the Word was with God, and the Word was God," etc. [2.] Therefore, with   Jn 1.1
respect to his divinity the Son is coequal and consubstantial with the Father; true God, not only in name or by adoption or by any merit, but in substance and nature,   Phil 2.11
as the apostle John has often said: "This is the true God and eternal life." Paul also   1 Jn 5.20
says: "He appointed the Son the heir of all things, through whom also he created the world. He reflects the glory of God and bears the very stamp of his nature, upholding all things by his word of power." For in the Gospel the Lord himself said: Heb 1.2–3
"Father, glorify thou me in thy own presence with the glory which I had with thee before the world was made." And in another place in the Gospel it is written: "The   Jn 17.5
Jews sought all the more to kill him because he . . . called God his Father making himself equal with God."   Jn 5.18

[3.] *The Sects.* We therefore abhor the impious doctrine of Arius and the Arians against the Son of God, and especially the blasphemies of the Spaniard, Michael Servetus, and all his followers, which Satan through them has, as it were, dragged up out of hell and has most audaciously and impiously spread abroad in the world.

[4.] *Christ Is True Man, Having Real Flesh.* We also believe and teach that the eternal Son of the eternal God was made the Son of man, from the seed of Abraham and David, not from the coitus of a man, as the Ebionites said, but was most chastely conceived by the Holy Spirit and born of the Ever-Virgin Mary, as the evangelical history carefully explains to us. And Paul says: "He took not on him the nature of angels, but of the seed of Abraham." Also the apostle John says that whoever does not believe that Jesus Christ has come in the flesh is not of God. Therefore, the flesh of Christ was neither imaginary nor brought from heaven, as Valentinus and Marcion wrongly imagined.

Mt 1
Heb 2.16

[5.] *A Rational Soul in Christ.* Moreover, our Lord Jesus Christ did not have a soul bereft of sense and reason, as Apollinaris thought, nor flesh without a soul, as Eunomius taught, but a soul with its reason, and flesh with its senses, by which in the time of his passion he sustained real bodily pain, as he himself testified when he said: "My soul is very sorrowful, even to death."[a] And, "Now is my soul troubled."[b]

[6.] *Two Natures in Christ.* We therefore acknowledge two natures or substances, the divine and the human, in one and the same Jesus Christ our Lord. And we say that these are bound and united with one another in such a way that they are not absorbed, or confused, or mixed, but are united or joined together in one person—the properties of the natures being unimpaired and permanent.

Heb 2

Not Two but One Christ. Thus we worship not two but one Christ the Lord. We repeat: one true God and man. With respect to his divine nature he is consubstantial with the Father, and with respect to the human nature he is consubstantial with us men, and like us in all things, sin excepted.

Heb 4.15

[7.] *The Sects.* And indeed we detest the dogma of the Nestorians, who make two of the one Christ and dissolve the unity of the person. Likewise we thoroughly execrate the madness of Eutyches and the Monothelites or Monophysites, who destroy the property of the human nature.

[8.] *The Divine Nature of Christ Is Not Passible, and the Human Nature Is Not Everywhere.* Therefore, we do not in any way teach that the divine nature in Christ has suffered or that Christ according to his human nature is still in the world and thus everywhere. For neither do we think or teach that the body of Christ ceased to be a true body after his glorification, or was deified, and deified in such a way

a. Mt 26.38
b. Jn 12.27

that it laid aside its properties as regards body and soul, and changed entirely into a divine nature and began to be merely one substance.

[9.] *The Sects.* Hence we by no means approve or accept the strained, confused, and obscure subtleties of Schwenckfeld and of similar sophists with their self-contradictory arguments; neither are we Schwenckfeldians.

[10.] *Our Lord Truly Suffered.* We believe, moreover, that our Lord Jesus Christ truly suffered and died for us in the flesh, as Peter says. We abhor the most impious madness of the Jacobites and all the Turks, who execrate the suffering of the Lord. At the same time we do not deny that the Lord of glory was crucified for us, according to Paul's words.   1 Pt 4.1

1 Cor 2.8

Interchange of Properties. We piously and reverently accept and use the interchange of properties, which is derived from Scripture and which has been used by all antiquity in explaining and reconciling apparently contradictory passages.

[11.] *Christ Is Truly Risen from the Dead.* We believe and teach that the same Jesus Christ our Lord, in his true flesh in which he was crucified and died, rose again from the dead, and that not another flesh was raised other than the one buried, or that a spirit was taken up instead of the flesh, but that he retained his true body. Therefore, while his disciples thought they saw the spirit of the Lord, he showed them them his hands and feet, which were marked by the prints of the nails and wounds, and added: "See my hands and my feet, that it is I myself; handle me, and see, for a spirit has not flesh and bones as you see that I have."   Lk 24.39

[12.] *Christ Is Truly Ascended into Heaven.* We believe that our Lord Jesus Christ, in his same flesh, ascended above all visible heavens into the highest heaven, that is, the dwelling-place of God and the blessed ones, at the right hand of God the Father. Although it signifies an equal participation in glory and majesty, it is also taken to be a certain place about which the Lord, speaking in the Gospel, says: "I go to prepare a place for you." The apostle Peter also says: "Heaven must receive Christ until the time of restoring all things." [13.] And from heaven the same Christ will return in judgment, when wickedness will then be at its greatest in the world and when the Antichrist, having corrupted true religion, will fill up all things with superstition and impiety and will cruelly lay waste the church with bloodshed and flames. But Christ will come again to claim his own, and by his coming to destroy the Antichrist, and to judge the living and the dead.[a] For the dead will rise again,[b] and those who on that day (which is unknown to all creatures) will be alive will be   Jn 14.2

Acts 3.21

Dn 11

Mk 13.32

a. Acts 17.31
b. 1 Thes 4.14ff.

changed "in the twinkling of an eye," and all the faithful will be caught up to meet

1 Cor 15.51-52 Christ in the air, so that then they may enter with him into the blessed dwelling-places to live forever. But the unbelievers and ungodly will descend with the devils

Mt 25.46 into hell to burn forever and never to be redeemed from torments.

[14.] *The Sects.* We therefore condemn all who deny a real resurrection of

2 Tm 2.18 the flesh, or who with John of Jerusalem, against whom Jerome wrote, do not have a correct view of the glorification of bodies. We also condemn those who thought that the devil and all the ungodly would at some time be saved, and that there would be an end to punishments. For the Lord has plainly declared: "Their fire is not

Mk 9.44 quenched, and their worm does not die." We further condemn Jewish dreams that there will be a golden age on earth before the day of judgment, and that the pious, having subdued all their godless enemies, will possess all the kingdoms of the earth.

Mt 24, 25; Lk 18 For evangelical truth in Matthew, chapters 24 and 25, and Luke 18, and apostolic

2 Thes 2; 2 Tm 3, 4 teaching in 2 Thessalonians 2, and 2 Timothy, chapters 3 and 4, present something quite different.

[15.] *The Fruit of Christ's Death and Resurrection.* Further by his passion and death and everything which he did and endured for our sake by his coming in the flesh, our Lord reconciled all the faithful to the heavenly Father, made expiation for our sins, disarmed death, overcame damnation and hell, and by his resurrection from the dead brought again and restored life and immortality. For he is our righteousness, life, and resurrection, in a word, the fullness and perfection of all the faithful, salvation, and all sufficiency. For the apostle says: "In him all the fullness

Col 1-2 of God was pleased to dwell," and, "You have come to fullness of life in him."

[16.] *Jesus Christ Is the Only Savior of the World, and the True Awaited Messiah.* For we teach and believe that Jesus Christ our Lord is the unique and eternal Savior of the human race, and thus of the whole world, in whom by faith are saved all who before the law, under the law, and under the gospel were saved, and however many will be saved at the end of the world. For the Lord himself says in the Gospel: "He who does not enter the sheepfold by the door but climbs in by another

Jn 10.1, 7 way, that man is a thief and a robber. . . . I am the door of the sheep." And also in

Jn 8.56 another place in the same Gospel he says: "Abraham saw my day and was glad." The apostle Peter also says: "There is salvation in no one else, for there is no other name under heaven given among men by which we must be saved." We therefore believe that we will be saved through the grace of our Lord Jesus Christ, as our fathers were.[a] For Paul also says: "All our fathers ate the same spiritual food and all drank the same spiritual drink. For they drank from the spiritual rock which fol-

a. Acts 4.12, 10.43, 15.11

lowed them, and the rock was Christ." And thus we read that John says: "Christ was   1 Cor 10.3-4
the Lamb which was slain from the foundation of the world," and John the Baptist   Rv 13.8
testified that Christ is that "Lamb of God, who takes away the sin of the world."   Jn 1.29
[17.] Wherefore, we quite openly profess and preach that Jesus Christ is the sole
Redeemer and Savior of the world, the King and High Priest, the true and awaited
Messiah, that holy and blessed one whom all the types of the law and predictions
of the prophets prefigured and promised; and that God appointed him beforehand
and sent him to us, so that we are not now to look for any other. Now there only
remains for all of us to give all glory to Christ, believe in him, rest in him alone,
despising and rejecting all other aids in life. For however many seek salvation in
any other than in Christ alone, have fallen from the grace of God and have rendered
Christ null and void for themselves.   Gal 5.4

[18.] *The Creeds of Four Councils Received*. And, to say many things with
a few words, with a sincere heart we believe, and freely confess with open mouth,
whatever things are defined from the Holy Scriptures concerning the mystery of
the incarnation of our Lord Jesus Christ, and are summed up in the creeds and decrees of the first four most excellent synods convened at Nicaea, Constantinople,
Ephesus, and Chalcedon—together with the creed of blessed Athanasius, and all
similar symbols; and we condemn anything contrary to these.

The Sects. And in this way we retain the Christian, orthodox, and catholic faith whole and unimpaired; knowing that nothing is contained in the aforesaid
symbols which is not agreeable to the word of God and does not altogether make
for a sincere exposition of the faith.

CHAPTER 12. OF THE LAW OF GOD

[1.] *The Will of God Is Explained for Us in the Law of God*. We teach that the will
of God is explained for us in the law of God, what he wills or does not will us to
do, what is good and just, or what is evil and unjust. Therefore, we confess that the
law is good and holy.

The Law of Nature. And this law was at one time written in the hearts of
men by the finger of God, and is called the law of nature (*the law of Moses is in two*   Rom 2.15
tables), and at another it was inscribed by his finger on the two tables of Moses, and
eloquently expounded in the books of Moses. For the sake of clarity we distinguish   Ex 20.1ff.; Dt 5.6ff.
the moral law, which is contained in the Decalogue or two tables and expounded in
the books of Moses, the ceremonial law, which determines the ceremonies and worship of God, and the judicial law, which is concerned with political and domestic
matters.

[2.] *The Law Is Complete and Perfect*. We believe that the whole will of God

and all necessary precepts for every sphere of life are taught in this law. For otherwise the Lord would not have forbidden us to add or to take away anything from
this law; neither would he have commanded us to walk in a straight path before this

Dt 4.2, 12.32   law, and not to turn aside from it by turning to the right or to the left.

[3.] *Why the Law Was Given.* We teach that this law was not given to men
that they might be justified by keeping it, but that rather from what it teaches we
may know [our] weakness, sin, and condemnation, and, despairing of our strength,
might be converted to Christ in faith. For the apostle openly declares: "The law

Rom 4.15, 3.20 brings wrath," and, "Through the law comes knowledge of sin," and, "If a law had
been given which could justify or make alive, then righteousness would indeed be
by the law. But the Scripture (that is, the law) has concluded all under sin, that the
promise which was of the faith of Jesus might be given to those who believe. . . .
Therefore, the law was our schoolmaster unto Christ, that we might be justified by

Gal 3.21–22, 24 faith."

The Flesh Does Not Fulfill the Law. For no flesh could or can satisfy the law
of God and fulfill it, because of the weakness in our flesh which adheres and remains
in us until our last breath. For the apostle says again: "God has done what the law,
weakened by the flesh, could not do: sending his own Son in the likeness of sinful

Rom 8.3   flesh and for sin." Therefore, Christ is the perfecting of the law and our fulfillment
of it,[a] who, in order to take away the curse of the law, was made a curse for us.[b]
Thus he imparts to us through faith his fulfillment of the law, and his righteousness
and obedience are imputed to us.

[4.] *How Far the Law Is Abrogated.* The law of God is therefore abrogated
to the extent that it no longer condemns us, nor works wrath in us. For we are under
grace and not under the law. Moreover, Christ has fulfilled all the figures of the law.
Hence, with the coming of the body, the shadows ceased, so that in Christ we now
have the truth and all fullness. But yet we do not on that account contemptuously
reject the law. For we remember the words of the Lord when he said: "I have not

Mt 5.17   come to abolish the law and the prophets but to fulfill them." We know that in the
law is delivered to us the patterns of virtues and vices. We know that the written law
when explained by the gospel is useful to the church, and that therefore its reading
is not to be banished from the church. For although Moses' face was covered with a
veil, yet the apostle says that the veil has been taken away and abolished by Christ.

The Sects. We condemn everything that heretics old and new have taught
against the law.

a. Rom 10.4
b. Gal 3.13

CHAPTER 13. OF THE GOSPEL OF JESUS CHRIST, OF THE PROMISES, AND OF THE SPIRIT AND LETTER

[1.] *The Ancients Had Evangelical Promises.* The gospel is indeed opposed to the law. For the law works wrath and announces a curse, whereas the gospel preaches grace and blessing. John says: "For the law was given through Moses; grace and truth came through Jesus Christ." Yet notwithstanding it is most certain that those who   Jn 1.17
were before the law and under the law, were not altogether destitute of the gospel. For they had extraordinary evangelical promises such as these are: "The seed of the woman shall bruise the serpent's head." "In thy seed shall all the nations of the earth   Gn 3.15
be blessed."ᵃ "The scepter shall not depart from Judah . . . until he comes."ᵇ "The Lord will raise up a prophet from among his own brethren," etc.   Dt 18.15; Acts 3.22

[2.] *The Promises Twofold.* And we acknowledge that two kinds of promises were revealed to the fathers, as also to us. For some were of present or earthly things, such as the promises of the land of Canaan and of victories, and as the promise today still of daily bread. Others were then and are still now of heavenly and eternal things, namely, divine grace, remission of sins, and eternal life through faith in Jesus Christ.

[3.] *The Fathers Also Had Not Only Carnal but Spiritual Promises.* Moreover, the ancients had not only external and earthly but also spiritual and heavenly promises in Christ. Peter says: "The prophets who prophesied of the grace that was to be yours searched and inquired about this salvation." Wherefore the apostle Paul   1 Pt 1.10
also said: "The gospel of God was promised beforehand through his prophets in the Holy Scriptures." Thereby it is clear that the ancients were not entirely destitute   Rom 1.2
of the whole gospel.

What Is the Gospel Properly Speaking? And although our fathers had the gospel in this way in the writings of the prophets by which they attained salvation in Christ through faith, yet the gospel is properly called glad and joyous news, in which, first by John the Baptist, then by Christ the Lord himself, and afterwards by the apostles and their successors, is preached to us in the world that God has now performed what he promised from the beginning of the world, and has sent, nay more, has given us his only Son and in him reconciliation with the Father, the remission of sins, all fullness and everlasting life. Therefore, the history delineated by the four evangelists and explaining how these things were done or fulfilled by Christ, what things Christ taught and did, and that those who believe in him have all fullness, is rightly called the gospel. The preaching and writings of the apostles,

a. Gn 22.18
b. Gn 49.10

in which the apostles explain for us how the Son was given to us by the Father, and in him everything that has to do with life and salvation, is also rightly called evangelical doctrine, so that not even today, if sincerely preached, does it lose its illustrious title.

[4.] *Of the Spirit and the Letter.* That same preaching of the gospel is also called by the apostle "the spirit" and "the ministry of the spirit" because by faith it becomes effectual and living in the ears, nay more, in the hearts of believers through the illumination of the Holy Spirit. For the letter, which is opposed to the spirit, signifies everything external, but especially the doctrine of the law which, without the spirit and faith, works wrath and provokes sin in the minds of those who do not have a living faith. For this reason the apostle calls it "the ministry of death." In this connection the saying of the apostle is pertinent: "The letter kills, but the spirit gives life." And false apostles preached a corrupted gospel, having combined it with the law, as if Christ could not save without the law.

The Sects. Such were the Ebionites said to be, who were descended from Ebion the heretic, and the Nazarites, who were formerly called Mineans. All these we condemn, while preaching the pure gospel and teaching that believers are justified by the Spirit[3] alone, and not by the law. A more detailed exposition of this matter will follow presently under the heading of justification.

[5.] *The Teaching of the Gospel Is Not New, but Most Ancient Doctrine.* And although the teaching of the gospel, compared with the teaching of the Pharisees concerning the law, seemed to be a new doctrine when first preached by Christ (which Jeremiah also prophesied concerning the New Testament), yet actually it not only was and still is an old doctrine (even if today it is called new by the papists when compared with the teaching now received among them), but is the most ancient of all in the world. For God predestinated from eternity to save the world through Christ, and he has disclosed to the world through the gospel this his predestination and eternal counsel. Hence it is evident that the religion and teaching of the gospel among all who ever were, are, and will be, is the most ancient of all. Wherefore we assert that all who say that the religion and teaching of the gospel is a faith which has recently arisen, being scarcely thirty years old, err disgracefully and speak shamefully of the eternal counsel of God. To them applies the saying of Isaiah the prophet: "Woe to those who call evil good and good evil, who put darkness for light and light for darkness, who put bitter for sweet and sweet for bitter!"

Margin references:
2 Cor 3.6
2 Cor 3.7
2 Cor 3.8
Jer [31.31]
2 Tm 1.9f.
Is 5.20

---

3. A Zurich manuscript has "Christ" instead of "Spirit."

CHAPTER 14. OF REPENTANCE AND THE CONVERSION OF MAN

[1.] The doctrine of repentance is joined with the gospel. For so has the Lord said in the Gospel: "Repentance and forgiveness of sins should be preached in my name to all nations." [2.] *What Is Repentance?* By repentance we understand the recovery of a right mind in sinful man awakened by the word of the gospel and the Holy Spirit, and received by true faith, by which the sinner immediately acknowledges his innate corruption and all his sins accused by the word of God; and grieves for them from his heart, and not only bewails and frankly confesses them before God with a feeling of shame, but also with indignation abominates them; and now zealously considers the amendment of his ways and constantly strives for innocence and virtue in which conscientiously to exercise himself all the rest of his life.

Lk 24.47

[3.] *True Repentance Is Conversion to God.* And this is true repentance, namely, a sincere turning to God and all good, and earnest turning away from the devil and all evil. *Repentance Is a Gift of God.* Now we expressly say that this repentance is a sheer gift of God and not a work of our strength. For the apostle commands a faithful minister diligently to instruct those who oppose the truth, if "God may perhaps grant that they will repent and come to know the truth." [4.] *Laments Sins Committed.* Now that sinful woman who washed the feet of the Lord with her tears, and Peter who wept bitterly and bewailed his denial of the Lord show clearly how the mind of a penitent man ought to be seriously lamenting the sins he has committed. [5.] *Confesses Sins to God.* Moreover, the prodigal son and the publican in the Gospel, when compared with the Pharisee, present us with the most suitable pattern of how our sins are to be confessed to God. The former said: "'Father, I have sinned against heaven and before you; I am no longer worthy to be called your son; treat me as one of your hired servants.'" And the latter, not daring to raise his eyes to heaven, beat his breast, saying, "God be merciful to me a sinner." And we do not doubt that they were accepted by God into grace. For the apostle John says "If we confess our sins, he is faithful and just, and will forgive our sins and cleanse us from all unrighteousness. If we say we have not sinned, we make him a liar, and his word is not in us."

2 Tm 2.25

Lk 7.38, 22.62

Lk 15.8ff.
Lk 18.13

1 Jn 1.9–10

[6.] *Sacerdotal Confession and Absolution.* But we believe that this sincere confession which is made to God alone, either privately between God and the sinner, or publicly in the church where the general confession of sins is said, is sufficient, and that in order to obtain forgiveness of sins it is not necessary for anyone to confess his sins to a priest, murmuring them in his ears, that in turn he might receive absolution from the priest with his laying on of hands, because there is neither a commandment nor an example of this in Holy Scriptures. David testifies and says: "I acknowledged my sin to thee, and did not hide my iniquity; I said, 'I will confess my transgressions to the Lord'; then thou didst forgive the guilt of my sin." And the Lord who taught us to pray and at the same time to confess our sins said: "Pray then like this: Our Father, who art in heaven, . . . forgive us our debts, as we also forgive our debtors." [7.] Therefore it is necessary that we confess our sins to God our Father, and be reconciled with our neighbor if we have offended him. Concerning this kind of confession, the apostle James says: "Confess your sins to one another." If, however, anyone is overwhelmed by the burden of his sins and by perplexing temptations, and will seek counsel, instruction, and comfort privately, either from a minister of the church, or from any other brother who is instructed in God's law, we do not disapprove; just as we also fully approve of that general and public confession of sins which is usually said in church and in meetings for worship, as we noted above, inasmuch as it is agreeable to Scripture.

[8.] *Of the Keys of the Kingdom of Heaven.* Concerning the keys of the kingdom of heaven which the Lord gave to the apostles, many babble many astonishing things, and out of them forge swords, spears, scepters and crowns, and complete power over the greatest kingdoms, indeed, over souls and bodies. Judging simply according to the word of the Lord, we say that all properly called ministers possess and exercise the keys or the use of them when they proclaim the gospel; that is, when they teach, exhort, comfort, rebuke, and keep in discipline the people committed to their trust.

Opening and Shutting (the Kingdom). For in this way they open the kingdom of heaven to the obedient and shut it to the disobedient. The Lord promised these keys to the apostles in Matthew 16,[a] and gave them in John 20, Mark 16, and Luke 24, when he sent out his disciples and commanded them to preach the gospel in all the world, and to remit sins.

The Ministry of Reconciliation. In the letter to the Corinthians the apostle says that the Lord gave the ministry of reconciliation to his ministers. And what this is he then explains, saying that it is the preaching or teaching of reconciliation. And explaining his words still more clearly he adds that Christ's ministers discharge the office of an ambassador in Christ's name, as if God himself through ministers exhorted the people to be reconciled to God, doubtless by faithful obedience. Therefore, they exercise the keys when they persuade [men] to believe and repent. Thus they reconcile men to God.

Ministers Remit Sins. Thus they remit sins. Thus they open the kingdom of

Ps 32.5

Mt 6[.9,] 12

Jas 5.16

2 Cor 5.18ff.

a. Mt 16; Jn 20; Mk 16; Lk 24

heaven, and bring believers into it: very different from those of whom the Lord said in the Gospel, "Woe to you lawyers! for you have taken away the key of knowledge; you did not enter yourselves, and you hindered those who were entering."   Lk 11.52

[9.] *How Ministers Absolve.* Ministers, therefore, rightly and effectually absolve when they preach the gospel of Christ and thereby the remission of sins, which is promised to each one who believes, just as each one is baptized, and when they testify that it pertains to each one peculiarly. Neither do we think that this absolution becomes more effectual by being murmured in the ear of someone or by being murmured singly over someone's head. We are nevertheless of the opinion that the remission of sins in the blood of Christ is to be diligently proclaimed, and that each one is to be admonished that the forgiveness of sins pertains to him.

[10.] *Diligence in the Renewal of Life.* But the examples in the Gospel teach us how vigilant and diligent the penitent ought to be in striving for newness of life and in mortifying the old man and quickening the new. For the Lord said to the man he healed of palsy: "See, you are well! Sin no more, that nothing worse befall you."[a] Likewise to the adulteress whom he set free he said: "Go, and sin no more."[b] To be sure, by these words he did not mean that any man, as long as he lived in the flesh, could not sin; he simply recommends diligence and a careful devotion, so that we should strive by all means, and beseech God in prayers lest we fall back into sins from which, as it were, we have been resurrected, and lest we be overcome by the flesh, the world, and the devil. Zacchaeus the publican, whom the Lord had received back into favor, exclaims in the Gospel: "Behold, Lord, the half of my goods I give to the poor; and if I have defrauded anyone of anything, I restore it fourfold."   Lk 19.8 Therefore, in the same way we preach that restitution and compassion, and even almsgiving, are necessary for those who truly repent, and we exhort all men everywhere in the words of the apostle: "Let not sin therefore reign in your mortal bodies, to make you obey their passions. Do not yield your members to sin as instruments of wickedness, but yield yourselves to God as men who have been brought from death to life, and your members to God as instruments of righteousness."   Rom 6.12–13

[11.] *Errors.* Wherefore we condemn all impious utterances of some who wrongly use the preaching of the gospel and say that "it is easy to return to God. Christ has atoned for all sins. Forgiveness of sins is easy. Therefore, what harm is there in sinning? Nor need we be greatly concerned about repentance, etc." Notwithstanding we always teach that an access to God is open to all sinners, and that he forgives all sinners of all sins except the one sin against the Holy Spirit.   Mk 3.29

a. Jn 5.14
b. Jn 8.11

[12.] *The Sects*. Wherefore we condemn both old and new Novatians and Cathars.

Papal Indulgences. We especially condemn the lucrative doctrine of the pope concerning penance, and against his simony and his simoniacal indulgences we avail ourselves of Peter's judgment concerning Simon: "Your silver perish with you, because you thought you could obtain the gift of God with money! You have neither part nor lot in this matter, for your heart is not right before God."

Acts 8.20–21

[13.] *Satisfactions*. We also disapprove of those who think that by their own satisfactions they make amends for sins committed. For we teach that Christ alone by his death or passion is the satisfaction, propitiation, or expiation of all sins. Yet as we have already said, we do not cease to urge the mortification of the flesh. We add, however, that this mortification is not to be proudly obtruded upon God as a satisfaction for sins, but is to be performed humbly, in keeping with the nature of the children of God, as a new obedience out of gratitude for the deliverance and full satisfaction obtained by the death and satisfaction of the Son of God.

Is 53; 1 Cor 1.30

CHAPTER 15. OF THE TRUE JUSTIFICATION
OF THE FAITHFUL

[1.] *What Is Justification?* According to the apostle in his treatment of justification, to justify means to remit sins, to absolve from guilt and punishment, to receive into favor, and to pronounce a man just. For in his epistle to the Romans the apostle says: "It is God who justifies; who is to condemn?" To justify and to condemn are opposed. And in the Acts of the Apostles the apostle states: "Through Christ forgiveness of sins is proclaimed to you, and by him everyone that believes is freed from everything from which you could not be freed by the law of Moses." For in the law and also in the prophets we read: "If there is a dispute between men, and they come into court . . . the judges decide between them, acquitting the innocent and condemning the guilty." And in Isaiah 5: "Woe to those . . . who acquit the guilty for a bribe."

Rom 8[.33–34]

Acts 13.38–39

Dt 25.1

Is 5.22, 23

[2.] *We Are Justified on Account of Christ*. Now it is most certain that all of us are by nature sinners and godless, and before God's judgment seat are convicted of godlessness and are guilty of death, but that, solely by the grace of Christ and not from any merit of ours or consideration for us, we are justified, that is, absolved from sin and death by God the Judge. For what is clearer than what Paul said: "Since all have sinned and fall short of the glory of God, they are justified by his grace as a gift, through the redemption which is in Christ Jesus."

Rom 3.23–24

[3.] *Imputed Righteousness*. For Christ took upon himself and bore the sins of the world, and satisfied divine justice. Therefore, solely on account of Christ's sufferings and resurrection God is propitious with respect to our sins and does not impute them to us, but imputes Christ's righteousness to us as our own,[a] so that now we are not only cleansed and purged from sins or are holy, but also, granted the righteousness of Christ, and so absolved from sin, death, and condemnation, are at last righteous and heirs of eternal life. Properly speaking, therefore, God alone justifies us, and justifies only on account of Christ, not imputing sins to us but imputing his righteousness to us.

[4.] *We Are Justified by Faith Alone.* But because we receive this justification, not through any works, but through faith in the mercy of God and in Christ, we therefore teach and believe with the apostle that sinful man is justified by faith alone in Christ, not by the law or any works. For the apostle says: "We hold that a man is justified by faith apart from works of law." Also: "If Abraham was justified   Rom 3.28 by works, he has something to boast about, but not before God. For what does the Scripture say? Abraham believed God, and it was reckoned to him as righteousness. . . . And to one who does not work but believes in him who justified the ungodly, his faith is reckoned as righteousness."[b] And again: "By grace you have been saved through faith; and this is not your own doing, it is the gift of God—not because of works, lest any man should boast," etc. Therefore, because faith receives Christ our   Eph 2.8–9 righteousness and attributes everything to the grace of God in Christ, on that account justification is attributed to faith, chiefly because of Christ and not therefore because it is our work. For it is the gift of God.

We Receive Christ by Faith. Moreover, the Lord abundantly shows that we receive Christ by faith, in John 6, where he puts eating for believing, and believing   Jn 6 for eating. For as we receive food by eating, so we participate in Christ by believing. [5.] *Justification Is Not Attributed Partly to Christ or to Faith, Partly to Us.* Therefore, we do not share in the benefit of justification partly because of the grace of God or Christ, and partly because of ourselves, our love, works, or merit, but we attribute it wholly to the grace of God in Christ through faith. For our love and our works could not please God if performed by unrighteous men. Therefore, it is necessary for us to be righteous before we may love and do good works. We are made truly righteous, as we have said, by faith in Christ purely by the grace of God, who does not impute to us our sins, but the righteousness of Christ, or rather, he imputes faith in Christ to us for righteousness. Moreover, the apostle very clearly derives love from faith when he says: "The aim of our command is love that issues from a pure heart, a good conscience, and a sincere faith."   1 Tm 1.5

a. 2 Cor 5.19ff.; Rom 4.25
b. Rom 4.2–3, 5; Gn 15.6

[6.] *James Compared with Paul.* Wherefore, in this matter we are not speaking of a fictitious, empty, lazy, and dead faith, but of a living, quickening faith. It is and is called a living faith because it apprehends Christ who is life and makes alive, and shows that it is alive by living works. And so James does not contradict anything in this doctrine of ours. For he speaks of an empty, dead faith of which some boasted but who did not have Christ living in them by faith. James said that works justify, yet without contradicting the apostle (otherwise he would have to be rejected) but showing that Abraham proved his living and justifying faith by works. This all the pious do, but they trust in Christ alone and not in their own works. For again the apostle said: "It is no longer I who live, but Christ who lives in me; and the life I now live in the flesh I live by faith in the Son of God, who loved me and gave himself for me. I do not reject the grace of God; for if justification were through the law, then Christ died to no purpose," etc.

Jas 2.14ff.

Gal 2.20–21

CHAPTER 16. OF FAITH AND GOOD WORKS, AND OF THEIR REWARD, AND OF MAN'S MERIT

[1.] *What Is Faith?* Christian faith is not an opinion or human conviction, but a most firm trust and a clear and steadfast assent of the mind, and then a most certain apprehension of the truth of God presented in the Scriptures and in the Apostles' Creed, and thus also of God himself, the greatest good, and especially of God's promise and of Christ who is the fulfillment of all promises.

[2.] *Faith Is the Gift of God.* But this faith is a pure gift of God which God alone of his grace gives to his elect according to his measure when, to whom, and to the degree he wills. And he does this by the Holy Spirit by means of the preaching of the gospel and steadfast prayer. *The Increase of Faith.* This faith also has its increase, and unless it were given by God, the apostles would not have said: "Lord, increase our faith." [3.] And all these things which up to this point we have said concerning faith, the apostles have taught before us. For Paul said: "For faith is the *hypostasis* or sure subsistence, of things hoped for, and the *elenchos,* that is, the clear and certain apprehension." And again he says that all the promises of God are Yes through Christ and through Christ are Amen. And to the Philippians he said that it has been given to them to believe in Christ. Again, God assigned to each the measure of faith.[a] Again: "Not all have faith," and, "Not all obey the gospel."[b] But Luke also bears witness, saying: "As many as were ordained to life believed." Wherefore Paul also calls faith "the faith of God's elect," and again: "Faith comes from hearing,

Lk 17.5

Heb 11.1

2 Cor 1.20

Phil 1.29

Acts 13.48

Ti 1.1

a. Rom 12.3
b. 2 Thes 3.2; Rom 10.16

and hearing comes by the word of God." Elsewhere he often commands men to pray for faith. Rom 10.17

[4.] *Faith Efficacious and Active.* The same apostle calls faith efficacious and active through love. It also quiets the conscience and opens a free access to God, so that we may draw near to him with confidence and may obtain from him what is useful and necessary. The same [faith] keeps us in the service we owe to God and our neighbor, strengthens our patience in adversity, fashions and makes a true confession, and in a word, brings forth good fruit of all kinds, and good works. Gal 5.6

[5.] *Concerning Good Works.* For we teach that truly good works grow out of a living faith by the Holy Spirit and are done by the faithful according to the will or rule of God's word. Now the apostle Peter says: "Make every effort to supplement your faith with virtue, and virtue with knowledge, and knowledge with self-control," etc. But we have said above that the law of God, which is his will, prescribes for us the pattern of good works. And the apostle says: "This is the will of God, your sanctification, that you abstain from immorality . . . that no man transgress, and wrong his brother in business." 2 Pt 1.5ff. 1 Thes 4.3–6

Works of Human Choice. And indeed works and worship which we choose arbitrarily are not pleasing to God. These Paul calls *ethelothrēskeias*, "self-devised worship." Of such the Lord says in the Gospel: "In vain do they worship me, teaching as doctrines the precepts of men." [6.] Therefore, we disapprove of such works, and approve and urge those that are of God's will and commission. Col 2.23 Mt 15.9

The End of Good Works. These same works ought not to be done in order that we may earn eternal life by them, for, as the apostle says, eternal life is the gift of God. Nor are they to be done for ostentation which the Lord rejects in Matthew 6, nor for gain which he also rejects in Matthew 23, but for the glory of God, to adorn our calling, to show gratitude to God, and for the profit of the neighbor. For our Lord says again in the Gospel: "Let your light so shine before men, that they may see your good works and give glory to your Father who is in heaven." And the apostle Paul says: "Lead a life worthy of the calling to which you have been called." Also: "And whatever you do, in word or deed, do everything in the name of the Lord Jesus, giving thanks to God and to the Father through him," and, "Let each of you look not to his own interests, but to the interests of others," and, "Let our people learn to apply themselves to good deeds, so as to help cases of urgent need, and not to be unfruitful." Rom 6.23 Mt 6[.1–6] Mt 23 Mt 5.16 Eph 4.1 Col 3.17 Phil 2.4 Ti 3.14

[7.] *Good Works Not Rejected.* Therefore, although we teach with the apostle that a man is justified by grace through faith in Christ and not through any good works, yet we do not think that good works are of little value and condemn them. We know that man was not created or regenerated through faith in order to be

idle, but rather that without ceasing he should do those things which are good and
useful. For in the Gospel the Lord says that a good tree brings forth good fruit,
and that "he who abides in me bears much fruit." The apostle says: "For we are
his workmanship, created in Christ Jesus for good works, which God prepared beforehand, that we should walk in them," and again: "Who gave himself for us to
redeem us from all iniquity and to purify for himself a people of his own who are
zealous for good deeds." [8.] We therefore condemn all who despise good works
and who babble that they are useless and that we do not need to pay attention to
them.

Mt 12.33
Jn 15.5
Eph 2.10
Ti 2.14

We Are Not Saved by Good Works. Nevertheless, as was said above, we do
not think that we are saved by good works, and that they are so necessary for salvation that no one was ever saved without them. For we are saved by grace and the
favor of Christ alone. Works necessarily proceed from faith. And salvation is improperly attributed to them, but is most properly ascribed to grace. The apostle's
sentence is well known: "If it is by grace, then it is no longer of works; otherwise
grace would no longer be grace. But if it is of works, then it is no longer grace,
because otherwise work is no longer work."

Rom 11.6

[9.] *Good Works Please God.* Now the works which we do by faith are pleasing to God and are approved by him. Because of faith in Christ, those who do good
works which, moreover, are done from God's grace through the Holy Spirit, are
pleasing to God. For St. Peter said: "In every nation anyone who fears God and does
what is right is acceptable to him." And Paul said: "We have not ceased to pray for
you that you may walk worthily of the Lord, fully pleasing to him, bearing fruit in
every good work."

Acts 10.35
Col 1.9–10

We Teach True, Not False and Philosophical Virtues. And so we diligently
teach true, not false and philosophical virtues, truly good works, and the genuine
service of a Christian. And as much as we can we diligently and zealously press them
upon all men, while censuring the sloth and hypocrisy of all those who praise and
profess the gospel with their lips and dishonor it by their disgraceful lives. In this
matter we place before them God's terrible threats and then his rich promises and
generous rewards—exhorting, consoling, and rebuking.

[10.] *God Gives a Reward for Good Works.* For we teach that God gives a
rich reward to those who do good works, according to that saying of the prophet:
"Keep your voice from weeping, . . . for your work shall be rewarded." The Lord
also said in the Gospel: "Rejoice and be glad, for your reward is great in heaven,"
and, "Whoever gives to one of these my little ones a cup of cold water, truly, I say to
you, he shall not lose his reward." However, we do not ascribe this reward, which
the Lord gives, to the merit of the man who receives it, but to the goodness, gen-

Jer 31.16; Is 4
Mt 5.12
Mt 10.42

erosity, and truthfulness of God who promises and gives it, and who, although he owes nothing to anyone, nevertheless promises that he will give a reward to his faithful worshipers; meanwhile he also gives them that they may honor him. Moreover, in the works even of the saints there is much that is unworthy of God and very much that is imperfect. But because God receives into favor and embraces those who do works for Christ's sake, he grants to them the promised reward. For in other respects our righteousnesses are compared to a filthy wrap. And the Lord says in the   Is 64.6 Gospel: "When you have done all that is commanded you, say, 'We are unworthy servants; we have only done what was our duty.'"   Lk 17.10

[11.] *There Are No Merits of Men.* Therefore, although we teach that God rewards our good deeds, yet at the same time we teach, with Augustine, that God does not crown in us our merits but his gifts. Accordingly we say that whatever reward we receive is also grace, and is more grace than reward, because the good we do, we do more through God than through ourselves, and because Paul says: "What have you that you did not receive? If then you received it, why do you boast as if you had not received it?" And this is what the blessed martyr Cyprian concluded   1 Cor 4.7 from this verse: We are not to glory in anything in us, since nothing is our own. We therefore condemn those who defend the merits of men in such a way that they invalidate the grace of God.

CHAPTER 17. OF THE CATHOLIC AND HOLY CHURCH OF GOD, AND OF THE ONE ONLY HEAD OF THE CHURCH

[1.] *The Church Has Always Existed and It Will Always Exist.* But because God from the beginning would have men to be saved, and to come to the knowledge of the truth, it is altogether necessary that there always should have been, and should be   1 Tm 2.4 now, and to the end of the world, a church.

What Is the Church? The church is an assembly of the faithful called or gathered out of the world; a communion, I say, of all saints, namely, of those who truly know and rightly worship and serve the true God in Christ the Savior, by the word and Holy Spirit, and who by faith are partakers of all benefits which are freely offered through Christ. *Citizens of One Commonwealth.* They are all citizens of the one city, living under the same Lord, under the same laws, and in the same fellowship of all good things. For the apostle calls them "fellow citizens with the saints and members of the household of God,"[a] calling the faithful on earth saints,[b] who

a. Eph 2.19
b. 1 Cor 6.11

are sanctified by the blood of the Son of God. The article of the creed, "I believe in the holy catholic church, the communion of saints," is to be understood wholly as concerning these saints.

[2.] *Only One Church for All Times.* And since there is always but one God, and there is one Mediator between God and men, Jesus the Messiah, and one Shepherd of the whole flock, one Head of this body, and, to conclude, one Spirit, one salvation, one faith, one testament or covenant, it necessarily follows that there is

1 Tm 2.5   only one church.

The Catholic Church. We, therefore, call this church catholic because it is universal, scattered through all parts of the world, and extended unto all times, and is not limited to any times or places. Therefore, we condemn the Donatists, who confined the church to I know not what corners of Africa. Nor do we approve of the Roman clergy, who have recently passed off only the Roman Church as catholic.

[3.] *Parts of Forms of the Church.* The church is divided into different parts or forms; not because it is divided or rent asunder in itself, but rather because it is distinguished by the diversity of the numbers that are in it. *Militant and Triumphant.* For the one is called the church militant, the other the church triumphant. The former still wages war on earth, and fights against the flesh, the world, and the prince of this world, the devil, against sin and death. But the latter, having been now discharged, triumphs in heaven immediately after having overcome all those things and rejoices before the Lord. Notwithstanding both have fellowship and union one with another.

[4.] *The Particular Church.* Moreover, the church militant upon the earth has always had many particular churches. Yet all these are to be referred to the unity of the catholic church. This [militant] church was set up differently before the law among the patriarchs; otherwise under Moses by the law; and differently by Christ through the gospel.

The Two Peoples. Generally two peoples are usually counted, namely, the Israelites and Gentiles, or those who have been gathered from among Jews and Gentiles into the church. There are also two Testaments, the Old and the New. *The Same Church for the Old and the New People.* Yet from all these people there was and is one fellowship, one salvation in the one Messiah; in whom, as members of one body under one Head, all united together in the same faith, partaking also of the same spiritual food and drink. Yet here we acknowledge a diversity of times, and a diversity in the signs of the promised and delivered Christ; and that now the ceremonies being abolished, the light shines unto us more clearly, and blessings are given to us more abundantly, and a fuller liberty.

[5.] *The Church the Temple of the Living God.* This holy church of God is called the temple of the living God, built of living and spiritual stones and founded upon a firm rock, upon a foundation which no other can lay, and therefore it is called "the pillar and bulwark of the truth." *The Church Does Not Err.* It does not 1 Tm 3.15 err as long as it rests upon the rock Christ, and upon the foundation of the prophets and apostles. And it is no wonder if it errs, as often as it deserts him who alone is the truth. *The Church as Bride and Virgin.* This church is also called a virgin and the bride of Christ, and even the only beloved. For the apostle says: "I betrothed you to Christ to present you as a pure bride to Christ." *The Church as a Flock of Sheep.* 2 Cor 11.2 The church is called a flock of sheep under the one shepherd, Christ, according to Ezekiel 34, and John 10. *The Church as the Body.* It is also called the body of Christ Ez 34; Jn 10 because the faithful are living members of Christ under Christ the Head.

[6.] *Christ the Sole Head of the Church.* It is the head which has the preeminence in the body, and from it the whole body receives life; by its spirit the body is governed in all things; from it, also, the body receives increase, that it may grow up. Also, there is one head of the body, and it is suited to the body. Therefore the church cannot have any other Head besides Christ. For as the church is a spiritual body, so it must also have a spiritual head in harmony with itself. Neither can it be governed by any other spirit than by the Spirit of Christ. Wherefore Paul says: "He is the Head of the body, the church; he is the beginning, the firstborn from the dead, that in everything he might be preeminent." And in another place: "Christ is the Col 1.18 head of the church, his body, and is himself its Savior." And again: he is "the head Eph 5.23 over all things for the church, which is his body, the fullness of him who fills all in all." Also: "We are to grow up in every way into him who is the Head, into Christ, Eph 1.22–23 from whom the whole body, joined and knit together, makes bodily growth." [7.] Eph 4.15–16 And therefore we do not approve of the doctrine of the Roman clergy, who make their pope at Rome the universal shepherd and supreme head of the church militant here on earth, and so the very vicar of Jesus Christ, who has (as they say) all fullness of power and sovereign authority in the church. [8.] *Christ the Only Pastor of the Church.* For we teach that Christ the Lord is, and remains the only universal pastor, the highest pontiff before God the Father; and that in the church he himself performs all the duties of a bishop or pastor, even to the world's end; *Vicar* and therefore does not need a substitute for one who is absent. For Christ is present with his church, and is its life-giving Head. *No Primacy in the Church.* He has strictly forbidden his apostles and their successors to have any primacy and dominion in the church. Who does not see, therefore, that whoever contradicts and opposes this Mt 20.25–28 plain truth is rather to be counted among the number of those of whom Christ's apostles prophesied: Peter in 2 Peter 2, and Paul in Acts 20.2, 2 Corinthians 11.2, 2 Thessalonians 2, and also in other places?[a]

[9.] *No Disorder in the Church.* However, by doing away with a Roman head we do not bring any confusion or disorder into the church, since we teach that the government of the church which the apostles handed down is sufficient to keep the church in proper order. In the beginning when the church was without any such Roman head as is now said to keep it in order, the church was not disordered or in confusion. The Roman head does indeed preserve his tyranny and the corruption that has been brought into the church, and meanwhile he hinders, resists, and with all the strength he can muster cuts off the proper reformation of the church.

[10.] *Dissensions and Strife in the Church.* We are reproached because there have been manifold dissensions and strife in our churches since they separated themselves from the church of Rome, and therefore cannot be true churches. As though there were never in the church of Rome any sects, nor contentions and quarrels concerning religion, and indeed, carried on not so much in the schools as from pulpits in the midst of the people. We know, to be sure, that the apostle said: "God is not a God of confusion but of peace," and, "While there is jealousy and strife among you, are you not of the flesh?" Yet we cannot deny that God was in the apostolic church and that it was a true church, even though there were wranglings and dissensions in it. The apostle Paul reprehended Peter, an apostle, and Barnabas dissented from Paul. Great contention arose in the church of Antioch between them that preached the one Christ, as Luke records in the Acts of the Apostles 15. And there have at all times been great contentions in the church, and the most excellent teachers of the church have differed among themselves about important matters without meanwhile the church ceasing to be the church because of these contentions. For thus it pleases God to use the dissensions that arise in the church to the glory of his name, to illustrate the truth, and in order that those who are in the right might be manifest.

1 Cor 14.33

1 Cor 3.3

Gal 2.11ff.

Acts 15

1 Cor 11.19

[11.] *Of the Notes or Signs of the True Church.* Moreover, as we acknowledge no other head of the church than Christ, so we do not acknowledge every church to be the true church which vaunts herself to be such; but we teach that the true church is that in which the signs or marks of the true church are to be found, especially the lawful and sincere preaching of the word of God as it was delivered to us in the books of the prophets and the apostles, which all lead us unto Christ, who said in the Gospel: "My sheep hear my voice, and I know them, and they follow me; and I give unto them eternal life. A stranger they do not follow, but they flee from him, for they do not know the voice of strangers."

Jn 10.5, 27, 28

a. 2 Pt 2; Acts 20.2; 2 Cor 11.2; 2 Thes 2

[12.] And those who are such in the church have one faith and one spirit; and therefore they worship but one God, and him alone they worship in spirit and in truth, loving him alone with all their hearts and with all their strength, praying unto him alone through Jesus Christ, the only Mediator and Intercessor; and they do not seek righteousness and life outside Christ and faith in him. Because they acknowledge Christ the only head and foundation of the church, and, resting on him, daily renew themselves by repentance, and patiently bear the cross laid upon them. Moreover, joined together with all the members of Christ by an unfeigned love, they show that they are Christ's disciples by persevering in the bond of peace and holy unity. At the same time they participate in the sacraments instituted by Christ, and delivered unto us by his apostles, using them in no other way than as they received them from the Lord. That saying of the apostle Paul is well known to all: "I received from the Lord what I also delivered to you." Accordingly, we condemn all   1 Cor 11.23ff. such churches as strangers from the true church of Christ, which are not such as we have heard they ought to be, no matter how much they brag of a succession of bishops, of unity, and of antiquity. Moreover, we have a charge from the apostles of Christ "to shun the worship of idols,"[a] and "to come out of Babylon," and to have no fellowship with her, unless we want to be partakers with her of all God's plagues.[b]

[13.] *Outside the Church of God There Is No Salvation.* But we esteem fellowship with the true church of Christ so highly that we deny that those can live before God who do not stand in fellowship with the true church of God, but separate themselves from it. For as there was no salvation outside Noah's ark when the world perished in the flood; so we believe that there is no certain salvation outside Christ, who offers himself to be enjoyed by the elect in the church; and hence we teach that those who wish to live ought not to be separated from the true church of Christ.

[14.] *The Church Is Not Bound to Its Signs.* Nevertheless, by the signs [of the true church] mentioned above, we do not so narrowly restrict the church as to teach that all those are outside the church who either do not participate in the sacraments, at least not willingly and through contempt, but rather, being forced by necessity, unwillingly abstain from them or are deprived of them; or in whom faith sometimes fails, though it is not entirely extinguished and does not wholly cease; or in whom imperfections and errors due to weakness are found. For we know that God had some friends in the world outside the commonwealth of Israel. We know what be-

a. 1 Cor 10.14; 1 Jn 5.21
b. Rv 18.4; 2 Cor 6.14ff.

fell the people of God in the captivity of Babylon, where they were deprived of their sacrifices for seventy years. We know what happened to St. Peter, who denied his Master, and what is wont to happen daily to God's elect and faithful people who go astray and are weak. We know, moreover, what kind of churches the churches in Galatia and Corinth were in the apostles' time, in which the apostle found fault with many serious offenses; yet he calls them holy churches of Christ.

1 Cor 1.2; Gal 1.2

[15.] *The Church Appears at Times to Be Extinct.* Yes, and it sometimes happens that God in his just judgment allows the truth of his word, and the catholic faith, and the proper worship of God to be so obscured and overthrown that the church seems almost extinct, and no more to exist, as we see to have happened in the days of Elijah, and at other times. Meanwhile God has in this world and in this darkness his true worshipers, and those not a few, but even seven thousand and more.[a] For the apostle exclaims: "God's firm foundation stands, bearing this seal, 'The Lord knows those who are his,'" etc. Whence the church of God may be termed invisible; not because the men from whom the church is gathered are invisible, but because, being hidden from our eyes and known only to God, it often secretly escapes human judgment.

1 Kgs 19.10, 14

2 Tm 2.19

[16.] *Not All Who Are in the Church Are of the Church.* Again, not all that are reckoned in the number of the church are saints, and living and true members of the church. For there are many hypocrites, who outwardly hear the word of God, and publicly receive the sacraments, and seem to pray to God through Christ alone, to confess Christ to be their only righteousness, and to worship God, and to exercise the duties of charity, and for a time to endure with patience in misfortune. And yet they are inwardly destitute of true illumination of the Spirit, of faith and sincerity of heart, and of perseverance to the end. But eventually the character of these men, for the most part, will be disclosed. For the apostle John says: "They went out from us, but they were not of us; for if they had been of us, they would indeed have continued with us." And although while they simulate piety they are not of the church, yet they are considered to be in the church, just as traitors in a state are numbered among its citizens before they are discovered; and as the tares or darnel and chaff are found among the wheat, and as swellings and tumors are found in a sound body, when they are rather diseases and deformities than true members of the body. And therefore the church of God is rightly compared to a net which catches fish of all kinds, and to a field, in which both wheat and tares are found.

1 Jn 2.19

Mt 13.24ff., 47ff.

[17.] *We Must Not Judge Rashly or Prematurely.* Hence we must be very careful not to judge before the time, nor undertake to exclude, reject, or cut off those

a. 1 Kgs 19.18; Rv 7.3ff.

whom the Lord does not want to have excluded or rejected, and those whom we cannot eliminate without loss to the church. On the other hand, we must be vigilant lest while the pious snore the wicked gain ground and do harm to the church.

The Unity of the Church Is Not in External Rites. Furthermore, we diligently teach that care is to be taken wherein the truth and unity of the church chiefly lies, lest we rashly provoke and foster schisms in the church. Unity consists not in outward rites and ceremonies, but rather in the truth and unity of the catholic faith. The catholic faith is not given to us by human laws, but by Holy Scriptures, of which the Apostles' Creed is a compendium. And, therefore, we read in the ancient writers that there was a manifold diversity of rites, but that they were free, and no one ever thought that the unity of the church was thereby dissolved. So we teach that the true harmony of the church consists in doctrines and in the true and harmonious preaching of the gospel of Christ, and in rites that have been expressly delivered by the Lord. And here we especially urge that saying of the apostle: "Let those of us who are perfect have this mind; and if in any thing you are otherwise minded, God will reveal that also to you. Nevertheless let us walk by the same rule according to what we have attained, and let us be of the same mind." Phil 3.15-16

CHAPTER 18. OF THE MINISTERS OF THE CHURCH, THEIR INSTITUTION AND DUTIES

[1.] *God Uses Ministers in the Building of the Church.* God has always used ministers for the gathering or establishing of a church for himself, and for the governing and preservation of the same; and still he does, and always will, use them so long as the church remains on earth. Therefore, the first beginning, institution, and office of ministers is a most ancient arrangement of God himself, and not a new one of men. *Institution and Origin of Ministers.* It is true that God can, by his power, without any means join to himself a church from among men; but he preferred to deal with men by the ministry of men. Therefore ministers are to be regarded, not as ministers by themselves alone, but as the ministers of God, inasmuch as God effects the salvation of men through them.

The Ministry Is Not to Be Despised. Hence we warn men to beware lest we attribute what has to do with our conversion and instruction to the secret power of the Holy Spirit in such a way that we make void the ecclesiastical ministry. For it is fitting that we always have in mind the words of the apostle: "How are they to believe in him of whom they have not heard? And how are they to hear without a preacher? So faith comes from hearing, and hearing comes by the word of God." Rom 10.14, 17 And also what the Lord said in the Gospel: "Truly, truly, I say to you, he who receives anyone whom I send receives me; and he who receives me receives him who

Jn 13.20   sent me." Likewise a man of Macedonia, who appeared to Paul in a vision while he
           was in Asia, secretly admonished him, saying: "Come over to Macedonia and help
Acts 16.9 us." And in another place the same apostle said: "We are fellow workmen of God;
1 Cor 3.9 you are God's tillage, God's building."

           [2.] Yet, on the other hand, we must beware that we do not attribute too
           much to ministers and the ministry; remembering here also the words of the Lord in
Jn 6.44   the Gospel: "No one can come to me unless my Father draws him," and the words
           of the apostle: "What then is Paul? What is Apollos? Servants through whom you
           believed, as the Lord assigned to each. I planted, Apollos watered, but only God
1 Cor 3.5-6 gives the growth." *God Moves the Hearts of Men.* Therefore, let us believe that God
           teaches us by his word, outwardly through his ministers, and inwardly moves the
           hearts of his elect to faith by the Holy Spirit; and that therefore we ought to render
           all glory unto God for this whole favor. But this matter has been dealt with in the
           first chapter of this exposition.

           [3.] *Who the Ministers Are and of What Sort God Has Given the World.* And
           even from the beginning of the world God has used the most excellent men in the
           whole world (even if many of them were simple in worldly wisdom or philosophy,
           but were outstanding in true theology), namely, the patriarchs, with whom he fre-
           quently spoke by angels. For the patriarchs were the prophets or teachers of their
           age whom God for this reason wanted to live for several centuries, in order that
           they might be, as it were, fathers and lights of the world. They were followed by
           Moses and the prophets renowned throughout all the world.

           [4.] *Christ the Teacher.* After these the heavenly Father even sent his only-
           begotten Son, the most perfect teacher of the world; in whom is hidden the wisdom
           of God, and which has come to us through the most holy, simple, and most perfect
           doctrine of all. For he chose disciples for himself whom he made apostles. These
           went out into the whole world, and everywhere gathered together churches by the
           preaching of the gospel, and then throughout all the churches in the world they
           appointed pastors or teachers according to Christ's command; through their succes-
           sors he has taught and governed the church unto this day. Therefore, as God gave
           unto his ancient people the patriarchs, together with Moses and the prophets, so
           also to his people of the New Testament he sent his only-begotten Son, and, with
           him, the apostles and teachers of the church.

           [5.] *Ministers of the New Testament.* Furthermore, the ministers of the new
           people are called by various names. For they are called apostles, prophets, evan-
           gelists, bishops, elders, pastors, and teachers.[a] *The Apostles.* The apostles did not

           a. 1 Cor 12.28; Eph 4.11

stay in any particular place, but throughout the world gathered together different churches. When they were once established, there ceased to be apostles, and pastors took their place, each in his church. *Prophets.* In former times the prophets were seers, knowing the future; but they also interpreted the Scriptures. Such men are also found still today. *Evangelists.* The writers of the history of the gospel were called Evangelists; but they also were heralds of the gospel of Christ; as Paul also commended Timothy: "Do the work of an evangelist." *Bishops.* Bishops are the over-   2 Tm 4.5
seers and watchmen of the church, who administer the food and needs of the life of the church. *Presbyters.* The presbyters are the elders and, as it were, senators and fathers of the church, governing it with wholesome counsel. *Pastors.* The pastors both keep the Lord's sheepfold, and also provide for its needs. *Teachers.* The teachers instruct and teach the true faith and godliness. Therefore, the ministers of the churches may now be called bishops, elders, pastors, and teachers.

[6.] *Papal Orders.* Then in subsequent times many more names of ministers in the church were introduced into the church of God. For some were appointed patriarchs, others archbishops, others suffragans; also, metropolitans, archdeacons, deacons, subdeacons, acolytes, exorcists, cantors, porters, and I know not what others, as cardinals, provosts, and priors; greater and lesser fathers, greater and lesser orders. But we are not troubled about all these, about how they once were and are now. For us the apostolic doctrine concerning ministers is sufficient.

[7.] *Concerning Monks.* Since we assuredly know that monks, and the orders or sects of monks, are instituted neither by Christ nor by the apostles, we teach that they are of no use to the church of God, nay rather, are pernicious. For, although in former times they were tolerable (when they were hermits, earning their living with their own hands, and were not a burden to anyone, but like the laity were everywhere obedient to the pastors of the churches), yet now the whole world sees and knows what they are like. They formulate I know not what vows; but they lead a life quite contrary to their vows, so that the best of them deserves to be numbered among those of whom the apostle said: "We hear that some of you are living an irregular life, mere busybodies, not doing any work," etc. Therefore, we neither have   2 Thes 3.11
such in our churches, nor do we teach that they should be in the churches of Christ.

[8.] *Ministers Are to Be Called and Elected.* Furthermore, no man ought to usurp the honor of the ecclesiastical ministry; that is, to seize it for himself by bribery or any deceits, or by his own free choice. But let the ministers of the church be called and chosen by lawful and ecclesiastical election; that is to say, let them be carefully chosen by the church or by those delegated from the church for that purpose in a proper order without any uproar, dissension, and rivalry. Not anyone may be elected, but capable men distinguished by sufficient consecrated learning, pious

eloquence, simple wisdom, lastly, by moderation and an honorable reputation, ac-
1 Tm 3 cording to that apostolic rule which is compiled by the apostle in 1 Timothy 3 and
Ti 1 Titus 1.

Ordination. And those who are elected are to be ordained by the elders with
public prayer and laying on of hands. Here we condemn all those who go off of their
Jer 23 own accord, being neither chosen, sent, nor ordained. We condemn unfit ministers
and those not furnished with the necessary gifts of a pastor.

[9.] In the meantime we acknowledge that the harmless simplicity of some
pastors in the primitive church sometimes profited the church more than the many-
sided, refined, and fastidious, but a little too esoteric learning of others. For this
reason we do not reject even today the honest, yet by no means ignorant, simplicity
of some.

[10.] *Priesthood of All Believers.* To be sure, Christ's apostles call all who
believe in Christ "priests," but not on account of an office, but because, all the faithful having been made kings and priests, we are able to offer up spiritual sacrifices
to God through Christ.[a] Therefore, the priesthood and the ministry are very different from one another. For the priesthood, as we have just said, is common to all
Christians; not so is the ministry. Nor have we abolished the ministry of the church
because we have repudiated the papal priesthood from the church of Christ.

[11.] *Priests and Priesthood.* Surely in the new covenant of Christ there is no
longer any such priesthood as was under the ancient people; which had an external
anointing, holy garments, and very many ceremonies which were types of Christ,
who abolished them all by his coming and fulfilling them. But he himself remains
the only priest forever, and lest we derogate anything from him, we do not impart
the name of priest to any minister. For the Lord himself did not appoint any priests
in the church of the New Testament who, having received authority from the suffra-
gan, may daily offer up the sacrifice, that is, the very flesh and blood of the Lord, for
the living and the dead, but ministers who may teach and administer the sacraments.

The Nature of the Ministers of the New Testament. Paul explains simply and
briefly what we are to think of the ministers of the New Testament or of the Christian church, and what we are to attribute to them. "This is how one should re-
1 Cor 4.1 gard us, as servants of Christ and stewards of the mysteries of God." Therefore,
the apostle wants us to think of ministers as ministers. Now the apostle calls them
hypēretas, rowers, who have their eyes fixed on the coxswain, and so men who do
not live for themselves or according to their own will, but for others—namely, their
masters, upon whose command they altogether depend. For in all his duties every

---

a. Ex 19.6; 1 Pt 2.9; Rv 1.6

minister of the church is commanded to carry out only what he has received in commandment from his Lord, and not to indulge his own free choice. And in this case it is expressly declared who is the Lord, namely, Christ; to whom the ministers are subject in all the affairs of the ministry.

[12.] *Ministers as Stewards of the Mysteries of God.* Moreover, to the end that he might expound the ministry more fully, the apostle adds that ministers of the church are administrators and stewards of the mysteries of God. Now in many passages, especially in Ephesians 3, Paul called the mysteries of God the gospel of Christ. And the sacraments of Christ are also called mysteries by the ancient writers. Therefore for this purpose are the ministers of the church called—namely, to preach the gospel of Christ to the faithful, and to administer the sacraments. We read, also, in another place in the Gospel, of "the faithful and wise steward," whom "his master will set over his household, to give them their portion of food at the proper time." Again, elsewhere in the Gospel a man takes a journey in a foreign country and, leaving his house, gives his substance and authority over it to his servants, and to each his work.

Eph 3

Lk 12.42

[Lk 19.12–13]

[13.] *The Power of Ministers of the Church.* Now, therefore, it is fitting that we also say something about the power and duty of the ministers of the church. Concerning this power some have argued industriously, and to it have subjected everything on earth, even the greatest things, and they have done so contrary to the commandment of the Lord, who has prohibited dominion for his disciples and has highly commended humility.[a] There is, indeed, another power that is pure and absolute, which is called the power of right. According to this power all things in the whole world are subject to Christ, who is Lord of all, as he himself has testified when he said: "All authority in heaven and on earth has been given to me," and again, "I am the first and the last, and behold I am alive for evermore, and I have the keys of Hades and death"; also, "He has the key of David, which opens and no one shall shut, who shuts and no one opens."

Mt 28.18

Rv 1.18

Rv 3.7

[14.] *The Lord Reserves True Power for Himself.* This power the Lord reserves to himself, and does not transfer it to any other, so that he might stand idly by as a spectator while his ministers work. For Isaiah says, "I will place on his shoulder the key of the house of David," and again, "The government will be upon his shoulders." For he does not lay the government on other men's shoulders, but still keeps and uses his own power, governing all things.

Is 22.22

Is 9.6

The Power of the Office and of the Minister. Then there is another power of an office or of ministry limited by him who has full and absolute power. And this is

a. Lk 22.24ff.; Mt 18.3–4, 20.25ff.

more like a service than a dominion. *The Keys.* For a lord gives up his power to the steward in his house, and for that cause gives him the keys, that he may admit into or exclude from the house those whom his lord will have admitted or excluded. In virtue of this power the minister, because of his office, does that which the Lord has commanded him to do; and the Lord confirms what he does, and wills that what his servant has done will be so regarded and acknowledged, as if he himself had done it. [15.] Undoubtedly, it is to this that these evangelical sentences refer: "I will give you the keys of the kingdom of heaven, and whatever you bind on earth shall Mt 16.19   be bound in heaven, and whatever you loose on earth shall be loosed in heaven." Again, "If you forgive the sins of any, they are forgiven; if you retain the sins of Jn 20.23   any, they are retained." But if the minister does not carry out everything as the Lord has commanded him, but transgresses the bounds of faith, then the Lord certainly makes void what he has done. Wherefore the ecclesiastical power of the ministers of the church is that function whereby they indeed govern the church of God, but yet so do all things in the church as the Lord has prescribed in his word. When those things are done, the faithful esteem them as done by the Lord himself. But mention has already been made of the keys above.

[16.] *The Power of Ministers Is One and the Same, and Equal.* Now the one and an equal power or function is given to all ministers in the church. Certainly, in the beginning, the bishops or presbyters governed the church in common; no man lifted up himself above another, none usurped greater power or authority over his fellow bishops. For remembering the words of the Lord: "Let the leader among you Lk 22.26   become as one who serves," they kept themselves in humility, and by mutual services they helped one another in the governing and preserving of the church.

Order to Be Preserved. Nevertheless, for the sake of preserving order some one of the ministers called the assembly together, proposed matters to be laid before it, gathered the opinions of the others, in short, to the best of man's ability took precaution lest any confusion should arise. [17.] Thus did St. Peter, as we read in the Acts of the Apostles, who nevertheless was not on that account preferred to the others, nor endowed with greater authority than the rest. Rightly then does Cyprian the Martyr say, in his *De simplicitate clericorum:* "The other apostles were assuredly what Peter was, endowed with a like fellowship of honor and power; but his primacy proceeds from unity in order that the church may be shown to be one."

When and How One Was Placed Before the Others. St. Jerome also in his commentary upon the Epistle of Paul to Titus, says something not unlike this: "Before attachment to persons in religion was begun at the instigation of the devil, the churches were governed by the common consultation of the elders; but after every one thought that those whom he had baptized were his own, and not Christ's, it was decreed that one of the elders should be chosen, and set over the rest, upon whom should fall the care of the whole church, and all schismatic seeds should be removed." Yet St. Jerome does not recommend this decree as divine; for he immediately adds: "As the elders knew from the custom of the church that they were subject to him who was set over them, so the bishops knew that they were above the elders, more from custom than from the truth of an arrangement by the Lord, and that they ought to rule the church in common with them." Thus far St. Jerome. Hence no one can rightly forbid a return to the ancient constitution of the church of God, and to have recourse to it before human custom.

[18.] *The Duties of Ministers.* The duties of ministers are various; yet for the most part they are restricted to two, in which all the rest are comprehended: to the teaching of the gospel of Christ, and to the proper administration of the sacraments. For it is the duty of the ministers to gather together an assembly for worship in which to expound God's word and to apply the whole doctrine to the care and use of the church, so that what is taught may benefit the hearers and edify the faithful. It falls to ministers, I say, to teach the ignorant, and to exhort; and to urge the idlers and lingerers to make progress in the way of the Lord. Moreover, they are to comfort and to strengthen the fainthearted, and to arm them against the manifold temptations of Satan; to rebuke offenders; to recall the erring into the way; to raise the fallen; to convince the gainsayers; to drive the wolf away from the sheepfold of the Lord; to rebuke wickedness and wicked men wisely and severely; not to wink at nor to pass over great wickedness. And, besides, they are to administer the sacraments, and to commend the right use of them, and to prepare all men by wholesome doctrine to receive them; to preserve the faithful in a holy unity; and to check schisms; to catechize the unlearned, to commend the needs of the poor to the church, to visit, instruct, and keep in the way of life the sick and those afflicted with various temptations. In addition, they are to attend to public prayers or supplications in times of need, together with common fasting, that is, a holy abstinence; and as diligently as possible to see to everything that pertains to the tranquillity, peace, and welfare of the churches.

[19.] But in order that the minister may perform all these things better and more easily, it is especially required of him that he fear God, be constant in prayer, attend to spiritual reading, and in all things and at all times be watchful, and by a purity of life to let his light to shine before all men.

[20.] *Discipline.* And since discipline is an absolute necessity in the church and excommunication was once used in the time of the early fathers, and there were ecclesiastical judgments among the people of God, wherein this discipline was exercised by wise and godly men, it also falls to ministers to regulate this discipline for edification, according to the circumstances of the time, public state, and necessity. At all times and in all places the rule is to be observed that everything is to be done for edification, decently and honorably, without oppression and strife. For the apostle testifies that authority in the church was given to him by the Lord for

2 Cor 10.8	building up and not for destroying. And the Lord himself forbade the weeds to be plucked up in the Lord's field, because there would be danger lest the wheat also

Mt 13.29–30	be plucked up with it.

[21.] *Even Evil Ministers Are to Be Heard*. Moreover, we strongly detest the error of the Donatists, who esteem the doctrine and administration of the sacraments to be either effectual or not effectual, according to the good or evil life of the ministers. For we know that the voice of Christ is to be heard, though it be out of the mouths of evil ministers; because the Lord himself said: "Practice and observe

Mt 23.3	whatever they tell you, but not what they do." We know that the sacraments are sanctified by the institution and the word of Christ, and that they are effectual to the godly, although they be administered by unworthy ministers. Concerning this matter, Augustine, the blessed servant of God, many times argued from the Scriptures against the Donatists.

[22.] *Synods*. Nevertheless, there ought to be proper discipline among ministers. In synods the doctrine and life of ministers is to be carefully examined. Offenders who can be cured are to be rebuked by the elders and restored to the right way, and if they are incurable, they are to be deposed, and like wolves driven away from the flock of the Lord by the true shepherds. For, if they be false teachers, they are not to be tolerated at all. Neither do we disapprove of ecumenical councils, if they are convened according to the example of the apostles, for the welfare of the church and not for its destruction.

[23.] *The Worker Is Worthy of His Reward*. All faithful ministers, as good workmen, are also worthy of their reward, and do not sin when they receive a stipend, and all things that be necessary for themselves and their family. For the apostle shows in 1 Corinthians 9, and in 1 Timothy 5,[a] and elsewhere that these things may rightly be given by the church and received by ministers. The Anabaptists, who condemn and defame ministers who live from their ministry, are also refuted by the apostolic teaching.

CHAPTER 19. OF THE SACRAMENTS OF THE CHURCH OF CHRIST

[1.] *The Sacraments [Are] Added to the Word and What They Are*. From the beginning, God added to the preaching of his word in his church sacraments or sacramental

a. 1 Cor 9[.13–14]; 1 Tm 5[.17]

signs. For thus does all Holy Scripture clearly testify. Sacraments are mystical symbols, or holy rites, or sacred actions, instituted by God himself, consisting of his word, of signs, and of things signified, whereby in the church he keeps in mind and from time to time recalls the great benefits he has shown to men; whereby also he seals his promises, and outwardly represents, and, as it were, offers unto our sight those things which inwardly he performs for us, and so strengthens and increases our faith through the working of God's Spirit in our hearts. Lastly, he thereby distinguishes us from all other people and religions, and consecrates and binds us wholly to himself, and signifies what he requires of us.

[2.] *Some Are Sacraments of the Old, Others of the New, Testaments.* Some sacraments are of the old, others of the new, people. The sacraments of the ancient people were circumcision, and the paschal lamb, which was offered up; for that reason it is referred to the sacrifices which were practiced from the beginning of the world.

The Number of Sacraments of the New People. The sacraments of the new people are baptism and the Lord's supper. There are some who count seven sacraments of the new people. Of these we acknowledge that repentance, the ordination of ministers (not indeed the papal but apostolic ordination), and matrimony are profitable ordinances of God, but not sacraments. Confirmation and extreme unction are human inventions which the church can dispense with without any loss, and indeed, we do not have them in our churches. For they contain some things of which we can by no means approve. Above all we detest all the trafficking in which the papists engage in dispensing the sacraments.

The Author of the Sacraments. The author of all sacraments is not any man, but God alone. Men cannot institute sacraments. For they pertain to the worship of God, and it is not for man to appoint and prescribe a worship of God, but to accept and preserve the one he has received from God. Besides, the symbols have God's promises annexed to them, which require faith. Now faith rests only upon the word of God; and the word of God is like papers or letters, and the sacraments are like seals which only God appends to the letters.

[3.] *Christ Still Works in Sacraments.* And as God is the author of the sacraments, so he continually works in the church in which they are rightly carried out; so that the faithful, when they receive them from the ministers, know that God works in his own ordinance, and therefore they receive them as from the hand of God; and the minister's faults (even if they be very great) cannot affect them, since they acknowledge the integrity of the sacraments to depend upon the institution of the Lord.

The Author and the Ministers of the Sacraments to Be Distinguished. Hence in the administration of the sacraments they also clearly distinguish between the Lord himself and the ministers of the Lord, confessing that the substance of the sacraments is given them by the Lord, and the outward signs by the ministers of the Lord.

[4.] *The Substance or Chief Thing in the Sacraments.* But the principal thing which God promises in all sacraments and to which all the godly in all ages direct their attention (some call it the substance and matter of the sacraments) is Christ the Savior—that only sacrifice, and the lamb of God slain from the foundation of the world; that rock, also, from which all our fathers drank, by whom all the elect are circumcised without hands through the Holy Spirit, and are washed from all their sins, and are nourished with the very body and blood of Christ unto eternal life.

[5.] *The Similarity and Difference in the Sacraments of Old and New Peoples.* Now, in respect of that which is the principal thing and the matter itself in the sacraments, the sacraments of both peoples are equal. For Christ, the only Mediator and Savior of the faithful, is the chief thing and very substance of the sacraments in both; for the one God is the author of them both. They were given to both peoples as signs and seals of the grace and promises of God, which should call to mind and renew the memory of God's great benefits, and should distinguish the faithful from all the religions in the world; lastly, which should be received spiritually by faith, and should bind the receivers to the church, and admonish them of their duty. In these and similar respects, I say, the sacraments of both people are not dissimilar, although in the outward signs they are different. [6.] And, indeed, with respect to the signs we make a great difference. For ours are more firm and lasting, inasmuch as they will never be changed to the end of the world. Moreover, ours testify that both the substance and the promise have been fulfilled or perfected in Christ; the former signified what was to be fulfilled. Ours are also more simple and less laborious, less sumptuous and involved with ceremonies. Moreover, they belong to a more numerous people, one that is dispersed throughout the whole earth. And since they are more excellent, and by the Holy Spirit kindle greater faith, a greater abundance of the Spirit also ensues.

[7.] *Our Sacraments Succeed the Old Which Are Abrogated.* But now since Christ the true Messiah is exhibited unto us, and the abundance of grace is poured forth upon the people of the New Testament, the sacraments of the old people are surely abrogated and have ceased; and in their stead the symbols of the New Testament are placed—baptism in the place of circumcision, the Lord's supper in place of the paschal lamb and sacrifices.

[8.] *In What the Sacraments Consist.* And as formerly the sacraments consisted of the word, the sign, and the thing signified; so even now they are composed, as it were, of the same parts. For the word of God makes them sacraments, which before they were not. *The Consecration of the Sacraments.* For they are consecrated by the word, and shown to be sanctified by him who instituted them. To sanctify or consecrate anything to God is to dedicate it to holy uses; that is, to take it from the common and ordinary use, and to appoint it to a holy use. For the signs in the sacraments are drawn from common use, things external and visible. For in baptism the sign is the element of water, and that visible washing which is done by the minister; but the thing signified is regeneration and the cleansing from sins. Likewise, in the Lord's supper, the outward sign is bread and wine, taken from things commonly used for meat and drink; but the thing signified is the body of Christ which was given, and his blood which was shed for us, or the communion of the body and blood of the Lord. Wherefore, the water, bread, and wine, according to their nature and apart from the divine institution and sacred use, are only that which they are called and we experience. But when the word of God is added to them, together with invocation of the divine name, and the renewing of their first institution and sanctification, then these signs are consecrated, and shown to be sanctified by Christ. For Christ's first institution and consecration of the sacraments remains always effectual in the church of God, so that those who do not celebrate the sacraments in any other way than the Lord himself instituted from the beginning still today enjoy that first and all-surpassing consecration. And hence in the celebration of the sacraments the very words of Christ are repeated.

[9.] *Signs Take Name of Things Signified.* And as we learn out of the word of God that these signs were instituted for another purpose than the usual use, therefore we teach that they now, in their holy use, take upon them the names of things signified, and are no longer called mere water, bread, or wine, but also regeneration or the washing of water, and the body and blood of the Lord or symbols and sacraments of the Lord's body and blood. Not that the symbols are changed into the things signified, or cease to be what they are in their own nature. For otherwise they would not be sacraments. If they were only the thing signified, they would not be signs.

The Sacramental Union. Therefore the signs acquire the names of things because they are mystical signs of sacred things, and because the signs and the things signified are sacramentally joined together; joined together, I say, or united by a mystical signification, and by the purpose or will of him who instituted the sacraments. [10.] For the water, bread, and wine are not common, but holy signs. And he that instituted water in baptism did not institute it with the will and intention that the faithful should only be sprinkled by the water of baptism; and he who commanded the bread to be eaten and the wine to be drunk in the supper did not want the faithful to receive only bread and wine without any mystery as they eat bread in their homes; but that they should spiritually partake of the things signified, and by faith be truly cleansed from their sins, and partake of Christ.

[11.] *The Sects.* And, therefore, we do not at all approve of those who attribute the sanctification of the sacraments to I know not what properties and formula or to the power of words pronounced by one who is consecrated and who has the intention of consecrating, and to other accidental things which neither Christ nor the apostles delivered to us by word or example. Neither do we approve of the doctrine of those who speak of the sacraments just as common signs, not sanctified and effectual. Nor do we approve of those who despise the visible aspect of the sacraments because of the invisible, and so believe the signs to be superfluous because they think they already enjoy the thing themselves, as the Messalians are said to have held.

The Thing Signified Is Neither Included in or Bound to the Sacraments. We do not approve of the doctrine of those who teach that grace and the things signified are so bound to and included in the signs that whoever participate outwardly in the signs, no matter what sort of persons they be, also inwardly participate in the grace and things signified.

[12.] However, as we do not estimate the value of the sacraments by the worthiness or unworthiness of the ministers, so we do not estimate it by the condition of those who receive them. For we know that the value of the sacraments depends upon faith and upon the truthfulness and pure goodness of God. For as the word of God remains the true word of God, in which, when it is preached, not only bare words are repeated, but at the same time the things signified or announced in words are offered by God, even if the ungodly and unbelievers hear and understand the words yet do not enjoy the things signified, because they do not receive them by true faith; so the sacraments, which by the word consist of signs and the things signified, remain true and inviolate sacraments, signifying not only sacred things, but, by God offering, the things signified, even if unbelievers do not receive the things offered. This is not the fault of God who gives and offers them, but the fault of men who receive them without faith and illegitimately; but whose unbelief Rom 3.3f. does not invalidate the faithfulness of God.

[13.] *The Purpose for Which Sacraments Were Instituted.* Since the purpose for which sacraments were instituted was also explained in passing when right at the beginning of our exposition it was shown what sacraments are, there is no need to be tedious by repeating what once has been said. Logically, therefore, we now speak severally of the sacraments of the new people.

CHAPTER 20. OF HOLY BAPTISM

[1.] *The Institution of Baptism.* Baptism was instituted and consecrated by God. First John baptized, who dipped Christ in the water in Jordan. From him it came to the apostles, who also baptized with water. The Lord expressly commanded them to preach the gospel and to baptize "in the name of the Father and of the Son and of the Holy Spirit." And in the Acts, Peter said to the Jews who inquired what they ought to do: "Be baptized every one of you in the name of Jesus Christ for the forgiveness of your sins; and you shall receive the gift of the Holy Spirit." Hence by some baptism is called a sign of initiation for God's people, since by it the elect of God are consecrated to God.

Mt 28.19

Acts 2.37–38

[2.] *One Baptism.* There is but one baptism in the church of God; and it is sufficient to be once baptized or consecrated unto God. For baptism once received continues for all of life, and is a perpetual sealing of our adoption.

What It Means to Be Baptized. Now to be baptized in the name of Christ is to be enrolled, entered, and received into the covenant and family, and so into the inheritance of the sons of God; yes, and in this life to be called after the name of God; that is to say, to be called a son of God; to be cleansed also from the filthiness of sins, and to be granted the manifold grace of God, in order to lead a new and innocent life. Baptism, therefore, calls to mind and renews the great favor God has shown to the race of mortal men. [3.] For we are all born in the pollution of sin and are the children of wrath. But God, who is rich in mercy, freely cleanses us from our sins by the blood of his Son, and in him adopts us to be his sons, and by a holy covenant joins us to himself, and enriches us with various gifts, that we might live a new life. All these things are assured by baptism. For inwardly we are regenerated, purified, and renewed by God through the Holy Spirit; and outwardly we receive the assurance of the greatest gifts in the water, by which also those great benefits are represented, and, as it were, set before our eyes to be beheld.

We Are Baptized with Water. And therefore we are baptized, that is, washed or sprinkled with visible water. For the water washes dirt away, and cools and refreshes hot and tired bodies. And the grace of God performs these things for souls, and does so invisibly or spiritually.

[4.] *The Obligation of Baptism.* Moreover, God also separates us from all strange religions and peoples by the symbol of baptism, and consecrates us to himself as his property. We, therefore, confess our faith when we are baptized, and obligate ourselves to God for obedience, mortification of the flesh, and newness of life. Hence, we are enlisted in the holy military service of Christ that all our life long we should fight against the world, Satan, and our own flesh. Moreover, we are baptized into one body of the church, that with all members of the church we might beautifully concur in the one religion and in mutual services.

[5.] *The Form of Baptism.* We believe that the most perfect form of baptism is that by which Christ was baptized, and by which the apostles baptized. Those things, therefore, which by man's device were added afterwards and used in the church we do not consider necessary to the perfection of baptism. Of this kind is exorcism, the use of burning lights, oil, salt, spittle, and such other things as that baptism is to be celebrated twice every year with a multitude of ceremonies. For we believe that one baptism of the church has been sanctified in God's first institution, and that it is consecrated by the word and is also effectual today in virtue of God's first blessing.

[6.] *The Minister of Baptism.* We teach that baptism should not be administered in the church by women or midwives. For Paul deprived women of ecclesiastical duties, and baptism has to do with these.

[1 Tm 2.13]

Anabaptists. We condemn the Anabaptists, who deny that newborn infants of the faithful are to be baptized. For according to evangelical teaching, of such is the kingdom of God, and they are in the covenant of God. Why, then, should the sign of God's covenant not be given to them? Why should those who belong to God and are in his church not be initiated by holy baptism? We condemn also the Anabaptists in the rest of their peculiar doctrines which they hold contrary to the word of God. We therefore are not Anabaptists and have nothing in common with them.

CHAPTER 21. OF THE HOLY SUPPER OF THE LORD

[1.] *The Supper of the Lord.* The supper of the Lord (which is called the Lord's table, and the eucharist, that is, a thanksgiving) is, therefore, usually called a supper, because it was instituted by Christ at his last supper, and still represents it, and because in it the faithful are spiritually fed and given drink.

The Author and Consecrator of the Supper. For the author of the supper of the Lord is not an angel or any man, but the Son of God himself, our Lord Jesus Christ, who first consecrated it to his church. And the same consecration or blessing still remains among all those who celebrate no other but that very supper which the Lord instituted, and at which they repeat the words of the Lord's supper, and in all things look to the one Christ by a true faith, from whose hands they receive, as it were, what they receive through the ministry of the ministers of the church.

[2.] *A Memorial of God's Benefits.* By this sacred rite the Lord wishes to keep in fresh remembrance that greatest benefit which he showed to mortal men, namely, that by having given his body and shed his blood he has pardoned all our sins, and redeemed us from eternal death and the power of the devil, and now feeds us with his flesh, and give us his blood to drink, which, being received spiritually by true faith, nourish us to eternal life. And this so great a benefit is renewed as often as the Lord's supper is celebrated. For the Lord said: "Do this in remembrance of me."[a] This holy supper also seals to us that the very body of Christ was truly given for us, and his blood shed for the remission of our sins, lest our faith should in any way waver.

[3.] *The Sign and Thing Signified.* And this is visibly represented by this sacrament outwardly through the ministers, and, as it were, presented to our eyes to be seen, which is invisibly wrought by the Holy Spirit inwardly in the soul. Bread is outwardly offered by the minister, and the words of the Lord are heard: "Take, eat; this is my body," and, "Take and divide among you. Drink of it, all of you; this is my blood." Therefore the faithful receive what is given by the ministers of the Lord, Mt 26.27–28 and they eat the bread of the Lord and drink of the Lord's cup. At the same time by the work of Christ through the Holy Spirit they also inwardly receive the flesh and blood of the Lord, and are thereby nourished unto life eternal. For the flesh and blood of Christ is the true food and drink unto life eternal; and Christ himself, since he was given for us and is our Savior, is the principal thing in the supper, and we do not permit anything else to be substituted in his place.

[4.] But in order to understand better and more clearly how the flesh and blood of Christ are the food and drink of the faithful, and are received by the faithful unto eternal life, we would add these few things. There is more than one kind of eating. There is corporeal eating whereby food is taken into the mouth, is chewed with the teeth, and swallowed into the stomach. In times past the Capernaites thought that the flesh of the Lord should be eaten in this way, but they are refuted by him in John 6. For as the flesh of Christ cannot be eaten corporeally without infamy Jn 6 and savagery, so it is not food for the stomach. All men are forced to admit this. We therefore disapprove of that canon in the pope's decrees, Ego Berengarius (*De consecratione*, distinction 2).[4] For neither did godly antiquity believe, nor do we believe, that the body of Christ is to be eaten corporeally and essentially with a bodily mouth.

[5.] *Spiritual Eating of the Lord.* There is also a spiritual eating of Christ's body; not such that we think that thereby the food itself is to be changed into spirit, but whereby the body and blood of the Lord, while remaining in their own essence and property, are spiritually communicated to us, certainly not in a corporeal but in a spiritual way, by the Holy Spirit, who applies and bestows upon us these things

a. Lk 22.19; 1 Cor 11.25

4. *Brngr 1059; Brngr 1079.*

which have been prepared for us by the sacrifice of the Lord's body and blood for us, namely, the remission of sins, deliverance, and eternal life; so that Christ lives in us and we live in him, and he causes us to receive him by true faith to this end that he may become for us such spiritual food and drink, that is, our life.

[6.] *Christ as Our Food Sustains Us in Life.* For even as bodily food and drink not only refresh and strengthen our bodies, but also keep them alive, so the flesh of Christ delivered for us, and his blood shed for us, not only refresh and strengthen our souls, but also preserve them alive, not in so far as they are corporeally eaten and drunken, but in so far as they are communicated unto us spiritually by the Spirit of God, as the Lord said: "The bread which I shall give for the life of the world is my flesh," and "the flesh" (namely what is eaten bodily) "is of no avail; it is the spirit that gives life." And: "The words that I have spoken to you are spirit and life."

Jn 6.51

Jn 6.63

Christ Received by Faith. And as we must by eating receive food into our bodies in order that it may work in us, and prove its efficacy in us—since it profits us nothing when it remains outside us—so it is necessary that we receive Christ by faith, that he may become ours, and he may live in us and we in him. For he says: "I am the bread of life; he who comes to me shall not hunger, and he who believes in me shall never thirst;" and also, "He who eats me will live because of me . . . he abides in me, I in him."

Jn 6.35

Jn 6.51, 56

[7.] *Spiritual Food.* From all this it is clear that by spiritual food we do not mean some imaginary food I know not what, but the very body of the Lord given to us, which nevertheless is received by the faithful not corporeally, but spiritually by faith. In this matter we follow the teaching of the Savior himself, Christ the Lord, according to John 6.

Jn 6

Eating Necessary for Salvation. And this eating of the flesh and drinking of the blood of the Lord is so necessary for salvation that without it no man can be saved. But this spiritual eating and drinking also occurs apart from the supper of the Lord, and as often and wherever a man believes in Christ. To which that sentence of St. Augustine's perhaps applies: "Why do you provide for your teeth and your stomach? Believe, and you have eaten."

[8.] *Sacramental Eating of the Lord.* Besides the higher spiritual eating there is also a sacramental eating of the body of the Lord by which not only spiritually and internally the believer truly participates in the true body and blood of the Lord, but also, by coming to the table of the Lord, outwardly receives the visible sacrament of the body and blood of the Lord. To be sure, when the believer believed, he first received the life-giving food, and still enjoys it. But therefore, when he now receives the sacrament, he does not receive nothing. For he progresses in continuing to communicate in the body and blood of the Lord, and so his faith is kindled and grows more and more, and is refreshed by spiritual food. For while we live, faith is continually increased. And he who outwardly receives the sacrament by true faith, not only receives the sign, but also, as we said, enjoys the thing itself. Moreover, he obeys the Lord's institution and commandment, and with a joyful mind gives thanks for his redemption and that of all mankind, and makes a faithful memorial to the Lord's death, and gives a witness before the church, of whose body he is a member. Assurance is also given to those who receive the sacrament that the body of the Lord was given and his blood shed, not only for men in general, but particularly for every faithful communicant, to whom it is food and drink unto eternal life.

[9.] *Unbelievers Take the Sacrament to Their Judgment.* But he who comes to this sacred table of the Lord without faith, communicates only in the sacrament and does not receive the substance of the sacrament whence comes life and salvation; and such men unworthily eat of the Lord's table. Whoever eats the bread or drinks the cup of the Lord in an unworthy manner will be guilty of the body and blood of the Lord, and eats and drinks judgment upon himself. For when they do not approach with true faith, they dishonor the death of Christ, and therefore eat and drink condemnation to themselves. 1 Cor 11.26–29

[10.] *The Presence of Christ in the Supper.* We do not, therefore, so join the body of the Lord and his blood with the bread and wine as to say that the bread itself is the body of Christ, except in a sacramental way; or that the body of Christ is hidden corporeally under the bread, so that it ought to be worshiped under the form of bread; or yet that whoever receives the sign, receives also the thing itself. The body of Christ is in heaven at the right hand of the Father; and therefore our hearts are to be lifted up on high, and not to be fixed on the bread, neither is the Lord to be worshiped in the bread. Yet the Lord is not absent from his church when she celebrates the supper. The sun, which is absent from us in the heavens, is notwithstanding effectually present among us. How much more is the sun of righteousness, Christ, although in his body he is absent from us in heaven, present with us, not corporeally, but spiritually, by his vivifying operation, and as he himself explained at his last supper that he would be present with us. Whence it follows that we do not have the supper without Christ, and yet at the same time have an unbloody and mystical supper, as it was universally called by antiquity. Jn 14–16

[11.] *Other Purposes of the Lord's Supper.* Moreover, we are admonished in the celebration of the supper of the Lord to be mindful of whose body we have become members, and that, therefore, we may be of one mind with all the brethren, live a holy life, and not pollute ourselves with wickedness and strange religions; but, persevering in the true faith to the end of our life, strive to excel in holiness of life.

Preparation for the Supper. It is therefore fitting that when we would come to the supper, we first examine ourselves according to the commandment of the apostle, especially as to the kind of faith we have, whether we believe that Christ has come to save sinners and to call them to repentance, and whether each man believes that he is in the number of those who have been delivered by Christ and saved; and whether he is determined to change his wicked life, to lead a holy life, and with the Lord's help to persevere in the true religion and in harmony with the brethren, and to give due thanks to God for his deliverance.

[12.] *The Observance of the Supper with Both Bread and Wine*. We think that rite, manner, or form of the supper to be the most simple and excellent which comes nearest to the first institution of the Lord and to the apostles' doctrine. It consists in proclaiming the word of God, in godly prayers, in the action of the Lord himself, and its repetition, in the eating of the Lord's body and drinking of his blood; in a fitting remembrance of the Lord's death, and a faithful thanksgiving; and in a holy fellowship in the union of the body of the church.

We therefore disapprove of those who have taken from the faithful one species of the sacrament, namely, the Lord's cup. For these seriously offend against

Mt 26.27   the institution of the Lord who says: "Drink ye all of this"; which he did not so expressly say of the bread.

[13.] We are not now discussing what kind of mass once existed among the fathers, whether it is to be tolerated or not. But this we say freely that the mass which is now used throughout the Roman Church has been abolished in our churches for many and very good reasons which, for brevity's sake, we do not now enumerate in detail. We certainly could not approve of making a wholesome action into a vain spectacle and a means of gaining merit, and of celebrating it for a price. Nor could we approve of saying that in it the priest is said to effect the very body of the Lord, and really to offer it for the remission of the sins of the living and the dead, and in addition, for the honor, veneration, and remembrance of the saints in heaven, etc.

CHAPTER 22. OF RELIGIOUS AND
ECCLESIASTICAL MEETINGS

[1.] *What Ought to Be Done in Meetings for Worship*. Although it is permitted all men to read the Holy Scriptures privately at home, and by instruction to edify one another in the true religion, yet in order that the word of God may be properly preached to the people, and prayers and supplication publicly made, also that the sacraments may be rightly administered, and that collections may be made for the poor and to pay the cost of all the church's expenses, and in order to maintain social intercourse, it is most necessary that religious or church gatherings be held. For it is certain that in the apostolic and primitive church, there were such assemblies frequented by all the godly.

[2.] *Meetings for Worship Not to Be Neglected.* As many as spurn such meetings and stay away from them, despise true religion, and are to be urged by the pastors and godly magistrates to abstain from stubbornly absenting themselves from sacred assemblies.

Meetings Are Public. But church meetings are not to be secret and hidden, but public and well attended, unless persecution by the enemies of Christ and the church does not permit them to be public. For we know how under the tyranny of the Roman emperors the meetings of the primitive church were held in secret places.

[3.] *Decent Meeting Places.* Moreover, the places where the faithful meet are to be decent, and in all respects fit for God's church. Therefore, spacious buildings or temples are to be chosen, but they are to be purged of everything that is not fitting for a church. And everything is to be arranged for decorum, necessity, and godly decency, lest anything be lacking that is required for worship and the necessary works of the church.

[4.] *Modesty and Humility to Be Observed in Meetings.* And as we believe that God does not dwell in temples made with hands, so we know that on account of God's word and sacred use places dedicated to God and his worship are not profane, but holy, and that those who are present in them are to conduct themselves reverently and modestly, seeing that they are in a sacred place, in the presence of God and his holy angels.

The True Ornamentation of Sanctuaries. Therefore, all luxurious attire, all pride, and everything unbecoming to Christian humility, discipline, and modesty, are to be banished from the sanctuaries and places of prayers of Christians. For the true ornamentation of churches does not consist in ivory, gold, and precious stones, but in the frugality, piety, and virtues of those who are in the church. Let all things be done decently and in order in the church, and finally, let all things be done for [1 Cor 14.40] edification.

Worship in the Common Language. Therefore, let all strange tongues keep silence in gatherings for worship, and let all things be set forth in a common language which is understood by the people gathered in that place.

CHAPTER 23. OF THE PRAYERS OF THE CHURCH, OF SINGING, AND OF CANONICAL HOURS

[1.] *Common Language.* It is true that a man is permitted to pray privately in any language that he understands, but public prayers in meetings for worship are to be made in the common language known to all. *Prayer.* Let all the prayers of the faithful be poured forth to God alone, through the mediation of Christ only, out of faith and love. The priesthood of Christ the Lord and true religion forbid the invocation of saints in heaven or to use them as intercessors. Prayer is to be made for magistracy, for kings, and all that are placed in authority, for ministers of the church, and for all needs of churches. In calamities, especially of the church, unceasing prayer is to be made both privately and publicly.

[2.] *Free Prayer.* Moreover, prayer is to be made voluntarily, without constraint or for any reward. Nor is it proper for prayer to be superstitiously restricted to one place, as if it were not permitted to pray anywhere except in a sanctuary. Neither is it necessary for public prayers to be the same in all churches with respect to form and time. Each church is to exercise its own freedom. Socrates, in his history, says, "In all regions of the world you will not find two churches which wholly agree in prayer" (*Ecclesiastical History* 5.22, 57). The authors of this difference, I think, were those who were in charge of the churches at particular times. Yet if they agree, it is to be highly commended and imitated by others.

[3.] *The Method to Be Employed in Public Prayers.* As in everything, so also in public prayers there is to be a standard lest they be excessively long and irksome. The greatest part of meetings for worship is therefore to be given to evangelical teaching, and care is to be taken lest the congregation is wearied by too lengthy prayers and when they are to hear the preaching of the gospel they either leave the meeting or, having been exhausted, want to do away with it altogether. To such people the sermon seems to be overlong, which otherwise is brief enough. And therefore it is appropriate for preachers to keep to a standard.

[4.] *Singing.* Likewise moderation is to be exercised where singing is used in a meeting for worship. That song which they call the Gregorian chant has many foolish things in it; hence it is rightly rejected by many of our churches. If there are churches which have a true and proper sermon but no singing, they ought not to be condemned. For all churches do not have the advantage of singing. And it is well known from testimonies of antiquity that the custom of singing is very old in the Eastern churches, whereas it was late when it was at length accepted in the West.

[5.] *Canonical Hours.* Antiquity knew nothing of canonical hours, that is, prayers arranged for certain hours of the day, and sung or recited by the papists, as can be proved from their breviaries and by many arguments. But they also have not a few absurdities, of which I say nothing else; accordingly they are rightly omitted by churches which substitute in their place things that are beneficial for the whole church of God.

CHAPTER 24. OF HOLY DAYS, FASTS, AND
THE CHOICE OF FOODS

[1.] *The Time Necessary for Worship.* Although religion is not bound to time, yet it cannot be cultivated and exercised without a proper distribution and arrangement of time. Every church, therefore, chooses for itself a certain time for public prayers, and for the preaching of the gospel, and for the celebration of the sacraments; and no one is permitted to overthrow this appointment of the church at his own pleasure. For unless some due time and leisure is given for the outward exercise of religion, without doubt men would be drawn away from it by their own affairs.

[2.] *The Lord's Day.* Hence we see that in the ancient churches there were not only certain set hours in the week appointed for meetings, but that also the Lord's Day itself, ever since the apostles' time, was set aside for them and for a holy rest, a practice now rightly preserved by our churches for the sake of worship and love.

Superstition. In this connection we do not yield to the Jewish observance and to superstitions. For we do not believe that one day is any holier than another, or think that rest in itself is acceptable to God. Moreover, we celebrate the Lord's Day and not the Sabbath as a free observance.

[3.] *The Festivals of Christ and the Saints.* Moreover, if in Christian liberty the churches religiously celebrate the memory of the Lord's nativity, circumcision, passion, resurrection, and of his ascension into heaven, and the sending of the Holy Spirit upon his disciples, we approve of it highly. But we do not approve of feasts instituted for men and for saints. Holy days have to do with the first table of the law and belong to God alone. Finally, holy days which have been instituted for the saints and which we have abolished, have much that is absurd and useless, and are not to be tolerated. In the meantime, we confess that the remembrance of saints, at a suitable time and place, is to be profitably commended to the people in sermons, and the holy examples of the saints set forth to be imitated by all.

[4.] *Fasting.* Now, the more seriously the church of Christ condemns surfeiting, drunkenness, and all kinds of lust and intemperance, so much the more strongly does it commend to us Christian fasting. For fasting is nothing else than the abstinence and moderation of the godly, and a discipline, care, and chastisement of our flesh undertaken as a necessity for the time being, whereby we are humbled before God, and we deprive the flesh of its fuel so that it may the more willingly and easily obey the Spirit. Therefore, those who pay no attention to such things do not fast, but imagine that they fast if they stuff their stomachs once a day, and at a certain or prescribed time abstain from certain foods, thinking that by having done this work they please God and do something good. Fasting is an aid to the prayers of the saints and for all virtues. But as is seen in the books of the prophets, the fast of the Jews who fasted from food but not from wickedness did not please God.

[5.] *Public and Private Fasting.* Now there is a public and a private fasting. In olden times they celebrated public fasts in calamitous times and in the affliction of the church. They abstained altogether from food till the evening, and spent all that time in holy prayers, the worship of God, and repentance. These differed little from mourning, and there is frequent mention of them in the prophets and especially by Joel in chapter 2. Such a fast should be kept at this day, when the church is in distress. Private fasts are undertaken by each one of us, as he feels himself withdrawn from the Spirit. For in this manner he withdraws the flesh from its fuel.

Jl 2

[6.] *Characteristics of Fasting.* All fasts ought to proceed from a free and willing spirit, and from genuine humility, and not feigned to gain the applause or favor of men, much less that a man should wish to merit righteousness by them. But let everyone fast to this end, that he may deprive the flesh of its fuel in order that he may the more zealously serve God.

[7.] *Lent.* The fast of Lent is attested by antiquity but not at all in the writings of the apostles. Therefore it ought not, and cannot, be imposed on the faithful. It is certain that formerly there were various forms and customs of fasting. Hence, Irenaeus, a most ancient writer, says: "Some think that a fast should be observed one day only, others two days, but others more, and some forty days. This diversity in keeping this fast did not first begin in our times, but long before us by those, as I suppose, who did not simply keep to what had been delivered to them from the beginning, but afterwards fell into another custom either through negligence or ignorance" (*Fragmenta* 3, 1.824f.). Moreover, Socrates, the historian says: "Because no ancient text is found concerning this matter, I think the apostles left this to every man's own judgment, that everyone might do what is good without fear or constraint" (*Ecclesiastical History* 5.22, 40).

[8.] *Choice of Food.* Now concerning the choice of foods, we think that in fasting all things should be denied to the flesh whereby the flesh is made more insolent, and by which it is greatly pleased, and by which it is inflamed with desire, whether by fish or meat or spices or delicacies and excellent wines. Moreover, we know that all the creatures of God were made for the use and service of men. All things which God made are good, and without distinction are to be used in the fear of God and with proper moderation. For the apostle says: "To the pure all things are pure," and also: "Eat whatever is sold in the meat market without raising any question on the ground of conscience." The same apostle calls the doctrine of those who

Gn 2.15–17
Ti 1.15
1 Cor 10.25

teach to abstain from meats "the doctrine of demons"; for "God created foods to be received with thanksgiving by those who believe and know this truth that everything created by God is good, and nothing is to be rejected if it is received with thanksgiving." The same apostle, in the Epistle to the Colossians, reproves those who want to acquire a reputation for holiness by excessive abstinence.

1 Tm 4.1, 3–4
Col 2.18ff.

Sects. Therefore we entirely disapprove of the Tatians and the Encratites, and all the disciples of Eustathius, against whom the Gangrian Synod was called.

CHAPTER 25. OF CATECHIZING AND COMFORTING AND VISITING THE SICK

[1.] *Youth to Be Instructed in Godliness.* The Lord enjoined his ancient people to exercise the greatest care that young people, even from infancy, be properly instructed. Moreover, he expressly commanded in his law that they should teach them, and that the mysteries of the sacraments should be explained. Now since it is well known from the writings of the evangelists and apostles that God has no less concern for the youth of his new people, when he openly testifies and says: "Let the children come to me; for to such belongs the kingdom of heaven," the pastors of the churches act most wisely when they early and carefully catechize the youth, laying the first grounds of faith, and faithfully teaching the rudiments of our religion by expounding the Ten Commandments, the Apostles' Creed, the Lord's Prayer, and the doctrine of the sacraments, with other such principles and chief heads of our religion. Here let the church show her faith and diligence in bringing the children to be catechized, desirous and glad to have her children well instructed.

Mk 10.14

[2.] *The Visitation of the Sick.* Since men are never exposed to more grievous temptations than when they are harassed by infirmities, are sick and are weakened by diseases of both soul and body, surely it is never more fitting for pastors of churches to watch more carefully for the welfare of their flocks than in such diseases and infirmities. Therefore let them visit the sick soon, and let them be called in good time by the sick, if the circumstance itself would have required it. Let them comfort and confirm them in the true faith, and then arm them against the dangerous suggestions of Satan. They should also hold prayer for the sick in the home and, if need be, prayers should also be made for the sick in the public meeting; and they should see that they happily depart this life. We said above that we do not approve of the popish visitation of the sick with extreme unction because it is absurd and is not approved by canonical Scriptures.

CHAPTER 26. OF THE BURIAL OF THE FAITHFUL,
AND OF THE CARE TO BE SHOWN FOR THE DEAD;
OF PURGATORY, AND THE APPEARING OF SPIRITS

[1.] *The Burial of Bodies.* As the bodies of the faithful are the temples of the Holy Spirit which we truly believe will rise again at the last day, Scriptures command that they be honorably and without superstition committed to the earth, and also that honorable mention be made of those saints who have fallen asleep in the Lord, and that all duties of familial piety be shown to those left behind, their widows and orphans. We do not teach that any other care be taken for the dead. Therefore, we greatly disapprove of the Cynics, who neglected the bodies of the dead or most carelessly and disdainfully cast them into the earth, never saying a good word about the deceased, or caring a bit about those whom they left behind them.

[2.] *The Care of the Dead.* On the other hand, we do not approve of those who are overly and absurdly attentive to the deceased; who, like the heathen, bewail their dead (although we do not blame that moderate mourning which the apostle 1 Thes 4.13   permits in 1 Thessalonians 4.13, judging it to be inhuman not to grieve at all); and who sacrifice for the dead, and mumble certain prayers for pay, in order by such ceremonies to deliver their loved ones from the torments in which they are immersed by death, and then think they are able to liberate them by such incantations.

[3.] *The State of the Soul Departed from the Body.* For we believe that the faithful, after bodily death, go directly to Christ, and, therefore, do not need the eulogies and prayers of the living for the dead and their services. Likewise we believe that unbelievers are immediately cast into hell from which no exit is opened for the wicked by any services of the living.

[4.] *Purgatory.* But what some teach concerning the fire of purgatory is opposed to the Christian faith, namely, "I believe in the forgiveness of sins, and the life everlasting," and to the perfect purgation through Christ, and to these words of Christ our Lord: "Truly, truly, I say to you, he who hears my word and believes him who sent me, has eternal life; he shall not come into judgment, but has passed Jn 5.24   from death to life." Again: "He who has bathed does not need to wash, except for Jn 13.10   his feet, but he is clean all over, and you are clean."

[5.] *The Apparition of Spirits.* Now what is related of the spirits or souls of the dead sometimes appearing to those who are alive, and begging certain duties of them whereby they may be set free, we count those apparitions among the laughing-stocks, crafts, and deceptions of the devil, who, as he can transform himself into an [2 Cor 11.14]   angel of light, so he strikes either to overthrow the true faith or to call it into doubt. In the Old Testament the Lord forbade the seeking of the truth from the dead, and Dt 18.11   any sort of commerce with spirits. Indeed, as evangelical truth declares, the glutton, being in torment, is denied a return to his brethren, as the divine oracle declares in the words: "They have Moses and the prophets; let them hear them. If they hear not Moses and the prophets, neither will they be convinced if someone should rise from the dead."

Lk 16.29, 31

CHAPTER 27. OF RITES, CEREMONIES, AND THINGS INDIFFERENT

[1.] *Ceremonies and Rites.* Unto the ancient people were given at one time certain ceremonies, as a kind of instruction for those who were kept under the law, as under a schoolmaster or tutor. But when Christ, the deliverer, came and the law was abolished, we who believe are no more under the law, and the ceremonies have disappeared; hence the apostles did not want to retain or to restore them in Christ's church to such a degree that they openly testified that they did not wish to impose any burden upon the church. Therefore, we would seem to be bringing in and restoring Judaism if we were to increase ceremonies and rites in Christ's church according to the custom in the ancient church. Hence, we by no means approve of the opinion of those who think that the church of Christ must be held in check by many different rites, as if by some kind of training. For if the apostles did not want to impose upon Christian people ceremonies or rites which were appointed by God, who, I pray, in his right mind would obtrude upon them the inventions devised by man? The more the mass of rites is increased in the church, the more is detracted not only from Christian liberty, but also from Christ, and from faith in him, as long as the people seek those things in ceremonies which they should seek in the only Son of God, Jesus Christ, through faith. Wherefore a few moderate and simple rites, that are not contrary to the word of God, are sufficient for the godly.

Rom 6.14

[Acts 15.10, 28]

[2.] *Diversity of Rites.* If different rites are found in churches, no one should think for this reason the churches disagree. Socrates says: "It would be impossible to put together in writing all the rites of churches throughout cities and countries. No religion observes the same rites, even though it embraces the same doctrine concerning them. For those who are of the same faith disagree among themselves about rites" (*Ecclesiastical History* 5.22, 30, 62). This much says Socrates. And we, today, having in our churches different rites in the celebration of the Lord's supper and in some other things, nevertheless do not disagree in doctrine and faith; nor is the unity and fellowship of our churches thereby rent asunder. For the churches have always used their liberty in such rites, as being things indifferent. We also do the same thing today.

[3.] *Things Indifferent.* But at the same time we admonish men to be on guard lest they reckon among things indifferent what are in fact not indifferent, as some are wont to regard the mass and the use of images in places of worship as things indifferent. "Indifferent," wrote Jerome to Augustine, "is that which is neither good nor bad, so that, whether you do it or not, you are neither just nor unjust." Therefore, when things indifferent are wrested to the confession of faith, they cease to be free; as Paul shows that it is lawful for a man to eat flesh if someone does not remind him that it was offered to idols, for then it is unlawful, because he who eats it seems to approve idolatry by eating it.

1 Cor 8.9ff., 10.25ff.

CHAPTER 28. OF THE POSSESSIONS OF THE CHURCH

[1.] *The Possessions of the Church and Their Proper Use.* The church of Christ possesses riches through the munificence of princes and the liberality of the faithful who have given their means to the church. For the church has need of such resources and from ancient time has had resources for the maintenance of things necessary for the church. Now the true use of the church's wealth was, and is now, to maintain teaching in schools and in religious meetings, along with all the worship, rites, and buildings of the church; finally, to maintain teachers, scholars, and ministers, with other necessary things, and especially for the succor and relief of the poor. *Management.* Moreover, God-fearing and wise men, noted for the management of domestic affairs, should be chosen to administer properly the church's possessions.

[2.] *The Misuse of the Church's Possessions.* But if through misfortune or through the audacity, ignorance, or avarice of some persons the church's wealth is abused, it is to be restored to a sacred use by godly and wise men. For neither is an abuse, which is the greatest sacrilege, to be winked at. Therefore, we teach that schools and institutions which have been corrupted in doctrine, worship, and morals must be reformed, and that the relief of the poor must be arranged dutifully, wisely, and in good faith.

CHAPTER 29. OF CELIBACY, MARRIAGE, AND THE MANAGEMENT OF DOMESTIC AFFAIRS

[1.] *Single People.* Those who have the gift of celibacy from heaven, so that from the heart or with their whole soul they are pure and continent and are not aflame with passion, let them serve the Lord in that calling, as long as they feel endued with that divine gift; and let them not lift up themselves above others, but let them serve the

1 Cor 7.7ff.

Lord continuously in simplicity and humility. For such are more apt to attend to divine things than those who are distracted with the private affairs of a family. But if, again, the gift be taken away, and they feel a continual burning, let them call to

1 Cor 7.9

mind the words of the apostle: "It is better to marry than to be aflame."

[2.] *Marriage.* For marriage (which is the medicine of incontinency, and continency itself) was instituted by the Lord God himself, who blessed it most bountifully, and willed man and woman to cleave one to the other inseparably, and to live together in complete love and concord. Whereupon we know that the apostle said: "Let marriage be held in honor among all, and let the marriage bed be undefiled." And again: "If a girl marries, she does not sin." *The Sects.* We therefore condemn polygamy, and those who condemn second marriages.

Mt 19.4ff
Heb 13.4
1 Cor 7.28

How Marriages Are to Be Contracted. We teach that marriages are to be lawfully contracted in the fear of the Lord, and not against the laws which forbid certain degrees of consanguinity, lest the marriages should be incestuous. Let marriages be made with consent of the parents, or of those who take the place of parents, and above all for that purpose for which the Lord instituted marriages. Moreover, let them be kept holy with the utmost faithfulness, piety, love, and purity of those joined together. Therefore let them guard against quarrels, dissensions, lust, and adultery.

Matrimonial Forum. Let lawful courts be established in the church, and holy judges who may care for marriages, and may repress all unchastity and shamefulness, and before whom matrimonial disputes may be settled.

[3.] *The Rearing of Children.* Children are to be brought up by the parents in the fear of the Lord; and parents are to provide for their children, remembering the saying of the apostle: "If anyone does not provide for his relatives, he has disowned the faith and is worse than an unbeliever." But especially they should teach their children honest trades or professions by which they may support themselves. They should keep them from idleness and in all these things instill in them true faith in God, lest through a lack of confidence or too much security or filthy greed they become dissolute and achieve no success.

1 Tm 5.8

[4.] And it is most certain that those works which are done by parents in true faith by way of domestic duties and the management of their households are in God's sight holy and truly good works. They are no less pleasing to God than prayers, fasting, and almsgiving. For thus the apostle has taught in his epistles, especially in those to Timothy and Titus. And with the same apostle we account the doctrine of those who forbid marriage or openly castigate or indirectly discredit it, as if it were not holy and pure, among the doctrine of demons.

[1 Tm 4.1–3]

[5.] We also detest an impure single life, the secret and open lusts and fornications of hypocrites pretending to be continent when they are the most incontinent of all. All these God will judge. We do not disapprove of riches or rich men, if they be godly and use their riches well. But we reject the sect of the Apostolicals, etc.

CHAPTER 30. OF THE MAGISTRACY

[1.] *The Magistracy Is from God*. Magistracy of every kind is instituted by God himself for the peace and tranquillity of the human race, and thus it should have the chief place in the world. If the magistrate is opposed to the church, he can hinder and disturb it very much; but if he is a friend and even a member of the church, he is a most useful and excellent member of it, who is able to benefit it greatly, and to assist it best of all.

[2.] *The Duty of the Magistrate*. The chief duty of the magistrate is to secure and preserve peace and public tranquillity. Doubtless he will never do this more successfully than when he is truly God-fearing and religious; that is to say, when, according to the example of the most holy kings and princes of the people of the Lord, he promotes the preaching of the truth and sincere faith, roots out lies and all superstition, together with all impiety and idolatry, and defends the church of God. We certainly teach that the care of religion belongs especially to the holy magistrate.

[3.] Let him, therefore, hold the word of God in his hands, and take care lest anything contrary to it is taught. Likewise let him govern the people entrusted to him by God with good laws made according to the word of God, and let him keep them in discipline, duty, and obedience. Let him exercise judgment by judging uprightly. Let him not respect any man's person or accept bribes. Let him protect widows, orphans, and the afflicted. Let him punish and even banish criminals, im-
Rom 13.4   postors, and barbarians. For he does not bear the sword in vain.

Therefore, let him draw this sword of God against all malefactors, seditious persons, thieves, murderers, oppressors, blasphemers, perjured persons, and all those whom God has commanded him to punish and even to execute. Let him suppress stubborn heretics (who are truly heretics), who do not cease to blaspheme the majesty of God and to trouble, and even to destroy the church of God.

[4.] *War*. And if it is necessary to preserve the safety of the people by war, let him wage war in the name of God; provided he has first sought peace by all means possible, and cannot save his people in any other way except by war. And when the magistrate does these things in faith, he serves God by those very works which are truly good, and receives a blessing from the Lord.

We condemn the Anabaptists, who, when they deny that a Christian may hold the office of a magistrate, deny also that a man may be justly put to death by the magistrate, or that the magistrate may wage war, or that oaths are to be rendered to a magistrate, and such like things.

[5.] *The Duty of Subjects*. For as God wants to effect the safety of his people by the magistrate, whom he has given to the world to be, as it were, a father, so all subjects are commanded to acknowledge this favor of God in the magistrate. Therefore let them honor and reverence the magistrate as the minister of God; let them love him, favor him, and pray for him as their father; and let them obey all his just and fair commands. Finally, let them pay all customs and taxes, and all other such dues faithfully and willingly. And if the public safety of the country and justice require it, and the magistrate of necessity wages war, let them even lay down their life and pour out their blood for the public safety and that of the magistrate. And let them do this in the name of God willingly, bravely, and cheerfully. For he who opposes the magistrate provokes the severe wrath of God against himself.

Sects and Seditions. We, therefore, condemn all who are contemptuous of the magistrate—rebels, enemies of the state, seditious villains, finally, all who openly or craftily refuse to perform whatever duties they owe.

We beseech God, our most merciful Father in heaven, that he will bless the rulers of the people, and us, and his whole people, through Jesus Christ, our only Lord and Savior; to whom be praise and glory and thanksgiving, for all ages. Amen.

Church of England, *The Thirty-Nine Articles*, 1571

The roots of *The Thirty-Nine Articles* go back at least as far as 1553, when Archbishop Thomas Cranmer drew up *The Forty-Two Articles* in the name of Edward VI. There were other steps along the way, however, including the *Thirteen Articles* of 1538 (never published or authorized), *The Six Articles* of 1543, and *The Eleven Articles* of 1559–60.[1] Over the years, the doctrinal positions of the Church of England had shifted from the traditionalist stance taken in → *The Ten Articles* (1536) to reflect a variety of influences from Lutheran, Calvinist, and Zwinglian thought.

Despite their significance as a source for *The Thirty-Nine Articles*, *The Forty-Two Articles* were of short-lived importance as a profession of faith. One month after mandating subscription to the articles, young King Edward VI died. His half-sister Queen Mary I quickly nullified *The Forty-Two Articles* and all other religious legislation of Edward's brief reign. When Elizabeth I came to the throne in 1558, she ordered a return to the second edition of Edward's prayer book, the 1552 *Book of Common Prayer*, for both worship and doctrinal instruction.

By 1563, however, the need for a doctrinal statement for the Church of England was apparent, and Matthew Parker, archbishop of Canterbury, prepared a revised version of *The Forty-Two Articles*, reducing it to thirty-nine articles. In addition to the work of his predecessor, he drew upon the Lutheran *Confession of Württemberg* of Johannes Brenz (1499–1570), especially for articles 2, 5, 6, 10, 11, 12, and 20.[2] Article 29 ("On the Wicked which do not eat the Body of Christ in the use of the Lord's Supper") was left out of the printed edition of 1563, therefore known as *The Thirty-Eight Articles*, but reintroduced in 1571. The removal of article 29 is usually attributed to Queen Elizabeth, although there is no certain evidence for this. The reasons given for its exclusion vary in the scholarship: some say Elizabeth did not wish to offend the Roman Catholic Church at that time,[3] others that she hoped to facilitate negotiations with Lutherans by leaving it out.[4] She eventually sanctioned all thirty-nine articles, however, and they were published in Latin

---

1. For an overview of the history of doctrinal statements of the Church of England in this period, see *Prayer Book Dictionary* 1918, 49–51. Complete texts and translations of all of the documents mentioned are included in Bray.
2. Heppe 1885, 491–554.
3. Dugmore 1980, 167.
4. *ODCC* 1161.

and English in 1571.[5] From that time to the present, subscription to—or, since 1975, acknowledgment of—the articles has been a requirement for all Anglican clergy.

In 1801 the Protestant Episcopal Church in the United States amended the text to reflect America's independence from the English monarchy and to omit the Athanasian Creed.[6] Since the mid-nineteenth century, however, the importance of *The Thirty-Nine Articles* has waned in both the Anglican and Episcopal Churches. Since 1977 the Episcopal Church in the United States has relegated the articles to a special section at the end of the *Book of Common Prayer* designated "Historical Documents of the Church."

Edition: *Anglican Book of Common Prayer* (1662), as authorized by the Anglican Church (includes some orthographic modernization). Changes established by the 1801 convention of the Protestant Episcopal Church in the United States of America, as printed in the 1979 *Book of Common Prayer*, are given in notes. The Latin text of 1571 is reproduced from Evans and Wright 1991, 155–228.

Note: For the English text of 1571, see Evans and Wright 1991, 155–228.

Literature: Applegate 1981; Bicknell 1955; Dugmore 1980; Evans and Wright 1991, 155–228; Hardwick 1876, 66–158; Haugaard 1968, 242–72; Marshall 1989; Newman 1841; *ODCC* 1611; O'Donovan 1986; *OER* 1:80–83 (Lytle); *Prayer Book Dictionary* 1918, 49–63; Reardon 1989; Ridley 1962, 214–15.

5. Both texts have equal authority.
6. Subscription to the articles has never been a requirement for priesthood in the United States.

Church of England, *The Thirty-Nine Articles,* 1571

[From the Book of Common Prayer, *1662]*

Articles whereupon it was agreed by the archbishops and bishops of both provinces and the whole clergy, in the convocation holden at London in the year of our Lord God 1562, according to the computation of the Church of England, for the avoiding of the diversities of opinions and for the establishing of consent touching true religion. Put forth by the Queen's authority.

1. OF FAITH IN THE HOLY TRINITY

There is but one living and true God, everlasting, without body, parts, or passions; of infinite power, wisdom, and goodness; the maker and preserver of all things both visible and invisible. And in unity of this Godhead there be three persons, of one substance, power, and eternity; the Father, the Son, and the Holy Ghost.

2. OF THE WORD, OR SON OF GOD, WHICH WAS MADE VERY MAN

The Son, which is the Word of the Father, begotten from everlasting of the Father, the very and eternal God, and of one substance with the Father, took man's nature in the womb of the Blessed Virgin, of her substance: so that two whole and perfect natures, that is to say, the Godhead and manhood, were joined together in one person, never to be divided, whereof is one Christ, very God, and very man, who truly suffered, was crucified, dead, and buried, to reconcile his Father to us, and to be a sacrifice, not only for original guilt, but also for all actual sins of men.

3. OF THE GOING DOWN OF CHRIST INTO HELL

As Christ died for us, and was buried, so also is it to be believed that he went down into hell.

4. OF THE RESURRECTION OF CHRIST

Christ did truly rise again from death, and took again his body, with flesh, bones, and all things appertaining to the perfection of man's nature, wherewith he ascended into heaven, and there sitteth until he return to judge all men at the last day.

5. OF THE HOLY GHOST

The Holy Ghost, proceeding from the Father and the Son, is of one substance, majesty, and glory with the Father and the Son, very and eternal God.

6. OF THE SUFFICIENCY OF THE
HOLY SCRIPTURES FOR SALVATION

Holy Scripture containeth all things necessary to salvation: so that whatsoever is not read therein, nor may be proved thereby, is not to be required of any man, that it should be believed as an article of the faith, or be thought requisite or necessary to salvation. In the name of the Holy Scripture, we do understand those canonical books of the Old and New Testament of whose authority was never any doubt in the church.

Of the names and number of the canonical books.

Genesis,
Exodus,
Leviticus,
Numbers,
Deuteronomy,
Joshua,
Judges,
Ruth,
The First Book of Samuel,
The Second Book of Samuel,
The First Book of Kings,
The Second Book of Kings,
The First Book of Chronicles,
The Second Book of Chronicles,
The First Book of Esdras,
The Second Book of Esdras,
The Book of Esther,
The Book of Job,
The Psalms,
The Proverbs,
Ecclesiastes or Preacher,
Cantica or Songs of Solomon,
Four Prophets the Greater,
Twelve Prophets the Less.

And the other books (as Jerome saith) the church doth read for example of life and instruction of manners; but yet doth it not apply them to establish any doctrine; such are these following:

> The Third Book of Esdras,
> The Fourth Book of Esdras,
> The Book of Tobias,
> The Book of Judith,
> The rest of the Book of Esther,
> The Book of Wisdom,
> Jesus the Son of Sirach,
> Baruch the Prophet,
> The Song of the Three Children,
> The Story of Susanna,
> Of Bel and the Dragon,
> The Prayer of Manasses,
> The First Book of Maccabees,
> The Second Book of Maccabees.

All the books of the New Testament, as they are commonly received, we do receive, and account them canonical.

7. OF THE OLD TESTAMENT

The Old Testament is not contrary to the New; for both in the Old and New Testament everlasting life is offered to mankind by Christ, who is the only mediator between God and man, being both God and man. Wherefore they are not to be heard which feign that the old fathers did look only for transitory promises. Although the law given from God by Moses, as touching ceremonies and rites, do not bind Christian men, nor the civil precepts thereof, ought of necessity to be received in any commonwealth; yet, notwithstanding, no Christian man whatsoever is free from the obedience of the commandments which are called moral.

8. OF THE THREE CREEDS[1]

The three creeds, Nicene Creed, Athanasius's Creed, and that which is commonly

---

1. The 1801 American revision reads: "VIII. Of the Creeds. The Nicene Creed, and that which is commonly called the Apostles' Creed, ought thoroughly to be received and believed: for they may be proved by most certain warrants of Holy Scripture."

called the Apostles' Creed, ought thoroughly to be received and believed; for they may be proved by most certain warrants of Holy Scripture.

9. OF ORIGINAL OR BIRTH-SIN

Original sin standeth not in the following of Adam (as the Pelagians do vainly talk), but is the fault and corruption of the nature of every man that naturally is engendered of the offspring of Adam; whereby man is very far gone from original righteousness, and is of his own nature inclined to evil, so that the flesh lusteth always contrary to the spirit; and therefore in every person born into this world, it deserveth God's wrath and damnation. And this infection of nature doth remain, yea, in them that are regenerated, whereby the lust of the flesh, called in Greek *phronēma*   [Rom 8.6–7] *sarkos,* which some do expound the wisdom, some sensuality, some the affection, some the desire of the flesh, is not subject to the law of God. And although there is no condemnation for them that believe and are baptized, yet the apostle doth confess that concupiscence and lust hath of itself the nature of sin.

10. OF FREE WILL

The condition of man after the fall of Adam is such, that he cannot turn and prepare himself, by his own natural strength and good works, to faith, and calling upon God: Wherefore we have no power to do good works pleasant and acceptable to God, without the grace of God by Christ preventing us that we may have a good will, and working with us when we have that good will.

11. OF THE JUSTIFICATION OF MAN

We are accounted righteous before God, only for the merit of our Lord and Savior Jesus Christ by faith, and not for our own works or deservings: Wherefore that we are justified by faith only is a most wholesome doctrine, and very full of comfort, as more largely is expressed in the Homily of Justification.

12. OF GOOD WORKS

Albeit that good works, which are the fruits of faith and follow after justification, cannot put away our sins and endure the severity of God's judgment, yet are they pleasing and acceptable to God in Christ, and do spring out necessarily of a true and lively faith, insomuch that by them a lively faith may be as evidently known as a tree discerned by the fruit.

13. OF WORKS BEFORE JUSTIFICATION

Works done before the grace of Christ, and the inspiration of his Spirit, are not pleasant to God, forasmuch as they spring not of faith in Jesus Christ, neither do they make men meet to receive grace, or (as the school authors say) deserve grace of congruity: yea, rather for that they are not done as God hath willed and commanded them to be done, we doubt not but they have the nature of sin.

14. OF WORKS OF SUPEREROGATION

Voluntary works besides, over and above, God's commandments which they call works of supererogation, cannot be taught without arrogancy and impiety. For by them men do declare that they do not only render unto God as much as they are bound to do, but that they do more for his sake than of bounden duty is required: whereas Christ saith plainly, When ye have done all that are commanded to do, say, [Lk 17.10]   We are unprofitable servants.

15. OF CHRIST ALONE WITHOUT SIN

Christ in the truth of our nature was made like unto us in all things, sin only except, from which he was clearly void, both in his flesh and in his spirit. He came to be [Jn 1.29]   the lamb without spot, who by sacrifice of himself once made, should take away [1 Jn 3.5] the sins of the world, and sin, as St. John saith, was not in him. But all we the rest, although baptized and born again in Christ, yet offend in many things; and if we [1 Jn 1.8] say we have no sin, we deceive ourselves, and the truth is not in us.

16. OF SIN AFTER BAPTISM

Not every deadly sin willingly committed after baptism is sin against the Holy Ghost, and unpardonable. Wherefore the grant of repentance is not to be denied to such as fall into sin after baptism. After we have received the Holy Ghost, we may depart from grace given and fall into sin, and by the grace of God we may arise again and amend our lives. And therefore they are to be condemned, which say, they can no more sin as long as they live here, or deny the place of forgiveness to such as truly repent.

17. OF PREDESTINATION AND ELECTION

Predestination to life is the everlasting purpose of God, whereby (before the foundations of the world were laid), he hath constantly decreed by his counsel secret to us, to deliver from curse and damnation those whom he hath chosen in Christ out of mankind, and to bring them by Christ to everlasting salvation as vessels made to honor. Wherefore, they which be endued with so excellent a benefit of God be called according to God's purpose by his Spirit working in due season; they through grace obey the calling; they be justified freely; they be made sons of God by adoption; they be made like the image of his only-begotten Son Jesus Christ; they walk religiously in good works; and at length, by God's mercy, they attain to everlasting felicity. As the godly consideration of predestination and our election in Christ is full of sweet, pleasant, and unspeakable comfort to godly persons and such as feel in themselves the working of the Spirit of Christ, mortifying the works of the flesh and their earthly members and drawing up their mind to high and heavenly things, as well because it doth greatly establish and confirm their faith of eternal salvation to be enjoyed through Christ, as because it doth fervently kindle their love towards God: so for curious and carnal persons, lacking the Spirit of Christ, to have continually before their eyes the sentence of God's predestination is a most dangerous downfall, whereby the devil doth thrust them either into desperation or into recklessness of most unclean living no less perilous than desperation. Furthermore, we must receive God's promises in such wise as they be generally set forth in Holy Scripture; and in our doings that will of God is to be followed which we have expressly declared unto us in the word of God.

18. OF OBTAINING ETERNAL SALVATION ONLY BY THE NAME OF CHRIST

They also are to be had accursed that presume to say that every man shall be saved by the law or sect which he professeth, so that he be diligent to frame his life according to that law and the light of nature. For Holy Scripture doth set out to us only the name of Jesus Christ, whereby men must be saved.   [Acts 4.12]

19. OF THE CHURCH

The visible church of Christ is a congregation of faithful men, in the which the pure word of God is preached and the sacraments be duly ministered according to Christ's ordinance in all those things that of necessity are requisite to the same. As the Church of Jerusalem, Alexandria, and Antioch have erred, so also the Church of Rome hath erred, not only in their living and manner of ceremonies, but also in matters of faith.

20. OF THE AUTHORITY OF THE CHURCH

The church hath power to decree rites or ceremonies and authority in controversies of faith. And yet it is not lawful for the church to ordain any thing that is contrary to God's word written, neither may it so expound one place of Scripture, that it be repugnant to another. Wherefore, although the church be a witness and a keeper of the Holy Writ: yet, as it ought not to decree anything against the same, so besides the same ought it not to enforce anything to be believed for necessity of salvation.

21. OF THE AUTHORITY OF GENERAL COUNCILS[2]

General councils may not be gathered together without the commandment and will of princes. And when they be gathered together (forasmuch as they be an assembly of men, whereof all be not governed with the Spirit and word of God), they may err, and sometimes have erred, even in things pertaining unto God. Wherefore things ordained by them as necessary to salvation have neither strength nor authority, unless it may be declared that they be taken out of Holy Scripture.

22. OF PURGATORY

The Romish doctrine concerning purgatory, pardons, worshiping and adoration, as well of images as of relics, and also invocation of saints, is a fond thing vainly invented, and grounded upon no warranty of Scripture, but rather repugnant to the word of God.

23. OF MINISTERING IN THE CONGREGATION

It is not lawful for any man to take upon him the office of public preaching or ministering the sacraments in the congregation, before he be lawfully called and sent to execute the same. And those we ought to judge lawfully called and sent, which be chosen and called to this work by men who have public authority given unto them in the congregation to call and send ministers into the Lord's vineyard.

24. OF SPEAKING IN THE CONGREGATION IN SUCH A TONGUE AS THE PEOPLE UNDERSTANDETH

It is a thing plainly repugnant to the word of God and the custom of the primitive church, to have public prayer in the church, or to minister the sacraments in a tongue not understanded of the people.

25. OF THE SACRAMENTS

Sacraments ordained of Christ be not only badges or tokens of Christian men's profession, but rather they be certain sure witnesses and effectual signs of grace and God's good will towards us, by the which he doth work invisibly in us, and doth not only quicken, but also strengthen and confirm, our faith in him. There are two sacraments ordained of Christ our Lord in the Gospel, that is to say, baptism and the supper of the Lord. Those five commonly called sacraments, that is to say, confirmation, penance, orders, matrimony, and extreme unction, are not to be counted

---

2. Article 21 is omitted in the 1801 American revision "because it is partly of a local and civil nature, and is provided for, as to the remaining parts of it, in other articles."

for sacraments of the Gospel, being such as have grown partly of the corrupt following of the apostles, partly are states of life allowed in the Scriptures; but yet have not the like nature of sacraments with baptism and the Lord's supper, for that they have not any visible sign or ceremony ordained of God. The sacraments were not ordained of Christ to be gazed upon or to be carried about, but that we should duly use them. And in such only as worthily receive the same, have they a wholesome effect or operation: but they that receive them unworthily, purchase to themselves damnation, as St. Paul saith. [1 Cor 11.26–29]

26. OF THE UNWORTHINESS OF THE MINISTERS, WHICH HINDERS NOT THE EFFECT OF THE SACRAMENTS

Although in the visible church the evil be ever mingled with the good, and sometime the evil have chief authority in the ministration of the word and sacraments; yet forasmuch as they do not the same in their own name, but in Christ's, and do minister by his commission and authority, we may use their ministry both in hearing the word of God and in the receiving of the sacraments. Neither is the effect of Christ's ordinance taken away by their wickedness, nor the grace of God's gifts diminished from such as by faith and rightly do receive the sacraments ministered unto them, which be effectual because of Christ's institution and promise, although they be ministered by evil men. Nevertheless it appertaineth to the discipline of the church that inquiry be made of evil ministers, and that they be accused by those that have knowledge of their offences; and finally, being found guilty by just judgment, be deposed.

27. OF BAPTISM

Baptism is not only a sign of profession and mark of difference whereby Christian men are discerned from other that be not christened, but is also a sign of regeneration or new birth, whereby, as by an instrument, they that receive baptism rightly are grafted into the church; the promises of forgiveness of sin, and of our adoption to be the sons of God, by the Holy Ghost are visibly signed and sealed; faith is confirmed, and grace increased by virtue of prayer unto God. The baptism of young children is in any wise to be retained in the church as most agreeable with the institution of Christ.

28. OF THE LORD'S SUPPER

The supper of the Lord is not only a sign of the love that Christians ought to have among themselves, one to another, but rather it is a sacrament of our redemption by Christ's death: insomuch that to such as rightly, worthily, and with faith receive the

same, the bread which we break is a partaking of the body of Christ, and likewise
[1 Cor 10.36] the cup of blessing is a partaking of the blood of Christ. Transubstantiation (or the
change of the substance of bread and wine) in the supper of the Lord, cannot be
proved by Holy Writ, but is repugnant to the plain words of Scripture, overthroweth
the nature of a sacrament, and hath given occasion to many superstitions. The body
of Christ is given, taken, and eaten in the supper, only after an heavenly and spiritual manner. And the mean whereby the body of Christ is received and eaten in the
supper is faith. The sacrament of the Lord's supper was not by Christ's ordinance
reserved, carried about, lifted up, or worshiped.

29. OF THE WICKED WHICH DO NOT EAT THE BODY OF CHRIST, IN THE USE OF THE LORD'S SUPPER

The wicked and such as be void of a lively faith, although they do carnally and visibly
press with their teeth (as St. Augustine saith) the sacrament of the body and blood of
Christ, yet in no wise are they partakers of Christ, but rather, to their condemnation,
do eat and drink the signs or sacrament of so great a thing.

30. OF BOTH KINDS

The cup of the Lord is not to be denied to the lay people; for both parts of the Lord's
sacrament, by Christ's ordinance and commandment, ought to be ministered to all
Christian men alike.

31. OF THE ONE OBLATION OF CHRIST FINISHED UPON THE CROSS

The offering of Christ once made is the perfect redemption, propitiation, and satisfaction for all the sins of the whole world, both original and actual, and there is
none other satisfaction for sin but that alone. Wherefore the sacrifices of masses,
in which it was commonly said that the priest did offer Christ for the quick and
the dead to have remission of pain or guilt, were blasphemous fables and dangerous
deceits.

32. OF THE MARRIAGE OF PRIESTS

Bishops, priests, and deacons are not commanded by God's law either to vow the
estate of single life or to abstain from marriage. Therefore it is lawful also for them,
as for all other Christian men, to marry at their own discretion, as they shall judge
the same to serve better to godliness.

33. OF EXCOMMUNICATE PERSONS, HOW THEY ARE TO BE AVOIDED

That person which by open denunciation of the church is rightly cut off from the unity of the church and excommunicated, ought to be taken of the whole multitude of the faithful as an heathen and publican, until he be openly reconciled by penance [Mt 18.17] and received into the church by a judge that hath authority thereto.

34. OF THE TRADITIONS OF THE CHURCH

It is not necessary that traditions and ceremonies be in all places one and utterly alike; for at all times they have been diverse, and may be changed according to the diversities of countries, times, and men's manners, so that nothing be ordained against God's word. Whosoever through his private judgment willingly and purposely doth openly break the traditions and ceremonies of the church which be not repugnant to the word of God, and be ordained and approved by common authority, ought to be rebuked openly that others may fear to do the like, as he that offendeth against common order of the church, and hurteth the authority of the magistrate, and woundeth the conscience of the weak brethren. Every particular or national church hath authority to ordain, change, and abolish ceremonies or rites of the church ordained only by man's authority, so that all things be done to edifying.

35. OF HOMILIES

The second Book of Homilies, the several titles whereof we have joined under this article, doth contain a godly and wholesome doctrine and necessary for these times, as doth the former Book of Homilies which were set forth in the time of Edward the Sixth: and therefore we judge them to be read in churches by the ministers diligently and distinctly, that they may be understanded of the people.

Of the Names of the Homilies.

1. Of the right use of the church.
2. Against peril of idolatry.
3. Of the repairing and keeping clean of churches.
4. Of good works: first of fasting.
5. Against gluttony and drunkenness.
6. Against excess of apparel.
7. Of prayer.
8. Of the place and time of prayer.
9. That common prayers and sacraments ought to be ministered in a known to tongue.

10. Of the reverend estimation of God's word.

11. Of alms-doing.

12. Of the nativity of Christ.

13. Of the passion of Christ.

14. Of the resurrection of Christ.

15. Of the worthy receiving of the sacrament of the body and blood
    of Christ.

16. Of the gifts of the Holy Ghost.

17. For the rogation-days.

18. Of the state of matrimony.

19. Of repentance.

20. Against idleness.

21. Against rebellion.

36. OF CONSECRATION OF BISHOPS AND MINISTERS[3]

The Book of Consecration of Archbishops and Bishops and Ordering of Priests and Deacons, lately set forth in the time of Edward the Sixth and confirmed at the same time by authority of Parliament, doth contain all things necessary to such consecration and ordering; neither hath it anything that of itself is superstitious or ungodly. And therefore whosoever are consecrated or ordered according to the rites of that book, since the second year of King Edward unto this time, or hereafter shall be consecrated or ordered according to the same rites, we decree all such to be rightly, orderly, and lawfully consecrated or ordered.

37. OF THE CIVIL MAGISTRATES[4]

The King's ["Queen's" in 1571 text] Majesty hath the chief power in this realm of England and other his dominions, unto whom the chief government of all estates

3. In the 1801 American revision, this article reads: "The Book of Consecration of Bishops, and Ordering of Priests and Deacons, as set forth by the General Convention of this Church in 1792, doth contain all things necessary to such consecration and ordering; neither hath it any thing that, of itself, is superstitious and ungodly. And, therefore, whosoever are consecrated or ordered according to said form, we decree all such to be rightly, orderly, and lawfully consecrated and ordered." Concerning the Homilies it specified: "All references to the constitution and laws of England are considered as inapplicable to the circumstances of this church."

4. In the 1801 American revision, this article reads: "The power of the civil magistrate extendeth to all men, as well clergy as laity, in all things temporal; but hath no authority in things

of this realm, whether they be ecclesiastical or civil, in all causes doth appertain, and is not nor ought to be subject to any foreign jurisdiction. Where we attribute to the King's Majesty the chief government, by which titles we understand the minds of some slanderous folks to be offended, we give not to our princes the ministering either of God's word or of sacraments, the which thing the injunctions also lately set forth by Elizabeth our Queen do most plainly testify: but only that prerogative which we see to have been given always to all godly princes in Holy Scriptures by God himself, that is, that they should rule all estates and degrees committed to their charge by God, whether they be temporal, and restrain with the civil sword the stubborn and evil-doers. The bishop of Rome hath no jurisdiction in this realm of England.

The laws of the realm may punish Christian men with death for heinous and grievous offenses.

It is lawful for Christian men at the commandment of the magistrate to wear weapons and serve in the wars.

38. OF CHRISTIAN MEN'S GOODS, WHICH ARE NOT COMMON

The riches and goods of Christians are not common, as touching the right, title, and possession of the same, as certain Anabaptists do falsely boast; notwithstanding every man ought, of such things as he possesseth, liberally to give alms to the poor, according to his ability.

39. OF A CHRISTIAN MAN'S OATH

As we confess that vain and rash swearing is forbidden Christian men by our Lord Jesus Christ, and James his apostle, so we judge that Christian religion doth not [Jas 5.12] prohibit but that a man may swear when the magistrate requireth in a cause of faith and charity, so it be done according to the prophet's teaching in justice, judgment, [Jer 4.2] and truth.

The Ratification[5]

This Book of Articles before rehearsed, is again approved, and allowed to be holden and executed within the realm, by the assent and consent of our Sovereign Lady

purely spiritual. And we hold it to be the duty of all men who are professors of the gospel, to pay respectful obedience to the civil authority, regularly and legitimately constituted."
5. Omitted in 1801 American revision.

ELIZABETH, by the grace of God, of England, France, and Ireland, Queen, Defender of the Faith, &c. Which articles were deliberately read, and confirmed again by the subscription of the hands of the archbishop and bishops of the upper-house, and by the subscription of the whole clergy of the nether-house in their convocation, in the year of our Lord 1571.

The King's Confession, 1581

When French influences threatened to revive Roman Catholicism in Scotland in the early 1580s, the Scottish Church responded with "A Short and General Confession of the True Christian Faith and Religion according to God's Word and Acts of our Parliaments" composed by John Craig (c. 1512–1600) in 1581. Because King James VI himself signed it, it is generally called *The King's Confession*. It is primarily a statement upholding belief in *The Scots Confession,* and all clergy were required to subscribe to it. The work is also known as *The Second Scots* or *The Negative Confession,* the latter designation referring to its rejection of any doctrine not outlined in → *The Scots Confession* and, perhaps, to the tone of its polemic catalog of what they "abhor and detest [in] all contrary religion and doctrine," which makes up more than half of the brief statement.

Edition (Latin and Scots-English): Henderson 1937, 102–11.

Translation: Prepared for this edition.

Literature: Cowan 1982, 89–130; Donaldson 1960, 29–75; Hazlett 1987; Henderson 1960; Knox 1949, 1:338–42; Niesel, 79–83; *OER* 4:33–36 (Kirk).

Each and every one of us undersigned protest that after long and due examination of our own consciences in matters of true and false religion, we are now thoroughly resolved in the truth by the word and spirit of God. And we believe, therefore, with our hearts, confess with our mouths, subscribe with our hands, and constantly affirm before God and the whole world, that this is the only true Christian faith and religion—pleasing God and bringing salvation to man—which is now, by the mercy of God, revealed to the world by the preaching of the blessed gospel. [This religion] which is received, believed, and defended by many and sundry notable churches and realms, but chiefly by the Kirk of Scotland, the king's majesty, and three estates of this realm, as God's eternal truth and as the only ground of our salvation. And as is expressed more particularly in the Confession of our Faith [→ *The Scots Confession,* 1560], established and publicly confirmed by sundry acts of parliament, and now, for a long time, openly professed by the king's majesty and the whole body of this kingdom, both in city and countryside. We willingly agree with this confession and form of religion in our consciences in all points, as unto God's undoubted truth and verity, grounded only upon his written word.

And therefore we abhor and detest all contrary religion and doctrine, but chiefly all kinds of papistry in general and particular even as they are now damned and confuted by the word of God and the Kirk of Scotland. But we especially detest and refuse: the usurped authority of that Roman Antichrist upon the Scriptures of God, upon the kirk, the civil magistrate, and consciences of men; all his tyrannous laws made upon adiaphora against our Christian liberty; his erroneous doctrine against the sufficiency of the written word, the perfection of the law, the office of Christ, and his blessed gospel; his corrupted doctrine concerning original sin, our natural inability and rebellion against God's law; and the nature, number, and use of the holy sacraments. [We also detest] his five illegitimate sacraments, with all his rites, ceremonies, and false doctrine added to the ministration of the true sacraments without the word of God. Also his cruel judgment against infants departing without the sacrament; his absolute necessity of baptism; his blasphemous opinion of transubstantiation or real presence of Christ's body in the elements, and receiving of the same by the wicked, or bodies of men; his dispensations with solemn oaths, perjuries, and degrees of marriage forbidden by the word; his cruelty against the innocent divorced; his devilish mass; his blasphemous priesthood; his profane sacrifice for the sins of the dead and the living; his canonization of men, calling upon

angels or saints departed; worshiping of imagery, reliquaries, and crosses; dedicat-
ing of churches, altars, and days; and his public pronouncing of vows. [We detest]
his purgatory; prayers for the dead; praying or speaking in a strange language; his
processions and blasphemous litany; his multitude of advocates or mediators with
his manifold orders; and auricular confessions. [We detest] his dispersed and uncertain repentance; his general and unfixed faith; his penances for men's sins; his
justification by works, *opus operatum,* works of supererogation, merits, pardons,
peregrinations, and stations; his holy water; baptizing of bells; conjuring of spirits;
crossing; signing; anointing; conjuring; and his hallowing of God's good creatures,
with the superstitious opinion joined therewith. [We detest] his worldly monarchy
and wicked hierarchy; his three solemn vows, with all his shavings of various orders;
and his erroneous and bloody decrees made at Trent, with all the subscribers and
approvers of that cruel and bloody band conjured against the church of God. And
finally, we detest all his vain allegories, rites, signs, and traditions brought into the
church without or against the word of God and against the doctrine of his true
reformed church, to which we join ourselves willingly in doctrine, faith, religion,
discipline, and the use of holy sacraments as lively members of the same, with Christ
as our Head. Promising and swearing by the great name of the Lord our God that
we shall persevere in obedience of the doctrine and discipline of this church and   [Jer 44.26]
shall defend the same, according to our vocation and power, all the days of our lives
under the pains contained in the law, and danger both to body and soul in the day
of God's fearful judgment.

  And seeing that many are roused by Satan and that Roman Antichrist to
promise, swear, subscribe, and sometimes use the holy sacraments in the church
deceitfully, against their own conscience, thus attempting, first under the external
cloak of religion, to corrupt and subvert secretly God's true religion within the
church, and afterward, when time may serve, to become open enemies and persecutors of the same, under the vain hope of the pope's dispensation, devised against the
word of God, to his greater confusion, and their double condemnation in the day of
the Lord Jesus, we, therefore, willingly to take away all suspicion of hypocrisy, and
of such double dealing with God and his church, protest and call the searcher of all   [Rom 8.27]
hearts for witness, that our mind and hearts do fully agree with this our confession,
promise, oath, and subscription. We are not moved with only worldly respect, but
are persuaded in our conscience alone, through the knowledge and love of God's
true religion printed in our hearts by the Holy Spirit, as we shall answer to him in
the day when the secrets of hearts shall be disclosed.

  And because we perceive that the quietness and stability of our religion and
church depends upon the safety and good behavior of the king's majesty, as upon

any comfortable instrument of God's mercy granted to this country for the maintaining of his church and ministration of justice among us, we protest and promise solemnly with our hearts, under the same signed oath, that we shall defend his person and authority with our weapons, bodies, and lives, in defense of Christ's gospel, liberty of our country, the administering of justice, and punishment of iniquity, against all enemies within this realm or without, since we desire our God to be a strong and merciful defender for us in the day of our death, and at the coming of our Lord Jesus Christ, to whom, with the Father and the Holy Spirit, be all honor and glory eternally. Amen.

The Lambeth Articles, 1595

Philip Schaff called *The Lambeth Articles* "a Calvinistic appendix to *The Thirty-Nine Articles*,"[1] and this was certainly the intent, although the articles never gained that level of authority. They were written in response to disputes on the nature of predestination at Cambridge University. In a sermon preached at Great St. Mary's in April 1595, William Barrett of Caius College, Cambridge, had publicly denied the indefectibility of grace and questioned the concept of double predestination. William Whitaker (1547/48–95), Regius Professor of Divinity, sought to suppress such anti-Calvinist (or Arminian) ideas, bringing the matter before the archbishop of Canterbury, John Whitgift (c. 1532–1604). Whitgift had written *The Eleven Articles* of 1583 and was theologically a Calvinist, though opposed to extreme Puritanism. The debating parties met at Lambeth Palace in November 1595, and Barrett was made to recant his positions. Soon thereafter, Whitaker submitted nine propositions to the archbishop for approval; these were modified somewhat and accepted by Whitgift as well as the archbishop of York and other bishops gathered at Lambeth. The articles maintained a strict and anti-Armininian view of predestination, declaring that God had predestined some for salvation and others for damnation, that the number of the elect was predetermined, and that irresistible grace and assurance are granted to the elect, who are saved not because of their individual merits but by the will of God alone.

Although the articles were approved at Lambeth, they were never authorized by Queen Elizabeth.[2] They had little lasting influence on the interpretation of *The Thirty-Nine Articles* in England but found a home in the Church of Ireland, where they provided the basis for → *The Irish Articles* of 1615 and enjoyed confessional status until 1634.

Edition: Schaff, 3:523–25.

Translation: Porter 1958, 371.

Literature: Bray, 399; Dawley 1954; Gilliam and Tighe 1992; Hardwick 1876, 159–77; Lake 1982, 201–42, and 1987; Lamont 1985; Miller 1994; Porter 1958, 364–75; Tyacke 1986, 23–25, 29–36.

1. Schaff, 3:523.
2. See Gilliam and Tighe 1992 for an attempt to explain the political undertones of the struggle between the archbishop and the queen over the articles.

1. God from eternity has predestined some men to life, and reprobated some to death.

2. The moving or efficient cause of predestination to life is not the fore-seeing of faith, or of perseverance, or of good works, or of anything innate in the person of the predestined, but only the will of the good pleasure of God.

3. There is a determined and certain number of predestined, which cannot be increased or diminished.

4. Those not predestined to salvation are inevitably condemned on account of their sins.

5. A true, lively, and justifying faith, and the sanctifying Spirit of God, is not lost nor does it pass away either totally or finally in the elect.

6. The truly faithful man—that is, one endowed with justifying faith—is sure by full assurance of faith of the remission of sins and his eternal salvation through Christ.

7. Saving grace is not granted, is not made common, is not ceded to all men, by which they might be saved, if they wish.

8. No one can come to Christ unless it be granted to him, and unless the Father draws him: and all men are not drawn by the Father to come to the Son.

9. It is not in the will or the power of each and every man to be saved.

The Remonstrance, or The Arminian Articles, 1610

As Calvinism developed in the late sixteenth and early seventeenth centuries, a kind of Protestant scholasticism arose in which the doctrinal boundaries of orthodoxy were defined more strictly within detailed and intricate theological systems. The Dutch theologian Jacob Arminius (1560–1609), although equally complex in his approach to systematics, advocated a shift away from Calvinist determinism. He rejected both supra- and sublapsarian approaches to predestination as unbiblical and proposed a view that incorporated free will and redefined the concept of the elect.

The year after Arminius died, his friend Johannes Uitenbogaert (1557–1644) and more than forty other ministers of the Dutch Reformed Church presented *The Remonstrance* (also known as *The Arminian Articles*) to the government of Holland, claiming that Calvinist teaching, as it was being practiced, was in error. They asked for a national synod to revise → *The Belgic Confession* and → *The Heidelberg Catechism*. They challenged Dutch Calvinism on five major issues: (1) instead of the total inability to effect one's spiritual fate, they allowed for some degree of free will or human ability to enable a sinner to repent; (2) instead of unconditional election, they took the view that before all time, God chose those whom he knew would, of their own free will, choose Christ; (3) instead of limited atonement, they argued for universal atonement, believing that Christ died for all, although only those who have faith will be saved; (4) instead of irresistible (or efficacious) grace, they allowed the possibility of resisting the Holy Spirit since free will limits the nonbeliever's ability to accept grace; and (5) instead of the perseverance of saints, they maintained that it is possible to lose salvation and fall from grace if faith is not strong enough.

The Remonstrance was presented to the states of Holland in July 1610 and achieved some measure of success. The government determined "that preachers of the opinions expressed in this *Remonstrance* being in the actual ministry should be free from the censure of other preachers" and that in the examination of new ministers, these views would be tolerated.[1] But Calvinists and Arminians (or Remonstrants, as they preferred to be called) did not coexist peacefully for long. The next eight years were marked by pamphlet wars, failed negotiations, and the growing power of the Calvinist party. In the end, the Remonstrants were condemned at the Synod of Dort in 1618–19. Two hundred Remonstrant ministers lost their positions,

---

1. Harrison 1937, 50.

and many went into exile to Schleswig-Holstein, where a small Remonstrant congregation still exists. One of their leaders, Hugo Grotius (1583–1645), best known for his contributions to jurisprudence, was condemned to life imprisonment but escaped to Paris hidden in a shipment of books. In the 1630s many Arminians returned to the Netherlands and settled in Antwerp, where they were tolerated and where the Remonstrant Brotherhood remains active.

The influence of Arminianism was most pronounced in England, where anti-Calvinist thought, especially after the Synod of Dort in the early reign of Charles I, identified with the tenets of the Remonstrants. Later, John Wesley (1703–91) incorporated some of these views into his theology. In fact, the Methodist movement itself soon split into Arminian and Calvinist camps, with John Wesley representing the Arminian Methodists and George Whitefield (1714–70), together with his patron Selina Hastings, the countess of Huntingdon ([†] 1791), representing Calvinist Methodism.

Edition: Hoenderdaal 1970–71 (Dutch), 74–75.

Translation: Bettenson and Munder 1999, 282–84 (based on Schaff). We have modified the translation to reflect the Hoenderdaal edition.

Note: The full text, included in Hoenderdaal 1970–71, 4–79, includes a preface, five negative articles, the Remonstrant articles, and a conclusion. We provide the five articles defining the beliefs of the Remonstrants.

Literature: Bangs 1985, 332–55; Boettner 1983; Brandt 1908, 220–22; Harrison 1926, 131–64, and 1937, 9–71; Hoenderdaal 1975; McCulloh 1962; Muller 1991, 31–51; *OER* 3:416–17 (Bangs), 4:301–2 (Hoenderdaal); Pinnock 1989; Smith 1997; *TRE* 4:63–69 (Hoenderdaal); Tideman 1851, 8–27; Tyacke 1986, 87–105.

The Remonstrance, or The Arminian Articles, 1610

1. That God, by an eternal and unchangeable purpose in Jesus Christ his Son, before the foundations of the world were laid, determined to save, out of the human race which had fallen into sin, in Christ, for Christ's sake, and through Christ, those who through the grace of the Holy Spirit shall believe on the same his Son and shall through the same grace persevere in this same faith and obedience of faith even to the end; and on the other hand to leave under sin and wrath the contumacious and unbelieving and to condemn them as aliens from Christ, according to the word of the Gospel in John 3.36: "He who believes in the Son has eternal life; he who does not obey the Son shall not see life, but the wrath of God rests upon him," and other passages of Scripture. Jn 3.36

2. That, accordingly, Jesus Christ, the Savior of the world, died for all and for every individual, so that he has obtained for all, by his death on the cross, reconciliation and remission of sins; yet so that no one is partaker of this remission except the believers, according to the word of the Gospel of John 3.16: "For God so loved the world that he gave his only Son that whoever believes in him should not perish, but have eternal life." And in the first letter of John, chapter 2, verse 2: "He is the expiation of our sins, and not for ours only but also for the sins of the whole world." Jn 3.16 / 1 Jn 2.2

3. That the human has not saving grace of himself, nor of the working of his own free will, inasmuch as in his state of apostasy and sin he can for himself and by himself think nothing that is good—nothing, that is, truly good, such as saving faith is, above all else. But that it is necessary that by God, in Christ, and through his Holy Spirit he be born again and renewed in understanding, affections and will, and in all his faculties, that he may be able to understand, think, will, and perform what is truly good, according to the word of Christ, John 15.5: "Apart from me you can do nothing." Jn 15.5

4. That this grace of God is the beginning, the progress, and the end of all good; so that even the regenerate human can neither think, will, nor effect any good, nor withstand any temptation to evil, without grace precedent (or prevenient), awakening, following, and cooperating. So that all good deeds and all movements towards good that can be conceived in thought must be ascribed to the grace of God in Christ. But with respect to the mode of operation, grace is not irresistible; for it is written of many "that they resisted the Holy Spirit," Acts 7 and elsewhere in many places. Acts 7[.51]

5. That those who are grafted into Christ by a true faith, and have thereby been made partakers of his life-giving Spirit, are abundantly endowed with power to strive against Satan, sin, the world, and their own flesh, and to win the victory; always, be it understood, with the help of the grace of the Holy Spirit, with Jesus Christ assisting them in all temptations, through his Spirit; stretching out his hand to them and (providing only that they are themselves prepared for the fight, that they entreat his aid and do not fail to help themselves) propping and upbuilding them so that by no guile or violence of Satan can they be led astray or plucked from Christ's hands, according to the word of Christ, John 10: "No one shall snatch them out of my hand." But for the question whether they are not able through sloth or negligence to forsake the beginning of their life in Christ, to embrace again this present world, to depart from the holy doctrine once delivered to them, to lose their good conscience, and to neglect grace—this must be the subject of more exact inquiry in the Holy Scriptures, before we can teach it with full confidence of our mind.

Jn 10[.28]

These articles thus set out and delivered the Remonstrants deem agreeable to the word of God, suitable for edification, and, on this subject, sufficient for salvation. So that it is not needful, and tends not to edification, to rise higher or to descend lower.

The Irish Articles, 1615

The Church of Ireland can trace its roots to 1536, when the Irish Parliament accepted Henry VIII as the supreme head of the church in Ireland. But the Reformation came to Ireland much later in the sixteenth century as immigration from England and Scotland increased. A stronghold of Protestantism and center for reformed theology took hold at Trinity College in Dublin in the early 1590s. *The Irish Articles* may have been written by the head of the theological faculty at Trinity, James Ussher (1581–1656), later archbishop of Armagh (1625) and famous for his chronological studies of the Bible.[1]

The author drew upon → *The Lambeth Articles* and → *The Thirty-Nine Articles* in an expansive doctrinal statement of 104 articles. The theology is Calvinist, as it developed in the scholastic period of the late sixteenth and early seventeenth centuries, with belief in absolute predestination, limited atonement, and the perseverance of the elect. They are strongly anti-Catholic, as one might expect in this time and place. *The Irish Articles* were presented to the first Convocation of Irish Reformed clergy at Dublin in 1615 and adopted as the confessional standard. It is not clear whether all Irish churchmen were expected to acknowledge their conformity with the articles, but it is known that Ussher required all ministers under his jurisdiction to subscribe to them. Their influence in Ireland was brief: *The Thirty-Nine Articles* replaced them in 1635. Yet their significance outlasted their tenure, for they were later incorporated, sometimes verbatim, into → *The Westminster Confession of Faith*.

Edition: Schaff, 3:526–44 (modernized orthography). See Hardwick 1876, 371–88, for original orthography.

Literature: Capern 1991; Ford 1996 and 1997, 156–64; Gaffney 1989; Hardwick 1876, 178–87; Knox 1967, 16–26, 49–52; Schaff, 1:662–65.

1. See Ford 1997, 157–59, for a recent refutation of Ussher's authorship.

Articles of Religion, Agreed upon by the Archbishops and Bishops, and the rest of the clergy of Ireland, in the convocation holden at Dublin in the year of our Lord God 1615, for the avoiding of diversities of opinions, and the establishing of consent touching true religion.

OF THE HOLY SCRIPTURE AND THE THREE CREEDS

1. The ground of our religion and the rule of faith and all saving truth is the word of God, contained in the Holy Scripture.

2. By the name of Holy Scripture we understand all the canonical books of the Old and New Testament, namely:

Of the Old Testament.
The Five Books of Moses.
Joshua.
Judges.
Ruth.
The First and Second of Samuel.
The First and Second of Kings.
The First and Second of Chronicles.
Ezra.
Nehemiah.
Esther.
Job.
Psalms.
Proverbs.
Ecclesiastes.
The Song of Solomon.
Isaiah.
Jeremiah, his Prophecy and Lamentation.
Ezekiel.
Daniel.
The Twelve lesser Prophets.

Of the New Testament.
The Gospels according to
Matthew,
Mark,
Luke,
John,
The Acts of the Apostles.
The Epistle of St. Paul to the Romans.
2 Corinthians.
Galatians.
Ephesians.
Philippians.
Colossians.
2 Thessalonians.
2 Timothy.
Titus.
Philemon.
Hebrews.
The Epistle of St. James.
St. Peter 2.
St. John 3.
St. Jude.
The Revelation of St. John.

All which we acknowledge to be given by the inspiration of God, and in that regard to be of most certain credit and highest authority.

3. The other books, commonly called *Apocryphal*, did not proceed from such inspiration, and therefore are not of sufficient authority to establish any point of doctrine; but the church doth read them as books containing many worthy things for example of life and instruction of manners.

Such are these following:
The Third Book of Esdras.
The Fourth Book of Esdras.
The Book of Tobias.
The Book of Judith.
Additions to the Book of Esther.
The Book of Wisdom.
The Book of Jesus, the Son of Sirach, called Ecclesiasticus.

Baruch, with the Epistle of Jeremiah.

The Song of the Three Children.

Susanna.

Bel and the Dragon.

The Prayer of Manasses.

The First Book of Maccabaeus.

The Second Book of Maccabaeus.

4. The Scriptures ought to be translated out of the original tongues into all languages for the common use of all men: neither is any person to be discouraged from reading the Bible in such a language as he doth understand, but seriously exhorted to read the same with great humility and reverence, as a special means to bring him to the true knowledge of God and of his own duty.

5. Although there be some hard things in the Scripture (especially such as have proper relation to the times in which they were first uttered, and prophecies of things which were afterwards to be fulfilled), yet all things necessary to be known unto everlasting salvation are clearly delivered therein; and nothing of that kind is spoken under dark mysteries in one place which is not in other places spoken more familiarly and plainly, to the capacity both of learned and unlearned.

6. The Holy Scriptures contain all things necessary to salvation, and are able to instruct sufficiently in all points of faith that we are bound to believe, and all good duties that we are bound to practice.

7. All and every the articles contained in the *Nicene Creed,* the *Creed of Athanasius,* and that which is commonly called the *Apostles' Creed,* ought firmly to be received and believed, for they may be proved by most certain warrant of Holy Scripture.

OF FAITH IN THE HOLY TRINITY

8. There is but one living and true God, everlasting, without body, parts, or passions; of infinite power, wisdom, and goodness; the Maker and Preserver of all things, both visible and invisible. And in unity of this Godhead, there be three persons of one and the same substance, power, and eternity: the Father, the Son, and the Holy Ghost.

9. The essence of the Father doth not beget the essence of the Son; but the person of the Father begetteth the person of the Son, by communicating his whole essence to the person begotten from eternity.

10. The Holy Ghost, proceeding from the Father and the Son, is of one substance, majesty, and glory with the Father and the Son, very and eternal God.

OF GOD'S ETERNAL DECREE AND PREDESTINATION

11. God from all eternity did, by his unchangeable counsel, ordain whatsoever in time should come to pass; yet so, as thereby no violence is offered to the wills of the reasonable creatures, and neither the liberty nor the contingency of the second causes is taken away, but established rather.

12. By the same eternal counsel God hath predestinated some unto life, and reprobated some unto death: of both which there is a certain number, known only to God, which can neither be increased nor diminished.[1]

13. Predestination to life is the everlasting purpose of God whereby, before the foundations of the world were laid, he hath constantly decreed in his sacred counsel to deliver from curse and damnation those whom he hath chosen in Christ out of mankind, and to bring them by Christ unto everlasting salvation, as vessels made to honor.

14. The cause moving God to predestinate unto life is not the foreseeing of faith, or perseverance, or good works, or of any thing which is in the person predestinated, but only the good pleasure of God himself.[2] For all things being ordained for the manifestation of his glory, and his glory being to appear both in the works of his mercy and of his justice, it seemed good to his heavenly wisdom to choose out a certain number towards whom he would extend his undeserved mercy, leaving the rest to be spectacles of his justice.

15. Such as are predestinated unto life be called according unto God's purpose (his Spirit working in due season), and through grace they obey the calling, they be justified freely; they be made sons of God by adoption; they be made like the image of his only-begotten Son Jesus Christ; they walk religiously in good works; and at length, by God's mercy, they attain to everlasting felicity. But such as are not predestinated to salvation shall finally be condemned for their sins.[3]

16. The godlike consideration of predestination and our election in Christ is full of sweet, pleasant, and unspeakable comfort to godly persons, and such as feel in themselves the working of the Spirit of Christ, mortifying the works of the flesh and their earthly members, and drawing up their minds to high and heavenly things: as well because it doth greatly confirm and establish their faith of eternal salvation, to be enjoyed through Christ, as because it doth fervently kindle their love towards God; and, on the contrary side, for curious and carnal persons lack-

---

1. *Lamb Art 1.3.*
2. *Lamb Art 2.*
3. *Lamb Art 4.*

ing the Spirit of Christ to have continually before their eyes the sentence of God's predestination is very dangerous.

17. We must receive God's promises in such wise as they be generally set forth unto us in Holy Scripture; and in our doings that will of God is to be followed which we have expressly declared unto us in the word of God.

OF THE CREATION AND GOVERNMENT OF ALL THINGS

18. In the beginning of time, when no creature had any being, God, by his word alone, in the space of six days, created all things, and afterwards, by his providence, doth continue, propagate, and order them according to his own will.

19. The principal creatures are angels and men.

20. Of angels, some continued in that holy state wherein they were created, and are by God's grace forever established therein; others fell from the same, and are reserved in chains of darkness unto the judgment of the great day.

[Gn 1.27] 21. Man being at the beginning created according to the image of God (which consisted especially in the wisdom of his mind and the true holiness of his free will), had the covenant of the law ingrafted in his heart, whereby God did promise unto him everlasting life upon condition that he performed entire and perfect obedience unto his commandments, according to that measure of strength wherewith he was endued in his creation, and threatened death unto him if he did not perform the same.

OF THE FALL OF MAN, ORIGINAL SIN, AND
THE STATE OF MAN BEFORE JUSTIFICATION

[Rom 5.12] 22. By one man sin entered into the world, and death by sin; and so death went over all men, forasmuch as all have sinned.

23. Original sin standeth not in the imitation of Adam (as the Pelagians dream), but is the fault and corruption of the nature of every person that naturally is engendered and propagated from Adam: where by it cometh to pass that man is deprived of original righteousness, and by nature is bent unto sin. And therefore, in every person born into the world, it deserveth God's wrath and damnation.

24. This corruption of nature doth remain even in those that are regenerated, whereby the flesh always lusteth against the spirit, and can not be made subject to the law of God. And howsoever, for Christ's sake, there be no condemnation to such as are regenerate and do believe, yet doth the apostle acknowledge that in itself
[Rom 7.8] this concupiscence hath the nature of sin.

25. The condition of man after the fall of Adam is such that he can not turn and prepare himself, by his own natural strength and good works, to faith, and

calling upon God. Wherefore, we have no power to do good works, pleasing and acceptable unto God, without the grace of God preventing us, that we may have a good will, and working with us when we have that good will.

26. Works done before the grace of Christ and the inspiration of his Spirit are not pleasing unto God, forasmuch as they spring not of faith in Jesus Christ, neither do they make men meet to receive grace, or (as the school authors say) deserve grace of congruity: yea, rather, for that they are not done in such sort as God hath willed and commanded them to be done, we doubt not but they are sinful.

27. All sins are not equal, but some far more heinous than others; yet the very least is of its own nature mortal, and, without God's mercy, maketh the offender liable unto everlasting damnation.

28. God is not the author of sin: howbeit, he doth not only permit, but also by his providence govern and order the same, guiding it in such sort by his infinite wisdom as it turneth to the manifestation of his own glory and to the good of his elect.

OF CHRIST, THE MEDIATOR OF THE SECOND COVENANT

29. The Son, which is the Word of the Father, begotten from everlasting of the Father, the true and eternal God—of one substance with the Father—took man's nature in the womb of the Blessed Virgin, of her substance, so that two whole and perfect natures—that is to say, the Godhead and manhood—were inseparably joined in one person, making one Christ very God and very man.

30. Christ, in the truth of our nature, was made like unto us in all things— sin only excepted—from which he was clearly void, both in his life and in his nature. He came as a lamb without spot to take away the sins of the world, by the sacrifice [Jn 1.29] of himself once made, and sin (as *St. John* saith) was not in him. He fulfilled the [1 Jn 3.5] law for us perfectly: For our sakes he endured most grievous torments immediately in his soul, and most painful sufferings in his body. He was crucified, and died to reconcile his Father unto us, and to be a sacrifice not only for original guilt, but also for all our actual transgressions. He was buried, and descended into hell, and the third day rose from the dead, and took again his body, with flesh, bones, and all things appertaining to the perfection of man's nature: wherewith he ascended into heaven, and there sitteth at the right hand of his Father, until he return to judge all men at the last day.

OF THE COMMUNICATING OF THE GRACE OF CHRIST

31. They are to be condemned that presume to say that every man shall be saved by the law or sect which he professeth, so that he be diligent to frame his life according

to that law and the light of nature. For Holy Scripture doth set out unto us only the
[Acts 4.12] name of Jesus Christ whereby men must be saved.

32. None can come unto Christ unless it be given unto him, and unless the
Father draw him. And all men are not so drawn by the Father that they may come
unto the Son. Neither is there such a sufficient measure of grace vouchsafed unto
every man whereby he is enabled to come unto everlasting life.[4]

33. All God's elect are in their time inseparably united unto Christ by the
effectual and vital influence of the Holy Ghost, derived from him as from the head
unto every true member of his mystical body. And being thus made one with Christ,
they are truly regenerated, and made partakers of him and all his benefits.

OF JUSTIFICATION AND FAITH

34. We are accounted righteous before God only for the merit of our Lord and Savior
Jesus Christ, applied by faith, and not for our own works or merits. And this righteousness, which we so receive of God's mercy and Christ's merits, embraced by
faith, is taken, accepted, and allowed of God, for our perfect and full justification.

35. Although this justification be free unto us, yet it cometh not so freely
unto us that there is no ransom paid therefore at all. God showed his great mercy in
delivering us from our former captivity without requiring of any ransom to be paid
or amends to be made on our parts; which thing by us had been impossible to be
done. And whereas all the world was not able of themselves to pay any part towards
their ransom, it pleased our heavenly Father of his infinite mercy, without any desert
of ours, to provide for us the most precious merits of his own Son, whereby our
ransom might be fully paid, the law fulfilled, and his justice fully satisfied. So that
Christ is now the righteousness of all them that truly believe in him. He, for them,
paid their ransom by his death. He, for them, fulfilled the law in his life; that now,
in him, and by him, every true Christian man may be called a fulfiller of the law:
forasmuch as that which our infirmity was not able to effect, Christ's justice hath
performed. And thus the justice and mercy of God do embrace each other: the grace
of God not shutting out the justice of God in the matter of our justification, but only
shutting out the justice of man (that is to say, the justice of our own works) from
being any cause of deserving our justification.

36. When we say that we are justified by faith only, we do not mean that
the said justifying faith is alone in man without true repentance, hope, charity, and
the fear of God (for such a faith is dead, and can not justify); neither do we mean
that this, our act, to believe in Christ, or this, our faith in Christ, which is within

4. *Lamb Art* 7, 8, 9.

us, doth of itself justify us or deserve our justification unto us (for that were to account ourselves to be justified by the virtue or dignity of something that is within ourselves); but the true understanding and meaning thereof is, that although we hear God's word, and believe it—although we have faith, hope, charity, repentance, and the fear of God within us, and add never so many good works thereunto—yet we must renounce the merit of all our said virtues, of faith, hope, charity, and all our other virtues and good deeds which we either have done, shall do, or can do, as things that be far too weak and imperfect and insufficient to deserve remission of our sins and our justification, and therefore we must trust only in God's mercy and the merits of his most dearly beloved Son, our only Redeemer, Savior, and Justifier, Jesus Christ. Nevertheless, because faith doth directly send us to Christ for our justification, and that by faith given us of God we embrace the promise of God's mercy and the remission of our sins (which thing none other of our virtues or works properly doth), therefore the Scripture useth to say that *faith without works*—and [Rom 11.6; Eph 2.8] the ancient fathers of the church to the same purpose—that *only faith* doth justify us.

37. By justifying faith we understand not only the common belief of the articles of Christian religion, and the persuasion of the truth of God's word in general, but also a particular application of the gracious promises of the gospel to the comfort of our own souls, whereby we lay hold on Christ, with all his benefits; having an earnest trust and confidence in God, that he will be merciful unto us for his only Son's sake. So that a true believer may be certain, by the assurance of faith, of the forgiveness of his sins, and of his everlasting salvation by Christ.[5]

38. A true, lively, justifying faith and the sanctifying Spirit of God is not extinguished nor vanished away in the regenerate, either finally or totally.[6]

OF SANCTIFICATION AND GOOD WORKS

39. All that are justified are likewise sanctified, their faith being always accompanied with true repentance and good works.

40. Repentance is a gift of God, whereby a godly sorrow is wrought in the heart of the faithful for offending God, their merciful Father, by their former transgressions, together with a constant resolution for the time to come to cleave unto God and to lead a new life.

41. Albeit that good works, which are the fruits of faith, and follow after justification, can not make satisfaction for our sins and endure the surety of God's

5. *Lamb Art 6.*
6. *Lamb Art 5.*

judgment; yet are they pleasing to God, and accepted of him in Christ, and do spring from a true and lively faith, which by them is to be discerned, as a tree by the fruit.

42. The works which God would have his people to walk in are such as he hath commanded in his Holy Scripture, and not such works as men have devised out of their own brain, of a blind zeal and devotion, without the warrant of the word of God.

43. The regenerate can not fulfill the law of God perfectly in this life. For in many things we offend all; and if we say we have no sin, we deceive ourselves, [1 Jn 1.8] and the truth is not in us.

44. Not every heinous sin willingly committed after baptism is sin against the Holy Ghost, and unpardonable. And therefore to such as fall into sin after baptism, place for repentance is not to be denied.

45. Voluntary works, besides over and above God's commandments, which they call works of supererogation, can not be taught without arrogancy and impiety; for by them men do declare that they do not only render unto God as much as they are bound to do, but that they do more for his sake than of bounden duty is required.

OF THE SERVICE OF GOD

46. Our duty towards God is to believe in him, to fear him, and to love him with [Lk 10.27] all our heart, with all our mind, and with all our soul, and with all our strength; to worship him, and to give him thanks; to put our whole trust in him, to call upon him, to honor his holy name and his word, and to serve him truly all the days of our life.

47. In all our necessities we ought to have recourse unto God by prayer: assuring ourselves that whatsoever we ask of the Father, in the name of his Son (our only Mediator and Intercessor) Christ Jesus, and according to his will, he will undoubtedly grant it.

48. We ought to prepare our hearts before we pray, and understand the things that we ask when we pray: that both our hearts and voices may together sound in the ears of God's majesty.

49. When Almighty God smiteth us with affliction, or some great calamity hangeth over us, or any other weighty cause so requireth, it is our duty to humble ourselves in fasting, to bewail our sins with a sorrowful heart, and to addict ourselves to earnest prayer, that it might please God to turn his wrath from us, or supply us with such graces as we greatly stand in need of.

50. Fasting is a withholding of meat, drink, and all natural food, with other outward delights, from the body, for the determined time of fasting. As for those

abstinences which are appointed by public order of our state, for eating of fish and forbearing of flesh at certain times and days appointed, they are noways meant to be religious fasts, nor intended for the maintenance of any superstition in the choice of meats, but are grounded merely upon politic considerations, for provision of things tending to the better preservation of the commonwealth.

51. We must not fast with this persuasion of mind, that our fasting can bring us to heaven, or ascribe holiness to the outward work wrought; for God alloweth not our fast for the work sake (which of itself is a thing merely indifferent), but simply respecteth the heart, how it is affected therein. It is, therefore, requisite that first, before all things, we cleanse our hearts from sin, and then direct our fast to such ends as God will allow to be good: that the flesh may thereby be chastised, the spirit may be more fervent in prayer, and that our fasting may be a testimony of our humble submission to God's majesty, when we acknowledge our sins unto him, and are inwardly touched with sorrowfulness of heart, bewailing the same in the affliction of our bodies.

52. All worship devised by man's phantasy besides or contrary to the Scriptures (as wandering on pilgrimages, setting up of candles, stations, and jubilees, pharisaical sects and feigned religions, praying upon beads, and such like superstition) hath not only no promise of reward in Scripture, but contrariwise threatenings and maledictions.

53. All manner of expressing God the Father, the Son, and the Holy Ghost in an outward form is utterly unlawful; as also all other images devised or made by man to the use of religion.

54. All religious worship ought to be given to God alone: from whom all goodness, health, and grace ought to be both asked and looked for, as from the very author and giver of the same, and from none other.

55. The name of God is to be used with all reverence and holy respect, and therefore all vain and rash swearing is utterly to be condemned. Yet, notwithstanding, upon lawful occasions, an oath may be given and taken, according to the word of God: *justice, judgment, and truth.*   [Jer 4.2]

56. The first day of the week, which is the *Lord's day,* is wholly to be dedicated unto the service of God; and therefore we are bound therein to rest from our common and daily business, and to bestow that leisure upon holy exercises, both public and private.

OF THE CIVIL MAGISTRATE

57. The king's majesty under God hath the sovereign and chief power within his realms and dominions, over all manner of persons, of what estate, either ecclesias-

tical or civil, soever they be; so as no other foreign power hath, or ought to have, any superiority over them.

58. We do profess that the supreme government of all estates within the said realms and dominions, in all cases, as well ecclesiastical as temporal, doth of right appertain to the king's highness. Neither do we give unto him hereby the administration of the word and sacraments, or the power of the keys, but that prerogative only which we see to have been always given unto all godly princes in Holy Scripture by God himself; that is, that he should contain all estates and degree committed to his charge by God, whether they be ecclesiastical or civil, within their duty, and restrain the stubborn and evil-doers with the power of the civil sword.

59. The pope, neither of himself, nor by any authority of the church or see of Rome, or by any other means with any other, hath any power or authority to depose the king, or dispose any of his kingdoms or dominions; or to authorize any other prince to invade or annoy him or his countries; or to discharge any of his subjects of their allegiance and obedience to his majesty; or to give license or leave to any of them to bear arms, raise tumult, or to offer any violence or hurt to his royal person, state, or government, or to any of his subjects within his majesty's dominions.

60. That princes which be excommunicated or deprived by the pope may be deposed or murdered by their subjects, or any other whatsoever, is impious doctrine.

61. The laws of the realm may punish Christian men with death for heinous and grievous offenses.

62. It is lawful for Christian men, at the commandment of the magistrate, to bear arms and to serve in just wars.

OF OUR DUTY TOWARDS OUR NEIGHBORS

63. Our duty towards our neighbors is, to love them as ourselves, and to do to all men as we would they should do to us; to honor and obey our superiors; to preserve the safety of men's persons, as also their chastity, goods, and good names; to bear no malice nor hatred in our hearts; to keep our bodies in temperance, soberness, and chastity; to be true and just in all our doings; not to covet other men's goods, but labor truly to get our own living, and to do our duty in that estate of life unto which it pleaseth God to call us.

64. For the preservation of the chastity of men's persons, wedlock is commanded unto all men that stand in need thereof. Neither is there any prohibition by the word of God but that the ministers of the church may enter into the state of matrimony: they being nowhere commanded by God's law either to vow the estate of single life or to abstain from marriage. Therefore it is lawful also for them, as

well as for all other Christian men, to marry at their own discretion, as they shall judge the same to serve better to godliness.

65. The riches and goods of Christians are not common, as touching the right, title, and possession of the same: as certain Anabaptists falsely affirm. Notwithstanding every man ought of such things as he possesseth liberally to give alms to the poor, according to his ability.

66. Faith given, is to be kept, even with heretics and infidels.

67. The popish doctrine of equivocation and mental reservation is ungodly, and tendeth plainly to the subversion of all human society.

OF THE CHURCH AND OUTWARD
MINISTRY OF THE GOSPEL

68. There is but one catholic church (out of which there is no salvation), containing the universal company of all the saints that ever were, are, or shall be, gathered together in one body, under one head, Christ Jesus: part whereof is already in heaven *triumphant*, part as yet *militant* here upon earth. And because this church consisteth of all those, and those alone, which are elected by God unto salvation, and regenerated by the power of his Spirit, the number of whom is known only unto God himself: therefore it is called the *catholic* or universal, and the *invisible* church.

69. But particular and visible churches (consisting of those who make profession of the faith of Christ, and live under the outward means of salvation) be many in number: wherein the more or less sincerely, according to Christ's institution, the word of God is taught, the sacraments are administered, and the authority of the keys is used, the more or less pure are such churches to be accounted.

70. Although in the visible church the evil be ever mingled with the good, and sometimes the evil have chief authority in the ministration of the word and sacraments: yet, forasmuch as they do not the same in their own name, but in Christ's, and minister by his commission and authority, we may use their ministry both in hearing the word and in receiving the sacraments. Neither is the effect of Christ's ordinance taken away by their wickedness, nor the grace of God's gifts diminished from such as by faith and rightly do receive the sacraments ministered unto them; which are effectual, because of Christ's institution and promise, although they be ministered by evil men. Nevertheless it appertaineth to the discipline of the church that inquiry be made of evil ministers, and that they be accused by those that have knowledge of their offenses, and finally, being found guilty, by just judgment be deposed.

71. It is not lawful for any man to take upon him the office of public preaching or ministering the sacraments in the church, unless he be first lawfully called

and sent to execute the same. And those we ought to judge lawfully called and sent which be chosen and called to this work by men who have public authority given them in the church to call and send ministers into the Lord's vineyard.

72. To have public prayer in the church, or to administer the sacraments in a tongue not understood of the people, is a thing plainly repugnant to the word of God and the custom of the primitive church.

73. That person which by public denunciation of the church is rightly cut off from the unity of the church, and excommunicate, ought to be taken of the whole [Mt 18.17] multitude of the faithful as a heathen and publican, until by repentance he be openly reconciled and received into the church by the judgment of such as have authority in that behalf.

74. God hath given power to his ministers, not simply to forgive sins (which prerogative he hath reserved only to himself), but in his name to declare and pronounce unto such as truly repent and unfeignedly believe his holy gospel the absolution and forgiveness of sins. Neither is it God's pleasure that his people should be tied to make a particular confession of all their known sins unto any mortal man: howsoever, any person grieved in his conscience upon any special cause may well resort unto any godly and learned minister to receive advice and comfort at his hands.

OF THE AUTHORITY OF THE CHURCH, GENERAL COUNCILS, AND BISHOP OF ROME

75. It is not lawful for the church to ordain any thing that is contrary to God's word: neither may it so expound one place of Scripture that it be repugnant to another. Wherefore, although the church be a witness and a keeper of Holy Writ, yet as it ought not to decree any thing against the same, so besides the same ought it not enforce any thing to be believed upon necessity of salvation.

76. General councils may not be gathered together without the commandment and will of princes; and when they be gathered together (forasmuch as they be an assembly of men not always governed with the Spirit and Word of God) they may err, and sometimes have erred, even in things pertaining to the rule of piety. Wherefore things ordained by them as necessary to salvation have neither strength nor authority, unless it may be shown that they be taken out of Holy Scriptures.

77. Every particular church hath authority to institute, to change, and clean to put away ceremonies and other ecclesiastical rites, as they be superfluous or be abused; and to constitute other, making more to seemliness, to order, or edification.

78. As the churches of *Jerusalem, Alexandria,* and *Antioch* have erred, so

also the church of *Rome* hath erred, not only in those things which concern matter of practice and point of ceremonies, but also in matters of faith.

79. The power which the bishop of *Rome* now challengeth to be supreme head of the universal church of Christ, and to be above all emperors, kings, and princes, is a usurped power, contrary to the Scriptures and word of God, and contrary to the example of the primitive church; and therefore is for most just causes taken away and abolished within the king's majesty's realms and dominions.

80. The bishop of *Rome* is so far from being the supreme head of the universal church of Christ, that his works and doctrine do plainly discover him to be *that man of sin,* foretold in the Holy Scriptures, *whom the Lord shall consume with the spirit of his mouth, and abolish with the brightness of his coming.*   [2 Thes 2.8]

OF THE STATE OF THE OLD AND NEW TESTAMENT

81. In the Old Testament the commandments of the law were more largely, and the promises of Christ more sparingly and darkly propounded, shadowed with a multitude of types and figures, and so much the more generally and obscurely delivered as the manifesting of them was further off.

82. The Old Testament is not contrary to the New. For both in the Old and New Testament everlasting life is offered to mankind by Christ, who is the only Mediator between God and man, being both God and man. Wherefore they are not to be heard which feign that the old fathers did look only for transitory promises. For they looked for all benefits of God the Father through the merits of his Son Jesus Christ, as we now do: only they believed in Christ which should come, we in Christ already come.

83. The New Testament is full of grace and truth, bringing joyful tidings unto mankind that whatsoever formerly was promised of Christ is now accomplished; and so, instead of the ancient types and ceremonies, exhibiteth the things themselves, with a large and clear declaration of all the benefits of the gospel. Neither is the ministry thereof restrained any longer to one circumcised nation, but is indifferently propounded unto all people, whether they be Jews or Gentiles. So that there is now no nation which can truly complain that they be shut forth from the communion of saints and the liberties of the people of God.

84. Although the law given from God by Moses as touching ceremonies and rites be abolished, and the civil precepts thereof be not of necessity to be received in any commonwealth, yet, notwithstanding, no Christian man whatsoever is freed from the obedience of the commandments which are called moral.

OF THE SACRAMENTS OF THE NEW TESTAMENT

85. The sacraments ordained by Christ be not only badges or tokens of Christian men's profession, but rather certain sure witnesses and effectual or powerful signs of grace and God's good will towards us, by which he doth work invisibly in us, and not only quicken, but also strengthen and confirm our faith in him.

86. There be two sacraments ordained of Christ our Lord in the Gospel: that is to say, *baptism* and the *Lord's supper.*

87. Those five which by the church of *Rome* are called sacraments, to wit: *confirmation, penance, orders, matrimony,* and *extreme unction,* are not to be accounted sacraments of the gospel; being such as have partly grown from corrupt imitation of the apostles, partly are states of life allowed in the Scriptures, but yet have not like nature of sacraments with *baptism* and the *Lord's supper,* for that they have not any visible sign or ceremony ordained of God, together with a promise of saving grace annexed thereto.

88. The sacraments were not ordained of Christ to be gazed upon, or to be carried about, but that we should duly use them. And in such only as worthily receive the same, they have a wholesome effect and operation; but they that receive them unworthily, thereby draw judgment upon themselves.

OF BAPTISM

89. Baptism is not only an outward sign of our profession, and a note of difference, whereby Christians are discerned from such as are no Christians; but much more a sacrament of our admission into the church, sealing unto us our new birth (and consequently our justification, adoption, and sanctification) by the communion which we have with Jesus Christ.

90. The baptism of infants is to be retained in the church, as agreeable to the word of God.

91. In the administration of baptism, *exorcism, oil, salt, spittle,* and superstitious *hallowing of the water,* are for just causes abolished; and without them the sacrament is fully and perfectly administered, to all intents and purposes, agreeable to the institution of our Savior Christ.

OF THE LORD'S SUPPER

92. The Lord's supper is not only a sign of the mutual love which Christians ought to bear one towards another, but much more a sacrament of our preservation in the church, sealing unto us our spiritual nourishment and continual growth in Christ.

93. The change of the substance of bread and wine into the substance of the

body and blood of Christ, commonly called *transubstantiation,* can not be proved by Holy Writ; but is repugnant to plain testimonies of the Scripture, overthroweth the nature of a sacrament, and hath given occasion to most gross idolatry and manifold superstitions.

94. In the outward part of the holy communion, the body and blood of Christ is in a most lively manner *represented;* being no otherwise present with the visible elements than things signified and sealed are present with the signs and seals —that is to say, symbolically and relatively. But in the inward and spiritual part the same body and blood is really and substantially *presented* unto all those who have grace to receive the Son of God, even to all those that believe in his name. And unto such as in this manner do worthily and with faith repair unto the Lord's table, the body and blood of Christ is not only signified and offered, but also truly exhibited and communicated.

95. The body of Christ is given, taken, and eaten in the Lord's supper only after a heavenly and spiritual manner; and the mean whereby the body of Christ is thus received and eaten is faith.

96. The wicked, and such as want a lively faith, although they do carnally and visibly (as St. Augustine speaketh) press with their teeth the sacrament of the body and blood of Christ, yet in nowise are they made partakers of Christ; but rather to their condemnation do eat and drink the sign or sacrament of so great a thing.

97. Both the parts of the Lord's sacrament, according to Christ's institution and the practice of the ancient church, ought to be ministered unto God's people; and it is plain sacrilege to rob them of the mystical cup, for whom Christ hath shed his most precious blood.

98. The sacrament of the *Lord's supper* was not by Christ's ordinance reserved, carried about, lifted up, or worshiped.

99. The sacrifice of the mass, wherein the priest is said to offer up Christ for obtaining the remission of pain or guilt for the quick and the dead, is neither agreeable to Christ's ordinance nor grounded upon doctrine apostolic; but contrariwise most ungodly and most injurious to that all-sufficient sacrifice of our Savior Christ, offered once forever upon the cross, which is the only propitiation and satisfaction for all our sins.

100. Private mass—that is, the receiving of the *eucharist* by the priest alone, without a competent number of communicants—is contrary to the institution of Christ.

OF THE STATE OF THE SOULS OF MEN AFTER THEY BE DEPARTED OUT OF THIS LIFE, TOGETHER WITH THE GENERAL RESURRECTION AND THE LAST JUDGMENT

101. After this life is ended the souls of God's children be presently received into heaven, there to enjoy unspeakable comforts; the souls of the wicked are cast into hell, there to endure endless torments.

102. The doctrine of the church of Rome concerning *limbus patrum, limbus puerorum, purgatory, prayer for the dead, pardons, adoration of images and relics,* and also *invocation of saints,* is vainly invented without all warrant of Holy Scripture, yea, and is contrary unto the same.

103. At the end of this world the Lord Jesus shall come in the clouds with the glory of his Father; at which time, by the almighty power of God, the living shall be changed and the dead shall be raised; and all shall appear both in body and soul before his judgment seat, to receive according to that which they have done in their bodies, whether good or evil.

[1 Cor 15.24, 28] 104. When the last judgment is finished, Christ shall deliver up the kingdom to his Father, and God shall be all in all.

THE DECREE OF THE SYNOD

If any minister, of what degree or quality soever he be, shall publicly teach any doctrine contrary to these articles agreed upon, if, after due admonition, he do not conform himself, and cease to disturb the peace of the church, let him be silenced, and deprived of all spiritual promotions he doth enjoy.

The Canons of the Synod of Dort, 1618–19

The theological disputes touched off by the presentation of → *The Remonstrance* in 1610 led, finally, to the convening of a national church conference in the city of Dort from November 1618 to May 1619. The Remonstrants had called for such a council in 1610, but by the time it took place, the Calvinist party controlled its agenda. The purpose of the synod had also changed. The Remonstrants' goal of negotiating a settlement that might accommodate theological differences had been replaced by the Calvinists' desire to define orthodoxy.

Johannes Bogerman (1576–1637) of Leeuwarden presided over a body of approximately eighty Dutch ministers and theologians and twenty-six representatives from Reformed Churches in England, Scotland, France, Switzerland, and Germany. Thirteen Remonstrants, led by Simon Episcopius (1583–1643) of Leiden, came before the synod. They attempted to discuss the issues as equals, claiming that their views, particularly on predestination, were biblically grounded. After five weeks they were dismissed and their beliefs were condemned in *The Canons of Dort*.

In its organization the document relies, interestingly enough, on the framework set forth in → *The Remonstrance*, refuting each of its five points in positive terms to define five chief articles of Dutch Calvinist doctrine on: (1) double predestination; (2) limited atonement; (3) the nature of sin; (4) the dispensation of grace; and (5) the perseverance of the saints. Each definition concludes with a "Rejection of Errors," condemning Remonstrant views.

The Canons of Dort, → *The Heidelberg Catechism,* and → *The Belgic Confession* became the doctrinal standards of the Dutch Reformed Church and remain so today. The Reformed Church in America and the Christian Reformed Church—descendants of the Dutch Church—also subscribe to these three confessional statements, although they sometimes omit the "Rejection of Errors" sections, presenting only the positive articles that define Calvinism.

The text was originally written in Latin but was issued simultaneously in Latin, Dutch, and French.

Edition: Bakhuizen van den Brink, 226–80 (Latin only).

Translation: *Ecumenical Creeds and Reformed Confessions* 1988, 122–45. This new translation from the Latin was authorized in 1986 by the Synod of the Christian Reformed Church and accepted by the Reformed Church in America. The text can also be found in *Liturgy and Confessions* 1990 and *The Psalter Hymnal* 1987.

Literature: Bakhuizen van den Brink, 41–56; De Jong 1968, esp. 1–52, 213–14; Dewar 1992; Girod 1978; Godfrey 1982; Hardwick 1876, 188–204; Harrison 1926, 300–383; Hoekema 1968a, 1968b, 1972; Hoenderdaal 1969, 1975; Kistemaker 1968; Klooster 1968; Praamsma 1968; Spijker 1987; Strehle 1989; *TRE* 9:140–47 (van Dooren); Tyacke 1986, 87–105.

The Canons of the Synod of Dort, 1618–19

The First Main Point of Doctrine Concerning Divine Predestination

ARTICLE 1. [GOD'S RIGHT TO CONDEMN ALL PEOPLE]

Since all people have sinned in Adam and have come under the sentence of the curse and eternal death, God would have done no one an injustice if it had been his will to leave the entire human race in sin and under the curse, and to condemn them on account of their sin. As the apostle says: The whole world is liable to the condemnation of God,[a] "All have sinned and are deprived of the glory of God,"[b] and "The wages of sin is death."

Rom 6.23

ARTICLE 2. [THE MANIFESTATION OF GOD'S LOVE]

But this is how God showed his love: he sent his only-begotten Son into the world, so that whoever believes in him should not perish but have eternal life.

1 Jn 4.9; Jn 3.16

ARTICLE 3. [THE PREACHING OF THE GOSPEL]

In order that people may be brought to faith, God mercifully sends proclaimers of this very joyful message to the people he wishes and at the time he wishes. By this ministry people are called to repentance and faith in Christ crucified. For "how shall they believe in him of whom they have not heard? And how shall they hear without someone preaching? And how shall they preach unless they have been sent?"

Rom 10.14–15

ARTICLE 4. [A TWOFOLD RESPONSE TO THE GOSPEL]

God's anger remains on those who do not believe this gospel. But those who do accept it and embrace Jesus the Savior with a true and living faith are delivered through him from God's anger and from destruction, and receive the gift of eternal life.

ARTICLE 5. [THE SOURCES OF UNBELIEF AND OF FAITH]

The cause or blame for this unbelief, as well as for all other sins, is not at all in God, but in man. Faith in Jesus Christ, however, and salvation through him is a free gift of God. As Scripture says, "It is by grace you have been saved, through faith, and this not from yourselves; it is a gift of God." Likewise: "It has been freely given to you to believe in Christ."

Eph 2.8
Phil 1.29

a. Rom 3.19
b. Rom 3.23

ARTICLE 6. [GOD'S ETERNAL DECISION]

The fact that some receive from God the gift of faith within time, and that others do not, stems from his eternal decision. For "all his works are known to God from eternity." In accordance with this decision he graciously softens the hearts, however hard, of his chosen ones and inclines them to believe, but by his just judgment he leaves in their wickedness and hardness of heart those who have not been chosen. And in this especially is disclosed to us his act—unfathomable, and as merciful as it is just—of distinguishing between people equally lost. This is the well-known decision of election and reprobation revealed in God's word. This decision the wicked, impure, and unstable distort to their own ruin, but it provides holy and godly souls with comfort beyond words.

Acts 15.18; Eph 1.11

ARTICLE 7. [ELECTION]

Election [or choosing] is God's unchangeable purpose by which he did the following:

Before the foundation of the world, by sheer grace, according to the free good pleasure of his will, he chose in Christ to salvation a definite number of particular people out of the entire human race, which had fallen by its own fault from its original innocence into sin and ruin. Those chosen were neither better nor more deserving than the others, but lay with them in the common misery. He did this in Christ, whom he also appointed from eternity to be the Mediator, the Head of all those chosen, and the foundation of their salvation. And so he decided to give the chosen ones to Christ to be saved, and to call and draw them effectively into Christ's fellowship through his word and Spirit. In other words, he decided to grant them true faith in Christ, to justify them, to sanctify them, and finally, after powerfully preserving them in the fellowship of his Son, to glorify them. "God did all this in order to demonstrate his mercy, to the praise of the riches of his glorious grace. As Scripture says, God chose us in Christ, before the foundation of the world, so that we should be holy and blameless before him with love; he predestined us whom he adopted as his children through Jesus Christ, in himself, according to the good pleasure of his will, to the praise of his glorious grace, by which he freely made us pleasing to himself in his beloved." And elsewhere, "Those whom he predestined, he also called; and those whom he called, he also justified; and those whom he justified, he also glorified."

Eph 1.4–6

Rom 8.30

ARTICLE 8. [A SINGLE DECISION OF ELECTION]

This election is not of many kinds; it is one and the same election for all who were to be saved in the Old and the New Testament. For Scripture declares that there is a single good pleasure, purpose, and plan of God's will, by which he chose us from eternity both to grace and to glory, both to salvation and to the way of salvation, which he prepared in advance for us to walk in.

ARTICLE 9. [ELECTION NOT BASED ON FORESEEN FAITH]

This same election took place, not on the basis of foreseen faith, of the obedience of faith, of holiness, or of any other good quality and disposition, as though it were based on a prerequisite cause or condition in the person to be chosen, but rather for the purpose of faith, of the obedience of faith, of holiness, and so on. Accordingly, election is the source of each of the benefits of salvation. Faith, holiness, and the other saving gifts, and at last eternal life itself, flow forth from election as its fruits and effects. As the apostle says, "He chose us [not because we were, but] so that we should be holy and blameless before him in love."

Eph 1.4

ARTICLE 10. [ELECTION BASED ON GOD'S GOOD PLEASURE]

But the cause of this undeserved election is exclusively the good pleasure of God. This does not involve his choosing certain human qualities or actions from among all those possible as a condition of salvation, but rather involves his adopting certain particular persons from among the common mass of sinners as his own possession. As Scripture says, "When the children were not yet born, and had done nothing either good or bad . . . , she [Rebecca] was told, 'The older will serve the younger.' As it is written, 'Jacob I loved, but Esau I hated.'" Also, "All who were appointed for eternal life believed."

Rom 9.11–13

Acts 13.48

ARTICLE 11. [ELECTION UNCHANGEABLE]

Just as God himself is most wise, unchangeable, all-knowing, and almighty, so the election made by him can neither be suspended nor altered, revoked, or annulled; neither can his chosen ones be cast off, nor their number reduced.

ARTICLE 12. [THE ASSURANCE OF ELECTION]

Assurance of this their eternal and unchangeable election to salvation is given to the chosen in due time, though by various stages and in differing measure. Such assurance comes not by inquisitive searching into the hidden and deep things of God, but by noticing within themselves, with spiritual joy and holy delight, the unmistakable fruits of election pointed out in God's word—such as a true faith in Christ, a childlike fear of God, a godly sorrow for their sins, a hunger and thirst for righteousness, and so on.

ARTICLE 13. [THE FRUIT OF THIS ASSURANCE]

In their awareness and assurance of this election God's children daily find greater cause to humble themselves before God, to adore the fathomless depth of his mercies, to cleanse themselves, and to give fervent love in return to him who first so greatly loved them. This is far from saying that this teaching concerning election, and reflection upon it, make God's children lax in observing his commandments or carnally self-assured. By God's just judgment this does usually happen to those who casually take for granted the grace of election or engage in idle and brazen talk about it but are unwilling to walk in the ways of the chosen.

ARTICLE 14. [TEACHING ELECTION PROPERLY]

Just as, by God's wise plan, this teaching concerning divine election has been proclaimed through the prophets, Christ himself, and the apostles, in Old and New Testament times, and has subsequently been committed to writing in the Holy Scriptures, so also today in God's church, for which it was specifically intended, this teaching must be set forth—with a spirit of discretion, in a godly and holy manner, at the appropriate time and place, without inquisitive searching into the ways of the Most High. This must be done for the glory of God's most holy name, and for the lively comfort of his people.

ARTICLE 15. [REPROBATION]

Moreover, Holy Scripture most especially highlights this eternal and undeserved grace of our election and brings it out more clearly for us, in that it further bears witness that not all people have been chosen but that some have not been chosen or have been passed by in God's eternal election—those, that is, concerning whom God, on the basis of his entirely free, most just, irreproachable, and unchangeable good pleasure, made the following decision: to leave them in the common misery into which, by their own fault, they have plunged themselves; not to grant them saving faith and the grace of conversion; but finally to condemn and eternally punish them (having been left in their own ways and under his just judgment), not only for their unbelief but also for all their other sins, in order to display his justice. And this is the decision of reprobation, which does not at all make God the author of sin (a blasphemous thought!) but rather its fearful, irreproachable, just judge and avenger.

ARTICLE 16. [RESPONSES TO THE
TEACHING OF REPROBATION]

Those who do not yet actively experience within themselves a living faith in Christ or an assured confidence of heart, peace of conscience, a zeal for childlike obedience, and a glorying in God through Christ, but who nevertheless use the means by which God has promised to work these things in us—such people ought not to be alarmed at the mention of reprobation, nor to count themselves among the reprobate; rather they ought to continue diligently in the use of the means, to desire fervently a time of more abundant grace, and to wait for it in reverence and humility. On the other hand, those who seriously desire to turn to God, to be pleasing to him alone, and to be delivered from the body of death, but are not yet able to make such progress along the way of godliness and faith as they would like—such people ought much less to stand in fear of the teaching concerning reprobation, since our merciful God has promised that he will not snuff out a smoldering wick and that he will not break a bruised reed. However, those who have forgotten God and their [Mt 12.20] Savior Jesus Christ and have abandoned themselves wholly to the cares of the world and the pleasures of the flesh—such people have every reason to stand in fear of this teaching, as long as they do not seriously turn to God.

ARTICLE 17. [THE SALVATION OF THE
INFANTS OF BELIEVERS]

Since we must make judgments about God's will from his word, which testifies that the children of believers are holy, not by nature but by virtue of the gracious covenant in which they together with their parents are included, godly parents ought not to doubt the election and salvation of their children whom God calls out of this life in infancy.

ARTICLE 18. [THE PROPER ATTITUDE TOWARD
ELECTION AND REPROBATION]

To those who complain about this grace of an undeserved election and about the severity of a just reprobation, we reply with the words of the apostle, "Who are you, O man, to talk back to God?" and with the words of our Savior, "Have I no right [Rom 9.20] to do what I want with my own?" We, however, with reverent adoration of these [Mt 20.15] secret things, cry out with the apostle: "Oh, the depths of the riches both of the wisdom and the knowledge of God! How unsearchable are his judgments, and his ways beyond tracing out! For who has known the mind of the Lord? Or who has been his counselor? Or who has first given to God, that God should repay him? For

Rom 11.33–36 from him and through him and to him are all things. To him be the glory forever! Amen."

Rejection of the Errors by Which the Dutch Churches Have for Some Time Been Disturbed

Having set forth the orthodox teaching concerning election and reprobation, the synod rejects the errors of those

1

Who teach that the will of God to save those who would believe and persevere in faith and in the obedience of faith is the whole and entire decision of election to salvation, and that nothing else concerning this decision has been revealed in God's word.

For they deceive the simple and plainly contradict Holy Scripture in its testimony that God does not only wish to save those who would believe, but that he has also from eternity chosen certain particular people to whom, rather than to others, he would within time grant faith in Christ and perseverance. As Scripture says, "I Jn 17.6 have revealed your name to those whom you gave me." Likewise, "All who were Acts 13.48 appointed for eternal life believed," and "He chose us before the foundation of the Eph 1.4 world so that we should be holy . . . ."

2

Who teach that God's election to eternal life is of many kinds: one general and indefinite, the other particular and definite; and the latter in turn either incomplete, revocable, nonperemptory (or conditional), or else complete, irrevocable, and peremptory (or absolute). Likewise, who teach that there is one election to faith and another to salvation, so that there can be an election to justifying faith apart from a peremptory election to salvation.

For this is an invention of the human brain, devised apart from the Scriptures, which distorts the teaching concerning election and breaks up this golden chain of salvation: "Those whom he predestined, he also called; and those whom Rom 8.30 he called, he also justified; and those whom he justified, he also glorified."

3

Who teach that God's good pleasure and purpose, which Scripture mentions in its teaching of election, does not involve God's choosing certain particular people rather than others, but involves God's choosing, out of all possible conditions (including the works of the law) or out of the whole order of things, the intrinsically unworthy act of faith, as well as the imperfect obedience of faith, to be a condition of salvation; and it involves his graciously wishing to count this as perfect obedience and to look upon it as worthy of the reward of eternal life.

For by this pernicious error the good pleasure of God and the merit of Christ are robbed of their effectiveness and people are drawn away, by unprofitable inquiries, from the truth of undeserved justification and from the simplicity of the Scriptures. It also gives the lie to these words of the apostle: "God called us with a holy calling, not in virtue of works, but in virtue of his own purpose and the grace which was given to us in Christ Jesus before the beginning of time."   2 Tm 1.9

4

Who teach that in election to faith a prerequisite condition is that man should rightly use the light of nature, be upright, unassuming, humble, and disposed to eternal life, as though election depended to some extent on these factors.

For this smacks of Pelagius, and it clearly calls into question the words of the apostle: "We lived at one time in the passions of our flesh, following the will of our flesh and thoughts, and we were by nature children of wrath, like everyone else. But God, who is rich in mercy, out of the great love with which he loved us, even when we were dead in transgressions, made us alive with Christ, by whose grace you have been saved. And God raised us up with him and seated us with him in heaven in Christ Jesus, in order that in the coming ages we might show the surpassing riches of his grace, according to his kindness toward us in Christ Jesus. For it is by grace you have been saved, through faith [and this not from yourselves; it is the gift of God] not by works, so that no one can boast."   Eph 2.3-9

5

Who teach that the incomplete and nonperemptory election of particular persons to salvation occurred on the basis of a foreseen faith, repentance, holiness, and godliness, which has just begun or continued for some time; but that complete and peremptory election occurred on the basis of a foreseen perseverance to the end in faith, repentance, holiness, and godliness. And that this is the gracious and evangelical worthiness, on account of which the one who is chosen is more worthy than the one who is not chosen. And therefore that faith, the obedience of faith, holiness, godliness, and perseverance are not fruits or effects of an unchangeable election to glory, but indispensable conditions and causes, which are prerequisite in those who are to be chosen in the complete election, and which are foreseen as achieved in them.

This runs counter to the entire Scripture, which throughout impresses upon our ears and hearts these sayings among others: "Election is not by works, but by him who calls";[a] "All who were appointed for eternal life believed";[b] "He chose us in himself so that we should be holy";[c] "You did not choose me, but I chose you";[d]

Rom 11.6   "If by grace, not by works"; "In this is love, not that we loved God, but that he loved
1 Jn 4.10 us and sent his Son."

6

Who teach that not every election to salvation is unchangeable, but that some of the chosen can perish and do in fact perish eternally, with no decision of God to prevent it.

By this gross error they make God changeable, destroy the comfort of the godly concerning the steadfastness of their election, and contradict the Holy Scrip-

Mt 24.24   tures, which teach that "the elect cannot be led astray," that "Christ does not lose
Jn 6.39   those given to him by the Father," and that "those whom God predestined, called,
Rom 8.30   and justified, he also glorifies."

7

Who teach that in this life there is no fruit, no awareness, and no assurance of one's unchangeable election to glory, except as conditional upon something changeable and contingent.

For not only is it absurd to speak of an uncertain assurance, but these things also militate against the experience of the saints, who with the apostle rejoice from an awareness of their election and sing the praises of this gift of God; who, as Christ

Lk 10.20   urged, rejoice with his disciples that "their names have been written in heaven"; and finally who hold up against the flaming arrows of the devil's temptations the awareness of their election, with the question, "Who will bring any charge against those

Rom 8.33   whom God has chosen?"

8

Who teach that it was not on the basis of his just will alone that God decided to leave anyone in the fall of Adam and in the common state of sin and condemnation or to pass anyone by in the imparting of grace necessary for faith and conversion.

a. Rom 9.11–12
b. Acts 13.48
c. Eph 1.4
d. Jn 15.16

For these words stand fast: "He has mercy on whom he wishes, and he hardens whom he wishes." And also: "To you it has been given to know the secrets of the kingdom of heaven, but to them it has not been given." Likewise: "I give glory to you, Father, Lord of heaven and earth, that you have hidden these things from the wise and understanding, and have revealed them to little children; yes, Father, because that was your pleasure." Rom 9.18

Mt 13.11

Mt 11.25–26

9

Who teach that the cause for God's sending the gospel to one people rather than to another is not merely and solely God's good pleasure, but rather that one people is better and worthier than the other to whom the gospel is not communicated.

For Moses contradicts this when he addresses the people of Israel as follows: "Behold, to Jehovah your God belong the heavens and the highest heavens, the earth and whatever is in it. But Jehovah was inclined in his affection to love your ancestors alone, and chose out their descendants after them, you above all peoples, as at this day." And also Christ: "Woe to you, Korazin! Woe to you, Bethsaida! for if those mighty works done in you had been done in Tyre and Sidon, they would have repented long ago in sackcloth and ashes." Dt 10.14–15

Mt 11.21

The Second Main Point of Doctrine: Christ's Death and Human Redemption Through It
ARTICLE 1. [THE PUNISHMENT WHICH GOD'S JUSTICE REQUIRES]

God is not only supremely merciful, but also supremely just. His justice requires (as he has revealed himself in the word) that the sins we have committed against his infinite majesty be punished with both temporal and eternal punishments, of soul as well as body. We cannot escape these punishments unless satisfaction is given to God's justice.

ARTICLE 2. [THE SATISFACTION MADE BY CHRIST]

Since, however, we ourselves cannot give this satisfaction or deliver ourselves from God's anger, God in his boundless mercy has given us as a guarantee his only-begotten Son, who was made to be sin and a curse for us, in our place, on the cross, in order that he might give satisfaction for us.

ARTICLE 3. [THE INFINITE VALUE OF CHRIST'S DEATH]
This death of God's Son is the only and entirely complete sacrifice and satisfaction
for sins; it is of infinite value and worth, more than sufficient to atone for the sins
of the whole world.

ARTICLE 4. [REASONS FOR THIS INFINITE VALUE]
This death is of such great value and worth for the reason that the person who suffered it is—as was necessary to be our Savior—not only a true and perfectly holy
man, but also the only-begotten Son of God, of the same eternal and infinite essence
with the Father and the Holy Spirit. Another reason is that this death was accompanied by the experience of God's anger and curse, which we by our sins had fully
deserved.

ARTICLE 5. [THE MANDATE TO PROCLAIM
THE GOSPEL TO ALL]
Moreover, it is the promise of the gospel that whoever believes in Christ crucified
shall not perish but have eternal life. This promise, together with the command to
repent and believe, ought to be announced and declared without differentiation or
discrimination to all nations and people, to whom God in his good pleasure sends
the gospel.

ARTICLE 6. [UNBELIEF MAN'S RESPONSIBILITY]
However, that many who have been called through the gospel do not repent or believe in Christ but perish in unbelief is not because the sacrifice of Christ offered on
the cross is deficient or insufficient, but because they themselves are at fault.

ARTICLE 7. [FAITH GOD'S GIFT]
But all who genuinely believe and are delivered and saved by Christ's death from
their sins and from destruction receive this favor solely from God's grace—which
he owes to no one—given to them in Christ from eternity.

ARTICLE 8. [THE SAVING EFFECTIVENESS
OF CHRIST'S DEATH]
For it was the entirely free plan and very gracious will and intention of God the
Father that the enlivening and saving effectiveness of his Son's costly death should
work itself out in all his chosen ones, in order that he might grant justifying faith
to them only and thereby lead them without fail to salvation. In other words, it was

God's will that Christ through the blood of the cross (by which he confirmed the new covenant) should effectively redeem from every people, tribe, nation, and language all those and only those who were chosen from eternity to salvation and given to him by the Father; that he should grant them faith (which, like the Holy Spirit's other saving gifts, he acquired for them by his death); that he should cleanse them by his blood from all their sins, both original and actual, whether committed before or after their coming to faith; that he should faithfully preserve them to the very end; and that he should finally present them to himself, a glorious people, without spot or wrinkle.

ARTICLE 9. [THE FULFILLMENT OF GOD'S PLAN]

This plan, arising out of God's eternal love for his chosen ones, from the beginning of the world to the present time has been powerfully carried out and will also be carried out in the future, the gates of hell seeking vainly to prevail against it. As a result the chosen are gathered into one, all in their own time, and there is always a church of believers founded on Christ's blood, a church which steadfastly loves, persistently worships, and—here and in all eternity—praises him as her Savior who laid down his life for her on the cross, as a bridegroom for his bride.

Rejection of the Errors

Having set forth the orthodox teaching, the synod rejects the errors of those

I

Who teach that God the Father appointed his Son to death on the cross without a fixed and definite plan to save anyone by name, so that the necessity, usefulness, and worth of what Christ's death obtained could have stood intact and altogether perfect, complete, and whole, even if the redemption that was obtained had never in actual fact been applied to any individual.

For this assertion is an insult to the wisdom of God the Father and to the merit of Jesus Christ, and it is contrary to Scripture. For the Savior speaks as follows: "I lay down my life for the sheep, and I know them." And Isaiah the prophet [Jn 10.15, 27] says concerning the Savior: "When he shall make himself an offering for sin, he shall see his offspring, he shall prolong his days, and the will of Jehovah shall prosper in his hand." Finally, this undermines the article of the creed in which we confess [Is 53.10.] what we believe concerning the church.

2

Who teach that the purpose of Christ's death was not to establish in actual fact a new covenant of grace by his blood, but only to acquire for the Father the mere right to enter once more into a covenant with men, whether of grace or of works.

Heb 7.22; 9.15   For this conflicts with Scripture, which teaches that Christ "has become the guarantee and mediator of a better—that is, a new covenant," and that "a will

Heb 9.17   is in force only when someone has died."

3

Who teach that Christ, by the satisfaction which he gave, did not certainly merit for anyone salvation itself and the faith by which this satisfaction of Christ is effectively applied to salvation, but only acquired for the Father the authority or plenary will to relate in a new way with men and to impose such new conditions as he chose, and that the satisfying of these conditions depends on the free choice of man; consequently, that it was possible that either all or none would fulfill them.

For they have too low an opinion of the death of Christ, do not at all acknowledge the foremost fruit or benefit which it brings forth, and summon back from hell the Pelagian error.

4

Who teach that what is involved in the new covenant of grace which God the Father made with men through the intervening of Christ's death is not that we are justified before God and saved through faith, insofar as it accepts Christ's merit, but rather that God, having withdrawn his demand for perfect obedience to the law, counts faith itself, and the imperfect obedience of faith, as perfect obedience to the law, and graciously looks upon this as worthy of the reward of eternal life.

For they contradict Scripture: "They are justified freely by his grace through the redemption that came by Jesus Christ, whom God presented as a sacrifice of

Rom 3.24–25   atonement, through faith in his blood." And along with the ungodly Socinus, they introduce a new and foreign justification of man before God, against the consensus of the whole church.

5

Who teach that all people have been received into the state of reconciliation and into the grace of the covenant, so that no one on account of original sin is liable to condemnation, or is to be condemned, but that all are free from the guilt of this sin.

For this opinion conflicts with Scripture which asserts that we are by nature

[Eph 2.3]   children of wrath.

6

Who make use of the distinction between obtaining and applying in order to instill in the unwary and inexperienced the opinion that God, as far as he is concerned, wished to bestow equally upon all people the benefits which are gained by Christ's death; but that the distinction by which some rather than others come to share in the forgiveness of sins and eternal life depends on their own free choice (which applies itself to the grace offered indiscriminately) but does not depend on the unique gift of mercy which effectively works in them, so that they, rather than others, apply that grace to themselves.

For, while pretending to set forth this distinction in an acceptable sense, they attempt to give the people the deadly poison of Pelagianism.

7

Who teach that Christ neither could die, nor had to die, nor did die for those whom God so dearly loved and chose to eternal life, since such people do not need the death of Christ.

For they contradict the apostle, who says: "Christ loved me and gave himself up for me," and likewise: "Who will bring any charge against those whom God has chosen? It is God who justifies. Who is he that condemns? It is Christ who died, that is, for them." They also contradict the Savior, who asserts: "I lay down my life for the sheep," and "My command is this: Love one another as I have loved you. Greater love has no one than this, that one lay down his life for his friends." Gal 2.20

Rom 8.33–34

Jn 10.15

Jn 15.12–13

The Third and Fourth Main Points of Doctrine: Human Corruption, Conversion to God, and the Way It Occurs

ARTICLE 1. [THE EFFECT OF THE FALL ON HUMAN NATURE]

Man was originally created in the image of God and was furnished in his mind with a true and salutary knowledge of his Creator and things spiritual, in his will and heart with righteousness, and in all his emotions with purity; indeed, the whole man was holy. However, rebelling against God at the devil's instigation and by his own free will, he deprived himself of these outstanding gifts. Rather, in their place he brought upon himself blindness, terrible darkness, futility, and distortion of judgment in his mind; perversity, defiance, and hardness in his heart and will; and finally impurity in all his emotions.

ARTICLE 2. [THE SPREAD OF CORRUPTION]

Man brought forth children of the same nature as himself after the fall. That is to say, being corrupt he brought forth corrupt children. The corruption spread, by God's just judgment, from Adam to all his descendants—except for Christ alone— not by way of imitation (as in former times the Pelagians would have it) but by way of the propagation of his perverted nature.

ARTICLE 3. [TOTAL INABILITY]

Therefore, all people are conceived in sin and are born children of wrath, unfit for any saving good, inclined to evil, dead in their sins, and slaves to sin; without the grace of the regenerating Holy Spirit they are neither willing nor able to return to God, to reform their distorted nature, or even to dispose themselves to such reform.

ARTICLE 4. [THE INADEQUACY OF THE LIGHT OF NATURE]

There is, to be sure, a certain light of nature remaining in man after the fall, by virtue of which he retains some notions about God, natural things, and the difference between what is moral and immoral, and demonstrates a certain eagerness for virtue and for good outward behavior. But this light of nature is far from enabling man to come to a saving knowledge of God and conversion to him—so far, in fact, that man does not use it rightly even in matters of nature and society. Instead, in various ways he completely distorts this light, whatever its precise character, and suppresses it in unrighteousness. In doing so he renders himself without excuse before God.

ARTICLE 5. [THE INADEQUACY OF THE LAW]

In this respect, what is true of the light of nature is true also of the Ten Commandments given by God through Moses specifically to the Jews. For man cannot obtain saving grace through the Decalogue, because, although it does expose the magnitude of his sin and increasingly convict him of his guilt, yet it does not offer a remedy or enable him to escape from his misery, and, indeed, weakened as it is by the flesh, leaves the offender under the curse.

ARTICLE 6. [THE SAVING POWER OF THE GOSPEL]

What, therefore, neither the light of nature nor the law can do, God accomplishes by the power of the Holy Spirit, through the word or the ministry of reconciliation. This is the gospel about the Messiah, through which it has pleased God to save believers, in both the Old and the New Testament.

ARTICLE 7. [GOD'S FREEDOM IN REVEALING THE GOSPEL]

In the Old Testament, God revealed this secret of his will to a small number; in the New Testament (now without any distinction between peoples) he discloses it to a large number. The reason for this difference must not be ascribed to the greater worth of one nation over another, or to a better use of the light of nature, but to the free good pleasure and undeserved love of God. Therefore, those who receive so much grace, beyond and in spite of all they deserve, ought to acknowledge it with humble and thankful hearts; on the other hand, with the apostle they ought to adore (but certainly not inquisitively search into) the severity and justice of God's judgments on the others, who do not receive this grace.

ARTICLE 8. [THE SERIOUS CALL OF THE GOSPEL]

Nevertheless, all who are called through the gospel are called seriously. For seriously and most genuinely God makes known in his word what is pleasing to him: that those who are called should come to him. Seriously he also promises rest for their souls and eternal life to all who come to him and believe.   [Mt 11.28–29]

ARTICLE 9. [HUMAN RESPONSIBILITY FOR
REJECTING THE GOSPEL]

The fact that many who are called through the ministry of the gospel do not come and are not brought to conversion must not be blamed on the gospel, nor on Christ, who is offered through the gospel, nor on God, who calls them through the gospel and even bestows various gifts on them, but on the people themselves who are called. Some in self-assurance do not even entertain the word of life; others do entertain it but do not take it to heart, and for that reason, after the fleeting joy of a temporary faith, they relapse; others choke the seed of the word with the thorns of life's cares and with the pleasures of the world and bring forth no fruits. This our Savior teaches in the parable of the sower.   Mt 13

ARTICLE 10. [CONVERSION AS THE WORK OF GOD]

The fact that others who are called through the ministry of the gospel do come and are brought to conversion must not be credited to man, as though one distinguishes himself by free choice from others who are furnished with equal or sufficient grace for faith and conversion (as the proud heresy of Pelagius maintains). No, it must be credited to God: just as from eternity he chose his own in Christ, so within time he effectively calls them, grants them faith and repentance, and, having rescued them from the dominion of darkness, brings them into the kingdom of his Son, in order   [Col 1.13]

that they may declare the wonderful deeds of him who called them out of dark-
[1 Pt 2.9] ness into this marvelous light, and may boast not in themselves, but in the Lord, as
[1 Cor 1.31] apostolic words frequently testify in Scripture.

ARTICLE 11. [THE HOLY SPIRIT'S WORK IN CONVERSION]
Moreover, when God carries out this good pleasure in his chosen ones, or works
true conversion in them, he not only sees to it that the gospel is proclaimed to them
outwardly, and enlightens their minds powerfully by the Holy Spirit so that they
may rightly understand and discern the things of the Spirit of God, but, by the effective operation of the same regenerating Spirit, he also penetrates into the inmost
being of man, opens the closed heart, softens the hard heart, and circumcises the
heart that is uncircumcised. He infuses new qualities into the will, making the dead
will alive, the evil one good, the unwilling one willing, and the stubborn one compli-
ant; he activates and strengthens the will so that, like a good tree, it may be enabled
to produce the fruits of good deeds.

ARTICLE 12. [REGENERATION A SUPERNATURAL WORK]
And this is the regeneration, the new creation, the raising from the dead, and the
making alive so clearly proclaimed in the Scriptures, which God works in us without our help. But this certainly does not happen only by outward teaching, by moral
persuasion, or by such a way of working that, after God has done his work, it remains in man's power whether or not to be reborn or converted. Rather, it is an
entirely supernatural work, one that is at the same time most powerful and most
pleasing, a marvelous, hidden, and inexpressible work, which is not lesser than or
inferior in power to that of creation or of raising the dead, as Scripture (inspired by
the author of this work) teaches. As a result, all those in whose hearts God works
in this marvelous way are certainly, unfailingly, and effectively reborn and do actually believe. And then the will, now renewed, is not only activated and motivated by
God but in being activated by God is also itself active. For this reason, man himself,
by that grace which he has received, is also rightly said to believe and to repent.

ARTICLE 13. [THE INCOMPREHENSIBLE
WAY OF REGENERATION]
In this life believers cannot fully understand the way this work occurs; meanwhile,
they rest content with knowing and experiencing that by this grace of God they do
believe with the heart and love their Savior.

ARTICLE 14. [THE WAY GOD GIVES FAITH]

In this way, therefore, faith is a gift of God, not in the sense that it is offered by God for man to choose, but that it is in actual fact bestowed on man, breathed and infused into him. Nor is it a gift in the sense that God bestows only the potential to believe, but then awaits assent—the act of believing—from man's choice; rather, it is a gift in the sense that he who works both willing and acting and, indeed, works all things in all people produces in man both the will to believe and the belief itself.

ARTICLE 15. [RESPONSES TO GOD'S GRACE]

God does not owe this grace to anyone. For what could God owe to one who has nothing to give that can be paid back? Indeed, what could God owe to one who has nothing of his own to give but sin and falsehood? Therefore the person who receives this grace owes and gives eternal thanks to God alone; the person who does not receive it either does not care at all about these spiritual things and is satisfied with himself in his condition, or else in self-assurance foolishly boasts about having something which he lacks. Furthermore, following the example of the apostles, we are to think and to speak in the most favorable way about those who outwardly profess their faith and better their lives, for the inner chambers of the heart are unknown to us. But for others who have not yet been called, we are to pray to the God who calls things that do not exist as though they did. In no way, however, are we to [Rom 4.17] pride ourselves as better than they, as though we had distinguished ourselves from them.

ARTICLE 16. [REGENERATION'S EFFECT]

However, just as by the fall man did not cease to be man, endowed with intellect and will, and just as sin, which has spread through the whole human race, did not abolish the nature of the human race but distorted and spiritually killed it, so also this divine grace of regeneration does not act in people as if they were blocks and stones; nor does it abolish the will and its properties or coerce a reluctant will by force, but spiritually revives, heals, reforms, and—in a manner at once pleasing and powerful—bends it back. As a result, a ready and sincere obedience of the Spirit now begins to prevail where before the rebellion and resistance of the flesh were completely dominant. It is in this that the true and spiritual restoration and freedom of our will consists. Thus, if the marvelous Maker of every good thing were not dealing with us, man would have no hope of getting up from his fall by his free choice, by which he plunged himself into ruin when still standing upright.

ARTICLE 17. [GOD'S USE OF MEANS IN REGENERATION]

Just as the almighty work of God by which he brings forth and sustains our natural life does not rule out but requires the use of means, by which God, according to his infinite wisdom and goodness, has wished to exercise his power, so also the aforementioned supernatural work of God by which he regenerates us in no way rules out or cancels the use of the gospel, which God in his great wisdom has appointed to be the seed of regeneration and the food of the soul. For this reason, the apostles and the teachers who followed them taught the people in a godly manner about this grace of God, to give him the glory and to humble all pride, and yet did not neglect meanwhile to keep the people, by means of the holy admonitions of the gospel, under the administration of the word, the sacraments, and discipline. So even today it is out of the question that the teachers or those taught in the church should presume to test God by separating what he in his good pleasure has wished to be closely joined together. For grace is bestowed through admonitions, and the more readily we perform our duty, the more lustrous the benefit of God working in us usually is and the better his work advances. To him alone, both for the means and for their saving fruit and effectiveness, all glory is owed forever. Amen.

Rejection of the Errors

Having set forth the orthodox teaching, the synod rejects the errors of those

1

Who teach that, properly speaking, it cannot be said that original sin in itself is enough to condemn the whole human race or to warrant temporal and eternal punishments.

Rom 5.12   For they contradict the apostle when he says: "Sin entered the world through one man, and death through sin, and in this way death passed on to all men because all sinned"; also: "The guilt followed one sin and brought condemnation";[a] likewise: "The wages of sin is death."[b]

2

Who teach that the spiritual gifts or the good dispositions and virtues such as goodness, holiness, and righteousness could not have resided in man's will when he was first created, and therefore could not have been separated from the will at the fall.

a. Rom 5.16
b. Rom 6.23

For this conflicts with the apostle's description of the image of God in Ephesians 4.24, where he portrays the image in terms of righteousness and holiness, which definitely reside in the will.

Eph 4.24

3

Who teach that in spiritual death the spiritual gifts have not been separated from man's will, since the will in itself has never been corrupted but only hindered by the darkness of the mind and the unruliness of the emotions, and since the will is able to exercise its innate free capacity once these hindrances are removed, which is to say, it is able of itself to will or choose whatever good is set before it—or else not to will or choose it.

This is a novel idea and an error and has the effect of elevating the power of free choice, contrary to the words of Jeremiah the prophet: "The heart itself is deceitful above all things and wicked"; and of the words of the apostle: "All of us also lived among them [the sons of disobedience] at one time in the passions of our flesh, following the will of our flesh and thoughts."

Jer 17.9

Eph 2.3

4

Who teach that unregenerate man is not strictly or totally dead in his sins or deprived of all capacity for spiritual good but is able to hunger and thirst for righteousness or life and to offer the sacrifice of a broken and contrite spirit which is pleasing to God.

For these views are opposed to the plain testimonies of Scripture: "You were dead in your transgressions and sins"; "The imagination of the thoughts of man's heart is only evil all the time." Besides, to hunger and thirst for deliverance from misery and for life, and to offer God the sacrifice of a broken spirit is characteristic only of the regenerate and of those called blessed.

Eph 2.1, 5

Gn 6.5, 8.21

Ps 51.17; Mt 5.6

5

Who teach that corrupt and natural man can make such good use of common grace (by which they mean the light of nature) or of the gifts remaining after the fall that he is able thereby gradually to obtain a greater grace—evangelical or saving grace—as well as salvation itself; and that in this way God, for his part, shows himself ready to reveal Christ to all people, since he provides to all, to a sufficient extent and in an effective manner, the means necessary for the revealing of Christ, for faith, and for repentance.

For Scripture, not to mention the experience of all ages, testifies that this is false: "He makes known his words to Jacob, his statutes and his laws to Israel;

Ps 147.19–20   he has done this for no other nation, and they do not know his laws"; "In the past
Acts 14.16   God let all nations go their own way"; "They [Paul and his companions] were kept
by the Holy Spirit from speaking God's word in Asia"; and "When they had come
Acts 16.6–7   to Mysia, they tried to go to Bithynia, but the Spirit would not allow them to."

6

Who teach that in the true conversion of man new qualities, dispositions, or gifts
cannot be infused or poured into his will by God, and indeed that the faith [or be-
lieving] by which we first come to conversion and from which we receive the name
"believers" is not a quality or gift infused by God, but only an act of man, and that
it cannot be called a gift except in respect to the power of attaining faith.

    For these views contradict the Holy Scriptures, which testify that God does
infuse or pour into our hearts the new qualities of faith, obedience, and the experi-
Jer 31.33   encing of his love: "I will put my law in their minds, and write it on their hearts"; "I
will pour water on the thirsty land, and streams on the dry ground; I will pour out
Is 44.3   my Spirit on your offspring"; "The love of God has been poured out in our hearts
Rom 5.5   by the Holy Spirit, who has been given to us." They also conflict with the continu-
ous practice of the church, which prays with the prophet: "Convert me, Lord, and
Jer 31.18   I shall be converted."

7

Who teach that the grace by which we are converted to God is nothing but a gentle
persuasion, or (as others explain it) that the way of God's acting in man's conversion
that is most noble and suited to human nature is that which happens by persuasion,
and that nothing prevents this grace of moral suasion even by itself from making
natural men spiritual; indeed, that God does not produce the assent of the will except in this manner of moral suasion, and that the effectiveness of God's work by
which it surpasses the work of Satan consists in the fact that God promises eternal
benefits while Satan promises temporal ones.

    For this teaching is entirely Pelagian and contrary to the whole of Scrip-
ture, which recognizes besides this persuasion also another, far more effective and
divine way in which the Holy Spirit acts in man's conversion. As Ezekiel 36.26 puts
it: "I will give you a new heart and put a new spirit in you; and I will remove your
Ez 36.26   heart of stone and give you a heart of flesh. . . ."

8

Who teach that God in regenerating man does not bring to bear that power of his
omnipotence whereby he may powerfully and unfailingly bend man's will to faith

and conversion, but that even when God has accomplished all the works of grace which he uses for man's conversion, man nevertheless can, and in actual fact often does, so resist God and the Spirit in their intent and will to regenerate him, that man completely thwarts his own rebirth; and, indeed, that it remains in his own power whether or not to be reborn.

For this does away with all effective functioning of God's grace in our conversion and subjects the activity of Almighty God to the will of man; it is contrary to the apostles, who teach that we believe by virtue of the effective working of God's mighty strength, and that God fulfills the undeserved good will of his kindness and the work of faith in us with power, and likewise that his divine power has given us everything we need for life and godliness.

Eph 1.19

2 Thes 1.11

2 Pt 1.3

9

Who teach that grace and free choice are concurrent partial causes which cooperate to initiate conversion, and that grace does not precede—in the order of causality—the effective influence of the will; that is to say, that God does not effectively help man's will to come to conversion before man's will itself motivates and determines itself.

For the early church already condemned this doctrine long ago in the Pelagians, on the basis of the words of the apostle: "It does not depend on man's willing or running but on God's mercy"; also: "Who makes you different from anyone else?" and "What do you have that you did not receive?" likewise: "It is God who works in you to will and act according to his good pleasure."

Rom 9.16

1 Cor 4.7

Phil 2.13

The Fifth Main Point of Doctrine: The Perseverance of the Saints

ARTICLE 1. [THE REGENERATE NOT ENTIRELY FREE FROM SIN]

Those people whom God according to his purpose calls into fellowship with his Son Jesus Christ our Lord and regenerates by the Holy Spirit, he also sets free from the reign and slavery of sin, though in this life not entirely from the flesh and from the body of sin.

ARTICLE 2. [THE BELIEVER'S REACTION TO SINS OF WEAKNESS]

Hence daily sins of weakness arise, and blemishes cling to even the best works of God's people, giving them continual cause to humble themselves before God, to flee for refuge to Christ crucified, to put the flesh to death more and more by the Spirit of supplication and by holy exercises of godliness, and to strain toward the goal of perfection, until they are freed from this body of death and reign with the Lamb of God in heaven.

ARTICLE 3. [GOD'S PRESERVATION OF THE CONVERTED]

Because of these remnants of sin dwelling in them and also because of the temptations of the world and Satan, those who have been converted could not remain standing in this grace if left to their own resources. But God is faithful, mercifully strengthening them in the grace once conferred on them and powerfully preserving them in it to the end.

ARTICLE 4. [THE DANGER OF TRUE BELIEVERS' FALLING INTO SERIOUS SINS]

Although that power of God strengthening and preserving true believers in grace is more than a match for the flesh, yet those converted are not always so activated and motivated by God that in certain specific actions they cannot by their own fault depart from the leading of grace, be led astray by the desires of the flesh, and give in to them. For this reason they must constantly watch and pray that they may not be led into temptations. When they fail to do this, not only can they be carried away by the flesh, the world, and Satan into sins, even serious and outrageous ones, but also by God's just permission they sometimes are so carried away—witness the sad cases, described in Scripture, of David, Peter, and other saints falling into sins.

[Mt 26.41]

ARTICLE 5. [THE EFFECTS OF SUCH SERIOUS SINS]

By such monstrous sins, however, they greatly offend God, deserve the sentence of death, grieve the Holy Spirit, suspend the exercise of faith, severely wound the conscience, and sometimes lose the awareness of grace for a time—until, after they have returned to the way by genuine repentance, God's fatherly face again shines upon them.

ARTICLE 6. [GOD'S SAVING INTERVENTION]

For God, who is rich in mercy, according to his unchangeable purpose of election does not take his Holy Spirit from his own completely, even when they fall grievously. Neither does he let them fall down so far that they forfeit the grace of adoption and the state of justification, or commit the sin which leads to death (the sin against the Holy Spirit), and plunge themselves, entirely forsaken by him, into eternal ruin.

ARTICLE 7. [RENEWAL TO REPENTANCE]

For, in the first place, God preserves in those saints when they fall his imperishable seed from which they have been born again, lest it perish or be dislodged. Secondly, [1 Pt 1.23] by his word and Spirit he certainly and effectively renews them to repentance so that they have a heartfelt and godly sorrow for the sins they have committed; seek and obtain, through faith and with a contrite heart, forgiveness in the blood of the Mediator; experience again the grace of a reconciled God; through faith adore his mercies; and from then on more eagerly work out their own salvation with fear and trembling. [Phil 2.12]

ARTICLE 8. [THE CERTAINTY OF THIS PRESERVATION]

So it is not by their own merits or strength but by God's undeserved mercy that they neither forfeit faith and grace totally nor remain in their downfalls to the end and are lost. With respect to themselves this not only easily could happen, but also undoubtedly would happen; but with respect to God it cannot possibly happen, since his plan cannot be changed, his promise cannot fail, the calling according to his purpose cannot be revoked, the merit of Christ as well as his interceding and preserving cannot be nullified, and the sealing of the Holy Spirit can neither be invalidated nor wiped out.

ARTICLE 9. [THE ASSURANCE OF THIS PRESERVATION]

Concerning this preservation of those chosen to salvation and concerning the perseverance of true believers in faith, believers themselves can and do become assured in accordance with the measure of their faith, by which they firmly believe that they are and always will remain true and living members of the church, and that they have the forgiveness of sins and eternal life.

ARTICLE 10. [THE GROUND OF THIS ASSURANCE]

Accordingly, this assurance does not derive from some private revelation beyond or outside the word, but from faith in the promises of God which he has very plentifully revealed in his word for our comfort, from the testimony of the Holy Spirit testifying with our spirit that we are God's children and heirs, and finally from a [Rom 8.16–17] serious and holy pursuit of a clear conscience and of good works. And if God's chosen ones in this world did not have this well-founded comfort that the victory will be theirs and this reliable guarantee of eternal glory, they would be of all people most miserable.

ARTICLE 11. [DOUBTS CONCERNING THIS ASSURANCE]

Meanwhile, Scripture testifies that believers have to contend in this life with various doubts of the flesh and that under severe temptation they do not always experience this full assurance of faith and certainty of perseverance. But God, the Father of all comfort, does not let them be tempted beyond what they can bear, but with the temptation he also provides a way out, and by the Holy Spirit revives in them the assurance of their perseverance.

1 Cor 10.13

ARTICLE 12. [THIS ASSURANCE AS AN INCENTIVE TO GODLINESS]

This assurance of perseverance, however, so far from making true believers proud and carnally self-assured, is rather the true root of humility, of childlike respect, of genuine godliness, of endurance in every conflict, of fervent prayers, of steadfastness in crossbearing and in confessing the truth, and of well-founded joy in God. Reflecting on this benefit provides an incentive to a serious and continual practice of thanksgiving and good works, as is evident from the testimonies of Scripture and the examples of the saints.

ARTICLE 13. [ASSURANCE NO INDUCEMENT TO CARELESSNESS]

Neither does the renewed confidence of perseverance produce immorality or lack of concern for godliness in those put back on their feet after a fall, but it produces a much greater concern to observe carefully the ways of the Lord which he prepared in advance. They observe these ways in order that by walking in them they may maintain the assurance of their perseverance, lest, by their abuse of his fatherly goodness, the face of the gracious God (for the godly, looking upon his face is sweeter than life, but its withdrawal is more bitter than death) turn away from them again, with the result that they fall into greater anguish of spirit.

ARTICLE 14. [GOD'S USE OF MEANS IN PERSEVERANCE]

And, just as it has pleased God to begin this work of grace in us by the proclamation of the gospel, so he preserves, continues, and completes his work by the hearing and reading of the gospel, by meditation on it, by its exhortations, threats, and promises, and also by the use of the sacraments.

ARTICLE 15. [CONTRASTING REACTIONS TO THE TEACHING OF PERSEVERANCE]

This teaching about the perseverance of true believers and saints, and about their assurance of it—a teaching which God has very richly revealed in his word for the glory of his name and for the comfort of the godly and which he impresses on the hearts of believers—is something which the flesh does not understand, Satan hates, the world ridicules, the ignorant and the hypocrites abuse, and the spirits of error attack. The bride of Christ, on the other hand, has always loved this teaching very tenderly and defended it steadfastly as a priceless treasure; and God, against whom no plan can avail and no strength can prevail, will ensure that she will continue to do this. To this God alone, Father, Son, and Holy Spirit, be honor and glory forever. Amen.

Rejection of the Errors Concerning the Teaching of the Perseverance of the Saints

Having set forth the orthodox teaching, the synod rejects the errors of those

1

Who teach that the perseverance of true believers is not an effect of election or a gift of God produced by Christ's death, but a condition of the new covenant which man, before what they call his "peremptory" election and justification, must fulfill by his free will.

For Holy Scripture testifies that perseverance follows from election and is granted to the chosen by virtue of Christ's death, resurrection, and intercession: The chosen obtained it; the others were hardened; likewise, He who did not spare his   Rom 11.7
own Son, but gave him up for us all—how will he not, along with him, grant us all things? Who will bring any charge against those whom God has chosen? It is God who justifies. Who is he that condemns? It is Christ Jesus who died—more than that, who was raised—who also sits at the right hand of God, and is also interceding for us. Who shall separate us from the love of Christ?   Rom 8.32–35

2

Who teach that God does provide the believer with sufficient strength to persevere and is ready to preserve this strength in him if he performs his duty, but that even with all those things in place which are necessary to persevere in faith and which God is pleased to use to preserve faith, it still always depends on the choice of man's will whether or not he perseveres.

For this view is obviously Pelagian; and though it intends to make men free it makes them sacrilegious. It is against the enduring consensus of evangelical teaching which takes from man all cause for boasting and ascribes the praise for this benefit only to God's grace. It is also against the testimony of the apostle: It is God who keeps us strong to the end, so that we will be blameless on the day of our Lord Jesus Christ.

1 Cor 1.8

3

Who teach that those who truly believe and have been born again not only can forfeit justifying faith as well as grace and salvation totally and to the end, but also in actual fact do often forfeit them and are lost forever.

For this opinion nullifies the very grace of justification and regeneration as well as the continual preservation by Christ, contrary to the plain words of the apostle Paul: "If Christ died for us while we were still sinners, we will therefore much more be saved from God's wrath through him, since we have now been justified by his blood"; and contrary to the apostle John: "No one who is born of God is intent on sin, because God's seed remains in him, nor can he sin, because he has been born of God"; also contrary to the words of Jesus Christ: "I give eternal life to my sheep, and they shall never perish; no one can snatch them out of my hand. My Father, who has given them to me, is greater than all; no one can snatch them out of my Father's hand."

Rom 5.8–9

1 Jn 3.9

Jn 10.28–29

4

Who teach that those who truly believe and have been born again can commit the sin that leads to death (the sin against the Holy Spirit).

For the same apostle John, after making mention of those who commit the sin that leads to death and forbidding prayer for them, immediately adds: "We know that anyone born of God does not commit sin [that is, that kind of sin], but the one who was born of God keeps himself safe, and the evil one does not touch him."

1 Jn 5.16–17

Jn 5.18

5

Who teach that apart from a special revelation no one can have the assurance of future perseverance in this life.

For by this teaching the well-founded consolation of true believers in this life is taken away and the doubting of the Romanists is reintroduced into the church. Holy Scripture, however, in many places derives the assurance not from a special and extraordinary revelation but from the marks peculiar to God's children and from God's completely reliable promises. So especially the apostle Paul: "Nothing

in all creation can separate us from the love of God that is in Christ Jesus our Lord"; $\quad$ Rom 8.39
and John: "They who obey his commands remain in him and he in them. And this
is how we know that he remains in us: by the Spirit he gave us." $\quad$ 1 Jn 3.24

6

Who teach that the teaching of the assurance of perseverance and of salvation is by
its very nature and character an opiate of the flesh and is harmful to godliness, good
morals, prayer, and other holy exercises, but that, on the contrary, to have doubt
about this is praiseworthy.

For these people show that they do not know the effective operation of
God's grace and the work of the indwelling Holy Spirit, and they contradict the
apostle John, who asserts the opposite in plain words: "Dear friends, now we are
children of God, but what we will be has not yet been made known. But we know
that when he is made known, we shall be like him, for we shall see him as he is.
Everyone who has this hope in him purifies himself, just as he is pure." Moreover, $\quad$ 1 Jn 3.2–3
they are refuted by the examples of the saints in both the Old and the New Testament, who though assured of their perseverance and salvation yet were constant in
prayer and other exercises of godliness.

7

Who teach that the faith of those who believe only temporarily does not differ from
justifying and saving faith except in duration alone.

For Christ himself in Matthew 13.20ff. and Luke 8.13ff.[a] clearly defines
these further differences between temporary and true believers: he says that the
former receive the seed on rocky ground, and the latter receive it in good ground, or
a good heart; the former have no root, and the latter are firmly rooted; the former
have no fruit, and the latter produce fruit in varying measure, with steadfastness,
or perseverance.

8

Who teach that it is not absurd that a person, after losing his former regeneration,
should once again, indeed quite often, be reborn.

For by this teaching they deny the imperishable nature of God's seed by
which we are born again, contrary to the testimony of the apostle Peter: "Born
again, not of perishable seed, but of imperishable." $\quad$ 1 Pt 1.23

---

a. Mt 13.20; Lk 8.13–15

9

Who teach that Christ nowhere prayed for an unfailing perseverance of believers in faith.

For they contradict Christ himself when he says: "I have prayed for you, Peter, that your faith may not fail"; and John the Gospel writer when he testifies in John 17 that it was not only for the apostles, but also for all those who were to believe by their message that Christ prayed: "Holy Father, preserve them in your name"; and "My prayer is not that you take them out of the world, but that you preserve them from the evil one."

Lk 22.32
Jn 17.20
Jn 17.11
Jn 17.15

Conclusion: Rejection of False Accusations

And so this is the clear, simple, and straightforward explanation of the orthodox teaching on the five articles in dispute in the Netherlands, as well as the rejection of the errors by which the Dutch churches have for some time been disturbed. This explanation and rejection the synod declares to be derived from God's word and in agreement with the confessions of the Reformed churches. Hence it clearly appears that those of whom one could hardly expect it have shown no truth, equity, and charity at all in wishing to make the public believe:

—that the teaching of the Reformed churches on predestination and on the points associated with it by its very nature and tendency draws the minds of people away from all godliness and religion, is an opiate of the flesh and the devil, and is a stronghold of Satan where he lies in wait for all people, wounds most of them, and fatally pierces many of them with the arrows of both despair and self-assurance;

—that this teaching makes God the author of sin, unjust, a tyrant, and a hypocrite; and is nothing but a refurbished Stoicism, Manichaeism, libertinism, and Mohammedanism;

—that this teaching makes people carnally self-assured, since it persuades them that nothing endangers the salvation of the chosen, no matter how they live, so that they may commit the most outrageous crimes with self-assurance; and that on the other hand nothing is of use to the reprobate for salvation even if they have truly performed all the works of the saints;

—that this teaching means that God predestined and created, by the bare and unqualified choice of his will, without the least regard or consideration of any sin, the greatest part of the world to eternal condemnation; that in the same manner in which election is the source and cause of faith and good works, reprobation is the cause of unbelief and ungodliness; that many infant children of believers are snatched in their innocence from their mothers' breasts and cruelly cast into hell so that neither the blood of Christ nor their baptism nor the prayers of the church at their baptism can be of any use to them; and very many other slanderous accusations of this kind which the Reformed churches not only disavow but even denounce with their whole heart.

Therefore this Synod of Dort in the name of the Lord pleads with all who devoutly call on the name of our Savior Jesus Christ to form their judgment about the faith of the Reformed churches, not on the basis of false accusations gathered from here or there, or even on the basis of the personal statements of a number of ancient and modern authorities—statements which are also often either quoted out of context or misquoted and twisted to convey a different meaning—but on the basis of the churches' own official confessions and of the present explanation of the orthodox teaching which has been endorsed by the unanimous consent of the members of the whole synod, one and all.

Moreover, the synod earnestly warns the false accusers themselves to consider how heavy a judgment of God awaits those who give false testimony against so many churches and their confessions, trouble the consciences of the weak, and seek to prejudice the minds of many against the fellowship of true believers.

Finally, this synod urges all fellow ministers in the gospel of Christ to deal with this teaching in a godly and reverent manner, in the academic institutions as well as in the churches; to do so, both in their speaking and writing, with a view to the glory of God's name, holiness of life, and the comfort of anxious souls; to think and also speak with Scripture according to the analogy of faith; and, finally, to refrain from all those ways of speaking which go beyond the bounds set for us by the genuine sense of the Holy Scriptures and which could give impertinent sophists a just occasion to scoff at the teaching of the Reformed churches or even to bring false accusations against it.

May God's Son Jesus Christ, who sits at the right hand of God and gives gifts to men, sanctify us in the truth, lead to the truth those who err, silence the mouths of those who lay false accusations against sound teaching, and equip faithful ministers of his word with a spirit of wisdom and discretion, that all they say may be to the glory of God and the building up of their hearers. Amen.

Signatories:

From the States of Gelderland

    Martinus Gregorius, Doctor of Law; Chief Justice of the Provincial Court

    Henricus van Essen, Justice of the Provincial Court

From The States of Holland and West-Friesland

    Walraven van Brederode, Baron of Vianen and Ameide; Lord of Noordeloos, Viscount of Utrecht

Hugo Muys van Holij, Knight; Sheriff of Dort; Bailiff of the lands of Strijen; Mayor of Dort

Jacob Boelens, Mayor of Amsterdam

Geraert Janszoon van Nyenburg, Mayor of Alkmaar

Rochum vanden Honert, Chief Justice of the High Court of Holland, Zeeland, and West Friesland; Curator of the Academy of Leiden

Nicolas Cromhout, Lord of Werkendam; Presiding Justice of the Court

From the States of Zeeland

Simon Schotte, Doctor of Law; Secretary of the City of Middleburg

Jacobus van Campen, Doctor of Law; Member of the States of Zeeland

From the States of Utrecht

Frederick van Zuylen van Nyevelt, Lord of Aartsbergen, Berkenwoude, etc.

Willem van Hartevelt, Mayor of Amersfoort

From the States of Friesland

Ernst van Aylav, Chief Officer of Oost-Dongeradeel

Ernst van Harinxma a Donia thoe Sloten, Chief Justice of the Provincial Court; Chief Officer of Leeuwarderadeel

From the States of Overijssel

Henricus Hagen, Nobleman of Volenhove

Johannes van Hemert, Mayor of Deventer

From the States of Groningen en Ommelanden

Hieronymus Ysbrants, Doctor of Law; Syndic of Groningen

Edzard Jacobs Clant, Lord of Ezinge and Landeweer

Here follow the names . . . of all the Members who were deputed to the Synod as the Representatives of their respective Churches; that is, of the Delegates from Great Britain, the Electoral Palatinate, Hessia, Switzerland, Wetteraw, the Republic and Church of Geneva, the Republic and Church of Bremen, the Republic and Church of Emden, the Duchy of Gelderland, and of Zutphen, South Holland, North Holland, Zealand, the Province of Utrecht, Friesland, Transisalania, the State of Groningen, and Omland, Drent, and the French Churches.

The Westminster Confession of Faith, 1647

The Westminster Confession of Faith is the last major confessional statement of the Reformation. Like many other doctrinal documents of the age, it is the product of political as well as theological circumstances. The Bishops' Wars of 1639 and 1640, provoked in part by Charles I's attempt to introduce the *Book of Common Prayer* in Scotland, and the start of the civil war in England in 1642 led to the seizure of power by the so-called Long Parliament. By order of this legislature—overwhelmingly Presbyterian in composition—an assembly of clergy was convened in July 1643 "to confer and treat among themselves of such matters and things, touching and concerning the liturgy, discipline, and government of the Church of England." The goal was to bring the Church of England more in line with the Church of Scotland and the Reformed churches of Europe.[1]

By an act of Parliament the assembly was charged with the preparation of a confessional statement for use in the Churches of England, Scotland, and Ireland. King Charles I refused to authorize the assembly, but this action merely kept those clergy committed to Anglicanism from contributing.[2] Scottish delegates were elected by their national church and served as an influential advisory body within the assembly, especially after the establishment of the Solemn League and Covenant. The Irish Church had only one representative, Professor Joshua Hoyle (†1654). Three ministers from the American colonies were invited—John Cotton, Thomas Hooker, and John Davenport—but did not make the long journey to attend.

The assembly of 121 members met, for the most part, in the Jerusalem Chamber of Westminster Abbey. Over the course of five and a half years, they partially revised → *The Thirty-Nine Articles*, replaced the *Book of Common Prayer* with a new order of public worship, adopted standards for Presbyterian church government, and composed *The Westminster Confession* and *Catechisms*.[3]

→ *The Irish Articles* of 1615 are often cited as a source for *The Westminster Confession*, although one can also detect influences from → *The Scots Confession*

---

1. Mitchell 1884, ix-xii.

2. James Ussher, archbishop of Armagh, and the bishops of Bristol, Exeter, and Worcester were invited to be members of the assembly along with a handful of university theologians and Church of England clergymen, but all were unable to attend because of the royal order. See Schaff, 1:733. Schaff also describes the leaders of the assembly in detail, 1:740-47.

3. For a description of the assembly, see Robert Baille's eyewitness account, reproduced in Schaff, 1:750-51, and Leith 1973, 50-52.

602   Reformed Confessions

and → *The Lambeth Articles*. There are also echoes from such earlier Reformed confessions as → *The Second Helvetic Confession* and → *The Heidelberg Catechism*. In its theology, *The Westminster Confession* reflects Calvinist thought as it evolved among Puritans in the seventeenth century. A significant development of this brand of Calvinism is that it upholds the doctrine of divine providence while avoiding what were taken to be the fatalistic consequences of double predestination. By elaborating upon the relation between God and human beings, who are instruments of divine purpose, this theology accentuates humankind's role in salvation without denying the teaching of "by grace alone." Two covenants are identified (chapter 7): the first, the covenant of works, is the covenant God made with Adam, promising salvation in return for obedience; the second, made after the first covenant had been broken, was the covenant of grace. Evidence for the covenant of grace appears throughout biblical history, from God's call to Abraham, to the giving of the law to Moses, to the incarnation of Jesus Christ. The covenant of grace is bestowed through the gospel, particularly the preaching of the word, and through the sacraments.

Although the supremacy of the Bible is emphasized by its position in the confession as chapter 1, the document was presented to Parliament for approval in late 1646 without any biblical proof texts. By order of the House of Commons, more than fifteen hundred proof texts were added before its first public printing on 29 April 1647.[4] In this form it served as the confession of the Churches of Ireland, England, and Scotland until the Restoration in 1660. In 1690 it was again adopted as a doctrinal standard by the Church of Scotland, and in 1729 it was adopted by the General Synod of the Presbyterian Church in colonial America.[5] It remains the official confession of the Church of Scotland, the Presbyterian Church (USA), and other Presbyterian churches in North America. With some modification, it was adopted by the Congregational Synods of Cambridge, Massachusetts, in 1648. It was revised into the Savoy Declaration of the English Congregational Churches in 1658, was accepted by the London Baptists in 1677, and reappeared, again somewhat altered, as → *The Philadelphia Confession* in 1742. It has been translated into numerous languages and has shaped, or at least influenced, Reformed churches throughout the world.

4. A small number of copies were printed for Parliament when the text was submitted for approval in late 1646 or early 1647, but the official text, with proof texts, first appeared on 29 April 1647. See Rogers 1967, 177. We have placed the proof texts immediately following each chapter to which they pertain.
5. The Adopting Act of 1729 excluded parts of chapters 20 and 23, however, which deal with the power of the civil magistrate over synods. See Barker 1984, 4–5.

Edition: Carruthers [1937] 1995, 89–157, with various American alterations in footnotes. See *Book of Confessions* 1996, 125–68, for the American text of the Presbyterian Church (USA) and for the differences between the texts used by the Presbyterian Church in the United States and the United Presbyterian Church.

Note: We have provided the proof texts that were added by order of Parliament in 1647. For the proof texts of the Presbyterian Church (USA), see *Book of Confessions* 1996, 169–77.

Literature: Barker 1984, 1994; Beveridge [1904] 1993; Carruthers [1937] 1995; Carson and Hall 1994; *Chr Trad* 4:241–44; Knight 1984; Leith 1982; Logan 1994; Rogers 1967; Schaff, 1:727–82; Spear 1994; Warfield 1901–2.

The Westminster Confession of Faith, 1647

The Humble Advice of the Assembly of Divines, Now by Authority of Parliament sitting at Westminster, Concerning A Confession of Faith: With Quotations and Texts of Scripture annexed. Presented by them lately to both Houses of Parliament.

CHAPTER 1. OF THE HOLY SCRIPTURE

1. Although the light of nature and the works of creation and providence do so far manifest the goodness, wisdom, and power of God, as to leave men inexcusable,[a] yet are they not sufficient to give that knowledge of God and of his will which is necessary unto salvation.[b] Therefore it pleased the Lord, at sundry times, and in diverse manners, to reveal himself, and to declare that his will unto his church;[c] and afterwards, for the better preserving and propagating of the truth, and for the more sure establishment and comfort of the church against the corruption of the flesh, and the malice of Satan and of the world, to commit the same wholly unto writing,[d] which maketh the Holy Scripture to be most necessary,[e] those former ways of God's revealing his will unto his people being now ceased.[f]

a. Rom 2.14-15; Rom 1.19-20; Ps 19.1-3; Rom 1.32 with 2.1
b. 1 Cor 1.21; 1 Cor 2.13, 14
c. Heb 1.1
d. Prv 22.19-21; Lk 1.3-4; Rom 15.4; Mt 4.4, 7, 10; Is 8.19-20
e. 2 Tm 3.15; 2 Pt 1.19
f. Heb 1.1-2

2. Under the name of Holy Scripture, or the word of God written, are now contained all the books of the Old and New Testament, which are these:

Of the Old Testament:
Genesis
Exodus
Leviticus
Numbers
Deuteronomy
Joshua
Judges
Ruth
1 Samuel
2 Samuel
1 Kings

2 Kings
1 Chronicles
2 Chronicles
Ezra
Nehemiah
Esther
Job
Psalms
Proverbs
Ecclesiastes
The Song of Songs
Isaiah
Jeremiah
Lamentations
Ezekiel
Daniel
Hosea
Joel
Amos
Obadiah
Jonah
Micah
Nahum
Habakkuk
Zephaniah
Haggai
Zechariah
Malachi

Of the New Testament:
The Gospels according to
Matthew
Mark
Luke
John
The Acts of the Apostles
Paul's Epistles

To the Romans
Corinthians 1
Corinthians 2
Galatians
Ephesians
Philippians
Colossians
Thessalonians 1
Thessalonians 2
To Timothy 1
To Timothy 2
To Titus
To Philemon
The Epistle to the Hebrews
The Epistle of James
The first and second Epistles of Peter
The first, second, and third Epistles of John
The Epistle of Jude
The Revelation of John

All which are given by inspiration of God, to be the rule of faith and life.[g]

g. Lk 16.29, 31; Eph 2.20; Rv 22.18–19; 2 Tm 3.16

3. The books commonly called Apocrypha, not being of divine inspiration, are no part of the canon of the Scripture; and therefore are of no authority in the church of God, nor to be any otherwise approved, or made use of, than other human writings.[h]

h. Lk 24.27, 44; Rom 3.2; 2 Pt 1.21

4. The authority of the Holy Scripture, for which it ought to be believed and obeyed, dependeth not upon the testimony of any man, or church, but wholly upon God (who is truth itself) the author thereof; and therefore it is to be received because it is the word of God.[i]

i. 2 Pt 1.19, 21; 2 Tm 3.16; 1 Jn 5.9; 1 Thes 2.13

5. We may be moved and induced by the testimony of the church to a high and reverent esteem of the Holy Scripture.[k] And the heavenliness of the matter, the efficacy of the doctrine, the majesty of the style, the consent of all the parts, the scope of the whole (which is, to give all glory to God), the full discovery it makes of the only way of man's salvation, the many other incomparable excellencies, and

the entire perfection thereof, are arguments whereby it doth abundantly evidence itself to be the word of God; yet notwithstanding, our full persuasion and assurance of the infallible truth and divine authority thereof, is from the inward work of the Holy Spirit bearing witness by and with the word in our hearts.[l]

k. 1 Tm 3.15

l. 1 Jn 2.20, 27; Jn 16.13–14; 1 Cor 2.10–12; Is 59.21

6. The whole counsel of God concerning all things necessary for his own glory, man's salvation, faith, and life, is either expressly set down in Scripture, or by good and necessary consequence may be deduced from Scripture, unto which nothing at any time is to be added, whether by new revelations of the Spirit, or traditions of men.[m] Nevertheless we acknowledge the inward illumination of the Spirit of God to be necessary for the saving understanding of such things as are revealed in the word:[n] and that there are some circumstances concerning the worship of God, and government of the church, common to human actions and societies, which are to be ordered by the light of nature and Christian prudence, according to the general rules of the word, which are always to be observed.[o]

m. 2 Tm 3.15–17; Gal 1.8–9; 2 Thes 2.2

n. Jn 6.45; 1 Cor 2.9–12

o. 1 Cor 11.13–14; 1 Cor 14.26, 40

7. All things in Scripture are not alike plain in themselves, nor alike clear unto all;[p] yet those things which are necessary to be known, believed, and observed for salvation, are so clearly propounded and opened in some place of Scripture or other, that not only the learned, but the unlearned, in a due use of the ordinary means, may attain unto a sufficient understanding of them.[q]

p. 2 Pt 3.16

q. Ps 119.105, 130

8. The Old Testament in Hebrew (which was the native language of the people of God of old), and the New Testament in Greek (which, at the time of the writing of it, was most generally known to the nations), being immediately inspired by God, and, by his singular care and providence kept pure in all ages, are therefore authentical,[r] so as, in all controversies of religion, the church is finally to appeal unto them.[s] But, because these original tongues are not known to all the people of God, who have right unto, and interest in the Scriptures, and are commanded, in the fear of God, to read and search them,[t] therefore they are to be translated into the vulgar language of every nation[1] unto which they come,[u] that the word of God

1. American edition: *into the language of every people.*

dwelling plentifully in all, they may worship him in an acceptable manner,[w] and, through patience and comfort of the Scriptures, may have hope.[x]

r. Mt 5.18

s. Is 8.20; Acts 15.15; Jn 5.39, 46

t. Jn 5.39

u. 1 Cor 14.6, 9, 11–12, 24, 27–28

w. Col 3.16

x. Rom 15.4

9. The infallible rule of interpretation of Scripture is the Scripture itself; and therefore, when there is a question about the true and full sense of any Scripture (which is not manifold, but one), it must be searched and known by other places that speak more clearly.[y]

y. 2 Pt 1.20–21; Acts 15.15–16

10. The supreme judge by which all controversies of religion are to be determined, and all decrees of councils, opinions of ancient writers, doctrines of men, and private spirits, are to be examined, and in whose sentence we are to rest, can be no other but the Holy Spirit speaking in the Scripture.[z]

z. Mt 22.29, 31; Eph 2.20 with Acts 28.25

CHAPTER 2. OF GOD, AND OF THE HOLY TRINITY

1. There is but one only,[a] living, and true God:[b] who is infinite in being and perfection,[c] a most pure spirit,[d] invisible,[e] without body, parts,[f] or passions,[g] immutable,[h] immense,[i] eternal,[k] incomprehensible,[l] almighty,[m] most wise,[n] most holy,[o] most free,[p] most absolute,[q] working all things according to the counsel of his own immutable and most righteous will,[r] for his own glory;[s] most loving,[t] gracious, merciful, long-suffering, abundant in goodness and truth, forgiving iniquity, transgression, and sin;[u] the rewarder of them that diligently seek him;[w] and with all,[2] most just and terrible in his judgments,[x] hating all sin,[y] and who will by no means clear the guilty.[z]

a. Dt 6.4; 1 Cor 8.4, 6

b. 1 Thes 1.9; Jer 10.10

c. Jb 11.7–9; Jb 26.14

d. Jn 4.24

e. 1 Tm 1.17

f. Dt 4.15, 16; Jn 4.24 with Lk 24.39

g. Acts 14.11, 15

h. Jas 1.17; Mal 3.6

i. 1 Kgs 8.27; Jer 23.23, 24

k. Ps 90.2; 1 Tm 1.17

l. Ps 145.3

2. American edition: *withal.*

m. Gn 17.1; Rv 4.8

n. Rom 16.27

o. Is 6.3; Rv 4.8

p. Ps 115.3

q. Ex 3.14

r. Eph 1.11

s. Prv 16.4; Rom 11.36

t. 1 Jn 4.8, 16

u. Ex 34.6–7

w. Heb 11.6

x. Neh 9.32–33

y. Ps 5.5–6

z. Na 1.2–3; Ex 34.7

2. God hath all life,[a] glory,[b] goodness,[c] blessedness,[d] in and of himself, and is alone in and unto himself all-sufficient, not standing in need of any creatures which he hath made,[e] nor deriving any glory from them,[f] but only manifesting his own glory in, by, unto, and upon them: He is the alone fountain of all being, of whom, through whom, and to whom are all things,[g] and hath most sovereign dominion over them, to do by them, for them, or upon them whatsoever himself pleaseth.[h] In his sight all things are open and manifest;[i] his knowledge is infinite, infallible, and independent upon the creature,[k] so as nothing is to him contingent, or uncertain.[l] He is most holy in all his counsels, in all his works, and in all his commands.[m] To him is due from angels and men, and every other creature, whatsoever worship, service, or obedience he is pleased to require of them.[n]

a. Jn 5.26

b. Acts 7.2

c. Ps 119.68

d. 1 Tm 6.15; Rom 9.5

e. Acts 17.24–25

f. Jb 22.2–3

g. Rom 11.36

h. Rv 4.11; 1 Tm 6.15; Dn 4.25, 35

i. Heb 4.13

k. Rom 11.33–34; Ps 147.5

l. Acts 15.18; Ez 11.5

m. Ps 145.17; Rom 7.12

n. Rv 5.12–14

3. In the unity of the Godhead there be three persons, of one substance, power, and eternity: God the Father, God the Son, and God the Holy Ghost.[o] The Father is of none, neither begotten, nor proceeding; the Son is eternally begotten of the Father;[p] the Holy Ghost eternally proceeding from the Father and the Son.[q]

o. 1 Jn 5.7; Mt 3.16–17; Mt 28.19; 2 Cor 13.14

p. Jn 1.14, 18

q. Jn 15.26; Gal 4.6

CHAPTER 3. OF GOD'S ETERNAL DECREE

1. God from all eternity did, by the most wise and holy counsel of his own will, freely, and unchangeably ordain whatsoever comes to pass:[a] yet so, as thereby neither is God the author of sin,[b] nor is violence offered to the will of the creatures, nor is the liberty or contingency of second causes taken away, but rather established.[c]

a. Eph 1.11; Rom 11.33; Heb 6.17; Rom 9.15, 18
b. Jas 1.13, 17; 1 Jn 1.5
c. Acts 2.23; Mt 17.12; Acts 4.27–28; Jn 19.11; Prv 16.33

2. Although God knows whatsoever may or can come to pass upon all supposed conditions,[d] yet hath he not decreed anything because he foresaw it as future, or as that which would come to pass upon such conditions.[e]

d. Acts 15.18; 1 Sm 23.11–12; Mt 11.21, 23
e. Rom 9.11, 13, 16, 18

3. By the decree of God, for the manifestation of his glory, some men and angels[f] are predestinated unto everlasting life, and others foreordained to everlasting death.[g]

f. 1 Tm 5.21; Mt 25.41
g. Rom 9.22–23; Eph 1.5–6; Prv 16.4

4. These angels and men, thus predestinated, and foreordained, are particularly and unchangeably designed, and their number so certain and definite, that it cannot be either increased or diminished.[h]

h. 2 Tm 2.19; Jn 13.18

5. Those of mankind that are predestinated unto life, God, before the foundation of the world was laid, according to his eternal and immutable purpose, and the secret counsel and good pleasure of his will, hath chosen, in Christ, unto everlasting glory,[i] out of his mere free grace and love,[3] without any foresight of faith or good works, or perseverance in either of them, or any other thing in the creature, as conditions, or causes moving him thereunto:[k] and all to the praise of his glorious grace.[l]

i. Eph 1.4, 9, 11; Rom 8.30; 2 Tm 1.9; 1 Thes 5.9
k. Rom 9.11, 13, 16; Eph 1.4, 9
l. Eph 1.6, 12

6. As God hath appointed the elect unto glory, so hath he, by the eternal and most free purpose of his will, foreordained all the means thereunto.[m] Wherefore they who are elected, being fallen in Adam, are redeemed by Christ,[n] are effectu-

---

3. American edition omits *mere*.

ally called unto faith in Christ by his Spirit working in due season, are justified, adopted, sanctified,[o] and kept by his power through faith, unto salvation.[p] Neither are any other redeemed by Christ, effectually called, justified, adopted, sanctified, and saved, but the elect only.[q]

m. 1 Pt 1.2; Eph 1.4, 5; Eph 2.10; 2 Thes 2.13

n. 1 Thes 5.9–10; Ti 2.14

o. Rom 8.30; Eph 1.5; 2 Thes 2.13

p. 1 Pt 1.5

q. Jn 17.9; Rom 8.28–39; Jn 6.64–65; Jn 10.26; Jn 8.47; 1 Jn 2.19

7. The rest of mankind God was pleased, according to the unsearchable counsel of his own will, whereby he extendeth or withholdeth mercy, as he pleaseth, for the glory of his sovereign power over his creatures, to pass by, and to ordain them to dishonor and wrath, for their sin, to the praise of his glorious justice.[r]

r. Mt 11.25–26; Rom 9.17–18, 21–22; 2 Tm 2.19–20; Jude 4; 1 Pt 2.8

8. The doctrine of this high mystery of predestination is to be handled with special prudence and care,[s] that men attending the will of God revealed in his word, and yielding obedience thereunto, may, from the certainty of their effectual vocation, be assured of their eternal election.[t] So shall this doctrine afford matter of praise, reverence, and admiration of God,[u] and of humility, diligence, and abundant consolation to all that sincerely obey the gospel.[w]

s. Rom 9.20; Rom 11.33; Dt 29.29

t. 2 Pt 1.10

u. Eph 1.6; Rom 11.33

w. Rom 11.5–6, 20; 2 Pt 1.10; Rom 8.33; Lk 10.20

CHAPTER 4. OF CREATION

1. It pleased God the Father, Son, and Holy Ghost,[a] for the manifestation of the glory of his eternal power, wisdom, and goodness,[b] in the beginning, to create, or make of nothing, the world, and all things therein whether visible or invisible, in the space of six days—and all very good.[c]

a. Heb 1.2; Jn 1.2, 3; Gn 1.2; Jb 26.13; Jb 33.4

b. Rom 1.20; Jer 10.12; Ps 104.24; Ps 33.5–6

c. Gn 1; Heb 11.3; Col 1.16; Acts 17.24

2. After God had made all other creatures, he created man, male and female,[d] with reasonable and immortal souls,[e] endued with knowledge, righteousness, and true holiness, after his own image,[f] having the law of God written in their hearts,[g] and power to fulfill it,[h] and yet under a possibility of transgressing, being left to the liberty of their own will, which was subject unto change.[i] Beside this law written in their hearts, they received a command, not to eat of the tree of the knowl-

edge of good and evil, which while they kept, they were happy in their communion with God,[k] and had dominion over the creatures.[l]

d. Gn 1.27

e. Gn 2.7 with Eccl 12.7, Lk 23.43, and Mt 10.28

f. Gn 1.26; Col 3.10; Eph 4.24

g. Rom 2.14-15

h. Eccl 7.29

i. Gn 3.6; Eccl 7.29

k. Gn 2.17; Gn 3.8-11, 23

l. Gn 1.26, 28

CHAPTER 5. OF PROVIDENCE

1. God the great Creator of all things doth uphold,[a] direct, dispose, and govern all creatures, actions, and things,[b] from the greatest even to the least,[c] by his most wise and holy providence,[d] according to his infallible foreknowledge,[e] and the free and immutable counsel of his own will,[f] to the praise of the glory of his wisdom, power, justice, goodness, and mercy.[g]

a. Heb 1.3

b. Dn 4.34-35; Ps 135.6; Acts 17.25-26, 28; Jb 38-41

c. Mt 10.29, 30, 31

d. Prv 15.3; Ps 104.24; Ps 145.17

e. Acts 15.18; Ps 94.8, 9-11

f. Eph 1.11; Ps 33.10-11

g. Is 63.14; Eph 3.10; Rom 9.17; Gn 45.7; Ps 145.7

2. Although, in relation to the foreknowledge and decree of God, the First Cause, all things come to pass immutably, and infallibly,[h] yet, by the same providence, he ordereth them to fall out, according to the nature of second causes, either necessarily, freely, or contingently.[i]

h. Acts 2.23

i. Gn 8.22; Jer 31.35; Ex 21.13 with Dt 19.5; 1 Kgs 22.28, 34; Is 10.6-7

3. God in his ordinary providence maketh use of means,[k] yet is free to work without,[l] above,[m] and against them at his pleasure.[n]

k. Acts 27.31, 44; Is 55.10-11; Hos 2.21-22

l. Hos 1.7; Mt 4.4; Jb 34.20

m. Rom 4.19-21

n. 2 Kgs 6.6; Dn 3.27

4. The almighty power, unsearchable wisdom, and infinite goodness of God so far manifest themselves in his providence, that it extendeth itself even to the first fall, and all other sins of angels and men[o]—and that not by a bare permission,[p] but such as hath joined with it a most wise and powerful bounding,[q] and otherwise ordering and governing of them, in a manifold dispensation, to his own holy

ends;[r] yet so, as the sinfulness thereof proceedeth only from the creature, and not from God, who, being most holy and righteous, neither is, nor can be, the author or approver of sin.[s]

o. Rom 11.32–34; 2 Sm 24.1 with 1 Chr 21.1; 1 Kgs 22.22–23; 1 Chr 10.4, 13–14; 2 Sm 16.10; Acts 2.23; Acts 4.27–28

p. Acts 14.16

q. Ps 76.10; 2 Kgs 19.28

r. Gn 50.20; Is 10.6–7, 12

s. Jas 1.13, 14, 17; 1 Jn 2.16; Ps 50.21

5. The most wise, righteous, and gracious God doth oftentimes leave for a season his own children to manifold temptations, and the corruption of their own hearts, to chastise them for their former sins, or to discover unto them the hidden strength of corruption, and deceitfulness of their hearts, that they may be humbled;[t] and, to raise them to a more close and constant dependence for their support unto[4] himself, and to make them more watchful against all future occasions of sin, and for sundry other just and holy ends.[u]

t. 2 Chr 32.25–26, 31; 2 Sm 24.1

u. 2 Cor 12.7–9; Ps 73; Ps 77.1–12; Mk 14.66–72 with Jn 21.15–17

6. As for those wicked and ungodly men whom God, as a righteous Judge, for former sins, doth blind and harden,[w] from them he not only withholdeth his grace, whereby they might have been enlightened in their understandings, and wrought upon in their hearts,[x] but sometimes also withdraweth the gifts which they had,[y] and exposeth them to such objects as their corruption makes occasions of sin,[z] and, withal, gives them over to their own lusts, the temptations of the world, and the power of Satan:[a] whereby it comes to pass that they harden themselves, even under those means which God useth for the softening of others.[b]

w. Rom 1.24, 26, 28; Rom 11.7, 8

x. Dt 29.4

y. Mt 13.12; Mt 25.29

z. Dt 2.30; 2 Kgs 8.12–13

a. Ps 81.11–12; 2 Thes 2.10–12

b. Ex 7.3 with Ex 8.15, 32; 2 Cor 2.15–16; Is 8.14; 1 Pt 2.7–8; Is 6.9–10 with Acts 28.26–27

7. As the providence of God doth in general reach to all creatures, so after a most special manner, it taketh care of his church, and disposeth all things to the good thereof.[c]

c. 1 Tm 4.10; Am 9.8–9; Rom 8.28; Is 43.3–5, 14

4. American edition: *upon.*

CHAPTER 6. OF THE FALL OF MAN, OF SIN,
AND OF THE PUNISHMENT THEREOF

1. Our first parents, being seduced by the subtilty and temptation of Satan, sinned, in eating the forbidden fruit.[a] This their sin God was pleased, according to his wise and holy counsel, to permit, having purposed to order it to his own glory.[b]

a. Gn 3.13; 2 Cor 11.3
b. Rom 11.32

2. By this sin they fell from their original righteousness and communion with God,[c] and so became dead in sin,[d] and wholly defiled in all the parts and faculties of soul and body.[e]

c. Gn 3.6–8; Eccl 7.29; Rom 3.23
d. Gn 2.17; Eph 2.1
e. Ti 1.15; Gn 6.5; Jer 17.9; Rom 3.10–19

3. They being the root of all mankind, the guilt of this sin was imputed,[f] and the same death in sin and corrupted nature conveyed, to all their posterity descending from them by ordinary generation.[g]

f. Gn 1.27–28 and Gn 2.16–17 and Acts 17.26 with Rom 5.12, 15–19, and 1 Cor 15.21–22, 49
g. Ps 51.5; Gn 5.3; Jb 14.4; Jb 15.14

4. From this original corruption, whereby we are utterly indisposed, disabled, and made opposite to all good,[h] and wholly inclined to all evil,[i] do proceed all actual transgressions.[k]

h. Rom 5.6; Rom 8.7; Rom 7.18; Col 1.21
i. Gn 6.5; Gn 8.21; Rom 3.10–12
k. Jas 1.14–15; Eph 2.2–3; Mt 15.19

5. This corruption of nature, during this life, doth remain in those that are regenerated;[l] and although it be, through Christ, pardoned and mortified, yet both itself and all the motions thereof are truly and properly sin.[m]

l. 1 Jn 1.8, 10; Rom 7.14, 17–18, 23; Jas 3.2; Prv 20.9; Eccl 7.20
m. Rom 7.5, 7–8, 25; Gal 5.17

6. Every sin, both original and actual, being a transgression of the righteous law of God, and contrary thereunto,[n] doth, in its own nature, bring guilt upon the sinner,[o] whereby he is bound over to the wrath of God,[p] and curse of the law,[q] and so made subject to death,[r] with all miseries spiritual,[s] temporal,[t] and eternal.[u]

n. 1 Jn 3.4
o. Rom 2.15; Rom 3.9, 19
p. Eph 2.3
q. Gal 3.10
r. Rom 6.23
s. Eph 4.18
t. Rom 8.20; Lam 3.39
u. Mt 25.41; 2 Thes 1.9

CHAPTER 7. OF GOD'S COVENANT WITH MAN

1. The distance between God and the creature is so great that although reasonable creatures do owe obedience unto him as their Creator, yet they could never have any fruition of him as their blessedness and reward, but by some voluntary condescension on God's part, which he hath been pleased to express by way of covenant.[a]

a. Is 40.13–17; Jb 9.32–33; 1 Sm 2.25; Ps 113.5–6; Ps 100.2–3; Jb 22.2–3; Jb 35.7–8; Lk 17.10; Acts 17.24–25

2. The first covenant made with man was a covenant of works,[b] wherein life was promised to Adam, and in him to his posterity,[c] upon condition of perfect and personal obedience.[d]

b. Gal 3.12
c. Rom 10.5; Rom 5.12–20
d. Gn 2.17; Gal 3.10

3. Man by his fall having made himself incapable of life by that covenant, the Lord was pleased to make a second,[e] commonly called the covenant of grace, wherein he freely offereth unto sinners life and salvation by Jesus Christ, requiring of them faith in him, that they may be saved,[f] and promising to give unto all those that are ordained unto life his Holy Spirit, to make them willing and able to believe.[g]

e. Gal 3.21; Rom 8.3; Rom 3.20–21; Gn 3.15; Is 42.6
f. Mk 16.15–16; Jn 3.16; Rom 10.6, 9; Gal 3.11
g. Ez 36.26–27; Jn 6.44–45

4. This covenant of grace is frequently set forth in Scripture by the name of a testament, in reference to the death of Jesus Christ the testator, and to the everlasting inheritance, with all things belonging to it, therein bequeathed.[h]

h. Heb 9.15–17; Heb 7.22; Lk 22.20; 1 Cor 11.25

5. This covenant was differently administered in the time of the law, and in the time of the gospel:[i] under the law, it was administered by promises, prophecies, sacrifices, circumcision, the paschal lamb, and other types and ordinances delivered to the people of the Jews, all foresignifying Christ to come,[k] which were, for that time, sufficient and efficacious, through the operation of the Spirit, to instruct and build up the elect in faith in the promised Messiah,[l] by whom they had full remission of sins, and eternal salvation; and is called, the Old Testament.[m]

i. 2 Cor 3.6–9
k. Heb 8–10; Rom 4.11; Col 2.11–12; 1 Cor 5.7
l. 1 Cor 10.1–4; Heb 11.13; Jn 8.56
m. Gal 3.7–9, 14

6. Under the gospel, when Christ, the substance,[n] was exhibited, the ordinances in which this covenant is dispensed are the preaching of the word, and the administration of the sacraments of baptism and the Lord's supper:[o] which, though fewer in number, and administered with more simplicity, and less outward glory,

yet, in them, it is held forth in more fullness, evidence, and spiritual efficacy,[p] to all nations, both Jews and Gentiles;[q] and is called the New Testament.[r] There are not therefore two covenants of grace, differing in substance, but one and the same, under various dispensations.[s]

n. Col 2.17

o. Mt 28.19–20; 1 Cor 11.23–25

p. Heb 12.22–28; Jer 31.33–34

q. Mt 28.19; Eph 2.15–19

r. Lk 22.20

s. Gal 3.14, 16; Rom 3.21–23, 30; Ps 32.1 with Rom 4.3, 6, 16–17, 23–24; Heb 13.8; Acts 15.11

CHAPTER 8. OF CHRIST THE MEDIATOR

1. It pleased God, in his eternal purpose, to choose and ordain the Lord Jesus, his only-begotten Son, to be the Mediator between God and man,[a] the Prophet,[b] Priest,[c] and King,[d] the Head and Savior of his church,[e] the Heir of all things,[f] and Judge of the world,[g] unto whom he did from all eternity give a people, to be his seed,[h] and to be by him in time redeemed, called, justified, sanctified, and glorified.[i]

a. Is 42.1; 1 Pt 19–20; Jn 3.16; 1 Tm 2.5

b. Acts 3.22

c. Heb 5.5, 6

d. Ps 2.6; Lk 1.33

e. Eph 5.23

f. Heb 1.2

g. Acts 17.31

h. Jn 17.6; Ps 22.30; Is 53.10

i. 1 Tm 2.6; Is 55.4–5; 1 Cor 1.30

2. The Son of God, the second person in the Trinity, being very and eternal God, of one substance and equal with the Father, did, when the fullness of time was come, take upon him man's nature,[k] with all the essential properties and common infirmities thereof, yet without sin,[l] being conceived by the power of the Holy Ghost, in the womb of the Virgin Mary, of her substance.[m] So that two whole, perfect, and distinct natures, the Godhead and the manhood, were inseparably joined together in one person, without conversion, composition, or confusion.[n] Which person is very God, and very man, yet one Christ, the only Mediator between God and man.[o]

k. Jn 1.1, 14; 1 Jn 5.20; Phil 2.6; Gal 4.4

l. Heb 2.14, 16–17; Heb 4.15

m. Lk 1.27, 31, 35; Gal 4.4

n. Lk 1.35; Col 2.9; Rom 9.5; 1 Pt 3.18; 1 Tm 3.16

o. Rom 1.3–4; 1 Tm 2.5

3. The Lord Jesus, in his human nature thus united to the divine, was sanc-

tified and anointed with the Holy Spirit, above measure,[p] having in him all the treasures of wisdom and knowledge,[q] in whom it pleased the Father that all fullness should dwell,[r] to the end that, being holy, harmless, undefiled, and full of grace and truth,[s] he might be thoroughly furnished to execute the office of a mediator and surety.[t] Which office he took not unto himself, but was thereunto called by his Father,[u] who put all power and judgment into his hand, and gave him commandment to execute the same.[w]

p. Ps 45.7; Jn 3.34
q. Col 2.3
r. Col 1.19
s. Heb 7.26; Jn 1.14
t. Acts 10.38; Heb 12.24; Heb 7.22
u. Heb 5.4–5
w. Jn 5.22, 27; Mt 28.18; Acts 2.36

4. This office the Lord Jesus did most willingly undertake;[x] which that he might discharge, he was made under the law,[y] and did perfectly fulfill it,[z] endured most grievous torments immediately in his soul,[a] and most painful sufferings in his body;[b] was crucified, and died;[c] was buried, and remained under the power of death; yet saw no corruption.[d] On the third day he arose from the dead,[e] with the same body in which he suffered,[f] with which also he ascended into heaven, and there sitteth at the right hand of his Father,[g] making intercession,[h] and shall return to judge men and angels at the end of the world.[i]

x. Ps 40.7–8 with Heb 10.5–10; Jn 10.18; Phil 2.8
y. Gal 4.4
z. Mt 3.15; Mt 5.17
a. Mt 26.37–38; Lk 22.44; Mt 27.46
b. Mt 26, 27
c. Phil 2.8
d. Acts 2.23–24, 27; Acts 13.37; Rom 6.9
e. 1 Cor 15.3–4
f. Jn 20.25, 27
g. Mk 16.19
h. Rom 8.34; Heb 9.24; Heb 7.25
i. Rom 14.9–10; Acts 1.11; Acts 10.42; Mt 13.40–42; Jude 6; 2 Pt 2.4

5. The Lord Jesus, by his perfect obedience, and sacrifice of himself, which he, through the eternal Spirit, once offered up unto God, hath fully satisfied the justice of his Father,[k] and purchased, not only reconciliation, but an everlasting inheritance in the kingdom of heaven, for all those whom the Father hath given unto him.[l]

k. Rom 5.19; Heb 9.14, 16; Heb 10.14; Eph 5.2; Rom 3.25–26
l. Dn 9.24, 26; Col 1.19–20; Eph 1.11, 14; Jn 17.2; Heb 9.12, 15

6. Although the work of redemption was not actually wrought by Christ till after his incarnation, yet the virtue, efficacy, and benefits thereof were communicated unto the elect in all ages successively from the beginning of the world, in and by those promises, types, and sacrifices, wherein he was revealed, and signified to be the seed of the woman which should bruise the serpent's head, and the Lamb slain from the beginning of the world, being yesterday and today the same, and forever.[m]

m. Gal 4.4–5; Gn 3.15; Rv 13.8; Heb 13.8

7. Christ, in the work of mediation, acteth according to both natures, by each nature doing that which is proper to itself;[n] yet, by reason of the unity of the person, that which is proper to one nature, is sometimes in Scripture attributed to the person denominated by the other nature.[o]

n. Heb 9.14; 1 Pt 3.18

o. Acts 20.28; Jn 3.13; 1 Jn 3.16

8. To all those for whom Christ hath purchased redemption, he doth certainly and effectually apply and communicate the same,[p] making intercession for them,[q] and revealing unto them, in and by the word, the mysteries of salvation,[r] effectually persuading them by his Spirit to believe and obey, and governing their hearts by his word and Spirit,[s] overcoming all their enemies by his almighty power and wisdom, in such manner, and ways, as are most consonant to his wonderful and unsearchable dispensation.[t]

p. Jn 6.37, 39; Jn 10.15–16

q. 1 Jn 2.1–2; Rom 8.34

r. Jn 15.13, 15; Eph 1.7–9; Jn 17.6

s. Jn 14.26; Heb 12.2; 2 Cor 4.13; Rom 8.9, 14; Rom 15.18–19; Jn 17.17

t. Ps 110.1; 1 Cor 15.25–26; Mal 4.2, 3; Col 2.15

CHAPTER 9. OF FREE WILL

1. God hath endued the will of man with that natural liberty, that[5] is neither forced, nor by any absolute necessity of nature determined to do[6] good or evil.[a]

a. Mt 17.12; Jas 1.14; Dt 30.19

2. Man, in his state of innocency, had freedom and power to will and to do that which was[7] good, and well pleasing to God,[b] but yet, mutably, so that he might fall from it.[c]

b. Eccl 7.29; Gn 1.26

5. American edition inserts *it* here.

6. American edition omits *do*.

7. American edition: *is*.

c. Gn 2.16–17; Gn 3.6

3. Man, by his fall into a state of sin, hath wholly lost all ability of will to any spiritual good accompanying salvation;[d] so as, a natural man, being altogether averse from that good,[e] and dead in sin,[f] is not able, by his own strength, to convert himself, or to prepare himself thereunto.[g]

d. Rom 5.6; Rom 8.7; Jn 15.5
e. Rom 3.10, 12
f. Eph 2.1, 5; Col 2.13
g. Jn 6.44, 65; Eph 2.2–5; 1 Cor 2.14; Ti 3.3–5

4. When God converts a sinner, and translates him into the state of grace, he freeth him from his natural bondage under sin,[h] and, by his grace alone, enables him freely to will and to do that which is spiritually good,[i] yet so, as that by reason of his remaining corruption, he doth not perfectly, nor only, will that which is good, but doth also will that which is evil.[k]

h. Col 1.13; Jn 8.34, 36
i. Phil 2.13; Rom 6.18, 22
k. Gal 5.17; Rom 7.15, 18–19, 21, 23

5. The will of man is made perfectly and immutably free to do good alone, in the state of glory only.[l]

l. Eph 4.13; Heb 12.23; 1 Jn 3.2; Jude 24

CHAPTER 10. OF EFFECTUAL CALLING

1. All those whom God hath predestinated unto life, and those only, he is pleased in his appointed and accepted time effectually to call,[a] by his word and Spirit,[b] out of that state of sin and death, in which they are by nature, to grace and salvation by Jesus Christ:[c] enlightening their minds spiritually and savingly to understand the things of God,[d] taking away their heart of stone, and giving unto them a heart of flesh;[e] renewing their wills, and, by his almighty power determining them to that which is good,[f] and effectually drawing them to Jesus Christ;[g] yet so, as they come most freely, being made willing by his grace.[h]

a. Rom 8.30; Rom 11.7; Eph 1.10, 11
b. 2 Thes 2.13–14; 2 Cor 3.3, 6
c. Rom 8.2; Eph 2.1–5; 2 Tm 1.9–10
d. Acts 26.18; 1 Cor 2.10, 12; Eph 1.17–18
e. Ez 36.26
f. Ez 11.19; Phil 2.13; Dt 30.6; Ez 36.27
g. Eph 1.19; Jn 6.44–45
h. Sg 1.4; Ps 110.3; Jn 6.37; Rom 6.16–18

2. This effectual call is of God's free and special grace alone, not from anything at all foreseen in man,[i] who is altogether passive therein, until being quickened

and renewed by the Holy Spirit,[k] he is thereby enabled to answer this call, and to embrace the grace offered and conveyed in it.[l]

i. 2 Tm 1.9; Ti 3.4–5; Eph 2.4–5, 8–9; Rom 9.11

k. 1 Cor 2.14; Rom 8.7; Eph 2.5

l. Jn 6.37; Ez 36.27; Jn 5.25

    3. Elect infants, dying in infancy, are regenerated, and saved by Christ through the Spirit,[m] who worketh when, and where, and how he pleaseth;[n] so also, are all other elect persons who are uncapable of being outwardly called by the ministry of the word.[o]

m. Lk 18.15–16; Acts 2.38–39; Jn 3.3, 5; 1 Jn 5.12; Rom 8.9

n. Jn 3.8

o. 1 Jn 5.12; Acts 4.12

    4. Others, not elected, although they may be called by the ministry of the word,[p] and may have some common operations of the Spirit,[q] yet they never truly come unto[8] Christ, and therefore can not be saved;[r] much less can men, not professing the Christian religion, be saved in any other way whatsoever, be they never so diligent to frame their lives according to the light of nature, and the law of that religion they do profess.[s] And to assert and maintain that they may, is very pernicious, and to be detested.[t] [9]

p. Mt 22.14

q. Mt 7.22; Mt 13.20–21; Heb 6.4–5

r. Jn 6.64–66; Jn 8.24

s. Acts 4.12; Jn 14.6; Eph 2.12; Jn 4.22; Jn 17.3

t. 2 Jn 9–11; 1 Cor 16.22; Gal 1.6–8

CHAPTER 11. OF JUSTIFICATION

1. Those whom God effectually calleth, he also freely justifieth,[a] not by infusing righteousness into them, but by pardoning their sins, and by accounting and accepting their persons as righteous, not for anything wrought in them, or done by them, but for Christ's sake alone; nor[10] by imputing faith itself, the act of believing, or any other evangelical obedience to them, as their righteousness, but by imputing the obedience and satisfaction of Christ unto them,[b] they receiving and resting on him and his righteousness by faith—which faith they have not of themselves, it is the gift of God.[c]

8. American edition: *to.*

9. American edition replaces this last phrase with: *is without warrant of the word of God.*

10. American edition: *not.*

a. Rom 8.30; Rom 3.24

b. Rom 4.5–8; 2 Cor 5.19, 21; Rom 3.22, 24–25, 27–28; Ti 3.5, 7; Eph 1.7; Jer 23.6; 1 Cor 1.30, 31; Rom 5.17–19

c. Acts 10.43; Gal 2.16; Phil 3.19; Acts 13.38–39; Eph 2.7–8

2. Faith, thus receiving and resting on Christ and his righteousness, is the alone instrument of justification;[d] yet is it not alone in the person justified, but is ever accompanied with all other saving graces, and is no dead faith, but worketh by love.[e]

d. Jn 1.12; Rom 3.28; Rom 5.1

e. Jas 2.17, 22, 26; Gal 5.6

3. Christ, by his obedience and death, did fully discharge the debt of all those that are thus justified, and did make a proper, real, and full satisfaction to his Father's justice in their behalf.[f] Yet, inasmuch as he was given by the Father for them,[g] and his obedience and satisfaction accepted in their stead,[h] and both freely, not for anything in them, their justification is only of free grace,[i] that both the exact justice, and rich grace of God, might be glorified in the justification of sinners.[k]

f. Rom 5.8–10, 19; 1 Tm 2.5, 6; Heb 10.10, 14; Dn 9.24, 26; Is 53.4–6, 10–12

g. Rom 8.32

h. 2 Cor 5.21; Mt 3.17; Eph 5.2

i. Rom 3.24; Eph 1.7

k. Rom 3.26; Eph 2.7

4. God did, from all eternity, decree to justify all the elect,[l] and Christ did, in the fullness of time, die for their sins, and rise again for their justification;[m] nevertheless, they are not justified, until the Holy Spirit doth, in due time, actually apply Christ unto them.[n]

l. Gal 3.8; 1 Pt 1.2, 19–20; Rom 8.30

m. Gal 4.4; 1 Tm 2.6; Rom 4.25

n. Col 1.21–22; Gal 2.16; Ti 3.3–7

5. God doth continue to forgive the sins of those that are justified.[o] And although they can never fall from the state of justification,[p] yet they may, by their sins, fall under God's fatherly displeasure, and not have the light of his countenance restored unto them, until they humble themselves, confess their sins, beg pardon, and renew their faith and repentance.[q]

o. Mt 6.12; 1 Jn 1.7, 9; 1 Jn 2.1–2

p. Lk 22.32; Jn 10.28; Heb 10.14

q. Ps 89.31–33; Ps 51.7–12; Ps 32.5; Mt 26.75; 1 Cor 11.30, 32; Lk 1.20

6. The justification of believers under the old testament was, in all these respects, one and the same with the justification of believers under the new testament.[r]

r. Gal 3.9, 13–14; Rom 4.22–24; Heb 13.8

CHAPTER 12. OF ADOPTION

All those that are justified, God vouchsafeth, in and for his only Son Jesus Christ, to make partakers of the grace of adoption:[a] by which they are taken into the number, and enjoy the liberties and privileges of the children of God,[b] have his name put upon them,[c] receive the spirit of adoption,[d] have access to the throne of grace with boldness,[e] are enabled to cry, Abba, Father,[f] are pitied,[g] protected,[h] provided for,[i] and chastened by him as by a father;[k] yet never cast off,[l] but sealed to the day of redemption,[m] and inherit the promises,[n] as heirs of everlasting salvation.[o]

a. Eph 1.5
b. Gal 4.4–5; Rom 8.17; Jn 1.12
c. Jer 14.9; 2 Cor 6.18; Rv 3.12
d. Rom 8.15
e. Eph 3.12; Rom 5.2
f. Gal 4.6
g. Ps 103.13
h. Prv 14.26
i. Mt 6.30, 32; 1 Pt 5.7
k. Heb 12.6
l. Lam 3.31
m. Eph 4.30
n. Heb 6.12
o. 1 Pt 1.3–4; Heb 1.14

CHAPTER 13. OF SANCTIFICATION

1. They who are once effectually called and regenerated, having a new heart and a new spirit created in them, are further sanctified, really and personally, through the virtue of Christ's death and resurrection,[a] by his word and Spirit dwelling in them:[b] the dominion of the whole body of sin is destroyed,[c] and the several lusts thereof are more and more weakened and mortified;[d] and they more and more quickened and strengthened in all saving graces,[e] to the practice of true holiness, without which no man shall see the Lord.[f]

a. 1 Cor 6.11; Acts 20.32; Phil 3.10; Rom 6.5–6
b. Jn 17.17; Eph 5.26; 2 Thes 2.13
c. Rom 6.6, 14
d. Gal 5.24; Rom 8.13
e. Col 1.11; Eph 3.16–19
f. 2 Cor 7.1; Heb 12.14

2. This sanctification is throughout, in the whole man,[g] yet imperfect in this life, there abiding still some remnants of corruption in every part;[h] whence ariseth a continual and irreconcilable war, the flesh lusting against the Spirit, and the Spirit against the flesh.[i]

g. 1 Thes 5.23
h. 1 Jn 1.10; Rom 7.18, 23; Phil 3.12
i. Gal 5.17; 1 Pt 2.11

3. In which war, although the remaining corruption, for a time, may much prevail,[k] yet through the continual supply of strength from the sanctifying Spirit of Christ, the regenerate part doth overcome;[l] and so, the saints grow in grace,[m] perfecting holiness in the fear of God.[n]

k. Rom 7.23
l. Rom 6.14; 1 Jn 5.4; Eph 4.15–16
m. 2 Pt 3.18; 2 Cor 3.18
n. 2 Cor 7.1

CHAPTER 14. OF SAVING FAITH

1. The grace of faith, whereby the elect are enabled to believe to the saving of their souls,[a] is the work of the Spirit of Christ in their hearts,[b] and is ordinarily wrought by the ministry of the word,[c] by which also, and by the administration of the sacraments, and prayer, it is increased and strengthened.[d]

a. Heb 10.39
b. 2 Cor 4.13; Eph 1.17–19; Eph 2.8
c. Rom 10.14, 17
d. 1 Pt 2.2; Acts 20.32; Rom 4.11; Lk 17.5; Rom 1.16–17

2. By this faith, a Christian believeth to be true whatsoever is revealed in the word, for the authority of God himself speaking therein,[e] and acteth differently upon that which each particular passage thereof containeth, yielding obedience to the commands,[f] trembling at the threatenings,[g] and embracing the promises of God for this life, and that which is to come.[h] But the principal acts of saving faith are accepting, receiving, and resting upon Christ alone for justification, sanctification, and eternal life, by virtue of the covenant of grace.[i]

e. Jn 4.42; 1 Thes 2.13; 1 Jn 5.10; Acts 24.14
f. Rom 16.26
g. Is 66.2
h. Heb 11.13; 1 Tm 4.8
i. Jn 1.12; Acts 16.31; Gal 2.20; Acts 15.11

3. This faith is different in degrees, weak or strong;[k] may be often and many ways assailed, and weakened, but gets the victory;[l] growing up in many to the attainment of a full assurance through Christ,[m] who is both the author and finisher of our faith.[n]

k. Heb 5.13–14; Rom 4.19–20; Mt 6.30; Mt 8.10
l. Lk 22.31–32; Eph 6.16; 1 Jn 5.4–5
m. Heb 6.11–12; Heb 10.22; Col 2.2
n. Heb 12.2

CHAPTER 15. OF REPENTANCE UNTO LIFE

1. Repentance unto life is an evangelical grace,[a] the doctrine whereof is to be preached by every minister of the gospel, as well as that of faith in Christ.[b]

a. Zec 12.10; Acts 11.18

b. Lk 24.47; Mk 1.15; Acts 20.21

2. By it, a sinner, out of the sight and sense not only of the danger, but also of the filthiness and odiousness of his sins, as contrary to the holy nature and righteous law of God, and upon the apprehension of his mercy in Christ to such as are penitent, so grieves for, and hates his sins, as to turn from them all unto God,[c] purposing and endeavoring to walk with him in all the ways of his commandments.[d]

c. Ez 18.30–31; Ez 36.31; Is 30.22; Ps 51.4; Jer 31.18–19; Jl 2.12–13; Am 5.15; Ps 119.128; 2 Cor 7.11

d. Ps 119.6, 59, 106; Lk 1.6; 2 Kgs 23.25

3. Although repentance be not to be rested in, as any satisfaction for sin, or any cause of the pardon thereof,[e] which is the act of God's free grace in Christ,[f] yet is it of such necessity to all sinners, that none may expect pardon without it.[g]

e. Ez 36.31–32; Ez 16.61–63

f. Hos 14.2, 4; Rom 3.24; Eph 1.7

g. Lk 13.3, 5; Acts 17.30–31

4. As there is no sin so small but it deserves damnation,[h] so there is no sin so great that it can bring damnation upon those who truly repent.[i]

h. Rom 6.23; Rom 5.12; Mt 12.36

i. Is 55.7; Rom 8.1; Is 1.16, 18

5. Men ought not to content themselves with a general repentance, but it is every man's duty to endeavor to repent of his particular sins, particularly.[k]

k. Ps 19.13; Lk 19.8; 1 Tm 1.13, 15

6. As every man is bound to make private confession of his sins to God, praying for the pardon thereof,[l] upon which, and the forsaking of them, he shall find mercy,[m] so, he that scandalizeth his brother, or the church of Christ, ought to be willing, by a private or public confession, and sorrow for his sin, to declare his repentance to those that are offended,[n] who are thereupon to be reconciled to him, and in love to receive him.[o]

l. Ps 51.4–5, 7, 9, 14; Ps 32.5, 6

m. Prv 28.13; 1 Jn 1.9

n. Jas 5.16; Lk 17.3–4; Jos 7.19; Ps 51

o. 2 Cor 2.8

CHAPTER 16. OF GOOD WORKS

1. Good works are only such as God hath commanded in his holy word,[a] and not such as, without the warrant thereof, are devised by men, out of blind zeal, or upon any pretence of good intention.[b]

a. Mi 6.8; Rom 12.2; Heb 13.21

b. Mt 15.9; Is 29.13; 1 Pt 1.18; Rom 10.2; Jn 16.2; 1 Sm 15.21-23

2. These good works, done in obedience to God's commandments, are the fruits and evidences of a true and lively faith;[c] and by them believers manifest their thankfulness,[d] strengthen their assurance,[e] edify their brethren,[f] adorn the profession of the gospel,[g] stop the mouths of the adversaries,[h] and glorify God,[i] whose workmanship they are, created in Christ Jesus thereunto,[k] that, having their fruit unto holiness, they may have the end, eternal life.[l]

c. Jas 2.18, 22

d. Ps 116.12-13; 1 Pt 2.9

e. 1 Jn 2.3, 5; 2 Pt 1.5-10

f. 2 Cor 9.2; Mt 5.16

g. Ti 2.5, 9-12; 1 Tm 6.1

h. 1 Pt 2.15

i. 1 Pt 2.12; Phil 1.11; Jn 15.8

k. Eph 2.10

l. Rom 6.22

3. Their ability to do good works is not at all of themselves, but wholly from the Spirit of Christ.[m] And that they may be enabled thereunto, besides the graces they have already received, there is required an actual influence of the same Holy Spirit, to work in them to will and to do of his good pleasure;[n] yet are they not hereupon to grow negligent, as if they were not bound to perform any duty, unless upon a special motion of the Spirit, but they ought to be diligent in stirring up the grace of God that is in them.[o]

m. Jn 15.4-5; Ez 36.26-27

n. Phil 2.13; Phil 4.13; 2 Cor 3.5

o. Phil 2.12; Heb 6.11-12; 2 Pt 1.3, 5, 10-11; Is 64.7; 2 Tim 1.6; Acts 26.6-7; Jude 20-21

4. They, who in their obedience attain to the greatest height which is possible in this life, are so far from being able to supererogate, and to do more than God requires, as[11] that they fall short of much which in duty they are bound to do.[p]

p. Lk 17.10; Neh 13.22; Jb 9.2-3; Gal 5.17

5. We cannot, by our best works, merit pardon of sin, or eternal life at the hand of God, by reason of the great disproportion that is between them and the glory to come, and the infinite distance that is between us and God, whom, by them,

11. American edition omits *as*.

we can neither profit, nor satisfy for the debt of our former sins,[q] but when we have done all we can, we have done but our duty, and are unprofitable servants;[r] and because, as they are good, they proceed from his Spirit,[s] and as they are wrought by us, they are defiled, and mixed with so much weakness and imperfection that they cannot endure the severity of God's judgment.[t]

q. Rom 3.20; Rom 4.2, 4, 6; Eph 2.8–9; Ti 3.5–7; Rom 8.18; Ps 16.2; Jb 22.2–3; Jb 35.7, 8
r. Lk 17.10
s. Gal 5.22–23
t. Is 64.6; Gal 5.17; Rom 7.15, 18; Ps 143.2; Ps 130.3

6. Yet notwithstanding, the persons of believers being accepted through Christ, their good works also are accepted in him,[u] not as though they were in this life wholly unblamable and unreprovable in God's sight,[w] but that he, looking upon them in his Son, is pleased to accept and reward that which is sincere, although accompanied with many weaknesses and imperfections.[x]

u. Eph 1.6; 1 Pt 2.5; Ex 28.38; Gn 4.4 with Heb 11.4
w. Jb 9.20; Ps 143.2
x. Heb 13.20–21; 2 Cor 8.12; Heb 6.10; Mt 25.21, 23

7. Works done by unregenerate men, although, for the matter of them, they may be things which God commands, and[12] of good use both to themselves and others,[y] yet, because they proceed not from a heart purified by faith,[z] nor are done in a right manner according to the word,[a] nor to a right end, the glory of God,[b] they are therefore sinful, and can not please God, or make a man meet to receive grace from God.[c] And yet, their neglect of them is more sinful, and displeasing unto God.[d]

y. 2 Kgs 10.30–31; 1 Kgs 21.27, 29; Phil 1.15–16, 18
z. Gn 4.5 with Heb 11.4; Heb 11.6
a. 1 Cor 13.3; Is 1.12
b. Mt 6.2, 5, 16
c. Hg 2.14; Ti 1.15; Am 5.22–23; Hos 1.4; Rom 9.16; Ti 3.5
d. Ps 14.4; Ps 36.3; Jb 21.14–15; Mt 25.41–43, 45; Mt 23.23

CHAPTER 17. OF THE PERSEVERANCE OF THE SAINTS

1. They whom God hath accepted in his Beloved, effectually called, and sanctified by his Spirit, can neither totally, nor finally, fall away from the state of grace, but shall certainly persevere therein to the end, and be eternally saved.[a]

a. Phil 1.6; 2 Pt 1.10; Jn 10.28–29; 1 Jn 3.9; 1 Pt 1.5, 9

2. This perseverance of the saints depends not upon their own free will, but upon the immutability of the decree of election, flowing from the free and unchangeable love of God the Father,[b] upon the efficacy of the merit and intercession

12. See *Book of Confessions* 1996, 143, for a slightly different rendering of this section.

of Jesus Christ,[c] the abiding of the Spirit, and of the seed of God within them,[d] and the nature of the covenant of grace,[e] from all which ariseth also the certainty and infallibility thereof.[f]

b. 2 Tm 2.18–19; Jer 31.3

c. Heb 10.10, 14; Heb 13.20–21; Heb 9.12–15; Rom 8.33–39; Jn 17.11, 24; Lk 22.32; Heb 7.25

d. Jn 14.16–17; 1 Jn 2.27; 1 Jn 3.9

e. Jer 32.40

f. Jn 10.28; 2 Thes 3.3; 1 Jn 2.19

3. Nevertheless, they may, through the temptations of Satan and of the world, the prevalency of corruption remaining in them, and the neglect of the means of their preservation, fall into grievous sins,[g] and, for a time, continue therein:[h] whereby they incur God's displeasure,[i] and grieve his Holy Spirit,[k] come to be deprived of some measure of their graces and comforts,[l] have their hearts hardened,[m] and their consciences wounded,[n] hurt and scandalize others,[o] and bring temporal judgments upon themselves.[p]

g. Mt 26.70, 72, 74

h. Ps 51 title and 14

i. Is 64.5, 7, 9; 2 Sm 11.27

k. Eph 4.30

l. Ps 51.8, 10, 12; Rv 2.4; Sg 5.2–4, 6

m. Is 63.17; Mk 6.52; Mk 16.14

n. Ps 32.3–4; Ps 51.8

o. 2 Sm 12.14

p. Ps 89.31–32; 1 Cor 11.32

CHAPTER 18. OF THE ASSURANCE OF GRACE AND SALVATION

1. Although hypocrites and other unregenerate men may vainly deceive themselves with false hopes, and carnal presumptions of being in the favor of God, and estate of salvation,[a] which hope of theirs shall perish,[b] yet such as truly believe in the Lord Jesus, and love him in sincerity, endeavoring to walk in all good conscience before him, may, in this life, be certainly assured that they are in a state of grace,[c] and may rejoice in the hope of the glory of God, which hope shall never make them ashamed.[d]

a. Jb 8.13–14; Mi 3.11; Dt 29.19; Jn 8.41

b. Mt 7.22–23

c. 1 Jn 2.3; 1 Jn 3.14, 18–19, 21, 24; 1 Jn 5.13

d. Rom 5.2, 5

2. This certainty is not a bare conjectural and probable persuasion, grounded upon a fallible hope,[e] but an infallible assurance of faith, founded upon the divine truth of the promises of salvation,[f] the inward evidence of those graces unto which these promises are made,[g] the testimony of the Spirit of adoption wit-

nessing with our spirits that we are the children of God:[h] which Spirit is the earnest of our inheritance, whereby we are sealed to the day of redemption.[i]

e. Heb 6.11, 19
f. Heb 6.17, 18
g. 2 Pt 1.4, 5, 10–11; 1 Jn 2.3; 1 Jn 3.14; 2 Cor 1.12
h. Rom 8.15–16
i. Eph 1.13–14; Eph 4.30; 2 Cor 1.21, 22

3. This infallible assurance doth not so belong to the essence of faith, but that a true believer may wait long, and conflict with many difficulties before he be partaker of it;[k] yet, being enabled by the Spirit to know the things which are freely given him of God, he may without extraordinary revelation, in the right use of ordinary means, attain thereunto.[l] And therefore it is the duty of every one to give all diligence to make his calling and election sure,[m] that thereby his heart may be enlarged in peace and joy in the Holy Ghost, in love and thankfulness to God, and in strength and cheerfulness in the duties of obedience, the proper fruits of this assurance;[n] so far is it from inclining men to looseness.[o]

k. 1 Jn 5.13; Is 50.10; Mk 9.24; Ps 88; Ps 77.1–12
l. 1 Cor 2.12; 1 Jn 4.13; Heb 6.11–12; Eph 3.17–19
m. 2 Pt 1.10
n. Rom 5.1–2, 5; Rom 14.17; Rom 15.13; Eph 1.3–4; Ps 4.6–7; Ps 119.32
o. 1 Jn 2.1–2; Rom 6.1–2; Ti 2.11–12, 14; 2 Cor 7.1; Rom 8.1, 12; 1 Jn 3.2–3; Ps 130.4; 1 Jn 1.6–7

4. True believers may have the assurance of their salvation diverse ways shaken, diminished, and intermitted: as, by negligence in preserving of it; by falling into some special sin, which woundeth the conscience and grieveth the Spirit; by some sudden or vehement temptation; by God's withdrawing the light of his countenance, and suffering even such as fear him to walk in darkness and to have no light.[p] Yet are they never so utterly destitute of that seed of God, and life of faith, that love of Christ and the brethren, that sincerity of heart, and conscience of duty, out of which, by the operation of the Spirit, this assurance may, in due time, be revived,[q] and by the which, in the mean time, they are supported from utter despair.[r]

p. Sg 5.2–3, 6; Ps 51.8, 12, 14; Eph 4.30–31; Ps 77.1–10; Mt 26.69–72; Ps 31.22; Ps 88; Is 50.10
q. 1 Jn 3.9; Lk 22.32; Jb 13.15; Ps 73.15; Ps 51.8, 12; Is 50.10
r. Mi 7.7–9; Jer 32.40; Is 54.7, 8–10; Ps 22.1; Ps 88

CHAPTER 19. OF THE LAW OF GOD

1. God gave to Adam a law, as a covenant of works, by which he bound him and all his posterity to personal, entire, exact, and perpetual obedience, promised life upon the fulfilling, and threatened death upon the breach of it, and endued him with power and ability to keep it.[a]

a. Gn 1.26–27 with Gn 2.17; Rom 2.14–15; Rom 10.5; Rom 5.12, 19; Gal 3.10, 12; Eccl 7.29; Jb 28.28

2. This law, after his fall, continued to be a perfect rule of righteousness, and, as such, was delivered by God upon Mount Sinai, in ten commandments, and written in two tables:[b] the four first commandments containing our duty towards God; and the other six our duty to man.[c]

b. Jas 1.25; Jas 2.8, 10–12; Rom 13.8–9; Dt 5.32; Dt 10.4; Ex 34.1

c. Mt 22.37–40

3. Beside this law, commonly called moral, God was pleased to give to the people of Israel, as a church under age, ceremonial laws, containing several typical ordinances, partly of worship, prefiguring Christ, his graces, actions, sufferings, and benefits,[d] and partly holding forth diverse instructions of moral duties.[e] All which ceremonial laws are now abrogated, under the New Testament.[f]

d. Heb 9; Heb 10.1; Gal 4.1–3; Col 2.17

e. 1 Cor 5.7; 2 Cor 6.17; Jude 23

f. Col 2.14, 16–17; Dn 9.27; Eph 2.15–16

4. To them also, as a body politic, he gave sundry judicial laws, which expired together with the state of that people, not obliging any other now, further than the general equity thereof may require.[g]

g. Ex 21; Ex 22.1–29; Gn 49.10 with 1 Pt 2.13–14; Mt 5.17, 38–39; 1 Cor 9.8–10

5. The moral law doth for ever bind all, as well justified persons as others, to the obedience thereof,[h] and that, not only in regard of the matter contained in it, but also in respect of the authority of God the Creator, who gave it;[i] neither doth Christ, in the gospel, any way dissolve, but much strengthen this obligation.[k]

h. Rom 13.8–10; Eph 6.2; 1 Jn 2.34, 7, 8

i. Jas 2.10, 11

k. Mt 5.17–19; Jas 2.8; Rom 3.31

6. Although true believers be not under the law, as a covenant of works, to be thereby justified, or condemned,[l] yet is it of great use to them, as well as to others, in that, as a rule of life informing them of the will of God, and their duty, it directs, and binds them to walk accordingly,[m] discovering also the sinful pollutions of their nature, hearts, and lives,[n] so as, examining themselves thereby, they may come to further conviction of, humiliation for, and hatred against sin,[o] together with a clearer sight of the need they have of Christ, and the perfection of his obedience.[p] It is likewise of use to the regenerate, to restrain their corruptions, in that it forbids sin;[q] and the threatenings of it serve to show what even their sins deserve, and what afflictions, in this life, they may expect for them, although freed from the curse thereof threatened in the law.[r] The promises of it, in like manner, show them God's approbation of obedience, and what blessings they may expect upon the performance thereof,[s] although not as due to them by the law, as a covenant of works.[t] So as, a man's doing good, and refraining from evil, because the law encourageth

to the one and deterreth from the other, is no evidence of his being under the law, and not under grace.[u]

l. Rom 6.14; Gal 2.16; Gal 3.13; Gal 4.4, 5; Acts 13.39; Rom 8.1

m. Rom 7.12, 22, 25; Ps 119.4–6; 1 Cor 7.19; Gal 5.14, 16, 18–23

n. Rom 7.7; Rom 3.20

o. Jas 1.23–25; Rom 7.9, 14, 24

p. Gal 3.24; Rom 7.24, 25; Rom 8.3, 4

q. Jas 2.11; Ps 119.101, 104, 128

r. Ezr 9.13, 14; Ps 89.30–34

s. Lv 26.1–14 with 2 Cor 6.16; Eph 6.2, 3; Ps 37.11 with Mt 5.5; Ps 19.11

t. Gal 2.16; Lk 17.10

u. Rom 6.12, 14; 1 Pt 3.8–12 with Ps 34.12–16; Heb 12.28, 29

7. Neither are the forementioned uses of the law contrary to the grace of the gospel, but do sweetly comply with it,[w] the Spirit of Christ subduing and enabling the will of man to do that, freely and cheerfully, which the will of God, revealed in the law, requireth to be done.[x]

w. Gal 3.21

x. Ez 36.27; Heb 8.10 with Jer 31.33

CHAPTER 20. OF CHRISTIAN LIBERTY, AND LIBERTY OF CONSCIENCE

1. The liberty which Christ hath purchased for believers under the gospel consists in their freedom from the guilt of sin, and condemning wrath of God, the curse of the moral law,[a] and, in their being delivered from this present evil world, bondage to Satan, and dominion of sin,[b] from the evil of afflictions, the sting of death, the victory of the grave, and everlasting damnation,[c] as also, in their free access to God,[d] and their yielding obedience unto him, not out of slavish fear, but a childlike love and [13] willing mind.[e] All which were common also to believers under the law.[f] But, under the new testament, the liberty of Christians is further enlarged, in their freedom from the yoke of the ceremonial law, to which the Jewish church was subjected,[g] and in greater boldness of access to the throne of grace,[h] and in fuller communications of the free Spirit of God, than believers under the law did ordinarily partake of.[i]

a. Ti 2.14; 1 Thes 1.10; Gal 3.13

b. Gal 1.4; Col 1.13; Acts 26.18; Rom 6.14

c. Rom 8.28; Ps 119.71; 1 Cor 15.54–57; Rom 8.1

d. Rom 5.1, 2

e. Rom 8.14–15; 1 Jn 4.18

f. Gal 3.9, 14

13. American edition inserts *a* after *and*.

g. Gal 4.1–3, 6–7; Gal 5.1; Acts 15.10–11
h. Heb 4.14, 16; Heb 10.19–22
i. Jn 7.38–39; 2 Cor 3.13, 17–18

2. God alone is Lord of the conscience,[k] and hath left it free from the doctrines and commandments of men, which are in any thing contrary to his word, or beside it, in matters of faith or worship.[l] So that, to believe such doctrines, or to obey such commands,[14] out of conscience,[m] is to betray true liberty of conscience; and the requiring of[15] an implicit faith, and an absolute and blind obedience is to destroy liberty of conscience, and reason also.[n]

k. Jas 4.12; Rom 14.4
l. Acts 4.19; Acts 5.29; 1 Cor 7.23; Mt 23.8–10; 2 Cor 1.24; Mt 15.9
m. Col 2.20, 22–23; Gal 1.10; Gal 2.4–5; Gal 5.1
n. Rom 10.17; Rom 14.23; Is 8.20; Acts 17.11; Jn 4.22; Hos 5.11; Rv 13.12, 16–17; Jer 8.9

3. They who, upon pretense of Christian liberty, do practice any sin, or cherish any lust, do thereby destroy the end of Christian liberty, which is, that being delivered out of the hands of our enemies, we might serve the Lord, without fear, in holiness and righteousness before him, all the days of our life.[o]

o. Gal 5.13; 1 Pt 2.16; 2 Pt 2.19; Jn 8.34; Lk 1.74–75

4. And because the power[16] which God hath ordained, and the liberty which Christ hath purchased, are not intended by God to destroy, but mutually to uphold and preserve one another, they who, upon pretense of Christian liberty, shall oppose any lawful power, or the lawful exercise of it, whether it be civil or ecclesiastical, resist the ordinance of God.[p] And, for their publishing of such opinions, or maintaining of such practices, as are contrary to the light of nature, or to the known principles of Christianity, whether concerning faith, worship, or conversation, or, to the power of godliness, or, such erroneous opinions or practices, as either in their own nature, or in the manner of publishing or maintaining them, are destructive to the external peace and order which Christ hath established in the church, they may lawfully be called to account, and proceeded against by the censures of the church,[q] and by the power of the civil magistrate.[r] [17]

p. Mt 12.25; 1 Pt 2.13–14, 16; Rom 13.1–8; Heb 13.17
q. Rom 1.32 with 1 Cor 5.1, 5, 11, 13; 2 Jn 10–11 and 2 Thes 3.14 and 1 Tm 6.3–5 and Ti 1.10–11, 13 and Ti 3.10 with Mt 18.15–17; 1 Tm 1.19–20; Rv 2.2, 14–15, 20; Rv 3.9
r. Dt 13.6–12; Rom 13.3, 4 with 2 Jn 10–11; Ezr 7.23, 25–28; Rv 17.12, 16–17; Neh 13.15, 17, 21–22, 25, 30; 2 Kgs 23.5, 6, 9, 20–21; 2 Chr 34.33; 2 Chr 15.12–13, 16; Dn 3.29; 1 Tm 2.2; Is 49.23; Zec 13.2, 3

14. American edition: *commandments.*
15. American edition omits *the* and *of.*
16. American edition: *powers.*
17. American edition omits *and by the power of the civil magistrate.*

CHAPTER 21. OF RELIGIOUS WORSHIP
AND THE SABBATH-DAY

1. The light of nature showeth that there is a God, who hath lordship and sovereignty over all, is good, and doth good unto all, and is therefore to be feared, loved, praised, called upon, trusted in, and served, with all the heart, and with all the soul, and with all the might.[a] But the acceptable way of worshiping the true God is instituted by himself, and so limited to[18] his own revealed will, that he may not be worshiped according to the imaginations and devices of men, or the suggestions of Satan, under any visible representations,[19] or any other way not prescribed in the Holy Scripture.[b]

a. Rom 1.20; Acts 17.24; Ps 119.68; Jer 10.7; Ps 31.23; Ps 18.3; Rom 10.12; Ps 62.8; Jos 24.14; Mk 12.33
b. Dt 12.32; Mt 15.9; Acts 17.25; Mt 4.9-10; Dt 4.15-20; Ex 20.4-6; Col 2.23

2. Religious worship is to be given to God, the Father, Son, and Holy Ghost; and to him alone,[c] not to angels, saints, or any other creature,[d] and since the fall, not without a mediator, nor in the mediation of any other but of Christ alone.[e]

c. Mt 4.10 with Jn 5.23 and 2 Cor 13.14
d. Col 2.18; Rv 19.10; Rom 1.25
e. Jn 14.6; 1 Tm 2.5; Eph 2.18; Col 3.17

3. Prayer, with thanksgiving, being one special part of religious worship,[f] is by God required of all men.[g] And that it may be accepted, it is to be made in the name of the Son,[h] by the help of his Spirit,[i] according to his will,[k] with understanding, reverence, humility, fervency, faith, love, and perseverance[l]—and, if vocal, in a known tongue.[m]

f. Phil 4.6
g. Ps 65.2
h. Jn 14.13-14; 1 Pt 2.5
i. Rom 8.26
k. 1 Jn 5.14
l. Ps 47.7; Eccl 5.1-2; Heb 12.28; Gn 18.27; Jas 5.16; Jas 1.6, 7; Mk 11.24; Mt 6.12, 14-15; Col 4.2; Eph 6.18
m. 1 Cor 14.14

4. Prayer is to be made for things lawful,[n] and for all sorts of men living, or that shall live hereafter,[o] but not for the dead,[p] nor for those of whom it may be known that they have sinned the sin unto death.[q] [20]

n. 1 Jn 5.14
o. 1 Tm 2.1-2; Jn 17.20; 2 Sm 7.29; Ru 4.12
p. 2 Sm 12.21-23 with Lk 16.25-26; Rv 14.13

18. American edition: *by.*
19. American edition: *representation.*
20. American edition omits this last phrase.

q. 1 Jn 5.16

5. The reading of the Scriptures with godly fear,[r] the sound preaching[s] and conscionable hearing of the word, in obedience unto God, with understanding, faith, and reverence,[t] singing of psalms with grace in the heart,[u] as also, the due administration and worthy receiving of the sacraments instituted by Christ, are all parts of the ordinary religious worship of God,[w] beside religious oaths,[x] vows,[y] [21] solemn fastings,[z] and thanksgivings, upon several[22] occasions,[a] which are, in their several times and seasons, to be used in a holy and religious manner.[b]

r. Acts 15.21; Rv 1.3

s. 2 Tm 4.2

t. Jas 1.22; Acts 10.33; Mt 13.19; Heb 4.2; Is 66.2

u. Col 3.16; Eph 5.19; Jas 5.13

w. Mt 28.19; 1 Cor 11.23–29; Acts 2.42

x. Dt 6.13 with Neh 10.29

y. Is 19.21 with Eccl 5.4, 5

z. Jl 2.12; Est 4.16; Mt 9.15; 1 Cor 7.5

a. Ps 107; Est 9.22

b. Heb 12.28

6. Neither prayer, nor any other part of religious worship, is now under the gospel either tied unto, or made more acceptable by any place in which it is performed, or towards which it is directed;[c] but God is to be worshiped everywhere,[d] in spirit and[23] truth,[e] as in private families[f] daily,[g] and in secret each one by himself;[h] so, more solemnly, in the public assemblies, which are not carelessly or willfully to be neglected, or forsaken, when God, by his word or providence, calls thereunto.[i]

c. Jn 4.21

d. Mal 1.11; 1 Tm 2.8

e. Jn 4.23–24

f. Jer 10.25; Dt 6.6–7; Jb 1.5; 2 Sm 6.18, 20; 1 Pt 3.7; Acts 10.2

g. Mt 6.11

h. Mt 6.6; Eph 6.18

i. Is 56.6, 7; Heb 10.25; Prv 1.20–21, 24; Prv 8.34; Acts 13.42; Lk 4.16; Acts 2.42

7. As it is the law of nature, that, in general, a due proportion of time be set apart for the worship of God, so, in his word, by a positive, moral, and perpetual commandment, binding all men, in all ages, he hath particularly appointed one day in seven, for a Sabbath, to be kept holy unto him,[k] which, from the beginning of the world to the resurrection of Christ, was the last day of the week, and, from the resurrection of Christ, was changed into the first day of the week,[l] which, in Scrip-

21. American edition reads: *and vows.*

22. American edition: *special.*

23. American edition inserts *in.*

ture, is called the Lord's Day,[m] and is to be continued to the end of the world, as the Christian Sabbath.[n]

k. Ex 20.8, 10–11; Is 56.2, 4, 6–7

l. Gn 2.2–3; 1 Cor 16.1–2; Acts 20.7

m. Rv 1.10

n. Ex 20.8, 10 with Mt 5.17, 18

8. This Sabbath is then kept holy unto the Lord, when men, after a due preparing of their hearts, and ordering of their common affairs beforehand, do not only observe a holy rest, all the day, from their own works, words, and thoughts about their worldly employments and recreations,[o] but also are taken up the whole time in the public and private exercises of his worship, and in the duties of necessity and mercy.[p]

o. Ex 20.8; Ex 16.23, 25–26, 29–30; Ex 31.15–17; Is 58.13; Neh 13.15–22

p. Is 58.13; Mt 12.1–13

CHAPTER 22. OF LAWFUL OATHS AND VOWS

1. A lawful oath is a part of religious worship,[a] wherein, upon just occasion, the person swearing solemnly calleth God to witness what he asserteth, or promiseth, and to judge him according to the truth or falsehood of what he sweareth.[b]

a. Dt 10.20

b. Ex 20.7; Lv 19.12; 2 Cor 1.23; 2 Chr 6.22–23

2. The name of God only is that by which men ought to swear, and therein it is to be used with all holy fear and reverence.[c] Therefore, to swear vainly or rashly, by that glorious and dreadful name, or, to swear at all by any other thing, is sinful, and to be abhorred.[d] Yet, as in matters of weight and moment, an oath is warranted by the word of God, under the new testament, as well as under the old,[e] so a lawful oath, being imposed by lawful authority, in such matters ought to be taken.[f]

c. Dt 6.13

d. Ex 20.7; Jer 5.7; Mt 5.34, 37; Jas 5.12

e. Heb 6.16; 2 Cor 1.23; Is 65.16

f. 1 Kgs 8.31; Neh 13.25; Ezr 10.5

3. Whosoever taketh an oath ought duly to consider the weightiness of so solemn an act, and therein to avouch nothing, but what he is fully persuaded is the truth.[g] Neither may any man bind himself by oath to any thing but what is good and just, and what he believeth so to be, and what he is able and resolved to perform.[h] Yet is it a sin to refuse an oath touching any thing that is good and just, being imposed by lawful authority.[i] [24]

24. American edition omits this last sentence.

g. Ex 20.7; Jer 4.2

h. Gn 24.2–3, 5–6, 8–9

i. Nm 5.19, 21; Neh 5.12; Ex 22.7–11

4. An oath is to be taken in the plain and common sense of the words, without equivocation, or mental reservation.[k] It cannot oblige to sin; but in any thing not sinful, being taken, it binds to performance, although to a man's own hurt.[l] Nor is it to be violated, although made to heretics, or infidels.[m]

k. Jer 4.2; Ps 24.4

l. 1 Sm 25.22, 32–34; Ps 15.4

m. Ez 17.16, 18–19; Jos 9.18–19 with 2 Sm 21.1

5. A vow is of the like nature with a promissory oath, and ought to be made with the like religious care, and to be performed with the like faithfulness.[n]

n. Is 19.21; Eccl 5.4–6; Ps 61.8; Ps 66.13–14

6. It is not to be made to any creature, but to God alone;[o] and that it may be accepted, it is to be made voluntarily, out of faith, and conscience of duty, in way of thankfulness for mercy received, or for the[25] obtaining of what we want, whereby we more strictly bind ourselves to necessary duties, or to other things, so far and so long as they may fitly conduce thereunto.[p]

o. Ps 76.11; Jer 44.25–26

p. Dt 23.21–23; Ps 50.14; Gn 28.20–22; 1 Sm 1.11; Ps 66.13–14; Ps 132.2–5

7. No man may vow to do anything forbidden in the word of God, or what would hinder any duty therein commanded, or which is not in his own power, and for the performance whereof he hath no promise of ability from God.[q] In which respect,[26] popish[27] monastical vows of perpetual single life, professed poverty, and regular obedience, are so far from being degrees of higher perfection, that they are superstitious and sinful snares, in which no Christian may entangle himself.[r]

q. Acts 23.12, 14; Mk 6.26; Nm 30.5, 8, 12–13

r. Mt 19.11–12; 1 Cor 7.2, 9; Eph 4.28; 1 Pt 4.2; 1 Cor 7.23

CHAPTER 23. OF THE CIVIL MAGISTRATE

1. God, the supreme Lord and King of all the world, hath ordained civil magistrates, to be, under him, over the people, for his own glory, and the public good, and, to this end, hath armed them with the power of the sword, for the defense and encouragement of them that are good, and for the punishment of evil-doers.[a]

a. Rom 13.1–4; 1 Pt 2.13–14

25. American edition omits *the*.

26. American edition: *respects*.

27. American edition omits *popish*.

2. It is lawful for Christians to accept and execute the office of a magistrate, when called thereunto;[b] in the managing whereof, as they ought especially to maintain piety, justice, and peace, according to the wholesome laws of each commonwealth,[c] so for that end, they may lawfully now, under the new testament, wage war, upon just and necessary occasion.[d] [28]

b. Prv 8.15–16; Rom 13.1–2, 4

c. Ps 2.10–12; 1 Tm 2.2; Ps 82.3–4; 2 Sm 23.3; 1 Pt 2.13

d. Lk 3.14; Rom 13.4; Mt 8.9–10; Acts 10.1–2; Rv 17.14, 16

3.[29] The civil magistrate may not assume to himself the administration of the word and sacraments, or the power of the keys of the kingdom of heaven;[e] yet he hath authority, and it is his duty, to take order, that unity and peace be preserved in the church, that the truth of God be kept pure and entire, that all blasphemies and heresies be suppressed, all corruptions and abuses in worship and discipline prevented or reformed, and all the ordinances of God duly settled, administrated, and observed.[f] For the better effecting whereof, he hath power to call synods, to be present at them, and to provide that whatsoever is transacted in them be according to the mind of God.[g]

e. 2 Chr 26.18 with Mt 18.17 and Mt 16.19; 1 Cor 12.28–29; Eph 4.11–12; 1 Cor 4.1–2; Rom 10.15; Heb 5.4

f. Is 49.23; Ps 122.9; Ezr 7.23, 25–28; Lv 24.16; Dt 13.5–6, 12; 1 Kgs 18.4; 1 Chr 13.1–9; 2 Kgs 23.1–26; 2 Chr 34.33; 2 Chr 15.12–13

g. 2 Chr 19.8–11; 2 Chr 29–30; Mt 2.4–5

4. It is the duty of people to pray for magistrates,[h] to honor their persons,[i] to pay them tribute or other dues,[k] to obey their lawful commands, and to be subject

28. American edition: *occasions*.

29. In the American edition, this section reads: *Civil magistrates may not assume to themselves the administration of the word and sacraments (2 Chr 26.8); or the power of the keys of the kingdom of heaven (Mt 16.19; 1 Cor 4.1–2); or, in the least, interfere in matters of faith (Jn 18.36; Mal 2.7; Acts 5.29). Yet as nursing fathers, it is the duty of civil magistrates to protect the church of our common Lord, without giving preference to any denomination of Christians above the rest, in such a manner that all ecclesiastical persons whatever shall enjoy full, free, and unquestioned liberty of discharging every part of their sacred functions, without violence or danger (Is 49.23). And, as Jesus Christ hath appointed a regular government and discipline in his church, no law of any commonwealth should interfere with, let, or hinder, the due exercise thereof, among the voluntary members of any denomination of Christians, according to their own profession and belief (Ps 105.15; Acts 18.14–16). It is the duty of civil magistrates to protect the person and the good name of all their people, in such an effectual manner as that no person be suffered, either upon pretense of religion or infidelity, to offer any indignity, violence, abuse, or injury to any other person whatsoever: and to take order, that all religious and ecclesiastical assemblies be held without molestation or disturbance (2 Sm 23.3; 1 Tm 2.1; Rom 13.4).*

to their authority, for conscience's sake.[l] Infidelity, or difference in religion, doth not make void the magistrates' just and legal authority, nor free the people from their due obedience to them,[m] from which ecclesiastical persons are not exempted,[n] much less hath the pope any power and jurisdiction over them in their dominions, or over any of their people, and, least of all, to deprive them of their dominions, or lives, if he shall judge them to be heretics, or upon any other pretense whatsoever.[o]

h. 1 Tm 2.1–2

i. 1 Pt 2.17

k. Rom 13.6–7

l. Rom 13.5; Ti 3.1

m. 1 Pt 2.13–14, 16

n. Rom 13.1; 1 Kgs 2.35; Acts 25.9–11; 2 Pt 2.1, 10–11; Jude 8–11

o. 2 Thes 2.4; Rv 13.15–17

CHAPTER 24.[30] OF MARRIAGE AND DIVORCE

1. Marriage is to be between one man and one woman; neither is it lawful for any man to have more than one wife, nor for any woman to have more than one husband at the same time.[a]

a. Gn 2.24; Mt 19.5–6; Prv 2.17

2. Marriage was ordained for the mutual help of husband and wife,[b] for the increase of mankind with a legitimate issue, and of the church with a holy seed,[c] and for preventing of uncleanness.[d]

b. Gn 2.18

c. Mal 2.15

d. 1 Cor 7.2, 9

3. It is lawful for all sorts of people to marry, who are able with judgment to give their consent.[e] Yet is it the duty of Christians to marry only in the Lord;[f] and therefore such as profess the true reformed religion should not marry with infidels, papists, or other idolaters; neither should such as are godly be unequally yoked, by marrying with such as are notoriously wicked in their life, or maintain damnable heresies.[g]

e. Heb 13.4; 1 Tm 4.3; 1 Cor 7.36–38; Gn 24.57–58

f. 1 Cor 7.39

g. Gn 34.14; Ex 34.16; Dt 7.3–4; 1 Kgs 11.4; Neh 13.25–27; Mal 2.11–12; 2 Cor 6.14

4. Marriage ought not to be within the degrees of consanguinity or affinity forbidden by the word;[h] nor can such incestuous marriages ever be made lawful by any law of man or consent of parties, so as those persons may live together as man and wife.[i] The man may not marry any of his wife's kindred nearer in blood than

30. See *Book of Confessions* 1996, 152–56, for two different American texts of this chapter.

he may of his own; nor the woman of her husband's kindred nearer in blood than of her own.[k]

h. Lv 18; 1 Cor 5.1; Am 2.7
i. Mk 6.18; Lv 18.24–28
k. Lv 20.19–21

5. Adultery or fornication committed after a contract, being detected before marriage, giveth just occasion to the innocent party to dissolve that contract.[l] In the case of adultery after marriage, it is lawful for the innocent party to sue out a divorce,[m] and, after the divorce, to marry another, as if the offending party were dead.[n]

l. Mt 1.18–20
m. Mt 5.31–32
n. Mt 19.9; Rom 7.2–3

6. Although the corruption of man be such as is apt to study arguments unduly to put asunder those whom God hath joined together in marriage, yet nothing but adultery, or such willful desertion as can no way be remedied by the church or civil magistrate, is cause sufficient of dissolving the bond of marriage:[o] wherein, a public and orderly course of proceeding is to be observed, and the persons concerned in it not left to their own wills and discretion, in their own case.[p]

o. Mt 19.8–9; 1 Cor 7.15; Mt 19.6
p. Dt 24.1– 4

CHAPTER 25. OF THE CHURCH

1. The catholic or universal church, which is invisible, consists of the whole number of the elect, that have been, are, or shall be gathered into one, under Christ the Head thereof, and is the spouse, the body, the fullness of him that filleth all in all.[a]

a. Eph 1.10, 22–23; Eph 5.23, 27, 32; Col 1.18

2. The visible church, which is also catholic or universal under the gospel (not confined to one nation as before under the law), consists of all those throughout the world that profess the true religion,[b] and of[31] their children,[c] and is the kingdom of the Lord Jesus Christ,[d] the house and family of God,[e] [32] out of which there is no ordinary possibility of salvation.[f]

b. 1 Cor 1.2; 1 Cor 12.12–13; Ps 2.8; Rv 7.9; Rom 15.9–12
c. 1 Cor 7.14; Acts 2.39; Ez 16.20–21; Rom 11.16; Gn 3.15; Gn 17.7
d. Mt 13.47; Is 9.7

31. American edition reads *together with,* instead of *and of.*
32. American edition completes this sentence with: *through which men are ordinarily saved and union with which is essential to their best growth and service.*

e. Eph 2.19; Eph 3.15

f. Acts 2.47

3. Unto this catholic visible church Christ hath given the ministry, oracles, and ordinances of God, for the gathering and perfecting of the saints, in this life, to the end of the world: and doth by his own presence and Spirit, according to his promise, make them effectual thereunto.[g]

g. 1 Cor 12.28; Eph 4.11–13; Mt 28.19–20; Is 59.21

4. This catholic church hath been sometimes more, sometimes less visible.[h] And particular churches, which are members thereof, are more or less pure, according as the doctrine of the gospel is taught and embraced, ordinances administered, and public worship performed more or less purely in them.[i]

h. Rom 11.3–4; Rv 12.6, 14

i. Rv 2 and 3; 1 Cor 5.6–7

5. The purest churches under heaven are subject both to mixture and error.[k] And some have so degenerated, as to become no churches of Christ, but synagogues of Satan.[l] [33] Nevertheless, there shall be always a church on earth, to worship God according to his will.[m]

k. 1 Cor 13.12; Rv 2 and 3; Mt 13.24–30, 47

l. Rv 18.2; Rom 11.18–22

m. Mt 16.18; Ps 72.17; Ps 102.28; Mt 28.19–20

6.[34] There is no other Head of the church, but the Lord Jesus Christ;[n] nor can the pope of Rome, in any sense, be head thereof, but is that Antichrist, that man of sin, and son of perdition, that exalteth himself, in the church, against Christ and all that is called God.[o]

n. Col 1.18; Eph 1.22

o. Mt 23.8–10; 2 Thes 2.3–4, 8–9; Rv 13.6

CHAPTER 26. OF THE COMMUNION OF THE SAINTS

1. All saints, that are united to Jesus Christ their Head by his Spirit and by faith, have fellowship with him in his grace, sufferings, death, resurrection, and glory.[a] And, being united to one another in love, they have communion in each other's gifts and graces,[b] and are obliged to the performance of such duties, public and private, as do conduce to their mutual good, both in the inward and outward man.[c]

a. Jn 1.3; Eph 3.16–17, 18–19; Jn 1.16; Eph 2.5–6; Phil 3.10; Rom 6.5–6; 2 Tm 2.12

33. American edition: *to become apparently no churches of Christ.*

34. In the American edition, this section reads: *The Lord Jesus Christ is the only head of the church, and the claim of any man to be the vicar of Christ and the head of the church is unscriptural, without warrant in fact, and is a usurpation dishonoring to the Lord Jesus Christ.*

b. Eph 4.15–16; 1 Cor 12.7; 1 Cor 3.21–23; Col 2.19

c. 1 Thes 5.11, 14; Rom 1.11–12, 14; 1 Jn 3.16–18; Gal 6.10

2. Saints by profession are bound to maintain a holy fellowship and communion in the worship of God, and in performing such other spiritual services as tend to their mutual edification,[d] as also in relieving each other in outward things, according to their several abilities, and necessities. Which communion, as God offereth opportunity, is to be extended unto all those who, in every place, call upon the name of the Lord Jesus.[e]

d. Heb 10.24–25; Acts 2.42, 46; Is 2.3; 1 Cor 11.20

e. Acts 2.44–45; 1 Jn 3.17; 2 Cor 8–9; Acts 11.29–30

3. This communion which the saints have with Christ, doth not make them, in any wise, partakers of the substance of his Godhead, or to be equal with Christ, in any respect, either of which to affirm is impious and blasphemous.[f] Nor doth their communion one with another, as saints, take away, or infringe the title or propriety[35] which each man hath in his goods and possessions.[g]

f. Col 1.18–19; 1 Cor 8.6; Is 42.8; 1 Tm 6.15–16; Ps 45.7 with Heb 1.8–9

g. Ex 20.15; Eph 4.28; Acts 5.4

CHAPTER 27. OF THE SACRAMENTS

1. Sacraments are holy signs and seals of the covenant of grace,[a] immediately instituted by God,[b] to represent Christ and his benefits; and to confirm our interest in him;[c] as also, to put a visible difference between those that belong unto the church, and the rest of the world,[d] and solemnly to engage them to the service of God in Christ, according to his word.[e]

a. Rom 4.11; Gn 17.7, 10

b. Mt 28.19; 1 Cor 11.23

c. 1 Cor 10.16; 1 Cor 11.25–26; Gal 3.17

d. Rom 15.8; Ex 12.48; Gn 34.14

e. Rom 6.3–4; 1 Cor 10.16, 21

2. There is in every sacrament a spiritual relation, or sacramental union, between the sign and the thing signified; whence it comes to pass, that the names and effects of the one are attributed to the other.[f]

f. Gn 17.10; Mt 26.27–28; Ti 3.5

3. The grace which is exhibited in or by the sacraments rightly used, is not conferred by any power in them; neither doth the efficacy of a sacrament depend upon the piety or intention of him that doth administer it:[g] but upon the work of

35. American edition: *property.*

the Spirit,[h] and the word of institution, which contains, together with a precept authorizing the use thereof, a promise of benefit to worthy receivers.[i]

g. Rom 2.28–29; 1 Pt 3.21
h. Mt 3.11; 1 Cor 12.13
i. Mt 26.27–28; Mt 28.19–20

4. There are only two sacraments ordained by Christ our Lord in the Gospel; that is to say, baptism and the supper of the Lord: neither of which may be dispensed by any but by a minister of the word lawfully ordained.[k]

k. Mt 28.19; 1 Cor 11.20, 23; 1 Cor 4.1; Heb 5.4

5. The sacraments of the old testament, in regard to the spiritual things thereby signified and exhibited, were, for substance, the same with those of the new.[l]

l. 1 Cor 10.1–4

CHAPTER 28. OF BAPTISM

1. Baptism is a sacrament of the New Testament, ordained by Jesus Christ,[a] not only for the solemn admission of the party baptized into the visible church,[b] but also, to be unto him a sign and seal of the covenant of grace,[c] of his engrafting into Christ,[d] of regeneration,[e] of remission of sins,[f] and of his giving up unto God through Jesus Christ, to walk in the newness of life.[g] Which sacrament is, by Christ's own appointment, to be continued in his church until the end of the world.[h]

a. Mt 28.19
b. 1 Cor 12.13
c. Rom 4.11 with Col 2.11–12
d. Gal 3.27; Rom 6.5
e. Ti 3.5
f. Mk 1.4
g. Rom 6.3, 4
h. Mt 28.19–20

2. The outward element to be used in this sacrament is water, wherewith the party is to be baptized, in the name of the Father, and of the Son, and of the Holy Ghost, by a minister of the gospel, lawfully called thereunto.[i]

i. Mt 3.11; Jn 1.33; Mt 28.19–20

3. Dipping of the person into the water is not necessary, but baptism is rightly administered by pouring or sprinkling water upon the person.[k]

k. Heb 9.10, 19–22; Acts 2.41; Acts 16.33; Mk 7.4

4. Not only those that do actually profess faith in and obedience unto Christ,[l] but also the infants of one or both believing parents, are to be baptized.[m]

l. Mk 16.15, 16; Acts 8.37, 38

m. Gn 17.7, 9–10 with Gal 3.9, 14, and Col 2.11–12 and Acts 2.38–39 and Rom 4.11–12; 1 Cor 7.14; Mt 28.19; Mk 10.13–16; Lk 18.15

5. Although it be a great sin to contemn or neglect this ordinance,[n] yet grace and salvation are not so inseparably annexed unto it, as that no person can be regenerated or saved without it,[o] or, that all that are baptized are undoubtedly regenerated.[p]

n. Lk 7.30 with Ex 4.24–26

o. Rom 4.11; Acts 10.2, 4, 22, 31, 45, 47

p. Acts 8.13, 23

6. The efficacy of baptism is not tied to that moment of time wherein it is administered;[q] yet notwithstanding, by the right use of this ordinance, the grace promised is not only offered, but really exhibited and conferred, by the Holy Ghost, to such (whether of age or infants) as that grace belongeth unto, according to the counsel of God's own will, in his appointed time.[r]

q. Jn 3.5, 8

r. Gal 3.27; Ti 3.5; Eph 5.25–26; Acts 2.38, 41

7. The sacrament of baptism is but once to be administered unto any person.[s]

s. Ti 3.5

CHAPTER 29. OF THE LORD'S SUPPER

1. Our Lord Jesus, in the night wherein he was betrayed, instituted the sacrament of his body and blood, called the Lord's supper, to be observed in his church, unto the end of the world, for the perpetual remembrance of the sacrifice of himself in his death, the sealing all benefits thereof unto true believers, their spiritual nourishment and growth in him, their further engagement in and to all duties which they owe unto him, and to be a bond and pledge of their communion with him, and with each other, as members of his mystical body.[a]

a. 1 Cor 11.23–26; 1 Cor 10.16–17, 21; 1 Cor 12.13

2. In this sacrament, Christ is not offered up to his Father; nor any real sacrifice made at all for remission of sins of the quick or dead,[b] but only a commemoration of that one offering up of himself, by himself, upon the cross, once for all, and a spiritual oblation of all possible praise unto God for the same;[c] so that the popish[36] sacrifice of the mass (as they call it)[37] is most[38] abominably in-

36. American edition: *so-called.*

37. American edition omits parenthetical comment.

38. American edition: *is most contradictory to Christ's one sacrifice, the only propitiation for all the sins of the elect.*

jurious to Christ's one, only sacrifice, the alone propitiation for all the sins of his elect.[d]

b. Heb 9.22, 25–26, 28

c. 1 Cor 11.24–26; Mt 26.26–27

d. Heb 7.23–24, 27; Heb 10.11–12, 14, 18

3. The Lord Jesus hath, in this ordinance, appointed his ministers to declare his word of institution to the people; to pray, and bless the elements of bread and wine, and thereby to set them apart from a common to a holy use; and to take and break the bread, to take the cup, and (they communicating also themselves) to give both to the communicants,[e] but to none who are not then present in the congregation.[f]

e. Mt 26.26–28 and Mk 14.22–24 and Lk 22.19–20 with 1 Cor 11.23–26

f. Acts 20.7; 1 Cor 11.20

4. Private masses, or receiving this sacrament by a priest or any other alone,[g] as likewise, the denial of the cup to the people,[h] worshiping the elements, the lifting them up or carrying them about for adoration, and the reserving them for any pretended religious use, are all contrary to the nature of this sacrament, and to the institution of Christ.[i]

g. 1 Cor 10.16

h. Mk 14.23; 1 Cor 11.25–29

i. Mt 15.9

5. The outward elements in this sacrament, duly set apart to the uses ordained by Christ, have such relation to him crucified, as that, truly, yet sacramentally only, they are sometimes called by the name of the things they represent, to wit, the body and blood of Christ;[k] albeit in substance and nature they still remain truly and only bread and wine, as they were before.[l]

k. Mt 26.26–28

l. 1 Cor 11.26–28; Mt 26.29

6. That doctrine which maintains a change of the substance of bread and wine into the substance of Christ's body and blood (commonly called transubstantiation) by consecration of a priest, or by any other way, is repugnant, not to Scripture alone, but even to common sense and reason, overthroweth the nature of the sacrament, and hath been, and is the cause of manifold superstitions, yea, of gross idolatries.[m]

m. Acts 3.21 with 1 Cor 11.24–26; Lk 24.6, 39

7. Worthy receivers outwardly partaking of the visible elements in this sacrament,[n] do then also, inwardly by faith, really and indeed, yet not carnally and corporally, but spiritually, receive and feed upon Christ crucified, and all benefits of his death: the body and blood of Christ being then, not corporally or carnally,

in, with, or under the bread and wine, yet, as really, but spiritually, present to the faith of believers in that ordinance, as the elements themselves are to their outward senses.[o]

n. 1 Cor 11.28

o. 1 Cor 10.16

8. Although ignorant and wicked men receive the outward elements in this sacrament, yet they receive not the thing signified thereby, but by their unworthy coming thereunto are guilty of the body and blood of the Lord to their own damnation.[39] Wherefore, all ignorant and ungodly persons, as they are unfit to enjoy communion with him, so are they unworthy of the Lord's table, and cannot, without great sin against Christ while they remain such, partake of these holy mysteries,[p] or be admitted thereunto.[q]

p. 1 Cor 11.27-29; 2 Cor 6.14-16

q. 1 Cor 5.6-7, 13; 2 Thes 3.6, 14-15; Mt 7.6

CHAPTER 30. OF CHURCH CENSURES

1. The Lord Jesus, as King and Head of his church, hath therein appointed a government, in the hand of church officers, distinct from the civil magistrate.[a]

a. Is 9.6-7; 1 Tm 5.17; 1 Thes 5.12; Acts 20.17-28; Heb 13.7, 17, 24; 1 Cor 12.28; Mt 28.18-20

2. To these officers the keys of the kingdom of heaven are committed: by virtue whereof, they have power respectively to retain, and remit sins; to shut that kingdom against the impenitent, both by the word and censures; and to open it unto penitent sinners, by the ministry of the gospel, and by absolution from censures, as occasion shall require.[b]

b. Mt 16.19; Mt 18.17-18; Jn 20.21-23; 2 Cor 2.6-8

3. Church censures are necessary, for the reclaiming and gaining of offending brethren, for deterring of others from the like offenses, for purging out of that leaven which might infect the whole lump, for vindicating the honor of Christ, and the holy profession of the gospel, and for preventing the wrath of God, which might justly fall upon the church, if they should suffer his covenant and the seals thereof to be profaned by notorious and obstinate offenders.[c]

c. 1 Cor 5; 1 Tm 5.20; Mt 7.6; 1 Tm 1.20; 1 Cor 11.27-34 with Jude 23

4. For the better attaining of these ends, the officers of the church are to proceed by admonition, suspension from the sacrament of the Lord's supper for a season, and by excommunication from the church, according to the nature of the crime, and demerit of the person.[d]

d. 1 Thes 5.12; 2 Thes 3.6, 14-15; 1 Cor 5.4-5, 13; Mt 18.17; Ti 3.10

39. American edition replaces *to their own damnation* with *and bring judgment on themselves.*

CHAPTER 31. OF SYNODS AND COUNCILS

1. For the better government, and further edification of the church, there ought to be such assemblies as are commonly called synods or councils.[a] [40]

a. Acts 15.2, 4, 6

2.[41] As magistrates may lawfully call a synod of ministers, and other fit persons, to consult and advise with, about matters of religion;[b] so, if magistrates be open enemies to the church, the ministers of Christ of themselves, by virtue of their office, or they, with other fit persons upon delegation from their churches, may meet together in such assemblies.[c]

b. Is 49.23; 1 Tm 2.1–2; 2 Chr 19.8–11; 2 Chr 29–30; Mt 2.4–5; Prv 11.14

c. Acts 15.2, 4, 22–23, 25

3.[42] It belongeth to synods and councils, ministerially to determine controversies of faith and cases of conscience; to set down rules and directions for the better ordering of the public worship of God, and government of his church; to receive complaints in cases of maladministration, and authoritatively to determine the same: which decrees and determinations, if consonant to the word of God, are to be received with reverence and submission; not only for their agreement with the word, but also for the power whereby they are made, as being an ordinance of God appointed thereunto in his word.[d]

d. Acts 15.15, 19, 24, 27–31; Acts 16.4; Mt 18.17–20

4.[43] All synods or councils, since the apostles' times, whether general or particular, may err; and many have erred. Therefore they are not to be made the rule of faith, or practice, but to be used as a help in both.[e]

e. Eph 2.20; Acts 17.11; 1 Cor 2.5; 2 Cor 1.24

5.[44] Synods and councils are to handle, or conclude, nothing, but that which is ecclesiastical, and are not to intermeddle with civil affairs which concern the commonwealth, unless by way of humble petition, in cases extraordinary; or by way of advice, for satisfaction of conscience, if they be thereunto required by the civil magistrate.[f]

f. Lk 12.13–14; Jn 18.36

40. American edition adds: *And it belongeth to the overseers and other rulers of the particular churches, by virtue of their office, and the power which Christ hath given them for edification, and not for destruction, to appoint such assemblies (Acts 15); and to convene together in them, as often as they shall judge it expedient for the good of the church (Acts 15.22–25).*

41. American edition omits this section.

42. Section 2 in American edition.

43. Section 3 in American edition.

44. Section 4 in American edition.

CHAPTER 32. OF THE STATE OF MEN[45] AFTER DEATH, AND OF THE RESURRECTION OF THE DEAD

1. The bodies of men, after death, return to dust and see corruption;[a] but their souls (which neither die nor sleep) having an immortal subsistence, immediately return to God who gave them;[b] the souls of the righteous, being then made perfect in holiness, are received into the highest heavens, where they behold the face of God, in light and glory, waiting for the full redemption of their bodies.[c] And the souls of the wicked are cast into hell, where they remain in torments and utter darkness, reserved to the judgment of the great day.[d] Beside these two places, for souls separated from their bodies, the Scripture acknowledgeth none.

a. Gn 3.19; Acts 13.36
b. Lk 23.43; Eccl 12.7
c. Heb 12.23; 2 Cor 5.1, 6, 8; Phil 1.23 with Acts 3.21 and Eph 4.10
d. Lk 16.23-24; Acts 1.25; Jude 6, 7; 1 Pt 3.19

2. At the last day, such as are found alive shall not die, but be changed;[e] and all the dead shall be raised up, with the selfsame bodies, and none other, although with different qualities, which shall be united again to their souls forever.[f]

e. 1 Thes 4.17; 1 Cor 15.51, 52
f. Jb 19.26, 27; 1 Cor 15.42, 43, 44

3. The bodies of the unjust shall, by the power of Christ, be raised to dishonor; the bodies of the just, by his Spirit, unto honor, and be made conformable to his own glorious body.[g]

g. Acts 24.15; Jn 5.28-29; 1 Cor 15.43; Phil 3.21

CHAPTER 33. OF THE LAST JUDGMENT

1. God hath appointed a day, wherein he will judge the world in righteousness, by Jesus Christ,[a] to whom all power and judgment is given of the Father.[b] In which day, not only the apostate angels shall be judged,[c] but likewise all persons that have lived upon earth shall appear before the tribunal of Christ, to give an account of their thoughts, words, and deeds, and to receive according to what they have done in the body, whether good or evil.[d]

a. Acts 17.31
b. Jn 5.22, 27
c. 1 Cor 6.3; Jude 6; 2 Pt 2.4
d. 2 Cor 5.10; Eccl 12.14; Rom 2.16; Rom 14.10, 12; Mt 12.36-37

2. The end of God's appointing this day is for the manifestation of the glory of his mercy, in the eternal salvation of the elect; and of his justice, in the damna-

45. American edition: *Man.*

tion of the reprobate who are wicked and disobedient. For then shall the righteous go into everlasting life, and receive that fullness of joy and refreshing, which shall come from the presence of the Lord; but the wicked who know not God, and obey not the gospel of Jesus Christ, shall be cast into eternal torments, and be punished with everlasting destruction from the presence of the Lord, and from the glory of his power.[e]

e. Mt 25.31–46; Rom 2.5–6; Rom 9.22–23; Mt 25.21; Acts 3.19; 2 Thes 1.7–10

3. As Christ would have us to be certainly persuaded that there shall be a day of judgment, both to deter all men from sin, and for the greater consolation of the godly in their adversity,[f] so will he have that day unknown to men, that they may shake off all carnal security, and be always watchful, because they know not at what hour the Lord will come; and may be ever prepared to say, Come, Lord Jesus, come quickly, Amen.[g]

f. 2 Pt 3.11, 14; 2 Cor 5.10–11; 2 Thes 1.5–7; Lk 21.27–28; Rom 8.23–25
g. Mt 24.36, 42–44; Mk 13.35–37; Lk 12.35–36; Rev 22.20

> Charles Herle, Prolocutor
> Cornelius Burges, Assessor
> Herbert Palmer, Assessor
> Henry Robroughe, Scriba
> Adoniram Byfield, Scriba

[In 1903, two chapters and a "Declaratory Statement" were added by the United Presbyterian Church in the United States of America. They are reproduced here as given in *Book of Confessions* 1996, 164–68.]

CHAPTER 34. OF THE HOLY SPIRIT

1. The Holy Spirit, the third person in the Trinity, proceeding from the Father and the Son, of the same substance and equal in power and glory, is, together with the Father and the Son, to be believed in, loved, obeyed, and worshiped throughout all ages.

2. He is the Lord and giver of life, everywhere present, and is the source of all good thoughts, pure desires, and holy counsels in men. By him the prophets were moved to speak the word of God, and all the writers of the Holy Scriptures inspired to record infallibly the mind and will of God. The dispensation of the gospel is especially committed to him. He prepares the way for it, accompanies it with his persuasive power, and urges its message upon the reason and conscience of men, so that they who reject its merciful offer are not only without excuse, but are also guilty of resisting the Holy Spirit.

3. The Holy Spirit, whom the Father is ever willing to give to all who ask

him, is the only efficient agent in the application of redemption. He regenerates men by his grace, convicts them of sin, moves them to repentance, and persuades and enables them to embrace Jesus Christ by faith. He unites all believers to Christ, dwells in them as their Comforter and Sanctifier, gives to them the spirit of adoption and prayer, and performs all these gracious offices by which they are sanctified and sealed unto the day of redemption.

4. By the indwelling of the Holy Spirit all believers being vitally united to Christ, who is the head, are thus united one to another in the church, which is his body. He calls and anoints ministers for their holy office, qualifies all other officers in the church for their special work, and imparts various gifts and graces to its members. He gives efficacy to the word and to the ordinances of the gospel. By him the church will be preserved, increased, purified, and at last made perfectly holy in the presence of God.

CHAPTER 35. OF THE GOSPEL OF THE
LOVE OF GOD AND MISSIONS

1. God in infinite and perfect love, having provided in the covenant of grace, through the mediation and sacrifice of the Lord Jesus Christ, a way of life and salvation, sufficient for and adapted to the whole lost race of man, doth freely offer this salvation to all men in the gospel.

2. In the gospel God declares his love for the world and his desire that all men should be saved; reveals fully and clearly the only way of salvation; promises eternal life to all who truly repent and believe in Christ; invites and commands all to embrace the offered mercy; and by his Spirit accompanying the word pleads with men to accept his gracious invitation.

3. It is the duty and privilege of everyone who hears the gospel immediately to accept its merciful provisions; and they who continue in impenitence and unbelief incur aggravated guilt and perish by their own fault.

4. Since there is no other way of salvation than that revealed in the gospel, and since in the divinely established and ordinary method of grace faith cometh [Rom 10.17] by hearing the word of God, Christ hath commissioned his church to go into all [Mt 28.19] the world and to make disciples of all nations. All believers are, therefore, under obligation to sustain the ordinance of the Christian religion where they are already established, and to contribute by their prayers, gifts, and personal efforts to the extension of the kingdom of Christ throughout the whole earth.

DECLARATORY STATEMENT

While the ordination vow of ministers, ruling elders, and deacons, as set forth in the form of government, requires the reception and adoption of the confession of faith only as containing the system of doctrine taught in the Holy Scriptures, nevertheless, seeing that the desire has been formally expressed for a disavowal by the church of certain inferences drawn from statements in the confession of faith, and also for a declaration of certain aspects of revealed truth which appear at the present time to call for more explicit statement, therefore the United Presbyterian Church in the United States of America does authoritatively declare as follows:

First, with reference to chapter 3 of the confession of faith: that concerning those who are saved in Christ, the doctrine of God's eternal decree is held in harmony with the doctrine of his love to all mankind, his gift of his Son to be the propitiation for the sins of the whole world, and his readiness to bestow his saving grace on all who seek it; that concerning those who perish, the doctrine of God's eternal decree is held in harmony with the doctrine that God desires not the death of any sinner, but has provided in Christ a salvation sufficient for all, adapted to all, and freely offered in the gospel to all; that men are fully responsible for their treatment of God's gracious offer; that his decree hinders no man from accepting that offer; and that no man is condemned except on the ground of his sin.

Second, with reference to chapter 10, section 3, of the confession of faith, that it is not to be regarded as teaching that any who die in infancy are lost. We believe that all dying in infancy are included in the election of grace, and are regenerated and saved by Christ through the Spirit, who works when and where and how he pleases.

The Westminster Shorter Catechism, 1648

The Westminster Assembly produced two catechisms based on → *The Westminster Confession*. *The Larger Catechism* was completed in October 1647. It is the basis for *The Shorter Catechism,* which seems to have been composed between 15 October and 25 November 1647, when it was presented to Parliament. Both catechisms were produced by committees.[1] Anthony Tuckney (1599–1670) played a significant role in the composition of both, serving as chairman of the committee that produced *The Shorter Catechism*.[2]

The need for two catechisms was explained in a pamphlet from 1646 entitled *The Moderate Presbyter:* "Let there be two sorts, one more large, applied to the delivering the sum of religion, by a suite and order of certain places of the Scriptures, according to which some part of the holy doctrine may be expounded every week. Another of the same sort, but shorter, fit for the examination of the rude and ignorant before they be admitted to the Lord's supper."[3]

As it has turned out, however, it has been the version for the "rude and ignorant" that has had the greater impact on the faith and that remains a beloved expression of Reformed doctrine. *The Shorter Catechism* is divided into two general categories. The first part (questions 1–38) deals with what one ought to believe and specifies doctrinal positions on the Trinity, providence, the covenants of works and grace, the incarnation, sanctification, and so on. The second part (questions 39–107) outlines the duties of the faithful as required by Scripture, including the moral law of the Ten Commandments, and proper understanding of the sacraments. Interestingly, neither *The Shorter Catechism* nor *The Larger Catechism* makes use of → *The Apostles' Creed* as a point of departure for teaching the tenets of the faith.[4]

1. Henry Palmer chaired the committee that produced *The Larger Catechism*. The other members were Thomas Hill, Stephen Marshall, Matthew Newcomen, and Anthony Tuckney. See Carruthers 1957, 3–4.
2. Tuckney became the chair after the death of Palmer in 1647. At that time the committee was reconstituted to include only Stephen Marshall, John Ward, and Tuckney. The only commissioner from Scotland who remained in the assembly, Samuel Rutherford, professor at St. Andrews, assisted until his departure on 9 November 1547. See Carruthers 1897, 33.
3. *The Moderate Presbyter, or, A Forme of Church-Government According to the Word of God* (London: Richard Cotes, 1646). Quoted in Carruthers 1957, 4.
4. The creed is appended at the end of the catechism, however, along with the text of the Ten Commandments and the Lord's Prayer.

Instead, the goal is to provide a systematic theology based on *The Westminster Confession*. The first edition of *The Shorter Catechism* appeared in November 1647. It was approved and accepted in 1648.

The Shorter Catechism is included in *The Book of Confessions* of the Presbyterian Church (USA) and remains a doctrinal standard for the Presbyterian Church in America, the Reformed Presbyterian Church, the Free Presbyterian Church, the Orthodox Presbyterian Church, and other Presbyterian and Reformed churches around the world.

Edition: *Book of Confessions* 1996, 179–97.

Note: Like *The Westminster Confession*, the first version of *The Shorter Westminster Catechism* appeared without proof texts. By order of Parliament, they were soon added and appeared in the printing of April 1648. Over the centuries, however, the proof texts—which are not merely references to quotations, but stimuli to interpretation—have been modified by various editors and denominations and now differ greatly among the churches that use the catechism as a standard. Hence, rather than give preference to any particular set of proof texts, we have reproduced the text as it was written in 1647 without these citations, including references only to biblical passages quoted in the text.

Literature: Carruthers 1897 and 1957, 1–16; Carson and Hall, 1994; Kelly 1994; Kendall 1981; Leith 1973; Paul 1985, 516–21; Schaff, 1:787–87; Torrance, xv, 261–62; Warfield 1931, 379–400; Willis-Watkins 1994.

Question 1. What is the chief end of man?

Answer. Man's chief end is to glorify God, and to enjoy him forever.

Q. 2. What rule hath God given to direct us how we may glorify and enjoy him?

A. The word of God, which is contained in the Scriptures of the Old and New Testaments, is the only rule to direct us how we may glorify and enjoy him.

Q. 3. What do the Scriptures principally teach?

A. The Scriptures principally teach, what man is to believe concerning God, and what duty God requires of man.

Q. 4. What is God?

A. God is a Spirit, infinite, eternal, and unchangeable, in his being, wisdom, power, holiness, justice, goodness, and truth.

Q. 5. Are there more gods than one?

A. There is but one only, the living and true God.

Q. 6. How many persons are there in the Godhead?

A. There are three persons in the Godhead; the Father, the Son, and the Holy Ghost; and these three are one God, the same in substance, equal in power and glory.

Q. 7. What are the decrees of God?

A. The decrees of God are, his eternal purpose, according to the counsel of his will, whereby, for his own glory, he hath foreordained whatsoever comes to pass.

Q. 8. How doth God execute his decrees?

A. God executeth his decrees in the works of creation and providence.

Q. 9. What is the work of creation?

A. The work of creation is, God's making all things of nothing, by the word of his power, in the space of six days, and all very good.

Q. 10. How did God create man?

A. God created man male and female, after his own image, in knowledge, righteousness, and holiness, with dominion over the creatures.

Q. 11. What are God's works of providence?

A. God's works of providence are, his most holy, wise, and powerful preserving and governing all his creatures, and all their actions.

Q. 12. What special act of providence did God exercise towards man in the estate wherein he was created?

A. When God had created man, he entered into a covenant of life with him, upon condition of perfect obedience; forbidding him to eat of the tree of the knowledge of good and evil, upon the pain of death.

Q. 13. Did our first parents continue in the estate wherein they were created?

A. Our first parents, being left to the freedom of their own will, fell from the estate wherein they were created, by sinning against God.

Q. 14. What is sin?

A. Sin is any want of conformity unto, or transgression of, the law of God.

Q. 15. What was the sin whereby our first parents fell from the estate wherein they were created?

A. The sin whereby our first parents fell from the estate wherein they were created, was their eating the forbidden fruit.

Q. 16. Did all mankind fall in Adam's first transgression?

A. The covenant being made with Adam, not only for himself, but for his posterity; all mankind, descending from him by ordinary generation, sinned in him, and fell with him, in his first transgression.

Q. 17. Into what estate did the fall bring mankind?

A. The fall brought mankind into an estate of sin and misery.

Q. 18. Wherein consists the sinfulness of that estate whereinto man fell?

A. The sinfulness of that estate whereinto man fell, consists in the guilt of Adam's first sin, the want of original righteousness, and the corruption of his whole nature, which is commonly called original sin; together with all actual transgressions which proceed from it.

Q. 19. What is the misery of that estate whereinto man fell?

A. All mankind, by their fall, lost communion with God, are under his wrath and curse, and so made liable to all miseries in this life, to death itself, and to the pains of hell forever.

Q. 20. Did God leave all mankind to perish in the estate of sin and misery?

A. God having, out of his mere good pleasure, from all eternity, elected some to everlasting life, did enter into a covenant of grace, to deliver them out of the estate of sin and misery, and to bring them into an estate of salvation by a Redeemer.

Q. 21. Who is the Redeemer of God's elect?

A. The only Redeemer of God's elect is the Lord Jesus Christ, who, being the eternal Son of God, became man, and so was, and continueth to be, God and man in two distinct natures, and one person, forever.

Q. 22. How did Christ, being the Son of God, become man?

A. Christ, the Son of God, became man, by taking to himself a true body and a reasonable soul, being conceived by the power of the Holy Ghost, in the womb of the Virgin Mary, and born of her, yet without sin.

Q. 23. What offices doth Christ execute as our Redeemer?

A. Christ, as our Redeemer, executeth the offices of a prophet, of a priest, and of a king, both in his estate of humiliation and exaltation.

Q. 24. How doth Christ execute the office of a prophet?

A. Christ executeth the office of a prophet, in revealing to us, by his word and Spirit, the will of God for our salvation.

Q. 25. How doth Christ execute the office of a priest?

A. Christ executeth the office of a priest, in his once offering up of himself a sacrifice to satisfy divine justice and reconcile us to God, and in making continual intercession for us.

Q. 26. How doth Christ execute the office of a king?

A. Christ executeth the office of a king, in subduing us to himself, in ruling and defending us, and in restraining and conquering all his and our enemies.

Q. 27. Wherein did Christ's humiliation consist?

A. Christ's humiliation consisted in his being born, and that in a low condition, made under the law, undergoing the miseries of this life, the wrath of God, and the cursed death of the cross; in being buried, and continuing under the power of death for a time.

Q. 28. Wherein consisteth Christ's exaltation?

A. Christ's exaltation consisteth in his rising again from the dead on the third day, in ascending up into heaven, in sitting at the right hand of God the Father, and in coming to judge the world at the last day.

Q. 29. How are we made partakers of the redemption purchased by Christ?

A. We are made partakers of the redemption purchased by Christ, by the effectual application of it to us by his Holy Spirit.

Q. 30. How doth the Spirit apply to us the redemption purchased by Christ?

A. The Spirit applieth to us the redemption purchased by Christ, by working faith in us, and thereby uniting us to Christ in our effectual calling.

Q. 31. What is effectual calling?

A. Effectual calling is the work of God's Spirit, whereby convincing us of our sin and misery, enlightening our minds in the knowledge of Christ, and renewing our wills, he doth persuade and enable us to embrace Jesus Christ, freely offered to us in the gospel.

Q. 32. What benefits do they that are effectually called partake of in this life?

A. They that are effectually called do in this life partake of justification, adoption, sanctification, and the several benefits which, in this life, do either accompany or flow from them.

Q. 33. What is justification?

A. Justification is an act of God's free grace, wherein he pardoneth all our sins, and accepteth us as righteous in his sight, only for the righteousness of Christ imputed to us, and received by faith alone.

Q. 34. What is adoption?

A. Adoption is an act of God's free grace, whereby we are received into the number, and have a right to all the privileges, of the sons of God.

Q. 35. What is sanctification?

A. Sanctification is the work of God's free grace, whereby we are renewed in the whole man after the image of God, and are enabled more and more to die unto sin, and live unto righteousness.

Q. 36. What are the benefits which in this life do accompany or flow from justification, adoption, and sanctification?

A. The benefits which in this life do accompany or flow from justification, adoption, and sanctification, are, assurance of God's love, peace of conscience, joy in the Holy Ghost, increase of grace, and perseverance therein to the end.

Q. 37. What benefits do believers receive from Christ at death?

A. The souls of believers are, at their death, made perfect in holiness, and do immediately pass into glory; and their bodies, being still united in Christ, do rest in their graves until the resurrection.

Q. 38. What benefits do believers receive from Christ at the resurrection?

A. At the resurrection, believers, being raised up to glory, shall be openly acknowledged and acquitted in the day of judgment, and made perfectly blessed in the full enjoying of God to all eternity.

Q. 39. What is the duty which God requireth of man?

A. The duty which God requireth of man, is obedience to his revealed will.

Q. 40. What did God at first reveal to man for the rule of his obedience?

A. The rule which God at first revealed to man for his obedience, was the moral law.

Q. 41. Where is the moral law summarily comprehended?

A. The moral law is summarily comprehended in the Ten Commandments.   [Ex 20; Dt 5.6–21]

Q. 42. What is the sum of the Ten Commandments?

A. The sum of the Ten Commandments is, to love the Lord our God, with all our heart, with all our soul, with all our strength, and with all our mind; and our neighbor as ourselves.

Q. 43. What is the preface to the Ten Commandments?

[Ex 20.2]   A. The preface to the Ten Commandments is in these words, "I am the Lord thy God, which have brought thee out of the land of Egypt, out of the house of bondage."

Q. 44. What doth the preface to the Ten Commandments teach us?

A. The preface to the Ten Commandments teacheth us, that because God is the Lord, and our God, and Redeemer, therefore we are bound to keep all his commandments.

Q. 45. Which is the first commandment?

[Ex 20.3]   A. The first commandment is, "Thou shalt have no other gods before me."

Q. 46. What is required in the first commandment?

A. The first commandment requireth us to know and acknowledge God to be the only true God, and our God, and to worship and glorify him accordingly.

Q. 47. What is forbidden in the first commandment?

A. The first commandment forbiddeth the denying, or not worshiping and glorifying, the true God as God, and our God; and the giving of that worship and glory to any other, which is due to him alone.

Q. 48. What are we specially taught by these words, "before me," in the first commandment?

A. These words, "before me," in the first commandment teach us, that God, who seeth all things, taketh notice of, and is much displeased with, the sin of having any other God.

Q. 49. Which is the second commandment?

[Ex 20.4-6]   A. The second commandment is, "Thou shalt not make unto thee any graven image, or any likeness of anything that is in heaven above, or that is in the earth beneath, or that is in the water under the earth; thou shalt not bow down thyself to them, nor serve them; for I the Lord thy God am a jealous God, visiting the iniquity of the fathers upon the children unto the third and fourth generation of them that hate me: and showing mercy unto thousands of them that love me, and keep my commandments."

Q. 50. What is required in the second commandment?

A. The second commandment requireth the receiving, observing, and keeping pure and entire, all such religious worship and ordinances as God hath appointed in his word.

Q. 51. What is forbidden in the second commandment?

A. The second commandment forbiddeth the worshiping of God by images, or any other way not appointed in his word.

Q. 52. What are the reasons annexed to the second commandment?

A. The reasons annexed to the second commandment are, God's sovereignty over us, his propriety in us, and the zeal he hath to his own worship.

Q. 53. Which is the third commandment?

A. The third commandment is, "Thou shalt not take the name of the Lord thy God in vain: for the Lord will not hold him guiltless that taketh his name in vain." [Ex 20.7]

Q. 54. What is required in the third commandment?

A. The third commandment requireth the holy and reverent use of God's names, titles, attributes, ordinances, word, and works.

Q. 55. What is forbidden in the third commandment?

A. The third commandment forbiddeth all profaning or abusing of anything whereby God maketh himself known.

Q. 56. What is the reason annexed to the third commandment?

A. The reason annexed to the third commandment is, that however the breakers of this commandment may escape punishment from men, yet the Lord our God will not suffer them to escape his righteous judgment.

Q. 57. Which is the fourth commandment?

A. The fourth commandment is, "Remember the Sabbath day, to keep it [Ex 20.8-11] holy. Six days shalt thou labor, and do all thy work: but the seventh day is the Sabbath of the Lord thy God: in it thou shalt not do any work, thou, nor thy son, nor thy daughter, thy manservant, nor thy maidservant, nor thy cattle, nor thy stranger that is within thy gates: for in six days the Lord made heaven and earth, the sea, and all that in them is, and rested the seventh day: wherefore the Lord blessed the Sabbath day, and hallowed it."

Q. 58. What is required in the fourth commandment?

A. The fourth commandment requireth the keeping holy to God such set times as he hath appointed in his word; expressly one whole day in seven, to be a holy Sabbath to himself.

Q. 59. Which day of the seven hath God appointed to be the weekly Sabbath?

A. From the beginning of the world to the resurrection of Christ, God appointed the seventh day of the week to be the weekly Sabbath; and the first day of the week, ever since, to continue to the end of the world, which is the Christian Sabbath.

Q. 60. How is the Sabbath to be sanctified?

A. The Sabbath is to be sanctified by a holy resting all that day, even from such worldly employments and recreations as are lawful on other days; and spending the whole time in the public and private exercises of God's worship, except so much as is to be taken up in the works of necessity and mercy.

Q. 61. What is forbidden in the fourth commandment?

A. The fourth commandment forbiddeth the omission, or careless performance, of the duties required, and the profaning the day by idleness, or doing that which is in itself sinful, or by unnecessary thoughts, words, or works, about our worldly employments or recreations.

Q. 62. What are the reasons annexed to the fourth commandment?

A. The reasons annexed to the fourth commandment are, God's allowing us six days of the week for our own employments, his challenging a special propriety in the seventh, his own example, and his blessing the Sabbath day.

Q. 63. Which is the fifth commandment?

A. The fifth commandment is, "Honor thy father and thy mother: that thy [Ex 20.12] days may be long upon the land which the Lord thy God giveth thee."

Q. 64. What is required in the fifth commandment?

A. The fifth commandment requireth the preserving the honor, and performing the duties, belonging to every one in their several places and relations, as superiors, inferiors, or equals.

Q. 65. What is forbidden in the fifth commandment?

A. The fifth commandment forbiddeth the neglecting of, or doing anything against, the honor and duty which belongeth to every one in their several places and relations.

Q. 66. What is the reason annexed to the fifth commandment?

A. The reason annexed to the fifth commandment is, a promise of long life and prosperity (as far as it shall serve for God's glory, and their own good) to all such as keep this commandment.

Q. 67. Which is the sixth commandment?

[Ex 20.13]   A. The sixth commandment is, "Thou shalt not kill."

Q. 68. What is required in the sixth commandment?

A. The sixth commandment requireth all lawful endeavors to preserve our own life, and the life of others.

Q. 69. What is forbidden in the sixth commandment?

A. The sixth commandment forbiddeth the taking away of our own life, or the life of our neighbor, unjustly, or whatsoever tendeth thereunto.

Q. 70. What is the seventh commandment?

[Ex 20.14]   A. The seventh commandment is, "Thou shalt not commit adultery."

Q. 71. What is required in the seventh commandment?

A. The seventh commandment requireth the preservation of our own and our neighbor's chastity, in heart, speech, and behavior.

Q. 72. What is forbidden in the seventh commandment?

A. The seventh commandment forbiddeth all unchaste thoughts, words, and actions.

Q. 73. Which is the eighth commandment?

A. The eighth commandment is, "Thou shalt not steal."   [Ex 20.15]

Q. 74. What is required in the eighth commandment?

A. The eighth commandment requireth the lawful procuring and furthering the wealth and outward estate of ourselves and others.

Q. 75. What is forbidden in the eighth commandment?

A. The eighth commandment forbiddeth whatsoever doth, or may, unjustly hinder our own, or our neighbor's, wealth or outward estate.

Q. 76. Which is the ninth commandment?

A. The ninth commandment is, "Thou shalt not bear false witness against thy neighbor."   [Ex 20.16]

Q. 77. What is required in the ninth commandment?

A. The ninth commandment requireth the maintaining and promoting of truth between man and man, and of our own and our neighbor's good name, especially in witness bearing.

Q. 78. What is forbidden in the ninth commandment?

A. The ninth commandment forbiddeth whatsoever is prejudicial to truth, or injurious to our own or our neighbor's good name.

Q. 79. Which is the tenth commandment?

A. The tenth commandment is, "Thou shalt not covet thy neighbor's house,   [Ex 20.17] thou shalt not covet thy neighbor's wife, nor his manservant, nor his maidservant, nor his ox, nor his ass, nor anything that is thy neighbor's."

Q. 80. What is required in the tenth commandment?

A. The tenth commandment requireth full contentment with our own condition, with a right and charitable frame of spirit toward our neighbor, and all that is his.

Q. 81. What is forbidden in the tenth commandment?

A. The tenth commandment forbiddeth all discontentment with our own estate, envying or grieving at the good of our neighbor, and all inordinate motions and affections to anything that is his.

Q. 82. Is any man able perfectly to keep the commandments of God?

A. No mere man since the fall is able in this life perfectly to keep the commandments of God, but doth daily break them in thought, word, and deed.

Q. 83. Are all transgressions of the law equally heinous?

A. Some sins in themselves, and by reason of several aggravations, are more heinous in the sight of God than others.

Q. 84. What doth every sin deserve?

A. Every sin deserveth God's wrath and curse, both in this life, and that which is to come.

Q. 85. What doth God require of us, that we may escape his wrath and curse, due to us for sin?

A. To escape the wrath and curse of God, due to us for sin, God requireth of us faith in Jesus Christ, repentance unto life, with the diligent use of all the outward means whereby Christ communicateth to us the benefits of redemption.

Q. 86. What is faith in Jesus Christ?

A. Faith in Jesus Christ is a saving grace, whereby we receive and rest upon him alone for salvation, as he is offered to us in the gospel.

Q. 87. What is repentance unto life?

A. Repentance unto life is a saving grace, whereby a sinner, out of a true sense of his sin, and apprehension of the mercy of God in Christ, doth, with grief and hatred of his sin, turn from it unto God, with full purpose of, and endeavor after, new obedience.

Q. 88. What are the outward and ordinary means whereby Christ communicateth to us the benefits of redemption?

A. The outward and ordinary means whereby Christ communicateth to us the benefits of redemption are, his ordinances, especially the word, sacraments, and prayer; all which are made effectual to the elect for salvation.

Q. 89. How is the word made effectual to salvation?

A. The Spirit of God maketh the reading, but especially the preaching, of the word, an effectual means of convincing and converting sinners, and of building them up in holiness and comfort through faith, unto salvation.

Q. 90. How is the word to be read and heard, that it may become effectual to salvation?

A. That the word may become effectual to salvation, we must attend thereunto with diligence, preparation, and prayer; receive it with faith and love, lay it up in our hearts, and practice it in our lives.

Q. 91. How do the sacraments become effectual means of salvation?

A. The sacraments become effectual means of salvation, not from any virtue in them, or in him that doth administer them; but only by the blessing of Christ, and the working of his Spirit in them that by faith receive them.

Q. 92. What is a sacrament?

A. A sacrament is a holy ordinance instituted by Christ; wherein, by sensible signs, Christ and the benefits of the new covenant are represented, sealed, and applied to believers.

Q. 93. Which are the sacraments of the new testament?

A. The sacraments of the new testament are baptism and the Lord's supper.

Q. 94. What is baptism?

A. Baptism is a sacrament, wherein the washing with water, in the name of the Father, and of the Son, and of the Holy Ghost, doth signify and seal our ingrafting into Christ, and partaking of the benefits of the covenant of grace, and our engagement to be the Lord's.

Q. 95. To whom is baptism to be administered?

A. Baptism is not to be administered to any that are out of the visible church, till they profess their faith in Christ, and obedience to him; but the infants of such as are members of the visible church are to be baptized.

Q. 96. What is the Lord's supper?

A. The Lord's supper is a sacrament, wherein, by giving and receiving bread and wine, according to Christ's appointment, his death is showed forth; and the worthy receivers are, not after a corporal and carnal manner, but by faith, made partakers of his body and blood, with all his benefits, to their spiritual nourishment, and growth in grace.

Q. 97. What is required for the worthy receiving of the Lord's supper?

A. It is required of them that would worthily partake of the Lord's supper, that they examine themselves, of their knowledge to discern the Lord's body, of their faith to feed upon him, of their repentance, love, and new obedience; lest, coming unworthily, they eat and drink judgment to themselves.

Q. 98. What is prayer?

A. Prayer is an offering up of our desires unto God, for things agreeable to his will, in the name of Christ, with confession of our sins, and thankful acknowledgment of his mercies.

Q. 99. What rule hath God given for our direction in prayer?

A. The whole word of God is of use to direct us in prayer, but the special rule of direction is that form of prayer which Christ taught his disciples, commonly called, The Lord's Prayer.

Q. 100. What doth the preface of the Lord's Prayer teach us?

A. The preface of the Lord's Prayer, which is, "Our Father which art in heaven," teacheth us to draw near to God with all holy reverence and confidence, [Mt 6.9] as children to a father, able and ready to help us; and that we should pray with and for others.

Q. 101. What do we pray for in the first petition?

A. In the first petition, which is, "Hallowed be thy name," we pray, that God would enable us, and others, to glorify him in all that whereby he maketh himself known, and that he would dispose all things to his own glory.

Q. 102. What do we pray for in the second petition?

[Mt 6.10]   A. In the second petition, which is, "Thy kingdom come," we pray, that Satan's kingdom may be destroyed; and that the kingdom of grace may be advanced, ourselves and others brought into it, and kept in it; and that the kingdom of glory may be hastened.

Q. 103. What do we pray for in the third petition?

[Mt 6.10]   A. In the third petition, which is, "Thy will be done in earth as it is in heaven," we pray, that God, by his grace, would make us able and willing to know, obey, and submit to his will in all things, as the angels do in heaven.

Q. 104. What do we pray for in the fourth petition?

[Mt 6.11]   A. In the fourth petition, which is, "Give us this day our daily bread," we pray, that of God's free gift we may receive a competent portion of good things of this life, and enjoy his blessing with them.

Q. 105. What do we pray for in the fifth petition?

[Mt 6.12]   A. In the fifth petition, which is, "And forgive us our debts, as we forgive our debtors," we pray, that God, for Christ's sake, would freely pardon all our sins; which we are the rather encouraged to ask, because by his grace we are enabled from the heart to forgive others.

Q. 106. What do we pray for in the sixth petition?

[Mt 6.13]   A. In the sixth petition, which is, "And lead us not into temptation, but deliver us from evil," we pray, that God would either keep us from being tempted to sin, or support and deliver us when we are tempted.

Q. 107. What doth the conclusion of the Lord's Prayer teach us?

A. The conclusion of the Lord's Prayer, which is, "For thine is the kingdom, and the power, and the glory, forever. Amen," teacheth us to take our encouragement in prayer from God only, and in our prayers to praise him, ascribing kingdom, power, and glory to him; and, in testimony of our desire and assurance to be heard, we say, Amen.

Confessions from the Radical Reformation

In addition to the Lutheran and the Reformed confessions—and in opposition to both—there were other Reformation groups and confessions that dissented much more sharply and fundamentally from the received traditions of the Catholic West.

The nomenclature for them has not been uniform. Common to most of them was the belief that neither the Lutheran nor the Reformed definitions of "reformation" had gone far enough on such issues as the sacraments or dogma or peace and war—or the relation to the political powers that be; hence the title "the continuing Reformation." To Lutheran and Reformed opponents, they were *Schwärmer*, or "Enthusiasts," because many of them appealed to religious experience and an inner light, not in place of the authority of the Bible but as a key to understanding and interpreting the Bible. Borrowing terminology from the taxonomy of political parties, Reformation historians such as John T. McNeill and Roland H. Bainton in the 1940s employed the classification "the left wing of the Reformation."

But the designation that seems to have stuck is "Radical Reformation," which became current, if not canonical, through the book of that name by George Huntston Williams, which was published in 1962 and came out in a greatly expanded third edition in 1992. As a counterpart to that designation, Williams introduced the term "Magisterial Reformation" to identify those versions of Protestantism that were in some sort of alliance with the political magistracy and/or were committed to conserving substantial portions of the "Catholic substance" of tradition even while asserting their "Protestant principle."

Although it sometimes appears to be an attempt to classify groups who by definition refused to be classified, "Radical" does seem to work as an appellation at least for these confessions, which came out of the more drastic reform in the very concept of the Christian faith and the Christian church.

Hans Denck, *Confession Before the Nuremberg Council*, 1525

Hans Denck (c. 1500–1527), a well-educated humanist schoolteacher, embraced the Lutheran cause early on but later joined the fledgling Anabaptist movement. Denck had studied at Ingolstadt and Basel and was praised for his knowledge of Scripture and biblical languages. Together with Ludwig Hätzer (c. 1500–1529), he published a translation of the Prophets from Hebrew in 1527, the first translation of that part of the Bible from the original language into German, preceding Luther by four years.[1] Early in his career he worked as an editor at a printing house in Basel. On the recommendation of Oecolampadius, however, he became the rector of St. Sebald's school in Nuremberg. It was in Nuremberg that Denck drifted toward the more radical elements in the Reform movement, influenced by the writings of Andreas Bodenstein von Carlstadt (c. 1480–1541) and Thomas Müntzer (c. 1489–1525). Müntzer probably stayed with Denck for about four weeks in the autumn of 1524.[2] Denck's theology, however, also draws on medieval mysticism, particularly the works of Johannes Tauler († 1361) and the anonymous *Theologia Deutsch.*

When the famous case of the three "godless painters" (Hans Sebald Beham, Barthel Beham, and Georg Pencz) came before the Nuremberg Council, Denck was implicated by Hans Sebald Beham (1500–1550), who claimed to have discussed his view of the sacrament with the schoolmaster.

The ministers of Nuremberg, chief among whom was the staunch Lutheran Andreas Osiander (1496/98–1552), questioned Denck and required him to submit a profession of faith. In his sometimes rambling statement, Denck emphasizes the role of faith in religious life and the supreme love of God for humankind. He did not question the validity of the Bible but viewed Scripture as a lantern that cannot remove the darkness unless one hears the inner call of the Holy Spirit to interpret it. External baptism, according to Denck, is not required for salvation and serves no purpose unless internal baptism—by which he means being filled with the Spirit— has taken place. Likewise the sacrament of the Lord's supper is merely a sign, efficacious only if one has faith.

---

1. The first edition, *Alle Propheten nach Hebraischer sprach verteütscht* (Worms: Peter Schöffer, 13 April 1527), was quickly followed by ten more printings and editions before the end of 1528.

2. Baring 1959, 154.

On 21 January 1525, Denck was ordered to leave Nuremberg and never to return. Over the course of the next year and a half, he suffered the same fate in other cities in southern Germany and Switzerland because of his radical spiritualism. He joined the southern German Anabaptists and became one of their most eloquent leaders until his early death from the plague in 1527. This branch of Anabaptists differed from the Swiss Brethren, and in fact, it is probably Denck and his followers who are referred to among the "false brethren" in the Swiss Anabaptist → *Schleitheim Confession.*[3]

Denck's *Confession Before the Nuremberg Council* became part of the doctrinal heritage of the Hutterite Brethren,[4] the Mennonites, and German Pietists, and Denck's writings influenced the work of such later spiritualists as Sebastian Frank (c. 1499–c. 1542) and Caspar Schwenckfeld (1490–1561).

Edition and translation: Bauman 1991, 54–67 (edition reprinted from Fellmann, *Quellen und Forschungen zur Reformationsgeschichte* 24/2).

Literature: Baring 1959; Bauman 1991, 51–53; Friedmann 1931–32; Hall 1961, 149–70; Keller 1882; Kiwiet 1957, 1958; Lohse 1968; Müsing 1977, 91–126; Ozment 1973, 116–36; Seebass 1976; Seguenny 1979; *TRE* 8:488–90 (Packull).

---

3. Kiwiet 1958, 24.

4. *The Five Articles* of the Hutterite Brethren have even been attributed to Denck. See Friedmann 1931–32.

Hans Denck, *Confession Before the Nuremberg Council*, 1525

I, Hans Denck, confess that I truly regard, feel, and perceive that by nature I am a poor in spirit person subject to every illness of body and soul.

Yet even so, I also sense, as well, something within me that powerfully resists my inborn willfulness and points me to a life or sanctity which appears as impossible to attain as it seems inconceivable for my body to ascend the visible heaven[s].

They say one comes to that life through faith. I let that be. But who gives me that faith? If it is inborn in me, then I must have that life by nature, [but] that is not so.

From childhood I learned the faith from my parents and used its language —thereafter also through reading mankind's books—and, what is much more, I boasted of having faith but never really considered its counterpart, which by nature is born within me, even though I have often been reproved by it.

This false [that is, traditional] faith decisively confronts the aforementioned inborn poverty of spirit. For I truly see that this inborn "sickness" or spiritual poverty does not the whole while fundamentally impoverish; the more I am preoccupied with myself, the more it necessarily increases.

Just as a diseased tree by nature does not become well but only worse, however much one binds and nurses it, if one does not attend to the root and master it.

He who would like to have money and yet has none would gladly say he has a thousand guilders if [only] it were true. But, since he does not have them, he should not say so lest by thus speaking he greatly deceive the people, himself most of all.

I dearly wish that I had faith, that is, life. But, since it is not thoroughly founded within me, I can deceive neither myself nor others.

Indeed, if I say today, I believe, I might, nevertheless, tomorrow reprove myself for lying, yet not I, but the truth [reproves] which I perceive imperfectly in me.

This I know in myself for certain that it is the truth, wherefore, God willing, I will listen to what it wishes to tell me; and I will not let anyone take it from me.

And where I discern what is lofty or low in a creature I will listen; whereto it directs me I will go according to his will, wherefrom it drives me I will flee.

Inasmuch as I presume [to discern] Scripture in my own power, I understand nothing. As much as that [truth] compels me, that much I thus comprehend, not through merit, but by grace.

By nature I cannot, indeed, believe the Scripture. But that [which is] in me, I do not say, of me, but that [which] compels me without any of my will and doing, that compels me to read the Scripture for the sake of [its] testimony.

Consequently, I read it and find in particular testimony which powerfully confirms that just that which thus compels me is [the] Christ whom Scripture testifies to be the Son of the Most High.

As for this faith, I dare not say I have it, for the reason stated. How well I see that my unbelief cannot stand before him. Therefore I say: Very well then, in God's almighty name, whom I fear from the depth of my heart. Lord, I believe, help

[Mk 9.24]   my [un]belief!

[2 Pt 1.19]   Thus with Peter I hold Scripture to be a lantern which shines in the dark. The darkness of my unbelief is by nature deep[-rooted] in (the) truth. The Scripture, the lantern, shines in the darkness, but it cannot of itself (as it is written with human hands, spoken with human mouth, seen with human eyes, and heard with human ears) entirely remove the darkness. But, when the day, that unending light dawns,

[Mt 17.20]   when the morning star—that faith like a mustard seed which presently announces the sun of Christ's righteousness—rises in our hearts, as Scripture also witnesses

[Gn 32.26]   concerning Jacob the patriarch, then only is the darkness of unbelief thus overcome. That is not yet in me.

While such darkness is in me, it is impossible that I should entirely understand the Scripture. But, if I do not understand it, how should I then draw (the) faith out of it? That would mean faith derives of itself if I claimed it before it were disclosed to me by God.

Indeed, he who will not await the revelation of God but presumes the work which solely belongs to the Spirit of God, he surely makes out of the mystery of God, documented in the Scripture, a dissolute abomination before God and perverts the grace of our God into licentiousness, as pointed out in the epistles of Jude

Jude [4]; 2 Pt 2[.18]   and 2 Peter 2.

From then on immediately after the apostles' death, there appeared very many divisions or sects all of whom armed themselves with Scripture badly understood. Why badly understood? Proceeding headlong according to their own presumption, they acquired a false faith before desiring from God a true one.

Therefore, Peter says further that Scripture "is not a matter of one's own in-

[2 Pt 1.20]   terpretation," but it belongs to the Holy Spirit to interpret [it], who also first gave it.

Of this interpretation of the Spirit everyone must beforehand be certain in himself. Where [this is] not [so], it is false and [worth] nothing. What is "false and nothing" one can refute with other testimony of Scripture.

That is my position to which I hold, freely, to the love and honor of God and to the harm and disgrace of no one, except what is not in the truth.

From this it is (in part) readily perceived what I hold regarding Scripture, sin, righteousness of God, law, and gospel. Yet, so as to briefly explain myself, I speak of the latter four thus:

Unbelief alone is sin, which the righteousness of God destroys through the law. As soon as the law has lost its function, the gospel takes its place. Through the hearing of the gospel comes faith. Faith has no sin. Where there is no sin, there the righteousness of God dwells. [Rom 10.17]

Thus, [the] righteousness of God is God himself. Sin is what raises itself up against God; it is in (the) truth nothing.

(The) righteousness works through the word that was from the beginning and is subsequently divided in two, law and gospel, on account of the twofold office which Christ as King of righteousness exercises, namely, to destroy the unbelievers and to bring to life the believers.

Now, all believers were once unbelievers. Consequently, in becoming believers, they thus first had to die in order that they might thereafter no longer live [for] themselves, as unbelievers do, but [for] God through Christ that their walk might indeed no longer be on earth but in heaven, as Paul says. [Phil 3.20]

David also verifies this where he says: The Lord leads down into hell and up again. [1 Sm 2.6]

All this I believe (Lord, crush my unbelief) in truth, await[ing] now whoever wishes to deny and overthrow it. Thereupon, I offer also to record what I believe about baptism and the Lord's supper. Now [my time] is too short. The Lord be with us. Amen.

[2.] CONCERNING BAPTISM

I, Hans Denck, confess further, that I in (the) truth comprehend, insofar as it has comprehended me, that all things which are unclean by nature, the more one washes them, the less one can accomplish with them.

For, who indeed would venture to wash the red off the brick and the black off the coal so long as they are not intrinsically otherwise? In any case, it would be useless work, because (the) nature is not basically changed and overcome.

Likewise, it is also futile to wash externally the man whose body and soul are by nature unclean if he is not initially penitent and won over from within.

The almighty word of God alone is able to descend and penetrate into the hard abyss of man's uncleanness, just as an arid soil is softened up by a good rain.

Where this happens, conflict arises in man before nature yields, and despair [ensues], so he supposes that he must perish in body and soul [and that] he might not sustain the work God commenced.

Just as one surmises when a great flood comes [that] the earth might not withstand but will be washed away.

In such despair David then says: "Lord God, help me, for the waters have risen up to my soul."

[Ps 69.2]

But such despair, whether great or small, lasts as long as the elect one is in this body, and the work of Christ begins therewith.

Therefore, not only John the Baptist but also the apostles of Christ baptized in water. [The] reason: whatever does not survive the water can indeed much less endure the fire, for the baptism of Christ is in Spirit, (and) the perfection of his work.

[1 Pt 3[.21]

This water or baptism makes blessed (1 Peter 3), not [in] that it removes the dirt from the body, but because of the covenant [for] a good conscience with God.

This covenant means that he who lets himself be baptized does so upon the death of Christ, that as he died this one also dies to Adam, as Christ is resurrected, this one also walks in a new life [of] Christ, according to Romans 6.

[Rom 6[.4]

Where this covenant is, there the Spirit of Christ also comes hither and ignites the fire of love which consumes fully what infirmity remains and completes the work of Christ. Thereafter befalls the Sabbath, the eternal rest in God, about which all tongues cease their speech.

Where external baptism transpires in the previously mentioned covenant, it is good. Where not, it serves no purpose for the reason indicated.

External baptism is not required for salvation; as Paul says, he was not sent to baptize, that being unnecessary, but to preach the gospel [that is] necessary.

[1 Cor 1.17]

But internal baptism, which is referred to above, is necessary. Thus it is written, he who believes and is baptized will be saved.

[Mk 16.16]

[3.] CONCERNING CHRIST'S SUPPER

I, Hans Denck, confess again as before that I find I am by nature unwell in body and soul, truly poisoned and feverish; and whatever I in this unhealthy, poisoned, and feverish body and soul eat does not drive away my illness but only worsens it.

I find also that that which drives and girds me, not as I will but as it wishes, advises and tells me as a faithful physician [that], because the poison runs in the blood, the fever cannot be alleviated except the blood be calmed and subdued.

And this may happen in two ways: through abstinence and bloodletting. Dieting means that one does not sustain oneself internally with unregulated eating, that is, with false satisfaction. Bloodletting means that one also should endure external suffering on the advice of the physician.

This is the work of Christ towards the death of Adam. Now, although that is not accomplished so long as I live in the body, it is nevertheless begun in the body [and] at times also suffered for the sake of the covenant with God as I place my will in God's will through Christ, the Mediator, as said above regarding baptism.

He who is thus minded and eats the living invisible bread, he will always be strengthened and empowered in the right life.

He who is thus minded and drinks from the invisible chalice the invisible wine, which God from the beginning has distilled through his Son, through the Word, he becomes ecstatic and no longer knows anything about himself but through the love of God becomes entirely deified and God in him humanized.

That is called having eaten the body of Christ and having drunk the blood of Christ, John 6.

Jn 6

Indeed, he who is thus minded, as often as he does what the Lord says, that is, as often as he eats of the bread and drinks from the cup, he commemorates and proclaims the death of the Lord.

[1 Cor 11.26]

Now, for him who thus also physically eats and drinks, it is truly wholesome and healthful for the body because the body has subjected itself to the Spirit and also serves [in] the truth.

Now if it is sound and hail, then it cannot differ from the word of God, as Paul often designates "sound" teaching. But since it is invisible in the visible bread and yet not different than the bread, therefore, it is indeed the invisible Word in the visible body, that is conceived by the Holy Spirit, born of Mary, the Virgin.

[2 Tm 4.3]

[As for] eating and drinking, neither can be without the other with proper benefit. Eating without drinking causes indigestion and does not nourish. This Paul intends when he says: "If I had faith so that I could move mountains with it, and had not love, it would still amount to nothing!"

[1 Cor 13.2]

Drinking without eating weakens and intoxicates. Love without faith deceives itself in that it purports to love everything for God's sake. For a time, indeed, it may appear thus, nevertheless, this does not in truth prevail. For suddenly it becomes evident that only that is loved by him which was loved before though it be evil and that [he] always hates what tells him the truth, even though it be good.

Eating and drinking, both together are beneficial. Eating cheers and strengthens, drinking kindles love and perfects that for which Christ came, which is the ablution of sin that transpired in the shedding of Christ's blood.

Now, what was said above concerning the visible bread, may also be said here concerning the cup.

[Mt 4.2]   One can live without this outer bread through the power of God wherever his praise requires it, as [did] Moses on Mount Sinai and Christ in the desert. Without the inner [bread] no one can live. For the righteous[a] live by faith. He who believes not, lives not.

All this I confess from the depth of my heart before the countenance of the invisible God, to whom through this confession I most humbly submit myself; I should not say I, but rather he himself subjects me to himself, not to him alone but to all creatures in him. Nevertheless,

I implore all creatures and your wisdom, which is in the hand of God, through the name of the terrible and great God to judge me and my imprisoned brethren, whom I love in [the] truth, not according to appearance but according to the truth. As also the Lord will judge when he will come in his glory on the day of the revelation of all mysteries. Amen. Amen.

a. [Heb 2.4; Rom 1.17]

Balthasar Hubmaier, *A Christian Catechism*, 1526

Balthasar Hubmaier (1480/85–1528) is one of the more prolific early Anabaptist writers. In twenty-five works written between 1524 and 1528, he put forward his views on Christian life and practice. Among his writings are statements of faith, including *The Eighteen Theses*, written at the very start of his career, and a conciliatory account of his faith composed with the goal of avoiding execution. Neither of these professions, however, reflects the more radical beliefs for which he is known from other writings. *A Christian Catechism*, by contrast, was written at the height of his success as an Anabaptist leader and in the safety of Moravia, where Anabaptists were tolerated.

Hubmaier began his religious life as an ordained priest. He was trained by Johannes Eck at the University of Freiburg and later studied at Ingolstadt, where he received the doctorate in theology and lectured in theology. In the early 1520s, as a parish priest in Waldshut, Hubmaier came into contact with Swiss reformers, especially Zwingli. He then successfully agitated for the Reformation of Waldshut. Following the model of → Ulrich Zwingli's *Sixty-Seven Articles,* Hubmaier published his *Eighteen Theses*—sometimes titled *Eighteen Dissertations*—in preparation for a religious disputation in Waldshut in April 1524.[1] He cites the Bible as the only authority for religious belief, scorns pilgrimages, rejects the notion of purgatory, acknowledges justification by faith alone, forbids the use of images, and takes a sacramentarian view of the eucharist. After the disputation, Catholic clerics left Waldshut. The townspeople embraced the newly reformed preacher, defending him against calls for his arrest from the Austrian Hapsburgs.

Within a year, Hubmaier had forsaken Zwinglian views, aligning himself with Anabaptists and defending believers' baptism in *Von der christlichen Taufe der Gläubigen (On the Christian Baptism of Believers).*[2] His radicalism soon brought him and the town of Waldshut into the Peasants' War. Hubmaier's willingness to take up the sword to defend Waldshut against imperial forces runs counter

---

1. See Pipkin and Yoder 1989, 31–34, for the English translation. For the original German, see Westin and Bergsten 1962, 71–74.
2. *Von der christenlichen Tauff der Gläubigen* (1525), edited by Westin and Bergsten 1962, 118–63.

to the pacifism of the Swiss Anabaptists as expressed in the later → *Schleitheim Confession*.[3]

Waldshut was taken by Catholic imperial forces in December 1525, causing Hubmaier to flee to Zurich, where he hoped to take refuge with coreligionists because Anabaptism was outlawed in that city. He was soon captured, tortured, and forced to recant. After his release in the spring of 1526, Hubmaier made his way to Nikolsburg (Mikulov) in Moravia, where Anabaptists were tolerated. During his stay in Nikolsburg he became a prominent leader of the movement and published most of his extant writings. His *Catechism* entitled *Ein christennliche Leertafel* (*A Christian Catechism* or, literally, *A Christian Instruction Tablet*) was completed in early 1527. It is presented as a dialogue between two members of the house of Liechtenstein, the ruling family in Moravia, but it reads very much like a traditional catechism with its question-and-answer format. Hubmaier says that one must know the *Catechism* before one can be baptized. Like any catechism, the work deals with the nature of God, the commandments, the Lord's Prayer, and → *The Apostles' Creed*. Not surprisingly, Hubmaier devotes a large section of the *Catechism* to baptism, but other Anabaptist tenets also appear, such as the ban. Missing from Hubmaier's brand of Anabaptism are injunctions against use of force and the swearing of oaths, as well as any notion of the community of goods.

After only twelve months in Nikolsburg, Hubmaier was extradited to Austria, where he was tried by Hapsburg authorities in Vienna. While imprisoned, he wrote another profession of faith, a pale reflection of his true views (*Rechenschaft des Glaubens*) addressed to Ferdinand of Austria.[4] Condemned to the stake, Hubmaier was executed on 10 March 1528. His motto, and the phrase printed at the end of most of his publications, was "Die warhait ist untödtlich [The truth is unkillable]."

Edition: Westin and Bergsten 1962, 71–74.

Translation: Pipkin and Yoder 1989, 31–34.

---

3. Hubmaier defended the use of military force in *Von dem Schwert* (1527), edited by Westin and Bergsten 1962, 434–57.
4. Westin and Bergsten 1962, 460–91; English translation in Pipkin and Yoder 1989, 525–68.

Literature: *ODCC* 798–99; *OER* 260–63 (Stayer); Pipkin and Yoder 1989, 15–30; Westin and Bergsten 1962, 9–57, 69–71; Windhorst 1978; Yoder 1959.

Balthasar Hubmaier, *A Christian Catechism*, 1526

A Christian Catechism that every person before he is baptized in water should previously know, in the form of a dialogue

Leonhart questions, Hans replies

1. *Leonhart:* What is your name?

Hans: My name is Hans.

2. *Leonhart:* Who gave you this name?

Hans: My father and mother.

3. *Leonhart:* For what purpose?

Hans: To tell me apart from other people.

4. *Leonhart:* What are you?

Hans: A corporeal reasonable creature, in body, soul, and spirit, created thus by God in his image.

5. *Leonhart:* What is God?

Hans: He is the highest good, almighty, all-wise, and all-merciful.

6. *Leonhart:* How do you recognize his omnipotence?

Hans: From the marvelous creation of the heaven, the earth, and all that is therein.

7. *Leonhart:* How his all-wisdom?

Hans: By the ingenious ordering and governing of all creatures.

8. *Leonhart:* How his all-mercifulness?

Hans: By his sending his only-begotten Son, our Lord Jesus Christ, into this world that it may not be lost because of sin, but through him attain to eternal life.

9. *Leonhart:* What is sin?

Hans: It is every movement or desire contrary to the will of God, whether in thought, in word, or in deed.

10. *Leonhart:* How do you recognize sin?

Hans: By the commandments of the law.

11. *Leonhart:* How many commandments are there?

Hans: Ten.

12. *Leonhart:* Recite them.

[Ex 20.2–17]   *Hans:* "I am the Lord your God, who brought you out of the land of Egypt, out of the house of bondage to sin.

"You shall have no other gods before me.

"You shall not make for yourself a graven image, or any likeness of anything that is in heaven above, or that is in the earth beneath, or that is in the water under the earth; you shall not worship them or serve them; for I the Lord your God am a jealous God, visiting the iniquity of the fathers upon the children to the third and fourth generation of those who hate me, but showing steadfast love to thousands of those who love me and keep my commandments.

"You shall not take the name of the Lord your God in vain; for the Lord will not hold him guiltless who takes his name in vain.

"Remember the Sabbath day, to keep it holy. Six days you shall labor, and do all your work; but the seventh day is a Sabbath to the Lord your God; in it you shall not do any work, you, or your son, or your daughter, your manservant, or your maidservant, or your cattle, or the sojourner who is within your city's gates; for in six days the Lord made heaven and earth, the sea, and all that is in them, and rested on the seventh day; therefore the Lord blessed the Sabbath day and hallowed it.

"Honor your father and your mother, that your days may be long in the land which the Lord your God shall give you.

"You shall not kill.

"You shall not commit adultery.

"You shall not steal.

"You shall not bear false witness against your neighbor.

"You shall not covet your neighbor's house; you shall not covet your neighbor's wife, or his manservant, or his maidservant, or his ox, or his ass, or anything that is your neighbor's."

13. *Leonhart:* But if you have fallen into sin, how do you get rid of it?

Hans: By repentance and prayer to God.

14. *Leonhart:* What is repentance?

Hans: Accusing oneself of sin before God, asking him for forgiveness, and thenceforth never again committing it; that is the highest form of repentance, namely, to guard oneself from sin and to walk henceforth according to God's word.

15. *Leonhart:* What is prayer?

Hans: It is lifting up the mind to God in spirit and in truth.

16. *Leonhart:* How do you pray?

Hans: As Christ taught his disciples, Matthew 6; Luke 11.[a]

17. *Leonhart:* What did he teach them to say?

Hans: Thus: Our Father who art in heaven,

Hallowed be thy name.

a. Mt 6[.9–13]; Lk 11[.2–4]

Thy kingdom come,

Thy will be done,

On earth as it is in heaven.

Give us this day our daily bread;

Forgive us our debts,

As we also forgive our debtors;

Lead us not into temptation,

But deliver us from evil. Amen.

18. *Leonhart:* How do you know that God hears your prayer?

Hans: From God's promises and from the gospel.

19. *Leonhart:* What is the difference between the two?

Hans: The promises comfort and preserve the confessing sinner, that he may not despair in his sins, for a Messiah will come to atone for the sins, to release the debtors from prison, and to lead them with him into the promised fatherland. It is as if one directed the sick man to a good physician who will surely make him well, but he is not yet well. The gospel, on the other hand, completely calms the person, helps him to rest in his conscience and makes him completely well, for it shows that the law is now fulfilled in Christ, who has paid the debt of sin for us and has already vanquished death, devil, and hell. Thus the patriarchs of old had the benefit of the promises of God as in Abraham's bosom; where they were preserved until the time of Christ's descent into hell. When the gospel was proclaimed to them there by the Spirit of Christ, only then did they really live in the Christ who had been given them and obtain redemption and eternal joy through the joyful message that he has vanquished sin, death, devil, and hell. Only then were the holy fathers freed of their pains in hell which they (but not the soul of Christ) had suffered there for a long time. Now the words of Peter are clearly understood, Acts 2; 1 Peter 3, 4.[a]

20. *Leonhart:* Point out to me a promise in the Bible.

Gn 3[.15]   *Hans:* The seed of the woman shall crush your head, serpent, Genesis 3. Likewise, through your seed, Abraham, shall all the peoples of the earth be blessed,

Gn 22[.18]   Genesis 22.

21. *Leonhart:* Show me also a message of the gospel.

Hans: Christ died for the sake of our sins, and arose for the sake of our

Rom 4[.25]   justification, Romans 4.

22. *Leonhart:* What follows from this message?

Hans: Faith.

---

a. Acts 2[.24]; 1 Pt 3[.19–22], 4[.6]

23. *Leonhart:* What is faith?

Hans: Faith is the realization of the unspeakable mercy of God, his gracious favor and goodwill, which he bears to us through his most beloved Son Jesus Christ, whom he did not spare and delivered him to death for our sakes that sin might be paid for, and we might be reconciled to him and with the assurance of our hearts cry to him: Abba, Father, our Father who are in heaven.

24. *Leonhart:* How many kinds of faith are there?

Hans: Two kinds, namely a dead one and a living one.

25. *Leonhart:* What is dead faith?

Hans: One that is unfruitful and without the works of love, James 2.   Jas 2[.17]

26. *Leonhart:* What is living faith?

Hans: One that produces the fruits of the Spirit and works through love, Galatians 5.   Gal 5[.22]

27. *Leonhart:* What are the fruits of the Spirit?

Hans: Love, joy, peace, patience, kindness, goodness, faith, gentleness, self-control, and the like.

28. *Leonhart:* What are the works of the flesh?

Hans: Adultery, whoring, impurity, licentiousness, idolatry, sorcery, enmity, strife, jealousy, anger, quarreling, dissension, party spirit, hatred, murder, drunkenness, gluttony, and the like.

29. *Leonhart:* How many articles of the Christian faith are there?

Hans: Twelve.

30. *Leonhart:* What are they?

Hans: I believe in God the Father Almighty, Maker of heaven and earth. I believe in Jesus Christ, his only Son our Lord, who was conceived by the Holy Spirit, born of the Virgin Mary. I believe he suffered under Pontius Pilate, was crucified, died, and was buried. He descended into hell; the third day he arose again from the dead. He ascended into heaven, where he sits at the right hand of God his Almighty Father, from whence he shall come to judge the quick and the dead. I believe in the Holy Spirit. I believe and confess the holy universal church, which is the fellowship of all holy and Christ-believing persons. I believe that by the command of Christ it has authority to forgive sins. I believe the resurrection of the body and the life everlasting.

31. *Leonhart:* After faith what do you desire?

Hans: Water baptism.

32. *Leonhart:* How many kinds of baptism are there?

Hans: Three kinds.

33. *Leonhart:* What are they?

Hans: A baptism of the Spirit, a baptism of water, and a baptism of blood.

34. *Leonhart:* What is the baptism of the Spirit?

Hans: It is an inner illumination of our hearts that takes place by the Holy Spirit, through the living word of God.

35. *Leonhart:* What is water baptism?

Hans: It is an outward and public testimony of the inner baptism in the Spirit, which a person gives by receiving water, with which one confesses one's sins before all people. One also testifies thereby that one believes in the forgiveness of his sins through the death and resurrection of our Lord Jesus Christ. Thereupon one also has himself outwardly enrolled, inscribed, and by water baptism incorporated into the fellowship of the church according to the institution of Christ, before which church the person also publicly and orally vows to God and agrees in the strength of God the Father, Son, and Holy Spirit that he will henceforth believe and live according to his divine word. And if he should trespass herein he will accept brotherly admonition, according to Christ's order, Matthew 18. This precisely is the true baptismal vow, which we have lost for a thousand years; meanwhile Satan has forced his way in with his monastic vows and priestly vows and established them in the holy place.

Mt 18[.15–17]

36. *Leonhart:* What is the baptism of blood?

Hans: It is a daily mortification of the flesh until death.

37. *Leonhart:* Where did Christ mention these baptisms?

Jn 3[.5]

Lk 12[.50]

Hans: Concerning Spirit baptism in John 3, concerning water baptism in Matthew 28, Mark 16,[a] and concerning the baptism of blood in Luke 12.

38. *Leonhart:* Why were you not baptized in infancy?

Hans: Because then I did not yet believe nor know what faith, Christ, or baptism is.

39. *Leonhart:* What is your opinion of the infant baptism which the water-priests use?

Hans: Nothing other than that the adult child gives a bath to the young child, thereby depriving it of the real water baptism of Christ.

40. *Leonhart:* If only believers are to be baptized who publicly confess with their mouth, as Christ instituted water baptism for believers alone, Matthew 28, Mark 16, must we submit to rebaptism? What seems right to you?

Hans: Our approving, supposing, and thinking are of no importance; we must ask advice of the mouth of the Lord who said: "Go therefore and teach all nations and baptize them; he who believes and is baptized will be saved." Since Christ commanded his disciples to preach and baptize, that very command orders

a. Mt 28[.18–20]; Mk 16[.15–16]

us to hear the preaching and to be baptized. For whoever then loosens one of the least of these commandments shall be called least in the kingdom of heaven, Matthew 5; James 2. But now water baptism is a very earnest command; it has been proclaimed to be performed in the name of the Father, the Son, and the Holy Spirit. If we accept this baptism, even though we were one hundred years old, it would still not be a rebaptism, because infant baptism is no baptism and is unworthy of being called baptism. For the infant knows neither good nor evil and cannot consent or vow either to the church or to God.

Mt 5[.19]; Jas 2[.10]

41. *Leonhart:* What is the baptismal pledge?

Hans: It is a commitment made to God publicly and orally before the congregation in which the baptized person renounces Satan and all his imaginations and works. He also vows that he will henceforth set his faith, hope, and trust solely in God and regulate his life according to the divine word, in the strength of Jesus Christ our Lord, and if he should fail to do so, he thereby promises the church that he would dutifully accept brotherly discipline from it and its members, as has been said above.

42. *Leonhart:* Which of the articles of the creed deal with baptism?

Hans: The ninth and tenth articles, where we confess the universal Christian church, the fellowship of the saints and forgiveness of sins, just as the Lord's supper is also included there. For with outward baptism the church opens her doors to all believers who confess their faith orally before her and receives them into her bosom, fellowship, and communion of saints for the forgiveness of their sins. Therefore, as one cares about the forgiveness of his sins and the fellowship of the saints outside of which there is no salvation, just so much should one value water baptism, whereby one enters and is incorporated into the universal Christian church. This is the understanding and decision Christianly issued by the Nicene Council, in these words: "I acknowledge one unique baptism for the remission of sins." Peter gives it the same meaning: "Be baptized every one of you in the name of Jesus Christ for the forgiveness of your sins," Acts 2.

Acts 2[.38]

43. *Leonhart:* Now that you have assured the church of your faith by your baptism, tell me, what is the church?

Hans: The church is sometimes understood to include all the people who are gathered and united in one God, one Lord, one faith, and one baptism, and have confessed this faith with their mouths, wherever they may be on earth. This, then, is the universal Christian corporeal church and fellowship of the saints, assembled only in the Spirit of God, as we confess in the ninth article of our creed. At other times the church is understood to mean each separate and outward meeting assembly or parish membership that is under one shepherd or bishop and assembles bodily for instruction, for baptism and the Lord's supper. The church as daughter has the same power to bind and to loose on earth as the universal church, her mother, when she uses the keys according to the command of Christ, her spouse and husband.

44. *Leonhart:* What is the difference between these two churches?

Hans: The particular congregation may err, as the papist church has erred in many respects. But the universal church cannot err. She is without spot, without wrinkle, is controlled by the Holy Spirit, and Christ is with her until the end of the world, Matthew 28. And God will through all time preserve to himself seven thousand who will not bend their knee to the idol Baal, 1 Kings 19; Romans 11.[a]

Mt 28[.20]

45. *Leonhart:* On what is the Christian church built?

Hans: On the oral confession of faith that Jesus is the Christ, the Son of the living God. This outward confession is what makes a church, and not faith alone; for the church that has the power to bind and to loose is outward and corporeal, not theoretical, and faith is inward. And although faith alone makes righteous, it does not alone give salvation, for it must be accompanied by public confession. Of this we have good testimony, Matthew 16. There Christ says, "You are Peter, and on this rock (meaning: which you confess) I will build my church." Likewise, he also says, "Everyone who acknowledges me before men, I will also acknowledge before my Father who is in heaven; but whoever denies me and is ashamed of my words before men I also will deny and be ashamed of him before my Father," Matthew 10; Luke 9, 12.[b] And Paul says, "For one believes with the heart and so is justified; but one confesses with the mouth and so is saved, Romans 10.

Mt 16[.18]

Rom 10[.10]

46. *Leonhart:* What authority do those in the church have over one another?

Hans: The power of fraternal admonition.

47. *Leonhart:* What is fraternal admonition?

Hans: One who sees his brother sin goes to him in love and admonishes him fraternally and quietly to abandon such sin. If he desists, he has won his soul. If he does not, then he takes two or three other witnesses with him and admonishes him once again. If he obeys him, all is well; if not he tells the church. The church calls him forward and admonishes him the third time. If he now leaves off his sin the church has won his soul, Matthew 18.

Mt 18[.15–17]

48. *Leonhart:* Whence does the church have this authority?

Hans: From Christ's command when he said to his disciples: "Whatever you bind on earth shall be bound in heaven, and whatever you loose on earth shall be loosed in heaven," Matthew 18; John 20.[c]

a. 1 Kgs 19[.18]; Rom 11[.4]

b. Mt 10[.32]; Lk 9[.26], 12[.5–6]

c. Mt 18[.18]; Jn 20[.23]

49. *Leonhart:* But what right has one brother to use this power against another?

Hans: From the baptismal pledge, in which one has made himself subject to the church and all her members, according to the word of Christ.

50. *Leonhart:* What if the admonished sinner refuses to reform?

Hans: In that case the church has the power and the right to excommunicate and ban him as a perjurer and perfidious.

51. *Leonhart:* What is the ban?

Hans: It is an exclusion and separation of such a nature that henceforth Christians may have no fellowship with such a person, either in word, eating, drinking, grinding, baking, or any other form, but treat him as a heathen and publican, that is, as an offensive, disorderly, and poisonous person, who is bound and handed over to the devil. He must be avoided and shunned so that the whole outward church may not be ill spoken of, shamed, and disgraced by fellowship with him or be corrupted by his evil example, but rather that it will be frightened and filled with fear by this punishment and henceforth die to sin. For as truly as God lives, what the church admits or excludes on earth is also admitted or excluded in heaven.

52. *Leonhart:* What are the causes for excommunication?

Hans: Refusal to be reconciled to the brother or to desist from sin.

53. *Leonhart:* Why is one excommunicated?

Hans: Not for petty offenses as our papists have been doing, but for an offensive sin; and it is done for the good of the sinner, that he may examine himself, know himself, and desist from the sin.

54. *Leonhart:* If he desists from his sin, avoids the ways and paths that might cause him to fall again, and reforms, what attitude does the church take toward him?

Hans: She receives him again with joy, as the father did his prodigal son, and as Paul did the Corinthians, Luke 15; 2 Corinthians 2.[a] She opens the door to heaven for him and lets him return to the communion of the Lord's supper. In sum: Where water baptism in accord with Christ's institution is not reestablished and practiced one does not know who is a brother or sister, there is no church, no brotherly discipline or reproof, no ban, no supper, nor anything that resembles the Christian stance and nature. God lives. So it must be, or heaven and earth must shatter.

a. Lk 15[.20]; 2 Cor 2[.10]

Second Part of the Dialogue

1. *Leonhart:* What is the Lord's supper?

 Hans: It is a public sign and testimonial of the love in which one brother obligates himself to another before the congregation that just as they now break and eat the bread with each other and share and drink the cup, likewise they wish now to sacrifice and shed their body and blood for one another; this they will do in the strength of our Lord Jesus Christ, whose suffering they are now commemorating in the supper with the breaking of bread and the sharing of the wine, and proclaiming his death until he comes. Precisely this is the pledge of love in Christ's supper that one Christian performs toward the other, in order that every brother may know what good deed to expect from the other.

2. *Leonhart:* Is the bread not the body of Christ and the wine his crimson blood, as the Maoz-priests have been telling us?

 Hans: By no means; the bread and wine are nothing but memorial symbols of Christ's suffering and death for the forgiveness of our sins. This on the basis of the institution by Christ on Maundy Thursday when he was about to go out and show us the greatest of all signs of love, on the next day giving his flesh and blood unto death on our account, which our forefathers consequently called Good Friday (*Karfreitag*) from *caritate,* that is, from love. Indeed, to state it bluntly, the Lord's supper is a sign of the obligation to brotherly love just as water baptism is a symbol of the vow of faith. The water concerns God, the supper our neighbor; therein lie all the law and the prophets. No other ceremonies were instituted by Christ and left behind on earth, and whoever correctly teaches these two signs teaches faith and love correctly.

3. *Leonhart:* Where do you worship Christ?

 Hans: Not at any one particular place. Even though someone says: "Look; there on the altar is Christ! There in the stone or silver tabernacle he sits!" I do not believe it. I worship him seated at the right hand of his heavenly Father; there he is my only Intercessor, Mediator, and Reconciler to God, as I have confessed above in the sixth article of the creed. There he remains seated, on the strength of the Scriptures, until the judgment day; and then he will come in his great majesty and judge the quick and the dead. Then we shall see him descend as he ascended; for this we wait and will not seek him in bread or wine.

4. *Leonhart:* Just what is the mass?

 Hans: It is the very idol and abomination, spoken of by the prophet Daniel in his prophecy, Daniel 11, to whom Christ so faithfully and earnestly directed us, that we read him and take heed, Matthew 24. This idol stands in the holy place and

Dn 11[.31]

Mt 24[.15]

is honored with gold, silver, gems, and all that is costly. By his honor he is recognized as the kind of God he is to the papists, maozites, mass-priests, sophists, and all belly-Christians.

5. *Leonhart:* Do you also confess your sins?

Hans: Yes, I confess them to God but not to a monk or priest.

6. *Leonhart:* How do you confess?

Hans: Thus: Father, I have sinned against heaven and before you; I am not worthy to be called your son, because I have not fulfilled your fatherly wish. But speak a word of comfort and my soul will be healed. God, be merciful to me a sinner. Amen; may this be true. [Lk 15.21]

7. *Leonhart:* Do you also fast?

Hans: I ought to fast daily, using food and drink in moderation, so that I do not overfeed the old Adam and he become insolent and cast the ark of the divine commands into the mud together with the stubborn ox.

8. *Leonhart:* Do you also bless the food and drink before you partake of them?

Hans: No. God blessed it long ago and created all things very good. It is not what goes into the mouth that defiles a man, but the evil that comes from it, [Mt 15.11] that defiles him; and to the pure all things are pure. Therefore I eat all kinds of food [Ti 1.15] without any difference whether it be fish or meat, but, as Christ and Paul teach me, with propriety and thankfulness.

9. *Leonhart:* How do you thank God before your meal?

Hans: Thus: Praise and honor be to you, God, Creator of the heaven and earth, who have created all things good and well, particularly food and drink, and ordained that we shall accept it with thanksgiving. Glory and honor be to God the Father and to the Son and to the Holy Spirit. As he was from the beginning, is now and ever shall be, world without end, God be praised in the heavens. Amen, so be it.

10. *Leonhart:* What do you do at the table?

Hans: I eat and drink with my household what God has given me. I speak to them about God's word. I restrain myself in order not to eat human flesh or drink human blood.

11. *Leonhart:* Who then eats human flesh and drinks human blood?

Hans: All who while eating swear, rave, and curse by the flesh, blood, pains, wounds, and suffering of Christ, take the name of God in vain, slander their neighbor's honor and good reputation, and speak ill of him, eat and drink the flesh and blood of men.

12. *Leonhart:* How do you thank God after the meal?

Hans: Thus: We thank and praise thee, Lord God, Creator of heaven and earth, for all the kindness thou hast shown unto us; especially since thou hast in this meal so graciously fed us in body and soul with our daily bread. Glory and honor be to God the Father, the Son, and the Holy Spirit, as he was in the beginning, is now, and ever shall be, world without end. May the almighty and merciful God grant us his eternal peace. Amen, may this come to pass.

13. *Leonhart:* Do you observe the Sabbath?

Hans: Yes. Man has an eternal Sabbath; this he should celebrate daily and without ceasing, keep himself from sin, and allow God to work in him.

14. *Leonhart:* What do you believe regarding Our Lady?

Hans: I believe that she was a pure, chaste, and spotless Virgin before, during, and after the birth; a Mother of God, and blessed, because she believed those things that were told her by God. I can give her no greater title, name, or praise than that.

15. *Leonhart:* Would you call on her or the other saints to pray to God for you that he would be gracious to you and save you from all your troubles?

Hans: At the marriage feast at Cana in Galilee, Mary said, "Do whatever my Son tells you," John 2. Her Son commanded us that when we are oppressed or in need of something we should all come to him and he will give us rest; he is the door, the way, the truth, and the life; no one comes to the Father except through him, Matthew 11, John 10, 14.[a] Anyone who does not do this dishonors Christ, and whoever dishonors Christ and does not follow his command dishonors Mary, his dear Mother, also. Such a man does not follow her teaching when she said, "Do whatever my Son tells you." Therefore, if you want to obey and honor Mary, do not call upon her or the other saints, but alone upon her Son, Christ Jesus, giving him the glory and honor, for he is the most gracious, kindest, and most merciful, unspeakably more than his own Mother and all the saints. Whoever runs to the saints and cries to them that they should ask Christ for them that he be gracious to him blasphemes Christ, for he does not believe that Christ is the most merciful and most gracious one in the heavens, our only Intercessor, Mediator, gracious one with the Father. That is a blasphemy against God contrary to all the Scriptures, 1 Timothy 2; 1 John 2,[b] whereby Christ and Mary are accused of lying as if they had not properly indicated to us the way to the heavenly Father.

16. *Leonhart:* Do you believe that the saints can perform wondrous signs and miracles?

Jn 2[.5]

a. Mt 11[.20]; Jn 10[.9], 14[.6]
b. [1 Tm 2[.5]; 1 Jn 2[.1]

Hans: No. God alone performs miracles through them. I find that in Mark 16; Acts 3, 14,[a] about the two cripples.

17. *Leonhart:* Do you also make and honor images of Christ, Mary, and the dear saints?

Hans: By no means. For images have been seriously forbidden by God and are of no benefit, Exodus 20; Deuteronomy 5, 7; Baruch 6; Galatians 4, 5; 1 Peter 4; 1 John 5; Acts 19.[b] But one should above all uproot such idols and images out of human hearts with the word of God, or the outward destruction of idols is futile.

18. *Leonhart:* Whom, then, do you honor?

Hans: God alone, and no one else in heaven or on earth, except inasmuch as God is in his creatures.

19. *Leonhart:* What is the highest honor to God?

Hans: To hear and believe his word.

20. *Leonhart:* Do you hear his word in the church?

Hans: Yes.

21. *Leonhart:* Why?

Hans: That my faith may constantly grow day by day as a mustard seed grows to the skies, and that I may perform my works in true faith, lest they lead to eternal damnation: for it is not enough to do something with good intentions; one must also be assured and convinced from God's word that God will accept from us the work done with good intentions. Peter, with truly good intentions, was unwilling to let Jesus wash his feet. But Christ wanted none of his good intentions, but said: "Peter, if I do not wash you, you have no part of me," John 13. Likewise, Uzzah, no doubt with good intentions, seized and held the ark of God which contained the commandments to keep it from being thrown into the mud by the stumbling oxen; but God was angry with him and smote him, and he died there beside the ark, 2 Samuel 6. He will never accept anything except only what he has commanded us; of his mouth we must ask for counsel. "Woe," he says, "to the same children who forsake me, who carry out a plan, but not mine," Isaiah 30.

Jn 13[.8]

2 Sm 6[.6–7]

Is 30[.1]

22. *Leonhart:* In what does the sum of all preaching lie?

Hans: In love.

23. *Leonhart:* In what way?

Hans: That I love the Lord my God with my whole heart, my whole soul,

a. Mk 16[.17–18]; Acts 3[.1–10], 14[.8–10]

b. Ex 20[.4]; Dt 5[.8], 7[.25]; Bar 6[.6]; Gal 4[.8], 5[.19–21]; 1 Pt 4[.3]; 1 Jn 5[.21]; Acts 19[.23–27]

and all my strength, and my neighbor as myself. If I do that, I have fulfilled all the law and the prophets.

24. *Leonhart:* Do you sing in church?

Hans: Yes, with my mouth I sing understandable words, and with my spirit I reflect on the words, so that I do not honor my God with my lips while my heart is far from it, as the Pharisees did. It is also better to speak or sing five words understandably before the church than ten thousand that cannot be understood, Mark 7; 1 Corinthians 14.[a]

25. *Leonhart:* Can you do good works of your own strength?

Hans: God alone is good, and he works in us to will and to do the good, Matthew 19; Philippians 2.[b]

26. *Leonhart:* Since man cannot do anything good, why does God condemn him?

Hans: God does not condemn him for doing, but for not doing, as a schoolmaster does not strike the boy for learning, but for not learning. Nor does a man strike his wife for doing, but for doing nothing. Likewise, God does not condemn a man on account of his works, but because he has neglected to do them or has not done them according to God's will and pleasure.

27. *Leonhart:* But after all, the Scriptures contain many verses that clearly indicate that doing good or evil is in our power and will, as Christ says, "If thou wilt enter into life, keep the commandments," Matthew 19.

Mt 19[.17]

Hans: Yes, that is true. But these Scriptures do nothing more than to reveal how man was created by God in the first place, how he lost his freedom through sin, and how he is reborn through the word sent to him. There is a vast difference between being and having been. We were, to be sure, free before sinning; but after sin we were not free until we were made truly free by the death and resurrection of Christ. One who falls and is crippled was straight before, but he is no longer straight until the physician helps him so that his lameness no longer handicaps him. Likewise, although there is indeed still something in us of God's likeness in which we were initially made, Genesis 1, still this likeness has been dimmed, captured, and bound by Adam's disobedience. We are thus mired there until Christ makes us free; that is, he renders flesh, sin, death, devil, and hell harmless. Here there is need to pray earnestly and to cry without ceasing to Christ with the apostles: Lord, help us! Lord, we are perishing! Lord, increase our faith! On the other hand, we find just as many Scriptures that reveal to us our human weaknesses, incapabilities,

Gn 1[.27]

a. Mk 7[.6–7]; 1 Cor 14[.19]
b. Mt 19[.17]; Phil 2[.13]

and lameness so that we—yes, in spite of our best performance of the divine commands—are unprofitable servants, and so that all our righteousness can be likened to the garment of a defiled woman, Luke 17; Isaiah 64. Wherefore one must ruminate these Scriptures, to make an exact distinction between human nature before the fall, after the fall, and after the restoration from the fall through Christ, carefully judging each and making distinctions; thereby one also very easily acquires a true distinction between the free will and the bound will. If before the fall God's likeness was free and unbound in us, since the fall it is held captive and the sin of the fall is damning. After the restoration of the fall through Christ, this likeness is made free again, although captive in the sinful and poisoned body; but the curse has been removed from the sin of the fall insofar as we do not by our own wickedness make it damning again by rebelliously walking in it. Thus Paul teaches us in Romans 8. Here you see clearly that the image or inbreathing of God is still in us all, although captive and as a live spark covered with cold ashes is still alive and will steam if heavenly water is poured on it. It also lights up and burns if one blows on it. That is the source of the conscience in the Jews, pagans, and Christians, as Paul writes about it, Romans 2. But Christ restored the quenched spark of flame on Easter Day when he breathed upon his disciples and said, "Receive the Holy Spirit," John 20. Now Christ has ordered his servants to inbreathe and blow by the proclaiming his holy word, that the wounded soul may be reawakened from sleep.

Lk 17[.10]; Is 64[.6]

Rom 8[.13]

Rom 2[.15]

Jn 20[.22]

From this you will note: If one says there is nothing good in man, that is saying too much. As Paul also said too much when he said, "I know that nothing good dwells within me." But he hastens to explain this by adding to this concept: "I know that nothing good dwells within me, that is, in my flesh," Romans 7. Likewise all the other Scriptures must be understood that indicate that there is nothing good in man, that is, in his flesh, for God's image has never yet been completely obliterated in us. How can it be evil, for (like the law) it shows and teaches us the good? Far be it from us then to call it evil. For we know that it is holy, makes us righteous, and is wholly good. Notice the Trinity in those three phrases. In sum: First God made us good and free in soul, body, and spirit. This goodness and freedom were through Adam's disobedience taken captive in our spirit, wounded in our soul, and completely corrupted in our flesh; therefore we are all conceived and born in sin and are by nature the children of wrath. If we are now again to become free in the spirit and healthy in the soul, and if this fall is to be made completely harmless in the flesh, then this must take place through a rebirth, as Christ said, or we shall not enter into the kingdom of God, John 3. But now God has given

Rom 7[.18]

Jn 3[.5]

birth to us of his own will, as James writes, James 1,[a] and Peter, 1 Peter 1,[b] by the word of his power in which we are really made whole and free again. Christ like-

Jn 8[.22] wise says, the truth will make you truly free, John 8, and David, "he sent forth his
Ps 107[.20] word and healed us," Psalms 107. Yes, to the present day through the word God sent, our souls are just as free in themselves to will good and evil as was Adam's soul in paradise.

28. *Leonhart:* How does it happen then that God at many places in the Scriptures promises a reward for our works?

Hans: That is due to his gracious kindness. He ascribes these to us as if we had done him a great favor out of ourselves and of our own [strength], whereas he, of course, has no need whatever of us and does not wish our service except for our own benefit. Then let God call it a reward, but woe to you if you should consider it a payment. Consider all God's dealing with you as pure grace. There is nothing that God's grace cannot tolerate or observe less than presumptuous merits of our
Rom 3, 4 own, as Paul teaches in Romans 3 and 4.

29. *Leonhart:* Give me a parable that I may know that you understand it correctly.

Hans: Yes, very gladly. If a serf performs a day's statute labor or socage for his lord, what can he expect from him except what is given out of mercy? A good son does not serve his father for pay, but out of love, even though the father wants to call the good he does for his son a payment. But if the son were to demand pay, it would rightly grieve the father. Therefore we should not conclude from these Scriptures that they indicate earnings or wages.

30. *Leonhart:* Why then do the Holy Scriptures attribute doing good and keeping God's commands to our will, as several passages seem to say, if we after all can do nothing good without him?

Hans: God wants to awaken us from sleep with them and give us the heart to resolve to do good and to accomplish this with the hope of divine help, because he asks it of us. Otherwise, we would not dare to be presumptuous in this, for it would be impossible for us in ourselves, without God's drawing which comes through his word. Therefore we must first beg him and say, "O Lord, give us what you command of us." We would not even dare to say "Our Father," if he had not commanded us to do so.

31. *Leonhart:* How does God draw or call a person?

Hans: In two forms, outwardly and inwardly. The outward drawing occurs

a. Jas 1[.18]
b. 1 Pt 1[.3]

through the public proclamation of his holy gospel, that Christ has commanded to preach to all creatures in the whole world, which is now proclaimed everywhere, Mark 16. The inward drawing is this, that God also illuminates the person's soul inwardly, so that it understands the incontrovertible truth, convinced by the Spirit and the preached word in such a way that one must in one's own conscience confess that this is the case and it cannot be otherwise.

Mk 16[.15]

32. *Leonhart:* Explain this by an example.

Hans: Gladly. Just as one hears outwardly with his ears and inwardly understands: All that enters into the mouth does not make one unclean. He knows too that Christ said this, Matthew 15. In his conscience he is now convinced that this must be true, and he cannot oppose it at all with clear Scripture. That is the outward and inward drawing of God, which everyone can safely believe and trust. But if he does not do this, God will abandon him and with just judgment give him over to a perverted mind, blind, harden, and strike him with a deceiving mind like Babylon, the Jews, and the Romans, Jeremiah 51; Matthew 13; Romans 1.[a]

Mt 15[.17]

33. *Leonhart:* No doubt many people hear God's word outwardly but do not understand it inwardly. What must they do?

Hans: Then they have to pray and in faith ask wisdom of God like Solomon, nothing doubting, and cry: Father, give us today our daily bread. Or like David, Lord, give me understanding that I may learn thy justification and thy commandments. One who prays thus is certain that God will enlighten him, even if he has to order a Peter from Joppa on the sea, or an angel from heaven. Here you can hear that the very highest theology is fervent unceasing prayer to God. He will give us a mouth and wisdom.

[Acts 10.5]

[Lk 21.15]

34. *Leonhart:* Some people do not want to hear the word of God. Some hear but do not comprehend. Some comprehend and do not obey. Some persecute the truth vehemently. What happens to them?

Hans: As one is saved in his own faith and not in that of someone else, so also are such people condemned in their own unbelief, for which condemnation they themselves are guilty and not God. For God has often desired to gather them with his word like a hen her chicks, but they of their own volition have freely and wickedly refused, nor do they recognize the day of their visitation. Therefore they cannot blame it on God, as he himself says, "The condemnation is thine, O Israel; only in me lies your salvation," Hosea 13.

Hos 13[.9]

35. *Leonhart:* Tell me what are the genuine good works.

Hans: The works of mercy, for which Christ will demand an account.

---

a. Jer 51[.7]; Mt 13[.15–17]; Rom 1[.18–20]

36. *Leonhart:* When?

Hans: On the day of judgment.

37. *Leonhart:* With what words?

Hans: With these: "Come here, blessed of my Father, inherit the kingdom prepared for you from the foundation of the world; for I was hungry and you fed me, I was thirsty and you gave me drink, I was a pilgrim and you took me in, I was naked and you clothed me, I was sick and you visited me, I was in prison and you

Mt 25[.34–36]   came to me," Matthew 25.

38. *Leonhart:* What are the evil works?

Hans: Those that Christ will reproach us for on the judgment day.

39. *Leonhart:* With what words?

Hans: Depart from me, you cursed, into the eternal fire prepared for the devil and his angels; for I was hungry and you did not feed me, I was thirsty and you gave me no drink, I was a pilgrim and you did not take me in, naked and you

[Mt 25.41–43]   did not clothe me, sick and in prison and you did not visit me.

40. *Leonhart:* You mentioned the judgment day. What is the judgment day?

Hans: It is the day on which the Lord shall come down from heaven with a battle cry and the voice of the archangel and the trumpets of God, and the dead in Christ will first be raised; that is, body, soul, and spirit will be reunited; then we who are living and surviving will immediately be snatched up into the clouds with them to meet the Lord in the air and will be with the Lord forever in everlasting life, yea, those who have done good. But those who have done evil will go forth to the resurrection of the judgment, 1 Thessalonians 4; John 5.[a]

41. *Leonhart:* What is eternal life?

Hans: It is an eternal, sure, and joyful vision of God's face, prepared from the foundation of the world for all believers in Christ who have performed works of mercy toward their neighbor, where there is nothing but bliss, joy, peace, rest, and all security throughout eternity.

42. *Leonhart:* Which is the shortest path of all to eternal life?

Hans: Through fear, distress, suffering, grief, persecution, and death for the sake of the name of Christ Jesus, who himself had to suffer and thus enter into his

Lk 24[.26]   glory, Luke 24. St. Paul also says: All who desire to live a godly life in Christ Jesus
2 Tm 3[.12]   will be persecuted, 2 Timothy 3. For where Christ is and dwells, there he brings the cross with him on his back from which he gives every Christian his own small cross to carry and to follow after him. We are to expect this small cross and if it comes accept it with joy and patience, and not pick and choose our own chips and

a. 1 Thes 4[.13–18]; Jn 5[.29]

bits of wood in false spirituality, selecting and gathering them up without divine understanding.

43. *Leonhart:* Who are these people?

Hans: The poor in spirit. Those that mourn. Those who are meek. Those who hunger and thirst after righteousness. The merciful. The pure in heart. The peacemakers. Those who are persecuted for righteousness' sake. Those who are reviled and despised on account of Christ's name. Also those against whom much evil is spoken falsely for Christ's sake, Matthew 5.   Mt 5[.3–12]

44. *Leonhart:* What is hell?

Hans: Hell is the eternally painful and unending deprivation of the contemplation of God's face; it has been prepared for the devil, his angels, and all unbelievers who have not performed deeds of mercy for their neighbor. There is nothing there but everlasting fire, outer darkness, weeping, and gnashing of teeth, from which may the almighty kind and merciful Father in heaven graciously preserve us throughout eternity through Jesus Christ, his only-begotten Son, our Lord, to whom be glory, praise, honor, and majesty always and forever.

45. *Leonhart:* Amen. The peace of God be with us all.

Hans: Amen. So be it.

Truth Is Unkillable.

The Schleitheim Confession, 1527

Commonly known as the first Anabaptist confession of faith, *The Schleitheim Confession* presents the beliefs of the Brüderliche Vereinigung, or Swiss Brethren, one of several groups labeled "Anabaptist" for their insistence on the believer's baptism. The diverse movements classified as Anabaptist also include Thomas Müntzer's followers and the Zwickau Prophets, the Hutterites, the Melchiorites, the Mennonites, and the radical Münster community. Under the leadership of Conrad Grebel (1498–1526) and Felix Mantz (1498–1527), the Swiss Brethren embraced the *sola scriptura* mandate of mainstream Reformers, claiming to draw upon the Bible alone for their doctrine.

A major schism between Zwingli and the more radical Reformers occurred in the aftermath of the second Zurich Disputation (October 1523). Causes of the rift included not only the Anabaptists' rejection of infant baptism but also their refusal to bear arms or take oaths. The different branches of Anabaptists, however, held a variety of views, including support of the Peasants' War, rejection of civic government, advocacy of the idea of communal property, and even polygamy. The societal implications of the extremes of Anabaptist thought alarmed political authorities and other religious leaders—both Roman Catholic and reform-minded. Consequently, many groups identified as Anabaptist were attacked and their proponents persecuted. Anabaptism was declared a capital offense in Zurich on 10 March 1525 and throughout the Holy Roman Empire at the second Diet of Speyer in 1529.[1]

The Schleitheim Confession was drafted in the face of such persecution. Grebel had died of the plague in 1526, Felix Mantz had been executed in January 1527, and other leaders had been forced to flee Switzerland. In February 1527, the remnants of the Swiss Brethren, led by Michael Sattler (c. 1490–1527), met in Schleitheim in the canton of Schaffhausen. The seven articles, probably drafted by Sattler, were intended for the instruction of Anabaptist congregations. The document focuses in particular on rules for replacement of pastors (when forced to flee or martyred for their faith) and congregational reprimand of those "who have turned away from the faith."[2] The internal threat from these "false brethren" is cited in the prefatory letter by Sattler. Other topics covered in the articles include baptism, the Lord's supper, and the need to separate oneself from worldly matters, particularly from participation in war and government.

1. See Williams, 358–60.
2. See Meihuizen 1967a.

Sebastian Franck first identified Sattler as the author of *The Schleitheim Confession* in 1531, an attribution generally accepted today. Michael Sattler was a former Benedictine monk who had come under the influence of Mantz and Grebel. He was rebaptized in 1526. In March 1527, just one month after the meeting in Schleitheim, he was arrested at Horb in southwest Germany. In May he was condemned, tortured, and burned at the stake in Rottenburg am Neckar for his Anabaptist beliefs. His wife, a former Beguine, was executed a few days later.

The text of the *Confession* is extant in a manuscript that was seized in April 1527 from Anabaptists in Bern and delivered to Ulrich Zwingli. Zwingli translated it into Latin and condemned it in his *In Catabaptistarum strophas elenchus* (1527). The manuscript does not contain the prefatory letter, which first appears in the three earliest printed versions (two undated, the other a 1533 imprint).[3] John Calvin also attacked the work in his *Brième instruction pour armer tous bons fidèles contre des erreurs de la secte commune des Anabaptistes* (1541).

Edition: *Quellen zur Geschichte der Täufer in der Schweiz* 1973, 2:26–36.

Translation: Yoder 1973, 34–43.

Note: Heinold Fast's edition, which we give here, is based on the 1527 Bern manuscript for the articles and the 1533 imprint for the prefatory letter.

Literature: Friedmann 1942; Haas 1982; Harder 1980; Jenny 1951; Köhler 1908; Meihuizen 1967a; Nienkirchen 1982; Payne 1952; Snyder 1984, 1985, 1989; Stauffer 1977; Wenger 1952, 71–77; Williams, 288–310; Winter 1991.

---

3. See Köhler 1908, 299–303, for a discussion of these imprints.

Brotherly Union of a Number of Children of God Concerning Seven Articles

[1 Cor 10.16] May joy, peace, mercy from our Father, through the atonement of the blood of Christ Jesus, together with the gifts of one Spirit—who is sent by the Father to all believers to [give] strength and consolation and constancy in all tribulation until the end, Amen, be with all who love God and all children of light, who are scattered everywhere, wherever they might have been placed by God our Father, wherever they might be gathered in unity of spirit in one God and Father of us all; grace and peace of heart be with you all. Amen.

[Eph 2.12] Beloved brothers and sisters in the Lord; first and primordially we are always concerned for your consolation and the assurance of your conscience (which was sometime confused), so that you might not always be separated from us as aliens and by right almost completely excluded, but that you might turn to the true implanted members of Christ, who have been armed through patience and the knowledge of self, and thus be again united with us in the power of a godly Christian spirit and zeal for God.

[Phil 1.6] It is manifest with what manifold cunning the devil has turned us aside, so that he might destroy and cast down the work of God, which in us mercifully and graciously has been partially begun. But the true Shepherd of our souls, Christ, who has begun such in us, will direct and teach the same unto the end, to his glory and our salvation, Amen.

Dear brothers and sisters, we who have been assembled in the Lord at Schleitheim on the Randen make known, in points and articles, unto all that love God, that as far as we are concerned, we have been united to stand fast in the Lord as obedient children of God, sons and daughters, who have been and shall be separated from the world in all that we do and leave undone, and (the praise and glory be to God alone) uncontradicted by all the brothers completely at peace. Herein we have sensed the unity of the Father and of our common Christ as present with us in their Spirit. For the Lord is a Lord of peace and not of quarreling, as Paul indi-

[1 Cor 14.33] cates. So that you understand at what points this occurred, you should observe and understand [what follows]:

A very great offense has been introduced by some false brothers among us, whereby several have turned away from the faith, thinking to practice and observe the freedom of the Spirit and of Christ. But such have fallen short of the truth and (to their own condemnation) are given over to the lasciviousness and license of the flesh. They have esteemed that faith and love may do and permit everything and that nothing can harm nor condemn them, since they are "believers."

Note well, you members of God in Christ Jesus, that faith in the heavenly Father through Jesus Christ is not thus formed: it produces and brings forth no such things as these false brothers and sisters practice and teach. Guard yourselves and be warned of such people, for they do not serve our Father, but their father, the devil.

But for you it is not so; for they who are Christ's have crucified their flesh with all its lusts and desires. You understand me well, and [know] the brothers [Gal 5.24] whom we mean. Separate yourselves from them, for they are perverted. Pray the Lord that they may have knowledge unto repentance, and for us that we may have constancy to persevere along the path we have entered upon, unto the glory of God and of Christ his Son. Amen.

The articles we have dealt with, and in which we have been united, are these: baptism, ban, the breaking of bread, separation from abomination, shepherds in the congregation, the sword, the oath.

[ARTICLE 1. *NOTICE CONCERNING BAPTISM*]

Baptism shall be given to all those who have been taught repentance and the amendment of life and [who] believe truly that their sins are taken away through Christ, and to all those who desire to walk in the resurrection of Jesus Christ and be buried with him in death, so that they might rise with him; to all those who with such an understanding themselves desire and request it from us; hereby is excluded all infant baptism, the greatest and first abomination of the pope. For this you have the reasons and the testimony of the writings and the practice of the apostles.[a] We wish simply yet resolutely and with assurance to hold to the same.

[ARTICLE 2. *WE HAVE BEEN UNITED AS FOLLOWS CONCERNING THE BAN*]

We have been united as follows concerning the ban. The ban shall be employed with all those who have given themselves over to the Lord, to walk after [him] in his commandments; those who have been baptized into the one body of Christ, and let themselves be called brothers or sisters, and still somehow slip and fall into error and sin, being inadvertently overtaken. The same [shall] be warned twice privately and the third time be publicly admonished before the entire congregation according

a. Mt 28[.19]; Mk 16[.6]; Acts 2[.38], 8[.36], 16[.31–33], 19[.4]

Mt 18[.15]   to the command of Christ. But this shall be done according to the ordering of the
[Mt 5.23ff.] Spirit of God before the breaking of bread, so that we may all in one spirit and in
one love break and eat from one bread and drink from one cup.

[ARTICLE 3. *CONCERNING THE BREAKING OF BREAD*]

Concerning the breaking of break, we have become one and agree thus: all those
who desire to break the one bread in remembrance of the broken body of Christ
and all those who wish to drink of one drink in remembrance of the shed blood of
Christ, they must beforehand be united in the one body of Christ, that is the con-
[1 Cor 10.21] gregation of God, whose Head is Christ, and that by baptism. For as Paul indicates,
we cannot be partakers at the same time of the table of the Lord and the table of
devils. Nor can we at the same time partake and drink of the cup of the Lord and
the cup of devils. That is: all those who follow the devil and the world, have no part
with those who have been called out of the world unto God. All those who lie in
evil have no part in the good.

So it shall and must be, that whoever does not share the calling of the one
[Eph 4.4-6] God to one faith, to one baptism, to one spirit, to one body together with all the
children of God, may not be made one loaf together with them, as must be true if
one wishes truly to break bread according to the command of Christ.

[ARTICLE 4. *WE HAVE BEEN UNITED CONCERNING THE SEPARATION THAT SHALL TAKE PLACE*]

We have been united concerning the separation that shall take place from the evil
and the wickedness which the devil has planted in the world, simply in this; that
we have no fellowship with them, and do not run with them in the confusion of
their abominations. So it is; since all who have not entered into the obedience of
faith and have not united themselves with God so that they will to do his will, are
a great abomination before God, therefore nothing else can or really will grow or
spring forth from them other than abominable things. Now there is nothing else
in the world and all creation than good or evil, believing and unbelieving, darkness
and light, the world and those who are [come] out of the world, God's temple and
[2 Cor 6.14-16] idols, Christ and Belial, and none will have part with the other.

To us, then, the commandment of the Lord is also obvious, whereby he
orders us to be and to become separated from the evil one, and thus he will be our
[2 Cor 6.17] God and we shall be his sons and daughters.

Further, he admonishes us therefore to go out from Babylon and from the
earthly Egypt, that we may not be partakers in their torment and suffering, which
[Rv 18.4-6] the Lord will bring upon them.

From all this we should learn that everything which has not been united with our God in Christ is nothing but an abomination which we should shun. By this are meant all popish and re-popish works and idolatry, gatherings, church attendance, winehouses, guarantees and commitments of unbelief, and other things of the kind, which the world regards highly, and yet which are carnal or flatly counter to the command of God, after the pattern of all the iniquity which is in the world. From all this we shall be separated and have no part with such, for they are nothing but abominations, which cause us to be hated before our Christ Jesus, who has freed us from the servitude of the flesh and fitted us for the service of God and the Spirit whom he has given us.

Thereby shall also fall away from us the diabolical weapons of violence—such as sword, armor, and the like, and all of their use to protect friends or against enemies—by virtue of the word of Christ: "you shall not resist evil."   [Mt 5.39]

[ARTICLE 5. WE HAVE BEEN UNITED AS FOLLOWS CONCERNING SHEPHERDS IN THE CHURCH OF GOD]

We have been united as follows concerning shepherds in the church of God. The shepherd in the church shall be a person according to the rule of Paul, fully and   [1 Tm 3.7] completely, who has a good report of those who are outside the faith. The office of such a person shall be to read and exhort and teach, warn, admonish, or ban in the congregation, and properly to preside among the sisters and brothers in prayer, and in the breaking of bread, and in all things to take care of the body of Christ, that it may be built up and developed, so that the name of God might be praised and honored through us, and the mouth of the mocker be stopped.

He shall be supported, wherein he has need, by the congregation which has chosen him, so that he who serves the gospel can also live therefrom, as the Lord has ordered. But should a shepherd do something worthy of reprimand, nothing   [1 Cor 9.14] shall be done with him without the voice of two or three witnesses. If they sin they   [Mt 18.16] shall be publicly reprimanded, so that others might fear.   [1 Tm 5.19]

But if the shepherd should be driven away or led to the Lord by the cross at the same hour another shall be ordained to his place, so that the little folk and the little flock of God may not be destroyed, but be preserved by warning and be consoled.

[ARTICLE 6. WE HAVE BEEN UNITED AS FOLLOWS CONCERNING THE SWORD]

We have been united as follows concerning the sword. The sword is an ordering of God outside the perfection of Christ. It punishes and kills the wicked and guards and protects the good. In the law the sword is established over the wicked for pun-

[Rom 13.1–6] ishment and for death and the secular rulers are established to wield the same.

But within the perfection of Christ only the ban is used for the admonition and exclusion of the one who has sinned, without the death of the flesh, simply the

[Jn 8.11] warning and the command to sin no more.

Now many, who do not understand Christ's will for us, will ask: whether a Christian may or should use the sword against the wicked for the protection and defense of the good, or for the sake of love.

The answer is unanimously revealed: Christ teaches and commands us to learn from him, for he is meek and lowly of heart and thus we shall find rest for our souls.[a] Now Christ says to the woman who was taken in adultery,[b] not that she should be stoned according to the law of his Father (and yet he says, "What the

[Jn 14.31] Father commanded me, that I do"), but with mercy and forgiveness and the warn-

[Jn 8.11] ing to sin no more, says: "Go, sin no more." Exactly thus should we also proceed, according to the rule of the ban.

Second, is asked concerning the sword: whether a Christian shall pass sentence in disputes and strife about worldly matters, such as the unbelievers have with one another. The answer: Christ did not wish to decide or pass judgment between

[Lk 12.13] brother and brother concerning inheritance, but refused to do so. So should we also do.

Third, is asked concerning the sword: whether the Christian should be a magistrate if he is chosen thereto. This is answered thus: Christ was to be made

[Jn 6.15] king, but he fled and did not discern the ordinance of his Father. Thus we should also do as he did and follow after him, and we shall not walk in darkness. For he himself says: "Whoever would come after me, let him deny himself and take up his cross and follow me."[c] He himself further forbids the violence of the sword when he says: "The princes of this world lord it over them etc., but among you it shall

[Mt 20.25] not be so." Further Paul says, "Whom God has foreknown, the same he has also

[Rom 8.30] predestined to be conformed to the image of his Son," etc. Peter also says: "Christ has suffered (not ruled) and has left us an example, that you should follow after in

[1 Pt 2.21] his steps."

Lastly, one can see in the following points that it does not befit a Christian to be a magistrate: the rule of the government is according to the flesh, that of the Christians according to the spirit. Their houses and dwelling remain in this

a. [Mt 11.29]
b. [Jn 8.11]
c. [Mt 16.24; Mk 8.34]

world, that of the Christians is in heaven. Their citizenship is in this world, that
of the Christians is in heaven. The weapons of their battle and warfare are carnal   [Phil 3.20]
and only against the flesh, but the weapons of Christians are spiritual, against the
fortification of the devil. The worldly are armed with steel and iron, but Christians   [2 Cor 10.4]
are armed with the armor of God, with truth, righteousness, peace, faith, salvation,
and with the word of God. In sum: as Christ our Head is minded, so also must be   [Eph 6.13–17]
minded the members of the body of Christ through him, so that there be no division in the body, through which it would be destroyed. Since then Christ is as is
written of him, so must his members also be the same, so that his body may remain whole and unified for its own advancement and upbuilding. For any kingdom
which is divided within itself will be destroyed.   [Mt 12.25]

[ARTICLE 7. WE HAVE BEEN UNITED AS FOLLOWS CONCERNING THE OATH]

We have been united as follows concerning the oath. The oath is a confirmation
among those who are quarreling or making promises. In the law it is commanded
that it should be done only in the name of God, truthfully and not falsely. Christ,   [Lv 19.12]
who teaches the perfection of the law, forbids his [followers] all swearing, whether
true or false; neither by heaven nor by earth, neither by Jerusalem nor by our head;
and that for the reason which he goes on to give: "For you cannot make one hair
white or black." You see, thereby all swearing is forbidden. We cannot perform   [Mt 5.33–36]
what is promised in the swearing, for we are not able to change the smallest part of
ourselves.

Now there are some who do not believe the simple commandment of God
and who say, "But God swore by himself to Abraham, because he was God (as he
promised him that he would do good to him and would be his God if he kept his
commandments). Why then should I not swear if I promise something to some-   [Gn 26.3]
one?" The answer: hear what the Scripture says: "God, since he wished to prove
overabundantly to the heirs of his promise that his will did not change, inserted an
oath so that by two immutable things we might have a stronger consolation (for it
is impossible that God should lie)." Notice the meaning of the passage: God has the   [Heb 6.17–18]
power to do what he forbids you, for everything is possible to him. God swore an
oath to Abraham, Scripture says, in order to prove that his counsel is immutable.
That means: no one can withstand and thwart his will; thus he can keep his oath.
But we cannot, as Christ said above, hold or perform our oath, therefore we should
not swear.

Others say that swearing cannot be forbidden by God in the New Testament when it was commanded in the Old, but that it is forbidden only to swear

by heaven, earth, Jerusalem, and our head. Answer: hear the Scripture. "He who

[Mt 23.22]   swears by heaven, swears by God's throne and by him who sits thereon." Observe: swearing by heaven is forbidden, which is only God's throne; how much more is it forbidden to swear by God himself. You blind fools, what is greater, the throne or

[Mt 23.17, 19]   he who sits upon it?

Others say, if it is then wrong to use God for truth, then the apostles Peter and Paul also swore. Answer: Peter and Paul only testify to that which God promised Abraham, whom we long after have received.[a] But when one testifies, one testifies concerning that which is present, whether it be good or evil. Thus Simeon spoke of Christ to Mary and testified: "Behold: this one is ordained for the falling and

[Lk 2.34]   rising of many in Israel and to be a sign which will be spoken against."

Christ taught us similarly when he says: "Your speech shall be yea, yea; and

[Mt 5.37]   nay, nay; for what is more than that comes of evil." He says, your speech or your word shall be yes and no, so that no one might understand that he had permitted

[2 Cor 1.19]   it. Christ is simply yea and nay, and all those who seek him simply will understand his word. Amen.

Dear brothers and sisters in the Lord: these are the articles which some brothers previously had understood wrongly and in a way not conformed to the true meaning. Thereby many weak consciences were confused, whereby the name of God has been grossly slandered, for which reason it was needful that we should be brought to agreement in the Lord, which has come to pass. To God be praise and glory!

Now that you have abundantly understood the will of God as revealed through us at this time, you must fulfill this will, now known, persistently and unswervingly. For you know well what is the reward of the servant who knowingly sins.

Everything which you have done unknowingly and now confess to have done wrongly, is forgiven you, through that believing prayer, which is offered among us in our meeting for all our shortcomings and guilt, through the gracious forgiveness of God and through the blood of Jesus Christ. Amen.

Watch out for all who do not walk in simplicity of divine truth, which has been stated by us in this letter in our meeting, so that everyone might be governed among us by the rule of the ban, and that henceforth the entry of false brothers and sisters among us might be prevented.

Put away from you that which is evil, and the Lord will be your God, and

[1 Cor 6.17]   you will be his sons and daughters.

a. [Rom 1.9; 2 Cor 1.23, 11.31; Phil 1.8]

Dear brothers, keep in mind what Paul admonished Titus. He says: "The saving grace of God has appeared to all, and disciplines us, that we should deny ungodliness and worldly lusts, and live circumspect righteous and godly lives in this world; awaiting the same hope and the appearing of the glory of the great God and of our Savior Jesus Christ, who gave himself for us, to redeem us from all unrighteousness and to purify unto himself a people of his own, that would be zealous of good works." Think on this, and exercise yourselves therein, and the Lord of peace [Ti 2.11–14] will be with you.

May the name of God be forever blessed and greatly praised, Amen. May the Lord give you his peace, Amen.

Done at Schleitheim, St. Matthew's Day [24 February] Anno 1527.

Laelius Socinus, *Confession of Faith*, 1555

Heinrich Bullinger urged Laelius Socinus (1525–62) to write this confession of faith. The reformer was reacting to letters he had received from Calvin and others expressing suspicions about the orthodoxy of Socinus, a young Italian exile in Zurich. At issue were his views of the Trinity, the immortality of the soul, and the divinity of Christ. Socinus, who is an important early figure in the history of Unitarianism, answered his critics in a carefully composed statement. He confessed his beliefs ambiguously, often using negative formulations to make clear what he did not believe without stating clearly what he did believe. The confession apparently satisfied Bullinger, who was at that time well disposed toward Socinus.

Socinus was born in Siena, the son of Mariano Sozzini (1482–1556), a prominent Italian lawyer and jurist.[1] The father wrote legal decisions for the celebrated cases of the divorce of Henry VIII and the bigamy of Philip of Hesse, two cases of enormous political and religious importance. Sozzini trained his son for the law, but Laelius was drawn to theological inquiry. The younger Sozzini became part of the Italian evangelical movement, moving to its center in Venice and later becoming one of the many reform-minded Italians who settled in Switzerland. He studied Hebrew with Sebastian Münster and knew and corresponded with Calvin, Melanchthon, Sebastian Castellio, and Ursinus, among others. Socinus questioned the reformers about matters of doctrine, so wearying Calvin with his inquiries that Calvin responded angrily, "Do not expect me to answer your outrageous questions."[2]

In 1551, Socinus's travels took him to Poland, where his ideas would take root in the proto-Unitarian community, both through his own writings and through the work of his nephew Faustus Socinus (1539–1604), who followed him. His most radical work, a commentary on the first chapter of John, was written around 1562, shortly before his death at thirty-two. In it, he claims that Christ, though Son of God and born of the Virgin, was not an eternal or cosmological principle existing before all time. His nephew would take this one step farther to deny openly the divinity of Christ.[3]

In his *Confession of Faith,* Socinus admits that he has known → *The Apostles'*

---

1. The name is Latinized as Socinus.

2. Rotondó 1986, epistola 35. For the correspondence between Calvin and Socinus, see *CR* 13–17, nos. 1191, 1212, 1231, 1323, 1341, 1361, 2219, 3100, and 3121.

3. Faustus Socinus wrote a similar work in 1562, *Explicatio primae partis primi capitis Johannis,* relying in part on his uncle's ideas. See Williams, 972, n. 68.

Creed since boyhood, and he "acknowledges it to be the most ancient," but he never says that he subscribes to it. Likewise, he is evasive but not overtly heterodox about the Trinity and the dual nature of Christ: "I do not assert that the Father is the same as the Son and the Holy Spirit. I do not suppose there to be three Jehovahs, our coessential gods; I do not divide the one person of Christ into two Christs, nor accept any confusion of his natures." Elsewhere he says he "recognizes" the terms *Trinity, hypostasis, consubstantiality,* and so on, yet he neglects to endorse them explicitly. Those terms were necessary for patristic authors, he maintains, implying that the Bible does not contain them and that they are perhaps not necessary for his understanding of God. He rejects the errors of the Anabaptists (whom he calls by Calvin's pejorative, Catabaptists) and the dogmas of Servetus, who had been recently executed in Geneva for his beliefs. Socinus's own beliefs, however, receive scant attention. Indeed, the phrase "I believe" (*credo*) does not occur in the text.

Edition: Rotondò 1986, 98–100.

Translation: Hulme [1931] 1968, 216–18.

Literature: Hulme [1931] 1968; *ODCC* 1512–13; Rotondò 1986; Wallace 1850, 1:63–95; Williams, 876–85, 965–72.

Laelius Socinus, *Confession of Faith*, 1555

I, Laelius Socinus, in my boyhood learned one creed, that which is called the Apostles' Creed, which I even now know and acknowledge to be the most ancient, accepted at all times in the church, though drawn up in various forms. But I have lately read others also, and attribute all the honor I can and ought to the very old creeds of Nicaea and Constantinople. Moreover, though ignorant men obstinately deny it, I recognize that the terms Trinity, persons, hypostasis, consubstantiality, union, distinction, and others of the kind are not recent inventions, but have been in use for the last thirteen hundred years, from the time of Justin Martyr, almost throughout the whole Christian world, and that too for the most convincing and cogent reasons. Yet I will say frankly what I think: I should be very glad if the Christian, apostolic and evangelical faith were still expounded to us in the words of Christ, the apostles, and the evangelists. I do not for that reason deny that those terms were necessary for the fathers, for the more splendid setting forth of those truths which are still handed down to us by the catholic faith; much less do I call in doubt the foundations of the Christian religion, which ought to be the most certain of all things to every orthodox believer. Would that they may be made more certain to me than they are! I do not assert that the Father is the same as the Son and the Holy Spirit. I do not suppose there to be three Jehovahs, our coessential gods; I do not divide the one person of Christ into two Christs, nor accept any confusion of his natures. I have a great dread of the wantonness and petulance of men's minds, and therefore ever shun such deadly paradoxes; moreover I avoid all the errors of the Catabaptists, and abominate and abhor the dogmas of Servetus and the whole Arian theology. The other fond imaginings of heretics, with which you charge me, I know nothing whatever of; I do not look for a new kind of doctrine, but I would have those things alone which are necessary to everlasting salvation, and which are taught by the common consent of all theologians, proved more clearly every day to be true, and be myself more firmly persuaded of them, that I may cleave the more closely to my God in love, and rest content with the simple truth of God, avoiding disputes about words, controversial opinions, thorny questions, and inextricable labyrinths. For I candidly confess that I have been more curious than certain Pythagorean zealots could bear, but now our heavenly Father has shown himself so gracious to me that I am quite confident that henceforward I shall behave myself with more discretion in holy concourses of men. Laying aside all the foolish speculations of imaginative persons, and bidding farewell to the quirks and fallacies of the sophists, I hope for

that great and excellent gift of God, resurrection from the dust of the earth. For he
that believeth in me, says he who never lies, though he be dead, yet shall he live; [Jn 11.25]
and what happier lot could befall us than to receive such a promise? There are profane races which have not this hope, and to whom these words bring no comfort. I
thank thee, therefore, Father of heaven and Lord of earth, that my soul is preserved
unto eternal life, and that though my body be killed no human power can kill my
soul. But I humbly beseech thee further that, if any over-great inquiry has arisen in
my mind concerning things which are contrary to nature and surpassing the understanding of us all, thou wilt forthwith banish it and, setting me in the clear light of
day, wilt make me blessed through Jesus Christ thy only Son, who is the one ambassador sent by thee to save from destruction beyond all their deserts and restore
those who believe in him. And so may the prophecy of Ezekiel 34 be in all respects Ez 34
fulfilled. Wherefore he is Almighty God, our Judge, Redeemer, and eternal Lord and
King, at whose name every knee doth bow of things in heaven and things on earth
and things under the earth, who is able to subdue all things unto himself. And so I [Phil 3.2]
tell you this from my heart, my very dear friends: I have hitherto believed nothing
appertaining to those things which need the testimony of the holy and divine Spirit,
which you all here alike do not teach ought to be believed; and, what is more, I
doubt no more than you to reveal that monstrous and horrible brute, which at last
shall be seized, together with the false prophet which doeth miracles in his sight,
whereby he deceives those who receive the mark of the beast, and those who worship his image. They both shall be cast alive into the lake that burneth with fire and [Rv 19.20–21]
brimstone. The rest shall be slain with the sword of him that sitteth on the horse,
from whose mouth a sword proceedeth, and all the birds shall batten on their flesh;
here we perceive their miserable fate and the sharp sword wherewith all those shall
be cut down who rebel against the Lamb. Why then should we punish otherwise
than by the Christian and apostolic law and sword those who break only the laws
and commandments of Christ and the apostles? However, my dear friend, I quite
understand that there is need of exceeding moderation, in order that all things may
be done for the best, and moreover that we shall have to give account for every evil
word of ours on the day of judgment. But we offend in many ways; if a man offend
not in words, he is a perfect man. Wherefore may God the giver of all true wisdom
rule and govern my tongue also, that from the same mouth there may not proceed
praise and reviling. But meanwhile I will never suffer myself to be deprived of this [Jas 3.10]
holy liberty of inquiring from my elders and disputing modestly and reverently in
order to enhance my knowledge of divine things; for there are not a few passages in
the Scripture the interpretation and exposition of which, by the doctors even who
are entitled to the homage of all ages, are by no means satisfactory. Moreover I am

not such a child that I am ignorant of my own childishness and do not know in how many respects I am wanting. Do you therefore pray without ceasing to the God of all mercy that he will finish the good work he has begun in your friend Laelius, that

[Eph 4.14–15]   he be no longer a boy, blown about by every wind of doctrine, but holding the truth
[Heb 12.1–2]   with charity may run the race that is set before him, forgetting those things that are
[Phil 3.13–14]   behind, and stretching forward to the mark may hasten to win the crown to which he has been called from on high by God through Jesus Christ. May all my desires be directed to this end—the resurrection from the dead, that caught up in the clouds

[1 Thes 4.17]   I may meet the Lord in the air and ever live with him, praising our God and Father world without end.

The Catechesis and Confession of Faith
of the Polish Brethren, 1574

Sometimes identified as the first Unitarian confession of faith, this early document of the Polish Brethren outlines their faith and practices before the influence of Laelius and Faustus Socinus.[1] The pre-Socinian brethren of Poland shared many of the moral and social beliefs of European Anabaptist groups, but they are distinguished by an anti-Nicene theology, which Williams calls "a scripturally grounded, eschatologically intense, Christocentric unitarian immersionist piety and discipline."[2]

The catechism was written by Georg Schomann (Jerzy Szoman), pastor of the Minor Church in Kraków. The Polish Minor Church arose from a schism within the Polish Reformed Church in 1563 over the nature of the Trinity. Following the thought of John Łaski (1499–1560), the *Catechesis* emphasizes the threefold office of Christ as prophet, priest, and king. God the Father, Christ the Son, whom God made incarnate, and the Holy Spirit are all part of this "Unitarian" creed. To the question, "What is Jesus Christ, the Son of God?" the *Catechesis* answers, "He is a man, our mediator with God, promised . . . by the prophets, and born at last from the seed of David."[3] Schomann enjoins belief in Jesus Christ, "most high after God," because he died for human sins and overcame death. The Holy Spirit is not a person but rather the power of God, which God gave to his Son "in order that we may take, as adopted sons, from his fullness."[4]

In addition to its definitions of God the Father, the Son, and the Holy Spirit, the *Catechesis* deals with justification by faith alone, ecclesiastical discipline (including the imposition of the ban), prayer, baptism by immersion, and the significance of the Lord's supper as a remembrance and commemoration of Christ's sacrifice. The work served as a model for the better-known *Racovian Catechism* of 1605,[5] although that work incorporated Socinian doctrines as well.

1. For an account of Socinianism, see Williams, 1157–75.

2. Lubieniecki 1994, 347.

3. Lubieniecki 1994, 32 (from the *Catechesis*, 1 B).

4. Lubieniecki 1994, 32 (from the *Catechesis*, 1 C).

5. For the text of the Racovian Catechism in English, see Rees [1818] 1962 (from English edition of 1680), 1–383.

Edition: Schomann 1574.

Translation: Lubieniecki 1994, 350–79 (translation by T. Corey Brennan).

Note: The dots in the translation do not imply editorial ellipsis, but are places where the translator has given the full text where Schomann conflated texts, reversed sequences, or abbreviated biblical citations. See Lubieniecki 1994, 350.

Literature: Bruckner 1979; Lubieniecki 1994, 345–50; Wallace 1850, 2:196–208; Williams 1990; Williams, 1142–47, 1232.

The Catechesis and Confession of Faith
of the Polish Brethren, 1574

Deuteronomy 6: "Hear, O Israel: The Lord our God is one Lord."   Dt 6[.4]

    John 8: "Jesus said, 'It is my Father . . . of whom you say that he is your God.'"   Jn 8[.54]

    At the press of Alexander Turobińczyk [Rodecki in Cracow] in the year of the birth of Jesus Christ, the Son of God, 1574

    Ecclesiastes 11: "Do not find fault before you investigate; first learn, then justly   Eccl 11[.7]
reprove."

    1 Corinthians 4: "Do not pronounce judgment before the time."   1 Cor 4[.5]

Preface to the Reader

The congregation (*coetus*) throughout Poland, baptized in the name of Jesus Christ the Nazarene, though meager and distressed, sincerely prays for grace and peace for all those who thirst after eternal salvation from the one God the Father, who is most high, through his only-begotten Son our Lord, Jesus Christ crucified.

Because the name of the Anabaptists, due to certain accursed men, is so disreputable and hated among all (just as it was among us a few years ago) so that as a result even the holy and salvation-giving oracles of God himself and his Christ clearly do not have a place among many men—even those who are not the worst sort—merely because the devil, that old imposter, besmirched the hated name of Anabaptism, and lest we appear to fail ourselves and yourselves before God and his Christ, we therefore present to you a confession of our faith and a catechism of our children (*puerorum*), frank and simple, produced insofar as it was possible from his Holy Scripture. We call to witness God, the Savior of hearts, and Jesus Christ, the righteous and terrible judge of the living and the dead, that we are not acting in a fraudulent, haughty, and high-handed manner, but do all things with a good conscience, as God inspires us with his Holy Spirit, and as far as Holy Scripture allows us, and we do this to the glory of God and his Son our Lord, for the correction of our life, and to attain eternal life. Moreover, if there is anything which escapes our notice, or "if in anything we are otherwise minded, God will reveal that also to us," as it says in Philippians 3. Indeed, these things which we now present to you we   Phil 3[.15] have drawn not from the cisterns of men that can hold no water but from the very clear fountains of the Savior. We are so sure and confident of these things that even "if an angel should try to thrust anything contrary on us, let him be accursed."   [Gal 1.8]

We make solemn appeal and entreaty to all by God and [for] your salvation to examine these [teachings] against the rule of the divine oracles and flee from a Babylonian faith and a life of Sodom, "having boarded the ark of Noah."

1 Pt 3[.19]

For the Lord is in a short time going to exact punishment from this accursed and ungrateful world, by means of a final flood, not of water, but of fire which will devour all those who are sinful and know not to repent. May God our Father who is most merciful avert this evil from us, for his own sake through the agency of his most charitable Son Jesus Christ, who was crucified and resurrected for our sake, and is now exalted above all the angels and blessed forever and ever. Amen.

Written at Cracow, Poland, in the 1574th year after the birth of Jesus Christ.

Catechism and Confession of Faith of the Congregation Gathered Throughout Poland, in the Name of Jesus Christ Our Lord Who Was Crucified and Resurrected

Q. Tell me, what things are especially necessary for the Christian man to know for salvation?

Jn 17[.3]

A. First and foremost is to know [A] the only true God, and [B] Jesus Christ whom he has sent . . . and this is eternal life, [C] and the Holy Spirit, John 17; second, [to know] about our justification; third, discipline; fourth, prayer; fifth, baptism; sixth, the Lord's supper.

[A] [ON THE ONLY TRUE GOD, THE FATHER, ON JESUS CHRIST, AND ON THE HOLY SPIRIT]

[Dt 6.4]

Q. What and what kind of God is it of whom Moses says: "Hear, O Israel, the Lord your God is one"?

[Dn 2.47]
[1 Tm 1.17]

A. The one God is Spirit,[a] Creator of heaven and earth,[b] our Father,[c] God of gods, Lord of lords, King of kings, "the one, only, wise God, immortal, [invisible]"; Head, God, and Father of Christ, to whom the Son and all are subject, he however to none;[d] our life, in whom as our God, with our whole heart, we ought above all to fear, to love ardently as our Father, to hear, to adore, to invoke, and with our lips and our pious life constantly to confess. [The remainder of the section, omitted, amplifies these ardent affirmations scripturally.]

a. [Jn 4.24]
b. [Gn 1.1]
c. [Gn 32; Mt 19]
d. [1 Cor 11.3, 15.27–28]

[B] ON JESUS CHRIST

Q. What is Jesus Christ, the Son of God?

    A. He is a man, our mediator with God, promised in the past to [our] fathers by the prophets, and born at last from the seed of David. God the Father made him Lord and Christ; that is, a most perfect prophet (*propheta*), a most holy priest (*sacerdos*), a most invincible king (*rex*). Through him [God] created a new world, restored, reconciled with himself, and pacified all things, and granted eternal life to those chosen by him. Thus let us believe him, most high after God. Let us adore him, let us invoke him, let us hear him, let us imitate him in our own small measure, and in him let us find rest for our souls.

    Q. Where does Holy Scripture call the Son of God a man?

    A. 1 Timothy 2, "For there is one God and there is one mediator between God and men, the man Christ Jesus"; Romans 5, "As sin came into the world through one man, . . . so much more is the grace of God, . . . which is of one man, Jesus Christ." 1 Corinthians 15, "As by a man came death, by a man has come also the resurrection of the dead. For as in Adam all die, so also in Christ shall all be made alive. . . . The first man Adam became a living being; the second man, the last Adam, became a life-giving spirit." And the Lord Jesus said of himself in John 8, "'You seek to kill me, a man, because I speak the truth to you . . . When you have lifted up the Son of a man,'" etc. Matthew 16, "'Who do men say that the Son of man is?' . . . 'You are the Christ, the Son of the living God.'" Daniel 7, "As I looked, thrones were placed and one that was ancient of days took his seat; . . . I looked then, and behold with the clouds of heaven there came one like the Son of man, and to him the ancient of days gave dominion and glory and kingdom, that all peoples, nations, and languages should serve him; his dominion is an everlasting dominion, which will not pass away, and his kingdom one that shall not be destroyed." *1 Tm 2[.5]* *Rom 5[.12, 15]* *1 Cor 15[.20, 45]* *Jn 8[.37, 28]* *Mt 16[.13, 16]* *Dn 7[.9, 13]*

    Q. Where is he called the mediator of God and men?

    A. 1 Timothy 2, "There is one God and there is one mediator between God and men, the man Christ Jesus." John 14, "Jesus himself said, 'I am the way, and the truth, and the life; no one comes to the Father, but by me!'" Ephesians 2, "Through Jesus we have access in one spirit to the Father." Romans 8, "It is Christ Jesus, who died and was raised from the dead who is at the right hand of God, interceding for us." 1 John 2, "My little children, . . . do not sin; but if anyone does sin, we have an advocate with the Father, Jesus Christ the righteous; and he is the expiation for our sins, and not for ours only but also for the sins of the whole world." *1 Tm 2[.5]* *Jn 14[.6]* *Eph 2[.18]* *Rom 8[.34]* *1 Jn 2[.1–2]*

    Q. To which fathers was Christ promised?

    A. To Adam, Abraham, David, and all of Israel.

    Q. Where is he first promised to Adam?

Gn 3[.14–15]   A. Genesis 3, "God said to the serpent . . . 'I will put enmity between your seed and her seed; he shall bruise your head, and you shall bruise his heel.'"

Q. Where are these things made clear?

1 Jn 3[.8]   A. 1 John 3, "He who commits sin is of the devil; for the devil has sinned from the beginning. The reason the Son of God appeared was to destroy the works

Heb 2[.14–15]   of the devil." Hebrews 2, "Jesus through death destroyed him who has the power of death, that is, the devil, and delivered all those who through fear of death were sub-

Rv 12[.7–10]   ject to lifelong bondage." Revelation 12, "Now war arose in heaven, Michael and his angels fighting against the dragon; and the dragon and his angels fought, but they were defeated and there was no longer any place for them in heaven. And the great dragon was thrown down, that ancient serpent, who is called the devil and Satan, the deceiver of the whole word—he was thrown down to earth, and his angels were thrown down with him. And I heard a loud voice in heaven, saying, 'Now the salvation and the power and the kingdom of our God and the authority of his Christ have come.'"

Q. Then how was Christ promised to Abraham?

Gn [22.18]   A. Genesis 12, 18, 22, 26, "'By your descendants shall all the nations of the

Gal 3[.16, 19, 24] earth bless themselves.'" Galatians 3, "Promises were made to Abraham and to his offspring (*semen*). It does not say 'and to his offsprings,' referring to many; but referring to one, 'and to offspring,' which is Christ. . . . The law was added because of transgressions, till the offspring should come. . . . The law was our custodian until

Gal 4[.4]   Christ came." Galatians 4, "When the time had fully come, God sent forth his Son, born under the law, to redeem those who were under the law."

Q. Where was he promised to all Israel?

Dt 18[.15, 18–19]   A. Deuteronomy 18, "Moses said, 'The Lord your God will raise up for you a prophet like me from among you, from your brethren—him you shall heed . . . and I will put my words in his mouth, and he shall speak to them all that I command him. And whoever will not give heed to my words which he shall speak in

Acts 3[.20, 22, 26] my name, I myself will require it of him.'" Acts 3, "God sent to you the one before promised for you, Jesus Christ. For Moses said to your fathers, 'Your Lord God from your brethren has raised up a prophet similar to me. . . .' God having raised up his Son Jesus, sent him to you first, to bless you in turning every one of you from wickedness."

Q. But where was he promised to David?

2 Sm 7[.12, 14]   A. 2 Samuel 7, "The Lord of hosts said, 'When your days are fulfilled and you lie down with your fathers, I will raise up your seed after you, who shall come

2 Sm 7[.14]   forth from your body, and I will establish his eternal kingdom. . . .' 'I will be his

Is 7[.14]   Father, and he shall be my Son.'" Psalm 89 and Isaiah 7, "Hear then, O house of

David! Your Lord God will give you a sign. Behold, a virgin shall conceive and bear a son, and shall call his Son Emmanuel." Isaiah 9, "for to us a child is born, and to us a son is given . . . and his name will be called 'wonderful counselor, mighty God, everlasting father, Prince of peace.' Of the increase of his government and of peace there will be no end, upon the throne of David, and over his kingdom he will sit for evermore, . . . the zeal of the Lord of Hosts will do this." Is 9[.6–7]

Q. In whom were all those things made complete?

A. In Jesus Christ our Lord, just as it was written in Matthew 1, "The book Mt 1[.1, 20, 23] of the genealogy of Jesus Christ, the son of David, the son of Abraham. . . . An angel of the Lord said, 'Joseph, son of David, do not fear to take Mary your wife, for that which is conceived in her is of the Holy Spirit. She will bear a son, and his name shall be called "Emmanuel" (which means, God with us).'" Luke 1 is even Lk 1[.26, 31–33] more expansive: "The angel Gabriel was sent from God to a virgin betrothed to a man whose name was Joseph, of the house of David. . . . And he said, 'Behold, you will conceive and bear a son, and you shall call his name Jesus. He will be great, and will be called the Son of the Most High, and the Lord God will give to him the throne of his father David, and he will reign over the house of Jacob forever, and of his kingdom there will be no end.'" Luke 2,[a] "In those days a decree went out from Caesar Augustus that all the world should be enrolled . . . and Joseph also went to Judaea, to the city of David, which is called Bethlehem, because he was of the lineage of David . . . with Mary, his betrothed, who was with child. . . . And she gave birth to her firstborn son. . . . And behold, an angel of the Lord said to shepherds, 'Be not afraid, I bring you good news of a great joy . . . to you is born this day in the city of David a Savior, who is Christ the Lord.' . . . And Simeon, looking for the consolation of Israel . . . received a revelation from the Holy Spirit that he should not see death before he had seen the Lord's Christ. . . . And when the parents brought the child Jesus into the temple, . . . he took him up in his arms and blessed God and said. . . . 'Mine eyes have seen thy salvation, . . . a light for revelation to the Gentiles, and for glory to thy people Israel.'"

Q. Where is God said to have created this Jesus Lord and Christ?

A. Psalm 45, "Your God has anointed you with the oil of gladness above Ps 45[.7] your fellows." Isaiah 61, "The Spirit of the Lord is upon me because God has Is 61[.1]; [Lk 4.18] anointed me to bring good tidings to the poor." Luke 4 and Daniel 9, "A most holy Dn 9[.26] man, Messiah and Prince, will be anointed, and the Messiah will be killed." John 3, Jn 3[.34] "It is not by measure that God gives the Spirit to this Jesus." Acts 2, "God has made Acts 2[.36]

---

a. Lk 2[.1, 4–5, 7, 10–11, 25–28, 30, 32]

Acts 10[.38]   him both Lord and Christ, this Jesus whom you crucified." Acts 10, "God anointed
Jesus of Nazareth with the Holy Spirit and with power." And Jesus himself said at
Mt 28[.18]   Matthew 28, "All authority in heaven and on earth has been given to me." Philip-
Phil 2[.5–11]   pians 2, "Jesus Christ, though he was in the form of God, . . . took the form of a
servant . . . and being found in human form he humbled himself and became obedient unto death, even death on a cross. Therefore God has highly exalted him and
bestowed on him the name which is above every name, that at the name of Jesus
every knee should bend, in heaven and on earth and under the earth, and every
tongue should confess that Jesus Christ is Lord, to the glory of God the Father."

Q. Where is Jesus said to be a *prophet* most high?

A. A little above something was quoted from the Deuteronomy of Moses,
chapter 18. But God himself, the heavenly Father, proclaims concerning Jesus: Mat-
[Mt 17.5]   thew 3 and 17, "'This is my Son, with whom I am well pleased. Listen to him.'"
Jn 1[.1, 17]   John 1, "In the beginning was the Word. . . . No one has ever seen God; the only
Mt 23[.10]   Son, who is in the bosom of the Father, he has made him known." Matthew 23,
"You are not to be called masters, for you have one Master, the Christ." Revelation
Rv 19[.11, 13]   19, "I saw a white horse, and he who sat upon it is called faithful and true. . . . He
is clad in a robe dipped in blood, and the name by which he is called is the Word
Heb 1[.1–2]   of God." Hebrews 1, "In many and various ways God spoke of old to our fathers
by the prophets; but in these last days he has spoken to us by a Son."

Q. Where is the *priesthood* of Christ written about?

Ps 110[.4]   A. Psalm 110, "The Lord has sworn and will not change his mind, 'You are
Heb 4[.14, 16]   a priest forever after the order of Melchizedek.'" Hebrews 4, "Since we have a High
Priest who has passed through the heavens. . . . Let us then with confidence draw
Heb 5[.7]   near to the throne of grace." Hebrews 5, "In the days of his flesh, Christ offered up
prayers and supplications, with loud cries and tears, to him who was able to save
Heb 9[.11–12, 14]   him from death, and he was heard for his [godly] fear." Hebrews 9, "Christ, the
High Priest of good things to come, . . . taking not the blood of goats and calves but
his own blood, entered once for all into the holy place, thus securing an eternal redemption. . . . Christ, who through the eternal Spirit offered himself without blemish to God, will purify our conscience from dead works to serve the living God."
Heb 10[.11–12]   Hebrews 10, "Every priest stands daily at his service, offering repeatedly the same
sacrifices, which can never take away sins. But when this man had offered a single
sacrifice for sins, he sat down at the right hand of God, . . . for by a single offering
he has perfected for all time those who are sanctified."

Q. What is the benefit which derives from his priesthood?

1 Pt 2[.9]   A. It is most great, concerning which there is 1 Peter 2, "You are a chosen

race, a royal priesthood, a holy nation, a people for God's possession." Revelation 5, Rv 5[.5, 9]
"The lion of the tribe of Judah, the root of David, has conquered . . . [to whom the
twenty-four elders sang,] 'Worthy art thou to take the scroll and to open its seals,
for thou wast slain and by thy blood didst ransom men for God, and hast made
them a kingdom and priests to our God.'"

Q. Where is it written concerning the kingdom of Jesus Christ?

A. Daniel 2, "And in the days of those kings the God of heaven will set Dn 2[.44]
up a kingdom which shall never be destroyed nor shall its sovereignty be left to
another people. It shall break in pieces all these kingdoms and bring them to an
end, and it will stand forever." Ezekiel 34, "I, the Lord, will be their God, and my Ez 34[.24]
servant David shall be prince among them." Ezekiel 37, "My servant David shall Ez 37[.24]
be king over them." Zechariah 9, "'Rejoice greatly, O daughter of Zion! . . . Lo, Zec 9[.9]
your king comes to you; triumphant and victorious is he, humble and riding an ass,
on a colt the foal of an ass.'" Matthew 21, "The disciples brought the ass and put Mt 21[.7, 9]
their garments on it, and sat him thereon. . . . and the crowds that went before him
and that followed him shouted 'Hosanna to the son of David! Blessed be he who
comes in the name of the Lord!'" Psalm 2, "The kings of the earth set themselves, Ps 2[.2, 6, 8]
and the rulers take counsel together, against the Lord and his anointed. . . . 'I, [the
Lord], set my king on Zion, my holy hill. . . . I will make the nations your heritage.'" Acts 4, "There were gathered together against thy holy child Jesus, whom Acts 4[.27]
thou didst anoint, both Herod and Pontius Pilate." John 1, "Nathaniel said to Jesus, Jn 1[.49]
'Rabbi, you are the Son of God! You are the king of Israel.'" John 18, "Pilate said Jn 18[.33, 36]
to Jesus, 'Are you the king of the Jews?' Jesus answered, "Do you say that I am a
king? . . . My kingship is not of this world.'" John 19, "Jesus of Nazareth, the king Jn 19[.19]
of the Jews." Colossians 1, "Give thanks to the Father, who has delivered us from Col 1[.13]
the dominion of darkness and transferred us to the kingdom of his beloved Son, in
whom we have redemption, through his blood, and the forgiveness of sins."

Q. But where is it written concerning this "new creation" of which you
speak?

A. Isaiah 65, "For behold, I create new heavens and a new earth; . . . for Is 65[.17–18]
behold, I create Jerusalem a rejoicing, and her people a joy." Isaiah 66, "'For as the Is 66[.22]
new heaven and the new earth which I will make shall remain before me,' says the
Lord." Ezekiel 36, "A new heart I will give you, . . . and I will take out the heart Ez 36[.26]
of stone." Psalm 51, "Create in me a clean heart, O God, and put a new and right Ps 51[.10]
spirit within me."

Q. Where is it written that all things have been created anew, restored, reconciled, and pacified by Jesus?

A. John 1,[a] "All things were made through him." 2 Corinthians 5,[b] "If anyone is in Christ, he is a new creation; the old has passed away, behold the new has come. . . . God, through Christ, reconciled us to himself; God was in Christ recon-

Heb 2[.2]
Col 1[.16–20]
ciling the world to himself." Hebrews 2, "Through a Son God created the world." Colossians 1, "In him all things were created, in heaven and on earth, visible and invisible. . . . In him all things hold together. He is the Head of the body, the church; he is the beginning. . . . Through him he reconciled to himself all things, whether on

Eph 1[.3, 10]
earth or in heaven, making peace by the blood of his cross." Ephesians 1, "Blessed be the God and Father of our Lord Jesus Christ. . . . who in the fullness of time unites all things in Christ, things in heaven and things on earth." Ephesians 2,[c] "And we were by nature children of wrath. . . . but God made us alive together with Christ. . . . for we are his workmanship created in Christ Jesus for good works. . . . He created in himself one new man in place of the two, so making peace, and reconciled us both. . . . For through him we both have access in one spirit to the Father." Ephesi-

Eph 4[.22]
ans 4, "Put on the new nature, created after the likeness of God in true righteousness and holiness."

Q. Where is it written that God shares eternal life with us through Jesus?

Jn 5[.26, 24]
A. John 5, "'As the Father has life in himself, so he has granted the Son also to have life in himself. . . . Truly, truly, I say to you, he who hears my word and believes him who sent me, has eternal life; he does not come into judgment, but

Jn 6[.47]
has passed from death to life.'" John 6, "'He who believes in me has eternal life.'" John 10,[d] "To my sheep I give eternal life." John 11,[e] "'He who believes in me shall never die.'" Colossians 3, "Your life is hid with Christ in God. When Christ who is

Col 3[.3–4]
1 Jn 5[.11]
our life appears, then you also will appear with him in glory." 1 John 5, "God gave us eternal life, and this life is in his Son."

Q. Where is it written that we, after God the Father who is most high, ought to believe in Christ Jesus the Mediator?

Ps 2[.11]
Is 28[.16]
A. Psalm 2, "Kiss the Son, lest he be angry, and you perish in the way; blessed are all who take refuge in him." Isaiah 28, "Behold, I am laying in Zion for a foundation a stone, a precious cornerstone. . . . 'He who believes will not be

Rom 9[.33]
in haste.'" Romans 9, "'Behold I am laying in Zion a stone that will make men stumble, a rock that will make them fall; and he who believes in him will not be put

1 Pt 2[.6–8]
to shame'"; 1 Peter 2, "'Behold, I am laying in Zion a stone, a cornerstone chosen

a. Jn 1[.3]
b. 2 Cor 5[.17–19]
c. Eph 2[.3–5, 10, 15, 18]
d. Jn 10[.28]
e. Jn 11[.25]

and precious, and he who believes in him will not be put to shame.' To you therefore who believe, he is precious, but for those who do not believe. . . . He is 'a stone
that will make men stumble.'" John 9, "Jesus said, 'Do you believe in the Son of   Jn 9[.35–38]
God?' He answered, 'And who is he, Sir, that I may believe in him?' Jesus said to
him, 'You have seen him, and it is he who speaks to you!' He said, 'Lord, I believe';
and he worshiped him." John 14, "Christ himself said to his disciples, 'Let not your   Jn 14[.1]
hearts be troubled; you believe in God; believe also in me.'" John 6, "This is the   Jn 6[.29, 47]
work of God, that you believe in him whom he has sent. . . . Truly, truly, I say to
you, he who believes in me has eternal life." John 11, "'I am the resurrection and   Jn 11[.25–26]
the life; he who believes in me, though he die, yet shall he live, and whoever lives
and believes in me shall never die.'"

Q. Why must one believe in Christ?

A. Matthew 28, "Because all authority in heaven and on earth has been   Mt 28[.18]
given to him." Hebrews 1, "He upholds the universe by his word of power." Mat-   Heb 1[.3]
thew 12 and John 2, "He knows the thoughts of men." Revelation 2, "He searches   Rv 2[.23]
mind and heart." Hebrews 7, "He holds the priesthood permanently, because he   Heb 7[.24–25]
continues forever. He is able for all time to save those who draw near to God through
him, since he always lives to make intercession for them."

Q. Where is it written concerning the adoration and invocation of Christ?

A. Daniel 7, "As I looked, thrones were placed and one that was ancient   Dn 7[.9, 13–14]
of days took his seat. . . . I also saw come with the clouds of heaven one like a son
of man, and he came to the ancient of days. And to him was given dominion and
glory and kingdom, that all peoples, nations, and languages should serve him; his
dominion is an everlasting dominion, and his kingdom one that shall not be destroyed." John 20,[a] "Thomas said to Jesus, 'My Lord and my God!'" Luke 23,[b]
"'Lord, remember me when you come into your kingdom.'" Luke 24, "Jesus blessed   Lk 24[.50]
the apostles, and was carried up into heaven. And they worshiped him, and returned
to Jerusalem with great joy." Acts 7,[c] "Stephen, full of the Holy Spirit, gazed into
heaven and saw the glory of God, and Jesus standing at the right hand of God; and
he said, 'Behold I see the heavens opened, and the Son of man standing at the right
hand of God. . . . Lord Jesus, receive my spirit.' And he knelt down and cried with
a loud voice, 'Lord do not hold this sin against them.'" And Paul always asks for
"grace and peace from God the Father and Lord Jesus Christ." Philippians 2, "Jesus   Phil 2[.5–6]
Christ, who, though he was in the form of God (that is, "although he was the image
of the invisible God," Colossians 1; and "he reflects the glory of God and bears the   Col 1[.15]

a. Jn 20[.28]
b. Lk 23[.42]
c. Acts 7[.55–56, 59–60]

Heb 1[.3, 7–11]   very stamp of his nature," Hebrews 1), did not count equality with God a thing to be grasped, but emptied himself, taking the form of a servant, being born in the likeness of men. And being found in human form (that is, "For our sake he made

2 Cor 5[.21]   him to be sin who knew no sin," 2 Corinthians 5, "Having become a curse for us,"

Gal 3[.13]   Galatians 3, he humbled himself and became obedient unto death, even death on a cross. Therefore God has highly exalted him and bestowed on him "the name which is above every name, that at the name of Jesus every knee should bow, in heaven and

[Phil 2.9–11]   on earth and under the earth, and every tongue confess that Jesus Christ is Lord, to

Ps 72[.9–11]   the glory of God the Father." Psalms 72, "May those who dwell in the wilderness bow before him, and his enemies lick the dust. . . . May all kings fall down be-

Heb 1[.6]   fore him, all nations serve him!" Hebrews 1, "'Let all God's angels worship him.'"

Rv 5[.11–13]   Revelation 5, "I looked, and I heard . . . the voice of many angels . . . saying with a loud voice, 'Worthy is the Lamb who was slain, to receive power and wealth and wisdom and might and honor and glory and blessing.' And I heard every creature in heaven and on earth and under the earth and in the sea, saying, 'To him who sits upon the throne and to the lamb be blessing and honor and glory and might for ever and ever, Amen!'"

    Q. What is the most important thing that we shall ask of the Son of God?

    A. What he himself gave the commandment to be asked, and what his true

Mt 9[.2, 6, 8]   worshipers once asked of him, that is, that he might forgive our sins. Matthew 9, "The Lord himself said, 'Take heart, my son; your sins are forgiven. . . . The Son of man has authority to forgive sins'. . . . Although the crowds were surprised at this, they glorified God, who had given such authority to men."

    [We shall ask him] "to build his own church, according to his promise," Mathew 16; "'I will build my church, to collect the sheep that are scattered into one

Jn 11[.52]   fold,'" John 10; "'to gather the children of God,'" John 11.

    [We shall ask him] "to sanctify his church, having cleansed her by the wash-

Eph 5[.26]   ing of water with the word," Ephesians 5.

    [We shall ask him] "'not to desert us but to be with us always, to the close

Mt 28[.20]   of the age,'" Matthew 28.

    [We shall ask him] "to send the promise of the Holy Spirit which he has

Acts 2[.33]   received from the Father," John 15 and Acts 2.

    [We shall ask him] "to give the church suitable ministers of the word,"

Eph 4[.11]   Ephesians 4, and "to give rest to all who labor and are heavy-laden," Matthew 11,[a] [and] "'to increase our faith,'" Luke 17,[b] [and] "'bless us and turn us from our

---

a. Mt 11[.28]

b. Lk 17[.5]

wickedness,'" Acts 3, [and] "to reveal the gospel to us just as he revealed it to Paul," Acts 3[.26]
Galatians 1,[a] [and] "to change our bodies on that day," Philippians 3,[b] [and] "to help
us in our temptation," Hebrews 2, [and] "to heal us in our sickness," Matthew 9[c]
and Acts 9, [and] "to raise up those who believe on the last day," John 6,[d] [and] "to
forgive our enemies for their wrong and to take our spirit into his hands," Acts 7;
and finally, "to give us the crown which does not languish on that day," 2 Timothy. 2 Tm [4.8]

Q. Why have all these things been written concerning the Son of God and
why must they be believed?

A. In order that we may hear him teaching, the only Master (*Magister*) from
God; and trusting in him and imitating his steps, in proportion to his giving that
we may find rest for our souls.

Q. Where is this commandment made?

A. Matthew 17[e] and 2 Peter 1,[f] "We heard the voice of God the Father, 'This
is my beloved Son, in whom I am well pleased.'" John 3, "God so loved the world Jn 3[.16]
that he gave his only Son, that whoever believes in him should not perish but have
eternal life."

Q. Where has instruction been given on imitating the Son of God?

A. Christ the Lord himself said, at Matthew 11, "Come to me, all who labor Mt 11[.28–29]
and are heavy-laden, and I will give you rest. Take my yoke upon you, and learn
from me; for I am gentle and lowly in heart, and you will find rest for your souls."
1 Peter 2, "Christ suffered for us, leaving us an example, that we should follow in his 1 Pt 2[.21–24]
steps. He committed no sin. No guilt was found on his lips. When he was reviled,
he did not revile in return; when he suffered, he did not threaten; but he trusted to
him who judges justly. He himself bore our sins in his body on the tree, that we
might die to sin and live to righteousness."

[C] ON THE HOLY SPIRIT

Q. Now discuss the Holy Spirit, because we are not able to cry, "Abba! Father!"
without the Holy Spirit, and "He who does not have the Spirit of Christ does not [Rom 8.15]
belong to him," Romans 8. Rom 8[.9]

A. "The Holy Spirit is the power of God, whose fullness God the Father
gave to his only-begotten Son, our Lord, in order that we may take, as adopted sons,

---

a. Gal 1[.12]

b. Phil 3[.20]

c. Heb 2[.18]; Mt 9[.18–31]

d. Acts 9[.34]; Jn 6[.40]

e. Mt 17[.30]

f. 2 Pt 1[.17]

Jn 1[.3]   from his fullness," John 1. The identity and character of the Spirit of God will be
apparent from his names, which follow.

      1. He is "The Spirit of God" because he is from God or, rather, proceeds

Jn 15[.26]   from God the Father. John 15, "The Spirit of truth, who proceeds from the Father."

1 Cor 2[.11] 1 Corinthians 2, "We have received not the Spirit, which is from God."

Acts 2[.38]   2. He is called "the gift of God." Acts 2, "'You shall receive the gift of the

Eph 4[.8]   Holy Spirit.'" Ephesians 4, "[When] he ascended on high, he gave gifts to men."

Ex 8[.19]   3. He is called "the finger of God." Exodus 8, "The magicians said to the

Lk 11[.20]   Pharaoh, 'This is the finger of God.'" Luke 11, "'It is by the finger of God that I cast
out demons.'"

Lk 1[.35]   4. He is called the "energy" or "power" of God. Luke 1, "'The Holy Spirit

Acts 1[.8]   will come upon you, and the power of the Most High will overshadow you.'" Acts 1,
"'You shall receive the power of the Holy Spirit, who will come upon you.'" Acts

Acts 10[.38] 10, "God anointed Jesus of Nazareth with the Holy Spirit and with power."

Mt 3[.11]   5. He is called "fire." Matthew 3, "He will baptize you with the Holy Spirit

Acts 2[.3]   and with fire." Acts 2, "There appeared to them tongues as of fire, distributed and
resting on each one of them, and they were all filled with the Holy Spirit."

Is 44[.3]   6. [He is called] "water." Isaiah 44, "I will pour water on the thirsty land

Ez 36[.25–26] . . . and I will pour my Spirit upon your descendants." Ezekiel 36, "'I will sprinkle
clean water upon you; . . . a new heart I will give you, and a new spirit I will put

Jn 7[.38–39] within you.'" John 7, "He who believes in me, as the Scripture has said, 'out of
his heart shall flow rivers of living water.' Now this he said about the Spirit, which
those who believed in him were to receive."

Eph 1[.13–14]   7. He is a seal and a guarantee of our inheritance. Ephesians 1, "You who
have believed in him were sealed with the promised Holy Spirit, which is the guar-

Eph 4[.30]   antee of our inheritance." Ephesians 4, "Do not grieve the Holy Spirit of God, in
whom you were sealed for the day of redemption." 2 Corinthians 1 and 2 Corinthians 5,[a] "But it is God who establishes us with you in Christ, and has commissioned
us; he has put his seal upon us and given us his Spirit in our hearts as a guarantee."

Ps 45[.7]   8. He is said to be "the anointing of God." Psalms 45, "Your God has

1 Jn 2[.27] anointed you with the oil of gladness above your fellows." 1 John 2, "The anointing
which you received from him abides in you . . . and his anointing teaches you about
everything."

Jn 14[.16, 26]   9. He is called "our counselor and teacher." John 14, "'I will pray the Father,
and he will give you another counselor, to be with you forever. . . . The counselor,
the Holy Spirit, whom the Father will send in my name, he will teach you all things,

a. 2 Cor 1[.21–22], 5[.5]

and bring to your remembrance all that I have said to you.'" John 16, "'If I do not Jn 16[.7, 13]
go away, the counselor will not come to you; but if I go, I will send him to you. . . .
When the Spirit of truth comes, he will guide you into all the truth.'"

Q. Why then does St. Paul call him "the Spirit of Christ" and "the Spirit
of the Son"?

A. Because God gave to his Son the fullness of the Holy Spirit to distribute to those who were chosen. John 1, "We have beheld his glory, glory as of the Jn 1[.14, 16]
only Son from the Father . . . full of grace and truth. . . . And from his fullness have
we all received." John 3, "'It was not by measure that he gave the Spirit to him!'" Jn 3[.34]
Colossians 1,[a] "In him all the fullness of God was pleased to dwell." Colossians 2,[b]
"In Christ are hid all the treasures of wisdom and knowledge. . . . In him the whole
fullness of deity lives bodily."

Q. Does there exist in Scripture a commandment and an example for worshiping and invoking the Holy Spirit?

A. In neither the old nor new covenant is there any mention of this matter.
But Christ gives the commandment that God the Father is to be asked for the Holy
Spirit: Luke 11, "'The Heavenly Father will give the Holy Spirit to those who ask Lk 11[.13]
him.'" He likewise orders that God is to be worshiped in spirit: John 4, "'God is Jn 4[.24, 23]
spirit, and those who worship him must worship in spirit and in truth. . . . For such
the Father seeks to worship him.'" Romans 8, "The Spirit of God dwells in you. Rom 8[.11, 15]
. . . Through whom we cry, 'Abba! Father!'" 1 Corinthians 12, "And no one can say 1 Cor 12[.3]
'Jesus is Lord,' except by the Holy Spirit."

2. ON OUR JUSTIFICATION BEFORE GOD

Q. What is justification?

A. It is the forgiveness in living faith of all our past trespasses by the pure
grace of God, through the agency of our Lord Jesus Christ, regardless of our works
and merits; [it is also] the most certain expectation of eternal life, and a true, not
artificial, correction of our life by the aid of the Spirit of God, to the glory of God
the Father and to the edification of our neighbors.

Q. Where has it been written concerning our sin?

A. Genesis 6, "The Lord saw the wickedness of men on earth, and that the Gn 6[.5]
imagination of the thoughts of his heart was only evil continually." Genesis 8, "The Gn 8[.21]
imagination of man's heart is evil from his youth." Job 15, "What is man that he can Jb 15[.14–16]
be clean? Or that he is born of a woman, that he can be righteous? Behold, God

a. Col 1[.19]
b. Col 2[.3, 9]

puts no trust in his holy ones, and the heavens are not clean in his sight, how much less one who is abominable and corrupt, a man who drinks iniquity like water!" Psalms 14, "The Lord looks down from heaven upon the children of men, to see if there are any who act wisely, that seek after God. They have all gone astray, they are all alike corrupt; there is none that does good, no, not one." Psalms 51, "Behold, I was brought forth in iniquity, and in sin did my mother conceive me." Psalms 130, "If thou, O Lord, shouldst mark iniquities, Lord, who could stand?" Psalms 143, "Enter not into judgment with thy servant; for no man living is righteous before thee." Isaiah 53, "All we like sheep have gone astray; we have turned every one to his own way." Romans 3, "All have sinned and fall short of the glory of God. . . . So that every mouth may be stopped, and the whole world may be held accountable to God. For no human being will be justified in his sight by works of the law, since through the law comes knowledge of sin." Romans 5, "Sin came into the world through one man and death through sin, and so death spread to all men." Ephesians 2, "We were all by nature children of wrath, like the rest of mankind." 1 John 1, "If we say we have no sin, we deceive ourselves, and the truth is not in us. . . . If we say we have not sinned, we make him a liar, and his word is not in us." Romans 7,[a] "If it had not been for the law, I should not have known sin. I should not have known what it is to covet if the law had not said, 'You shall not covet'. . . . So the law is holy, and the commandment is holy and just and good. . . . The law is spiritual, but I am carnal, sold under sin. I do not understand my own actions. For I do not do what I want, but I do the very thing I hate. . . . Sin dwells within me: for I know that nothing good dwells within me, that is, in my flesh. . . . I find it to be a law that when I want to do right, evil lies close at hand. For I delight in the law of God, in my inmost self, but I see in my members another law at war with the law of my mind and making me captive to the law of sin which dwells in my members. Wretched man that I am! Who will deliver me from this body of death? Thanks be to God through Jesus Christ our Lord!"

Q. Where has it been written concerning the grace of God and the forgiveness of our sins?

A. Numbers 14, "The Lord is slow to anger, and abounding in steadfast love, forgiving iniquity and transgression." Psalms 103, "The Lord is merciful and gracious, slow to anger and abounding in steadfast love. He will not always chide, nor will he keep his anger forever. He does not deal with us according to our sins, nor requite us according to our iniquities. For as the heavens are high above the earth, . . . as far as the East is from the West, so far does he remove our transgres-

Marginal references:
Ps 14[.2–3]
Ps 51[.5]
Ps 130[.3]
Ps 143[.2]
Is 53[.6]
Rom 3[.23, 19–20]
Rom 5[.12]
Eph 2[.3]
1 Jn 1[.8, 10]
Nm 14[.18]
Ps 103[.8–14]

---

a. Rom 7[.7, 12, 14–15, 17, 21–25]

sions from us. As a father pities his children, so the Lord pities those who fear him. For he knows our frame; he remembers that we are dust." Isaiah 43, "I, I am the Lord, and besides me there is no Savior. . . . I, I am he who blots out your transgressions for my own sake, and I will not remember your sins. Put me in remembrance, let us argue together; set forth your case, that you may be proved right." Isaiah 42, "Behold my servant, . . . my chosen, in whom my soul delights; I have put my Spirit upon him, he will bring forth justice to the nations. . . . A bruised reed he will not break, and a dimly burning wick he will not quench; he will faithfully bring forth justice." Isaiah 49, "You are my servant Israel. . . . It is too light a thing that you should be my servant to raise up the tribes of Jacob. . . . I have given you as a light to the nations, that my salvation may reach to the end of the earth." Isaiah 53,[a] "By his knowledge shall the righteous one, my servant, make many to be accounted righteous. He was wounded by our transgressions. . . . The Lord has laid on him the iniquity of us all. . . . He made his soul an offering for sin. . . . and made intercession for the transgressors." Jeremiah 31, "The Lord says, 'I will forgive their iniquity, and I will remember their sin no more.'" Jeremiah 23, "Behold, the days are coming, says the Lord, when I will raise up for David a righteous branch. . . . In his day Judah will be saved. . . . And this is the name by which he will be called: 'The Lord is our righteousness.'" Ezekiel 18, "If a wicked man turns away from all his sins which he has committed and keeps all my statutes and does what is lawful and right, he shall surely live; he shall not die. None of the transgressions which he has committed shall be remembered against him. . . . 'Have I any pleasure in the death of the wicked,' says the Lord God, 'and not rather that he should turn from his way and live?'" Ezekiel 37, "I will save them from all the backslidings in which they have sinned, and will cleanse them; and they shall be my people, and I will be their God. My servant David shall be king over them; and they shall all have one shepherd. They shall follow my ordinances and be careful to observe my statutes. . . . David my servant shall be their prince forever." Romans 3, "All have sinned and fall short of the glory of God. But they are justified by his grace as a gift, through the redemption which is in Jesus Christ, whom God put forward as an expiation by his blood, to be received by faith. This was to show God's righteousness, because . . . he had passed over former sins. . . . A man is justified by faith apart from works of law." Romans 5, "Since we are justified by faith, we have peace with God through our Lord Jesus Christ." 1 Corinthians 1, "Christ Jesus, whom God made our wisdom, our righteousness and sanctification and redemption." Ephesians 2, "God, who is rich in mercy, out of the great love with which he loved us, even when we were dead

Is 43[.11, 25–26]

Is 42[.1, 13]

Is 49[.3, 6]

Jer 31[.34]
Jer 23[.5–6]

Ez 18[.21–23]

Ez 37[.23–25]

Rom 3[.23–25, 28]

Rom 5[.1]
1 Cor 1[.30]
Eph 2[.4–5, 8–9]

a. Is 53[.11, 5–6, 10, 12]

through our trespasses, made us alive together with Christ. . . . by whose grace you have been saved by faith; and this is not your own doing, it is the gift of God not because of works, lest any man should boast." Titus 3, "We ourselves were once foolish, disobedient, led astray, slaves to various passions and pleasures, passing our days in malice and envy, hated by men and hating one another; but when the goodness and loving kindness of God our Savior appeared, he saved us, not because of deeds done by us in righteousness, but in virtue of his own mercy, by the washing of regeneration and renewal in the Holy Spirit, which he poured out upon us richly through Jesus Christ our Savior, so that we might be justified by his grace and become heirs in hope of eternal life." 1 John 1, "If we confess our sins, he is faithful and just, and will forgive our sins and cleanse us from all unrighteousness. . . . And the blood of Jesus his Son cleanses us from all sin." 1 John 2, "My little children, . . . do not sin; but if anyone does sin, we have an advocate with the Father, Jesus Christ the righteous; and he is the expiation for our sins, . . . and for the sins of the whole world."

Ti 3[.3–6]

1 Jn 1[.9, 7]

1 Jn 2[.1–2]

 Q. Where has instruction been given concerning the correction of our life?

 A. John the Baptist said at Matthew 3, "Bear fruit that befits repentance. . . . Even now the ax is laid to the root of the trees; every tree therefore that does not bear good fruit is cut down and thrown into the fire." Matthew 5, Jesus said to his disciples, "Let your light so shine before men, that they may see your good works and give glory to your Father who is in heaven. . . . I have come not to abolish the law but to complete it. . . . Unless your righteousness exceeds that of the scribes and Pharisees, you will not enter the kingdom of heaven."

Mt 3[.8, 10]

Mt 5[.16–17, 20]

 1. "You have heard that it was said to the men of old, 'You shall not kill; and whoever kills shall be liable to judgment.' But I say to you that everyone who is angry with his brother shall be liable to judgment; . . . and whoever says, 'you fool!' shall be liable to the Gehenna of fire."

[Mt 5.21–22]

 2. "You have heard that it was said to the men of old, 'You shall not commit adultery.' But I say to you that everyone who looks at a woman lustfully has already committed adultery with her in his heart."

[Mt 5.27–28]

 3. "You have heard that it was said to the men of old, 'You shall not swear falsely, but shall perform to the Lord what you have sworn.' But I say to you, do not swear at all, either by heaven . . . or by the earth. . . . Let what you say be simply 'yes' or 'no'; anything more than this comes from evil."

[Mt 5.33–35, 37]

 4. "You have heard that it was said, 'An eye for an eye and a tooth for a tooth.' But I say to you, do not resist one who is evil. But if anyone strikes you on the right cheek, turn to him the other also; and if anyone would sue you and take your coat, let him have your cloak as well; and if anyone forces you to go one mile, go with him two miles. . . . Love your enemies, and bless those who curse you. . . . Do

[Mt 5.38–41, 44]

[Lk 6.28]

good to those who hate you . . .[a] and pray for those who abuse you." Galatians 5,[b] "Walk by the Spirit, and do not gratify the desires of the flesh. . . . Now the works of the flesh are plain: immorality, impurity, licentiousness, idolatry, sorcery, enmity, strife, jealousy, anger, selfishness, dissension, party spirit, envy, murder, drunkenness, carousing, and the like. I warn you . . . that those who do such things shall not inherit the kingdom of God. But the fruit of the Spirit is love, joy, peace, patience, kindness, goodness, faithfulness, gentleness, self-control; against such things is no law. And those who belong to Christ have crucified the flesh with its passions and desires." Ephesians 2, "We are the workmanship of God, created in Christ Jesus for good works, which God prepared beforehand, that we should walk in them." Ephesians 4 and 5, "This I testify in the Lord, that you must no longer live as the Gentiles do. . . . Put off your old nature which belongs to your former manner of life. . . . And put on the new nature, created after the likeness of God in true righteousness and holiness." [Eph 2.10] [Eph 4.17, 22, 24]

1. Therefore, putting away falsehood, let everyone speak the truth with his neighbor. . . . [Eph 4.25]

2. If you be angry, do not sin. . . . Let all bitterness and wrath and anger and clamor and slander be put away from you, with all malice, and be kind to one another, tenderhearted, forgiving one another, as God in Christ forgave you. . . . [Eph 4.26, 31–32]

3. Let the thief no longer steal, but rather let him labor, doing honest work with his hands. . . . [Eph 4.28]

4. Let no evil talk come out of your mouths, but only such as is good for edifying. . . . Let there be no filthiness, nor silly talk, nor levity. . . . [Eph 4.29] [Eph 5.4]

5. Impurity or covetousness must not even be named among you, as is fitting among saints. . . . [Eph 5.3]

6. Do not get drunk with wine, for that is debauchery; but be filled with the Spirit. . . . No immoral or impure man, or one who is covetous (that is, an idolater) has any inheritance in the kingdom of Christ and of God. Let no one deceive you with empty words, for it is because of these things that the wrath of God comes upon the sons of disobedience. Therefore do not associate with them, for once you were darkness, but now you are light in the Lord. [Eph 5.18, 5–8]

7. Titus 2, "The grace of God has appeared for the salvation of all men, training us to renounce irreligion and worldly passions, and to live sober, upright, and godly lives in this world, . . . as a people of his own who are zealous for good deeds." 1 Peter 1, "As he who called you is holy, be holy yourselves in all your conduct. . . . You know that you were ransomed from the futile ways inherited from [Ti 2[.11–12, 14] [1 Pt 1[.15, 18–19]

a. [Lk 6.27–28]
b. Gal 5[.16, 19–24]

your fathers, not with perishable things such as silver or gold, but with the precious

1 Pt 2[.21, 24] blood of Christ, like that of a lamb without blemish or spot." 1 Peter 2, "Christ suffered for us, leaving us an example, that we should follow in his steps. . . . He himself bore our sins in his body on the tree, that we might die to sin and live to

1 Jn 3[.1, 3, 7–8] righteousness." 1 John 3, "Beloved, what love the Father has given us, that we should be called children of God. . . . and everyone who thus hopes in him purifies himself as he is pure. . . . Little children, let no one deceive you. He who does right is righteous, as he is righteous. He who commits sin is of the devil. . . . the reason the

Jas 2[.14, 19, 26] Son of God appeared was to destroy the works of the devil." James 2, "What does it profit, my brethren, if a man says he has faith but has not works? Can his faith save him . . . ? Even the demons believe—and shudder. . . . For as the body apart from the spirit is dead, so faith apart from works is dead."

3. ON ECCLESIASTICAL DISCIPLINE

Q. What is discipline?

A. It is the frequent recital of the duty (*officium*) of individuals, and the duty of those sinning against God or a neighbor, first in private, then also in public, before the whole congregation having been called together, and finally the duty of those stubborn men who are alienated from the communion of the holy, in order that they, one filled with shame, may change, or, if they are unwilling to do this, be

[Mt 18.15–18] damned forever.

Q. What is the office of the bishop (*episcopus*)?

1 Tm 3[.1–7] A. 1 Timothy 3, "If anyone aspires to the office of bishop, he desires a noble task. Now a bishop must be above reproach, temperate, sensible, dignified, hospitable, an apt teacher, no drunkard, not violent but gentle, not quarrelsome, and no lover of money. He must manage his own household well, keeping his children submissive and respectful in every way; for if a man does not know how to manage his own household, how can he care for God's church? He must not be a recent convert, or he may be puffed up with conceit and fall into the condemnation of the slanderer; moreover he must be well thought of by outsiders, or he may fall into reproach and the snare of the devil."

Q. Where is the duty of deacons (*diaconi*) described?

Acts 6[.1–6] A. Acts 6, "Now in those days when the disciples were increasing in number, the Hellenists murmured against the Hebrews because their widows were neglected in the daily distribution. And the twelve summoned the body of the disciples and said, 'It is not right that we should give up preaching the word of God to serve tables. Therefore, brethren, pick out from among you seven men of good repute, full of the Spirit and of wisdom, whom we may appoint to this duty. But we will devote ourselves to prayer and to the ministry of the word.' And what they said pleased the whole multitude. . . . They set the men whom they chose before the apostles, and they prayed and laid their hands upon them." 1 Timothy 3, "Deacons must be serious, not double-tongued, not addicted to much wine, not greedy for gain; they must hold the mystery of the faith. . . . And let them also be tested first; then if they prove themselves blameless let them serve as deacons. The women likewise must be serious, no slanderers, but temperate, faithful in all things. Let deacons be married only once, and let them manage their children and their households well." 1 Tm 3[.8–12]

Q. Where is the office of elders (*seniores*) described?

A. 1 Timothy 5, "Let the elders who rule well be considered worthy of a double honor, especially those who labor in preaching and teaching; for the Scripture says, 'You shall not muzzle an ox when it is treading out the grain,' and 'the laborer deserves his wages.' Never admit any charge against an order except on the evidence of two or three witnesses. As for those who persist in sin, rebuke them in the presence of all, so that the rest may stand in fear." 1 Tm 5[.17–20]

Q. Where has instruction been given concerning widows?

A. 1 Timothy 5,[a] "She who is a real widow, and is left all alone, has set her hope on God and continues in supplications and prayers night and day. . . . let no one be enrolled as a widow who is under sixty years of age, or has been married more than once; and she must be well attested for her good deeds, whether she has brought up children, shown hospitality, washed the feet of the saints, received the afflicted, and devoted herself to doing good in every way. . . . I would have younger widows marry, bear children, rule their households, and give the enemy no occasion to revile us. . . . But if any believing woman has relatives who are widows, let her assist them; let the church not be burdened, so that it may assist those who are real widows."

Q. Where has the commandment been made concerning husbands and wives?

A. Ephesians 5,[b] "Wives, be subject to your husbands, as to the Lord. For the husband is the head of the wife as Christ is the head of the church, . . . As the church is subject to Christ, so let wives also be subject in everything to their husbands. Husbands, love your wives, as Christ loved the church and gave himself up for her. . . . Even so husbands should love their wives as their own bodies. . . . For no man ever hates his own flesh, but nourishes it and cherishes it. . . . 'For this reason a man shall leave his father and mother and be joined to his wife, and the two

a. 1 Tm 5[.5, 9–10, 14, 16]
b. Eph 5[.22–25, 28–29, 31, 33]

shall become one. . . .' However, let each one of you love his wife as himself, and 1 Tm 2[.8–15] let the wife see that she respects her husband." 1 Timothy 2, "I desire then that in every place the men should pray, lifting holy hands without anger or quarreling; also that women should adorn themselves modestly and sensibly in seemly apparel, not with braided hair, or gold or pearls or costly attire but by good deeds, as befits women who profess religion. Let a woman learn in silence with all submissiveness. I permit no woman to teach or to have authority over men; she is to keep silent. For Adam was formed first, then Eve. And Adam was not deceived, but the woman was deceived and became a transgressor. Yet woman will be saved through bearing children, if she continues in faith and love and holiness, with modesty."

Q. Where are old men and women, girls and boys taught their office?

Ti 2[.1–6]   A. Titus 2, "Teach what befits sound doctrine. Bid the older men be temperate, serious, sensible, sound in faith, in love, and in steadfastness. Bid the older women likewise to be reverent in behavior, not to be slanderers or slaves to drink; they are to teach what is good, and so train the young women to love their husbands and children, to be sensible, chaste, domestic, kind, and submissive to their husbands that the word of God may not be discredited. Likewise urge the younger men to control themselves."

Q. Where has a statement been made concerning the office of children and parents?

Eph 6[.1–4]   A. Ephesians 6, "Children, obey your parents in the Lord, for this is right. 'Honor your father and mother'; (this is the first commandment with a promise), 'that it may be well with you, and that you may live long on the earth.' Fathers, do not provoke your children to anger, but bring them up in the discipline and instruction of the Lord."

Q. Where have commandments been given concerning servants and masters?

Eph 6[.5–9]   A. Ephesians 6 says also, "Slaves, be obedient to those who are your earthly masters, with fear and trembling, in singleness of heart; . . . not in the way of eye-service, as men-pleasers, but as servants of Christ, doing the will of God from the heart, rendering service with a good will as to the Lord and not to men, knowing that whatever good anyone does, he will receive the same again from the Lord, whether he is a slave or free. Masters, do the same to them, and forbear threatening, knowing that he who is both their master and yours is in heaven, and that there is no partiality with him."

Q. And how ought those who are subjects behave toward the magistracy (*magistratus*)?

Rom 13[.1–5, 7]   A. Romans 13, "Let every person be subject to the governing authorities.

For there is no authority except from God, and those that exist have been instituted by God. Therefore he who resists the authorities resists what God has appointed, and those who resist will incur judgment. For rulers are not a terror to good conduct, but to bad. Would you have fear of him who is in authority? Then do what is good, and you will receive his approval, for he is God's servant for your good. But if you do wrong, be afraid, for he does not bear the sword in vain; he is the servant of God to execute his wrath on the wrongdoer. Therefore one must be subject, not only to avoid God's wrath but also for the sake of conscience. . . . Pay all of them their due, revenues to whom revenue is due, respect to whom respect is due, honor to whom honor is due."

Q. Where are commandments laid down concerning wives, widows, and unmarried girls?

A. 1 Corinthians 7. Read the entire chapter.

Q. Where is instruction given concerning the office of the rich as regards those who are truly poor?

A. Luke 6, "Jesus said, 'Give to everyone who begs from you. . . . and lend,   Lk 6[.30, 35–36, 38] expecting nothing in return; and your reward will be great. . . . Be merciful, even as your Father is merciful. . . . Give, and it will be given to you.'" And Matthew 25, "Come, O blessed of my Father, inherit the kingdom prepared for you; . . . for   Mt 25[.34–36, 40] I was hungry and you gave me food, I was thirsty and you gave me drink, I was a stranger and you welcomed me, I was naked and you clothed me, I was sick and you visited me, I was in prison and you came to me. . . . Truly, I say to you, as you did it to one of the least of these my brethren, you did it to me." 1 Corinthians 16, "Now   1 Cor 16[.1–2] concerning the contribution for the saints; as I directed the churches [of Galatia] so you also are to do. On the first day of every week, each of you is to put something aside and store it up." 2 Corinthians 9, "He who sows sparingly will also reap spar-   2 Cor 9[.6, 9] ingly, and he who sows bountifully will also reap bountifully. . . . Each one must do as he has made up his mind, not reluctantly or under compulsion, for God loves a cheerful giver." 1 Timothy 6, "As for the rich in this world, charge them not to   1 Tm 6[.17–19] be haughty, nor to set their hopes on uncertain riches but on the living God. . . . They are to do good, to be rich in good deeds, liberal and generous, thus laying up for themselves a good foundation for the future, so that they may take hold of the life which is life indeed." James 1, "Religion that is pure and undefiled before God   Jas 1[.25, 27] and the Father is this: to visit orphans and widows in their affliction, and to keep oneself unstained from the world."

Q. Finally, how ought individuals behave toward their neighbor?

A. Romans 13, "Owe no one anything, except to love one another; for he   Rom 13[.8–10] who loves his neighbor has fulfilled the law. The commandments, 'You shall not commit adultery, you shall not kill, you shall not steal, you shall not covet' and any other commandment, are summed up in this sentence, 'You shall love your neighbor as yourself.' Love does no wrong to a neighbor; therefore love is the fulfilling of the law."

[Lv 19.18]

Q. What must be done if one does not behave according to the rules which have been ordained?

Mt 18[.15–22]

A. This must be done, what Christ the Lord has ordered: Matthew 18, "'If your brother sins against you, go and tell him his fault, between you and him alone. If he listens to you, you have gained your brother. But if he does not listen, take one or two others along with you, that every word may be confirmed by the evidence of two or three witnesses. If he refuses to listen to them, tell it to the church; and if he refuses to listen to the church, let him be to you as a Gentile and a tax collector. Truly, I say to you, whatever you bind on earth shall be bound in heaven, and whatever you loose on earth shall be loosed in heaven. Again I say to you, if two of you agree on earth about anything they ask, it will be done for them by my Father in heaven. For where two or three are gathered in my name, there am I in the midst of them.' Then Peter said to him, 'Lord, how often shall my brother sin against me, and I forgive him? As many as seven times?' Jesus said to him, 'I do not say to you seven times, but seventy times seven.'"

Q. Where have his disciples carried out this commandment of the Lord?

1 Cor 5[.1–5, 11]

A. 1 Corinthians 5, "It is actually reported that there is immortality among you. . . . And you are arrogant! Ought you not rather to mourn? Let him who has done this be removed from among you. . . . I have already pronounced judgment, 'So that when you are assembled in the name of our Lord Jesus Christ, . . . with the power of our Lord Jesus Christ, this man who has done such a thing is to be delivered to Satan for the destruction of the flesh, that his spirit may be saved in the day of the Lord Jesus.' . . . If anyone bears the name of brother, if he is guilty of immorality or greed, or is an idolater, reviler, drunkard, or robber—do not even eat

1 Cor 6[.9–10]

with such a one." 1 Corinthians 6, "Do you not know that the unrighteous will not inherit the kingdom of God? Do not be deceived; neither the immoral, nor idolaters, nor adulterers, nor homosexuals, nor thieves, nor the greedy, nor drunkards, nor revilers, nor robbers will inherit the kingdom of God."

Q. What is the destruction of the flesh?

Rom 6[.6]

A. It is the same as the death of the old man. Romans 6, "Our old self was crucified with Christ, so that the sinful body might be destroyed, and we might

Col 3[.5–6]

no longer be enslaved to sin." Colossians 3, "Put to death what is earthly in you: immorality, impurity, passion, evil desire, and covetousness, which is idolatry. On account of these the wrath of God is coming upon the sons of disobedience."

Q. Are there not more examples pertaining to this matter?

A. 1 Timothy 1, "Certain persons have made shipwreck of their faith,   1 Tm 1[.19]
among them Hymenaeus and Alexander, whom I have delivered to Satan so that
they may learn not to blaspheme." Titus 3, "As for a man who is factious, after ad-   Ti 3[.10]
monishing him once or twice, have nothing more to do with him." 2 John 1, "If   2 Jn 1[.10, 11]
anyone comes to you and does not bring this doctrine, do not receive him into the
house or give him any greeting; for he who greets him shares his wicked work."
2 Thessalonians 3,[a] "Now we command you, brethren, in the name of our Lord Jesus
Christ, that you keep away from any brother who is living in idleness and not in
accord with the tradition that you received from us. . . . For we hear that some of
you are living in idleness, mere busybodies, not doing any work. Now such persons
we command and exhort in the Lord Jesus Christ to do their work in quietness and
to earn their own living. . . . [But] if anyone will not work, let him not eat."

Q. But what ought to be done, if a fallen brother should change his ways?

A. The church ought to do what the Lord himself did, who rejoiced after
finding his sheep which was lost,[b] and what the father did after his prodigal son
returned and found welcome.   [Lk 15.11–32]

Q. Where is this commandment?

A. 2 Corinthians 2, "For such a one this punishment by the majority is   2 Cor 2[.6–8]
enough; so you should rather turn to forgive and comfort him, or he may be overwhelmed by excessive sorrow, so I beg you to reaffirm your love for him."

Q. What must be thought of a man if right up to the time of death he does
not come to his senses?

A. "It would have been better for that man if he had not been born," for to   [Mt 26.24]
him will apply that commandment stated above in Matthew 25: "He will not inherit   Mt 25[.41, 30]
the kingdom of heaven, but he will be sent into the eternal fire, . . . where there will
be weeping and gnashing of teeth."

4. ON PRAYER

Q. What is prayer?

A. It is the serious and ardent conversation of a faithful believer, when he
or a neighbor is in need, with God the Father. That is to say, prayer is either a giving
of thanks for benefits received in the past, or a plea for help in time of distress, with
the full assurance of faith that God wishes to help (as the Father is most loving of

a. 2 Thes 3[.6, 11–12, 10]
b. [Mt 18.12–14; Lk 15.4–7]

us), that he knows how to help (as he alone is wise), and that he is able to help (as the Lord is all-powerful).

Q. Who has taught us this?

Rom 8[.26]   A. "We by nature do not know how to pray as we ought," Romans 8. But God himself, our Father, and his beloved Son, our Lord Jesus Christ, commanded this to us, promising that we will surely be heard and made free.

Q. Where has this been written?

Ps 50[.14]   A. Psalms 50, "Says the God of gods, 'Offer to God a sacrifice of thanksgiving; . . . and call upon me in the day of trouble. I will deliver you, and you shall
Mt 7[.7]   glorify me.'" And this Son of God says in Matthew 7, "Ask, and it will be given you;
Ps 145[.18–19]   seek and you will find; knock, and it will be opened to you." Psalm 145, "The Lord is near to all who call upon him, . . . in truth he fulfills the desire of all who fear him."
Is 65[.24]   Isaiah 65, "Before they call I will answer, while they are yet speaking I will hear."
Sir 35[.17]   Ecclesiasticus 35, "The prayer of a man in distress passes through the clouds."

Deut 7.2   Q. Yet because "The one God is a terrible God" and "he dwells in unap-
1 Tm 6[.15]   proachable light," how shall we approach him?

1 Tm 2[.5]   A. Through the one Mediator, the man Jesus Christ, our Lord, 1 Timothy 2. And the Lord himself says at John 14 and 10, "I am the way[a] and the door,[b] no one comes to the Father but by me."[c] John 16,[d] "If you ask anything of the Father, he will give it to you in my name."

Q. What is "to pray in the name of Jesus"?

Jn 15[.7]   A. Our Lord himself explains at John 15, "If you abide in me, and my words abide in you, ask whatever what you will, and it shall be done for you." Hebrews 10,[e] "Since we have confidence to enter the sanctuary by the blood of Jesus, by the . . . way which he opened for us, . . . let us draw near with a true heart in full assurance of faith, with our hearts sprinkled clean from an evil conscience and our bodies washed with pure water. Let us hold fast the confession of our hope, . . . for he who promised is faithful; and let us consider how to stir up one another to love and good works, not neglecting to meet together, . . . but encouraging one another."

Q. Therefore "God does not listen to sinners, but if anyone is a worshiper
Jn 9[.31]   of God and does his will, God listens to him," John 9?
Ps 50[.16–19]   A. Most certainly. For so it is written in Psalms 50: "to the wicked God

a. Jn [14.6]
b. Jn [10.9]
c. Jn [14.6]
d. Jn 16[.23]
e. Heb 10[.19–20, 22–25]

says, 'What right have you to recite my statutes, or take my covenant on your lips? For you hate discipline, and you cast my words behind you. If you see a thief, you are a friend of his; and you keep company with adulterers. . . . and your tongue frames deceit.'"

Q. Therefore what qualities does one especially need for prayer?

A. Faith in God, and love toward [one's] neighbor.

Q. Where is instruction given concerning faith?

A. Hebrews 11, "Whoever would draw near to God must believe that he   Heb 11[.6] exists. . . . and without faith it is impossible to please him." James 1, "If any of you   Jas 1[.5–6, 8] lacks wisdom, let him ask God . . . and it will be given him. But let him ask in faith, with no doubting, for he who doubts. . . . must not suppose that . . . he will receive anything from the Lord."

Q. Where is instruction given on charity toward one's neighbor?

A. Matthew 5, "If you are offering your gift at the altar, and there remem-   Mt 5[.23–24] ber that your brother has something against you, leave your gift there before the altar and go; first be reconciled to your brother and then come and offer your gift." Isaiah 1, "Even though you make many prayers, I will not listen: your hands are full   Is 1[.15] of blood."

Q. How must we feel about those who are "weak" and "frail"?

A. The Lord does not reject their prayers if they do not indulge in a sin in violation of their conscience, but having fallen, grieve in earnest and raise themselves up again. Thus the case of the taxpayer in Luke 18 and that of Cornelius in Acts 10.

Q. What about the place and time of prayer?

A. John 4, "Neither on this mountain nor in Jerusalem. . . . but in spirit and   Jn 4[.21, 23] in truth . . . will true worshipers worship the Father." 1 Timothy 2, "I desire that   1 Tm 2[.8] in every place the man should pray." Concerning the time, the Lord says: Luke 18,   Lk 18[.1] "They ought always to pray and not lose heart." 1 Thessalonians 5, "Pray constantly,   1 Thes 5[.17–18] give thanks in all circumstances."

Q. For how long must one pray?

A. Although the Lord prohibits at Matthew 6, "heaping up empty phrases,"   Mt 6[.7] yet if the need be pressing and the heart is in agony it is permitted to pray more urgently, as the Lord himself does at Luke 22.   Lk 22[.44]

Q. What things ought to be asked of God in prayer?

A. Good things which pertain to both the spirit and the flesh. These things are spiritual: the forgiveness of sins, the gift of the Holy Spirit, increases in the glory of God, good order in the church, a good conscience, a correction of [one's] life, and eternal life. These things pertain to the flesh: peace in the state, good magistrates, a fair amount of money, success in crops, food, friendship, freedom from enemies. We ought to ask for the spiritual things without using a condition: John

Jn 12[.28] 12, "'Father, glorify thy name.' Then a voice came from heaven, 'I have glorified it, and I will glorify it again.'" But the things of the flesh must be sought conditionally,

2 Sm 15[.25–26] [with the formula] "if God be willing." As David says: 2 Samuel 15, "If I find favor in the eyes of the Lord, he will bring me back. . . . But if he says, 'I have no pleasure

Dn 3[.17–18] in you,' . . . let him do to me what seems good to him." Daniel 3, "Our God . . . is able to deliver us from the burning fiery furnace; . . . but if not, be it known to you

Mt 26[.39] . . . that we will not serve your gods." Matthew 26, "My Father, if it be possible, let this cup pass from me; nevertheless, not as I will, but as thou wilt."

Q. With what words must one pray?

A. It is best that Christian boys be trained in the prayers of the prophets, Christ, and the apostles, but the adult Christian ought to pray as he is inspired by

Rom 8[.26] the Holy Spirit, who, Romans 8, "helps us in our weakness . . . and intercedes for us with sighs too deep for words."

Q. In what manner must one pray?

A. God is mindful of the heart, but in order that the heart may be stirred up, it is best, when [our] conscience calls us to account, to lower our eyes and beat

Lk 18[.13] our breast, as the taxpayer does in Luke 18. When we cast ourselves down before

Ex 17[.12] God, it is best to raise our hands, as Moses did in Exodus 17. When we prostrate ourselves [falling] onto our knees and face, it is best to let the hands fall, as the Lord

Mt 26[.39] Jesus did in the garden, Matthew 26. When we are joyful in spirit, it is best to lift

Jn 17[.1] the hands up to heaven as the Lord does in John 17.

Q. Ought a man pray alone or with another?

A. Both alone and with the congregation. The Lord speaks about private

Mt 6[.6] prayers at Matthew 6, "When you pray, go into your room"; and public prayer at

Mt 18[.19] Matthew 18, "If two of you agree on earth about anything they ask, it will be done

Acts 1[.14] for them." Acts 1, "All these with one accord devoted themselves in prayer."

5. ON BAPTISM

Q. What is baptism?

A. Baptism is the immersion (*immersio*) and emersion (*emersio*) of a man believing in the gospel and doing penance in the name of the Father and Son and Holy Spirit,[a] or in the name of Jesus Christ,[b] in which he publicly declares that he has been cleansed of sin by the grace of God the Father, in the blood of Christ,

a. [Mt 28.19]
b. [Acts 2.38]

by the assistance of the Holy Spirit, that, having been introduced into the body of Christ, he will put to death the old Adam, and will be transformed into the heavenly Adam, certain that after the resurrection he will gain eternal life.

Q. Who instituted baptism?

A. It was God our Father, who instituted baptism and his beloved Son, our Lord Jesus Christ [who] confirmed it.

Q. Where is this written?

A. Matthew 21,[a] "The baptism of John was from heaven." Luke 7,[b] "The baptism of John was the purpose of God." Luke 3, "The word of God came to John the son of Zechariah in the wilderness and he went . . . preaching a baptism of repentance for the forgiveness of sins." John 1, "There was a man sent from God, whose name was John."   *Lk 3[.2–3]*   *Jn 1[.6]*

Q. But where is Christ, the Son of God, said to have confirmed baptism?

A. Matthew 28, "Jesus said, 'All authority in heaven and on earth has been given to me. Go therefore and make disciples of all nations, baptizing them in the name of the Father and of the Son and of the Holy Spirit, teaching them to observe all that I have commanded you; and lo, I am with you always, to the close of the age.'" Mark 16, "Go into all the world and preach the gospel to the whole creation. He who believes and is baptized will be saved; but he who does not believe will be condemned."   *Mt 28[.18–20]*   *Mk 16[.14, 16]*

Q. Where do we read that John and the apostles followed these mandates?

A. Matthew 3, Mark 1, Luke 3,[c] "John appeared in the desert, preaching a baptism of repentance for the forgiveness of sins.[d] And all went out to him . . .[e] and were baptized by him in the River Jordan, confessing their sins. And he said to them,[f] 'Bear fruit that befits repentance. . . .[g] Even now the ax is laid to the root of the trees; every tree therefore that does not bear good fruit is cut down and thrown into the fire.' And the multitudes asked him, 'What then shall we do?' And he answered them, 'He who has two coats, let him share with him who has none; and he who has food, let him do likewise.' Tax collectors also came to be baptized, and said to him, 'Teacher, what shall we do?' And he said to them, 'Collect no more than is appointed you.' Soldiers also asked him, 'And us, what shall we do?' And he   *[Mt 3.7]*   *[Lk 3.10–14]*

a. Mt 21[.25]

b. Lk 7[.29–30]

c. [Mt 3.5; Mk 1.4; Lk 3.3]

d. [Mt 3.6]

e. [Mt 3.6; Mk 1.5]

f. [Mt 3.8; Lk 3.8]

g. [Mt 3.10; Lk 3.9]

said to them, 'Rob no one by violence or by false accusation, and be content with your wages.'"

Q. So even Jesus himself has been baptized?

Mt 3[.13–17]   A. Most definitely. Matthew 3, "Jesus came . . . to John, to be baptized by him. John would have prevented him, saying, 'I need to be baptized by you, and do you come to me?' But Jesus answered him, 'Let it be so now; for thus it is fitting for us to fulfill all righteousness.' Then he consented. And when Jesus was baptized he went up immediately from the water, and behold, the heavens were opened to him, and he saw the Spirit of God descending like a dove, and alighting on him and lo, a voice from heaven, saying, 'This is my beloved Son, with whom I am well pleased.'"

Q. So were the apostles also baptized?

Acts 2[.36–38, 41]   A. Most definitely. Acts 2, the extensive speech of Peter, which was given to him as a gift by the Holy Spirit, who, by the agency of God through Jesus of Nazareth, had filled the apostles, concludes, "'Let all the house of Israel therefore know assuredly that God has made him both Lord and Christ, this Jesus whom you crucified.' Now when they heard this they were cut to the heart, and they said . . . 'What shall we do?' And Peter said to them, 'Repent, and be baptized every one of you in the name of Jesus Christ for the forgiveness of your sins; and you shall receive the gift of the Holy Spirit' . . . So those who received his word were baptized, and there were added that day about three thousand souls. And they devoted themselves to the apostles' teaching and fellowship, to the breaking of bread and the prayers."

Q. Christ commands that baptism be made in the name of the Father and the Son and the Holy Spirit; the apostles however baptized only in the name of Jesus What is the significance of this difference?

Jn 8[.42]   A. There is no difference, for . . . Jesus did not come on his own accord but the Father sent him. . . . John 8, "He does not seek his own glory, but that of his Father," John 7.[a] Finally, at John 12,[b] he cries out in a deep voice, "He who believes in me, believes not in me, but in him who sent me. And he who sees me," etc.

Q. Therefore what does it mean to be baptized in the name of the Father and the Son and the Holy Spirit, or in the name of Jesus?

Rom 8[.15]   A. It means to believe and to confess that God is your Father, [and to believe] in his beloved Son Jesus Christ who gives to you the Spirit of sonship, through whom we cry, "Abba! Father!" Romans 8.

a. Jn 7[.18]
b. Jn 12[.44–45]

Q. Therefore all ought to be baptized, and ought to hear the word of God, and ought to believe, confess, and do penance?

A. Most definitely. Acts 8, "Philip told the eunuch of the good news of Jesus reading from a passage of Isaiah.[a] And as the eunuch and Philip came to some water, the eunuch said . . . 'What is to prevent my being baptized?' And Philip said, 'If you believe with all your heart, you may.' And he replied, 'I believe that Jesus Christ is the Son of God. . . .' And they both went down into the water, . . . and he baptized him.'" Hebrews 6, "Let us leave the elementary doctrines of Christ and go onto maturity, not laying again a foundation of repentance from dead works and of faith toward God, with instruction about ablutions, the laying on of hands, the resurrection of the dead, and eternal judgment." Galatians 3, "In Christ Jesus you are all sons of God, through faith. For as many of you as were baptized into Christ have put on Christ." Acts 8, "The Samaritans believed Philip as he preached good news about the kingdom of God and the name of Jesus Christ, [and] they were baptized, both men and women." Heb 6[.1–2] Gal 3[.26–27] Acts 8[.12]

Q. But did they baptize whole families by the faith of the heads of the families?

A. No, for the righteous man lives by his own faith, not another's. In Acts 16,[b] where they are said to have baptized families, they only baptized those hearing the word and believing. "The Lord opened the heart of Lydia to give heed to what was said by Paul. And she was baptized, with her household, and the jailor said, 'Men, what must I do to be saved?' And they said, 'Believe in the Lord Jesus, and you will be saved, you and your household.' And they spoke the word of the Lord to him and to all that were in his house. . . . And he was baptized at once, with all his family. . . . And he rejoiced with all his household that he had believed in God."

Q. Where is it written concerning the death of the old Adam through baptism?

A. Romans 6,[c] "All of us who have been baptized into Christ Jesus have been baptized into his death. We were buried therefore with him by baptism into death, so that as Christ was raised from the dead by the glory of the Father, we too might walk in newness of life. . . . We know that our old self was crucified with him . . . so that we might no longer be enslaved to sin. . . . Let not sin therefore reign in your mortal bodies, . . . Do not yield your members to sin as instruments of wickedness, but yield yourselves to God as men who have been brought from death

a. Is [53.7–8]; Acts 8[.32–33, 36–38]
b. Acts 16[.14–15, 30–34]
c. Rom 6[.3–4, 6, 12–13]

to life, and your members to God as instruments of righteousness." Colossians 2,[a] "In him you were circumcised with a circumcision made without hands, by putting off the body of flesh in the circumcision of Christ; and you were buried with him in baptism, in which you were also raised with him through faith in the working of God, who raised him from the dead." 1 Peter 3, "Our baptism, which corresponds to the ark of Noah, now saves us, not as a removal of dirt from the body but as an appeal to God for a clear conscience."

1 Pt 3[.21]

Q. What must a man do if he sins after baptism?

A. He ought not despair of the grace of God in Christ, but ought to pray fervently, "Forgive us our sins." And the church ought to deal with him as was stated above on discipline.

Q. How must one feel about the man who renounces faith in God and Christ?

Heb 6[.4–6]

A. This is what is said in Hebrews 6, "It is impossible to restore again to repentance those who have once been enlightened, who have tasted the heavenly gift, and have become partakers of the Holy Spirit, and have tasted the goodness of the word of God and the powers of the age to come, if they then commit apostasy, since they crucify the Son of God on their own account and hold him up to contempt." Hebrews 10,[b] "For if we sin deliberately after receiving the knowledge of the truth, there no longer remains a sacrifice for sins, but a fearful prospect of judgment, and a fury of fire which will consume the adversaries. . . . How much worse punishment do you think will be deserved by the man who has spurned the Son of God, and profaned the blood of the covenant by which he was sanctified, and outraged the spirit of grace . . . ? It is a fearful thing to fall into the hands of the living God."

6. ON THE LORD'S SUPPER

Q. What is the Lord's supper?

A. It is the holy action, instituted by Christ the Lord himself, in which proven disciples of Christ sitting at the table of the Lord in holy congregation, sincerely give thanks to God the Father for his benefits in Christ, and breaking bread eat it, and they drink from the chalice of the Lord, to the devout recollection of the body of Christ our Lord, handed over to death for our sake, and of his blood poured out in the forgiveness of our sins, stirring ourselves up in turn to constant endurance under the cross and to sincere brotherly love.

Q. Where is this taught?

a. Col 2[.11–12]
b. Heb 10[.26–27, 29, 31]

A. Matthew 26. Mark 14. Luke 22. "And when the hour came, Jesus sat [at the table] and the twelve apostles with him. And he said to them, 'I have earnestly desired to eat this Passover with you before I suffer; for I tell you I shall not eat it until it is fulfilled in the kingdom of God. . . .' And he took bread, and when he had given thanks he broke it and gave it to them, saying, 'This is my body, which is given for you. Do this in remembrance of me.' And likewise the cup after supper, saying, 'This cup which is poured out for you is the new covenant in my blood.'ᵃ [Mt 26.29] 'Truly, I tell you, I shall not drink again of this fruit of the vine until that day when I drink it new with you in my Father's kingdom.' And all drank from it.ᵇ And he said, 'You are those who have continued with me in my trials; as my Father appointed a kingdom for me, so do I appoint for you that you may eat and drink at my table in my kingdom, and sit on thrones judging the twelve tribes of Israel.'"ᶜ Acts 2, [Acts 2[.42]] "The baptized devoted themselves to the apostles' teaching and fellowship, to the breaking of bread and the prayers." 1 Corinthians 11, "When you meet together, it [1 Cor 11[.20–29]] is not the Lord's supper that you eat. For in eating, each one goes ahead with his own meal, and one is hungry and another is drunk. What! Do you not have houses to eat and drink in? Or do you despise the church of God and humiliate those who have nothing? What shall I say to you? Shall I command you in this? No, I will not. For I received from the Lord what I also delivered to you, that the Lord Jesus on the night when he was betrayed took bread, and when he had given thanks, he broke it, and said, 'This is my body which . . . is broken for you. Do this in remembrance of me.' In the same way also the cup, after supper, saying, 'This cup is the new covenant in my blood. Do this, as often as you drink it, in remembrance of me.' For as often as you eat this bread and drink this cup, you proclaim the Lord's death until he comes. Whoever, therefore, eats the bread or drinks the cup of the Lord in an unworthy manner will be guilty of profaning the body and blood of the Lord. Let a man examine himself, and so eat of the bread and drink of the cup. For anyone who eats and drinks without discerning the body eats and drinks judgment upon himself."

Q. But why is the remembrance of the body and blood of Christ made with bread and wine?

A. Because just as "bread strengthens man's heart, and wine gladdens it," Psalms 104, so Jesus Christ our Lord is given to us starved sinners by God the Father, [Ps 104[.15]] as a bread which nourishes us to eternal life.

a. [Lk 22.14–16, 19–20]
b. [Mk 14.23]
c. [Lk 22.28–30]

Q. Where is this written?

A. John 6,[a] "Do not labor for the food which perishes, but for the food which endures to eternal life, which the Son of man will give to you; for on him has God the Father set his seal. . . . I am the bread of life; . . . . which comes down from heaven, that a man may eat of it and not die, ... but will live forever; and the bread which I shall give for the life of the world is my flesh. . . . Truly, truly, I say to you, unless you eat the flesh of the Son of man and drink his blood, you have no life in you; he who eats my flesh and drinks my blood has eternal life, and I will raise him up at the last day. For my flesh is food indeed, and my blood is drink indeed."

Q. What is it, to drink and eat Christ?

A. Hear the Lord Jesus himself speaking:[b] "The words that I speak to you are spirit and life. . . . This is the work of God, that you believe in him whom he has sent. . . . He who comes to me shall not hunger, and he who believes in me shall not thirst. . . . For this is the will of my Father, that everyone who . . . believes in the Son should have eternal life; and I will raise him up at the last day. . . . He who believes in me has eternal life. . . . He who eats my flesh and drinks my blood abides in me, and I in him. As the living Father sent me, and I live because of the Father, so he who eats me will live because of me."

Q. Is not this action, then, a sacrifice for sin?

A. No. But it is the grateful remembrance and a commemoration of that sacrifice once offered, on which there is Hebrews 9, "Christ has entered, not into a sanctuary made with hands, a copy of the true one, but into heaven itself, now to appear in the presence of God on our behalf. Nor was it to offer himself repeatedly, ... for then he would have had to suffer repeatedly since the foundation of the world, but as it is, he has appeared once for all at the end of the age to put away sin by the sacrifice of himself. . . . So Christ, having been offered once to bear the sins of many, will appear a second time, not to deal with sin but to save those who are eagerly waiting for him."

Heb 9[.25–26, 28]

Q. How is Christ present at this action, when "heaven must receive him until the time for establishing all things?" Acts 3. "And he will come in the same way as he was seen to go into heaven?" Acts 1.

Acts 3[.21]
Acts 1[.11]

Mt 28[.20]

A. He is most certainly present to his faithful, as Matthew 28 promised, "Lo, I am with you always, to the close of the age." I say that he is not present in the flesh, but by his Holy Spirit, as John 14 states, "I will pray the Father, and he will give you another counselor, to be with you forever. . . . I will not leave you deso-

Jn 14[.16, 18, 26]

a. Jn 6[.27, 35, 50–51, 53–55]
b. [Jn 6.63, 29, 35, 40, 47, 56–57]

late. . . . The counselor, the Holy Spirit, whom the Father will send in my name, he
will teach you all things." John 16, "When the counselor comes, he will convince   Jn 16[.8, 13–14]
the world of sin. . . . He will guide you into all the truth. . . . He will glorify me."

Q. Where does Christ at the supper rouse his followers to steadfastness and
endurance?

A. John 16,ª "I say this to you to keep you from falling away. They will put
you out of the synagogues; indeed, the hour is coming when whoever kills you will
think he is offering service to God. . . . You will be sorrowful . . . you will weep
and lament, but the world will rejoice . . . but your sorrow will turn into joy. . . . I
will see you again and your hearts will rejoice, and no one will take your joy from
you. . . . I have said this to you, that in me you may have peace. In the world you
have tribulation; but be of good cheer, I have overcome the world." John 15, "If the   Jn 15[.18–20, 23]
world hates you, know that it has hated me before it hated you. If you were of the
world, the world would love its own; but because you are not of the world, but I
chose you out of the world, therefore the world hates you. . . ." "A servant is not
greater than his master. If they persecuted me, they will persecute you; . . . . He
who hates me hates my Father also." Luke 22, "Jesus said, 'Simon, Simon; behold,   Lk 22[.31–32]
Satan demanded to have you, that he might sift you like wheat, but I have prayed
for you that your faith may not fail; and when you have turned again, strengthen
your brethren.'"

Q. Where in the supper does the Lord command brotherly love?

A. John 13. "Jesus said to his disciples, 'If I then, your Lord and teacher,   Jn 13[.14–15, 34–35]
have washed your feet, you also ought to wash one another's feet. For I have given
you an example, that you also should do as I have done to you. . . . A new commandment I give to you, that you love one another, even as I have loved you. . . . By
this all men will know that you are my disciples.'" 1 Corinthians 10,ᵇ "The cup of
blessing which we bless, is it not a communion of the blood of Christ? The bread
which we break, is it not a communion in the body of Christ? Because there is one
loaf, we who are many are one body, for we all partake of the same loaf. . . . You
cannot drink the cup of the Lord and the cup of demons. You cannot partake of the
table of the Lord and the table of demons."

Q. What is a worthy preparation and examination (*probatio*) for the Lord's
supper?

A. The church ought to keep careful watch lest it admit to the sacred meal
anyone who has been contaminated with manifest crimes and does not do penance.

a. Jn 16[.1–2, 20, 22, 33]
b. 1 Cor 10[.16–17, 21]

[The section] above, "On Discipline," is more expansive on this matter. But if anyone is not notorious for a heinous crime, the Holy Spirit commands him to put himself to this test:

    1. If he believes with his heart and confesses with his mouth that he is a sinner before God the Father, and by nature a son of wrath, and a slave of death. [The section] above, "On Justification," is more expansive on this matter.

    2. If he believes that "God so loved the world that he gave his only Son, that whoever believes in him should not perish but have eternal life," John 3.

Jn 3[.16]

    3. If he has resolved for the future to conduct a pious and guiltless life. 1 Peter 4, "Since therefore Christ suffered in the flesh for us, arm yourselves with the same thought; for whoever has suffered in the flesh has ceased from sin, so as to live for the rest of the time in the flesh no longer by human passions but by the will of God."

1 Pt 4[.1–2]

    Q. Must absolute perfection in this test of faith be expected?

    A. There will at last be absolute perfection in the other life. "For here our knowledge is imperfect," 1 Corinthians 13; and often we are compelled to shout, with the apostles, "Lord, increase our faith," Luke 17;[a] 1 Corinthians 5,[b] "Cleanse out the old leaven that you may be fresh dough, as you really are unleavened. For Christ, our passover lamb, has been sacrificed. Let us, therefore, celebrate the festival, not with the old leaven, the leaven of malice and evil, but with the unleavened bread of sincerity and truth." Thus, if we handle even one talent faithfully, to the glory of God, to the one who has will more be given, and we will hear that most joyful voice, "Well done, faithful servant . . . enter into the joy of your master," Matthew 25. May God, our one Father, through Jesus Christ his Son our Lord, grant this to us. Amen.

1 Cor 13[.9]

Mt 25[.21]

a. Lk 17[.5]
b. 1 Cor 5[.7–8]

The Transylvanian Confession of Faith, 1579

Much of Transylvania had been reformed in the 1530s, with the larger cities, especially those with ethnic ties to Saxony, becoming Lutheran. The Hungarian portions of the country, influenced by the Swiss Reformation, adopted Calvinism, especially in their sacramentarian view of the eucharist. In the 1560s, antitrinitarianism found favor with the king, John Sigismund, largely through the efforts of Giorgio Biandrata (c. 1515–88), an Italian physician. Biandrata rejected the existence of a common substance for the three persons of God, the Son, and the Holy Spirit. The shifts in religious sentiments in sixteenth-century Transylvania are remarkable. Indeed, one important leader, Francis Dávid (c. 1520–79), whose mother was Hungarian and whose father was Saxon, began as a Lutheran, developed into a Calvinist, published an Anabaptist tract, and finally became a Unitarian leader.

King John Sigismund, son of John Zápolya and Isabelle, daughter of King Sigismund I of Poland, followed his mother's policy of maintaining religious liberty[1] and issued a law requiring toleration in 1568.[2] His own Unitarian Reformed preference led many of the upper classes to convert. But John Sigismund died in 1571, and his successor, Stephen Báthory, decreed that Unitarians must hold to the faith of the late king and would be punished if they introduced new reforms.[3] This injunction came in the face of radicalization of the movement under Francis Dávid, who was promoting nonadorantism (denial of Christ's divinity) and the abolishment of infant baptism. Dávid was eventually tried in 1579 at a diet in Torda. He was found guilty and died in prison within a half-year of the verdict.

The popularity of Dávid's innovations was short-lived. Most Unitarians probably did not hold Dávid's radical views, or at least they abandoned such radicalism after his trial. In July 1579, the party of the more conservative Biandrata

---

1. Isabelle, as the queen mother during John Sigismund's minority, issued an edict in response to the Diet of Torda (1557), granting religious freedom to all: "Each person [may] maintain whatever religious faith he wishes, with old or new rituals, while we . . . leave it to their judgment to do as they please in the matter of their faith . . . so long . . . as they bring no harm to bear on anyone." For the entire text, see Williams, 1104–5. For the original Latin, see Szilágyi 1875–99, 2:78.

2. See Williams, 1113, for an English translation of the law.

3. Stephen Báthory, though Catholic himself, permitted freedom of religion in his realm. It was not until supporters of a rival leader—a Unitarian—opposed his rule that he imposed sanctions against individual Unitarians.

composed a christocentric Unitarian confession of faith. The following year infant baptism was restored and commemoration of the Lord's supper was sanctioned.

The confession, with its emphasis on Christ as the Son of God, certainly does not reflect a strong antitrinitarian position, although belief in the Trinity is nowhere expressed. It remained the standard of the Unitarian Church in this region until the end of the nineteenth century.

Edition: Wallace 1850, 3:556–57.

Translation: Williams, 1131–33.

Literature: Szczucki 1982; Szilágyi 1875–99, 2:78; Wallace 1850, 1:140–47, 2:368; Wilbur 1942, 12–15; Williams, 1098–1133.

The Transylvanian Confession of Faith, 1579

1. We believe and confess that this Jesus of Nazareth is the Son of the Most High, the only-begotten Son, and to be called God in accordance with the genuine sense of Holy Scripture on account of these reasons: (1) Since he was conceived by the Holy Spirit;[a] (2) Since he was anointed by the Holy Spirit before all others,[b] he received the Holy Spirit without measure; (3) On account of the majesty and glory which in heaven and on earth the Father fully gave after he rose from the dead; (4) Since God the Father in the fullness of time will restore and establish all things by him, and he gave him to us that we by him might be saved and might receive the inheritance of eternal life.

[Col 1.19]

[Acts 2.31–36]

[Acts 3.21]

[Eph 1.13–14]

    2. We believe this same Jesus Christ is to be worshiped and adored since the Father gave all things to the Son, and prescribed that we hear him, that we believe him, and the same praise and adore. Therefore he has hidden in him all the treasures of knowledge and wisdom in order that out of his fullness we all receive all things; namely, that worshiping the Son, we might worship the Father, that believing the Son, we might believe in the Father, which Father is honored in the Son.

[Eph 1.22]

[Col 2.3]

    3. We confess that this same Jesus, the true Messiah, while he was on earth conferred and even now confers spiritual goods on the faithful by word and spirit, and for that reason he is to be invoked, for by God the Father, all good things are brought together in the same that from him we might pray and hope confidently for them in our necessities. Thus after he came revealed (*exhibitus*) into the world many fled to him for refuge, saying "Jesus, Son of David, have mercy on me";[c] again, "Lord Jesus! receive my spirit"; but in neither instance is invoked as God the Father, in whom are all things, nor again even in that form of invocation by which we invoke the Father, saying, "Our Father," etc., but for that reason that what God the Father conferred *on him,* we might be certain Christ would bestow it more richly on us just as he himself promised, "Whatsoever you ask in my name, I will do it"; and similarly, "I will give you eternal life."[d] Nor is he our Mediator[e] in such fashion that he confers nothing on us or that there is nothing that might be asked, expected, or even hoped for from him. For to this very end he accepted all things from God his

[Jn 1.1]

Acts 7[.59]

1 Cor 8[.4]

[Mt 6.9–13]

Jn 14[.13]

a. [Mt 1.20]
b. [Ps 2.2; Acts 4.25–26]
c. Mt 15 [.22]; Mk 10[.47–48]
d. Jn 10[.19]
e. [1 Tm 2.5]

747

heavenly Father in order that from himself all things in us should be derived as his members.

    4. For we say with the Sacred Scriptures that this Jesus the Christ, who is said to be our Head, is now King of the churches and reigns by his Spirit those faithful to him, "for he rules over the living and the dead," or, again, that "He rules all things by the word of his power." For to this end our Father gave Christ to us, that he might reign in those faithful to him, and that he might confer on them eternal life, and "He himself is alone under heaven, in whose name we might be saved." And although it is said this kingdom will come to an end when Christ delivers up the kingdom to God and the Father, and when all things will be subject to him; nevertheless, it does not follow from this that Christ our God is not now King, because there it is said that he must reign until all things are subjected to him.

Rom 14[.10–12]

Heb 1[.2, 8–13]

Acts 4[.12]

1 Cor 15[.24–28]

The Concept of Cologne, 1591

It is curious, as C. J. Dyck has observed, "that the Anabaptists, who considered themselves anticreedal, produced as many confessions as Calvinism and many more than the Lutheran movement during the first one hundred years of their history."[1] Their earliest "confessions," such as → Hans Denck's *Confession,* Pilgrim Marpeck's *Rechenschaft,* and Peter Riedemann's *Account of Our Religion,* were not so much creeds as personal statements and defenses of the faith in the face of persecution. The first outline of beliefs written to express the distinctive views of a group of Anabaptists was → *The Schleitheim Confession* of 1527. The Mennonites, like the Melchiorites, the Hutterites, and the Amish, have their roots in the Anabaptist movement of the sixteenth century. Throughout the sixteenth and seventeenth centuries, various groups of Anabaptist-Mennonites composed confessions of faith, although the man from whom the Mennonites derive their name, Menno Simons (1496–1561), is not responsible for any of the authoritative confessions of the movement.[2]

Toward the end of Simons's life, divisions arose in the movement over the use of the ban. Dutch congregations applied the ban (withholding communion or banning entirely from the community of worship) to their members with greater severity than the churches in southern Germany and parts of Switzerland. *The Concept of Cologne* is the product of a synod of Dutch (mostly Frisian) and High German ministers who hoped to unite the splintered movement.[3] The agreement was drawn up by Leenaerd Clock (c. 1565–1606) and signed by fifteen participants on 1 May 1591 in Cologne. By 1601 another group of Dutch Mennonites, the Waterlanders, had signed this confessional document, and the union became known as the Bevredigde Broederschap (Satisfied or Conciliated Brotherhood). But this union was short-lived; for divisions soon developed among the Frisians, some of whom departed with the Waterlanders in 1613. Nonetheless, *The Concept of Cologne* is an important document for understanding the Mennonite movements in the late six-

---

1. Dyck 1964, 5.

2. He did write a summary of his theology, however, in *Dat fundament des christelycken leers* (1539/1540). Edited by Meihuizen 1967b. English translation, Wenger and Verduin 1978, 103–226.

3. The group met in Cologne in spite of that city's officially sanctioned suppression of Anabaptists. As late as January 1591, a city ordinance made the employment of "Wiedertäufer" illegal in Cologne; see Hege 1908, 149.

teenth century because it emphasizes the common theological beliefs and church practices of Dutch and German Mennonites.

As *The Concept of Cologne* makes clear in its teachings, the term *Anabaptist* was a misnomer for the descendants of that movement, since rebaptism was strictly forbidden. Other matters of doctrine include an affirmation of the Trinity and a view of the eucharistic bread and wine solely as a memorial of Christ's love and suffering. Significantly, the Holy Spirit is said to proceed from the Father *through* the Son; this teaching, which reflects the formulation used at the Council of Florence (1439), does not appear in later Mennonite confessions. A milder stance on the ban prevailed, although the practice was retained. Communities are enjoined, however, "to act with love in disciplining the offender, according to the anointing of the Holy Spirit, so that they might improve and be rectified" (article 7). On another issue that divided the movement—marriage outside the community—they take a more rigid view, imposing the ban on those who marry outside the faith. *The Concept of Cologne* also prescribes other Mennonite practices, such as foot washing, pacifism, refusal to take oaths, and modesty in dress.

Edition: Rembert 1899, 615–18.

Translation: *Mennonite Yearbook* 1990–91, 8–10 (translated by Leonard Gross and Jan Gleysteen).

Literature: Coggins 1986, 129; Hege 1908, 149–52; *ME* 1:663–64; *ML* 1:364–65, 2:545–47; Rembert 1899, 495–513.

[1. THE TRINITY]

First of all, we believe in the divine Trinity—Father, Son, and Holy Spirit—that there is one, sole, eternal, and omnipotent God.

[2. JESUS CHRIST]

We believe Jesus Christ to be the sole Son of the Father from eternity, born of Mary in the fullness of time, through the power of the Most High and through the participation of the Holy Spirit, and who became flesh through the eternal Word of the Father.

[3. THE HOLY SPIRIT]

We also believe in the Holy Spirit, as a power of God, proceeding from the Father through the Son, promised by Christ, and sent to comfort the believers.

[4. SALVATION]

Whoever believes in this Son of God as the promised Redeemer and Savior sent by God, the same is free of all sins.

[5. BAPTISM]

The person who acknowledges himself or herself to be sinful, who demonstrates worthy fruits of repentance, who gladly embraces the word of Christ, and who desires and requests baptism: that person is to be baptized with water by an irreproachable chosen minister, in the name of the Father, the Son, and the Holy Spirit. Furthermore, whoever is so minded, and who is already baptized in the manner mentioned above, shall not be baptized again.

[6. COMMUNION]

All who in this manner have been baptized through one Spirit into one body shall [1 Cor 12.13] celebrate communion together, using common bread and wine, in memory of Christ's great love and his bitter death.

[7. CONGREGATIONAL DISCIPLINE]

This community of the saints has the power through the keys of the kingdom of heaven to bind and to loose, and in this manner, the rule of Matthew 18 is to be   Mt 18[.15–20] observed, when a sin is committed between brother and brother.

751

1 Cor 5[.9–13] However, public acts of the flesh are to be disciplined, according to God's word, with mature judgment. According to the teachings of Paul, 1 Corinthians 5, one is to have nothing to do with such persons, including not eating with them. To be sure, in carrying out such strict discipline, there is to be no misuse, which unfortunately has taken place many times, through which the misuse of marital avoidance and other such disorders also followed. Much more, according to the anointing of the Holy Spirit, one is to act with love in working with those being disciplined, that they may mend their ways.

Even if this judgment of Paul is understood by some in a more complex manner, and by others in a simpler manner, we still, as God-fearing people, until [Phil 3.15] further indication from God to the contrary, shall at all times be reconciled with one another in love, listening to each other's views in the spirit of love, without strife and quarreling.

Individuals who sin shall be avoided if they were admonished once or twice.

[8. MARRIAGE]

We also confess from Holy Scripture, both Old and New Testaments, that believers do not have the freedom to marry, except among those who through faith have become a member of the body of Christ, who are thus a spiritual brother or sister — namely, two free persons according to the first charter as initiated with Adam and Eve. Transgressors of the same are deserving of discipline by the congregation, and no spiritual unity is to be maintained with them, unless one detects in them worthy fruits of regret and repentance; they then are to be admonished to hold faithfully to their marriage vows, neither to forsake their spouse, nor to enter into a second marriage. All this is to be administered correctly according to the anointing [of the Holy Spirit].

[9. FOOT WASHING]

We also want to practice the foot washing of the saints. If fellow believers ask this of us, we want to comply: their washing our feet, but also our washing their feet, in humility.

[10. LEADERSHIP]

A bishop or a preacher is to be blameless. After he has been tested, he is to be allowed to serve. He is to be installed in his office through the laying on of hands by the elders, in agreement with the congregation, and elected in this manner.

[11. DEACONS]

According to the example of the apostolic congregations, deacons are also to be chosen, to whom the care of the needy is entrusted. They are to distribute the gifts donated for those in need in such a manner that the distributions also remain confidential, according to the teachings of Christ.

[Mt 6.3]

[12. CONCERNING OATHS]

According to Christ's and James's teachings, one is not to swear oaths; much more, all words and deeds are to be confirmed with a truthful yes or no, and nothing in addition—which in truth is to be held to, in the same manner as that of a sworn oath.

[Mt 5.34; Jas 5.12]

[13. CONCERNING USURY]

Since usury is an abomination before God, and seen as damaging to humanity, therefore everything that according to Holy Scripture can be identified as being usury is not to be permitted.

[14. CONCERNING REVENGE]

No revenge is permitted, whether with outward weapons, or in requiting verbal abuse with verbal abuse.

[15. THE RESURRECTION]

We also believe in a bodily resurrection of the dead, both for the righteous and unrighteous, and believe that at the last judgment each will be received accordingly as he or she has lived.

[16. SEPARATION FROM THE WORLD]

Furthermore, another proper concern was discussed, namely, that the freedom the merchants exercise in running their businesses tends to increase temporal greed, and that the fashions of dress resemble more the ways of the world than they do the way of Christian humility. Since these sins can creep in unnoticed, and since it is to be feared that the same will bring damage to many souls, and since it is not easy to set exact standards in this regard—how much profit a merchant may earn and what a person is to wear—we still desire that everyone be content with a modest profit and with simple clothing: indeed, in every way, proving oneself to be a light to the world, neither following the fashions of the world, nor comparing self to those who are insatiable, forever wanting more and more. It was agreed in this regard that all guardians of God's household are to warn their people, in all faithfulness to—and empowered by—the word, that they together may remain pure, and escape from the corruption of the disobedient. In this manner one member is to admonish and warn the other in a kindhearted way, so that the admonition may be all the more agreeable.

This was signed by many hands.

[*The agreement was signed by the elders and servants of Anabaptist congregations in Alsace, the Breisgau, the Palatinate, Strasbourg, Wissembourg, Landau, Neustadt, Lambsheim, Worms, and Kreuznach, as well as by representatives from Cologne, Odenkirche, Gladbeck, Rees, and the duchy of Berg.*]

The Short Confession of Faith, 1610

Because the Mennonite movement is congregationally based, with no central organizing body, theological differences naturally developed among the autonomous churches. Distinct groups arose in the seventeenth century, defined largely by their location: (1) the so-called High Germans, including southern Germans and some of the Swiss Brethren; (2) the Frisians made up of three Dutch parties from Friesland in the north; (3) the Flemish from the south; and (4) the Waterlanders from the area around Amsterdam, as well as various splinter groups within each affiliation.

In spite of their different theological positions, especially on the issue of the ban, the groups regularly attempted alliances, coming together in various constellations, as, for example, the 1591 union of High Germans and Frisians in → *The Concept of Cologne*.[1]

In *The Short Confession of Faith* by Hans de Ries (1553–1638), however, Mennonite efforts at union and reconciliation are expanded to an attempt at an alliance between the Waterlanders and English Separatists who had settled in Amsterdam. Hans de Ries, a leader of the Waterlanders in Alkmaar, and his colleague Lubbert Gerritsz (1534–1612) in Amsterdam drew up the *Short Confession* at the request of John Smyth († 1612), the pastor of the English congregation.

On matters of doctrine, the confession affirms free will and rejects the notion of a predetermined elect (articles 5 and 7); follows Menno Simons's teaching on the miraculous nature of Christ's mortality, which dissociated Mary from his humanity (article 8); develops a Christology based on the offices of Christ (articles 9–18); maintains that justification is by faith alone (article 21); acknowledges two sacraments—baptism and the Lord's supper (article 30); and rejects infant baptism (article 31). Excommunication and avoidance (the ban) are described in articles 35 and 36, and marriage outside the faith is forbidden (article 39). In all matters of faith and doctrine, the Bible is the chief authority.

Although forty-one of the English signed the confession, as translated by John Smyth, true union was never achieved. Because it elucidated the core beliefs of the largest group of Dutch Mennonites, however, the Waterlanders' *Short Confession of Faith* became a defining document of the movement. It was published in many edi-

---

1. Other alliance creeds include *The Olive Branch* of 1627 for a union of Frisian and Flemish congregations and the *Jan Cents' Confession* of 1630, which was signed by High German and Frisian ministers. For English translations, see Braght 1985, 27–38.

tions throughout the seventeenth and eighteenth centuries and was translated into English, French, German, and Latin.

Edition: Ries 1686, 1–123.

Translation: Dyck 1964, 11–19.

Note: Dyck's translation follows the 1618 edition with comparative references to the edition of 1686. The confession may have been published as early as 1610, but no copy of that edition exists (see Coggins 1986).

Literature: Coggins 1986, 1991; Dyck 1964, 5–10; *ME* 4:554–55, 895–96; *ML* 3:509–11.

The Short Confession of Faith, 1610

1. GOD

We believe and confess, by the power and instruction of Holy Scripture, that there is one God alone, a spirit or spiritual being, eternal, incomprehensible, everlasting, invisible, immutable, almighty, merciful, righteous, perfect, wise, alone good, a fountain of life, the source of all good, the Creator and Sustainer of heaven and earth, of all things visible and invisible. [Dt 6.4; 1 Cor 8.4]

2. THE TRINITY

This one only God is revealed and discerned in the Holy Scriptures as Father, Son, and Holy Spirit, being three yet, nevertheless, one God. [1 Jn 5.7]

3. THE TRINITY

The Father is the origin and beginning of all things, having brought forth his Son from eternity, before all creation, in an incomprehensible manner. The Son is the [Col 1.17] eternal Word and wisdom of the Father, in whom all things consist. The Holy Spirit is God's power and might, proceeding from the Father and the Son. The three are neither divided nor different in nature, essence, or essential attributes: to wit, eternal, omnipotent, invisible, immortal, glorious, and the like.

4. CREATION, FALL, AND REDEMPTION OF MAN

This only God created man good, in his own image, for happiness and salvation. The first man fell into sin and disgrace. Nevertheless, he has been saved by God and [Rom 5.17] given eternal life, together with all those who had fallen in him, according to the comforting promises of God. Consequently none of his descendants, being included in this redemption, are born with sin or guilt.

5. FREEDOM OF THE WILL

Because man was created good he had in himself the ability to hear, accept, or reject the wrong with which he was tempted by the spirit of evil. Thus when man fell he still had the ability, though standing in this evil, to hear, accept, or reject the good which the Lord himself placed before him. Even as he was able to hear and accept the evil before the fall, so also he is able to hear and accept the good that is before him after the fall. This ability to accept or reject the grace of God has remained with the posterity of the first man as a gift of grace.

6. THE ORIGIN OF SIN

God has foreseen and foreknown all things that have occurred, occur, and will occur, both good and bad, from all eternity. Since he is the only good and perfect
fountain of life, we confess him to be the only author, source, and creator of the
things that are good, holy, clean, pure, and conformable to his nature. In no sense,
however, is he the origin of sin or evil unto damnation. God commands the good,
desires obedience to the good, counsels and admonishes to do the good, giving great
promises to those who obey. On the other hand he forbids evil, warns evildoers
and pleads with them, announcing to them eternal punishment and sometimes punishing them in this life. In this he testifies that he is the enemy of the sinner, that
all unrighteousness is contrary to his holy nature. Thus not the good God but evil
man, through his free choice of sin, together with the spirit of evil within him, is
the author, source, and worker of sin and evil, being thereby guilty and punishable.

7. PREDESTINATION

The cause of man's calamity and damnation is his own free choice of darkness, his
affirming of sins and his willingness to live in them. Destruction comes from man,
not from the good Creator. God, being perfect good and love itself (according to
the nature of perfect love and goodness), desired the best for his creatures—healing, salvation. Therefore he neither predestined, determined, nor created anyone for
damnation, neither willing nor ordaining their sinful life in order to bring them to
destruction. Rather (since as a good God he had no desire, as surely as he lives, that
[Jn 3.16]   any man should perish but that all might be saved), he created all men for salvation.
When they fell he restored them, with infinite love, through Christ who has become
for all men a medicine of life. This Christ was given over to judgment, sacrificed
and died for the reconciliation of all men, affirming his desire that all creatures and
nations should hear, and have offered to them through evangelical preaching, the
grace, love, and compassion which he brings. All those who now receive this grace
of God in Christ (who came for the salvation of the world) with penitent and believing hearts and remain in him are and remain the elect whom God has ordained
before the foundation of the world that they should share his glory. Those, how-
[Jn 3.19]   ever, who despise or reject this grace of God, who love darkness more than light,
who remain unrepentant and unbelieving, make themselves unworthy of salvation
through their own perversity, and are therefore justly rejected by God because of
their own evil. These will not reach the end for which they were created and for
which they were ordained in Christ, neither shall they taste the supper of the Lord,
to which they had been invited, in all eternity.

8. THE INCARNATION

The eternal intention of God to reconcile the world which he saw falling into wrath and disgrace has been accomplished in the fullness of time through the sending of his Son, the eternal Word from heaven, as the fulfillment of the promise to the fathers. Born of the Holy Virgin Mary he became flesh and blood through the miraculous work of the Holy Spirit. This, however, not in a manner by which a part of the eternal essence of the Word was changed into visible, mortal flesh or man and thereby ceasing to be spirit or God; rather, the eternal Son of God, remaining what he had been before, namely God and spirit, became that which he had formerly not been, flesh or man. Thus Jesus Christ, our Emmanuel, is at the same time in one person true God and man born of Mary, visible and invisible, external and internal, very Son of the living God.

9. THE THREEFOLD OFFICE OF CHRIST

Being then both God and man, Son of the living God, Christ came into the world to save sinners, to reconcile the sinful world to God the Father. Therefore we confess him to be our only Mediator, Prophet, Priest, and King, a lawgiver and teacher whom God had promised to send into the world. Him we hear, believe, and must follow. [1 Tm 1.15]

10. CONCERNING THE LAW

Christ has brought to an end and removed from among his people the unbearable burden of the law of Moses with its shadows and figures, the priestly office of the temple, altar, sacrifice, and all else that was a part of the priestly office. Likewise he brought to an end the kingly office and what came with it, the kingdom, sword, the wrath of the law, war, and whatever prefigured his person and office. These were the image, the shadow of him who was to come. [Col 2.17]

11. THE PROPHETIC OFFICE OF CHRIST

As the true prophet of the promise Christ has revealed and proclaimed to us the will of God, that which God requires of the people of the New Testament. Even as God spoke to the people of the Old Testament through Moses and the prophets, declaring his will to them, so in the last days he has spoken to us through this prophet (his Son), proclaiming that which had been hidden during all time. Thus he preached to us the good news, instituted and ordered the sacraments, offices, and services provided by God. With his life and teaching he pointed out the law of Christ, the rule of life, and the path to eternal life. [Heb 1.1–2]

12. THE PRIESTLY OFFICE OF CHRIST

Beyond this, as the only High Priest and Mediator of the New Testament he interceded with his heavenly Father for all believers as well as for all those who crucified

[Lk 23.34]   and killed him. Finally he himself entered into the extremity of suffering, offering himself to the Father through his death upon the cross, an offering and gift of sweet savor and eternal worth.

13. THE OBEDIENCE OF CHRIST

We confess that the obedience of the Son of God, his bitter suffering, death, shed blood, and sacrifice upon the cross is the reconciliation and satisfaction for all our sins and the sins of the world. Therefore we have been reconciled with God and are at peace, having a certain high hope and assurance of entry into eternal life.

14. THE OFFICE OF CHRIST AS KING

As the promised spiritual king Jesus Christ, our Prophet and Priest, has also established a spiritual kingdom, having gathered a multitude of believing and spiritual people whom he has provided with spiritual laws and weapons in the manner of his heavenly kingdom. In this kingdom he has ordained righteousness and those who dwell therein as servants of righteousness. He himself is the preserver, protector, fortress, castle, and rock, and shall remain king of this kingdom forever.

15. THE RESURRECTION OF CHRIST

After he had completed his work here upon earth through his death upon the cross he was buried as a certain sign of his death. On the third day he arose again from the dead, showing himself thereby as Lord and conqueror over death, one who could no longer be held by the grave. In this he became to all believers a comforting assurance of their redemption and final resurrection from the dead.

16. THE ASCENSION AND GLORIFICATION OF CHRIST

Following this he walked among his disciples forty days, showing himself to them in order that no doubt should remain concerning his resurrection. Then, surrounded

[Eph 4.8]   by a cloud, he ascended to heaven and entered into his glory. Thus he led captivity captive, establishing a glorious triumph over his enemies. Seated at the right hand of the majesty of God he has been made both Lord and Christ, glorified in his body, exalted, crowned with praise and honor, remaining priest and king over Mount Zion in all eternity.

17. THE PRIESTLY OFFICE OF CHRIST

The holy office of this glorified priest, king, Lord, and Christ in his heavenly being consists in serving, guiding, and ruling his holy church amidst the storms of this world by the strength of his Spirit. According to his priestly office, as servant of the sacred things, the true tabernacle, he is our intercessor, spokesman, and mediator with the Father. He teaches, comforts, strengthens, and baptizes us with the Holy Spirit and with fire, bringing us heavenly gifts. He celebrates his spiritual supper with believing souls, making them partakers of the living food and drink of the soul. In these sacraments alone is the fruit, power, and worth of his work upon the cross appropriated.

18. THE ROYAL OFFICE OF CHRIST

According to his royal, heavenly office Christ rules over the hearts of the believers through his word and Holy Spirit. He takes them into his care, covers them with the shadow of his wings, arms them with spiritual weapons for a spiritual warfare against all their enemies, the spirits of evil with their associates upon earth. This glorious, almighty, and heavenly king stands by the faithful believers in every need, delivering and freeing them from the hands of their spiritual enemies, conquering the enemy, and winning the field of battle, thus preparing for his own a heavenly kingdom of righteousness. These are the redeemed of the Lord, living in the house of the Lord and on Mount Zion. They have changed their carnal weapons. Their swords have been changed into plowshares and their spears into sickles. They [Is 2.4] neither lift a sword, nor teach, nor participate in carnal warfare.

19. TO KNOW CHRIST ACCORDING TO THE SPIRIT

From what has thus been said concerning the ascension, glorification, office, and service of Christ in glory we believe and confess that he must not only be known according to the flesh, or confessed literally according to historical knowledge, or only in his incarnation, birth, manifestation in the flesh, his life, miracles, suffering, death, cross, and other events. Rather we must rise higher and confess Christ also according to the Spirit, in his exaltation and glory, according to his glorious office and, as the Scriptures teach, receive this knowledge with a believing heart. Continuing in fervent prayer to God, we must seek to have his holy office according to the Spirit, and a knowledge of him revealed to us through his infinite patience and love.

All this must be sought to the end that his image and likeness may be born within us, that he himself may be revealed in us, living, walking, teaching, and preaching; that the miracles he performed in the flesh may be worked in us according to the Spirit, healing us of the sickness of the soul, deafness, blindness, leprosy, uncleanness, sin, and death. We must know Christ according to the Spirit that he may baptize us with the Holy Spirit and with fire, feed us with heavenly food and [Mt 3.11] drink, making us partakers of the divine nature. In this power we may crucify the [2 Pt 1.4] old man in us, becoming like Christ in his suffering and death. In this power we are resurrected to new life according to his own resurrection, to the glory and honor of God our heavenly Father. This we call a knowledge of Christ according to the Spirit, without which the knowledge of Christ according to the flesh is not sufficient for salvation.

20. CONCERNING SAVING FAITH

All the spiritual gifts and mercies which Jesus Christ won for the salvation of sinners through his own merit, we enjoy by grace through a living faith active in love. This faith is a certain heartfelt assurance or inner knowledge of God, of Christ, and other heavenly things received by grace out of the word of God. This knowledge, together with the love of God, a sincere trust in the one, only God as gracious, heavenly Father who provides all our physical and spiritual needs for Christ's sake, is necessary for salvation.

21. JUSTIFICATION

Through this living faith we are truly justified, that is, we are declared free of all past and present sins through the shed blood of Jesus Christ, receiving the true righ- [Rom 5.1] teousness which he works in us in cooperation with the Holy Spirit. Thus we are transformed from being evil to being good, from a carnal to a spiritual state, from selfishness to mildness, from pride to humility, being changed from unrighteousness to righteousness. This justification proceeds from the new birth.

22. THE NEW BIRTH

The new birth is an act of God effected in the soul of the truly repentant, a restoring of the image of God in man, a renewing of the mind and heart, an enlightening of reason through an acknowledgment of the truth. This new birth brings with it a transformation of the will, of carnal desires and lust, a sincere putting to death of all evil within, of the old man with his desires and life of sin and rebellion. At the same time the new birth brings an awakening of new life in God, in true goodness, righteousness, and holiness. It is a taking away of the heart of stone with its pride, ignorance, blindness, sin, and sinful lusts, and a gracious granting of the promised fleshly heart filled with the law of God, light, wisdom, understanding, virtue, and holy desires. This new birth comes from God through Christ. It is worked in us by the Holy Spirit with his fire and power, not by a creaturely means. Therefore the regenerate person also testifies to his being born again or not, not by natural means. Hereby we become children of God, spiritual-minded, righteous, and holy. We believe and teach that this new birth is necessary for salvation according to the words of Christ: "Truly, truly, I say to you, unless one is born anew, he cannot see the kingdom of God," and again, "unless one is born of water and the Spirit, he cannot enter the kingdom of God."

[Jn 3.3]

[Jn 3.5]

23. GOOD WORKS

When man has thus been born again and justified of God through Jesus Christ, he lives in love (which the Holy Spirit has poured into his heart), rejoicing in all good works, in the law, commandments, and morality given him by God through Christ. Thus he thanks God from a pure heart through a holy life, for all his gifts, particularly the spiritual gifts to the soul. This soul is a sacred plant of the Lord, a tree of righteousness honoring God through good works, awaiting the blessed reward which God in his abundant goodness has promised to it.

[Rom 5.5]

24. THE CHURCH

All who believe and are born again, though scattered to the ends of the earth, are the true church of God, or church of Jesus Christ upon earth. These he has loved and given himself for them that they be holy. Yes, he has sanctified them through the water and the word of life. Of this church Jesus Christ is the foundation, the Head, the Shepherd, Leader, Lord, King, Master. She alone is his beautiful bride, his holy body, clothing, and people who through the new birth have become part of his flesh and body. While there are among these many hypocrites and pretenders, those who have been born again in Christ and sanctified are true members of the body of Christ and will inherit the promises. Of these great blessings the pretenders and hypocrites, through their own fault, will have no part.

25. THE MINISTRY

In this his holy church God has ordained the evangelical office of teaching the divine word, administering the sacraments, and aiding the poor. Likewise God intended the servants of these offices to admonish the brethren, to chastise, and finally to separate the unrepentant from the brotherhood. These holy ordinances are contained in, and must be administered according to, the word of God.

26. THE MINISTRY AND THE LAITY

Even as a body consists of many members of which each has its own particular function since not every member is the hand, eye, or foot, so also in the church of God.

[1 Cor 12.12]

Though every believer is a member, not every one is a teacher, elder, or deacon, but only those who have been designated to these offices. Therefore the administration of these offices belongs only to those who have been ordained, not to every layman.

27. THE CALLING OF MINISTERS

The calling or selecting of servants to these offices takes place through the ministers of the church together with the congregation. They call upon the name of the Lord, for he alone knows the hearts of men, he is in the midst of the believers gathered in his name, guiding them by his Holy Spirit. Thus he knows the minds and hearts of his own, bringing into service those who will best serve his church.

28. ORDINATION

Although the calling and selection of these servants occurs as stated, the installation of these men into their office is the work of the elders of the church through the laying on of hands.

29. CONCERNING TRUE DOCTRINE

The doctrine taught by ordained servants of the church is the same as Jesus brought from heaven, which he taught by word (that is, with life and teaching) and which was taught by the apostles at the command of Christ and by his Spirit. The doctrine we find described (as much as is necessary for salvation) in the writings of the New Testament, to which we add all that is contained in the canonical books of the Old Testament and which is in harmony with the teaching of Christ and his apostles, which conforms to the rule of his spiritual kingdom.

30. THE SACRAMENTS

Jesus Christ has instituted two sacraments in his holy church, baptism and the Lord's supper, attaching their administration to the office of the ministry. These are external, visible signs of the invisible divine grace given to us by God. They are the invisible, spiritual act of God through Christ (in cooperation with the Holy Spirit), bringing the new birth, justification, spiritual nourishment, and sustenance to repentant and believing souls. Likewise we testify thereby [in partaking of the sacraments] to our repentance, faith, and obedience, committing ourselves in good conscience to the service of God.

31. EXTERNAL BAPTISM

Holy baptism is an external, visible, evangelical act in which the believer is baptized with water in the name of the Father, Son, and Holy Spirit according to the com-

mand of Christ and the practice of the apostles. All who hear, believe, and gladly   [Mt 28.19–20]
receive the good news of the gospel are thus commanded by Jesus to be baptized,
but not children.

32. THE INNER SIGNIFICANCE OF BAPTISM

The external act of baptism places before us the fact that Jesus Christ himself baptizes the repentant believer inwardly in the bath of the new birth and renewal
through the Holy Spirit, washing the soul from all filth and sin through the merit   [Ti 3.5]
and shed blood of Christ. Through the power and work of the Holy Spirit the heavenly, spiritual, and living water washes the soul, making it heavenly, spiritual, alive
in goodness and righteousness. Therefore water baptism points us to Christ and to
his office in glory, brings this to our remembrance, and certifies the effectiveness of
his work to the hearts of the faithful. Thus external baptism admonishes us not to
rely upon the external but in holy prayer to ascend to Christ, seek the gifts he graciously bestows and multiplies in the hearts of those who receive the sacraments in
true faith.

33. THE LORD'S SUPPER

The Lord's supper, even as baptism, is an external, visible, evangelical act in which,
according to the command of Christ and the example of the apostles, bread and
wine is received for a holy purpose. The bread is broken, the wine poured out and
given to those who have been baptized upon their faith according to the ordinance
of Christ. In eating the bread and drinking the wine Christ's death, passion, and
bitter suffering is proclaimed. All this is done in remembrance of him.

34. THE INNER SIGNIFICANCE OF THE LORD'S SUPPER

The external, visible administration of the Lord's supper witnesses and signifies to
us that Christ's holy body was broken upon the cross, his blood shed for the forgiveness of our sins, that in his glorified state he is the living bread, food, and drink
of the soul. The external supper brings to our mind the office and function of Christ
in glory, his institution of the spiritual supper with believing souls, feeding them
with truly spiritual food. Likewise the external supper teaches us to rise above the
external in holy prayer, longing for the reality of the gift of Christ. It teaches us to
be thankful to God, to live in love and unity with each other.

35. CHURCH DISCIPLINE

Church discipline or the extreme penalty is an external act among the believers
by which the unrepentant sinner, after due admonition and exhortation, is denied

the fellowship of the faithful and the external gifts because of his sin, the wrath of God being announced to him unless he repent. Thus through external separation is shown how God deals with the unrepentant. The initiative in judgment remains with God, the church remains his servant. Therefore we teach herewith that no one should be judged by the church who has not previously been judged by the word of God.

36. AVOIDANCE

Unless they repent, those separated from the fellowship are in no case allowed to partake of the Lord's supper or other ordinances of the church. These and all fellowship or spiritual communion are withdrawn from them. Thus their ungodly life and conversation, which is detrimental to the faithful as an irritation and temptation, is rejected to the preservation of holiness and the honor of the name of the Lord. All this, however, must be done in keeping with the word of God. Thus married persons may not be separated. None may be encouraged to act contrary to the command of love, mercy, and Christian humility nor to ignore need and other requirements of daily living.

37. GOVERNMENT

Government, or secular authority, is ordained of God as necessary for the maintenance of public life, of orderly citizenship, for the protection of the good and punishment of evil. We confess our obligation according to the word of God, to fear, honor, and obey the secular powers in all things not contrary to the word of God. We are called upon to pray for these powers, to thank God for good and Christian government, to give to her without complaint the taxes and assessments which are her due.

[Rom 13.1–2]

This office of secular power has not been given by the Lord Jesus in his spiritual kingdom to the members of his church. He has not called his disciples to be secular kings, princes, dukes, or authorities, nor instructed them to seek and assume such office, nor to rule the world in a worldly manner. Neither has he given to his disciples a law which would establish such a service. Rather, with a continuing voice from heaven, they are called to lead a nonresistant life to become cross-bearers, following in the footsteps of the Master. Nothing is further from this call than to rule this world with the sword.

All this then, together with the many other things which are attached to worldly office—the waging of war, the destroying of life and property of the enemy, etc., which things do not harmonize with the new life in Christ—lead us to avoid these offices and services. With this, however, we in no way seek to despise honest government nor give it a lesser place than that given by the Holy Spirit through the writings of the apostle Paul.

38. THE OATH

Jesus Christ, King and Lawgiver of the New Testament, has forbidden all swearing of oaths to Christians. Therefore the swearing of oaths is also forbidden to all believers of the New Testament.

39. MARRIAGE

We hold marriage to be an ordinance of God, instituted in such manner that every husband shall have his own wife and every wife her own husband. These may not be separated except for reasons of adultery. Neither do we believe that one of our brotherhood may marry an ungodly, unbelieving, carnal person outside of the church without being judged, as other sins are, by the word of God, and, according to the circumstances, [by the church].

40. CONCERNING LAST THINGS

Finally we believe and teach that Jesus Christ, our glorified Lord and King, will come again, visibly, in a manner like unto his ascension, in power and glory with his holy angels, to reveal himself in his holy ones and all who believe, to judge the living and the dead. Then all people who have lived upon the earth, both good and bad, shall arise imperishable from the grave. Their soul shall be united with the body in which they lived sinfully or virtuously. Those who have not died but remain alive upon earth shall be changed in a moment into an eternal state, and all mankind shall appear before the judgment seat of Christ to receive their reward according to their works, either good or evil. Then Jesus shall separate the sheep from the goats as a shepherd divides his flock, putting the sheep to his right, the goats to [Mt 25.32–46] his left, and pronouncing judgment upon them. The righteous, who led a holy life on earth, who did works of love and mercy, he shall separate and take to himself as a bridegroom. They shall enter with him into eternal life, into their heavenly rest, remaining always in the presence of the Lord and inheriting the kingdom prepared for them from the foundation of the world. The unrighteous, however, who did not know God nor obeyed the gospel of our Lord Jesus Christ, shall be sent into fire prepared for the devil and his angels. These shall suffer torment, eternal damnation before the glory and majesty of the Lord.

     The Almighty God, full of grace and mercy, preserve us from the judgment of the ungodly and grant us grace to live a holy life, to die blessedly, and to arise joyfully at the last day with all true believers. Amen.

The Dordrecht Confession, 1632

The Dordrecht Confession is the central statement of faith of most Mennonites. It was adopted in 1632 as a union document between the conservative Old Flemish and the more liberal Young Flemish congregations. Adriaan Cornelisz († 1632), an elder in the Old Flemish congregation of Dordrecht (Dort), probably drafted the eighteen articles of the agreement. Thereafter, however, *The Dordrecht Confession* was adopted by other Mennonite groups, including the Alsatian Mennonites, some of the Swiss Brethren, German Mennonites, and the Mennonites of Pennsylvania.

Theologically, the confession reflects more traditionalist views, with emphases on the ban and shunning (articles 16–17). Other defining doctrines include the baptism of believers, a sacramentarian view of the eucharist, foot washing, strict pacifism, a proscription on oath swearing, and an insistence on marriage within the faith community.

The confession was printed in 1633 and reprinted many times in the seventeenth and eighteenth centuries. It appeared in T. J. van Braght's *Martyrs' Mirror* (1660) and in the earliest collection of Mennonite creeds, *Algemeene Belydenissen* (1665). There also exist early translations into German (1664), English (1712), and French (1771).

Edition: Brüsewitz and Krebber 1982, 31–58.

Translation: Horst, 19–38.

Note: For a facsimile of the 1633 edition, which exists in only one copy, see Horst, 41–72.

Literature: Brüsewitz and Krebber 1982, 7–16 (Horst); Dyck 1993, 128–30; Horst, 9–14; Horst, 1982; Loewen, 24–27, 62–70; *ME* 2:92–93; *ML* 1:468–69; Studer 1984; Wenger 1952, 77–87.

The Dordrecht Confession, 1632

Confession and Peace Agreement

Reached at Dordrecht, Anno 1632, on the 21st of April, between the Mennonites [Doops-gezinden] called the Flemish: in which everyone can see and perceive how and on what this peace has been made and established.

Blessed are the peacemakers: for they shall be called the children of God. Mt 5.9

Follow peace with all men, and holiness, without which no man shall see the Lord. Heb 12.14

God hath called us to peace. 1 Cor 7.15

Preface to the Peace Agreement Reached Among the Mennonites Called the Flemish on 21 April 1632 at Dordrecht

Mindful and peace-loving reader, seeker after happiness and truth, we hear daily of some persons who are not favorable to our peace agreement. Failing to comply with the nature of love, which sees the best in everything, they do not speak well of it. Thereby they cause innocent and unlearned persons—who regrettably at times are more impressed by men of today than by the teaching and life of our Savior Jesus Christ and his beloved apostles—to shy off and to turn away from it. These opponents not only reject us but also the peace so highly commended by the Son of God and his apostles. They do not obey, it seems, the exhortation of Christ: "Blessed are the peacemakers: for they shall be called the children of God," Matthew 5.9. "Fol- Mt 5.9 low peace with all men, and holiness, without which no man shall see the Lord," Hebrews 12.14.[a] "Have peace one with another," Mark 9.[b] "On earth peace," Luke 2.14.[c] "Peace I leave with you, my peace I give unto you." John 14.27.[d] "How beautiful are the feet of them that preach the gospel of peace, and bring glad tidings of good things," Romans 10.15 and Isaiah 52.7. "Behold, how good and how pleasant Rom 10.15; Is 52.7 it is for brethren to dwell together in unity! It is like the precious ointment upon the beard, even Aaron's beard: that went down to the skirts of his garments; as the

a. Heb 12.14
b. Mk 9[.50]
c. Lk 2.14
d. Jn 14.27

769

dew of Hermon, and as the dew that descended upon the mountains of Zion: for

Ps 133 there the Lord commanded the blessing, even life for evermore," Psalms 133. "If it

Rom 12.18 be possible, as much as lieth in you, live peaceably with all men," Romans 12.18.

"For the kingdom of God is not meat and drink, but righteousness and peace, and

Rom 14[.17] joy in the Holy Ghost," Romans 14. "Let us therefore follow after the things which

Rom 14.[19] make for peace, and things wherewith one may edify another," Romans 14. "God

1 Cor 7.15 hath called us to peace," 1 Corinthians 7.15. "Finally, brethren, farewell. Be perfect,

be of good comfort, be of one mind, live in peace; and the God of love and peace

2 Cor 13.11 shall be with you," 2 Corinthians 13.11.

Taking these and other Scriptures for our learning to heart and consider-

ing them in the fear of God, we found that we had strayed from them and, in so

Ps 119.59 doing, had left the way of peace. Like David in Psalms 119.59 we thought about

our ways and found it high time to return to the instruction of the Lord, to humble

ourselves before God and our brethren, and to say with Jeremiah in Lamentations

Lam 3.42 3.42: "We have transgressed and have rebelled: thou hast not pardoned." With our

Acts 16.14 minds kindled by this and opening our hearts with Lydia, Acts 16.14, we sensed that

the time had come to re-establish the broken peace. We desired to live and walk

again in peace and love with each other, with the scattered sheep—of whom we

were not the least—who are one with us in faith, doctrine, and practice and in this

way magnify God's great and holy name. We undertook this then for the upbuilding

and betterment of our own ways, for the edification of our fellowmen, and finally

for the common salvation of our souls. We trust that the merciful God—who is a

God of peace rather than of wrangling and discord—will give his gracious blessing

through his blessed Son, our Savior and Lord. Apart from him we can do nothing,

Jn 15.5 John 15.5. Amen.

For the reason mentioned at the beginning of this preface, we could not

neglect to inform all true lovers of peace and at the same time to make public in

what capacity and upon what articles of faith the peace is again built and estab-

lished—at Dordrecht on 21 April 1632 the peace was renewed and took place by

a mutual, complete forgiving of, freeing from, and acquittal of all previous faults

and mistakes, wrong actions, and restrictions—that no one from now on through

ignorance should speak unjustly about something of which he is not informed. Use

what follows for your profit.

—In Haarlem as of 8 April [1633] by a Lover of Peace

Introduction

Brethren, we along with our elders and ministers (unworthy as we are) of the united church of God here at Dordrecht; also, we, the undersigned elders, ministers, and brethren—who as coworkers were invited, delegated, and came, each for himself and for his church—are gathered in the Lord's name in the church at this place and are one with it: wish heavenly wisdom, divine enlightenment from the almighty, eternal, and incomprehensible God for all churches, coworkers, brethren, and partakers of our common Christian faith in all towns and places where this—our brotherly union, appeasement, and agreement—will be presented and read. May this divine wisdom enable you to test, discern, and pursue what is necessary for our common peace and mutual improvement. Such peace is pleasing to God, agreeable to men, and enables us to walk as becomes our calling. In order that we and you with us after this life, along with all God's chosen, holy, and beloved saints, may be eternally saved through our Lord Jesus Christ. To this end may the kind and faithful God help us and grant his gracious blessing to make you and us worthy and acceptable. Amen.

Further, this must be mentioned: it is public knowledge for quite some time in many or at least some places that for various reasons an unhappy contention leading to confusion—yes, even separation and schism—rose and continued among fellow believers of the same persuasion and brotherhood of faith. Not the least among these contentions was the division of the House-Buyers which continued for many years. As a result of this and all that developed from it, God's worthy name was slandered and disgraced, and the church became an object of reproach and contempt. Along with this there was much giving and taking of offense as well as provocation and insult, especially in the church at Franeker but also elsewhere. One might well lament such matters with regret and remorse and wish they had never happened. Mistakes are usually better seen and discerned afterwards than before, as is the case with these contentions. The more one considers them, especially with an impartial mind, the stronger one is convinced that the cause as well as the unfortunate results cannot entirely be laid at the feet of one side. Both sides have been greatly at fault; both have been overzealous and immoderate in the use of discipline, or rejection and separation from each other.

Both sides lacked a recognition of love as the principal garb and characteristic of the true followers of Christ. Love is the sum of the great commandments, the fulfillment of the law. Love is indeed the bond of perfection; it binds believers   Jn 13.35; Col 3.14
in a harmonious relationship with the Lord; it binds believers as one heart and soul to each other in peace and unity. As members of one body they are closely related

to each other at all times and in every way: to bear and forgive the shortcomings

Lk 6.36 of each other, to cover the failures of neighbors. They deal gently with each other, showing compassion and mercy; they do not increase the hurt of the injured nor

2 Cor 5.11; Ez 34.4 oppress or reject the weak. Instead each esteems the other person more than himself,[a] and in this way the weaker members receive attention and respect.[b] Indeed, love was too much lacking on the part of both sides and much unhappiness, strife, and contention were the result.

      If this bond of love becomes weak and cold—or actually broken by many—

Mt 13.25 the enemy sows tares in the hearts of many dozing members which take root in bit-

Heb 12.15 terness. All kinds of confusion and error result and bear fruit such as envy, discord, backbiting, hate, and strife. As a tiny spark, if it is fanned and not extinguished in time, can cause great destruction, so it has gone in this matter. Also, one may truthfully say that not the House-Buyers only, nor only the results of this affair and all that was attached to it, but much rather the sins of both sides should be acknowledged as contributing to the cause of the contention.

      All of this we here at Dordrecht as well as brethren at many other places have taken to heart and given thought and considered. In this we profit from the many excellent examples in Scripture, how the patriarchs and prophets, along with the apostles as shepherds, fathers, and leaders in the church, truly sought the unity of fellow believers. Their instruction is given to us as pointers so that we can see as in a mirror how we ought to act and treat each other in matters of contention and disagreement. We see in this mirror their endeavors to meet each other with respect. These fathers and leaders have highly recommended all Christian believ-

Heb 13.20 ers to follow them in such matters as they followed the great Shepherd. With these examples before us to follow, quarreling, wrangling, backbiting, and destruction ought finally to cease. We should now accept each other in loving kindness and in

Sg 1.6; Ps 85.11 trust. Yes, meet each other in love and peace. As much as possible should be done

Mt 18.12 to seek the lost, to bring together those scattered and gone astray, to bind up the wounded,[c] to repair the breaches,[d] to level the hills and remove the rocks of offense, to repair the roads and make a straight path so that on it the wayfaring man shall

[Is 35.8] not err. Always on every occasion we must seek what is pleasing to God, what is necessary for the welfare of the church, as well as what makes for peace and healing among each other.

a. Phil 2.3
b. 1 Cor 12.23
c. Ez 34.16
d. Is 58.12

We of both sides have earnestly prayed to God and constantly labored that what happened and continues to happen in the dispute over the House-Buyers be brought to an end: that following the example of the patriarchs, according to the teaching of Scripture, we might again meet each other in love, reconciliation, and unity. Finally, by the grace of God and with his help it was possible that we together in mutual agreement, representing both sides, the one as well as the other from many different places, were called by letter to come to Dordrecht.

And so both sides assembled here in the Lord's name (unworthy as we were) in love and friendship. Insofar as it was fitting, we have spoken about and discussed these matters in the fear of the Lord. After this we turned to prayer and supplication, for which the Lord had prepared our hearts so that we were inclined towards each other. For this be the praise and thanksgiving only to him. Unshackled, free, and unbound as we had now been made, with sincere confession of guilt in regard to the matter mentioned above, we also set free and unbound all those whom we   Is 58.6
and our former leaders, together with their congregations, had bound, banned, or burdened in any way.

And moreover, in sincere repentance and contrition we begged each other for forgiveness; thereafter we forgave each other and acquitted each other of everything which had been done by us or our former leaders or the congregations involved, specifically or in a general way in regard to the matter of the House-buying at Franeker. This included everything connected with it, whether words, acts, books, letters, or any form of mistreatment or indebtedness—nothing excepted—wherever up until now we together as a group or separately as individuals of either side had grieved, hurt, or offended others.

In regard to this matter we have also at the same time together in sincere and earnest confession prayed and implored our merciful God and heavenly Father in the name of his dear Son, our Lord Jesus Christ, for complete forgiveness of everything done until now in this matter by us and our brethren on both sides. We desired   Mt 6.12; Prv 28.8
complete forgiveness for everything we have in any way done against God in his majesty or against each other or any other person.

In evidence and confirmation of this complete agreement, reconciliation, and unity, we have received each other with the hand and with the brotherly kiss of peace. Each accepted the other in the name of the Lord as is becoming for those who are bound to each other in one fellowship with him.

In this union we have accepted and included all fellow members, present and absent, both as a group and as individuals, those residing here as elsewhere, those invited as well as all others—excluding none. Just as we included those who were with us, the invited and their proxies, and who stand with us united in good-

will, doctrine, and practice, we have not overlooked those who hereafter wish to
follow our example and thus live to the honor of God and for the upbuilding, edification, and improvement of the church so that together we might with heart and

Acts 4.12 soul live and walk peaceably. Such a walk becomes our calling and is in keeping
with our common Christian faith, the principal articles of which are briefly drawn
up—from the word of God—and here added.

The Principal Articles of Our Common Christian Faith as Taught and Practiced by Our Church

ARTICLE 1. [GOD AND THE CREATION]

Heb 11.6 Scripture testifies that without faith it is impossible to please God, for everyone who
comes to him must believe that he is and that he rewards those who seek him. Therefore, we confess with the mouth and believe with the heart—in company with all
devout men and women and in keeping with Scripture—in one eternal,[a] almighty,
and incomprehensible God: the Father, Son, and Holy Ghost. There is only one
God—none other before him and none other after him—for from, by, and in him

Rom 11.36 are all things. All praise and honor be to him forever. Amen.

1 Cor 12.6   We believe and confess that this one God is the creator of all things, visible
and invisible. During six days he[b] created the heaven and earth, the sea,[c] and everything in them. We also believe that he continues to rule and maintain his creation
by his wisdom and by the power of his word.

        And when he had completed his work in keeping with his good pleasure
and had ordered it as perfect and right, each part in keeping with its nature and

Gn 1.27 being, he also created the first man, Adam, the father of us all. He gave him a body

Gn 2.7 made from a lump of clay and breathed into his nostrils the breath of life. Thus

Gn 5.1 Adam became a living soul from God, created in his own image and likeness in true
righteousness and holiness unto eternal life. God regarded him as above all other
creatures and adorned him with many great and glorious gifts. He placed him in the

Gn 2.17 delightful garden, or paradise, and gave him a command and a prohibition. After

Gn 2.22 this he took a rib from Adam, made a woman of it, brought her to him, and gave her

Gn 2.18 to him as a helper, companion, and wife. Accordingly, God caused that from this

Acts 17.26 first man, Adam, all men living on the entire earth have generated and descended.

---

a. Dt 6.4; Gn 17.1; Is 45.9; 1 Jn 5.7

b. Gn 1

c. Acts 14.15

ARTICLE 2. [THE FALL OF MAN]

We believe and confess, according to Scripture, that our first parents, Adam and
Eve, did not continue long in the happy state in which they had been created. They
became disobedient and broke God's high command, for they were seduced and   Gn 3.6
misled by the snake and the malice of the devil. In this way sin entered the world,   4 Ezr 3.7
and death by sin has passed upon all men, for all have sinned and incurred the wrath Rom 5.12, 18
of God and fallen under his condemnation. Therefore, Adam and Eve were driven
by God from paradise or the delightful garden to cultivate the earth, in sorrow to   Gn 3.23
provide for themselves, and to eat their bread in the sweat of their faces — until they
returned to the earth from which they came. We believe that through this one sin
they fell so deeply, became estranged and separated from God, that neither they   Ps 49.8
themselves, nor any of their posterity, nor angels, nor any other creature in heaven Rv 5
or earth could help them, redeem them, or reconcile them to God. They would have
been eternally lost had not God in compassion for his creatures intervened in his
love and mercy.   Jn 3.16

ARTICLE 3. [THE RESTORATION OF MAN]

We believe and confess that God — notwithstanding the fall of the first man and his
descendants, their sin and wrongdoing, and their helplessness to save themselves —
did not abandon men and women to be cast off entirely nor to be eternally lost. No,
God called them back to himself again; he comforted them and showed them that
there was yet a means of reconciliation. This was the unspotted Lamb, the Son of
God, who was prepared for this purpose before the foundation of the world. While   Jn 1.29
our first parents were still in paradise, he was promised for consolation, redemption, and salvation to man and his posterity.[a] In truth, he was granted to them by
faith from that time on so that all of the devout patriarchs, to whom this promise
was often renewed,[b] have longed for, desired,[c] and seen by faith its fulfillment. They
knew that his coming would save and free men and women from their sins, guilt,
and unrighteousness and restore them again to God's favor.

ARTICLE 4. [THE COMING OF CHRIST]

We also believe and confess that when the time of the promise came and was fulfilled — the time so much longed for and awaited by all the devout patriarchs — then   Jn 4.25

a. 1 Pt 1.19; Gn 3.15; 1 Jn 3.8; 1 Jn 2.1
b. Heb 11.13; Ps 39
c. Gal 4.4

Jn 16.28 the promised Messiah, Redeemer, and Savior, going out from God, was sent into the world. This was in keeping with the prediction of the prophets and the witness
1 Tm 3.15; Jn 1.14 of the Gospel writers. Yes, came in the flesh and revealed himself: the Word itself
Mt 1.22 became flesh and man. He was conceived in the Virgin Mary (who was engaged to
Lk 2.7, 21 Joseph of the house of David); and when she gave birth to him as her firstborn at Bethlehem, she wrapped him in swaddling clothes and laid him in a manger.

Mi 5.2 We believe and confess that he is the same one whose origin is from of old,
Heb 7.3 from the days of eternity; his years have no beginning, his life no end. Of him it is
Rv 1.8, 18 testified that he is the Alpha and the Omega, who is, was, and is to come. He is the one who was foreseen, promised, sent, and came into the world; he is God's own, first, and only Son.[a] He was before John the Baptist, before Abraham, before the
Mt 22.41 world; yes, he was David's Lord and the God of all the world. He is the firstborn of all creatures who[b] was sent into the world and yielded up the body prepared[c] for him as an offering and sacrifice whose fragrance was pleasing to God. This was for the solace, redemption, and salvation of all men and women, for the whole human race.

But as to how and in what manner this body was prepared, how the Word became flesh, and he himself man, we are content with the explanation[d] given by the faithful Gospel writers. Therefore, we confess with all the saints that he is the
Mt 16.16 Son of the living God. In him is all our hope, comfort, redemption, and salvation, and we should not seek the same in any other.

Further, we believe and confess with Scripture that, when he had finished the work for which he had been sent into the world, he was—in keeping with the
Lk 22.53 providence of God—delivered into the hands of evil men; that he suffered under the magistrate Pontius Pilate;[e] that he was crucified, died, and was buried.[f] On the third
Lk 24.50 day he rose from the dead and ascended to heaven and took his seat at the right hand of the throne of majesty in the heavens. From that place he shall come again to judge the living and the dead.

The Son of God also died, tasted death, and shed his precious blood for
Gn 3.15; 1 Jn 3.8 all men; in this way he bruised the serpent's head, destroyed the works of the devil,
Col 2.14 canceled the bond which pledged us to the decrees of the law, and achieved the for-

a. Jn 3.16; Heb 1.6; Rom 8.32; Jn 1.30
b. Col 1.15
c. Heb 10.5
d. Lk 1.30–31; Jn 20.31
e. Lk 23.1
f. Lk 24.5–6

giveness of sins for the entire human family. Thus he effected salvation for all, from the time of Adam to the end of the world, who believe in and obey him.

Rom 5.18

ARTICLE 5. [THE LAW OF CHRIST]

We also believe and confess that before his ascension Christ set up and instituted his new covenant. And because it was to remain an eternal covenant—which he confirmed and sealed with his own precious blood[a]—he highly charged and commissioned that it not be altered, neither by angels nor men, nor be added to nor diminished. And since it contained the whole counsel and will of his heavenly Father as far as is necessary for salvation, he has caused it to be published by his dear apostles, messengers, and servants, whom he has called and chosen for that purpose. He sent them to every part of the world to preach in his name to all nations, people, and tongues, proclaiming repentance and forgiveness of sins. Accordingly, he has declared in his covenant that all men without distinction as his children and lawful heirs, insofar as they follow and live up to its precepts by faith, are not excluded from this glorious inheritance of salvation. Excepted are the unbelieving and disobedient, the obstinate and unrepentant, who despise such salvation by their sinful actions and thus make themselves unworthy of eternal life.

Jer 31.31

Gal 1.8; 2 Tm 6.3

Jn 15.15

Mt 28.19; Mk 16.13

Lk 24.46–47

Rom 8.17

Acts 13.46

ARTICLE 6. [REPENTANCE AND AMENDMENT OF LIFE]

We believe and confess, since man is by nature inclined to do evil from his youth and is prone to sin and wickedness, that, therefore, the first lesson of the new covenant of the Son of God is repentance and amendment of life. Men and women with ears to hear and minds to understand should show the fruits of repentance and amend their lives. It means to believe the gospel, to depart from evil and do good, to cease to be unjust, and to reject sin. In short, it implies a discarding of the old nature[b] with its deeds and putting on the new nature, which is created after God in righteousness and true holiness. For neither baptism, nor the Lord's supper, nor church membership, nor any other outward ceremony can without faith, the new birth, and the amendment of life make it possible for us to please God and to receive the solace and promise of salvation. With sincere hearts and completely by faith we must come to God and believe in Jesus Christ as Scripture speaks and testifies of him. By this faith we receive forgiveness of sins, are justified and sanctified, and are made children of God—yes, partakers of his image, nature, and being: born again from above by the incorruptible seed.

Gn 8.21

Mk 1.15; Ez 12.1

Mk 1.15

Heb 10.21–22

Jn 7.38

a. Heb 9.15–17; Mt 26.27
b. Col 3.9–10; Eph 4.21–24

ARTICLE 7. [BAPTISM]

With regard to baptism we believe and confess that all penitent believers who by
faith, the new birth, and the renewing of the Holy Ghost are made one with God,
their names written in heaven—upon a scriptural confession of faith and amendment of life—ought to be baptized with water in the name of the Father, the Son,
and the Holy Ghost. This is in keeping with the doctrine and command of Christ
and the practice of his apostles: for the burial of their sins and in order to become incorporated into the fellowship of the saints.[a] In consequence of this they must learn
to keep all that the Son of God taught and commanded his followers.

Acts 2.38

Mt 28.19–20

ARTICLE 8. [THE CHURCH OF CHRIST]

We also believe and confess: a visible church of God—namely, of those who, as explained above, truly repent, believe rightly, and have received true baptism. They
are united with God in heaven and incorporated into the fellowship of the saints
on earth. These persons we hold to be the chosen race, the royal priesthood, the
holy people, who have the witness that they are the spouse and bride of Christ.[b]
Indeed, they are children and heirs of eternal life, a tent, a tabernacle, and house
of God in the Spirit, built upon the foundation of the apostles and the prophets—
Christ being the chief cornerstone.[c] This church of the living God[d] he bought and
redeemed with his own precious blood. According to his promise, he will always
stand by this church: to comfort and protect even to the end of the world. He will
dwell and walk with her and keep her so that neither floods, nor tempests, nor even
the gates of hell shall ever move or conquer her. This church is to be known by her
scriptural faith, doctrine, love, and godly life; also by a fruitful living up to, use, and
observance of the ordinances of Christ which he so highly commended and enjoined
upon his followers.

1 Cor 12.13

1 Pt 2.9

Ti 3.6–7

Eph 2.19–21

Mt 28.20

2 Cor 6.16

Mt 7.25, 16.18

ARTICLE 9 [THE CHOOSING AND MINISTRY OF THE TEACHERS, DEACONS, AND DEACONESSES IN THE CHURCH]

With regard to offices and election in the church, we believe and confess—since
the church can neither exist and grow nor continue as a structure without offices
and ordination—the Lord Christ himself as a father in his own house has instituted
offices and ordinations and regulated how each should walk in this respect in keep-

Eph 4.10–12

---

a. Rom 6.4; Mk 16.15; Mt 3.15; Acts 2.28, 8.11, 9.18, 10.47, 16.33; Col 2.11–12
b. Jn 3.29; Rv 19.7
c. Mt 16.18
d. 1 Pt 1.18–19

ing with his own work and calling and do that which is right and necessary. For Christ himself as the faithful, chief shepherd and bishop of our souls was sent and came into the world, not to wound or to break or to destroy the souls of men but to heal and cure, to seek the lost,[a] to break down the barrier and dividing wall,[b] to make one out of two, and thus to gather Jews, Gentiles, and people of all nations into one fold—that is, one fellowship in his name. For this he gave his life so that none should go astray; thus he made a way for their salvation by redeeming and releasing them when there was no one to help or assist.

      We also believe that before his departure Christ provided for his church faithful ministers, apostles, evangelists, pastors, and teachers—whom he had chosen by the Holy Ghost with prayer and supplication—to feed his flock, to govern the church, to watch over and nurture her, and in every way care for her—yes, to do in all things as he had done before them by way of example and precept.

      Also, that the apostles likewise, as faithful followers of Christ and leaders in the church, were diligent with prayer and supplication to God to provide from among the brethren: bishops, pastors, and leaders for all the cities and places where churches existed; to ordain such persons who took heed to themselves, to the doctrine, to the church and who were sound in the faith, godly in life and conduct with a good reputation within as well as without the church. That so they might be an example, light, and pattern in all godliness and good works; that they might worthily administer the ordinances of baptism and the Lord's supper. And that they might appoint in all places faithful men and elders capable of teaching others, ordaining them by the laying on of hands in the name of the Lord to enable them to minister to the church according to their ability that as faithful servants they might invest their Lord's talent, gain by it, and consequently save both themselves and those who hear them.

      And that they also should diligently see to it, each where he has oversight, to provide in all places deacons to look after and minister to the poor that they might receive gifts and alms and in turn faithfully distribute them, with all honesty as is becoming, to the saints in need.

      Also, that honorable, older widows should be chosen and ordained as deaconesses for the purpose of assisting the deacons to visit, comfort, and provide for the poor, infirm, ill, and distressed. Also, they should visit widows and orphans in order to comfort and care for them; further, to help look after the necessities of the church according to the best of their ability.

---

a. Mt 18.11
b. Eph 2.13

Marginal references:

1 Pt 2.29
Mt 12.19
Gal 3.28
Jn 10.9, 11.15
Ps 49.7
Eph 4.11; Lk 10.1
Lk 6.12–13
Jn 2.15
Mt 28.20
1 Tm 3.1
Acts 1.23–24
Ti 1.5
1 Tm 4.16
Ti 2.1–2
1 Tm 3.7
2 Tm 2.2
1 Tm 4.14, 5.2
Lk 19.13
Acts 6.3–6
1 Tm 5.9
Rom 16.1
Jas 1.27

What further concerns the deacons, that they, especially those gifted and chosen from the church for this purpose and ordained—to help lighten the work of the bishops—may also admonish and assist in word and doctrine in order to serve one another in love with the gift they have received from the Lord. So that through the mutual service and assistance of every member, according to his ability, the body of Christ may be improved and the Lord's vineyard and church may increase in growth while keeping the structure properly in order.

ARTICLE 10. [THE LORD'S SUPPER]

We also believe in and observe a breaking of bread or Lord's supper such as the Lord Christ Jesus instituted with bread and wine before his suffering.[a] He ate it with his apostles and commanded it to be done in remembrance of himself. Accordingly, his apostles also taught and observed it in the churches and commanded the believers to do it in memory of the Lord's death and suffering, that his body was broken and his precious blood shed for us and for all mankind. Remembering also its effect— namely, the redemption and salvation he accomplished—which showed us sinful men such a love whereby we are highly admonished to love and forgive each other and our neighbor as he has done unto us. Also, to keep in mind and to practice
Acts 2.46   the unity and fellowship we have with God and each other, a unity represented and signified in the breaking of the bread.

ARTICLE 11. [FOOTWASHING]

We also confess a washing of the saints' feet just as the Lord Christ instituted and commanded[b] but also exemplified by washing his apostles' feet himself even though he was their Lord and Master. This was an example that they should wash each other's feet. They followed this example and taught the believers to observe it as
Gn 18.4, 19.2   a sign of true humility; also as a special sign of the true washing by which we are washed in his precious blood and our souls are cleansed.

ARTICLE 12. [THE STATE OF MARRIAGE]

We believe and confess that in the church of God there is an honorable state of mar-
Gn 1.26   riage between two free and believing persons in keeping with and as God originally
Gn 2.18–24   ordained in paradise and established himself between Adam and Eve. And likewise the Lord Christ approved it and removed all the abuses which had gradually crept
Mt 19.4–6   in by restoring it to its first order. The apostle Paul also taught and permitted mar-

---

a. Mt 26.25; Mk 14.22; Acts 2.42; 1 Cor 10.16, 11.22–26
b. Jn 13.4–17; 1 Tm 5.10; Gn 18.4, 19.2

riage[a] in the church leaving it to everyone's free choice to marry in the Lord[b] in keeping with the original plan. By the phrase "in the Lord" we think it ought to be understood that, as the patriarchs were to marry among their own relatives or kin- Gn 24, 28 dred, no other liberty is granted to the believers of the new covenant. They are to marry among the chosen generation and the spiritual kindred of Christ (and none other), those who have been united to the church as one heart and soul, having received baptism and standing in the same fellowship, faith, doctrine, and walk before they are united in marriage. Such are then joined together in his church, according to the original ordinance of God. This is called "marrying in the Lord." 1 Cor 7.39

ARTICLE 13. [THE OFFICE OF CIVIL GOVERNMENT]

We also believe and confess that God instituted civil government for the punishment of evil and the protection of the good as well as to govern the world and to Rom 13.1–7 provide good regulations and policies in cities and countries. Therefore, we may not resist, despise,[c] or condemn the state. We should recognize it as a minister of God.[d] Further, we ought to honor and obey it and be ready to perform good works in its behalf insofar as it is not in conflict with God's law and commandment. Also, we should be faithful in the payment of taxes and excises, giving what is due to the Mt 17.27, 22.17–21 state as the Son of God taught, practiced, and commanded his disciples to do. Besides, we should constantly and earnestly pray for the state and the welfare of the 1 Tm 2.1–2 country that under its protection we may lead a quiet and peaceful life in all godliness and honesty. And further, that the Lord may be pleased to reward them here and in eternity for all of the privileges and benefits as well as the liberty we enjoy here under their laudable rule.

ARTICLE 14. [DEFENSE BY FORCE]

With regard to revenge and resistance to enemies with the sword, we believe and confess that our Lord Christ as well as his disciples and followers have forbid- Mt 5.39, 44 den and taught against all revenge. We have been commanded to recompense no man with evil for evil, not to return curse for cursing, but to put the sword into its Rom 12.14 sheath[e] or in the words of the prophet beat the swords into plowshares.[f] From this we understand that following the example, life, and doctrine of Christ, we may not

a. 1 Cor 7
b. 1 Cor 9.5
c. Ti 3.1
d. 1 Pt 2.17
e. Jn 18.11
f. Is 2.4; Mi 4.3; Zec 9.8–9

cause offense or suffering but should instead seek to promote the welfare and happiness of others. If necessary for the Lord's sake, we should flee from one city or country to another; we should suffer the loss of goods rather than bring harm to another. If we are slapped, we should turn the other cheek rather than take revenge or strike back. In addition, we should pray for our enemies and, if they are hungry or thirsty, feed and refresh them and thus assure them of our goodwill and desire to overcome evil with good. In short, we ought to do good, commending ourselves to every man's and woman's conscience, and, according to the law of Christ, do unto others as we would wish them to do unto us.

Mt 5.39
Rom 12.19–21

2 Cor 4.2

Mt 7.12

ARTICLE 15. [THE SWEARING OF OATHS]

Concerning the swearing of oaths, we believe and confess that our Lord Christ forbade it and taught his followers that they should not swear at all. Rather, they should let their yes be yes and no, no. From this we understand that all oaths, great or small, are prohibited. Instead, all our promises, commitments, and contracts, yes, also our statements and bearing of witness, ought to be confirmed only with our word—yes in what is yes, no in what is no— provided that at all times we keep our word and live faithfully as if we had confirmed and established it with an oath. And if we do this, we have confidence that no man, not even the magistrate, will have just reason to lay a heavier burden on our mind and conscience.

Mt 5.34–35
Jas 5.12

2 Cor 1.17–18

ARTICLE 16. [EXCOMMUNICATION OR SEPARATION FROM THE CHURCH]

We also believe and confess a ban, separation, and Christian punishment in the church for amendment and not for destruction: whereby the pure may be distinguished from the impure. In other words, if anyone, after he is enlightened, has attained knowledge of the truth, and has been received into the fellowship of the saints and afterward either willfully or out of presumption against God or otherwise falls back into the unfruitful works of darkness[a] by which he is separated from God— so that the kingdom of God is denied him—that such a person, after the matter is made public and sufficiently known in the church, may not remain in the congregation of the righteous. As an offensive member and public sinner he ought to be set aside, punished before all,[b] and purged as bad leaven:[c] this for his amendment and as an example and warning to others; also that the church may be kept pure and

Is 59.2

a. 1 Cor 5.5–6, 12; 1 Tm 5.20
b. 1 Tm 5.20; 1 Cor 5.6
c. 2 Cor 10.8, 13.10

free of scandals so that the name of the Lord be not dishonored and the church be not an offense to those who are without. Finally, a sinner should not be condemned along with the world but that he may be convinced in his heart and mind and again brought to contrition, repentance, and amendment of life.

Concerning brotherly reproof and exhortation and also the instruction of those who err, it is necessary to use all diligence and care in watching over them and admonishing them with all meekness with a view to their correction and amendment; and in case any should remain obstinate and unconverted, to reprove them as seems fit. In short, the church ought to put away from their company those who are evil—whether in doctrine or in life—but no other. Jas 5.19–20

Ti 3.10

1 Cor 5.12

ARTICLE 17. [THE SHUNNING OF THE EXCOMMUNICATED]

With regard to the withdrawal from or shunning of the separated, we believe and confess that, when someone has so far fallen away either by his wicked life or false doctrine so that he is estranged from God and as a consequence justly separated from and punished by the church, such a person must be shunned according to the doctrine of Christ and his apostles and avoided without partiality by all members of the church (especially by those to whom it is known). In eating and drinking and other similar fellowship such a person should be shunned and avoided so that one is not involved with his way of life or a partaker of his sins. This should be done so that the sinner may be ashamed, struck in his heart and conscience, and thus be induced to an amendment of his ways. Such a shunning, we believe, ought to be used in Christian moderation so that it may have the effect not of destroying but of healing the sinner. If he is in need, hungry, thirsty, naked, ill, or in any form of want, then we ought—according to the love and teaching of Christ and his apostles—to help and give him assistance. Otherwise, the shunning leads to ruin instead of correction or amendment. Such persons should not be considered enemies but should be admonished as brethren. Again, the purpose is to bring them to acknowledgment, contrition, and repentance of their sins in order that they may be reconciled to God and again received into the church. In this way love can have its way with them as is becoming.

1 Cor 5.9–11

2 Thes 3.14; Ti 3.10

2 Thes 3.14

ARTICLE 18. [THE RESURRECTION OF THE DEAD
AND THE LAST JUDGMENT]

As to the resurrection of the dead we believe and confess in keeping with Scripture that all men who have died[a] and fallen asleep shall be awakened, made alive, and Mt 22.30–31

a. Dn 12.12; Jb 19.26–27; Mt 25.31; Jn 5.28; 2 Cor 5.10; 1 Cor 15; Rv 12.4; 1 Thes 4.13

raised up on the last day by the incomprehensible power of God. These together with those who are then alive shall be changed at the sound of the last trumpet and appear before the judgment seat of Christ. There the good shall be separated from the evil so that everyone may receive in his own body according to his deeds whether they be good or evil. The good or the devout shall be taken up with Christ as the blessed, enter into life eternal, and receive that joy which no eye has seen nor ear heard to reign and triumph with Christ forever. On the other hand, the wicked or the ungodly shall be driven away as accursed and thrown into great darkness, into the eternal pains of hell, where in the words of Scripture the worm dieth not and the fire is not quenched. There they shall never have any hope, comfort, or redemption. May the Lord by his mercy make all of us fit and worthy that no such thing befall any of us but that we may take heed to ourselves and be diligent so that at that time we may be found before him in peace, without spot, and blameless. Amen.

These now, as briefly stated above, are the principal articles of our common Christian faith as in our church and among our people are taught and practiced. They are, according to our judgment, the only true Christian faith, which the apostles in their time believed and taught. Yes, they testified to this faith with their lives and confirmed it with their death; some of them sealed it with their blood. With them and all godly men and women we seek in our weakness to abide by the same in life and death that by the grace of the Lord with them we may obtain salvation.

It was decided that two exact copies, signed by us as principals of the meeting, should be kept as a matter of record—one to be retained here at Dordrecht and the other, at Amsterdam. Also, that all elders now present at this meeting should receive a copy to show at home. Furthermore, that each elder obtain a copy for the congregations he serves.

So, beloved fellow workers, brothers and sisters, and all companions in Christ, we trust that with this short, written explanation our efforts and work in this matter, carried out in love, will be understood. To this end we humbly pray and sincerely request that you will accept this from us (unworthy as we are) for the good and will follow the same in love and that you willingly and in good faith will let it serve you together for your deepest peace and betterment. So that in this way also, the God of peace will dwell in and abide with you and us together, according to his promise; and that the good work begun may continue to bring honor and glory to the Lord, that it may serve for the growth and upbuilding of his church. To this end and further in everything that is necessary and pleasing to him, the good and merciful God will help us and you, granting his gracious blessing and strengthening and approving our efforts that we together may be made worthy and able. Amen.

Marginal references:
1 Cor 2.9
Mk 9.44
Rv 14.11

We request, pray, and desire in all friendliness that everyone, and in particular those who receive our above-mentioned statement in their hands or obtain knowledge about it by way of seeing, hearing, or reading—and find they cannot accept, approve, or see through it in all its parts—that in such cases you still will always speak well of it to others. One should recall that it has been written: he who speaks well of a matter (and explains all with a good interpretation) such a one in turn is well spoken of. To recall also that God's Son has charged and commanded: "whatsoever ye would that men should do to you, do ye even so to them."   [Mt 7.12]

As notice, witness, and full confirmation of what was transacted and done here by the congregation and our countrymen together as stated above: Thus we the undersigned elders, ministers, and brethren as such and in the name of and in behalf of the request of this, our as now united congregation at this place, as also for ourselves and in behalf of each congregation, the same as our public and general Brotherly Union, Pacification, and Agreement, have endorsed and undersigned. Use it for your benefit. And hereby we commend you to God Almighty in his gracious keeping unto salvation. Sincere greetings with the everlasting peace of the Lord from all of us and from the congregation here. Amen.

Transacted and concluded in our united congregation in the town of Dordrecht, 21 April, Anno 1632. New Style. Farewell.

And was signed by

Dordrecht.

Isack de Coningh, and in behalf of our ministers, Ian Jacobs.

Middelburg.

Bastiaen Willemsen.

Ian Winckelmans.

Vlissingen.

Oillaert Willeborts.

By Iacob Pennen.

Lieven Marijness.

Amsterdam.

Tobias Govertsz.

Pieter Iansen Moijer.

Abraham Dirckxsz.

Haarlem.

Ian Doom.

Pieter Grijspeer.

Bommel.

Willem Iansen van Exselt.

Ghisiert Spiering.

Rotterdam.

Balten Centen Schoenmaker.

Michiel Michielsz.

Dordrecht.

By me, Hans Cobrijssen.

By me, Iacuis Terwen.

Claes Dircksen.

Mels Ghijsbaerts.

Aeriaen Cornelissoon.

From the Upper Country.

Peeter van Borsel.

Antonij Hansz.

Crefeld, ditto

Herman op den Graff.

Weylm Kreynen.

Zeeland.

Cornelis de Moir.

Isaac Claessen.

Haarlem.

Dirck Wouters Kolenkamp.

Pieter Ioosten.

Rotterdam.

Israel van Halmael.

Heyndrick Dircksz. Apeldoren.

Andies Lucken, de Jonghe.

Schiedam.

Cornelis Bom.

Lambrecht Paeldinck.

Leyden.

Mr. Christaen de Coninck.

Ian Weyns.

Blokzijl.

Claes Claessen.

Pieter Peters.

Zierkzee.

Anthuenis Cornelisz.

Pieter Iansen Timmerman.

Utrecht.

 Herman Segerts.

 Ian Hendricksen Hoochvelt.

 Daniel Lhorens.

Amsterdam.

 David ter Haer.

 Pieter Iansen van Singel.

Gorinchem.

 Iacob van der Heyde Sebrechts

 Ian Iansz. vande Cruysen.

Arnhem.

 Cornelijes Iansen.

 Derojck Rendersen.

Utrecht.

 Abraham Spronck.

 Willem van Broeckhuysen.

Confessions of Attempts at Reconciliation and Alliance

It was a source of consternation to the first generation of Reformation Protestants, and a source of glee and *Schadenfreude* to their Roman Catholic adversaries, that as soon as the Reformation began, it started to divide into several species of Protestantism. In 1530, at the very Diet of the Holy Roman Empire in Augsburg from which the premier Lutheran → *Augsburg Confession* takes its name, there were two other Protestant statements of faith, → *The Tetrapolitan Confession* and Ulrich Zwingli's → *Reckoning of the Faith* (*Fidei ratio*) that spoke to the assembled political and ecclesiastical authorities on behalf of their constituencies.

Beyond the obvious embarrassment that this fissiparous tendency occasioned in Protestant camps, everyone was, at least in principle, committed to preserving, or recovering, Christian unity: *The Augsburg Confession* was speaking for all the parties when it expressed the hope that "our differences may be reconciled, and we may be united in one, true religion, even as we are all under one Christ and should confess and contend for Christ."

The documents of such "confessing and contending for Christ" are the particularistic confessions that fill these volumes. But in addition, the confessional format likewise became the medium for articulating various attempts at reconciliation and alliance, either within or between the major divisions.

Some of these were strongly political in inspiration, coming out of the desire to form a common front and alliance, usually of Protestant princes and magistrates against Catholic powers. But by the nature of the case, they could not be "purely political" (if anything can): everyone's copy of the Gospels contained the prayer of Jesus Christ on the eve of his crucifixion (John 17.20), "that they may all be one, *ut omnes unum sint*." Out of the tension between that imperative and the imperative "to contend for the faith which was once for all delivered to the saints" (Jude 3) came the confessions that follow.

The Marburg Articles, 1529

At the invitation of Landgrave Philip of Hesse, Zwingli and Luther met at Marburg in October 1529 with the goal of achieving an alliance between the Reformed and Lutheran movements. Though a Lutheran, Philip had been influenced by reformers in Strasbourg and hoped to encourage understanding between those holding Zwinglian and Lutheran positions. He also had political reasons for this peacemaking role, however, because he was seeking allies among other Protestants against the Catholic Hapsburgs.

Luther and Melanchthon reluctantly agreed to meet with Zwingli, Oecolampadius, and Bucer. There are several eyewitness reports of the discussions, which took place over four days (1–4 October 1529).[1] Some degree of accord was reached on the doctrine of the Trinity, the nature of Christ and the Holy Spirit, the sacrament of baptism, justification by faith, good works, confession, and the role of secular government. But on the central issue of the eucharist, the two sides could not agree. Luther maintained the literal meaning of "hoc est corpus meum" (this is my body; Luke 22.19) which he had written in chalk on the table at the start of the colloquy, and throughout the discussions he remained steadfast on the concept of the real presence. Zwingli argued that "est" means "signifies" and claimed that Christ spoke the words of institution in a figurative sense. He offered as evidence the fact that Jesus could not be "at the right hand of the Father" and in the host at the same time. He also gave examples of Christ's propensity for metaphors, as in the phrase "I am the vine" (John 15.1). When he cited John 6.63, a favorite proof text of sacramentarians in which Christ says, "It is the spirit that quickens; the flesh profits nothing: the words that I speak unto you, they are spirit, and they are life," Zwingli taunted Luther, saying that this passage would break his neck. But Luther only joked that necks were not so easily broken in Hesse as in Zurich.

Although the discussions devolved into insult-hurling at times, Philip of Hesse prevailed on both sides to draw up an account of their agreements. Luther drafted the articles, outlining fifteen fundamental tenets of faith.[2] Amazingly, the

1. These sources include letters by Luther and Melanchthon and Zwingli's notes, as well as accounts by Andreas Osiander, Johannes Brenz, Rudolf Collin (a friend of Zwingli), and Caspar Hedio of Strasbourg. An attempt to reconstruct the colloquy from these and other sources can be found in WA 30/3:110–59. For a similar account in English, see Sasse 1959, 223–69.

2. These articles later became the basis for *The Schwabach Articles,* which in turn influenced the text of → *The Augsburg Confession.*

participants were able to agree on fourteen of the fifteen articles. Even in the fifteenth article on the eucharist, they expressed some common beliefs, including the view that the sacrament is not a sacrifice, support of communion in both kinds, and the necessity of spiritual eating. But on the nature of presence of the body and blood of Christ, the differences were too great to be resolved. Nonetheless, an irenic tone prevails: "At present we are not agreed as to whether the true body and blood are bodily present in the bread and wine, nevertheless each party should show Christian love to the other, so far as conscience can permit, and both should fervently pray Almighty God that he, by his Spirit, would confirm us in the right understanding. Amen."

The two sides drifted further apart after the colloquies, however, and remained polemical in their opposition to one another. After Zwingli's death, Reformed and Lutheran parties came together again in 1536, at Bucer's urging, to draw up another alliance, → *The Wittenberg Concord*. And later, under Heinrich Bullinger, Zwingli's successor in Zurich, the extreme sacramentarian position was sufficiently modified to allow for an agreement with Calvin in → *The Consensus Tigurinus* of 1549.

Edition: *WA* 30/3:160–71.

Translation: Sasse 1959, 269–72.

Note: We give the German text from the Kassel manuscript (K) as signed by the participants. There is another signed manuscript in Zurich (Z). Both are given in *WA* 30/3:160–71, as is the text of a 1529 Wittenberg imprint (D) that may reflect a lost manuscript mentioned by Osiander. See *WA* 30/3: 101–6.

Literature: Bainton 1949; Brecht 1985–93, 1:325–34; *Chr Trad* 4:151; Congar 1985; Davies 1979; Delius 1983; Gäbler 1983b; Green 1976; Hausammann 1966; Miller 1982; *OER* 3:2–5 (May); Sasse 1959, 187–268; Snavely 1994; *TRE* 1:106–22 (Staedtke); *WA* 30:92–109; Wright 1985.

The Marburg Articles, 1529

[ARTICLE 1]

That we on both sides unanimously believe and hold that there is only one true natural God, Maker of all creatures, and that this same God is one in essence and nature and triune in the persons, namely Father, Son, and Holy Ghost, as it was decreed in the Council of Nicaea, and is sung and read in the Nicene Creed by the entire Christian church throughout the world.

[ARTICLE 2]

We believe that not the Father, nor the Holy Ghost, but the Son of God the Father, true and natural God himself, became man through the working of the Holy Ghost, without the agency of male seed, born of the pure Virgin Mary, complete in body and soul as another man, but without sin.

[ARTICLE 3]

That this Son of God and Mary, undivided in person, Jesus Christ, was crucified for us, died, was buried, rose from the dead, ascended into heaven, sitteth at the right hand of God, Lord over all creatures, and will come to judge the quick and the dead.

[ARTICLE 4]

We believe that original sin is innate, and inherited by us from Adam, and is such a sin as condemns all men. And if Jesus Christ had not come to help us by his death and life, we would of necessity have died eternally and could not have entered God's kingdom and salvation.

[ARTICLE 5]

We believe that we are saved from this sin and from all other sins, as well as from eternal death, if we believe in this Son of God, Jesus Christ, who died for us, and that beyond this faith no works, station, or order can make us free from any sin.

[ARTICLE 6]

That this faith is a gift of God which we cannot obtain by any preceding works or merit, nor acquire by our own strength, but the Holy Ghost gives and creates this faith in our hearts, as it pleases him, when we hear the gospel or word of Christ.

[ARTICLE 7]

That this faith is our righteousness before God, on account of which God reckons and regards us as righteous, godly, and holy, without all works and merit, and
thereby delivers us from sin, death, and hell, and receives us into grace and saves
us, for the sake of his Son, in whom we accordingly believe and thereby enjoy and
partake of righteousness, life, and all possessions. Therefore, all monastic life and
vows, when they are reckoned as aids to salvation, are altogether condemned.

[ARTICLE 8]

That the Holy Ghost normally gives this faith or his gift to no one without preaching, or the oral word, or the gospel of Christ preceding, but by and with such oral
Rom 10[.17]   word he works and creates faith where and in whom it pleases him.

[ARTICLE 9]

That holy baptism is a sacrament that has been instituted by God as an aid to such
[Mt 28.19]   faith, and because God's command "Go ye, baptize," and God's promise "He that
[Mk 16.16]   believes" are therein, it is not a mere empty sign or watchword among Christians,
but rather a sign and work of God by which our faith grows and through which we
are regenerated to eternal life.

[ARTICLE 10]

That such faith, when we have been reckoned and made righteous and holy by it,
by the efficacy of the Holy Ghost exercises good works through us, namely, to love
our neighbor, to pray to God, and to suffer all persecution.

[ARTICLE 11]

That confession or the seeking of counsel from one's pastor or neighbor should indeed be unconstrained and free, but nevertheless is very helpful to consciences that
are distressed, troubled, or burdened with sins, or that have fallen into error, especially on account of the absolution or consolation of the gospel, which is the true
absolution.

[ARTICLE 12]

That all magistrates and secular laws, courts, and ordinances, wherever they are, are
a truly good estate, and are not forbidden, as some papists and Anabaptists teach
and hold. On the contrary, that a Christian who is born or called thereto, can certainly be saved through faith in Christ, just as in the estate of father or mother,
husband or wife, and so on.

[ARTICLE 13]

What is called tradition or human ordinance in spiritual or ecclesiastical matters, provided they do not obviously contradict God's word, may freely be kept or abolished according to (the needs of) the people with whom we deal, in order to prevent unnecessary offense in practicing love toward the weak and to preserve peace. Also that the doctrine forbidding marriage to priests is a doctrine of the devil.   [1 Tm 4.1–3]

[ARTICLE 14]

That baptism of infants is right, and that they are thereby received into God's grace and into Christendom.

[ARTICLE 15]

We all believe and hold concerning the supper of our dear Lord Jesus Christ that both species should be used according to the institution of Christ; also that the mass is not a work whereby one obtains grace for another, dead or living; also that the sacrament of the altar is a sacrament of the true body and blood of Jesus Christ, and that the spiritual partaking of this body and blood is especially necessary for every true Christian. In like manner that the use of the sacrament, like the word, is given and ordained by Almighty God in order that weak consciences may thereby be excited to faith by the Holy Ghost. And although at present we are not agreed as to whether the true body and blood are bodily present in the bread and wine, nevertheless each party should show Christian love to the other, so far as conscience can permit, and both should fervently pray Almighty God that he, by his Spirit, would confirm us in the right understanding. Amen.

    Martinus Luther
    Justus Jonas
    Philippus Melanchthon
    Andreas Osiander
    Stephanus Agricola
    Johannes Brentius
    Johannes Oecolampadius
    Huldrychus Zwinglius
    Martinus Butzerus
    Caspar Hedio

The Wittenberg Concord, 1536

The Wittenberg Concord attempted to bridge the differences between the Reformed and Lutheran Churches. The primary goal was to reach a common understanding, or at least a compromise, on the nature of Christ's presence in the eucharist, the very issue that had kept the two sides apart at Marburg in 1529 and that remained the chief obstacle to Protestant union in the sixteenth century and beyond.

Martin Bucer, the reformer from Strasbourg who had participated in → *The Marburg Articles* and devoted much of his life to conciliatory efforts, was the driving force behind the negotiation of *The Wittenberg Concord*. For his willingness to compromise, Bucer has been labeled a political opportunist and a fence-straddler by both his contemporaries and modern scholars. Heinrich Bullinger even mockingly coined the word *bucerisare*, meaning "to vacillate."[1] But Bucer's writings and actions show him to have been consistent in his belief that Christians could and should find common ground. As he wrote in 1530 when drafting → *The Tetrapolitan Confession*:

> It is enough for Christians that they be assured by the Holy Spirit and free from all doubt that God, through our Lord Jesus Christ, wishes eternally to be a Father to them. . . . This faith produces children and heirs of God; and, therefore, it must be maintained. Beyond that, even those who already are holy and pious may be burdened with many grievous errors. . . . No one, no matter how holy he may be, lives here on earth without error, and one often errs just when one is most certain of something. . . . One must always keep in view the main points: faith and love. Where these are found, do not doubt that this is the Spirit of God. Thus we must acknowledge as brothers and comrades in Christ all in whom we perceive true faith and love, regardless of their errors and flaws.[2]

Given his adiaphorism, it is not surprising that Bucer was a lifelong friend of Melanchthon.

1. See Pauck 1950, 96.
2. From Ratschlag A. Quoted, in part, from English translation in Brady 1973, 188. For the complete text in original German, see Bucer 1969, 3:325, 327.

The *Wittenberg Concord* was negotiated by Bucer and Wolfgang Capito (1478–1541), representing the southern Germans (with hopes of extending the agreement to their Swiss brethren), and Luther and Melanchthon in May 1536 in Wittenberg. Melanchthon drafted the text, which comprises three sections: part 1 on the eucharist was signed by twenty-one ministers who were present; parts 2 and 3 deal with the less contentious issues of baptism and absolution. Both sides made compromises. The Reformed party agreed to a definition of the eucharist that did not state clearly its function as a "memorial," and they let stand the view that even the unworthy truly receive the body and blood of Christ. Because "unworthy" was not defined, Bucer could later divide the unworthy into two categories in his interpretation of the concord: unworthy communicants whose faith, though deficient, allows them to receive the sacrament; and the completely unworthy, who receive only bread and wine (a distinction not made in the concord, and not acceptable to Lutherans).[3] In the description of the eucharist, Luther allowed the wording: "that *with* [*cum*] the bread and wine the body and blood are truly and substantially present, offered, and received," a change Melanchthon would also make in the *Variata* edition of → *The Augsburg Confession*.[4] The success of the agreement on the eucharist is in its careful phrasing, which allowed each side to agree with the words while holding differing views of their meaning. In the concluding section, however, *The Augsburg Confession* (obviously the *Invariata* at this date) is cited as a standard of doctrine, imposing on the document a distinctly Lutheran character.[5]

The concord's Lutheran flavor resulted in its being rejected in Ulm, in Constance, and by the Swiss Reformers in general.[6] The eucharistic definition was later incorporated into → *The Formula of Concord* in 1577,[7] a sign of its orthodoxy. In the end, the connections forged by *The Wittenberg Concord* led not to Protestant union but to Strasbourg's adoption of Lutheranism, officially declared in 1598.

Edition: *CR* 3:75–81.

Translation: Jacobs 1893, 2:283–88.

---

3. Bucer's position on the "unworthy" is basically Zwinglian. For the Strasbourg position on this issue, see → *The Tetrapolitan Confession* 20.

4. *The Augsburg Confession* 10.1 leaves out the preposition.

5. Bucer had already subscribed personally to *The Augsburg Confession* in 1532.

6. It was accepted by Strasbourg, Frankfurt, Worms, Landau, Weißenburg, Esslingen, Augsburg, Memmingen, Kempten, and Reutlingen.

7. *Solid Declaration* 7.12–16.

Literature: Backus 1990; Bornkamm 1952; Brecht 1983, 507–14; Eells 1931, 190–224, 471–77; Göszwein 1886; Greschat 1985; Hazlett 1994; Kittelson and Schurb 1986; Köhler 1953, 2:432–55; Pauck 1950, 73–83; Poll 1954; Schiess 1908–12, 2:308; Stephens 1970; Stupperich 1938.

The Wittenberg Concord, 1536

Formula of Concord between the Wittenberg doctors and the doctors of the states of the empire in Upper Germany concerning the presence of the body and blood of Christ in the Lord's supper. Written by the order and request of both parties by Philipp Melanchthon, in the year of Christ 1536.

We have heard Dr. Bucer explaining his opinion, and that of others who have been with him, concerning the sacrament of Christ's body and blood, in this way:

1.

We confess that, according to the words of Irenaeus, the eucharist consists of two things, an earthly and a heavenly. They hold and teach, therefore, that with the bread and wine the body and blood of Christ are truly and substantially present, offered and received.

2.

And although they deny that transubstantiation occurs, and do not hold that a local inclusion in the bread occurs, or any lasting connection without the use of the sacrament, yet they concede that, by the sacramental union, the bread is the body of Christ; that is, they hold that when the bread is held out the body of Christ is at the same time present and truly tendered. For, apart from use, when it is laid by in the pyx or displayed in processions, as occurs among the papists, they hold that the body of Christ is not present.

3.

Then, too, they hold that this institution of the sacrament is efficacious in the church, and depends upon the worth neither of minister nor communicant. Wherefore, as Paul says that the unworthy also eat, so they hold that the body and blood of the Lord are truly extended also to the unworthy, and that the unworthy receive, where the words and institution of Christ are retained. But these partake for judgment, as Paul says, because they abuse the sacrament when they use it without re- [1 Cor 11.27] pentance and faith. For it has been set forth for the purpose of witnessing that the benefits of Christ are applied to those, and that they become members of Christ and are washed by the blood of Christ, who repent and sustain themselves by faith in Christ.

Since, however, only a few of us have met, and it is necessary on both sides to refer this matter to other preachers and superiors, it is not yet allowable for us to come to terms concerning an agreement before we have referred it to the rest.

Since, however, all profess that in all articles they want to hold and teach according to the Confession and Apology of the princes professing the gospel, we are especially anxious that harmony be sanctioned and established. And we have the hope that, if the rest, on both sides, would so agree, there would be thorough harmony.

Dr. Wolfgang Capito, minister of the church at Strasbourg.

M. Martin Bucer, minister of the church at Strasbourg.

Lic. Martin Fecht, minister of the word of the church at Ulm.

Lic. Jacob Other, minister of the church at Esslingen.

M. Boniface Lycosthenes [Wolfhardt], minister of the word of the church at Augsburg.

Wolfgang Musculus, minister of the word of the church at Augsburg.

M. Gervasius Scholasticus, pastor of the church at Memmingen.

M. John Bernhardi, minister of the church at Frankfort.

Martin Germani, minister of the church at Fürfeldt.

M. Matthew Aulbert, pastor of the church of Reutlingen.

John Sebradinus, deacon of Reutlingen.

Martin Luther, Wittenberg doctor.

Dr. Justus Jonas.

Dr. Caspar Cruciger.

Dr. John Bugenhagen, Pomeranus.

Philipp Melanchthon.

Justus Menius, of Eisenach.

Frederick Myconius, of Gotha.

Dr. Urban Regius, superintendent of the churches of the duchy of Luneburg.

George Spalatin, pastor of the church at Altenburg.

Dionysius Melander, minister of the church at Cassel; and many others.

4. OF BAPTISM

Of the baptism of infants, all without doubt agreed that it is necessary that infants be baptized. For since the promise of salvation pertains also to infants, and does not pertain to those who are outside the church, it is necessary that it be applied to infants by the ministry and to add them to the members of the church. And since [Mt 18.13-15] of such infants as are in the church it is said: "It is not the will of your Father that

one of them perish,"it is manifest that through baptism there come to infants the [Mt 18.14]
forgiveness of original sin and the gift of the Holy Ghost, who is efficacious in them
according to their measure. For we reject the error of those who imagine that infants please God and are saved without any action of God, since Christ says clearly:
"Except a man be born of water and of the Spirit, he cannot enter into the kingdom [Jn 3.5]
of God." Although, therefore, we do not understand of what nature that action of
God in infants is, nevertheless it is certain that in them new and holy movements [Lk 1.41]
are wrought, just as in John, when in the womb, new movements occurred. For although we must not imagine that infants understand, nevertheless these movements
and inclinations to believe Christ and love God are in a measure like the movements
of faith and love. This is what we say when we say that infants have faith. For we
speak thus that it may be understood that infants cannot become holy and be saved
without a divine action in them.

Although, therefore, it is the custom in some places that baptism be publicly administered on certain days, nevertheless men should be taught that if there be
danger to the life of infants they have them meanwhile baptized, and that ministers
ought to grant baptism to such.

5. OF ABSOLUTION

Concerning absolution, all desire that private absolution also be preserved in the
church, both on account of the consolation to consciences and because the discipline is very useful to the church, in which men are heard privately, so that the
inexperienced may be instructed. For, indeed, the more uncultivated have need of
such conversation and examination. But for this reason the old confession and enumeration of offenses are neither to be approved nor required, but this conversation
is preserved, because of the absolution and institution.

All subscribed as above. Done the second day after *Exaudi*, 29 May 1536.

The Zurich Agreement (Consensus Tigurinus), 1549

More than any other issue, the interpretation of the eucharist prevented the establishment of a unified Protestant Reformation. And yet, many reformers found that their views on this crucial doctrine of the faith changed and evolved over time. In *The Zurich Agreement,* Calvin, representing the French-speaking Protestants, came to an agreement on the nature of the eucharist with Heinrich Bullinger and the German-speaking Protestants of Switzerland. The statement of consensus was possible only because Bullinger had developed his sacramentarianism beyond the basic Zwinglian view and because Calvin, though closer to Luther in his understanding, was willing to make concessions, at least in his theological terminology, in order to accommodate the doctrinal concerns of the Zurich reformers.

After a lengthy correspondence between Bullinger and Calvin, negotiations began in earnest in November 1548, when Bullinger sent Calvin twenty-four propositions on the Lord's supper.[1] Although critical of his sacramentarianism, Calvin continued the discussions with Bullinger by letter and finally arrived in Zurich—unexpectedly—with Guillaume Farel in late May 1549, hoping to conclude the agreement. Calvin presented his twenty articles on the sacrament, which he had recently submitted to the Synod of Bern, as a basis for the consensus.[2] Working with that document and Bullinger's twenty-four propositions, the representatives from Geneva and Zurich hammered out *The Zurich Agreement*. It was eventually accepted, albeit unenthusiastically and with some changes, by Bern, Lausanne, and Basel, thereby achieving its aim of uniting the two Reformed traditions of Switzerland.

It is a minimalist document, not reflecting the full eucharistic doctrine of either Bullinger or Calvin, but rather emphasizing the core beliefs on which both sides could agree. In brief, they were united in their rejection of transubstantiation and their opposition to the real presence in a Catholic or Lutheran sense; they maintained that the sacraments themselves do not confer grace; and they repudiated any veneration of the eucharist.

Although Calvin claimed that he and Bullinger put together the final form of the agreement in a mere two hours,[3] there had been struggles over language and meaning before Calvin's visit. For greater theological clarity they composed

---

1. CR 35 (= *Calvini Opera 7*), 693–700.
2. CR 35:701–8.
3. In a letter to Myconius from December 1549; see CR 41:457 (no. 1309).

the agreement in Latin, and its precise terminology was the key to its success. For example, the Zwinglian notion of the sacraments as signs or symbols is stressed throughout, but the idea that these symbols may serve as "implements" or "organs" of grace for the faithful is also expressed. Thus, the instrumentalist view of Calvin is represented, but modified somewhat by the substitution of "implements" (*organa*) for Calvin's preferred "instruments" (*instrumenta*).[4] Other linguistic solutions include a statement that Christ is present (*praesens*) in the sacraments, but only *per spiritum* (through the Spirit), and the ingenious use of the preposition *in* to express the view that "Christ communicates himself to Christians in the supper [*in coena*]." Calvin surely understood this as "through the supper" (with the eucharist as an agent of grace), whereas Bullinger and his followers could interpret the phrase more symbolically as "during the supper" (with the eucharist serving only to remind the faithful of Christ's sacrifice).[5]

The Zurich Agreement was successful as a unifying document for Swiss Protestantism, although each branch of the Reformed tradition tended (and tends) to put more or less emphasis on the symbolic or the instrumental nature of the sacraments depending on its heritage. Not surprisingly, *The Zurich Agreement* put an end to any discussions of accord between Calvinists and Lutherans.

After the text had undergone some alterations to satisfy the cities of Bern, Basel, and Lausanne, and some additions (articles 5 and 23) to ease Calvin's mind about the concessions he had made, it was published in 1551 almost simultaneously in Zurich (at the press of Rudolf Wysenbach) and Geneva (by Jean Crispin). Later the same year it appeared in German and French translations.

Edition: Calvin 1926–59, 2:246–58.

Translation: Bunting 1966, 48–61.

Note: A preface and conclusion agreed upon in Zurich were soon replaced by a letter from Calvin at the beginning of the document and one from the

---

4. Again and again in his letters to Calvin, Bullinger insists that the sacraments are testimonies or signs of God's grace, but not instruments. The use of *organa* secured the success of the agreement, although critics on both sides expressed dissatisfaction: Zwinglians said it smacked of instrumentalism, and Calvinists thought that sacramentarianism was implied in the absence of the word *instrumentum*. See Bunting 1966, 76–77, and Rorem 1994.

5. See Rorem 1988 and 1994 for a discussion of the language and theology of *The Zurich Agreement*.

pastors of Zurich at the end. It was in this final form that the first edition appeared in 1551.

Literature: Bizer 1962; Bunting 1966; *Chr Trad* 4:189–95; Gäbler 1979; George 1988; Kolfhaus 1909; Mueller 1949; Pruett 1975; Rorem 1988, 1994; Sanders 1992; Strasser 1949; *TRE* 7:75–87 (Büsser), 189–92 (Gäbler).

The Zurich Agreement (Consensus Tigurinus), 1549

Agreement of the Ministers of the Church of Zurich and of John Calvin, Minister of the Church of Geneva, on the Subject of the Sacrament

John Calvin sends greetings to his well-loved colleagues and respected brothers, most excellent men and faithful servants of Jesus Christ, the pastors and doctors of the church at Zurich.

Although I often discuss the same subject with you, yet I do not think I need fear being considered irksome by you. When we are in agreement, you can hardly disapprove of what I do. As for the suggestion that I am a little too keen, I am urged on by the earnest pleadings of good men.

I have already warned you on a number of occasions, not without cause, that many are offended because I seem to hold some view of the sacraments other than your own. They justly reverence your church which is adorned with so many excellent gifts: and they also defer somewhat to our church and perhaps even to me too as an individual. And so they want to be assisted in learning holy doctrine from our writings in order that no appearance of division may retard their own progress. For this reason, I thought there could be no fitter remedy for removing this scandal than a friendly conference for the purpose of testifying to our agreement. You know that it was in the pursuit of this end that I came to you. And our venerable colleague, William Farel, that indefatigable soldier of Christ, did not refuse to come with me. He was, moreover, the prompter of my visit and my guide. On both sides then we can now certainly and confidently affirm that we are in agreement. However because I am unable to persuade all of this fact, it greatly grieves me that there are some who remain in doubt or anxiety. And it is their peace of mind that I would rather consider. Hence, as I said at the beginning, I do not think that I am acting out of season when I urge that there should be some public testimony of the agreement we have now concluded.

In fact, I thought it would be worthwhile briefly to collect and set in order the heads upon which we have conferred, so that if my plan approves itself to you, each may discern for himself, in tabular form, what was done and transacted between us. I feel sure that you will bear witness that I have recounted in good faith the details of our discussions which I now set down. For the rest, I hope that Christian readers will notice that we (that is Farel and myself) have desired, with a zeal like yours, a sincere clarity of expression free from all pretense and guile. At the same time I would have it understood that this work contains nothing which has not been officially approved by our colleagues who serve Christ in the republic of Geneva or the canton of Neuchâtel. Farewell, most excellent men and brethren, to whom I owe heartfelt respect. May the Lord continue to direct you by his Spirit for the building up of the church; and may he bless your labors. Geneva, 1 August 1549.

The Articles of the Agreement Follow

[1.] THE WHOLE SPIRITUAL GOVERNMENT OF THE CHURCH LEADS US TO CHRIST.

Since Christ is the end of the law, and knowledge of him comprehends, in itself, the sum total of the gospel, there is no doubt that the whole spiritual government of the church aims to bring us to Christ: for it is through him alone that a man comes to God, who is the ultimate end of a blessed life. And so whoever draws away from this in the slightest point will never be able to speak rightly or appositely of any of God's ordinances.

[2.] THE TRUE KNOWLEDGE OF THE SACRAMENTS FROM THE KNOWLEDGE OF CHRIST.

Since the sacraments are appendixes to the gospel, one can only speak fittingly and usefully of their nature, force, office, and fruit when one starts from Christ. And one is not only to touch lightly upon the name of Christ, but one is to hold true to the purpose for which he was given to us by the Father and to those good things which he has brought us.

[3.] THE NATURE OF THE KNOWLEDGE OF CHRIST.

Thus it is to be maintained that Christ, being the eternal Son of God of the same glory and essence with the Father, has taken upon himself our flesh to bring to us, by right of adoption, what belonged to him by nature; namely, that we may be sons of God. This happens when we, engrafted by faith into the body of Christ and that by virtue of the Holy Spirit, are first accounted just by a free imputation of righteousness and then are regenerated into new life, whereby being formed again in the image of our heavenly Father, we renounce the old man.

[4.] CHRIST AS PRIEST: CHRIST AS KING.

Thus we have to consider Christ in his flesh as priest, who expiated our sins by the unique sacrifice of his own death. It is he who has put away all our iniquities by his obedience, who has acquired for us perfect righteousness and who now intercedes for us to give us access to God. He must be reckoned too as an expiatory victim by which God is reconciled to the world. He is also to be reckoned a brother who has made us blessed sons of God who were once miserable sons of Adam. He is also to be reckoned as a repairer who reforms whatever is vicious in us by the virtue of his Spirit, so that we may cease to live after the world and the flesh and so that God himself may abide in us. He must be reckoned as king, who enriches us with every kind of good thing, who rules and protects us by his power, who provides us with spiritual weapons that we may stand unconquered against the world and the devil, who frees us from all harm and who governs and guides us by the scepter of his mouth. And he is to be so reckoned in all his qualities that he may bring us to himself as true God and to the Father, until that which will be at the end is fulfilled; namely, until God is all in all.   [1 Cor 15.28]

[5.] HOW CHRIST COMMUNICATES HIMSELF TO US.
Moreover, in order that Christ may exhibit himself to us in this way and produce these effects in us, we must be made one with him and grow together into his body. For he does not pour out his life into us unless he is our head from which the whole body, compacted and connected through every joint of supply, makes for the increase of each member of the body by proportion according to his working.[1]   [Eph 4.15]

[6.] SPIRITUAL COMMUNION. THE SACRAMENTS INSTITUTED.
This spiritual communion which we have with the Son of God, when he lives in us by his Spirit, makes every believer a partaker of all the blessings which reside in him. To testify to this, the preaching of the gospel was instituted and the use of the sacraments was entrusted to us, namely the sacraments of holy baptism and the holy supper.

[7.] THE ENDS OF THE SACRAMENTS.
The ends of the sacraments are that they may be marks and badges of Christian profession and of our community or brotherhood, to incite us to thanksgiving and exercises of faith and godly living and to be contracts binding us to this. But the end which is first among the others is that through them God may testify, represent, and seal his grace to us. For although they signify nothing that is not announced by the word, yet it is a great benefit that there are cast before our eyes, as it were,

---

1. This article was missing in the original versions of *The Consensus Tigurinus*. It was included at the request of Calvin and with the agreement of Bullinger. See *CR* 41:305 (1211).

living pictures which influence our senses in a deeper way, as if leading up to the thing itself; while they recall to our memory the death of Christ and all his benefits so that our faith may better be exercised. It is also a great benefit that what God has pronounced with his mouth, is confirmed and ratified as if by seals.

[8.] THE LORD TRULY PRESENTS WHAT THE SACRAMENTS TRULY FIGURE. THANKSGIVING.

Since the testimonies and seals, which God has given us of his grace, are true; there can be no doubt that God grants within us by his Spirit that which the sacraments figure to our eyes and other senses. That is: that we may receive Christ, as the fountain of all good, both that we may be reconciled to God by means of his death and renewed by the Spirit to holiness of life, and that we may obtain righteousness and finally salvation. At the same time we give thanks for these benefits once exhibited on the cross, which we now perceive daily by faith.[2]

[9.] THE SIGNS AND THE THINGS SIGNIFIED ARE DISTINCT.

Therefore although we draw a distinction, as we must, between the signs and the things signified, yet we do not disjoin the truth from the signs. But we acknowledge that all who embrace in faith the promises there offered, receive Christ spiritually with his spiritual gifts, and even those who for a long time have been partakers of Christ continue and renew that communion.

[10.] IT IS PRINCIPALLY THE PROMISE THAT IS TO BE REGARDED IN THE SACRAMENTS.

One must not look to the bare signs but rather to the promise attached to them. Inasmuch, therefore, as our faith profits from the promise offered, so that force and efficacy of which we speak displays itself. Thus the element of water, bread, or wine by no means offers us Christ, nor makes us possessors of his spiritual gifts. Rather, one must look at the promise, whose office it is to lead us to Christ by the true way of faith, which makes us partakers of Christ.

2. This clause originally read: "and truly perceived by us through faith." It was changed at the request of Calvin; see *CR* 41:306 (1211), "afterwards I noticed that the unevenness of the work could be mitigated somewhat in this way: *et quae quotidie fide percipimus*. Thus the meaning will be more complete."

[11.] WE ARE NOT TO GAZE IN BEWILDERMENT
AT THE ELEMENTS.

This defeats the error of those who gaze in bewilderment at the elements and attach
to them their confidence of salvation. For the sacraments, separated from Christ,
are nothing but empty masks: yet in them all a voice clearly resounds, telling us to
hold fast to none other than Christ alone and to seek the grace of salvation nowhere
else.

[12.] THE SACRAMENTS ACHIEVE NOTHING OF THEMSELVES.
EVERY SAVING ACT IS TO BE ATTRIBUTED TO GOD ALONE.

Besides, if any good thing is bestowed upon us through the sacraments, it is not
because of any inherent virtue, not even if you understand by that the promise by
which they are distinguished. For it is God alone who works by his Spirit. And although he uses the ministry of the sacraments, he neither infuses his own power into
them nor does he derogate in any way from the efficacy of his Spirit: but according
to our ignorance, he uses them as helps, yet so that all the power remains with him
alone.

[13.] GOD USES THE INSTRUMENT, BUT ONLY IN SUCH
A WAY THAT ALL THE VIRTUE IS HIS.

And so, as Paul warns us, he who sows or waters is nothing, but it is God alone who
gives the increase. The same must be said of the sacraments, that they are nothing,   [1 Cor 3.7]
because they will profit nothing unless God in all things makes them effective. They
are indeed organs by which God acts efficaciously, when he so pleases; yet in such
a way that the whole work of our salvation must be ascribed to him alone.

[14.]

We conclude therefore that it is Christ alone who truly baptizes within and who
in the supper makes us partakers of himself. In brief, it is he who fulfills what the
sacraments figure, and he uses these aids in such a way that the whole effect rests
in his Spirit.

[15.] HOW THE SACRAMENTS CONFIRM.

In this way the sacraments are sometimes called seals, and are said to nourish, confirm, and promote faith: and yet in the proper sense the Spirit alone is the seal,
inasmuch as he is the one who begins and perfects faith. For all these attributes
of the sacraments take an inferior place, so that not even the smallest portion of

our salvation may be transferred from the single author of it, to the creatures or elements.

[16.] NOT ALL PARTAKERS IN THE SACRAMENT RECEIVE THE THING ITSELF.

Besides, we are careful to teach that God does not exert his power indiscriminately in all who receive the sacraments, but only in the elect. For as he only illuminates into faith those whom he has foreordained to life; so by the secret virtue of his Spirit, he works that the elect may receive what the sacraments offer.

[17.] THE SACRAMENTS DO NOT CONFER GRACE.

By this doctrine, that fiction of the sophists is refuted which teaches that the sacraments of the new law confer grace on all who do not interpose the obstacle of mortal sin. For besides the fact that nothing is received in the sacraments except by faith, it is also necessary to hold that the grace of God is certainly not so tied to them that whoever has the sign receives the thing itself. For the signs are administered to the reprobate as well as to the elect, but the reality only reaches the latter.

[18.] THE GIFTS OF GOD ARE OFFERED TO ALL BUT IT IS THE FAITHFUL WHO RECEIVE THEM.

It is quite certain that Christ, with his gifts, is offered communely to all, and that the truth of God is not overthrown by the unfaithfulness of men: the sacraments always retain their power, but all are not capable of Christ and his gifts. And so on God's part, nothing is changed; but as for men, each receives according to the measure of his faith.

[19.] THE FAITHFUL COMMUNICATE IN CHRIST BOTH BEFORE AND OUTSIDE THE USE OF THE SACRAMENTS.

And as the use of the sacraments is no more profitable to the unfaithful than if they abstained, yet is rather destructive to them: so on the other hand even outside the use of the sacraments the reality which is figured remains firm for the faithful. Thus the sins of Paul were washed away by baptism, although they had already been washed before baptism. Likewise for Cornelius, baptism was the laver of re-

[Acts 10.44–48]   generation, although he had already received the Holy Spirit. Thus in the supper Christ communicates himself to us, although he has imparted himself to us before and dwells within us forever. For since all are commanded to examine themselves,

[1 Cor 11.28]   it follows that faith is required of all before they approach the sacrament. And faith cannot exist without Christ; but inasmuch as faith is confirmed and increased by the sacraments, the gifts of God are confirmed in us and so, in a manner of speaking, Christ grows in us and we in him.

[20.] THE GRACE IS NOT SO TIED TO THE ACTION OF THE SACRAMENTS THAT THE FRUIT OF THEM MAY NOT BE RECEIVED SOMETIME AFTER THE ACTION.

Moreover the benefit which we receive from the sacraments ought not to be restricted to the time at which they are administered to us, as though the visible sign, when it is offered, brought with it at that very moment the grace of God. For those who were baptized in first infancy God regenerates in childhood or at the start of adolescence or even sometimes in old age. So the benefit of baptism stretches through the whole course of life, because the promise contained within it lives forever. And sometimes it can happen that the use of the holy supper, which in the action itself profits very little because of our thoughtlessness or slowness of heart, yet afterwards bears its fruit.

[21.] THE IDEA OF A LOCAL PRESENCE IS TO BE REJECTED.

It is particularly necessary to reject every idea of a local presence. For as the signs are present in this world and are perceived with the eyes and touched with the hands, so Christ, as man, is nowhere but in heaven and is to be sought in no other way than by the mind and the understanding of faith. For this reason it is a perverse and impious superstition to enclose him under elements of this world.

[22.] AN EXPOSITION OF THE WORDS OF THE LORD'S SUPPER: THIS IS MY BODY.

We reject therefore those ridiculous interpreters who insist on what they call the precise literal sense of the solemn words of the supper—This is my body, this is my blood. For without question we hold that they are to be taken figuratively, so that the bread and wine are said to be that which they signify. And it ought not to be thought new or insolent that by metonymy the name of the thing signified is transferred to the sign, since in the Scriptures the same modes of expression occur, and in speaking in this way we affirm nothing which is not prominent in the most ancient and famous writers of the church.

[23.] CONCERNING THE EATING OF CHRIST'S FLESH.

Because Christ feeds our souls through faith by virtue of his Spirit, by the eating of his flesh and the drinking of his blood which are here figured, it is not therefore to be understood as though there was an intermingling or transfusion of substance.

But we draw life from the flesh once offered in sacrifice and the blood poured out for expiation.[3]

[24.] AGAINST TRANSUBSTANTIATION AND OTHER MADNESSES.

In this way not only the fiction of the papists about transubstantiation is refuted, but also all stupid fantasies and worthless quibbles which either derogate from his heavenly glory or do not really agree with the truth of his human nature. And we judge that it is not less absurd to place Christ under the bread or to couple him with the bread than to transubstantiate the bread into his body.

[25.] THE BODY OF CHRIST IS IN HEAVEN AS IN A PLACE.

And in order that no ambiguity may remain; when we say that Christ is to be sought in heaven, this saying implies and expresses to us separation in space. For although, speaking philosophically, there is no place above the skies, yet the body of Christ, bearing the nature and fashion of a human body, is finite and is contained in heaven as in a place. It is necessary that it be separated from us by such an interval of space, in the same way as the heaven is separated from the earth.

[26.] CHRIST IS NOT TO BE ADORED IN THE BREAD OR IN THE SACRAMENT.

And if it is not right to affix Christ to the bread and the wine by our imagination, much less is it lawful to adore him in the bread. For although the bread is given to us as a symbol and pledge of that communion which we have with Christ yet it is a sign and not the thing itself, and because it does not have the thing included in it or

---

3. This article was added at the request of Calvin with Bullinger's approval. See CR 41:306 (1211), "After the 18th paragraph, where we give a figurative exposition of the words of the Supper: This is my body, This is my blood, I thought it would not be inappropriate if all access to uncertainty be removed. For without doubt there are certain good men who will take it ill that there is no mention of the reality, when thus far it is called a sign and when moreover there is no mention of the eating of the flesh in the whole work. Inasmuch therefore as we cannot be too careful that our words do not smell of contact with worthless opinions, we must be diligent that reasonable men may not justly find here anything which is less than satisfactory. It would not be difficult to give satisfaction if some explanation like this were to be included: *Quod autem . . . hauriamus.* I think that this also contains nothing that will displease you or that can be suspected by others or that in the future will become subject to misinterpretation."

attached to it, therefore those who turn their minds to the thing, in adoring Christ, make an idol of it.

The Reply of the Zurichers to Calvin's Writing

The pastors, doctors, and ministers of the church of Zurich send greetings to their dear brother John Calvin, faithful pastor of the church of Geneva.

Calvin, most reverend brother in the Lord, your great zeal and careful labors daily to illuminate the doctrine of the sacraments and to remove from the church the offenses which seem to have arisen from some rather obscure explanation of the mysteries, are so far from being irksome to us that we judge them not only worthy of proclamation with praise, but also worthy to be emphasized and imitated by us to the best of our ability. For while the holy laws of our prince Jesus Christ set down all actions for the purpose of cultivating charity or zeal for brotherly love, there is nothing they prohibit more severely than for anyone to cause offense to another so that he cannot make a right judgment concerning these things, the knowledge of which is necessary or at least useful and salutary for men, or so that he cannot perform that duty which he owes to God first and then to his neighbors. With the same weight these laws command us to remove, as far as we can, those obstacles over which men continually stumble. For this reason the coming of both William Farel, our revered brother, and yourself seemed to us most creditable and specially worthy of leading churchmen. The first object in this friendly colloquium was to expound to each other, as simply as possible, our position with regard to the sacraments especially on those heads where admittedly there has been some controversy until now among those who on other points have handed on the pure doctrine of the gospel with full agreement. A further purpose was to publish our *Consensus* in writing, as a witness. For we see no other way or more fitting course by which we may abolish religious controversy or suppress empty suspicions where now no divisions exist, or by which offenses may be removed which are sometimes born in the church from the controversial opinions of the teachers, than if those who seem to disagree, or do in fact disagree, explain their view openly and in turn, both by word of mouth and written document. However it would be worth little if, when the truth has been sought out and established, it should be retained among them and not be made available also to other men by fuller explanation of those things which had been barely introduced and obscurely expressed, by expounding with clarity what was set forth ambiguously and by making a declaration in definite, appropriate, and significant statements. This method was always approved by our fathers in the church, was very often used in settling religious controversies, and was never without salutary effect for the church: in short, it was approved by the supreme example of the apostles of Christ, our Lord and God. For as we read in Acts 15, a very great dissension was dissolved in no other way than this when the apostles and their own disciples taught that hearts were purified by faith in the name of Christ and men were saved by his grace alone; but others argued for circumcision and the keeping of the Mosaic Law. And so, dear brother Calvin, we cannot but thoroughly approve your holy efforts and those of all pious men who work by suitable arguments to remove offenses and to repair the tottering peace and harmony of the church, attempting by simple and accurate explanation to make Christian doctrine more and more lucid and plain and attempting to rid minds of empty and divisive conjectures; and attempting also to bring into true, lasting, and holy concord even those who have been in some disagreement of words or opinions.

For the rest, we wanted our published agreement to be witnessed, alike by the pious and the enemies of the truth; and we are led to hope that when it has passed its present test, it will bear the fruit which you foretell in your letter. For we have sent the formula of our mutual agreement to a number of brethren and have shown it here to a number of persons who love Christ and the truth and who are experienced in matters of doctrine. They have not only acknowledged our agreement on those points on which it was commonly reported that we disagreed, but they have also offered thanks to Christ our Savior, entertaining great hopes of more abundant fruit in the church, as they discern that we are agreed in God and in the truth. Some, however, have wanted a fuller treatment of the argument on account of certain subtle men who, when they heard of our agreement, found it somewhat difficult to admit satisfaction. But what purpose would it serve—an explanation in multitudinous words, that God is author of the sacraments and instituted them for the lawful sons of the church; or that just so many sacraments were given to the church by Christ and the others were devised by men; or what are the parts of the sacrament; or in what place, at what time, and by what sacred means the mysteries ought to be celebrated? Our published treatises on the sacraments, or those of our tutors of blessed memory, adequately prove that there has been no appearance or shadow of an argument between us on these or any other points of a similar nature. Indeed we have spoken so fully, plainly, and simply of the bodily presence of our Lord Christ, of the genuine meaning of the solemn words, of the manducation of the body of Christ, and of the purpose, use, and effect of the sacrament (on which issues many have thought our opinions, or certainly our words, to have been hitherto in conflict); of these things we have so spoken that we hope men, anxious for brotherly concord and clear truth, will not find in our work either a lack of fullness or a lack of lucid expression. And we are not diffident that the ministers of the other churches of Christ in Switzerland will also easily admit that we have expressed the same doctrine of the sacraments which has been received by Christian people for many generations, so that in the acknowledged truth they will be the last to disagree with us. Not without good reason, we promise ourselves this too for all pious men throughout the churches of other nations.

However, if anyone produces a clearer explanation of the sacraments, we would prefer to use it among the saints, rather than urge one man to subscribe to our agreement; in which nevertheless we have employed the words of Sacred Scripture and expounded openly in what sense we understand it: indeed we are clearly persuaded that we are in agreement with the catholic church. Moreover, if this document has not removed all the offenses which apparent disagreement interposed between us in the ways of the Lord, we will still think, however, that it has admirably borne fruit because we have witnessed to all without obscurity or pretense that we, to whom it has been given by Christ to think and speak in the same terms with regard to the faith, do not differ at all even in the explanation of these mysteries. Farewell, dearest brother. Zurich, 30 August 1549.

Creeds and Dogmas of the Catholic Reformation

Even more ambiguous than the designations "Reformed" and "Radical" for those two versions of Reformation confessions is the problem of the best terminology for the Roman Catholic participation in the phenomenon of sixteenth-century confessionalism.

Traditional textbooks of church history and theology, both Roman Catholic and Protestant, used to call it "the Counter-Reformation": the Council of Trent, the founding of the Society of Jesus, the Wars of Religion up to and including the Thirty Years' War, even the missionary expansion of the sixteenth and seventeenth centuries—all of these could be seen as components of the reaction of church and papacy to the split within Western Christendom. But increasingly, this way of reading the history seemed to be excessively reactive and negative.

Therefore that standard term has been widely superseded by "the Catholic Reformation." Although it, too, entails other difficulties of classification and designation—which have given rise to alternative proposals, such as John W. O'Malley's nomination of "Early Modern Catholicism"—it does have the great advantage of coordinating what the third session of the Council of Trent itself called "the dual purpose on account of which the council was primarily brought together: the rooting out of heresy and the reform of conduct."

For our purposes, that advantage of the name "the Catholic Reformation" applies especially to its two confessional formulations as given here, *The Canons and Decrees of the Council of Trent* and *The Tridentine Profession of Faith*. For on one doctrine after another these confessions are addressed both to the Protestant challenge (or, rather, the several Protestant challenges) and to the crisis of doctrinal pluralism inherited from earlier centuries, and they do not make sense unless they are seen in both of these contexts.

817

Dogmatic Decrees of the Council of Trent, 1545–63

As the reform movement took shape in the early sixteenth century, theologians, churchmen, and even the emperor repeatedly called for a general church council to address disputed issues of doctrine and to stem the problems of ecclesiastical corruption. Finally, Pope Paul III convoked a council in Mantua in 1537. It was the announcement of this council that inspired Luther to compose → *The Smalcald Articles*. But the meeting in Mantua did not occur, nor did another that was to be held in Vicenza in 1538. Both were thwarted more by the political situation in the empire than by any hesitation on the part of the papacy.

After more postponements, the council eventually convened in Trent in December 1545. By this time the schism between Catholics and Protestants was complete and there was no serious plan for attempting to reconcile the two sides, as there had been in earlier designs for a council. German Protestants were invited and offered safe conduct in session 13 (October 1551), however, and attended from January to April 1552, but neither side made any earnest steps toward union.

Nonetheless, the participants clearly had the issues of the Reformation in mind when they discussed and decreed upon matters of dogma and introduced moral and administrative reforms. Over the course of nearly two decades of sporadic meetings, the council clarified the Catholic position on such central issues as the Bible, tradition, and the sacraments. It also put into perspective other tenets of the faith (such as the invocation of saints, veneration of relics, and indulgences) that had acquired exaggerated importance in the polemical writings of both Protestants and Catholics in the sixteenth century.

The council lasted from 1545 to 1563 and can be divided into three distinct periods. During the first period (1545–47; sessions 1–8) the council issued decrees on faith (session 3), Scripture and tradition (session 4), original sin (session 5), justification[1] and good works (session 6), and the theology of the sacraments (session 7). Reforms were also mandated, especially in the areas of benefices and ecclesiastical management.

The second gathering met from 1551 to 1552 under a new pope, Julius III. It issued decrees on the eucharist, penance, and the last rites. In the decree on the eucharist (session 13), Lutheran, Calvinist, and Zwinglian views are described and anathematized.

---

1. For discussions of the doctrine of justification at the Council of Trent, see Brunner 1963; *Chr Trad* 4:280–89; Joest 1962; and Peter 1985.

The third period of the Council of Trent did not take place until 1561–63 (sessions 17–25), when it was summoned by Pius IV. The sacraments, in particular the eucharist, were again the subjects of the decrees. Session 21 addressed the issue of lay communion in both kinds, decreeing that it was not necessary to receive both bread and wine, but not forbidding the practice. The sacrificial nature of the mass was defined (session 22), and the sacraments of holy orders (session 23) and marriage (session 24) were affirmed. The council also ordered further ecclesiastical reforms, dealt with issues of discipline, and established theological seminaries and schools.

Addressing issues unresolved by patristic and medieval theologians, the Council of Trent clarified Catholic doctrine and identity. The participants were reacting, in part, to the ideas and criticism of the Reformation. But on another level, the new realities of the divided Christian church in the West necessitated intense self-reflection and study to define just what it meant to be Roman Catholic.

Edition and translation: *DEC* 2:662–*667, 671–*681, 684–*686, 693–*698, 703–*711, 726–*727, 732–*736, 742–*744, 753–*754, 774–*776.

Note: The dogmatic degrees from sessions 3–7, 13–14, and 21–25 are included here. For the complete texts of all decrees and canons, see *DEC* 2:660–*799.

Literature: Alberigo 1959, 1988; Bäumer 1979; Bedouelle 1989; Brunner 1963; *Chr Trad* 4:245–46, 253–57, 274–303; Duval 1985; Frost 1975; Ganzer 1985; Holstein 1976; Jedin 1941, 1948, 1948–75; Joest 1962; Kolb 1984; McHugh 1995; Montgomery 1976; *ODCC* 1639–40; *OER* 4:173–77 (Alberigo); Pas 1954; Peter 1985; Venard 1992; Wright 1975.

Session 3. 4 February 1546
ACCEPTANCE OF THE CREED OF THE CATHOLIC FAITH

In the name of the holy and undivided Trinity, the Father and the Son and the Holy Spirit. This holy, ecumenical, and general Council of Trent, lawfully assembled in the Holy Spirit, with the same three legates of the apostolic see presiding, has considered the tremendous nature of the matters to be treated, especially those which fall within the dual purpose on account of which the council was primarily brought together: the rooting out of heresy and the reform of conduct. The council recognizes with the apostle that we are not contending against flesh and blood, but against spiritual hosts of wickedness in the heavenly places; with him, likewise, it [Eph 6.12] exhorts each and every one in the first place to be strong in the Lord, in the strength of his might, in all things taking the shield of faith with which you can quench all [Eph 6.10] the flaming darts of the evil one, and take the helmet of salvation with the sword of the spirit which is the word of God. Consequently, that this loving care of the [Eph 6.16–17] council may both begin and continue by the grace of God, it determines and decrees first of all to begin with a creed of the faith. In this it follows the example of the fathers of the more revered councils who, at the beginning of their proceedings, were accustomed to make use of this shield against all heresies, and in some cases by this means alone they have drawn unbelievers to the faith, defeated heretics, and strengthened the faithful. Hence the council voted that the creed which the Holy Roman Church uses as that basic principle on which all who profess the faith of Christ necessarily agree as the firm and sole foundation against which the powers of death shall never prevail, should be expressed in the words in which it is read in [Mt 16.18] all the churches. It runs as follows:

I believe in one God, the Father Almighty, Maker of heaven and earth, of all that is, seen and unseen. And in one Lord, Jesus Christ, the only Son of God, eternally begotten of the Father, God from God, light from light, true God from true God, begotten, not made, of one being with the Father. Through him all things were made. For us and for our salvation he came down from heaven: by the power of the Holy Spirit he became incarnate from the Virgin Mary, and was made man. For our sake he was crucified under Pontius Pilate; he suffered death and was buried. On the third day he rose again in accordance with the Scriptures; he ascended into heaven and is seated at the right hand of the Father. He will come again in glory to judge the living and the dead, and his kingdom will have no end. I believe in the

Holy Spirit, the Lord, the giver of life, who proceeds from the Father and the Son. With the Father and the Son he is worshiped and glorified. He has spoken through the prophets. I believe in one holy, catholic, and apostolic church. I acknowledge one baptism for the forgiveness of sins. I look for the resurrection of the dead, and the life of the world to come. Amen.

Session 4. 8 April 1546
FIRST DECREE: ACCEPTANCE OF THE SACRED BOOKS
AND APOSTOLIC TRADITIONS

The holy, ecumenical, and general Council of Trent, lawfully assembled in the Holy Spirit, with the same three legates of the apostolic see presiding, keeps ever before its eyes this purpose: that the purity of the gospel, purged of all errors, may be preserved in the church. Our Lord Jesus Christ, the Son of God, first proclaimed with his own lips this gospel, which had in the past been promised by the prophets in the Sacred Scriptures; then he bade it be preached to every creature through his apostles as the source of the whole truth of salvation and rule of conduct. The council clearly perceives that this truth and rule are contained in written books and in unwritten traditions which were received by the apostles from the mouth of Christ himself, or else have come down to us, handed on as it were from the apostles themselves at the inspiration of the Holy Spirit. Following the example of the orthodox fathers, the council accepts and venerates with a like feeling of piety and reverence all the books of both the Old and the New Testament, since the one God is the author of both, as well as the traditions concerning both faith and conduct, as either directly spoken by Christ or dictated by the Holy Spirit, which have been preserved in unbroken sequence in the Catholic Church.

The council has decided that a written list of the sacred books should be included in this decree in case a doubt should occur to anyone as to which are the books which are accepted by this council. They are as follows. The Old Testament: the five books of Moses, namely Genesis, Exodus, Leviticus, Numbers, Deuteronomy; Joshua, Judges, Ruth, four books of Kings, two of Paralipomenon, Esdras 1 and 2 (which is also named Nehemiah), Tobit, Judith, Esther, Job, 150 Psalms of David, Proverbs, Ecclesiastes, Song of Songs, Wisdom, Ecclesiasticus, Isaiah, Jeremiah with Baruch, Ezekiel, Daniel; the twelve minor prophets, namely Hosea, Joel, Amos, Obadiah, Jonah, Micah, Nahum, Habakkuk, Zephaniah, Haggai, Zechariah, Malachi; two books of the Maccabees, 1 and 2. The New Testament: the four Gospels according to Matthew, Mark, Luke, and John; the Acts of the Apostles written by the evangelist Luke; fourteen letters of Paul the apostle, to the Romans, two to the Corinthians, to the Galatians, to the Ephesians, to the Philippians, to the Colossians, two to the Thessalonians, two to Timothy, to Titus, to Philemon, to the Hebrews; two letters of the apostle Peter; three of the apostle John; one of the apostle James; one of the apostle Jude; the Apocalypse of the apostle John.

If anyone should not accept as sacred and canonical these entire books and all their parts as they have, by established custom, been read in the Catholic Church, and as contained in the old Latin Vulgate edition, and in conscious judgment should reject the aforesaid traditions: let him be anathema. Hence, let all understand the order and manner by which the council will proceed after laying down the foundation of the profession of faith, and what witnesses and supports it will especially use in strengthening its teachings and renewing conduct in the church.

SECOND DECREE: ACCEPTANCE OF THE LATIN VULGATE EDITION OF THE BIBLE; RULE ON THE MANNER OF INTERPRETING SACRED SCRIPTURE, ETC.

Moreover, the same holy council considers that noticeable benefit can accrue to the church of God if, from all the Latin editions of the sacred books which are in circulation, it establishes which is to be regarded as authentic. It decides and declares that the old well-known Latin Vulgate edition which has been tested in the church by long use over so many centuries should be kept as the authentic text in public readings, debates, sermons, and explanations; and no one is to dare or presume on any pretext to reject it.

The council further decrees, in order to control those of unbalanced character, that no one, relying on his personal judgment in matters of faith and customs which are linked to the establishment of Christian doctrine, shall dare to interpret the Sacred Scriptures either by twisting its text to his individual meaning in opposition to that which has been and is held by Holy Mother Church, whose function is to pass judgment on the true meaning and interpretation of the Sacred Scriptures; or by giving it meanings contrary to the unanimous consent of the fathers, even if interpretations of this kind were never intended for publication. Whoever acts contrary to this decision is to be publicly named by religious superiors and punished by the penalties prescribed by law.

In this regard, as is right, the council wishes to impose a restriction also on printers who, thinking they have a right to do what they wish without restraint and without the permission of ecclesiastical superiors, print the texts of Sacred Scripture with added notes and commentaries of anyone at all; and this they often do without stating the name or with a false name of the press and, what is more serious, without the name of the author; and they have books of this kind, printed in other places, on sale without permission. Hence the council decrees and determines that hereafter the Sacred Scriptures, particularly this ancient Vulgate edition, shall be printed after a thorough revision; that no one may print or have printed any books on sacred subjects without the name of the author, nor in future sell them or even keep them in his possession, unless they have first been examined and approved by the local ordinary, under pain of anathema and fine as determined in the regulation of the most recent Lateran Council. If they are regulars, in addition to the above examination and approval, they must also obtain permission from their own superiors and have the books acknowledged by the latter, in accordance with the formula of their own institutes. Those who make written copies of or publish those books without their having previously been examined and approved, are liable to the same penalties as the printers. Those who possess or read them, if they have not disclosed the author, are to be regarded as the authors. The actual approval of such books is to be given in written form and should be authoritatively displayed at the front of a book, whether it be written or printed. All this, namely the approval and assessment, is to be done without fee, so that approval may be given to what deserves to be approved, and rejection to what has to be condemned.

In addition, the council wishes to check the lack of discretion by which the words and sentiments of Sacred Scripture are turned and twisted to scurrilous use, to wild and empty fancies, to flattery, detraction, superstitions, godless and devilish magical formulas, fortune-telling, lotteries, and also slanderous pamphlets. So as to banish this kind of irreverence and contempt, and so that no one may in future dare in any way to make use of the words of Sacred Scriptures for these or similar purposes, the council orders and prescribes that all persons in that category, violators, and profaners of the word of God, should be checked by the bishops by legal and imposed penalties.

Session 5. 17 June 1546
DECREE ON ORIGINAL SIN

The aim of the holy, ecumenical, and general Council of Trent, lawfully assembled in the Holy Spirit, with the same three legates of the apostolic see presiding, is that

[Heb 11.6]   our Catholic faith without which it is impossible to please God may, after it has been cleansed of errors, remain complete and unsoiled in its integrity, and that the Chris-

[Eph 4.14]   tian people may not be carried about with every wind of doctrine. For, amid the many evils by which the church of God is troubled in our times that ancient serpent, the undying enemy of the human race, is stirring up not only new disagreements but also old ones about original sin and its remedy. The council now wishes to call back those who are going astray and to strengthen the hesitant. And so, following the witness of the Sacred Scriptures, of the holy fathers, and of the most authoritative councils, as well as the agreement and judgment of the church, it determines, confesses, and declares as follows with regard to original sin.

1. If anyone does not acknowledge that the first man, Adam, when he acted against God's command in paradise, immediately lost that holiness and justice in which he had been created and, because of the sin of such a transgression, incurred the anger and displeasure of God and consequently death, with which God had previously threatened him, and with death a captivity under the power of him who, thenceforth, had the power of death, that is, the devil; and that the whole Adam, [Heb 2.14] because of that sinful disobedience, was changed in body and soul for the worse: let him be anathema.

2. If anyone declares that the sin of Adam damaged him alone and not his descendants, and that the holiness and justice received from God, which he lost, he lost for himself alone and not for us; or that, while he was stained by the sin of disobedience, he transmitted only death and bodily pains to the whole human race, but not that sin which is the death of the soul: let him be anathema, for he contradicts the apostle saying, "Sin came into the world through one man, and death through sin, and so death spread through the whole human race because everyone [Rom 5.12] has sinned."

3. If anyone asserts that this sin of Adam which, one by origin and passed on to all by propagation and not by imitation, inheres in everyone as something proper to each, is removed by human and natural powers, or by any remedy other than the merit of the one Mediator, our Lord Jesus Christ, who has reconciled us to God in his own blood, being made our righteousness and sanctification and redemption;[a] or if anyone denies that the actual merit of Christ Jesus is applied to both adults and infants through the sacrament of baptism duly administered in the form of the church: let him be anathema; for there is no other name under heaven given among people by which we must be saved. Hence that saying: "Behold the [Acts 4.12] Lamb of God, behold him who takes away the sins of the world." And that other: [Jn 1.29] "For as many of you as were baptized, have put on Christ." [Gal 3.27]

4. If anyone says that recently born babies should not be baptized even if they have been born to baptized parents; or says that they are indeed baptized for the remission of sins, but incur no trace of the original sin of Adam needing to be cleansed by the water of rebirth for them to obtain eternal life, with the necessary consequence that in their case there is being understood a form of baptism for the

a. [Rom 5.9–10; 1 Cor 1.30]

remission of sins which is not true, but false: let him be anathema. For the saying of the apostle, "Sin came into the world through one man and death through sin, [Rom 5.12] and so death spread through the whole human race because everyone has sinned," must be understood not otherwise than as the Catholic Church in its entire extent has always understood it. For, according to the rule of faith transmitted from the apostles, even small children, who could not yet of themselves have committed any kind of sin, are truly baptized for the remission of sins in order that what they contracted by generation may be cleansed in them by regeneration. For, unless one is [Jn 3.5] born again of water and of the Holy Spirit, he cannot enter the kingdom of God.

5. If anyone says that the guilt of original sin is not remitted through the grace of our Lord Jesus Christ which is given in baptism, or even asserts that all which pertains to the true essence of sin is not removed, but declares it is only erased and not attributed: let him be anathema. For God hates nothing in the reborn, because there is no condemnation for those who are truly buried with Christ by bap- [Rom 8.1] tism into death, who do not walk according to the flesh but, putting off the old person and putting on the new person created according to God, become innocent, stainless, pure, blameless, and beloved children of God, heirs indeed of God and [Rom 8.17] fellow heirs with Christ, so that nothing at all impedes their entrance into heaven. The holy council confesses and perceives that in the baptized, concupiscence or a tendency to sin remains; since this is left as a form of testing, it cannot harm those who do not give consent but, by the grace of Christ, offer strong resistance; indeed, [2 Tm 2.5] that person will be crowned who competes according to the rules. This concupis- [Rom 7.14, 17, 20] cence the apostle sometimes calls sin, but the holy council declares that the Catholic Church has never understood it to be called sin in the sense of being truly and properly such in those who have been regenerated, but in the sense that it is a result of sin and inclines to sin. If anyone holds a contrary view: let him be anathema.

6. The same holy council, however, also declares that it is not its intention to include in this decree, when it is dealing with original sin, the blessed and immaculate Virgin Mary, mother of God, but rather that observance must be given to the constitutions of Pope Sixtus IV of happy memory, in accord with the penalties included in those constitutions, which the council renews.

Session 6. 13 January 1547
DECREE ON JUSTIFICATION
Introduction

At this time there has been spread an erroneous doctrine about justification, with resulting loss of many souls and serious damage to the unity of the church. Because of this, the holy, ecumenical, and general Council of Trent, lawfully assembled in the Holy Spirit for the praise and glory of Almighty God, the peace of the church, and the salvation of souls, sets down its intention: those presiding in the name of our father and lord in Christ, Paul III by divine providence pope, being John Mary bishop of Palestrina de Monte and Marcellus priest of the holy cross in Jerusalem, cardinals of the Holy Roman Church and legates *a latere* of the Holy See. Its intention is to set out for all the Christian faithful the true and sound doctrine on justification which the sun of justice, Jesus Christ, pioneer and perfecter of our faith, [Mal 4.2; Heb 12.2] taught, the apostles handed down, and the Catholic Church under the prompting of the Holy Spirit has always retained. This it does by imposing a strict check on anyone who dares to believe, preach, or teach otherwise than is defined and declared in the present decree.

Chapter 1. On the Powerlessness of Nature and Law to Justify

First of all, for a true and genuine understanding of the doctrine of justification, the holy council declares that everyone must acknowledge and confess that, since all lost their innocence in the sin of Adam, became unclean and (in the words of the apostle) by nature children of wrath, as is set out in the decree on original sin, [Eph 2.3] they were so far slaves of sin and under the power of the devil and death, that not only could the Gentiles not be freed from or rise above it by the force of nature, but neither could the Jews even by the letter of the law of Moses, though their free will, for all that it had been weakened and sapped in strength, was in no way extinct.

Chapter 2. The Ordering and the Mystery of Christ's Coming

Wherefore it came about that the Father in heaven, the Father of mercies and God of all comfort, when that blessed fullness of time came, sent Jesus Christ his Son, an- [2 Cor 1.3] nounced and promised both before the law and in the time of the law by many holy fathers, in order to redeem the Jews who were under the law, and that the Gentiles [Gal 4.5] who did not pursue righteousness might attain it, so that all might receive adoption [Rom 9.30] as sons. Him God put forward as an expiation by his blood, to be received by faith, [Rom 3.25] for our sins, and not for ours only, but also for the sins of the whole world. [1 Jn 2.2]

Chapter 3. Who Are Justified Through Christ

But though he died for all, yet not all receive the benefit of his death, but only those [2 Cor 5.15] to whom the merit of his passion is imparted. For just as men and women would not actually be born unjust if they were not bred and born from the seed of Adam, since by that descent they incur through him their own state of injustice while they are being conceived; so, if not reborn in Christ, they would never be justified, because by that rebirth there is granted to them, through the merit of his passion, his grace by which they become just. For this gift the apostle enjoins on us always to give thanks to the Father who has qualified us to share in the inheritance of the saints in [Col 1.12–14] light. He has delivered us from the dominion of darkness and transferred us to the kingdom of his beloved Son, in whom we have redemption, the forgiveness of sins.

Chapter 4. Suggested Description of the Justification of a Sinner and Its Character in the State of Grace

By those words there is suggested a description of the justification of a sinner: how there is a transition from that state in which a person is born as a child of the first Adam to the state of grace and of adoption as children of God through the agency of the second Adam, Jesus Christ our Savior; indeed, this transition, once the gospel has been promulgated, cannot take place without the waters of rebirth or the desire for them, as it is written: "Unless a person is born again of water and the [Jn 3.5] Holy Spirit, he cannot enter the kingdom of God."

Chapter 5. On the Need of Preparation for Justification in Adults and Its Source

The council further declares that actual justification in adults takes its origin from a predisposing grace of God through Jesus Christ, that is, from his invitation which calls them, with no existing merits on their side; thus, those who had been turned away from God by sins are disposed by God's grace inciting and helping them, to turn towards their own justification by giving free assent to and cooperating with this same grace. Consequently, though God touches a person's heart through the light of the Holy Spirit, neither does that person do absolutely nothing in receiving that movement of grace, for he can also reject it; nor is he able, by his own free will and without God's grace, to move himself towards justice in God's sight. Hence, [Zec 1.3] when Scripture says, "Return to me and I will return to you," we are being reminded of our freedom; when we answer, "Restore us to yourself, O Lord, that we may be [Lam 5.21] restored," we are admitting that we are forestalled by the grace of God.

Chapter 6. The Manner of Preparation

People are disposed for that justice when, roused and helped by divine grace and attaining the faith that comes from hearing, they are moved freely towards God and [Rom 10.17] believe to be true what has been divinely revealed and promised, and in particular that the wicked are justified by God by his grace through the redemption which is in [Rom 3.24] Christ Jesus. At the same time, acknowledging that they are sinners, they turn from fear of divine justice, which profitably strikes them, to thoughts of God's mercy; they rise to hope, with confidence that God will be favorable to them for Christ's sake; and they begin to love him as the fount of all justness. They are thereby turned against sin by a feeling of hatred and detestation, namely by that repentance which must occur before baptism. Finally, when they are proposing to receive baptism, they are moved to begin a new life and to keep God's commandments. Of this attitude of mind, Scripture says: "Whoever would draw near to God must believe that he exists and that he rewards those who seek him"; and, "Take heart, son, your sins [Heb 11.6] are forgiven";ᵃ and, "Fear of the Lord drives out sin";ᵇ and, "Repent and be baptized every one of you in the name of Jesus Christ for the forgiveness of your sins, and you shall receive the gift of the Holy Spirit"; and, "Go, therefore, and make [Acts 2.38] disciples of all nations, baptizing them in the name of the Father, and of the Son, and of the Holy Spirit, teaching them to observe all that I have commanded you"; [Mt 28.19–20] finally, "Direct your hearts to the Lord." [1 Kgs 7.3]

Chapter 7. What the Justification of the Sinner Is and What Are Its Causes

This disposition and preparation precede the actual justification, which consists not only in the forgiveness of sins but also in the sanctification and renewal of the inward being by a willing acceptance of the grace and gifts whereby someone from being unjust becomes just, from being an enemy becomes a friend, so that he is an heir in hope of eternal life. The causes of this justification are: final cause, the glory [Ti 3.7] of God and of Christ, and eternal life; efficient cause, the God of mercy who, of his own free will, washes and sanctifies, placing his seal and anointing with the prom- [1 Cor 6.11] ised Holy Spirit who is the guarantee of our inheritance; meritorious cause, his most [Eph 1.13–14] beloved and only-begotten Son, our Lord Jesus Christ who, when we were at enmity with him, out of the great love with which he loved us, merited justification [Eph 2.4]

a. [Mt 9.2]
b. [Sir 1.27]

for us by his most holy passion on the wood of the cross, and made satisfaction to God the Father on our behalf; instrumental cause, the sacrament of baptism, which is the sacrament of faith, without which justification comes to no one. Finally, the one formal cause is the justness of God: not that by which he himself is just, but that by which he makes us just and endowed with which we are renewed in the spirit of our mind, and are not merely considered to be just but we are truly named and are just, each one of us receiving individually his own justness according to the measure which the Holy Spirit apportions to each one as he wills, and in view of each one's dispositions and cooperation. For though no one can be just unless the merits of the passion of our Lord Jesus Christ are communicated to him; nevertheless, in the justification of a sinner this in fact takes place when, by the merit of the same most holy

[Rom 5.5]   passion, the love of God is poured out by the agency of the Holy Spirit in the hearts of those who are being justified, and abides in them. Consequently, in the process of justification, together with the forgiveness of sins a person receives, through Jesus Christ into whom he is grafted, all these infused at the same time: faith, hope, and charity. For faith, unless hope is added to it and charity too, neither unites him perfectly with Christ nor makes him a living member of his body. Hence it is very truly

[Jas 2.17]   said that faith without works is dead and barren, and in Christ Jesus neither cir-
[Gal 5.6]   cumcision is of any avail nor uncircumcision, but faith working through love. From apostolic tradition, catechumens seek this faith from the church before the sacrament of baptism when they ask for the faith that gives eternal life; and this, without hope and charity, faith cannot give. Consequently, they immediately hear the word

[Mt 19.17]   of Christ: "If you would enter life, keep the commandments." Thus, receiving true and Christian justness in exchange for that which Adam, by his disobedience, lost for himself and for us, the reborn are immediately ordered to preserve the justice freely granted to them through Jesus Christ in a pure and spotless state like a best robe, so that they may carry it before the tribunal of our Lord Jesus Christ and possess eternal life.

Chapter 8. How Justification of the Sinner Freely Granted Through Faith Is to Be Understood

When the apostle says that a person is justified by faith and as a gift, those words are to be understood in the sense which the perennial consent of the Catholic Church has maintained and expressed, namely, that we are said to be justified by faith because faith is the first stage of human salvation, the foundation and root of all justi-

[Heb 11.6]   fication, without which it is impossible to please God and come to the fellowship of his children. And we are said to receive justification as a free gift because nothing

that precedes justification, neither faith nor works, would merit the grace of justification; for if it is by grace, it is no longer on the basis of works; otherwise (as the
same apostle says) grace would no longer be grace. [Rom 11.6]

Chapter 9. Against the Vain Confidence of the Heretics

But though it is necessary to believe that sins are not forgiven, nor have they ever
been forgiven, save freely by the divine mercy on account of Christ; nevertheless, it
must not be said that anyone's sins are or have been forgiven simply because he has a
proud assurance and certainty that they have been forgiven, and relies solely on that.
For this empty and ungodly assurance may exist among heretics and schismatics,
as indeed it does exist in our day, and is preached most controversially against the
Catholic Church. Neither should it be declared that those who are truly justified
must determine within themselves beyond the slightest hesitation that they are justified, and that no one is absolved from sin and justified except one who believes
with certainty that he has been absolved and justified, and that absolution and justification are effected by this faith alone—as if one who does not believe this is casting doubts on God's promises and on the efficacy of the death and resurrection of
Christ. For, just as no devout person ought to doubt the mercy of God, the merit
of Christ, and the power and efficacy of the sacraments; so it is possible for anyone, while he regards himself and his own weakness and lack of dispositions, to be
anxious and fearful about his own state of grace, since no one can know, by that
assurance of faith which excludes all falsehood, that he has obtained the grace of
God.

Chapter 10. On the Increase of Justification Received

So those justified in this way and made friends and members of the household of
God, going from strength to strength,[a] are (as the apostle says) renewed from day[b]
to day by putting to death what is earthly in themselves and yielding themselves as
instruments of righteousness for sanctification by observance of the commandments
of God and of the church. They grow and increase in that very justness they have
received through the grace of Christ, by faith united to good works, as it is written:
"Let him who is holy become more holy"; and again, "Do not wait until death to [Rv 22.11]
be justified"; again, "You see that a person is justified by works and not by faith [Sir 18.22]

a. [Ps 83.8]
b. [2 Cor 4.16]

[Jas 2.24]   alone." Indeed, holy church asks for this increase in justice when it prays, "Lord, give us an increase in faith, hope, and charity."

Chapter 11. The Keeping of the Commandments: Its Necessity and Possibility

But no one, however much justified, ought to think that he is exempt from the observance of the commandments, nor should he use that rash statement, forbidden by the fathers under anathema, that the commandments of God are impossible of observance by one who is justified. For God does not command the impossible, but by commanding he instructs you both to do what you can and to pray for what you cannot, and he gives his aid to enable you; for his commandments are not heavy, his

[Mt 11.30]   yoke is sweet and his burden light. Those who are children of God love Christ; and

[Jn 14.23]   those who love him (as he himself bears witness) keep his words which, of course, they can do with the divine help. For in this mortal life men and women, however holy and just, will sometimes fall into sin, at least light and everyday sins which are also called venial, but they do not therefore cease to be just. For the voice that says,

[Mt 6.12]   "Forgive us our trespasses," is the voice of the just and it is humble and truthful. Hence it is the just who should feel themselves bound to walk in the path of justice

[Rom 6.22]   all the more because, now that they are set free from sin and are become slaves of

[Ti 2.12]   God, and are living sober and upright lives, they can make progress through Jesus Christ, through whom they had access to that state of grace. For God does not abandon those once justified by his grace, unless he is first deserted by them. Therefore, no one should yield to complacency in faith alone, thinking that by faith alone he has been established as an heir, and that he will obtain that inheritance even if he has not suffered with Christ so as to be glorified with him. For (as the apostle says) even Christ himself, though he was the Son of God, learned obedience through what he suffered, and being made perfect, he became the source of eternal salvation to

[Heb 5.8–9]   all who obey him. Consequently, the apostle himself warns those who are justified saying, "Do you not know that in a race all the runners compete, but only one receives the prize; so run that you may obtain it. I do not run aimlessly, I do not box as one beating the air; but I pummel my body and subdue it, lest after preaching to

[1 Cor 9.24, 26–27]   others, I myself should be disqualified." Likewise Peter, the prince of the apostles: "Be more zealous by good works to confirm your call and election, for if you do

[2 Pt 1.10]   this you will never fall." Hence it is certain that they are opponents of the orthodox teaching of religion who say that in every good work the just person sins at least venially; or (which is more intolerable), that he deserves eternal punishment; likewise, those who hold that the just sin in all their works if, when arousing their sloth and encouraging themselves to run in the race, in addition to the aim that above all God may be glorified, they are also looking to an eternal reward; since it is written: "I have inclined my heart to perform your statutes for the sake of the reward," and the apostle said of Moses that he looked to the reward.

[Ps 119.112 Vulg]

[Heb 11.26]

Chapter 12. Rash Presumption About Predestination Must Be Avoided

In addition, no one, so long as he remains in this present life, ought so to presume about the hidden mystery of divine predestination as to hold for certain that he is unquestionably of the number of the predestined, as if it were true that one justified is either no longer capable of sin or, if he sins, may promise himself sure repentance. For, apart from a special revelation, it is impossible to know whom God has chosen for himself.

Chapter 13. On the Gift of Perseverance

Similarly, concerning the gift of perseverance, it is written: "He who endures to the end will be saved" (and indeed, the gift can have no other source save him who has the power to uphold one who stands so that he may continue, and to restore him who falls). Even though all should place an unshaken hope in God's help and rest in it, let no one promise himself with absolute certainty any definite outcome. For, unless they themselves neglect his grace, as God has begun the good work, so he will bring it to completion, bringing about both the will and the performance. Nevertheless, let those who think themselves to stand, take heed lest they fall, and work out their own salvation with fear and trembling, in labors, watchings, almsdeeds, prayers, and offerings, in fastings and chastity. For, knowing that they are reborn to the hope of glory, and not yet to glory itself, they ought to tremble about the struggle with the flesh, with the world, with the devil, which still remains and in which they cannot be victors unless, with the grace of God, they do what the apostle says: "We are debtors not to the flesh, to live according to the flesh, for if you live according to the flesh you will die; but if by the Spirit you put to death the deeds of the body, you will live."

[Mt 10.22, 24.13]

[1 Cor 10.12]

[Phil 12.12]

[Rom 8.12–13]

Chapter 14. On the Fallen and Their Restoration

Those who fall away by sin from the grace of justification which they had received, can again be justified when at God's prompting they have made the effort through the sacrament of penance to recover, by the merit of Christ, the grace which was lost. For this kind of justification is a restoration of the fallen, which the holy fathers suitably call a second plank for the grace shattered in a storm. It was for the sake of those who fall into sin after baptism that Jesus Christ instituted the sacrament of penance, when he said: "Receive the Holy Spirit; if you forgive the sins of any,

[Jn 20.22–23]   they are forgiven; and if you retain the sins of any, they are retained." Hence it must be taught that the repentance of a Christian after a fall is very different from repentance at baptism: it includes not only ceasing from sins and detestation of them,

[Ps 51.17]   or a humble and contrite heart, but also confession of them in the sacrament of penance, to be made at least in desire and in due season, absolution by a priest, and also satisfaction by fasting, almsgiving, prayers, and other devout exercises of the spiritual life; these take the place, not indeed of eternal punishment which is remitted together with the guilt either by the sacrament or the desire of the sacrament, but of temporal punishment which (as Scripture teaches) is not wholly discharged—as happens in baptism—by those who, lacking gratitude for the grace of God which they have received, have grieved the Holy Spirit and not feared to violate the temple of God. Of this repentance it is written: "Remember, then, from what

[Rv 2.5]   you have fallen; repent and do the works you did at first"; and again, "For godly

[2 Cor 7.10]   grief produces a repentance that leads to salvation and brings no regret"; and again, "Repent"[a] and, "Bear fruit that befits repentance."[b]

Chapter 15. Grace, but Not Faith, Is Lost by Every Mortal Sin

It must be asserted, against the subtle modes of thinking of certain people, who by fair and flattering words deceive the hearts of the simple-minded, that the grace of

[Rom 16.18]   justification once received is lost not only by apostasy, by which faith itself is lost, but also by any other mortal sin, though faith is not lost. Thus is defended the teaching of the divine law which excludes from God's kingdom not only unbelievers, but also the faithful if they are guilty of fornication, adultery, wantonness, sodomy, theft, avarice, drunkenness, slander, plundering, and all others who commit mortal sins from which, with the help of divine grace, they can refrain, and because of which they are severed from the grace of Christ.

a. [Mt 3.2, 4.17]
b. [Lk 3.8; Mt 3.8]

Chapter 16. On the Fruit of Justification, Namely Merit from Good Works, and on the Nature of That Merit

Hence, to those justified by this means, whether they have continued to preserve the grace received or have recovered it once lost, the words of the apostle should be addressed: "Always abound in the work of the Lord, knowing that in the Lord your [1 Cor 15.58] labor is not in vain." "For God is not so unjust as to overlook your work and the [Heb 6.10] love which you showed for his sake." And, "Do not throw away your confidence, [Heb 10.35] which has a great reward." Thus, to those who work well right to the end and keep [Mt 10.22] their trust in God, eternal life should be held out, both as a grace promised in his mercy through Jesus Christ to the children of God, and as a reward to be faithfully bestowed, on the promise of God himself, for their good works and merits. This, then, is that crown of righteousness which the apostle says is laid up for him after his fight and his race, and will be awarded by the righteous judge not only to him but to all who love his appearing. For Jesus Christ himself continually imparts [2 Tm 4.8] strength to those justified, as the head to the members and the vine to the branches, [Jn 15.5] and this strength always precedes, accompanies, and follows their good works, and without it they would be wholly unable to do anything meritorious and pleasing to God; hence it must be believed that nothing more is needed for the justified to be considered to have fully satisfied God's law, according to this state of life, by the deeds they have wrought in him and to have truly deserved to gain eternal life in their time (provided they die in a state of grace). For Christ our Savior says: "Whoever drinks of the water that I shall give him will never thirst, but it will become in him a spring of water welling up to eternal life." Thus our own personal justice is [Jn 4.13–14] not established as something coming from us, nor is the justice of God disregarded or rejected; what is called our justice, because we are justified by its abiding in us, is that same justice of God, in that it is imparted to us by God through the merit of Christ. However, it must not be overlooked that, though so much is attributed in Scripture to good works (Christ indeed promises that anyone who gives a cup of cold water to one of the least of his little ones will not lack his reward; and the [Mt 10.42] apostle bears witness: "This slight momentary affliction is preparing for us an eter- [2 Cor 4.17] nal weight of glory beyond comparison"), yet no Christian should ever either rely on or glory in himself and not in the Lord, whose goodness towards all is so great that he desires his own gifts to be their merits. And because we all make many mistakes, each of us ought to keep before his eyes the severity and judgment as much as [Jas 3.2] the mercy and goodness; and even if he is not aware of anything in himself, a person ought not to pronounce judgment on himself, for our whole life must be examined and judged not by our judgment but by that of God, who will bring to light the [1 Cor 4.5]

things now hidden in darkness and disclose the purposes of the heart; then every-
[Mt 16.27] one will receive his commendation from God, who, as it is written, will render to
everyone according to his works.[a]

After this Catholic teaching about justification—and unless each one faithfully and firmly accepts it, he cannot be justified—the holy council decided to attach
these canons, so that all may know not only what they must hold and obey, but
what they must totally avoid.

CANONS CONCERNING JUSTIFICATION

1. If anyone says that a person can be justified before God by his own works, done
either by the resources of human nature or by the teaching of the law, apart from
divine grace through Jesus Christ: let him be anathema.

2. If anyone says that divine grace through Jesus Christ is given solely to
enable a person to live justly and to merit eternal life more easily, as if each could
be done through free will without grace, even though with a struggle and with difficulty: let him be anathema.

3. If anyone says that, without preceding inspiration of the Holy Spirit and
without his help, a person can believe, hope, love, and repent, as he ought, so that
the grace of justification may be granted to him: let him be anathema.

4. If anyone says that a person's free will when moved and roused by God,
gives no cooperation by responding to God's summons and invitation to dispose
and prepare itself to obtain the grace of justification; and that it cannot, if it so
wishes, dissent but, like something inanimate, can do nothing at all and remains
merely passive: let him be anathema.

5. If anyone says that, after the sin of Adam, human free will was lost and
blotted out, or that its existence is purely nominal, a name without substance, indeed
a fiction introduced into the church by Satan: let him be anathema.

6. If anyone says that it is not in human power to adopt evil ways, but that
God is the agent for evil acts just as for good, not only by permitting them but also
in a full sense and by personal act, so that the betrayal of Judas no less than the call
of Paul is an act fully his: let him be anathema.

7. If anyone says that all acts done prior to justification, no matter for what
reason, are either truly sins or deserve God's hatred; or that the more earnestly
one strives to dispose oneself for grace, the more gravely does one sin: let him be
anathema.

8. If anyone says that the fear of hell, because of which we seek refuge in

a. [Rom 2.6; Rv 22.12]

God's mercy by expressing sorrow for sins, or refrain from committing sin, is itself a sin or makes sinners worse: let him be anathema.

9. If anyone says that the sinner is justified by faith alone, meaning thereby that no other cooperation is required for him to obtain the grace of justification, and that in no sense is it necessary for him to make preparation and be disposed by a movement of his own will: let him be anathema.

10. If anyone says that people are justified without the justice of Christ by which he gained merit for us; or that they are formally just by his justness itself: let him be anathema.

11. If anyone says that people are justified either solely by the attribution of Christ's justice, or by the forgiveness of sins alone, to the exclusion of the grace and charity which is poured forth in their hearts by the Holy Spirit and abides in them; or even that the grace by which we are justified is only the goodwill of God: let him be anathema.

12. If anyone says that the faith which justifies is nothing else but trust in the divine mercy, which pardons sins because of Christ; or that it is that trust alone by which we are justified: let him be anathema.

13. If anyone says that to secure pardon of his sins, everyone must believe, with certainty and without any hesitation about his own weakness and lack of dispositions, that his sins have been forgiven: let him be anathema.

14. If anyone says that a person is absolved from sins and is justified by the fact that he certainly believes he is absolved and justified; or that no one is truly justified except one who believes that he is justified, and that by that faith alone are forgiveness and justification effected: let him be anathema.

15. If anyone says that a person reborn and justified is bound to believe as a matter of faith that he is certainly in the number of the predestined: let him be anathema.

16. If anyone says with absolute and infallible certitude (unless he shall have learned this by special revelation) that he will certainly have that great gift of final perseverance: let him be anathema.

17. If anyone says that the grace of justification is the lot only of those predestined to life, but that all the rest who are called are indeed called, but do not receive the grace, as they are predestined to evil by God's power: let him be anathema.

18. If anyone says that the commandments of God are impossible of observance even by a person justified and established in grace: let him be anathema.

19. If anyone says that in the gospel nothing but faith is prescribed, while other matters are indifferent, neither prescribed nor forbidden, but free; or that the Ten Commandments in no way apply to Christians: let him be anathema.

20. If anyone says that a justified person, of whatever degree of perfection, is not bound to keep the commandments of God and of the church but only to believe, as if the gospel were simply a bare and unqualified promise of eternal life without the condition of observing the commandments: let him be anathema.

21. If anyone says that Jesus Christ was given to men and women by God as a redeemer to trust, and not also as a lawgiver to obey: let him be anathema.

22. If anyone says either that one justified can persevere in the justice received without the special help of God; or that, even with that help, he cannot: let him be anathema.

23. If anyone says that a person, once justified, cannot sin any more or lose grace, and therefore that one who falls and sins has never been truly justified; or, on the other hand (apart from a special privilege from God such as the church holds in the case of the Blessed Virgin), that he can avoid all sins, even venial sins, throughout his life: let him be anathema.

24. If anyone says that justice once received is neither preserved nor increased in the sight of God by good works, but that the works themselves are no more than the effects and signs of the justification obtained, and not also a cause of its increase: let him be anathema.

25. If anyone says that in any good work a just person sins at least venially, or (which is more intolerable) mortally, and thus deserves eternal punishments, and is not thereby damned only because God does not impute those works unto damnation: let him be anathema.

26. If anyone says that the just ought not, in return for good works wrought in God, to expect and hope for an eternal reward from God through his mercy and the merit of Jesus Christ, if by acting rightly and keeping the divine commandments they persevere to the end: let him be anathema.

27. If anyone says that there is no mortal sin save that of unbelief; or that grace, once received, is lost by no other sin, however serious and enormous, than that of unbelief: let him be anathema.

28. If anyone says that when grace is lost by sin, faith too is always lost; or that the faith that remains is not true faith, even if it is not a living faith; or that one who has faith without charity is not a Christian: let him be anathema.

29. If anyone says that one who has fallen after baptism cannot rise again by the grace of God; or that he can recover the lost justice by faith alone, and without the sacrament of penance as the Holy Roman and Universal Church, taught by Christ and his apostles, has to this day professed, maintained, and taught: let him be anathema.

30. If anyone says that once the grace of justification has been received, the fault of any repentant sinner is forgiven and the debt of eternal punishment is wiped out, in such a way that no debt of temporal punishment remains to be discharged, either in this world or later on in purgatory, before entry to the kingdom of heaven can lie open: let him be anathema.

31. If anyone says that a justified person commits sin when he does something good with a view to an eternal reward: let him be anathema.

32. If anyone says that the good deeds of a justified person are the gifts of God, in the sense that they are not also the good merits of the one justified; or that the justified person, by the good deeds done by him through the grace of God and the merits of Jesus Christ (of whom he is a living member), does not truly merit an increase in grace, eternal life, and (so long as he dies in grace) the obtaining of his own eternal life, and even an increase in glory: let him be anathema.

33. If anyone says that this Catholic doctrine concerning justification, set out in this present decree by the holy council, detracts in any way from the glory of God or the merits of Jesus Christ our Lord, and does not rather make clear the truth of our faith, and the glory alike of God and of Jesus Christ: let him be anathema.

Session 7. 3 March 1547
FIRST DECREE [ON THE SACRAMENTS]
Introduction

For the completion of the doctrine of salvation concerning justification which was promulgated at the immediately preceding session by the unanimous consent of the fathers, there was general agreement to treat the most holy sacraments of the church by means of which all true justness either begins, or once received gains strength, or if lost is restored. Therefore the holy, ecumenical, and general Council of Trent, lawfully assembled in the Holy Spirit, with the same legates of the apostolic see presiding, set as its aim the removal of errors and the rooting out of heresies, which have arisen at the present time concerning the most holy sacraments: some, which have revived, concern heresies condemned in the past by our fathers; others more recently devised greatly oppose the purity of the Catholic Church and the salvation of souls. By adhering to the teaching of the Holy Scriptures, the apostolic traditions, and the common opinion of other councils and of the fathers, this council has established and formally decreed the canons here set out; later (with the help of the Divine Spirit) it will publish others which remain for the completion of the work begun.

Canons on the Sacraments in General

1. If anyone says that the sacraments of the new law were not all instituted by our Lord Jesus Christ; or that there are more or fewer than seven: namely, baptism, confirmation, eucharist, penance, last anointing, order, matrimony; or that one or other of these seven is not truly and in the full sense a sacrament: let him be anathema.

2. If anyone says that those same sacraments of the new law are no different from the sacraments of the old law, except by reason of a difference in ceremonies and in external rites: let him be anathema.

3. If anyone says that these seven sacraments are so equal to each other that on no ground is one of greater dignity than another: let him be anathema.

4. If anyone says that the sacraments of the new law are not necessary for salvation but are superfluous, and that people obtain the grace of justification from God without them or a desire for them, by faith alone, though all are not necessary for each individual: let him be anathema.

5. If anyone says that these sacraments have been instituted only to nourish faith: let him be anathema.

6. If anyone says that the sacraments of the new law do not contain the grace which they signify; or do not confer that grace on those who place no obstacle in the way, as if they were only external signs of grace or justice received by faith, and some kind of mark of the Christian profession by which believers are distinguished from unbelievers in the eyes of people: let him be anathema.

7. If anyone says that grace is not given by sacraments of this kind always and to all, as far as depends on God, even if they duly receive them, but only sometimes and to some: let him be anathema.

8. If anyone says that grace is not conferred by the sacraments of the new law through the sacramental action itself, but that faith in the divine promise is by itself sufficient for obtaining the grace: let him be anathema.

9. If anyone says that in the three sacraments, namely, baptism, confirmation, and order, a character, namely a spiritual and indelible mark, is not imprinted on the soul, because of which they cannot be repeated: let him be anathema.

10. If anyone says that all Christians have the power to exercise the ministry of the word and of all the sacraments: let him be anathema.

11. If anyone says that, when ministers effect or confer the sacraments, they do not need the intention of at least doing what the church does: let him be anathema.

12. If anyone says that a minister in a state of mortal sin, even if he observes all the essentials which belong to the effecting or administering of a sacrament, does not effect or administer it: let him be anathema.

13. If anyone says that the received and approved rites of the Catholic Church in customary use in the solemn administration of the sacraments may, without sin, be neglected or omitted at choice by the ministers, or can be changed to other new ones by any pastor whatever: let him be anathema.

Canons on the Sacrament of Baptism

1. If anyone says that the baptism of John had the same effect as the baptism of Christ: let him be anathema.

2. If anyone says that true and natural water is not a necessary element in baptism, and therefore twists those words of our Lord Jesus Christ, "unless one is born of water and the Holy Spirit," into some form of metaphor: let him be anathema. [Jn 3.5]

3. If anyone says that in the Roman Church (which is the mother and mistress of all the churches) there is not the true teaching on the sacrament of baptism: let him be anathema.

4. If anyone says that the baptism which is given by heretics in the name of the Father and of the Son and of the Holy Spirit, with the intention of doing what the church does, is not a true baptism: let him be anathema.

5. If anyone says that baptism is optional, namely that it is not necessary for salvation: let him be anathema.

6. If anyone says that one who is baptized cannot, even if he wishes, lose grace however much he sins, unless he refuses to believe: let him be anathema.

7. If anyone says that those baptized are obliged to faith alone, but not to the observance of the whole law of Christ: let him be anathema.

8. If anyone says that those baptized are exempt from all the precepts of holy church, whether they are in writing or handed down, so that they are not bound to observe them, unless of their own free will they wish to submit themselves to them: let him be anathema.

9. If anyone says that people must be recalled to the memory of the baptism they received, thereby understanding that all vows made after baptism become of no effect by the force of the promise already made in their actual baptism, as if such vows detract from the faith they have professed and from the baptism itself: let him be anathema.

10. If anyone says that, solely by the remembrance of receiving baptism and of its faith, all sins committed after baptism are forgiven or become venial: let him be anathema.

11. If anyone says that, if anyone has denied the faith of Christ among unbe-

lievers, his true and rightly conferred baptism must be repeated when he has turned back to repentance: let him be anathema.

12. If anyone says that no one should be baptized except at that age at which Christ was baptized, or at the point of death: let him be anathema.

13. If anyone says that little children, because they make no act of faith, should not after the reception of baptism be numbered among the faithful; and that, therefore, when they reach the age of discretion, they should be rebaptized; or that it is better that their baptism be omitted than that they be baptized while believing not by their own faith but by the faith of the church alone: let him be anathema.

14. If anyone says that, when they grow up, those baptized as little children should be asked whether they wish to ratify what their godparents promised in their name when they were baptized; and that, when they reply that they have no such wish, they should be left to their own decision and not, in the meantime, coerced by any penalty into the Christian way of life, except that they be barred from the reception of the eucharist and the other sacraments, until they have a change of heart: let him be anathema.

Canons on the Sacrament of Confirmation

1. If anyone says that confirmation of the baptized is an empty ceremony, and not rather a true and proper sacrament; or that at one time it was nothing but a form of religious instruction in which those approaching adolescence presented an account of their faith publicly to the church: let him be anathema.

2. If anyone says that they are slighting the Holy Spirit who assign some special power to the holy chrism of confirmation: let him be anathema.

3. If anyone says that the ordinary minister of holy confirmation is not a bishop only but any simple priest: let him be anathema.

Session 13. 11 October 1551

DECREE ON THE MOST HOLY SACRAMENT OF THE EUCHARIST

The holy, ecumenical, and general Council of Trent, lawfully assembled in the Holy Spirit, and having as presidents the same legate and nuncios of the holy apostolic see, has come together under the special guidance and direction of the Holy Spirit in order that it may set out the true and ancient teaching on faith and the sacraments, and supply a remedy for all the heresies and other serious troubles by which the church is now miserably disturbed and torn apart in a great variety of divisions; yet it had among its chief aims right from the beginning to tear up root and branch the tares of those detestable errors and schisms which the enemy in these calamitous times has sown in the teaching of faith in the most holy eucharist and its use and liturgy, the very sacrament which the Savior left in his church as a symbol of its unity and love, whereby he wished all Christians to be mutually linked and united. Consequently, the same most holy council, handing on that sound and uncontaminated teaching concerning this venerable and divine sacrament of the eucharist which the Catholic Church, instructed by our Lord Jesus Christ himself and his apostles, and taught by the Holy Spirit as he daily proposes to her all truth, has always retained and will preserve till the end of the world, prohibits all Christians from venturing to believe, teach, or preach otherwise concerning the most holy eucharist than as has been explained and defined in this present decree.

Chapter 1. On the Real Presence of Our Lord Jesus Christ in the Most Holy Sacrament of the Eucharist

In the first place, the holy council teaches and openly and without qualification professes that, after the consecration of the bread and the wine, our Lord Jesus Christ, true God and true man, is truly, really, and substantially contained in the propitious sacrament of the holy eucharist under the appearance of those things which are perceptible to the senses. Nor are the two assertions incompatible, that our Savior is ever seated in heaven at the right hand of the Father in his natural mode of existing, and that he is nevertheless sacramentally present to us by his substance in many other places in a mode of existing which, though we can hardly express it in words, we can grasp with minds enlightened by faith as possible to God and must most firmly believe. For thus did all our forefathers, as many as were in the true church of Christ and treated of this most holy sacrament, most clearly profess: namely, that our Redeemer at the last supper instituted this so admirable sacrament when he bore witness in express and unambiguous words that, after the blessing of the bread and the wine, he was offering to them his own body and his own blood. Since those words, recorded by the holy evangelists and afterwards repeated by St. Paul, bear that proper and very clear meaning which the fathers understood them to have, it is surely a most intolerable and shameful deed for some base and argumentative persons to twist them to false and imaginary meanings that deny the reality of Christ's flesh and blood, against the universal understanding of the church which, as the pillar and bulwark of the truth, detests these contrived theories of evil people as the [1 Tm 3.15] work of the devil, and constantly recalls and confesses with gratitude this outstanding favor of Christ.

Chapter 2. The Reason for the Institution of
This Most Holy Sacrament

Therefore, our Savior, about to depart from this world to the Father, instituted this sacrament in which he as it were poured out the riches of his divine love towards

[Ps 111.4]   humanity, causing his wonderful works to be remembered, and he bade us cherish

[1 Cor 11.26] his memory as we partook of it and to proclaim his death until he comes to judge the world. He wished this sacrament to be taken as the spiritual food of souls, to nourish and strengthen them as they lived by his life who said, he who eats me will

[Jn 6.58]   live because of me, and as an antidote to free us from daily faults and preserve us from mortal sins. He further wished it to be a pledge of our future glory and unending happiness, and thus a sign of that one body of which he is the head and to which he wished us all to be united as members by the closest bonds of faith, hope, and love, so that we should all speak with one voice and there might be no division

[1 Cor 1.10]   among us.

Chapter 3. On the Excellence of the Most Holy Eucharist
over the Other Sacraments

There is indeed this which is common to the most holy eucharist along with the other sacraments: it is a sign of sacred reality and the visible form of invisible grace. But in it there is found the excelling and unique quality that, whereas the other sacraments first have the force of sanctifying at the moment when one uses them, in the eucharist the author of holiness himself is present before their use. For the apostles had not yet received the eucharist from the hand of the Lord when he declared with all truth that it was his own body which he was offering. And it has at all times been the belief in the church of God that immediately after the consecration the true body of our Lord and his true blood exist along with his soul and divinity under the form of bread and wine. The body is present under the form of bread and the blood under the form of wine, by virtue of the words. The same body, however, is under the form of wine and the blood under the form of bread, and the soul under either form, by virtue of that natural link and concomitance by which the parts of Christ the Lord, who has now risen from the dead and will die no more, are mutually united. The divinity, too, is present by that marvelous hypostatic union with his body and soul. Hence it is entirely true that as much is contained under one of the forms as under both; for Christ exists whole and entire under the form of bread and under any part of that form, and likewise whole under the form of wine and under its parts.

Chapter 4. On Transubstantiation

But since Christ our Redeemer said that it was truly his own body which he was offering under the form of bread, therefore there has always been complete conviction in the church of God—and so this holy council now declares it once again—that, by the consecration of the bread and wine, there takes place the change of the whole substance of the bread into the substance of the body of Christ our Lord, and of the whole substance of the wine into the substance of his blood. And the Holy Catholic Church has suitably and properly called this change transubstantiation.

Chapter 5. On the Worship and Reverence to Be Shown to This Most Holy Sacrament

Hence there is no room for doubting that all Christians, by a custom always accepted in the Catholic Church, should reverently express for this most holy sacrament the worship of adoration which is due to the true God. For it is not less worthy of adoration because it was instituted by Christ the Lord in order to be consumed. For we believe that the same God is present therein of whom the eternal Father declared when introducing him into the created world, "Let all God's angels worship [Heb 1.6] him"; he whom the Magi, falling down, worshiped; he who, finally, as the Scrip- [Mt 2.11] tures bear witness, was adored by the apostles in Galilee. The holy council further [Mt 28.17] declares that it was with true religious devotion that the custom was introduced into the church of God whereby every year, on a special fixed day of festival, this sublime and venerable sacrament should be hailed with particular veneration and solemnity, and carried with reverence and honor in processions through streets and public places. For it is most reasonable that some days have been set aside on which all Christians may manifest, with some noteworthy and unusual tokens, their thoughts of gratitude and remembrance towards the Lord and Redeemer they share, for a favor so much beyond words and clearly divine by which his victory and triumph over death are recalled. And thus indeed must truth, the victor, celebrate a triumph over falsehood and heresy so that, confronted with so much splendor and such great joy of the universal church, her enemies weakened and broken may fall into decline or, touched by shame and confounded, may in time come to repentance.

Chapter 6. On Reserving the Sacrament of the Holy Eucharist and Taking It to the Sick

The custom of reserving the eucharist in a sacred place is so ancient that even the age of the Council of Nicaea recognized it. In addition, the practice of carrying the holy eucharist to the sick, and hence its careful reservation for that purpose in the churches, is not only consonant with right and proper understanding, but can be shown to be enjoined in many councils, and has been observed by longstanding custom of the Catholic Church. And so this holy council rules that this salutary and necessary practice is to be universally retained.

Chapter 7. On the Preparation to be Observed for the Worthy Reception of the Holy Eucharist

If it is unfitting for anyone to approach any sacred functions except in a spirit of holiness, then surely the more the sacred quality and divinity of this heavenly sacrament are understood by a Christian, the more carefully ought he or she to be on guard against approaching to receive it without great reverence and holiness, especially since we read those awesome words of the apostle: "Anyone who eats and drinks

[1 Cor 11.29]   unworthily without discerning the body of the Lord, eats and drinks judgment upon himself." Consequently anyone desiring to communicate should be reminded of his

[1 Cor 11.28]   injunction: "Let a person examine himself." The practice of the church declares that examination necessary, so that no one who is aware of personal mortal sin, however contrite he may feel, should approach the holy eucharist without first having made a sacramental confession. The holy council has decreed that this practice should always be retained by all Christians, even by those priests who may have the obligation to celebrate mass, so long as they do not lack an available confessor. But if a priest should celebrate in urgent need without previous confession, let him confess at the first opportunity.

Chapter 8. On the Use of This Wonderful Sacrament

With respect to the use, however, our fathers rightly and wisely distinguished three types of reception of this holy sacrament. For they taught that some, being sinners, receive it only sacramentally; others receive only spiritually, namely those who have the desire to eat the heavenly food that is set before them, and so experience its

[Gal 5.6]   effect and benefit by a lively faith working through love; the third group, who receive both sacramentally and spiritually, are those who so test and train themselves

[Mt 22.11]   beforehand, that they approach this divine table clothed in a wedding garment. In the reception of the sacrament, there has always been a custom in the church of God that the laity receive communion from priests, but that priests, when celebrating, administer communion to themselves; this custom, coming down as from apostolic tradition, should rightly and deservedly be retained. Finally, the holy council with

true paternal affection enjoins, exhorts, begs, and entreats through the tender mercy
of our God that each and all who are marked by the name of Christian should now,   [Lk 1.78]
at long last, join together and agree in this sign of unity, this bond of love, this symbol of harmony; and that, mindful of the so great majesty and surpassing love of
our Lord Jesus Christ, who gave his own dear life as the price of our salvation and
his own flesh for us to eat, they should believe and reverence these sacred mysteries
of his body and blood with such constancy and firmness of faith, such dedication
of mind, such devotion and worship, that they may be able to receive frequently
that life-supporting bread, and that it may be for them truly the life of the soul
and the unending health of the mind; thus, strengthened by its force, may they be
able after the journey of this wretched pilgrimage to reach the heavenly fatherland,
there to eat without veil the same bread of angels which they now eat beneath the
sacred veils.   [Ps 78.25]

But since it is not enough to declare the truth unless errors are exposed
and refuted, it is the will of the holy council to affix these canons so that, with the
Catholic teaching already recognized, all may also understand which heresies they
must guard against and avoid.

CANONS ON THE MOST HOLY SACRAMENT
OF THE EUCHARIST

1. If anyone denies that in the most holy sacrament of the eucharist there are contained truly, really, and substantially, the body and blood of our Lord Jesus Christ
together with the soul and divinity, and therefore the whole Christ, but says that he
is present in it only as in a sign or figure or by his power: let him be anathema.

2. If anyone says that in the venerable sacrament of the eucharist the substance of the bread and wine remains together with the body and blood of our Lord
Jesus Christ, and denies that marvelous and unique change of the whole substance
of the bread into the body, and of the whole substance of the wine into the blood,
while only the appearance of bread and wine remains, a change which the Catholic
Church most aptly calls transubstantiation: let him be anathema.

3. If anyone denies that the whole Christ is contained in the venerable sacrament of the eucharist under each form, and under each part of each form when it
is divided: let him be anathema.

4. If anyone says that the body and blood of our Lord Jesus Christ are not
present in the wondrous sacrament of the eucharist after the completion of the consecration, but only in its use, while it is being consumed, but not before or after; and

that the true body of the Lord does not remain in the hosts or consecrated particles which are reserved or remain over after the communion: let him be anathema.

5. If anyone says either that the principal fruit of the most holy eucharist is the forgiveness of sins, or that other effects do not result from it: let him be anathema.

6. If anyone says that Christ, the only-begotten Son of God, is not to be adored in the holy sacrament of the eucharist by the worship of adoration, including its outward expression; and therefore is not to be reverenced by the celebration of a special festival nor carried round solemnly in procession, as is the praiseworthy rite and custom everywhere of holy church; nor exposed publicly to the people that he may be adored; and that those who so adore are idolaters: let him be anathema.

7. If anyone says that it is unlawful to reserve the holy eucharist in a sacred place, but that it must of necessity be distributed to those present immediately after the consecration; or that it is unlawful for it to be carried with due honor to the sick: let him be anathema.

8. If anyone says that Christ, when presented in the eucharist, is consumed only spiritually, and not also sacramentally and really: let him be anathema.

9. If anyone denies that each and all of Christ's faithful of both sexes, when they have reached the age of discretion, are bound in accordance with the commandment of Holy Mother Church to receive communion every year, at least at Easter time: let him be anathema.

10. If anyone says that it is unlawful for a priest, when celebrating, to give himself communion: let him be anathema.

11. If anyone says that faith alone is sufficient preparation for receiving the sacrament of the most holy eucharist: let him be anathema. And, in order that so great a sacrament may not be received unworthily, and hence unto death and condemnation, the holy council establishes and declares that, granted the availability of a confessor, those burdened by an awareness of mortal sin, however much they may feel themselves to be contrite, must first avail themselves of sacramental confession. But if anyone presumes to teach, preach, or obstinately assert the contrary, or even defend it in public debate, by that very act he shall be excommunicated.

Session 14. 25 November 1551
TEACHING CONCERNING THE MOST HOLY SACRAMENTS
OF PENANCE AND LAST ANOINTING

The holy, ecumenical, and general Council of Trent, lawfully assembled in the Holy Spirit, with the same legate and nuncios of the holy apostolic see as its presidents,

realizes that in the decree on justification a good deal about the sacrament of penance was introduced for a reason which seemed necessary, namely the close connection between the two subjects. Nevertheless, so great is the accumulation of errors
about that sacrament during our time that no small public advantage will come from
giving a more detailed and full definition concerning this sacrament in which, once
the widespread errors have been disclosed and uprooted with the assistance of the
Holy Spirit, the catholic truth will become more clear and distinct. This holy council
now lays before all Christians this truth to be forever observed.

Chapter 1. On the Need for the Sacrament of Penance and Its Institution

If thanksgiving to God in all the regenerated was such that they unfailingly preserved the justice received by his favor and grace in baptism, there would have been
no need for a sacrament other than baptism to be instituted for the forgiveness of
sins. But since God, rich in mercy, knows our frame, he has also bestowed a remedy   [Eph 2.4; Ps 103.14]
of life on those who have subsequently surrendered to the slavery of sin and the
power of the devil, namely the sacrament of penance by which the benefit of Christ's
death is applied to those who have fallen away after baptism. Repentance, indeed,
was necessary at all times for all who had stained themselves by some mortal sin so
as to gain grace and justice, including those who had asked to be cleansed by the
sacrament of baptism, in order that, rejecting and correcting their perversity, they
might with a hatred of sin and a genuine sorrow of mind detest so great an offense
against God. Hence the prophet says: "Repent and turn from all your transgressions lest iniquity be your ruin." The Lord also said: "Unless you repent, you will all   [Ez 18.30]
likewise perish." And Peter, prince of the apostles, commending penance to those   [Lk 13.3]
sinners about to be baptized, said: "Repent, and be baptized every one of you."   [Acts 2.38]
Moreover, before the coming of Christ penance was not a sacrament, nor after his
coming does anyone receive it prior to baptism. But the Lord instituted the sacrament of penance at that particular moment when, after his resurrection from the
dead, he breathed on his disciples, saying: "Receive the Holy Spirit; if you forgive
the sins of any, they are forgiven; if you retain the sins of any, they are retained."   [Jn 20.22–23]
The universal consent of the fathers has always understood that by this remarkable
act and by these clear words the power to forgive and retain sins, and so to reconcile those who had fallen after baptism, was communicated to the apostles and
to their lawful successors; and the Catholic Church with sound reason denounced
and condemned the Novatians as heretics when they obstinately denied the power

to forgive. Consequently this holy council, approving and accepting the literal and true meaning of those words of the Lord, condemns the fraudulent interpretation of those who, opposing the institution of this sacrament, falsely twist the words to mean the power of preaching the word of God and of proclaiming the gospel of Christ.

Chapter 2. The Difference Between the Sacraments of Penance and Baptism

But in fact this sacrament is seen to differ in many respects from baptism. For, apart from the fact that the matter and form, by which the essence of a sacrament is constituted, are totally distinct, there is certainly no doubt that the minister of baptism ought not to be a judge, since the church exercises judgment on no one who has [1 Cor 5.12] not previously entered it by the gate of baptism. "For what have I to do with judging outsiders?" says the apostle. It is otherwise with those of the household of the faith whom Christ has once made members of his body by the font of baptism; for if these should afterwards defile themselves by some fault, the church does not wish them to be cleansed by a repetition of baptism (since this is under no circumstances lawful in the Catholic Church), but to stand as culprits before this tribunal in order that they may be set free through the decision of the priests, not once but as often as, in repentance of sins admitted, they have recourse to it. Besides, the fruit of bap- [Gal 3.27] tism is something other than the fruit of penance. For by baptism we put on Christ [2 Cor 5.17] and become in him an entirely new creature, gaining full and complete remission of all sins; this newness and wholeness, however, we can in no way reach by the sacrament of penance without great weeping and labor on our part, as the divine justice demands, and so penance has rightly been called by the holy fathers a laborious kind of baptism. But this sacrament of penance is necessary for salvation for those who have fallen after baptism, just as baptism itself is for those not yet regenerated.

Chapter 3. On the Parts and Fruit of This Sacrament

In addition, the holy council teaches that the form of the sacrament of penance, in which its effectiveness chiefly lies, is expressed in those words of the minister, "I absolve you," etc. To these indeed, by a praiseworthy custom of holy church, some prayers are added, but they in no way affect the essence of the form, nor are they necessary for the administration of the sacrament. The acts of the penitent, namely contrition, confession, satisfaction, are as it were the matter of this sacrament. These are called parts of penance, in that, by God's institution, they are required in the penitent for the integrity of the sacrament, and for the full and complete forgiveness of sins. Of course, the meaning and fruit of this sacrament, so far as its force and efficacy are concerned, is reconciliation with God, which in devout persons who are receiving this sacrament with devotion is often followed by a peace and a serenity of conscience accompanied by an intense consolation of spirit. While handing on these teachings on the parts and effect of this sacrament, the holy council at the same time condemns the opinions of those who insist that the constituent parts of penance are the fears which afflict conscience and faith.

Chapter 4. On Contrition

Contrition, which holds the first place among the above-mentioned acts of the penitent, is a grief and detestation of mind at the sin committed, together with the resolution not to sin in the future. This movement of sorrow has been necessary at all times to obtain the pardon of sins and, in a person who has fallen after baptism, it finally prepares for the forgiveness of sin if it is linked with trust in the divine mercy and the desire to provide all the other requirements for due reception of the sacrament. The holy council therefore declares that this contrition includes not only ceasing from sin, the resolve of a new life, and a beginning of it, but also a hatred of the old in accordance with the words: "Cast away from you all the transgres- [Ez 18.31] sions which you have committed against me, and get yourselves a new heart and a new spirit." And certainly one who has pondered those exclamations of the saints, "Against you only have I sinned and done what is evil in your sight"; "I am weary [Ps 51.4] with my moaning, every night I flood my bed with tears"; "in my bitterness of soul I [Ps 6.6] recall all my years before you"; and others like them, will easily understand that they [Is 38.15] have sprung from an intense hatred of the past life and a very deep hatred of sins. The council further teaches that, though it sometimes happens that this contrition is made perfect by love, and a person is reconciled with God before this sacrament is actually received; nevertheless, the reconciliation is not to be attributed to the contrition without a desire for the sacrament being included in it. But of that imperfect contrition, which is called attrition since it is generally conceived either out of a consideration of the baseness of sin or from a fear of hell and punishments, as long as it excludes the will to sin and hopes for pardon, the council declares that not only does it not make a person a hypocrite and even more of a sinner, but that it is even a gift of God and an impulse of the Holy Spirit, not yet actually dwelling in the penitent, but only moving him, helped by which he prepares for himself a path towards justice; and although it cannot of itself and without the sacrament of penance lead the sinner to justification, yet it disposes him to beg and obtain the

[Jon 3.5] grace of God in this sacrament of penance. For, struck to their advantage by this fear, the Ninivites at the terrifying preaching of Jonah did penance and obtained mercy from the Lord. For that reason some make false accusations against Catholic writers, as if they have taught that the sacrament of penance confers grace without a good impulse on the part of its recipients, something which the church of God has never taught nor imagined. But they also teach falsely that contrition is wrested or forced from people, not freely willed.

Chapter 5. On Confession

From the time of the institution of the sacrament of penance already explained, the universal church has always understood that there was also instituted by the Lord the complete confession of sins, and that this is necessary by divine law for all who have fallen after baptism. For our Lord Jesus Christ, when about to ascend from earth to heaven, left priests as his own vicars, as overseers and judges, to whom all mortal sins into which Christ's faithful might have fallen were to be referred, so that by the power of the keys they might declare the decision of forgiveness or retention of sins. For it is clear that priests could not have exercised this judgment if the case were unknown, nor could they have preserved fairness in imposing penances if the faithful had declared their sins only in general, and not rather specifically and in detail. Hence it follows that all mortal sins that penitents are aware of after a careful self-examination have to be related in the confession, even if they are very private and committed only against the last two commandments of the Decalogue, since these may often quite seriously damage the soul and are more dangerous than those which are openly admitted. For venial sins, by which we are not cut off from the grace of God and into which we more frequently fall, although they may be admitted in confession (as the practice of devout persons shows), can nevertheless be passed over in silence without fault and expiated by many other remedies. But since

[Eph 2.3] mortal sins, even those of thought, make people children of wrath and enemies of God, it is essential to seek pardon of God by an open and humble confession of all of them. Thus, when Christ's faithful endeavor to confess all sins which come to mind, they are beyond doubt setting them before the divine mercy for all to be pardoned. Those, however, who do otherwise and knowingly hold some things back, are presenting nothing to the divine goodness for forgiveness through the priest; for if a sick man is ashamed to disclose his wound, the doctor does not heal with medicine what he is unaware of. It further follows that the circumstances which change the sin's nature must also be explained in confession because, without them, the sins themselves are not being completely revealed by the penitents nor made known to the judges, and it is impossible for the latter rightly to estimate the gravity of the faults and to impose on the penitents the penance appropriate to them. Hence it is completely unreasonable to teach that these circumstances have been thought out by idle minds or that only one circumstance need be confessed, namely a sin against a brother. And it is impious to say that confession according to these rules is impossible, or to call it a tormentor of consciences; for it is clear that the church requires nothing more of penitents than that, after each has examined himself diligently and explored all the nooks and crannies of his conscience, he confess those sins by which he recalls that he has mortally offended his Lord and God; but the other sins, which do not come to mind when he is carefully examining himself, are understood to have been included in a general form in the same confession; for those we say confidently with the prophet, "Lord, clear me from hidden faults." The difficulty of this kind [Ps 19.12] of confession and the shame at uncovering sins could seem to be burdensome, were it not lightened by so many advantages and consolations which will most certainly be granted through the absolution to all who approach the sacrament worthily. For the rest, with regard to the manner of confessing secretly to a priest alone, though Christ has not forbidden anyone to confess his sins publicly—in expiation for his offenses and in self-humiliation, both as an example to others and for the edification of the church which has been offended—yet this is not commanded by divine precept, nor would it be really well-considered to enjoin by human law that sins, especially secret ones, must be revealed by public confession. The fact that secret sacramental confession, which Holy Church has used from its beginning and still uses, has always been commended by the most venerable and most ancient fathers with great and unanimous agreement, clearly refutes that empty calumny of those who do not fear to teach that it is a human invention foreign to the divine command, originating from the fathers assembled in the Lateran Council; for the church did not establish through the Lateran Council that Christ's faithful should confess, which it had understood to be a necessary institution of divine law, but that the precept of confession should be discharged by one and all at least once a year on their reaching the age of discretion. Hence, throughout the whole church, at that sacred and most acceptable season of Lent, the salutary custom of confessing is observed with very great fruit for the souls of the faithful; and this custom the present holy council thoroughly approves and cherishes as holy and deserving to be retained.

Chapter 6. On the Minister of the Sacrament and on Absolution

Concerning the minister of the sacrament, however, the holy council declares false and completely alien to the truth of the gospel all teachings which destructively extend the ministry of the keys to all persons indiscriminately, in addition to bishops and priests, and maintain against the institution of this sacrament that those words [Mt 18.18] of the Lord, "Whatever you bind on earth shall be bound in heaven, and whatever you loose on earth shall be loosed in heaven," and, "If you forgive the sins of any, [Jn 20.23] they are forgiven; if you retain the sins of any, they are retained," were spoken to all Christ's faithful without distinction and discrimination, so that anyone has the power to forgive sins, public sins by reproof if the one reproved agrees to this, secret sins by a voluntary confession made to anyone. The council also teaches that even priests who are in mortal sin discharge as ministers of Christ the function of forgiving sins by the power of the Holy Spirit conferred in ordination, and that those think wrongly who insist that bad priests do not have this power. And although a priest's absolution is a stewardship of another's gift, nevertheless it is not only a bare service, either of proclaiming the gospel or of declaring that sins have been forgiven; but it is like a judicial act in which a verdict is pronounced by him as a judge; and therefore the penitent should not so flatter himself about his own faith that, even if he has no contrition or the priest has no intention of acting seriously and truly absolving, he may yet think he is truly absolved in the sight of God on the grounds of his faith alone. For faith without repentance would not secure any forgiveness of sins, nor would anyone be other than most careless of his salvation who, though aware that a priest was absolving jokingly, made no serious effort to find another acting with due care.

Chapter 7. On Reservation of Cases

Since the nature and meaning of the judicial process require that a verdict be passed only over those subject to it, the church of God has always maintained, and this council confirms its complete truth, that an absolution should be considered to have no value if pronounced by a priest over someone over whom he has neither ordinary nor delegated jurisdiction. Our most holy fathers judged that it was very important for the discipline of the Christian people that certain more heinous and more serious offenses should be absolved, not by any priest whatever, but only by those of highest rank; hence popes, in virtue of the supreme power committed to them in the universal church, could rightly reserve to their own particular decision some more serious classes of offense. And (since all that is from God is well ordered) there can be no doubt that this same procedure is lawful for all bishops, each in his own dio-[2 Cor 10.8, 13.10] cese, for building up, however, not for destroying, in virtue of that greater authority committed to them over their subjects than that of other priests of lesser rank, especially with regard to those offenses to which the penalty of excommunication is attached. It is in harmony with divine authority that this reservation of sins has force not only in external administration but also in the sight of God. Nevertheless, lest anyone perish on that account, it has always been most devoutly observed in the same church of God that there be no reservation in immediate danger of death, and so all priests may then absolve all penitents without distinction from every kind of sin and censure; outside this particular case, since priests have no power in reserved cases, their one endeavor should be to persuade the penitents to approach judges of higher rank who have legal power to grant absolution.

Chapter 8. On the Necessity and the Fruit of Satisfaction

Finally, there is satisfaction. Of all the parts of penance, it has at all times been commended to the Christian people by our fathers; yet in our day it is the one thing particularly attacked under the lofty pretext of devotion by those who maintain the appearance of devotion but have denied its inner reality. The holy council consequently declares that it is completely false and alien to the word of God that a fault is never forgiven by God without all penalty being condoned as well; for manifest and famous examples are found in Scripture which, apart from divine tradition, refute this error beyond all question. Surely the nature of divine justice itself demands that those who, prior to baptism, have failed through ignorance, should be received by God into grace in one manner; but in another manner those who, after once being freed from slavery to sin and to the devil and after receiving the gift of the Holy Spirit, have not feared knowingly to violate the temple of God and to grieve the Holy Spirit. It also befits the divine clemency not to free us from sins without any satisfaction with the result that, given the opportunity and thinking sins of small importance, we become neglectful and insolent towards the Holy Spirit and fall into more serious faults, storing up anger against ourselves in the day of wrath. For it is [Rom 2.5] beyond doubt that penances imposed in satisfaction very much deter people from sin, hold them in check by a kind of rein, and make those doing penance more cautious and more watchful for the future; they also heal the remaining effects of sins and, by the practice of the contrary virtues, remove vicious habits acquired by evil living. Nor has any path ever been considered more secure in the church of God for removing the threat of punishment by the Lord than that people should make regular use of these works of penance with genuine sorrow of mind. Moreover, while by making satisfaction we suffer for our sins, we become like Christ Jesus who made satisfaction for our sins, and from whom is all our sufficiency, and we also have a most sure pledge thereby that, if we suffer with him, we shall also be glorified with

[Rom 8.17]   him. For this satisfaction which we offer in payment for our sins is not so much ours that it is not also done through Christ Jesus; for we can do nothing of ourselves as of ourselves; with his cooperation we can do everything in him who strengthens

[Phil 4.13]   us. Thus we have nothing of which to boast; but all our boasting is in Christ, in whom we live, in whom we merit, in whom we make satisfaction and yield fruits

[Lk 3.8; Mt 3.8]   that will benefit repentance, which have their worth from him, are offered by him to the Father, and through him are accepted by the Father. The priests of the Lord, therefore, as the spirit of prudence shall suggest, must enjoin salutary and appropriate penances in keeping with the type of offense and the ability of the penitent, so as not to become sharers in the sins of others by imposing very light tasks for very serious faults, and perhaps thereby conniving at the sins by acting with too great indulgence towards the penitents. Let them rather bear in mind that the satisfaction they impose should not only be aimed at protecting the new life and at being a remedy against weakness, but also be for the atonement and punishment of past sins; for the ancient fathers believe and teach that the keys were granted to priests not only for releasing but also for binding. Nor for that reason did they think that the sacrament of penance is a forum of wrath or penalties, just as no Catholic ever supposed that the value of the merit and satisfaction of our Lord Jesus Christ was either obscured or in some way diminished as a result of acts of satisfaction on our part. Because the innovators refuse to acknowledge this, they so emphasize that a new life is the best penance as to take away the whole force and practice of satisfaction.

Chapter 9. On the Works of Satisfaction

The council further teaches that the abundance of the divine generosity is so great that through Jesus Christ we are able to make satisfaction before the Father not only by penances voluntarily undertaken by us to atone for sin, or those imposed by the judgment of the priest according to the extent of the fault, but also (and this is the greatest proof of love) by the temporal afflictions imposed by God and borne by us with patience.

TEACHING ON THE SACRAMENT OF LAST ANOINTING

The holy council, however, decided to attach to the above teaching on penance the following points about the sacrament of last anointing, which was regarded by the fathers as the final complement not only of penance but also of the whole Christian life, which ought to be an ever-continuing penance. So, first of all, it states its teaching about that sacrament's institution. Our most merciful Redeemer wished provision to be made for his servants of salutary remedies against all the darts of all enemies for every occasion in life. Just as he has prepared by other sacraments very important supports by which Christians may be able to keep themselves safe from all the more serious spiritual disquiets during their lifetime, so likewise by the sacrament of last anointing he has guarded the end of life by a very strong defense. For though our adversary seeks and seizes opportunities through the whole of life of finding ways to devour our souls, yet there is no time at which he draws more strongly on every shred of his skill to destroy us utterly, and to deprive us, if he can, of our confidence in the divine mercy, than when he sees that our departure from life is at hand.

Chapter 1. On the Institution of the Sacrament of Last Anointing

This holy anointing of the sick was instituted as a true and proper sacrament of the New Testament by Christ our Lord, as is suggested in Mark's Gospel, and recom- [Mk 6.13] mended and announced to the faithful through James, the apostle and brother of the Lord. He says: "Is anyone among you sick? Let him call for the elders of the church, and let them pray over him, anointing him with oil in the name of the Lord; and the [Jas 5.14–15] prayer of faith will save the sick person and the Lord will raise him up; and if he has committed sins, he will be forgiven." By these words, as the church has learned by an apostolic tradition that has been handed on, he is teaching the matter, the form, the official minister and the effect of this sacrament. The church has understood the matter to be oil blessed by a bishop, for anointing very fittingly manifests the grace of the Holy Spirit by which the soul of the sick person is invisibly anointed; and, finally, that the form is the words, "By this anointing," and so on.

Chapter 2. On the Effect of This Sacrament

Moreover the reality and effect of this sacrament is explained in the words: "And the prayer of faith will save the sick person, and the Lord will raise him up; and if [Jas 5.15] he has committed sins, he will be forgiven." For the reality is the grace of the Holy Spirit, whose anointing takes away sins, if there are any still to be expiated, and the remains of sin, and comforts and strengthens the soul of the sick person, by arousing in him great trust in the divine mercy; supported by this the sick person bears more lightly the inconveniences and trials of his illness, and resists more easily the temptations of the devil who lies in wait for his heel; and sometimes he regains bodily health when it is expedient for the salvation of his soul.

Chapter 3. On the Minister of This Sacrament and the Time at Which It Ought to Be Given

The words quoted above also give a very clear rule about those who should receive and those who should administer this sacrament. For they show that the proper ministers of this sacrament are "presbyters" of the church, and by this title in the text are to be understood, not the elders or leading figures among the people, but [1 Tm 4.14] either bishops or priests duly ordained by them by the laying on of hands of the presbyterate. It is also stated that this anointing is to be used for the sick, in particular those who are so dangerously ill that they seem to be about to depart from life; and consequently it is also called the sacrament of the departing. If the sick persons should recover after receiving the anointing, they may be helped again by the support of this sacrament when they incur another similar risk to life. Hence there is no reason to listen to those who teach, against the open and clear meaning of the apostle James, that this anointing is either a human fabrication or a rite received from the fathers which includes neither a command from God nor a promise of grace; nor to those who assert that it has now ceased, as though it belonged only to the grace of healings in the primitive church; nor to those who say that the rite and usage observed by the Holy Roman Church in the administration of this sacrament are at odds with the statement of the apostle James, and so should be changed to something else; nor, finally, to those who declare that this final anointing can, without sin, be treated as negligible by the faithful. For all these views are very clearly in conflict with the clear words of this leading apostle. Indeed, in administering this anointing the Roman Church, mother and mistress of all others, only does (in matters which constitute the substance of this sacrament) what the blessed James prescribed. Nor, indeed, could there be any slighting of so great a sacrament without immense impiety and an insult to the Holy Spirit himself.

These are the truths concerning the sacraments of penance and last anointing which this holy ecumenical council openly confesses, teaches, and proposes to all Christ's faithful to be believed and maintained.

Session 21. 16 July 1562
TEACHING ON COMMUNION UNDER BOTH KINDS AND OF CHILDREN
Introduction

The holy, ecumenical, and general Council of Trent, lawfully assembled in the Holy Spirit, with the same legates of the apostolic see as presidents, seeing that various horrifying errors about the most awesome and holy sacrament of the eucharist are being spread in different places by the tricks of the most evil spirit, because of which many people in some provinces seem to have fallen away from the faith and obedience of the Catholic Church, has judged that the subjects of communion under both kinds and that of children should be set out here. It therefore forbids all the faithful to presume to believe or teach or preach on these matters otherwise than is explained and defined in these decrees.

Chapter 1. Laity and Nonconsecrating Clergy Are Not Bound by Divine Command to Communion Under Both Kinds

Hence this holy council, taught by the Holy Spirit, who is the Spirit of wisdom and understanding, the Spirit of counsel and piety, and following the judgment and custom of the church itself, declares and teaches that laity, and clergy who are not consecrating, are under no divine command to receive the sacrament of the eucharist under both kinds; and that it can in no way be doubted (with integrity in faith) that communion under either kind is sufficient for their salvation. For, though Christ the Lord instituted this revered sacrament at the last supper and gave it to the apostles in the forms of bread and wine, this institution and gift do not mean that all the faithful are bound by a precept of the Lord to receive both forms. Nor is it correct to deduce from that saying in the sixth chapter of John that communion in both kinds was commanded by the Lord, however it may be understood from different interpretations of the holy fathers and doctors. For he who said, "unless you eat the flesh of the son of man and drink his blood, you have no life in you," also said, "if [Jn 6.52] anyone eats of this bread, he will live forever." And he who said, "he who eats my flesh and drinks my blood has eternal life," also said, "the bread which I shall give [Jn 6.55] for the life of the world is my flesh." And finally, he who said, "he who eats my flesh [Jn 6.52] and drinks my blood abides in me, and I in him," said as well, "he who eats this [Jn 6.57] bread will live forever." [Jn 6.59]

Chapter 2. The Power of the Church in Administering the Sacrament of the Eucharist

The council further declares that the church always had the power in administering the sacraments of making dispositions and changes it judged expedient for the well-being of recipients, or for the reverence due to the sacraments themselves, provided their essentials remained intact, in view of changing affairs, times, and places. This the apostle seems to have indicated plainly enough when he said: "This is how one

[1 Cor 4.1] should regard us, as servants of Christ and stewards of the mysteries of God"; and it is surely clear that he himself used this power, not only in many other matters, but over this sacrament too, when after giving some instructions for its conduct he

[1 Cor 11.34] said: "About the other things I will give directions when I come." Although from the beginning of Christian worship the use of both kinds was common, yet that custom was very widely changed in the course of time; and so Holy Mother Church, acknowledging her authority over the administration of the sacraments and influenced by good and serious reasons, has approved this custom of communicating in one form and has decreed this to be its rule, which is not to be condemned nor freely changed without the church's own authority.

Chapter 3. Christ Is Received Whole and Entire Under Either Kind, As Is the True Sacrament

The council also declares that, although our Redeemer instituted this sacrament at the last supper and gave it to the apostles in two forms, as was said above; it must nevertheless be asserted that Christ is also received whole and entire, as is the true sacrament, under either kind alone, and that therefore, as far as the effect is concerned, those who receive only one form are not cheated of any grace necessary for salvation.

Chapter 4. Children Are Not Bound to Sacramental Communion

Finally, the same holy council teaches that children under the age of discernment are not bound by any obligation to sacramental holy communion, seeing that after rebirth by the water of baptism and incorporation in Christ they are not at that age able to lose the grace they have received of being children of God. Nor are times past to be condemned if they sometimes observed that custom in some places. For those holy fathers had good reason for their practice in the situation of their time, and we must certainly believe without dispute that they did not do this for any necessity of salvation.

Session 22. 17 September 1562
TEACHING AND CANONS ON THE MOST HOLY SACRIFICE OF THE MASS

In order that the ancient faith and the teaching on the great mystery of the eucharist may be retained in the Holy Catholic Church unqualified and complete in every detail, and be preserved in its purity by the rejection of all errors and heresies; the holy, ecumenical, and general Council of Trent, lawfully assembled in the Holy Spirit, with the same legates of the apostolic see as presidents, and taught by the light of the Holy Spirit, teaches and declares all that follows concerning the eucharist in so far as it is a true and unique sacrifice, and decrees that it is to be preached to the faithful.

Chapter 1

As there was no fulfillment under the old covenant because of the powerlessness of the Levitical priesthood (as the apostle Paul testifies), it was necessary (God the Father of mercies thus ordaining) for another priest to arise according to the order of Melchizedek, our Lord Jesus Christ, who was able to bring to completion all due to be sanctified and to lead them to perfection. And so he, our Lord and God, was to offer himself once to God the Father on the altar of the cross, a death thereby occurring that would secure for them eternal redemption. But his priesthood was not to be eliminated by death. So, in order to leave to his beloved spouse the church a visible sacrifice (as human nature requires), by which that bloody sacrifice carried out on the cross should be represented, its memory persist until the end of time, and its saving power be applied to the forgiveness of the sins which we daily commit; therefore, at the last supper on the night he was betrayed, as the Catholic Church has always understood and taught, he announced that he had been appointed forever a second priest in the order of Melchizedek, offered his body and blood to God the Father under the forms of bread and wine, and handed them to the apostles under the same material symbols to be received by them (whom at that point he was making priests of the new covenant), and he commanded them and their successors in the priesthood to offer them by the words: "Do this in remembrance of me,"[a] and

[Heb 7.11, 19]

a. [Lk 22.19; 1 Cor 11.24]

so on. For after celebrating the old passover which the whole people of the children of Israel offered in memory of their departure from Egypt, he instituted a new passover, namely the offering of himself by the church through its priests under visible signs, in memory of his own passage from this world to the Father, when he redeemed us by the shedding of his blood, rescued us from the power of darkness [Col 1.13] and transferred us to his kingdom. And this is none other than that clean oblation that can be soiled by no unworthiness or evil on the part of those offering, which [Mal 1.11] the Lord foretold through Malachi as being offered in purity in every place to his name, which would be great among the nations. And the apostle Paul indicates the same clearly enough in writing to the Corinthians, when he says that those contami- 1 Cor [10.21] nated by sharing in the table of demons cannot be sharers in the table of the Lord, by "table" meaning "altar" in both places. Finally this is the offering, prefigured by many images of sacrifice in the age of nature and the law, which was to embrace all the values signified by them, as the fulfillment and consummation of them all.

Chapter 2

In this divine sacrifice which is performed in the mass, the very same Christ is contained and offered in bloodless manner who made a bloody sacrifice of himself once for all on the cross. Hence the holy council teaches that this is a truly propitiatory sacrifice, and brings it about that if we approach God with sincere hearts and up- [Heb 4.16] right faith, and with awe and reverence, we receive mercy and find grace to help in time of need. For the Lord is appeased by this offering, he gives the gracious gift of repentance, he absolves even enormous offenses and sins. For it is one and the same victim here offering himself by the ministry of his priests, who then offered himself on the cross: it is only the manner of offering that is different. For the benefits of that sacrifice (namely the sacrifice of blood) are received in the fullest measure through the bloodless offering, so far is this latter in any way from impairing the value of the former. Therefore it is quite properly offered according to apostolic tradition not only for the sins, penalties, satisfactions, and other needs of the faithful who are living, but also for those who have died in Christ but are not yet fully cleansed.

Chapter 3

It has been the custom in the church to celebrate masses from time to time in honor and memory of the saints; the council, however, teaches that the sacrifice is not offered to them, but only to God who gave them their crown. So the priest does not say, "Peter and Paul, I offer sacrifice to you," but, thanking God for their triumph, he implores their patronage, that they may deign to intercede for us in heaven, whose memory we recall on earth.

Chapter 4

Holy things must be treated in a holy way, and this sacrifice is the holiest of all things. Hence, so that it might be offered worthily and with reverence, the Catholic Church has for many centuries fixed a venerable eucharistic prayer quite free from error, and containing only what savors in the highest degree of that holiness and devotion which raises the minds of those offering to God. For it contains both the Lord's very own words and elements from apostolic tradition and the devout enactments of saintly popes.

Chapter 5

And as human nature is such that it cannot easily raise itself up to the meditation of divine realities without external aids, Holy Mother Church has for that reason duly established certain rites, such as that some parts of the mass should be said in quieter tones and others in louder; and it has provided ceremonial such as symbolic blessings, lights, incense, vestments, and many other rituals of that kind from apostolic order and tradition, by which the majesty of this great sacrifice is enhanced, and the minds of the faithful are aroused by those visible signs of religious devotion to contemplation of the high mysteries hidden in it.

Chapter 6

The holy council would certainly like the faithful present at each mass to communicate in it not only by spiritual devotion but also by sacramental reception, so that the fruits of this sacrifice could be theirs more fully. But, if this does not always happen, the council does not for that reason condemn as private and illicit masses in which only the priest communicates. Rather, it approves and commends them, for they too should be considered truly communal masses, partly because the people communicate spiritually in them, and partly because they are celebrated by an official minister of the church, not for his own good alone but for all the faithful who belong to the body of Christ.

Chapter 7

The holy council draws the attention of priests to the rule of the church that they should mix water with the wine to be offered in the chalice, both because Christ the Lord is believed to have done so, and because water came from his side together [Jn 19.34] with blood and this sacred sign is recalled by this mixing. Further, when in the Reve- [Rv 17.15] lation of blessed John the peoples are said to be waters, the union of Christ the head with his faithful people is signified.

Chapter 8

Although the mass is full of instruction for the faithful people, the council fathers did not think it advantageous that it should everywhere be celebrated in the vernacular. Each church in its place should retain its ancient rite, approved by the Holy Church of Rome, mother and teacher of all the churches. At the same time, lest the sheep of Christ go hungry or the children ask for bread and there is no one to break it for them, the holy synod instructs the shepherds and all who have responsibility for souls frequently to explain during the celebration of mass, either personally or through another, some of what is recited in the course of the mass, and in addition to give some explanation of this mysterious and most holy sacrifice, especially on Sundays and feast days.

Chapter 9

But as in these days many errors are being spread abroad, and much is being taught or argued by many people against this ancient faith founded on the holy gospel, the traditions of the apostles, and the teaching of the holy fathers; this holy council, after holding many weighty and mature discussions of these matters, has decided by unanimous agreement of the fathers to condemn and banish from holy church all that is contrary to this most pure faith and sacred teaching, by the canons which follow.

CANONS ON THE MOST HOLY SACRIFICE OF THE MASS

1. If anyone says that a true and proper sacrifice is not offered to God in the mass, or that the offering is nothing but the giving of Christ to us to eat: let him be anathema.

[1 Cor 11.25]   2. If anyone says that by the words, "Do this in remembrance of me," Christ did not make the apostles priests, or did not lay down that they and other priests should offer his body and blood: let him be anathema.

3. If anyone says that the sacrifice of the mass is only one of praise and thanksgiving, or that it is a mere commemoration of the sacrifice enacted on the cross and not itself appeasing; or that it avails only the one who receives and should not be offered for the living and the dead, for their sins, penalties, satisfactions, and other needs: let him be anathema.

4. If anyone says that by the sacrifice of the mass blasphemy is committed against the most holy sacrifice of Christ enacted on the cross, or that it devalues that sacrifice: let him be anathema.

5. If anyone says that it is an imposture for masses to be celebrated in honor of the saints and to secure their intercession with God, as is the mind of the church: let him be anathema.

6. If anyone says that the canon of the mass contains errors and should therefore be abolished: let him be anathema.

7. If anyone says the ceremonial, vestments, and external signs used by the Catholic Church in the celebration of mass are incitements to impiety rather than instruments of devotion: let him be anathema.

8. If anyone says that masses in which only the priest communicates sacramentally are unlawful, and so should be abolished: let him be anathema.

9. If anyone says the rite of the Roman Church, in which the words of consecration and parts of the eucharistic prayer are said in a low voice, should be condemned; or that mass should only be celebrated in the vernacular; or that water should not be mixed with the wine to be offered in the chalice, on the grounds that this is against Christ's institution: let him be anathema.

Session 23. 15 July 1563
THE TRUE AND CATHOLIC DOCTRINE OF THE SACRAMENT OF ORDER, TO CONDEMN THE ERRORS OF OUR TIME
Chapter 1

Sacrifice and priesthood are so joined together by God's foundation that each exists in every law. And so, since in the new covenant the Catholic Church has received the visible sacrifice of the eucharist from the Lord's institution, it is also bound to profess that there is in it a new, visible, and external priesthood into which the old has been changed. The Sacred Scriptures show, and the tradition of the Catholic Church has always taught, that this was instituted by the same Lord our Savior, and that power was given to the apostles and their successors in the priesthood to consecrate, offer, and administer his body and blood, as also to remit or retain sins.

Chapter 2

But as the ministry of so holy a priesthood is a godly service, it was altogether fitting, so as to ensure its exercise in a more worthy and reverent manner, that in the careful organization of the church there should be other and varied orders of ministers to give official assistance to priests, so arranged that those already distinguished by the clerical tonsure should ascend through the minor to the major orders. For Scripture not only speaks of priests but also of deacons, and teaches in weighty words what [1 Tm 3.8–13] must chiefly be looked to in ordaining them. And from the very beginning of the church the names and proper functions of each of the following orders are known to have been in use (though not of equal rank), namely: subdeacon, acolyte, exorcist, reader, and doorkeeper. For the subdiaconate is included among major orders by fathers and holy councils, and we often read in them of the other lower orders.

Chapter 3

As it is quite clear from the witness of Scripture, apostolic tradition, and the unanimous consent of the fathers, that grace is conferred in sacred ordination carried out by words and external signs, no one can doubt that in a proper and true sense order is one of the seven sacraments of holy church. For the apostle says: "I remind you to rekindle the gift of God that is within you through the laying on of my hands; [2 Tm 1.6–7] for God did not give us a spirit of timidity but a spirit of power and love and self-control."

Chapter 4

In the sacrament of order, as in baptism and confirmation, a character is imprinted, which cannot be deleted or removed. Hence the holy synod justifiably condemns the opinion of those who assert that priests of the new covenant have only temporary power, and when duly ordained can be made laity once more if they do not exercise the ministry of the word of God. And if anyone maintains that all Christians without distinction are priests of the new covenant, or that all are equally endowed with the same spiritual power, he appears to be openly overthrowing the church's hier- [Sg 6.3, 9] archy, which is drawn up as a battle line, just as if (against the teaching of blessed [1 Cor 12.29] Paul) all were apostles, all prophets, all evangelists, all pastors, all teachers. The holy council further declares that, apart from the other ranks in the church, bishops in particular belong to this hierarchical order and (as the same apostle says) have been [Acts 20.28] made by the Holy Spirit rulers of the church of God; and that they are higher than priests and are able to confer the sacrament of confirmation, to ordain the ministers of the church and to fulfill many other functions, whereas those of lower order have no power to perform any of these acts. The holy council further teaches that in the ordination of bishops, priests, and other ministers neither the consent nor calling nor authority of the people or of any secular power or functionary is so required that without it the ordination would be invalid. On the contrary, it declares that those who are raised to the exercise of these ministries when called and appointed only by a secular power and functionary, and those who have the temerity to assume such office themselves, are to be regarded one and all, not as ministers of the church, but as thieves and robbers who have not entered by the sheepgate. [Jn 10.8]

These are the general truths which the holy council has decided to teach to the Christian faithful about the sacrament of order. But it has determined to condemn contrary teachings by certain appropriate censures in the following manner, so that all may use the rule of faith with Christ's help, and may more easily recognize and hold to Catholic truth amid the darkness of so many errors.

CANONS ON THE SACRAMENT OF ORDER

1. If anyone says that in the new covenant there is no visible and external priesthood; or that there exists no power to consecrate and offer the true body and blood of the Lord, and to forgive or retain sins, but only a duty and a mere service of preaching the gospel; or that those who do not preach are simply not priests: let him be anathema.

2. If anyone says that apart from the priesthood there do not exist other orders in the Catholic Church, both major and minor, by which one reaches the priesthood as by successive steps: let him be anathema.

3. If anyone says that order and holy ordination are not a true and proper sacrament instituted by Christ; or that they are a human fabrication devised by men who know nothing of church affairs; or that they are simply a rite for choosing ministers of the word of God and of the sacraments: let him be anathema.

4. If anyone says the Holy Spirit is not given through holy ordination, and so bishops say "Receive the Holy Spirit" in vain; or that no character is imprinted [Jn 20.22] by it; or that someone who was once a priest can become a layman again: let him be anathema.

5. If anyone says the sacred anointing which the church uses in holy ordination is not only unnecessary but despicable and destructive, as are the other ceremonies of holy order: let him be anathema.

6. If anyone denies that there exists in the Catholic Church a hierarchy con-

sisting of bishops, priests, and ministers, instituted by divine appointment: let him be anathema.

7. If anyone says that bishops are not of higher rank than priests, or have no power to confirm and ordain, or that the power they have is common to them and the priests; or that orders conferred by them are invalid without the consent or calling of the people or of secular authority; or that those are legitimate ministers of the word and sacraments who have neither been duly ordained nor commissioned by ecclesiastical and canonical authority, but have other origins: let him be anathema.

8. If anyone says that bishops who are elevated by the authority of the pope are not legitimate and true bishops, but a human fabrication: let him be anathema.

Session 24. 11 November 1563
[TEACHING ON THE SACRAMENT OF MARRIAGE]

Inspired by the Holy Spirit, the forefather of the human race pronounced marriage to be a perpetual and indissoluble bond when he said: "This at last is bone of my bones and flesh of my flesh. . . . Therefore a man will leave his father and mother and cleave to his wife, and the two will become one flesh."ᵃ

Christ our Lord taught more openly that two alone are to be coupled and joined by this bond when, referring to the words just quoted as spoken by God, he said, "So they are no longer two but one flesh," and went on at once to confirm the lasting nature of the same bond, previously declared only by Adam, with the words, "What therefore God has joined together, let no one put asunder."ᵇ

Christ himself, the instituter and perfecter of the most holy sacraments, merited for us by his passion the grace that would perfect natural love, strengthen the unbreakable unity, and sanctify the spouses. This the apostle Paul indicated [Eph 5.25] when he said, "Husbands love your wives, as Christ loved the church and gave himself up for her," and went on to add, "This is a great mystery and I take it to mean [Eph 5.32] Christ and the church."

Since grace received through Christ raises marriage in the dispensation of the gospel above the unions of the old law, our holy fathers and councils and the universal tradition of the church have always taught that it is rightly to be counted among the sacraments of the new law. Against this teaching wicked and wild people of our time have not only thought basely about this revered sacrament but, as is their wont, smuggling in the license of the flesh on pretext of the gospel, they have said

a. [Gn 2.23–24; Mt 19.5; Eph 5.31]
b. [Mt 19.6; Mk 10.8–9]

and written a great deal that is foreign to the mind of the Catholic Church and to custom from apostolic times, bringing great damage to the Christian faithful. Desiring to confront their rash opinions, the holy and universal council has decided to root out the more glaring errors and heresies of these schismatics, so that their noxious infection may not spread.

Session 25. 3–4 December 1563
DECREE ON PURGATORY

As the Catholic Church, instructed by the Holy Spirit, has taught from Holy Scripture and the ancient tradition of the fathers in its holy councils and most recently in this ecumenical council that purgatory exists, and that the souls detained there are helped by the prayers of the faithful and most of all by the acceptable sacrifice of the altar; the holy council charges bishops to ensure that sound teaching on purgatory, handed down by the holy fathers and sacred councils, is believed and held by the Christian faithful and everywhere preached and expounded. In homilies to uninstructed people the more difficult and subtle questions, which do nothing to sustain faith and give rise to little or no increase of devotion, should be excluded. They should not allow uncertain speculation or what borders on falsehood to be publicly treated. And they should prohibit all that panders to curiosity and superstition, or smacks of base gain, as scandalous stumbling-blocks to the faithful. Bishops should see to it that the offerings of the faithful who are living, namely masses, prayers, alms, and other works of piety, customarily done by the faithful for those of the faithful who have died, should be performed piously and with devotion according to the laws of the church, and that whatever is due for these purposes from testamentary bequests or any other sources should be discharged by priests and ministers of the church and others bound to this duty in no perfunctory manner but with diligence and accuracy.

ON INVOCATION, VENERATION, AND RELICS OF
THE SAINTS, AND ON SACRED IMAGES

The holy council charges all bishops and others with the office and responsibility of teaching, according to the practice of the Catholic and Apostolic Church received from the earliest times of the Christian religion, to the consensus of the holy fathers and to the decrees of the sacred councils, as follows: they are first of all to instruct the faithful carefully about the intercession of the saints, invocation of them, reverence for their relics, and the legitimate use of images of them; they should teach them that the saints, reigning together with Christ, offer their prayers to God for people; that it is a good and beneficial thing to invoke them and to have recourse to their prayers and helpful assistance to obtain blessings from God through his Son our Lord Jesus Christ, who is our sole Redeemer and Savior; and that those hold impious opinions who deny that the saints who enjoy eternal happiness in heaven should be invoked, or who say either that they do not pray for people, or that calling on them to pray for all of us is idolatry, or contrary to the word of God, or impugns the honor of the one Mediator between God and humankind, Jesus Christ, or that it is foolish to invoke those reigning in heaven with mind and voice. And they should teach that the holy bodies of the blessed martyrs and others who live with Christ, in that they were living members of Christ and a temple of the Holy Spirit, due to be raised by him to eternal and glorified life, are to be venerated by the faithful, and that through them many blessings are given to us by God: and hence that those are altogether to be condemned, as Holy Church has formerly condemned them and now condemns them again, who assert that no veneration or honor is owed to the relics of the saints, or that it is futile for people to honor them and other sacred memorials, and that they rehearse the memory of the saints in vain when seeking to gain their help.

And they must also teach that images of Christ, the Virgin Mother of God, and the other saints should be set up and kept, particularly in churches, and that due honor and reverence is owed to them, not because some divinity or power is believed to lie in them as reason for the cult, or because anything is to be expected from them, or because confidence should be placed in images as was done by the pagans of old; but because the honor showed to them is referred to the original which they represent: thus, through the images which we kiss and before which we uncover our heads and go down on our knees, we give adoration to Christ and veneration to the saints, whose likeness they bear. And this has been approved by the decrees of councils, especially the Second Council of Nicaea, against the iconoclasts.

Bishops should teach with care that the faithful are instructed and strengthened by commemorating and frequently recalling the articles of our faith through the expression in pictures or other likenesses of the stories of the mysteries of our redemption; and that great benefits flow from all sacred images, not only because people are reminded of the gifts and blessings conferred on us by Christ, but because the miracles of God through the saints and their salutary example is put before the eyes of the faithful, who can thank God for them, shape their own lives and conduct in imitation of the saints, and be aroused to adore and love God and to practice devotion. If anyone teaches or holds what is contrary to these decrees: let him be anathema.

The holy council earnestly desires to root out utterly any abuses that may have crept into these holy and saving practices, so that no representations of false doctrine should be set up which give occasion of dangerous error to the unlettered. So if accounts and stories from Holy Scripture are sometimes etched and pictured, which is a help to uneducated people, they must be taught that the Godhead is not pictured because it can be seen with human eyes or expressed in figures and colors. All superstition must be removed from invocation of the saints, veneration of relics, and use of sacred images; all aiming at base profit must be eliminated; all sensual appeal must be avoided, so that images are not painted or adorned with seductive charm; and people are not to abuse the celebration of the saints and visits to their relics for the purpose of drunken feasting, as if feast days in honor of the saints were to be celebrated with sensual luxury. And lastly, bishops should give very great care and attention to ensure that in this matter nothing occurs that is disorderly or arranged in an exaggerated or riotous manner, nothing profane and nothing unseemly, since holiness befits the house of God.

That these points may be carried out more faithfully, the holy synod lays down that no one may erect or see to the erection of any unusual image in any church or site, however exempt, unless it has been approved by the bishop. Nor are any new miracles to be accepted, or new relics recognized, without the bishop similarly examining and approving them. And as soon as he learns of something of this kind, he should consult with theologians and other devout men and decide as truth and devotion suggest. But if some doubtful or resistant abuse has to be rooted out, or some far more serious problem arises in these matters, then before deciding the issue the bishop should await the opinion of the metropolitan and his fellow bishops in the provincial synod, but ensuring that no new and unprecedented decree be passed in the church without the pope being consulted beforehand.

The Tridentine Profession of Faith, 1564

The Council of Trent's general decree on reform (session 25, 3–4 December 1563), mandated that all patriarchs, primates, archbishops, bishops, professors at the church's universities, and holders of papal benefices openly and formally "accept each and all of the decisions and instructions of this holy council."[1] To aid these officeholders in this requirement, Pius IV issued an authorized profession of faith in the bull "Iniunctum nobis" on 13 November 1564. Also known as the Creed of Pius IV or *The Tridentine Profession of Faith*, the creed was probably drafted by the Jesuit Peter Canisius (1521–97). The creed opens with an affirmation of → *The Niceno-Constantinopolitan Creed* before summarizing the chief decrees of the Council of Trent. From 1564 until 1967, *The Tridentine Profession of Faith* remained the standard statement for all bishops, beneficed clergy, and theological faculty. The only modification over four hundred years was the addition, in 1877, of a statement of subscription to the decrees of the First Vatican Council. This creed was also the standard profession of faith required of all Catholic converts until 1967.

Edition: Denzinger, 1862–70.

Translation: Neuner and Dupuis 2001, 21–23.

Literature: Fenlon 1980; Venard 1992, 262–63.

---

1. *DEC* 2:785.

The Tridentine Profession of Faith, 1564

1. I, N., with firm faith believe and profess each and every article contained in the symbol of faith which the Holy Roman Church uses:

[*The Latin text of the Niceno-Constantinopolitan Creed follows.*]

2. I most firmly accept and embrace the apostolic and ecclesiastical traditions, and all other observances and constitutions of the same church. I likewise accept Holy Scripture according to that sense which Holy Mother Church has held and does hold, to whom it belongs to judge of the true meaning and interpretation of the Sacred Scriptures; I shall never accept or interpret them otherwise than according to the unanimous consent of the fathers.

3. I also profess that there are truly and properly speaking seven sacraments of the new law, instituted by Jesus Christ our Lord and necessary for the salvation of the human race, though not all are necessary for each individual person: (they are) baptism, confirmation, the eucharist, penance, extreme unction, order, and matrimony. And (I profess) that they confer grace, and that of these, baptism, confirmation, and order cannot be repeated without sacrilege. I also admit and accept the rites received and approved in the Catholic Church for the administration of all the sacraments mentioned above.

4. I embrace and accept each and all the articles defined and declared by the most holy synod of Trent concerning original sin and justification.

5. I also profess that in the mass there is offered to God a true sacrifice, properly speaking, which is propitiatory for the living and the dead, and that in the most holy sacrament of the eucharist the body and blood together with the soul and the divinity of our Lord Jesus Christ are truly, really, and substantially present, and that there takes place a change of the whole substance of bread into the body and of the whole substance of wine into the blood; and this change the Catholic Church calls transubstantiation. I also confess that under each species alone the whole and entire Christ and the true sacrament is received.

6. I steadfastly hold that there is a purgatory, and that the souls detained there are helped by the acts of intercession of the faithful; likewise, that the saints reigning together with Christ should be venerated and invoked, that they offer prayers to God for us, and that their relics should be venerated. I firmly declare that the images of Christ and of the Mother of God Ever-Virgin and of the other saints as well are to be kept and preserved, and that due honor and veneration should be

given to them. I also affirm that the power of indulgences has been left by Christ to the church, and that their use is very beneficial to the Christian people.

7. I acknowledge the holy, catholic, and apostolic, Roman Church as the mother and the teacher of all the churches, and I promise and swear true obedience to the Roman pontiff, successor of blessed Peter, chief of the apostles, and vicar of Christ.

8. I unhesitantly accept and profess also all other things transmitted, defined, and declared by the sacred canons and the ecumenical councils, especially by the most holy council of Trent [and by the ecumenical Vatican Council, mostly as regards the primacy of the Roman pontiff and his infallible teaching authority]. At the same time, all contrary propositions and whatever heresies have been condemned, rejected, and anathematized by the church, I too condemn, reject, and anathematize.

9. This true Catholic faith, outside of which no one can be saved, which of my own accord I now profess and truly hold, I, N., do promise, vow, and swear that, with the help of God, I shall most faithfully keep and confess entire and inviolate, to my last breath, and that I shall take care, as far as it lies in my power, that it be held, taught, and preached by those under me, or those over whom I have charge by virtue of my office. So help me God and these his Holy Gospels.

Bibliography

Aalen, Leiv. 1981. "Confessio Augustana, 1530–1980: Jubilaeum oder Mausoleum? Zur Bedeutung des Schrifttheolgen Luther für die Augsburgische Konfession und das lutherische Bekenntnis." In *Luther und die Bekenntnisschriften 1981*, 20–45.

Abate, Eshetu. 1989. "Confessing Christ in the Apostles' Creed." *East Africa Journal of Evangelical Theology* 8/1:29–40.

Abramowski, Luise. 1975. "Die Synode von Antiochien 324/25 und ihr Symbol." *ZKG* 86/3: 356–66.

———. 1976. "Das Bekenntnis des Gregor Thaumaturgus bei Gregor von Nyssa und das Problem seiner Echtheit." *ZKG* 87/2–3:145–66.

Acta et scripta theologorum Wirtembergensium et Patriarchae Constantinopolitani D. Hieremiae quae utrique ab anno M.D.LXXVI. usque ad annum M.D. LXXXI. 1584. Wittenberg: Johannes Crato.

Afanas'ev, Nikolaj. 1931. *Provincialnija sobranija rimskoj imperii i vselenskie sobory* [Provincial gatherings of the Roman Empire and the ecumenical councils]. Belgrade: Zapiski Russkago Otdělný ottisk.

Ahlers, Rolf. 1986. *The Barmen Theological Declaration of 1934: The Archeology of a Confessional Text.* Lewiston, N.Y.: Edwin Mellen Press.

Ahlstrom, Sydney E. 1972. *A Religious History of the American People.* New Haven and London: Yale University Press.

Aktensammlung zur Geschichte der Berner-Reformation, 1521–1532. 1918–23. 2 vols. Edited by R. Steck and G. Tobler. Bern: K. J. Wyss Erben.

Alberigo, G. 1959. *I vescovi italiani al concilio di Trento (1545–47).* Florence: G. C. Sansoni.

———. 1988. "The Council of Trent." In *Catholicism in Early Modern History*, 211–26. Edited by John W. O'Malley. Saint Louis, Mo.: Center for Reformation Research.

———, ed. 1991. *Christian Unity: The Council of Ferrara-Florence, 1438/39–1989.* Bibliotheca Ephemeridum Theologicarum Lovaniensium, 97. Louvain: Peeters.

———. 1995. *Announcing and Preparing Vatican Council II: Toward a New Era in Catholicism.* English version edited by Joseph A. Komonchak. Maryknoll, N.Y.: Orbis.

Aldama, J. A. de. 1934. *El Simbolo Toledano I.* Analecta Gregoriana, 8. Rome: Pontificia Universitas Gregoriana.

Alexakis, Alexander. 1997. "Before the Lateran Council of 649: The Last Days of Herakleios the Emperor and Monotheletism." In *Synodus*, 93–101. Edited by Remigius Bäumer, Evangelos Chrysos, et al. Paderborn, Germany: Ferdinand Schöningh.

Alliance of Confessing Evangelicals. 1996. *The Cambridge Declaration.* [Anaheim, Calif.: Alliance of Confessing Evangelicals.]

Altaner, B., and A. Stuiber. 1978. *Patrologie: Leben Schriften und Lehre der Kirchenväter.* 8th ed. Freiburg: Herder.

Amato, Angelo. 1983. "La dimension 'thérapeutique' du sacrement de la pénitence dans la théologie et la praxis de l'Eglise greco-orthodoxe." *Revue des sciences philosophiques et théologiques* 67:233–54.

Anabaptism Revisited: Essays on Anabaptist/Mennonite Studies in Honor of C. J. Dyck. 1992. Edited by Walter Klaassen. Scottdale, Pa.: Herald Press.

Anderson, David, tr. 1980. *On the Holy Spirit by Basil of Caesarea.* Crestwood, N.Y.: Saint Vladimir's Seminary Press.

Andrews, Theodore. 1953. *The Polish National Catholic Church in America and Poland.* London: S.P.C.K.

Androutsos, Chrēstos. 1930. *Symbolikē ex epopseōs Orthodoxou.* [Symbolics from an Orthodox perspective]. 2d ed. Athens: Typois I. A. Aleuropoulou.

———. 1956. *Dogmatikē tēs Orthodoxou Anatolikēs Ekklēsias.* Athens: Aster.

Aoanan, Melanio La Guardia. 1996. *Pagkakaisa at Pagbabago: Ang Patotoo ng United Church of Christ in the Philippines.* Quezon City, Philippines: New Day Publishers.

The Apocryphal New Testament. 1993. Edited and translated by J. K. Elliott. Oxford: Oxford University Press.

The Apostolic Fathers. 1999. 3d ed. Edited and translated by J. B. Lightfoot and J. R. Harmer; updated and revised by Michael W. Holmes. Grand Rapids, Mich.: Baker Book House.

Applegate, Stephen H. 1981. "The Rise and Fall of the Thirty-Nine Articles: An Inquiry into the Identity of the Protestant Episcopal Church in the United States." *Historical Magazine of the Protestant Episcopal Church* 50/4:409–21.

Arens, Heribert. 1982. *Die christologische Sprache Leos des Grossen: Analyse des Tomus an den Patriarchen Flavian.* Freiburg: Herder.

Armand-Hugon, A., and G. Gonnet. 1953. *Bibliografia Valdese.* Torre Pellice, Italy: Tipografia Subalpina.

Armstrong, Maurice W., Lefferts A. Loetscher, and Charles A. Anderson, eds. 1956. *The Presbyterian Enterprise: Sources of American Presbyterian History.* Philadelphia: Westminster.

Arpee, Leon. 1909. *The Armenian Awakening: A History of the Armenian Church, 1820–1860.* Chicago: University of Chicago Press.

———. 1946. *A History of Armenian Christianity from the Beginning to Our Own Time.* New York: Armenian Missionary Association of America.

Arquillière, Henri Xavier. 1926. *Le plus ancien traite de l'Eglise: Jacques de Viterbe "De regimine christiano" (1301–1302). Etude des sources et edition critique.* Paris: Beauchesne.

Arx, Urs von. 1989. *Koinonia auf altkirchlicher Basis: Deutsche Gesamtausgabe der gemeinsamen Texte des orthodox-altkatholischen Dialogs 1975–1987 mit französischer und englischer Übersetzung.* Bern: n.p.

———. 1994. "Der ekklesiologische Charakter der Utrechter Union." *Internationale Kirchliche Zeitschrift* 84:20–61.

Ascough, Richard S. 1994. "An Analysis of the Baptismal Ritual of the Didache." *Studia Liturgica* 24/2:201–13.

Aston, Margaret. 1984. *Lollards and Reformers: Images and Literacy in Late Medieval England.* London: Hambledon Press.

———. 1987. "Wyclif and the Vernacular." In *From Ockham to Wyclif,* 281–330. Edited by Anne Hudson and Michael Wilks. Oxford: Basil Blackwell.

———, and Colin Richmond, eds. 1997. *Lollardy and the Gentry in the Later Middle Ages.* New York: St. Martin's Press.

Atkinson, James. 1983. "Luthers Beziehungen zu England." In Junghans 1983, 1:677–87.

Attwater, Donald. 1935. *The Catholic Eastern Churches*. Milwaukee, Wis.: Bruce Publishing.

Aturan ni Huria Kristen Batak Protestan (H.K.B.P.). 1962. Pearadja, Tarutung, Indonesia: H.K.B.P.

Audisio, Gabriel. 1989. *Les "Vaudois": Naissance, vie et mort d'une dissidence (XIIme–XVIme siècles)*. Turin: Albert Meynier.

Ayer, Joseph C. [1913] 1970. *A Source Book for Ancient Church History from theApostolic Age to the Close of the Conciliar Period*. Reprint, New York: AMS Press.

Azevedo, Marcello de C. 1985. "Basic Ecclesial Communities: A Meeting Point of Ecclesiologies." *Theological Studies* 46:601–20.

Backus, Irena. 1990. "Polemic, Exegetical Tradition, and Ontology: Bucer's Interpretation of John 6:52, 53, and 64 Before and After the Wittenberg Concord." In *The Bible in the Sixteenth Century*, 167–80. Edited by David C. Steinmetz. Durham, N.C.: Duke University Press.

———, and Claire Chimelli, eds. 1986. *"La vraie piété": Divers traités de Jean Calvin et Confession de foi de Guillaume Farel*. Geneva: Labor et Fides.

Bainton, Roland H. 1949. "Luther and the *via media* at the Marburg Colloquy." *Lutheran Quarterly* 1:394–98.

Baker, J. Wayne. 1988. "Church, State and Dissent: The Crisis of the Swiss Reformation, 1531–1536." *Church History* 57:135–52.

Bakhuizen van den Brink, J. N., ed. 1974. *Ratramnus, De corpore et sanguine Domini*. Amsterdam: North-Holland Publishing.

Balcomb, Raymond E. 1967. "United Presbyterian General Assembly." *Christian Century* 84:788–90.

Balić, Carolus. 1948. *Tractatus de immortalitate beatae virginis Mariae*. Rome: Academia Mariana.

Balmas, Enea, and Menascé, Esther. 1981. "L'opinione pubblica inglese e le 'Pasque Piemontesi': Nuovi documenti." *Bollettino della Società di Studi Valdesi* 150:3–26.

Balthasar, Hans Urs von, ed. 1984. *Sedet ad dexteram Patris*. Special issue of *Internationale Katholische Zeitschrift "Communio"* 13:1–34.

———. 1990. *Credo: Meditations on the Apostles' Creed*. Introduction by Medard Kehl; translated by David Kipp. New York: Crossroad.

Bangs, Carl. 1985. *Arminius: A Study in the Dutch Reformation*. 2d ed. Grand Rapids, Mich.: Asbury Press.

Baptism, Eucharist, and Ministry. 1982. Faith and Order Paper 111. 35th printing. Geneva: World Council of Churches Publications.

Barbour, Hugh Christopher. 1993. *The Byzantine Thomism of Gennadios Scholarios*. Vatican City: Libreria Editrice Vaticana.

Barclay, Robert. [1673]. *A Catechism and Confession of Faith*. Urie, Scotland: n.p.

———. 1857. *A Catechism and Confession of Faith*. Philadelphia: n.p.

Bardy, Gustave. 1926. "Saint Alexandre d'Alexandrie a-t-il connu la *Thalie* d'Arius?" *Revue des sciences religieuses* 6:527–32.

Baring, Georg. 1959. "Hans Denck und Thomas Müntzer in Nürnberg 1524." *ARG* 50:145–81.

Barker, William S. 1984. "Subscription to the Westminster Confession of Faith and Catechisms." *Presbyterion* 10/1–2:1–19.

——. 1994. "The Men and Parties of the Assembly." In Carson and Hall 1994, 47–61.

Bârlea, Octavian. 1948. *De Confessione Orthodoxa Petri Mohilae*. Frankfurt: Josef Knecht.

——. 1989. *Die Konzile des 13.-15. Jahrhunderts und die ökumenische Frage*. Wiesbaden: Harrassowitz.

Barnard, Leslie William. 1962. "The Problem of Saint Polycarp's Epistle to the Philippians." *Church Quarterly Review* 163:421–30.

——. 1967. *Justin Martyr: His Life and Thought*. Cambridge: Cambridge University Press.

——. 1974. *The Graeco-Roman and Oriental Background of the Iconoclastic Controversy*. Leiden: Brill.

——. 1980. "Marcellus of Ancyra and the Eusebians." *GOTR* 25:63–76.

——. 1983. *The Council of Serdica, 343 A.D.* Sofia: Synodal Publishing House.

——, tr. 1997. *St. Justin Martyr: The First and Second Apologia*. New York: Paulist Press.

Barnes, Michel R., and Daniel H. Williams, eds. 1993. *Arianism After Arius: Essays on the Development of the Fourth-Century Trinitarian Conflicts*. Edinburgh: T. and T. Clark.

Barnes, T. D. 1990. "The Consecration of Ulfila." *JTS* 41:541–45.

Barr, O. Sydney. 1964. *From the Apostles' Faith to the Apostles' Creed*. New York: Oxford University Press.

Barrus, Ben M., Milton L. Baughn, and Thomas H. Campbell. 1972. *A People Called Cumberland Presbyterians*. Memphis, Tenn.: Frontier Press.

Barth, Karl. 1948a. *Die christliche Lehre nach dem Heidelberger Katechismus*. Zurich: Evangelischer Verlag. [Translated, together with *Einführung in den Heidelberger Katechismus* (1960) in *The Heidelberg Catechism for Today*. London: Epworth Press, 1964.]

——. 1948b. *Credo: Die Hauptprobleme der Dogmatik dargestellt im Anschluss an das Apostolische Glaubensbekenntnis; 16 Vorlesungen, gehalten an der Universität Utrecht im Februar und März 1935*. Zöllikon, Switzerland: Evangelischer Verlag. [English translation by J. Strathearn McNab. New York: C. Scribner's Sons, 1936.]

——. 1953. *Dogmatique: La doctrine de la parole de Dieu*. Geneva: Labor et Fides.

——. 1959. *Protestant Thought from Rousseau to Ritschl*. Translated by Brian Cozens. Introduction by Jaroslav Pelikan. New York: Harper and Brothers.

Bate, Herbert Newell. 1928. *Faith and Order: Proceedings of the World Conference Lausanne, August 3–21, 1927*. Garden City, N.Y.: Doubleday.

Batiffol, P. 1925/1927. "Les sources de l'histoire du Concile de Nicée." *Echos d'Orient* 24:385–402, 26:5–17.

Bauer, Johannes B. 1995. *Die Polykarpbriefe*. Göttingen: Vandenhoeck und Ruprecht.

Bauman, Clarence, ed. and trans. 1991. *The Spiritual Legacy of Hans Denck*. Leiden: E. J. Brill.

Baumer, Franklin Le Van. 1960. *Religion and the Rise of Scepticism*. New York: Harcourt, Brace and World.

Bäumer, Remigius, ed. 1979. *Concilium Tridentinum*. Darmstadt: Wissenschaftliche Buchgesellschaft.

Baur, August. 1883. *Die erste Zürcher Disputation*. Halle: Niemeyer.

Bavaud, Georges. 1956. *La Dispute de Lausanne (1536): Une étape de l'évolution doctrinale de réformateurs romands*. Fribourg, Switzerland: Editions Universitaires.

Baxter, Anthony. 1989. "Chalcedon and the Subject of Christ." *Downside Review* 107:1–21.

Bayne, Stephen Fielding. 1960. *Ceylon, North India, Pakistan: A Study in Ecumenical Decision.* London: S.P.C.K., 1960.

Bays, Daniel H., ed. 1996. *Christianity in China: From the Eighteenth Century to the Present.* Stanford, Calif.: Stanford University Press.

Bazaar of Heraclides. 1925. Edited and translated by Godfrey Rolles Driver and Leonard Hodgson. Oxford: Clarendon Press.

Beaupère, René. 1979. "La réunion piénière de Foi et Constitution à Bangalore." *Istina* 24: 352–65, 391–412.

Beck, Hildebrand. 1937. *Vorsehung und Vorherbestimmung in der theologischen Literatur der Byzantiner.* Rome: Pontificale Institutum Orientalium Studiorum.

Becker, Karl Josef. 1967. *Die Rechtfertigungslehre nach Domingo de Soto: Das Denken eines Konzilstellnehmers vor, in und nach Trient.* Rome: Gregorian University.

Bedouelle, Guy. 1989. "L'eglise du Concile de Trente." In *Visages de l'eglise: Cours d'ecclésiologie,* 9–23. Edited by Patrick de Laubier. Fribourg, Switzerland: Editions Universitaires.

Beggiato, Fabrizio, ed. 1977. *Le lettere di Abelardo ed Eloisa nella traduzione di Jean de Meun.* Modena: S.T.E.M. Mucchi.

Békés, Gerard J., and Harding Meyer, eds. 1982. *Confessio fidei: International Ecumenical Colloquium, Rome, 3-8 November 1980.* Rome: Pontificio Ateneo S. Anselmo.

Benrath, Gustav Adolf. 1963. "Die Eigenart der Pfälzischen Reformation und die Vorgeschichte des Heidelberger Katechismus." *Heidelberger Jahrbuch* 7:13–32.

———. 1965. "Wyclif und Hus." *Zeitschrift für Theologie und Kirche* 62/2:196–216.

Bente, F. [1921] 1965. *Historical Introductions to the Symbolical Books of the Evangelical Lutheran Church.* Reprint, Saint Louis, Mo.: Concordia Publishing House.

Benz, Ernst. 1949. *Wittenberg und Byzanz: Zur Begegnung und Auseinandersetzung der Reformation und der Östlich-orthodoxen Kirche.* Marburg: L. Elwert-Gräfe und Unzer.

Berkhof, Hendrikus. 1963. "The Catechism in Historical Context" and "The Catechism as an Expression of Our Faith." In *Essays on the Heidelberg Catechism,* 76–92, 93–123. A collection of essays by Bard Thompson, Hendrikus Berkhof, Eduard Schweizer, and Howard Hageman. Philadelphia: United Church Press.

Bergman, Jerry. 1984. *Jehovah's Witnesses and Kindred Groups: A Historical Compendium and Bibliography.* New York: Garland.

Berryman, Phillip. 1986. "El Salvador: From Evangelization to Insurrection." In *Religion and Political Conflict in Latin America,* 58–78. Edited by Daniel H. Levine. Chapel Hill: University of North Carolina Press.

Bettenson, Henry Scowcroft, ed. 1963. *Documents of the Christian Church.* 2d ed. London; New York: Oxford University Press.

Bettenson, Henry Scowcroft, and Chris Maunder. 1999. *Documents of the Christian Church.* 3d ed. Edited by Chris Maunder. Oxford: Oxford University Press.

Beveridge, William. [1904] 1993. *A Short History of the Westminster Assembly.* Reprint, Greenville, S.C.: A Press.

Bicknell, E. J. 1955. *A Theological Introduction to the Thirty-Nine Articles of the Church of England.* 3d ed. revised by H. J. Carpenter. London: Longmans.

Biel, Pamela. 1991. *Doorkeepers at the House of Righteousness: Heinrich Bullinger and the Zurich Clergy, 1535-1575*. Bern: Peter Lang.

Bieler, Ludwig. 1986. *Studies on the Life and Legend of St. Patrick*. Edited by Richard Sharpe. London: Variorum Reprints.

Bienert, Wolfgang A. 1981. "The Significance of Athanasius of Alexandria for Nicene Orthodoxy." *Irish Theological Quarterly* 48:181-95.

Bierma, Lyle D. 1982. "Olevianus and the Authorship of the Heidelberg Catechism: Another Look." *Sixteenth Century Journal* 13:17-28.

Bindley, T. Herbert. 1950. *The Oecumenical Documents of the Faith*. 4th ed., revised by F. W. Green. London: Methuen.

Birnbaum, Philip, tr. 1977. *Daily Prayer Book*. New York: Hebrew Publishing.

Bitterman, M. G. F. 1973. "The Early Quaker Literature of Defense." *Church History* 42:203-28.

Bizer, Ernest. 1955-56. "Zum geschichtlichen Verständnis von Luthers Schmalkaldischen Artikeln." *ZKG* 67/1-2:61-92.

———. 1957. "Noch einmal: Die Schmalkaldischen Artikel." *ZKG* 68:287-94.

———. 1962. *Studien zur Geschichte des Abendmahlsstreits im 16. Jahrhundert*. Darmstadt: Wissenschaftliche Buchgesellschaft.

Blanke, Fritz. 1966. "Zwingli's 'Fidei Ratio' (1530)." *ARG* 57:96-102. Abbreviated form of introduction in *CR* 93/2:754-89.

———, and Immanuel Leuschner. 1990. *Heinrich Bullinger: Vater der reformierten Kirche*. Zurich: Theologischer Verlag.

Blankenship, Paul F. 1964. "The Significance of John Wesley's Abridgement of the Thirty-Nine Articles as Seen from His Deletions." *Methodist History* 3:34-47.

Blumhofer, Edith Waldvogel. 1993. *Restoring the Faith: The Assemblies of God, Pentecostalism, and American Culture*. Urbana: University of Illinois Press.

Board of Christian Education of the United Presbyterian Church of America. 1956. *The Confessional Statement and the Book of Government and Worship of the United Presbyterian Church of North America*. Pittsburgh, Pa.: Board of Christian Education of the United Presbyterian Church of North America.

Boase, T. S. R. 1933. *Boniface VIII*. London: Constable.

Boccassini, Daniela. 1984. "Il massacro dei Valdesi di Provenza per una rilettura." *Bollettino della Societa di Studi Valdesi* 154:59-73.

Boelens, Wim L. 1964. *Die Arnoldshainer Abendmahlsthesen: Die Suche nach einem Abendmahlskonsens in der Evangelischen Kirche in Deutschland, 1947-1957, und eine Würdigung aus katholischer Sicht*. Assen, Netherlands: Van Gorcum.

Boespflug, François, and Nicolas Lossky, eds. 1987. *Nicée II, 787-1987: Douze siècles d'images religieuses*. Paris: Editions du Cerf.

Boettner, Loraine. 1983. *The Reformed Faith*. Phillipsburg, Pa.: Presbyterian and Reformed Publishing.

Bogolepov, Aleksandr Aleksandrovich. 1963. "Which Councils Are Recognized as Ecumenical?" *Saint Vladimir's Seminary Quarterly* 7/2:54-72.

Boice, James Montgomery. 1996. *Here We Stand: A Call from Confessing Evangelicals*. Grand Rapids, Mich.: Baker Book House.

Boisvert, Robert G. 1964. *The Scheme of Church Union in Ceylon and the Problems It Presents to the Anglican Community*. Rome: Catholic Book Agency.

Bolink, Peter. 1967. *Towards Church Union in Zambia*. Franeker, Netherlands: T. Wever.

The Book of Confessions. Part I: The Constitution of the Presbyterian Church (U.S.A.). 1996. Louisville, Ky.: Office of the General Assembly.

Book of Worship: United Church of Christ. 1986. New York: United Church of Christ Office for Church Life and Leadership.

Bornkamm, Heinrich. 1952. *Martin Bucers Bedeutung für die europäische Reformationsgeschichte*. Schriften des Vereins für Reformationsgeschichte, 169. Gütersloh, Germany: C. Bertelsmann.

Botte, Bernard. 1984. *La tradition apostolique*. 2d ed. Paris: Editions du Cerf.

Bouman, Walter R. 1969. "The Gospel and the Smalcald Articles." *Concordia Theological Monthly* 40:407–18.

Bouwsma, William James. 1989. *John Calvin: A Sixteenth-Century Portrait*. New York: Oxford University Press.

Bovon-Thurneysen, Annegreth. 1973. "Ethik und Eschatologie im Philipperbrief des Polycarp von Smyrna." *Theologische Zeitschrift* 29:241–56.

Bowman, Robert M. 1991. *Understanding Jehovah's Witnesses: Why They Read the Bible the Way They Do*. Grand Rapids, Mich.: Baker Book House.

Bradow, Charles King. 1960. "The Career and Confession of Cyril Loukaris: The Greek Orthodox Church and Its Relations with Western Christians (1543–1638)." Ph.D. diss., Ohio State University.

Brady, Thomas A. 1973. "Jacob Sturm of Strasbourg and the Lutherans at the Diet of Augsburg, 1530." *Church History* 42/2:183–202.

Braekman, Emile-Michel. 1988. "Les interventions de Calvin." In *La Dispute de Lausanne 1988*, 170–77.

————, and J. F. Gilmont. 1971. "Les écrits de Guy de Brès: Editions des XVe et XVIIe siècles. *Annales. Société d'Histoire du Protestantisme Belge*, 5th ser., 8:265–75.

Braght, Thieleman J. van, comp. 1985. *The Bloody Theater or Martyrs Mirror*. Translated from the 1660 edition by Joseph F. Sohm. Scottdale, Pa.: Herald Press.

Brandi, Karl. 1965. *The Emperor Charles V*. London: J. Cape.

Brändle, Werner. 1989. "Hinabgestiegen in das Reich des Todes." *Kerygma und Dogma* 35:54–68.

Brandt, Caspar. 1908. *Life of James Arminius*. Translated by John Guthrie. Nashville, Tenn.: Publishing House of the Methodist Episcopal Church South.

Bray, Gerald. 1983. "The *filioque* Clause in History and Theology." *Tyndale Bulletin* 34:91–144.

Brecht, Martin. 1983. "Luthers Beziehungen zu den Oberdeutschen und Schweizern von 1530–1531 bis 1546." In Junghans 1983, 1:497–517.

————. 1985–93. *Martin Luther*. 3 vols. Translated by James L. Schaaf. Minneapolis, Minn.: Fortress Press.

————, and Reinhard Schwarz, eds. 1980. *Bekenntnis und Einheit der Kirche: Studien zum Konkordienbuch*. Stuttgart: Calwer Verlag.

———. 1990. *Martin Luther: Shaping and Defining the Reformation, 1521-1532.* Translated by James L. Schaaf. Minneapolis, Minn.: Fortress Press.

Bréhier, Louis. [1904] 1969. *La querelle des images (VIIIe-IXe siècles).* Reprint, New York: Burt Franklin.

Brennecke, Hanns Christof. 1988. *Studien zur Geschichte der Homöer.* Tübingen: Mohr.

———. 1993. "Lukian von Antiochien in der Geschichte der arianischen Streites." In *Logos: Festschrift für Luise Abramowski,* 170-92. Edited by Hanns Christof Brennecke, Ernst Ludwig Grasmück, and Christoph Markschies. Beihefte zur Zeitschrift für die neutestamentliche Wissenschaft und die Kunde der älteren Kirche, 67. Berlin: W. de Gruyter.

Brent, Allen. 1992. "The Ignatian Epistles and the Threefold Ecclesiastical Order." *Journal of Religious History* 17:18-32.

———. 1995. *Hippolytus and the Roman Church in the Third Century: Communities in Tension Before the Emergence of a Monarch Bishop.* Leiden: E. J. Brill.

Bretscher, Paul M. 1959. "The Arnoldshain Theses on the Lord's Supper." *Concordia Theological Monthly* 30:83-91.

Brewer, Priscilla J. 1986. *Shaker Communities, Shaker Lives.* Hanover, N.H.: University Press of New England.

Brightman, F. E. 1896. *Liturgies, Eastern and Western, Being the Texts, Original or Translated, of the Principal Liturgies of the Church.* Edited with introductions and appendices on the basis of former work by C. E. Hammond. Oxford: Clarendon Press.

Brinton, Howard H. 1973. *The Religious Philosophy of Quakerism: The Beliefs of Fox, Barclay, and Penn as Based on the Gospel of John.* Wallingford, Pa.: Pendle Hill Publications.

Brost, Eberhard. 1979. *Abaelard: Die Leidensgeschichte und der Briefwechsel mit Heloisa.* Heidelberg: Lambert Scheider.

Brouwer, Christian. 1996. "Les condamnations de Bérenger de Tours (XIe siècle)." In *Le penseur, la violence, la religion,* 9-23. Edited by Alain Dierkens. Brussels: Editions de l'Université de Bruxelles.

Brown, G. Thompson. 1986. *Christianity in the People's Republic of China.* Atlanta, Ga.: John Knox Press.

Brown, Peter. 1973. "A Dark Age Crisis: Aspects of the Iconoclastic Controversy." *English Historical Review* 88:1-34.

Brown, Robert McAfee. 1979. "Confession of Faith of the Presbyterian-Reformed Church in Cuba, 1977." *Religion in Life* 48:268-82.

Brown, Thomas. [1812] 1977. *An Account of the People Called Shakers: Their Faith, Doctrines, and Practice.* Reprint, New York: AMS Press.

Bruckner, Aleksander. 1979. "The Polish Reformation in the Sixteenth Century." In *Polish Civilization,* 68-87. Edited by Mieczyslaw Giergielewicz and Ludwik Krzyzanowski. New York: New York University Press.

Brunner, Peter. 1963. "Die Rechtfertigungslehre des Konzils von Trient." In *Pro veritate: Ein theologischer Dialog,* 59-96. Edited by Edmund Schlink and Hermann Volk. Münster: Aschendorffsche Verlagsbuchhandlung.

Brüsewitz, J., and M. A. Krebber, eds. 1982. *Confessie van Dordrecht, 1632.* Introduction by Irvin B. Horst. Amsterdam: Doopgezinde Historische Kring.

Bucer, Martin. 1969. *Martin Bucers Deutsche Schriften*. Vol. 3. Edited by Bernd Moeller. Series editor, Robert Stupperich. Gütersloh, Germany: Gerd Mohn.

Bucke, Emory Stevens, ed. 1964. *History of American Methodism*. 3 vols. Nashville, Tenn.: Abingdon Press.

Buehrens, John A., ed. 1999. *The Unitarian Universalist Pocket Guide*. 3d ed. Boston: Skinner House Books.

Bunting, Ian D. 1966. "The *Consensus Tigurinus*." *Journal of Presbyterian History* 44:45–61.

Burchill, Christopher J. 1986. "On the Consolation of a Christian Scholar: Zacharias Ursinus (1534–1583) and the Reformation of Heidelberg." *Journal of Ecclesiastical History* 37/4:568–83.

Burckhardt, Paul. 1946. *Basel in den ersten Jahren nach der Reformation*. Basler Neujahrsblatt, 124. Basel: R. Reich.

Burckhardt-Biedermann, Thomas. 1896. "Zur Publikation des ersten Basler Glaubensbekenntnisses." *Anzeiger für schweizerische Geschichte*, 359.

Burg, B. R. 1974. "The Cambridge Platform: A Reassertion of Ecclesiastical Authority." *Church History* 43:470–87.

Burgess, Joseph A., ed. 1980. *The Role of the Augsburg Confession: Catholic and Lutheran Views*. Philadelphia: Fortress Press.

Burgess, Stanley M., and Gary B. McGee, eds. 1988. *Dictionary of Pentecostal and Charismatic Movements*. Grand Rapids, Mich.: Regency Reference Library.

Burgsmüller, Alfred, and Rudolf Weth, eds. 1983. *Die Barmer Theologische Erklärung: Einführung und Dokumentation*. Foreword by Eduard Lohse. Neukirchen-Vluyn, Germany: Neukirchener Verlag des Erziehungsvereins.

Burkhardt, C. A. H. 1879. *Geschichte der sächsischen Kirchen- und Schulvisitationen von 1524–45*. Leipzig: F. W. Grunow.

Burn, Andrew Ewbank. 1906. *The Apostles' Creed*. New York: E. S. Gorham.

———. 1909. *Facsimiles of the Creeds from Early Manuscripts*. Paleographic notes by Ludwig Traube. London: Harrison and Sons.

———. 1925–26. "The Authorship of the *Quicumque Vult*." *JTS* 27:19–28.

———. 1930. *The Athanasian Creed*. London: Rivingtons.

———. [1896] 1967. *The Athanasian Creed and Its Early Commentaries*. Texts and Studies: Contributions to Biblical and Patristic Literature, 4/1. Reprint, Nendeln, Liechtenstein: Kraus Reprint.

Burnett, Charles S. F. 1986. "Confessio fidei ad Heloisam." *Mittellateinisches Jahrbuch* 21:147–55.

Burrage, Champlin. 1906. *The True Story of Robert Browne (1550?–1633), Father of Congregationalism*. Oxford: Oxford University Press.

Bury, J. B. 1964. *History of the Papacy in the Nineteenth Century: Liberty and Authority in the Roman Catholic Church*. Augmented ed. New York: Schocken Books.

Büsser, Fritz. 1985. *Wurzeln der Reformation in Zürich: Zum 500ten Geburtstag des Reformators Huldrych Zwingli*. Leiden: E. J. Brill.

Butterworth, G. W., tr. 1966. *On First Principle, Being Koetschau's Text of the De principiis of Origen*. New York: Harper and Row.

Butterworth, Robert, ed. and tr. 1977. *Contra Noetum*. London: Heythrop College, University of London.

Bwalya, Musonda. 2000. "The Present State of Theological Education in Zambia: With a Focus on the United Church of Zambia." Presented at the United Church of Zambia Theological College Golden Jubilee Celebrations. Kitwe, Zambia, August 2000. Supplied by the author.

Calvin, John. 1926–59. *Opera Selecta*. 5 vols. Edited by Petrus Barth, Wilhelm Niesel, and Dora Scheuner. Munich: Kaiser.

Camelot, P.-Th. 1962. *Ephèse et Chalcédoine*. Mainz: Matthias-Grünewald-Verlag.

Camenisch, Emil. 1920. *Bündnerische Reformationsgeschichte*. Chur, Switzerland: Bischofberger und Hotzenköcherle.

Capelle, B. 1922. "La lettre d'Auxence sur Ulfila." *Revue Bénédictine* 34:224–33.

Capern, Amanda. 1991. "'Slipperye times and dangerous dayes': James Ussher and the Calvinist Reformation of Britain, 1560–1660." Ph.D. diss., University of New South Wales, 1991.

Cappuyns, M. 1934. "L'origine des 'Capitula' d'Orange 529." *Recherches de théologie ancienne et médiévale* 6:121–42.

Carcione, Filippo. 1985. "Enérgheia, Thélema, e Theokínetos nella lettera Sergio, Patriarca di Constantinopolim a Papa Onorio Primo." *Orientalia Christiana perodica* 51/2:263–76.

Cariño, Feliciano V., ed. 1987. *Like a Mustard Seed: Commentaries on the Statement of Faith of the United Church of Christ in the Philippines*. Quezon City, Philippines: United Church of Christ in the Philippines.

Carrington, Philip. 1940. *The Primitive Christian Catechism: A Study in the Epistles*. Cambridge: Cambridge University Press.

Carruthers, Samuel William. 1897. *The Shorter Catechism of the Westminster Assembly of Divines*. London: Publication Office of the Presbyterian Church of England.

———. 1957. *Three Centuries of the Westminster Shorter Catechism*. Fredericton: University of New Brunswick.

———. [1937] 1995. *The Westminster Confession of Faith*. Reprint, Greenville, S.C.: Reformed Academic Press.

Carson, John L., and David W. Hall, ed. 1994. *To Glorify and Enjoy God: A Commemoration of the 350th Anniversary of the Westminster Assembly*. Carlisle, Pa.: Banner of Truth Trust.

Cartellieri, A., and W. Stechele, eds. 1909. *Chronicon universale anonymi Laudunensis*. Leipzig: Dyksche Buchhandlung.

Carton, Raoul. 1930. "Le christianisme et l'Augustinisme de Boéce." *Revue de philosophie*, n.s., 1:573–659.

Caspar, E. 1932. "Die Lateransynod von 649." *ZKG* 51:75–137.

Caspari, C. P. [1866] 1964. *Ungedruckte, unbeachtete und wenig beachtete Quellen zur Geschichte des Taufsymbols und der Glaubensregel*. 3 vols. Reprint, Brussels: Culture et Civilisation.

Cather, Willa, and Georgine Milmine. 1993. *The Life of Mary Baker G. Eddy and the History of Christian Science*. Introduction and afterword by David Stouck. Lincoln: University of Nebraska Press.

Catto, Jeremy. 1987. "Some English Manuscripts of Wyclif's Latin Works." In *From Ockham*

to Wyclif, 353–59. Edited by Anne Hudson and Michael Wilks. Studies in Church History,
Subsidia, 5. Oxford: Basil Blackwell.

———. 1992. "Theology After Wycliffism." In *The History of the University of Oxford.* Volume 2 of *Late Medieval Oxford,* 263–80. Edited by J. I. Catto and T. A. R. Evans. Oxford: Clarendon Press.

Cavadini, John. 1993. *The Last Christology of the West: Adoptionism in Spain and Gaul, 785–820.* Philadelphia: University of Pennsylvania Press.

Cazacu, M. 1984. "Pierre Mohyla (Petru Movil) et la Roumanie: Essai historique et bibliographique." *Harvard Ukrainian Studies* 8:188–221.

Cegna, Romolo. 1982. *Fede ed etica Valdese nel Quattrocento.* Turin: Editrice Claudiana.

Chadwick, Henry. 1955. "Exile and Death of Flavian of Constantinople: A Prologue to the Council of Chalcedon." *JTS* 6:17–34.

———. 1958. "Ossius of Cordova and the Presidency of the Council of Antioch, 325." *JTS* 9:292–304.

———. 1965. "Justin Martyr's Defence of Christianity." *Bulletin of the John Rylands Library* 47:275–97.

———. 1966. *Early Christian Thought and the Classical Tradition: Studies in Justin, Clement, and Origen.* New York: Oxford University Press.

———. 1980. "The Authenticity of Boethius' Fourth Tractate *De fide catholica.*" *JTS,* n.s., 31:551–56.

———. 1981. *Boethius: The Consolations of Music, Logic, Theology, and Philosophy.* Oxford: Clarendon Press.

———. 1990. "Symbol and Reality: Berengar and the Appeal to the Fathers." In Ganz, Huygens, and Niewöhner 1990, 29–46.

Chao, Jonathan, ed. 1983. *Zhonggong yu Jidujiao de Zhengce* [Chinese Communist policy toward Christianity]. Hong Kong: Chinese Church Research Center.

———, and Richard Van Houten, interviewers. 1988. *Wise as Serpents, Harmless as Doves: Christians in China Tell Their Story.* Pasadena, Calif.: Chinese Church Research Center.

Chatzēantōniou, Georgios A. 1954. *Kyrillos Loukaris.* Athens: n.p.

Chenu, Marie-Dominique. 1964. *Toward Understanding Saint Thomas.* Translated by A.-M. Landry and D. Hughes. Chicago: Henry Regnery.

Chrestou, Panagiotes. 1982. "The Ecumenical Character of the First Synod of Constantinople, 381." *GOTR* 27:359–74.

Christensen, Carl C. 1984. "John of Saxony's Diplomacy, 1529–1530: Reformation or Realpolitik?" *Sixteenth Century Journal* 15/4:419–30.

Cicognani, A. G. 1951. "The Assumption—and Devotion to Mary in America." *Thomist* 14:22–30.

Clapsis, Emmanuel. 1982. "The *filioque* Question." *Patristic and Byzantine Review* 1/2:127–36.

Clark, Donald N. 1986. *Christianity in Modern Korea.* New York: University Press of North America.

Clark, E. A. 1992. *The Origenist Controversy.* Princeton, N.J.: Princeton University Press.

Cochrane, Arthur C. 1962. *The Church's Confession Under Hitler.* Philadelphia: Westminster Press.

Cochrane, Charles Norris. 1944. *Christianity and Classical Culture: A Study of Thought and Action from Augustus to Augustine*. London: Oxford University Press.

Codrington, H. W. 1952. *Studies of the Syrian Liturgies*. London: Coldwell.

Coggins, James R. 1986. "A Short Confession of Hans de Ries: Union and Separation in Early Seventeenth-Century Holland." *MQR* 60:128–38.

———. 1991. *John Smyth's Congregation: English Separatism, Mennonite Influence and the Elect Nation*. Scottdale, Pa.: Herald Press.

Colish, Marcia L. 1994. *Peter Lombard*. 2 vols. Leiden: E. J. Brill.

Comba, Emilio. 1889. *History of the Waldenses of Italy*. London: Truslove and Shirley.

Confesión de fe 1977 de la Iglesia Presbiteriana Reformada en Cuba. 1978. Havana: Editorial Orbe.

The Confession of Faith and the Eleven Great Principles of the Polish National Catholic Church. 1975. [Scranton, Pa.]: [Polish National Catholic Church].

Congar, Yves. 1972. "Reception as an Ecclesiological Reality." In *Election and Consensus in the Church*, 43–68. Edited by Giuseppe Alberigo and Anton Weiler. New York: Herder and Herder.

———. 1985. "De Marburg (1529) à Leuenberg (1971): Lutheriens et Reformes au temps de l'opposition et sur la voie d'une union." *Istina* 30:47–65.

Constantelos, Demetrios J. 1962–63. "Justinian and the Three Chapters Controversy." *GOTR* 8/1–2:71–94.

———. 1982. "Toward the Convocation of the Second Ecumenical Synod." *GOTR* 27:395–405.

Constitution and Bylaws of the United Church of Christ in the Philippines. 1996. [Quezon City], Phillipines: United Church of Christ in the Philippines.

Constitution and Discipline for the American Yearly Meetings of Friends. 1925. Boston: Permanent Board of the Yearly Meeting of the Friends for New England.

Constitution and Laws of the Polish National Church. 1991. Scranton, Pa.: Polish National Catholic Church.

Constitution, Rules and Regulations of the United Church of Zambia. 1994. Kitwe, Zambia: United Church Publications.

Conzemius, Victor. 1969. *Katholizismus ohne Rom: Die altkatholische Kirchengemeinschaft*. Zurich: Benziger.

Cook, William R. 1973. "John Wyclif and Hussite Theology, 1415–1436." *Church History* 42:335–49.

———. 1975. "The Eucharist in Hussite Theology." *ARG* 66:23–35.

Corpus juris canonici. [1879] 1959. 2 vols. Edited by E. Friedberg. Reprint, Graz: Akademische Druck- u. Verlagsanstalt.

Corwin, Virginia. 1960. *St. Ignatius and Christianity in Antioch*. New Haven: Yale University Press.

Countryman, L. William. 1974. "Monothelite Kontakion of the Seventh Century." *GOTR* 19:23–36.

———. 1982. "Tertullian and the Regula Fidei." *Second Century* 2/4:208–27.

Courvoisier, Jaques. 1944. *La confession helvétique postérieure: Texte français de 1566*. Neuchâtel: Editions Delachaux et Niestlé.

Cowan, Ian Borthwick. 1982. *The Scottish Reformation: Church and Society in Sixteenth-Century Scotland.* New York: St. Martin's Press.

Crabbe, Anna M. 1981. "The Invitation List to the Council of Ephesus and Metropolitan Hierarchy in the Fifth Century." *JTS* 32:369–400.

Creed and Constitution of the Cumberland Presbyterian Church. 1892. Nashville, Tenn.: Cumberland Presbyterian Publishing House.

Creighton, Mandell. 1901–2. "Introductory Note." *The Cambridge Modern History*, 1:1–6. Cambridge: Cambridge University Press.

Cross, Frank Leslie. 1939. "The Council of Antioch, AD 325." *Church Quarterly Review* 128: 49ff.

———, ed. [1960] 1986. *St. Cyril of Jerusalem's Lectures on the Christian Sacraments: The Procatechesis and the Five Mystagogical Catecheses.* Translated by R. W. Church. Reprint, Crestwood, N.Y.: Saint Vladimir's Seminary Press.

Crouzel, Henri. 1971. *Bibliographie critique d'Origèneis. Instrumenta Patristica*, 8 and 8A. Supplement published in 1982. Steenbrugge, Netherlands: Abbey of St. Peter, and The Hague: Nijhoff.

———. 1980. "La cristologia in Gregorio Taumaturgo." *Gregorianum* 61/4:745–55.

———. 1989. *Origen.* Translated by A. S. Worrall. San Francisco: Harper and Row.

Cullmann, Oscar. 1949. *The Earliest Christian Creeds.* Translated by J. K. S. Reid. London: Lutterworth.

Curtius, Ernst Robert. 1953. *European Literature and the Latin Middle Ages.* Translated from the German by Willard R. Trask. New York: Pantheon Books.

Daily Prayer Book [Ha-Siddur Ha-Shalem]. 1977. Translated by Philip Birnbaum. New York: Hebrew Publishing.

Daley, Brian E. 1998. *On the Dormition of Mary: Early Patristic Homilies.* Crestwood, N.Y.: Saint Vladimir's Seminary Press.

Davey, Colin. 1987. *Pioneer for Unity: Metrophanes Kritopoulos (1589–1639) and Relations Between the Orthodox, Roman Catholic and Reformed Churches.* London: British Council of Churches.

Davies, Andrew A. 1979. "The Marburg Colloquy." In *Union and Communion*, 92–101. Edited by Philip H. Eveson et al. London: Westminster Conference.

Davis, J. F. 1982. "Lollardy and the Reformation in England." *ARG* 73:217–36.

Davis, Leo Donald. 1987. *The First Seven Ecumenical Councils (325–787).* Wilmington, Del.: Michael Glazer.

Dawley, Powel Mills. 1954. *John Whitgift and the English Reformation.* New York: Scribner.

DeClercq, V. C. 1954. *Ossius of Cordova: A Contribution to the History of the Constantinian Period.* Washington, D.C.: Catholic University of America Press.

DeFerrari, Roy J, tr. [1957] 2002. *The Sources of Catholic Dogma: From the Thirtieth Edition of Henry Denzinger's Enchiridion Symbolorum.* Reprint, Fitzwilliam, N.H.: Loreto Publications.

Definite Platform, Doctrinal and Disciplinarian, for Evangelical Lutheran District Synods: Construed in Accordance with the Principles of the General Synod. 1856. 2d ed. Philadelphia: Miller and Burlock.

Dehandschutter, Boudewijn. 1989. "Polycarp's Epistle to the Philippians: An Early Example of 'Reception.'" In *The New Testament in Early Christianity*, 275–91. Edited by J. M. Sevrin. Leuven: Leuven University Press.

De Jong, Peter Y., ed. 1968. *Crisis in the Reformed Churches: Essays in Commemoration of the Great Synod of Dort, 1618–19*. Grand Rapids, Mich.: Reformed Fellowship.

Delagneau, G. 1931. "Le Concil de Sens de 1140: Abélard et Saint Bernard." *Revue apologétique* 52:385–408.

Delius, Hans Ulrich. 1983. "Die Marburger Artikel, 1529." In *Martin Luther Studienausgabe*, 3:463–76. Berlin: Evangelische Verlagsanstalt.

Deluz, René, and Henri Meylan. 1936. *La Dispute de Lausanne (Octobre 1536)*. Lausanne: Bibliothèque de la Faculté de Théologie.

DeSimone, Russell J. 1970. *The Treatise of Novatian the Roman Presbyter on the Trinity*. Studia Ephemeridis Augustinianum, 4. Rome: Institutum Patristicum Augustinianum.

Dewar, Michael Willoughby. 1992. "The British Delegation at the Synod of Dort: Assembling and Assembled, Returning and Returned." *Churchman* 106/2:130–46.

Dewart, Leslie. 1966. *The Future of Belief: Theism in a World Come of Age*. New York: Herder and Herder.

de Zwaan, J. 1933. "Date and Origin of the Epistle of the Eleven Apostles." In *Amicitiae Corolla*, 344–55. Edited by H. G. Wood. London: University of London Press.

Diekamp, Franz. 1899. *Die Origenistischen Streitigkeiten im sechsten Jahrhundert und das fünfte allgemeine Concil*. Münster: Aschendorff.

Dieter, Hans Jörg. 1991. *Leben wie es Gott gefällt: Confessio Taboritarum von 1434*. Berlin: Alektor Verlag.

Dinkha, K. Mar. 1994. "A Common Christological Declaration Between the Roman Catholic Church and the Assyrian Church of the East." *Ecumenical Trends* 23:173–74.

Discipline of the Korean Methodist Church [Korean]. 1931. Seoul: General Board of the Korean Methodist Church.

Discipline of the Korean Methodist Church. 1932. Translated by E. M. Cable. Seoul: General Board of the Korean Methodist Church.

La Dispute de Lausanne, 1536: La théologie réformée après Zwingli et avant Calvin. 1988. Edited by Eric Junod. Bibliothèque historique vaudoise, 90. [Proceedings of the Colloque international sur la Dispute de Lausanne, 1986.] Lausanne: Presses Centrales Lausanne.

Dix, Gregory, ed. and tr. 1992. *The Treatise on the Apostolic Tradition of St. Hippolytus of Rome*. Reissued with corrections, preface, and bibliography by Henry Chadwick. London: S.P.C.K.

Doctrines and Discipline of the Free Methodist Church. 1866. Rochester, N.Y.: General Conference.

Dods, Marcus. 1883. *The Works of Aurelius Augustine*. Volume 9: *On Christian Doctrine; The Enchiridion; On Catechising and On Faith and The Creed*. Edinburgh: T. and T. Clark.

Donaldson, Gordon. 1960. *The Scottish Reformation*. Cambridge: Cambridge University Press.

Dondaine, A. 1946. "Aux orignines du valdéisme: Une profession de foi de Valdès." *Archivum Fratrum Praedicatorum* 16:191–235.

Donfried, Karl P. 2000. "Augsburg, 1999: By Grace Alone, Some Reflections by a Participant." *Pro Ecclesia* 9/1:5–7.

Dowey, Edward A. 1966. "Der theologische Aufbau des Zweiten Helvetischen Bekenntnisses." In *Glauben und Bekennen: Vierhundert Jahre Confessio Helvetica Posterior*, 205–34. Edited by Joachim Staedtke. Zurich: Zwingli Verlag.

————. 1968. *A Commentary on the Confession of 1967 and an Introduction to the Book of Confessions*. Philadelphia: Westminster Press.

Drickamer, John M. 1982. "The Religion of 'The Large Catechism.'" *Concordia Journal* 8:139–42.

Duensing, Hugo. 1925. *Epistula Apostolorum*. Kleine Texte für Vorlesungen und Übungen, 152. Bonn: Marcus and Weber.

Duggan, Paul E. 1989. *The Assumption Dogma: Some Reactions and Ecumenical Implications in the Thought of English-Speaking Theologians*. [Cleveland, Ohio: Emerson Press].

Dugmore, C. W. 1980. "Foundation Documents of the Faith, VI: The Thirty-Nine Articles." *Expository Times* 91:164–67.

Duke, Alastair. 1990. *Reformation and Revolt in the Low Countries*. London: Hambledon Press.

Dulles, Avery. 1980. "The Augsburg Confession and Contemporary Catholicism." In Burgess 1980, 131–38.

————. 1998. "Two Languages of Salvation: The Lutheran-Catholic Joint Declaration." *First Things* 98:25–30.

Dummville, David N., ed. 1993. *Saint Patrick, A.D. 493-1993*. Rochester, N.Y.: Boydell Press.

Duval, André. 1985. *Des Sacrements au Concile de Trente*. Paris: Editions du Cerf.

Dvornik, Francis. 1948. *The Photian Schism, History and Legend*. Cambridge: Cambridge University Press.

————. 1958. *The Idea of Apostolicity in Byzantium and the Legend of the Apostle Andrew*. Cambridge, Mass.: Harvard University Press.

————. 1970. *Byzantine Missions Among the Slavs: SS. Constantine-Cyril and Methodius*. New Brunswick, N.J.: Rutgers University Press.

Dwight, H. G. O. 1854. *Christianity in Turkey: A Narrative of the Protestant Reformation in the Armenian Church*. London: J. Nesbit.

Dyck, C. J. 1964. "A Short Confession of Faith by Hans de Ries." *MQR* 38:5–19.

————, ed. 1993. *An Introduction to Mennonite History: A Popular History of the Anabaptists and the Mennonites*. Scottdale, Pa.: Herald Press.

Ebel, Jobst Christian. 1978. "Jacob Andreae (1528–1590) als Verfasser der Konkordienformel." *ZKG* 89/1–2:78–119.

————. 1980. "Die Herkunft des Konzeptes der Konkordienformel: Die Funktionen der 5 Verfasser neben Andreae beim Zustandekommen der Formel." *ZKG* 91/2–3:237–82.

————. 1981. *Wort und Geist bei den Verfassern der Konkordienformel*. Munich: Kaiser.

Eberhard, Winifried. 1981. *Konfessionsbildung und Stände in Böhmen, 1478-1530*. Munich: R. Oldenbourg.

Eck, Johannes. 1530. *Repulsio articulorum Zwinglii Ceas. Maiestati oblatorum*. [Augsburg: Alexander Weissenhorn].

Ecumenical Creeds and Reformed Confessions. 1988. Grand Rapids, Mich.: CRC Publications.

Eddy, Mary Baker. 1906. *Manual of the Mother Church, The First Church of Christ, Scientist in Boston, Massachusetts*. Boston: J. Armstrong.

————. 1906. *Science and Health, with Key to the Scriptures*. Boston: Joseph Armstrong.

Eeg-Olofsson, Ansgar. 1954. *The Conception of the Inner Light in Robert Barclay's Theology*. Lund, Sweden: C. W. K. Gleerup.

Eells, Hastings. 1931. *Martin Bucer*. New Haven: Yale University Press.

Ehrenström, Nils, and Günther Gassmann. 1979. *Confessions in Dialogue: Survey of Bilateral Conversations Among World Confessional Families*. 4th ed. Geneva: World Council of Churches.

Ehrhardt, A. A. T. 1964. "Judaeo-Christians in Egypt: The *Epistula Apostolorum* and the Gospel to the Hebrews." *Studia Evangelica* 3, 360–82. Edited by F. L. Cross. [2d International Conference on New Testament Studies, Oxford.] Berlin: Akademie-Verlag.

Eichenseer, Caelestis. 1960. *Das Symbolum apostolicum beim heiligen Augustinus: Mit Berücksichtigung des dogmengeschichtlichen Zusammenhangs*. Kirchengeschichtliche Quellen und Studien, 4. St. Ottilien, Germany: EOS.

Eire, Carlos M. N. 1986. *War Against the Idols: The Reformation of Worship from Erasmus to Calvin*. Cambridge: Cambridge University Press.

Elbogen, Ismar. [1931] 1962. *Der jüdische Gottesdienst in seiner geschichtlichen Entwicklung*. 3d ed. Reprint, Hildesheim: Georg Olms.

Elliger, Walter. 1931. "Zur bilderfeindlichen Bewegung des achten Jahrhunderts." In *Forschungen zur Kirchengeschichte und zur christlichen Kunst*, 40–60. Festschrift für Johannes Ficker. Edited by Walter Elliger. Leipzig: Dieterich.

Elliott, J. K. 1993. *The Apocryphal New Testament*. Oxford: Clarendon Press.

Encyclical Epistle of the One Holy Catholic and Apostolic Church, to the Faithful Everywhere: Being a Reply to the Epistle of Pius IX to the Easterns, Dated January 6, 1848. 1867. Papers of the Russo-Greek Committee of the Orthodox Eastern Church, 2d ser., no. 1. New York: John F. Trow.

Endriss, J. 1931. *Das Ulmer Reformationsjahr 1531 in seinem entscheidenen Vorgängen*. Ulm: K. Höhn.

Erickson, Scott E., ed. 1996. *American Religious Influences in Sweden*. Uppsala: Svenska kyrkans forskningsråd och fösfattarna.

Esbroeck, Michel van. 1989. "The Credo of Gregory the Wonderworker and Its Influence Through Three Centuries." In *Studia Patristica*, 19: *Historica, Theologica, Gnostica, Biblica et Apocrypha* [Tenth International Conference on Patristic Studies, Oxford, 1987], 255–66. Edited by Elizabeth A. Livingstone. Louvain: Peeters.

Esser, Helmut Hans. 1992. "Die Stellung des 'Summaire' von Guillaume Farel innerhalb der frühen reformierten Bekenntnisschriften." In *Reformiertes Erbe: Festschrift für Gottfried W. Locher zu seinem 80. Geburtstag*, 92–114. Edited by Heiko A. Oberman, Ernst Saxer, et al. Zurich: Theologischer Verlag Zurich.

Essig, K.-G. 1986. "Erwägungen zum geschichtlichen Ort der Apologie des Aristides." *ZKG* 97:163–88.

Ettlinger, Gerard H. 1982. "The Holy Spirit in the Theology of the Second Ecumenical Synod and in the Undivided Church." *GOTR* 27:431–40.

Eutudjian, Stepan. 1914. *Dzakoumn yev Entazn Avedaranagan Ee Hais*. Constantinople: Arax Press.

Evans, G. R., and J. Robert Wright, eds. 1991. *The Anglican Tradition: A Handbook of Sources.* London: S.P.C.K.; Minneapolis, Minn.: Fortress Press.

Ewing, John W. 1946. *Goodly Fellowship: A Centenary Tribute to the Life and Work of the World's Evangelical Alliance, 1846-1946.* London: Marshall, Morgan, and Scott.

Eynde, Damien van den. 1933. *Les normes de l'enseignement chrétien dans la littérature patristique des trois premiers siècles.* Gembloux, Belgium: J. Duculot; Paris: Gabalda et Fils.

Fagley, Frederick L., and Henry Wilder Foote. 1948. *The Cambridge "Platform of Church Discipline," 1648.* Boston: Joint Commission of the Congregational Christian Churches of the United States and the American Unitarian Association.

Farel, Guillaume. 1980. *Sommaire et brève déclaration, 1525.* Edited by Arthur L. Hofer. Neuchâtel: Editions Belle Rivière.

Fasciculi Zizaniorum magistri Johannis Wyclif cum tritico [1858] 1965. Attributed to Thomas Netter. Edited by Walter Waddington Shirley. Reprint, Wiesbaden: Kraus.

Fatio, Olivier, ed. 1986. *Confessions et Catechismes de la foi Reformée.* Paris: Labor et Fides.

Fenlon, Dermot. 1980. "Foundation Documents of the Faith, V: The Tridentine Profession of Faith [1564]." *Expository Times* 91:133-37.

Ferm, Vergilius Ture Anselm, ed. 1945. *An Encyclopedia of Religion.* New York: Philosophical Library.

Festugière, André J., ed. 1982. *Ephèse et Chalcédoine: Actes des conciles.* Paris: Beauchesne.

Fiangonan' i Jesoa Kristy eto Madagasikara. 1968. Antananarivo, Madagascar: F.J.K.M. Imarivolanitra.

Flavian. 1903. *Appellatio Flaviani: The Letters of Appeal from the Council of Ephesus, 449, Addressed by Flavian and Eusebius to St. Leo of Rome.* Edited by T. A. Lacey. London: S.P.C.K.

Florovsky, Georges. 1972-89. *Collected Works of Georges Florovsky.* 14 vols. Belmont, Mass.: Nordland Publishing.

Ford, Alan. 1996. "The Origins of Irish Dissent." In *The Politics of Irish Dissent, 1650-1800,* 9-30. Edited by Kevin Herlihy. Dublin: Four Courts Press.

———. 1997. *The Protestant Reformation in Ireland, 1590-1641.* 2d ed. Dublin: Four Courts Press.

Förstmann, Karl Eduard, ed. [1833] 1966. *Urkundenbuch zu der Geschichte des Reichstages zu Augsburg im Jahre 1530.* Reprint, Osnabrück, Germany: Biblio Verlag.

Frank, Franz Hermann Reinhold. 1858-65. *Die Theologie der Concordienformel historisch-dogmatisch entwickelt und beleuchtet.* 4 vols. Erlangen, Germany: T. Blaesing.

Frank, G. L. C. 1991. "The Council of Constantinople II as a Model Reconciliation Council." *Theological Studies* 52:636-50.

Freeman, Ann. 1957. "Theodulf of Orleans and the *Libri Carolini.*" *Speculum* 32:663-70.

———. 1965. "Further Studies in the *Libri Carolini:* I. Palaeographical Problems in Vaticanus Latinus 7207, II." *Speculum* 40:203-89.

———. 1994. "Scripture and Images in the Libri Carolini." In *Testo e immagine nell'altomedioevo,* 1:163-95. Edited by Giovanni Tabacco et al. Spoleto: Centro Italiano di Studi sull'Alto Medioevo.

Frei, Hans W. 1974. *The Eclipse of Biblical Narrative: A Study in Eighteenth- and Nineteenth-Century Hermeneutics.* New Haven and London: Yale University Press.

Frend, W. H. C. 1972. *The Rise of the Monophysite Movement*. Cambridge: Cambridge University Press.

———. 1991. *The Early Church: From the Beginnings to 461*. 3d ed. London: SCM Press.

Friedmann, Robert. 1931–32. "Eine dogmatische Hauptschrift der hutterischen Täufergemeinschaften in Mähren." *ARG* 28:80–111, 207–41, 29:1–17.

———. 1942. "The Schleitheim Confession (1527) and Other Doctrinal Writings of the Swiss Brethren in a Hitherto Unknown Edition." *MQR* 16/2:82–87.

Fries, Paul R., and Tiran Nersoyan, eds. 1987. *Christ in East and West*. Macon, Ga.: Mercer University Press.

Froehlich, Karlfried. 1992. "The Libri Carolini and the Lessons of the Iconoclastic Controversy." In *The One Mediator, the Saints, and Mary*, 193–208. Edited by H. George Anderson, J. Francis Stafford, and Joseph A. Burgess. Lutherans and Catholics in Dialogue, 8. Minneapolis, Minn.: Augsburg Publishing House.

Froidevaux, L. 1929. "Le Symbole de Saint Grégoire le Thaumaturge." *Recherches de science religieuse* 19:193–247.

Froom, LeRoy Edwin. 1946–54. *The Prophetic Faith of Our Fathers: The Historical Development of Prophetic Interpretation*. 4 vols. Washington, D.C.: Review and Herald.

Frost, Francis. 1975. "Le Concile de Trente et la doctrine protestante." In *Culpabilité fondamentale: Péché originel et anthropologie moderne*, 80–105. Edited by Paul Guilluy. Gembloux, Belgium: J. Duculot; Lille: Centre des Facultés Catholiques.

Fudge, Thomas A. 1998. *The Magnificent Ride: The First Reformation in Hussite Bohemia*. St. Andrews Studies in Reformation History. Aldershot, England: Ashgate.

Funk, F. X. 1901. *Das Testament unseres Herrn und die verwandten Schriften*. Mainz: Kirchheim.

Furcha, E. J., trans. 1984. *The Defense of the Reformed Faith*. Volume 1 of *Huldrych Zwingli: Writings*. Allison Park, Pa.: Pickwick Publications.

Gäbler, Ulrich. 1979. "Das Zustandekommen des Consensus Tigurinus im Jahre 1549." *Theologische Literatur-Zeitung* 104:321–32.

———. 1983a. *Huldrych Zwingli: Eine Einführung in sein Leben und sein Werk*. Munich: Beck.

———. 1983b. "Luthers Beziehungen zu den Schweizern und Oberdeutschen von 1526 bis 1530–31." In Junghans 1983, 1:481–96.

Gaffney, Declan. 1989. "The Practice of Religious Controversy in Dublin, 1600–1641." In *The Churches, Ireland and the Irish*, 145–58. Edited by William J. Sheils and Diana Wood. Studies in Church History, 25. Oxford: Blackwell.

Galbreath, Paul. 1996. "The Apostles' Creed in Liturgy." *Reformed Liturgy and Music* 30/4:189–92.

Galot, Jean. 1989. "Une seule personne, une seule hypostase: Origine et sens de la formule de Chalcédoine." *Gregorianum* 70:251–76.

Gams, Pius Bonifatius. [1862–79] 1956. *Die Kirchengeschichte von Spanien*. Reprint, Graz: Akademische Druck- u. Verlagsanstalt.

Ganz, Peter, R.B. C. Huygens, and Friedrich Niewöhner, eds. *Auctoritas und Ratio: Studien zu Berengar von Tours*. Wiesbaden: Harrassowitz.

Ganzer, Klaus. 1985. "Das Konzil von Trient und die theologische Dimension der katholischen Konfessionalisierung." In *Die katholische Konfessionalisierung: Wissenschaftliche*

Symposion der Gesellschaft zur Herausgabe des Corpus Catholicorum und des Vereins für Reformationsgeschichte, 50–69. Edited by Wolfgang Reinhard and Heinz Schilling. Münster: Aschendorff.

Garegin II, Catholicos of Cilicia. 1965. *The Council of Chalcedon and the Armenian Church*. London: S.P.C.K.

Garfiel, Evelyn. 1989. *Service of the Heart: A Guide to the Jewish Prayer Book*. Northvale, N.J.: Jason Aronson.

Garrison, Winfred Ernest, and Alfred T. DeGroot. 1958. *The Disciples of Christ: A History*. Saint Louis, Mo.: Bethany Press.

Gassmann, Günther. 1985. "Towards Common Confession of Apostolic Faith: Ecumenical Investigation into Fundamentals of Faith." *Centro Pro Unione Bulletin* 28:38–44.

———. 1988. "100 Jahre Lambeth-Quadrilateral: Die anglikanische Einheitscharta und ihre ökumenische Wirkung." *Ökumenische Rundschau* 37:301–11.

Gaudemet, Jean, and Brigitte Basdevant-Gaudemet. 1989. *Les Canons des Conciles Mérovingiens (VIe–VIIe siècles)*. Paris: Editions du Cerf.

Gauss, J. 1940. "Die Dictatusthesen Gregors VII. als Unionsforderungen: Ein historischer Erklärungsversuch." *Zeitschrift der Savigny-Stiftung für Rechtsgeschichte*. Kanonistische Abteilung, 29:1–115.

Geanakoplos, Deno J. 1966. "The Council of Florence (1438–39) and the Problem of Union Between the Byzantine and Latin Churches." In *Byzantine East and Latin West: Two Worlds of Christendom in Middle Ages and Renaissance; Studies in Ecclesiastical and Cultural History*, 84–109. New York: Harper Torchbooks.

———. 1982. "The Second Ecumenical Synod of Constantinople (381): Proceedings and Theology of the Holy Spirit." *GOTR* 27:407–29.

Gee, Henry, and William John Hardy. 1896. *Documents Illustrative of English Church History*. London: Macmillan.

Geisberg, Max. 1923. "Cranach's Illustrations to the Lord's Prayer and the Editions of Luther's Catechism." *Burlington Magazine* 43:84–87.

George, Timothy. 1988. "John Calvin and the Agreement of Zurich (1549)." In *Calvin Studies* 4, 25–40. Edited by W. Stacy Johnson and John H. Leith. Davidson, N.C.: Davidson College.

———, and Denise George, eds. 1996. *Baptist Confessions, Covenants, and Catechisms*. Nashville, Tenn.: Broadman and Holman.

Georgi, Curt Robert Armin. 1940. *Die Confessio Dosithei (Jerusalem 1672): Geschichte, Inhalt und Bedeutung*. Munich: Ernst Reinhardt.

Gerhardsson, Birger. 1992. "The Shema in Early Christianity." In *The Four Gospels*, 1:275–93. Festschrift for Frans Neirynck. Edited by Frans van Segbroeck, Christopher M. Tuckett, et al. Bibliotheca Ephemeridum Theologicarum Lovaniensium, 100. Louvain: Peeters.

Gero, Stephen. 1973a. *Byzantine Iconoclasm During the Reign of Leo III, with Particular Attention to the Oriental Sources*. Louvain: Corpus Scriptorum Christianorum Orientalium.

———. 1973b. "Libri Carolini and the Image Controversy." *GOTR* 18:7–34.

———. 1977. *Byzantine Iconoclasm During the Reign of Constantine V, with Particular Attention to the Oriental Sources*. Louvain: Corpus Scriptorum Christianorum Orientalium.

Ghellinck, Joseph de. 1946. *Les recherches sur les origines du symbole des apôtres*. Volume 1 of *Patristique et moyen âge: Etudes d'histoire littéraire et doctrinale*. Museum Lessianum. Section historique, 6. Gembloux, Belgium: J. Duculot.

Giakalis, Ambrosios. 1994. *Images of the Divine: The Theology of Icons at the Seventh Ecumenical Council*. Leiden: E. J. Brill.

Gibbon [1776–88] 1896–1900. *The History of the Decline and Fall of the Roman Empire*. Edited by J. B. Bury. 7 vols. London: Methuen.

Gibellini, Rosino, ed. 1979. *Frontiers of Theology in Latin America*. Translated by J. Drury. Maryknoll, N.Y.: Orbis Books.

Gibson, Margaret T., ed. 1981. *Boethius: His Life, Thought and Influence*. Oxford: Blackwell.

Giet, Stanislas. 1955. "Saint Basile et le Concile de Constantinople de 360." *JTS* 6:94–99.

Gil, Juan. 1973. *Corpus Scriptorum Muzarabicorum*. 2 vols. Madrid: Instituto Antonio de Nebrija.

Gill, Joseph. 1964. *Personalities of the Council of Florence*. Oxford: Oxford University Press.
———. [1959] 1982. *The Council of Florence*. Reprint, New York: AMS Press.

Gillespie, George. [1846] 1991. *Notes of Debates and Proceedings of the Assembly of Divines at Westminster, February 1644 to January 1645*. Reprint, Edmonton: Still Waters Revival Books.

Gillet, Lev. 1987. *The Jesus Prayer*. 2d ed. Foreword by Kallistos Ware. Crestwood, N.Y.: Saint Vladimir's Seminary Press.

Gillett, Ezra Hall. 1863.*The Life and Times of John Huss: or, The Bohemian Reformation of the Fifteenth Century*. 2 vols. New York: AMS Press.

Gilliam, Elizabeth, and W. J. Tighe. 1992. "To 'Run with the Time': Archbishop Whitgift, the Lambeth Articles, and the Politics of Theological Ambiguity in Late Elizabethan England." *Sixteenth Century Journal* 23:325–40.

Gilmont, Jean-François. 1990. *La Réforme et le livre: L'Europe de l'imprimé (1517–v. 1570)*. Paris: Editions du Cerf.

Gilson, Etienne. 1953. *Heloise and Abelard*. Translated by L. K. Shook. London: Hollis and Carter.
———. [1951] 1957. "Historical Research and the Future of Scholasticism." In *A Gilson Reader*, 156–67. Edited with an introduction by Anton C. Pegis. Garden City, N.Y.: Hanover House.

Gindely, Antonin. 1857–58. *Geschichte der Böhmischen Brüder*. Prague: C. Bellmann.

Girod, Gordon H. 1978. *The Deeper Faith: An Exposition of the Canons of the Synod of Dort*. Grand Rapids, Mich.: Baker Book House.

Giving Account of the Hope Together. 1978. Compiled by the World Council of Churches, Commission on Faith and Order. Geneva: World Council of Churches.

Gloer, W. Hulitt. 1984. "Homologies and Hymns in the New Testament: Form, Content and Criteria for Identification." *Perspectives in Religious Studies* 11:115–32.

Godfrey, W. Robert. 1982. "Calvin and Calvinism in the Netherlands." In *John Calvin: His Influence in the Western World*, 95–120. Edited by W. Stanford Reid. Grand Rapids, Mich.: Zondervan.

Golubev, Stefan Timofeevich. 1883–98. *Kievskii mitropolit Petr Mogila i ego spodvizhniki: Opyt istoricheskago izsliedovaniia*. 2 vols. Kiev: Tip. G. T. Korchak-Hovitskago.

González, Justo L. 1987. *A History of Christian Thought*. Revised ed. 3 vols. Nashville, Tenn.: Abingdon Press.

Goodenough, E. R. 1923. *The Theology of Justin Martyr*. Jena, Germany: Frommann.

Goodsell, Daniel A., Joseph B. Hingeley, and James M. Buckley, eds. 1908. *The Doctrines and Discipline of the Methodist Episcopal Church*. New York: Eaton and Mains.

Gorrell, Donald K. 1988. "The Social Creed and Methodism Through Eighty Years." *Methodist History* 26:213–28.

Göszwein, G. 1886. *Eine Union in der Wahrheit*. Saint Louis, Mo.: Concordia Publishing House.

Gould, Graham. 1988. "Cyril of Alexandria and the Formula of Reunion." *Downside Review* 106:235–52.

Grabmann, Martin. [1909] 1957. *Die Geschichte der scholastischen Methode: Nach den gedruckten und ungedruckten Quellen*. 2 vols. Graz: Akademische Druck- und Verlagsanstalt.

Grant, Robert M. 1966. *Ignatius of Antioch*. Camden, N.J.: Nelson.

——. 1988. *Greek Apologists of the Second Century*. Philadelphia: Westminster Press.

Gray, G. F. S. 1996. *Anglicans in China: A History of the Zhonghua Shenggong Hui*. New Haven: Episcopal China Mission History Project.

Gray, Patrick T. R. 1979. *The Defense of Chalcedon in the East (451–553)*. Leiden: Brill.

——. 1987. "Ecumenical Dialogue, Ecumenical Council, and Constantinople II." *Toronto Journal of Theology* 3:50–59.

——, and Michael W. Herren. 1994. "Columbanus and the Three Chapters Controversy: A New Approach." *JTS* 45:160–70.

Green, Lowell C. 1976. "What Was the True Issue at Marburg in 1529?" *Springfielder* 40:102–6.

——. 1977. *The Formula of Concord: An Historical and Bibliographical Guide*. Saint Louis, Mo.: Center for Reformation Research.

Gregg, Robert C., ed. 1985. *Arianism: Historical and Theological Reassessments*. [Ninth International Conference on Patristic Studies, Oxford, 1983.] Patristic Monograph Series, 11. Philadelphia: Philadelphia Patristic Foundation.

Gregory of Nyssa. 1960. *Contra Eunomium*. Edited by Werner Jaeger. Leiden: Brill.

Greschat, Martin. 1985. "Martin Bucers Anteil am Bericht der oberländischen Prediger über den Abschluß der Wittenberger Konkordie (1536)." *ARG* 76:296–98.

Grillmeier, Aloys. 1964. *Christ in Christian Tradition*. Volume 1 of *From the Apostolic Age to Chalcedon*. Translated by J. S. Bowden. London: A. R. Mowbray.

——. 1975. *Christ in Christian Tradition*. Volume 1 of *From the Apostolic Age to Chalcedon (451)*. 2d revised ed. Translated by John Bowden. London: Mowbrays.

——. 1980. *Nicaea (325) und Chalcedon (451): Um das christliche Gottes- und Menschenbild*. Donauwörth, Germany: Ludwig Auer.

——. 1987. *Christ in Christian Tradition*. Vol. 2/1: *Reception and Contradiction from Chalcedon to Justinian I*. Translated by Pauline Allen and John Cawte. Atlanta, Ga.: John Knox Press.

——, and Heinrich Bacht. 1951–54. *Das Konzil von Chalcedon: Geschichte und Gegenwart*. 4th ed. 3 vols. Würzburg: Echter-Verlag.

Gritsch, Eric W., and Robert Jenson. 1976. *Lutheranism: The Theological Movement and Its Confessional Writings.* Philadelphia: Fortress Press.

Grumel, A. A. 1928–30. "Recherches sur l'histoire du monothélisme." *Echos d'Orient* 27:6–16, 257–77, 28:19–34, 272–82, 29:16–28.

Grüneisen, Ernst. 1938. "Grundlegendes für die Bilder in Luthers Katechismen." *Luther-Jahrbuch* 20:1–44.

Guerra, A. J. 1992. "The Conversion of Marcus Aurelius and Justin Martyr: The Purpose, Genre, and Context of the First Apology." *Second Century* 9:129–87.

Guerrier, Louis, and L. Grébaut, eds. and trans. 1913. *Le Testament en Galilée de Notre-Seigneur Jesus-Christ.* Paris: Firmin-Didot.

Guggisberg, Hans. 1982. *Basel in the Sixteenth Century: Aspects of the City Republic Before, During, and After the Reformation.* Saint Louis, Mo.: Center for Reformation Research.

Guggisberg, Kurt. 1958. *Bernische Kirchengeschichte.* Bern: P. Haupt.

Guillaume Farel, 1489–1565: Biographie nouvelle écrite d'après les documents originaux. 1930. Edited by the Comité Farel. Neuchâtel: Delachaux et Niestlé.

Gussmann, Wilhelm, ed. 1911. *Quellen und Forschungen zur Geschichte des Augsburgischen Glaubensbekenntnisses.* Volume 1 of *Die Ratschläge der evangelischen Reichstände zum Reichstag von Augsburg 1530.* Leipzig: Teubner.

Haas, Martin. 1969. *Huldrych Zwingli und seine Zeit: Leben und Werk des Züricher Reformators.* Zurich: Zwingli Verlag.

————. 1982. "Michael Sattler: On the Way to Anabaptist Separation." In *Profiles of Radical Reformers: Biographical Sketches from Thomas Müntzer to Paracelsus,* 132–43. Edited by Hans J. Goertz. Scottdale, Pa.: Herald Press.

Hadjiantoniou, Georgios A. 1961. *Protestant Patriarch: The Life of Cyril Lucaris, 1572–1638, Patriarch of Constantinople.* Richmond, Va.: John Knox Press.

Haelst, J. van. 1970. "Le Papyrus der Balizeh: Une nouvelle interprétation." In *Ecclesia a spiritu sancto edocta,* 201–12. Edited by Joseph C. Coppens et al. Bibliotheca Ephemeridum Theologicarum Lovaniensium, 27. Gembloux, Belgium: J. Duculot.

Hagen, Kenneth. 1987. "The Historical Context of the Smalcald Articles." *Concordia Theological Quarterly* 51:245–53.

Hagenbach, K. R. 1827. *Kritische Geschichte der Entstehung und der Schicksale der ersten Basler Confession und der auf sie gegründeten Kirchenlehre.* Basel: Neukirch.

Hägglund, Bengt. 1958. "Die Bedeutung der *Regula fidei* als Grundlage theologischer Aussagen." *Studia Theologica* 12:1–44.

————. 1980. "Melanchthon versus Luther: The Contemporary Struggle." *Concordia Theological Quarterly* 44:123–33.

————. 1981. "Die Rezeption Luthers in der Konkoridenformel." In *Luther und die Bekenntnisschriften,* 107–20. Edited by Joachim Heubach, Maurice Schild, Leiv Aalen, et al. Erlangen, Germany: Martin Luther-Verlag.

Haidostian, Paul. 1996. "Armenian Evangelical Vision and Revision." *Near East School of Theology Theological Review* 17:52–60.

Hajjar, Joseph. 1962. *Le synode permanent dans l'Eglise byzantine des origines au iie siècle.* Rome: Pontificium Institutum Orientalium Studiorum.

————. 1995. *Les Chrétiens uniates du Proche-Orient.* Damascus: Dar Tlass.

Halecki, Oskar. 1958. *From Florence to Brest (1439-1596)*. New York: Fordham University Press.

Hall, Stuart G. 1965. *Christ in the Christian Tradition: From the Apostolic Age to Chalcedon (451)*. Translated by J. S. Bowden. New York: Sheed and Ward.

———. 1980. "Nicaea (325) und Chalcedon (451): Um das christliche Gottes- und Menschenbild." In *Wegmarken der Christologie*, 43-80. Edited by Anton Ziegenaus. Donauwörth, Germany: Verlag Ludwig Auer.

———. 1987. "The Understanding of the Christological Definitions of Both (Oriental Orthodox and Roman Catholic) Traditions in the Light of the Post-Chalcedonian Theology." In Fries and Nersoyan 1987, 65-82.

———. 1989. "The Creed of Sardica." In *Studia Patristica, 19: Historica, Theologica, Gnostica, Biblica et Apocrypha* [Tenth International Conference on Patristic Studies, Oxford, 1987], 173-84. Edited by Elizabeth A. Livingstone. Louvain: Peeters.

———. 1991. *Doctrine and Practice in the Early Church*. London: S.P.C.K.

Hall, Thor. 1961. "Possibilities of Erasmian Influence on Denck and Hubmaier and Their Views on the Freedom of the Will." *MQR* 35:149-70.

Halleux, André de. 1985. "La réception du symbole oecuménique, de Nicée à Chalcédoine." *Ephemerides Theologicae Lovanienses* 61/1:5-47.

———. 1993. "La première session du Concile d'Ephèse." *Ephemerides Theologicae Lovanienses* 69:48-87.

Hamann, Henry P. 1988. "The Smalcald Articles as a Systematic Theology: A Comparison with the Augsburg Confession." *Concordia Theological Quarterly* 52:29-40.

Hamilton, John Taylor. 1900. *A History of the Church Known as the Moravian Church, or, The Unitas Fratrum, or, The Unity of the Brethren, During the Eighteenth and Nineteenth Centuries*. Bethlehem, Pa.: Times Publishing.

Handlingar vid de Svenska Baptistförsamlingarnas: Tredje allmäna Konferens. [1861?]. [Stockholm]: n.p.

Handy, Robert T., ed. 1966. *The Social Gospel in America, 1870-1920*. New York: Oxford University Press.

Hanson, Richard P. C. 1954. *Origen's Doctrine of Tradition*. London: S.P.C.K.

———. 1983. "The Doctrine of the Trinity Achieved in 381." *Scottish Journal of Theology* 36:41-57.

———. 1985. *Studies in Christian Antiquity*. Edinburgh: T. and T. Clark.

———. 1988. *The Search for the Christian Doctrine of God: The Arian Controversy, 318-381*. Edinburgh: T. and T. Clark.

Harder, Leland. 1980. "Zwingli's Reaction to the Schleitheim Confession of Faith of the Anabaptists." *Sixteenth Century Journal* 11/4:51-66.

Hardon, John A. 1968. *The Spirit and Origins of American Protestantism: A Source Book in Its Creeds*. Dayton, Ohio: Pflaum Press.

Hardwick, Charles. 1876. *A History of the Articles of Religion*. 3d ed. London: George Bell and Sons.

Harman, Allan M. 1973. "Speech About the Trinity: With Special Reference to Novatian, Hilary and Calvin." *Scottish Journal of Theology* 26:385-400.

Harmon, Nolan B., and John W. Bardsley. 1953. "John Wesley and the Articles of Religion." *Religion in Life* 22:280–91.

Harnack, Adolf von. 1897. *Die Chronologie der altchristlichen Litteratur bis Eusebius.* 2 vols. Leipzig: J. C. Hinrichs.

———. 1901. *The Apostles' Creed.* Translated by Stewart Means from article in Herzog's *Real-Encyclopädie,* 3d ed. London: A. and C. Black.

———. 1931–32. *Lehrbuch der Dogmengeschichte.* 3 vols. Tübingen: J. C. B. Mohr (Paul Siebeck).

———. [1900] 1957. *What Is Christianity?* Translated by Thomas Bailey Saunders. Introduction by Rudolf Bultmann. Reprint, New York: Harper Torchbooks.

———. [1898] 1958. *History of Dogma.* Translated by J. Millar, Neil Buchanan, E. B. Speirs, and W. M. Gilchrist from the 3d ed. 7 vols. Reprint, New York: Russell and Russell.

———. [1908] 1961a. *The Mission and Expansion of Christianity in the First Three Centuries.* Translated by James Moffatt. Reprint ed. Introduction by Jaroslav Pelikan. New York: Harper Torchbooks.

———. [1893] 1961b. *History of Dogma.* Translated from the third German edition by Neil Buchanan. 7 vols. Reprint, New York: Dover.

Harnack, Theodosius. 1856. *Der Kleine Katechismus Dr. Martin Luthers in seiner Urgestalt.* Stuttgart: S. G. Liesching.

Harris, James Rendel, ed. 1887. *The Teaching of the Apostles (Didache ton Apostolon).* Baltimore: C. J. Clay and Sons.

———, ed. and tr. [1893] 1967. *The Apology of Aristides on Behalf of the Christians, from a Syriac Ms. Preserved on Mount Sinai.* Greek text edited by J. Armitage Robinson. 2d ed. Reprint, Nendeln, Liechtenstein: Kraus.

Harrison, A. W. 1926. *The Beginnings of Arminianism to the Synod of Dort.* London: University of London Press.

———. 1937. *Arminianism.* London: Duckworth.

Hartfelder, Karl. [1889] 1964. *Philipp Melanchthon als Praeceptor Germaniae.* Reprint, Nieuwkoop, Netherlands: B. de Graaf.

Hartman, Lars. 1994. "Obligatory Baptism—But Why? On Baptism in the *Didache* and in the *Shepherd of Hermas.*" *Svensk Exegetisk Årsbok* 59:127–43. Uppsala: Uppsala Exegetiska Sällskap.

Hasler, August. 1981. *How the Pope Became Infallible: Pius IX and the Politics of Persuasion.* Translated by Peter Heinegg. Garden City, N.Y.: Doubleday.

Haugaard, William P. 1968. *Elizabeth and the English Reformation: The Struggle for a Stable Settlement of Religion.* London: Cambridge University Press.

Haugh, Richard. 1975. *Photius and the Carolingians: The Trinitarian Controversy.* Belmont, Mass.: Nordland Publishers.

Hausammann, Susi. 1966. "Die Marburger Artikel: Eine echte Konkordie." *ZKG* 77/3–4: 288–321.

Hausherr, Irénée. 1966. *Hésychasme et prière.* Rome: Pontificale Institutum Orientalium Studiorum.

Hauzenberger, Hans. 1985. *Einheit auf evangelischer Grundlage: Von Werden und Wesen der Evangelischen Allianz.* Giessen, Germany: Brunnen Verlag.

Hazlett, W. Ian P. 1987. "The Scots Confession 1560: Context, Complexion and Critique." *ARG* 78:287–320.

———. 1994. "Eucharistic Communion: Impulses and Directions in Martin Bucer's Thought." In *Martin Bucer: Reforming Church and Community*, 72–82. Edited by D. F. Wright. Cambridge: Cambridge University Press.

Heather, P. J., and John Matthews. 1991. *The Goths in the Fourth Century.* Liverpool: Liverpool University Press.

Hebart, Friedemann, ed. and tr. 1983. *Luther's Large Catechism: Anniversary Translation.* Adelaide, Australia: Lutheran Publishing House.

Hefele, Karl Joseph von. 1869–90. *Conciliengeschichte. Nach den Quellen bearbeitet.* 9 vols. Vols. 1–6 in 2d ed.; vols. 5–6 edited by Alois Knöpfler; vols. 8–9 edited by Cardinal Hergenröther. Freiburg: Herder.

Hefner, Philip J. 1963. "Saint Irenaeus and the Hypothesis of Faith." *Dialog* 2:300–306.

Hege, Christian. 1908. *Die Täufer in der Kurpfalz.* Frankfurt: Hermann Minjon.

The Heidelberg Catechism: Four Hundredth Anniversary Edition, 1563-1963. 1963. Philadelphia: United Church Press.

Heideman, Eugene P. 1975. *Our Song of Hope: A Provisional Confession of Faith of the Reformed Church in America.* Grand Rapids, Mich.: Eerdmans.

Heijting, Willem. 1989. *De catechismi en confessies in de Nederlandse reformatie tot 1585.* 2 vols. Nieuwkoop: De Graaf.

Heil, Gunther, ed. 1990– . *Gregorii Nysseni Opera. Sermones.* Leiden: E. J. Brill.

Heiner, Franz Xavier. 1908. *Der neue Syllabus Pius' X. oder Dekret des Heiligen Offiziums "Lamentabili" vom 3. Juli 1907, dargestellt und kommentiert.* 2d ed. Mainz: Verlag von Kirchheim.

Heinrich, Wilhelm, and Rudolf Walter de Moos. 1942. *Petitiones de assumptione corporea B.V. Mariae in caelum definienda ad Sanctam Sedem delatae: Propositae secundum ordinem hierarchicum dogmaticum, geographicum, chronologicum ad consensum ecclesiae manifestandum.* 2 vols. Rome: Typis Polyglottis Vaticanis.

Henderson, George D., ed. 1937. *The Scots Confession, 1560 (Confessio Scoticana), and Negative Confession, 1581 (Confessio Negativa).* Edinburgh: Church of Scotland, Committee on Publications.

———, ed. [1960]. *The Scots Confession.* Rendering into modern English by James Bulloch. Edinburgh: Saint Andrew Press.

Hendricks, Dan L. 1978. "The Bern Disputation: Some Observations." *Zwingliana* 14:565–75.

Hennecke, Edgar. [1896] 1990. *Altchristliche Malerei und altkirchliche Literatur: Eine Untersuchung über den biblischen Cyklus der Gemälde in den römischen Katakomben.* Reprint, Leipzig: Veit.

Hennessey, Lawrence R. 1998. "A Moment of Grace: Some Reflections on the Common Christological Declaration Between the Assyrian Church of the East and the Roman Catholic Church." *Ecumenical Trends* 27:26–29.

Henry, Patrick. 1974. "The Formulators of Icon Doctrine." In *Schools of Thought in the Christian Tradition*, 75–89. Edited by Patrick Henry. Philadelphia: Fortress Press.

———. 1977. "Images of the Church in the Second Nicene Council and the Libri Carolini."

In *Law, Church, and Society: Essays in Honor of Stephan Kuttner*, 237–52. Edited by Kenneth Pennington and Robert Somerville. Philadelphia: University of Pennsylvania Press.

Heppe, Heinrich. 1885. *Die Bekenntnisschriften der altprotestantischen Kirche Deutschlands.* Kassel: T. Fischer.

Hergenröther, Joseph Adam Gustav. 1867–69. *Photius, Patriarch von Konstantinopel.* 3 vols. Regensburg: G. J. Manz.

Herrin, Judith. 1987. *The Formation of Christendom.* Oxford: Basil Blackwell.

Hertz, Joseph H. 1948. *The Authorized Daily Prayer Book.* Revised ed. New York: Bloch.

Hess, H. 1958. *The Canons of the Council of Sardica, A.D. 343: A Landmark in the Early Development of Canon Law.* Oxford: Clarendon Press.

Heymann, Frederick Gotthold. 1955. *John Zizka and the Hussite Revolution.* Princeton, N.J.: Princeton University Press.

———. 1961. "The Hussite-Utraquist Church in the Fifteenth and Sixteenth Centuries." *ARG* 52/1:1–16.

Hicks, Eric. 1991. *La vie et les epistres: Pierres Abaelart et Heloys sa fame.* Paris: Champion.

Higman, Francis. 1988. "La Dispute de Lausanne, carrefour de la Réformation française." In *La Dispute de Lausanne 1988*, 23–35.

Hildebrandt, Walter, and Rudolf Zimmermann. 1938. *Bedeutung und Geschichte des zweiten Helvetischen Bekenntnisses.* Zurich: Zwingli-Verlag.

———. 1966. *Das Zweite Helvetische Bekenntnis.* Zurich: Zwingli-Verlag.

Hillman, Eugene. 1993. *Toward an African Christianity: Inculturation Applied.* New York: Paulist Press.

Hinson, E. Glenn. 1979. "Confessions or Creeds in Early Christian Tradition." *Review and Expositor* 76:5–16.

Hirsch, Emanuel. 1960. *Geschichte der neuern evangelischen Theologie im Zusammenhang mit den allgemeinen Bewegungen des europäischen Denkens.* 5 vols. Gütersloh, Germany: C. Bertelsmann Verlag.

Hitchcock, F. R. Montgomery. 1932. "The Creeds of SS. Irenaeus and Patrick." *Hermathena* 48:232–37.

Hobbs, Herschel H. 1979. "Southern Baptists and Confessionalism: A Comparison of the Origins and Contents of the 1925 and 1963 Confessions." *Review and Expositor* 76/1:55–68.

Hodgson, Leonard G., ed. 1934. *Convictions: A Selection from the Responses of the Churches to the Report of the World Conference on Faith and Order, Held at Lausanne in 1927.* London: SCM Press.

———, ed. 1938. *The Second World Conference on Faith and Order Held at Edinburgh, August 3–18, 1937.* New York: Macmillan.

Hoekema, Anthony A. 1968a. "Needed: A New Translation of the Canons of Dort." *Calvin Theological Journal* 3:41–47.

———. 1968b. "New English Translation of the Canons of Dort." *Calvin Theological Journal* 3:133–61.

———. 1972. "Missionary Focus of the Canons of Dort." *Calvin Theological Journal* 7:209–20.

Hoenderdaal, J. 1969. "De Kerkorderlijke Kant van de Dortse Synode." *Nederlands Theologisch Tijdschrift* 23:349–63.

———. 1970–71. "Remonstrantie en Contraremonstrantie." *Nederlands Archief voor Kerk-geschiedenis*, n.s., 51:49–92.

———. 1975. "The Debate About Arminius Outside the Netherlands." In *Leiden University in the Seventeenth Century: An Exchange of Learning*, 137–59. Edited by Th. H. Lunsingh Scheurleer and G. H. M. Posthumus Meyjes. Leiden: Brill.

Hofmann, Georg, ed. 1935–51. *Documenta Concilii Florentini de unione Orientalium*. 3 vols. Rome: Pontificia Università Gregoriana.

Hofmann, Johann Christian Konrad von. 1857. *Das Bekenntniss der lutherischen Kirche von der Versöhnung und die Versöhnungslehre*. Erlangen, Germany: T. Bläsing.

Hofmann, Karl. 1933. *Der "Dictatus papae" Gregors VII: Eine Rechtsgeschichtliche Erklärung*. Paderborn, Germany: Ferdinand Schöningh.

Hofmann, Rudolph. 1857. *Symbolik oder systematische Darstellung des symbolischen Lehrbe-griffs der verschiedenen christlichen Kirchen und namhaften Sekten*. Leipzig: Friedrich Voigt.

Holl, Karl. 1898. *Enthusiasmus und Bussgewalt beim griechischen Mönchtum: Eine Studie zu Symeon dem neuen Theologen*. Leipzig: J. C. Hinrichs.

———. [1919] 1928. "Zur Auslegung des 2. Artikels des sog. Apostolischen Glaubensbe-kenntnisses." In *Gesammelte Aufsätze zur Kirchengeschichte*, 2:115–28. Tübingen: J. C. B. Mohr (Paul Siebeck).

Holland, David Larrimore. 1965. "The Earliest Text of the Old Roman Symbol: A Debate with Hans Lietzmann and J. N. D. Kelly." *Church History* 34:262–81.

———. 1969. "Creeds of Nicaea and Constantinople Reexamined." *Church History* 38:248–61.

———. 1970. "Die Synode von Antiochien (324/25) und ihre Bedeutung für Eusebius von Caesarea und das Konzil von Nizäa." *ZKG* 81/2:163–81.

Hollis, Michael. 1966. *The Significance of South India*. London: Lutterworth.

Hollweg, Walter. 1968. *Neue Untersuchungen zur Geschichte und Lehre des Heidelberger Kate-chismus*. Neukirchen, Germany: Verlag des Erziehungsverein.

Holstein, Henri. 1976. "Cène et la messe dans la doctrine du sacrifice eucharistique du Con-cile de Trente." In *Humanisme et foi chrétienne*, 649–62. Edited by Charles Kannengiesser and Yves Marchasson. Paris: Beauchesne.

Hopkins, C. H. 1940. *The Rise of the Social Gospel in American Protestantism*. New Haven: Yale University Press.

Hörcsik, Richard. 1994. "John Calvin in Geneva, 1536–38: Some Questions About Calvin's First Stay at Geneva." In *Calvinus Sacrae Scripturae professor: Calvin as Confessor of Holy Scriptures*, 155–65. Edited by Wilhelm H. Neuser. Grand Rapids, Mich.: W. B. Eerdmans.

Hornschuh, M. 1965. *Studien zur Epistula Apostolorum*. Patristische Texte und Studien, 5. Berlin: De Gruyter.

Horst, Irvin B. 1982. "The Dordrecht Confession of Faith: 350 Years." *Pennsylvania Menno-nite Heritage* 5:2–8.

———, tr. and ed. 1988. *Mennonite Confession of Faith*. Mennonite Sources and Documents, 2. Lancaster, Pa.: Lancaster Mennonite Historical Society.

Horton, Douglas. 1962. *The United Church of Christ: Its Origins, Organization, and Role in the World Today*. New York: T. Nelson.

Houssiau, A. 1955. *La Christologie de saint Irénée*. Gembloux, Belgium: J. Duculot.

Howlett, D. R. 1994. *Liber epistolarum sancti Patricii episcopi. The Book of Letters of Saint Patrick the Bishop*. Dublin: Four Courts Press.

Hrejsa, Ferdinand. 1912. *Česká konfesse, její vznik, podstata a dějiny*. Prague: Česká Akademie Císaře Františka Josefa.

Hudson, Anne. 1978. *Selections from English Wycliffite Writings*. Cambridge: Cambridge University Press.

Hüffmeier, Wilhelm, and Christine-Ruther Müller, eds. 1995. *Wachsende Gemeinschaft in Zeugnis und Dienst: Reformatorische Kirchen in Europa*. Frankfurt: Otto Lembeck.

Huhn, Joseph. 1954. *Das Geheimnis der Jungfrau-Mutter Maria nach dem Kirchenvater Ambrosius*. Würzburg: Echter-Verlag.

Huizing, Petrus, and Knut Walf. 1983. *The Ecumenical Council: Its Significance in the Constitution of the Church*. Edinburgh: T. and T. Clark.

Hulme, Edward M. [1931] 1968. "Lelio Sozzini's Confession of Faith." In *Persecution and Liberty: Essays in Honor of George Lincoln Burr*. Reprint, Freeport, N.Y.: Books for Libraries Press.

Hunt, E. 1957. *St. Leo the Great: Letters*. Fathers of the Church, 34. New York: Fathers of the Church.

Hunter, Alan, and Kim-Kwong Chan. 1993. *Protestantism in Contemporary China*. Cambridge: Cambridge University Press.

Hussey, Joan Mervyn. 1986. *The Orthodox Church in the Byzantine Empire*. Oxford: Clarendon Press.

Idelsohn, A. Z. 1932. *Jewish Liturgy and Its Development*. New York: Henry Holt.

Ihm, Claudia Carlen. 1981. *The Papal Encyclicals, 1939-1958*. Raleigh, N.C.: McGrath Publishing.

Immenkötter, Herbert, ed. 1979. *Die Confutatio der Confessio Augustana von 3. August 1530*. Münster: Aschendorff.

Ionesco, Teofil. 1944. *La vie et l'oeuvre de Pierre Movila, Métropolite de Kiev*. Paris: Nidot.

Jackson, Samuel Macauley. [1901] 1972. *Huldreich Zwingli: The Reformer of German Switzerland, 1484-1531*. 2d ed. Reprint, New York: AMS Press.

Jacobs, Henry E., ed. and trans. 1893. *The Book of Concord; or, The Symbolic Books of the Evangelical Lutheran Church*. Philadelphia: G. W. Frederick.

Jacobs, Paul. 1959. *Theologie reformierter Bekenntnisschriften in Grundzügen*. Neukirchen, Germany: Neukirchener Verlag.

Jahr, Hannelore. 1964. *Studien zur Überlieferungsgeschichte der Confession de foi von 1559*. Neukirchen, Germany: Verlag des Erziehungsverein.

James, M. R. 1900-1904. *Western Manuscripts in the Library of Trinity College, Cambridge: A Descriptive Catalogue*. 4 vols. Cambridge: Cambridge University Press.

Jamison, Wallace N. 1958. *The United Presbyterian Story: A Centennial Study, 1858-1958*. Pittsburgh, Pa.: Geneva Press.

Janetzki, Elvin W. 1980. "Teaching Luther's *Small Catechism* as Law and Gospel." *Lutheran Theological Journal* 14:73-79.

Jecker, G. 1927. *Die Heimat des heiligen Pirmin: Des Apostels der Alamannen*. Münster: Aschendorff.

Jedin, Hubert. 1941. *Krisis und Wendpunkt des Trienter Konzils, 1562–1563*. Würzburg: Rita-Verlag und -Druckerei der Augustiner.

———. 1946. *Katholische Reformation oder Gegenreformation? Ein Versuch zur Klärung der Begriffe nebst einer Jubiläumsbetrachtung über das Trienter Konzil*. Lucerne: Josef Stocker.

———. 1948. *Das Konzil von Trient: Eine Überblick über die Erforschung seiner Geschichte*. Rome: Edizioni di Storia e letteratura.

———. 1948–75. *Geschichte des Konzils von Trient*. 4 vols. Freiburg: Herder.

———. 1957–61. *A History of the Council of Trent*. Translated by Ernest Graf. Saint Louis, Mo.: Herder.

———, and John Dolan, eds. 1980. *History of the Church*. 10 vols. New York: Seabury Press.

Jefford, Clayton N., ed. 1995. *The Didache in Context: Essays on Its Text, History, and Transmission*. Supplements to *Novum Testamentum*, 77. Leiden: Brill.

———. 1996. *Reading the Apostolic Fathers: An Introduction*. With Kenneth J. Harder and Louis D. Amezaga. Peabody, Mass.: Hendrickson.

Jenny, Beatrice. 1951. *Das Schleitheimer Täuferbekenntnis, 1527*. Thayngen, Switzerland: Karl Augustin.

Jobert, Ambroise. 1974. *De Luther à Mohila: La Pologne dans la crise de la chretienté, 1517–1648*. Collection historique de l'Institut d'études slaves, 21. Paris: Institut d'Etudes Slaves.

Joest, Wilfried. 1962. "The Doctrine of Justification of the Council of Trent." *Lutheran World* 9:204–18.

John Paul II, Pope. 1992. "Déclaration du pape Jean-Paul II sur la Procession du Saint-Esprit." [Reprint from *L'Osservatore Romano*, French ed. 13 November 1990] *Istina* 37:78–83.

———. 1998. "Ad Tuendam Fidem." *L'Osservatore Romano* 28 (1550), 15 July 1998.

John, Jeffrey, ed. 1994. *Living the Mystery: Affirming Catholicism and the Future of Anglicanism*. London: Darton, Longman and Todd.

Johnson, John F. 1989. "Polemicism or Ecumenism: Another Look at the Smalcald Articles." In *Promoting Unity: Themes in Lutheran-Catholic Dialogue*, 39–49. Edited by H. George Anderson and James R. Crumley, Jr. Minneapolis, Minn.: Augsburg Publishing House.

Johnson, Morris R. 1999. *Archbishop Daniel William Alexander and the African Orthodox Church*. San Francisco: International Scholars.

Johnston, Paul. 1993. "Reu's Understanding of *The Small Catechism*." *Lutheran Quarterly*, n.s., 7:425–50.

Jones, Charles Edwin. 1974. *A Guide to the Study of the Holiness Movement*. Metuchen, N.J.: Scarecrow Press.

Jones, Francis Price. 1962. *The Church in Communist China: A Protestant Appraisal*. New York: Friendship Press.

———, consultant and ed. 1963. *Documents of the Three-Self Movement: Source Materials for the Study of the Protestant Church in Communist China*. New York, N.Y.: Far Eastern Office, Division of Foreign Missions, National Council of the Churches of Christ in the U.S.A.

Jones, Joe R. 1980. "A Theological Analysis of the Design." *Mid-Stream* 19/3:309–21.

Jones, Rufus M. [1927] 2002. *The Faith and Practice of the Quakers*. Reprint, Richmond, Ind.: Friends United Press.

Jordan, H. William. 1977. "A Model for the Church in Conflict: The Smalcald Articles and

the Treatise on the Power and Primacy of the Pope." *Currents in Theology and Mission*
4/1:22–27.

Junghans, Helmar, ed. 1983. *Leben und Werk Martin Luthers von 1526 bis 1546. Festgabe zu
seinem 500. Geburtstag.* 2 vols. Göttingen: Vandenhoeck und Ruprecht.

Jungkuntz, Theodore R. 1977a. *Formulators of the Formula of Concord: Four Architects of
Lutheran Unity.* Saint Louis, Mo.: Concordia Publishing House.

———. 1977b. "Sectarian Consequences of Mistranslation in Luther's Smalcald Articles."
Currents in Theology and Mission 4/3:166–67.

Kahle, Paul Eric, ed. 1954. *Bala'izah: Coptic Texts from Deir el Bala'izah in Upper Egypt.*
London: Griffith Institute; Oxford: Oxford University Press.

Kaminsky, Howard. 1967. *A History of the Hussite Revolution.* Berkeley: University of Califor-
nia Press.

Kandler, Karl-Hermann. 1970. *Luther, Arnoldshain, und das Abendmahl: Die Herausforderung
der lutherischen Abendmahlslehre durch die Arnoldshainer Abendmahlsthesen.* Berlin: Evangelische Verlagsanstalt.

Kannengiesser, Charles. 1970. *Traité sur l'incarnation du Verbe et sur sa manifestation corpo-
relle en notre faveur.* Paris: Institut Catholique.

———. 1981. "Athanasius of Alexandria and the Holy Spirit Between Nicaea I and Constantinople I." *Irish Theological Quarterly* 48:166–80.

Karmirēs, Ioannēs, ed. 1937. *Mētrophanēs ho Kritopoulos kai hē anekdotos allēgographia autou.*
Athens: Paraskeua Lēonē.

———. 1949. *Heterodoxoi epidraseis epi tas homologias tou IZ' Aiōnos.* Jerusalem: Typois Hie-
rou Koinou P. Taphou.

Kartašev, Anton Vladimirovič. 1932. *Na put'ach k vselenskomu soboru* [On the way to an
ecumenical council]. Paris: YMCA Press.

Kasper, Walter. 2000. "The Joint Declaration on the Doctrine of Justification: Cause for
Hope." *Centro Pro Unione Bulletin* 57:3–6.

Keller, Ludwig. 1882. *Ein Apostel der Wiedertäufer.* Leipzig: Hirzel.

Keller-Hüschemenger, Max. 1967. "Die Wittenberger Artikel von 1536." *Kergyma und Dogma*
22/2:149–61.

Kellock, James. 1965. *Breakthrough for Church Union in North India and Pakistan.* Madras:
Christian Literature Society.

Kelly, Douglas F. 1994. "The Westminster Shorter Catechism." In Carson and Hall 1994,
101–26.

Kelly, J. N. D., tr. 1955. *A Commentary on the Apostles' Creed* by Rufinus. Westminster, Md.:
Newman Press.

———. 1958. *Early Christian Doctrine.* New York: Harper and Brothers.

———. 1964. *The Athanasian Creed.* The Paddock Lectures for 1962–3. New York: Harper
and Row.

———. 1983. "The Nicene Creed: A Turning Point." *Scottish Journal of Theology* 36/1:29–39.

———. 1986. *The Oxford Dictionary of the Popes.* Oxford: Oxford University Press.

Kendall, R. T. 1981. *Calvin and English Calvinism to 1649.* New York: Oxford University
Press.

Kessler, Juan B. A. 2001. *Limits of Spiritual Unity: A History of the Evangelical Alliance in Great Britain from Origins to 1960s*. Denver, Colo.: Academic Books.

Kidd, B. J. 1911. *The Thirty-Nine Articles: Their History and Explanation*. 5th ed. 2 vols. London: Rivingtons.

Kilpatrick, Thomas B. 1928. *Our Common Faith, with a Brief History of the Church Union Movement in Canada*. Toronto: Ryerson Press.

King, N. G. 1957. "The 150 Holy Fathers of the Council of Constantinople 381." *Studia Patristica* 1:635–41.

Kingdon, Robert M. 1974. "Was the Protestant Reformation a Revolution? The Case of Geneva." In *Transition and Revolution: Problems and Issues of European Renaissance and Reformation History*, 53–76. Edited by Robert M. Kingdon. Minneapolis, Minn.: Burgess Publishing.

———, ed. 1977. *Formula of Concord: Quadricentennial Essays*. Special issue of *Sixteenth Century Journal* 8/4:9–123.

———. 1985. *Church and Society in Reformation Europe*. London: Variorum Reprints.

Kinzig, Wolfram, Christoph Markschies, and Markus Vinzent. 1999. *Tauffragen und Bekenntnis: Studien zur sogenannten "Traditio apostolica," zu den "Interrogationes de fide" und zum "Römischen Glaubensbekenntnis."* Berlin: W. de Gruyter.

Kirchner, Hubert. 1983. "Luther und das Papsttum." In Junghans 1983, 1:441–56.

Kistemaker, Simon. 1968. "Leading Figures at the Synod of Dort." In *Crisis in the Reformed Churches: Essays in Commemoration of the Great Synod of Dort, 1618–1619*, 39–51. Edited by Peter Y. De Jong. Grand Rapids, Mich.: Reformed Fellowship.

Kitamori, Kazo. 1968. *Nihon Kirisuto Kyodan Shinko Kokuhaku*. Tokyo: Nihon Kirisuto Kyodan Shuppan Kyoku.

Kittelson, James M. 1973. "Martin Bucer and the Sacramentarian Controversy: The Origins of His Policy of Concord." *ARG* 64:166–83.

———. 1975. *Wolfgang Capito: From Humanist to Reformer*. Leiden: Brill.

———. 1993. "Martin Bucer: Forgotten Man in the Late Sixteenth Century?" In *Martin Bucer and Sixteenth-Century Europe: Actes du colloque de Strasbourg*, 2:705–14. Edited by Christian Krieger and Marc Lienhard. Leiden: Brill.

———, and Ken Schurb. 1986. "The Curious Histories of the Wittenberg Concord." *Concordia Theological Quarterly* 50/2:119–37.

Kiwiet, Jan J. 1957. "The Life of Hans Denck." *MQR* 31:227–59.

———. 1958. "The Theology of Hans Denck." *MQR* 32:3–27.

Klooster, Fred H. 1986. "The Priority of Ursinus in the Compostion of the Heidelberg Catechism." In Visser 't Hooft 1986, 73–100.

———. 1994. "Calvin's Attitude to the Heidelberg Catechism." In *Later Calvinism: International Perspectives*, 311–31. Edited by W. Fred Graham. Sixteenth Century Essays and Studies, 22. Kirksville, Mo.: Sixteenth Century Journal Publishers.

Klug, Eugene F. 1980. "Luther's Contribution to the Augsburg Confession." *Concordia Theological Quarterly* 44:155–72.

Knight, George W. 1984. "A Response to Dr. William Barker's Article 'Subscription to the Westminster Confession of Faith and Catechisms.'" *Presbyterion* 10/1–2:56–63.

Knoch, Otto. 1981. "Petrus und Paulus in den Schriften der Apostolischen Väter." In *Kon-*

tinuität und Einheit: Für Franz Mussner, 240–60. Edited by Paul G. Mueller. Freiburg: Herder.

Knox, John. 1949. *John Knox's History of the Reformation in Scotland*. Edited by William Croft Dickinson. 2 vols. London: Thomas Nelson and Sons.

Knox, R. Buick. 1967. *James Ussher, Archbishop of Armagh*. Cardiff: University of Wales Press.

Knox, Ronald A. 2000. *Enthusiasm: A Chapter in the History of Religion, with Special Reference to the Seventeenth and Eighteenth Centuries*. Oxford: Clarendon Press.

Kobong, Theodorus. 1992. *Aluk, adat, dan kebudayaan Toraja dalam perjumpaannya dengan Injil*. [Rantepao, Indonesia]: Pusbang, Badan Pekerja Sinode, Gereja Toraja.

Koch, Ernst. 1966. "Die Textüberlieferung der Confessio Helvetica Posterior und ihre Vorgeschichte." In *Glauben und Bekennen: Vierhundert Jahre Confessio Helvetica Posterior*, 13–40. Edited by Joachim Staedtke. Zurich: Zwingli Verlag.

———. 1968. *Die Theologie der Confessio Helvetica Posterior*. Neukirchen, Germany: Neukirchener Verlag des Erziehungsvereins.

———. 1992. "Beobachtungen zur Vorgeschichte der Confessio Helvetica Posterior." In *Reformiertes Erbe*, 223–32. Edited by Heiko Oberman, Ernst Saxer, Alfred Schindler, et al. Special issue of *Zwingliana* (19/1). Zurich: Theologischer Verlag.

———. 1995. "Zwingli und die Berner Reformation." *Theologische Rundschau* 60/2:131–51.

Koelpin, Arnold J., ed. 1980. *No Other Gospel: Essays in Commemoration of the Four Hundredth Anniversary of the Formula of Concord, 1580-1980*. Milwaukee, Wis.: Northwestern Publishing House.

Koestlin, Julius. 1875. *Martin Luther: Sein Leben und Seine Schriften*. Elberfeld, Germany: R. L. Friedrichs.

Köhler, Walther, ed. 1908. *Brüderlich Vereinigung etzlicher Kinder Gottes Sieben Artikel betreffend: Item ein Sendbrief Michael Sattlers an eine gemeine Gottes samt seinem Martyrium (1527)*. Halle: R. Haupt.

———. 1953. *Zwingli und Luther: Ihr Streit über das Abendmahl nach seinen politischen und religiösen Beziehungen*. Vol. 2. Vol. 7 of *Quellen und Forschungen zur Reformationsgeschichte*. Edited by Ernst Kohlmeyer and Heinrich Bornkamm. Gütersloh, Germany: C. Bertelsmann.

Kolb, Robert. 1977. *Andreae and the Formula of Concord: Six Sermons on the Way to Lutheran Unity*. Saint Louis, Mo.: Concordia Publishing House.

———. 1979. "The Layman's Bible: The Use of Luther's Catechisms in the German Late Reformation." In Scaer and Preus 1979, 16–26.

———. 1980. "Augsburg 1530: German Lutheran Interpretations of the Diet of Augsburg to 1577." *Sixteenth Century Journal* 11/3:47–61.

———. 1984. "The German Lutheran Reaction to the Third Period of the Council of Trent." *Lutherjahrbuch* 1984:63–95.

———. 1988. "Luther's Smalcald Articles: Agenda for Testimony and Confession." *Concordia Journal* 14:115–37.

———. 1995. "'That I May Be His Own': The Anthropology of Luther's Explanation of the Creed." *Concordia Journal* 21:28–41.

———, and James A. Nestingen, eds. 2001. *Sources and Contexts of the Book of Concord*. Minneapolis, Minn.: Fortress Press.

Kolfhaus, W. 1909. "Der Verkehr Calvins mit Bullinger." In *Calvinstudien: Festschrift zum 400. Geburtstage Johann Calvins*, 27–125. Edited by J. Bohatec. Leipzig: Rudolf Haupt.

Konidaris, G. 1971. "The Christological Decisions of Chalcedon: Their History down to the Sixth Ecumenical Synod (451–680/1)." *GOTR* 16:63–78.

Koop, Karl Peter. 1999. "Early Seventeenth Century Mennonite Confessions of Faith: The Development of an Anabaptist Tradition." Ph.D. diss., University of St. Michael's College, Toronto.

Kopecek, Thomas A. 1979. *A History of the Neo-Arianism.* 2 vols. Patristic Monograph Series, 8. Philadelphia: Philadelphia Patristic Foundation.

Koren, Henry J. 1958. *The Spiritans: A History of the Congregation of the Holy Ghost.* Pittsburgh, Pa.: Duquesne University.

Kraft, Heinrich. 1980. "Das Apostolicum—Das apostolische Symbol." In *Studien zur Bekenntnisbildung,* 16–29. Edited by Peter Meinhold. Wiesbaden: Steiner.

Krauth, Charles Porterfield. [1899] 1963. *The Conservative Reformation and Its Theology.* Reprint, Minneapolis, Minn.: Augsburg.

Krummel, Leopold. 1871. *Ultraquisten und Taboriten.* Gotha: Friedrich Andreas Perthes.

Kruse, Martin. 1975. "Abendmahl im Wandel." *Evangelische Theologie* 35:481–96.

Kubiak, Hieronim. 1982. *The Polish National Catholic Church in the United States of America from 1897 to 1980.* Kraków: Jagiellonian University.

Kucharek, Casimir A. 1971. *The Byzantine-Slav Liturgy of St. John Chrysostom: Its Origin and Evolution.* Allendale, N.J.: Alleluia Press.

Küng, Hans, and Jürgen Moltmann, eds. 1979. *An Ecumenical Confession of Faith?* New York: Seabury Press.

———. 1992. *Credo: Das Apostolische Glaubensbekenntnis-Zeitgenossen erklärt.* Munich: Piper. [English translation: *Credo: The Apostles' Creed Explained for Today.* Translated by John Bowden. London: SCM Press, 1993.]

Künstle, Karl. 1900. *Eine Bibliothek der Symbole und theologischer Tractate zur Bekämpfung des Priscillianismus und westgothischen Arianismus aus dem 6. Jahrhundert: Ein Beitrag zur Geschichte der theologischen Litteratur in Spanien.* Mainz: F. Kirchheim.

Küppers, Werner. 1978. "Verbindliches Lehren im Lichte des Verständnisses und der Ausübung von Autorität in der alten Kirche." In *Verbindliches Lehren der Kirche Heute,* 79–93. Frankfurt: Otto Lembeck.

———, Peter Hauptmann, and Friedrich Baser. 1964. *Symbolik der kleineren Kirchen, Freikirchen und Sekten des Westens.* Stuttgart: A. Hiersemann.

Küry, Urs, and Christian Oeyen. 1982. *Die altkatholische Kirche: Ihre Geschichte, Ihre Lehre, Ihr Anliegen.* Frankfurt: Evangelisches Verlagswerk.

Kuttner, Stephen Georg. 1947. "Liber canonicus: A Note on the 'Dictatus Pape' c. 17." In *Studi Gregoriani: Per la storia di Gregorio VII e della Riforma Gregoriana,* 2:387–401. Edited by G. B. Borino. Rome: Abbazia di San Paolo di Roma.

Kydd, Ronald. 1977. "Novatian's *De trinitate,* 29: Evidence of the Charismatic?" *Scottish Journal of Theology* 30/4:313–18.

Labunka, Miroslav. 1990. *Mitropolit Ilarion I joho pisannja* [Metropolitan Ilarion and his writings]. Rome: Ukrainian Catholic University.

Lacko, Michael. 1966. *The Union of Užhorod.* Cleveland, Ohio: Slovak Institute.

Lagorio, Valerie. M. 1974. "The Text of the *Quicunque vult* in Codex Ottob. Lat. 663." *JTS* 25:127–28.

Lake, Kirsopp, tr. 1959. *The Apostolic Fathers.* 2 vols. Cambridge, Mass.: Harvard University Press.

Lake, Peter. 1982. *Moderate Puritans and the Elizabethan Church.* Cambridge: Cambridge University Press.

———. 1987. "Calvinism and the English Church, 1570–1635." *Past and Present* 114:22–76.

Lambert, Malcolm. 1977. *Medieval Heresy: Popular Movements from Bogomil to Hus.* New York: Holmes and Meier.

The Lambeth Conference 1930: Encyclical Letter from the Bishops with Resolutions and Reports. 1930. London: S.P.C.K; New York: Macmillan.

Lamm, Norman. 1998. *The Shema: Spirituality and Law in Judaism.* Philadelphia: Jewish Publication Society.

Lamont, William. 1985. "The Rise of Arminianism Reconsidered." *Past and Present* 107:227–31.

Lampe, Geoffrey William Hugo. 1960. "The Evidence in the New Testament for Early Creeds, Catechisms and Liturgy." *Expository Times* 71:359–63.

Land, Gary, ed. 1998. *Adventism in America: A History.* Revised ed. Barren Springs, Mich.: Andrews University Press.

Landgraf, Artur Michael. 1952–56. *Dogmengeschichte der Frühscholastik.* 4 vols. Regensburg: Verlag Friedrich Pustet.

Lane, Grace. 1974. *Brief Halt at Mile "50": A Half Century of Church Union.* [N.p.:United Church Publishing House].

Lange, Albert de, ed. 1990. *Dall'Europa alle Valli Valdesi.* Turin: Editrice Claudiana.

Langton, Edward. 1956. *History of the Moravian Church: The Story of the First International Protestant Church.* London: Allen and Unwin.

Lankshear, David W., and Leslie J. Francis. 1991. "The Use of the Revised Catechism in Anglican Churches." *British Journal of Religious Education* 13:95–100.

Lanne, Emmanuel. 1977. "Eglise une." *Irénikon* 50:46–58.

———. 1984. "The Apostolic Faith as Expressed in the Apostles' Creed, Especially Compared with the Nicene Creed." In *The Roots of Our Common Faith: Faith in the Scriptures and in the Early Church,* 95–105. Edited by Hans-Georg Link. Faith and Order Paper, 119. Geneva: World Council of Churches.

Latourette, Kenneth Scott. 1937–45. *A History of the Expansion of Christianity.* 7 vols. New York: Harper and Brothers.

———. 1967. *A History of Christian Missions in China.* New York: Russell and Russell.

Lavater, Hans Rudolf. 1980. "Zwingli und Bern." In *450 Jahre Berner Reformation: Beiträge zur Geschichte der Berner Reformation und zu Niklaus Manuel,* 60–103. Edited by Hans A. Michel, Rudolf Dellsperger, Hans Rudolf Lavater, et al. Bern: Historische Verein des Kantons Bern.

Lawson, John. 1974. "Articles of Religion." *The Encyclopedia of World Methodism,* 1:146–58, s.v. "American Methodism." Edited by Nolan B. Harmon. Nashville, Tenn.: United Methodist Publishing House.

Lecoy de la Marche, A., ed. 1877. *Anecdotes historiques légendes et apologues tirés du recuiel inédit d'Etienne de Bourbon, dominicain du XIIIe siècle.* Paris: Société de l'Histoire de France.

Leduc-Fayette, Denise. 1996. *Fénelon et l'amour de Dieu.* Paris: Presses Universitaires de France.

Leff, Gordon. 1967. *Heresy in the Later Middle Ages.* 2 vols. Manchester: Manchester University Press; New York: Barnes and Noble.

———. 1986. *Wyclif in His Times.* Oxford: Clarendon Press.

Leger, Jean. 1669. *Histoire generale des Eglises evangeliques des vallees de Piemont; ou Vaudoises.* 2 vols. Leyde: Le Carpentier.

Leith, John H. 1973. *Assembly at Westminster.* Richmond, Va.: John Knox Press.

———. 1982. *Creeds of the Churches.* 3d ed. Atlanta, Ga.: John Knox Press.

Lennerz, H. 1924. "Wurde die 11. Synode von Toledo (675) von Innozenz III als 'authentisch' erklärt?" *ZfkT* 48:322-23.

Leonard, Emile G. 1959. "Légende et histoire du synode de 1559." *Etudes évangéliques de la Faculté de théologie d'Aix* 1959:12-27.

Lewis, Jack P. 1983. "Baptismal Practices of the Second- and Third-Century Church." *Restoration Quarterly* 26/1:1-17.

Lewis, Keith D. 1985. "Johann Faber and the First Zürich Disputation,1523: A Pre-Tridentine Catholic Response to Ulrich Zwingli and His Sixty-Seven Articles." Ph.D. diss., Catholic University of America.

L'Huillier, Peter. 1982. "Faits et fiction à propos du deuxième concile oecuménique." *Eglise et théologie* 13:135-56.

———. 1996. *The Church of the Ancient Councils: The Disciplinary Work of the First Four Ecumenical Councils.* Crestwood, N.Y.: Saint Vladimir's Seminary Press.

Lietzmann, Hans. 1921. "Die Anfänge des Glaubensbekenntnisses." In *Festgabe für D. Dr. A. von Harnack . . . zum siebzigsten Geburtstag dargebracht von Fachgenossen und Freunden,* 226-42. Tübingen: J. C. B. Mohr (Paul Siebeck).

———. [1925] 1963. *Die Entstehung der christlichen Liturgie nach den ältesten Quellen.* Reprint, Darmstadt: Wissenschaftliche Buchgesellschaft.

———. 1966. *Symbolstudien I-XIV.* Sonderausgabe. Darmstadt: Wissenschaftliche Buchgesellschaft.

———, and Martin Dibelius. [1910] 1921. *Die Briefe des Apostels Paulus.* Tübingen: J. C. B. Mohr (P. Siebeck).

Lightfoot, J. B., ed. and tr. [1889-90] 1981. *The Apostolic Fathers: Clement, Ignatius, and Polycarp.* 2d ed. Reprint, Grand Rapids, Mich.: Baker Book House.

Limberis, Vasiliki. 1995. "The Council of Ephesos: The Demise of the See of Ephesos and the Rise of the Cult of the Theotokos." In *Ephesos: Metropolis of Asia: An Interdisciplinary Approach to Its Archaeology, Religion, and Culture,* 321-40. Edited by Helmut Koester. Harvard Theological Studies, 41. Valley Forge, Pa.: Trinity Press International.

Linde, Simon van der. 1966. "Die Lehre von der Kirche in der *Confessio Helvetica Posterior.*" In *Glauben und Bekennen: Vierhundert Jahre Confessio Helvetica Posterior,* 337-67. Edited by Joachim Staedtke. Zurich: Zwingli Verlag.

Link, Hans-Georg. 1985. *Apostolic Faith Today: A Handbook for Study.* Geneva: World Council of Churches.

Lippy, Charles H., and Peter Williams, eds. 1988. *Encyclopedia of the American Religious Experience: Studies of Traditions and Movements*. 3 vols. New York: Charles Scribner's Sons.

Littell, Franklin Hamlin. 1958. *The Anabaptist View of the Church: A Study in the Origins of Sectarian Protestantism*. Boston: Starr King Press.

Little, Edward. 1973. "Bernard and Abelard at the Council of Sens, 1140." In *Bernard of Clairvaux: Studies Presented to Dom Jean Leclerq*, 67–71. Edited by Henri Rochais. Spencer, Mass.: Cistercian Publications.

———. 1977. "Relations Between St. Bernard and Abelard Before 1139." In *Saint Bernard of Clairvaux: Studies Commemorating the Eighth Centenary of His Canonization*, 155–68. Edited by M. Basil Pennington. Kalamazoo, Mich.: Cistercian Publications.

Liturgienbuch der evangelischen Brüdergemeine. 1873. Gnadau: C. H. Pemsel.

Liturgy and Confessions. 1990– . Looseleaf collection issued by the Reformed Church in America. [New York]: Reformed Church Press.

Locher, Gottfried W. 1978. "Die deutsche Reformation aus Schweizer Sicht." *ZKG* 89/1–2:31–35.

———. 1980a. "Von der Standhaftigkeit: Zwinglis Schlusspredigt an der Berner Disputation als Beitrag zu seiner Ethik." In *Humanität und Glaube: Gedenkschrift für Kurt Guggisberg*, 29–41. Edited by Ulrich Neuenschwander and Rudolf Dellsperger. Bern: Paul Haput.

———. 1980b. "Die Berner Disputation 1528." In *450 Jahre Berner Reformation: Beiträge zur Geschichte der Berner Reformation und zu Niklaus Manuel*, 138–55. Edited by Hans A. Michel, Rudolf Dellsperger, Hans Rudolf Lavater, et al. Bern: Historische Verein des Kantons Bern.

———. 1988. "Die Lausanne Disputationsthesen als Dokument Zwinglischer Theologie." In *La Dispute de Lausanne 1988*, 91–103.

———. 1990. "Huldrych Zwingli an Karl V: Das Vorwort zur *Fidei Ratio* 1530." *Theologische Zeitschrift* 46/3:205–18.

Lochman, Jan M. 1975. "Not Just One Reformation: The Waldensian and Hussite Heritage." *Reformed World* 33:218–24.

Logan, Samuel T. 1994. "The Context and Work of the Assembly." In Carson and Hall 1994, 27–46.

Lo Grasso, Giovanni B. 1939. *Ecclesia et status: De mutuis officiis et iuribus, fontes selecti*. Rome: Apud Aedes Universitatis Gregorianae.

Lohse, Bernhard. 1968. "Hans Denck und der 'linke Flügel' der Reformation." In *Humanitas-Christianitas*, 74–83. Edited by G. M. Beyschlag and E. Wölfel. Festschrift for Walther von Loewenich. Witten, Germany: Luther Verlag.

———. 1979. "Augsburger Bekenntnis I." In *TRE* 4:616–27.

———. 1980a. "Luther und das Augsburger Bekenntnis." In *Das Augsburger Bekenntnis von 1530: Damals und Heute*, 144–63. Edited by Bernhard Lohse and Otto Hermann Pesch. Munich: Kaiser, and Mainz: Grünewald.

———. 1980b. "Lehrentscheidungen ohne Lehramt: Die Konkordienformel als Modell theologischer Konfliktbewältigung." *Kerygma und Dogma* 26:174–87.

———. 1983. "Philipp Melanchthon in seinen Beziehungen zu Luther." In Junghans 1983, 1:403–18.

———. 1986. "Die ökumenische Bedeutung von Luthers Schmalkaldischen Artikeln." In

Kirchengemeinschaft: Anspruch und Wirklichkeit, 165–75. [Festschrift für Georg Kretschmar zum 60. Geburtstag.] Edited by Wolf-Dieter Hauschild et al. Stuttgart: Calwer Verlag.

Loofs, F. 1909. "Das Glaubensbekenntnis der Homousianer von Sardica." *Abhandlungen der königlichen preußischen Akademie der Wissenschaften,* Phil.-hist. Klaße 1:3–39.

———. 1914. *Nestorius and His Place in the History of Christian Doctrine.* Cambridge: Cambridge University Press.

Lossky, Vladimir. 1976. *The Mystical Theology of the Eastern Church.* Translated by members of the Fellowship of Saint Alban and Saint Sergius. Crestwood, N.Y.: Saint Vladimir's Seminary Press.

Lovisa, Barbro. 1994. *Italienische Waldenser und das protestantische Deutschland, 1655–1989.* Göttingen: Vandenhoeck und Ruprecht.

Lubac, Henri de. 1950. *Histoire et esprit: L'intelligence de l'Ecriture d'après Origène.* Paris: Aubier.

———. 1959. *Exégèse médiéval: Les quatres sens de l'ecriture.* 2 vols. [Paris]: Aubier. [English: *Medieval Exegesis.* Translated by Mark Sebanc. Grand Rapids, Mich.: Eerdmans, 1998–2000.]

———. 1969. *L'Eglise dans la crise actuelle.* Paris: Editions du Cerf.

———. 1970. *La foi chrétienne: Essai sur la structure de symbole des apôtres.* Paris: Aubier-Montaigne. [English: *The Christian Faith: An Essay on the Structure of the Apostles' Creed.* Translated by Richard Arnandez. San Francisco: Ignatius Press, 1986.]

———. 1975. "Das apostolische Glaubensbekenntnis." *Internationale Katholische Zeitschrift "Communio"* 4:1–9.

Lubieniecki, Stanislas. 1994. *History of the Polish Reformation.* Translated and interpreted by George Hunston Williams. Minneapolis, Minn.: Fortress Press.

Lueker, Erwin L., ed. 1954. *Lutheran Cyclopedia.* Saint Louis, Mo.: Concordia Publishing House.

Luibhéid, Colm. 1981. *Eusebius of Caesarea and the Arian Crisis.* Dublin: Irish Academic Press.

———. 1982. *The Council of Nicaea.* Galway: Galway University Press.

———. 1983. "The Alleged Second Session of the Council of Nicaea." *Journal of Ecclesiastical History* 34:165–74.

Lumpkin, William Latane, ed. 1959. *Baptist Confessions of Faith.* Chicago: Judson Press.

Luther und die Bekenntnisschriften. 1981. Edited by R. Heinrich Foerster. Erlangen, Germany: Martin Luther-Verlag.

McBeth, H. Leon. 1990. *A Sourcebook for Baptist Heritage.* Nashville, Tenn.: Broadman Press.

McCallum, James Ramsay. 1948. *Abelard's Christian Theology.* Oxford: Basil Blackwell.

Maccarrone, Michele. 1961. *Papato e Impero dalla elezione di Federico I alla morte di Adriano IV, 1152–1159.* Rome: Pontificia Universitas Lateranensis, Facultas Theologica.

McCarthy, Timothy. 1998. *The Catholic Church: The Church in the Twentieth Century.* 2d ed. Chicago: Loyola University Press.

McComish, William. 1981. "Reazioni inglesi alla 'primavera di sangue' valdese del 1655." Translated by Giorgio Vola. *Bollettino della Società di Studi Valdesi* 149:3–10.

McCulloh, Gerald O., ed. 1962. *Man's Faith and Freedom: The Theological Influences of Jacobus Arminius.* Nashville, Tenn.: Abingdon Press.

McElrath, Damian. 1964. *The Syllabus of Pius IX: Some Reactions in England*. Louvain: Bibliothèque de l'université.

McGrath, Alister E. 1990. *Life of John Calvin: A Study in the Shaping of Western Culture*. Grand Rapids, Mich.: Baker Book House.

McHardy, A. K. 1987. "The Dissemination of Wyclif's Ideas." In *From Ockham to Wyclif*, 361–68. Edited by Anne Hudson and Michael Wilks. Studies in Church History, Subsidia, 5. Oxford: Basil Blackwell.

Macholz, Waldemar Karl Ludwig. 1902. *Spuren binitarischern Denkweise im Abendlande seit Tertullian*. Jena: A. Kämpfe.

McHugh, J. F. 1995. "The Sacrifice of the Mass at the Council of Trent." In *Sacrifice and Redemption*, 157–81. Edited by Stephen W. Sykes. Cambridge: Cambridge University Press.

McNeill, John Thomas. 1964. *Unitive Protestantism: The Ecumenical Spirit and Its Persistent Expression*. Revised ed. Richmond, Va.: John Knox Press.

McShane, Philip. 1983. "Leo the Great, Guardian of Doctrine and Discipline." *Eglise et théologie* 14:9–24.

Macy, Gary. 1984. *The Theologies of the Eucharist in the Early Scholastic Period: A Study of the Salvific Function of the Sacrament According to the Theologians, c. 1080–c. 1220*. New York: Oxford University Press.

———. 1990. "Berengar's Legacy as Heresiarch." In *Auctoritas und Ratio*, 47–68. Edited by Peter Ganz, R. B. C. Huygens, and Friedrich Niewöhner. Wiesbaden: Harrassowitz.

Madoz, Joseph. 1938. *Le Symbole du XIe Concile de Tolèdo, ses sources, sa date, sa valeur*. Louvain: Spicilegium Sacrum Lovaniense.

Magee, John. 1988. "Note on Boethius, Consolatio I, 1:5, 3:7: A New Biblical Parallel." *Vigiliae Christianae* 42/1:79–82.

Maichle, Albert. 1929. *Der Kanon der biblischen Bücher und das Konzil von Trient*. Freiburg: Herder.

Maloney, George A. 1976. *A History of Orthodox Theology Since 1453*. Belmont, Mass.: Nordland.

Malvy, Antoine, and Marcel Viller. 1927. *La confession orthodoxe de Pierre Moghila, métropolite de Kiev (1633-1646), approuvée par les patriarches grecs du XVIIe siècle*. Rome: Pontificale Institutum Orientalium Studiorum.

Manns, Peter. 1981. "Luther auf der Koburg das Reichstagsgeschehen von Augsburg und die Entstehung der *Confessio Augustana*." In *Luther und die Bekenntnisschriften* 1981, 121–30.

Manschreck, Clyde L. 1957. "The Role of Melanchthon in the Adiaphora Controversy." *ARG* 48:165–82.

Mantzaridēs, Gēorgios I. 1984. *The Deification of Man: St. Gregory Palamas and the Orthodox Tradition*. Translated by Liadain Sherrard. Foreword by Bishop Kallistos of Diokleia. Crestwood, N.Y.: Saint Vladimir's Seminary Press.

The Manual. 2000. London: United Reformed Church.

Manual of the Church of the Nazarene: History, Constitution, Government, Ritual. 1952. Kansas City, Mo.: Nazarene Publishing House.

Marcel, Pierre, ed. 1952. *La confession de foi des Eglises réformés en France dite Confession de La Rochelle*. [St.-Germain-en-Laye (Seine-et-Oise)]: La Revue Réformée.

Marcovich, Miroslav, ed. 1994. Justin Martyr. *Apologiae pro Christianis*. Patristische Texte und Studien, 38. Berlin: W. De Gruyter.

Marsden, George M. 1970. *The Evangelical Mind and the New School Presbyterian Experience: A Case Study of Thought and Theology in Nineteenth-Century America*. New Haven and London: Yale University Press.

Marshall, Paul V. 1989. *Prayer Book Parallels*. 2 vols. New York: Church Hymnal Corp.

Mastrantonis, George. 1982. *Augsburg and Constantinople: The Correspondence Between the Tübingen Theologians and Patriarch Jeremiah II of Constantinople on the Augsburg Confession*. Brookline, Mass.: Holy Cross Orthodox Press.

Mathisen, Ralph W. 1989. *Ecclesiastical Factionalism and Religious Controversy in Fifth-Century Gaul*. Washington, D.C.: Catholic University of America.

Matthews, A. G., ed. 1959. *The Savoy Declaration of Faith and Order, 1658*. With an additional notice by Daniel T. Jenkins. London: Independent Press.

Maurer, Wilhelm. 1962. "Confessio Augustan Variata." *ARG* 53:97–151.

———. 1986. *Historical Commentary on the Augsburg Confession*. Translated by H. George Anderson. Philadelphia: Fortress Press.

Mehl, Roger. 1959. *Explication de la confession de foi de La Rochelle*. Paris: Les Bergers et les Mages.

———. 1977. "Strasbourg et Luther: La Tétrapolitaine." In *Strasbourg au coeur religieux du XVIe siècle: Actes du colloque international de Strasbourg, 1975*, 145–52. Edited by Georges Livet and Francis Rapp. Strasbourg: Librairie Istra.

Mehlhausen, Joachim. 1980. "Der Streit um die Adiaphora." In *Bekenntnis und Einheit der Kirche: Studien zum Konkordienbuch*, 105–28. Edited by Martin Brecht and Reinhard Schwarz. Stuttgart: Calwer Verlag.

Meigs, Samantha A. 1997. *The Reformations in Ireland: Tradition and Confessionalism, 1400–1690*. New York: St. Martin's Press.

Meihuizen, Hendrick W. 1967a. "Who Were the False Brethren Mentioned in the Schleitheim Articles?" *MQR* 41:200–222.

———, ed. 1967b. Menno Simons. *Dat Fundament des Christelycken leers*. The Hague: Martin Nijhoff.

Meijering, E. P. 1987. *Augustine: De Fide et Symbolo*. Amsterdam: J. C. Gieben.

Meinhold, Peter. 1971. "Christologie und Jungfrauengeburt bei Ignatius von Antiochien." In *Studia mediaevalia et mariologica*, 465–76. Edited by Pedro Capkun-Delic. Rome: Edizione Antonianum.

———. 1979. *Studien zu Ignatius von Antiochien*. Veröffentlichungen des Institus für Europäische Geschichte, Mainz. Wiesbaden: Steiner.

Melia, Pius. 1870. *The Origin, Persecutions, and Doctrine of the Waldenses*. London: James Toovey.

Mentz, Georg, ed. [1905] 1968. *Die Wittenberger Artikel von 1536*. Darmstadt: Wissenschaftliche Buchgesellschaft.

Menzies, William W. 1971. *Anointed to Serve: The Story of the Assemblies of God*. Springfield, Mo.: Gospel Publishing House.

Merdinger, J. E. 1997. *Rome and the African Church in the Time of Augustine*. New Haven and London: Yale University Press.

Meridith, Anthony. 1981. "The Pneumatology of the Cappadocian Fathers and the Creed of Constantinople." *Irish Theological Quarterly* 48:197–211.

Merwin, Wallace C. 1974. *Adventure in Unity: The Church of Christ in China*. Grand Rapids, Mich.: Eerdmans.

Mews, Constant J. 2002. *Reason and Belief in the Age of Roscelin and Abelard*. Aldershot, England: Ashgate.

Meyendorff, John. 1964–65. "Chalcedonians and Monophysites After Chalcedon." *GOTR* 10/2:16–36.

———. 1966. *Orthodoxy and Catholicity*. New York: Sheed and Ward.

———. 1969. *Christ in Eastern Thought*. Washington, D.C.: Corpus Books.

———. 1974. *Byzantine Hesychasm: Historical, Theological, and Social Problems*. London: Variorum Reprints.

———. 1982. *The Byzantine Legacy in the Orthodox Church*. Crestwood, N.Y.: Saint Vladimir's Seminary Press.

———. 1989. *Imperial Unity and Christian Divisions: The Church, 450–680 A.D.* Crestwood, N.Y.: Saint Vladimir's Seminary.

———. 1996. *Rome, Constantinople, Moscow: Historical and Theological Studies*. Crestwood, N.Y.: Saint Vladimir's Seminary Press.

———. 1998. *Saint Gregory Palamas and Orthodox Spirituality*. Translated by Adele Fiske. Crestwood, N.Y.: Saint Vladimir's Seminary Press.

———, ed. 1983. Gregory Palamas. *The Triads*. Translated by Nicholas Gendle. Preface by Jaroslav Pelikan. New York: Paulist Press.

Meyendorff, Paul, ed. and tr. 1984. *Saint Germanus of Constantinople on the Divine Liturgy*. Crestwood, N.Y.: Saint Vladimir's Seminary Press.

———. 1989. "Reflections on Russian Liturgy: A Retrospective on the Occasion of the Millennium." In *Saint Vladimir's Theological Quarterly* 33/1:21–34.

Meyer, Carl S. 1972. "Melanchthon's Visitation Articles of 1528." *Journal of Ecclesiastical History* 23:309–22.

Michel, Anton. 1924–30. *Humbert und Kerullarios*. 2 vols. Paderborn, Germany: F. Schöningh.

Miller, Allen O., and M. Eugene Osterhaven. 1963. *The Heidelberg Catechism: Four Hundredth Anniversary Edition, 1563–1963*. Philadelphia: United Church Press.

Miller, Ed L. 1982. "Oecolampadius: The Unsung Hero of the Basel Reformation." *Iliff Review* 39:5–25.

Miller, Russell E. 1979–85. *The Larger Hope*. 2 vols. Boston: Unitarian Universalist Association.

Miller, Victoria C. 1994. *The Lambeth Articles: Doctrinal Development and Conflict in Sixteenth-Century England*. Oxford: Latimer House.

Millet, Robert L., ed. 1989. *Joseph Smith: Selected Sermons and Writings*. New York: Paulist Press.

Minear, Mark. 1987. *Richmond, 1987: A Quaker Drama Unfolds*. Richmond, Ind.: Friends United Press.

Minutes of the Auburn Convention, Held August 17, 1837, to Deliberate upon the Doings of the Last General Assembly in Relation to the Synods of Western Reserve, Utica, Geneva and Genesee, and the Third Presbytery of Philadelphia. 1837. Auburn, N.Y.: Auburn Convention.

Mirbt, Carl. 1924. *Quellen zur Geschichte des Papsttums und des römischen Katholizismus.* 4th ed. Tübingen: J. C. B. Mohr [Paul Siebeck].

Mitchell, Alexander F. 1884. *The Westminster Assembly: Its History and Its Standards.* Philadelphia: Board of Publications.

———, and John Struthers, eds. 1874. *Minutes of the Sessions of the Westminster Assembly of Divines.* Edinburgh: William Blackwood and Sons.

Moberly, R. 1990. "Yahweh Is One: The Translation of the Shema." In *Studies in the Pentateuch,* 209–15. Edited by J. A. Emerton. Supplements to Vetus Testamentum, 41. Leiden: E. J. Brill.

Möhler, Johann Adam. [1832] 1958–61. *Symbolik: Oder Darstellung der dogmatischen Gegensätze der Katholiken und Protestanten nach ihren öffentlichen Bekenntnisschriften.* Reprint, Cologne: Jakob Hegner.

Molnar, Amedeo. 1973. "Czech Confession of 1575." *Communio-Viatorum* 16/4:241–47.

———. 1983. "Luthers Beziehungen zu den Böhmischen Brüdern." In Junghans 1983, 1:627–39.

Montclos, Jean de. 1993. "Lanfranc et Bérenger: Les origines de la doctrine de la transsubstantiation." In *Lanfranco di Pavia e l'Europa del secolo XI nel IX centenario della morte (1089–1989),* 297–326. Rome: Herder.

Montgomery, John W. 1976. "Chemnitz on the Council of Trent." In *Soli Deo Gloria: Essays in Reformed Theology,* 73–94. Edited by Robert C. Sproul. Nutley, N.J.: Presbyterian and Reformed Publishing.

Moreton, M. 1989. "Commandment and Remembrance in the Shema and in the Eucharistic Prayer." In *Studia Patristica,* 20: *Critica, Classica, Orientalia, Ascetica, Liturgica* [Tenth International Conference on Patristic Studies, Oxford, 1987], 384–88. Edited by Elizabeth A. Livingstone. Louvain: Peeters.

Morin, G. 1901. "Le Symbole d'Athanase et son premier témoin, S. Césaire d'Arles." *Revue Bénédictine* 18:337–62.

———. 1932. "L'Origine du symbole d'Athanase: témoignage inédit de S. Césaire d'Arles." *Revue Bénédictine* 44:207–19.

Morris, Kenneth R. 1994. "'Pure Wheat of God' or Neurotic Deathwish? A Historical and Theological Analysis of Ignatius of Antioch's Zeal for Martyrdom." *Fides et Historia* 26:24–41.

Morrow, Hubert W. 1970. "Cumberland Presbyterian Theology: A Nineteenth-Century Development in American Presbyterianism." *Journal of Presbyterian History* 48:203–20.

Moss, C. B. 1964. *The Old Catholic Movement: Its Origins and History.* 2d ed. London: S.P.C.K.

Muelder, Walter G. 1961. *Methodism and Society in the Twentieth Century.* New York: Abingdon Press.

Mueller, John T. 1949. "Notes on the Consensus Tigurinus of 1549." *Concordia Theological Monthly* 20:894–909.

Mueller, William A. 1959. *A History of Southern Baptist Theological Seminary.* Nashville, Tenn.: Broadman Press.

Müller, Ewald. 1934. *Das Konzil von Vienne, 1311-1312: Seine Quellen und seine Geschichte.* Münster: Aschendorff.

Müller, Gerhard. 1968. "Pius IX. und die Entwicklung der römisch-katholischen Mariologie." *Neue Zeitschrift für systematische Theologie und Religionsphilosophie* 10:111-30.

Müller, Joseph Theodor. 1922-31. *Geschichte der Böhmischen Brüder.* 3 vols. Herrnhut, Germany: Missionsbuchhandlung.

Muller, Richard A. 1991. *God, Creation, and Providence in the Thought of Jacob Arminius: Sources and Directions of Scholastic Protestantism.* Grand Rapids, Mich.: Baker Book House.

Muralt, Leonhard von. 1930. "Stadtgemeinde und Reformation in der Schweiz." *Zeitschrift für schweizerische Geschichte* 10:349-84.

———. 1969. "Der Anfang der Reformation in Zurich." *Reformatio* 18:3-9.

Murphy, Francis X., and P. Sherwood. 1974. *Constantinople II et Constantinople III.* Vol. 3 of *Histoire des conciles oecuméniques.* Paris: Orante.

Müsing, Hans-Werner. 1977. "The Anabaptist Movement in Strasbourg from Early 1526 to July 1577." *MQR* 51:91-126.

My People's Prayer Book: Traditional Prayers, Modern Commentaries. 1997. Edited by Lawrence A. Hoffman. Woodstock, Vt.: Jewish Lights Publishing.

Nacpil, Emerito P. 1976. "A Gospel for the New Filipino." In Anderson, 117-45.

Navè, Pnina. 1974. "Höre Israel: Talmudische und liturgische Traditionen über Dt 6, 4-9, 11, 13-21; Nm 15, 37-41." In *Das Vaterunser: Gemeinsames im Beten von Juden und Christen,* 56-76. Edited by Michael Brocke, Jakob J. Petuchowski, and Walter Strolz. Frieburg: Herder.

Nelson, E. Clifford, ed. 1980. *The Lutherans in North America.* 2d ed. Philadelphia: Fortress Press.

Nelson, Stanley A. 1994. "Reflecting on Baptist Origins: The London Confession of Faith of 1644." *Baptist History and Heritage* 29:33-46.

Nestorius. 1925. *The Bazaar of Heraclides.* Edited and translated by G. R. Driver and L. Hodgson. Oxford: Clarendon Press.

Netter, Thomas. 1858. *Fasciculi Zizaniorum magistri Johannis Wyclif cum tritico.* London: Longman, Brown, Green, Longmans, and Roberts.

Neuner, J., and J. Dupuis. 2001. *The Christian Faith in the Doctrinal Documents of the Catholic Church.* New York: Alba House.

Newbigin, Lesslie, J. E. [1948] 1960. *The Reunion of the Church: A Defence of the South India Scheme.* 2d ed. Reprint, London: SCM Press.

Newman, John Henry. 1841. *Tract Ninety* [Remarks on Certain Passages in the Thirty-Nine Articles]. London: J. G. F. and J. Rivington.

Nichols, Robert L., and Theofanis George Stavrou. 1978. *Russian Orthodoxy Under the Old Regime.* Minneapolis: University of Minnesota Press.

Niederwimmer, Kurt, ed. 1993. *Die Didache.* 2d ed. Göttingen: Vandenhoeck und Ruprecht. Also published with English translation of commentary, Minneapolis, Minn.: Fortress Press, 1998.

Niemöller, Gerhard, ed. 1959. *Die erste Bekenntnissynode der Deutschen Evangelischen Kirche zu Barmen.* Göttingen: Vandenhoeck und Ruprecht.

Nienkirchen, Charles. 1982. "Reviewing the Case for a Non-Separatist Ecclesiology in Early Swiss Anabaptism." *MQR* 56:227–41.

Nihon Kirisuto Kyodan Kyouken Kyouki oyobi syokisoku. 2001. Tokyo: Nihon Kirisuto Kyodan Shyuppankyoku.

Niles, D. T. 1962. "Church Union in North India, Pakistan, and Ceylon." *Ecumenical Review* 14: 305–22.

Noko, Ishmael. 2000. "The Joint Declaration on the Doctrine of Justification: Some Observations." *Centro Pro Unione Bulletin* 57:7–9.

Nordström, N. J. 1928. *Svenska Baptistsamfundets Historia.* Stockholm: Baptistmissionens Bokförlags.

Norris, Frederick W. 1978. "Apostolic, Catholic, and Sensible: The *Consensus Fidelium.*" In *Essays on New Testament Christianity,* 15–29. Edited by C. Robert Wetzel. Cincinnati, Ohio: Standard Publishing.

Norris, R. A. 1990. "Irenaeus' Use of Paul in His Polemic Against the Gnostics." In *Paul and the Legacies of Paul,* 79–98, 337–40. Edited by William S. Babcock. Dallas: SMU Press.

Nulman, Macy. 1993. "Shema." In *The Encyclopedia of Jewish Prayer: Ashkenazic and Sephardic Rites,* 294–98. Northvale, N.J.: Jason Aronson.

Oberdorfer, Bernd. 2001. *Filioque: Geschichte und Theologie eines ökumenischen Problems.* Göttingen: Vandenhoeck und Ruprecht.

Oberman, Heiko A. 1981. *Masters of the Reformation.* Cambridge: Cambridge University Press.

———. 1994. "Initia Calvini: The Matrix of Calvin's Reformation." In *Calvinus Sacrae Scripturae professor: Calvin as Confessor of Holy Scripture,* 113–54. Edited by Wilhelm H. Neuser. Grand Rapids, Mich.: W. B. Eerdmans.

O'Connell, Timothy E., ed. 1986. *Vatican II and Its Documents: An American Reappraisal.* Wilmington, Del.: Michael Glazier.

O'Connor, Edward D. 1958. *The Dogma of the Immaculate Conception: History and Significance.* Notre Dame, Ind.: University of Notre Dame Press.

O'Dea, Thomas F. 1957. *The Mormons.* Chicago: University of Chicago Press.

Odložilik, Otakar. 1940. "Two Reformation Leaders of the Unitas Fratrum." *Church History* 9:253–63.

O'Donnell, James J. 1985. *Augustine.* Boston: Twayne.

O'Donovan, Oliver. 1986. *On the Thirty Nine Articles: A Conversation with Tudor Christianity.* Exeter, England: Paternoster Press for Latimer House, Oxford.

Ogudo, Donatus Emeka Onyemaobi. 1988. *The Catholic Missionaries and the Liturgical Movement in Nigeria: An Historical Overview.* Paderborn, Germany: Verlag Bonifatius-Druckerei.

Olbricht, Thomas H., and Hans Rollmann, eds. 2000. *The Quest for Christian Unity, Peace, and Purity in Thomas Campbell's "Declaration and Address": Text and Studies.* Lanham, Md.: Scarecrow Press.

Olmsted, Wendy Raudenbush. 1989. "Philosophical Inquiry and Religious Transformation in Boethius's *The Consolation of Philosophy* and Augustine's *Confessions.*" *Journal of Religion* 69:14–35.

Onasch, Konrad, and Annemarie Schnieper. 1997. *Icons: The Fascination and the Reality.* New York: Riverside Book.

Oosthuizen, Gerhard Cornelis. 1958. *Theological Discussions and Confessional Developments in the Churches of Asia and Africa.* Franeker, Netherlands: T. Wever.

Opitz, Hans-Georg, ed. 1934–41. *Athanasius. Werke.* 3 vols. Berlin: Walter de Gruyter.

Opitz, Peter, trans. 1995. *Rechenschaft über den Glauben* [translation of Zwingli's "Fidei ratio"]. Vol. 4 of *Huldrych Zwingli Schriften.* Edited by Thomas Brunnschweiler and Samuel Lutz. Zurich: Theologischer Verlag Zurich.

Ordo Missae Cum Populo / The Ordinary of the Mass in Eight Languages. 1992. Collegeville, Minn.: Liturgical Press.

Orthodox Church in America. 1967. *The Divine Liturgy, According to St. John Chrysostom, with Appendices.* New York: Orthodox Eastern Church.

Ortiz de Urbina, Ignacio. 1963. *Nicée et Constantinople.* Paris: Editions de l'Orante.

Osborn, Eric F. 1989. "Reason and the Rule of Faith in the Second Century A.D." In *The Making of Orthodoxy: Essays in Honour of Henry Chadwick,* 40–61. Edited by Rowan Williams. Cambridge: Cambridge University Press.

Osborn, Ronald E. 1979. *The Faith We Affirm: Basic Beliefs of Disciples of Christ.* St. Louis, Mo.: Bethany Press.

Oulton, John Ernest Leonard. 1940. *The Credal Statements of St. Patrick.* Dublin: Hodges, Figgis.

Our Lady. 1961. Selected and arranged by the Benedictine monks of Solesmes. Translated by the Daughters of St. Paul. Boston: St. Paul Editions.

Outler, Albert C. 1991. *The Wesleyan Theological Heritage.* Edited by Thomas C. Oden and Leicester R. Longden. Grand Rapids, Mich.: Zondervan.

Overduin, Daniel C. 1980. *Reflections on Luther's Small Catechism.* Saint Louis, Mo.: Concordia Press.

Ozment, Steven. 1973. *Mysticism and Dissent.* New Haven and London: Yale University Press.

Packull, Werner O. 1982. "Hans Denck: Fugitive from Dogmatism." In *Profiles of Radical Reformers: Biographical Sketches from Thomas Müntzer to Paracelsus,* 62–71. Edited by Hans Goertz. Scottdale, Pa.: Herald Press.

Palacký, František, ed. 1829. *Staří letopisové čeští, 1378–1527. Scriptorum rerum bohemicarum,* vol. 3. Prague: J. H. Pospissila.

———. 1844–67. *Geschichte von Böhmen.* 5 vols. Prague: Kronberger und Weber.

Pallath, Paul, ed. 1994. *Catholic Eastern Churches: Heritage and Identity.* Rome: Mar Thoma Yogam (The St. Thomas Christian Fellowship in Rome).

Palmer, Paul F., ed. 1952. *Mary in the Documents of the Church.* Westminster, Md.: Newman Press.

Palmieri, Aurelio. 1909. *Dositeo, patriarca greco di Gerusalemme (1641–1707): Contributo alla storia della teologia greco-ortodossa nel secolo XVII.* Florence: Libreria Editrice Fiorentina.

Panindangion Haporseaon (Confessie) ni Huria Kristen Batak Protestant (H.K.B.P.). 1966. Pearadja Tarutung, Indonesia: H.K.B.P. Pusat.

Pannenberg, Walter. 1979. "Faith and Disorder in Bangalore." *Worldview* 22:37–40.

Pannier, Jacques. 1936. *Les origines de la confession de foi et la discipline des Eglises réformées de France.* Paris: F. Alcan.

Papademetriou, George C., ed. 1989. *Photian Studies*. Brookline, Mass.: Holy Cross Orthodox Press.

Papadopoulos, Chrysostomos. 1939. *Kyrillos Loukaris*. Edited by Grēgorios Papamichaēl. 2nd ed. Athens: Phoinikos.

Paret, Friedrich. 1891. *Priscillianus, ein Reformator des vierten Jahrhunderts: Eine Kirchengeschichtlich Studie, zugleich ein Kommentar zu den erhaltenen Schriften Priscillians*. Würzburg: A. Stuber.

Parker, G. Keith. 1982. *Baptists in Europe: History and Confessions of Faith*. Nashville, Tenn.: Broadman Press.

Pas, P. 1954. "La doctrine de la double justice au Concile de Trent." *Ephemerides Theologicae Lovanienses* 30:5–53.

Patch, Howard Rollin. 1935. *The Tradition of Boethius: A Study of His Importance in Medieval Culture*. New York: Oxford University Press.

Patschovsky, Alexander, and Kurt-Victor Selge. 1973. *Quellen zur Geschichte der Waldenser*. Gütersloh, Germany: Gerd Mohn.

Patterson, Lloyd G. 1982. "Nikaia to Constantinople: The Theological Issues." *GOTR* 27: 375–93.

Pauck, Wilhelm. 1950. *The Heritage of the Reformation*. Glencoe, Ill.: Free Press.

Paul, Robert S. 1985. *The Assembly of the Lord: Politics and Religion in the Westminster Assembly and the "Grand Debate."* Edinburgh: T. and T. Clark.

Paulsen, Henning. 1985. *Die Briefe des Ignatius von Antiochia und der Brief des Polykarp von Smyrna*. 2d ed. Tübingen: Mohr.

Payne, Ernest A. 1952. "Michael Sattler and the Schleitheim Confession, 1527." *Baptist Quarterly* 14:337–44.

Peel, Robert. 1958. *Christian Science: Its Encounter with American Culture*. New York: Henry Holt.

Peitz, W. M. 1917. "Martin I und Maximus Confessor: Beiträge zur Geschichte des Monotheletenstreits in den Jahren 642–68." *Historisches Jahrbuch* 38:213–36, 429–58.

Pelikan, Jaroslav. 1948. "Luther's Attitude Toward John Hus." *Concordia Theological Monthly* 19:747–63.

———. 1949a. "Luther's Endorsement of the *Confessio Bohemica*." *Concordia Theological Monthly* 20:829–43.

———. 1949b. "Luther's Negotiations with the Hussites." *Concordia Theological Monthly* 20:496–517.

———. 1951a. "Chalcedon After Fifteen Centuries." *Concordia Theological Monthly* 22:926–36.

———. 1951b. "Church and Church History in the Confessions." *Concordia Theological Monthly* 22:305–20.

———. 1967. "Verius Servamus Canones: Church Law and Divine Law in the Apology of the Augsburg Confession." In *Studia Gratiana* 11, special issue, *Collectanea Stephan Kuttner*, 1:367–88. Edited by Alphons M. Stickler.

———. 1971. *Historical Theology: Continuity and Change in Christian Doctrine*. New York: Corpus.

———. 1974. "The Doctrine of *filioque* in Thomas Aquinas and Its Patristic Antecedents:

An Analysis of *Summa theologiae*, Part I, Question 36." In *St. Thomas Aquinas, 1274-1974*, 1:315-36. Edited by Etienne Gilson et al. Toronto: Pontifical Institute of Mediaeval Studies.

———. 1985. *Jesus Through the Centuries: His Place in the History of Culture*. New Haven and London: Yale University Press.

———. 1990a. *Imago Dei: The Byzantine Apologia for Icons*. The A. W. Mellon Lectures in the Fine Arts, 1987. Princeton, N.J.: Princeton University Press.

———. 1990b. *Eternal Feminines: Three Theological Allegories in Dante's "Paradiso."* New Brunswick, N.J.: Rutgers University Press.

———. 1990c. *Confessor Between East and West*. Grand Rapids, Mich.: Eerdmans.

———. 1993. *Christianity and Classical Culture: The Metamorphosis of Natural Theology in the Christian Encounter with Hellenism*. New Haven and London: Yale University Press.

———. 1996. *Mary Through the Centuries: Her Place in the History of Culture*. New Haven and London: Yale University Press.

———. 1997. *The Reformation of the Bible/The Bible of the Reformation*. Catalogue of the exhibition by David Price and Valerie R. Hotchkiss. New Haven and London: Yale University Press.

Pengakuan Gereja Toraja dalam bahasa Toraja. 1994. 2d ed. Rantepao, Indonesia: Pusbang-Badan Pekerja Sinode Gereja Toraja.

Perkins, Carl M. 1994. "The Evening Shema: A Study in Rabbinic Consolation." *Judaism* 43:26-36.

Peronnet, Michel. 1988. "Guillaume Farel à Lausanne en 1536." In *La Dispute de Lausanne 1988*, 133-41.

Perosanz, J. M. 1976. *El simbolo atanasiano*. Madrid: Palabra.

Péry, Andé. 1959. *Le Catéchisme de Heidelberg*. Geneva: Labor et Fides.

Peter, Carl J. 1985. "The Decree on Justification in the Council of Trent." In *Justification by Faith*, 218-29. Edited by H. George Anderson, T. Austin Murphy, and Joseph A. Burgess. Minneapolis, Minn.: Augsburg Publishing House.

Peters, Albrecht. 1981. "Die Bedeutung der Katechismen Luthers innerhalb der Bekenntnis-schriften." In *Luther und die Bekenntnisschriften 1981*, 46-89.

Petersen, Peter. [1921] 1964. *Geschichte der aristotelischen Philosophie im protestantischen Deutschland*. Reprint, Stuttgart: Frommann.

Petit, Louis, Xénophon Sidéridès, and Martin Jugie, eds. 1928-36. *Georgiou tou Skolariou Apanta ta euriskomena = Oeuvres complètes de Georges Scholarios*. Paris: Maison de la Bonne Presse.

Pfister, Rudolf. 1966. "Die Zweite Helvetische Bekenntnis in der Schweiz." In *Glauben und Bekennen: Vierhundert Jahre Confessio Helvetica Posterior*, 54-80. Edited by Joachim Staedtke. Zurich: Zwingli Verlag.

Pfnür, Vinzenz. 1970. *Einig in der Rechtfertigungslehre? Die Rechtfertigungslehre der "Confessio Augustana" (1530) und die Stellungnahme der katholischen Kontroverstheologie zwischen 1530 und 1533*. Wiesbaden: Franz Steiner.

Pharantos, Mega L. 1969. *Hē theologia Gennadiou tou Scholariou* [The theology of Gennadius Scholarius]. Athens: University of Athens.

Phougias, Methodios G. 1990. *Hē ekklēsiastikē antiparathesis Hellēnōn kai Latinōn: Apo tēs epochēs tou Megalou Phōtiou mechri tēs Synodou tēs Phlōrentias, 853-1439.* Athens: Heptalophos.

Piaget, Arthur, ed. 1928. *Les actes de la Dispute de Lausanne, 1536.* Neuchâtel: Secrétariat de l'Université.

Piepkorn, Arthur Carl. 1993. *The Church: Selected Writings of Arthur Carl Piepkorn.* Edited by Michael P. Plekon and William S. Wiecher. Afterword by Richard John Neuhaus. Delhi, N.Y.: ALPB Books.

Pii IX Pontificis Maximi Acta. 1854-78. 9 vols. [Rome]: Ex Typographia Bonarum Artium.

Pillinger, Renate. 1975. "Die Taufe nach der Didache: Philologisch-archäologische Untersuchung der Kapitel 7, 9, 10 und 14." *Wiener Studien; Zeitschrift für Klassische Philologie und Patristik* 88:152-60.

Pin, Jean-Pierre. 1979. "Pour une analyse textuelle du catechisme (1542) de Jean Calvin." In *Calvinus ecclesiae doctor,* 159-70. Edited by W. H. Neuser. Kampen, Netherlands: J. H. Kok.

Pinnock, Clark H., ed. 1989. *The Grace of God, the Will of Man: A Case for Arminianism.* Grand Rapids, Mich.: Zondervan.

Pipkin, H. Wayne, and John H. Yoder, trans. and eds. 1989. *Balthasar Hubmaier, Theologian of Anabaptism.* Scottdale, Pa.: Herald Press.

Plan of Church Union in North India and Pakistan. 1965. 4th ed. Madras: Christian Literature Society for the Negotiating Committee.

Plantinga, Cornelius, Jr. 1979. *A Place to Stand: A Reformed Study of Creeds and Confessions.* Board of Publications of the Christian Reformed Church.

Podskalsky, Gerhard. 1988. *Griechische Theologie in der Zeit der Türkenherrschaft (1453-1821): Die Orthodoxie im Spannungsfeld der nachreformatorischen Konfessionen des Westens.* Munich: C. H. Beck.

Poitras, Edward. 1997. "How Korean Is the Methodist 'Korean Creed'?" *Methodist History* 36:3-16.

Polish National Catholic Church of America. 1975. *The Confession of Faith and the Eleven Great Principles of the Polish National Catholic Church.* [Scranton, Pa.]: [Polish National Catholic Church].

Poll, G. J. van de. 1954. *Martin Bucer's Liturgical Ideas.* Assen: Van Gorcum.

Pollard, John E. 1995. "Patristic Sources of the Catechism of the Catholic Church." *Josephinum Journal of Theology,* n.s., 2:18-42.

Pollet, Jacques V. 1963. *Huldrych Zwingli et la Réforme en Suisse.* Paris: Presses Universitaires de France.

Pont, A. D. 1991. "Confession of Faith in Calvin's Geneva." In *Calvin: Erbe und Auftrag,* 106-16. Edited by Willem van 't Spijker. Kampen, Netherlands: Kok Pharos.

Pontal, Odette. 1986. *Die Synoden im Merowingerreich.* Paderborn, Germany: Ferdinand Schöningh.

Popescu, T., ed. 1935. *Enciclica Patriarhilor Ortodocsi dela 1848: Studiu introductive, text si traducere.* Bucharest: n.p.

Popivchak, Ronald Peter. 1975. "Peter Mohila, Metropolitan of Kiev (1633-47): Translation and Evaluation of His 'Orthodox Confession of Faith' (1640)." Ph.D. diss., Catholic University of America.

Porter, Harry Culverwell. 1958. *Reformation and Reaction in Tudor Cambridge*. Cambridge: Cambridge University Press.

Potter, G. R. 1976. *Zwingli*. Cambridge: Cambridge University Press.

Pottmeyer, Hermann Joseph. 1968. *Der Glaube vor dem Anspruch der Wissenschaft: Die Konstitution über den katholischen Glauben, Dei Filius des 1. Vatikanischen Konzils*. Freiburg: Herder.

————. 1975. *Unfehlbarkeit und Souveränität: Die päpstliche Unfehlbarkeit im System der ultramontanischen Ekklesiologie des 19. Jahrhunderts*. Mainz: Matthias-Grünewald-Verlag.

Potz, Richard. 1971. *Patriarch und Synode in Konstantinopel: Das Verfassungrecht des ökumenischen Patriarchates*. Vienna: Herder.

Poythress, Vern S. 1976. "Is Romans 1:3–4 a Pauline Confession After All?" *Expository Times* 87:180–83.

Praamsma, Louis. 1968. "Background of the Arminian Controversy (1586–1618)." In *Crisis in the Reformed Churches: Essays in Commemoration of the Great Synod of Dort, 1618–1619*, 22–38. Edited by Peter Y. De Jong. Grand Rapids, Mich.: Reformed Fellowship.

The Prayer Book Dictionary. [1918]. Edited by George Harford, Morley Stevenson, and J. W. Tyrer. London: Waverly Book.

Praying Together. 1988. Prepared by the English Language Liturgical Consultation. Revised ed. Nashville, Tenn.: Abingdon Press.

Prestige, George Leonard. 1956. *St. Basil the Great and Apollinaris of Laodicea*. Edited by Henry Chadwick. London: S.P.C.K.

Principe, Walter Henry. 1963–75. *The Theology of the Hypostatic Union in the Early Thirteenth Century*. 4 vols. Toronto: Pontifical Institute of Mediaeval Studies.

Pritsak, Omeljan, et al. 1984. *The Kiev Mohyla Academy: Commemorating the 350th Anniversary of Its Founding (1632)*. Cambridge, Mass.: Ukrainian Research Institute, Harvard University.

Prokurat, Michael, Alexander Golitzin, and Michael D. Peterson. 1996. *Historical Dictionary of the Orthodox Church*. Lanham, Md.: Scarecrow Press.

Proposed Basis of Union. 1965. [Accra]: Ghana Church Union Committee.

Proposed Scheme of Church Union in Ceylon. 1955. 3d revised ed. Madras: Christian Literature Society.

Provost, James H. 1998. "Safeguarding the Faith." *America* 179/3:8.

Pruett, Gordon E. 1975. "A Protestant Doctrine of the Eucharistic Presence." *Calvin Theological Journal* 10:142–74.

Psalter Hymnal: Including the Psalms, Bible Songs, Hymns, Ecumenical Creeds, Doctrinal Standards, and Liturgical Forms of the Christian Reformed Church in North America. 1988. Grand Rapids, Mich.: CRC Publications.

Quellen zur Geschichte der Täufer in der Schweiz. 1973. Edited by Heinold Fast. 4 vols. Zurich: Theologischer Verlag.

Raabe, Paul R. 1989. "Children's Sermons and Luther's *Small Catechism*." *Concordia Journal* 15:100–102.

Radice, Betty, tr. 1974. *The Letters of Abelard and Heloise*. Baltimore: Penguin.

Railton, Nicholas. 2000. *No North Sea: The Anglo-German Evangelical Network in the Middle of the Nineteenth Century*. Leiden: Brill.

Rand, E. K. 1928. *Founders of the Middle Ages*. Cambridge, Mass.: Harvard University Press.

Rankin, D. 1995. *Tertullian and the Church*. Cambridge: Cambridge University Press.

Ratzinger, Joseph, Cardinal, and Tarcisio Bertone. 1998. "Commentary on the Profession of Faith." *L'Osservatore Romano,* 15 July 1998, 3-4.

Rauschenbusch, Walter. 1907. *Christianity and the Social Crisis*. Reprint, New York: Macmillan.

Reardon, Bernard M. G. 1989. "The Thirty-Nine Articles and the Augsburg Confession." *Lutheran Quarterly* 3/1:91-106.

Reed, Stephen D. 1983. "The Decalogue in Luther's *Large Catechism*." *Dialog* 22:264-69.

Rees, Thomas. [1818] 1962. *The Racovian Catechism*. Reprint, Lexington, Ky.: American Theological Library Association.

Reinhard, Wolfgang. 1977. "Gegenreformation als Modernisierung? Prolegomena zu einer Theorie des konfessionellen Zeitalters." *ARG* 68:226-52.

———, and Heinz Schilling, eds. 1995. *Die katholische Konfessionalisierung*. Gütersloh, Germany: Gütersloher Verlagshaus.

Rembert, Karl. 1899. *Die "Wiedertäufer" im Herzogtum Jülich*. Berlin: R. Gaertners Verlagsbuchhandlung.

Renihan, James M. 1996. "An Examination of the Possible Influence of Menno Simons' *Foundation Book* upon the Particular Baptist Confession of 1644." *American Baptist Quarterly* 15:190-207.

Resolutions of the First Synod of Old Catholics of the German Empire: Articles Adopted by the Conference Held at Bonn, 14-16 Sept. 1874. 1874. Cambridge: J. Palmer.

Reu, Johann Michael. [1904] 1976. *Quellen zur Geschichte des kirchlichen Unterrichts in der evangelischen Kirche Deutschlands zwischen 1530 und 1600*. Reprint, Hildesheim: Olms.

———. 1929. *Dr. Martin Luther's Small Catechism: A History of Its Origin, Its Distribution, and Its Use*. Chicago: Wartburg.

Rhee, Jong Sung. "The Significance of the Lausanne Covenant." *Northeast Asia Journal of Theology* 15:26-37.

Řičan, Rudolf. 1992. *The History of the Unity of Brethren: A Protestant Hussite Church in Bohemia and Moravia*. Translated by C. Daniel Crews. Bethlehem, Pa.: Moravian Church in America.

Richmond, Mary L. Hurt. 1977. *Shaker Literature: A Bibliography*. Hancock, Mass.: Shaker Community; distributed by the University Press of New England.

Ridley, Jasper. 1962. *Thomas Cranmer*. Oxford: Oxford University Press.

Riedinger, Rudolf. 1976. "Aus den Akten der Lateran-Synode von 649." *Byzantinische Zeitschrift* 69:17-29.

———. 1981. "Das Bekenntnis des Gregor Thaumaturgus bei Sophronius von Jerusalem und Macarius von Antiocheia." *ZKG* 92/2-3:311-14.

———. 1982. "Die Lateransynode von 649 und Maximos der Bekenner." In *Maximus Confessor,* 111-21. Edited by Felix Heinzer and Christoph Schönborn. Fribourg, Switzerland: Editions Universitaires.

Ries, Hans de. 1686. *Corte belijdenisse des geloofs*. Edited by Pieter Jansz. Amsterdam: Joannes van Veen.

Ris, Cornelis. 1766. *De geloofsleere der waare Mennoniten of Doopsgezinden*. Hoorn: T. Tjallingius.

——. 1904. *Mennonite Articles of Faith as Set Forth in Public Confession of the Church: A Translation*. Berne, Iowa: Mennonite Book Concern.

Ritschl, Dietrich. 1979. "The History of the *filioque* Controversy." Translated by R. Nowell. In *Conflicts About the Holy Spirit*, 3–14. Edited by Hans Küng and Jürgen Moltmann. New York: Seabury Press.

——. 1981. "Historical Development and Implications of the *filioque* Controversy." In *Spirit of God, Spirit of Christ: Ecumenical Reflections on the filioque Controversy*, 46–65. Edited by Lukas Vischer. Geneva: World Council of Churches.

——. 1982. "Warum wir Konzilien feiern: Konstantinopel 381." *Theologische Zeitschrift* 38:213–25.

Ritter, Adolf Martin. 1965. *Das Konzil von Konstantinopel und sein Symbol: Studien zur Geschichte und Theologie des II. Ökumenischen Konzils*. Göttingen: Vandenhoeck und Ruprecht.

——. 1981. "The Dogma of Constantinople (381) and Its Reception Within the Churches of the Reformation." *Irish Theological Quarterly* 48:228–32 [Special issue commemorating 1600th anniversary of the first council of Constantinople].

Rivera, Juan Francisco. 1940. *Elipando de Toledo: Nueva aportación a los estudios Mozárabes*. Toledo: Editorial Católica Toledana.

Rivière, Jean. 1926. *Le problème de l'Eglise et de l'Etat au temps de Philippe le Bel: Etude de théologie positive*. Louvain: Spicilegium Sacrum Lovaniense.

Roberg, Burkhard. 1990. *Das Zweite Konzil von Lyon [1274]*. Paderborn, Germany: Ferdinand Schöningh.

Roberts, Benjamin Titus. 1984. *Why Another Sect?* New York: Garland.

Roberts, C. H., and Dom B. Capelle, eds. 1949. *An Early Euchologium: The Dêr-Balizeh Papyrus Enlarged and Reedited*. Louvain: Bureaux du Muséon.

Robertson, J. N. W. B. 1899. *The Acts and Decrees of the Synod of Jerusalem in 1672*. London: Baker.

Robinson, Elmo Arnold. 1970. *American Universalism: Its Origins, Organization, and Heritage*. New York: Exposition Press.

Robinson, J. Armitage, ed. 1920. *The Demonstration of the Apostolic Preaching of St. Irenaeus*. London: S.P.C.K.

Robson, J. A. 1961. *Wyclif and the Oxford Schools*. Cambridge: Cambridge University Press.

Rogers, Jack Bartelett. 1967. *Scripture in the Westminster Confession: A Problem of Historical Interpretation for American Presbyterianism*. Grand Rapids, Mich.: W. B. Eerdmans.

——. 1985. *Presbyterian Creeds: A Guide to the Book of Confessions*. Philadelphia: Westminster Press.

Rohls, Jan. 1987. *Theologie reformierter Bekenntnisschriften: Von Zürich bis Barmen*. Göttingen: Vandenhoeck und Ruprecht.

Roloff, Hans-Gert. 1988 "Die Funktion von Hus-Texten in der Reformations-Polemik." In *De captu lectoris: Wirkungen des Buches im 15. und 16. Jahrhundert*, 219–56. Edited by Wolfgang Milde and Werner Schuder. Berlin: de Gruyter.

Romanides, John S. 1987. "St. Cyril's 'One Physis or Hypostasis of God the Logos Incarnate' and Chalcedon." In Fries and Nersoyan 1987, 15–34.

The Roman Missal, Revised by Decree of the Second Vatican Ecumenical Council. The Sacramentary. 1995. Collegeville, Minn.: Liturgical Press.

Rordorf, Willy. 1972. "Le baptême selon la Didaché." In *Mélanges liturgiques offerts à Bernard Botte de l'Abbaye du Mont César,* 499–509. Edited by Jean J. von Allmen et al. Louvain: Abbaye du Mont César.

———, and André Tuilier, eds. and trans. 1998. *La doctrine des douze apôtres (Didachè).* Source chrétiennes, 248. Paris: Editions du Cerf.

Rorem, Paul. 1988. "Calvin and Bullinger on the Lord's Supper: The Agreement." *Lutheran Quarterly,* n.s., 2:357–89.

———. 1994. "The Consensus Tigurinus (1549): Did Calvin Compromise?" In *Calvinus Sacrae Scripturae professor: Calvin as Confessor of Holy Scripture,* 72–90. Edited by Wilhelm H. Neuser. Grand Rapids, Mich.: W. B. Eerdmans.

Rothschild, Fritz 1964. *The Shema.* New York: Burning Bush Press.

Rotondò, Antonio, ed. 1986. *Lelio Sozzini: Opere.* Florence: L. S. Olschki.

Rouse, Ruth, and Stephen C. Neill, eds. 1986. *A History of the Ecumenical Movement, 1517–1948.* 3d ed. Geneva: World Council of Churches.

Rousseau, Adelin, and Louis Doutreleau, eds. and trans. 1952–82. *Contre les hérésies.* 5 vols. in 11. Paris: Editions du Cerf.

Routley, Erik. 1963. *Creeds and Confessions: From the Reformation to the Modern Church.* Philadelphia: Westminster Press.

Rückert, Hanns. 1925. *Die Rechtfertigungslehre auf dem Tridentinischen Konzil.* Bonn: A. Marcus und E. Weber.

Rusch, William G., and Daniel F. Martensen, eds. 1989. *The Leuenberg Agreement and Lutheran-Reformed Relationships: Evaluations by North American and European Theologians.* Minneapolis, Minn.: Augsburg Publishing House.

Russell, William. 1991a. "A Theological Guide to the Smalcald Articles." *Lutheran Quarterly,* n.s., 5:469–92.

———. 1991b. "The Smalcald Articles, Luther's Theological Testament." *Lutheran Quarterly,* n.s., 5:277–96.

———. 1994. "Martin Luther's Understanding of the Pope as the Antichrist." *ARG* 85:32–44.

———. 1995. *Luther's Theological Testament: The Schmalkald Articles.* Minneapolis, Minn.: Fortress Press.

Ryang, J. S. 1934. *Fiftieth Anniversary of Korean Methodism.* [Seoul?]: Korean Methodist Church.

Sahas, Daniel J. 1986. *Icon and Logos: Sources in Eighth-Century Iconoclasm.* Toronto: University of Toronto Press.

Sahu, Dhirendra Kumar. 1994. *The Church of North India: A Historical and Systematic Theological Inquiry into an Ecumenical Ecclesiology.* Frankfurt: P. Lang.

Samuel, Vinay C. 1984. "The Nicene Creed: Compared to the Apostles' Creed, the Quicunque Vult and the New Testament." In *The Roots of Our Common Faith: Faith in the*

Scriptures and in the Early Church, 81–93. Edited by Hans-Georg Link. Faith and Order Paper, 119. Geneva: World Council of Churches.

Sandall, Robert. [1947–73] 1979. *The History of the Salvation Army*. 6 vols. Vols. 4–5 by Arch R. Wiggins; vol. 6 by Frederick Coutts. Reprint, New York: Salvation Army.

Sanders, Paul. 1992. "Heinrich Bullinger et le Zwinglianisme tardif aux lendemains du 'Consensus Tigurinus.'" In *Reformiertes Erbe*, 307–23. Festschrift für Gottfried W. Locher zu seinem 80. Geburtstag. Edited by Heiko Oberman, Ernst Saxer, Alfred Schindler, et al. Special issue of *Zwingliana* (19/1). Zurich: Theologischer Verlag.

Sansbury, Christopher J. 1985. "Athanasius, Marcellus, and Eusebius of Caesarea: Some Thoughts on Their Resemblances and Disagreements." In Gregg 1985, 281–86.

Sarkissian, Karekin. 1965. *The Council of Chalcedon and the Armenian Church*. London: S.P.C.K.

Sasse, Herman. 1959. *This Is My Body: Luther's Contention for the Real Presence*. Minneapolis, Minn.: Augsburg Publishing House.

The Savoy Declaration of Faith and Order, 1658. 1971. With an extract from the original preface by John Owen, and a foreword by Derek Swann. London: Evangelical Press.

Scaer, David P., and Robert D. Preus, eds. 1979. *Luther's Catechisms—450 Years: Essays Commemorating the Small and Large Catechisms of Dr. Martin Luther*. Fort Wayne, Ind.: Concordia Theological Seminary Press.

Schaaf, James L. 1969. "The Smalcald Articles and Their Significance: Luther's Own Confession." In *Interpreting Luther's Legacy: Essays in Honor of Edward C. Fendt*, 68–82. Edited by Fred W. Meuser and Stanley D. Schneider. Minneapolis, Minn.: Augsburg Publishing House.

———. 1979. "*The Large Catechism*: A Pastoral Tool." In Scaer and Preus 1979, 41–46.

Schäferdiek, Knut. 1967. *Die Kirche in den Reichen der Westgoten und Suewen bis zur Errichtung der westgotischen katholischen Staatskirche*. Berlin: de Gruyter.

———. 1979. "Wulfila: Vom Bischof von Gotien zum Gotenbischof." *ZKG* 90/1:107–46.

Scheele, Paul W. 1981. "1600 Jahre Konzil von Konstantinopel: Ein ökumenisches Signal." *Catholica* 35/4:249–64.

Scheible, Heinz. 1997. *Melanchthon: Eine Biographie*. Munich: C. H. Beck.

Schermann, Theodor. 1910. *Der liturgische Papyrus von Dêr-Balyzeh eine Abendmahlsliturgie des Ostermorgens*. Leipzig: J. C. Hinrichs.

Schiess, Traugott, ed. 1908–12. *Briefwechsel der Brüder Ambrosius und Thomas Blaurer, 1509–1548*. 3 vols. Freiburg: F. E. Fehsenfeld.

Schindler, Alfred. 1965. *Wort und Analogie in Augustins Trinitätslehre*. Tübingen: J. C. B. Mohr.

Schmaus, Michael. 1927. *Die psychologische Trinitätslehre des heiligen Augustinus*. Münster: Aschendorff.

Schmidt, Carl. [1919] 1967. *Gespräche Jesu mit seinen Jüngern nach der Auferstehung*. Reprint, Hildesheim: Georg Olms.

Schmidt, Kurt Dietrich, 1939–41. *Die Bekehrung der Germanen zum Christentum*. 2 vols. Göttingen: Vandenhoeck und Ruprecht.

Schneemelcher, Wilhelm, ed. 1991. *New Testament Apocrypha*. English translation edited by R. McL. Wilson. Revised ed. 2 vols. Cambridge: James Clark; Louisville, Ky.: Westminster.

Schoedel, William R. 1985. *Ignatius of Antioch: A Commentary on the Letters of Ignatius of Antioch.* Edited by Helmut Koester. Hermeneia. Philadelphia: Fortress Press.

Schomann, Georg. 1574. *Catechesis et confessio fidei coetus per Poloniam congregati in nomine Iesu Christi, domini nostri crucifixi et resuscitati.* Kraków: Typis Alexandri Turobini.

Schönborn, Christoph von. 1982. "681–1981: Ein vergessenes Konzilsjubiläum, eine versäumte ökumenische Chance." *Freiburger Zeitschrift für Philosophie und Theologie* 29:157–74.

Schrader, Clemens. 1865. *Pius IX. als Papst und als Koenig, dargestellt aus den Acten seines Pontificates von den Verfasser der Broschüre: Der Papst und die modernen Ideen, mit einem Päpstlichen Belobungschreiben.* Vienna: C. Sartori.

Schreiner, Lothar. 1966. *Das Bekenntnis der Batak Kirche: Entstehung, Gestalt, Bedeutung und eine revidierte Übersetzung.* Munich: Chr. Kaiser Verlag.

Schroeder, Gustavus W. 1898. *History of the Swedish Baptists in Sweden and America.* New York: Schroeder.

Schulz, Frieder. 1966. "Communio Sanctorum: Apostolisches Symbol und Arnoldshainer Thesen." *Kerygma und Dogma* 12/2:154–79.

Schummer, Leopold. 1982. "La Communio Sanctorum dans les confessions de foi et les Catechismes reformes du XVIme siècle." In *Communio Sanctorum: Mélanges offerts à Jean-Jacques von Allmen*, 114–27. Edited by Boris Bobrinskoy et al. Geneva: Labor et Fides.

Schwartz, Eduard. 1905/1908. "Zur Geschichte des Athanasius, VI and VII." In *Nachrichten von der (königlichen) Gesellschaft (Akademie) der Wissenschaften zu Göttingen* 1905:271ff., 1908:305ff.

Schwarzlose, Karl. [1890] 1970. *Der Bilderstreit: Ein Kampf der griechischen Kirche um ihre Eigenart und um ihre Freiheit.* Reprint, Amsterdam: Rodopi.

Schwarzwäller, Klaus. 1989. "Rechtfertigung und Ekklesiologie in den Schmalkaldischen Artikeln: Eine dogmatische Studie." *Kergyma und Dogma* 35:84–105.

Schweinitz, Edmund de. 1901. *The History of the Church Known as the Unitas Fratrum or the Unity of the Brethren.* Bethlehem, Pa.: Moravian Publication Concern.

Schweitzer, Albert. [1906] 1961. *The Quest of the Historical Jesus: A Critical Study of Its Progress from Reimarus to Wrede.* Translated by W. Montgomery. Reprint, New York: Macmillan.

Schwöbel, Heide. 1982. *Synode und König im Westgotenreich: Grundlagen und Formen ihrer Beziehung.* Cologne: Böhlau.

Scott, S. Herbert. 1928. *The Eastern Churches and the Papacy.* London: Sheed and Ward.

Seebass, Gottfried. 1976. "Hans Denck." *Frankische Lebensbilder* 6:107–29.

———. 1984. "The Importance of Luther's Writings in the Formation of Protestant Confessions of Faith in the Sixteenth Century." In *Luther's Ecumenical Significance: An Interconfessional Consultation*, 71–80. Edited by Peter Manns and Harding Meyer. Philadelphia: Fortress Press; New York: Paulist Press.

———. 1993. "Martin Bucer und die Reichsstadt Augsburg." In *Martin Bucer and Sixteenth-Century Europe: Actes du colloque de Strasbourg*, 2:478–91. Edited by Christian Krieger and Marc Lienhard. Leiden: E. J. Brill.

Seeberg, Alfred. [1903] 1966. *Der Katechismus der Urchristenheit.* Reprint, Munich: Kaiser.

Seguenny, André. 1979. "Hans Denck et ses disciples." In *L'humanisme allemand (1480–1540),*

441–54. Edited by Georges Livet, William Melczer, Pierre Aquilon, et al. Munich: Fink Verlag; Paris: J. Vrin.

Sehling, Emil. 1902– . *Die evangelischen Kirchenordnungen des XVI Jahrhunderts*. Leipzig: O. R. Reisland.

Selge, Kurt-Victor. 1967. *Die ersten Waldenser*. Berlin: Walter de Gruyter.

Sellers, R. V. 1961. *The Council of Chalcedon: A Historical and Doctrinal Survey*. London: S.P.C.K.

Selwyn, D. G. 1964. "Neglected Edition of Cranmer's Catechism." *JTS* 15:76–91.

Ševčenko, Ihor. [1984] 1992. "The Many Worlds of Peter Mohyla." In *Byzantium and the Slavs in Letters and Culture*, 651–87. Cambridge, Mass.: Harvard Ukrainian Research Institute.

Sha'are tefilah [Siddur]. 1975. *The Gates of Prayer: The New Union Prayerbook*. New York: Central Conference of American Rabbis.

Sharing in One Hope: Bangalore 1978. Reports and Documents from the Meeting of the Faith and Order Commission, 15–30 August, 1978, Ecumenical Christian Centre, Bangalore, India. 1979. Geneva: World Council of Churches.

Shinn, Roger L. 1990. *Confessing Our Faith: An Interpretation of the Statement of Faith of the United Church of Christ*. New York: Pilgrim Press.

Sider, Robert D. 1982. "Approaches to Tertullian: A Study of Recent Scholarship." *Second Century* 2:228–60.

Sieben, Hermann J. 1979. "Die früh- und hochmittelalterliche Konzilsidee im Kontext der *Filioque*-Kontroverse." *Traditio* 35:173–207.

Simpson, Robert. 1965. *The Interpretation of Prayer in the Early Church*. Philadelphia: Westminster Press.

Sitompul, A. A., and Arne Sovik, eds. 1986. *Horas HKBP! Essays for a 125-Year-Old Church*. Pematangsiantar, North Sumatra: Sekolah Tinggi Teologia HKBP.

Skarsaune, O. 1976. "The Conversion of Justin Martyr." *Studia theologica* 30:53–73.

Sladeczek, Franz Josef. 1988. "'Die götze in miner herren chilchen sind gerumpt." *Theologische Zeitschrift* 44/4:289–311.

Slusser, Michael. 1990. "The Issues in the Definition of the Council of Chalcedon." *Toronto Journal of Theology* 6:63–69.

Smend, Julius. 1898. *Kelchversagung und Kelchspendung im Abendland: Ein Beitrag zur Kultusgeschichte*. Göttingen: Vandenhoeck und Ruprecht.

Smith, Mahlon H. 1978. *And Taking Bread: Cerularius and the Azyme Controversy of 1054*. Paris: Editions Beauchesne.

Smith, Page. 1964. *The Historian and History*. New York: Alfred A. Knopf.

Smith, Wanda Willard. 1997. *Selina Hastings: The Countess of Huntingdon*. Dallas: Bridwell Library.

Smolík, Josef. 1981. "*Filioque* in the Reformed Tradition." *Communio Viatorum* 24/4:219–22.

Smulders, Pieter. 1975. "The Sitz im Leben of the Old Roman Creed: New Conclusions from Neglected Data." *Studia Patristica* 13/2:409–21.

Snavely, Iren. 1994. "'The Evidence of Things Unseen': Zwingli's Sermon on Providence and the Colloquy of Marburg [1529]." *Westminster Theological Journal* 56:399–407.

Snyder, Arnold. 1984. *The Life and Thought of Michael Sattler*. Studies in Anabaptist and Mennonite History, 27. Scottdale, Pa.: Herald Press.

———. 1985. "The Schleitheim Articles in Light of the Revolution of the Common Man: Continuation or Departure?" *Sixteenth Century Journal* 16/4:419–30.

———. 1989. "The Influence of the Schleitheim Articles on the Anabaptist Movement: An Historical Evaluation." *MQR* 63:323–44.

Somerset, Fiona. "Answering the Twelve Conclusions: Dymmok's Halfhearted Gestures Towards Publication." In Aston and Richmond 1997, 52–76.

Soysa, Harold de. 1962. *Suggested Amendments to Scheme of Church Union in Ceylon*. N.p.

Spear, Wayne R. 1994. "The Westminster Confession of Faith and Holy Scripture." In Carson and Hall 1994, 85–100.

Spijker, W. van 't, et al. 1987. *De Synode van Dordrecht in 1618 en 1619*. Houten, Netherlands: Hertog.

Spindler, Marc Robert. 1990. "Creeds and Credibility in the Philippines: Introductory Notes to the Statement of Faith and Other Statements of the UCC in the Philippines." *Exchange* 19:152–71.

Spinka, Matthew. 1956. "Paul Krava and the Lollard-Hussite Relations." *Church History* 25: 16–26.

———. 1966. *John Hus' Concept of the Church*. Princeton, N.J.: Princeton University Press.

Spitz, Lewis W. 1954. "The Schism of the Eastern and Western Churches." *Concordia Theological Monthly* 25:881–91.

———, and Wenzel Lohff, eds. 1977. *Discord, Dialogue, and Concord: Studies in the Lutheran Reformation's Formula of Concord*. Philadelphia: Fortress Press.

Staats, Reinhart. 1981. "The Nicene-Constantinopolitan Creed as a Foundation for Church Unity? Protestant Thoughts on Its Centenary, 1981." *Irish Theological Quarterly* 48:212–27.

Stacy, Kevin M. 1993. "Augustine on Language and the Nature of Belief." In *Augustine: Presbyter Factus Sum*, 305–16. Edited by Joseph T. Lienhard, Earl C. Muller, and Roland J. Teske. New York: P. Lang.

Staedtke, Joachim. 1963. "Gibt es einen offiziellen Text der Confessio Helvetica Posterior?" *Theologische Zeitschrift* 19:29–41.

———. 1965. "Entstehung und Bedeutung des Heidelberger Katechismus." In *Warum Wirst Du Ein Christ Genannt*, 11–23. Edited by Walter Herrenbruck and Udo Smidt. Neukirchen, Germany: Neukirchener Verlag des Erziehungsvereins.

———. 1966. "Bibliographie des Zweiten Helvetischen Bekenntnisses." In *Glauben und Bekennen: Vierhundert Jahre Confessio Helvetica Posterior*, 41–53. Edited by Joachim Staedtke. Zurich: Zwingli Verlag.

———, and Gottfried W. Locher. 1967. *Vierhundert Jahre Confessio Helvetica Posterior; Akademische Feier*. Bern: P. Haupt.

Staehlin, Ernst, ed. 1929. *Das Buch der Basler Reformation*. Basel: Helbing and Lichtenhahn.

Starke, Elfriede. 1983. "Luthers Beziehungen zu Kunst und Künstlern." In Junghans 1983, 1:531–48.

Starowieyski, Marek. 1990. "La plus ancienne description d'une mariophanie par Grégoire de Nysse [Vita Gregorii Thaumaturgi]." In *Studien zu Gregor von Nyssa und der christlichen Spätantike*, 245–53. Festschrift for Andreas Spira. Edited by Hubertus R. Drobner and Christoph Klock. Vigiliae Christianae, Supplements, 12. Leiden: E. J. Brill.

Stassen, Glen H. 1962. "Anabaptist Influence in the Origin of the Particular Baptists." *MQR* 36:322–48.

Statut der Internationalen Altkatholischen Bischofkonferenz: Offizielle Ausgabe in fünf Sprachen. 2001. Edited and translated by Urs von Arx and Maja Weyermann. Bern: Stampfli.

Stauffer, Richard. 1977. "Zwingli et Calvin: Critiques de la confession de Schleitheim." In *Origins and Characteristics of Anabaptism / Les débuts et les caracteristiques de l'Anabaptisme,* 126–47. Edited by Marc Lienhard. The Hague: Martinus Nijhoff.

———. 1983. "Farel à la Dispute de Lausanne: Sa défense de la doctrine de la justification par la foi." *Cahiers de la Revue de théologie et de philosophie* 9/1:107–23.

Stead, George Christopher. 1973. "Eusebius and the Council of Nicaea." *JTS* 24:85–100.

Steck, Rudolf, and G. Tobler. 1923. *Aktensammlung zur Geschichte der Berner-reformation, 1521–1532.* Bern: K. J. Wyss Erben.

Steere, Douglas V. 1955. *Where Words Come From: An Interpretation of the Ground and Practice of Quaker Worship and Ministry.* London: Allen and Unwin.

Stegmüller, Friedrich, ed. 1947. *Repertorium commentariorum in sententias Petri Lombardi.* 2 vols. Würzburg: Schöningh.

Steinen, W. von den. 1929–30. "Entstehungsgeschichte der Libri Carolini." *Quellen und Forschungen aus italienischen Archiven und Bibliotheken* 21:1–93.

Stephens, John Vant. 1941. *The Genesis of the Cumberland Presbyterian Church.* Cincinnati, Ohio: n.p.

Stephens, Prescott. 1998. *The Waldensian Story: A Study in Faith, Intolerance, and Survival.* Lewes, Sussex: Book Guild.

Stephens, W. P. 1970. *The Holy Spirit in the Theology of Martin Bucer.* London: Cambridge University Press.

———. 1986. *Theology of Huldrych Zwingli.* Oxford: Oxford University Press.

———. 1992. *Zwingli: An Introduction to His Thought.* Oxford: Clarendon Press.

Stephenson, A. A. 1961. "The Text of the Jerusalem Creed." In *Studia Patristica* 3:303–13. Edited by F. L. Cross [Papers presented at the Third International Conference on Patristic Studies, Oxford 1959]. Berlin: Akademie Verlag.

Stevenson, J. [1966] 1989. *Creeds, Councils and Controversies: Documents Illustrating the History of the Church, AD 337–461.* Revised and enlarged by W. H. C. Frend. London: S.P.C.K.

Stewart, H. F., E. K. Rand, and S. J. Tester, trans. 1973. *The Theological Tractates of Boethius.* Cambridge, Mass.: Harvard University Press.

Stiglmayr, J. 1925. "Das 'Quicunque' und Fulgentius von Ruspe." *ZfKT* 49:341–57.

Stock, Konrad. 1980. *Cubanisches Glaubensbekenntnis: Einführung Text, Interpretation.* Munich: Kaiser; Mainz: Grünewald.

Stocking, Rachel L. 2000. *Bishops, Councils, and Consensus in the Visigothic Kingdom, 589–633.* Ann Arbor, Mich.: University of Michigan Press.

Stockmeier, Peter. 1972. "Zum Verhaltnis von Glaube und Religion bei Tertullian." *Studia Patristica* 11:242–46.

———. 1981. "Bemerkungen zur Christianisierung der Goten im 4. Jahrhundert." *ZKG* 92/1:315–24.

———. 1982. "Das Konzil von Chalkedon: Probleme der Forschung." *Freiburger Zeitschrift für Philosophie und Theologie* 29:140–56.

————. 1985. "Anmerkungen zum 'in' bzw. 'ex duabus naturis' in der Formel von Chalkedon." In *Studia Patristica* 18/1: 213-20.

————. 1986. "Universalis ecclesia: Papst Leo der Grosse und der Osten." *Kirchengemeinschaft—Anspruch und Wirklichkeit: Festschrift für Georg Kretschmar zum 60. Geburtstag,* 83-91. Edited by Wolf Dieter Hauschild, Carsten Nicolaisen, and Dorothea Wendebourg. Stuttgart: Calwer Verlag.

————. 1987. "Glaubenssymbol, Lehrschreiben und Dogma im Umfeld von Chalkedon." In *Weisheit Gottes—Weisheit der Welt: Festschrift für Joseph Kardinal Ratzinger zum 60. Geburtstag,* 689-96. Edited by Walter Baier, Stephan Otto Horn, Vinzenz Pfnür, et al. St. Ottilien, Germany: EOS Verlag.

Stoevesandt, Hinrich. 1970. *Die Bedeutung des Symbolums in Theologie und Kirche: Versuch einer dogmatisch-kritischen Ortsbestimmung aus evangelischer Sicht.* Munich: Christian Kaiser Verlag.

Stott, John R. W. 1975. "The Significance of Lausanne." *International Review of Missions* 64:288-94.

Strasser, Otto Erich. 1949. "Der Consensus Tigurinus." *Zwingliana* 9/1:1-16.

Strauss, Gerald. 1978. *Luther's House of Learning: Indoctrination of the Young in the German Reformation.* Baltimore: Johns Hopkins University Press.

Strehle, Stephen. 1989. "The Extent of the Atonement and the Synod of Dort." *Westminster Theological Journal* 51:1-23.

Strothmann, Jürgen. 1995. "Das Konzil von Sens 1138 und die Folgeereignisse 1140." *Theologie und Glaube* 85:238ff., 396ff.

Strupl, Milos. 1964. "Confessional Theology of the Unitas Fratrum." *Church History* 33:279-93.

Strype, John, ed. 1842-54. *Memorials of the Most Reverend Father in God Thomas Cranmer, Sometime Lord Archbishop of Cantebury.* Oxford: Ecclesiastical History Society.

Studer, Basil. 1990. "La recezione del concilio di Efeso del 431." *Studia Ephemeridis Augustinianum* 31:427-42.

Studer, Gerald C. 1984. "The Dordrecht Confession of Faith, 1632-1982." *MQR* 58:503-19.

Studien zur Bekenntnisbildung. 1980. Edited by Peter Meinhold. Wiesbaden: Steiner.

Stupperich, Robert. 1938. "Die Kirche in Martin Bucers theologischer Entwicklung." *ARG* 35:81-101.

Sullivan, Francis. 1998. "A New Obstacle to Anglican-Roman Catholic Dialogue." *America* 179/3:6.

Sundkler, Bengt. 1954. *Church of South India: The Movement Towards Union, 1900-1947.* London: Lutterworth Press.

Supplementa Melanchthoniana. 1915. Vol. 1. Edited by D. Ferdinand Cohrs. Leipzig: Rudolf Haupt.

Sysyn, F. E. 1984. "Peter Mohyla and the Kiev Academy in Recent Western Works: Divergent Views on Seventeenth-Century Ukrainian Culture." *Harvard Ukrainian Studies* 8:155-87.

Szczucki, Lech. 1982. "Polish and Transylvanian Unitarians." In *Antitrinitarianism in the Second Half of the Sixteenth Century,* 238-41. Edited by Róbert Dán and Antal Pirnát. Budapest: Akadémiai Kiadó; Leiden: E. J. Brill.

————, ed. 1983. *Socinianism and Its Role in the Culture of XVI-th to XVIII-th Centuries.*

Edited by Lech Szczucki in cooperation with Zbigniew Ogonowski and Janusz Tazbir. Warsaw: Polish Academy of Sciences, Institute of Philosophy and Sociology.

Szilágyi, Sandor, ed. 1875-99. *Monumenta Hungariae Historica*. 22 vols. Budapest: A.M.T. Akadémia Könyvkiadó-Hivatala.

Taft, Robert F. 1991. *The Diptychs*. Volume 4 of *A History of the Liturgy of St. John Chrysostom*. Rome: Pontificium Institutum Studiorum Orientalium.

Tangl, Georgine. 1992. *Die Teilnehmer an den allgemeinen Konzilien des Mittelalters*. Weimar: H. Böhlaus Nachfolger.

Tavard, George H. 1959. *Holy Writ or Holy Church: The Crisis of the Protestant Reformation*. New York: Harper and Brothers.

Terry-Thompson, Arthur Cornelius. 1956. *The History of the African Orthodox Church*. New York: Beacon Press.

Tetz, Martin. 1973. "Markellianer und Athanasios von Alexandrien: Die markellianische *Expositio fidei ad Athanasium* des Diakons Eugenios von Ankyra." *Zeitschrift für die Neutestamentliche Wissenschaft und die Kunde der Älteren Kirche* 64/1-2:75-112.

———. 1985. "Ante omnia de sancta fide et de integritate veritatis: Glaubensfragen auf der Synode von Serdika (342)." *Zeitschrift für die neutestamentliche Wissenschaft* 76:243-69.

Themel, Karl. 1973. "Dokumente von der Entstehung der Konkordienformel." *ARG* 64:287-313.

Theurer, Wolfdieter. 1967. *Die trinitarische Basis des Ökumenischen Rates der Kirchen*. Bergen-Enkheim: G. Kaffke.

Thomas Aquinas. 1954. *Opuscula theologica*. 2 vols. Turin: Marietti.

Thompson, Bard. 1963. "Historical Background of the Catechism" and "The Reformed Chruch in the Palatinate." In *Essays on the Heidelberg Catechism*, 8-30, 31-52. A Collection of Essays by Bard Thompson, Hendrikus Berkhof, Eduard Schweizer, and Howard Hageman. Philadelphia: United Church Press.

Thompson, David M., ed. 1990. *Stating the Gospel: Formulations and Declarations of Faith from the Heritage of the United Reformed Church*. Edinburgh: T. and T. Clark.

Thompson, E. A. 1960. "The Conversion of the Visigoths to Catholicism." *Nottingham Mediaeval Studies* 4:4-35.

———. 1966. *The Visigoths in the Time of Ulfila*. Oxford: Clarendon Press.

———. 1985. *Who Was Saint Patrick?* New York: St. Martin's Press.

Thomson, R. M. 1980. "The Satirical Works of Berengar of Poitiers." *Mediaeval Studies* 42:89-138.

Thomson, S. Harrison. 1932. "John Wyclif's 'Lost' *De fide sacramentorum*." *JTS* 33:359-65.

———. 1953. "Luther and Bohemia." *ARG* 44/2:160-81.

Thurian, Max. 1983. *Ecumenical Perspectives on Baptism, Eucharist, and Ministry*. Geneva: World Council of Churches.

———, and Geoffrey Wainwright. 1984. *Baptism and Eucharist: Ecumenical Convergence in Celebration*. Grand Rapids, Mich.: Eerdmans.

Tideman, J. 1851. *De remonstrantie en het remonstrantisme: Historisch onderzoek*. Te Haarlem: Bij de Erven F. Bohn.

Tidner, E. 1963. *Didascalia Apostolorum, Canonum Ecclesiasticorum, Traditionis Apostolicae Versiones Latinae*. Berlin: Akademie-Verlag.

Tierney, Brian. 1972. *Origins of Papal Infallibility, 1150–1350: A Study on the Concepts of Infallibility, Sovereignty, and Tradition in the Middle Ages.* Leiden: E. J. Brill.

———. 1988. *Origins of Papal Infallibility, 1150–1350: A Study on the Concepts of Infallibility, Sovereignty, and Tradition in the Middle Ages.* 2d ed. Leiden: E. J. Brill.

———. 1998. *Foundations of the Conciliar Theory: The Contribution of the Medieval Canonists from Gratian to the Great Schism.* Enlarged new ed. Leiden: Brill.

Tjernagel, N. S. 1965. *Henry VIII and the Lutherans: A Study in Anglo-Lutheran Relations from 1521 to 1547.* Saint Louis, Mo.: Concordia Publishing House.

Tokuzen, Yoshikazu. 1983. "Pädagogik bei Luther." In Junghans 1983, 1:323–30.

Tootikian, Vahan H. 1982. *The Armenian Evangelical Church.* Detroit, Mich.: Armenian Heritage Committee.

Torrance, Thomas Forsyth. 1983. "The Deposit of Faith." *Scottish Journal of Theology* 36/1:1–28.

———. 1985. "The Trinitarian Foundation and Character of Faith and of Authority in the Church." In *Theological Dialogue Between Orthodox and Reformed Churches,* 1:79–120. Edited by T. F. Torrance. Edinburgh: Scottish Academic Press.

———. 1988. *The Trinitarian Faith: The Evangelical Theology of the Ancient Catholic Church.* Edinburgh: T. and T. Clark.

Tourn, Giorgio. 1980. *The Waldensians: The First Eight Hundred Years.* Translated by Camillio P. Merlino. Turin: Editrice Claudiana.

———. 1989. *You Are My Witnesses: The Waldensians Across Eight Hundred Years.* Turin: Editrice Claudiana.

Trakatellis, Demetrios. 1991. "God Language in Ignatius of Antioch." In *The Future of Early Christianity: Essays in Honor of Helmut Koester,* 422–30. Edited by Birger A. Pearson et al. Minneapolis, Minn.: Fortress Press.

Trevett, Christine. 1992. *A Study of Ignatius of Antioch in Syria and Asia.* Lewiston, N.Y.: E. Mellen.

Trilling, Lionel. [1950] 2000. "Wordsworth and the Rabbis." In Leon Wieseltier, ed., *The Moral Obligation to Be Intelligent: Selected Essays,* 188–202. New York: Farrar, Straus, Giroux.

Trimua, Ekom Dake. 1984. "Naissance et développement de l'Eglise Evangélique au Togo, de 1847 à 1980." Ph.D. diss., University of Strasbourg.

Troeltsch, Ernst. 1891. *Vernunft und Offenbarung bei Johann Gerhard und Melanchthon: Untersuchung zur Geschichte der altprotestantischen Theologie.* Göttingen: Vandenhoeck und Ruprecht.

Tschackert, Paul. 1910. *Die Entstehung der lutherischen und der reformierten Kirchenlehre: Samt ihren innerprotestantischen Gegensätzen.* Göttingen: Vandenhoeck und Ruprecht.

Turner, C. H. 1910. "A Critical Text of the *Quicunque vult.*" *JTS* 11:401–11.

———. 1921–22. "The 'Blessed Presbyters' Who Condemned Noetus." *JTS* 23:28–35.

Tyacke, Nicholas. 1986. *Anti-Calvinists: The Rise of English Arminianism, c. 1590–1640.* Oxford: Clarendon Press.

Uhlirz, Mathilde. 1914. *Die Genesis der vier Prager Artikel.* Sitzungsberichte der Kaiserlichen Akademie der Wissenschaften, 175/3. Vienna: Kaiserliche Akademie der Wissenschaften.

Ullrich, Lothar. 1985. "Die Bedeutung des Symbolum Chalcedonense für die Christologie:

Eine dogmengeschichtliche Übersicht zu den trinitarischen und christologischen Entscheidungen der Alten Kirche in systematischer Absicht." *Theologische Versuche* 15:135–49. Edited by Joachim Rogge and Gottfried Schille. Berlin: Evangelische Verlagsanstalt.

Ulrich, Jörg. 1994. *Die Anfänge der abendländischen Rezeption des Nizänums*. Berlin: W. de Gruyter.

The United Church of Canada Yearbook 1928, Including Record of Proceedings of Third General Council, Winnipeg, September, 1928, Statistics of the Church, April 1st–December 31st, 1927, Pastoral Charges and the Ministers at June 30th, 1927. 1928. Toronto: United Church of Canada General Offices.

Urban, Hans Jörg. 1972. *Bekenntnis, Dogma, kirchliches Lehramt: Die Lehrautorität der Kirche in heutiger evangelischer Theologie*. Wiesbaden: F. Steiner.

Vaggione, Richard Paul, ed. and tr. 1987. *Eunomius, the Extant Works*. Oxford: Clarendon Press.

Vajta, Vilmos. 1983. "Luther als Beter." In Junghans 1983, 1:279–95.

———, and Hans Weissgerber. 1963. *The Church and the Confessions: The Role of the Confessions in the Life and Doctrine of the Lutheran Churches*. Philadelphia, Pa.: Fortress Press.

Van Dam, Raymond. 1982. "History and Hagiography: The Life of Gregory Thaumaturgus." *Classical Antiquity* 1:272–308.

Van Engen, John. 1993. "Anticlericalism Among the Lollards." In *Anticlericalism in Late Medieval and Early Modern Europe*, 53–63. Edited by Peter A. Dykema and Heiko A. Oberman. Leiden: E. J. Brill.

Van Halsema, Thea Bouma. 1961. *Glorious Heretic: The Story of Guido de Brès*. Grand Rapids, Mich.: Eerdmans.

van Unnik, W. C. 1961. "Die Gotteslehre bei Aristides und in gnostischen Schriften." *Theologische Zeitschrift* 17:166–74.

Vasileiadēs, Nikolaos P. 1983. *Markos ho Eugenikos kai hē henōsis tōn ekklēsiōn* [Markos Eugenikos and the union of the churches]. 3d ed. Athens: Adelphotēs Theologōn "Ho Sōtēr."

Vasiliev, A. A. 1964. *History of the Byzantine Empire, 324–1453*. 2 vols. Madison: University of Wisconsin Press.

Veijola, Timo. 1992. "Das Bekenntnis Israels: Beobachtungen zur Geschichte und Theologie von Dtn 6,4–9." *Theologische Zeitschrift* 48/3–4:369–81.

Venard, Marc, ed. 1992. *Histoire du christianisme des origines à nos jours*. Vol. 8 of *Le temps des confessions (1530–1620/30)*. Paris: Desclée.

Vercruysse, Jos E. 1983. "Schlüsselgewalt und Beichte bei Luther." In Junghans 1983, 153–69.

Verghese, Paul. 1968. "The Monothelete Controversy: A Historical Survey." *GOTR* 13/2:196–211.

———. 1971. "Ecclesiological Issues Concerning the Relation of Eastern Orthodox and Oriental Orthodox Churches." *GOTR* 16/1–2:133–43.

Vida è Missão: Decisoes do XIII Concílio Geral da Igreja Metodista e Credo social da Igreja Metodista. 1982. Piracicaba, Brazil: Editora Unimep.

Vidler, Alexander R. 1976. *The Modernist Movement in the Roman Church, Its Origins and Outcome*. New York: Gordon Press.

450 Jahre Zürcher Reformation. 1969. Sonderdruck aus *Zwingliana* 13/1. Zurich: Buchdruckerei Berichthaus.

Vigil, J. M., and A. Torrellas. 1988. *Misas Centroamericanas*. Managua: CAV-CEBES.

Vinay, Valdo. 1975. *Le Confessione di Fede dei Valdesi riformati*. Turin: Editrice Claudiana.

———. 1983. "Waldes." In *Gestalten der Kirchengeschichte*, 3:238–48. Edited by Martin Greschat. Stuttgart: Kohlhammer.

Vinogradský, Nicolaj Fedorovič. 1899. *Cerkovný sobor v Moskvě 1682 goda* [The ecclesiastical synod in Moscow of the year 1682]. Smolensk: Ja. N. Podzemský.

Vischer, Lukas, ed. 1981. *Spirit of God, Spirit of Christ: Ecumenical Reflections on the filioque Controversy*. Faith and Order Paper, 103. Geneva: World Council of Churches.

———, ed. 1987. *Was bekennen die evangelischen Kirchen in der Schweiz?* Bern: Evangelische Arbeitsstelle Oekumene Schweiz.

Visser, Derk. 1983. *Zacharias Ursinus: The Reluctant Reformer, His Life and Times*. New York: United Church Press.

———, ed. 1986. *Controversy and Conciliation: The Reformation and the Palatinate, 1559–1583*. Allison Park, Pa.: Pickwick Publications.

Visser, Dirk, comp. 1975. *A Checklist of Dutch Mennonite Confessions of Faith to 1800*. Amsterdam: Commissie tot de uitgave van Documenta Anabaptistica Neerlandica.

Visser 't Hooft, W. A. 1949. *The First Assembly of the World Council of Churches, Held at Amsterdam, August 22nd to September 4th, 1948*. Volume 5 of *Man's Disorder and God's Design*. New York: Harper.

———, et al. 1977. *Lausanne 77, Fifty Years of Faith and Order (1927–1977)*. Geneva: World Council of Churches.

Voelz, James W. 1979. "Luther's Use of Scripture in the *Small Catechism*." In Scaer and Preus 1979, 55–64.

Vogel, Cornelia J. de. 1973. "The Problem of Philosophy and Christian Faith in Boethius' Consolatio." In *Romanitas et Christianitas*, 357–70. Edited by W. den Boer. Amsterdam: North-Holland Publishing.

Vogt, Hermann Josef. 1968. *Coetus Sanctorum: Der Kirchenbegriff des Novatian und die Geschichte seiner Sonderkirche*. Bonn: Peter Hanstein.

———. 1993. "Unterschiedliches Konzilsverständnis der Cyrillianer und der Orientalen beim Konzil von Ephesus 431." In *Logos: Festschrift für Luise Abramowski*, 429–51. Edited by Hanns Christof Brennecke, Ernst Ludwig Grasmück, and Christoph Markschies. Beihefte zur Zeitschrift für die neutestamentliche Wissenschaft und die Kunde der älteren Kirche, 67. Berlin: W. de Gruyter.

Voices United: The Hymn and Worship Book of the United Church of Canada. 1996. Ontario: United Church Publishing House.

Vola, Giorgio. 1984. "Mais où sont les neiges d'antan: La colletta inglese del 1655 per i Valdesi." *Bollettino della Società di studi valdesi* 155:3–20.

Volz, Hans. 1957. "Luthers Schmalkaldische Artikel." *ZKG* 68:259–86.

———. 1963. "Zur Entstehungsgeschichte von Luthers Schmalkaldischen Artikeln." *ZKG* 74/3–4:316–20.

Vries, Wilhelm de. 1987. "The Reasons for the Rejection of the Council of Chalcedon by the Oriental Orthodox Churches." In Fries and Nersoyan 1987, 3–13.

Wagner, Georg. 1973. *Der Ursprung der Chrysostomusliturgie*. Münster: Aschendorff.

Wainwright, Geoffrey, ed. 1986. *Baptism, Eucharist, and Ministry: A Liturgical Appraisal of the Lima Text.* Rotterdam: Liturgical Ecumenical Center Trust.

Wakefield, Walter L., and Austin P. Evans. 1969. *Heresies of the High Middle Ages.* New York: Columbia University Press.

Walker, Peter W. L. 1990. *Holy City, Holy Places: Christian Attitudes to Jerusalem and the Holy Land in the Fourth Century.* Oxford: Clarendon Press.

Wallace, R. S. 1988. *Calvin, Geneva and the Reformation.* Grand Rapids, Mich.: Baker Book House.

Wallace, Robert. 1850. *Antitrinitarian Biography.* 3 vols. London: E. T. Whitfield.

Wallace-Hadrill, D. S. 1961. *Eusebius of Caesarea.* Westminster, Md.: Canterbury Press.

Wandel, Lee Palmer. 1995. *Voracious Idols and Violent Hands: Iconoclasm in Reformation Zurich, Strasbourg, and Basel.* Cambridge: Cambridge University Press.

Ward, Harry Frederick, ed. 1912. *The Social Creed of the Churches.* New York: Eaton and Maine; Cincinnati, Ohio: Jennings and Graham.

Warfield, Benjamin Breckinridge. 1901-2. "The Printing of the Westminster Confession." Extract from *The Presbyterian and Reformed Review* (October 1901, January 1902, April 1902). Philadelphia: MacCalla.

———. 1931. *The Westminster Assembly and Its Work.* New York: Oxford University Press.

———. 1956. *Calvin and Augustine.* Edited by Samuel G. Craig. Philadelphia: Presbyterian and Reformed Publishing.

Wartenberg, Günther. 1983a. "Unterricht der Visitatoren an die Pfarrherrn im Kurfürstentum Sachsen, 1528 und spätere Ausgaben." In *Martin Luther Studienausgabe,* 3:402-62. Edited by Hans Ulrich Delius. Berlin: Evangelische Verlagsanstalt.

———. 1983b. "Luthers Beziehungen zu den sächsischen Fürsten." In Junghans 1983, 1:549-71.

Waterland, Daniel. 1724. *A Critical History of the Athanasian Creed.* Cambridge: Cambridge University Press.

Webb, Henry E. 1990. *In Search of Christian Unity: A History of the Restoration Movement.* Cincinnati, Ohio: Standard Publishing.

Weber, Georg Gottlieb. 1783-84. *Kritische Geschichte der Augspurgischen Confession aus archivalischen Nachrichten nebst einigen diplomatischen Zeichnungen.* 2 vols. Frankfurt: Varrentrapp Sohn und Wenner.

Weingart, Richard E. 1970. *The Logic of Divine Love: A Criticial Analysis of the Soteriology of Peter Abailard.* London: Clarendon Press.

Weischer, Bernd M. 1977. "Die Glaubenssymbole des Epiphanios von Salamis und des Gregorios Thaumaturgos im Qerello." In *Oriens Christianus,* 61:20-40. Edited by Joseph Molitor. Wiesbaden: Otto Harrassowitz.

Weismann, Christoph, ed. 1995. *Eine Kleine Biblia: Die Katechismen von Luther und Brenz.* Stuttgart: Calwer Verlag.

Welch, Claude. 1972-85. *Protestant Thought in the Nineteenth Century.* 2 vols. New Haven and London: Yale University Press.

Welch, Herbert. [1946]. *The Story of a Creed.* Reprinted with slight changes from the *Nashville Christian Advocate,* 1 August 1946, 937-44.

Wells, Patricia. 1992. *Welcome to the United Church of Canada*. [Toronto]: Division of Mission in Canada, United Church of Canada.

Wendenbourg, Dorothea. 1986. *Reformation und Orthodoxie (Der ökumenische Briefwechsel zwischen der Leitung der Würtembergischen Kirche und Patriarch Jeremias II von Konstantinopel, 1573-1581)*. Göttingen: Vandenhoeck und Ruprecht.

Wenger, John Christian. 1952. *The Doctrines of the Mennonites*. Scottdale, Pa.: Mennonite Publishing House.

———. 1966. *The Mennonite Church in America*. Scottdale, Pa.: Herald Press.

———, and Leonard Verduin, eds. and trans. 1978. *The Complete Writings of Menno Simons, c. 1496-1561*. Corrected ed. Scottdale, Pa.: Herald Press.

Wenz, Gunther. 1996. *Theologie der Bekenntnisschriften der evangelisch-lutherischen Kirche: Eine historische und systematische Einführung in das Konkordienbuch*. Berlin: Walter de Gruyter.

Westin, Gunnar, and Torsten Bergsten. 1962. *Balthasar Hubmaier: Schriften*. Gütersloh, Germany: Gerd Mohn.

White, B. R. 1968. "The Doctrine of the Church in the Particular Baptist Confession of 1644." *JTS*, n.s., 19:570-90.

———. 1996. *The English Baptists of the Seventeenth Century*. Oxford: Baptist Historical Society.

Whitehead, Alfred North. [1925] 1952. *Science and the Modern World*. Lowell Lectures for 1925. Reprint, New York: New American Library.

Whitley, W. T. 1923. *A History of British Baptists*. London: Charles Griffin.

Whitson, Robley Edward, ed. 1983. *The Shakers: Two Centuries of Spiritual Reflection*. New York: Paulist Press.

Wilbur, Earl Morse. 1942. *A History of Unitarianism in Transylvania, England, and America*. Cambridge, Mass.: Harvard University Press.

Wilckens, Ulrich. 1961. *Die Missionsreden der Apostelgeschichte; Form- und traditionsgeschichtliche Untersuchungen*. Neukirchen, Germany: Neukirchener Verlag.

Wiles, Maurice. 1989. "Eunomius: Hair-Splitting Dialectician or Defender of the Accessibility of Salvation?" *The Making of Orthodoxy: Essays in Honour of Henry Chadwick*, 157-72. Edited by Rowan Williams. Cambridge: Cambridge University Press.

———. 1996. *Archetypal Heresy: Arianism Through the Centuries*. Oxford: Clarendon Press.

Wilken, Robert L. 1979. "Introducing the Athanasian Creed." *Currents in Theology and Mission* 6:4-10.

Wilks, M. J. 1969. "The Early Oxford Wyclif: Papalist or Nominalist?" In *Studies in Church History*, 5:69-98. Edited by G. J. Cuming. Leiden: E. J. Brill.

Will, Cornelius. 1861. *Acta et scripta quae de controversies ecclesiae Graecae et Latinae saeculo undecimo composita extant*. Paris: n.p.

Williams, Daniel H. 1996. "Another Exception to Later Fourth-Century 'Arian' Typologies: The Case of Germinius of Sirmium." *Journal of Early Christian Studies* 4:335-57.

Williams, George Hunston. 1951. "Christology and Church-State Relations in the Fourth Century." *Church History* 20/3:3-33, 20/4:3-26.

———. 1960. *Anselm: Communion and Atonement*. Saint Louis, Mo.: Concordia.

————. 1990. "Radicalization of the Reformed Church in Poland, 1547–1574: A Regional Variant of Sixteenth-Century Anabaptism." *MQR* 65:54–68.

Williams, Rowan. 2002. *Arius: Heresy and Tradition*. Revised ed. Grand Rapids, Mich.: Eerdmans.

Willis-Watkins, David. 1994. "The Third Part of Christian Freedom Misplaced, Being an Inquiry into the Lectures of the Late Rev. Samuel Willard on the Assembly's Shorter Catechism." In *Later Calvinism: International Perspectives*, 471–88. Edited by W. Fred Graham. Kirksville, Mo.: Sixteenth Century Journal Publishing.

Wilson, N. G., ed. 1994. *The "Bibliotheca" of Photius: A Selection*. London: Duckworth.

The Winchester Centennial, 1803–1903: Historical Sketch of the Universalist Profession of Belief: Adopted at Winchester, N.H., September 22, 1803, with the Address and Sermons at the Commemorative Services Held in Winchester, Rome City, Ind., and Washington, D.C., September and October, 1903. 1903. Boston: Universalist Publishing House.

Windhorst, Christof. 1978. "Balthasar Hubmaier: Professor, Prediger, Politiker." In *Radikale Reformatoren*. Edited by Hans-Jürgen Goertz, 125–36. Munich: Beck.

Winter, Sean F. 1991. "Michael Sattler and the Schleitheim Articles: A Study in the Background to the First Anabaptist Confession of Faith." *Baptist Quarterly* 34:52–66.

Witte, John. 1997. *From Sacrament to Contract: Marriage, Religion, and Law in the Western Tradition*. Louisville, Ky.: Westminster John Knox Press.

Wolf, Ernst, ed. 1959. *Christusbekenntnis im Atomzeitalter?* Munich: Christian Kaiser Verlag.

————. 1962. "Die Schmalkaldischen Artikel und die Gegenwart." *Communio Viatorum* 5:88–102.

Wolfson, Harry Austryn. 1947. *Philo: Foundations of Religious Philosophy in Judaism, Christianity, and Islam*. 2 vols. Cambridge, Mass.: Harvard University Press.

Wolter, H., and H. Holstein. 1967. *Lyon I et Lyon II*. Histoire des conciles oecuméniques, 7. Paris: Editions de l'Orante.

Wood, Edward. 1961. *Whosoever Will; Quicunque vult*. London: Faith Press.

World Council of Churches, Commission on Faith and Order. 1984. "The Apostolic Faith in the Scriptures and in the Early Church: Report of the Faith and Order Consultation Held in Rome, 1–8 October 1983." *Ecumenical Review* 36:329–37.

————. 1986. "Nous croyons en Dieu, le Père, le Fils et l'Esprit Saint: Une explication oecuménique de la foi apostolique exprimée dans le Symbole de Nicée-Constantinople (381)." *Istina* 31/1:63–129.

Wouk, Herman. 1978. *War and Remembrance*. Boston: Little, Brown.

Wozniak, Casimir J. 1997. *Hyphenated Catholicism: A Study of the Polish-American Model of Church, 1890–1908*. San Francisco: International Scholars Publications.

Wright, A. D. 1975. "The Significance of the Council of Trent." *Journal of Ecclesiastical History* 26:353–62.

Wright, David F. 1982. "Christian Faith in the Greek World: Justin Martyr's Testimony." *Evangelical Quarterly* 54:77–87.

Wright, J. Robert, ed. 1988. *Quadrilateral at One Hundred: Essays on the Centenary of the Chicago-Lambeth Quadrilateral, 1886/88–1986/88*. Cincinnati, Ohio: Forward Movement Publications.

Wright, Susan J. 1988. "Catechism, Confirmation and Communion: The Role of the Young in the Post-Reformation Church." In *Parish Church and People: Local Studies in Lay Religion, 1350-1750*, 203-27. Edited by Susan J. Wright. London: Hutchinson.

Wright, William. 1985. "Philip of Hesse's Vision of Protestant Unity and the Marburg Colloquy." In *Pietas et Societas: New Trends in Reformation Social History*, 163-79. Edited by Kyle C. Sessions and Phillip N. Bebb. Kirksville, Mo.: Sixteenth Century Journal Publishers.

Wyschogrod, Michael. 1984. "The 'Shema Israel' in Judaism and the New Testament." In *The Roots of Our Common Faith: Faith in the Scriptures and in the Early Church*, 23-32. Edited by Hans-Georg Link. Faith and Order Paper, 119. Geneva: World Council of Churches.

Wyznanie wiary Kościoła Polskiego Narodowego Katolickiego w Ameryce. 1936. Scranton, Pa.: Drukiem "Straczy."

Yoder, John H. 1959. "Balthasar Hubmaier and the Beginnings of Swiss Anabaptism." *MQR* 33:5-17.

———, tr. and ed. 1973. *The Legacy of Michael Sattler*. Scottdale, Pa.: Herald Press.

Young, Frances M. 1983. *From Nicaea to Chalcedon: A Guide to the Literature and Its Background*. Philadelphia: Fortress Press.

Zahn-Harnack, Agnes von. 1951. *Adolf von Harnack*. 2d ed. Berlin: Walter de Gruyter.

Zdenek, David V. 1999. "Utraquists, Lutherans, and the Bohemian Confession of 1575." *Church History* 68/2:294-336.

Zerbi, Piero. 1975. "San Bernardo e il Concilio di Sens." In *Studi su S Bernardo di Chiaravalle nell'ottavo centenario della canonizzazione*, 49-73. Rome: Editiones Cistercienses.

Zēsēs, Theodōros. 1980. *Gennadios B' Scholarios—Bios, syngrammata, didaskalia* [Gennadius II Scholarius—life, writings, doctrine]. Thessalonica: Patriarchikon Idryma Paterikōn Meletōn.

Ziegenaus, Anton. 1989. "Die Jungfrauengeburt im Apostolischen Glaubensbekenntnis: Ihre Interpretation bei Adolf von Harnack." In *Divergenzen in der Mariologie: Zur ökumenischen Diskussion um die Mutter Jesu*, 35-55. Edited by Heinrich Petri. Regensburg, Germany: Friedrich Pustet.

Ziegler, Aloysius K. 1930. *Church and State in Visigothic Spain*. Washington, D.C.: Catholic University of America.

Zimmermann, Gunter. 1989. "Die pneumatologische Tradition in der reformierten Bekenntnisbildung." *Theologische Zeitschrift* 45:352-74.

Zimmermann, Rudolf, and Walter Hildebrandt, trans. 1967. *Das Zweite Helvetische Bekenntnis*. Zurich: Zwingli Verlag.

Zovatto, Pietro. 1968. *La polemica Bossuet-Fénelon: Introduzione critico-bibliografica*. Padua: Gregoriana.

Žukovský, Arkadij. 1997. *Petro Mohyla j pytannja ednosty cerkov* [Petro Mohyla and the problem of the unity of the churches]. Kiev: Mystectvo.

Zwingli, Ulrich. 1994. *Huldrych Zwingli: Schriften*. Edited by Thomas Brunnschweiler, Samuel Lutz, et al. 4 vols. Zurich: Theologischer Verlag.

A Comparative Creedal Syndogmaticon,
with Alphabetical Index

Although it is, lamentably, still true, as Robert L. Collison observed in his hand-book of 1962, *Indexing Books: A Manual of Basic Principles*, that "few indexes make a conscientious attempt to index ideas," precisely that must be the chief business of an index to *Creeds and Confessions of Faith in the Christian Tradition*. The title "Syndogmaticon" is adapted from "Syntopicon," which was coined to identify the comprehensive index of "102 Great Ideas," constructed for *Great Books of the Western World* under the editorship of Mortimer J. Adler and published in 1952 by *Encyclopaedia Britannica*. But here it is "Syn*dogmati*con," because the "topics" with which this index deals are in fact the *dogmata* and doctrines of the Christian tradition as these appear in the various creeds and confessions of faith. The problem is that not every dogma appears in every creed or confession, and that even when they do appear, the doctrines do not always employ the same terminology or follow in the same sequence. Instead of a conventional index, therefore, what is needed here is a doctrinal roadmap, a Syndogmaticon, to serve not as a substitute for, but as a guide to, the close reading of the creedal and confessional texts themselves. This Comparative Creedal Syndogmaticon does not pretend to be a comprehensive concordance to all the topics and theological opinions that happen to have been touched on somewhere in the thousands of pages of creeds and confessions, espe-cially in texts as bulky and discursive as *The Westminster Confession of Faith* or *The Solid Declaration* of *The Formula of Concord* or *The Doctrinal Decrees of the Second Vatican Council*. Nor does it aspire to be used as a miniature *summa theologica*, as may be possible for indexes that confine themselves to the more or less homogene-ous confessions coming out of a single tradition, the most notable of these being the "Index Systematicus Rerum" to the Denzinger *Enchiridion*. The Syndogmaticon is "comparative": it does not itself work out a point-by-point comparison, as a textbook or course in Comparative Symbolics might; but, by locating where a par-ticular doctrine is treated in a particular confession, it does make such comparison and contrast possible across the boundaries of confessions, denominations, and historical periods, documenting the sometimes surprising convergences as well as the striking divergences among them. And it is "creedal," both because the texts it indexes are all creeds and confessions of faith and because it is organized on the basis of the text of *The Niceno-Constantinopolitan Creed* of 381 (more commonly, though less precisely, known as *The Nicene Creed*). The Alphabetical Index serves, in turn, as an "index to the index."

In the roster of all the hundreds and even thousands of creeds and confessions of faith that have been composed over a span of two millennia, *The Niceno-Constanti-nopolitan Creed* must hold pride of place. It has a special standing *among* all the creeds and confessions of faith of Christian history as the only truly ecumenical creed, one that is shared by West and East: including under "West" not only Western Catholicism but much (though by no means all) of Western Protestantism; and including under "East" not only the Eastern Orthodox Church but the Oriental Orthodox Churches and the Assyrian Church of the East. Though often linked with *The Apostles' Creed* and *The Athanasian Creed* as one of "the three ecumenical creeds," particularly in the West, this creed also occupies an authoritative place that is distinctive *within* many of the subsequent confessions of those several traditions (see Ecclesiastical Index, s.v. *Niceno-Constantinopolitan Creed*). Thus it represents an outstanding instance of what indexers refer to as a "controlled vocabulary": all, or virtually all, the authors of subsequent creeds and confessions for over sixteen centuries have known its text; most of them have ascribed greater or lesser authority to it; and many of them have prayed its words in their liturgies. Therefore it is uniquely suited to provide, phrase by phrase, the outline for this Comparative Creedal Syndogmaticon. Even what later generations have sometimes perceived to be its lacunae—its silence on the doctrines of election (3.2), justification (3.5), and atonement (4.1); its evident indifference to particular questions of ethics and society (7.3; 8.4); its failure to affirm the inspiration and inerrancy of Holy Scripture (8.14); its lack of specific prescriptions about polity, ministry, and church order (9.8); its reference only to baptism among the sacraments (10.2)—may serve to emphasize this unparalleled position of *The Niceno-Constantinopolitan Creed*. Explicating the text of an ancient creed phrase by phrase to present a summary of Christian doctrine follows ecumenical precedent across the confessions and across the centuries, for example: *The Catechetical Lectures* by Cyril of Jerusalem for the Greek church fathers; *A Commentary on the Apostles' Creed* by Rufinus of Aquileia for the Latin fathers; *The Heidelberg Catechism* for the Protestant Reformation; *The Orthodox Confession of the Catholic and Apostolic Eastern Church by Peter Mogila* for Eastern Orthodoxy; and the *Catechism of the Catholic Church* for Roman Catholicism.

Basically, the Syndogmaticon reproduces and follows the text of *The Niceno-Constantinopolitan Creed* just as Part One of *Creeds and Confessions of Faith in the Christian Tradition* has presented it, dividing it into the traditional twelve articles. But on account of their historical importance, the two most significant of the later divergences from that original text of the First Council of Constantinople in 381 have been added, in brackets: the substitution—or, if it was originally a baptismal creed, actually the restoration—in both Eastern and Western Christendom, of the singular "I believe" in place of the council's original plural "We believe" as the opening of article 1 (which carries through to the other plural verbs, in articles 11 and 12 of the creed); and, in article 8, the addition, by Western Christendom, of "and from the Son [*Filioque*]" to the original phrase about the Holy Spirit, "proceeding forth from the Father," as this *Western Recension* appears at the beginning of Part Three.

Because *The Niceno-Constantinopolitan Creed* serves as the outline of the Syndogmaticon, it would have been redundant to include its individual articles among the references; the same applies to the "creeds" in the Bible, which go on to serve as proof texts for other creeds. Certain other brief creedal formulas, too, especially from the early period and then the modern period, are indexed sometimes according to the individual doctrines in them when these are distinctive or unusually emphatic or prominent (which in the early period is usually the Trinity or the incarnation, and in the modern period often the church and the ministry) or sometimes (as in the case of most early creeds, or of the one-sentence *Doctrinal Basis* of the World Council of Churches of 1948 and other ecumenical affirmations) simply under "1.1. The Faith and Creed of the Church." This heading is therefore also the place to look for early references to such teachings as "6.1. The Ascension of Christ" and others that did not become controversial questions and therefore creedal and confessional issues until later. For similar reasons, as the cross-references and the Alphabetical Index indicate but cannot of course indicate exhaustively, it is always necessary to look up not only a specific doctrinal subject but others that are adjacent or closely related to it (for instance, not only 8.1 on the person of the Holy Spirit, but 1.8 on the Trinity); otherwise, it would be easy to miss what a particular creed or confession teaches on that subject, or even to draw the mistaken conclusion that it says nothing about it.

1. WE BELIEVE [I BELIEVE] IN ONE GOD THE FATHER ALL-POWERFUL, MAKER OF HEAVEN AND EARTH, AND OF ALL THINGS BOTH SEEN AND UNSEEN.

2. AND IN ONE LORD JESUS CHRIST, THE ONLY-BEGOTTEN SON OF GOD, BEGOTTEN FROM THE FATHER BEFORE ALL THE AGES, LIGHT FROM LIGHT, TRUE GOD FROM TRUE GOD, BEGOTTEN NOT MADE, CONSUBSTANTIAL WITH THE FATHER; THROUGH WHOM ALL THINGS CAME TO BE,

3. WHO FOR US HUMANS AND FOR OUR SALVATION CAME DOWN FROM THE HEAVENS AND BECAME INCARNATE FROM THE HOLY SPIRIT AND THE VIRGIN MARY, BECAME HUMAN

4. AND WAS CRUCIFIED ON OUR BEHALF UNDER PONTIUS PILATE; HE SUFFERED AND WAS BURIED

5. AND ROSE UP ON THE THIRD DAY IN ACCORDANCE WITH THE SCRIPTURES.

6. AND HE WENT UP INTO THE HEAVENS AND IS SEATED AT THE FATHER'S RIGHT HAND;

7. HE IS COMING AGAIN WITH GLORY TO JUDGE THE LIVING AND THE DEAD; HIS KINGDOM WILL HAVE NO END.

8. AND IN THE SPIRIT, THE HOLY, THE LORDLY AND LIFE-GIVING ONE, PROCEEDING FORTH FROM THE FATHER [AND THE SON], CO-WORSHIPED AND CO-GLORIFIED WITH FATHER AND SON, THE ONE WHO SPOKE THROUGH THE PROPHETS;

9. IN ONE, HOLY, CATHOLIC, AND APOSTOLIC CHURCH.

10. WE CONFESS [I CONFESS] ONE BAPTISM FOR THE FORGIVING OF SINS.

11. WE LOOK FORWARD [I LOOK FORWARD] TO A RESURRECTION OF THE DEAD

12. AND LIFE IN THE AGE TO COME.

1. WE BELIEVE

1.1 . The Faith and Creed of the Church: Believing "that"
[*fides quae creditur*]

I: *Ign; Just; Tert; Hipp; Orig; Dêr Bal; Novat; Greg Thaum; Cyr Jer; Ant 325; Ant 341; N*

II: *Jer II 1.2; Metr Crit 1; Mogila 1.4–5; Dosith* decr 9; *Vald*

III: *Ap 1; Ath 1–2, 42; No Afr; Patr; Fid cath; Lat 1215*

IV: *17 Art 1; Luth Sm Cat 3.5; Apol Aug 4.337–38, 4.383; Form Conc Epit 3.6; Heid 22–24; Denck 1; Ries 19; Witt Art 4; Trid Prof 9*

V: *Geloof 20.5; Dec Addr 6–7; Vat I 3.3,* can 3.2; *Sacr ant 6; Br St Luth 20; WCC; Un Ch Japan 5; Sri Lanka 3; Zambia 1; Un Ref Ch 12; Laus Cov 1; F&O Ban; Un Ch Can: Crd; Chile; BEC*

1.2. Knowledge of God and of the Will of God Through Creation, History, Conscience, and Reason

II: *Gennad 12.2, 4; Metr Crit 4.2–6; Dosith* decr 14

III: *Tol XI 9; Petr Ab 1*

IV: *17 Art 12; Apol Aug 18.9; Form Conc Epit 1.9; Form Conc Sol Dec 2.9; Genv Cat 113; Helv II 9.6, 12.1, 16.9; Dort 3/4.4; West 1.1, 16.7*

V: *Gen Bap 4–10, 28; Sav 1.1, 16.7; Geloof 1, 11.1; Cumb Pres 38, 67; Syl 3–6, 8–9, 15–16, 56; Vat I 3.2, 3.4, 3* can 2.1, can 3.1–3; *Com Cr 4; Richmond 3; Sacr ant 2; Pol Nat 1; Un Ch Can: Union 2; Un Pres 2; Barm 1; Munif 12; Vat II 8.6, 9.3; Menn Con 2.1; Pres USA 9.13, 9.41–42; Laus Cov 9–10; Toraja 2.2, 7.4*

1.3. The Revelation of Divine Mystery, Its Scope and Language
(*see also* 8.11–15)

I: *Alex; Eph 431 Form Un*

II: *CP 1351 15; Metr Crit 1.3; Mogila 1.8–10*

IV: *Gall 2; Scot I 4; Belg 2; West 1.1*

V: *London I 1; Sav 1.1; Friends I 11; Geloof 2.1–2, 9.4, 17.5; Aub 1; Syl 5; Vat I 3.2, 3.4, 3* can 2.2–3, 3 can 4.1; *Com Cr 4; Lam 20–26, 58–65; Pol Nat 1; Assem 13b; Un Ch Can: Union 2; Un Pres 2, 15; Br St Luth 14–16; Madag* pr 3; *Vat II 8.2–6; Menn Con 1.2, 2.1; PRCC 1a; Toraja* pr, 1.1, 2.2, 7.4; *Bap Conf 1; Morav Am 1, 3*

1.4. The Rule of Faith; Authority of Creeds and Confessions
(*see also* 8.11-12, 9.6, 9.8, Ecclesiastical Index)

I: *Iren; Tert; Tome* 1-2

II: *Phot* 8; *Dosith* decr 9; *Jer II* 1.1

III: *Boh I* 2

IV: *Apol Aug* 27.60; *Form Conc Epit* int; *Form Conc Sol Dec* int; *Irish* 1; *Witt Art* 1; *Trid Prof* 1

V: *Dec Addr* 3; *Def Plat* 1.1, 2 pr; *Adv* pr; *Lamb Quad* 2; *Utrecht* 1; *Lam* 62; *Assem* pr; *Afr Orth* 2; *So Bap* pr; *Un Ch Can: Union* pr; *Un Pres* pr; *F&O Laus* 4; *Chin Un* 3; *Ess* 14; *Meth Kor* pr; *Br St Luth* 29, 45-48; *Wash*; *CSI 1947* 1; *Philip Ind* 2.3, 2.21; *Bat* pr; *Un Ch Japan* 5; *Madag* pr 2; *Sri Lanka* 3; *CNI* 3; *Ghana* 3.3-4; *Zambia* 2; *Pres USA* 9.01-05; *Togo* pr; *Un Ref Ch* 18; *Leuen* 4, 12, 37; *RCA* 7; *Toraja* pr; *Bap Conf* pr; *Morav Am* 4; *Camb Dec* 1; *Ad tuendam* 1

1.5. The One Faith: Confession of Orthodox Doctrine and Anathema
Against Heresy (*see also* Ecclesiastical Index)

I: *Iren; Tome* 14; *Edict* 2, 56, 62-63, 77-78, anath 1-13; *Chal* ecth; *CP II* 1, 7, 12, anath 11; *CP III* 10

II: *Phot* 1; *CP 1351* 7, 51; *Mark Eph* 5; *Mogila* 1.91

III: *Lat 649* 18-20; *Sens* 1-19

IV: *Aug* 21 con; *Smal Art* 3.3.40; *Form Conc Epit* 12; *Form Conc Sol Dec* int 14-20, 12; 67 *Art* 5; 10 *Art* 1; *Ries* 29; *Trent* 3

V: *Sav* pr; *Cum occas; Dec Addr* 7; *Ev All* con; *Resp Pius IX* 1-3, 21; *Syl* 15-18; *Vat I* 3.pr; *Lam* 7-8, 22-24, 26; *Naz* pr; *Sacr ant* 1, 5, 7; *Br St Luth* 28-29, 44; *Barm* pr; *Munif* 12, 36; *Bap Assoc* 20; *Bat* pr 4, 9.4; *Madag* 1, 4; *Vat II* 5.3.11, 5.3.24; *CNI* 4-5; *Leuen* 2, 20, 23, 26, 27; *PRCC* pr, 1b; *Chr Dec* 4-5; *Morav Am* 3-4; *Camb Dec* pr; *Ad tuendam; LuRC Just* 7, 42

[I BELIEVE]

1.6. Saving Faith: Believing "in" [*fides qua creditur*] (*see also* 3.5)

II: *Jer II* 1.4, 6; *Lucar* 9, 13; *Mogila* 1.1-3; *Dosith* decr 9

III: *Ap* 1; *Ath* 1-2, 42; *R* 1; *Orange* 5-6; *Lat 1215*

IV: 17 *Art* 2; *Luth Sm Cat* 1.1; *Luth Lg Cat* 1.1-29; *Aug* 20.8-26; *Apol Aug* 4.48-121, 4.153, 12.45; *Form Conc Epit* 3.5-6; *Form Conc Sol Dec* 3.11-14, 4.35; *Tetrapol* 3; *Bas Bek* 9; *Helv I* 13; *Genv Con* 11; *Genv Cat* III-14; *Belg* 23; *Heid* 21; *Helv II* 16.1-4; *Irish* 37; *Dort* 3/4.14; *West* 11.2, 14.1-3, 18.2-4; *West Sh Cat* 86; *18 Diss* 1-3, 8; *Denck* 1; *Ries* 19, 20; *Marburg* 5; *Witt Art* 4; *Trent* 6 can 12-14

V: *London I* 22–24; *Camb Plat* 12.2–3; *Sav* 11.2, 14.1–3, 18.2–4; *Friends I* 12; *Morav* 1; *Geloof* 18, 20.3; *Meth Art* 9, 12; *Dec Addr* 8–9; *Cumb Pres* 45–47, 62–65; *New Hamp* 6, 8; *Aub* 11; *LDS* 4; *Abst Prin* 10; *Swed Bap* 6; *Vat I* 3.3, 3.4; *Bonn I* 5; *Salv Arm* 8–9; *Richmond* 6; *Sacr ant* 6; *So Bap* 8; *Un Ch Can: Union* 10; *Un Pres* 17, 19, 24; *Ess* 1–2; *Br St Luth* 9; *F&O Edin* 1.2; *Philip Ind* 2.1; *Bat* 7, 15; *Arn* 8a; *UCC* 1; *Vat II* 8.5, 9.9–10; *Menn Con* 6; *Un Ref Ch* 3; *PRCC* 1; *Toraja* 5.4; *BEM* 1.8–10; *Morav Am* 2; *Camb Dec* 4; *LuRC Just* 25–27

IN ONE GOD

1.7. The Monotheistic Faith and Its Confession (*see also* 1.8)

I: *Tert; Smyr*

II: *Gennad* 1

III: *Ath* 3, 6, 16; *Tol I* 1; *Tol XI* 7

IV: *Genv Con* 2; *Helv II* 3.1–2; *West* 2.1; *West Sh Cat* 5, 46–47; *Ries* 1; *Dordrecht* 1

V: *True Con* 1; *Sav* 2.1; *Friends I* 1; *Morav* 1; *Geloof* 4.1,5; *New Hamp* 2; *Winch* 2; *Arm Ev* 1; *Ev All* 3; *Abst Prin* 2; *Swed Bap* 2; *Free Meth* 1; *Vat I* 3.1, 3 can 1.1; *Adv* 1; *Salv Arm* 2; *Chr Sci* 2; *Com Cr* 1; *Richmond* 1; *Naz* 1; *Assem* 2; *So Bap* 2; *Un Ch Can: Union* 1; *Un Pres* 1; *Meth Kor* 1; *Br St Luth* 4; *Philip Ind* 1.1; *Madag* 1, 4; *Menn Con* 1.1; *Zambia* 1; *Un Ref Ch* 17.1; *Laus Cov* 1; *Toraja* 1.1; *Bap Conf* 2; *Philip UCC* 1

THE FATHER

1.8. The Trinity of Father, Son, and Holy Spirit (*see also* 1.9, 2.1, 8.1)

I: *Iren; Orig* 4; *Greg Thaum; Ar; Alex; Eus; Ant* 341; *Sard; Sirm; CP* 360; *Ulph; Epiph; Eun; Aug; Edict* 3, anath 1; *Ecth* 1; *N; CP I; CP II* anath 1, 10

II: *Lit Chrys; Phot* 8–23; *CP* 1351 9, 44; *Greg Palam* 1; *Gennad* 2–3; *Jer II* 1.1; *Metr Crit* 1; *Lucar* 1; *Mogila* 1.7–11; *Dosith* decr 1

III: *Ap; Ath; R; Tol I* 1–11, anath 2–4; *Fid cath; Tol III; Lat* 649 1; *Tol XI; Rom Syn* 1; *Fréjus* 1–5; *Sens* 1–2, 4, 14, 17; *Petr Ab* 2; *Lat* 1215 1; *Lyons; Flor Un; Flor Arm; Vald Boh I* 3

IV: *Aug* 1; *Apol Aug* 1; *Smal Art* 1.1–2; *Tetrapol* 2; *Fid rat* 1; *Bas Bek* 1; *Helv I* 6; *Genv Cat* 19–20; *Gall* 6; *Scot I* 1; *Belg* 8–9; *Heid* 25; *Helv II* 3.3–4; *39 Art* 1; *Irish* 8–10; *West* 2.3; *West Sh Cat* 6; *Cologne* 1; *Ries* 2–3; *Dordrecht* 1; *Marburg* 1

V: *True Con* 2; *London I* 2, 27; *Sav* 2.3; *Friends I* 1; *Morav* 1; *Geloof* 4; *Meth Art* 1; *Winch* 2; *Cumb Pres* 7; *New Hamp* 2; *LDS* 1; *Arm Ev* 2; *Ev All* 3; *Resp Pius IX* 5; *Abst Prin* 3; *Swed Bap* 2; *Free Meth* 1, 4; *Salv Arm* 3; *Chr Sci* 2; *Com Cr* 1; *Richmond* 1; *Am Bap* 2; *Naz* 1–2; *Assem* 2, 13; *So Bap* 2; *Un Ch Can: Union* 1; *Un Pres* 1, 11–13; *Meth Kor* 1–3; *Br St Luth* 4; *CSI* 1947 1; *Philip Ind* 1.1; *Bap Assoc* 1; *Bat* 2; *Un Ch Japan* 2;

Madag 1–3; *Menn Con* 1; *CNI* 1; *Ghana* 3.1; *Zambia* 1, 4; *Pres USA* 9.07; *Meth Braz* 2.1–3; *Un Ref Ch* 12, 17.1; *Laus Cov* 1; *RCA* pr; *Toraja* 1.1–6; *Bap Conf* 2; *Philip UCC* 1; *Morav Am* 1; *Com Dec* 2

ALL-POWERFUL

1.9. The Attributes, Hypostases, and "Energies" of God (*see also* 3.9–10)

I: *Edict* 33–41

II: *CP 1341* 8–46; *CP 1351* 9–11, 17–22, 27, 29–30, 32–35, 38, 40; *Greg Palam* 7; *Mogila* 1.11–17

III: *Tol I* 10; *Lat 649* 1; *Boh I* 3

IV: *Aug* 1.2; *Form Conc Epit* 2.8, 8.7, 11.2–4; *Form Conc Sol Dec* 4.16, 11.4–7; *Fid rat* 2; *Genv Cat* 9, 23–24, 271–74; *Gall* 1; *Scot I* 1; *Belg* 1; *Heid* 11; *Irish* 8; *Dort* 1.11; *West* 2.1–2; *West Sh Cat* 4; *Ries* 3

V: *True Con* 2; *London I* 2; *Gen Bap* 1; *Sav* 2.1–2; *Geloof* 1.1, 3.1; *Winch* 2; *Cumb Pres* 5–6; *Arm Ev* 1; *Resp Pius IX* 5; *Abst Prin* 3; *Syl* 1–2; *Free Meth* 1; *Vat I* 3.1, 3 can 1.3–5; *Adv* 1; *Richmond* 1; *Naz* 1; *Pol Nat* 1; *So Bap* 2; *Un Ch Can: Union* 1; *Un Pres* 1, 11; *Wash*; *Philip Ind* 1.1; *Bat* 1; *Madag* 1; *Menn Con* 1.1; *Pres USA* 9.15; *Meth Braz* 2.1; *Bap Conf* 2

MAKER OF HEAVEN AND EARTH AND OF ALL THINGS BOTH SEEN

1.10. God the Creator: Creation, Preservation, and Providence

I: *Ep Ap*; *Tert*; *Orig* 7; *Novat*

II: *CP 1351* 26; *Metr Crit* 2; *Lucar* 4–5; *Mogila* 1.18, 1.29–31; *Dosith* decr 5

III: *Ap* 1; *Tol I* 1, anath 1, 9, 14; *Lat 1215* 1

IV: *Luth Sm Cat* 2.2; *Luth Lg Cat* 2.9–24; *Bas Bek* 1, 3; *Genv Cat* 25–27; *Gall* 7–8; *Belg* 12; *Heid* 26–28; *Helv II* 6, 7.1–2; *Irish* 18; *West* 4–5; *West Sh Cat* 9, 11–12; *Dordrecht* 1

V: *Gen Bap* 2–3; *Sav* 4–5; *Geloof* 6.1; *Cumb Pres* 8–9, 10, 12–16; *Abst Prin* 4; *Syl* 1–2; *Vat I* 3.1, 3 can 1.1–5; *Salv Arm* 2; *Com Cr* 2; *Am Bap* pr, 3; *Sacr ant* 3; *So Bap* 11; *Un Ch Can: Union* 3–4; *Un Pres* 4–6; *Br St Luth* 5; *CSI 1947* 1; *Sheng Kung* 2; *Bap Assoc* 3; *Bat* 3A; *Madag* 1; *UCC* 2; *Masai* 1; *Menn Con* 1.2, 3.1–2; *Ref All* 1; *Pres USA* 9.16; *Design* 1.3; *Meth Braz* 2.1, 2.10; *Togo* 1; *PRCC* 1; *Hond* pr; *Pres So Afr* 1; *Toraja* 1.2–3, 7.1, 7.11; *Bap Conf* 2a; *Philip UCC* 1

1.11. God and the Powers of Evil (*see also* 1.14, 3.4, 4.1)

I: *Orig* 6; *CP III* 4

II: *Phot* 1; *CP 1054* 3; *CP 1351* 1; *Greg Palam* 5; *Jer II* 1.19; *Metr Crit* 2.4–5, 2.10; *Lucar* 4; *Mogila* 1.21; *Dosith* decr 3, 4, 5

III: *Sens* 7, 16; *Lat 1215* 1

IV: *Aug* 19; *Apol Aug* 19; *Form Conc Epit* 11.4; *Form Conc Sol Dec* 11.7; *Genv Cat* 28–29; *Gall* 8; *Belg* 13; *Helv II* 8.8–10; *Irish* 28; *Ries* 6; *Trent* 6 can 6

V: *True Con* 4; *Geloof* 36.4; *Cumb Pres* 14–15; *Chr Sci* 3; *Un Pres* 4, 7; *Wash*; *Bap Assoc* 4; *Bat* 5; *Menn Con* 3.2; *Laus Cov* 12; *Toraja* 7.3; *Bap Conf* 3

1.12. Creation of the Human Race in the Image of God (*see also* 3.4)

II: *Metr Crit* 2.6–8; *Mogila* 1.22–23

III: *Orange* 8; *Lat 1215* 1; *Vienne* 2

IV: *17 Art* 12; *Aug* 18; *Apol Aug* 2.18–22, 4.27, 18.4–8; *Form Conc Epit* 6.2; *Form Conc Sol Dec* 1.34–42, 2.1–90; *Bas Bek* 2; *Helv I* 7, 9; *Gall* 9; *Scot I* 2; *Belg* 14; *Heid* 6; *Helv II* 7.5–7, 9.1; *Irish* 21; *Dort* 3/4.1; *West* 4.2; *West Sh Cat* 10; *Ries* 4; *Dordrecht* 1

V: *True Con* 4; *London I* 4; *Gen Bap* 11–13; *Sav* 4.2; *Geloof* 5.1–3, 7.1; *Cumb Pres* 11; *Aub* 4; *Abst Prin* 6; *Swed Bap* 3; *Vat I* 3.1; *Chr Sci* 2; *Com Cr* 3; *Richmond* 5; *So Bap* 3; *Un Pres* 4, 11; *Br St Luth* 6; *UCC* 2; *Masai* 1; *Vat II* 9.2–3; *Menn Con* 3.1–2; *Pres USA* 9.17; *Meth Braz* 2.6, 3.1; *PRCC* 2a; *Hond* 1; *Toraja* 3.1–4; *Bap Conf* 3; *Philip UCC* 2

1.13. Freedom of the Will and the Sovereignty of God (*see also* 3.2, 8.5)

I: *Orig*

II: *Jer II* 1.18; *Lucar* 14; *Mogila* 1.27; *Dosith* decr 3

III: *Orange; Sens* 5

IV: *Aug* 18; *Apol Aug* 18; *West* 9; *Ries* 5; *Trent* 6 can 2, 4, 5

V: *Cum occas* 3; *Sav* 9; *Geloof* 11; *Meth Art* 8; *Cumb Pres* 34–37; *Aub* 14, 16; *Free Meth* 8; *Naz* 7; *So Bap* 9; *F&O Edin* 1.3; *Bat* 3A; *Menn Con* 3.2, 4.1

AND UNSEEN

1.14. The Doctrine of Angels (*see also* 1.11)

II: *CP 1341* 20–21; *Metr Crit* 2.2; *Lucar* 4; *Mogila* 1.19–20; *Dosith* decr 4

III: *Tol I* 11

IV: *Apol Aug* 21.8; *Gall* 7; *Helv II* 7.3–4; *Irish* 20; *Menn Con* 20

V: *Geloof* 5.1; *Vat I* 3.1; *Afr Orth* 6; *Un Pres* 7; *Bat* 17; *Bap Conf* 3

2. AND IN ONE LORD JESUS CHRIST, THE ONLY-BEGOTTEN SON OF GOD, BEGOTTEN FROM THE FATHER BEFORE ALL THE AGES, LIGHT FROM LIGHT, TRUE GOD FROM TRUE GOD, BEGOTTEN NOT MADE, CONSUBSTANTIAL WITH THE FATHER; THROUGH WHOM ALL THINGS CAME TO BE

2.1. Jesus Christ as Lord: Titles, Offices, States, Deeds, and Teachings

I: *Arist; Ep Ap; Tert; Smyr; N; Chal 9*

II: *Greg Palam 2; Mogila 1.34–36*

III: *Ap 2; Ath 22, 29–41; R 2; Tol I 12–13,* anath 3; *Lat 649 2; Tol XI 2; Boh I 6*

IV: *Luth Lg Cat 3.27–31; Apol Aug 4.69, 21.17–20; Laus Art 2; Genv Cat 30–47, 54; Gall 13; Scot I 7–8; Belg 10, 26; Heid 29–31, 33–34; Helv II 5, 11, 18.4; 39 Art 18; Irish 31; West 8; West Sh Cat 21, 23–26; Cologne 2; Ries 9, 11, 12, 17; Tig 4*

V: *True Con 9–15; London I 9–20; Gen Bap 20–23; Friends I 4; Sav 8; Morav 2; Geloof 4.3, 12–16; Meth Art 2; Shkr 3; Cumb Pres 27; Abst Prin 7; Syl 7; Free Meth 2; Vat I 3.3, 3 can 3.4; Richmond 2; Am Bap 5; Lam 13–18, 27–38; Naz 2; Pol Nat 2–3; Assem 13e–j; Witness 7; Afr Orth 3; So Bap 8; Un Ch Can: Union 2, 7; Un Pres 12; Chin Un 1; Meth Kor 2; Barm 2; F&O Edin 2.1–2; Wash; CSI 1947 1; Philip Ind 1.2, 2.16; Bap Assoc 6; Bat 9; Madag 2; Masai 2; Menn Con 5; CNI 1; Ghana 3.1; Zambia 5; Ref All 2; Pres USA 9.08–11, 9.19; Design 1.1–2; Meth Braz 2.2; Togo 2; Leuen 21; Laus Cov 3; PRCC 1a; Pres So Afr 2; Toraja pr, 1.4, 2.1, 4.3; Philip UCC 1*

3. WHO FOR US HUMANS AND FOR OUR SALVATION

3.1. The Divine Economy of Salvation

I: *Iren; Tert; Orig 4; Tome 6*

II: *Metr Crit 3; Lucar 7*

III: *Ath 38; Sens 3; Lat 1215 2; Unam 8*

IV: *Form Conc Epit 11.17–19; Form Conc Sol Dec 11.28; Sax Vis 1.4.2; Belg 17; West 7; Cologne 4; Dordrecht 3; Trent 6.2*

V: *True Con 5–6; London I 5–6; Sav 7; Friends I 10; Geloof 10; Shkr 1; Dec Addr 8; Cumb Pres 22–25; New Hamp 4; Assem 4; So Bap 4; Un Ch Can: Union 3, 6; Philip Ind 2.1; UCC 3; Masai 1; Vat II 8.2–4, 8.14–16; Menn Con 1.2; Pres USA 9.18; PRCC 3b; Chr Dec 6*

3.2. Election, Predestination, and Divine Foreknowledge

II: *Metr Crit* 4; *Lucar* 3; *Mogila* 1.25–26, 1.30; *Dosith* decr 3

IV: *Form Conc Epit* 11; *Form Conc Sol Dec* 11; *Sax Vis* 1.4, 2.4; *Fid rat* 3; *Bas Bek* 1; *Helv I* 10; *Gall* 12; *Scot I* 8; *Belg* 16; *Lamb Art* 1–4; *Helv II* 10; *39 Art* 17; *Remon* 1; *Irish* 11–17; *Dort* 1; *West* 3.1–8, 17.2; *West Sh Cat* 7; *Ries* 7; *Trent* 6.12, 6 can 15, 17

V: *True Con* 3; *London I* 3, 21; *Sav* 3.1–8, 17.2; *Morav* 1; *Geloof* 9; *New Hamp* 9; *Aub* 2; *Abst Prin* 5; *Swed Bap* 6; *So Bap* 9; *Un Pres* 10; *Afr Orth* 11; *Br St Luth* 35–40; *Munif* 40; *Un Ch Japan* 3; *Vat II* 5.1.2–3; *Menn Con* 6; *Leuen* 24–26

3.3. Plan of Salvation; Gospel and Law; Preaching and Evangelization
(*see also* 8.5, 10.1)

II: *Metr Crit* 3.3–4
III: *Prague* 1; *Boh I* 10
IV: *Apol Aug* 4.5–6, 36–39, 43, 12.53–58; *Smal Art* 3.2, 3.4; *Form Conc Epit* 5; *Form Conc Sol Dec* 4.17, 5.3, 5.20; *67 Art* 1–2; *Helv I* 12; *Genv Con* 6; *Heid* 19, 65; *Helv II* 13; *Dort* 3/4.6–8; *West* 7.5–6; *18 Diss* 12; *Ries* 10; *Dordrecht* 5; *Marburg* 8; *Tig* 1

V: *London I* 24–25; *Sav* 7.5, 20.1–4; *Shkr* 2; *Cumb Pres* 69; *New Hamp* 12; *Arm Ev* 12; *Swed Bap* 7; *Richmond* 5; *So Bap* 23; *Un Ch Can: Union* 14; *Un Pres* 9, 15, 25; *F&O Laus* 2; *Barm* 6; *Bat* 9.1; *UCC* 7; *Vat II* 5.1.16–17, 5.1.25, 5.1.35, 8.18–19; *Menn Con* 8.2, 9; *CNI* 1; *Pres USA* 9.06, 9.49; *Meth Braz* 6; *Leuen* 13; *Laus Cov* pr, 1, 4, 6–10; *Pres So Afr* 3; *Toraja* 1.1, 2.1, 6.3; *Bap Conf* 5; *Morav Am* pr, 7; *LuRC Just* 31–33

3.4. The Need for Salvation: Sin and the Fall (*see also* 1.11, 1.13)

II: *Jer II* 1.3; *Metr Crit* 2.9–12; *Lucar* 6; *Mogila* 1.24–25; *Dosith* decr 6, 14
III: *Orange* 1–2, 8, 15, 21–22, con; *Sens* 8–10, 19; *Boh I* 4
IV: *Luth Lg Cat* 2.28; *Aug* 2; *Apol Aug* 2.3–6, 4.169–71; *Smal Art* 3.1; *Form Conc Epit* 1; *Form Conc Sol Dec* 1; *Fid rat* 2, 4–5; *Bas Bek* 2; *Helv I* 7–8; *Genv Con* 4–5; *Genv Cat* 197, 214–16; *Gall* 9–11; *Scot I* 3; *Belg* 15; *Heid* 3–10; *Helv II* 8.1–5, 9.2–12; *39 Art* 9–10, 15–16; *Remon* 3; *Irish* 22–24, 27, 43–44; *Dort* 3/4; *West* 6; *West Sh Cat* 13–19, 82–84; *Ries* 4; *Dordrecht* 2; *Marburg* 4; *Witt Art* 2; *Trent* 5, 6.1, 6 can 27–29; *Trid Prof* 4

V: *True Con* 4–5; *London I* 4–5; *Gen Bap* 14–16; *Cum occas* 2; *Sav* 6; *Geloof* 8; *Meth Art* 7; *Dec Addr* 8; *Cumb Pres* 17–21, 36; *New Hamp* 3; *Aub* 1, 3–7, 9; *LDS* 2; *Ev All* 4; *Abst Prin* 6; *Swed Bap* 3; *Free Meth* 7; *Salv Arm* 5; *Com Cr* 3; *Richmond* 5; *Naz* 5; *Assem* 3; *Arm Ev* 4; *So Bap* 3; *Un Ch Can: Union* 5; *Un Pres* 8; *Ess* 3, 9; *Br St Luth* 7; *Bap Assoc* 5; *Bat* 5–6; *Madag* 5; *Menn Con* 4.1–2; *Zambia* 5; *Pres USA* 9.12–14; *Togo* 2; *PRCC* 3a; *RCA* 2; *Toraja* 3.5–8, 7.2–3; *Bap Conf* 4; *Morav Am* 1

3.5. Salvation as Forgiveness, Adoption, Justification
(*see also* 1.6, 4.1, 8.2–3)

II: *Jer II* 1.4; *Metr Crit* 6.5; *Lucar* 9, 13; *Dosith* decr 13

III: *Ap* 10; *R* 10; *Boh I* 6

IV: *Luth Sm Cat* 3.16; *Luth Lg Cat* 3.85–98; *Aug* 4; *Apol Aug* 4; *Smal Art* 2.1.4, 3.13; *Form Conc Epit* 3; *Form Conc Sol Dec* 3; *Tetrapol* 3; *Genv Con* 7, 9; *Genv Cat* 101–5, 114–20, 280–86; *Gall* 18–20; *Belg* 22, 23; *Heid* 56, 59–64; *Lamb Art* 5–6; *Helv II* 15; *39 Art* 13; *Irish* 34–35; *West* 11; *West Sh Cat* 32–33; *Ries* 21; *Marburg* 7; *Witt Art* 4; *Tig* 3; *Trent* 6; *Trid Prof* 4

V: *London I* 28; *Sav* 11–12; *Friends I* 12; *Geloof* 20; *Meth Art* 9; *Shkr* 5; *Cumb Pres* 48–50; *New Hamp* 5; *Aub* 15; *Arm Ev* 7; *Ev All* 6; *Abst Prin* 11; *Free Meth* 9; *Vat I* 3.3; *Adv* 15; *Bonn I* 5; *Salv Arm* 8; *Chr Sci* 3; *Richmond* 6; *Naz* 9.9; *Assem* 4a; *Afr Orth* 11; *So Bap* 5; *Un Ch Can: Union* 11; *Un Pres* 19–20; *Ess* 2; *Meth Kor* 4; *Br St Luth* 9, 17–19; *F&O Edin* 1.2; *CSI 1947* 1; *Bap Assoc* 10; *Bat* 7; *UCC* 8; *Masai* 3; *Leuen* 6–8, 10, 12; *PRCC* 3c; *Toraja* 4.7, 5.3–4; *Bap Conf* 5; *Camb Dec* 4; *LuRC Just*

CAME DOWN FROM THE HEAVENS
AND BECAME INCARNATE

3.6. The Incarnation of the Son of God

I: *Tert*; *Tome* 7–10; *Edict* 4, anath 2; *Ecth* 2; *Eph* 431 ecth; *Chal* 13–15; *CP II* anath 2

II: *Greg Palam* 2; *Gennad* 4–5; *Metr Crit* 3.4–5; *Mogila* 1.38

III: *Ap* 3; *Ath* 29–37; *R* 3; *Tol I* 12–19, anath 5; *Lat 649* 2; *Tol XI* 9–15; *Rom Syn* 2; *Fréjus* 6–8; *Sens* 3; *Petr Ab* 3; *Lat 1215* 2; *Vienne* 1; *Vald*

IV: *Aug* 3; *Apol Aug* 3; *Smal Art* 1.3–4; *Form Conc Epit* 8; *Form Conc Sol Dec* 8.6; *Tetrapol* 2; *Fid rat* 1; *Bas Bek* 4; *Helv I* 11; *Genv Cat* 50–53; *Gall* 14; *Scot I* 6; *Belg* 18; *Heid* 35; *Helv II* 11; *39 Art* 2; *Irish* 29; *West* 8.2–3; *Ries* 8; *Dordrecht* 4; *Marburg* 2

V: *Sav* 8.2–3; *Friends I* 5; *Morav* 2; *Geloof* 12; *Meth Art* 2; *Cumb Pres* 28; *Ev All* 5; *Free Meth* 2; *Adv* 2; *Richmond* 2; *Naz* 2; *Witness* 8; *So Bap* 4; *Un Pres* 12; *Br St Luth* 8; *CSI 1947* 1; *Philip Ind* 2.16; *Bat* 3B; *Masai* 2; *Vat II* 8.4; *Menn Con* 1.3, 5.1; *Meth Braz* 2.3; *Leuen* 9; *PRCC* 1b; *RCA* 3; *Hond* 1; *Toraja* 1.4, 4.1; *Bap Conf* 2b; *Chr Dec* 1

FROM THE HOLY SPIRIT AND
THE VIRGIN MARY

3.7. Mary Virgin Mother and Theotokos;
Other Titles and Privileges of Mary

I: *Ign; Ep Ap; Tert; Tome* 4; *Edict* anath 5; *Ecth* 3; *Eph 431; Chal; CP II* 11, anath 6; *Nic II*

II: *Lit Chrys* I.A.2, II.F.5; *Greg Palam* 6; *Metr Crit* 9.5, 17.7–9; *Mogila* 1.39–42; *Dosith* decr 1.6, 8, q 4; *Rom Syn* 2

III: *Ap* 3; *R* 3; *Tol I* 12; *Lat 649* 3; *Tol XI* 9, 13; *Boh I* 17

IV: *Apol Aug* 21.27–28; *Smal Art* 1.4; *Trent* 5.6, 6 can 23; *Form Conc Epit* 8.12; *Form Conc Sol Dec* 8.24; *Genv Cat* 49

V: *Ineff; Bonn I* 10; *Utrecht* 3; *Am Bap* 4; *Afr Orth* 6; *Philip Ind* 2.14; *Munif; Bap Assoc* 6; *Bat* 3B1; *Vat II* 5.1.52–69, 5.3.15; *Hond* 1; *Chr Dec* 3

3.8. The Saints: Veneration and Invocation

II: *Jer II* 1.15, 1.21; *Metr Crit* 17; *Dosith* decr 8

III: *Ap* 9; *Boh I* 17

IV: *Aug* 21; *Apol Aug* 21; *Smal Art* 2.2; *67 Art* 19–21; *Bern* 6; *Tetrapol* 11; *10 Art* 7–8; *Genv Con* 12; *Genv Cat* 238–39; *Gall* 24; *Belg* 26; *Helv II* 5.4–6; *West* 21.2, 26.1–3; *Witt Art* 16; *Trent* 25.2

V: *Sav* 22.2; *Meth Art* 14; *Arm Ev* 9; *Bonn I* 7; *Afr Orth* 6–7; *Philip Ind* 2.15; *Vat II* 5.1.50–51, 5.1.66–69, 5.3.15

BECAME HUMAN

3.9. Fully Divine Nature and Fully Human Nature (*see also* 1.8–9, 3.10)

I: *Ign; Tome* 5; *Edict* 5–7, 13–18, 23–32, anath 8; *Ecth* 3–4; *Eph 431* ecth; *Chal* 5–12, 16–20; *Nic II*

II: *CP 1351* 13; *Greg Palam* 2; *Gennad* 6–7; *Metr Crit* 3.6–7

III: *Ath* 30–37; *Tol I* 13–15; *Lat 649* 4–5; *Rom Syn* 3; *Sens* 4; *Lat 1215* 2

IV: *Form Conc Epit* 8.8; *Form Conc Sol Dec* 1.43–44; *Sax Vis* 1.2, 2.2; *Fid rat* 1; *Gall* 15; *Belg* 19; *Helv II* 11.6–10

V: *Meth Art* 2; *Cumb Pres* 29; *Arm Ev* 5; *Swed Bap* 4; *Free Meth* 2; *Com Cr* 6; *Naz* 2; *Assem* 13f–g; *Witness* 8; *Un Pres* 12; *Ess* 8; *Bat* 3B; *Menn Con* 1.3; *Leuen* 22; *Hond* 2; *Toraja* 4.2; *Bap Conf* 2b; *Chr Dec* 2–3; *Com Dec* 3

3.10. Hypostatic Union of Two Natures, with Two Wills and Two "Energies" (*see also* 1.9, 3.9)

I: *Edict* 8–12, 19–22, anath 4, 9; *Ecth* 4–6; *Eph* 431 ecth; *Chal* 19–24; *CP II* anath 3–5, 7–9; *CP III* 7–9; *Nic II*

II: *CP 1351* 14

III: *Tol I* anath 13; *Lat 649* 6–16; *Rom Syn* 3; *Flor Arm* 7–9

IV: *Form Conc Epit* 3.3, 3.12–13, 8.1–18; *Form Conc Sol Dec* 8.31–87; *Sax Vis* 1.2, 2.2; *Fid rat* 1; *Gall* 15; *Belg* 19; *Helv II* 11.6–10

V: *Def Plat* 2.7; *Free Meth* 2; *Salv Arm* 4; *Naz* 2; *Un Pres* 12; *Leuen* 22

4. AND WAS CRUCIFIED ON OUR BEHALF UNDER PONTIUS PILATE

4.1. Reconciliation, Redemption, and Atonement

II: *Gennad* 9; *Mogila* 1.50–51

III: *Ath* 38; *Vienne* 1; *Boh I* 6

IV: *17 Art* 9; *Luth Sm Cat* 2.4; *Luth Lg Cat* 2.31; *Aug* 3.3; *Apol Aug* 4.179, 24.22–24, 58–59; *Smal Art* 2.1; *Form Conc Sol Dec* 5.20–22; *67 Art* 54; *Bern* 3; *Fid rat* 3 *Helv I* 11; *Genv Cat* 56–61, 71; *Gall* 17; *Scot I* 9; *Heid* 12–18, 37–39; *Helv II* 11.15; *39 Art* 31; *Remon* 2; *Irish* 30; *Dort* 2; *West* 8.4–7; *West Sh Cat* 25; *18 Diss* 9; *Ries* 13; *Dordrecht* 4; *Marburg* 3; *Trent* 22.2

V: *True Con* 14; *London I* 17–18; *Gen Bap* 17–19; *Cum occas* 5; *Sav* 8.4–7; *Friends I* 6, 10; *Geloof* 13, 15.2; *Meth Art* 2, 20; *Cumb Pres* 31–33; *Aub* 8, 10; *LDS* 3; *Arm Ev* 5; *Swed Bap* 4; *Free Meth* 2, 20; *Adv* 2; *Salv Arm* 6; *Chr Sci* 4; *Com Cr* 6; *Richmond* 2, 6; *Utrecht* 6; *Am Bap* 6; *Lam* 38; *Naz* 2, 6; *Pol Nat* 3; *Assem* 12; *Un Ch Can: Union* 7; *Un Pres* 9, 12, 14; *F&O Laus* 2; *Ess* 8–9; *Br St Luth* 4, 8, 18; *F&O Edin* 1.1; *Bap Assoc* 7; *Bat* 3B; *Un Ch Japan* 2; *Arn* 3d; *Madag* 5; *UCC* 5; *Menn Con* 5.2; *Ref All* 2; *Pres USA* 9.09; *Meth Braz* 2.4; *Un Ref Ch* 17.2; *Leuen* 9; *PRCC* 1b; *RCA* 4; *Toraja* 4.4–5; *Bap Conf* 2b; *Camb Dec* 2

HE SUFFERED AND WAS BURIED

4.2. Events of the Passion: Transfiguration, Crucifixion, Death, and Descent into Hades

I: *Ign*; *Tert*; *Tome* 12–13

II: *CP 1341*; *CP 1351* 46; *Metr Crit* 3.8–11; *Mogila* 1.43–49

III: *Ap* 4; *Ath* 38; *R* 4; *Tol I* 16, anath 6–7; *Sens* 18; *Lat 1215* 2

IV: *Form Conc Epit* 9; *Form Conc Sol Dec* 9; *Genv Cat* 55, 65–70; *Heid* 40–44; *Helv II* 11.10; *39 Art* 3; *West Sh Cat* 2

V: *Geloof* 15.2; *Cumb Pres* 30; *Free Meth* 2; *Chr Sci* 5; *Com Cr* 6; *Richmond* 2; *Naz* 2; *Un Pres* 12; *Masai* 2; *Hond* 2; *Toraja* 4.5

5. AND ROSE UP ON THE THIRD DAY IN ACCORDANCE WITH THE SCRIPTURES

5.1. The Resurrection of Christ (*see also* 11.4)

I: *Polyc*; *Tert*; *Tome* 11; *CP II* anath 12
II: *Metr Crit* 3.12; *Mogila* 1.52–53
III: *Ap* 5; *Ath* 38; *R* 5; *Tol I* 16–17
IV: *Aug* 3.4; *Lu Sm Cat* 2.4; *Lu Lg Cat* 2.31; *Tetrapol* 2; *Bas Bek* 4; *Helv I* 11; *Genv Cat* 73–74; *Scot I* 10; *Heid* 45; *Helv II* 11.11; *39 Art* 4; *West Sh Cat* 28; *Ries* 15
V: *Geloof* 15.3; *Meth Art* 3; *Free Meth* 3; *Chr Sci* 5; *Com Cr* 7; *Richmond* 2; *Am Bap* 7; *Lam* 36–37; *Naz* 2; *Witness* 10; *So Bap* 16; *Un Pres* 12; *Ess* 8; *Bap Assoc* 8; *Bat* 3B; *Madag* 7; *Masai* 2; *Pres USA* 9.26; *RCA* 4; *Hond* 3; *Toraja* 4.6; *Bap Conf* 2b; *Philip UCC* 6

6. AND HE WENT UP INTO THE HEAVENS AND IS SEATED AT THE FATHER'S RIGHT HAND

6.1. The Ascension of Christ into Heaven

II: *Gennad* 10; *Metr Crit* 3.13; *Lucar* 8; *Mogila* 1.55–56
III: *Ap* 6; *Ath* 39; *R* 6; *Tol I* 18; *Tol XI* 17
IV: *Form Conc Sol Dec* 7.93–103; *Genv Cat* 75–82; *Scot I* 11; *Heid* 46–51; *Helv II* 11.12; *39 Art* 4; *Ries* 16; *Tig* 25
V: *Meth Art* 3; *Com Cr* 7; *Richmond* 2; *Am Bap* 7; *Un Pres* 12; *Bap Assoc* 8; *Bat* 3B; *Masai* 2; *RCA* 5; *Toraja* 4.8–9; *Bap Conf* 2b

7. HE IS COMING AGAIN WITH GLORY TO JUDGE THE LIVING AND THE DEAD

7.1. The Second Coming of Christ to Judgment (*see also* 11–12)

I: *Tert*
II: *Gennad* 10; *Jer II* 1.17; *Mogila* 1.57–68

III: *Ap* 7; *Ath* 39–41; *R* 7; *Tol XI* 17; *Sens* 17; *Lat 1215* 2

IV: *Aug* 17; *Apol Aug* 17; *Bas Bek* 10; *Helv I* 11.5; *Genv Cat* 83–87; *Scot I* 11; *Heid* 52; *Helv II* 11.13; *Irish* 104; *West* 33.1; *Ries* 40

V: *Sav* 32.1; *Geloof* 33.3–4, 34.4; *Shkr* 3–4; *Cumb Pres* 114–15; *New Hamp* 18; *Ev All* 8; *Abst Prin* 20; *Swed Bap* 12; *Free Meth* 14; *Adv* 17–18; *Com Cr* 12; *Richmond* 2; *Am Bap* 8; *Naz* 11.14; *Assem* 15; *Witness* 2; *Afr Orth* 13; *So Bap* 17; *Un Ch Can: Union* 19; *Un Pres* 12, 40; *Br St Luth* 42; *Bap Assoc* 22; *Bat* 3B, 18; *Madag* 7; *Masai* 2; *Menn Con* 20; *Leuen* 9; *Laus Cov* 15; *RCA* con; *Toraja* 4.8, 8.2–3; *Bap Conf* 9; *Philip UCC* 6

HIS KINGDOM WILL HAVE NO END

7.2. The Kingdom of Christ and of God

II: *Jer II* 1.5

III: *Tol XI* 18

IV: *Luth Sm Cat* 3.7–8; *Luth Lg Cat* 3.51–58; *Aug* 17.5; *Genv Cat* 37, 42, 268–70; *Heid* 123; *Helv II* 11.14; *Irish* 104; *West Sh Cat* 26, 102; *Ries* 14, 18; *Tig* 4

V: *True Con* 15–16; *London I* 19–20; *Geloof* 16; *Com Cr* 9, 12; *Lam* 52; *Assem* 15; *So Bap* 25; *Un Ch Can: Union* 20; *Un Pres* 12, 37–38, 40, 43–44; *Chin Un* 1; *Meth Kor* 7; *Br St Luth* 42; *Barm* 5; *F&O Edin* 9; *Vat II* 5.1.3–5, 5.1.9–10, 5.1.36; *Pres USA* 9.53–55; *Design* 1.8; *Meth Braz* 2.5; *Korea* pr; *Laus Cov* 15; *PRCC* 4; *Hond* 3; *Pres So Afr* 3; *Toraja* 4.3, 5.2, 6.6; *BEM* 1.7, 2.22; *Philip UCC* 5

7.3. The Kingdoms of This World: Civil Government and Civil Society; Church and State

I: *Edict* 1; *Ecth* con; *CP II* 2; *CP III* 1, 5

II: *CP 1351* con; *Jer II* 1.14, 1.16

III: *Dict Pap* 9, 12, 19, 27; *Unam* 4–6; *Loll* 6, 10; *Prague* 3; *Boh I* 16

IV: *17 Art* 3, 4, 14; *Luth Sm Cat* pr 13, 21–22; *Aug* 16, 28; *Apol Aug* 16; *67 Art* 35–43; *Tetrapol* 23; *Fid rat* 11; *Bas Bek* 8; *Helv I* 26; *Laus Art* 8; *10 Art* pr 1; *Genv Con* 20; *Gall* 39–40; *Scot I* 24; *Belg* 36; *Helv II* 30; *39 Art* 37; *Irish* 57–62; *West* 22–23; *Schleit* 4, 6, 7; *Cologne* 12; *Ries* 37–38; *Dordrecht* 13–15; *Marburg* 12; *Witt Art* 11

V: *True Con* 39–44; *London I* 48–53; *Camb Plat* 17; *Sav* 23–24; *Friends I* 21–22; *Geloof* 28–30; *Meth Art* 23–25; *Cumb Pres* 81–88; *New Hamp* 16; *Swed Bap* 11; *Free Meth* 23; *LDS* 10, 12; *Syl* 20, 23–32, 39–55, 75–77; *Richmond* 12, 14, 15; *Soc Meth*; *Soc Ch*; *So Bap* 18–19; *Un Pres* 31, 37–38; *Ess* 12–13; *Br St Luth* 34; *Barm* pr, 4–5; *Philip Ind* 2.19; *Chin Man*; *Sheng Kung* 2, 6; *Bat* 8.3, 12; *Vat II* 5.3.12, 9.3, 9.6–7, 9.11–15; *Menn Con* 9, 17–19; *Pres USA* 9.43–47; *Meth Braz* 3; *Korea* 2–3; *Laus Cov* 5, 13; *PRCC* 2b, 3e; *RCA* 10–12; *Pres So Afr* 2; *Toraja* 7.5–8; *Bap Conf* 7; *Morav Am* con

8. AND IN THE SPIRIT, THE HOLY, THE LORDLY

8.1. The Divine Person of the Holy Spirit (*see also* 1.8)

I: *Tert; CP I*
II: *CP 1341* 30–31; *Greg Palam* 3; *Mogila* 1.69–70
III: *Ap* 8; *Ath* 23; *R* 8; *Tol I* anath 4; *Tol XI* 3; *Sens* 1–2
IV: *Belg* 11; *Heid* 53; *39 Art* 5; *Cologne* 3
V: *Morav* 3; *Geloof* 4.4, 14.4; *Meth Art* 4; *Free Meth* 4; *Richmond* 3; *Naz* 3; *Pol Nat* 4; *Witness* 9; *Un Ch Can: Union* 8; *Un Pres* 13; *F&O Laus* 1; *Meth Kor* 3; *CSI 1947* 1; *Philip Ind* 1.3; *Bap Assoc* 9; *Madag* 3; *Menn Con* 1.4; *Meth Braz* 2.3; *Laus Cov* 14; *Toraja* 1.5, 4.9, 5.1–3; *Philip UCC* 1

AND LIFE-GIVING ONE

8.2. Life in the Spirit: Conversion, Regeneration, Sanctification, Restoration of the Divine Image, Participation in the Divine Nature

II: *CP 1341* 19, 35–38; *CP 1351* 36–37
III: *Orange* 4, 6
IV: *Luth Sm Cat* 2.6; *Luth Lg Cat* 2.35–45; *Apol Aug* 4.126; *Form Conc Sol Dec* 2.25–27, 3.19–23, 8.34; *Helv I* 11; *Genv Con* 8; *Genv Cat* 88–91; *Gall* 21; *Scot I* 12; *Belg* 24; *Dort* 3/4.11–13; *West* 10, 12–13, 26.3; *West Sh Cat* 29–39; *Denck* 3; *Ries* 19; *Marburg* 6
V: *Sav* 10, 13, 27.1; *Friends I* 1–2, 7–8; *Geloof* 19; *Cumb Pres* 51–54; *New Hamp* 7, 10; *Aub* 12; *Arm Ev* 6; *Ev All* 7; *Abst Prin* 8, 12; *Adv* 5, 14; *Salv Arm* 7, 10; *Richmond* 3, 6; *Naz* 9.10, 10.13; *Assem* 4b, 19; *So Bap* 7, 10; *Un Ch Can: Union* 8–9, 12; *Un Pres* 11, 13, 16, 21; *Br St Luth* 10–16; *F&O Edin* 1.2; *Bap Assoc* 11; *Bat* 3C; *Madag* 3; *UCC* 6; *Masai* 3; *Vat II* 5.1.4; *Menn Con* 6–7; *Zambia* 6; *Ref All* 3; *Pres USA* 9.20; *Design* 1.5; *Meth Braz* 2.3; *Leuen* 10; *RCA* 6–9; *Hond* 3; *Toraja* 5.1–3

8.3. The Gifts of the Holy Spirit; Divine Grace and Human Merit

II: *Metr Crit* 3.14; *Mogila* 1.73–81; *Dosith* decr 3
III: *Orange* 3, 5–7, 12, 18–21, con; *Sens* 5
IV: *Apol Aug* 4.17, 4.19–20, 4.288, 4.316, 4.356–77; *Form Conc Sol Dec* 2.25–27; *Genv Cat* 115; *Lamb Art* 7; *Helv II* 16.11; *Remon* 4; *Irish* 26; *West* 7.3–6; *West Sh Cat* 20; *18 Diss* 16; *Witt Art* 5; *Trent* 6.15–16
V: *Gen Bap* 25–26, 29–33; *Cum occas* 1–4; *Sav* 7.3–5; *Geloof* 17; *Cumb Pres* 39–40; *Aub* 13; *LDS* 4, 7; *Adv* 15–16; *Bonn I* 6; *Naz* 7; *Pol Nat* 5; *Assem* 6; *Un Pres* 13; *Meth Kor* 4; *F&O Edin* 1.1, 1.6; *Bat* 7; *Un Ch Japan* 3; *Vat II* 8.8; *Menn Con* 6–7; *Pres So Afr* 3; *BEM* 1.5; *Camb Dec* 3; *LuRC Just* 19–21, 25–27

8.4. Sanctification as a Life of Love, Christian Service, Virtue, and Good Works

II: *Jer II* 1.2, 1.5, 1.6, 1.20; *Lucar* 13; *Mogila* 1.3; *Dosith* decr 13
III: *Orange* 17; *Sens* 13; *Boh I* 7
IV: *Luth Sm Cat* 1, 9; *Luth Lg Cat* 1; *Aug* 20; *Apol Aug* 4.111–16, 4.122–58, 4.189–94, 20; *Form Conc Epit* 4; *Form Conc Sol Dec* 4; *67 Art* 22; *Tetrapol* 4–6; *10 Art* 3.8–10; *Genv Con* 10; *Genv Cat* 121–27; *Gall* 22; *Scot I* 13–14; *Belg* 24; *Heid* 86–91; *Helv II* 16; *Remon* 5; *Irish* 39–45, 63–67; *West* 16.1–6; *West Sh Cat* 39–84; *18 Diss* 4, 18; *Cologne* 13, 14, 16; *Ries* 22–23; *Dordrecht* 14; *Marburg* 10; *Witt Art* 4, 5; *Trent* 6.11, 6 can 18–21, 24–26, 31–32
V: *Gen Bap* 33–42; *Sav* 16; *Friends I* 13–14, 21; *Geloof* 20.6, 21.1–5, 22.4; *Meth Art* 10–11; *Winch* 3; *Cumb Pres* 55–59; *LDS* 13; *Arm Ev* 8; *Syl* 56–64; *Free Meth* 10–11, 13; *Chr Sci* 6; *Com Cr* 8; *Naz* 10.13; *Assem* 7; *So Bap* 21, 24; *Un Ch Can: Union* 12; *Un Pres* 44; *Br St Luth* 20; *F&O Edin* 2.8–10; *Philip Ind* 2.12; *Sheng Kung* 5; *Bat* 15; *Un Ch Japan* 3; *Masai* 3; *Vat II* 5.1.39–42; *Pres USA* 9.22–25; *Meth Braz* 9; *Leuen* 11; *PRCC* 1c; *RCA* 10–14; *Toraja* 5.5–6; *Bap Conf* 2c, 8; *Morav Am* 7–9; *LuRC Just* 37–39

8.5. Sanctification as Free Obedience to the Law of God
(*see also* 1.13, 3.3, 8.4)

II: *Metr Crit* 6; *Mogila* 1.86–95
III: *Orange* 13
IV: *17 Art* 2; *Luth Sm Cat* pr 17–18, 1; *Luth Lg Cat* 1; *Aug* 6; *Form Conc Epit* 6; *Form Conc Sol Dec* 6; *Genv Con* 3; *Genv Cat* 131–232; *Gall* 23; *Scot I* 15; *Heid* 92–115; *Helv II* 12; *Irish* 84; *West* 19–20; *Witt Art* 5
V: *London I* 29; *Gen Bap* 28; *Cum occas* 1; *Sav* 19, 21; *Meth Art* 6; *Cumb Pres* 37, 66–74; *New Hamp* 12; *Abst Prin* 18; *Adv* 11; *Un Ch Can: Union* 14; *Un Pres* 25; *Bat* 15

PROCEEDING FORTH FROM THE FATHER [AND THE SON]

8.6. The Procession of the Holy Spirit

I: *Tert*
II: *Phot* 8–23; *CP 1054* 3, 4; *Greg Palam* 3; *Mark Eph* 1–2, 6; *Metr Crit* 1.5–31; *Mogila* 1.71
III: *Ath* 23; *Tol XI* 3; *Fréjus* 4; *Lyons*; *Flor Un* 5–9; *Flor Arm* 6
IV: *Smal Art* 1.2; *Form Conc Sol Dec* 8.73; *Gall* 6; *Belg* 9, 11; *39 Art* 5; *Helv II* 3.3; *Irish* 10; *West* 2.3; *West Lg Cat* 10; *Cologne* 3; *Ries* 3
V: *True Con* 2; *Morav* 3; *Geloof* 4.4; *Meth Art* 4; *Free Meth* 4; *Resp Pius IX* 5–7;

Bonn I pr; *Bonn II*; *Richmond* 1; *Witness* 9; *Afr Orth* 2, 5; *Un Ch Can: Union* 8; *Un Pres* 11, 13; *F&O Laus* 4.1; *Philip Ind* 1.3

CO-WORSHIPED AND CO-GLORIFIED WITH FATHER AND SON

8.7. Worship

II: *Lit Chrys*; *Phot* 5, 29–30; *Jer II* 1.13, 1.24, 1.26; *Metr Crit* 9.2–6, 14–16, 18, 22.1–2, 23.9; *Mogila* 1.87–88, 1.93; *Dosith* q 4

III: *Ath* 27; *Tol I* anath 17; *Flor Arm* 27; *Loll* 5; *Boh I* 18

IV: *Luth Lg Cat* 1.79–102; *Aug* 15, 21, 24, 26; *Apol Aug* 4.10–11, 4.155, 15, 24.27–33, 24.81–83, 27.55–56; *Form Conc Epit* 10, *Form Conc Sol Dec* 10; *67 Art* 24–26; *Fid rat* 9; *Tetrapol* 7–10, 21; *Bas Bek* 11; *Helv I* 23–24; *Laus Art* 10; *10 Art* 9; *Genv Con* 13, 17; *Gall* 33; *Genv Cat* 141–42, 163–65, 183; *Helv II* 17, 22, 24.1–7, 27.1–3; *Irish* 49–56, 77; *West* 21; *18 Diss* 4–7, 10; *Denck* 3; *Cologne* 9; *Dordrecht* 11; *Marburg* 13; *Witt Art* 10, 12; *Tig* 26; *Trent* 13.5

V: *True Con* 30–31, 33; *Camb Plat* 1.3; *Gen Bap* 21, 35, 46; *Sav* 22; *Friends I* 17, 20; *Geloof* 23.7; *Meth Art* 15, 22; *Dec Addr* 5, 12–13; *Cumb Pres* 72, 75–80; *New Hamp* 15; *LDS* 11; *Arm Ev* 1, 9; *Resp Pius IX* 5.12; *Def Plat* 1.1, 1.3, 2.1, 2.2, 2.4; *Abst Prin* 17; *Swed Bap* 9–10; *Syl* 78–79; *Free Meth* 15, 19, 21; *Adv* 12–13; *Bonn I* 4; *Com Cr* 11; *Richmond* 10, 16; *Assem* 13j; *Afr Orth* 12; *So Bap* 14; *Un Ch Can: Union* 15, 20; *Un Pres* 28–29; *Ess* 3–6, 11; *Br St Luth* 41; *F&O Edin* 7; *CSI 1947* 1, 5; *Philip Ind* 2.5, 2.8–11; *Munif* 15–20, 23; *Bat* 11, 13, 14, 16; *Arn* 3; *Vat II* 5.3.8, 5.3.23, 5.3.66–67; *Menn Con* 8.4–5, 13–14; *Sri Lanka* 4–5; *CNI* 3; *Ghana* 11; *Ref All* 4; *Pres USA* 9.50; *Meth Braz* 2.11; *Un Ref Ch* 17.1, 17.4; *RCA* 17; *Toraja* 1.2, 6.7; *Camb Dec* 5

8.8. Prayer

II: *CP 1341* 13; *Jer II* 1.13, 1.15; *Metr Crit* 21; *Mogila* 1.92

III: *Orange* 3, 11; *Loll* 7; *Boh I* 2

IV: *17 Art* 3; *Luth Sm Cat* 3, 7–8; *Luth Lg Cat* 3; *67 Art* 44–46; *Tetrapol* 7; *Genv Cat* 233–95; *Heid* 116–29; *Helv II* 23; *Irish* 47–48; *West* 21.3–6; *West Sh Cat* 98–107; *Witt Art* 5

V: *True Con* 45; *Sav* 22.3–6; *Cumb Pres* 76; *Richmond* 11; *Un Ch Can: Union* 13; *Un Pres* 27; *Meth Kor* 4; *Sheng Kung* con; *Vat II* 5.1.15, 5.3.8; *Zambia* 6; *Toraja* 5.4; *Bap Conf* 2a

8.9. Prayer for the Departed (*see also* 12.1)

II: *Lit Chrys* I.D.1; *Jer II* 1.15; *Metr Crit* 20
III: *Loll* 7
IV: *Apol Aug* 24.89–98
V: *Cumb Pres* 76; *Arm Ev* 9; *Bonn I* 13; *Afr Orth* 10; *Vat II* 5.1.50; *Toraja* 8.5

8.10. Images in the Church

I: *Nic II* ecth, anath 1–3
II: *Phot* 43; *Greg Palam* 4; *Metr Crit* 15; *Lucar* q 4; *Dosith* q 4
III: *Loll* 8, 12; *Boh I* 17
IV: *Bern* 8; *Tetrapol* 22; *Laus Art* 7; 10 *Art* 6; *Genv Cat* 143–49; *Heid* 96–98; *Helv II* 4; *Irish* 53; *West Sh Cat* 49–52; 18 *Diss* 7; *Witt Art* 17; *Trent* 25.2; *Trid Prof* 6
V: *Meth Art* 14; *Arm Ev* 9; *Afr Orth* 7; *Madag* 1

THE ONE WHO SPOKE THROUGH THE PROPHETS

8.11. The Authority of Scripture as the Word of God
(*see also* 1.4, 8.12, 9.6, 9.8)

I: *Chal* 25
II: *Gennad* 12.1; *Jer II* 1 int; *Metr Crit* 7.6, 7.9; *Lucar* 2, q 1–2; *Mogila* 1.54, 1.72; *Dosith* decr 2, q 1–2
III: *Tol I* anath 8; *Prague* 1; *Boh I* 1
IV: *Form Conc Epit* int 3; *Form Conc Sol Dec* int 1–8; *Tetrapol* 1; *Helv I* 1, 5; *Genv Con* 1; *Genv Cat* 300–306; *Scot I* 5, 19; *Belg* 5; *Helv II* 1, 13.2; 39 *Art* 6; *West* 1.4–6; *West Sh Cat* 3; 18 *Diss* 8, 11–12
V: *True Con* 7–8; *London I* 7–8; *Gen Bap* 46; *Sav* 1.4–6; *Friends I* 3; *Geloof* 2, 14.3; *Meth Art* 5–6; *Winch* 1; *Dec Addr* 4; *Cumb Pres* 2, 68; *LDS* 8–9; *Arm Ev* 3; *Abst Prin* 1; *Swed Bap* 1; *Free Meth* 5–6; *Vat I* 3.pr; *Adv* 3, 6–7; *Bonn I* 2–3; *Salv Arm* 1; *Chr Sci* 1; *Com Cr* 5; *Lamb Quad* 1; *Richmond* 4; *Naz* 4; *Sacr ant* 3; *Afr Orth* 1; *So Bap* pr 4, 1; *Un Ch Can: Union* pr, 2; *Un Pres* 3, 26; *Chin Un* 2; *Meth Kor* 5; *Br St Luth* 2; *CSI* 1947 1; *Philip Ind* 2.2; *Munif* 12; *Bat* 4; *Un Ch Japan* 1; *Arn* 4; *Madag* pr 2, art 4; *Vat II* 8.7– 10, 8.21–26; *Menn Con* pr, 2.1; *Sri Lanka* 3; *CNI* 2; *Ghana* 3.2; *Zambia* 2–3; *Pres USA* 9.27–28; *Design* 1.7; *Meth Braz* 1.1; *Un Ref Ch* 12; *Leuen* 4; *Laus Cov* 2; *RCA* 1; *Toraja* 2.3, 2.6; *Bap Conf* 1; *Philip UCC* 4; *Morav Am* 3; *Camb Dec* 1

8.12. The Authority of Church and Tradition (*see also* 1.4, 8.11, 9.6, 9.8)

I: *Iren; CP II* 7; *Nic II*

II: *Phot* 5; *Jer II* 1.26; *Metr Crit* 7.5, 7.10, 14.1–4; *Dosith* decr 2, 12

III: *Rom Syn* 4; *Boh I* 15

IV: *Aug* 26, *Apol Aug* pr 11, 4.393, 15.1–4; *Smal Art* 3.15; *Form Conc Sol Dec* 2.52; 67 *Art* 11, 16; *Bern* 2; *Tetrapol* 14; *Helv I* 3–4; *Gall* 5; *Belg* 7; *Helv II* 2.2, 2.5; 39 *Art* 34; *Scot II*; *Irish* 6; *Trent* 4.1; *Trid Prof* 2

V: *Dec Addr* 11; *Resp Pius IX* 17; *Vat I* 3.2, 4.4; *Bonn I* 9.1; *Utrecht* 1; *Lam* 1–8; *Sacr ant* 10–11; *Afr Orth* 1; *F&O Laus* 3A; *Ess* 10; *CSI* 1947 1; *Munif* 12; *Vat II* 5.1.20–21, 8.7–10, 8.24, 9.1, 9.14; *Com Dec* 2; *Ad tuendam* 4

8.13. The Canon of Scripture

II: *Metr Crit* 7.6–8; *Lucar* q 3; *Dosith* q 3

III: *Tol I* anath 12

IV: *Gall* 3–4; *Belg* 4, 6; *Helv II* 1.9; 39 *Art* 6; *Irish* 2–3; *West* 1.2–3; *Trent* 4.1

V: *Sav* 1.2–3; *Geloof* 2.3; *Meth Art* 5; *Cumb Pres* 1; *Free Meth* 5; *Vat I* 3.2, 3 can 2.4; *Bonn I* 1; *Vat II* 8.8; *Sri Lanka* 3.3; *RCA* 7; *Toraja* 2.3

8.14. The Inspiration and Inerrancy of Scripture

II: *Gennad* 12.2

IV: *Belg* 3; *West* 1.8

V: *Gen Bap* 46; *Sav* 1.8; *Geloof* 2.3–4; *Cumb Pres* 1; *New Hamp* 1; *Arm Ev* 3; *Ev All* 1; *Abst Prin* 1; *Syl* 7; *Vat I* 3.2; *Salv Arm* 1; *Am Bap* 1, 3; *Lam* 9–19; *Naz* 4; *Assem* 1; *So Bap* 1; *Un Pres* 3, 13; *Ess* 7; *Br St Luth* 1, 3; *Bap Assoc* 2–3; *Un Ch Japan* 1; *Vat II* 5.3.21, 8.7–8, 8.11, 8.14, 8.20; *Menn Con* 2.1; *Pres USA* 9.29; *Laus Cov* 2; *RCA* 6; *Toraja* 2.7; *Bap Conf* 1, 2c; *Philip UCC* 4; *Camb Dec* 1

8.15. Criteria of Scriptural Interpretation

I: *Orig* 8; *Tome* 1–2

II: *Dosith* decr 2

IV: *Apol Aug* 24.35; *Helv I* 2; *Scot I* 18; *Helv II* 2; *Irish* 5; *West* 1.7–10; 18 *Diss* 8, 10; *Denck* 1; *Trent* 4.2; *Trid Prof* 2

V: *True Con* 34; *Sav* 1.7–10; *Cumb Pres* 3–4; *Ev All* 2; *Syl* 22; *Vat I* 3.2; *Richmond* 4; *Lam* 1–8; *Sacr ant* 10; *Munif* 26; *Vat II* 8.10, 8.12; *Zambia* 9; *Pres USA* 9.29–30; *Leuen* 39; *Toraja* 2.5

9. IN ONE

9.1. Unity, Union, and Reunion with the Church of Christ

II: *Metr Crit* 7.2; *Mogila* 1.82–83
III: *Unam* 2–3; *Flor Un; Flor Arm; Boh I* 8
IV: *Aug* 7.2–4; *Apol Aug* 7/8.30–46; *Bas Bek* 5; *Helv II* 17.2–4; *Dordrecht* int
V: *Friends I* 9; *Geloof* 23.2; *Dec Addr* 1; *Vat I* 4 pr; *Lamb Quad* 4; *Pol Nat* 6, 9; *So Bap* 22; *Un Pres* 22, 32, 35; *F&O Laus* 1; *Br St Luth* 29; *Barm* pr; *F&O Edin* 1 pr, 2.1–10; *CSI 1947* 7–8; *Philip Ind* 2.18; *Bat* 8D; *Madag* 6; *Sri Lanka* 1, 11; *CNI* 4; *Ghana* 1; *Meth Braz* 1.4, 2.7; *Leuen* 1, 29–49; *Laus Cov* 7; *Balamand* 6–18; *Chr Dec* 8–10; *BEM* 1.15–16; *Morav Am* 5; *Com Dec* 5–6

9.2. Schism, Separation, and Division

II: *Phot; CP 1054*
III: *Flor Un*
IV: *Apol Aug* 23.59; *Helv I* 25; *Helv II* 17.10; *Schleit* 4
V: *True Con* 36; *London I* 46; *Camb Plat* 13.5, 14.9; *Dec Addr* 2, 10–11; *Resp Pius IX* 9; *Syl* 18, 38; *F&O Laus* 1; *Br St Luth* 28; *F&O Edin* 2.3–5; *Bat* 8.1; *Vat II* 5.1.15, 5.3.1, 5.3.3; *Pres USA* 9.34; *Morav Am* 5–6

HOLY

9.3. The Holiness of the Church and of the Means of Grace

II: *Jer II* 1.8
III: *Ap* 9; *R* 9; *Loll* 1; *Prague* 4; *Boh I* 11
IV: *Luth Lg Cat* 5.15–19; *Aug* 8; *Apol Aug* 7/8.47–50; *Genv Cat* 96, 99; *Gall* 28; *Helv II* 1.4, 18.21, 19.12; *39 Art* 26; *Irish* 70; *West* 27.3; *Witt Conc* 3; *Trent* 7 can 1.12
V: *Geloof* 23.3, 8; *Un Ch Can: Union* 18; *Sheng Kung* 4; *Bat* 8B; *Vat II* 5.1.8, 5.1.39–42

9.4. Church Discipline (*see also* 10.10)

III: *Boh I* 14
IV: *17 Art* 16; *Aug* 26.33–39; *Apol Aug* 15.45–48; *Smal Art* 3.7, 3.9; *Form Conc Epit* 4.17–18; *67 Art* 31–32; *Bas Bek* 7; *Genv Con* 19; *Belg* 29, 32; *Heid* 83–85; *Helv II* 18.15, 20; *39 Art* 33; *Irish* 73; *West* 30; *Schleit* 2; *Cologne* 7; *Ries* 35–36; *Dordrecht* 16–17
V: *True Con* 23–25; *London I* 42–43; *Camb Plat* 14; *Gen Bap* 55–56, 67–72; *Geloof* 27; *Bat* 8D, 9.4; *Vat II* 5.3.6; *Menn Con* 8.3

CATHOLIC

9.5. Catholicity of the Church

I: *Iren*
II: *Mogila* 1.84; *Dosith* decr 10
III: *Ap* 9
IV: *Genv Cat* 97; *Belg* 27; *Helv II* 17.2; *West* 25.1
V: *Camb Plat* 2.1; *Sav* 26.1–2; *Geloof* 23.4; *Un Pres* 32; *Sheng Kung* 4; *Madag* 6; *Vat II* 5.1.13; *Toraja* 6.13

AND APOSTOLIC

9.6. Apostolic Authority in the Church (*see also* 1.4, 8.11–12, 9.8)

II: *Jer II* 1.int
III: *Dict Pap; Sens* 12; *Unam* 3, 7–8; *Flor Un* 14–15
IV: *Helv I* 16; *Helv II* 17.6–8; *39 Art* 20; *Scot II; Irish* 79–80
V: *Gen Bap* 51; *Cumb Pres* 108–11; *LDS* 5; *Resp Pius IX* 11–14; *Ineff; Syl* 21–23, 33; *Vat I* 4.4; *Utrecht* 1–2, 4; *Lam* 55–56; *Sacr ant* 1; *Afr Orth* 3; *Br St Luth* 30; *Barm* 4; *Munif* 12; *Bat* 3B3, 8.2; *Vat II* 5.1.12, 5.1.25; *Pres USA* 9.10

9.7. Apostolic Church Order and Polity; Hierarchy (*see also* 10.12)

II: *Jer II* 1.14, 1.28; *Metr Crit* 11.5–7, 11.9, 23.7–8; *Mogila* 1.84–85; *Dosith* decr 10
III: *Dict Pap; Boh I* 9
IV: *17 Art* pr; *Aug* 5, 14, 28; *Apol Aug* 14, 28; *Helv I* 15, 17, 19; *Laus Art* 5; *Genv Cat* 307–8; *Gall* 25–26, 29–32; *Belg* 30–32; *Helv II* 18; *39 Art* 23; *Irish* 71; *Schleit* 5; *Cologne* 10–11; *Ries* 25–28; *Dordrecht* 9; *Witt Art* 9; *Trent* 23 can 7
V: *True Con* 19–27; *London I* 44–45; *Camb Plat* 1, 4, 6, 7, 8; *Sav* con 1–30; *Dec Addr* 3; *Cumb Pres* 108–9; *LDS* 6; *Resp Pius IX* 6; *Vat I* 4.1–3; *Bonn I* 9.2; *Lamb Quad* 4; *Un Ch Can: Union* 17–18, con; *Un Pres* 33; *F&O Laus* 5; *CSI 1947* 3–4, 6; *Philip Ind* 2.6; *Bat* 11; *Vat II* 5.1.10, 5.1.18–29; *Sri Lanka* 7; *Ghana* 5.2; *Pres USA* 9.38–40; *BEM* 3.34–38

9.8. Authority of Church Councils and Synods
(*see also* 1.4, 8.11–12, 9.7, Index B)

I: *Eph 431* can 7; *CP II* 4, 5, con; *Nic II*
II: *Phot* 40–44; *Greg Palam* 6–7; *Mark Eph* 4; *Jer II* 1.int, 1.29; *Metr Crit* 15.4; *Mogila* 1.4–5; *Dosith* decr 12

III: *Lat 649* 17, 20; *Dict Pap* 4, 16, 25

IV: *Smal Art* pr 1, 10–13; *Scot I* 20; *Helv II* 2.4; *39 Art* 21; *Irish* 76; *West* 31; *18 Diss* pr; *Trid Prof* 8

V: *Camb Plat* 16; *Resp Pius IX* 3, 5; *Syl* 23, 35–36; *Vat I* 3 pr, 4.4; *Utrecht* 1, 5; *Lam* 31; *Afr Orth* 1; *Philip Ind* 2.17; *Vat II* 5.1.22, 5.1.25; *Camb Dec* pr, 1

CHURCH

9.9. Definition of the True Church

II: *Jer II* 1.7, 1.8; *Metr Crit* 7; *Lucar* 10–12; *Mogila* 1.82–96; *Dosith* decr 10–12
III: *Ap* 9; *Tol XI* 18; *Unam* 1; *Boh I* 8
IV: *Luth Sm Cat* 2.6; *Luth Lg Cat* 2.47–56; *Aug* 7; *Apol Aug* 7/8.5–29; *Smal Art* 3.12; *67 Art* 8; *Tetrapol* 15; *Fid rat* 6; *Bas Bek* 5; *Helv I* 14; *Laus Art* 3; *Genv Con* 18; *Genv Cat* 93–95; *Gall* 27; *Scot I* 5, 16, 18; *Belg* 27, 29; *Heid* 54–55; *Helv II* 17; *39 Art* 19; *Irish* 68–69; *West* 25–26; *Ries* 24; *Dordrecht* 8; *Trid Prof* 7
V: *True Con* 17–18; *Camb Plat* 2–3; *Sav* 26–27; *Friends I* 16; *Morav* 3–4; *Meth Art* 13; *Shkr* 3; *Dec Addr* 1; *Cumb Pres* 93–97; *New Hamp* 13; *Arm Ev* 11; *Abst Prin* 14; *Swed Bap* 9; *Syl* 19; *Free Meth* 16; *Vat I* 3.3; *Com Cr* 10; *Richmond* 2; *Am Bap* 10–12; *Lam* 52–57; *Pol Nat* 6–8; *Assem* 8; *Witness* 1; *So Bap* 12; *Un Ch Can: Union* 15; *Un Pres* 32; *F&O Laus* 3; *Meth Kor* 6; *Br St Luth* 24–30; *Barm* 3; *F&O Edin* 1.4; *CSI 1947* 4; *Philip Ind* 1.4; *Chin Man*; *Bap Assoc* 15–19; *Bat* 8D; *Un Ch Japan* 4; *Arn* 6–7; *UCC* 7; *Vat II* 5.1; *Menn Con* pr, 8.1; *Sri Lanka* 2; *Ghana* 2; *Zambia* 7; *Pres USA* 9.31–33; *Design* 2; *Togo* 4; *Un Ref Ch* 17.4; *Laus Cov* 6; *PRCC* 1c; *RCA* 15–19; *Toraja* 6; *Bap Conf* 6; *Philip UCC* 3

10. WE CONFESS ONE BAPTISM FOR THE FORGIVING OF SINS

10.1. Word, Sacraments, and Means of Grace

II: *Jer II* 1.7, 1.13; *Metr Crit* 5; *Lucar* 15; *Mogila* 1.97–101; *Dosith* decr 10, 15
III: *Flor Arm* 10–20; *Boh I* 11
IV: *Luth Sm Cat* 4.10; *Luth Lg Cat* 4.21–22, 5.10–14; *Aug* 7.2, 13.1–3; *Apol Aug* 13, 24.69; *67 Art* 14; *Tetrapol* 16; *Fid rat* 7, 10; *Helv I* 16, 19–20; *Laus Art* 4; *Genv Con* 14; *Genv Cat* 309–20; *Gall* 34; *Scot I* 21–22; *Belg* 33; *Heid* 65–68; *Helv II* 17.7, 19, 25; *39 Art* 25; *Irish* 85–88; *West* 21.5, 27; *West Sh Cat* 88–93; *Ries* 17, 30; *Witt Art* 8; *Tig* 2, 6–20; *Trent* 5.2.9–10, 7, 13.3; *Trid Prof* 3
V: *True Con* 35; *Gen Bap* 47–52; *Sav* 28; *Meth Art* 16; *Cumb Pres* 25, 40–41, 98; *Arm Ev* 11; *Syl* 65–66; *Free Meth* 17; *Bonn I* 8; *Com Cr* 11; *Lamb Quad* 3; *Richmond* 10; *Lam* 39–51; *Afr Orth* 8; *Un Ch Can: Union* 16; *Un Pres* 16, 26, 30; *F&O Laus* 6; *Br St*

Luth 21–23; *F&O Edin* 1.5; *CSI* 1947 2; *Philip Ind* 2.4; *Bat* 8D, 9.2, 10; *Un Ch Japan* 4; *Arn* 2b; *UCC* 7; *Masai* 3; *Vat II* 5.1.11; *Sri Lanka* 5; *Ghana* 4; *Zambia* 6, 8; *Pres USA* 9.48–52; *Leuen* 13; *RCA* 15–16; *Toraja* 2.4–5, 6.8–11; *Morav Am* 1

10.2 Baptism

I: *Did; Just; Hipp*

II: *Jer II* 1.3, 1.7, 1.9; *Metr Crit* 5.2–3, 7.10, 8.2; *Lucar* 16; *Mogila* 1.102–4; *Dosith* decr 16

III: *Tol I* anath 18; *Orange* 8, 13; *Tol XI* 18; *Petr Ab* 3; *Lat 1215* 3; *Vienne* 3; *Flor Arm* 14; *Boh I* 12

IV: *17 Art* 5; *Luth Sm Cat* 4; *Luth Lg Cat* 4; *Aug* 9; *Apol Aug* 2.35–45, 9.1–3; *Smal Art* 3.5; *Sax Vis* 1.3, 2.3; *Tetrapol* 17; *Bas Bek* 5; *Helv I* 21; *10 Art* 2; *Genv Con* 15; *Genv Cat* 323–39; *Gall* 28, 35, 38; *Scot I* 21; *Belg* 34; *Heid* 69–74; *Helv II* 20; *39 Art* 27; *Irish* 89–91; *West* 28; *West Sh Cat* 94; *18 Diss* 8–9; *Denck* 2; *Schleit* 1; *Cologne* 5; *Ries* 31–32; *Dordrecht* 7; *Marburg* 9; *Witt Art* 3; *Trent* 7 can 1.9, 7 can 2.1–14

V: *London I* 39–41; *Camb Plat* 12.7; *Sav* 29; *Friends I* 18; *Morav* 4; *Geloof* 25; *Meth Art* 17; *Cumb Pres* 99–103; *New Hamp* 14; *LDS* 4; *Arm Ev* 11; *Ev All* 9; *Def Plat* 1.4, 2.5; *Abst Prin* 15; *Free Meth* 18; *Adv* 4; *Com Cr* 11; *Lamb Quad* 3; *Richmond* 8; *Lam* 42–43; *Naz* 13.18; *Assem* 11; *So Bap* 13; *Un Ch Can: Union* 16.1; *Un Pres* 30; *F&O Laus* 6; *Ess; Br St Luth* 21; *CSI* 1947 2; *Philip Ind* 2.4.2; *Bap Assoc* 12, 21; *Bat* 10A; *Masai* 3; *Vat II* 5.1.7, 5.1.40, 5.3.22; *Menn Con* 11; *Sri Lanka* 2, 5.1; *Pres USA* 9.36, 9.51; *Design* 1.4; *Un Ref Ch* 14; *Leuen* 14; *RCA* 18; *Toraja* 6.8–10; *Bap Conf* 6; *BEM* 1.1–23; *Chr Dec* 7; *LuRC Just* 28

10.3. The Mode and the Subject of Baptism

I: *Did; Hipp*

II: *Mogila* 1.103; *Dosith* decr 16

III: *Vienne* 3; *Boh I* 12

IV: *Luth Lg Cat* 4.47–86; *Apol Aug* 9.2–3; *Smal Art* 3.5.4; *Form Conc Epit* 11.6–8; *Form Conc Sol Dec* 12.11–13; *Sax Vis* 2.3.6; *Tetrapol* 17; *Fid rat* 7; *Bas Bek* 12; *10 Art* 2.2–4; *Genv Con* 15; *Genv Cat* 333–39; *Gall* 35; *Scot I* 23; *Belg* 34; *Heid* 74; *Helv II* 20.6; *39 Art* 27.2; *Irish* 90; *West* 28.3–4; *West Sh Cat* 95; *18 Diss* 8; *Ries* 31; *Marburg* 14; *Witt Conc* 4; *Witt Art* 3; *Trent* 5.4, 7 can 2.13–14

V: *True Con* 35; *London I* 39–41; *Sav* 29.3–4; *Gen Bap* 48; *Geloof* 25.2, 5–6; *Meth Art* 17; *Cumb Pres* 26, 102–3; *New Hamp* 14; *LDS* 4; *Resp Pius IX* 5.11; *Def Plat* 2.5–6; *Abst Prin* 15; *Swed Bap* 8; *Free Meth* 18; *Adv* 4; *Com Cr* 11; *Lam* 43; *Naz* 13.18; *Un Ch Can: Union* 16.1; *Un Pres* 30; *Bap Assoc* 12; *Bat* 10A; *Menn Con* 11; *Pres USA* 9.51; *Un Ref Ch* 14; *Leuen* 15–16, 18–20; *Toraja* 6.10; *Bap Conf* 6; *BEM* 1.11–12

10.4. Confirmation/Chrismation

II: *Phot 6–7, 32; Jer II 1.3, 1.7; Metr Crit 8; Mogila 1.104–5*
III: *Flor Arm 15*
IV: *Apol Aug 13.6; Genv Cat pr; Trent 7 can 1.9, 7 can 3.1–3*
V: *Lam 44; Philip Ind 2.4.3; Sri Lanka 5.1; BEM 1.14; Chr Dec 7*

10.5. The Eucharist/Lord's Supper

II: *Jer II 1.7, 1.10, 1.13; Metr Crit 5.2–3, 9.1–13; Lucar 17; Mogila 1.106–7; Dosith* decr 17

III: *Brngr 1059; Brngr 1079; Lat 1215 3; Flor Arm 16; Wyclif; Boh I 13*

IV: *Luth Sm Cat 6; Luth Lg Cat 5; Aug 10; Apol Aug 10; Smal Art 3.6; Form Conc Epit 7; Form Conc Sol Dec 7; Sax Vis 1.1; Tetrapol 18; Fid rat 8; Bas Bek 6; Helv I 22; 10 Art 4; Genv Con 16; Genv Cat 340–73; Gall 36; Belg 35; Heid 75–82; Helv II 21; 39 Art 28; Irish 92–100; West 29; West Sh Cat 96–97; Denck 3; Schleit 3; Cologne 6; Ries 33–34; Dordrecht 10; Marburg 15; Trent 13*

V: *True Con 35; Camb Plat 12.7; Sav 30; Friends I 19; Morav 4; Geloof 26; Meth Art 18; Cumb Pres 104–7; New Hamp 14; Arm Ev 11; Ev All 9; Abst Prin 16; Free Meth 19; Com Cr 11; Lamb Quad 3; Richmond 9; Lam 45, 49; Naz 14.19; Assem 10; So Bap 13; Un Ch Can: Union 16.2; Un Pres 30; F&O Laus 6; Br St Luth 21; CSI 1947 2; Philip Ind 2.4.5, 2.5; Bap Assoc 13; Bat 10B; Arn 1–8; Menn Con 12; Sri Lanka 5.2; Pres USA 9.36; Design 1.6; Un Ref Ch 15; RCA 19; Toraja 6.9,11; Bap Conf 6; BEM 2.1–33*

10.6. The Real Presence of the Body and Blood of Christ

II: *Dosith decr 17*
III: *Brngr 1059; Brngr 1079; Lat 1215 3; Boh I 13*
IV: *17 Art 6; Luth Sm Cat 6.2; Luth Lg Cat 5.8–14; Aug 10; Apol Aug 10; Form Conc Epit 7.6–20; Form Conc Sol Dec 7.45–58; Sax Vis 1.1.1–6, 2.1.6; Bern 4; Fid rat 8; Genv Cat 354–55; Gall 37; Belg 35; Helv II 21.4, 10; Irish 94–96; Marburg 15; Witt Conc 1; Witt Art 6; Tig 21–22; Trent 13.1, 13 can 1, 3–4; Trid Prof 5*
V: *Cumb Pres 105; Def Plat 1.5, 2.9; Utrecht 6; Afr Orth 9; F&O Laus 6; Bat 10B; Arn 4; Leuen 19; BEM 2.14–15, 2.32*

10.7. Change of the Eucharistic Elements into the Body and Blood of Christ

II: *Lit Chrys II.F.5; Jer II 1.10; Metr Crit 9.11; Mogila 1.107; Dosith decr 17*
III: *Brngr 1059; Brngr 1079; Lat 1215 3; Flor Un 10; Flor Arm 16; Loll 4*

IV: *Smal Art* 3.6.5; *Form Conc Epit* 7.22; *Form Conc Sol Dec* 7.108; *Scot I* 21; *Helv II* 19.9–10; *39 Art* 28.2; *Irish* 93; *West* 29.6; *Marburg*; *Witt Conc* 2; *Tig* 24; *Trent* 13.4, 13 can 2; *Trid Prof* 5

V: *Sav* 30.6; *Meth Art* 18; *Cumb Pres* 105; *Free Meth* 19; *Afr Orth* 9; *Arn* 5a

10.8. The Lord's Supper as Memorial and Communion

II: *Jer II* 1.22; *Metr Crit* 9.9–10; *Mogila* 1.107; *Dosith* decr 17
III: *Prague* 2
IV: *Aug* 22; *Apol Aug* 22; *Smal Art* 3.6.2–4; *Form Conc Epit* 7.24; *Form Conc Sol Dec* 7.110; *Genv Cat* 351–52; *Helv II* 21.2, 12; *39 Art* 30; *Irish* 97; *West* 29.2, 4; *18 Diss* 6–7; *Denck* 3; *Marburg* 15; *Witt Art* 12–13; *Trent* 21.1–3, 21 can 1–3; *Trid Prof* 5

V: *Gen Bap* 53; *Sav* 30.2, 4; *Meth Art* 19; *Cumb Pres* 104–5; *Resp Pius IX* 5.12; *Def Plat* 2.8; *Abst Prin* 16; *Utrecht* 6; *Naz* 14.19; *So Bap* 13; *Un Ch Can: Union* 16.2; *Un Pres* 30; *Vat II* 5.1.26, 5.3.2; *Pres USA* 9.52; *Bap Conf* 6; *Chr Dec* 8; *BEM* 2.5–13, 2.19–22

10.9. The Sacrifice of the Mass

II: *Mogila* 1.107; *Dosith* decr 17
III: *Flor Un* 11
IV: *Aug* 24; *Apol Aug* 24.9–77; *Smal Art* 2.2; *Form Conc Epit* 7.23; *67 Art* 18; *Bern* 5; *Tetrapol* 19; *Genv Con* 16; *Genv Cat* 350; *Scot I* 22; *Heid* 80; *Helv II* 21.13; *Irish* 99–100; *West* 30.2; *18 Diss* 5; *Witt Art* 12; *Trent* 22.1–9, 22 can 1–9; *Trid Prof* 5

V: *Sav* 30.2; *Meth Art* 20; *Free Meth* 20; *Bonn I* 14; *Utrecht* 6; *Bat* 3B2, 10B; *Arn* 5b; *Vat II* 5.1.3; *Chr Dec* 7; *BEM* 2.8

10.10. Penance/Repentance: Contrition, Confession, Absolution, Satisfaction

II: *Jer II* 1.4, 5, 7, 11–12, 25; *Metr Crit* 5.2–3, 10.1–4; *Mogila* 1.90, 1.112–14
III: *Flor Arm* 17; *Loll* 9; *Boh I* 5, 14
IV: *17 Art* 2, 7–9; *Luth Sm Cat* 5; *Luth Lg Cat* 6; *Aug* 11, 12, 25; *Apol Aug* 4.258–68, 4.272–74, 11, 12.11–12, 12.13–17, 35–38, 41, 98–177; *Smal Art* 3.3.1–8, 3.3.15–18, 3.3.39–45; *Form Conc Sol Dec* 5.7; *10 Art* 3; *Tetrapol* 20; *Laus Art* 6; *Genv Cat* 128; *Helv II* 14; *Irish* 74; *West* 15; *West Sh Cat* 87; *Dordrecht* 6; *Marburg* 11; *Witt Conc* 4; *Witt Art* 4, 7; *Trent* 14.1.1–9, 14 can 1.1–15

V: *Camb Plat* 12.5–7; *Gen Bap* 44–45; *Sav* 15; *Geloof* 19.3, 27.2–10; *Meth Art* 12; *Cumb Pres* 42–44; *New Hamp* 8; *LDS* 4; *Def Plat* 1.2, 2.3; *Abst Prin* 9; *Swed Bap* 5; *Bonn I* 11–12; *Salv Arm* 7; *Lam* 43, 46–47; *Naz* 8; *So Bap* 8; *Un Ch Can: Union* 10; *Un Pres* 18; *Philip Ind* 2.4.4; *Camb Dec* 6

10.11. The Anointing of the Sick/Extreme Unction

II: *Jer II* 1.7; *Metr Crit* 13; *Mogila* 1.117–19
III: *Flor Arm* 18
IV: *Apol Aug* 13.6; *Trent* 14.2, 14 can 2.1–4
V: *Lam* 48; *Friends I* 19; *Philip Ind* 2.4.6

10.12. Holy Orders/Ordination; Ordained Ministry and Priesthood (*see also* 9.7)

II: *Jer II* 1.7, 1.14; *Metr Crit* 11; *Mogila* 1.89, 1.108–11
III: *Flor Arm* 19; *Loll* 2; *Boh I* 9
IV: *Apol Aug* 13.12, 24.52–55; *Smal Art* 3.10; *67 Art* 61–63; *Tetrapol* 13; *Genv Con* 20; *Helv II* 18.8, 18.10–11; *39 Art* 36; *18 Diss* 12; *Trent* 7 can 1.9, 23.1–4, 23 can 1–8
V: *True Con* 19–27; *London I* 44–45; *Camb Plat* 9; *Gen Bap* 58–67, 73; *Sav* con 15; *Friends I* 16; *Geloof* 24; *Ev All* 9; *Syl* 30–32; *Lam* 50; *Assem* 9; *So Bap* 12; *Un Ch Can: Union* 17; *Un Pres* 34; *F&O Laus* 5; *Ess* 11; *Br St Luth* 31–33; *CSI 1947* 3–4, 6; *Philip Ind* 2.4.7, 2.6; *Bat* 9; *Vat II* 5.1.18–29; *Menn Con* 10; *Sri Lanka* 1, 6–8; *Ghana* 5; *Pres USA* 9.38–40; *Design* 1.7; *Toraja* 6.12; *BEM* 3.7–25, 3.39–50

10.13. Clerical Celibacy

II: *Phot* 5, 31; *CP 1054* 3; *Jer II* 1.23; *Metr Crit* 11.6
III: *Loll* 3; *Prague* 4; *Boh I* 9, 19
IV: *Aug* 23; *Apol Aug* 23; *Smal Art* 3.11; *67 Art* 28–30; *Bern* 9–10; *Helv I* 27; *Helv II* 29; *39 Art* 32; *Irish* 64; *Witt Art* 14; *Trent* 24.9
V: *Meth Art* 21; *Philip Ind* 2.7; *Vat II* 5.1.29, 5.1.42

10.14. Asceticism and Monasticism

II: *Jer II* 1.16, 1.20, 1.27; *Metr Crit* 19
III: *Loll* 11
IV: *Aug* 27; *Apol Aug* 27; *Smal Art* 3.14; *Tetrapol* 12; *Helv II* 18.7; *Witt Art* 15
V: *Sav* 23.6; *Vat II* 5.1.43–47, 5.3.15

10.15. Matrimony; Christian Marriage and the Family

II: *Jer II* 1.7; *Metr Crit* 12; *Mogila* 1.115–16
III: *Tol I* 16; *Flor Arm* 20

IV: *Luth Lg Cat* 1.200–221; *Apol Aug* 13.14–15; *Helv I* 27; *Laus Art* 9; *Helv II* 29.2–4; *Irish* 64; *West* 24; *Cologne* 8; *Ries* 39; *Dordrecht* 12; *Trent* 7.1.1–2, 24 decr

V: *Sav* 25; *Geloof* 31; *Cumb Pres* 89–92; *Syl* 65–74; *Richmond* 13; *Lam* 51; *Un Pres* 36; *Philip Ind* 2.4.8; *Vat II* 5.1.35, 9.5; *Menn Con* 16; *Sri Lanka* 9; *Pres USA* 9.47; *RCA* 13; *Toraja* 7.9

11. WE LOOK FORWARD TO A RESURRECTION OF THE DEAD

11.1. The Eschatological Hope (*see also* 7.1)

II: *Mogila* 1.120–24
III: *R* 11
IV: *Ries* 40; *Dordrecht* 18; *Trent* 6 can 26
V: *Morav* 5–6; *LDS* 10; *Syl* 17; *Adv* 8–10; *Pol Nat* 11–12; *Assem* 14; *Witness* 4, 6; *Meth Kor* 8; *UCC* 8; *Masai* 3; *Vat II* 5.1.48–51, 5.1.68; *Menn Con* 20; *Un Ref Ch* 17.5; *RCA* 21; *Bap Conf* 9

11.2. Final Preservation and Perseverance

III: *Boh I* 20
IV: *Remon* 5; *Dort* 5; *West* 17, 18.2–3; *Trent* 6.13, 6 can 16, 22–23
V: *London I* 23, 26; *Gen Bap* 43; *Sav* 17; *Friends I* 15; *Geloof* 22; *Cumb Pres* 60–61; *New Hamp* 11; *Abst Prin* 13; *So Bap* 11; *Un Pres* 23–24; *Bap Assoc* 15; *LuRC Just* 34–36

11.3. Antichrist

II: *Metr Crit* pr 3, 10.4, 23.2–4
III: *Boh I* 8
IV: *Apol Aug* 7/8.4, 15.18–19, 23.25; *Smal Art* 2.4.10–11; *Irish* 80; *West* 25.6
V: *True Con* 28; *Sav* 26.4–5; *Shkr* 3–4; *Adv* 13; *Br St Luth* 43; *Laus Cov* 15

11.4. The General Resurrection (*see also* 5.1)

II: *Gennad* 11
III: *Ap* 11; *Tol I* 20, anath 10; *Tol XI* 17; *Petr Ab* 4; *Lat 1215* 2
IV: *Luth Lg Cat* 2.60; *Form Conc Sol Dec* 1.46–47; *Genv Cat* 106–10; *Belg* 37; *Heid* 57; *Helv II* 11.14; *West* 32.2–3; *Cologne* 15
V: *Sav* 31.2–3; *Friends I* 23; *Morav* 5–6; *Geloof* 33; *Cumb Pres* 112–13; *New Hamp*

18; *Arm Ev* 10; *Ev All* 8; *Abst Prin* 19; *Swed Bap* 12; *Adv* 21–22; *Salv Arm* 11; *Com Cr* 12; *Richmond* 7; *Am Bap* 7; *Naz* 12.15; *Assem* 14; *So Bap* 16; *Un Ch Can: Union* 19; *Un Pres* 41; *Bap Assoc* 23; *Madag* 7; *Menn Con* 20; *Toraja* 4.6, 8.4; *Bap Conf* 9

11.5. Immortality of the Soul

II: *Gennad* 11; *Mogila* 1.28
III: *Tol I* 21, anath 11
IV: *Scot I* 17; *West* 32.1
V: *Sav* 31.1; *Geloof* 5.1, 32.3; *Cumb Pres* 112; *Ev All* 8; *Adv* 19–20; *Salv Arm* 11; *Un Pres* 5; *Bat* 16; *Toraja* 3.4

12. AND LIFE IN THE AGE TO COME

12.1. Life Everlasting; Heaven, Hell, and Purgatory

I: *Orig* 5
II: *Jer II* 1.17; *Metr Crit* 20.4; *Lucar* 18; *Mogila* 1.60–68, 1.124–26; *Dosith* decr 18
III: *Ap* 12; *Ath* 41; *Sens* 15; *Lat 1215* 2; *Flor Un* 11–13
IV: *Smal Art* 2.2.12–15; *67 Art* 57–60; *Bern* 7; *Fid rat* 12; *10 Art* 10; *Genv Cat* 110; *Gall* 24; *Scot I* 17, 25; *Heid* 58; *Helv II* 26.4; *39 Art* 22; *Irish* 101–2; *West* 33.1–2; *18 Diss* 14; *Trent* 6 can 30, 25; *Trid Prof* 6
V: *Sav* 32.1–2; *Geloof* 35–36; *Meth Art* 14; *Winch* 2; *Cumb Pres* 113–15; *New Hamp* 17–18; *Arm Ev* 10; *Ev All* 8; *Abst Prin* 20; *Swed Bap* 12; *Syl* 17; *Free Meth* 14; *Adv* 23–25; *Salv Arm* 11; *Com Cr* 12; *Richmond* 7; *Am Bap* 9; *Naz* 12.16–17; *Pol Nat* 11–12; *Assem* 16–17; *So Bap* 15; *Un Ch Can: Union* 19; *Un Pres* 39, 42–43; *Meth Kor* 8; *Bap Assoc* 24–25; *Bat* 16, 18; *Menn Con* 20; *RCA* 20–21; *Toraja* 8.6–8; *Bap Conf* 9; *Philip UCC* 6; *Camb Dec* 6

Alphabetical Index to the Comparative Creedal Syndogmaticon

Ecclesiastical Index: Churches, Heresies, Creeds, Confessions, Councils

What is a "church" (or even "*the* church") in one creed or confession is, of course, often a "heresy" for another. "Heresies" here are only those that are explicitly named as such (under one or another label) in a confession. Likewise, "creeds," "confessions," and "councils" are those that are expressly cited or quoted by another creed, confession, or council. Confessional references that speak in the name of a separate church, rather than about it (or against it), appear here in *italicized ALL CAPS.*

V: *Resp Pius IX; INEFF; Def Plat* 1.1–2, 5, 2.1–3, 7; *VAT I; Bonn I* 8b, 10; *Utrecht* 2–5; *LAM; SACR ANT; MUNIF; Bat* pr, 3.Bst; *Masai; VAT II; HOND; BEC; BALAMAND; CHR DEC; COM DEC; AD TUENDAM; LURC JUST*

Rus, Church of
  II: *Phot* 35

Sabellianism
  I: *Ar; Ecth* 1
  II: *CP 1351* 1
  III: *Lat 649* 18; *Petr Ab* 2
  IV: *Belg* 9; *Helv II* 3.5
Sacramentarianism
  IV: *Form Conc Epit* 7.2–5, 25–42; *Form Conc Sol Dec* 7; *Gall* 38
Salvation Army
  V: *SALV ARM*
Samosatenism
  II: *CP 1351* 47
  III: *Lat 649* 18
  IV: *Aug* 1.5; *Form Conc Sol Dec* 8.15–16; *Belg* 9; *Helv II* 3.5
Savoy Declaration (1658)
  V: *Un Ref Ch* 18
Schwenkfeldianism
  IV: *Form Conc Epit* 12.20–27; *Form Conc Sol Dec* 12.28–35; *Helv II* 11.9
Semipelagianism (*see also* Pelagianism)
  IV: *Form Conc Epit* 2.10
  V: *Cum occas* 4–5
Seventh-Day Adventist Church
  V: *ADV; Bat* pr
Shaker Church
  V: *SHKR*
Smalcald Articles (1537)
  IV: *Form Conc Epit* int 4; *Form Conc Sol Dec* int 7, 1.8, 1.52, 2.33–35, 5.14, 7.17–19, 10.18–23
Synergism
  IV: *Form Conc Sol Dec* 2.77–78

Tatianism
  IV: *Helv II* 24.8
Tetrapolitan Confession (1530)
  IV: *Form Conc Sol Dec* 7.1
Thirty-Nine Articles of the Church of England (1571)
  V: *Lamb Quad* 1; *Morav Am* 5
Three Chapters (Theodore of Mopsuestia, Theodoret, Ibas)

Index of References to Scripture

Index of Names of Persons

Abelard, Peter (1079-1142/43), III 647, 655, 679, 733, 734, 735-36, 737-38

Adam, Karl (1876-1966), V 397

Agatho (c. 577-681), Pope, I 216, 223; III 722

Akindynos († c. 1349), II 334, 335, 336, 337, 338, 339, 345, 368

Alexander, St. († 328), Bp. of Alexandria, I 75, 79, 80-81

Alexander I (early 2d c.), Pope, III 760

Alexander III († 1181), Pope, III 769

Alexander VIII (1610-91), Pope, V 101

Ambrose, Pseudo. See Prosper of Aquitaine

Ambrose, St. (c. 339-97), Bp. of Milan, I 13, 102; II 260; III 667; IV 72, 74, 86, 266

Anastasius, St. († c. 700), II 357

Anastasius Bibliothecarius (9th c.), V 268

Anastasius I († 598), Patr. of Antioch, II 351

Anderson, David, I 13

Andreae, Jakob (1528-86), IV 166, 168-203

Andrew of Crete, St. (c. 660-740), II 324-25

Androutsos, Chrestos, II 250

Anselm, St. (c. 1033-1109), Abp. of Canterbury, III 639, 654-55, 658

Anselm of Laon († 1117), III 735

Antoninus Pius, Roman Emperor 138-61, I 19, 22, 45

Antony of Egypt, St. (251?-356), I 23

Apollinaris. See Apollinarius, "the Younger"

Apollinarius, "the Younger" (c. 310-c. 390), I 146, 203, 219

Aquinas, Thomas. See Thomas Aquinas, St.

Argyrus, military governor of Byzantine Italy, II 313, 316

Aristides of Athens (2d c.), I 51, 52

Aristotle (384-322 B.C.), II 353, 505; IV 23

Arius († 336), I 75, 77-78, 87, 134, 136, 156, 219, 235; II 334, 353, 368; III 701, 737

Arminius, Jacob (1560-1609), IV 547

Arsenios, Metropolitan of Cyzicus, II 373

Asbury, Francis (1745-1816), V 201

Asmussen, Hans, V 504, 505-8

Athanasius, St. (c. 296-373), Bp. of Alexandria, I 11, 18, 20, 23, 41, 87, 142, 145, 225; II 302, 327, 351, 352, 357, 360, 365-66, 369, 482-83, 491, 566, 592; III 646, 665, 673, 762, 765; IV 241, 300

Augusta, Jan († 1572), III 797

Augustine, Pseudo-, V 301-2, 303

Augustine of Hippo, St. (354-430), I 6, 21, 110-11, 112, 192; II 260-61, 491, 627; III 643-46, 647-48, 670, 683, 728, 767, 802, 807; IV 15-16, 17, 68, 69, 72, 73, 92, 100, 108, 128, 142, 224-25, 234, 266-67, 461, 465, 466, 467, 468, 470, 472, 474, 504, 512; V 26-27, 101, 289, 304, 606

Barclay, Robert (1648-90), V 136, 137-48, 377, 399

Barlaam of Calabria († 1350), II 318, 320, 322, 329, 332, 334, 336, 337, 338, 339, 345

Barrett, William, IV 545

Barth, Karl (1886-1968), V 18-19, 504, 505-8

Basil, St., "the Great" (c. 330-79), I 6, 9, 13, 105, 132; II 302, 326-27, 327, 338, 341, 344, 349-50, 351, 352-53, 354-55, 357, 358, 359-60, 362, 365, 381, 384, 401, 402, 419, 431, 434, 443, 452, 460, 462-63, 464, 465-68, 469, 470-72, 532, 543, 575; V 273

Báthory, Stephen (1533-86), King of Transylvania, IV 745

Beck, Hans-Georg, II 379

Becket, St. Thomas (?1120-70), Abp. of Canterbury, III 789

Beham, Hans Sebald (1500-1550), IV 665

Benedict, St. (c. 480-c. 550), of Nursia, I 4

Benedict VIII, Pope 1012-24, III 645, 671

Berengar of Tours (c. 1010-88), III 650, 728, 729

Credits

We are grateful to the publishers, individuals, church bodies, religious organizations, and ecumenical agencies listed below for allowing us to reproduce texts and translations that appear in this work. The particular editions and translations we have used are acknowledged in the introductory note for each text. All possible care has been taken to trace ownership of every work. If any errors or omissions have accidentally occurred, they will be corrected in subsequent editions provided notification is sent to the publisher.

Abingdon Press; Academie Verlag; Akademische Druck- u. Verlagsanstalt; Alba House, a division of the Society of St. Paul; The Alliance of Confessing Evangelicals; American Bible Society; Andrews University Press; Arbeitsstelle Mittellateinisches Jahrbuch; *Archivum Fratrum Praedicatorum;* Urs von Arx; Augsburg/ Fortress Publishers; Baker Book House; Bayerische Akademie der Wissenschaften; Beacon Press; Verlag Hermann Böhlaus Nachfolger; Ton Bolland; Charles King Bradow; Brepols Editions; Brill Academic Publishers; Broadman and Holman Publishers; Cambridge University Press; Catholic University of America Press; Les Editions du Cerf; The Christian Church (Disciples of Christ); The Church of Jesus Christ in Madagascar; The Church of North India; The Church of Scotland; The Church of South India; The Church of Toraja, Indonesia; Clarendon Press; Columbia University Press; Concordia Publishing House; Continuum International Publishing Group; CRC Publications; Deutsche Bibelstiftung; Doopsgezinde Historische Kring; Eerdmans Publishing Company; The Evangelical Church of Togo; The Evangelical Presbyterian Church in South Africa; The Evangelical Presbyterian Church of Chile; Forward Movement Publications; Friends United Meeting; Friendship Press; General Secretariat of the Nihon Kirisuto Kyodan (United Church of Christ in Japan), Tokyo; Georgetown University Press; Verlagshaus Gerd Mohn; HarperCollins Publishers; *Harvard Theological Review;* Harvard University Press; Herald Press; Herder Verlag; Historical Committee of the Mennonite Church; Holy Cross Orthodox Press; Huria Kristen Batak Protestant Church; Ignatius Press; Jewish Lights Publishing; J. C. Gieben, Publisher; *Journal of Presbyterian History;* Judson Press; K. G. Saur Verlag; The Korean Methodist Church; Labor et Fides; Lancaster Mennonite Historical Society; Liverpool University Press; Longman Group, Ltd.; Loreto Publications; *L'Osservatore Romano;* L. S. Olschki; Mennonite Publishing House, Inc.; The Methodist Church of Brazil; Moravian Church in America; National Christian Council, Sri Lanka; Nazarene Publishing House; The North American Baptist Conference; *Noticias Aliadas;* Office of the General Assembly of the Presbyterian Church (USA); The Old Catholic Church–Utrecht Union; Openbook Publishers; Orbis Books; The Orthodox Church in America; Oxford University Press; Paulist Press; Pearson Education, Ltd.; Peeters Publishers and Booksellers; Penguin Group (U.K.); The Philippine Independent Church; The Polish National Catholic Church; Pontificia Università Gregoriana; The Presbyterian Church (USA); Presbyterian Publishing Corporation; The Presbyterian-Reformed Church in Cuba; The Reformed Church in America; Routledge; Rowman and Littlefield Publishers, Inc.; Saint Andrew Press; Saint Paul Editions; Saint Vladimir's Seminary Press; The Salvation Army; SCM-Canterbury Press, Ltd.; Scarecrow Press, Inc.; Sixteenth Century Journal Publishers; The Society for Promoting Christian Knowledge; *Spicilegium Sacrum Lovaniense;* Theologischer Verlag Zürich; Thomas Nelson Publishers; The Unitarian Universalist Association; The United Church of Canada; The United Church of Christ; The United Church of Christ in Japan; The United Church of Christ in the Philippines; The United Church of Zambia; The United Reformed Church; University Press Fribourg; Vandenhoeck und Ruprecht; Walter de Gruyter and Company; Westminster/John Knox Press; Rowan Williams, Archbishop of Canterbury; The World Council of Churches; *Zeitzeichen;* Zondervan Publishing House.